Writer's Guide to Book Editors, Publishers, and Literary Agents

1997–1998

D1403041

Writer's Guide to Book Editors, Publishers, and Literary Agents

1997–1998

JEFF HERMAN

edited by
JAMIE FORBES

PRIMA PUBLISHING

© 1997 by Jeff Herman

All rights reserved. No part of this book may be reproduced or transmitted in any form or by any means, electronic or mechanical, including photocopying, recording, or by any information storage or retrieval system, without written permission from Prima Publishing, except for the inclusion of quotations in a review.

PRIMA PUBLISHING and colophon are registered trademarks of Prima Communications, Inc.

ISBN: 0-7615-0508-3
ISSN: 1089-3369

96 97 98 99 00 01 BB 10 9 8 7 6 5 4 3 2 1
Printed in the United States of America

How to Order:

Single copies may be ordered from Prima Publishing, P.O. Box 1260BK, Rocklin, CA 95677; telephone (916) 632-4400. Quantity discounts are also available. On your letterhead, include information concerning the intended use of the books and the number of books you wish to purchase.
                    Visit us online at http://www.primapublishing.com

The power to publish is the power to destroy as well as to create. No one is inherently entitled to publication. Nor should anyone be arbitrarily blinded at the gates. It is not for the publishers to issue the call; that is determined by a source beyond them. By merits granted or earned, some will be chosen. The gates should therefore never be sealed, and those with the power to publish revealed.

—An Anonymous Literary Agent

About the Author

Jeff Herman is founder of the Jeff Herman Literary Agency, Inc., in New York City. One of the youngest and most innovative agents in the book business, he represents more than 100 writers and has sold nearly 300 titles. Herman has been extensively written and talked about in numerous print publications and broadcast programs.

Herman is the co-author with Deborah Adams of *Write the Perfect Book Proposal*.

About the Editor

Jamie M. Forbes specializes in the interlocking media arenas that emphasize the written and spoken word. He has worked with award-winning creators and performers of popular fiction, literary nonfiction, poetry, drama, performance art, the kitchen arts, clinical and popular psychology, business and communications, compositional and improvisational music, film, video, and computer-based multimedia.

Acknowledgments

Once more, Jamie Forbes has dedicated countless sleepless nights researching and deftly composing each publisher's description. No other book tells you so much; nor do they match Jamie's special style. Thank you, Mr. Forbes.

My significant other, Deborah Levine, has again provided the inspiration and energy that tedious tasks hunger for.

Gene Gusnar; Bill Hamilton; and Greg Ionou's essays are an invaluable contribution.

Meredith Browne and Jennifer Tropp have often been the arms and legs of this agency. At this printing they are enjoying new challenges. But I cherish the time I've had with them, and will miss them. And of course, Lillian Moon Lee has always been indispensable.

Books don't get published without publishers. Thank you Prima! And thank you for your wonderful people: Jennifer Sander, Georgia Hughes, and Brenda Nichols.

Books don't live unless people buy them. I pray that this book serves those who need it, and thank those who serve me by buying it.

Contents

Introduction

Welcome to the *Writer's Guide to Book Editors, Publishers, and Literary Agents*. Each new edition of this handbook (this is the seventh) blooms in size, stature, comprehensiveness—and value to you the reader. The *Guide* surely does seem to have a life and calling all its own. Our mission is to ensure that you, whether a new reader or an old-timer, can find the information you need to build a productive and successful writing career.

The talent is yours. Never let it be said that you did not realize your goals because you could not find the right editor to whom to direct your query letter. And never let it be said that you did not have a chance because you didn't know the best way to reach a literary agent.

The original *Writer's Guide* was published when I was a relative newcomer to the business. I wanted to punch through the closed walls of the clandestine world of book publishing and let in the light. I'm glad to see the *Guide* is still punching away—successfully, to judge from the gracious reports we receive from our readers. Although there are some editors, publishers, and agents who would rather the industry remain the province of a select elite, with the *Writer's Guide* you have as much information at your fingertips as do many of the most powerful figures in the book world.

Yes, you are in possession of the tools you need to contend with the best. And, to be sure, the writers who have already staked their turf in the publishing industry *are* the best. So don't be discouraged if you find the going is not easy. With talent, drive, and mastery of a few fine tricks of the trade, you have a solid shot to join those chosen few. You are a professional.

Sincerely,

Jeffrey H. Herman

Jeffrey H. Herman

The Jeff Herman Literary Agency, Inc.
140 Charles Street, Suite, 15A
New York, NY 10014
212-941-0540

Contributors to *Writer's Guide*

Deborah Levine is a vice president of The Jeff Herman Agency, and a writer and coauthor of numerous works including *Write the Perfect Book Proposal: 10 Proposals That Sold and Why* (John Wiley & Sons).

Gene Busnar is an author, collaborator, ghostwriter, and publishing consultant with dozens of books to his credit.

Jamie M. Forbes is a publishing and media consultant based in New York.

William Hamilton is the publisher at University of Hawaii Press.

Greg Ioannou is director of the Editorial Centre in Toronto, Ontario, Canada.

How to Get the Most
from *Writer's Guide*

If you are familiar with previous editions of the *Writer's Guide,* you will appreciate the value of this new updated release. The editor listings are the most complete and current possible at press time, many more superb literary agents have chosen to join our roster, and the essay section is revised and expanded in light of recent trends and events.

This book holds a colossal amount of information—there is so much data, so varied in detail, that judging from the range of response we receive each year there are almost as many ways to read *Writer's Guide* as there are readers. In addition to writers, our many friends include publishing-industry professionals from editors to agents to literary consultants, from job-searchers to researchers to media buffs.

If you're a writer who wants to keep abreast of the changing face of the industry and the opportunities available for you, here's one way to use the *Writer's Guide* for excellent results:

Start by reading some or all of the essays in Part Three: Writer's Guide Road Maps to Your Success. Here you'll probe the sum and substance of the book business and gain an overview of how to navigate your way through the publishing world.

Next, it might be best to evaluate Part Two: Writer's Guide Directory of Literary Agents. There's no better way to get commercially published than to be represented by a good agent. In this directory, over 100 qualified agents tell us about themselves—and some of them offer precious and encouraging words of wisdom gleaned from personal experience. If you need an agent, and virtually all writers do, here's where you may find her or him.

Finally, jump into Part One: Writer's Guide Directory of Book Editors and Publishers. Here more than 500 United States and Canadian houses are profiled. These include the vast media conglomerates, the lean-and-mean, and the in-between. We cover the upstarts as well as the traditional old guard. We present houses with finely focused lists, those with sweeping scope, and those downright wild and woolly.

Within this directory there are special sections for university presses and houses with a religious, spiritual, or inspirational emphasis, as well as a section geared to the Canadian market. Then there are the editor listings—you'll discover well over 1,000 editors listed. You'll know who they are, and what they want to publish.

With this book, writers can get what *they* want.

Writer's Guide to
Book Editors, Publishers,
and Literary Agents

1997–1998

PART ONE

Writer's Directory of Book Publishers and Editors

SECTION ONE

United States Publishers

ABBEVILLE PUBLISHING GROUP

488 Madison Avenue
New York, NY 10022
212-888-1969

Abbeville is renowned for finely produced award-winning volumes in the areas of fine arts, art history, architecture, graphic arts, design, lifestyle, cuisine, handicrafts, nature, collectibles, popular culture, sports, and illustrated historical works. Abbeville also produces calendars; stationery items; pop-up children's books; artists' portfolios; and titles in biography, letters, literature, and humor. Abbeville issues hardcover and trade paperback editions—all published with attention to quality in design, illustration, and production standards.

Abbeville Kids is their children's imprint (see subentry below). Tiny Folios is a line of small, handsome, reasonably priced volumes. The Cross River Press imprint offers literary titles with a worldwide cultural horizon. Editions Abbeville is the house's ambitious French imprint. Aerospace Publishing offers a short list of specialty titles. Artabras is a house imprimatur for promotional/premium volumes.

Abbeville Publishing Group is an international firm with offices in New York and Paris. Abbeville upholds a tradition of bookmaking established by the publisher Harry N. Abrams, who with his son Robert E. Abrams started Abbeville Press (in 1977) subsequent to the purchase of the eponymous publishing house Harry N. Abrams, Inc., by the Times Mirror Company (see entry for Abrams in this directory).

Titles from Abbeville: *Do Not Disturb* by Gianni Versace, *Modern Masters: Max Beckman* by Peter Selz, *Norwegian Folk Art* (edited by Marion Nelson); *Beer: A Connoisseur's Guide to the World's Best* by Gordon Brown; *Contemporary American Folk Art: A Collector's Guide* by Chuck and Jan Rosenak; *Elegant New York* by John Tauranac (photography by Christopher Little); *Piaget: Watches and Wonders Since 1874* by Franco Cologni and Giampero Negretti; and *Architects' Dream Houses* by Jean-Claude Delorme (photography by Thibault Cuisset).

Abbeville's colleagues at Paris-based Flammarion publish a vigorous list that includes *Beat Culture and the New America: 1950–1965* (copublished with the Whitney Museum of American Art), with a prologue by Allen Ginsberg and lead essay by Lisa Phillips; *The Office* by Elizabeth Pelegrin-Grenel; and *The Book of Chocolate*, with a preface by Jeanne Bourin.

Abbeville Press distributes its own books throughout the United States, and also distributes for Flammarion. International distribution is handled by regional representatives including John Murray Ltd., for the United Kingdom.

ABBEVILLE KIDS

Abbeville Kids produces a stunning lineup designed to introduce younger folk to the world of art and design, as well as to hone the tastes of younger artists and connoisseurs. In addition, Abbeville Kids offers books that deal with some of the finer pleasures of living and life.

Titles here include the *How Artists See* Series, *My New Friends: A Funny Fingers Book* by Karin Blume and Brigitte Pokornik, *The Jungle: A Big, Bigger, Biggest Book* by Marie Aubinais (illustrated by Jean-Francois Martin), and *Cartas de Félix* by Annette Langren (illustrated by Constanza Droop).

Query letters and SASEs should be directed to:

Susan Costello, Editorial Director
Gardening, nature, folk art.

Jackie Decter, Senior Editor
Russian interest, general.

Nancy Grubb, Executive Editor
Fine arts, women's interests.

ABC-CLIO

130 Cremona Drive
Santa Barbara, CA 93117
812-357-8011

Acquisitions department:
50 South Steele Street
Suite 805
Denver, CO 80209

ABC-CLIO produces high-quality reference books and serial publications in the fields of history, social sciences, political science, humanities, bibliographical reference, art bibliographies, subject bibliographies, directories, guides, and handbooks. ABC-CLIO also produces video guides, CD-ROMs, and serials for professionals. ABC-CLIO is an independent house geared toward the educational market (including curriculum-support materials and references).

The main market for ABC-CLIO books is school, public, and academic libraries, with single books and series keyed to a variety of subjects, including history, politics, social issues, ethics and philosophy, women's studies, mythology, literature, and anthropology. Almost all ABC-CLIO publications are in hardcover. The house actively pursues subrights and foreign rights (with paperback reprint sales going to such houses as Oxford University Press and W. W. Norton). ABC-CLIO series include Contemporary World Issues, Literary Companions, American Leaders, and Global Studies.

Representing the ABC-CLIO list: *Encyclopedia of Sport: From Ancient Times to the Present* (a three-volume set edited by David Levinson and Karen Christensen), *Dictionary of Native American Healing* by William S. Lyon, *Encyclopedia of Utopian Literature* by Mary Ellen Snodgrass, *Computer Revolution* by Paul Ceruzzi, *Women in the Workplace* by Dorothy Schneider and Carl J. Schneider, *Sports Ethics* by Lawrence H. Berlow, *Rape in America* by Rob Hall, *Animal Rights* by Clifford J. Sherry, and *Goddesses in World Mythology* by Martha Ann and Dorothy Myers Imel. The house produces *Exegy*, an electronic encyclopedia of current world information.

Publishing opportunities are open for practitioners and researchers in all branches of the social sciences and humanities; ABC-CLIO welcomes proposals from authors working on projects that fit the publishing program. Writer's guidelines are available from the publisher.

ABC-CLIO (founded in 1946) instituted its publishing program with a series of abstracts and indexes in 1955; the house launched its book program in 1967.

ABC-CLIO handles its own distribution.

Query letters and SASEs should be directed to:

Henry Rasof, Senior Acquisitions Editor

ABINGDON PRESS

(See Directory of Religious, Spiritual, and Inspirational Publishers)

ABRAMS

100 Fifth Avenue
New York, NY 10011
212-206-7715

Abrams was founded in 1950 as an independent house (then known as Harry N. Abrams, Inc.) and has been a subsidiary of the Times Mirror Company since 1977. Abrams has from its inception published fine, illustrated volumes in the fields of art, architecture, design, ethnology and culture, gardening, literary and art criticism, and the natural sciences. Many Abrams books are published in cooperation with institutions such as museums, foundations, or art galleries; these works bring together top-quality illustrative materials and expert text. Abrams maintains an extensive backlist.

Books from Abrams: *Perpetual Mirage: Photographic Narratives of the Desert West* by May Castleberry; *Platinum by Cartier: Triumphs of the Jeweler's Art* by Franco Cologni and Eric Nussbaum; *Contemporary Art of Africa* (edited by André Magnin with Jacques Soulillou); *The Parthenon and Its Impact in Modern Times* (general editor: Panayotis Tournikiotis); *The Olmec World: Ritual and Rulership* (in conjunction with the Princeton Museum of Art, with essays by Michael D. Coe, Richard A. Diehl, and others); *The United States of Poetry* by Joshua Blum, Bob Holman, and Mark Pellington; and *Cézanne: A Biography* by John Rewald.

The Discoveries series comprises paperback editions in a full range of the house's subject areas of interest. Titles here include *Angkor: Heart of an Asian Empire* by Bruno Dagens, *Birth of the Motion Picture* by Emmanuelle Toulet, and *Voodoo: Search for the Spirit* by Laënnec Hurbon.

Abrams series in trade paperback include Cameo Books, Great Modern Masters (volumes about individual artists), Perspectives (keyed to arts of specific periods or styles), and Discoveries (books covering history, archeology, natural history, and culture and the arts).

It should be noted that Abrams is a specialist house and acquires projects on a highly selective basis that gives particular weight to such factors as the national or international renown and credentials of participant artists, photographers, and writers.

Abrams distributes its own books in the United States, and utilizes regional representatives worldwide. Abrams also has a European subsidiary headquartered in the Netherlands as well as a Japanese branch with offices in Tokyo.

Query letters and SASEs should be directed to:

Margaret Chase, Managing Editor

ACADEMY CHICAGO PUBLISHERS

213 West Institute Place
Chicago, IL 60610
312-751-7302

Academy Chicago produces a pointed list in fiction (including mysteries), general nonfiction, art, history, and gender and cultural studies. The publisher also offers a line of classic reprints. Established in 1975, it is a small house with an inspired list, and is a major player in American letters.

The Academy Chicago program in fiction and letters encompasses English-language originals, often with a historical or cultural hook, with a significant portion featuring the mystery and suspense genres. Academy Chicago also publishes a variety of contemporary and vintage novels in translation.

Representing Academy Chicago fiction and literary works: *The Fat Woman's Joke* by Fay Weldon, *Circling Eden* by Carol Magun, *The Life and Times of Deacon A. L. Wiley* by Gregory Alan-Williams (drama/African-American studies), *Case for Three Detectives* by Leo Bruce, and *The Perfect Murder* by H. R. F. Keating. Academy Chicago is the American publisher of the successful British series of humorous and profound Miss Read novels, including *Fresh from the Country*.

Nonfiction includes popular works with an emphasis on contemporary culture, current events, and historical interpretation. Academy Chicago nonfiction highlights: *The Methuselah Factors: Learning from the World's Longest-Living People* by Dan

Georgakas, *No Tears for Mao* by Niu-Niu (memoir first published in France; translated by Enne and Peter Amann), *Titanic: A Survivor's Story* by Colonel Archibald Gracie, and *The Age of Agony: The Art of Healing, 1700–1800* by Guy Williams.

Academy Chicago handles its own distribution.

Query letters and SASEs should be directed to:

Anita Miller, Senior Editor

Jordan Miller, Vice President and Editor

ADAMS MEDIA CORPORATION
260 Center Street
Holbrook, MA 02343
617-767-8100

Adams emphasizes business and careers, popular psychology, self-improvement and awareness, pets, parenting and the family, lifestyle and cuisine, gift items (such as annotated datebooks), sports and games, and humor. The publisher's extensive backlist is particularly strong in the fields of sales how-to, professional exam preparation, job hunting, and personal finance.

Adams Media Corporation was begun in 1980 as Bob Adams, Inc., Publishers. The current corporate tag reflects the increased diversity, continued growth, and marketing success that the enterprise has earned over the years.

Among the fastest-growing midsize book publishers in the United States, Adams is recognized throughout the industry for aggressive promotion of its books. The house is interested in nonfiction book proposals and concentrates on personal finance, regional and local interest, interpersonal relationships, and women's studies, as well as book/software packages.

The Adams' program offers the perennially successful *Knock 'Em Dead* career books by Martin Yate, which detail techniques in résumé writing and employment interviews.

The Adams Business Advisors are designed to help new and growing private enterprises start right, solve problems, and endure successfully. Titles here include *The Small Business Legal Kit*, *Do-It-Yourself Advertising*, and *Managing People*.

Among Adams' titles: *Famous Friends of the Wolf Cookbook* by Nancy Reid and Sheila Liermann (photographs by Jim Brandenburg and Jim Dutcher), *365 Excuses for Being Late to Work* by Andy Sharpe, *101 Reasons Why Cats Make Great Kids* by Allia Zobel (illustrated by Nicole Hollander), *You Know You're Drinking Too Much Coffee When . . .* by Aviv and Davide Ilan, *The Everything Baby Names Book* by Lisa Shaw, *The Lost Lennon Interviews* by Geoffrey and Brenda Giuliano, *Josephine: The Josephine Baker Story* by Jean-Claude Baker and Chris Chase, *Happy Days Were Here Again: Reflections of a Libertarian Journalist* by William F. Buckley Jr., *Life, Liberty, and the Pursuit of Happiness* by Peggy Noonan, *Just Do It: The Nike Spirit in the Corporate World* by Donald Katz, and *Streetwise Small Business Start-Up* by Bob Adams.

Representative of Adams' books geared to children: *The Museum of Science Activities for Kids* by Tanya Gregoire, Joan Wilcox, and Boston's Museum of Science; and *365 TV-Free Activities You Can Do with Your Child* and *365 Outdoor Activities You Can Do with Your Child* (both by Steve and Ruth Bennett).

Adams distributes directly to bookstore chains, wholesalers, and independent jobbers in the United States—and to the United Kingdom and elsewhere in the world via overseas distributors. The house also sells to the gift trade, the office trade, and the computer software trade.

Query letters and SASEs should be directed to:

Pam Altschul Liflander, Editor
Popular culture, humor, performing arts, history, biography, and a variety of women's issues. Projects include *365 Excuses for Being Late to Work*, *The Book of African-American Women*, and *Your Healing Potential*.

Laura Morin, Editor
Nonfiction with broad consumer appeal in such areas as how-to, self-help, careers, humor, parenting, women's issues, cooking, and weddings. Projects include *Famous Friends of the Wolf Cookbook* and *The Lost Lennon Interviews*.

Edward Walters, Editor in Chief
Wide range of commercial nonfiction, especially self-help, relationships, popular reference, business, women's issues, and parenting. Acquisitions include the New York Public Library's *Around the American Table*, *King of the Cowboys*, *The Museum of Science's Book of Answers & Questions*, and *Sally Edwards' Heart Zone Training*.

Ann Weaver, Editor
Various self-help/how-to subjects.

ADDISON-WESLEY PUBLISHING COMPANY
General Books Division
Route 128
One Jacob Way
Reading, MA 01867
617-944-3700

The Addison-Wesley trade division incorporates a number of imprints and subsidiaries. It publishes in hardcover and paperback with a general trade focus on health care, psychology, management, general business, and computer books, as well as titles in sports and current affairs. Addison-Wesley imprints include Merloyd Lawrence Books, Helix Books (titles in the sciences), and Planet Dexter (children's books).

Addison-Wesley offers a full range of computer books. For the most part, titles on the Developers Press imprint are directed toward programmers and the technical end. A-W trade computer books are geared to the Apple and Windows realms, covering such areas as business computing, graphics, and database management. In late 1994 Addison Wesley acquired consumer computer book specialist Peachpit Press, thus increasing house presence in this burgeoning arena. (Please see separate main entry in this section under Peachpit Press.)

Addison-Wesley Publishing Company produces an enterprising trade line as well as an established educational and textbook program. In addition to the Massachusetts office, Addison-Wesley has a New York editorial address (see subentry listings for New York editors).

Prominent among Addison-Wesley trade titles: *The Sibling Society* by Robert Bly (author of *Iron John*), *The Temple Bombing* by Melissa Fay Greene, *True Love Waits: Essays and Criticism* by Wendy Kaminer, *The Politics of Meaning Affirming Hope and Possibility in an Age of Cynicism* by Michael Lerner, *The Essential Neoconservative Reader* (edited by Mark Gerson; foreword by James Q. Wilson), *Manifesto for a New Medicine: Your Guide to Healing Partnerships and the Wise Use of Alternative Therapies* by James S. Gordon, *Blind Watchers of the Sky: The People and Ideas That Shaped Our View of the Universe* by Rocky Kolb, and *Customer-Centered Growth: Five Proven Strategies for Building Competitive Advantage* by Richard Whiteley and Diane Hessan.

Addison-Wesley handles distribution for its list, as well as for its subsidiaries and imprints (see subentries).

Query letters and SASEs should be directed to:

John Bell, Editor
Health, American history and culture, trade paperbacks.
Popular business-related subjects.

Heather Mimnaugh, Helix Books
The sciences.

Beth Wolfensberger, Planet Dexter
Children's activity books.

Kathleen Tibbets, Editor
Computer books.

MERLOYD LAWRENCE BOOKS

102 Chestnut Street
Boston, MA 02108
617-523-5895

Merloyd Lawrence Books produces a list focusing on issues of contemporary interest, child development, psychology, and education. The imprint is home to the Radcliffe Biography Series, a collection of historical biographies of notable women.

From the Merloyd Lawrence list: *The Challenging Child: How to Understand, Raise, and Enjoy Your "Difficult" Child* by Stanley I. Greenspan with Jacqueline Salmon; *Bonding: Building the Foundations of Secure Attachment and Independence* by Marshall H. Klaus, John H. Kennell, and Phyllis H. Klaus; and *Dr. Susan Love's Breast Book* by Susan Love with Karen Lindsey.

Query letters and SASEs should be directed to:

(Ms.) Merloyd Lawrence

ADDISON-WESLEY

New York office:
170 Fifth Avenue
New York, NY 10010
212-463-8440

Query letters and SASEs should be directed to:

Henning Gutmann, Senior Editor
Politics, history, current events.

Elizabeth Maguire, Executive Editor
Women's studies, psychology, biography/memoir, current affairs.

ALGONQUIN BOOKS OF CHAPEL HILL

(See Workman Publishing Company)

ALYSON PUBLICATIONS

6922 Hollywood Boulevard
Suite 1000
Los Angeles, CA 90028
213-871-1225

Alyson Publications is a midsize publisher geared to topnotch expressions of the gay and lesbian cultural arenas. It also catalogs a list with multicultural, bisexual, and transgender appeal, as well as crossover titles of mainstream interest and social import. Alyson offers a preferred seasonal list of fiction and nonfiction, published in trade paperback editions, selected hardcovers, and mass-market paperbacks. The press tends a heady backlist.

The house accents both issues and lifestyle in such categories as current affairs, history, biography and memoirs, games and puzzles, cartoon collections, popular reference (including books of anecdotes and lists), and mainstream and genre fiction. Works of literary note are offered in all areas.

Alyson Publications was founded in 1977 by Sasha Alyson (reputedly with an initial outlay of $500) and was headquartered in Boston for its first decade and a half, during which time the house released many prominent titles in the lesbian and gay publishing arena. In 1995 Alyson Publications was purchased by the publishers of *The Advocate* magazine and its editorial offices were relocated from the east coast to the west coast.

Alyson nonfiction: *School's Out: The Impact of Gay and Lesbian Issues on America's Schools* by Dan Woog, *The Lesbian Sex Book: A Guide for Women Who Love Women* by Wendy Caster, *A Lotus of Another Color: An Unfolding of the South Asian Gay and Lesbian Experience* (edited by Rakesh Ratti), and *Bi Any Other Name* (edited by Loraine Hutchins and Lani Kaahumanu).

Fictional and literary works embrace novels and story collections, literary memoirs, essays, and category-keyed anthologies. Representative works: *The Femme Mystique* (edited by Lesléa Newman), *Amnesty* by Louise A. Blum, *My First Time: Gay Men Describe Their First Same-Sex Experience* (edited by Jack Hart), *Rattler!* by Cap Iverson (part of the Dakota series of Westerns), *The Hadra* (lesbian fantasy adventure) by Diana Rivers, *Embracing the Dark* (tales of horror; edited by Eric Garber), *Rapture and the Second Coming* by Wendy Borgstrom, *Macho Sluts* (pansexual erotica) by Pat Califia, *Below the Belt and Other Stories* by Phil Andros, and *Dykescapes* (edited by Tina Portillo). A poetry slam is presented in print through the pages of *Gents, Bad Boys, and Barbarians* (edited by Rudy Kikel).

Educational and younger readers' titles include *Two Teenagers in Twenty: Writings by Gay and Lesbian Youth* (edited by Ann Heron), *Heather Has Two Mommies* by Lesléa Newman (illustrated by Diana Souza), and *Daddy's Roommate* by Michael Willhoite.

Alyson Publications distributes through Consortium.

Query letters and SASEs should be directed to:

Tom Radko, Publisher, Editor in Chief

AMACOM BOOKS

American Management Association
1601 Broadway
New York, NY 10019
212-586-8100

AMACOM publishes business and management books for a primarily professional readership. AMACOM trade nonfiction specialty lines include works in the fields of computing, management, marketing and sales, information technology, finance and accounting, project management, small businesses, human resources, teams, customer service, career, quality and manufacturing, personal finance, self-development, and human issues in the work environment. AMACOM Books (founded in 1923) is the book-publishing division of the American Management Association.

Prospective writers might keep in mind the following AMACOM readership profile—not to typecast, but rather to offer guidelines. AMACOM readers are definitely not mass-market consumers; they want specialized materials and information on business issues that concern them most. AMACOM book buyers want more than a quick fix. They crave in-depth ideas and practical approaches they can try out on the job. They like to be on the leading edge and get a jump on the competition. They do not want secondhand information, but want to go straight to the source. AMACOM readers appreciate value and a good deal.

With this prospectus in mind, the AMACOM booklist includes: *Redefining Diversity* by R. Roosevelt Thomas Jr., *Wisdom for Earthlings: How to Make Better Choices and Take Action in Your Life and in Your Work* by John Newman, *Multimedia Tools for*

Managers by Bohdan Szuprowicz, *How to Price a Profitable Company* by Paul B. Baron, *From Secretary Track to Fast Track: The Get Ahead Guide for Administrative Assistants, Secretaries, Office Managers, Receptionists, and Everyone Who Wants More* by Kate Lizotte and Barbara A. Litwak, and *Getting Employees to Fall in Love with Your Company* by Jim Harris.

AMACOM distributes its own products in a program that features an especially strong direct-marketing arm. AmaCorp is a wing that promotes special-sales innovations for corporate consumers.

Query letters and SASEs should be directed to:

Adrienne Hickey, Senior Acquisitions Editor
General and human resource management, marketing/advertising.

Mary Glenn, Senior Acquisitions Editor
Career skills, small business, sales, customer service, self-development.

Tony Vlamis, Senior Acquisitions Editor
Information systems, quality, manufacturing, research/development, finance.

AMERICAN BAR ASSOCIATION BOOK PUBLISHING

750 North Lake Shore Drive
Chicago, IL 60611
312-988-5000

The American Bar Association publishes in a variety of specialty legal fields. The prospective writer should note that the American Bar Association publishes for the professional market, and each ABA division publishes its own line of books.

Please inquire as to which divisional line your project fits before querying. For general-interest professional–legal projects, query letters and SASEs may be directed to:

Joseph Weintraub, Manager

Alan Eastcott, Law Practice Management Division

AMERICAN FEDERATION OF ASTROLOGERS

(See Directory of Religious, Spiritual, and Inspirational Publishers)

AMERICAN MEDICAL ASSOCIATION

AMA Books
515 North State Street
Chicago, IL 60610
312-464-5983

American Medical Association books cover areas of professional information and reference in the healthcare field, as well as a growing concentration in patient information and related materials intended for a popular general readership.

American Medical Association (founded in 1847), in addition to being a preeminent professional organization in the field of medicine, is the world's largest medical publisher. The focus of this organization's publishing program is professional information and reference. In addition, the house has expanded its line of publications for the commercial trade market.

Books that bear the AMA logo (based on the serpent staff of Aesculapius) satisfy rigorous editorial and professional standards. In addition to medical-specialist works, AMA Books considers proposals from qualified authors on topics of interest to the broad and diversified patient market. AMA looks for materials that are supported by sound medical research and that can withstand the demands of AMA's review process; these works should also be user friendly, aimed at an audience with no formal medical training.

For particular trade-oriented projects, AMA functions as copublisher; these titles are marketed and distributed through the offices of the partner publishers or independent trade-distribution specialists. For example, AMA has combined with Random House on several selected titles (including *AMA Pocket Guide to Back Pain* and *AMA Pocket Guide to Calcium*). These books are cataloged and marketed with the Random House list.

Query letters and SASEs should be directed to:

Gail L. Cassel, Manager, Product Line Development

AMERICAN PSYCHIATRIC PRESS, INC.

1400 K Street Northwest
Washington, DC 20005
800-368-5777

American Psychiatric Press (founded in 1981) publishes professional, reference, and trade books, as well as college textbooks. The press's spheres of interest include the behavioral and social sciences, psychiatry, and medicine. The house publishes a mid-size booklist in hardcover and trade paper and also produces a number of professional journals. Selected reference works are issued in electronic formats, such as diskettes and CD-ROM.

Although by far the major portion of the American Psychiatric list is geared toward the professional and academic markets, the house catalogs a number of books in the areas of patient information and books for the general public, among which are selected titles marketed through trade channels.

Representative of the American Psychiatric popular-interest list: *Wrestle with Demons: A Psychiatrist Struggles to Understand His Patients and Himself* by Keith Russell Ablow, *Lies! Lies! Lies! The Psychology of Deceit* by Charles V. Ford, *Bad Men Do What Good Men Dream* by Robert I. Simon, *Coping with Trauma* by Jon G.

Allen, *Talking about Sex* by Derek C. Polonsky, *How to Help Your Child Overcome Your Divorce* by Elissa P. Benedek and Catherine F. Brown, *Surviving Childhood Cancer: A Guide for Families* by Margot Joan Fromer, and *The Preteen's First Book about Love, Sex, and AIDS* by Michelle Harrison (illustrated by Lynn Beckstrom).

American Psychiatric Press is the publisher of the psychiatric profession's accredited clinical guidebook, *Diagnostic and Statistical Manual of Mental Disorders* (fourth edition), also known as *DSM-IV*.

American Psychiatric Press distributes through a number of regional distribution services.

Query letters and SASEs should be directed to:

Claire Reinburg, Editorial Director

AMERICAN PSYCHOLOGICAL ASSOCIATION, INC.

750 First Street Northeast
Washington, DC 20002
202-336-5636

Areas of American Psychological Association publishing interest include virtually all aspects of the field of psychology: methodology, history, student aids, teaching, health, business strategies, violence, personality, and clinical issues. APA publications include books, journals, publishing resources, continuing-education/home-study programs, audiotapes, videotapes, and databases.

The information resources produced by APA are grounded in a long publishing tradition of scholarly and professional works that encompass diverse topics and applications in the arena of human behavior. APA offerings range from basic research to practical therapies, including the teaching curriculum of psychology as well as the contributions of psychology to progressive education, and from personality disorders to implications for psychology of public policies. The American Psychological Association (founded in 1892) is the major psychological organization in the United States.

On the APA list: *Abused Women and Survivor Therapy: A Practical Guide for the Psychotherapist* by Lenore E. A. Walker; *Attention-Deficit/Hyperactivity Disorder: Abstracts of the Psychological and Behavioral Literature, 1971–1994* (edited by Robert J. Resnick and Kathleen McEvoy); *Constructivism in Psychotherapy* (edited by Robert A. Neimeyer and Michael J. Mahoney); *Elder Suicide: Research, Theory, and Treatment* by John L. McIntosh, John F. Santos, Richard W. Hubbard, and James C. Overholser; *Jeopardy in the Courtroom: A Scientific Analysis of Children's Testimony* by Stephen J. Ceci and Maggie Bruck; *Job Stress in a Changing Workforce: Investigating Gender, Diversity, and Family Issues* (edited by Gwendolyn Puryear Keita and Joseph J. Hurrell Jr.); *Sleep Onset: Normal and Abnormal Processes* (edited by Robert Ogilvie and John Harsh); *Solving Your Problems Together: Family Therapy for the Whole Family* by Joe Annunziata and Phyllis Jacobson-Kram; *Testifying in Court: Guidelines and Maxims for the Expert Witness* by Stanley L. Brodsky; *The*

Disturbed Violent Offender by Hans Toth and Kenneth Adams; and *Understanding AIDS: A Guide for Mental Health Professionals* by Seth C. Kalichman.

A publication of the American Psychological Association that has wide influence in all areas of scholarly publishing, especially the social and behavioral sciences, is the *Publication Manual of the American Psychological Association* (now in its fourth edition), which guides writers and editors through manuscript preparation and production.

APA handles its own distribution.

Query letters and SASEs should be directed to:

Julia Frank-McNeil, Director, APA Books

AMERICAN SOCIETY FOR TRAINING AND DEVELOPMENT (ASTD) ASTD BOOKS

Box 1443
1640 King Street
Alexandria, VA 22313
703-683-8100

The American Society for Training and Development/ASTD Books is a business-information specialist. Among ASTD's major categories are customer service, sales and marketing, quality, training basics, performance appraisals and improvement, multicultural and women's issues, America and the new economy, workforce issues, consulting, teamwork, technology, games, and problem solving and creativity. In addition to books, ASTD offers training kits, diagnostic tools, presentation materials, games and simulations, videos, audiotapes, and computer software. ASTD publishes selected titles in conjunction with other business-oriented houses, such as Irwin Professional Publications, Jossey-Bass, and McGraw-Hill.

ASTD Books (founded in 1944) is the book-publishing wing of American Society for Training and Development, a nonprofit membership organization. The house's professional books cover such areas as employee education, training, and development; human resource development; organization management; and career development. Within this business arena, ASTD strives to put forth a list that represents the most current topics, the most innovative techniques, and the most gifted authors in the field.

Titles from ASTD: *A Manager's Guide to Globalization: Six Keys to Success in a Changing World* by Stephen A. Rhinesmith, *Corporate Quality Universities: Lessons in Building a Work-Class Work Force* by Jeanne C. Meister, *Evaluation: A Tool for Improving HRD Quality* by Nancy M. Dixon, *Performance Appraisal: Perspectives on a Quality Management Approach* (edited by Gary N. McLean, Susan R. Damme, and Richard A. Swanson), *Women's Network Professional Resource Guide* (edited by Rita I. McCullough), and *Training Cost Analysis* by Glenn E. Head.

Author's guidelines are available from the publisher upon request.

ASTD Books distributes its own list via an in-house easy-ordering program. Selected ASTD books are available through other publishing houses, for which ASTD returns the favor by cataloging business titles from such houses as John Wiley; Random House; Scott, Foresman; and Van Nostrand Reinhold.

Query letters and SASEs should be directed to:

Nancy Olson, Vice President, Publications

ANDREWS AND MCMEEL

4520 Main Street
Kansas City, MO 64111
816-932-6700

Andrews and McMeel (founded in 1970) is a Universal Press Syndicate company that publishes a wide assortment of general trade nonfiction books and consumer references, children's nonfiction, humor (including cartoon books), and calendars. Areas of interest include journalism and current affairs, popular culture and lifestyles, politics, psychology and self-help, health and medicine, business, sports and fitness, travel, biography, new age and inspiration, women's issues, nature, gift books (including highly illustrated and full-color titles), and children's interactive and book-plus products. Andrews and McMeel publishes over 100 calendars each year in day-to-day, wall, and desk-diary format.

From Andrews and McMeel: *Lessons from the Trial* by Gerald Uelman, *Running in Place: How Bill Clinton Disappointed America* by Richard Reeves, *Fuzzy Memories* by Jack Handley, *Hug the Monster* by David Smith, *Roger Ebert's Video Companion* by Roger Ebert, *Far Side Gallery 5* by Gary Larson, *Still Pumped from Using the Mouse* by Scott Adams, *Flashbacks* by Gary Trudeau, *I Got Married—If You Can Believe That* (a Jim's Journal collection) by Jim (aka Scott Dikkers), *The Revolutionary Cholesterol Breakthrough* by Robert Kowalski, *Together We Were Eleven Foot Nine* by Jim Palmer with Jim Dale, *The Unauthorized Anne Rice Companion* (edited by George Beahm), *Say It in Six: How to Say Exactly What You Mean in Six Minutes or Less* by Ron Hoff, *Midwest Weekends: Memorable Getaways in the Upper Midwest* by Beth Gauper, and *The Universal Almanac 1996*.

Andrews and McMeel distributes its own list, which is also handled by regional sales representatives. Andrews and McMeel also distributes for Turner Publishing and Cumberland house, and copublishes two imprints, Cader Books and buzz boxx books.

Agents, please query. No unsolicited manuscripts are accepted. Query letters and SASEs should be directed to:

Christine Schillig, Vice President and Editorial Director
General nonfiction, all categories.

Dorothy O'Brien, Executive Managing Editor
Humor and general nonfiction.

Jean Lowe, Executive Editor
Psychology, self-help, new age, inspiration.

Jake Morrissey, Senior Editor and Director, Newspaper Publishing
Journalism and current affairs, politics, general nonfiction.

Patty Rice, Editor
Childcare, parenting, careers.

THE ANONYMOUS PRESS

332 Bleecker Street
New York, NY 10014
888-2Write2 (888-297-4832)

The Anonymous Press, Inc. specializes in high-velocity projects that tap the current cultural pulse. The house is on the lookout for commercial, inherently marketable non-ficiton in such areas as investigative and journalistic accounts; issues-oriented human-interest stories; celebrity biographies, ultimate conspiracies, exposés, and scandalous affairs; and popular reference works (including single-volume encyclopedias, personal and professional how-to, looking good, feeling good, making money, and awareness).

The Anonymous Press (founded in 1996) featured as its initial release *Sleeping with the President: My Intimate Years with Bill Clinton* by Gennifer Flowers, a personal memoir of an extraordinarily powerful political love story.

Anonymous wishes to create its own marketing vision and break through to new publishing frontiers, and is open to a wide variety of creative projects. It is essential that submitted materials be imaginatively conceived and in professional book-proposal format. Authors must demonstrate expertise in the chosen topic area, and must offer thorough and credible documentation.

Do not send materials via registered mail, overnight express delivery, or any other means requiring a recipient's signature. Please query first.

Query letters and SASEs should be directed to:

(Mr.) Chris Bonner, Acquisitions

THE APEX PRESS
THE BOOTSTRAP PRESS

Council on International and Public Affairs
777 United Nations Plaza, Suite 3C
New York, NY 10017
212-953-6920 (catalog requests)

Branch office:
Box 337
Croton-on-Hudson, NY 10520
914-271-6500

Apex accents nonfiction titles in such fields as corporate accountability, grassroots and worker participation, and intercultural understanding. One special publishing focus is on economic and social justice, human rights, and the impact of technology on contemporary society.

The Apex Press (established in 1985) is an imprint of the nonprofit research, education, and publishing group Council on International and Public Affairs (CIPA). Apex publishes hardcover and paperback books that provide critical analyses of and new approaches to significant economic, social, and political issues in the United States, other industrialized nations, and the Third World.

On the Apex list: *The Community Land Trust Legal Manual* by the Institute for Community Economics, *Ecological Tax Reform: A Policy Proposal for Sustainable Development* by Ernt Ulrich von Weiszäcker and Jochen Jesinghaus, *International Directory of Youth Internships* (edited by Michael Culigan), *The Maximum Wage: A Common-Sense Prescription for Revitalizing America—by Taxing the Very Rich* by Sam Pizzigati (with illustrations by Howard Saunders), and *Development Dictionary: A Guide to Knowledge as Power* (edited by Wolfgang Sachs).

The Apex Press handles its own distribution; the house catalog includes books and additional resources (including videos) from a number of publishers worldwide.

THE BOOTSTRAP PRESS

Intermediate Technology Development Group of North America
777 United Nations Plaza, Suite 3C
New York, NY 10017
914-271-6500

Bootstrap's publishing interest focuses on social economics and community economic change. The house covers small- and intermediate-scale or appropriate technology in both industrialized and emerging countries, with an aim to promote more just and sustainable societies. Its books explore business and industry theory and how-to, gardening and agriculture, building and construction, and communications.

The Bootstrap Press (inaugurated in 1988) is an imprint of Intermediate Technology Development Group of North America (ITDG/North America) in cooperation with Council on International and Public Affairs.

Bootstrap titles include *The Gross National Waste Product* by Larry Martin, *Another American Dilemma: What to Do About the Crisis in Affordable Housing* by Peter Werwath, *The Barefoot Book: Economically Appropriate Services for the Rural Poor* (edited by Marilyn Carr), *After the Crash: The Emergence of the Rainbow Economy* by Guy Dauncey, *Chicken Little, Tomato Sauce and Agriculture: Who Will Produce Tomorrow's Food?* by Joan Dye Gussow, and *Worker Empowerment: The Struggle for Workplace Democracy* (edited by Jon Wisman).

Bootstrap publications are distributed in tandem with those of its sibling house Intermediate Press Limited (UK).

Query letters and SASEs should be directed to:

Ward Morehouse, President

Judi Rizzi, Publications Manager

APPLAUSE THEATRE BOOK PUBLISHERS

211 West 71st Street
New York, NY 10023
212-496-7511

Applause Theatre Book Publishers (established in 1983) produces a list geared to the fields of stage, cinema, and the entertainment arts. Applause produces collections, compendiums, biographies, histories, resource books, reference works, and guides keyed to the needs of the house's wide readership of seasoned pros, rookies, and aficionados.

The Applause program covers hardback and paperback editions, among them a number of generously illustrated and well-produced works. Applause issues stage plays and screenplays (many in translation and many in professional working-script format) that run the gamut from the classical repertory to contemporary works in drama, comedy, and musicals. Applause also offers audio works and a video library. The publisher's backlist is comprehensive.

Special-production volumes encompass works that detail the background and history behind the creation of works for stage and screen in addition to containing complete scripts.

Highlighting the Applause list: *David Merrick: The Abominable Showman* by Howard Kissel, *The Collected Works of Harold Clurman: Six Decades of Commentary on Theatre, Dance, Music, Film, Art, Letters and Politics* (edited by Marjorie Loggia and Glenn Young), and *Womenswork: Five New Plays from the Women's Project* (edited by Julia Miles).

For theatrical professionals and students as well, Applause offers *Acting in Film* (from the Applause Acting Series) by Michael Caine, *Telling Moments: 15 Gay Monologues* by Robert C. Reinhart, *The Actor and the Text* by Cicely Berry and *The Secret of Theatrical Space* by Josef Svoboda.

Applause Annuals include *Applause/Best Plays Theater Yearbook*, *The Best American Short Plays*, *Screen World*, and *Theatre World*. Also periodically revised and updated are *Applause: New York's Guide to the Performing Arts* and *Applause: The Los Angeles Guide to the Performing Arts*.

Applause handles its own distribution.

Query letters and SASEs should be directed to:

Glenn Young, President and Publisher

ARCADE PUBLISHING

141 Fifth Avenue
New York, NY 10010
212-475-2633

Arcade Publishing (founded in 1988 by Jeannette and Richard Seaver) produces commercial and literary fiction and nonfiction, both American and foreign. Arcade's fiction list includes high-quality entrants in such categories as mystery, and suspense.

Nonfiction standouts include issues-oriented titles, contemporary human-interest stories, and cultural historical works. Arcade's program maintains a marked bent toward learned and enlightened reading.

Representative Arcade nonfiction: *Leading with My Left: One Woman's Life in the Political Arena* by Elizabeth Holtzman with Cynthia L. Cooper, *Journey to My Father, Isaac Bashevis Singer* by Israel Zamir (translated from the Hebrew by Barbara Harshav), *Wounded Titans: American Presidents and the Perils of Power* by Max Lerner, *Harry's Bar: Watering Hole of the Rich and Famous* by Harry Cipriani, *The Laundrymen: Money Laundering: The World's Third Largest Business—the Inside Story* by Jeffrey Robinson, and *Ivy League Stripper* by Heidi Mattson.

Arcade fiction and literature includes *Trying to Save Peggy Sneed* by John Irving, *The Pyramid* by Ismail Kadare (translated by Jusuf Vrioni and David Bellos), *Murder Chez Proust* by Estelle Monbrun (translated from the French by David Martyn), *Our Lady of Babylon* by John Rechy, and *The Ego Makers* by Donald Everett Axinn.

Arcade Publishing is distributed by Little, Brown.

Prospective authors please note that Arcade does not accept unsolicited submissions. Query letters and SASEs should be directed to:

Calvert Barksdale, Senior Editor
All areas of house interest.

Timothy Bent, Senior Editor
All areas of house interest.

Jeannette Seaver, Associate Publisher
Fiction: literary. Nonfiction: History, politics, literary criticism.

Richard Seaver, President
Fiction: literary. Nonfiction: history, politics, literary criticism, illustrated books.

JASON ARONSON INC., PUBLISHERS

230 Livingston Street
Northvale, NJ 07647
201-767-4093

Jason Aronson Inc., Publishers (started in 1965) maintains two areas of publishing concentration: One Aronson line comprises psychotherapy, offering professional books (as well as some trade-oriented titles) in psychiatry, psychoanalysis, counseling (including pastoral care), and the behavioral sciences. The other Aronson publishing arena is Judaica (please see Aronson listing in Directory of Religious, Spiritual, and Inspirational Publishers). Aronson's strong backlist encompasses a wide range of publications well-regarded in the field of psychotherapy.

Among Aronson highlights in psychotherapy: *Attack on the Self: Adolescent Behavioral Disturbances and their Treatment* by Derek Miller, *Reparative Therapy of Male Homosexuality: A New Clinical Approach* by Joseph Nicolosi, *Treatment of Alcoholism and Other Addictions: A Self-Psychology Approach* by Jerome D. Levin, *Crisis: Psychological First Aid* by Ann S. Kliman, *Family Play Therapy* by Charles

Schaefer and Lois Carey, *Borderline Conditions and Pathological Narcissism* by Otto Kernberg, *A Curious Calling: Unconscious Motivations for Practicing Psychotherapy* by Michael R. Sussman, and *Feminist Psychoanalytic Psychotherapy* by Charlotte Krause Prozan.

Jason Aronson Inc., Publishers oversees a distribution network that utilizes its own in-house services as well as independent trade-fulfillment services. Aronson also features a direct-mail catalog that includes special-interest titles from other presses.

Query letters and SASEs should be directed to:

Arthur Kurzweil, Publisher

ARTE PÚBLICO PRESS

University of Houston
Houston, TX 77204-2090
713-743-2841

Arte Público Press (founded in 1979) publishes books of fiction, poetry, drama, literary criticism, reference works, and children's literature by and about Americans with roots in Mexico, Cuba, Puerto Rico, and the American Southwest, as well as by other American Latino writers. In addition, the press has a particular focus on women's literature. Arte Público is the oldest and largest publisher of Spanish-American writing of the United States.

The house publishes works in both the English and Spanish languages, as well as in bilingual editions. Arte Público's Piñata Books imprint is devoted to books for children and young adults that address the Hispanic experience in the United States. Arte Público issues a full roster of new titles each season and maintains a steadfast backlist.

On the Arte Público list: *Holy Radishes* by Roberto Fernández, *Havana Thursdays: A Documentary Novel* by Virgil Suárez, *The Candy Vendor's Boy and Other Stories* by Beatriz de la Garza, *A Fabricated Mexican* by Rick P. Rivera, *Cactus Blood* by Lucha Corpi, *A Fire in the Earth* by Marcos McPeek Villatoro, *Handbook of Hispanic Cultures of the United States* by Nicolás Kanellos and Claudio Esteva Fabregat, *In Other Words: Literature by Latinas of the United States* (edited by Roberta Fernández), and *Memories of Ana Calderón* by Graciela Limón.

Arte Público was the original publisher of *The House on Mango Street* by Sandra Cisneros (in 1985), and published *The Last of the Menu Girls* by Denise Chavez, as well as the works of Victor Villaseñor, Rolando Hinojosa, and Luis Valdez.

Arte Público handles its own distribution and distributes Hispanic literature for smaller presses, in addition to publishing *The Americas Review* literary journal.

PIÑATA BOOKS

Piñata Books publishes books for children and young adults that deal with Hispanic experience in the United States. The list is selected with the intention to promote writing that will thrill and inspire.

On the Piñata Books list: *The Secret of Two Brothers* by Irene Beltrán Hernández, *¡Aplauso! Hispanic Children's Theater* (edited by Joe Rosenberg), *Mexican Ghost Tales of the Southwest* by Alfred Avila (edited by Kat Avila), *In Nueva York* by Nicolasa Mohr, and *Hispanic, Female and Young: An Anthology* (edited by Phyllis Tashlik).

Query letters and SASEs should be directed to:

Nicolás Kanellos, Publisher

ASTD BOOKS

(See American Society for Training and Development [ASTD])

ATHENEUM PUBLISHERS

(See Simon & Schuster)

ATLANTIC MONTHLY PRESS

(See Grove/Atlantic, Inc.)

AUGSBURG FORTRESS PUBLISHING

(See Directory of Religious, Spiritual, and Inspirational Publishers)

AUTONOMEDIA
SEMIOTEXT(E)

P.O. Box 568 Williamsburgh Station
55 South Eleventh Street
Brooklyn, NY 11211
718-387-6471

Areas of Autonomedia/Semiotext(e) publishing scope include art and music; gender and ethnicity; fiction and belles-lettres; and contemporary, futurist, and historical criticism. The two divisional imprints overlap in their respective areas of interest; however, Autonomedia and Semiotext(e) remain distinctive entities with regard to editorial approach and featured series lines.

Autonomedia/Semiotext(e) is a publisher with a vision and a mission. Begun in 1983, this double-barreled house produces a powerful list of what is portrayed as movement literature. Whatever the dog tag—traditional book-publishing labels simply don't stick—Autonomedia and Semiotext(e) are antiauthoritarian publishers; they show a bent literature that "examines culture from a perspective that is against work and all forms of exploitation, and promotes actively the abolition thereof."

Although Autonomedia/Semiotext(e) publications are not intended for specialist market sectors, individual titles are of particular appeal to media buffs, political watchers, pop-culture hounds, and aficionados of the arts as well as artistic practitioners. The list also includes works that speak distinctly to an academic audience.

The house oversees its own distribution.

AUTONOMEDIA

Autonomedia is active in the arenas of cultural theory and criticism. The house emphasizes original artistic and literary expression, issues of ethnicity and race (Black radical), and viewpoints that radiate from gender and sexual perspectives (gay, lesbian, feminist). Autonomedia produces a gamut of creative thought that, though perhaps implicitly political, is essentially unfettered by conventional notions of partisanship.

Indicative of the Autonomedia list: *Arcane of Reproduction: Housework, Prostitution, Labor and Capital* by Leopoldina Fortunati, *TAZ: The Temporary Autonomous Zone, Ontological Anarchy, Poetic Terrorism* by Hakim Bey, *Cassette Mythos: The New Music Underground* (edited by Robin James), *Magpie Reveries* by James Koehnline, *The New Fuck You: Adventures in Lesbian Reading* (edited by Eileen Myles and Liz Kotz), *About Face: Race in Postmodern America* by Maliqalim Simone, *Columbus and Other Cannibals* by Jack Forbes, and *Horsexe: Essay on Transsexuality* by Catherine Millot.

New Autonomy is a series of anarchist and antihierarchical works in the areas of literature, politics, and culture. Bob Black (author of the successful title *Friendly Fire*) and Tad Kepley are coeditors of *ZeroWork: The Anti-Work Anthology*—a collection of writings that in large measure epitomizes the publisher's primary stance.

Query letters and SASEs should be directed to:

Jim Fleming, Editor

Peter Lamborn Wilson, Editor

SEMIOTEXT(E)

Semiotext(e) offers a concentrated list, with series keyed to fields such as radical European continental philosophy (including works by Jean Beaudrillard, Pierre Clastres, and Michel Foucault), social and cultural theory, gender expression and sexuality, artistic and political affairs, and native Asian feminist and gay literature (including fiction and poetry).

Representative titles from Semiotext(e): *Assassination Rhapsody* by Derek Pell, *The Cutmouth Lady* by Romy Ashby, *Whore Carnival* by Shannon Bell, *I Shot Mussolini* by Eldon Garnet, *Madame Realism Comples* by Lynne Tillman, *Unholy Bible: Hebrew Literature of the Kingdom Period* by Jacob Rabinowitz, *Sick Burn Cut* by Deran Ludd, *Hannibal Lecter, My Father* by Kathy Acker, *If You're a Girl* by Ann Rower, *Polysexuality* (edited by François Peraldi), *Semiotext(e): Architecture* (edited by Hraztan Zeitlian), and *Speed and Politics* by Paul Virilio.

A major release features the insider lowdown on the world's first postmodern revolution, fresh from the jungles of Chiapas: *¡Zapatistas! Documents of the New Mexican Revolution* by the Emiliano Zapata Liberation Army.

Query letters and SASEs should be directed to:

Jim Fleming, Editor

Sylvere Lotringer, Editor

AVALON BOOKS

401 Lafayette Street
New York, NY 10003
212-598-0222

Avalon Books produces wholesome family stories in the following categories: traditional mysteries, mainstream romance, career romance, and traditional genre Westerns.

Avalon Books (a subsidiary of Thomas Bouregy & Company, founded in 1950) publishes a primarily hardcover fiction list. The house concentrates on library sales, with emphasis on new original novels of high interest to the patrons of this core readership market. Avalon also produces a line of literary classics in reprint (on the Airmont Classics imprint).

Distribution is primarily through library sales.

Query letters and SASEs should be directed to:

Marcia Markland, Publisher

Eleanor Wickland, Associate Editor

AVERY PUBLISHING GROUP

120 Old Broadway
Garden City Park, NY 11040
516-741-2155

New Jersey office:
89 Baldwin Terrace
Wayne, NJ 07470

Avery's publishing scope includes a broad range of topical nonfiction, accenting such areas as health and nutrition, parenting, spirituality, science and technology, business, education, gardening, government, and history.

Avery Publishing Group (founded in 1976) produces a freewheeling list of high-interest commercial nonfiction in hardcover and trade paperback. Avery also catalogs fantasy-theme art from Paper Tiger Books, as well as college textbooks and professional reference works. Avery is the publisher of the West Point Military History series.

Avery books are designed to take readers back to where they've been, mirror who they are today, and show what they can aspire to be. Avery's authors and conceptual hooks often lead with an alternative edge or reach out to challenge with fresh views on current readership and cultural trends.

General-interest highlights from the Avery list: *Dressed to Kill: The Link Between Breast Cancer and Bras* by Sydney Ross Singer and Soma Grismaijer, and *Medicine, Monopolies, and Malice: How the Medical Establishment Tried to Destroy Chiropractic* by Chester A. Wilk.

Health and nutrition titles include: *What's Really Wrong with You? A Revolutionary Look at How Muscles Affect Your Health* by Thomas Griner, and *How to Start a Romantic Encounter* by Larry Glanz and Robert H. Phillips, *Reverse the Aging Process of Your Face: A Simple Technique That Works* by Rachel Perry, *Sexual Nutrition* by Morton Walker, *Lemon Tree Very Healthy Cookbook: Zestful Recipes with Just the Right Twist of Lemon* by Michelle Sbraga and Sunny Baker, *The Harvest Collection Cookbook: A Vegetarian Cookbook for All Seasons* by Gardner Merchant, and *The Sensuous Vegetarian Barbecue: A Hot and Healthful Collection of Recipes, Marinades, and Grilling Tips* by Vicki Rae Chelf and Dominique Biscotti.

Parenting and the family are represented by: *How to Cut Your Child's Hair at Home: A Simple Guide to Giving Your Child a Professional Looking Haircut at Home* by Laura DeRosa, *How to Multiply Your Baby's Intelligence* by Glenn Doman and Janet Doman, *Kids Who Start Ahead, Stay Ahead: What Actually Happens When Home-Taught Early Learners Go to School* by Neil Harvey, and *The Treasure of Trash: A Recycling Story for Children* by Linda Mandel and Heidi M. Mandel.

Avery Publishing Group distributes its own books and those of Ashgrove Press, W. Foulsham & Company, Paper Tiger Books, and Prism Press. Avery uses traditional trade bookseller channels as well as health food and nutritional store outlets within a network that includes Publishers Group West and Whole Health Books.

Query letters and SASEs should be directed to:

Rudy Shur, President

Joanne Abrams, Editorial Coordinator

AVON BOOKS
(See William Morrow & Company)

BAEN PUBLISHING ENTERPRISES
BAEN BOOKS

5020 Henry Hudson Parkway
Riverdale, NY 10421
212-532-4111

Baen publishes science fiction and fantasy writing. The house's new releases are generally published in mass-market paperback format, with special editions of targeted lead titles produced in trade paper and hardcover. Baen is a prominent publisher of series lines in science fiction and fantasy, and also publishes collections and anthologies geared to various subgenre traditions and the works of individual writers. The Baen program aims a significant portion of its list toward a younger readership.

Baen Publishing Enterprises (founded in 1984) concentrates its concise list on proven categories of publishing strength. Baen's roster of writers includes Poul and Karen Anderson, Piers Anthony, Margaret Ball, Marion Zimmer Bradley, Lois McMaster Bujold, John Dalmas, Robert A. Heinlein, Mercedes Lackey, Anne McCaffrey, Frederik Pohl, Spider and Jeanne Robinson, and Melissa Scott.

On the Baen booklist: *1945* by Newt Gingrich and William R. Forstchen, *Allies and Aliens* by Roger McBride Allen, *Doc Sidhe* by Aaron Allston, *Mall, Mayhem, and Magic* by Holly Lisle and Chris Guin, *Nanodreams* (edited by Elton Elliot), *Proteus in the Underworld* by Charles Sheffield, *The Magnificent Wilf* by Gordon R. Dickson, *The Printer's Devil* by Chico Kidd, *The Shattered Oath* by Josepha Sherman, and *Winning Colors* by Elizabeth Moon.

Baen Books is distributed by Simon & Schuster.

Query letters and SASEs should be directed to:

Toni Weisskopf, Executive Editor

BALLANTINE/DEL REY/FAWCETT/COLUMBINE/IVY

(See Random House)

BANTAM DOUBLEDAY DELL PUBLISHING GROUP

1540 Broadway
New York, NY 10036
212-354-6500

Bantam Doubleday Dell Publishing Group is a colossal enterprise that comprises a number of formerly independent major houses under one canopy. Bantam Doubleday Dell is itself owned by the German-based communications conglomerate Bertelsmann Publishing Group International.

Broadway Books is a dynamic new trade division that accents highly marketable nonfiction projects, as well as selected titles in fiction. (Please see subentry below for Broadway Books).

The group addresses the entire mainstream book-publishing spectrum from frontlist commercial products to specialty nonfiction titles and genre fiction, and issues titles published in hardcover, trade paperback, and mass-market paperback rack editions. Bantam Doubleday Dell publishes for adult and children's markets and catalogs an audio-publishing specialty list (BDD Audio Cassette). Bantam Doubleday Dell Books for Young Readers hosts the house's children's program. (Please see separate subentries below.)

Bantam Doubleday Dell Publishing Group handles its own distribution.

BANTAM BOOKS

Bantam is active in virtually every nonfiction and fiction category, including literary works. The fighting-cock logo of Bantam Books (founded in 1945) was for decades synonymous with paperbacks in mass-market editions. Bantam currently publishes hardcover and paperback originals, while carrying on its mass-market tradition, in both originals and reprints. Special Bantam frontlist titles enjoy simultaneous release on BDD Audio Cassette.

Bantam nonfiction encompasses titles such as *The Fine Art of Erotic Talk: How to Entice, Excite, and Enchant Your Lover with Words* by Bonnie Gabriel, *The Corporate Mystic: A Guidebook for Visionaries with Their Feet on the Ground* by Gay Hendricks and Kate Ludeman, *Sex, Power, and Boundaries: Understanding and Preventing Sexual Harassment* by Peter Rutter, *The Republican War against Women: An Insider's Report from Behind the Lines* by Tanya Melich, *Loving Each One Best: A Caring and Practical Approach to Raising Siblings* by Nancy Samalin with Catherine Whitney, *'Scuse Me While I Kiss the Sky: The Life of Jimi Hendrix* by David Henderson, *Red Hot Mamas: Coming into Our Own at Fifty* by Colette Dowling, *Protein Power* by Michael Eades and Mary Dan Eades, and *Family Secrets: The Path to Self-Acceptance and Reunion* by John Bradshaw.

Bantam fiction encompasses commercial novels; mysteries, suspense, and thrillers; science fiction and fantasy; romance and women's fiction; and select literary works. Crime Line is the Bantam imprint for topnotch suspense and detective fiction. Titles include *The Web* by Jonathan Kellerman, *Two Crowns for America* by Katherine Kurtz, *Guilty as Sin* by Tami Hoag, *F2F* by Philip Finch, *Riding Shotgun* by Rita Mae Brown, *Brothers* by Ben Bova, *Jane and the Unpleasantness at Scargrave Manor: Being the First Jane Austen Mystery* by Stephanie Barron, *The Outspoken Princess and the Gentle Knight: A Treasury of Modern Fairy Tales* (edited by Jack Zipes; illustrations by Stéphane Poulin), and *Cherokee Rose: A Novel of America's First Cowgirl* by Judy Alter. A highly conceptualized approach to verse is exemplified by *The Book of Birth Poetry* (edited by Charlotte Otten).

Query letters and SASEs should be directed to:

(Ms.) Toni Burbank, Executive Editor
New Age, addiction/recovery, health.

Tom Dupree, Senior Editor
Fiction: Science fiction. Acquires for the Bantam Spectra science fiction/fantasy imprint

Harry Helm, Editor
Fiction: Westerns. Nonfiction: military history, current events.

Anne Lesley Groell, Associate Editor
Works with Tom Dupree (see above). Fiction: Bantam Spectra science fiction/fantasy imprint.

Beth de Guzman, Senior Editor
Romance, general fiction, suspense, women's fiction.

Cassie Goddard, Assistant Editor
Women's fiction; mysteries, suspense, and thrillers. Commercial nonfiction, popular culture. Works with Beth de Guzman.

Emily Heckman, Senior Editor
Popular reference and general nonfiction.

Stephanie Kip, Assistant Editor
Women's fiction. Commercial nonfiction, popular culture.

Fran McCullough, Consulting Editor
Cookbooks.

Wendy McCurdy, Senior Editor
Women's fiction, romance. Commercial nonfiction, popular culture.

Kate Burke Miciak, Associate Publisher, Crime Line
Mysteries, thrillers, true crime.

Elisa Petrini, Senior Editor
Varied nonfiction interests, especially popular science and women's issues. Popular fiction, especially mysteries and thrillers.

Shauna Summers, Editor
Women's fiction, romance. Commercial nonfiction, popular culture.

Brian Tart, Editor
New Age, spirituality, popular religion, inspiration, health/fitness.

Nita Taublib, Deputy Publisher
Projects consistent with the Bantam list.

DOUBLEDAY

Doubleday (founded in 1897) is one of America's cherished publishing names; the house's emblematic colophon (a dolphin entwined around a ship's anchor) is equally beloved among book buyers, booksellers, and critics. Doubleday is known for its potent commercial list in fiction and nonfiction, with major concentration in mainstream popular nonfiction and genre fiction (Double D Westerns, Perfect Crime, Loveswept), as well as works of literary note.

Doubleday publishes hardcover and paperback editions. The Anchor imprint features original nonfiction and fiction in hardcover and trade paper, as well as paperback reprints. Doubleday/Currency produces a list of high-interest books in business, finance, management, and human relations. Doubleday Equestrian Library publishes top-of-the-line titles in the art and sport of horsemanship. Doubleday is also the home of Nan A. Talese's personalized trade imprint (see separate subentry below).

Doubleday spins off many of its lead titles on BDD Audio Cassette.

Doubleday's fiction list includes *Pandora's Clock* by John J. Nance, *Some Love, Some Pain, Sometime* (stories) by J. California Cooper, *Parsley, Sage, Rosemary, and Crime: A Pennsylvania Dutch Mystery with Recipes* by Tamar Myers, *Wilderness of Mirrors* by Linda Davies, *The War Trail North: A New Novel of the Cherokee People* by Robert J. Conley, and *St. Famous* by Jonathan Dee.

Doubleday is the publisher of *The Runaway Jury* by John Grisham, as well as his earlier works *The Firm, The Pelican Brief, The Client, The Chamber*, and *The Rainmaker*. A notable lineup by the 1988 winner of the Nobel Prize for literature, Naguib Mahfouz, includes *The Cairo Trilogy*: (I) *Palace Walk*, (II) *Palace of Desire*, and (III) *Sugar Street*.

Representing Doubleday nonfiction: *The Sixth Extinction: Patterns of Life and the Future of Humankind* by Richard Leakey and Roger Lewin, *The '21' Cookbook: Recipes and Lore from New York's Fabled Restaurant* by Michael Lomonaco with Donna Forsman, *The Way of Woman: Awakening the Perennial Feminine* by Helen Luke, *Animalogies* (humor) by Michael Macrone, *The Last Word on Power: Reinvention for Executives Who Want to Change Their World* by Tracy Goss (edited by Betty Sue Flowers), and *Racial Healing: Confronting the Fear between Blacks and Whites* by Harlon L. Dalton.

On the Anchor Books list: *Virtual Equality: The Mainstreaming of Gay and Lesbian Liberation* by Urvashi Vaid, *Dark Carnival: The Secret World of Tod Browning— Hollywood's Master of the Macabre* by David J. Skal and Elias Savada, *Sister to Sister: Women Write about the Unbreakable Bond* (edited by Patricia Foster), *Nine Poets of Desire: The Hidden World of Islamic Women* by Geraldine Brooks, and *Backlash* by Susan Faludi.

Query letters and SASEs should be directed to:

Charles Conrad, Editor in Chief, Anchor Books
Popular culture, social history, literary nonfiction. Contemporary literary and quality fiction.

Jackie Gill, Editor, Doubleday Books for Young Readers
Fiction and nonfiction for children to age ten; seeking primarily illustrated volumes.

Judith Kern, Senior Editor
Fiction: quality commercial, historical romance. Nonfiction: cookbooks, diet books, self-help and how-to, illustrated.

Elizabeth Lerner, Executive Editor
Fiction: literary and women's. Nonfiction: popular psychology, social/cultural history, anthropology.

Martha Levin, Publisher and Vice President, Anchor Books
Fiction: quality prose and poetry. Nonfiction: upscale, academically oriented titles in human behavior, biography, history, and contemporary issues. Also reprints.

Bruce Tracy, Executive Editor, Main Street Books
Practical nonfiction (health, psychology, fitness), how-to, popular culture, humor.

Eric Major, Director, Religious Publishing
Scholarly and popular works on religion and spirituality; titles likely to provoke religious controversy; books covering a wide range of religious thought, including Hinduism and Buddhism; Judaica.

Arabella Meyer, Editor, Anchor Books
Women's studies, politics, history.

(Ms.) Pat Mulcahy, Vice President and Editor in Chief, Doubleday
Commercial and literary fiction. Does a lot of suspense, thriller, and mystery fiction. General nonfiction; special interests include music and other popular culture.

Harriet Rubin, Publisher, Currency
Acquires business-oriented titles for Currency imprint.

Roger Scholl, Senior Editor, Anchor Books
History, women's studies, Black studies, biography, popular science, sociology.

Bill Thomas, Editor
General nonfiction, politics, current affairs.

NAN A. TALESE BOOKS

The personalized imprint of Nan A. Talese concentrates on topical issues of widespread interest addressed through frontlist nonfiction and selected fiction. The Talese roster is particularly strong in works that tie in with areas of contemporary cultural themes.

Representative of the Talese list are *"Feminism Is Not the Story of My Life" : How Today's Feminist Elite Has Lost Touch with the Real Concerns of Women* by Elizabeth Fox-Genovese, *The Voyage* (fiction) by Robert MacNeil, *Beach Music* (fiction) by Pat Conroy, *Choices* (a novel) by Mary Lee Settle, *How the Irish Saved Civilization: The Untold Story of Ireland's Historic Role from the Fall of Rome to the Rise of Medieval Europe* by Thomas Cahill, *Follow Your Heart* by Susanna Tamaro (translated by Avril Bardoni), and *Skin Deep: Black Women and White Women Write about Race* (edited by Marita Golden and Susan Richards Shreve).

Query letters and SASEs should be directed to:

Nan A. Talese, Publisher

Jesse Cohen, Editor
Fiction: literary (particularly women authors on a variety of female issues); occasional commercial works. Nonfiction: biographies of fine and performing artists, essays, subjects of popular or contemporary cultural interest. Not interested in unagented/ unsolicited submissions.

BANTAM DOUBLEDAY DELL NEW MEDIA

Computer-based works including multimedia properties.

Query letters and SASEs should be directed to:

Jonathan Guttenberg, Senior Editor

DELL PUBLISHING
DELACORTE PRESS

Dell currently produces trade and mass-market paperbacks in virtually all fiction and nonfiction categories, along with selected hardcover originals. Delacorte concentrates on hardcover frontlist releases. Among Delacorte's nonfiction areas of interest are popular psychology, self-help, childcare, humor, politics, true crime, and current issues and events. Delacorte trade fiction includes commercial novels, mystery, romance, historical sagas, and occasional high-concept horror and futurist works. A good number of Delacorte's frontlist titles are presented with simultaneous release on BDD Audio Cassette.

Dell (founded in 1921) upholds a traditional position as one of the major players in paperback publishing. The DTP imprint covers practical and inspirational nonfiction in trade paperback. Delta Trade Paperbacks include serious (and fun) contemporary fiction, narrative nonfiction, popular culture, popular science, and issues-oriented psychology. The Laurel imprint includes literary and reference titles in trade paper and mass-market paperback. Dell mass-market paperbacks feature reprints of Delacorte hardcovers, as well as paperback originals. Dell Abyss accents new directions in horror and dark suspense.

The Dial Press is a revived presence in the Dell Publishing division of Bantam Doubleday Dell Publishing Group. Dial offers a short, selective commercial-literary list (fiction and serious nonfiction) published primarily in hardcover editions under its own lion-and-cupid logo.

Delacorte Press nonfiction books include *Bad As I Wanna Be* by Dennis Rodman with Tim Keown, *In Sickness and Health: Sex, Love, and Chronic Illness* by Lucille Carlton, *Wild Steps of Heaven* by Victor Villaseñor, *Tricks in the Wilderness of Dreaming: Exploring Interior Landscape through Practical Dreamwork* by Robert Bosnak, *Men Like Women Who Like Themselves (and Other Secrets That the Smartest Women Know)* by Steven Carter and Julia Sokol, and *Rush Limbaugh Is a Big Fat Idiot (and Other Observations)* by Al Franken.

Delacorte frontlist fiction includes *Malice* by Danielle Steel, *Sacred Dust* by David Hill, *Buzz Cut* by James W. Hall, *Promises* by Belva Plain, *The Last Sanctuary* by Craig Holden, *Sudden Exposure* (a Jill Smith mystery) by Susan Dunlap, *Women On the Case* (introduced and edited by Sara Paretsky), and *Murder for Love* (edited by Otto Penzler). Notable backlist items: *Riding the Rap* by Elmore Leonard, *The Horse Whisperer* by Nicholas Evans, the Carlotta Carlyle mysteries by Linda Barnes, novels by Maeve Binchy, and Sara Paretsky's series of V. I. Warshawski detective fiction.

The Dial Press literary purview is represented by such fiction as *The Giant's House: A Romance* by Elizabeth McCracken, *Fast Greens* by Turk Pipkin, and *Veronica* by Nicholas Christopher. Creative nonfiction from Dial includes *Drinking: A Love Story* by Caroline Knapp, and *Light Fantastic: Adventures in Theatre* by John Lahr.

Delta trade paperbacks embrace both originals and reprints in mainstream nonfiction and in popular and cutting-edge fiction. Representing the Delta line: *When Elephants Weep: The Emotional Lives of Animals* by Jeffrey Moussieff Masson and Susan McCarthy, *Blown Sideways through Life: A Hilarious Tour de Résumé* (autobiography) by Claudia Shear, *Letters from Motherless Daughters: Words of Courage, Grief, and Healing* (edited by Hope Edelman), *M31: A Family Romance* by Stephen Wright, *A Day in the Life: The Music and Artistry of the Beatles* by Mark Hertsgaard, *Rolling Stone's Alt-Rock-a-Rama: An Outrageous Compendium of Fact, Fiction, Trivia and Critiques on Alternative Rock* by Scott Schinder and the editors of Rolling Stone Press, and *The Paperboy* (fiction) by Pete Dexter.

DTP trade paperbacks accent up-to-the-minute trends in mainstream commercial readership interest—primarily nonfiction areas—with a list that also hits specialty sectors such as humor and puzzles. The DTP nonfiction program covers such titles as *I Am the Walrus: Confessions of a Blue-Collar Golfer* by Craig Stadler with John Andrisani, *Rock the Casbah: The Ultimate Guide to Hosting Your Own Theme Party* by Ellen Hoffman (illustrations by Louise Farrell), *White Moon, Red Dragon* (science fiction) by David Wingrove, *Seven Weeks to Better Sex* by Domeena Renshaw, and *I Am Not a Corpse! and Other Quotes Never Actually Said* (humor) by Mark Katz.

Laurel publishes the writing and editing reference *The 21st Century Manual of Style* (edited by the Princeton Language Institute).

Query letters and SASEs should be directed to:

Marjorie Braman, Executive Editor, Dell
Women's fiction, mystery and suspense, general fiction. Nonfiction: women's issues and general nonfiction.

Betsy Bundschuh, Editor
Trade paperbacks.

(Ms.) Jackie Cantor, Executive Editor, Delacorte Press
Fiction: women's fiction, mysteries, historical romance, and quality/literary fiction.

Laura Cifelli, Editor, Dell
Romance fiction. Nonfiction: women's issues, general self-help.

(Ms.) Jackie Farber, Executive Editor
Quality/literary fiction.

Stephanie Gunning, Editor, Dell
Spirituality, health, environment.

Jacob Hoye, Editor

Kathleen Jayes, Associate Editor, Dell
Commercial and popular projects in fiction and nonfiction. From new writers: a fresh voice, unique point of view, personal style with something new to say.

Susan Kamil, Editorial Director, Dial Press
Literary fiction. Quality nonfiction.

Mary Ellen O'Neill, Senior Editor, Dell
Women's fiction: contemporaries, historical romances.

Maureen O'Neal, Editor
In charge of nonfiction and paperback program.

Leslie Schnur, Vice President and Editor in Chief, Dell Publishing/Delacorte Press
Strong projects consistent with the house list.

Eric Wybenga, Associate Editor
Commercial, popular, and quality nonfiction and fiction.

BANTAM DOUBLEDAY DELL BOOKS FOR YOUNG READERS

Bantam Doubleday Dell Books for Young Readers brings out a lively list of fiction and nonfiction geared toward the preschool through young-adult markets. This division encompasses numerous lines and imprints, including Doubleday Books for Young Readers, Bank Street (Ready-to-Read Books and Museum Books), Audubon One Earth Books, Delacorte Press Middle Readers, Skylark, Delacorte Press Young Adult, Starfire, Laurel, Little Rooster, Rooster, and Yearling. This division issues books in hardcover, trade paperback, and economically priced paper editions.

Representative projects: *Big David, Little David* by S. E. Hinton (illustrated by Alan Daniel), *Thwonk* by Jon Bauer, *Weird on the Outside* by Shelley Stoehr, *Music in the Wood* by Cornelia Cornelissen (photographs by John MacLachlan), *Yo, Hungry Wolf* by David Vozar (illustrated by Betsy Lewin), *A Season for Goodbye* by Lurlene McDaniel, *Sweet Valley High* by Francine Pascal (in monthly volumes; series spin-off on television), and *Camp Dracula* by Tom B. Stone.

Query letters and SASEs should be directed to:

Beverly Horowitz, Editor in Chief, Vice President, Deputy Publisher

Michelle Poploff, Editorial Director

Mary Cash, Editorial Director

Kathleen Squires, Editor

Karen Wojtyla, Editor

BROADWAY BOOKS

Broadway's core program consists of commercial nonfiction in the areas of celebrity autobiography and biography, biography, memoirs, politics and current affairs, multicultural, popular culture, cookbooks, diet and nutrition, consumer reference, business, personal finance, psychology, spirituality, and women's issues. The house also produces selective literary frontlist fiction, primarily by established and/or highly promotable authors.

Overall, Broadway strategy involves publishing unique, marketable books of the highest editorial quality by authors who are authorities in their field and who use their credibility and expertise to promote their work.

Broadway Books swung into operation with a mission to publish high-quality nonfiction hardcovers and trade paperbacks. William Shinker was named president and publisher of the Broadway Books adult trade division in late 1994, joined by John Sterling as Editor in Chief, and Janet Goldstein as the wing's executive editor.

Among Broadway's inaugural nonfiction projects: *Bare Knuckles and Back Rooms: My Life in American Politics* by Ed Rollins and Tom DeFrank, *With God on Our Side: The Rise of the Religious Right in America* by William Martin, *Picture This: A Visual Diary* by Tipper Gore, *Let's Pave the Stupid Rainforests & Give School Teachers Stun Guns and Other Ways to Save America* by Ed Anger, and *The Unshredded Files of Hillary and Bill Clinton* by Henry Beard and John Boswell.

Also on tap: *The Kingdom of Shivas Irons* by Michael Murphy (author of *Golf in the Kingdom*); *What It Means to Be a Libertarian* by Charles Murray (coauthor of *The Bell Curve*); a memoir from Bob Costas (written with Pulitzer Prize winner H. G. "Buzz" Bissinger); two books (inspiration and autobiography) from Bernice King, youngest daughter of Martin Luther King Jr. and Coretta Scott King; and a narrative nonfiction account of one student's heroic effort to leave the inner city by Pulitzer Prize winner Ron Suskind (who also reports for *The Wall Street Journal*).

Broadway's general nonfiction program includes kitchen-arts and lifestyle; relationships, parenting and the family; popular business; and popular psychology, inspirational, and self-help/self-awareness works. Sample projects: *Eat Your Way across the U.S.A.* by Jane and Michael Stern, *A Fresh Taste of Italy* by Michele Scicolone, *Bake and Freeze Chocolate Desserts* by Elinor Klivans, *Polenta* by Michele Anna Jordan, *The Simple Living Guide* by Janet Luhrs, *Becoming the Parent You Want to Be* by Laura Davis and Janis Keyser, *The Roller Coaster Years* by Charlene Canape Giannetti and Margaret Sagarese, *A Family Like Any Other* (a work on stepfamilies in America) by James Bray, *Big Bertha and Me* by Ely Callaway (founder of Callaway Golf), *It's Here Now (Are You?)* by Bhagavan Das, and *The Wise Woman's Guide to Erotic Videos*.

On Broadway's select fiction list: A new crime/suspense novel from Richard Price (author of *Clockers*, as well as *The Wanderers* and *Bloodbrothers*); *A Face at the Window* by Pulitzer Prize winning novelist Dennis McFarland (described as a literary ghost story); a novel from National Book Award winner Tim O'Brien; *Eat Me* a (down-under sensation) from Sydney-based author Linda Jaivin, as well as Linda's new work, *Rock 'n' Roll Babes from Outer Space*; and *As Francesca*, a first novel from Martha Baer (features editor for *Wired* magazine and a member of the V-Girls performance group), an erotic work that has been serialized as a work-in-progress on the Internet.

The publishing house's namesake street and logo (a diagonally bisected letter B) are emblematic of the publisher's mandate. Broadway is New York's oldest thoroughfare and runs obliquely through the diversity of Manhattan's multicultural neighborhoods, from the original harbor and the financial district, along the city's centers of government, literature, music, theater, communications, retail shops, to educational and medical institutions.

Please query the house's acquisition stance prior to submitting projects—Broadway wishes to receive no unsolicited manuscripts; only agented works will be considered. Query letters and SASEs may be directed to:

Harriet Bell, Executive Editor
Cookbooks and the kitchen arts.

Janet Goldstein, Vice President and Executive Editor; Editorial Director for Trade Paperbacks
Women's and feminist issues; relationships and popular psychology; social trends, parenting, and family issues.

John Sterling, Vice President and Editor in Chief
Literary fiction and nonfiction.

Lauren Marino, Editor
Nonfiction, especially popular culture, entertainment, humor, spirituality.

Suzanne Oaks, Editor
Business-related titles.

BARRICADE BOOKS INC.

1530 Palisade Avenue
Fort Lee, NJ 07020
201-592-0926

Editorial offices:
150 Fifth Avenue, Suite 700
New York, NY 10011
212-627-7000

Barricade's publishing interests include arts and entertainment; cookbooks; fiction (including topflight mainstream novels, genre anthologies, and tales of mystery and suspense); how-to/self-help; biography, history, politics, and current events; humor; natural sciences; new age, occult, and religion; psychology, health, and sexuality; recreation; and true crime.

Barricade Books was founded in 1991 by Carole Stuart and Lyle Stuart (formerly of the publishing house Lyle Stuart, which is now a component of Carol Publishing Group). Barricade Books was launched in order to continue the tradition begun in 1956 when Lyle Stuart became a publisher—to specialize in books other publishers might hesitate to publish because they were too controversial.

Barricade publisher Carole Stuart is the author of a number of successful books including *I'll Never Be Fat Again* and *Why Was I Adopted?* She has worked in book publishing her entire adult life. Lyle Stuart is a former newspaper reporter who launched his career as a book publisher with $8,000 that he won in a libel action against Walter Winchell. Stuart sold that company three decades later for $12 million.

The Barricade catalog expands this tradition with a roster of freethinking writers that is perhaps unrivaled in the international commercial-publishing arena. Barricade's list is exemplary of publishing courage in action.

Among Barricade's books: *Hollywood Lesbians* by Boze Hadleigh, *Jokes for Your John: The Full Bathroom Reader* by Omri Bar-Lev and Joe Weis, *Injustice for All: How Our Adversary System of Law Victimizes Us and Subverts True Justice* by Anne Strick, *Mark It with a Stone: A Moving Account of a Young Boy's Struggle to Survive the Nazi Death Camps* by Joseph Horn, *The Complete Book of Devils and Demons* by Leonard R. N. Ashley, *Killer Kids, Bad Law: Tales of the Juvenile Court System* by Peter Reinharz, *The King of Clubs: The Story of Scores—the Famed Topless Club—and the Lurid Life behind the Glitter* by Jay Bildstein (as told to Jery Schmetter), *My Struggle: The Explosive Views of Russia's Most Controversial Political Figure* by Vladimir Zhirnovsky, and *Great Big Beautiful Doll: The Anna Nicole Smith Story* by Eric and D'Eva Redding

Indicative of the Barricade tradition in fiction and the literary arts are *Gasp! A Novel of Revenge* by Frank Freudberg, *The Best Japanese Science Fiction Stories* (edited by John Apostolou and Martin Greenberg), *Orion: The Story of a Rape* by Ralph Graves, *Norman Corwin's Letters* (edited by A. J. Langguth), and *The George Seldes Reader* (edited by Randolph T. Holhut).

Among other notable Barricade projects are the revised and updated version of *L. Ron Hubbard: Messiah or Madman?—The Book That Survived Every Attempt to Suppress Its Publication* by Brent Corydon, and William Powell's radical classic *The Anarchist Cookbook*—now in well over three dozen printings with more than 2 million volumes sold.

Barricade Books manages its own sales and distribution services.

Query letters and SASEs should be directed to:

(Ms.) Carole Stuart, Publisher

BARRON'S
BARRON'S EDUCATIONAL SERIES, INC.

250 Wireless Boulevard
Hauppauge, NY 11788
516-434-3311

Barron's hosts a broad publishing operation that encompasses books in business and finance, gift books, cooking, family and health, gardening, nature, pets, and retirement lifestyle, as well as selected titles in arts, crafts, and hobbying. Barron's also produces computer books and software, and highlights a children's line.

Barron's (founded in 1945) was originally known for its comprehensive line of study notes and test-preparation guides in business, literature, and languages, and standardized tests in individual subject and professional fields. The house offers a number of practical business series, retirement and parenting keys, programs on skills develop-

ment in foreign languages (as well as in English), and specialty re
areas of interest.

Barron's cookbooks address international cuisines as well as areas
such as chocolate, pasta, and ice cream. Family and health books cover he
first aid, baby care, and dictionaries of health-related terms, as well as gene
works. Under the rubric of special-interest titles, Barron's produces series on a
crafts techniques, biographies of well-known artists, fashion traditions and trends,
home and garden. Books on pets and pet care include numerous titles keyed to partic
lar breeds and species of birds, fish, dogs, and cats.

Children's and young-adult books include series on pets, nature and the environment, dinosaurs, sports, fantasy, adventure, and humor. Many of these are picture storybooks, illustrated works, and popular reference titles of general interest.

On the Barron's list: *Being There: The Benefits of a Stay-at-Home Parent* by Isabelle
Fox with Norman M. Lobsenz, *Trattoria Pasta* by Loukie Werle (photos by Peter
Johnson), *Mini Fact Finder: Stars* by Joachim Ekrutt, *Easy Painting and Drawing
Series* (four individual volumes from Parramon Studios), *Barron's Business Thesaurus*
by Mary DeVries, *Ferrets* by Chuck Morton and Fox Morton, *The Water Gardener* by
Anthony Archer-Wills, and *Household Spanish: How to Communicate with Your
Spanish Employees* by William C. Harvey.

Barron's handles its own distribution.

Query letters and SASEs should be directed to:

Grace Freedson, Acquisitions Manager

BASIC BOOKS
(See HarperCollins)

BASKERVILLE PUBLISHERS
7616 LBJ Freeway, Suite 220
Dallas, TX 75251
214-934-3451

Baskerville publishes literary fiction and trade nonfiction in hardcover and softcover
editions. Baskerville series include Great Voices (biographies of vocalists) and Basset
Books (trade paperbacks).

Baskerville Publishers (first list issued in 1992) presents creative, individualist writing voices that sing in the American idiom. What sets Baskerville's writers apart is a
combination of hooks derived from mainstream or popular culture. Often unexpectedly
laced with humor, Baskerville's storytellers present tales that emerge from a dark-
tinged web.

aldi: The Voice of an Angel (biography by
ie Mandracchia DeCaro), *Bad Housekeeping*
tnam, Brooklyn Boy by Alan Lelchuk, *Eyes
a* by Lynn Stegner, *Graveyard Working* by
*lman, Opportunities in Alabama Agriculture
e Crawlspace Conspiracy* by Thomas Keech,

through major wholesalers.
cted to:

25 Beacon Street
Boston, MA 02108
617-742-2110

Beacon is primarily a publisher of nonfiction works (along with some literary fiction and poetry). Among the house's areas of publishing interest are contemporary affairs; gender, ethnic, and cultural studies; the life of the mind and spirit; history; science; and the spectrum of global and environmental concerns. The publisher also hosts a short, strong list of titles in fiction, literary essays, and poetry. The house no longer publishes children's titles. Beacon Press tenders an extensive backlist.

Beacon Press has been a light of independent American publishing since 1854, when the house was established by the Unitarian Universalist Church. The Beacon Press list is presented as a complement to corporate publishing's rapt attention to commercially correct topics and as a publishing platform for those whose search for meaning draws them to fresh points of view. Indeed, the house's estimable reputation thrives on the diversity and divergence of the ideas and stances advanced by Beacon authors.

Emblematic of Beacon's list: *Transgender Warriors: Making History from Joan of Arc to RuPaul* by Leslie Feinberg, *Meeting the Great Bliss Queen: Buddhists, Feminists, and the Art of the Self* by Anne Corolyn Klein, *Seeing and Believing: Religion and Values in the Movies* by Margaret R. Miles, *A Fire in the Bones: Reflections on African-American Religious History* by Albert J. Raboteau, *Queer Spirits: A Gay Men's Myth Book* (edited by Will Roscoe), *Fist Stick Knife Gun: A Personal History of Violence in America* by Geoffrey Canada, *Remembering the Bone House: An Erotics of Place and Space* by Nancy Mairs, *Women in the Trees: U.S. Women's Short Stories of Battering and Resistance, 1839–1994* (edited by Susan Koppelman), *Tasting Food, Tasting Freedom: Excursions into Eating, Culture, and the Past* by Sidney W. Mintz, and *Beyond Pro-Life and Pro-Choice: Moral Diversity in the Abortion Debate* by Kathy Rudy.

A scholarly highlight is Beacon's edition of the seventeenth-century classic *Lieutenant Nun: Memoir of a Transvestite in the New World* by Catalina de Erauso (translated by Michele Stepto and Gabriele Stepto; foreword by Marjorie Garber).

And please note these titles that bring the literary landscape into benevolent focus: *Ruined by Reading: A Life in Books* by Lynne Sharon Schwartz, *Facing the Lion: Writers on Life and Craft* (edited by Kurt Brown), and *Talking to Angels: A Life Spent at High Latitudes* by Robert Perkins.

Beacon Press is distributed to the trade by Farrar Straus & Giroux.

Query letters and SASEs should be directed to:

Helene Atwan, Director

Deborah Chasman, Executive Editor
Gay/lesbian studies; African-American, Jewish, and Native American studies.

Deanne Urmy, Executive Editor
Environmental and nature studies, family issues.

Andrew Hrycyna, Editor
Philosophy, politics, education.

Susan Worst, Editor
Religion, guidance.

Marya Van't Hul, Editor
Science and society; women's studies; Asian-American studies.

BEAR & COMPANY PUBLISHING
(See Directory of Religious, Spiritual, and Inspirational Publishers)

PETER BEDRICK BOOKS
2112 Broadway, Suite 318
New York, NY 10023
212-496-0751

Peter Bedrick Books was established in 1983, following the founder's long and successful association with Schocken Books. Today a midsized publishing house with a fetching swan logo, Bedrick still has a personal touch—evident from the first Bedrick list, which featured adult and children's books and introduced the initial three titles in the Library of the World's Myths and Legends, which remain in print in both hardcover and paperback editions.

Bedrick's adult list has focused on popular reference works in such areas as history, folklore and mythology, and women's studies. The children's list accents highly illustrated nonfiction, with several ongoing series in world history and cultures, including numerous educational titles. Bedrick also issues a line of children's books in cooperation with Blackie & Sons under the Bedrick/Blackie imprint.

Features from Peter Bedrick: *The Impressionists: The Origins of Modern Painting* by Francesco Salvi (illustrated by L. R. Galante and Andrea Riccardi), *The Rise of Islam* by John Child, *Demons, Gods, and Holy Men from Indian Myths and Legends* by Shahrukh Husain (illustrated by Durga Prasad Das), *What Do We Know about the Inuit?* by Brian and Cherry Alexander, and *Amazing Spacefacts* by Susan Goodman.

The Inside Story series offers fascinating titles filled with full-color cutaway illustrations and informative text. Notable entrants here include *A 16th Century Galleon* by Richard Humble with illustrations by Mark Bergin and *A Medieval Cathedral* by Fiona Macdonald with illustrations by John James.

Peter Bedrick Books handles its own sales, with distribution via Publishers Group West.

Query letters and SASEs should be directed to:

Peter Bedrick, President and Publisher

MATTHEW BENDER AND COMPANY

11 Pennsylvania Plaza
New York, NY 10001
212-967-7707

Bender produces works in the fields of law, accounting, banking, insurance, and related professions. Areas of Bender catalog concentration include general accounting, administrative law, admiralty, civil rights law, computer law, employment/labor, environmental, estate and financial planning, government, health care, immigration, insurance, intellectual property, law-office management, personal injury/medico-legal, products liability, real estate, securities, taxation, and worker's compensation.

Matthew Bender (founded in 1887), a subsidiary of Times Mirror, is a specialist publisher of professional information in print and electronic format. Bender publishes general references as well as state-specific works. Bender produces treatises, textbooks, manuals, and form books, as well as newsletters and periodicals. Many Matthew Bender publications are available in the CD-ROM format.

Representing the Bender list: *A Practical Guide to the Federal Acquisition Regulation* by Darrell J. Oyer, *Recreational Boating Law* (edited by C. Peter Theut), *The Law of Electronic Funds Transfer* by Benjamin Geva, *Collier on Bankruptcy Taxation* (edited by Lawrence P. King), *California Guide to Reporting Hazardous Releases—Rules and Procedures* by Albert M. Cohen, *Equipment Leasing* (edited by Jeffrey J. Wong), *State Constitutional Law: Litigating Individual Rights, Claims, and Defenses* by Jennifer Freisen, *Proving Criminal Defenses* (edited by Gene P. Schultz), *Drafting Employment and Termination Agreements* by Laurie E. Leader, *The Lender's Guide to Environmental Law: Risk and Liability* by Barbara Pfeffer Billauer and Margaret V. Hathaway, and *New York Intellectual Property Handbook* by Hugh C. Hansen.

Matthew Bender handles its own distribution.

Query letters and SASEs should be directed to:

Ken Halajian, Vice President, Professional Relations

BERKLEY PUBLISHING GROUP

(See Putnam Berkley Publishing Group)

BERRETT-KOEHLER PUBLISHERS

155 Montgomery Street
San Francisco, CA 94104-4109
415-288-0260

Berrett-Koehler is active in nonfiction publishing, with an accent in the areas of work and the workplace, business, management, leadership, career development, entrepreneurship, human resources, and global sustainability. Berrett-Koehler Publishers (instituted in 1992) is an independent press that produces books, periodicals, journals, newsletters, and audiocassettes.

The house aims to support the movement toward a more enlightened world of work through an approach to publishing that features innovative guidance, thought, and technique. The Berrett-Koehler booklist is produced in well-crafted, ecologically aware hardcover and softcover editions.

Representing the B-K book-publishing spectrum: *Corporate Tides: The Inescapable Laws of Organizational Structure* by Robert Fritz, *Synchronicity: The Inner Path of Leadership* by Joseph Jaworsku, *Managers As Mentors: Building Partnerships for Learning* by Chip R. Bell, *A Complaint Is a Gift: Using Customer Feedback As a Strategic Tool* by Janelle Barlow and Claus Møller, *Stewardship: Choosing Service Over Self-Interest* by Peter Block, and *Repacking Your Bags: Lighten Your Load for the Rest of Your Life* by Richard J. Leider and David A. Shapiro.

Berrett-Koehler orchestrates its own distribution through multiple channels including bookstores; direct-mail brochures; catalogs; a toll-free 800 telephone-order number; book clubs; association book services; and special sales to business, government, and nonprofit organizations. The house is distributed to the trade via Publishers Group West.

Query letters and SASEs should be directed to:

Steven Piersanti, President and Publisher

BETHANY HOUSE PUBLISHERS

(See Directory of Religious, Spiritual, and Inspirational Publishers)

BETTERWAY BOOKS
(See Writer's Digest Books)

BIRCH LANE PRESS
(See Carol Publishing Group)

BLACK SPARROW PRESS
24 Tenth Street
Santa Rosa, CA 95401
707-579-4011

Black Sparrow offers a select group of new seasonal titles in the literary zones of original poetry and prose, literary reprints, scholarly bibliography, and academic—though not necessarily scholastic in tone—literary criticism.

Black Sparrow Press (begun in 1966) is a small house with a succinct list that features some dazzling and visionary writing. The press maintains a doughty backlist of titles, featuring works by some of the most distinguished modern and contemporary writers.

Among Black Sparrow's releases: *Prodigious Thrust* (memoir) by William Everson, *Mythologies of the Heart* (poems) by Gerard Malanga, *Betting on the Muse: Poems & Stories* by Charles Bukowski, *Enchanted Men* (stories) by Thaisa Frank, and *Junkets on a Sad Planet: Scenes from the Life of John Keats* by Tom Clark.

Featured on the Black Sparrow backlist are *Chekov* (a biography in verse) by Edward Sanders, *Maxfield Parrish: Early and New Poems* by Eileen Myles, *The Emerald City of Las Vegas* (epic poetry) by Diane Wakoski, *African Sleeping Sickness* (poetry and stories) by Wanda Coleman, *According to Her Contours* (stories and poems) by Nancy Boultier, and *Bitches Ride Alone* (stories) by Laura Chester.

Black Sparrow Press handles its own distribution.

The publisher concentrates first and foremost on its established roster of authors; Black Sparrow does not wish to receive unsolicited manuscripts. Query letters and SASEs should be directed to:

John Martin, President

BLAST BOOKS
P.O. Box 51 Cooper Station
New York, NY 10276

Blast Books (established in 1989) is a small independent press with an offbeat, eclectic nonfiction list. Whatever category Blast titles fall into—or through—the house remains on the lookout for perversely compelling properties. Blast founder Ken Sweezy formerly partnered Amok Press with Adam Parfrey (now of Feral House; see separate entry).

On the Blast list: *Alone With the President* by John Strausbaugh (a canny selection of celebrity photographs with United States presidents along with accompanying documentation), *Grace Beats Karma: Letters from Prison 1958–1960* by Neal Cassady (with foreword by Carolyn Cassady), *Guillotine: Its Legend and Lore* by Daniel Gerould, *Mr. Arashi's Amazing Freak Show: A Graphic Novel* by Suehiro Maruo, and *Venus in Furs and Selected Letters* by Leopold von Sacher-Masoch (a Literary Guild pick. Features correspondence of the author with Emilie Mataja; translated by Uwe Moeller and Laura Lindgren).

Generally, Blast acquires new books through networking and personal contact with the authors; the publisher cannot recall ever having acquired a book through an unsolicited submission. In addition, Blast traditionally has not bought works through agents—primarily on account of the publisher's relatively small advances, which naturally serves to lessen an agent's interest. However, in order to stem the tide of unsolicited manuscripts, the house's stance is to accept agented manuscripts only when there does not already exist a previous relationship.

Potential Blast authors should note: If you believe you must get this publisher's attention, pay careful attention to the publisher's list and preferences, and then definitely query via *letter* and SASE *only*—rather than by sending a complete manuscript or even a proposal. Though Blast has published fictional works (primarily in reprint), the house does not wish to receive fiction submissions.

Blast Books is distributed by Publishers Group West.

Query letters and SASEs should be directed to:

Ken Sweezy, Publisher

BLUE MOON BOOKS

61 Fourth Avenue
New York, NY 10003
212-505-6880

Blue Moon's erotica includes some of the finest novels and stories in the field. Blue Moon Books also publishes selected trade fiction and nonfiction. The North Star Line offers a discriminating literary list.

Blue Moon Books was established in 1987 by Barney Rosset, the trailblazing publisher who earlier founded Grove Press and developed that enterprise into a house of international literary, cultural, and commercial renown.

Blue Moon/North Star highlights: *Goa Freaks: My Hippie Years in India* by Cleo Odzer, *Brazen* by Ghislaine Dunant (translated by Rosette Lamont), *The Mad Club* (in a new edition) by Michael McClure, and *Seventeen (The Political Being) and J (The Sexual Being)* (two novellas) by Kenzaburo Oe.

In addition to classical fervid romances, Blue Moon offers erotic works with contemporary themes such as psychosexual suspense thrillers. The house also offers a significant listing of erotic fiction by women.

Blue Moon's erotic fiction embraces works such as *A Brief Education* by Denise Hall, *Sundancer* by Briony Shilton, *Shades of Singapore* by Angus Balfour, *The Afternoons of a Woman of Leisure* by Elizabeth Bennett, *The Love Run* by Jay Parini, *What Love* by Maria Madison, *Birch Fever* by Martin Pyx, *Fantasy Line* by Michelle St. John, and *Mistress of Instruction* by Christine Kerr.

Blue Moon Books oversees its own distribution.

North Star Line

The North Star Line has produced volumes of fine writing in both hardcover and paperback. North Star hosts literary anthologies, poetic works, and short and long fiction, as well as general trade titles.

On the North Star list: *Stirrings Still* by Samuel Beckett, *The Man Sitting in the Corridor* by Marguerite Duras, *The Correct Sadist* by Terence Sellers, *Lament: A Novel about How the West Was Blown* by David (Sunset) Carson, *The Ghost Ship* (poems) by Henry Hart, *Triangulation from a Known Point* by Ruth Danon, *New and Selected Poems 1930–1990* by Richard Eberhart, *The Colors of Infinity* by Donald E. Axinn, and *Two Dogs and Freedom: The Open School in Soweto* (schoolchildren from South Africa's Open School speak out).

A North Star Line highlight is the republished set of classics *The Olympia Reader* and *The New Olympia Reader*. These volumes are filled with ribald and erotic writings first published in Paris by the germinal publisher of Olympia Press, Maurice Girodias. They feature the work of authors like Jean Genet, Henry Miller, Chester Himes, Lawrence Durrell, William S. Burroughs, Gregory Corso, George Bataille, John Cleland, Pauline Réage, Samuel Beckett, and the Marquis de Sade. Publisher Barney Rosset, along with associates, has edited *Evergreen Review Reader 1957–1966*, featuring selections from *Evergreen*, America's fabled journal of literary provocateurism.

Query letters and SASEs should be directed to:

Barney Rosset, President

Louella DiZon, Editorial Coordinator

Bonus Books, Inc.
160 East Illinois Street
Chicago, IL 60611
312-467-0580

Bonus produces a strong list of general nonfiction, including titles in sports, gambling, automotive, broadcasting, business and careers, collectibles, consumer, legal, self-help, humor and nostalgia, health and fitness, cooking, autobiography and biography, books of regional interest (including the Chicago area), and current affairs. Precept Press titles are written by and for fund-raising professionals and physicians.

Bonus Books, Inc. (founded in 1985) had an original focus on sports titles and grew quickly into a trade book publisher with nationwide prominence. Strong Bonus growth categories have been sports books and gambling books. As remarked in a letter to booksellers from Bonus publisher Aaron Cohodes: "I don't know what this says about our society, but perhaps that's just as well."

Highlights from Bonus include *Best Blackjack* by Frank Scoblete, *Silver Linings* by Herschell Gordon Lewis, *Buttermilk Cookbook: The Rest of the Carton* by Susan Costello and Anna Heller, *Selling Your Valuables* by Jeanne Siegel, *Sampras: A Legend in the Works* by H. A. Branham, *Woulda, Coulda, Shoulda* (new expanded edition) by Dave Feldman with Frank Sugano, *Do Well by Doing Good* by Keith E. Gregg, and *Handbook of Commonly Used Chemotherapy Regimens* (edited by F. Anthony Greco).

Bonus's watershed title, *Ditka: An Autobiography* by Mike Ditka with Don Pierson, remains in print on a sturdy backlist. Other Bonus backlist favorites: *Overlay: How to Bet Horses Like a Pro* by Bill Heller, *Break the One-Armed Bandits: How to Come Out When You Play the Slots* by Frank Scoblete, *101 Ways to Make Money in the Trading-Card Market Right Now!* by Paul Green and Kit Kiefer, *Settle It Yourself: When You Need a Lawyer—and When You Don't* by Fred Benjamin and Dorothea Kaplan, and *Quarterblack: Shattering the NFL Myth* by Doug Williams with Bruce Hunter.

Bonus Books distributes its own list and utilizes a number of national sales representatives.

Query letters and SASEs should be directed to:

Aaron Cohodes, President and Publisher

Aili Bresnahow, Assistant Editor

Deborah Flapow, Managing Editor

THE BOOTSTRAP PRESS
(See listing for The Apex Press)

MARION BOYARS PUBLISHING
237 East 39th Street
New York, NY 10016
212-697-1599

The Marion Boyars publishing program gives preeminence to fine writing, considering the highest level of expression in virtually any category. Areas of particular Marion Boyars accomplishment are in the fields of fiction, poetry, belles lettres, memoirs, literary criticism, biography, music, theater, sociology, and travel.

Marion Boyars Publishing (founded in 1978) has achieved international renown and commercial presence in letters with an individualist precision and personalized disposition. Marion Boyars releases a medium-sized seasonal list; the house tends a strong backlist.

Though not technically a United States publishing house (projects emanate editorially from the London base), Boyars presents writers whose works may have more of an international appeal than a strictly commercial American flavor. The publisher acquires on the basis of enthusiasm for a given work—which is not necessarily based on projections of huge initial sales. Indeed, Marion Boyars herself has remarked that overlooked books and translations are often the house's jewels.

A representative coup is the English-language publication of *Nip the Buds, Shoot the Kids* by Nobel laureate Kenzaburo Oe.

Marion Boyars Publishing is distributed by Rizzoli International.

Query letters and SASEs should be directed to:

(Ms.) Marion Boyars, President, Editor in Chief
Marion Boyars Publishing
24 Lacy Road
London SW15 INL, England, U.K.

BOYDS MILLS PRESS

910 Church Street
Honesdale, PA 18431
717-253-1164

Boyds Mills offers storybooks, picture books, rhyming books, craft books, gamebooks, posters, and poetry—nonsensical verse as well as more serious fare. The press produces a solid seasonal list and hosts a hefty backlist. Boyds Mills Press (founded in 1990) is a subsidiary of Highlights for Children. From its headquarters in the mountains of Pennsylvania, this house issues books for children of all ages.

Boyds Mills wants books that challenge, inspire, and entertain young people the world over. Boyds Mills has published such international best-sellers as *Dougal Dixon's Dinosaurs* (over a dozen editions in ten languages, plus multivolume spinoffs). Among Boyds Mills authors is the award-winning writer Jane Yolen, whose books from Boyds Mills include *Sleep Rhymes Around the World* and *An Invitation to the Butterfly Ball*.

On the Boyds Mills Press list: *I Don't Want to Go to Camp* by Eve Bunting (illustrated by Maryann Cocca-Leffler), *Taking Care of the Earth: Kids in Action* by

Laurence Pringle (illustrated by Bobbie Moore), *Leah's Pony* by Elizabeth Friedrich (illustrated by Michael Garland), *Mother Earth, Father Sky: Poems of Our Planet* (selected by Jane Yolen; illustrations by Jennifer Hewitson), *Baseball, Snakes, and Summer Squash: Poems about Growing Up* by Donald Graves, *The Hidden Picture Book of Aesop's Fables* (retold by Christine San José; illustrated by Charles Jordan), *Puppet and Theater Activities: Theatrical Things to Do and Make* (edited by Beth Murray; illustrated by Anni Matsick), and *The Distant Talking Drum: Poems from Nigeria* by Isaac Olaleye (paintings by Frané Lessac).

Boyds Mills Press handles its own distribution.

Query letters and SASEs should be directed to:

Kent L. Brown Jr., Publisher

Clay Winters, President

GEORGE BRAZILLER, INC.

60 Madison Avenue
New York, NY 10010
212-889-0909

George Braziller (founded in 1955) is known for fine books in art and architecture. George Braziller also publishes literary works, philosophy, science, history, and biographical works. The house hosts a solid backlist.

Much of Braziller's fiction is foreign literature in translation, although the publisher does publish original literary novels (such as works by Janet Frame), and works in the English language that have received initial publication elsewhere. Braziller also has a strong interest in literary criticism and writing relating to the arts, in addition to a noteworthy list of contemporary poetry. Braziller markets the series Essential Readings in Black Literature featuring world-class writers from around the globe. Other Braziller series include Library of Far Eastern Art and New Directions in Architecture.

On the Braziller list: *The Future Eaters: An Ecological History of the Australasian Lands and People* by Timothy Flannery, *Celtic Goddesses: Warriors, Virgins, and Mothers* by Miranda Green, *Samuel Beckett* (photographs by John Minihan; introduction by Aidan Higgins), *Annibale Carracci: The Farnese Palace, Rome* by Charles Dempsey, *Constructivism: Origins and Evolution* by George Rickey, *Georgia O'Keefe: Canyon Suite* by Barbara J. Bloeink, and *Multiples: From Duchamp to the Present* (edited by Zdenek Felix).

Braziller fiction and literary works: *Poetry of the American Renaissance* (edited by Paul Kane), *The First Century after Beatrice* (novel) by Amin Malouf, *The Game in Reverse: Poems and Essays* by Taslima Nasrin, and *Papa's Suitcase* (a comic tale) by Gerhard Köpf.

Braziller handles its own distribution, as well as that of Persea Books and Persea's imprint Ontario Review Press.

Query letters and SASEs should be directed to:

Adrienne Baxter, Fine Arts Editor
Fine arts.

George Braziller, Publisher
All areas consistent with publisher description.

BROADMAN PRESS

(See Directory of Religious, Spiritual, and Inspirational Publishers)

BRUNNER/MAZEL

19 Union Square West
New York, NY 10003
212-924-3344

Brunner/Mazel's publishing scope includes such fields as psychology, psychiatry, psychotherapy, psychoanalysis, neurology, social work, special education, child development, couples, marriage, family therapy, and group therapy.

Brunner/Mazel (instituted in 1945) publishes primarily for a professional market. The house also offers a number of titles geared toward general readers. Brunner/Mazel publishes a juveniles line, highlighting the publisher's pertinent topic areas, as well as a limited number of gift books. The house maintains a comprehensive backlist.

The publishing program at Brunner/Mazel keeps abreast of developments in this active professional sector; the house has frontlisted titles in fields of family therapy, child sexual abuse, sex therapy, self-psychology, stress and trauma, substance abuse, eating disorders, hypnosis, art therapy, and parenting.

Representative Brunner/Mazel projects: *Acting for Real: Drama Therapy Process, Technique, and Performance* by Renee Emunha; *Aging into the 21st Century: The Exploration of Aspirations and Values* by Rachelle A. Dorfman; *Eating Disorders and Marriage: The Couple in Focus* by D. Blake Woodside, Lorie Shekter-Wolfson, Jack S. Brandes, and Jan B. Lackstrom; *Family Therapy: Fundamentals of Theory and Practice* by William A. Griffin; *Magazine Photo Collage: A Multicultural Assessment and Treatment Technique* by Helen B. Landgarten; *Self-Hypnosis: The Complete Manual for Health and Self-Change* by Brian M. Alman and Peter D. Lambrou; *Sex, Priests, and Power: Anatomy of a Crisis* by A. W. Richard Sipe; *The Illustrated Manual of Sex Therapy* by Helen Singer Kaplan; *Therapists Who Have Sex with Their Patients* by Herbert S. Strean; and *Vampires, Werewolves, and Demons: Twentieth-Century Reports in the Psychiatric Literature* by Richard Noll.

Magination Press is an imprint for books that help parents help their children. Titles here are *Luna and the Big Blur: A Story for Children Who Wear Glasses* by Shirley

Day (illustrated by Don Morris), *You Can Call Me Willy: A Story for Children about AIDS* by Joan C. Verniero (illustrated by Verdon Flory), and *Proud of Our Feelings* by Lindsay Leghorn.

Brunner/Mazel oversees its own distribution services, including a strong mail-order operation directed toward the professional market; the publisher's books may also be ordered through Publishers Group West.

Query letters and SASEs should be directed to:

Natalie Gilman, Editorial Vice President
Psychology, behavioral sciences, hypnosis, family therapy, psychoanalysis, psychiatry, child and adolescent development, eating disorders, marriage and family therapy, sex therapy, and related fields.

Suzi Tucker, Senior Editor

BULFINCH PRESS
(See Little, Brown)

BUSINESS ONE IRWIN
(See Irwin Professional Publishing)

BUTTERWORTH-HEINEMANN
(See listing for Heinemann)

CAMBRIDGE UNIVERSITY PRESS
(See Directory of University Presses)

CAPRA PRESS
P.O. Box 2068
Santa Barbara, CA 93210
805-966-4590

The Capra list presents topflight nonfiction and contemporary literary fiction. Noteworthy Capra concentration is found in art and architecture, letters, mysteries, travel and American regional, natural history, and specialty items including postcard series.

Capra Press (founded in 1970) is a small house with a highly select catalog of titles for the general trade. Capra's respected mountain goat colophon mascot was initially representative of fine books on the American West. The Capra interest has since expanded, and the current backlist features a solid assortment of the house's own originals as well as literary works in reprint.

Representing the Capra Press general nonfiction list: *Fitness Lite: A Guide for Those Who Have Never Taken Fitness Seriously* by William Burleigh (illustrated by Shell Fisher), *Seeing Europe Again: Secrets from a First-World Traveler* by Elaine Kendall, *Great Hot Springs of the West* by Bill Kaysing, *How to Protect Your Heart from Your Doctor* by Howard Wayne, and *In Praise of Wine: An Offering of Hearty Toasts, Quotations, Witticisms, Poetry and Proverbs Throughout History* (edited by Joni McNutt).

Cultural and literary works include: *Art & Fear: Observations on the Perils (and Rewards) of Artmaking* by David Bayles and Ted Orland, *Edna's Nudes: A Celebration of the Photography of Edna Bullock* (text by Barbara Bullock-Wilson and Karen Sinsheimer), *Robert Stacy-Judd: Maya Architecture, the Creation of a New Style* (text by David Gebhard and photography by Anthony Peres), *Portable Kisses: Love Poems* by Tess Gallagher, *Short Cuts: The Screenplay* by Robert Altman and Frank Barhydt, *The Mystic of Sex: Uncollected Writings, 1930–1974* by Anaïs Nin, and *Wolverine Creates the World: Labrador Indian Tales* by Lawrence Millman.

The Capra imprint Perseverance Press focuses on mystery and suspense fiction, often with a West Coast twist. Capra Western Classics series offers such titles as *The Happy Man: A Novel of California Ranch Life* by Robert Easton. Capra also publishes a roster of cat books, crossword puzzle collections, and books of Santa Barbara regional focus.

Capra Press titles are distributed to the book trade by Consortium Book Sales and Distribution. Titles are also available to individuals via mail order.

Query letters and SASEs should be directed to:

Noel Young, President

CAREER PRESS

3 Tice Road
P.O. Box 687
Franklin Lakes, NJ 07417
201-848-0310

With its reputation established as a hard-driving, entrepreneurial business and financial publisher, Career Press currently offers an expanded program that features a wide variety of titles in such fields as business and financial how-to, small business operation, financial planning, retirement, and general nonfiction (where the list includes lifestyle, recreation, parenting, and popular reference). The publisher also produces specialty educational titles (including study series). Career tends a select, fast-moving backlist.

Career Press (founded in 1985) originally secured a publishing niche for its career-related titles with a short list of practical business books for the professional market (career planning, job search, how-to résumé and interview books).

The staunch Career Press product line is no accident. The house promotes aggressively and resourcefully, and prompts booksellers with titles geared to receive major review attention; national print, radio, and TV exposure; and radio phone-in shows nationwide.

Representative Career Press titles in business, careers, and finance (including backlist highlights and updated editions): *Get Rich Slow* by Tama McAleese, *Superstar Sales Secrets* by Barry J. Farber, *50 Powerful Ideas You Can Use to Keep Your Customers* by Paul R. Timm, *CyberPower for Business: How to Profit from the Information Superhighway* by Walter H. Bock and Jeff Senne, *The Dolphin Dynamic: Make a Splash in Today's Shark-Infested Business Waters* by Laura Laaman with Lilly Walters, *Hiring: More Than a Gut Feeling* by Richard S. Deems, *Business Letters for Busy People* by Jim Dugger, *The Smart Woman's Guide to Interviewing and Salary Negotiation* by Julie Adair King, *Fast Cash for Kids* by Bonnie and Noel Drew, *Our Emperors Have No Clothes* by Alan Weiss, *Warning: Dying May Be Hazardous to Your Wealth* by Adriane Berg, and *Win the Value Revolution* by Robert B. Tucker.

A Career Press frontlist favorite has been *Roger Dawson's Secrets of Power Negotiating*, a hardcover book version of the best-selling Nightingale-Conant audio series by Roger Dawson. One of Career's perennial sellers is a two-volume business-reference hardback edition of the United States government's reference tome *Dictionary of Occupational Titles*.

In the general nonfiction area, including health and fitness, lifestyle and recreation, and popular reference, Career offers: *The Best Wedding Ever* by Diane Warner, *The Silva Method: Think and Grow Fit* by José Silva with Ed Bernd Jr., *Alternative Healing: Nontraditional Therapies* by Arnold Fox and Barry Fox, and *50 Fabulous Places to Retire in America* by Lee and Saralee Rosenberg.

Career Press distributes its own list.

Query letters and SASEs should be directed to:

Ronald Fry, President

CAROL PUBLISHING GROUP
122 East 42nd Street
New York, NY 10168
212-557-3300

Editorial offices:
120 Enterprise Avenue
Secaucus, NJ 07094
201-866-0490

The Carol list covers essentially all popular trade nonfiction categories. Among the several Carol imprints, Birch Lane Press highlights general trade nonfiction (and occasional lead fiction), and Citadel Press accents film, popular culture, and titles in self-awareness/improvement. The Carol Publishing Group publishes hardcover books, as well as trade and mass-market paperbacks.

Carol is a large independent publisher that comprises a number of lines, with Birch Lane Press the featured frontlist imprint. Many Carol/Birch Lane books veer toward the provocative—some are intentionally controversial—and authors with this sort of publicity edge are prime candidates for publication opportunities.

Carol Publishing Group was established in 1989 when Steven Schragis acquired several formerly independent presses, including Citadel Press, University Books, and the publishing house Lyle Stuart.

Citadel was (and remains) the second largest publisher of entertainment books in the country. The Lyle Stuart list represents a high reputation for hard-hitting, serious commercial vehicles with lively sales potential in areas of topical interest eminently appropriate for talkshow debate, a tradition in which Carol participates. Citadel Stars is an imprint created for books that pertain to trends and personalities of the mass-media arena.

Though Carol has successfully produced commercial fiction—often positioned to tap into current topics within a novelistic framework or to tie in with a celebrity-author—at this point Carol publishes virtually no fiction.

Indicative of the Carol list: *The Titanic Conspiracy: Cover-Ups and Mysteries of the World's Most Famous Sea Disaster* by Robin Gardiner and Dan Van Der Vat, *Little Girl Lost: The Troubled Childhood of Princess Diana by the Woman Who Raised Her* by Mary Clark, *Jodie Foster: A Life On Screen* by Philippa Kennedy, *The Woman in the White House: The Remarkable Story of Hillary Rodham Clinton* by Norman King, *Do We Need another Baby? Helping Your Child Welcome a New Arrival—with Love and Illustrations* by Cynthia MacGregor (illustrated by David Roth), and *The Man in the Red Velvet Dress: Inside the World of Cross-Dressing* by J. J. Allen.

Highlights from the Carol backlist: *Liz: An Intimate Biography of Elizabeth Taylor* by C. David Heymann; *Wannabe: A Would-Be Player's Misadventures in Hollywood* by Everett Weinberger; *Continue Laughing* (a novel) by Carl Reiner; *The Hispanic Cookbook: Traditional and Modern Recipes in English and Spanish* by Nilda Luz Rexach; *Total Exposure: The Movie Buff's Guide to Celebrity Nude Scenes* by Jami Bernard; and *The Psychedelic Experience: A Manual Based on the Tibetan Book of the Dead* by Timothy Leary, Ralph Metzner, and Richard Alpert.

Carol Publishing Group distributes its own list domestically, as well as handling titles from Dr. Who, Gambling Times Books, High-Top Sports Audio, the National Hemlock Society, and Virgin Publishing. International sales are handled by a worldwide network of regional representatives.

All Carol editors acquire in the following areas: popular culture, business, current events, biography, history, controversial subjects, and entertainment. Listed below are editors with specific or additional individual interests.

Query letters and SASEs should be sent to the New Jersey editorial address. Project submissions from agents, as well as query letters and SASEs, should be directed to:

Hillel Black, Editor in Chief
General nonfiction, celebrity fiction, current affairs, history, biography, popular culture, music, film.

Jim Ellison, Editor
Popular culture, film, entertainment, current affairs, parenting.

Marcy Swingle, Associate Editor
Biography, pop culture, music, film, general nonfiction.

Alan Wilson, Executive Editor
Fiction: mainstream. Nonfiction: biography, books about film.

CARROLL & GRAF PUBLISHERS

260 Fifth Avenue
New York, NY 10001
212-889-8772

Carroll & Graf publishes general trade nonfiction and literary and commercial fiction (including a strong list in mystery and suspense).

Carroll & Graf (founded in 1983) is a compact house with a list as select and well targeted as it is diverse. In addition to its original titles, Carroll & Graf reprints American classics and foreign literature in translation, issues a full raft of genre-specific anthologies, and offers a topflight lineup of erotic literature. The house publishes hardcover, trade paper, and mass-market paperback editions.

Carroll & Graf nonfiction covers issues-oriented journalistic perspectives (including true crime), business, contemporary culture, and current events, as well as self-improvement, humor, and high-interest topical reference.

In nonfiction, Carrol & Graf lists: *My Real Name Is Lisa* by David Alexander, *Genius and Lust: The Creative and Sexual Lives of Cole Porter and Noel Coward* by Joseph Morella and George Mazzei, *Love at Second Sight: Strange Romantic Encounters* by Paul McLaughlin, *Men Are from Heaven, Women Are from Hell: And Other Misconceptions about Human Behavior* by Gary Null, *Mind Control and the Assassination of President Kennedy* by Dick Russell, *The Letterman Wit: His Life and Humor* by Bill Adler, *The Machiavellian's Guide to Womanizing* by Nick Casanova, and *Outposts: A Catalog of Rare and Disturbing Information* by Russ Kick.

In fiction and the literary arts, Carroll & Graf produces mainstream novels, tales of the supernatural, fantasy, and science fiction, and is particularly adventuresome in suspense categories, publishing an array of titles that runs from traditional mysteries to future-horror crime thrillers with a literary bent.

Highlights in fiction and literature from Carroll & Graf: *Dead Man Falling* by Randall Silvis, *Sentinels* by Bill Pronzini, *The Mammoth Book of Pulp Fiction* (edited by Maxim Jakubowski), *The Nightmare Factory* (stories) by Thomas Ligotti, *Grave Doubt* by Michael Allegretto, *Bad Dreams* by Kim Newman, *Louisiana Purchase* by A. E. Hotchner, *A Dead Man in Deptford* by Anthony Burgess, *Black Hornet* by James Sallis (author of *Long-Legged Fly* and *Moth*), *Murder Live at Five* by David Debin, and *The Tiger in the Smoke* by Margery Allingham.

Works with an amatory inclination include: *Erotica III: An Illustrated Anthology of Sexual Art and Literature* (edited by Charlotte Hill and William Wallace), *Love's Theater* (edited by Esther Selsden), *The Pleasures of Jessicalynn* by Joan Elizabeth Lloyd, and *Tart Tales: Elegant Erotic Stories* by Carolyn Banks.

Carroll & Graf books are distributed to the trade by Publishers Group West (which owns 20 percent of Carroll & Graf).

Query letters and SASEs should be directed to:

Kent Carroll, Publisher and Executive Editor

CATBIRD PRESS
GARRIGUE BOOKS

16 Windsor Road
North Haven, CT 06473
800-360-2391

Catbird Press (founded in 1987), along with its Garrigue Books imprint, is a small publisher with specialties in the areas of citizen-action reference, American fiction, general humor, travel humor, legal humor, and Central European literature.

Fiction and humor: *Human Resources: A Corporate Nightmare* (fiction) by Floyd Kemske, *I'm Right Here, Fish-Cake* (humor) by Jeffrey Shaffer, *The Four Arrows Fe-as-ko* (fiction) by Randall Beth Platt, *Was That a Tax Lawyer Who Just Flew Over? From Outside the Offices of Fairweather, Winters & Sommers* (fiction/humor) by Arnold B. Kanter, and *Trials and Tribulations: Appealing Legal Humor* (edited by Daniel R. White).

Nonfiction includes: *Jewish Voices, German Words: Growing Up Jewish in Postwar Germany and Austria* (edited by Elena Lapin), *Talks with T. G. Masaryk* (biography) by Karel Capek (translated and edited by Michael Henry Heim), and *The Giver's Guide: Making Your Charity Dollars Count* by Philip English Mackey.

This house is emblematic of small-press savvy in its pursuit of publicity and promotion: Catbird was among the first presses to post selected novels-in-progress via the electronic Online Bookstore.

Catbird Press and Garrigue Books are distributed to the trade by Independent Publishers Group.

Query letters and SASEs should be directed to:

Robert Wechsler, Publisher

Christine C. Schmitt, Promotion and Marketing Director

CELESTIAL ARTS

(See Ten Speed Press/Celestial Arts)

CHAPMAN AND HALL

One Penn Plaza
41st Floor
New York, NY 10019
212-254-3232

Chapman and Hall is an academic-science publisher that produces professional, technical, and reference titles in a variety of fields. C&H subject areas include medicine, life sciences, chemistry, earth science, food science and technology, statistics, mathematics, computer science, and engineering. A former division of Routledge and Chapman and Hall, this house is currently an independent firm. (Please see entry for Routledge, Inc. in this directory.)

Query letters and SASEs should be directed to:

(Ms.) Dana Dreibelbis, President
Medical.

Margaret Cummins, Acquisitions Editor
Engineering.

Lauren Enk, Associate Editor
Medical.

Henry Flesh, Projects Editor
Life sciences.

Dean Smith, Publisher, New Business and Media

Tracy Tucker, Editor
Medical.

Joanna Turtletaub, Associate Editor
Food science and technology.

CHAPTERS PUBLISHING

2031 Shelburne Road
Shelburne, VT 05482
802-985-8700

Chapters Publishing specializes in the fields of cooking and nutrition, health and fitness, gardening, nature, country living, and home and family. The house offers a line of calendars with themes linked to its overall publishing interests. Chapters features excellent book design and top-quality paper and binding.

Chapters Publishing (founded in 1991) is a compact, bustling enterprise. The house publishes a limited number of new titles each season and tends toward larger print runs; many Chapters titles enjoy sales through established book clubs. The house's advances are generally comparable with those of major publishers.

From Chapters: *Fresh & Fast: Inspired Cooking for Every Season and Every Day* by Marie Simmons, *Lean and Lovin' It: Exceptionally Delicious Recipes for Low-Fat Living and Permanent Weight Loss* by Don Mauer, *Help! My Apartment Has a Kitchen Cookbook: 100+ Great Recipes with Foolproof Instructions* by Kevin Mills and Nancy Mills, *How to Spot Hawks & Eagles* by Clay and Patricia Sutton, *The Basement Book: Upstairs Downstairs—Reclaiming the Wasted Space in Your Basement* by Tom Carpenter and Jeff Taylor, and *Landscaping with Native Trees* (Northeast, Midwest, Midsouth, and Southeast editions) by Guy Sternberg and Jim Wilson.

A major trade-publishing program is the nature/ecology Curious Naturalist series, which has highlighted such writers as Peter Mathiessen, R. D. Lawrence, Adrian Forsyth, and Sy Montgomery in handsome trade paperback editions.

From the Curious Naturalist series: *A Natural History of Sex: The Ecology and Evolution of Mating Behavior* by Adrian Forsyth, *Birds of Tropical America* by Steven J. Hilty, *Nature's Everyday Mysteries: A Field Guide to the World in Your Backyard* by Sy Montgomery, *Shark! Nature's Masterpiece* by R. D. Lawrence, and *The Wind Birds: Shorebirds of North America* by Peter Mathiessen.

Chapters is distributed by W. W. Norton; Canadian distribution is handled by Key Porter Books.

Query letters and SASEs should be directed to:

James Lawrence, Publisher

Barry Estabrook, Editor in Chief

Russ Martin, Senior Editor

Sandy Taylor, Consulting Editor

Cristen Brooks, Acquisitions Editor

CHELSEA GREEN PUBLISHING COMPANY

205 Gates-Briggs Building
White River Junction, VT 05001
802-295-6300

Chelsea Green publishes adult trade nonfiction in natural gardening and food, energy/shelter, nature and the environment, and regional books (including travel, social issues, and history and culture). Chelsea Green projects include a publishing coventure with Real Goods Trading Company, designated by the imprimatur Real Goods Independent Living Book. Chelsea Green also issues titles geared to children's activities.

Chelsea Green Publishing Company (founded in 1984) is a compact, independent firm, of individualistic spirit, that continues to hone its publishing program through a small number of new seasonal releases (in hardcover and trade paper formats) and by maintaining a hardy backlist.

On the Chelsea Green list: *A Patch of Eden: America's Inner-City Gardeners* by H. Patricia Hynes; *The Rammed Earth House: Rediscovering the Most Ancient Building Material* by David Easton (photographs by Cynthia Wright); *Baba á Louis Bakery Bread Book: The Secret Book of the Bread* by John McLure; *In the Northern Forest* by David Dobbs and Richard Ober; *The Safari Companion: A Guide to Watching African Mammals* by Richard D. Estes (illustrated by Daniel Otte); and *Beyond the Limits: Confronting Global Collapse, Envisioning a Sustainable Future* by Donella H. Meadows, Dennis L. Meadows, and Jørgen Randers.

Chelsea Green handles its own distribution, and distributes for the Canadian publisher Nimbus (books and calendars), as well as NatureSound Studios (environmental booklet/audiocassette packets), and other small, innovative independent presses such as Orwell Cove, OttoGraphics, Ecological Design Press, Harmonious Press, and Seed Savers Exchange.

Query letters and SASEs should be directed to:

Ian Baldwin Jr., President, Cofounder

Stephen Morris, Publisher

Jim Schley, Editor in Chief

Donella Meadows, Consulting Editor

Noel Perrin, Consulting Editor

Michael Potts, Consulting Editor

Joni Praded, Consulting Editor

Ben Watson, Consulting Editor

CHELSEA HOUSE PUBLISHERS

1974 Sproul Road, Suite 400
Broomall, PA 19008
800-848-2665

Chelsea House (founded in 1967) is an established publisher of books for older children and young adults. Chelsea House Publishers was originally instituted as a small press (located in New York City) devoted to trade and reference titles on American history and popular culture. The company was bought in 1983 by Main Line Book Company, a library distributor based in suburban Philadelphia—whereupon the house's emphasis turned toward nonfiction for a young-adult readership.

Books on the Chelsea House list are most often produced in library-bound hardcover volumes, with some titles offered in trade paperback editions. The Chelsea House program accents the educational and institutional market in history, young-adult fiction and nonfiction, reference works, and literary criticism, as well as some works of broader appeal.

The Chelsea House horizon encompasses biography, culture, and history (American and worldwide). The editorial focus is on developmental marketing of series such as the Asian-American Experience, Folk Tales and Fables, the Immigrant Experience, Issues in Gay and Lesbian Life, Lives of the Physically Challenged, Milestones in Black American History, Mysterious Places, Pop Culture Legends, Science Discoveries, Sports Legends, and different series of theme-oriented fiction.

Chelsea House distributes its own books and is particularly strong in the library and institutional market.

Chelsea House is moving through a transitional phase, and editorial address and contacts should be checked before submitting publishing projects for consideration. Administrative and warehousing facilities are currently located in the Philadelphia area.

Query letters and SASEs should be directed to:

Rick Rennert, Editor in Chief

CHILTON BOOK COMPANY

One Chilton Way
Radnor, PA 19089
610-964-4743

Chilton Book Company (founded in 1968), a subsidiary of Capital Cities/ABC, is a large publisher of trade books with a concentration in the areas of antiques, collectibles, sewing, ceramics, and crafts and hobbies, as well as technical (such as engineering) and automotive topics. Chilton series include Contemporary Quilting, Creative Machine Arts, and consumer/trade titles that list current market values (usually in periodically updated editions).

Chilton offers *Warman's Antiques and Their Prices* by Harry L. Rinker, *Collecting Carnival Glass: A Wallace-Homestead Price Guide* by Marion Quentin-Baxendale, *Art for All: How to Buy Fine Art for Under $300* by Alan S. Bamberger, *Daddy's Ties* by Shirley Botsford, *Scenery for Model Railroads, Dioramas, and Miniatures* by Robert Schleicher, *Subaru 1970–1984, Exotic Beads* by Sara Withers, and *Working Safe: How to Change Behaviors and Attitudes* by E. Scott Geller.

Chilton Book Company distributes its own list via a network of regional sales representatives.

Query letters and SASEs should be directed to:

Kerry Freeman, Publisher and Editor in Chief, Automotive Division

Susan Clarey, Acquisitions Editor

Mary Green, Acquisitions Editor

CHRONICLE BOOKS

Address after December 1, 1996:
85 Second Street
San Francisco, CA 94105

Address through November, 1996:
275 Fifth Street
San Francisco, CA 94103
415-777-7240

Chronicle's areas of interest include architecture and fine arts, design, photography, history and popular culture, travel and the outdoors (including nationwide regional guides), lifestyle (cuisine, pets, travel, home, and family), related business titles, and sports. The house issues a separate catalog for its children's books and for the GiftWorks list.

Chronicle Books (founded in 1966) was initially best known for its glossy hardcover series of illustrated theme cookbooks. Since that early era Chronicle has gradually ventured further afield and currently publishes general nonfiction in both hardback and paperback. Chronicle Books also publishes selected fiction.

The Chronicle backlist features many selections of California regional interest (food, architecture, outdoors), with a focus on San Francisco and the Bay Area in particular. The publisher has grown more expansive in its regional scope: Chronicle is open to an increasing variety of titles keyed to areas and travel destinations worldwide. Chronicle scored major best-seller hits with Nick Bantock's Griffin & Sabine fiction trilogy: *Griffin & Sabine*, *Sabine's Notebook*, and *The Golden Mean*.

Representative Chronicle titles: *On the Edge of Magic: Petroglyphs and Rock Paintings of the Ancient Southwest* by Salvatore Mancini, *The Blues: Album Cover Art* (edited by Graham Marsh and Barrie Lewis), *Freak Show: Sideshow Banner Art* by Carl Hammer and Gideon Bosker, *The Secret Life of the Stars and Planets: A Visual Key to the Heavens* by Geoffrey Cornelius, *Yiddish Wisdom: In Yiddish and English* (collected and illustrated by Kristina Swarner), *Festive Tarts: Splendid Fare for Fun and Fanciful Occasions* by Sylvia Thompson (illustrated by Brooke Scudder), *Eternal Mexico* by Robert Frerck, and *The Mediterranean Cat* by Hans Silvester.

Literary projects include *Dancer with Bruised Knees* (novel) by Lynne McFall, *Lies of the Saints* (stories) by Erin McGraw, *Texas Stories: Tales from the Lone Star State* (edited by John and Kirsten Miller), and *White Rabbit: A Psychedelic Reader* (edited by John Miller and Randall Koral).

CHRONICLE CHILDREN'S BOOKS

Chronicle's children's lineup has a reputation for high quality and innovation in traditional and not-so-traditional formats. From the Chronicle children's list: *Honey Paw and Lightfoot* by Jonathan London (illustrated by Jon Van Zyle), *Eye Count: A Book of Counting Puzzles* by Linda Bourke, *The Great Bird Detective* by David Elcome (illustrations by John Cox and Spike Gerrell), *Bears at Work: A Book of Bearable Jobs* by Gage Taylor, and *Tyrannosaurus Rex: The Tyrant King* (a pop-up book) by John Sibbick.

Chronicle distributes its own publications.

Query letters and SASEs should be directed to:

Annie Barrows, Editor
All publisher's described areas, with special interest in art, illustrated, and photography books.

Christine Carswell, Executive Editor and Associate Publisher
All publisher's described areas.

Caroline Herter, Associate Publisher
Illustrated and visual books. GiftWorks.

Bill LeBlond, Senior Editor and Cookbook Editor
Acquires in all publisher's described areas, with special interest in cookbooks and design books (all book types).

(Mr.) Nion McEvoy, Editor in Chief and Associate Publisher
All publisher's described areas, with special interest in New Age, business, and multimedia books.

Victoria Rock, Director, Children's Books, and Associate Publisher
Children's books.

Jay Schaefer, Senior Editor, Fiction
Send complete manuscript, synopsis, and SASE. No queries, please.

Karen Silver, Associate Editor
All publisher's described areas, with special interest in regional books.

CHRONIMED PUBLISHING

Ridgedale Office Center, Suite 250
13911 Ridgedale Drive
Minneapolis, MN 55343
612-541-0239

Chronimed catalogs such topic areas as nutrition, healthful cookbooks, health, parent-ing, general health, chronic health challenges, transplants, psychology, fitness, diabetes, and health resources and professional needs. The publisher also offers health-education videos, slides, and cassettes.

Chronimed Publishing (formerly known as DCI Publishing) was founded in 1985 as a publishing division of Diabetes Institute, Inc. The house trade banner runs: "The best in health, wellness, and nutrition." Chronimed Publishing is dedicated to new life-enhancing, breakthrough titles on a wealth of health topics—from self-improvement to fitness, healthy eating, and coping with a chronic illness.

Representative titles: *Taking the Work Out of Working Out: A Revolutionary Approach for Making Exercise More Exciting and Easier to Stick To* by Charles Roy Schroeder, *Muscle Pain Relief in 90 Seconds* by Dale Anderson, *Fast Food Facts* by Marion Franz, *International Travel Health Guide* by Stuart R. Rose, *The Fight Fat and Win Cookbook* by Elaine Moquette-Magee, *Whole Parent, Whole Child: A Parent's Guide to Raising a Child with a Chronic Illness* by Patricia M. Moynihan and Broatch Haig, *Transplants: Unwrapping the Second Gift of Life* by Pat Steve Helmberger, and *You're in Control: A Guide for Teens with Diabetes* by Jean Betschart and Susan Thom (illustrated by P. S. Mueller).

The publisher offers a series of publications (including a particularly strong line of patient-information books and pamphlets) from the International Diabetes Center and the Joslin Diabetes Center.

Chronimed Publishers distributes its own list.

Query letters and SASEs should be directed to:

David Wexler, Associate Publisher

CITY LIGHTS PUBLISHERS

261 Columbus Avenue
San Francisco, CA 94133
415-362-1901

The City Lights list covers literary fiction (including first novels), literary essays and criticism, biography, philosophy, and poetry, as well as artistically ecumenical volumes featuring both words and visual images.

City Lights Booksellers and Publishers (founded in 1953 by the poet–publisher Lawrence Ferlinghetti) is a San Francisco treasure, its bookstore a North Beach landmark, and above all else a resolute cultural institution and self-embodied tradition. City Lights initially featured the Pocket Poets series, which introduced writers such as Gregory Corso, Allen Ginsberg, Jack Kerouac, and other Beats to a wider audience. Since then, as successive literary generations have commenced and terminated, City Lights remains most assuredly commercially viable.

Titles from City Lights: *Dirty Truths* (essays) by Michael Parenti, *The New World Border: Prophecies, Poems, and Loqueras for the End of the Century* by Guillermo Gómez-Peña, *Blues and the Poetic Spirit* by Paul Garon, *Fast Speaking Woman and*

Other Chants by Anne Waldman, *First World, Ha Ha Ha!: The Zapatista Challenge* (edited by Elaine Katzenberger), *Annie Oakley's Girl* (stories) by Rebecca Brown, *Light from a Nearby Window: Contemporary Mexican Poetry* (edited by Juvenal Acosta), *Macumba: The Teachings of Maria-José Mother of the Gods* by Serge Bramly, *Red-Haired Android* (poetry) by Jeremy Reed, *Resisting the Virtual Life* (edited by James Brook and Iain A. Boal), and *Sacred Drift: Essays on the Margins of Islam* by Peter Lamborn Wilson.

City Lights nurtures a backlist that encompasses many of this publishing house's classic publications, such as *Howl and Other Poems* by Allen Ginsberg (available in the original Pocket Poets format as well as a lavish trade-paper reprint), *Gasoline* (poetry) by Gregory Corso, *Scripture of the Golden Eternity* (literary writings) by Jack Kerouac, William S. Burroughs's *Yage Letters* (creative essays and imaginative correspondence with Allen Ginsberg), and *Shock Treatment* (monologues from performance artist Karen Finley). Each fall, the publisher issues *City Lights Review: Annual Journal of Literature and Politics*, which brims with original poetry, essays, and fiction.

City Lights is distributed by the Subterranean Company of Monroe, Oregon, and has its own in-house mail-order-fulfillment department.

Query letters and SASEs should be directed to:

Nancy J. Peters, Executive Editor

CLEIS PRESS

P.O. 8933
Pittsburgh, PA 15221
412-937-1555

branch office:
Cleis West
P.O. Box 14684
San Francisco, CA 94114
415-864-3385

Cleis Press publishes books in sexual politics and self-help, lesbian and gay studies and culture, feminism, fiction, erotica, humor, and translations of world-class women's literature. Cleis titles cross the market niches of gender and sexuality to reach the widest possible audiences.

Projects from Cleis Press (founded in 1980) garner numerous awards and reviews—and include many best-selling books. The house is committed to publishing the most original, creative, and provocative works by women (and a few men) in the United States and Canada.

From the Cleis list: *Different Daughters: A Book by Mothers of Lesbians* (edited by Louise Rafkin), *I Am My Own Woman: The Outlaw Life of Charlotte von Mahlsdorf, Berlin's Most Distinguished Transvestite* by Charlotte von Mahlsdorf (translated by Jean Hollander), *1 in 3: Women with Cancer Confront an Epidemic* (edited by Judith

Brady), *Good Sex: Real Stories from Real People* by Julia Hutton, *Susie Bright's Sexwise* by Susie Bright (billed as America's Favorite X-Rated Intellectual), and *Dyke Strippers: Lesbian Cartoonists A to Z* (edited by Roz Warren).

Cleis fiction includes: *A Ghost in the Closet* (mystery featuring Nancy Clue and the Hardly Boys) by Mabel Maney, *Half a Revolution: Contemporary Fiction by Russian Women* (edited by Masha Green), *Only Lawyers Dancing* (literary thriller) by Jan McKemmish, *Dark Angels: Lesbian Vampire Stories* (edited by Pam Keesey, a sequel to the popular *Daughters of Darkness: Lesbian Vampire Stories*), *Best Gay Erotica* (edited by Michael Ford; selected and introduced by Scott Heim), *Best Lesbian Erotica* (edited by Tristan Taormino; selected and introduced by Heather Lewis), and *Switch Hitters: Lesbians Write Gay Male Erotica and Gay Men Write Lesbian Erotica* (edited by Carol Queen and Lawrence Schimel).

Cleis Books is represented to the book trade by Publishers Group West.

Query letters and SASEs should be directed to:

Frederique Delacoste, Acquisitions Editor (San Francisco)

Felice Newman, Publisher and Marketing (Pittsburgh)

CLEVELAND STATE UNIVERSITY POETRY CENTER

(See Directory of University Presses)

COBBLEHILL BOOKS

(See Penguin USA)

COFFEE HOUSE PRESS

27 North Fourth Street, Suite 400
Minneapolis, MN 55401
612-338-0125

Coffee House Press produces contemporary poetry, short fiction, and novels. Coffee House remains a source of contemporary writing that is challenging and thought provoking, funny and furious, wildly diverse, even downright wacky, vibrant, and lyrical.

This small publishing house descends from what was originally (in the 1970s) a letterpress specialty firm, with a small list and an intimate circle of readers. The publisher then introduced titles geared toward an expanded readership; happily, conviviality and craft remain in strong evidence.

Coffee House Press (established in 1984) is a publisher of trade titles and fine editions in a program that features a creative approach to the publishing arts. The house colophon is a steaming book, which is chosen to let the reader know (as the Coffee House motto runs) "where good books are brewing."

Fiction from Coffee House: *The Ivory Crocodile* by Eileen Drew, *American Heaven* by Maxine Chernoff, *Her Wild American Self* (stories) by M. Evelina Galang, *The Worldwide Church of the Handicapped* by Marie Sheppard Williams, *A Place Where the Sea Remembers* by Sandra Benitez, *Bone Truth* by Annie Finger, *Elvis Presley Calls His Mother After the Ed Sullivan Show* by Samuel Charters, *For Keepsies* (stories) by Gary Fincke, *Gunga Din Highway* by Frank Chin, and *A Robber in the House* by Jessica Treat (in the Coffee-to-Go Short-Short Story series).

Poetry includes *Avalanche* (poems by Quincy Troupe; illustrations by José Bédia), *Can't Be Wrong* by Michael Lally, *Decoy* by Elaine Equi, *Sesame* by Jack Marshall, *The Book of Medicines* by Linda Hogan, *Returning a Borrowed Tongue* (Asian-American poets; edited by Nick Carró), *Atomic Ghost: Poets Respond to the Nuclear Age* (edited by John Bradley), and *Iovis* (book-length poem) by Ann Waldman.

Coffee House books are printed on acid-free paper stock and have sewn bindings for comfortable reading and long life—as well they might, for the house features a comprehensive and enduring backlist.

Coffee House Press oversees its own marketing and sales network with the assistance of regional representatives; trade distribution is handled by Consortium.

Query letters and SASEs should be directed to:

Chris Fischbach, Editorial Assistant

Allan Kornblum, Publisher

COLUMBIA UNIVERSITY PRESS
(See Directory of University Presses)

COLLECTOR BOOKS
5801 Kentucky Dam Road
Paducah, KY 42001
502-898-6211

Mailing address:
P.O. Box 3009
Paducah, KY 42002
800-626-5420

Collector Books concentrates on the fields of antiques, arts, and crafts. Interest areas include Depression-era glassware; pottery, porcelain, and figurines; furniture; bottles;

quilts and quilting; North American Indian crafts; U.S. guns, knives, tools, and primitives; paper collectibles, records, and books; and jukeboxes and slot machines. Collector Books also produces inventory ledgers for professional dealers and avid collectors.

Collector's publications are liberally illustrated editions, generally filled with histories, production facts and lore, research sources, and identification information

Collector Books (founded in 1969) is a division of Schroeder Publishing Company. Collector specializes in books on antiques and collectibles; the house produces a mid-sized list of new offerings each year and maintains a sizeable backlist. By remaining committed to its original principles of offering quality products, ensuring customer satisfaction, giving customers the most for their dollars, and providing one-day sudden service, Collector Books has grown from a single book on fruit jars to over 500 titles, and from a firm of two employees to over sixty. Fueled by strong customer support, the publisher's list of new releases continues its recent growth.

Collector offerings are particularly wide ranging in the house's Identification & Value Guide series. Among these titles: *Christmas Collectibles* by Margaret and Kenn Whitmeyer, *Modern Collector's Dolls* by Patricia Smith, *The Collector's Encyclopedia of Niloak*, and *Toy and Miniature Sewing Machines* by Glenda Thomas.

Also from Collector: *American Oak Furniture* by Kathryn McNerney, *Collector's Guide to Snow Domes* by Helen Guarnaccia, *Golf Antiques & Other Treasures of the Game* by John M. Olman and Morton W. Olman, *Matchbox Toys, 1948 to 1993* by Dana Johnson, *Pocket Guide to Handguns, Rifles & Shotguns* (in three volumes) by Steve and Russell Quertermous, and *The World of Barbie Dolls* by Paris and Susan Manos.

Collector Books looks for its authors to be knowledgeable people considered experts within their fields. Writers who feel there is a real need for a book on their collectible subject and have available a comprehensive collection are invited to contact the publisher at the house's mailing address.

Collector Books distributes its own list, targeting particularly bookstore buyers and antiques-trade professionals. Collector operates an especially strong mail-order program and purveys selected works from other publishers, including out-of-print titles in the collectibles and antiques field.

Query letters and SASEs should be directed to:

Bill Schroeder, Publisher

Lisa Stroup, Editor

COMPCARE PUBLISHERS

(See listing for Hazelden Publishing Group in Directory of Religious, Spiritual, and Inspirational Publishers)

COMPUTE BOOKS

Compute Books (a computer-book specialist founded in 1979) is no longer doing business.

COMPUTER SCIENCE PRESS

(See W.H. Freeman and Company)

CONARI PRESS

2550 Ninth Street, Suite 101
Berkeley, CA 94710
510-649-7183

Conari Press (founded in 1987) accents works in relationships, self-awareness, spirituality, and the family. In addition to books, Conari produces a select line of audiotapes, project packets, buttons, and posters. The house began as a small press and has grown step-by-step, expanding cogently on its strong backlist base. Conari is one of the most successful regional independent publishers.

Conari titles: *Facing Fear, Finding Courage: Your Path to Peace of Mind* by Sarah Quigley with Marilyn Shroyer, *So You Want to Be a Shaman: A Creative and Practical Guide to the History, Wisdom and Rituals of This Ancient Tradition* by David Lawson, *Heart Centered Marriage: Fulfilling Our Natural Desire for Sacred Partnership* by Sue Patton Thoele, *The Web of Life: Weaving the Values That Sustain Us* by Richard Louv, *Our Power As Women: Wisdom and Strategies of Highly Successful Women* by Helene Lerner-Robbins, *The Natural Artistry of Dreams: Creative Ways for Bringing the Wisdom of Dreams to Waking Life* by Jill Mellick, and *Wonderful Ways to Love a Teen...Even When It Seems Impossible* by Judy Ford.

A high-profile Conari project is *The Practice of Kindness: Meditations for Bringing More Peace, Love and Compassion into Daily Life* by the editors of *Random Acts of Kindness* (foreword by Harold Kushner). It involves an all-out national media assault as well as a hefty first printing and sizeable advertising and publicity commitment.

Conari Press seeks to be a catalyst for profound change by providing enlightening books on topics that range from spirituality and women's issues to sexuality, relationships, and personal growth. Conari values integrity, process, compassion, and receptivity in publishing projects as well as in the house's internal workings.

Conari is distributed to the trade by Publishers Group West; giftstore distribution is handled through Sourcebooks, Inc.

Query letters and SASEs should be directed to:

Mary Jane Ryan, Acquisitions

CONSUMER REPORTS BOOKS

101 Truman Avenue
Yonkers, NY 10703
914-378-2000

Consumer Reports Books is active in a number of consumer-information spheres. Among them are product-buying guides and consumer reference; automotive; children and teenagers; consumer issues; food, cooking, and nutrition (including cookbooks); general interest; health and fitness; home and environment; law for consumers; personal finance; and travel.

Consumer Reports Books is the book-publishing wing of the Consumers Union (founded in 1936), which also publishes *Consumer Reports* magazine. Consumer Reports Books specializes in nonfiction works (most of them in trade paperback format with a few hardcovers) designed as guides (some of which are periodically revised) for consumers as they make purchasing decisions or participate in the demands of contemporary corporate and commercial society—such as healthcare, personal finance, and the law. Some Consumer Reports titles hone a controversial edge.

The publisher typically offers a small number of new books each season and maintains a full backlist. Many Consumer Reports titles originate in-house and are researched and written by Consumer Reports editors; however, the house acquires and produces a limited number of works from independent authors.

Representative Consumer Reports titles: *Mind/Body Medicine*; *Health Schemes, Scams and Frauds*; *101 Health Questions*; *AIDS: Trading Fears for Facts*; *Women's Sexual Health*; *Sumptuous Desserts*; *Homeowner's Legal Guide*; *Complete Book of Bathroom Design*; *Easy Lawn and Garden Care*; *Yard and Garden Buying Guide*; *How to Avoid Auto Repair Rip-Offs*; *Travel Buying Guide*; *Audio/Video Buying Guide*; *Consumer Reports Money Book: How to Get It, Save It, and Spend It Wisely*; and *Below the Line: Living Poor in America*.

Consumer Reports Books are distributed to the trade by St. Martin's Press.

Query letters and SASEs should be directed to:

Mark Hoffman, Executive Editor

CONTEMPORARY BOOKS

2 Prudential Plaza, Suite 1200
Chicago, IL 60601
312-540-4500

Contemporary Books offers a list tailored to general nonfiction areas such as self-improvement, personal finance, popular biography, health, and lifestyle. Contemporary Books also has a major concentration in materials for adult education. Contemporary Books (established in 1947) is part of the Tribune New Media organization. Contemporary has branched out from a former emphasis on sports titles to a program broad in scope that includes hardcover and trade paperback editions.

Titles from Contemporary: *Cocktail Hour: A Mixer of Quips and Quotations* by Jess M. Brallier and Sally Chabert, *Parenting the Strong-Willed Child* by Rex Forehand and

Nicholas Long, *The Knitter's Companion* by Jody Korch, *Fat-Burning Foods and Other Weight-Loss Secrets: New Discoveries That Help You Lose Weight Quickly, Safely, and Permanently* by Judy Jameson, *Value-Added Customer Service* by Tom Reilly, *Our Fascinating Earth* by Philip Seff and Nancy R. Seff, *Nick Bollettieri's Mental Efficiency Program for Playing Great Tennis* by Nick Bolletieri and Charles A. Maher, *Be the Target: How to Let Go and Play the Game of Golf* by Byron Huff, and *Primetime Bodies* by Cynthia Tivers and Kathy Kaehler.

Contemporary is also on the lookout for titles of topical cultural interest, including works with an investigative or issues-oriented edge. For example: *Camilla: The King's Mistress—a Love Story* by Caroline Graham.

Contemporary Books distributes its own list and also handles distribution for other publishers including Lowell House, the Sporting News, Singer Sewing Reference Library, Marlor Press, FASA Corporation, IMG Publishing, and Interweave Press.

Query letters and SASEs should be directed to:

Nancy Crossman, Editorial Director, Associate Publisher
Sports, lifestyles, cookbooks, child care, health and fitness, biographies, travel, reference, self-help, women's issues.

Linda Gray, Senior Editor
Popular culture, popular psychology, entertainment, humor, cookbooks, fun/game books.

Kara Leverte, Senior Editor (New York)
Health and fitness, child care, self-help.

Susan Schwartz, Senior Editor (New York)
General commercial nonfiction.

New York address:
712 Fifth Avenue
New York, NY 10019
212-903-3840

CONTINUUM PUBLISHING GROUP

370 Lexington Avenue
New York, NY 10017
212-953-5858

Continuum's broad focus integrates the fields of literature and criticism, psychology and counseling, women's studies, and social issues of contemporary public interest. The house also produces a select line of books in the areas of religion and philosophy. The Frederick Ungar imprint specializes in literature, film, and the performing arts.

Continuum Publishing Group (founded in 1979) hosts a burgeoning trade list as it serves scholarly, professional, and educational markets. Continuum and Crossroad Publishing Company were editorially independent components of the Crossroad/Continuum Publishing Group from 1980 into the early 1990s, since which time Continuum has pursued its own independent publishing trajectory. (For Crossroad Publishing, see entry in the Directory of Religious, Spiritual, and Inspirational Publishers.)

Representing the Continuum list: *The Perfectible Body: The Western Ideal of Male Physical Development* by Kenneth R. Dutton, *Her Father's Daughter* by Mary E. Loomis, *The Scent of Eros: Mysteries of Odor in Human Sexuality* by James Vaughn Kohl and Robert T. Francoeur, *Nazi Germany: A New History* by Klaus P. Fischer, and *Dictionary of Teleliteracy: A Personal Guide to Television from 1948 to the Present* by David Bianculli.

Continuum has an especially strong presence in the religious-trade arena. Some titles here: *Christianity: Essence, History, and Future* by Hans Kung, *Crisis and the Renewal of Creation: The World Church in the Age of Ecology* (edited by Jeffrey Golliher and William Bryant Logan), *Crisis of Faith, Crisis of Love* by Thomas Keating, *I Am My Body: A Theology of Embodiment* by Elizabeth Moltmann-Wendel, *Jesus the Healer: Possession, Trance and the Origins of Christianity* by Stevan L. Davies, *Odyssey with the Goddess: A Spiritual Quest in Crete* by Carol P. Christ, *The Truth about the Virgin: Sex and Ritual in the Dead Sea Scrolls* by Ita Sheres and Anne Kohn Blau, *Their Stories/Our Stories: Women of the Bible* by Rose Sallberg Kam, and *World Scripture: A Comparative Anthology of Sacred Texts* (edited by Andrew Wilson).

Continuum is distributed through Publisher Resources.

Query letters and SASEs should be directed to:

(Mr.) Evander Lomke, Managing Editor
Psychological counseling, history and the arts, literary criticism, current affairs, women's studies.

Justus George Lawler, Senior Editor
Literary criticism, religion.

Frank Oveis, Publishing Director
Academic religious and biblical studies, world religions, spirituality.

Cynthia Eller, Associate Editor
Women's studies.

John Heidenry, Associate Editor
Social research.

DAVID C. COOK PUBLISHING COMPANY
(See Directory of Religious, Spiritual, and Inspirational Publishers)

COPPER CANYON PRESS

P.O. Box 271
Port Townsend, WA 98368
360-385-4925

The Copper Canyon mission is to publish poetry distinguished in both content and design, with the belief that the publisher's art—like the poet's—is sacramental. Copper Canyon Press (founded in 1973) publishes a literary list in hardcover and paperback as well as special fine editions.

Copper Canyon's commitment is demonstrated through its program to further the exposure of and enthusiasm for contemporary poetry. Copper Canyon also offers selected belletristic offerings that include essays, critiques, and forays into diverse fictional forms.

Within this ambitious vision, there are limitations; Copper Canyon generally does not sign many new writers. The house assigns its resources to furthering its established roster. The publisher's success in its aim is proven through abundant and continuing recognition of its authors via honors, awards, grants, and fellowships.

Copper Canyon Press is the publisher of *The Landlady in Bangkok* by Karen Swenson, *Soul Make a Path Through Shouting* by Cyrus Cassells, *Sappho's Gymnasium* by Olga Broumas and T Begley, *My Town* by David Lee, *The Book of Light* by Lucille Clifton, *Lethal Frequencies* by James Galvin, *Infanta* by Erin Belieu, *Collected Longer Poems* by Hayden Carruth, *August Zero* by Jane Miller, *Armored Hearts* by David Bottoms, and *The Second Four Books of Poems* by W. S. Merwin,

Copper Canyon is distributed to the trade by Consortium.

Query letters and SASEs should be directed to:

Sam Hamill, Editor

CORNELL UNIVERSITY PRESS

(See Directory of University Presses)

CRAIN BOOKS

(See NTC Publishing Group)

CRESCENT BOOKS

7325 Delaware Road, Suite 195
Town of Tonawanda, NY 14223

Crescent Books (founded in 1996) publishes mainstream and literary fiction, genre fiction (especially horror), and all categories of nonfiction. Crescent emphasizes trade paperback editions.

Contact publisher for information regarding writer's guidelines, editorial policy and contacts, and marketing direction for this new enterprise. The publisher requests complete manuscripts and SASE with all submissions.

CRISP PUBLICATIONS

1200 Hamilton Court
Menlo Park, CA 94025
415-949-4988

Crisp Publications produces books and media packages in the areas of management, personal improvement, human resources and wellness, communications and creativity, customer service, sales, small businesses, financial planning, adult literacy and learning, careers, and retirement and life planning.

Crisp Publications (founded in 1985) is a specialist in business publishing. Crisp offers an extensive selection of training programs (including self-study formats) that incorporate books, manuals, and audiovisual materials. The house's aim is to provide high-quality cost-effective books and videos that can help business organizations succeed in competitive times. Crisp also offers a specialized speaker/trainer referral service.

The 50-Minute Book is Crisp's signature designation for books produced with the concept of being concise, easily read, and readily understood through personal involvement with exercises, activities, and assessments. Other Crisp lines are the Quick Read Series, the Small Business and Entrepreneurship Series, and Crisp Computer Series. A significant portion of the Crisp list is available in Spanish-language editions.

Highlights from Crisp: *The New Supervisor* by Elwood N. Chapman, *The Art of Communicating* by Bert Decker, *Motivating at Work: Empowering Employees to Give Their Best* by Twyla Dell, *Training Managers to Train* by Brother Herman Zaccarelli, *Preventing Job Burnout* by Beverly A. Potter, *Measure and Manage Stress* by Herbert Kindler and Marilyn Ginsburg, *Preventing Workplace Violence* by Marianne Minor, *Organizing Your Workspace* by Odette Pollar, *A Legal Guide for Small Business* by Charles Lickson, and *Writing Fitness: Practical Exercises for Better Business Writing* by Jack Swenson.

Crisp Publications distributes through the National Book Network, and also catalogs on a title-selective basis for several other business-related publishing houses.

Query letters and SASEs should be directed to:

Michael G. Crisp, Publisher

THE CROSSING PRESS

P.O. Box 1048
Freedom, CA 95019
408-722-0711

The publishing program at Crossing Press is particularly strong in the areas of cooking and cuisine, alternative healthcare and self-awareness (special focus on herbalism), poetry, relationships, spiritualism, women's and feminist literature and general nonfiction (including a focus on the lesbian arena), and men's studies and the men's movement (including titles of gay orientation).

The Crossing Press produces a range of hardcover and trade paperback editions, as well as a line of notecards, postcards, calendars, and journals.

The Crossing Press was established in upstate New York in 1972 as a modest house, indeed a veritable cottage press run from the farmhouse of the founders, Elaine Goldman-Gill and John Gill, who were at the time teaching at Cornell University. Relocated to the central California coastal region and with a new office building adjacent to the warehouse, the expanded scope of Crossing Press nevertheless retains its personalized editorial touch and small-press savvy.

The Crossing Press has particular commercial success with its series of distinguished recipe books and is well known for its anthologies and collections (including fiction and essays) relevant to those fields in which it specializes. The house nurtures a solid backlist.

Crossing Press general nonfiction: *Natural Healing for Babies and Children* by Aviva Jill Romm, *Transsexuals: Candid Answers to Private Questions* by Gerald Ramsey, *An Astrological Herbal for Women* by Elisabeth Brooke, *Breaking Convention with Intercultural Romances* (edited by Dianne Dicks), *Psychic Healing with Spirit Guides and Angels* by Diane Stein, *Nudes* (photography) by Amy Sibiga, *Reach for Joy: How to Find the Right Therapist and Therapy for You* by Lynne D. Finney, *A Loving Testimony: Remembering Loved Ones Lost to AIDS* (edited by Lesléa Newman), *Revolutionary Laughter: The World of Women Comics* (edited by Roz Warren), and *The Wiccan Path: A Guide for the Solitary Practitioner* by Rae Beth.

Titles in the kitchen arts: *The Hot Sauce Bible* by Dave DeWitt and Chuck Evans, *Pocket Guide to Good Food: A Shopper's Resource* by Margaret M. Wittenberg, *Traveling Jamaica with Knife, Fork & Spoon: A Righteous Guide to Jamaican Cooking* by Robb Walsh and Jay McCarthy, *New Vegetarian Classics: Entrées* by Mary F. Taylor, *Meltdown! The Official Fiery Foods Show Cookbook and Chilehead Resource Guide* by Dave DeWitt and Mary Jane Wilan, *Jungle Feasts & Dangerous Dining: Adventures and Recipes from a Culinary Rogue* by Richard Sterling, and *Good Food: The Complete Guide to Eating Well* by Margaret M. Wittenberg.

Calendars and posters from Crossing include *The Chilehead Art Calendar* by Ron Genta (along with a Chilehead line of poster art), *Women Writers Engagement Calendar* (edited by Dena Taylor), *The Black Woman's Perpetual Calendar: Our Names Are Many* (edited by Terri Jewell), and *The Goddess Book of Days: A Perpetual 366-Day Engagement Calendar* by Diane Stein.

Fiction and literature from Crossing has run the spectrum of traditional categories. Current activity in this arena is limited, though the house hosts a noteworthy backlist in science fiction and fantasy, mystery, poetry, and special-interest anthologies. A title here is *Poems of Passion, Poems of Love* (edited by Elaine Goldman-Gill and John Gill). Other fiction and literary works: *When Warhol Was Alive* by Margaret McMullan,

Hog Heaven: Erotic Lesbian Stories by Caressa French, and *Breaking Up Is Hard to Do: Stories by Women* (edited by Amber Coverdale Sumrall).

Crossing Press distributes to the trade through a group of regional services and a network of independent sales representatives.

Query letters and SASEs should be directed to:

Elaine Gill, Publisher and Editor

Dennis Hayes, Acquisitions Editor

CROSSROAD PUBLISHING COMPANY

See Directory of Religious, Spiritual, and Inspirational Publishers)

CROWN PUBLISHING GROUP

(See Random House)

DA CAPO PLENUM INSIGHT

233 Spring Street
New York, NY 10013
212-620-8000

Da Capo Plenum Insight comprises three primary lines under the auspices of a single house. The individual lists of Da Capo Press, Plenum Publishing Corporation, and Insight Books do show a bit of topical overlap, but each imprint stakes claim to an identifiable primary domain. The firm thereby achieves an overall purview that encompasses popular, scholarly, and academic works in the areas of art, music, and culture (Da Capo's emphasis); medicine, science, and technology (the Plenum arena); and public-interest issues, psychology, and self-awareness (under the Insight aegis).

Da Capo Plenum Insight handles its own distribution via a network of regional sales and distribution services.

DA CAPO PRESS

Da Capo emphasis is on classical music; jazz, blues, and popular music; dance; theater; film and television; photography; art and architecture; crafts and antiques; literature; African-American studies; the American Civil War; history; true crime; science and technology; popular culture; and sports. Da Capo produces new titles and reprints in hardcover and trade paperback.

Da Capo nonfiction reprint editions are primarily trade paper, with some special clothbound editions. The imprint specializes in making out-of-print and hard-to-find books available again. Many Da Capo books are firsthand accounts by artists, musicians, and historical figures and are often revised editions of classic writings in their fields. Though much of Da Capo's list has a learned slant, these works are by no means of strictly academic appeal; included among these are a deck of popular reference works in education, health, history, and literature.

Indicative of the Da Capo list: *Good Morning Blues: The Autobiography of Count Basie* (as told to Albert Murray), *Tap! The Greatest Tap Dance Stars and Their Stories, 1900–1955* by Rusty Frank (revised edition with foreword by Gregory Hines), *A Dreamer of Pictures: Neil Young—a Man and His Music* by David Downing, *The Military Maxims of Napoleon* (edited by William E. Cairnes), *A Civil War Treasury* by Albert A. Nofi, and *The Black Panthers Speak* (edited by Philip S. Foner).

Query letters and SASEs should be directed to:

Yuval Taylor, Senior Editor, Da Capo Press

Michael Dorr, Editor, Da Capo Press
All Da Capo subject areas.

PLENUM PUBLISHING CORPORATION

Plenum trade-publishing scope includes popular biography, criminology, health, and popular renditions of vanguard scientific theory. Plenum remains a potent producer of journals in the fields of biosciences (including biology and medicine) and environmental sciences.

Plenum Publishing Corporation (trade motto: "the language of science") was originally established as a publisher of professional, scholarly, and academic works—including a noteworthy line of journals and monographs that provided western academia with a window into the scientific and scholarly scene dominated by the former Soviet Union. The house currently has a broad base of interest that includes related commercial veins of its traditional subject areas.

From the Plenum frontlist: *Impact Jupiter: The Crash of Comet Shoemaker-Levy 9* by David H. Levy (codiscoverer of the comet); *Genius Talk: Conversations with Nobel Scientists and Other Luminaries* by Denis Brian; *Raising Your Child's Self-Esteem: The Authoritative Guide from Infancy through the Teen Years* by Karen Owens; *Creativity and the Mind: Discovering the Genius Within* by Thomas B. Ward, Ronald A. Finke, and Steven M. Smith; *The Cyclical Serpent: Prospects for an Ever-Repeating Universe* by Paul Halpern; *Protecting Your Life, Home, and Property: A Cop Shows You How* by Robert L. Snow; *Nazi Science: Myth, Truth, and the German Atomic Bomb* by Mark Walker; *Figures of Light: Actors and Directors Illuminate the Art of Film Acting* by Carole Zucker; and *The Sea of Galilee Boat: An Extraordinary 2000 Year Old Discovery* by Shelley Wachsmann.

Query letters and SASEs should be directed to:

Mariclaire Cloutier, Editor, Plenum
Medicine.

Amelia McNamara, Senior Editor, Plenum
Physical sciences.

Lucien S. Marchand, Senior Editor, Plenum
Engineering, mathematics, computer science.

Linda Greenspan Regan, Executive Editor, Plenum Trade
Nonfiction in popular science, social science, criminology, mathematics, anthropology.

Eliot Werner, Executive Editor, Plenum

INSIGHT BOOKS

The publishing outlook of Insight Books (a trade imprint of Plenum Publishing Corporation) exemplifies a comprehensive popular- and professional-market approach to social and interpersonal psychology, self-improvement, current events, relationships, gender studies, and issues that reflect currents of thought in behavioral science. Insight publishes most titles solely in hardcover at a length of approximately 300 pages (about 90,000–100,000 words).

Representing the Insight list: *My Body: Women Speak Out about Their Health Care* by Marion Crook, *Mind Your Own Business: The Battle for Personal Privacy* by Gini Graham Scott, *HIV-Negative: How the Uninfected Are Affected by AIDS* by William I. Johnston, *American Prejudice: With Liberty and Justice for Some* by Richard H. Ropers and Dan J. Pence, and *The New Poverty: Homeless Families in America* by Ralph de Costa Nuñez.

Query letters and SASEs should be directed to:

Frank K. Darmstadt, Editor, Insight Books
Popular psychology, personal finance, lifestyle issues, contemporary sociology, marriage and family situations.

DALKEY ARCHIVE PRESS

Illinois State University
Box 4241
Normal, IL 61790
309-438-7555

Dalkey Archive (founded in 1984) is dedicated to breakthrough artistic expression in fiction and creative voices in all fields of letters. Dalkey's writers are among the most influential stylists on the printed page. The house's production forte is finely designed, innovatively conceived softcover editions. Dalkey Archive Press is a division of the Review of Contemporary Fiction.

Representing the Dalkey Archive list: *Island People* by Coleman Dowell, *The Poor Mouth: A Bad Story about the Hard Life* by Flann O'Brien (translated by Patrick C. Power; illustrated by Ralph Steadman), *Storytown* by Susan Daitch, *Palinuro of*

Mexico by Fernando del Paso (translated by Elisabeth Plaister), *Sabbatical* by John Barth, and *The Red Shoes and Other Tattered Tales* by Karen Elizabeth Gordon.

Dalkey Archive distributes through Chicago Distribution Center.

Query letters and SASEs should be directed to:

Steven Moore, Senior Editor

John O'Brien, Publisher

THE DARTNELL CORPORATION

4660 North Ravenswood Avenue
Chicago, IL 60640
312-561-4000

Dartnell is a business-specialist house that publishes practical books, handbooks, manuals, periodicals, planners, and business how-to and education programs, including audiocassettes, film, videotapes, and computer software. Dartnell's major publishing concentration is in the areas of sales, marketing, and office administration and management.

The Dartnell Corporation (established in 1917) is a privately owned, international business information and training publisher dedicated to supplying diverse business audiences with instructional and motivational materials—presented under the Dartnell banner, which reads: "Helping You Compete Through Better Training."

Dartnell prides itself on its ability to reach corporate audiences at all levels in a variety of businesses and industries with products that target members of the business community from factory line workers to executive officers. Topical highlights of the Dartnell list include sales skills, sales motivation, sales management, leadership, communication, team building and teamwork, customer service, quality, general motivation, influence and persuasion, and sexual harassment and gender-based issues.

Dartnell's approach encompasses not only the production and publication of their varied media products, the publisher is also a service organization. Dartnell invites corporate and business clients to contact the house representatives and determine what promotions, programs, or training tools can be worked into a customized package that will best serve that particular client's needs.

Dartnell's list reflects a simple, steadfast commitment to how-to, results-oriented training, and accents publications that often incorporate components within a number of different media formats.

Representative Dartnell titles: *A Team of Eagles* by Mike Singletary, *How Leaders Lead: The Essential Skills for Career and Personal Success* by Ken Blanchard and Brian Tracy, *How to Negotiate Anything with Anyone Anywhere in the World* by Frank L. Acuff, *Take Charge of Your Life* by Les Brown, *Connecting with Your Customers* by Bill Bethel, *Winning with Promotion Power* by Frank Caci and Donna Howard, *Super Selling Skills* by Tony Alessandra, *Cracking New Accounts* by Terry L. Booton,

Creative Training and Presentation Techniques by Robert Pike, and *Psyched to Sell* by Art Mortell.

Dartnell distributes its own books and other media products.

Query letters and SASEs should be directed to:

Scott B. Pemberton, Vice President of Editorial Division

DAW BOOKS INC.

375 Hudson Street
New York, NY 10014
212-366-2096

DAW Books (founded in 1971) is at the forefront of literary categories and genres such as science fiction, fantasy, science fantasy, future fiction and future fantasy, dark suspense, and horror. DAW publishes mass-market paperbound originals and reprints, as well as hardcovers and trade paperbacks. The DAW backlist is replete with successful individual titles, along with a host of series offerings. The DAW line includes masterful genre-keyed anthologies that showcase some of the most respected writers in their respective literary provinces. The house is affiliated with Penguin USA.

Representative titles from DAW Books: *The Winds of Darkover* by Marion Zimmer Bradley, *Northlight* by Deborah Wheeler, *Murder at the Galactic Writers' Society* by Janet Asimov, *Fire in the Sky* by Jo Clayton, *Death Watch* by Elizabeth Forrest, and *Vampire Detectives* (edited by Martin H. Greenberg).

DAW distributes through an affiliation with Penguin USA.

Query letters and SASEs should be directed to:

Elizabeth Wollheim, Publisher

Sheila Gilbert, Publisher

Peter Stampfl, Submissions Editor

DCI PUBLISHING

(See Chronimed Publishing)

DEACONESS PRESS

(See Fairview Press)

DEARBORN PUBLISHING GROUP, INC.

155 North Wacker Drive
Chicago, IL 60606
312-836-4400

Founded in 1982 as Longman Financial Services Publishing, and subsequently operating as Dearborn Financial Publishing, Inc., this house has grown and metamorphosed into Dearborn Publishing Group, Inc. It is a diverse business-oriented house with a number of imprints and affiliates that include Dearborn Trade, Commodity Trend Service, Dearborn R&R Newkirk, Real Estate Education Company, and Vernon Publishing. Upstart Publishing Company was acquired in full and moved to Chicago, after having been an editorially independent affiliate with a New Hampshire base for the previous few years.

After thirty-five years at its previous location, Dearborn moved corporate headquarters in late 1994. Settled in at the new, more expansive address, Dearborn is actively developing audio, CD-ROM, video, and software products in addition to its print publishing program.

DEARBORN TRADE
DEARBORN FINANCIAL PUBLISHING, INC.

Dearborn Trade and Dearborn Financial Publishing, Inc., produce trade and professional books and training materials in the areas of entrepreneurship, real estate, financial planning, investments, personal finance, insurance, management, careers, small business, and banking. Dearborn offers titles intended for corporate and institutional markets in addition to books aimed primarily toward the individual book buyer. Dearborn also produces career and college guides, reference books, and regional real estate guides.

Entrepreneurship receives special Dearborn emphasis, with titles cataloged for the emerging entrepreneur, the growing business, the maturing business, and the established entrepreneur. The Upstart imprint specializes in entrepreneurship and small-business management.

Through its Real Estate Education Company division, Dearborn offers a wealth of practical training materials (including books, audio, video, and computer-based training products). These items cover fields such as real estate licensing, property management, new homes and renovation, advertising and marketing, and sales skills.

Highlights from Dearborn include *The Under-35 Guide to Starting and Running Your Business* by Lisa Shaw, *Beating the Paycheck-to-Paycheck Blues* by John Ventura, *Wall Street's Picks* (an annual) by Kick Kazanjian, *The Budget Kit* by Judy Lawrence, *Successfully Self-Employed* by George Brennan, *The Personal Finance Kit* by Ellen Norris Gruber, *How Good Guys Grow Rich* by Adriane G. Berg and Milton Gralla, *Be Your Own Contractor and Save Thousands* by James Shepherd, and *How to Avoid the 10 Biggest Homebuying Traps* by A. M. Watkins and Patrick Hogan.

The Dearborn Multimedia imprint offers personal-productivity book/CD-ROM packages of best-selling titles in small business, personal finance/investments, home ownership/real estate, and careers. Titles on this imprint include: *Starting a Home-Based Business*, *How to Form Your Own Corporation without a Lawyer for Under $75*, *The Budget Kit*, *The Mortgage Kit*, and *The Credit Repair Kit*.

Dearborn distributes its own list, as well as books by a number of smaller business-oriented houses.

Query letters and SASEs should be directed to:

Anita A. Constant, Senior Vice President
All areas covered in house description.

Kevin Commins, Editorial Director
All areas covered in house description.

Christine Litavsky, Acquisitions Editor
Real estate, Personal finance.

(Ms.) Bobbye Middendorf, Executive Editor
Small business, careers.

UPSTART PUBLISHING COMPANY

The Upstart imprint specializes in entrepreneurship and small-business management.

Upstart Publishing (incorporated in 1979) became an independent division of Dearborn Publishing Group in 1991. In early 1995, Upstart's editorial operations were transferred from its original New Hampshire habitat to the expanded Dearborn corporate environs in Chicago.

"A small business is one where you can bring your dog to work." This philosophical statement is from the best-selling Upstart book, *The Business Planning Guide* by David H. Bangs, founder of Upstart and author of the Planning Guide Series. Other Upstart series are Small Business Basics and Common Sense (with the editors of *Common Sense*).

Representative Upstart titles: *Restaurant Planning Guide* by Peter Rainsford and David H. Bangs Jr., *From Kitchen to Market: Selling Your Gourmet Food Specialty* by Stephen F. Hall, *On Your Own: A Woman's Guide to Building a Business* by Laurie B. Zuckerman, *100 Best Retirement Businesses* by Lisa Agnowski Rogak and David H. Bangs Jr., *The Entrepreneur's Guide to Going Public* by James B. Arkebauer and Ron Schultz, *The Complete Guide to Selling Your Business* by Paul S. Sperry and Beatrice H. Mitchell, *Media Power: How Your Business Can Profit from the Media* by Peter G. Miller, *Sit and Grow Rich: Petsitting and Housesitting for Profit* by Patricia A. Doyle, and *The Language of Small Business* (a dictionary of business usage) by Carl O. Trautmann.

Query letters and SASEs should be directed to:

Jere Calmes, Publisher

DELACORTE PRESS
(See Bantam Doubleday Dell)

DELL BOOKS
(See Bantam Doubleday Dell)

DIGITAL PRESS
(See Heinemann)

DISNEY PRESS
(See Hyperion)

DOUBLEDAY
(See Bantam Doubleday Dell)

DOVE BOOKS
301 North Canon Drive, Suite 207
Beverly Hills, CA 90210
310-273-7722

Dove Books is centrally located to be a major player in the arena of high-interest topical titles that tie in with current events and trends of popular culture. Dove currently issues a select fiction list. The house also offers a line of children's titles. Dove Audio features a high-interest lineup of audio books.

Indicative of the Dove list: *You'll Never Make Love in This Town Again* by Robin, Liza, Linda, and Tiffany (as told to Jennie Louise Frankel, Terrie Maxine Frankel, and Joanne Parrent); *Fatal Subtraction: The Inside Story of Buchwald vs. Paramount* by Pierce O'Donnell and Dennis McDougal (introduction by Art Buchwald); *Everything I Ever Needed to Know about Succeeding in Hollywood I Learned from My Pit Bull: A Hollywood Handbook* by David Chasman; *On Negotiating* by Mark H. McCormack;

The Answer: A Fable for Our Times by Philip Wylie; and *A Gift of Sharing: A Celebration of Christmas and Hanukkah* (edited by Deborah Raffin).

Backlist favorites: *Nicole Brown Simpson: The Private Diary of a Life Interrupted* by Faye D. Resnick, *Iron Rose: A Biography of Rose Fitzgerald Kennedy* by Cindy Adams and Susan Crimp, and *The Private Diary of Lyle Menendez: In His Own Words—Unauthorized* (as told to Norma Novelli with Mike Walker).

From Dove Kids: *Enchanted Tales* (adapted by Mary Sheldon; illustrations by Guadalupe Mernandez), *Megan's Two Houses: A Story of Adjustment* by Erica Jong, and *The Long Journey of the Little Seed* (written and illustrated by Annie Reiner).

Dove Books is distributed by Penguin USA.

Query letters and SASEs should be directed to:

Michael Viner, Publisher

Beth Leiberman, Acquisitions

(Ms.) Lee Montgomery, Acquisitions

DUTTON
(See Penguin USA)

THE ECCO PRESS
100 West Broad Street
Hopewell, NJ 08525
609-466-4748

The Ecco list is redolent of literary fiction, poetry, and essays, along with selected general nonfiction including imaginative and practical works on travel, food, culture, and sports. The Ecco Press (founded in 1970) is a small, distinguished publisher of trade books (many in special fine editions).

Popular titles on the Ecco Press list: *Paris Bistros and Wine Bars: A Select Guide* by Robert and Barbara Hamburger, *The Vines of San Lorenzo: The Making of Great Wine in the New Tradition* by Edward Steinberg, *The Compleat Angler* by Izaak Walton, *Reckless Appetites: A Culinary Romance* by Jacqueline Deval, *Bull Cook and Authentic Historical Recipes and Practices* (survival tips and cookery) by George and Berthe Herter, *The Progressive Puzzler: A Crossword Puzzle Book* by Susannah B. Mintz, and *I Never Had It Made: An Autobiography* by Jackie Robinson.

Fiction and literary writing from Ecco includes: *Women on Hunting: Essays, Fiction, and Poetry* (edited by Pam Houston), *The Culture of Bruising: Essays on Prizefighting, Literature, and Modern American Culture* by Gerald Early, *The Perfectionist and Other Plays* by Joyce Carol Oates, *Manic Pop Thrill* (contemporay fiction) by Rachel

Felder, *The Primitive* (psychological suspense) by Stephen Amidon, and *Diary of a Rapist* (fiction) by Evan S. Connell.

Stalwarts on Ecco's roster of poets include Louise Glück, Robert Hass, Zbigniew Herbert, Carolyn Kizer, Czeslaw Milosz, Robert Pinsky, and Charles Simic. The house also offers classic reprints in the Essential Poets series. In addition, Ecco publishes the literary journal *Antæus*.

Books of the Ecco Press are distributed by W. W. Norton.

Query letters and SASEs should be directed to:

Daniel Halpern, President and Editor in Chief

WILLIAM B. EERDMANS PUBLISHING COMPANY

(See Directory of Religious, Spiritual, and Inspirational Publishers)

M. EVANS AND COMPANY

216 East 49th Street
New York, NY 10017
212-688-2810

The M. Evans frontlist features high-profile offerings in investigative public interest and popular biography. The main portion of the house's program accents popular nonfiction books in the areas of health and fitness, human relationships, business and finance, and lifestyle and cuisine. Evans also issues a small market-targeted fiction list (including Westerns), and a line of books for children. The house tends a strong and varied backlist.

M. Evans and Company (founded in 1963) thrives as a selective trade publisher (in hardcover and trade paperback) with a clear, constantly honed commercial focus in its favored market niches.

Evans nonfiction titles include *Ablaze! A Study of Spontaneous Human Combustion* by Larry E. Arnold, *How to Rear a Successful Child* by Lendon Smith, *A Handbook for Wilderness Survival* by Bob Harris, *Lost Gold and Buried Treasure: A Treasure Hunter's Guide to 100 Fortunes Waiting to Be Found* by Kevin D. Randle, *Spies: A Narrative Encyclopedia of Dirty Tricks and Double Dealing from Biblical Times to Today* by Jay Robert Nash, *Dr. Atkins' New Diet Cookbook* by Robert C. Atkins and Fran Gare, *The Artist in the Marketplace: Making Your Living in the Fine Arts* by James Adams and Patricia Frischer, *Hawk Woman Dancing with the Moon: The Last Female Shaman* by Tela Starhawk Lake, and *Prospero's Kitchen: Mediterranean Cooking of the Ionian Islands from Corfu to Kythera* by Diana Farr Louis and June Marinos.

Evans fiction is exemplified by *A Fine Italian Hand* (a Shifty Lou Anderson mystery) by William Murray. Evans novels of the West include *The Sons of Grady Rourke* by Douglas Savage, *Buckskinner* by R. C. House, and *Wolfer* by Mac McKee.

M. Evans is the distributor for the Masters Press list; M. Evans books are distributed to the trade via National Book Network and Kampmann.

Query letters and SASEs should be directed to:

George C. de Kay, President
Popular psychology, health, cookbooks.

F&W PUBLICATIONS
(See Writer's Digest Books)

FABER AND FABER

53 Shore Road
Winchester, MA 01890
617-721-1427

Faber and Faber, Inc., publishes adult fiction and nonfiction; much of the Faber fiction list has a distinguished literary bent. Nonfiction strengths include history, biography, health, women's interest, gay and lesbian issues, popular science, cooking, music, film, and drama.

Faber and Faber (instituted in 1976) is the American subsidiary of the British publisher Faber and Faber Ltd. In addition to producing original books by American authors, FF also handles North American distribution for its parent company.

On the Faber fiction and literary list: *Empire Under Glass* by Julian Anderson, *The Life Stone of Singing Bird* by Melodie Stevenson, *The Tempest of Clemenza* by Glenda Adams, *Bailey's Beads* by Terry Wolverton, *Twilight at the Equator* by Jaime Manrique, and *Ladies, Start Your Engines* (edited by Elinor Nauen). Forthcoming on Faber's list is the second set of paired anthologies (edited by Robert Drake and Terry Wolverton), tentatively titled *His 2: More Brilliant New Fiction by Gay Writers* and *Hers 2: More Brilliant New Fiction by Lesbian Writers* (the first *His* volume was nominated for a Lambda Literary Award).

On the Faber nonfiction list: *Knowing Hepburn* by Jim Prideaux (about the later years of Katharine Hepburn's life); *Demand and Get the Best Health Care for You: An Eminent Doctor's Practical Advice* by Curtis Prout, M.D.; *Tourists: How the Fastest Growing Industry Is Changing the World* by Larry Krotz; *Counterpoint* by Paul Brodeur; *Impersonating Elvis* by Leslie Rubinkowski; and *Savoring the East: Feasts and Stories from Istanbul to Bali* by David Burton.

Performance—whether stage and screen or in the musical arena—represents one of Faber and Faber's strongest areas. FF publishes an array of accessible titles on film actors and directors, music producers and performers, and life in the theater, as well as plays and screenplays. Titles in these areas include *A Year with Swollen Appendices* by Brian Eno; *Magic Hour: The Life of a Cameraman* by Jack Cardiff; *Fargo* by the Coen brothers; *Leaving Las Vegas* by Mike Figgis; *The General from America* by Richard Nelson; and the most recent installment in the Projections series, *Projections 6* (edited by John Boorman and Walter Donohue).

Although there are a number of children's books and volumes of poetry published by Faber and Faber, the majority of these titles are acquired by the London office.

Faber and Faber utilizes a number of independent regional sales representatives; the house's book orders are fulfilled through Cornell University Press Services (CUP Services).

Unsolicited query letters from authors must include SASE. Query letters and SASEs should be directed to:

Dan Weaver, Editor in Chief

Valerie Cimino, Senior Editor

FACTS ON FILE

11 Penn Plaza
15th Floor
New York, NY 10001
212-967-8800

Facts On File specializes in reference and information titles in a broad popular range, including business, popular culture, art and architecture, design, sports, health, history, current affairs and politics, the environment, and young adult lines—in addition to general reference works. Facts On File offers a broad selection of historical and cultural atlases, dictionaries, and encyclopedias geared toward professional as well as popular interests and is one of the pioneers of the CD-ROM multimedia-publishing frontier.

Facts On File (founded in 1940) is a dynamic popular-reference publisher. The house has a full skein of award-winning titles to its credit, and many Facts On File publications feature an innovative production approach. The publisher is extremely well tuned to specific category markets, which it targets with marked commercial consistency.

Business books include guides to telecommunications, franchising, and the business aspects of the health care industry, as well as business history and biography.

Young adult books cover cultural history worldwide—with emphasis on United States and ethnic heritage—as well as series in science and technology, the natural environment, and space exploration.

Representative Facts On File projects: *Career Opportunities in the Food and Beverage Industry* by Barbara Sims-Bell; *Crusades* by Terry Jones and Alan Ereira; *In Vitro Fertilization: The Art of Making Babies* by Geoffrey Sher, Virginia A. Marriage, and Jean Stoess; *The Atlas of Endangered Peoples* by Steve Pollock; *The Home Health Guide to Poisons and Antidotes* by Carol Turkington; *The Parents' Financial Survival Guide* by Theodore E. Hughes and David Klein; and *Women for a Change: A Grassroots Guide to Activism and Politics* by Thalia Zepatos and Elizabeth Kaufman.

Facts On File utilizes individualized marketing and distribution programs that are particularly strong in the areas of corporate, institutional, and library sales.

Query letters and SASEs should be directed to:

Jeffrey Golick, Project Editor
Science, music, history.

Gary Krebs, Associate Editor
Reference books: entertainment subjects, TV, movies, Broadway, sports.

James Warren, Senior Editor
Nonfiction young-adult reference books about military history, sports, American culture and history, music.

FAIRVIEW PRESS

2450 Riverside Avenue South
Minneapolis, MN 55454
612-672-4228; 612-672-4858; 800-544-8207

Fairview Press is a specialist publisher and distributor of nonfiction books on relationships, parenting, domestic violence, divorce, family activities, aging, health, self-esteem, social issues, and addictions.

Fairview is a small house committed to publishing advice and support that individuals and families need to face stressful situations, difficult choices, and the trials and changes of everyday life. In addition, Fairview Press books are tools to help families enjoy and appreciate each other and strengthen family bonds. Fairview Press (formerly Deaconess Press; founded in 1988) is a division of Fairview Riverside Medical Center.

From the Fairview list: *Raising Strong Daughters* by Jeanette Gadeberg, *When Nothing Makes Sense: Disaster, Crisis, and Their Effects on Children* by Gerald Deskin and Greg Steckler, *The Fairview Guide to Positive Quotations* (compiled and arranged by John Cook), *Divorced Dads: In Their Own Words* (authored and edited by C. Stephen Fouquet), *Torn Togas: The Dark Side of Greek Life* by Esther Wright, *Family-by-Choice* by Susan Ahern with Kent Bailey, and *Breaking the Age Barrier* by Linda Meyers.

Of special interest to younger readers: *Alligator in the Basement* by Bob Keeshan (illustrated by Kyle Corkum); *Clover's Secret* by Christine M. Winn with David Walsh (illustrated by Christine M. Winn); and *My Dad Has HIV* by Earl Alexander, Sheila Rudin, and Pam Sejkora (illustrated by Ronnie Walter Shipman).

Fairview handles its own distribution.

Query letters and SASEs should be directed to:

Edward A. Wedman, Publisher

Robin Hansen, Editor

Julie Smith, Senior Editor

FANTAGRAPHICS BOOKS

7563 Lake City Way Northeast
Seattle, WA 98115
206-524-1967

Fantagraphics produces comics and comic art. The house accents a list of mainstream, classic, and borderline offerings in this specialty arena, and also purveys a strong line of erotic comics. Fantagraphics Books (inaugurated in 1976) produces trade paperbacks, hardbound editions, and quality fine-art album editions of graphic productions, in addition to comic books, comics-related magazines, and a line of gift items dedicated to this most accessible literary form.

The Fantagraphics roster features some of the finest cartoonists of America and around the world—underground masters, political satirists, artists in the realms of science fiction and fantasy, and reprints of classic newspaper comic-strip series—as well as works from the emerging young turks in the field.

Comics creators cataloged by Fantagraphics include Peter Bagge, Vaughn Bode, Daniel Clowes, Guido Crepax, Robert Crumb, Kim Deitch, Julie Doucet, Jules Feiffer, Frank Frazetta, Drew Friedman, Rick Geary, Los Bros. Hernandez, Peter Kuper, Terry LeBan, Douglas Michael, Joe Sacco, Gilbert Shelton, Art Spiegelman, Ralph Steadman, Basil Wolverton, and Wallace Wood.

Among Fantagraphics projects: *A Bitch Is Born* by Roberta Gregory, *Trip to Tulum* by Milo Manara and Federico Fellini, *Grit Bath* by Renée French, *Omaha the Cat Dancer* by Reed Waller and Kate Worley, *Yummy Fur: Fuck & Matthew* by Chester Brown, *Guttersnipe* by Glenn Head, *Nurture the Devil* by Jeff Johnson, *Peepshow* by Joe Matt, *Real Smut* by Dennis Eichhorn, and *The New American Splendor Anthology* by Harvey Pekar.

Fantagraphics also offers Burne Hogarth's set of art-instruction books.

Fantagraphics distributes its own list and catalogs selections from a number of other comics- and graphics-oriented publishers.

Query letters (accompanied by short, carefully selected samples) and SASEs should be directed to:

Ezra Mark, Submissions Editor

FARRAR STRAUS & GIROUX

19 Union Square West
New York, NY 10003
212-741-6900

Farrar Straus & Giroux (founded in 1946) is a trade house that produces top-of-the-line fiction and literature as well as a wide range of general-interest and specialist nonfiction on its commercial list of finely designed hardcover and trade paperback editions. Long a mainstay among independently owned American publishing houses, Farrar Straus & Giroux was bought by Verlagsgruppe Georg von Holtzbrinck. In this new multinational corporate phase, FS&G retains an affluent spirit that seeks to represent writing at its commercial-literary best, presented under the esteemed and widely recognized FS&G logo of three abstract fish.

Among FS&G divisions and imprints are Hill and Wang and North Point Press (see separate subentries below), the primarily trade paper imprint Noonday Press for adult titles, and Sunburst Books for young readers. FS&G tends a solid backlist and issues a line of classic works in reprint.

FS&G literary areas include novels, short stories, drama (and other theatrical works), essays, biography, memoirs, and poetry. In this arena, the house's offerings have often exhibited an adventuresome approach to both form and content.

FS&G publishes works from diverse writers such as Joseph Brodsky, Carlos Fuentes, John McPhee, Philip Roth, Aleksandr Solzhenitsyn, Calvin Trillin, Scott Turow, Mario Vargas Llosa, Tom Wolfe, and Susan Sontag. In addition to the FS&G roster of established and marketable literary talent, the house is alert to hitherto lesser appreciated literary voices primed for the commercial spotlight.

Farrar Straus & Giroux fiction and literature: *Flesh and Blood* (literary family saga) by Michael Cunningham, *Lytton Strachey: The New Biography* by Michael Holroyd, *The Chess Garden or the Twilight Letters of Gustav Uyterhoeven* by Brooks Hansen, *The Autobiography of My Mother* by Jamaica Kincaid, *A Little Too Much Is Enough* by Kathleen Tyau, *The Golden Plough* (thriller) by James Buchan, *Galatea 2.2* by Richard Powers, *Panama* (historical international thriller) by Eric Zencey, and *Hunters and Gatherers* (satire of the sexes) by Francine Prose.

Poetry from FS&G includes *Red Sauce, Whiskey, and Snow* by August Kleinzahler, *Chickamauga* by Charles Wright, *Gilgamesh: A New Rendering in English Verse* by David Ferry, *Madoc: A Mystery* by Paul Muldoon, and *The Man With Night Sweats* by Thom Gunn.

FS&G nonfiction offerings encompass such works as *The Snarling Citizen* (essays) by Barbara Ehrenreich, *The French Secret Service: From the Dreyfus Affair to the Gulf War* by Douglas Porch, *Smokestack Lightning: Adventures in the Heart of Barbecue Country* by Lolis Eric Elie (photographs by Frank Stewart), *Breaking Free: A Memoir of Love and Revolution* by Susan Eisenhower, *Jackie Under My Skin: Interpreting an Icon* by Wayne Koestenbaum, and *"It's Not Fair, Jeremy Spencer's Parents Let Him Stay Up All Night!" A Guide to the Tougher Parts of Parenting* by Anthony E. Wolf.

Trade distribution for FS&G is handled by the Putnam Publishing Group, while FS&G's catalog and promotional endeavors include services for a number of small quality houses, such as Beacon and Soho.

Query letters and SASEs should be directed to:

Elizabeth Dyssegaard, Executive Editor, Noonday Press
Fiction: literary, German and Scandinavian translations. Nonfiction: open to many areas.

Jonathan Galassi, Editor in Chief
Acquires in areas consistent with house description.

John Glusman, Executive Editor
Acquires titles per house description.

Linda Healey, Editor
Current events, politics.

FARRAR STRAUS & GIROUX BOOKS
FOR YOUNG READERS

Farrar Straus & Giroux Books for Young Readers publishes for a wide-ranging readership under several individualized imprints: Sunburst Books for younger and middler readers, Aerial Fiction for teenagers, and Mirasol *libros juveniles* (children's books in Spanish). Among FS&G children's authors are William Steig, Maurice Sendak, and Madeleine L'Engle.

Titles here: *The Library* by Sarah Stewart (illustrated by David Small), *Carl's Birthday* by Alexandra Day, *Troubling a Star* by Madeleine L'Engle, *Falling into Glory* (young-adult novel) by Robert Westall, *Brainstorm! The Stories of Twenty Kid Inventors* by Tom Tucker (pictures by Richard Loehle), *Saturday Sancocho* by Leyla Torres, *Lost Summer* by Elizabeth Feuer, *Paper Dinosaurs* (a cut-out book) by Satoshi Kitamura, *Dear Elijah* (a Passover story) by Miriam Bat-Ami, and *In the Back Seat* by Deborah Durland Desaix.

Query letters and SASEs should be directed to:

Margaret Ferguson, Editorial Director

Wes Adams, Senior Editor

HILL AND WANG

Hill and Wang highlights general-interest trade nonfiction as well as selected titles in drama as literature. Otherwise (and traditionally) viewed as part of the scholarly academic publishing scene, the house is increasingly active commercially with an eclectic and lively list that features titles with public-interest and popular cultural hooks.

Representative Hill and Wang titles: *Going All the Way: Teenager Girls' Tales of Sex, Romance, and Pregnancy* by Sharon Thompson, *Manifest Destiny: American Expansionism and the Empire of Right* by Anders Stephanson, *Village Journey: The Report of the Alaska Native Review Commission* (in an updated edition) by Thomas R. Berger, *Abandoned in the Wasteland: Children, Television, and the First Amendment* by Newton Minow and Craig LaMay, *The Organic Machine* by Richard White, and *Cracking Up: The Work of Unconscious Experience* by Christopher Bollas.

Query letters and SASEs should be directed to:

Elisabeth Sifton, Publisher, Hill and Wang
History, politics, current events and issues. Literary fiction.

NORTH POINT PRESS

North Point Press publishes literary nonfiction, including nature writing and natural history; literary food, travel, and sports writing; Asian literature; books about spirituality and religion; as well as biographies, memoirs, and essays.

Among North Point authors are Gary Snyder (*Practice of the Wild*, *Riprap* and *Cold Mountain Poems*), Wendell Berry (*What Are People For?*, *The Gift of the Good Land*), Beryl Markham (*West with the Night*), M. F. K. Fischer (*The Gastronomical Me*, *How to Cook a Wolf*), and Robert Aitken (*Taking the Path of Zen*). New titles include *Swamp*

Screamer: At Large with the Florida Panther by Charles Fergus, and *But Beautiful: A Book about Jazz* by Geoff Dyer.

Founded in Berkeley, California in 1980, North Point Press is now a Division of Farrar Straus & Giroux.

Query letters and SASEs should be directed to:

Ethan Nosowsky, Editor

FELDHEIM PUBLISHERS/FELDHEIM BOOKS

(See Directory of Religious, Spiritual, and Inspirational Publishers)

THE FEMINIST PRESS AT THE CITY UNIVERSITY OF NEW YORK

(See Directory of University Presses)

FERAL HOUSE

P.O. Box 3466
Portland, OR 97208
503-222-4902

Feral House publishes cultural critiques, individualistic essays, investigative and journalistic accounts, and popular reference works. The press publishes a variety of carefully designed and produced hardcover and trade paperback formats, including limited-edition signed clothbound volumes and illustrated paperbound books, in addition to a select audio library. Feral House typically issues several new titles per season and maintains a frothy backlist.

Feral House (founded in 1988) glides proudly through a brainscape of expression that traditional media have hitherto been slow—or fearful—to address. Feral House has proved the commercial viability of its creators' visions with a slate of successful releases.

Feral founder Adam Parfrey formerly fronted the celebrated Amok Press (house now deceased—RIP) in tandem with Ken Sweezy (publisher of Blast Books; please see separate Blast Books entry in this directory).

Picks of Feral House litter: *Cad: A Handbook for Heels* (edited by Charles Schneider), *Crying Wolf: Hate Crime Hoaxes in America* by Laird Wilcox, *I Cried, You Didn't Listen: A Survivor's Exposé of the California Youth Authority* by Dwight Edgar Abbott with Jack Carter, *Influencing Minds: A Reader in Quotations* (edited by Leonard Roy Frank), *Kooks: A Guide to the Outer Limits of Human Belief* by Donna Kossy, *Loser: The Real Seattle Music Story* by Clark Humphrey (coffee-table edition, designed by Art Chantry), *Psychic Dictatorship in the USA* by Alex Constantine, *Secret and Suppressed: Banned Ideas and Hidden History* (edited by Jim Keith), *Tortures and Torments of the Christian Martyrs: Illuminated by Contemporary Artists & Loathsome*

Criminals by Antonio Gallonio, a series of works by and about Anton LaVey (founder of the Church of Satan), and the sumptuous retrospective volume *Cosmic Retribution: The Infernal Art of Joe Coleman.*

On the all-important subsidiary-rights front: Feral's *Nightmare of Ecstasy: The Life and Art of Edward D. Wood, Jr.* by Rudolph Gray became the basis for the Academy Award-winning film *Ed Wood* (directed by Tim Burton). Reanimated title: Feral House has resuscitated Josh Alan Friedman's *Tales of Times Square* in an affordable photo-illustrated edition (after the original work was killed through neglect by a major trade publisher).

Feral's own homegrown tome, *Cult Rapture: Revelations of the Cosmic Mind* by Adam Parfrey, is an instant classic, a worthy follow-up to the renowned *Apocalypse Culture* (edited by Adam Parfrey), which has earned an enlarged and revised edition.

Potential Feral authors should note, and direct their queries accordingly: This house is very selective. Though the published materials may seem weird, wild, and extreme, the writing has to be thoughtful and accomplished. Subjects currently addressed are the more unusual aspects of popular culture, crime, the occult, film, and music. The house seeks manuscripts for its new imprint Funeral Home, which is devoted to rock and popular culture.

Feral House is distributed to the trade by Publishers Group West.

Query letters and SASEs should be directed to:

Adam Parfrey, President

FICTION COLLECTIVE TWO

Publications Center
Box 494
University of Colorado
Boulder, CO 80309
303-492-8947

Fiction Collective Two (founded in 1974) publishes innovative works of fiction; the house is among the most renowned small literary operations in the nation. Fiction Collective Two (FC2) considers finely honed projects that feature stylistic experimentation and challenging subject material. FC2 imprints include Black Ice Book series, On the Edge, and New Women's Fiction.

Fiction Collective Two oversees its own distributional network, including regional and national trade representatives.

Query letters and SASEs should be directed to:

Ronald Sukenick, Director

Curtis White, Director

DONALD I. FINE, INC.

(See under listings for Penguin USA)

FIREBRAND BOOKS

141 The Commons
Ithaca, NY 14850
607-272-0000

Firebrand is a publisher of award-winning titles in feminist and lesbian literature. The house publishes fiction (including genre categories, short stories, and literary novels), poetry, and general nonfiction (including informational works, personal tales, historical and cultural studies). Among Firebrand's strong suits is writing from an ethnic or cultural perspective, including African-American, American Indian, Latina, Italian-American, Jewish, and the American South.

Firebrand Books (founded in 1984 by Nancy K. Bereano) is notably inventive in its pursuit of new avenues for marketing and sales; the house maintains a solid backlist.

Firebrand nonfiction includes: *Eight Bullets: One Woman's Story of Surviving Anti-Gay Violenc*e by Claudia Brenner with Hannah Ashley, *My Mama's Dead Squirrel: Lesbian Essays on Southern Culture* by Mab Segrest, *Parker & Hulme: A Lesbian View* by Julie Glamuzina and Alison J. Lurie, *Politics of the Heart: A Lesbian Parenting Anthology* (edited by Sandra Pollack and Jeanne Vaughn), *S/he* by Minnie Bruce Pratt, and *Skin: Talking About Sex, Class and Literature* by Dorothy Allison (author of *Bastard Out of Carolina* and *Trash*).

Firebrand fiction and literary works: *Horseshoe Sky* (novel) by Catherine Koger, *Legal Tender: A Mystery* by Marion Foster, *The Other Sappho* by Ellen Frye, *A Gathering of Spirit: A Collection by North American Indian Women* (edited by Beth Brant), *The Gilda Stories* (time-traveling African-American vampire account) by Jewelle Gomez, and *Moll Cutpurse* (an Elizabethan picaresque) by Ellen Galford.

Poetry on the Firebrand list showcases diversity of approach and content. Representative works: *Artemis in Echo Park* by Eloise Klein Healey, *Beneath My Heart* by Janice Gould, *Normal Sex* by Linda Smukler, *Oral Tradition: Poems Selected & New* by Jewelle Gomez, and *The Black Back-Ups* by Kate Rushin.

Firebrand is the publisher of the renowned *Lesbian (Out)law: Survival Under the Rule of Law* by Ruthann Robson, and the cultural classic *Diamonds Are a Dyke's Best Friend* by Yvonne Zipter (an in-depth look at the lesbian national pastime of baseball).

Firebrand publishes the resource guide *Words to the Wise: A Writer's Guide to Feminist and Lesbian Periodicals & Publishers* by Andrea Fleck Clardy.

Humor on Firebrand's list features the *Dykes to Watch Out For* cartoon series by Alison Bechdel.

Firebrand is strong in direct-mail marketing and offers an 800 number for credit card orders; Firebrand titles are distributed to the trade by Inland.

Query letters and SASEs should be directed to:

Nancy K. Bereano, Editor and Publisher

FOCAL PRESS

(See Heinemann)

FOUR WALLS EIGHT WINDOWS

39 West 14th Street, Suite 503
New York, NY 10011
212-206-8965

Four Walls Eight Windows offers a compact seasonal list in literary fiction and creative nonfiction oriented toward issues and culture. The house is known for experimental fiction that features a stylistic and intellectual edge, American and world culture portrayed through artistic renditions of the essay, journalistic forays into progressive politics, literary and critical studies, and poetry.

This is a publisher with a list far from the norm: Four Walls Eight Windows catalogs cultural artifacts in book form. The house hosts a healthy backlist laden with critically acclaimed, accomplished sellers, as well as an array of literary reprints.

Four Walls Eight Windows (established in 1986) was dubbed descriptively—for the initial editorial environs—by founders John Oakes and Daniel Simon. Contrary to widespread speculation, when Dan Simon split to found the independent press Seven Stories (in early 1996; see separate entry in this directory), John Oakes *did not even contemplate* a name change to Two Walls Four Windows.

Fiction, literary works, and creative publishing ventures from Four Walls Eight Windows include *Ribofunk* (interconnected short stories) by Paul Di Filippo (author of *The Steampunk Trilogy*), *Hypnotism Made Easy* (novel) by Marie Nimier, *Eluthéria* (dramatic work) by Samuel Beckett, *Illuminated Poems* by Allen Ginsberg (illustrations by Eric Drooker), *American Poets Say Goodbye to the Twentieth Century* (edited by Andrei Codrescu and Laura Rosenthal), *The Sweet-Scented Manuscript* (novel) by Tito Perdue, and *No Entry* (novel) by Edward A. Nagel.

Four Walls Eight Windows nonfiction offerings: *Blood Season: Mike Tyson and the World of Boxing* by Phil Berger, *The Trials of Maria Barbella: The True Story of a 19th Century Crime of Passion* by Idanna Pucci, *Thomas Paine: Apostle of Freedom* (biography) by Jack Fruchtman Jr., and *The Enemy Within: The High Cost of Living Near Nuclear Reactors* by Jay Gould.

Four Walls Eight Windows books are distributed to the trade by Publishers Group West; foreign rights are administered by Writers House.

Query letters and SASEs should be directed to:

John Oakes, Publisher

FREE SPIRIT PUBLISHING

400 First Avenue North, Suite 616
Minneapolis, MN 55401
612-338-2068

Free Spirit Publishing (founded in 1983) produces trade nonfiction in a variety of arenas keyed to parenting, human development, the family, education, and relationships. Areas of special concentration: creative learning, healthy families, school success, self-esteem, gifted education, LD (learning differences), and good humor.

Free Spirit publications include education guides for students, educators, parents, and mental health professionals, as well as self-help for parents, educators, children, and teens. The publisher has been particularly successful with its Self-Help for Kids line of books and educational materials. Free Spirit also catalogs posters and other creative learning wares.

Free Spirit highlights: *The Families Book* by Arlene Erlbach, *Holding Steady* (novel) by Stephen Schwandt, *Write from the Edge: A Creative Borders Book* by Ken Vinton, *Helping Children Cope with the Loss of a Loved One: A Guide for Grownups* by William C. Kroen, *Win the Whining War & Other Family Skirmishes: A Family Peace Plan* by Cynthia Whitham, and *How to Reach and Teach ADD/ADHD Children: Practical Techniques, Strategies, and Interventions for Helping Children with Attention Problems and Hyperactivity* by Sandra F. Rief.

Free Spirit's distribution has been primarily in the educational arena; the house intends to tackle the broader book-trade market.

Query letters and SASEs should be directed to:

Judy Galbraith, Publisher

W. H. FREEMAN AND COMPANY PUBLISHERS
SCIENTIFIC AMERICAN BOOKS/COMPUTER SCIENCE PRESS

41 Madison Avenue
New York, NY 10010
212-576-9400

W. H. Freeman represents outstanding and innovative publishing in mathematics and the sciences, featuring trade titles of general interest, textbooks, and professional books. Areas of trade interest include anthropology, astronomy, current issues, nature and the environment, health and medicine, life sciences, parenting, and psychology.

Freeman books—especially the popular works—often display superb graphics and fine design. W. H. Freeman and Company (established in 1946) is a subsidiary of Scientific American, Inc. The house logs a trusty backlist.

Freeman books include *Drugs and the Brain* by Solomon H. Snyder, *The Science of Words* by George A. Miller, *Power Unseen: How Microbes Run the World* by Benard Dixon, and *Self-Traps: The Elusive Quest for Higher Self-Esteem* by William B. Swann Jr.

From Scientific American Library, a line of trade-oriented books authored by celebrated scientists, comes titles geared to particular fields in addition to works of general-readership appeal. Sample titles: *Beyond the Third Dimension: Geometry, Computer Graphics, and Higher Dimensions* by Thomas F. Banchoff, *Conservation and Biodiversity* by Andrew Dobson, *Perception* by Irvin Rock, and *Gravity's Fatal Attraction: Black Holes in the Universe* by Mitchell Begelman and Martin Rees.

A special coproduction of Infon, Inc., Scientific American, and W. H. Freeman is *Molecular Cell Biology* (CD-ROM).

W. H. Freeman oversees its own distribution.
Query letters and SASEs should be directed to:

Deborah Allen, Acquisitions Editor
Biology, biochemistry.

Richard Bonacci, Acquisitions Editor
Mathematics.

Susan Brennan, Acquisitions Editor
Psychology.

Jonathan Cobb, Acquisitions Editor
Trade Scientific American Library series.

Holly Hodder, Acquisitions Editor
Astronomy, anthropology, geosciences, physics, statistics.

Michelle Juliet, Acquisitions Editor
Chemistry.

Elizabeth Knoll, Acquisitions Editor
Trade areas of house interest.

COMPUTER SCIENCE PRESS

The focus of Current Computer Science Press is on computer science and information technology, with an eye on emerging areas within these quickly moving fields. The house offers introductory- to advanced-level books in computer science, and professional, trade, and college texts in computer sciences, telecommunications, and computer mathematics, as well as related areas. Computer Science Press, founded in 1974, became an imprint of W. H. Freeman in 1988.

Representing popularly oriented Computer Science Press offerings: *The New Turing Omnibus* by A. K. Dewdney, *Computer Power and Human Reason: From Judgment to Calculation* by Joseph Weizenbaum, and *The Digital Connection: A Layman's Guide to the Information Age* by Irwin Lebow.

Query letters and SASEs should be directed to:

Richard Bonacci, Publisher

FRIENDSHIP PRESS

(See Directory of Religious, Spiritual, and Inspirational Publishers)

FROMM INTERNATIONAL PUBLISHING CORPORATION

560 Lexington Avenue
New York, NY 10022
212-308-4010

Fromm International is a small-size house with a strong literary list. In addition to modern and contemporary fiction from around the globe, Fromm publishes diverse, high-quality writings in nonfiction categories such as history, biography, memoirs, belles-lettres, essays, cultural and performing arts, analytical psychology, and issues of contemporary interest. The house produces hardcovers and trade paperbacks. Fromm International (founded in 1982) has branch offices in Germany and Switzerland.

Query letters and SASEs should be directed to:

Leo V. Fromm, President

Thomas Thornton, Executive Editor

Kelley Williams, Assistant Editor

FULCRUM PUBLISHING

350 Indiana Street, Suite 350
Golden, CO 80401
303-277-1623

Fulcrum features books in general trade nonfiction, with an emphasis in gardening, nature and the outdoors, food, travel guides, business and the environment, Colorado and the Rockies, parenting, health, humor, and American history,

Imprints and lines include the Library of Congress series of Americana, educational books (for children and adults), and the Starwood line of books and calendars. The house also issues selected audiocassettes on the Fulcrum Audio Book imprint. Native American writers and subjects are a vital part of the Fulcrum program.

Fulcrum Publishing (founded in 1984) is a growing firm with an ambitious list. It is the Fulcrum vision to produce works that provide a link to the experiences and wisdom of the past. This image fits in neatly with the publisher's characterization of himself as a biblioholic who shares the notion expressed by Thomas Jefferson in a letter to John Adams: "I cannot live without books." This is good news for Fulcrum readers, and good news for writers too. Fulcrum supports a hefty backlist.

Titles from Fulcrum: *Edible Flowers: From Garden to Palate* by Cathy Wilkinson Barash, *Bagging Big Bugs* by Whitney Cranshaw and Boris Kondratieff, *Basic Gardening: A Handbook for Beginning Gardeners* by Louise Carter, *Americans on the Move: The History of Waterways, Railways, and Highways* by Russell Bourne, *Treasure Islands: The Fascinating World of Pirates, Buried Treasure, and Fortune Hunters* by Cameron Platt and John Wright, *Earth Warrior: Overboard with Paul Watson and the Sea Shepherd Conservation Society* by David B. Morris, *The Utah Guide* by Allan Kent Powell, *God Is Red: A Native View of Religion* by Vine Deloria Jr., and *Keepers of Life: Discovering Plants Through Native American Stories and Earth Activities for Children* by Michael J. Caduto and Joseph Bruhac (illustrated book; accompanying set of audiocassettes).

Fulcrum Publishing handles its own distribution.

Query letters and SASEs should be directed to:

T. J. Baker, Acquisitions Editor
Or send prospective projects in care of the Submissions Department.

GALE

835 Penobscot Building
Detroit, MI 48226
313-961-2242

Gale catalogs professional and popular reference and information works with an accent in fields such as technological innovation, international business, environmental issues, literature and author biographies, multicultural studies, and women's studies. Gale also produces titles in the additional areas of arts and entertainment, religion and occultism, education, careers, business, nation and world, government and law, science and medicine, the electronic information industry, publishing and information science, general reference, and sports.

Gale is a stalwart specialist in reference products, including books and databases for businesses, consumers, students, and general information seekers. Gale's list embraces directories, biographical works, specialty dictionaries, and series in literary and cultural criticism. The house catalog includes products from imprints and subsidiaries such as Visible Ink Press, St. James Press, and the Taft Group. Gale (formerly Gale Research) was begun in 1954; the firm is currently a subsidiary of the Thomson Corporation.

As an information publisher, Gale constantly courts new topic arenas and information-delivery systems to address the ever-widening range of reader requests and needs as well as to take advantage of the burgeoning reservoir of information sources. Gale titles are available through on-line delivery services, and on diskette, magnetic tape, CD-ROM, and the Internet.

From Gale: *Worldwide Government Directory*; *European Wholesalers and Distributors Directory*; *National Housing Directory for People with Disabilities*; *Cemeteries of the U.S.*; *Statistical Record of Religion in America*; *Encyclopedia of College Basketball*; *Chronology of Native North American History*; *Divorce Help Sourcebook*; *The Vampire Book: The Encyclopedia of the Undead*; *The Student Contact Book; Pop Culture Landmarks*; *Major 20th-Century Writers*; and *Directory of Online Databases*.

Gale oversees its own trade and library distribution, as well as its own electronic distribution. The house catalog includes products from Visible Ink Press, St. James Press, the Taft Group, and UXL.

Query letters and SASEs should be directed to:

Dedria Bryfonski, President and Chief Operating Officer

GALLAUDET UNIVERSITY PRESS

(See Directory of University Presses)

THE GAMMON PRESS

P.O. Box 294
Arlington, MA 02174
617-641-2091

Gammon publishes works that deal with games of skill and chance, primarily in the domain of backgammon, with additional titles in areas such as hyper-backgammon, poker, theory of gambling, blackjack, video poker, sports betting, horse racing, and (very occasionally) chess. The Gammon Press emphasizes practical instruction, strategy, and game improvement; the house also produces profiles of players, match analyses, and techniques of the masters.

The Gammon Press is a specialty house that produces a select number of new products each year. In addition to books, Gammon offers computer software, backgammon sets and supplies, calendars, periodicals (including *Inside Backgammon*), and videotapes. The house maintains a hardy backlist.

The Gammon catalog includes these works in its core backgammon publishing program: *The Backgammon Handbook* by Enno Heyken and Martin Fischer, *Hyper-Backgammon: Game of Lightning Speed* by Hugh Sconyers, *How to Play Tournament Backgammon* by Kit Woolsey, *In the Game Until the End: Winning in Ace-Point Endgames* by Bob Wachtel, and *Learning From the Machine: Robertie vs. TD-Gammon* by Bill Robertie.

Also from Gammon: *Basics of Sports Betting* by Avery Cardoza, *Poker Essays* by Mason Malmuth, *Winning Poker* by David Slansky, *Basics of Horse Racing* by Whitney Cobb, and *MatchQuiz: Annotated Matches on Computer Diskettes* (compiled by Hal Heinrich; commentary by Kit Woolsey).

The Gammon Press handles the distribution of its own list.

Query letters and SASEs should be directed to:

William Robertie, President

GARRETT PUBLISHING

384 South Military Trail
Deerfield Beach, FL 33442
305-480-8543

Garrett focuses on business, finance, law, and personal finance. Garrett books are practical and embody a self-help/how-to approach that features sample forms, ready-to-use templates, checklists, instructions, resources, and informative examples. A major Garrett imprint is E•Z Legal Books.

Garrett Publishing (founded in 1990) is on the lookout for authors with marketable projects—authors who are experts in their fields and who know how to get their point across clearly and enthusiastically. Garrett's marketing department is staffed with professionals skilled in publicity, promotions, advertising, and editorial services. Garrett promotes its authors' books through print advertising, television appearances, and radio spots. The house offers competitive advances and royalties.

With sales representatives located strategically across the United States, Garrett's books are available in the giant trade bookseller chains and are obtainable from major wholesalers and distributors. Over the past several seasons, the publisher has expanded its retail distribution.

Representative titles from Garrett: *Super Savvy* by Robert E. Levinson, *Pay Zero Estate Taxes* by Milton Corey, *How I Made Millions (With Just a Few Simple Ideas)* by Robert M. Hayes, *Cash for Your Business* by Garrett Adams, *Asset Protection Secrets* by Arnold S. Goldstein, and *The E•Z Legal Advisor*.

Garrett Publishing distributes through its own house operation as well as via outlets such as Quality Book Distributors, Ingram, and Baker and Taylor.

Query letters and SASEs should be directed to:

Arnold Goldstein, Editor/Owner

GENERAL PUBLISHING GROUP

2701 Ocean Park Boulevard, Suite 140
Santa Monica, CA 90405
310-314-4000
800-745-9000

General Publishing produces commercial nonfiction covering the high-interest areas of film, television, music, popular culture, global issues, politics, personalities, self-improvement and fitness, sports, history, humor, and popular inspiration. General publishes in hardcover, quality trade paper, and mass-market paperback editions, in addition to producing a strong selection of illustrated gift books.

General Publishing Group (founded in 1991) accents entertainment and the media; General projects by and large share an emphasis on instantly recognizable, celebrity- and media-oriented topics and subjects (including tie-in publications).

Sample General titles: *Pamela Anderson in Pictures* (photographed by Stephen Wayda; text by Bibi Jordan), *As the World Turns: The Complete Family Scrapbook* by Julie Poll, *Jacqueline Kennedy Onassis: The Making of a First Lady* by James Lowe (introduction by Letitia Baldridge), *The Simpson Trial in Black and White* by Tom Elias and Dennis Schatzman, *How to Be a Hollywood Superstar* by Barry Dutter and Rich Hoover, and *Nips and Tucks: Everything You Must Know before Having Cosmetic Surgery* by Diana Barry.

Among the house's initial successes were a lavish biography of Hugh Hefner and *The Bettie Page Book*. Daytime television drama is featured in *General Hospital* and *All My Children* (both by Gary Warner). Big hits from the General list include *Frank Sinatra* by Nancy Sinatra (in editions featuring a lineup of collector's CD recordings), *100 Greatest Moments in Olympic History* by Bud Greenspan, and *Top 40 Years of Rock & Roll* by Casey Kasem.

General Publishing Group oversees its own distribution.

Query letters and SASEs should be directed to:

Quay Hays, Publisher

Murray Fisher, Editor

GLENEIDA PUBLISHING GROUP

(See Baker Book House and Liguori Publications, both in the Directory of Religious, Spiritual, and Inspirational Publishers)

THE GLOBE PEQUOT PRESS

6 Business Park Road
Old Saybrook, CT 06475
203-395-0440

mailing address:
P.O. Box 833
Old Saybrook, CT 06475

Globe Pequot is a specialist in travel and outdoor recreation, with additional interest in cooking, personal finance, and home-based business. The publisher accents titles marketed to both trade and specialty market slots.

Within this program, Globe Pequot looks for works in a number of important categories: travel books, regional and special-interest travel guides; family adventure guides; travel annuals, accommodations guides, itinerary-format guides, and travel how-tos; outdoor recreation—any outdoor sport; how-to and where-to guides; home-based business—authors should have firsthand experience running the featured business; source books (almanac-style books that combine informational essays with source information on specific avocations and areas of interest).

In the travel arena, Globe Pequot is well regarded for several best-selling series and also distributes for a number of travel-specialist houses. Among Globe Pequot lines: Discover Historic America, Quick Escapes (weekend and day trips keyed to metropolitan areas or regions), Recommended Country Inns, the Bed & Breakfast guidebook series, Family Adventure Guides, Cadogan Guides to destinations worldwide for the discriminating traveler, Karen Brown Travel Press personalized guides, and the popular Off-the-Beaten-Path series. Globe Pequot also updates a variety of annuals, among them *Europe by Eurail*. Globe Pequot's regionally keyed books also cover interest areas such as biking, hiking, mountaineering, skiing, and family activities in wilderness areas and on the beach.

Globe Pequot catalogs the following representative titles: *Family Adventure Guide: Illinois* by Lori Meek Schuldt, *Stepping Lightly on Australia: A Traveler's Guide to Ecotourism* by Shirly LaPlanche, *Getting the Most for Your Travel Dollar* by Herbert Teison and Nancy Dunnan, *Pirates & Patriots of the Revolution: An Illustrated Encyclopedia of Colonial Seamanship* by C. Keith Wilbur, *Enduring Harvests: Native American Foods and Festivals for Every Season* by E. Barrie Kavasch, *The 100 Best Honeymoon Resorts of the World* by Katharine D. Dyson, *Guide to Ancient Native American Sites* by Michael Durham, *Kayaking Made Easy: A Manual for Beginners with Tips for the Experienced* by Dennis O. Stuhaug, and *Beautiful Easy Lawns and Landscapes* by Laurence Sombke.

The Globe Pequot Press (originated in 1947) operates from publishing and warehouse headquarters in Old Saybrook. The press distributes its own list through its home-office facilities as well as a network of regional sales representatives. The house handles distribution for houses such as Appalachian Mountain Club Books, Berlitz Publishing, Karen Brown Travel Press, Cadogen Guides, Corkscrew Press, and Moorland Publishing.

Query letters and SASEs should be directed to:

Laura Strom, Acquisitions Editor

DAVID R. GODINE, PUBLISHER, INC.

Box 9103
9 Lewis Street
Lincoln, MA 01773
617-259-0700

Godine accents trade nonfiction in areas such as history and criticism, typography and graphic arts, art and architecture, horticulture, cooking, Americana, and regional interest. The house also publishes fiction (including mysteries), literature and essays, and poetry, as well as children's books. Godine offers a line of classic works in reprint as well as works in translation.

The Godine program is committed to quality. Godine specializes in attentively produced hardcover and trade paperback editions. The house issues a small catalog of new titles each year while maintaining an active backlist. Godine's imprints include Country Classics, Double Detectives, and Nonpareil Books.

David R. Godine, Publisher (founded in 1969) was started in an abandoned cow barn, where David R. Godine both worked and lived; the expanding operation later moved to Boston. Now relocated to Lincoln, Massachusetts, Godine has an increasingly successful distribution arrangement and a stronger concentration on titles with backlist potential (particularly nonfiction).

Representative of Godine nonfiction: *Tyranny of the Normal: Essays on Bioethics, Theology, and Myth* by Leslie Fiedler, *The Art of the Printed Book, 1455–1955* by Joseph Blumenthal, *Into Print: Selected Writings on Printing History, Typography, and Book Production* by John Dreyfus, *Calligraphic Flourishing: A New Approach to an Ancient Art* by Bill Hildebrandt, *Growing Up in New York* (photographs by Arthus Leipzig; foreword by Gordon Parks), *Landmarks in the Landscape: Historic Architecture in the Western National Parks* by Harvey H. Kaiser, *Giving Up the Gun: Japan's Reversion to the Sword, 1545–1879* by Noel Perrin, and *Reading in Bed: Personal Essays on the Glories of Reading* (edited by Steven Gilbar).

Indicative of fiction and literary writing on the Godine list: *Eclipse Fever* by Walter Abish, *Famine* by Liam O'Flaherty, *Little Jordan* by Marly Youmans, *Diary of a Humiliated Man* by Félix de Azúa, *Ghost Wrestling* (poetry) by Roger Weingarten, *Vain Empires* (poetry) by William Logan, and *Make the Cobra Talk* (poetry) by Mark Cox.

Mystery and suspense titles are represented by *The Man Who Liked Slow Tomatoes* by K. C. Constantine and *The Woman in Black* by Susan Hill.

Godine's children's books backlist includes: *We Didn't Mean to Go to the Sea* by Arthur Ransome, *Crime and Puzzlement: 24 Solve-Them-Yourself Picture Mysteries* by Lawrence Treat (illustrated by Leslie Cabarga), *The Empty Creel* by Geraldine Pope (illustrations by Dennis Cunningham), and *Ned Kelly and the City of Bees* by Thomas Keneally.

Godine distributes through National Book Network; the house distributes for Eridanos Press, which publishes foreign literature in translation.

Query letters and SASEs should be directed to:

Mark Polizzotti, Editorial Director

GOODFELLOW PRESS

7710 196th Avenue Northeast
Redmond, WA 98053
206-868-7323

Goodfellow specializes in character-driven mainstream trade paperback fiction of all kinds. Categories and genres include love stories and romances, mysteries, suspense novels, and strong contemporary stories with mainstream-readership appeal.

Distribution is primarily through mail-order and library markets.

Writer guidelines are available from the publisher. Please query first. Query letters and SASEs should be directed to:

Sally Astridge, Acquisitions Editor

Pamela R. Goodfellow, Editorial Director

Kay Morison, Acquisitions Editor

Sharon Plowman, Acquisitions Editor

C. J. Wycoff, Acquisitions Editor

GRAYWOLF PRESS

2402 University Avenue, Suite 203
Saint Paul, MN 55114
612-641-0077

Graywolf publishes poetry, fiction, and belletristic nonfiction and essays. Graywolf produces works by writers past and present, with particular emphasis on the scene of contemporary international letters as well as a line of literary anthologies and reissues. The Graywolf Discovery series focuses on reprint gems in paperback. Graywolf hosts a solid backlist of featured titles.

Graywolf backs up its authors and its literary claims with publishing prowess: the Graywolves have been successful in finding an audience for their works, and the Graywolf Press list has been augmented, confirming the achievement of a program that runs contrary to the stream of contemporary commercial publishing.

Begun in 1974, Graywolf Press exemplifies the small-scale independent American literary house. The publisher's wolfpack logo marks a list rippling with award-winners and critical endorsement.

Fiction and literary works: *Watershed* by Percival Everett, *The Last Studebaker* by Robin Hemley, *Places in the World a Woman Could Walk* by Janet Kauffman, *Beachcombing for a Shipwrecked God* by Joe Coomer, and *The True Subject: Writers on Life and Craft* (edited by Kurt Brown).

Poetry from Graywolf includes: *Otherwise* (new and selected poems) by Jane Kenyon, *Wild Kingdom* by Vijay Seshadri, *The Misunderstanding of Nature* by Sophie Cabot Black, and *The Owl in the Mask of the Dreamer* by John Haines.

Indicative of Graywolf nonfiction are selections in essays, criticism, history, biography, and memoirs. Among them: *A Song of Love and Death: The Meaning of Opera* by Peter Conrad, *Jack and Rochelle: A Story of Love and Resistance* by Jack Sutin and Rochelle Sutin (as told to Lawrence Sutin), *South Wind Changing* by Ngoc Quang Huynh, *Voices Over Water* by Dennis Nurkse, and *Episodes* by Pierre Delattre.

Graywolf Press utilizes a network of regional sales representatives; books are proffered to the trade through Consortium Book Sales and Distribution.

Query letters and SASEs should be directed to:

Anne Czarniecki, Managing Editor

Fiona McCrae, Director and Publisher

Scott M. Walker, Publisher and Editor

GREENWOOD PUBLISHING GROUP
AUBURN HOUSE/BERGIN & GARVEY/GREENWOOD PRESS/
PRAEGER PUBLISHERS/QUORUM BOOKS

88 Post Road West
P.O. Box 5007
Westport, CT 06881
203-226-3571

The Greenwood publishing program encompasses general trade nonfiction, along with a traditional emphasis on professional, academic, and reference books in economics, business, social sciences and humanities, law enforcement, business, law, and current affairs. It also offers special series of reference works. In addition, Greenwood produces reprints of scholarly monographs and journals. The house issues editions in hardcover and trade paperback.

Greenwood Publishing Group (instituted in 1967) comprises a number of imprints and divisions that include Auburn House, Bergin & Garvey, Greenwood Press, Quorum

Books, and Praeger Publishers. (See separate subentries below.) Greenwood imprints generally maintain extensive backlists.

Greenwood Publishing Group orchestrates its own distribution. A major portion of Greenwood's sales are aimed at the library, institutional, and corporate markets.

GREENWOOD ACADEMIC AND TRADE PUBLISHING
AUBURN HOUSE
BERGIN & GARVEY
PRAEGER PUBLISHERS

Greenwood Publishing Group's general nonfiction trade books and academic works are published under the imprints Auburn House, Bergin & Garvey, and Praeger Publishers. Each imprint has its own individual publishing orbit and distinct editorial approach.

Auburn House concentrates on professional and academic works in economics, business, healthcare, labor relations, and public policy.

Bergin & Garvey accents scholarly monographs in the social sciences and humanities, as well as general nonfiction works in a similar subject range geared toward a popular audience.

Praeger Publishers evidences a vigorous approach to trade nonfiction and areas of scholarly specialist attention. Categories of publishing interest include history (including cultural history), military studies (including history, espionage, and military operations), political science and international relations, women's studies, business and economics, psychology, and urban affairs.

Representing the trade-oriented portion of the list are *Putting America's House in Order: The Nation As a Family* by David Abshire and Brock Brower, *Our Mothers, Our Selves: Writers and Poets Celebrating Motherhood* (edited by Karen J. Donnelly and J. B. Bernstein), *Killing Ground on Okinawa: The Battle for Sugar Loaf Hill* by James H. Hallas, *Drug Warriors and Their Prey: From Police Power to Police State* by Richard Lawrence Miller, *The Golden Years: A 12-Step Anti-Aging Plan for a Longer, Healthier, and Happier Life* by Lawrence B. Slobody (edited by David Oliphant), and *Zero Fighter* (a technohistory) by Akira Yoshimura (translated by Retsu Kaiho and Michael Gregson).

Query letters and SASEs should be directed to:

James Dunton, Publisher

Lynn Taylor, Assistant Vice President for Editorial

James Ice, Editor
Business, Economics.

Alan Sturmer, Editor
Textbooks.

Daniel Eades, Senior Editor
Political science, history, and military studies.

Elizabeth Murphy, Editor
Anthropology, education, women's studies, ethnic studies.

Nick Street, Editor
Sociology and psychology.

Nina Pearlstein, Editor
Humanities.

GREENWOOD REFERENCE PUBLISHING

The Greenwood Reference Publishing imprint offers popular, educational, scholarly, and professional reference works. The house counts among its other specialty areas library and information sciences; social sciences, humanities, and the arts; and works covering contemporary trends in cultural studies and criticism.

A good number of these reference series are authored primarily by academics, including the Music Reference Collection, Bio-Bibliographies in Music, Contributions in Economics and Economic History, Contributions in Women's Studies, Contributions to the Study of Science Fiction and Fantasy, and Contributions to the Study of World History.

Query letters and SASEs should be directed to:

Cynthia Harris, Executive Editor

Alicia Merrit, Acquisitions Editor
Humanities.

Barbara Rader, Senior Editor
School and public library reference.

Nita Romer, Editor
Social and behavioral science.

George Butler, Associate Editor
Library and information science.

Emily Michic, Assistant Editor
School and Public Library Reference.

GREENWOOD BUSINESS AND PROFESSIONAL PUBLISHING QUORUM BOOKS

At Greenwood Business and Professional Publishing and Quorum Books the accent is on titles keyed to areas of current topical issues in business, finance, and law. Sectors of this division's scope are management issues and trends; business ethics; international business and economics; business, law, and public policy; environment and energy; information and corporate communications; human resource management; organizational behavior and development; finance, investment, and banking; accounting and taxation; marketing, advertising, and sales; and public and not-for-profit management.

Indicative of the Quorum list: *Scenario-Driven Planning: Learning to Manage Strategic Uncertainty* by Nicholas C. Georgantzas and William Acar; *The Music Business—a Legal Perspective: Music and Live Performances* by Peter Muller;

Mediating Environmental Conflicts: Theory and Practice   (edited by J. Walton Blackburn and Willa Marie Bruce); *Futurework: The Revolution Reshaping American Business* by Edward E. Gordon, Ronald R. Morgan, and Judith A. Ponticell; and *How Women Executives Succeed: Lessons and Experiences from the Federal Government* by Danity Little.

Query letters and SASEs should be directed to:

Eric Valentine, Publisher

GROLIER CHILDREN'S PUBLISHING
GROLIER INCORPORATED
ORCHARD BOOKS
FRANKLIN WATTS

Grolier Incorporated is a subsidiary of the Matra Hachette international multimedia communications empire. Grolier Children's Publishing is the umbrella under which the separate book-publishing houses Franklin Watts and Orchard Books operate their independent, distinctive lists geared to children's and young-adult markets. (See separate subentries below.)

FRANKLIN WATTS

Sherman Turnpike
Danbury, CT 06813
203-797-3500

Franklin Watts produces a comprehensive array of school and library books for grades 4–12, and offers a line of Spanish-language titles. Emphasis at Franklin Watts is on historical and contemporary biography, nature and the environment, social issues, health and the human body, science and technology, and language arts.

Franklin Watts (founded in 1942) publishes a few trade projects, in addition to its core concentration on scholarly and educational titles for a school-age readership, as well as a select reference list.

Franklin Watts handles its own distribution.

Franklin Watts does not consider fiction or adult titles. Query letters and SASEs should be directed to:

Melissa Stewart, Editor
Science.

Scott Prentzas, Editor
Young-adult nonfiction.

Russell Prim, Executive Editor
All other areas of house interest.

ORCHARD BOOKS

95 Madison Avenue
New York, NY 10016
212-951-2649

Orchard Books produces mainstream trade-oriented fiction and nonfiction books for children, many of them copiously illustrated works. Here, award-winning titles and authors abound. Storybooks and picture books for children are among areas of particular house emphasis.

Orchard titles include *Counting Our Way to Maine* by Maggie Smith, *Jennifer's Room* by Peter Utton, *The Moonglow Roll-O-Rama* by Dav Pilkey, *Homeless* (written and photographed by Bernard Wolf), and *1,000 Miles in 12 Days: Pro Cyclists on Tour* by David Hautzig.

Query letters and SASEs should be directed to:

Neal Porter, President and Publisher

Maggie Herold, Executive Editor

GROVE/ATLANTIC, INC.

841 Broadway
New York, NY 10003
212-614-7850

Grove/Atlantic publishes trade nonfiction and fiction, often with a contemporary cultural bent or an issues-oriented edge. Grove Press and Atlantic Monthly Press, two previously independent houses, are united under the Grove/Atlantic, Inc., corporate crest. Grove/Atlantic operates from the former Grove headquarters on Broadway (with Atlantic having relocated from its previous digs at nearby Union Square West). Grove/Atlantic operates essentially as one house while maintaining the distinction of two major imprints.

Subsequent to the above-noted merger—with Atlantic most decidedly the major partner—speculation was that Atlantic had bought Grove essentially for Grove's extensive, internationally renowned backlist. Atlantic would presumably vampirize, cannibalize, then cast aside the bare bones of Grove to any interested bidders. Happily, such baleful prognostications have not come to pass; the publishing image of Grove/Atlantic is, if anything, more finely honed under the auspices of the umbrella house. (See separate subentries below.)

Grove/Atlantic books are distributed by Publishers Group West.

ATLANTIC MONTHLY PRESS

Atlantic Monthly Press produces a list that embraces the spectrum of commercial categories, publishing hardcover and trade paperback editions in fiction, memoirs, belles-lettres, history, social sciences, current affairs, natural history, ethnology, lifestyle, fashion, and cuisine. AMP authors have over the years garnered an enormous wealth of recognition for their work, including Pulitzers, Nobels, and National Book Awards. The AMP Traveler series encompasses nonfiction works that offer unstinting looks at nations, cultures, and peoples of the world.

Atlantic Monthly Press has long been representative of the highest aims of American publishing—with a list that features quality writing, fine production, and strong commercial presence. Atlantic Monthly Press was inaugurated originally (in 1917) to be primarily a book-publishing vehicle for writers associated with *Atlantic Monthly* magazine. From 1925 through 1984 the press was an imprint of Boston's Little, Brown. Atlantic Monthly Press was bought by Carl Navarre in 1985, and under current owner-publisher Morgan Entrekin (who bought out Navarre in 1991) AMP (now in consort with Grove) continues as a leading force in American letters.

Atlantic nonfiction includes *The Price of Experience: Money, Power, Image, and Murder in Los Angeles* by Randall Sullivan, *The Enemies List* by P. J. O'Rourke (with contributions from the readers of *The American Spectator* magazine), *Mukiwa: A White Boy in Africa* by Peter Godwin, *Victory: The Reagan Administration's Secret Strategy That Hastened the Collapse of the Soviet Union* by Peter Schweitzer, *When the Phone Doesn't Ring, It'll Be Me!* by Cynthia Heimel, *Secret Soldier: The True Life Story of Israel's Greatest Commando* by Muki Betser with Robert Rosenberg, *The Road to Hell: The True Story of George Jackson, Stephen Bingham, and the San Quentin Massacre* by Paul Liberatore, *Yakuza Diary: Doing Time in the Japanese Underworld* by Christopher Seymour, *A Flyfisher's World* by Nick Lyons (drawings by Mari Lyons), and *The Little Book of Weddings: Anthology* (a keepsake/gift book) edited by Will Balliett.

Representing AMP fiction and literature are *Let's Put the Future Behind Us* by Jack Womack, *Learning to Drive* by William Norwich, *Worst Fears* by Fay Weldon, *Dead Folks* (a Detective Sergeant Mulheisen mystery) by Jon A. Jackson, and *Sewer, Gas & Electric* by Matt Ruff.

GROVE PRESS

Grove Press accents fiction and nonfiction with a sharp cultural consciousness and literary flair. The house continues to expand on its strong backlist base by engaging at the forefront of publishing trends: Grove publishes a line of feature-film screenplays and has instituted a new poetry series.

Grove Press was founded in 1952 by literary pathfinder Barney Rosset, who established a tradition of adventuresome lists featuring some of the finest and most fearless writing from around the globe. This literary institution was purchased by Ann Getty in 1985; in league with the British-based house of Weidenfeld & Nicholson, the publisher (briefly) operated under the sobriquet Grove Weidenfeld. With the early retreat of the Weidenfeld interests, the fate of Grove was a popular topic of publishing tattle—rumored by some to be perpetually on the block prior to the house's merger with Atlantic Monthly Press.

Throughout these corporate shifts, Grove nevertheless extended its distinguished reputation, with a masterly mix of backlist fiction and nonfiction as well as worthy new titles that are commercially successful and stimulating (cerebrally as well as sensually)—as befits the Grove tradition.

In fiction, Grove owns a historic commitment to literature that pushes at boundaries, having published such authors as Kathy Acker, William S. Burroughs, Robert Coover, Thulani Davis, Jack Kerouac, Milan Kundera, Henry Miller, Bharati Mukherjee, Hubert Selby Jr., and Diane Williams. Grove publishes a wide variety of world literature in translation and has a strong drama list.

Indicative of Grove fiction and literary works: *Shooting Elvis* by Robert Eversz, *Chairman Mao Would Not Be Amused: Fiction from Today's China* (edited by Howard Goldblatt), *The Dream Police* by Dennis Cooper, *The Water Buddha Drinks* by Banana Yoshimoto, *Leaving Las Vegas* by John O'Brien, *Bongwater* by Michael Hornburg, *Behind Closed Doors* and *The Butcher and Other Erotica* by Alina Reyes (both volumes translated from the French by David Watson), *Meeting the Master* by Elissa Ward, *Pussy, King of the Pirates* by Kathy Acker (which ties in with independently produced grunge/punk musical version on CD, featuring Kathy and the Mekons and graphics by S. Clay Wilson), *Wild at Heart* by Barry Gifford, and *The Ages of Lulu* by Almudena Grandes.

Grove nonfiction areas include biography and memoirs, popular culture worldwide, literary criticism, history and politics, fine crafts and art, and cuisine. Titles include *Please Kill Me: The Uncensored History of Punk* by Legs McNeil and Gillian McCain, *Bound and Gagged: Pornography and the Politics of Fantasy in America* by Laura Kipnis, *ClitNotes: A Sapphic Sampler* (memoir) by Holly Hughes, *New Orleans: Behind the Masks of America's Most Exotic City* by Carol Flake, and *The Language of Vision: Meditations on Myth and Metaphor* by Jamake Highwater.

Grove/Atlantic Monthly editors acquire in all areas consistent with house description. Prospective authors please note that Grove/Atlantic no longer accepts unsolicited material. However, you may still send a query or (occasionally) talk directly with an editor before sending a manuscript. Query letters and SASEs should be directed to:

Morgan Entrekin, Publisher

Joan Bingham, Editor

Jim Moser, Executive Editor

Anton Muller, Senior Editor

Colin Dickerman, Associate Editor

GULF PUBLISHING COMPANY

P.O. Box 2608
Houston, TX 77252
713-529-4301
713-529-4444

Gulf Publishing Company (founded in 1916) is a leading publisher in the areas of recreation and travel, business and management, training and adult education, and science and technology. As a large and varied media enterprise, Gulf also produces audiotapes, videotapes, and computer software.

Gulf Publishing's regional-interest list covers North America in general as well as the Gulf Coast belt and Texas. A house specialty line offers regional business and legal guides that supplement a strong selection of travel, recreational, and historical works.

In addition, Gulf publishes selectively throughout the gamut of general trade categories, with seasonal lists that include current affairs, political stories, lifestyle and cuisine, some children's books for kids ages nine and up, and occasional fiction. Gulf offers a robust backlist, and a significant portion of Gulf's travel-guide titles are released in periodically updated versions.

Gulf's imprints include Pisces Books (diving and snorkeling guides, as well as titles in history), Mariner's Atlas Series (maps, charts, and cartographic guides to cruising waters for mariners, anglers, and divers), Texas Monthly Guidebooks and the Texas Monthly Field Guides, and Ray Miller's Eyes of Texas historical travel guides. Gulf publishing also offers a software catalog, videotape training programs, and professional reference books in engineering.

Gulf Publishing is always on the lookout for new manuscripts in its areas of interest.

The Gulf trade list has featured such titles as *Good Food Afloat: Tasty and Nutritious Recipes for Healthy Shipboard Meals* by Joan Betterly, *The Chinese Microwave Cookbook* by Pearly Hoh, *The Denver Chronicle: From a Golden Past to a Mile-High Future* by David Kent Ballast, *Backroads of New England* by Bob Howells, *Space Satellite Handbook* (edited by Anthony R. Curtis), *International Business Case Studies for the Multicultural Marketplace* (edited by Robert T. Moran, David Braaten, and John Walsh), *Solution Selling* by Robert R. Blake and Rachel Kelly McKee, and the children's title *Hank the Cowdog: The Case of the Double Bumblebee Sting* by John R. Erickson.

Gulf Publishing Company's customer-service team manages regional, national, and international sales and distribution, both in-house and through a network of regional sales representatives.

Query letters and SASEs should be directed to:

William J. Lowe, Editor in Chief

HARCOURT BRACE & COMPANY

San Diego office:
525 B Street, Suite 1900
San Diego, CA 92101
619-699-6816

New York office:
15 East 26th Street
New York, NY 10010
212-592-1120

The Harcourt Brace trade division publishes the gamut of serious and commercial fiction and nonfiction in both hardcover and paperback. Of special note are HB's Judaica backlist, literary works in translation, the Harvest imprint (which accents American and international literature and culture in trade paper originals and reprints), Gulliver Books (popular works in hardcover and trade paper for readers of all ages), and HB Miller Accounting Publications.

Harcourt Brace & Company (founded in 1919) has through the decades evolved into a publishing house of prodigious reach. HB's multidimensional sprawl encompasses offices in such diverse locations as Orlando, San Diego, Toronto, and New York. Although the trade-publishing program has been trimmed markedly of late, Harcourt Brace (formerly Harcourt Brace Jovanovich) remains particularly potent in the arena of educational materials and texts, as well as professional reference. Among HB subsidiaries are Academic Press; HB Legal and Professional Publications; Johnson Reprint (scholarly and special-interest titles); W. B. Saunders (professional and academic medical publications); and Holt, Rinehart, & Winston (focusing on the educational market from elementary through university levels).

On the Harcourt Brace nonfiction trade list: *Tomorrow's War: The Threat of High-Technology Weapons* by David Shukman, *The Walls of Jericho: Lyndon Johnson, Hubert Humphrey, Richard Russell, and the Struggle for Civil Rights* by Robert Mann, *Matisse: A Portrait* by Hayden Herrera, *Homosexuality in History* by Colin Spencer, *Shoot Out the Lights: The Amazing, Improbable, Exhilarating Saga of the 1969–70 New York Knicks* by Bob Spitz, and *Citizen Turner: The Wild Rise of an American Tycoon* by Robert and Gerald Jay Goldberg.

Harcourt Brace fiction and literature: *Pushing the Bear: A Novel of the Trail of Tears* by Diane Glancy, *A History Maker* by Alasdair Gray (with illustrations by the author), *Butterfly Weed* by Donald Harrington, *The King of Babylon Shall Not Come Against You* by George Garrett, *Lonesome Standard Time* by Dana Andrew Jennings, *But I Love You Anyway* by Sara Lewis, *Shipwrecks* by Akira Yoshimura (translated from the Japanese by Mark Ealey), *Blameless in Abaddon* (science fiction) by James Morrow, and *Nebula Awards 30: SFWA's Choices for the Best Science Fiction and Fantasy of the Year* (edited by Pamela Sargent).

Harcourt Brace handles its own distribution.

Although Harcourt Brace has greatly reduced its acquisitions, the house is still active in the trade arena. Query letters and SASEs should be directed to:

Daniel H. Farley, Vice President and Publisher (New York and San Diego)
Adult trade books.

Walter Bode, Editor (New York)

Candace Hodges, Assistant Editor (San Diego)

Christa Malone, Editor (San Diego)

(Ms.) Drenka Willen, Editor (New York)
Literary fiction, translations; some poetry.

Vick Austin-Smith, Senior Editor (San Diego)
Serious and general fiction and nonfiction in hardcover and softcover, with emphasis on backlist titles. Some humor.

Diane Sterling, Senior Editor (San Diego)
Translations. Test-preparation books.

Yoji Yamaguchi, Associate Editor (New York)

HARCOURT BRACE CHILDREN'S BOOKS

Harcourt Brace children's categories include picture books, easy readers, nonfiction, fiction, poetry, big books, older readers, and reference books.

Harcourt Brace produces a full offering of children's books in hardcover and paperback. Many HB titles are presented as books for all ages—intended to embrace a wide readership range.

The house features several distinct imprints for young readers. Among them: Jane Yolen Books, Gulliver Books, HB Big Books, HB Creative Curriculum Connections, and the paperback lines Odyssey and Voyager—along with a lineup of author videos. Libros Viajeros is the Voyager line of Spanish-language books.

From the HB children's list: *Runaway Opposites* by Richard Wilbur (illustrated by Henrik Drescher), *A Prayer for the Opening of the Little League Season* by Willie Morris (illustrated by Barry Moser), and *Bad Behavior* (collection of crime fiction; edited by Mary Higgins Clark). On the staunch backlist: *Fishy Facts* by Ivan Chermayeff, *Rio Grande Stories* by Carolyn Meyer, *Drummers of Jericho* by Carolyn Meyer, *Crews: Gang Members Talk to Maria Hinojosa* (photographs by German Perez), and *The Harcourt Brace Student Dictionary*.

Unsolicited manuscripts are no longer accepted. Editors now work exclusively through literary agents. Query letters and SASEs should be directed to:

Diane D'Andrade, Senior Editor (San Diego)

Allyn Johnson, Senior Editor (San Diego)

Karen Grove, Editor (San Diego)

HARLEQUIN BOOKS
SILHOUETTE BOOKS

300 East 42nd Street, 6th Floor
New York, NY 10017
212-682-6080

The Harlequin Books New York office issues several Harlequin series; the rest of the list is published from the Harlequin Enterprises base in Ontario, Canada (please see directory of Canadian publishers and editors), and the house's United Kingdom branch (contact information listed under the Canadian section). The Silhouette Books (a division of Harlequin) editorial offices are in New York and the Silhouette line is listed here in a separate subentry.

Both Harlequin and Silhouette issue editorial guidelines for writers who wish to submit manuscripts for publishing consideration. Included in the material are series requirements—including tips for authors on plotting and character (some of which are applicable to other fiction-genre areas)—as well as nuts-and-bolts advice pertaining to the preferred physical properties of manuscripts they review.

HARLEQUIN BOOKS

Harlequin Books is an innovator not only in the romance category but also in defining and refining the market for women's fiction and in continuing to access that market through diverse venues such as direct marketing, wire book racks in discount department stores, and the wood-grained shelves of major book-chain superstores. A précis of the Harlequin Books American lines follows.

Harlequin American Romance offers a lineup of contemporary, upbeat, action-packed novels set in a world where everything is possible; they are not problem-based or introspective. These stories feature a characteristically self-assured, perceptive American woman as heroine. The hero is a dynamic American man who is irresistible, whether he's rough around the edges, earthy, slick, or sophisticated. Sizzling repartee and one-upmanship are hallmarks of the characters' attraction.

Harlequin Intrigue is an exciting presentation of contemporary romance within a format of mystery, suspense, espionage, woman-in-jeopardy, adventure, and puzzles. The love story is central to the mystery at the level of the novel's premise. The heroine and her hero must be indispensable in solving the mystery or completing whatever adventure they undertake. Their lives are on the line, as are their hearts.

Harlequin Historicals are sweeping period romances and range from Medieval sagas to lighthearted Westerns and everything in between. These romance titles should be authentically detailed and realistic (to provide atmosphere, rather than a history lesson). Heroes and heroines are equally strong willed; their relationship is the focus of the story. The writing should be rich and evocative, with the characters bringing the material alive so that the reader may connect with and appreciate the attributes of the historical setting. The story focus is on the heroine and how one man changes her life forever; the stories must have depth and complexity: subplots and important secondary characters are necessary items here.

Length of manuscript and level of sensuality vary from series to series; contact Harlequin for detailed editorial guidelines.

Harlequin is distributed to the book trade by Simon & Schuster.

When corresponding with Harlequin, please specify the series for which your manuscript is intended. Query letters and SASEs should be directed to:

Debra Matteucci, Senior Editor and Editorial Coordinator
Harlequin American Romance and Harlequin Intrigue.

Tracy Farrell, Senior Editor
Harlequin Historicals.

Julianne Moore, Editor

Bonnie Crisalli, Associate Editor

Denise O'Sullivan, Associate Editor

SILHOUETTE BOOKS

300 East 42nd Street
New York, NY 10017
212-682-6080

Silhouette Books publishes adult category romances set in a contemporary milieu. Authors must indicate with their submissions for which series their work is intended. Silhouette Books was previously a major competitor of Harlequin Enterprises, its current parent company. A summary of the Silhouette romance lines follows.

Silhouette Romance tales are contemporary stories of change and challenge, often in exotic settings. They focus on women who must choose between their desire for the man they love and their romantic ideal. Although the hero and heroine do not make love unless married, continuing sexual tension keeps the reader engaged. Silhouette encourages writers to come up with new twists, and new writers are welcome.

Silhouette Desire accents the sensuous side of romance. These books are written for today's woman, whether innocent or experienced. The conflict should be emotional, springing naturally from within the characters. They don't have to be married to make love, but lovemaking is not taken lightly. New slants on tried-and-true formulas are welcome. Secondary characters and subplots must blend with the core story.

Silhouette Special Edition romances are sophisticated and substantial contemporary tales that probe deeply into their characters. The complexity of the characters heightens the drama of the plot—the issues that are important to the characters should be important to the reader. Sensuality may be sizzling or subtle. The plot can run the gamut from the wildly innovative to the comfortably traditional. The novel's depth and emotional vividness should contribute to the overall effect of a very special romance.

Silhouette Intimate Moments features characters swept into a magical world larger than life. These works explore new directions by setting the romantic fiction within the framework of today's mainstream novels: glamour, melodrama, suspense, and adventure. Let your imagination be your guide.

Silhouette Yours Truly features short, sassy tales with a contemporary, modern tone; the story opens with some form of written communication, such as a personal ad, invitation, or letter—leading unexpectedly to meeting, dating, and marrying Mr. Right.

Manuscript length and other series requirements vary; detailed editorial guidelines are available from the publisher.

Silhouette is distributed through Simon & Schuster.

When querying, please specify the series for which your work is intended. Query letters and SASEs should be directed to:

Isabel Swift, Editorial Director

Melissa Senate, Senior Editor
Silhouette Romance.

Tara Gavin, Senior Editor
Silhouette Special Edition.

Lucia Macro, Senior Editor
Silhouette Desire.

Leslie Wainger, Senior Editor and Editorial Coordinator
Silhouette Intimate Moments and Silhouette Yours Truly.

Gail Chasan, Editor

Marcia Book Adirim, Editor
Silhouette contact for Love and Laughter (published through Harlequin Canadian offices).

Mary Theresa Hussey, Associate Editor

Karen Taylor Richman, Associate Editor

Melissa Jeglinski, Associate Editor

Cathleen Treacy, Associate Editor

Cristine Niessner, Associate Editor

Lynda Cumyn, Assistant Editor

Angela Catalano, Assistant Editor

HARMONY BOOKS

(See Crown Publishing Group under Random House)

HARPERCOLLINS PUBLISHERS

10 East 53rd Street
New York, NY 10022
212-207-7000

HarperCollins Publishers offers a program that spans a full spectrum of commercial, trade, professional, and academic interests within a number of interlocked divisions (located on both the east and the west coasts, as well as in the Rockies). HarperCollins projects are issued in hardcover and softcover, as well as in multimedia editions.

Among the HarperCollins east coast American components are Harper Perennial (trade paper originals and reprints), Harper Paperback (mass-market), and Basic Books (scholarly and professional academic with significant commercial trade crossover). A special high-concept HarperCollins program is the Regan Books imprint.

HarperInteractive is the house's electronic-publishing division. HarperLibros publishes a wide range of works in the Spanish language. HarperCollins is home to a number of children's-book and reference divisions. (See separate subentries below.)

The HarperCollins San Francisco wing is evolving a mainstream commercial profile accenting lifestyle titles, general trade nonfiction, and occasional literary works (in addition to the Harper San Francisco emphasis in spirituality, self-awareness, and healing; please see Harper San Francisco entry in the directory of Religious, Spiritual, and Inspirational publishers). These west coast programs enjoy centralized marketing, production, finance, administration, rights, and inventory control, while maintaining editorial independence.

Westview Press accents scholarly and academic works, with some trade crossover. HarperCollins also owns Hazelden Publishing Group and Zondervan (see entries in the directory of Religious, Spiritual, and Inspirational publishers).

HarperCollins Publishers is the current corporate embodiment of the venerable firm (founded in 1817) previously known as Harper & Row. HarperCollins is part of Rupert Murdoch's transnational communications empire, which includes the *New York Post* newspaper and Twentieth Century Fox. For all its international divisions, imprints, and subsidiaries, HarperCollins is a publishing colossus with a well-defined image: The house's flaming-torch logo signifies a reputation for superior editorial quality and mighty commercial carriage.

HarperCollins handles its own distribution.

HARPERCOLLINS TRADE DIVISION

HarperCollins produces adult hardcover books, trade paperbacks, and mass-market paperback editions that cover the breadth of trade publishing categories including feature biographies (celebrity, sports, and historical), business books, mysteries and thrillers, popular culture, humor, inspiration, and how-to (including cookbooks and health), in addition to works across most popular reference categories. Harper Style specializes in illustrated works keyed to contemporary lifestyle, design, and culture. Many HarperCollins frontlist titles are also available on HarperAudio.

Representing HarperCollins general nonfiction and popular titles: *To Save My Child: The Elizabeth Morgan Story* by Elizabeth Morgan, *The Sephardic Kitchen: The Healthy Food and Rich Culture of the Mediterranean Jews* by Robert Sternberg, *Jane Austen's Little Advice Book* by Cathryn Michon and Pamela Norris, *Hell-Bent: The Inside Story of a "Win" or Else Dallas Cowboy Season* by Skip Bayless, *Red, White, and Greens: The Italian Way with Vegetables* by Faith Willinger, *Bouncing Back: How to Survive Anything . . . and I Mean Anything* by Joan Rivers, and *All Madden: Boom! Bam! Boink* by John Madden with Dave Anderson.

Representative backlist hits: *Breakthrough* by Whitley Streiber, *Driving Under the Affluence* by Julia Phillips, *Mars and Venus in the Bedroom* by John Gray, *Your Sacred Self* by Wayne Dyer, *To Renew America* by Newt Gingrich, and *The Erotic Mind* by Jack Morin.

HarperCollins offers fiction and literary works on a diversified program that includes commercial novels and standout category titles, in addition to select literary works. HarperCollins has published such authors as Anne Rivers Siddons, Ursula K. LeGuin, Sue Miller, Len Deighton, Allen Ginsberg, Barbara Taylor Bradford, Oscar Hijuelos, Tony Hillerman, Leon Uris, and William Lashner. Harper Prism is the imprint designation for selected high-concept titles in science fiction, fantasy, horror, and thrillers.

Representative titles include *The Trouble with a Bad Fit: A Novel of Food, Fashion, and Mystery* by Camilla T. Crespi, *Stainless* by Todd Grimson (Harper Prism), *The Only World* (poems) by Lynda Hull (edited by David Wojahn), *Obscene Bodies* by Kim Benabib, *Naked Sleeper* by Sigrid Nunez, *Death in High Water* (a Guido Brunetti mystery) by Donna Leon, *Dirt* by Stuart Woods, *A Secret Affair* by Barbara Taylor Bradford, *96 Tears* (suspense) by Doug J. Swanson, *Heat Wave* by Penelope Lively, and *What Keeps Me Here* (stories) by Rebecca Brown.

The Harper Paperbacks program includes a strong lineup in mystery, suspense, and thrillers (primarily reprints, along with a few originals). Harper Paperbacks also publishes a select number of mass-market true crime titles, as well as a few hardcover originals in commercial fiction genres. Harper Monogram is a mass-market imprint that specializes in women's fiction, including historical romances, time travel, and commercial contemporaries.

HARPERBUSINESS

HarperBusiness heralds the latest trends of thought in fields such as management, finance, and international business. Business books from HarperCollins are most often (but not always) presented under the HarperBusiness banner. The HarperCollins business list is distinguished by gifted, individualistic authors geared to attract a wide popular readership in addition to interested business professionals. HarperCollins also releases comprehensive and specifically targeted professional reference works and career how-tos.

On the HarperCollins business list: *The Individualized Corporation: A New Doctrine for Managing People* by Sumantra Ghoshal and Christopher A. Bartlett; *An Eye for Winners: How I Built America's Greatest Direct-Mail Business* by Lillian Vernon; *Beyond Reengineering: How the Process-Centered Organization Will Change Our Work and Our Lives* by Michael Hammer; *Hidden Order: The Economics of Everyday Life* by David D. Friedman; *The Executive in Action* (a set of three classic books) by Peter F. Drucker; *Everyone's a Coach* by Don Shula and Ken Blanchard; *Clicking* by Faith Popcorn with Lys Marigold; *How the Cadillac Got Its Fins* by Jack Mingo; and *Cracking the Corporate Closet* by Daniel B. Baker, Sean O'Brien Strub, and Bill Henning (in association with the National Gay and Lesbian Task Force Policy Institute).

Query letters and SASEs should be directed to:

Lawrence Ashmead, Executive Editor
Fiction: mysteries, thrillers. Nonfiction: biographies and autobiographies, gardening, general self-help.

Cynthia Barrett, Editor
Fiction: literary and commercial. Nonfiction: biographies and memoirs, military and general history, nutrition, medicine, celebrity stories, popular culture, true crime, sports, current events, business. Works with Gladys Justin Carr (see below).

(Mr.) Cass Canfield Jr., Publisher, Icon Editions
Nonfiction: history; social and intellectual issues; gardening; foods, wine, and cookery; art, design, and architecture. Fiction: Latin American translations.

Gladys Justin Carr, Associate Publisher
Fiction: literary and commercial. Nonfiction: biographies and memoirs, military and general history, nutrition, medicine, celebrity stories, popular culture, true crime, sports, current events, business.

(Mr.) Eamon Dolan, Editor
Fiction: literary and suspense. Nonfiction: science, social issues, cyberculture, health, humor, ethnic interest.

John Douglas, Senior Editor
Fiction: science fiction, adventure, military, mystery, horror. Nonfiction: UFOs, history.

Susan Friedland, Senior Editor
Food, cookbooks, literary history.

Mitchell Ivers, Editor and Publishing Coordinator
Fiction and nonfiction for trade hardcover and paperbacks. Commercial fiction, popular culture, and social issues. Nonfiction with an inspirational edge, including but not limited to self-help and stories of personal growth and recovery. Interest in the lesbian-and-gay market.

Robert Jones, Senior Editor, Harper Perennial
Quality literary fiction. Nonfiction: social issues, current affairs, psychology.

(Ms.) Terry Karten, Executive Editor
Quality literary fiction. Nonfiction: biographies and autobiographies, history, current issues, women's issues.

(Ms.) Trena Keating, Associate Editor
Fiction: literary and commercial, women's; especially interested in contemporary western American settings. Nonfiction: contemporary issues, inspirational, spiritual, self-improvement, memoir.

Eric Steel, Editor
Select literary fiction. Nonfiction: current issues, politics, culture, history, memoirs, biographies.

Mauro DiPreta, Editor
Fiction: thrillers. Nonfiction: pop-culture, humor, commercial nonfiction.

Kirsten D. Sandberg, Editor
Business books.

Christopher Schelling, Executive Editor, Harper Prism
Science fiction/fantasy, some horror.

John Silbersack, Vice President, Harper Prism
Science fiction/fantasy, some horror.

Peternelle Van Arsdale, Editor, Harper Perennial
Fiction: literary and commercial. Nonfiction: African-American and multicultural studies, gender studies, current issues.

Hugh Van Dusen, Executive Editor, Harper Perennial
History, biography, spirituality, self-help. Fiction and nonfiction reprints and originals in quality paperback.

Buz Wyeth, Executive Editor
Fiction: commercial and literary. Nonfiction: biography, history, inspiration, human interest, popular reference, nature and outdoor activities, military affairs.

(Mr.) Adrian Zackheim, Executive Editor
Business books; general nonfiction.

David Conti, Executive Editor
Investment subjects and nonficiton business stories.

HARPERPAPERBACKS

Query letters and SASEs should be directed to:

Abigail Kamen Holland, Editor, Harper Paperbacks
Mass-market fiction: women's stories in mystery and suspense, romances, Westerns.

Jessica Lichtenstein, Senior Editor, Harper Paperbacks
Wide range of interests in fiction and nonfiction. Commercial nonfiction, including true crime originals. Young-adult fiction is a specialty. Fiction also includes mysteries and commercial women's fiction.

Carolyn Marino, Editor in Chief, Editorial Director, Harper Paperbacks
Mass-market fiction: women's stories in mysteries, suspense, historical romances; some Westerns.

Sharon Morey, Assistant Editor, Harper Paperbacks
Women's fiction, romances.

Gretchen Young, Editor, Harper Paperbacks
Mass-market nonfiction originals.

HARPERREFERENCE

Harper Reference encompasses general-interest territory as well as special fields of interest. HarperReference lists titles in areas such as popular how-to/self-help guides, contemporary culture, college and career sourcebooks, family resources, sports books, hobbies and recreation, consumer guides, business references, and specialized dictionaries.

Titles from Harper Reference: *Parenting A to Z: A Guide to Everything from Conception to College* by Irene Franck and David Brownstone, *Bill Rodgers' Lifetime Running Plan: Definitive Programs for Runners of All Ages and Levels* by Bill Rodgers, *Simpson's Contemporary Quotations: The Most Notable Quotes from 1950 to the Present* by James B. Simpson, *Be Your Own Literary Agent* by Martin P. Levin, *Erotic Literature* (edited by Jane Mills), and *The Used Car Book* by Jack Gillis.

Additional titles in the lineup include those in the Born to Shop series by Suzy Gershman. HarperCollins also publishes foreign-language dictionaries, books in computer application, and several travel series including Jerry Levitin's Country Inns and Back Roads and Birnbaum Travel Guides.

Query letters and SASEs should be directed to:

Rob Kaplan, Senior Editor
General-reference titles, word books, atlases, travel, health, popular culture, education.

BASIC BOOKS

Basic is particularly bold in the trade areas of current affairs and civic issues, historical and cultural studies, and the sciences; many popular titles exhibit a public-interest stance. Basic Books offers a roster of authors who are leaders in contemporary thought, and Basic titles have proven potent commercially as well as on the book awards circuit.

The house catalogs a distinctive academic, professional, and popular topical list in the burgeoning fields of psychiatry, psychology, psychotherapy, and current trends in counseling—indeed, Basic Books was originally an independent publisher that specialized in the behavioral sciences. Basic Books is now a HarperCollins division distinguished as a publisher of well-polished trade nonfiction (in hardcover and trade paper editions) that addresses cultivated spheres traditionally more characteristic of the academic arena than trade publishing.

Titles from Basic: *The Medicine of ER: How We Almost Die* by Alan Duncan Ross and Harlan Gibbs, *Rosa Lee: A Generational Tale of Poverty and Survival in Urban America* by Leon Dash (photographs by Lucian Perkins), *How Brains Think: Evolving Intelligences, Then and Now* by William H. Calvin, *Sperm Wars: The Science of Sex* by Robin Baker, *A Mood Apart: Depression, Manic Depression and Other Afflictions of the Self* by Peter Whybrow, *Sixty Miles from Contentment: Traveling the Nineteenth-Century American Interior* by M. H. Dunlop, and *Art Lessons: Learning from the Rise and Fall of Public Arts Funding* by Alice Goldfarb Marquis.

Query letters and SASEs should be directed to:

John Donatich, Deputy Publisher
Projects consistent with house interest.

Paul Golob, Senior Editor
Politics, current events, journalism, international relations.

Kermit Hummel, President and Publisher
Projects consistent with house interest.

Linda Kahn, Senior Editor
Gender issues, multicultural topics, memoirs.

Susan Rabiner, Editorial Director
Popular science, history, law.

Gail Winston, Executive Editor
Psychology, memoirs, social issues.

Eric Wright, Associate Editor
Professional books in psychology and psychiatry.

REGAN BOOKS

10 East 53rd Street
New York, NY 10022
212-207-7400

Regan Books hosts a selective list of general nonfiction and commercial fiction. The house scouts properties with best-seller and high commercial potential. Nonfiction tends to be tailored toward celebrity, personality, and topical issues. In fiction, the house accents extremely commercial big-concept works, especially projects with performance-rights potential.

Nonfiction and popular works include: *In Contempt* by Christopher Darden with Jess Walter, *Enter Whining* by Fran Drescher, *The Zone* (health and fitness) by Barry Sears with Bill Lawren, *Slouching towards Gomorrah: Modern Liberalism and American Decline* by Robert H. Bork, and *A Babe in Boyland* by the Fabulous Sports Babe with Neal Karlen.

Fiction includes: *Fatal Convictions* (thriller/suspense) by Shari P. Geller, *Hunger Point* (seriocomic novel) by Jillian Medoff, and *Microserfs* by Douglas Coupland (author of *Generation X*).

Publishing virtuoso Judith Regan set the literary world alight with publishing feats such as extraordinarily popular titles from contemporary cultural icons like Howard Stern, Rush Limbaugh, and Beavis and Butthead. HarperCollins launched the Regan Books enterprise as a way to fully realize Regan's manifold talents. Thus another publishing star was born.

Query letters and SASEs should be directed to:

Judith Regan, President and Publisher

Kristin Kiser, Associate Editor

HARPERCOLLINS CHILDREN'S BOOKS

HarperCollins Children's Books produces hardcovers, trade paperbacks, and mass-market titles in fiction and nonfiction for all readership levels, from preschool through young adult. The HarperFestival and HarperTrophy lines issue primarily novelty publications and paperbacks.

HarperCollins Children's is interested in hardcover picture books, fiction, nonfiction, and poetry, as well as in novelty projects. The Harper Arco Iris program of books in the Spanish language covers a wide range of products aimed at children and young adults.

On the list: *Falling Up* (poems and drawings) by Shel Silverstein, *Mine's the Best Cow* (written and illustrated by Crosby Bonsall), *Falcons Nest on Skyscrapers* by Priscilla Belz Jenkins (illustrated by Megan Lloyd), *Tornado* by Betsy Byars (pictures by Doron Ben-Ami), *Zoe Rising* by Pam Conrad, *Thump, Thump, Rat-a-Tat-Tat* by Gene Baer (pictures by Lois Ehlert).

Representative backlist items: *Inch by Inch: The Garden Song* by David Mallett (pictures by Ora Eitan), *Street Music: City Poems* by Arnold Adoff (pictures by Karen Barbour), *Making Music: 6 Instruments You Can Create* by Eddie Herschel Oates (pictures by Michael Koelsch), and *The Camp Survival Handbook* by Katy Hall and Lisa Eisenberg (pictures by David Neuhaus).

Query letters and SASEs should be directed to:

Kate Morgan Jackson, Vice President, Associate Publisher, and Editor in Chief

Stephanie Spinner, Vice President and Editorial Director, HarperTrophy

Mary Alice Moore, Editorial Director, HarperFestival

Sally Doherty, Executive Editor

Robert Warren, Executive Editor

Joanna Cotler, Editorial Director, Joanna Cotler Books

Michael DiCapra, Editorial Director, Michael DiCapra Books

Laura Geringer, Editorial Director, Laura Geringer Books

HARPERCOLLINS SAN FRANCISCO

1160 Battery Street
San Francisco, CA 94111
415-477-4400

HarperCollins San Francisco incorporates California-based divisions. HarperCollins San Francisco International Editions publishes imported original titles and reprints originating from HarperCollins divisions outside the U.S. sphere (Australia, New Zealand, South Africa, Canada, and the United Kingdom).

The former imprint Collins Publishers San Francisco is slated in the fall of 1996 to move to New York to combine with Harper Style to form the illustrated division of Adult Trade.

Harper San Francisco (please see Directory of Religious, Spiritual, and Inspirational Publishers) is a general publishing house with a list that accents books that inspire the mind, body, and spirit, as well as trends in world culture.

HarperCollins San Francisco issues theme-specific volumes that in general feature discerning graphics and astute accompanying text, primarily in such lifestyle areas of popular culture and art, pets, entertaining, the home, the garden, travel, family life, and cuisine. Much of the list projects an international or sophisticated-traveler twist within a program that also offers coffee-table books, calendars, book-and-audio products, and gift-type publications.

Query letters and SASEs should be directed to:

Tom Grady, Vice President and Publisher

WESTVIEW PRESS

5500 Central Avenue
Boulder, CO 80301
303-444-3541

Westview Press produces trade titles as well as scholarly and academic works, primarily in the social and political sciences. Westview catalogs areas such as politics, Europe and Russia/Eurasia, Asia and the Pacific, Middle East and North Africa, Africa, Latin America and the Caribbean, economics, psychology, philosophy, religion, communication, history, anthropology, criminology, sociology, law, agriculture, and entomology.

In addition to its Colorado operation, the Westview operation includes a vast United Kingdom division and has additional offices in San Francisco.

Highlights from the Westview trade list: *Betrayed: A History of Presidential Failure to Protect Black Lives* by Earl Ofari Hutchinson, *Present Imperfect: Stories by Russian Women* (edited by Ayesha Kagal and Natasha Perova), *Dressing in Feathers: The Construction of "The Indian" in American Popular Culture* (edited by S. Elizabeth Bird), *Opera in the Flesh: Sexuality in Operatic Performance* by Sam Abel, and *Scarlet Memorial: Tales of Cannibalism in Modern China* by Zheng Yi (edited and translated by T. P. Sym).

Query letters and SASEs should be directed to:

Dean Birkenkamp, Editorial Director

Spencer Carr, Editorial Director

Jennifer Knerr, Senior Acquisitions Editor

Susan McEachern, Senior Acquisitions Editor

HARPER SAN FRANCISCO
(See Directory of Religious, Spiritual, and Inspirational Publishers)

HARVARD BUSINESS SCHOOL PRESS
(See Directory of University Presses)

THE HARVARD COMMON PRESS
535 Albany Street
Boston, MA 02118
617-423-5803

Harvard Common publishes in the nonfiction trade areas of home and the family, small-business guides, travel, cuisine, and lifestyle, as well as a select list of children's books.

The Harvard Common Press (founded in 1976) is a small house devoted to the publication of general nonfiction in hardcover and trade paperback; the press maintains a solid backlist.

Parenting and the family are sectors where Harvard Common shows particular traditional success. Titles: *A Good Birth, a Safe Birth* by Diana Korte and Roberta Scaer, *You and Your Newborn Baby: A Guide to the First Months After Birth* by Linda Todd, *The Nursing Mother's Guide to Weaning* by Kathleen Huggins and Linda Zeidrich, *Tough Questions: Talking Straight with Your Kids about the Real World* by Sheila Kitzinger and Celia Kitzinger, and *Helping Children Cope With Separation and Loss* by Claudia Jewett Jarratt.

Representative Harvard Common titles in lifestyle and travel: *The Border Cookbook: Authentic Home Cooking of the American Southwest and Northern Mexico* by Cheryl Alters Jamison and Bill Jamison, *J. Bildner & Sons Cookbook: Casual Feasts, Food on the Run, and Special Celebrations* by Jim Bildner, *The Best Things in New York Are Free* by Marian Hamilton, *Where to Eat in Canada* by Anne Hardy, *A Guide to Public Art in Greater Boston* by Marty Carlock, and *Travel Writer's Markets: Where to Sell Your Travel Articles and Place Your Press Releases* by Elaine O'Gara.

Harvard Common issues the Best Places to Stay series as part of its travel line. The press lists how-to business titles geared to starting up and operating small restaurants, newspapers, and theaters. It also offers titles on alternative careers for teachers, and *Buller's Professional Course in Bartending for Home Study* by Jon Buller.

The Harvard Common Press distributes its own books.

Query letters and SASEs should be directed to:

Dan Rosenberg, Managing Editor

Bruce Shaw, President

HARVARD UNIVERSITY PRESS

(See Directory of University Presses)

HAZELDEN PUBLISHING GROUP/
HAZELDEN EDUCATIONAL MATERIALS

(See Directory of Religious, Spiritual, and Inspirational Publishers)

HEALTH COMMUNICATIONS, INC.

3201 Southwest 15th Street
Deerfield Beach, FL 33442
305-360-0909

Health Communications accentuates nonfiction trade titles in relationships, finance, spirituality, health, empowerment, esteem, and social issues. Subject areas of notable Health Communications emphasis include personal growth, women's issues, addiction and other compulsive behaviors, abuse and trauma, family relationships, and healing.

Health Communications (founded in 1976) publications provide direction for the journey of living. The publisher's issues orientation is apparent in a list that addresses a family spectrum of interest, encompassing books geared to be read by early readers through adults, as well as targeted market interest segments. Health Communications publishes books in affordable hardcover and trade paperback editions and also produces a line of audiobooks.

Health Communications operates in tandem with sister companies U.S. Journal, U.S. Journal Training, A & D Publications, and Children Are People Too! in a program that brings together professional caregivers and the broader community in a publishing forum that embraces books, journals, pamphlets, and conferences.

Representative of the Health Communications list: *Garden of the Soul: Lessons on Living in Peace, Happiness and Harmony* by Sri Chinmoy, *Living Simply: Timeless Thoughts for a Balanced Life* by Sara Orem and Larry Demarest, *Make an Appointment With Yourself: Simple Steps to Positive Self-Esteem* by Maida Berenblatt and Alena Joy Berenblatt, *Memory and Abuse: Remembering and Healing the Effects of Trauma* by Charles L. Whitfield, *Reclaiming Pride: Daily Reflections on Gay and Lesbian Life* by Joseph H. Neisen, *Recovery of the Sacred: Lessons in Soul Awareness* by Carlos Warter, *The Myth of the Maiden: On Being a Woman* by Joan E. Childs, and *We'd Have a Great Relationship If It Weren't for You: Regaining Love and Intimacy through Mutuality* by Bruce Derman with Michael Hauge.

The house has huge success with its best-selling *Chicken Soup* group of books. The first of these well-received works was *Chicken Soup for the Soul: 101 Stories to Open the Heart and Rekindle the Spirit* (written and compiled by Jack Canfield and Mark Victor Hansen).

Health Communications hosts a hardy backlist that includes *Change Your Life Now: Get Out of Your Head, Get Into Your Life* by Gary Null, and *Appearance Obsession: Learning to Love the Way You Look* by Joni E. Johnston.

Health Communications distributes its own list, as well as those of its sister companies U.S. Journal, Children Are People Too!, U.S. Journal Training, and A&D Publications.

Query letters and SASEs should be directed to:

Christine Belleris, Editorial Director

Mark Colucci, Editorial Assistant

Matthew Diener, Acquisitions Editor

HEINEMANN
BUTTERWORTH-HEINEMANN
FOCAL PRESS
DIGITAL PRESS

361 Hanover Street
Portsmouth, NH 03801
800-541-2086

Legal-publishing office:
8 Industrial
Unit C
Salem, NH 03079

Heinemann offers a varied, general-interest, primarily nonfiction trade list, with selected fiction and literary works. Recent frontlist offerings accent titles in drama and the performing arts, education, creative writing, and the humanities. This publisher's books are offered under such logos as Heinemann, Butterworth, as well as Butterworth-Heinemann. In addition, the house comprises several specialist subsidiaries and imprints that produce professional titles in architecture; business management and operations, technique, and theory; computer technology; state and regional law books and periodicals; and medical, scientific, and security books and journals. Heinemann (founded in 1976) is a wing of the internationally based Reed Elsevier Group.

Many of the corporate subsidiaries operate primarily through editorial offices based outside North America. The subentries for Focal Press and Digital Press below are keyed to imprints with acquisitions functions centered in the United States. The core trade list—usually cataloged to booksellers as Heinemann and Butterworth-Heinemann books—often includes selections from the internationally based specialty imprints.

On the Heinemann trade list: *The Audition Process: A Guide for Actors* by Bob Funk, *Hi Concept–Lo Tech: Theatre for Everyone in Any Place* by Barbara Carlisle and Don Drapeau, *Fight Directing for the Theatre* by J. Allen Suddeth, *The Last Closet: The Real Lives of Lesbian and Gay Teachers* by Rita Kissen, *The Career Novelist: A Literary Agent Offers Strategies for Success* by Donald Maass. Heinemann series include African Studies, Caribbean Writers, African Writers, and Creative Sparks (titles about the creative process).

Heinemann distributes the lists of its various components via an international network of book trade representatives and distribution offices.

FOCAL PRESS

80 Montvale Avenue
Stoneham, MA 02180
617-438-8464

Focal Press publishes professional titles and textbooks in fields such as communications, cinematography, photography, and television. Since 1938 Focal Press has been publishing works geared to the media arts. The house intends for its titles to make a difference in the lives and careers of its readers by keeping them in the forefront of technological and creative innovation in the arenas of photography, broadcast, audio, film, video, computer media, and theater. The press looks for outstanding new book and audiovisual projects that can help media professionals and students achieve their potential. A number of Focal handbooks and manuals are classics in their fields and head a potent backlist.

Among Focal Press highlights: *Working in Commercials: A Complete Sourcebook for Adult and Child Actors* by Elaine Keller Beardsley, *Film Production Management* by Bastian Cleve, *Playwriting: The First Workshop* by Kathleen E. George, *Photography and the Performing Arts* by Gerry Kopelow, *Gum-Oil Photographic Printing* by Karl Koenig, *Electronic Media Criticism: Applied Perspectives* by Peter B. Orlick, and *Corporate Video Directing* by Howard Hall.

For Butterworth-Heineman and Focal Press, all query letters and SASEs should be directed to:

Karen M. Speerstra, Editorial Director

DIGITAL PRESS

313 Washington Street
Newton, MA 02158
617-928-2500

Digital Press, the former book-publishing group of Digital Equipment Corporation, is now part of the Butterworth-Heinemann division of the Reed Elsevier Group. Digital Press publishes books for the information-technology community, from absolute beginner to seasoned pro. Among the press's titles are those that relate directly to Digital products and services, whereas the major portion of the list addresses broader interests. The company strives to provide its readership with the latest technical information—presented in readable and useful formats—and is on the lookout for projects that reflect imminent advances in the computer universe.

Digital catalogs titles in the areas of networking and data communications, windowing, artificial intelligence, policy and strategy, organizational design, software development, computer technology, and Alpha/VAX/VMS operating systems. In addition, Digital Press marketing services handle computing titles published under the auspices of the umbrella company.

On the Digital Press list: *Open VMS Performance Management* by Joginder Sethi, *The Middleware Source Book* by Kohn Colonna-Romani and Patricia Srite, *The Unix Philosophy* by Mike Gancarz, *Open VMS AXP Internals and Data Structures* by Ruth Goldenberg and Saro Saravanan, *The Art of Technical Documentation* by Katherine Haramandanis, and *The Human Factor: Designing Computer Systems for People* by Richard Rubinstein and Harry M. Hersh.

Query letters and SASEs should be directed to:

Frank Satlow, Publisher

HIPPOCRENE BOOKS

171 Madison Avenue
New York, NY 10016
212-685-4371

Hippocrene's areas of special interest are history, military science, international literature, music, travel, cuisine, and scholarly Judaica and Polonica. Hippocrene offers selected works in the area of current affairs and popular culture in addition to comprehensive lines of foreign-language dictionaries, maps, and atlases—the house publishes dictionaries and instruction books in over 100 languages. Hippocrene Books (founded in 1971) publishes hardcovers and trade paperbacks. The house also produces a line of audiobooks.

Hippocrene's Treasury of Love Poems, Quotations and Proverbs is a bilingual series with traditional and historical sources. Hippocrene has undertaken publication of the works of Polish writer Henryk Sienkiewicz (1905 Nobel laureate in literature) in English translation.

Features from Hippocrene: *Daedalus Book of Medieval Literature: The Grin of the Gargoyle* (edited and translated by Brian Murdoch), *Torture Garden* by Octave Mirbeau, *The Art of Irish Cooking* by Monica Sheridan, *Language and Travel Guide to Indonesia* by Gary Chandler, *Victory Must Be Ours: Germany in the Great War, 1914–1918* by Laurence V. Moyer, *A Collector's Guide to the Waffen-SS* by Robert Lumsden, *Towards an Indefinite Shore: The Final Months of the Civil War, December 1864–May 1865* (the final book of a four-volume study of Ulysses S. Grant's campaigns) by Don Lowry, *The Glassmakers: An Odyssey of the Jews* by Samuel Kurinsky, and *Gridiron Greats: A Century of Polish Americans in College Football* by Ben Chestowski.

Hippocrene distributes its own list.

Query letters and SASEs should be directed to:

George Blagowidow, President and Editorial Director

HOLIDAY HOUSE

425 Madison Avenue
New York, NY 10017
212-688-0085

Holiday House specializes in quality trade hardcover children's and young-adult books in a program that encompasses picture books, short-chapter books, and middle-grade readers, as well as selected novels for young adults. Holiday House publishes general nonfiction works for all age levels, ethnic stories and nonfiction, fast-paced adventure stories, historical fiction, boys' books, humorous stories, folktales, fairy tales, poetry, and fantasy for ages eight to twelve.

Holiday House (established in 1935) is a small independent publisher with a large and varied list of fiction and nonfiction children's books. The publisher is open to inspired, well-written, new ideas—the house may be worth a shot for writers who have developed keenly original projects.

Holiday House titles include: *Festivals* by Myra Cohn Livingston (illustrated by Leonard Everett Fisher), *Antonio's Apprenticeship: Painting a Fresco in Renaissance Italy* (written and illustrated by Taylor Morrison), *Old Bag of Bones: A Coyote Tale* (retold and illustrated by Janet Stevens), *Rimonah of the Flashing Sword: A North African Tale* (retold by Eric A. Kimmel; illustrated by Omar Rayyan), *The Reason for All Seasons* (written and illustrated by Gail Gibbons), *The Treasure Chest: A Chinese Tale* (retold by Rosalind C. Wang; illustrated by Will Hillenbrand), and *Wagon Train: A Family Goes West in 1865* by Courtni C. Wright (illustrated by Gershom Griffith).

Authors' guidelines from Holiday House contain concise advice that all authors of children's books should be aware of; contact the publisher for detailed information regarding manuscript submissions.

Holiday House handles its own distribution.

Query letters and SASEs should be directed to:

Regina Griffin, Editor in Chief

Ashley Mason, Associate Editor

HOLLOWAY HOUSE PUBLISHING GROUP

8060 Melrose Avenue
Los Angeles, CA 90046
213-653-8060

Holloway House (founded in 1960) is the world's largest publisher of paperbacks representing the American Black experience. Holloway House produces a varied list in fiction and nonfiction within its areas of publishing interest, including African-American, American Indian, and Hispanic literature, as well as selected titles in games and gambling.

The publisher is noted for hard-hitting novels, historical anthologies and biographical series (including the Educator's Library), and selected public-interest nonfiction. The house is also known for reprint editions of classic works by such authors as Donald Goines and Iceberg Slim. Among Holloway House imprints are Avanti, Heartline Romances, Mankind, and Melrose Square. Holloway also produces calendars, postcard books, and posters. The publisher typically publishes a midsized list of new titles each year and maintains a strong backlist.

On the Holloway House fiction list: *Buffalo Soldier* by C. R. Goodman, *Shack Town* by Glen T. Brock, *Black Bait* by Leo Guild, *Daddy Must Die* by William O. Brown, *Coming of Age* by Lorri Hewett, and *Black Cheyenne* by Charles R. Goodman.

Nonfiction of note includes: *Women in History* by D. L. Shepherd, *To Kill a Black Man* (dual biography of Martin Luther King and Malcolm X) by Louis E. Lomax, *Dizzy Gillespie* by Tony Gentry, and *Kathleen Dunham* by Darlene Donloe.

The Holloway House list is handled by All America Distributors Corporation.

Query letters and SASEs should be directed to:

Ray Locke, Senior Editor

HENRY HOLT AND COMPANY

115 West 18th Street
New York, NY 10011
212-886-9200

Henry Holt and Company publishes a full range of hardcover and paperback trade books in fiction and nonfiction. In addition, Holt maintains a number of individualized imprints and divisions.

Metropolitan Books is an imprint that features an international lineup of topical-interest nonfiction and literary fiction. Metropolitan is open to different genres, unconventional points of view, controversial opinions, and new voices in fiction. Other Holt trade imprints include John MacRae Books, Marian Wood Books, and Owl trade paperbacks.

Computer titles are the specialty at Holt subsidiaries MIS: Press, Inc. and M & T Books (please see subentry for MIS: Press/M & T Books).

The house presents several fine children's and young-adult lines under the aegis of Henry Holt's Books for Young Readers (please see subentry below). Trade paperbacks are produced under the Owl imprint. Henry Holt and Company nurtures a healthy backlist.

Henry Holt and Company (founded in 1866) is part of the German-based international Verlagsgruppe Georg von Holtzbrinck. The house was previously a thriving independent publisher, subsequent to the sale of former umbrella operation Holt Rinehart & Winston's textbook division to Harcourt Brace in 1987.

Henry Holt's offerings come stamped with the house's bookish owl colophon (a symbol of the wise goddess Athena), one of the most respected mascot logos in book publishing.

The Henry Holt nonfiction scope spans the trade spectrum, including such offerings as *Maximum Leadership* by Chuck Farkas and Phillipe DeBacker, *Sex, Laws, and Cyberspace: Freedom and Regulation on the Frontiers of the Online Revolution* by Jonathan Wallace and Mark Mangan, *The Spirits Speak: One Woman's Mystical Journey into the African Spirit World* by Nicky Arden, *Better with Buttermilk: The Secret Ingredient in Old-Fashioned Cooking* by Lee Edwards Benning, *No Hands: The Rise and Fall of the Schwinn Bicycle Company, an American Institution* by Judith Crown and Glenn Coleman, *The Body's Edge: Our Cultural Obsession with Skin* by Mark Lappé, *Topspin: Ups and Downs in Big-Time Tennis* by Eliot Berry, *The Interior Design Style Guide: America's Designing Duo Helps You Find Your Ideal Decorating Style* by Mars Jaffe and Ron Jaffe, and *The New Perennial Garden* by Noël Kingsbury.

Henry Holt fiction includes frontlist commercial novels and literary works, as well as a number of topflight mysteries. Representative titles here: *Edisto Revisited* by Padgett Powell, *The Debt to Pleasure* by John Lanchester, *Amnesiascope* by Steve Erickson, *The Death of Frank Sinatra* by Michael Ventura, *Sandra Nichols Found Dead* (a Jerry Kennedy novel) by George V. Higgins, *Kink* by Kathe Koja, *Angel Maker: The Collected Short Stories of Sara Maitland* by Sara Maitland, *Cheap Ticket to Heaven* by Charlie Smith, *Go the Way Your Blood Beats: An Anthology of Gay and Lesbian Literary Writings by African Americans* (edited by Shawn Stewart Ruff).

Holt has also featured John Harvey's Charlie Resnick mysteries, John Lutz's Fred Carver mysteries, Collin Wilcox's San Francisco police procedurals, and Sue Grafton's alphabetically titled Kinsey Millhone detective series.

Henry Holt and Company handles its own distribution.

Query letters and SASEs should be directed to:

Sara Bershtel, Associate Publisher, Metropolitan Books

Tracy Brown, Executive Editor
Literary fiction, current issues, politics, biography, literary memoir, nature, and travel.

Theresa Burns, Senior Editor
Nonfiction paperback originals and hardcovers in women's issues, health, psychology, Black and Hispanic history and culture, social history, religion, politics.

Elizabeth Crossman, Editor-at-Large
Cookbooks, gardening, and crafts.

Tom Engelhardt, Consulting Editor, Metropolitan Books
Expressive, inventive, and creative nonfiction and literary fiction.

Stephen Hubbell, Senior Editor, Metropolitan Books
International fiction and affairs, politics, biography, literary memoir, travel essays.

Albert LaFarge, Associate Editor, John Macrae Books
General nonfiction, literary works.

Jack Macrae, Editorial Director, John Macrae Books
American history and biography, scientific inquiry, travel and nature.

Bryan Oettel, Editor at Large
Alternative and general health, outdoor activity and nature, popular culture, American history; selected commercial literary works.

Allen Peacock, Senior Editor
Literary fiction.

Ray Roberts, Senior Editor
Gardening, design, biography; literary detective fiction.

Tracy Sherrod, Editor
Nonfiction and fiction written by and/or for African-Americans and lesbians and gays.

David Sobel, Senior Editor
Science, natural history, popular reference, health, history, sports, popular culture.

William Strachan, Editor in Chief, Associate Publisher
History, current events, natural history, biography.

Cynthia Vartan, Editor at Large
Practical how-to books, women's health, family, relationships, popular business.

(Ms.) Marian Wood, Associate Publisher, Marian Wood Books
History, biography, travel essays, nature, military subjects, Judaica. Popular and literary fiction.

HENRY HOLT AND COMPANY BOOKS FOR YOUNG READERS

Henry Holt and Company Books for Young Readers offers categories ranging from the youngest readers through young-adult. The list includes illustrated storybooks, specialty items and kits, fiction, and nonfiction volumes of popular educational appeal. Imprints include Books by Michael Hague, Books by Bill Martin Jr. and John Archambault, W5 (Who What Where When Why) Reference, Edge Books, Redfeather Books, and Owlet Paperbacks. The hardcover young-adult Edge imprint features multicultural titles from around the world. Among Holt productions in the children's arena are those issued in finely crafted, elegantly understated editions.

Representative of the Holt Books for Young Readers list: *Where Once There Was a Wood* by Denise Sleming, *Clown* by Quentin Blake, *The Trouble with Wishes* by Susan Beth Pfeffer (illustrated by Jennifer Plecas), *Stopping for Death: Poems of Death and Loss* (edited by Carol Ann Duffy; illlustrated by Trisha Rafferty), *Barrio Streets, Carnival Dreams: Three Generations of Latino Artistry* (edited by Lori M. Carlson), and *Tutu Much Ballet* by Gabrielle Charbonnet (illustrated by Abby Carter).

Query letters and SASEs should be directed to:

Brenda Bowen, Editor in Chief

MIS: PRESS/
M & T BOOKS

115 West 18th Street
New York, NY 10011
212-886-9200

Offerings from MIS: Press, Inc. and M & T Books constitute the main computer-book list for Henry Holt and Company. The house goal in publishing computer books is to inspire confidence while building competence. Achievement and continued growth come from the combined efforts of talented authors, editors, a strong sales and marketing team, and customer support.

MIS: Press, Inc. (established in 1980) is a subsidiary of Henry Holt & Company. The press offers a carefully crafted list of books that appeals to every major segment of the computer market. MIS is recognized for books that offer complete, accurate, and easy to understand information (including packages with accompanying diskettes), particularly geared to some of the most popular computer hardware and software. Expanded areas of MIS interest include CD-ROM, multimedia, and PC sound. Noteworthy MIS series include Welcome to . . . and Teach Yourself . . . , with many of the house's titles geared to proprietary products.

M & T Books (founded in 1984 as a division of M & T Publishing) was acquired by MIS: Press in April of 1993. After the transition from its former California location, the house is at home in its New York abode, out of which all titles are produced, edited, and marketed. M & T is a publisher of high-quality books for the serious computer user. M & T has traditionally supported its publishing program via aggressive advertising campaigns directed at driving the consumer into the bookstore to buy M & T titles—a success that in part derives from the house's association with some of the most potent computer magazines.

M & T offers a complete line of titles for technical professionals as well as advanced end-users. The list has focused on emerging developments in such areas as multimedia, artificial life and intelligence, networking, programming languages, graphics programming, and desktop publishing.

MIS: Press and M & T Books are distributed through the parent organization Henry Holt & Company. MIS: Press books combine with those of sibling imprint M & T Books to qualify for bookseller discount.

Query letters and SASEs should be directed to:

Paul Farrell, Editor in Chief, Computer Book Group

THE JOHNS HOPKINS UNIVERSITY PRESS
(See Directory of University Presses)

HORIZON PUBLISHERS
(See Directory of Religious, Spiritual, and Inspirational Publishers)

HOUGHTON MIFFLIN COMPANY
Boston office:
222 Berkeley Street
Boston, MA 02116-3764
617-725-5000

New York office:
215 Park Avenue South
New York, NY 10003
212-420-5800

Houghton Mifflin produces general trade nonfiction and fiction in hardcover and paperback. Houghton Mifflin's trade and reference program includes the imprints Peter Davison Books, Marc Jaffe Books, and Richard Todd Books; the Ticknor & Fields lineup has been incorporated into the core Houghton Mifflin trade list. Children's divisions include Houghton Mifflin Books for Children and the editorially independent juveniles imprint Clarion Books (see subentries below).

Houghton Mifflin (founded in 1832) is one of the grand names of American publishing tradition. The house's renowned leaping-dolphin emblem embellishes a distinguished list.

Houghton Mifflin nonfiction encompasses mainstream titles in areas such as current events, international affairs, business, journalism, lifestyle and travel, and natural history.

Reference works include the *American Heritage Dictionary of the English Language* (an excellent resource for American writers), *The Columbia Encyclopedia* (copublished with Columbia University), and *Cannon's Concise Guide to Rules of Order.*

Also on the Houghton Mifflin list are travel and nature series that include the Apa Insight Guides, Peterson Field Guides, and Best Places to Stay Guides.

Representative Houghton Mifflin nonfiction: *Guerrilla Marketing Online: The Entrepreneur's Guide to Earning Profits on the Internet* by Jay Conrad and Charles Rubin, *The Good Marriage: How and Why Love Lasts* by Judith S. Wallerstein and Sandra Blakeslee, *Tasha Tudor's Engagement Calendar* (photographs by Richard W. Brown; text by Tovah Martin), *Headache Help: A Complete Guide to Understanding Headaches and the Medicines That Relieve Them* by Lawrence Robbins and Susan S. Lang, *Listening to America: Twenty-Five Years in the Life of a Nation as Told to National Public Radio* (edited by Linda Wertheimer), and *A Who's Who of Sports Champions: Their Stories and Their Records* by Ralph Hickok.

Fiction and literary works from Houghton Mifflin: *Evelyn Waugh: A Biography* by Selina Hastings, *Split Horizon* by Thomas Lux, *Gringa Latina: A Woman of Two Worlds* by Gabriella De Ferrari, *Slippage: Previously Uncollected, Precariously Poised Stories* by Harlan Ellison, *In the Loyal Mountains: Stories* by Rick Bass, and *Inventing the Truth: The Art and Craft of Memoir* (edited by William Zinsser). The Houghton fiction backlist includes Richard Price's *Clockers*, Antonya Nelson's *Family Terrorists: Seven Stories and a Novella,* and *The Love Letter* by Cathleen Schine. The publisher also issues selected works of poetry, including *Time & Money: New Poems* by William Matthews, and *Nature: Poems Old and New* by May Swenson.

Houghton Mifflin distributes its own list.

Query letters and SASEs should be directed to:

Alan Andres, Editor (Boston)
Paperback reprints.

Peter Davison, Peter Davison Books (Boston)
Poetry.

Harry L. Foster Jr., Senior Editor (Boston)
Science and nature subjects.

Marc Jaffe, Marc Jaffe Books (New York)
Serious nonfiction, religion, politics.

Dawn Seferian, Senior Editor (New York)
Literary fiction—African-American, Asian-American, Latino. Gay and lesbian fiction and nonfiction. Literary criticism and biography.

Janet Silver, Senior Editor (Boston)
Literary fiction. Nonfiction: biographies, arts and culture, women's issues.

Frances Tenenbaum, Editor (Boston)
Gardening.

Richard Todd, Richard Todd Books (Boston)
Mostly serious nonfiction.

HOUGHTON MIFFLIN BOOKS FOR CHILDREN

This division stands out with a broad list of books that address topics of wide import, including works of thematic complexity and emotional depth at all reading levels. The program encompasses hardcover and paperback titles from picture books for the youngest readers to fiction for young adults, audiotapes, foldout books—many by a brace of successful authors as well. Caldecott and Newbery medallions abound in the tradition of Houghton Mifflin Books for Children.

Representing the Houghton Mifflin approach: *Cat and Cat-Face* by Chyng Feng Sun (illustrated by Lesley Liu), *Cry of the Benu Bird: An Egyptian Creation Story* (adapted and illustrated by C. Shana Greger), *Child of the Wolves* by Elizabeth Hall, and *In the Days of the Salem Witchcraft Trials* (written and illustrated by Marilynne K. Roach).

Sandpiper Paperbacks include *Elvira* (written and illustrated by Margaret Shannon), *El Chino* (written and illustrated by Allen Say), *Mommy Doesn't Know My Name* by Suzanne Williams (illustrated by Andrew Shachat), and *Amish Home* (written and photographed by Raymond Bial).

Query letters and SASEs should be directed to:

Matilda Welter, Senior Juvenile Editor (Boston)

Audrey Bryant, Editor (Boston)

Norma Jean Sawicki, Editor (New York)

CLARION BOOKS

Houghton Mifflin
215 Park Avenue South
New York, NY 10003
212-420-5800

Clarion publishes books, audiocassettes, and videos geared for the youngest readers up through the early teen years. Clarion's fiction includes serious, topical works and time-less classics. Clarion Books is an award-winning children's book division that is editorially independent of Houghton Mifflin's other lines.

On Clarion's list: *Good Night, Dinosaurs* by Judy Sierra (illustrated by Victoria Chess), *Temple Cat* by Andrew Clements (illustrated by Kate Kiesler), *Magid Fasts for Ramadan* by Mary Matthews (illustrated by E. B. Lewis), *Would My Fortune Cookie Lie?* by Stella Pevsner, *Nursery Tales Around the World* (selected and retold by Judy Sierra; illustrated by Stefano Vitale), and *Winston Churchill: Soldier, Statesman, Artist* by John B. Severance.

Query letters and SASEs should be directed to:

Dorothy Briley, Editor in Chief and Publisher
Juvenile to young adult.

HOWARD UNIVERSITY PRESS

(See Directory of University Presses)

HRD PRESS

Human Resource Development Press
23 Amherst Road
Amherst, MA 01002
413-253-3488

HRD Press (also known as Human Resource Development Press) specializes in a business list, with emphasis in the areas of training—resource books, management, professional interest, and finance. Catalog designations include customer service, tools for trainers, teams, change and problem solving, situational leadership, leadership and empowerment, performance-skills series, performance, games and activities, sexual harassment, management and supervision, employee selection, and diversity.

From the HRD list: *Fieldbook of Team Interventions: Step-by-Step Guide to High Performance Teams* by Judy C. Rice and C. Harry Eggleston, *The Visionary Leader: Leader Behavior Questionnaire* by Marshall Sashkin, *How to Hire the Right Person* by Denis Cauvier, *Are Your Employees Stealing You Blind?* by Robert Cameron New, and *Advertising Is a Waste of Money* by Robert Ranson.

HRD Press distributes to the trade through National Book Network.

Query letters and SASEs should be directed to:

Barry Davis, President

HUMANICS PUBLISHING GROUP

1482 Mecaslin Street Northwest
Atlanta, GA 30309
404-874-2176

Humanics's fields of publishing interest include self-help, how-to, psychology, human relations, health and nutrition, creative expression (in art, crafts, literature), education, humor, and spirituality. Special emphasis is on such topics as personal growth, love and relationships, environment and peace, and Taoism.

Humanics offers concentrations in the areas of elementary child and child development, teachers' resource books, childcare, and the family. The publisher produces children's books under the Humanics Children's House imprint. The Humanics line of teachers' resource books and materials in child development are directed in part to colleges and institutional markets; popular works in this subject area are published under the Humanics Learning imprint.

Humanics Publishing Group (founded in 1976) publishes a small- to medium-sized list of paperback trade books, a line of special fine editions, and audiocassettes.

Humanics titles: *A Goddess in My Shoes: Seven Steps to Peace* by Rickie Moore, *Balance of Body, Balance of Mind: A Rolfer's Vision of Buddhist Practice in the West* by Will Johnson, *Empowerment: Vitalizing Personal Energy* by William G. Cunningham, *Life Trek: The Odyssey of Adult Development* by John Stockmyer and

Robert Williams, *Shades of Love: A Collection of Poetry* by JoAnne Berkow, *The Best Chance Diet* by Joe D. Goldstritch, *The Tao of Learning* by Pamela Metz, and *Working and Managing in a New Age* by Ron Garland.

Humanics oversees its own distribution.

Query letters and SASEs should be directed to:

Arthur Bligh, Acquisitions Editor
Adult trade books.

HUMANICS CHILDREN'S HOUSE
HUMANICS LEARNING

Humanics Children's House publishes primarily illustrated works; the general accent is on original stories and tales targeted for younger readers. The Fun E. Friends series is one of the house's popular lines. Humanics also produces guides for caregivers and educators under the Humanics Learning logo.

Representing the Children's House list: *The Planet of the Dinosaurs* by Barbara Carr (illustrated by Alice Bear), *Fibber E. Frog* by Al Newman (illustrated by Jim Doody), *Creatures of an Exceptional Kind* by Dorothy B. Whitney, and *Cambio Chameleon* by Mauro Magellan.

Titles for teachers and caregivers issued under the Learning imprint: *Parental Classroom: A Parent's Guide for Teaching Your Baby in the Womb* by Rene Van De Carr and Marc Lehrer, *Teaching Terrific Twos* by Terry Graham and Linda Camp, *The Infant and Toddler Handbook* by Kathryn Castle, and *Toddlers Learn by Doing* by Rita Schrank.

Query letters and SASEs should be directed to:

Arthur Bligh, Humanics Children's House

HUMAN KINETICS

P.O. Box 5076
Champaign, IL 61825
217-351-5076
800-747-4457

Human Kinetics (founded in 1974) offers a list of trade and academic works (including college textbooks) that cover a wide range of athletic pursuits, with specialty areas in physical education, sports medicine, and fitness. Human Kinetics offers books geared for professional-level coaches, trainers, and participants, in addition to serious recreational athletes. A noteworthy HK imprint is YMCA of America Books. Human Kinetics books are issued primarily in trade softcover editions, although some are published as hardcovers. The press also publishes a number of periodicals in its areas of interest. Human Kinetics bills itself as the premier publisher for sports and fitness.

Representative titles: *Better Runs: 25 Years' Worth of Lessons for Running Faster and Farther* by Joe Henderson, *Snowshoeing* by Sally Edwards and Melissa McKenzie, *Basketball for Women: Becoming a Complete Player* by Nancy Lieberman-Cline and Robin Roberts, *Winning Racquetball: Drills, Skills, Strategies* by Ed Turner and Woody Clouse, *Your Child's Fitness: Practical Advice for Parents* by Susan Kalish, *Ice Skating: Steps to Success* by Karin Künzle-Watson and Steve DeArmond, *LifeFit* by Ralf S. Paffenbarger and Eric Olsen, *Offensive Baseball Drills* by Rod Delmonico, and *Water Fun and Fitness* by Terri Elder.

Human Kinetics oversees its own distribution.

Query letters and SASEs should be directed to:

Rainer Martens, Publisher and President

HYPERION

114 Fifth Avenue
New York, NY 10011
212-633-4400

Hyperion (founded in 1992) publishes commercial fiction and literary works, and frontlist nonfiction in the areas of popular culture, international affairs, current topical interest, popular psychology and self-help, and humor. The house publishes books in hardcover and trade paperback formats. Hyperion operates a strong children's program that encompasses Hyperion Books for Children and Disney Press. (See separate subentry below.) Miramax Books (see separate subentry below) concentrates on projects that tie in with the world of film.

Hyperion is part of Disney—the transnational corporate entity noted for its bountiful theme parks, hotels, and resorts, as well as its considerable ledger of film enterprises (including Touchstone, Miramax, and Disney studios). Disney launched Hyperion as a full-fledged, well-funded book-publishing division, and the house's top-of-the-line reputation commenced with its initial well-chosen list.

Exemplifying the arrangements available for coveted properties via major media enterprises, Hyperion acquired publishing rights to *Takedown: The Pursuit and Capture of America's Most Wanted Computer Criminal* by cybersleuth Tsutomu Shinomura and journalist John Markoff (of the New York *Times*); Miramax Films simultaneously consummated a contract for dramatic (stage and screen) rights, as well as CD-ROM/interactive (computer game) rights to the project.

Representing Hyperion nonfiction: *The Path: Creating Your Mission Statement for Work and for Life* by Laurie Beth Jones, *A Separate Creation: The Search for the Biological Origins of Sexual Orientation* by Chandler Burr, *In Heaven As on Earth: A Vision of the Afterlife* by M. Scott Peck, *Disney's Family Cookbook: Irresistible Recipes That Make Mealtime Fun* by Deanna Cook and the Experts at Family Fun Magazine, *Living the Simple Life: 100 Steps to Scaling Down and Enjoying More* by Elaine St. James, *Foxworthy* by Jeff Foxworthy, *Lucille's Car Care: Everything You*

Need to Know from Under the Hood—by America's Most Trusted Mechanic by Lucille Treganowan with Gina Catanzarite, *My Road to the Sundance: One Man's Journey into Native Spirituality* by Manny Twofeathers, *Think Yourself Thin: The Visualization Technique That Will Make You Lose Weight Without Exercise or Diet* by Debbie Johnson, and *The Inner Elvis: A Psychological Biography of Elvis Aaron Presley* by Peter O. Whitmer.

More media-related hits include: *Go, Cat, Go! The Life and Times of Carl Perkins, the King of Rockabilly* by Carl Perkins and David McGee, *Knee Deep in Paradise* (memoir) by Brett Butler, *I'm Only One Man* by Regis Philbin with Bill Zehme, *I Am Spock* by Leonard Nimoy, *Spike, Mike, Slackers and Dykes: A Guided Tour through a Decade of American Cinema* by John Pierson, *We Played the Game: 65 Players Remember Baseball's Greatest Era, 1947–1964* (edited by Danny Peary), and *Ismail Merchant's Passionate Meals: The New Indian Cuisine for Fearless Cooks and Adventurous Eaters* by Ismail Merchant.

Emblematic of Hyperion fiction and literary works: *Sunset Express* (an Elvis Cole novel) by Robert Crais, *The Free Fall of Webster Cummings* by Tom Bodett, *The Gettin Place* by Susan Straight, *Going Local* (mystery) by Jamie Harrison, *The Triggerman's Dance* by T. Jefferson Parker, *Crows Over a Wheatfield* by Paula Sharp, and *Cadillac Jukebox* by James Lee Burke. Other noteworthy projects have included *Myst: The Book of Atrus* (based on the best-selling CD-ROM game) by Robyn and Rand Miller, *Act of Betrayal* by Edna Buchanan, *Tropical Depression* by Laurence Shames, *Ain't Gonna Be the Same Fool Twice* by April Sinclair, and *Arise and Walk* by Barry Gifford.

Hyperion hardcover and trade paperback books are distributed to the trade by Little, Brown; Warner Books handles special sales as well as the mass-market paperback list.

The Hyperion editors listed (unless otherwise noted) acquire fiction and nonfiction titles consistent with the house description. Query letters and SASEs should be directed to:

Laurie Abkemeier, Editor
Nonfiction concentration; no fiction.

Jennifer Barth, Editor

David Cashion, Associate Editor

Brian DeFiore, Editor in Chief

Rick Kot, Executive Editor

Wendy Lefkon, Executive Editor

(Ms.) Leslie Wells, Executive Editor
Does a lot of suspense/thriller/mystery books.

HYPERION BOOKS FOR CHILDREN
DISNEY PRESS

The children's book division of Hyperion produces titles for younger readers through young adult via a number of series, imprints, and lines. Hyperion Books for Children accentuates illustrated fairy tales, picture storybooks, poetry, illustrated fiction, calendars, and activity books. Disney Press concentrates on illustrated works that tie in with Disney children's cinema classics, old and new—including series novelizations and lavishly illustrated formats. On the Hyperion children's division list are volumes that are finely designed and luxuriously produced.

Titles from Hyperion Books for Children: *Fireworks: The Science, the Art, the Magic* (written and photographed by Susan Kuklin), *Pamela's First Musical* by Wendy Wasserstein (illustrated by Andrew Jeckness), *Hostage* by Edward Myers, *Spooky Stories for a Dark and Stormy Night* (edited by Alice Low; illustrated by Gahan Wilson), and *Racetrack Robbery* by Ellen Leroe (illustrated by Bill Basso).

Disney Press produces a lineup that includes picture books, board books, pop-up books, novels, and activity books. These works are derived from such successful Disney cinematic productions as *The Hunchback of Notre Dame*, *101 Dalmatians*, *Beauty and the Beast*, *James and the Giant Peach*, *Aladdin*, *Pocahontas*, *Lady and the Tramp*, *Bambi*, *The Mighty Ducks*, and *The Little Mermaid*.

Hyperion Books for Children and products from Disney Press are distributed to the trade by Little, Brown.

Query letters and SASEs should be directed to:

Andrea Cascardi, Associate Publisher

Lisa Holton, Vice President and Publisher

MIRAMAX BOOKS

Miramax Books accents titles keyed to cinema—as a profession, industry, lifestyle, or avocation. The Miramax imprint develops a wide range of markets within this interest area. The Miramax list includes select original fiction, reprints of novels that serve as the basis for films, and other movie tie-in projects.

From Miramax Books: *From Dusk Till Dawn* (a script by Quentin Tarantino); *The Last of the High Kings* (novel keyed to a film project) by Ferdia MacAnna; a new dark-comic novel by David Lipsky (author of *The Pallbearer*); *The Piano* (a script by Jane Campion); *The Postman* (a script by Antonio Skarmeta); *Jane Eyre* by Charlotte Brontë (in a film tie-in reprint edition); and *Pulp Fiction* (a script by Quentin Tarantino and Roger Avary).

Query letters and SASEs should be directed to:

Susan Dalsimer, Vice President of Publishing
Film-related projects.

IDG BOOKS WORLDWIDE

919 East Hillsdale Boulevard, Suite 400
Foster City, CA 94404
415-655-3000
800-762-2974 (catalog requests)

IDG Books produces titles for the computer user and general nonfiction reader that cover a broad range of popular topics. The IDG computer list is keyed primarily to proprietary applications software and operating systems, and the house produces several prominent series in this vein.

IDG has well over 50 selections in the popular . . . For Dummies series; Hot . . . Secrets titles accent such areas as Windows, DOS, and network security; Macworld Books concentrates on the universe of Apple users; and PC World handbooks are hands-on tutorial reference works. Many IDG books come packaged with bonus software that features some of the best in shareware, freeware, and macros.

IDG Books Worldwide (founded in 1990) is a subsidiary of International Data Group. Expanding beyond its original sphere of computer titles, IDG is interested in authors and/or potential projects that are appropriate for series in all areas of business and general reference. IDG takes pride in issuing books chock full of information and valuable advice the reader is not likely to encounter anywhere else—brought together with attention to quality, selection, value, and convenience.

Representative general computing titles from IDG Books Worldwide: *Macworld QuarkXPress Bible* by Barbara Assadi and Galen Gruman; *PC Secrets* by Caroline M. Halliday; *PC World DOS Handbook* by John Socha, Clint Hicks, and Devra Hall; and *Security Network Secrets* by David Stang and Sylvia Moon.

On the expanding and highly successful . . . For Dummies list: *Windows for Dummies* by Andy Rathbone, *The Internet for Dummies* by John Levine and Carol Baroudi, *Sex for Dummies* by Dr. Ruth Westheimer, *Selling for Dummies* by Tom Hopkins, *Macs for Dummies* by David Pogue, *Job Hunting for Dummies* by Max Messmer, *Investing for Dummies* by Eric Tyson, and *DOS for Dummies* by Dan Gookin.

IDG Books Worldwide directs its own distribution services.

Query letters and SASEs should be directed to:

Suki Gear, Editorial Assistant (computer books)

Milissa Koloski, Senior Vice President Group Publisher, Dummies, Inc. (computer books)

Kathleen A. Welton, Vice President and Publisher (Chicago)
Business books (does not do computer titles).

Contact at:
  645 North Michigan Ave.
  Chicago, IL 60611
  312-482-8460

INDIANA UNIVERSITY PRESS
(See Directory of University Presses)

INDUSTRIAL PRESS
200 Madison Avenue
New York, NY 10016
212-889-6330

Industrial Press categories include scientific works, technical handbooks, professional guides, and reference books in the areas of engineering and the law, manufacturing processes and materials, design engineering, and quality control, as well as plant and industrial engineering interface with management and logistics. They also include basic references in these fields.

Industrial Press (founded in 1883) is a leading specialist house in the professional, scientific, and scholarly publishing arenas. The publisher typically offers several hand-picked new titles a year in addition to its ongoing backlist of established sellers.

Industrial Press continues to offer its classic *Machinery's Handbook* by Erik Oberg, Franklin D. Jones, Holbrook L. Horton, and Henry H. Ryffel, along with its companion guidebook (in fully revised formats).

Other titles representative of the Industrial Press list: *Engineering Formulas, Conversions, Definitions, and Tables* by Frank Sims, *Blueprint Reading Basics* by Warren Hammer, *Why Systems Fail: And How to Make Sure Yours Doesn't* by David A. Turbide, *Rapid Automated Prototyping* by Lamont Wood, *Application of Metal Cutting Theory* by Fryderyk E. Gorczyca, *Modern Manufacturing Processes* by James Brown, *Handbook of Dimensional Measurement* by Francis Fargo and Mark Curtis, *Computerized Maintenance Management Systems* by Terry Wireman, *Microbiologically Influenced Corrosion Handbook* by Susan Watkins Borenstein, *Fundamentals of Product Liability Law for Engineers* by Linda K. Enghagen, and *Pipefitter's Handbook* by Forrest R. Lindsey.

Industrial Press handles its own distribution.

Query letters and SASEs should be directed to:

Woodrow W. Chapman, Editorial Director

INNER TRADITIONS INTERNATIONAL
(See Directory of Religious, Spiritual, and Inspirational Publishers)

INTERVARSITY PRESS
(See Directory of Religious, Spiritual, and Inspirational Publishers)

IRWIN PROFESSIONAL PUBLISHING
1333 Burr Ridge Road
Burr Ridge, IL 60521
708-789-4000

Irwin Professional produces a comprehensive lineup of business and professional publications. Areas of Irwin interest include accounting, banking, corporate finance, employee benefits, entrepreneurship, financial advising, futures and options, general business, healthcare management, individual investing, institutional investing, management, manufacturing, marketing, quality, and sales.

Irwin's topical concentration hits niches such as business economics, international trade, real estate, small business, personal finance, fixed income, lending and retail banking, global investing, mutual funds, stocks, portfolio management, business strategy, communication, customer satisfaction, diversity, global management, executive management, sales management, operations, auditing, compliance, human resources, fraud prevention/security, insurance, leadership, teams, and training.

Irwin Professional Publishing (a subsidiary of the Times Mirror Company) gears its titles to the needs of the contemporary business community and produces an array of books, video seminars, and other media products of interest to seasoned corporate veterans as well as to rookie recruits—keyed to professional business readership markets worldwide.

The publisher has a strong sales focus on the corporate and institutional market (featuring quantity discounts); of particular interest is the house's customer advisory service that involves working with individual companies to develop specially tailored in-house training programs that feature Irwin Professional Publishing products. In addition, Irwin Professional Publishing has a section that specializes in custom-published and copublished corporate projects.

ASQC Quality Press and Irwin Professional Publishing have a conjoint arrangement; the fruits of this endeavor include the Malcolm Baldridge National Quality Award Series as well as a line that focuses on issues of quality.

Irwin Professional (founded in 1965) went by the name of Dow Jones–Irwin until Dow Jones sold its interest in 1990; for a few years subsequently the house published under the Business One Irwin imprint. Irwin merged with formerly independent Probus Publishing Company in late 1994.

Prior to its acquisition by Irwin Professional, Probus Publishing Company (founded in 1984) was a privately held house specializing in trade and professional books for investors, business professionals, and entrepreneurs. Combining the complementary strengths of Irwin and Probus creates a market leader with increased publishing savvy and financial strength—of potential benefit to authors and booksellers alike. The plan goes forward with a large and varied publishing program dedicated to the development and marketing of business and financial books—as well as other information of significance to professionals around the world.

Irwin Professional Publishing highlights: *Forensic Accounting: How to Investigate Financial Fraud* by William T. Thornhill; *The Accountant's Guide to Legal Liability and Ethics* by Marc Epstein and Albert Spalding; *SuperCommunity Banking: A Super-Strategy for Success* by Anat Bird; *Valuing a Business: The Analysis and Appraisal of Closely Held Companies* by Shannon P. Pratt, Robert F. Reilly, and Robert P. Schweihs; *The Handbook of Executive Benefits* by Towers Perrin; *Getting the Money You Need: Practical Solutions for Financing Your Small Business* by Gibson Heath; *How to Start Your Own Money Management Business* by Douglas K. Harmon; *Implementing Diversity: Best Practices for Making Diversity Work in Your Organization* by Marilyn Loden; and *The Secret Empire: How 25 Multinationals Rule the World* by Janet Lowe.

Irwin Professional Publishing handles its own distribution as well as that of books published conjointly with Quality Press, APICS, and Pfeiffer & Company.

Query letters and SASEs should be directed to:

Mark Butler, Acquisitions Editor
Banking.

Caroline Carney, Editor
Management and marketing.

Michael Desposito, Associate Publisher, Investments, Manufacturing, & Quality Management

Jeffrey Krames, Associate Publisher, Trade Publishing
Individual investing, personal finance, management, sales and marketing management, employee benefits.

Amy Hollands Gaber, Executive Editor
Corporate finance, personal finance, financial planning, employee benefits.

James McNeil, Associate Publisher, Banking, Corporate Finance & Accounting/ Healthcare Management

Amy Ost, Acquisitions Editor
Corporate finance, accounting.

Ralph Rieves, Executive Editor
Institutional investing, portfolio management.

Kristine Rynne, Acquisitions Editor
Healthcare management.

Cindy Zigmund, Senior Editor
Manufacturing, management, quality.

JEWISH LIGHTS PUBLISHING
(See Directory of Religious, Spiritual, and Inspirational Publishers)

THE JEWISH PUBLICATION SOCIETY
(See Directory of Religious, Spiritual, and Inspirational Publishers)

KENSINGTON PUBLISHING CORPORATION
ZEBRA BOOKS/PINNACLE BOOKS

850 Third Avenue
16th Floor
New York, NY 10022
212-407-1500

The Kensington, Zebra, and Pinnacle programs cover all major categories of commercial and popular trade fiction and nonfiction. Areas of fiction concentration include romance fiction (historical and contemporary), horror, mystery and suspense, Westerns, thrillers, action-adventure, and women's fiction. Nonfiction is strong in areas such as topical interest, humor, health, self-help and awareness, true crime, and popular biography.

Kensington is one of the largest independently owned book publishers. Kensington Publishing Corporation is home to such divisional imprints as Kensington Books (primarily hardcover and trade paperback originals), along with Zebra and Pinnacle (mainly mass-market paperback editions, as well as selected hardcovers). Long a leader in the paperback arena, the house has expanded its publishing emphasis along the commercial spectrum; under the Kensington and Zebra/Pinnacle banners the house is a vital hardcover presence.

The Kensington mass-market imprint publishes quality and commercial fiction and nonfiction, both original titles and reprints.

Zebra Books (founded in 1975) and its sibling house Pinnacle Books (acquired in 1987) publish a colossal list of mass-market paperback originals that span the spectrum of mainstream and genre categories. Zebra and Pinnacle also produce mass-market reprints of hardcover originals, as well as fiction and nonfiction in trade paper and designated high-profile titles in original hardcover editions.

The paperback-originals division of the house maintains a firm backlist of books—however, in keeping with the mass-market rack tradition, titles that don't move are soon gone.

Kensington continues its romance program under imprints, series, and lines such as Lovegram Romance, Regency Romance, Historical Romance, Denise Little Presents, and Arabesque (a line of multicultural romances).

Indicative of the house roster within the various fiction genres and categories: *Shadow and Silk* by Ann Maxwell, *Vegas Heat* by Fern Michaels, *Infernal Affairs* by Jane Heller, *Murder Among Friends* (a Kate Austen mystery) by Jonnie Jacobs (from Partners in Crime), *Gray Matter* by Shirley Kennett, *Back\Slash: A Cyber Thriller* by William H. Lovejoy, *Wake Up to Murder* by Steve Allen, and *Pig Town* by William Caunitz.

Nonfiction entrants include: *Bad Blood: Crisis in the American Red Cross* by Judith Reitman, *Baby: An Owner's Manual* by Bud Zukow, *The Unauthorized X-Files Challenge: Everything You Ever Wanted to Know about TV's Most Incredible Show!* by James Hatfield and George Burt, *Stepparenting* by Jeanette Lofus, *Wildly Gross Jokes* by Julius Alvin, *The Dinosaur Heresies: New Theories Unlocking the Mystery of the Dinosaurs and Their Extinction* by Robert T. Bakker, and *Star Stalkers* by George Mair.

Kensington oversees its own distributional operations.

All listed Kensington editors have a wide range of interests in fiction and nonfiction; some of their personal specialties are noted below. Query letters and SASEs should be directed to:

Tracy Bernstein, Executive Editor, Kensington (trade paper)
Nonfiction; mysteries/suspense, mainstream commercial fiction.

Paul Dinas, Editor in Chief
Supervises all hardcover trade and mass-market titles, as well as the Zebra and Pinnacle imprints. Specialties: True crime, nonfiction, humor, thrillers.

Kate Duffy, Senior Editor
Commercial fiction; women's stories, romance—especially Regencies, mysteries. Nonfiction.

Sarah Gallick, Executive Editor, Kensington (hardcover)
Fiction, nonfiction.

Amy Garvey, Assistant Editor
Wide range of commercial interests, including women's fiction.

Karen Haas, Consulting Editor
Commercial women's fiction, including romance.

Monica Harris, Editor
Romance, women's fiction, Arabesque.

Ann LaFarge, Executive Editor, Zebra
Women's fiction.

Denise Little, Senior Editor
Romances, women's fiction, Denise Little Presents, mystery.

Carin Cohen Ritter, Consulting Editor
Commercial women's fiction, including romance.

John Scognamiglio, Senior Editor
Horror, psychological suspense, mysteries, romance.

Michael Kesend Publishing, Ltd.

1025 Fifth Avenue
New York, NY 10028
212-249-5150

Kesend's publishing accent is on travel, leisure, animals, pets, the outdoors, hiking, nature, and sports—as well as literary works and biographies (often with themes related to the core house focus). Kesend also publishes select serious new fiction in addition to literary reprints, along with some general trade nonfiction (especially in healthcare).

Michael Kesend Publishing (begun in 1979) is an intimate house that offers personalized attention to the authors and books on its choice list. Kesend produces a small number of new hardcover and trade paperback titles each year; Kesend maintains a backlist featuring the publisher's many perennial sellers.

Kesend has been extremely successful with its national and regional travel guidebooks. Representing the Kesend list in travel, leisure, and the outdoors: *Art on Site: Country Artwalks from Maine to Maryland* by Marina Harrison and Lucy D. Rosenfeld, *A Guide to the Sculpture Parks and Gardens of America* by Jane McCarthy and Laurily K. Epstein, *Walks in Welcoming Places: Outings in the Northeast for Strollers of All Ages and the Disabled* by Marina Harrison and Lucy D. Rosenfeld, *The Essential Guide to Wilderness Camping and Backpacking in the United States* by Charles Cook, *Mountainsigns/Mountain Life* (in the illustrated Pocket Nature Guidebook series) by Gerald Cox, and *Care of the Wild, Feathered and Furred: Treating and Feeding Injured Birds and Animals* by Mae Hickman and Maxine Guy (with foreword by Cleveland Amory).

A novel with a travel theme is *Season of the Migration to the North* by Tayeb Salih (translated from the Arabic by Denys Johnson-Davies). Literary travel writing includes a reprint of the classic *A Poet's Bazaar: A Journey to Greece, Turkey, and Up the Danube* by Hans Christian Andersen.

Kesend books in sports and athletics: *The Historical Dictionary of Golfing Terms: From 1500 to the Present* by Peter Davies, *Swee'pea and Other Playground Legends: Tales of Drugs, Violence and Basketball* by John Valenti with Ron Naclerio, and *Butch Beard's Basic Baseball: The Complete Player* by Butch Beard with Glenn Popowitz and David Samson (with foreword by Julius Erving).

Health and popular medicine titles from Kesend include: *Hysterectomy: Learning the Facts, Coping With the Feelings, Facing the Future* by Wanda Wigfall-Williams, and *Understanding Pacemakers* by David Sonnenburg, Michael Birnbaum, and Emil A. Naclerio.

Michael Kesend Publishing handles its own distribution.

Query letters and SASEs should be directed to:

Michael Kesend, Publisher

KITCHEN SINK PRESS
320 Riverside Drive
Northampton, MA 01060
413-586-7822

Kitchen Sink Press (founded in 1969) publishes graphic novels, collections of contemporary comic masters, and classic reprints in editions that encompass hardcovers, paperbacks, magazines, and comic books. The house also sells t-shirts, posters, serigraphs, portfolios, postcards, mugs, cloisonné pins, neckties, beach towels, satin jackets, finger puppets, statuettes, and other merchandise—all related to pictorial literary forms.

Along with publishers such as Fantagraphics (please see separate entry in this directory), KSP is at the forefront of the movement to generate increased marketing of comics-related works (especially graphics novels and hardcover or trade paper collections) via traditional publishing-trade venues (independent bookstores as well as chain outlets) in addition to comics specialty shops. After Kitchen Sink acquired Tundra, another comics publisher, KSP relocated to Massachusetts from its previous headquarters in Wisconsin.

Highlights from the Kitchen Sink catalog: *Blab* (edited by Monte Beauchamp), *Voodoo Child: The Illustrated Legend of Jimi Hendrix* (written by Martin I. Green; painted by Bill Seinkiewicz—plus bonus music CD, *Jimi by Himself*), *The Collected Crow* by James O'Barr, *Twisted Sisters* (edited by Diane Noomin), *Now, Endsville* by Carol Lay, *Cherry Collection* by Larry Welz, *Introducing Kafka* by Robert Crumb and David Zane Mairowitz, *New York* by Will Eisner ("Father of the Graphic Novel"), *Black Hole* by Charles Burns, *A Century of Women Cartoonists* (edited by Trina Robbins), and *The Comic Strip Art of Lyonel Feininger* (edited by Bill Blackbeard).

Kitchen Sink Press distributes its own line of products; the house also maintains distribution arrangements with mass-market and trade book establishments such as Berkley Books.

Query letters (with samples) and SASEs should be directed to:

Denis Kitchen, Publisher

KIVAKÍ PRESS

585 East 31st Street
Durango, CO 81301
303-385-1767
800-578-5904

Kivakí Press is a small publishing company with a focus on three editorial areas: environmental restoration; community renewal and education; and personal and holistic healing. Kivakí exists to provide people with practical strategies for restoring their ecosystems, for reconnecting with their places and local cultures, and for renewing their bodies holistically. Kivakí addresses academic, holistic health, and environmental book markets. Located in the San Juan mountains of southwestern Colorado, the press produces a small number of new titles on a seasonal basis to add to a strong backlist.

Indicative of Kivakí interest are *A Wilder Life: Essays from Home* by Ken Wright, *The Company of Others: Essays in Celebration of Paul Shepard* (edited by Max Oelschlaeger), *Look to the Mountain: An Ecology of Indigenous Education* by Gregory Cajete, *Seasons of Change: Growing through Pregnancy and Birth* by Suzanne Arms, *Restoration Forestry: An International Guide to Sustainable Forestry Practices* (edited by Michael Pilarski), *Flora of the San Juans: A Field Guide to the Mountain Plants of Southwestern Colorado* by Sue Komarek, *Sacred Land Sacred Sex: Rapture of the Deep—Concerning Deep Ecology and Celebrating Life* by Dolores LaChapelle, and *Neuropathic Handbook of Herbal Formulas: A Practical and Concise Herb User's Guide* by Richard Scalzo (in an updated edition).

Kivakí oversees its own distribution, including direct mail order, and a trade distribution network that utilizes the facilities of several national fulfillment and distribution firms.

Query letters and SASEs should be directed to:

Greg Cumberford, Publisher

KNOPF PUBLISHING GROUP/ALFRED A. KNOPF

(See Random House)

KODANSHA AMERICA

Kodansha International
114 Fifth Avenue
New York, NY 10011
212-727-6460

Kodansha America produces hardcover and trade paperback books in English by a variety of authors in a diverse array of subject areas. Interests include autobiography and biography, business and psychology, garden and design, health and lifestyle, parenting, self-help, history and sociology, natural history, world culture, religion and spirituality, and women's studies.

Kodansha America is the wholly owned United States subsidiary of Kodansha Ltd., Japan's largest publishing company (started in 1963 and headquartered in Tokyo). Kodansha America also acts as distributor and marketing representative for its sister company, Kodansha International. Kodansha America maintains the Kodansha Globe Trade Paperbacks imprint and offers a strong backlist.

The house list, including distribution/marketing clients Kodansha International and Japan Publications, has a sizable selection of individual works relating to Japanese cultural tradition.

Kodansha America's nonfiction includes: *Empires of Time: Calendars, Clocks, and Cultures* by Anthony Aveni, *Healing Essence: A Cancer Doctor's Practical Program for Physical and Spiritual Well-Being* by Mitchell L. Gaynor, *International Excellence: Seven Breakthrough Strategies for Personal and Professional Success* by Christopher Engholm and Diana Rowland, *Living Color: Master Lin Yun's Guide to Feng Shui and the Art of Color* by Sarah Rossbach and Lin Yun, *Moscow Days: Life and Hard Times in the New Russia* by Galina Dutkina, *Pussyfooting: Essential Dance Procedures for Cats* (written and illustrated by Viv Quillan), *The Book of Everyday Wisdom* by Sarah and A. Elizabeth Delany with Amy Hill Heath, *The Heart of the Sky: Travels Among the Maya* by Peter Canby, and *What Is Japan? Contradictions and Transformations* by Taichi Sakaiya.

Kodansha fiction and literary writing (much of it in translation) includes works from authors such as Kobo Abe, Sawako Ariyoshi, Takeshi Kaiko, Saiichi Maruya, Yukio Mishima, and Nobel laureate Kenzaburo Oe, as well as critical works in art, culture, and letters. Titles: *Coin Locker Babies* by Ryu Murakami, *Trash* by Amy Yamada, *The Art of Peter Voulkos* by Rose Slivka and Karen Tsujimoto, *Japan, the Ambiguous, and Myself: The Nobel Prize Speech and Other Lectures* by Kenzaburo Oe, and *A Cultural History of Intoxicants in Society* by Richard Rudgley.

Books on the Japan Publications list specialize in the interrelationship of physical and mental well-being in the contexts of health and fitness, cuisine and nutrition, and lifestyle.

Kodansha is distributed in the United States by Farrar Straus & Giroux.

Query letters and SASEs should be directed to:

Paul De Angelis, Editor at Large
Special interest in history, culture, Eastern philosophy.

Deborah Baker, Senior Editor
Women's issues, autobiography, personal growth and development, health, cross-cultural narratives.

Nancy Cooperman, Senior Editor
Health and lifestyle, science, parenting, natural history, world cultures, religion and spirituality—in both narrative and how-to formats.

H. J. KRAMER INC.

(See Directory of Religious, Spiritual, and Inspirational Publishers)

KTAV PUBLISHING HOUSE INC.

(See Directory of Religious, Spiritual, and Inspirational Publishers)

LAST GASP ECO-FUNNIES, INC.

777 Florida Street
San Francisco, CA 94110
415-824-6636

Last Gasp produces an array of goods that cover the fields of popular and cult comics, underground comics, punk rock (recordings and print publications), popular and diverse subcultures, and marijuana literature. In addition to trade paperbacks and comics folios, the house catalogs merchandise such as poster art, decorative and illustrated cards, t-shirts and other apparel, and audio and visual items. Imprints include Gentzer & Gonif.

Last Gasp Eco-Funnies, Inc. (founded in 1970) is distributed to the trade through Publishers Group West; the house shows heavy catalog sales through direct marketing.

Query letters and SASEs should be directed to:

Ron Turner, Owner

LATIN AMERICAN LITERARY REVIEW PRESS

121 Edgewood Avenue
Pittsburgh, PA 15218
412-371-9023

Latin American Literary Review Press produces reference books, trade books, and specialty publications in Latin American interest and studies. The press produces books in art, architecture, literature, and poetry; history, biography, and natural science; country studies, Spain, Europe, United States, Latin America; and children's books.

Latin American Literary Review Press (founded in 1980) is an independent house that is particularly vigorous in fields such as Latin American literature in English translation, Spanish-language art books, and literary criticism in Spanish. The press also publishes the journal *Latin American Literary Review*.

Representative titles in fiction and literature: *When New Flowers Bloomed: Short Stories by Women Writers from Costa Rica and Panama* (edited and with a prologue by Enrique Jaramillo Levi), *A Bag of Stories* (short stories) by Edla Van Steen (translated from the Portuguese by David George), *Bazaar of the Idiots* (stories) by Gustavo Alvarez Gardeazábal (translated by Jonathan Titler and Susan F. Hill), *The Pink Rosary* (novel) by Ricardo Means Ybarra, *Beatle Dreams and Other Stories* by Guillermo Samperio (translated by Russell M. Cluff and L. Howard Quackenbush), and *Borinqueña: Puerto Rico in the Sixties* (fiction) by Flora Becker.

Nonfiction and critical works: *XVIII Century Spanish Music Villancicos of Juan Francés de Iribarren* by Marta Sánchez, *Mexican American Theater: Legacy and Reality* by Nicolás Kanellos, and *The Art of Mariano Azuela* by Eliud Martínez.

Latin American Literary Review Press has its own in-house distribution operation; in addition, the house markets through direct-mail catalog dissemination and utilizes a variety of national and regional distribution houses. Major markets include public libraries, trade booksellers, and university and college libraries. Latin American Literary Review Press handles distribution for a number of domestic and international presses.

Query letters and SASEs should be directed to:

Connie Matthews, Assistant to the Editor

Yvette E. Miller, President and Editor

LEISURE BOOKS

276 Fifth Avenue
Suite 1008
New York, NY 10001
212-725-8811

Leisure's publishing program centers on mass-market paperback originals in fiction and nonfiction, with a short list of hardcover reprints. Leisure's category fiction embraces contemporary women's fiction, horror, mysteries and detective fiction, suspense, thrillers, and Westerns.

Leisure hosts a fine list from established genre writers, and also offers works from newer authors; the house publishes several brand-name category series and issues a notable number of deluxe double editions. The innovative Love Spell line has defined new market territory with experimental marketing slates in contemporary, historical, futuristic, and time-travel romance. Leisure Books (founded in 1970) is a division of Dorchester Publishing Company.

Sample titles: *Apache Runaway* by Madeline Baker, *Savage Embers* by Cassie Edwards, *A Fire in the Blood* by Shirl Henke, *Fancy* by Norah Hess, *Sheik's Promise* by Carole Howey, *The Outlaw Viking* by Sandra Hill, *Timbal Gulch Trail* by Max Brand, *Renegade Nation* by Judd Cole, and *Captive Legacy* by Theresa Scott.

Leisure Books handles its own distribution.

Query letters and SASEs should be directed to:

Alicia Condon, Editorial Director

Joanna Cagan, Editor

Don D'Auria, Editor
Westerns and technothrillers; horror.

Jennifer Eaton, Editorial Assistant

Chris Keeslar, Editorial Assistant

Kimberly Waltemyer, Editorial Director

Edith Wilson, Editor

LEXINGTON BOOKS

(See Jossey-Bass under Simon & Schuster listing)

LITTLE, BROWN AND COMPANY

New York office:
Time & Life Building
1271 Avenue of the Americas
New York, NY 10020
212-522-8700

Boston office:
34 Beacon Street
Boston, MA 02108
617-227-0730
800-343-9204 (catalog requests)

Little, Brown publishes trade nonfiction and fiction. Nonfiction concentration includes popular and literary biography, history, travel, art, medicine and allied health education, law, science, cuisine and lifestyle, reference, inspiration, and keepsake volumes/gift books. Little, Brown also produces commercial and literary fiction, essays, and memoirs; cultural, literary, and art criticism; and selected poetry. Little, Brown publishes in hardcover, trade paper, and mass-market paperback editions, and produces deluxe editions as well as calendars.

Back Bay Books is a Little, Brown trade paperback imprint that specializes in contemporary fiction; Back Bay titles are generally cataloged with the core Little, Brown list. Little, Brown and Company Books for Young Adults is among the strongest and most respected imprints in its field. (Please see separate subentry below.)

Little, Brown and Company (founded in 1837) originated as an independent house with a Boston home base. Little, Brown earned renown as a publisher with a dynamic, commercially successful as well as literary list. Little, Brown, now a subsidiary of Time Warner, functions autonomously from within the Time Life building (where its main trade offices reside), and publishes under its stately colophon image of an eagle-topped column. Bulfinch Press (still based in Boston; see subentry below) hones its own fine-arts specialist program.

Representing Little, Brown nonfiction and popular works: *Last Night in Paradise: Sex and Morals at the Century's End* by Katie Roiphe, *Five Against One: The Saga of Eddie Vedder and Pearl Jam* by Kim Neely, *A World without Jews: Is There a Future for Us?* by Alan Dershowitz, *Bordering on Chaos: Guerillas, Stockbrokers, Politicians, and Mexico's Road to Prosperity* by Andres Oppenheimer, *Sex and Spirit* (in the Living Wisdom series) by Clifford Bishop, *Virus-X: Tracking the New Killer Plagues out of the Present and into the Future* by Frank Ryan, *Nothing to Lose: Fitness for All Shapes and Sizes* by Dee Hakala and Michael D'Orso, *The Fugitive Game: Online with Kevin Mitnick* by Jonathan Littman, *The Coming Race War in America: A Wake-Up Call* by Carl T. Rowan, *Oz Clarke's Wine Advisor* (updated annually) by Oz Clarke, *X-Files Confidential: The Unauthorized X-Philes Compendium* by Ted Edwards, *Parenting the Fussy Baby and High-Need Child: Everything You Need to Know—from Birth to Age Five* by William Sears and Martha Sears, *Hello, He Lied: And Other Truths from the Hollywood Trenches* by Lynda Obst, and *How Good Do We Have to Be? A New Understanding of Guilt and Forgiveness* by Harold Kushner.

Little, Brown fiction and letters encompasses topnotch thrillers, suspense, and mystery works as well as mainstream novels and compositions of literary note. Featured titles: *Jack and Jill* (suspense) by James Patterson, *Trunk Music* (a Harry Bosch novel) by Michael Connelly, *The Hottest State* (novel) by Ethan Hawke, *Love and Longing in Bombay* (stories) by Vikram Chandra, *Infinite Jest* by David Foster Wallace, *On with the Story* (stories) by John Barth, *Let's Face the Music and Die* (a Lauren Laurano mystery) by Sandra Scoppettone, *Snakebite's Sonnet* (novel) by Max Phillips, *Playing the Bones* by Louise Reed, *The Prophetess* by Barbara Wood, *Naked* by David Sedaris, *Best American Gay Fiction* (new annual series; edited by Brian Bouldrey), and *Miracle on the 17th Green* (novelistic golf fable) by James Patterson and Peter de Jonge.

Little, Brown maintains an extensive backlist and is especially strong in literary fiction and nonfiction. Little, Brown distributes its own titles as well as those of a changing list of other publishing houses both large and small (currently including Hyperion and Arcade).

Please note: There are currently no Little, Brown adult-trade editors in Boston full-time. Query letters and SASEs should be directed to these New York editors:

Catherine Crawford, Assistant Editor
General nonfiction. Literary and serious commercial fiction.

Fredrica Friedman, Vice President, Associate Publisher, Editorial Director
Commercial fiction, celebrity books, and social history; general nonfiction. Projects have included: *The Day After Tomorrow* by Allan Folson, *Hide and Seek* by James Patterson, *Dream Makers, Dream Breakers* by Carl Rowan, *Tangled Vines* by Janet Dailey, *The Best Cat Ever* by Cleveland Amory, *New York Days* by Willie Morris, *Life of the Party* by Christopher Ogden, *Chutzpah* by Alan Dershowitz, and books with Henry Kissinger, Victoria Glendening, and Letty Cottin Pogrebin.

Jennifer Josephy, Senior Editor
General nonfiction, some literary fiction, cookbooks.

Jordan Pavlin, Editor
General nonfiction; literary fiction.

William D. Phillips, Editor in Chief
General nonfiction; some literary fiction.

Michael Pietsch, Vice President and Executive Editor
Music-related books, pop culture, and literary fiction; general nonfiction. Projects have included *A Good Walk Spoiled: Days and Nights on the PGA Tour* by John Feinstein, *The Poet* by Michael Connelly, *Cobain and Garcia* by the editors of *Rolling Stone*, *Last Train to Memphis* by Peter Guralnick, *Faithfull* by Marianne Faithfull and David Dalton, *Hank Williams* by Colin Escott, and books by David Mamet, David Foster Wallace, Anita Shreve, Rick Moody, Tony Early, Peter Guralnick, and Brock Yates.

Geoffrey Kroske, Assistant Editor
General nonfiction; some fiction.

BULFINCH PRESS

Bulfinch Press is a Little, Brown and Company division (based in Boston) that produces titles in art, architecture, photography, and design, as well as collections of literary works and illustrated volumes with a historical, cultural, or geographic accent. The house produces graphically lush hardcovers and paperbacks, as well as specialty lines including posters and calendars.

Among noteworthy Bulfinch projects: *Crimes and Splendors: The Desert Cantos of Richard Misrach* (text by Anne Tucker; essay by Rebecca Solnit), *Roadworks* by Linda McCartney, *The Kings and Queens of England* by Nicholas Best, *Romantic Needlepoint: 20 Needlepoint Designs Inspired by Love* by Candace Bahouth (photography by Linda Burgess), *Medieval Cats* by Susan Hebert, *Royal Blood: Fifty Years of*

Classic Thoroughbreds (portraits by Richard Stone Reeves; text by Jim Bolus), *Pump and Circumstance: Thirty Gas Station Postcards* by John Margolies, *Library of Interior Detail* by Elizabeth Hilliard, *Cecil Beaton* (photographs by Cecil Beaton; essays by David Allen Mellor and Philippe Garner), and *A Walk in Monet's Garden: A Pop-Up Book* (illustrated by Francesco Crespi).

Query letters and SASEs should be directed to:

Carol Judy Leslie, Publisher (Bulfinch Press; Boston)
Illustrated gift/coffee-table books.

LITTLE, BROWN AND COMPANY BOOKS FOR CHILDREN AND YOUNG ADULTS

Little, Brown's children's books division (headquartered in Boston) produces picture books, springboard books, flip books, book-and-toy packages, activity books and kits, pop-up editions, and titles for middle and young-adult readers. The house distributes Sierra Club Books for Children, a line of fine nature-theme picture books. This division also issues resource guides and reference titles in careers, social issues, and intellectual topics for higher grade levels and the college bound. The *Where's Waldo?* series is an especially successful project. The house also offers volumes in the Spanish language and in dual Spanish/English editions and is on the lookout for an increasing list in the multicultural arena.

Sample titles: *Fairy Wings* by Lauren Mills and Dennis Nolan, *The Jolly Pocket Postman* by Janet and Allen Ahlberg, *Monster's Lunch Box* by Marc Brown, *SLUGS: Pet Slug and Book* by David Greenberg, *The Kid Detective's Handbook and Scene-of-the-Crime Kit* by William Vivian Butler, and *Papa Gatto* by Ruth Sanderson.

Prospective authors please note that Little, Brown's children's division no longer accepts unsolicited manuscripts directly from authors. Manuscripts go through an agent to:

Erica Stahler, Senior Editorial Assistant (Boston)

LODESTAR BOOKS

(Imprint of Dutton/NAL; see Penguin USA)

LONELY PLANET PUBLICATIONS

155 Filbert Street
Suite 251
Oakland, CA 94607
510-893-8555

Lonely Planet Publications (founded in 1975) specializes in travel guides and phrase-books for the practical traveler, city guides, walking guides, and guides for those on a shoestring budget. A significant portion of Lonely Planet's list offers travel survival kits that provide in-depth coverage of a single country or group of countries with travel options for a range of budgets and styles. Lonely Planet has begun a line of literary travel narratives.

On the Lonely Planet list are works geared to travel in North America from the West Coast to New England; through Europe (north to south, east to west, via highway, rail-ways, and on foot); treks through the Sahara and across equatorial Africa and the Middle East; journeys along the Karakorum Highway and through China; wanderings in Southeast Asia, Indonesia, and Micronesia; travels in Baja California, central Mexico, and the Maya area; tours through the Caribbean and through Central and South America; and visits to the polar zones. Many of these publications are decidedly for the adventuresome wayfarer rather than the casual tourist.

Lonely Planet produces an anecdotal and informative travel newsletter and distrib-utes its own list in America through its United States office. The Lonely Planet editor-ial division is located in Australia—though manuscripts and proposals are given preliminary consideration at the stateside contact address.

Query letters and SASEs should be directed to:

Eric Kettunen, U.S. Manager (at United States office)

LONGMEADOW PRESS

Longmeadow Press, begun in 1984, is no longer operating as a publisher. The house was a proprietary publishing division of the powerful retail bookstore chain WaldenBooks.

LOOMPANICS UNLIMITED

Box 1197
Port Townsend, WA 98368

Loompanics Unlimited produces books of trade interest in addition to professional and special-interest nonfiction. The Loompanics list accents practical self-help and how-to, contemporary and historical culture, and sociopolitical and issues-oriented works. The house offers a selective fiction list (primarily reprints of hitherto overlooked masterworks).

Loompanics offers books in categories such as underground economy; tax avoid-ance; money-making opportunities; individual privacy; fake identification; Big Brother is watching you; conducting investigations; crime and police science; locks and lock-smithing; self-defense; revenge; guns, weapons, bombs and explosives; guerrilla war-fare; murder and torture; survival, self-sufficiency, head for the hills, gimme shelter; health and life extension; paralegal skills; sex, drugs, rock and roll; intelligence increase; science and technology; heresy/weird ideas; anarchism and egoism; work; mass media; censorship; reality creation; self-publishing; and an enigmatic category of works classified solely under the designation of miscellaneous.

Since its foundation in 1973, Loompanics titles have been among the most controversial and unusual publications available, and the publishing program (which includes books, audiotapes, and videocassettes) has produced recognized classics in a number of fields.

Many Loompanics publications test the edge of the free-speech envelope—and often do so with humorous subversiveness and literary zest; some of the more treacherous materials are clearly intended exclusively for amusement, information, or scholarly reference purposes.

Loompanics features: *Community Technology* by Karl Hess, *Free Space: Real Alternatives for Reaching Outer Space* by B. Alexander Howerton, *How to Obtain a Second Passport and Citizenship and Why You Want To* by Adam Starchild, *How to Sneak into the Movies* by Dan Zamudio, *Practical LSD Manufacture* by Uncle Fester, *Secondhand Success: How to Turn Discards into Dollars* by Jordan L. Cooper, *The Hitchhiker's Handbook* by James MacLaren, *The Politics of Consciousness: A Practical Guide to Personal Freedom* by Steve Cubby, *The Rape of the American Constitution* by Chuck Shiver, *Stoned Free: How to Get High Without Drugs* by Patrick Wells with Douglas Rushkoff, *The Wild and Free Cookbook* by Tom Squire, *Travel-Trailer Homesteading Under $5000* by Brian D. Kelly, and *You Are Going to Prison* (a survival guide) by Jim Hogshire.

From the literary arena: *Freak Show* (a classic literary novel in reprint) by Jacquin Sanders, and *The Gas* (another classic literary work in reissue) by Charles Platt.

Some backlist favorites: *Bad Girls Do It! An Encyclopedia of Female Murderers* by Michael Newton, *Psychedelic Shamanism* by Jim DeKorne, *Secrets of a Superhacker* by an incognito information superhighwayman known as the Knightmare, *Shadow Merchants: Successful Retailing Without a Storefront* by Jordan L. Cooper, *The Art & Science of Dumpster Diving* by John Hoffman (with original comix by Ace Backwords), *The Emperor Wears No Clothes—Hemp and the Marijuana Conspiracy* by Jack Herer, and *Screw the Bitch: Divorce Tactics for Men* by Dick Hart.

Loompanics Unlimited is editorially a reclusive house. Writers who wish to work with Loompanics should note that their business is the printed word, and potential authors should approach Loompanics through the printed word (via mail—do not telephone). The publisher also notes that the press tends toward small advances and works through literary agents only on occasion.

The Loompanics Unlimited direct-order catalog (emblazoned with the publisher's freebooter-spaceship colophon) depicts a wealth of titles from its own list as well as select offerings from other houses in a luscious newsprint format that includes graphics, essays, and short fiction, as well as blurbs from reviewers and satisfied customers testifying to the potency of the house's list and the efficacy of the Loompanics distribution and fulfillment services.

Query letters and SASEs should be directed to:

Michael Hoy, President

Dennis Eichhorn, Editorial Director

LOTHROP, LEE & SHEPARD BOOKS
(See William Morrow & Co.)

LOUISIANA STATE UNIVERSITY PRESS
(See Directory of University Presses)

LOWELL HOUSE
2029 Century Park East, Suite 3290
Los Angeles, CA 90067
310-552-7555

Lowell House is dedicated to publishing quality nonfiction in fields such as medicine and health, self-help and improvement, cuisine, parenting, and areas of women's interest, in addition to a list for children. Lowell House specialty imprints include Anodyne, Extension Press, Global Gourmet, Legacy Press, and Woman to Woman. Lowell House (established in 1988) is a division of RGA Publishing Group.

The Anodyne line addresses contemporary health and medical issues and concerns; Anodyne offers titles with an overall emphasis on innovative approaches in prevention, acceptance, and action.

Extension Press helps those who want to help themselves; the Extension list accents entertaining and practical works to help readers master the skills that make life interesting.

Global Gourmet purveys a line of cookbooks, most of which feature healthy lowfat fare: The imprint concentrates on unusual recipes from creative cooks featuring the world's cuisines so that the reader may indulge in gourmet without guilt.

Legacy Press addresses concerned parents who have an interest in raising a healthy family, through books that exemplify the human side of parenting—top-quality advice by experts in the field.

The Woman to Woman imprint issues titles primarily authored by women (as well as by an occasional qualified man). These works are directed toward women readers and are about concerns such as career, health, and relationships; the imprint embodies a veritable support group between book covers.

Titles bearing the Lowell House imprint are less category specific and include more general trade books encompassing timely and timeless topics.

Representative of the Lowell House program: *The Sizzling Southwestern Cookbook* by Lynn Nusom; *Overcoming the Legacy of Overeating* by Nan Kathryn Fuchs; *Domestic Violence Sourcebook* by Dawn Bradley Berry; *How to Develop Your Child's Gifts and Talents in Reading* by Martha Cheney; *Making the Prostate Therapy Decision* by Jeff Baggish; *Financial Tips for Teachers* by Alan Jay Weiss and Larry Strauss; *The Diabetes Sports and Exercise Book* by Claudia Graham, June Biermann, and Barbara Toohey; and *Eve of Destruction: Prophecies, Theories, and Preparations for the End of the World* by Eva Shaw.

Lowell House titles are distributed through Contemporary Books; special sales are handled by the Lowell House/RGA Publishing Group home office.

LOWELL HOUSE JUVENILE

The Lowell House Juvenile division issues well-designed lines that appeal to youthful readers. Beanstalk Books make learning fun through the vehicle of high-quality illustrated and photographic titles—picture books, board books, and activity books for kids ages two to six. FRESH stands for Friendly, Real, Esteem-building, Smart, and Honest; the FRESH line of nonfiction books explores topical issues that affect today's young females. Gifted & Talented books are designed by experts in the field of early childhood education to bring out every child's gifts via workbooks, beginning readers, picture books, and reference works. Periscope Press brings the mysteries and wonders of the natural world into sharp focus for readers ages five to thirteen; in addition to science titles, Periscope offers reference works in language arts, writing, and more.

Lowell House Juvenile titles include *Draw Science: Cockroaches, Stinkbugs, and Other Creepy Crawlers* by Christine Becker, *More Scary Stories for Stormy Nights* by Scott Ingram, *60 Super Simple Crafts* by Holly Hebert, and *The Ultimate Sleep-Over Book* by Kayte Kuch.

Query letters and SASEs should be directed to:

Bud Sperry, Editor
All described areas.

M & T BOOKS
(See Henry Holt)

MACMILLAN PUBLISHING GROUP
(See Simon & Schuster)

MANIC D PRESS
1853 Stockton
San Francisco, CA 94133
415-788-6459

Manic D Press (founded in 1984) produces a short list of contemporary fiction, poetry, literary works, and creative nonfiction. Emphasis is on innovative styles and nontraditional writers and artists. The house publishes primarily in trade paperback editions and offers a line of recordings.

Featured on the Manic D list: *Alibi School* by Jeffrey McDaniel, *King of the Roadkills* by Bucky Sinister, and *The Underground Guide to San Francisco* (edited by Jennifer Joseph).

Manic D Press distributes through Publishers Group West.

Query letters and SASEs should be directed to:

Jennifer Joseph, Publisher

MARLOWE & THUNDER'S MOUTH
MARLOWE AND COMPANY/THUNDER'S MOUTH PRESS

632 Broadway
New York, NY 10012
212-780-0380

Marlowe & Thunder's Mouth emphasizes trade nonfiction in current events, contemporary culture, biography/personality, the arts, and popular reference. Marlowe & Thunder's Mouth combines two previously independent firms, Thunder's Mouth Press and Marlowe & Company, each with overlapping fields of concentration and a distinct publishing persona.

Thunder's Mouth Press (founded in 1980) upholds a tradition of producing high-interest nonfiction (as well as selected fiction), with an accent on works of quirky ambiance and decidedly popular appeal. An overview of the Thunder's Mouth nonfiction program provides a list particularly strong in the areas of topical issues, popular culture, and specialty reference. In fiction, Thunder's Mouth spouts modern and contemporary literary writing in addition to classic genre fiction, poetry, and works for stage and screen. There is an additional focus on the African-American tradition, works from the Beat generation, and hitherto underappreciated women authors in reprint editions.

During early 1995, Thunder's Mouth initiated a radical restructuring. Thunder's Mouth publisher Neil Ortenberg announced that substantially all assets of the house had been acquired by Avalon Publishing Group, an affiliate of Publishers Group West (the distribution house with an East Coast office located conveniently adjacent to the Thunder's Mouth digs). The Thunder's Mouth program was downsized dramatically—everyone was fired, leaving Ortenberg the sole crew. The house was poised for consolidation and regrowth, with a projected scenario reminiscent of that at Grove/Atlantic.

Thunder's Mouth merged with Marlowe & Company (previously part of Universal Sales and Marketing, a promotional and remaindering operation), a new, independent house headed by John Webber, which purchased the Paragon Publishing backlist. In tandem with the Thunder's Mouth literary resources, the new publishing entity (known corporately as Marlowe & Thunder's Mouth) features two main imprints (Marlowe and Thunder's Mouth) and covers the publishing spectrum from commercial to controversial.

Representative general nonfiction: *The Canary Syndrome: The Complete Guide for Diagnosing, Treating, and Preventing Environmental Illness* by Dana Godbout Laake and Cindy Sharon Spitzer, *The Big White Lie: The Inside Story of the Deep Cover Sting Operation That Exposes the Drug War* by Michael Levine with Laura Kavanau-Levine, *The Baby Name Countdown: Meanings and Popularity Ratings for 50,000 Names* by Janet Schwegel, *Synchronicity: Science, Myth, and the Trickster* by Allan Combs and Mark Holland, *Murder in Memphis: The FBI and the Martin Luther King Assassination* by Mark Lane and Dick Gregory, *Judgment at the Smithsonian: The Bombing of Hiroshima and Nagasaki* by Philip Nobile, *Information Warfare: Chaos on the Electronic Superhighway* by Winn Schwartau, *Hot Copy: Behind the Scenes at the Daily News* by Theo Wilson, and *Doctors Are Gods: Corruption and Unethical Practices in the Medical Profession* by David Jacobsen and Eric D. Jacobsen.

Works with a cultural/personality tilt: *The Velvet Years, 1965–1967: Warhol's Factory* by Stephen Shore and Lynne Tillman, *To Be, or Not . . . to Bop: Memoirs—the Autobiography of Dizzy Gillespie* by Dizzy Gillespie and Al Fraser, *Fear and Loathing: The Strange and Terrible Saga of Hunter S. Thompson* by Paul Percy, *John Lennon: In My Life* by Pete Shotton with Nicholas Shaffner, and *Captain Trips: A Biography of Jerry Garcia* by Sandy Troy.

Sample fiction and literary works: *A Treasury of African Folklore* (edited, retold, and with commentary by Harold Courlander), *Life is Hot in Cracktown* by Buddy Giovinazzo, *Goodbye, Sweetwater: New and Selected Stories* by Henry Dumas, *City of Light* by Cyrus Colter, and *Panther* by Melvin Van Peebles (who authored the screenplay for the film of the same name, directed by his son Mario Van Peebles—whose first movie appearance was as a kid in Melvin's classic *Sweet Sweetback's Baadasssss Song*).

Another event of media interest was the publication of *Marita* (a memoir) by Marita Lorenz, Fidel Castro's former mistress. In a related development, Thunder's Mouth publisher Ortenberg was wed to Lorenz's daughter Monica Mercedes.

Meanwhile: What has the name Thunder's Mouth got to do with all this? William Shakespeare's *King John* provides the source: "O that my tongue were in the thunder's mouth! Then with a passion would I shake the world."

Marlowe & Thunder's Mouth Press is distributed by Publishers Group West.

Query letters and SASEs should be directed to:

Neil Ortenberg, Senior Editor and Publisher, Thunder's Mouth

John Webber, Publisher, Marlowe

MASQUERADE BOOKS

801 Second Avenue
New York, NY 10017
212-661-7878

Masquerade Books (founded in 1989) is dedicated to vanguard publishing in a number of breakthrough literary arenas. Masquerade is known for writers with original voices whose works in dark romance, horror, futurist fiction, erotica, and crime, as well as creative/niche high-interest nonfiction and literary works, are issued through mass-market paperback originals as well as hardcovers and trade paperbacks.

Masquerade Books lets this be known: Send a manuscript in; if we like it, we'll want to publish it. Areas of interest are open, as is format: hardcover, trade paper, mass-market paperback. "If we can make money on it, we'll publish it."

Masquerade imprints include Badboy, Hard Candy, Rhinoc*Eros*, a Richard Kasak Book, and Rosebud. Writers who wish to submit works to the house should request a set of guidelines (include SASE with your guideline query).

Here's an overview of some of Masquerade's special-imprint series (primarily mass-market paperback releases, with some trade-paper editions and occasional hardcovers).

Masquerade: Straight erotica, usually with an SM bent. Includes Victorian titles.

Badboy: Erotica for gay men.

Rosebud: Erotica for gay women. Includes the Leatherwomen series.

Hard Candy: Literary works by gay men and women with a strong emphasis on sexuality and sexual themes.

Rhinoc*Eros*: Pansexual literary works with a strong emphasis on sexuality and sexual themes. Includes the Marketplace series.

Sample titles: *Pirate's Slave* by Erica Bronte, *Ask Isadora* by Isadora Alman, *The Velvet Tongue* by Mercedes Kelly, *Silk and Steel* by Michael Drax, *Cinderella* by Titian Beresford, *Thrill City* by Jean Stine, *The Repentance of Lorraine* by Andrei Codrescu, *Diary of a Vampire* by Gary Bowen, *Flesh* by Philip José Farmer, *Chains* by Larry Townsend, *The Sexpert* by Pat Califia, *F/32* by Eurydice, *Dryland's End* by Felice Picano, *Unnatural Acts* by Lucy Taylor, and *The Motion of Light in Water* by Samuel R. Delany.

Masquerade also publishes a bimonthly erotic newsletter.

Masquerade orchestrates its own sales and distribution; orders are handled in house as well as through a network of regional distributors and wholesalers.

Query letters and SASEs should be directed to:

Richard Kasak, Publisher

Jennifer Reut, Managing Editor

Kiri Blakely, Editor

McGraw-Hill Publishing Group

11 West 19th Street
New York, NY 10011
212-512-2000

McGraw-Hill operates specialty programs in journals and books covering a variety of professional, business, and educational fields, such as law, healthcare, high-tech industries, and college textbooks. McGraw-Hill officially disbanded its adult general trade book-publishing operation in 1989; since then, the house's lineup of professional and reference book divisions has continued to thrive. Still geared primarily toward business and professional titles, McGraw-Hill is again venturing into the broader range of commercial trade arenas. In the United States, this international house publishes titles in business, trades and technical fields, computing, architecture, engineering/electronics, science, and leisure.

An area of particular McGraw-Hill presence is business and personal computing and computer science—many titles are published from within the McGraw-Hill list and that of the Osborne/McGraw-Hill subsidiary. (See separate subentries below.)

McGraw-Hill distributes for all its divisions.

BUSINESS McGRAW-HILL

Business McGraw-Hill produces trade and professional titles in areas including business, finance, entrepreneurship, marketing, training, human resources, investing, management, advertising, sales, self-help, and communication.

Indicative of the Business McGraw-Hill list: *Selling to the World: Your Fast and Easy Guide to Exploring and Importing* by L. Fargo Wells, *Power Schmoozing: The New Etiquette for Social and Business Success* by Terri Mandel, *Heart at Work: Stories and Strategies for Building Self-Esteem and Reawakening the Soul at Work* by Jack Canfield and Jacqueline Miller, *Get a Life without Sacrificing Your Career* by Dianna Booher, *Airline Odyssey: The Airline Industry's Turbulent Flight into the Future* by James D. Ott and Raymond E. Neidl, *Be-All End-All Get Me a Job Book* by Kelly Barrington, *Secrets of the Street: The Dark Side of Making Money* by Gene G. Marcial, *How to Pay Zero Taxes: Your Guide to Every Tax Break the IRS Allows* by Jeff A. Schnepper, *Techno Vision: The Executive's Survival Guide to Understanding and Managing Information Technology* by Charles Wang, and *The Eloquent Executive: Mastering the Fine Art of Speaking* by Granville N. Toogood.

Query letters and SASEs should be directed to:

Susan Barry, Executive Editor
Management, current events, investing.

Betsy Brown, Senior Editor
Career, self-help, executive skills, communications.

Richard Narramore, Editor
Training and development, organizational development, management.

Philip Ruppel, Publisher
All areas indicated in house description, including marketing, management, quality, human resources, training, operations management.

COMPUTING McGRAW-HILL

Computing McGraw-Hill is the trade designation (used widely in advertising and promotional venues) for titles in computing that arise from the various McGraw-Hill divisions, including projects acquired through the trade/business wing as well as the Osborne/McGraw-Hill subsidiary (please see separate subentry below).

Computing titles from McGraw-Hill: *The Year 2000 Computing Crisis: A Millennium Date Conversion Plan* by Jerome T. Murray and Marilyn J. Murray, *Client/ Server Architecture* by Alex Benson, *Finding a Job on the Internet* by Alfred Glossbrenner, and *The Woman's Guide to Online Services* by Judith Broadhurst.

OSBORNE/MCGRAW-HILL

2600 Tenth Street
Berkeley, CA 94710
510-549-6600

Osborne/McGraw-Hill publishes a list that targets primarily the hands-on user approach to computer software and hardware systems, with many titles geared toward specific types of projects or proprietary systems and programs.

Interest areas include spreadsheets, accounting, integrated software, graphics, word processing, desktop publishing, computer-aided design, telecommunications, networking, operating systems, hardware, programming languages, databanks, and business applications, as well as games and entertainment. The house also frontlists titles of broader appeal among a wide range of computer-friendly readers.

Sample titles: *Beyond HTML* by Richard Karpinski, *PCs for Busy People* by David Einstein, and *Internet Kids Yellow Pages* by Jean Armour Polly.

Osborne/McGraw-Hill distributes its titles via the order-services center shared with and operated through TAB/McGraw-Hill.

Query letters and SASEs should be directed to:

Larry Levitsky, Editor in Chief

MCGRAW-HILL, INC./TAB BOOKS

13311 Monterey Lane
Blue Ridge Summit, PA 17294
717-794-2191

This division of McGraw-Hill publishes books in a growing number of specialty areas—notably aviation, boating, business, professional design and architecture, electronics, residential construction, science, and travel and recreation. Among McGraw-Hill's imprints are the outdoorsy Ragged Mountain Press, Design Press, International Marine, and the Aero series (aeronautics).

Ragged Mountain Press is dedicated to "books that take you off the beaten path," and for every unit sold, a contribution is made to an environmental cause. Subjects here are travel, sport, recreation, the environment and nature, and outdoor discovery.

Representative of this McGraw-Hill division's list: *Transit Villages in the Twenty-First Century* by Michael S. Bernick and Robert Burke Cervero, *Chicago in and around the Loop: Walking Tours of Architecture and History* by Gerard R. Wolfe, *Everyday Math for Contractors: A Timesaving Field Guide* by James Gerhart, *Mathematics Beyond Measure: Essays on Nature, Myth, and Number* by Jay Kappraff, *Unheeded Warning: The Inside Story of American Eagle Flight 4184* by Stephen A.

Fredrick, *Sailor's Secrets: Advice from the Masters* by Mike Badham and Bobby Robinson, *Lasers, Ray Guns, and Light Cannons! Projects from the Wizard's Workbench* by Gordon McComb, and *Encyclopedia of Electronic Circuits* by Rudolf F. Graf and William Sheets.

From Ragged Mountain: *The Dayhiker's Handbook: An All-Terrain, All-Season Guide* by John Long, *The Art of Trolling: A Complete Guide to Freshwater Methods* by Ken Schultz, and *Adventure New England: An Outdoor Vacation Guide* by Diane Bair and Pamela Wright.

McGraw-Hill handles distribution through its own order-services operation.

Query letters and SASEs should be directed to:

Jon Eaton, Editor
International Marine Books series.

Larry Hager, Editor
Electrical, mechanical, and civil engineering.

Roland Phelps, Editor
Electronics, adult-level science.

Jennifer DiGiovanna, Editor
Computer books.

April Nolan, Editor
Trades and technical.

Brad Schepp, Senior Editor
Computer books.

Kim Tabor, Editor in Chief
General science (K–12).

Shelley Chevalier, Editor
Aviation.

MEADOWBROOK PRESS

18318 Minnetonka Boulevard
Deerhaven, MN 55391
612-473-5400

Meadowbrook Press (established in 1975) is a small trade-oriented house with emphasis in areas of family interest, including pregnancy and childcare, parenting, health, the environment, business, travel, cooking, reference, party-planning, children's-activity books, and humor. Within the scope of its family orientation, Meadowbrook pinpoints special fields of reader interest that include baby names, family humor, and the facts of life.

From the Meadowbrook list: *The Very Best Baby Name Book in the Whole Wide World* by Bruce Lansky, *Eating Expectantly* by Bridget Swinney, *Feed Me! I'm Yours* by Vicki Lansky, *First-Year Baby Care* (edited by Paula Kelly), *Gentle Discipline* by Dawn Leighter, *The Joy of Grandparenting* by Audrey Sherins and Joan Holleman, *Baby and*

Child Emergency First Aid Handbook by Mitchell J. Enzig, *The Working Woman's Guide to Breastfeeding* by Nancy Dana and Anne Price, *The Joy of Marriage* by Monica and Bill Dodds, *Birth Partner's Handbook* by Carl Jones, *The Baby Journal* by Matthew Bennett (illustrated by Breck Wilson), and *Kids' Holiday Fun* by Penny Warner.

Indicative of the further range of Meadowbrook publishing interest: *Golf: It's Just a Game* (selected by Bruce Lansky), *Sizzling Southwestern Cookery* by Lisa Golden Schroeder, *Weird Wonders and Bizarre Blunders* by Brad Schreiber, and *European Customs and Manners* by Nancy L. Braganti and Elizabeth Devine.

Meadowbrook Press is distributed by Simon & Schuster.

Query letters and SASEs should be addressed to:

Bruce Lansky, President and Publisher

MECKLERMEDIA CORPORATION

20 Ketchum Street
Westport, CT 06880
203-226-6967

Mecklermedia (founded in 1971, and formerly known as Meckler Publishing) specializes in the electronic arena, with emphasis on books and directories keyed to management of information technology, computer science and applications, directories and databases, and library and information sciences. The house has in the past published some Americana, as well as books in the areas of history, business, law, literature, and sports. Meckler also organizes conferences, produces periodicals and general reference titles, and generates and markets computer software and videotapes.

From Mecklermedia: *Directory of Directories on the Internet: A Guide to Information Sources* by Gregory Newby, *Electronic Journal Literature: Implications for Scholars* by Jan Olsen, *Electronic Style: A Guide to Citing Electronic Information* by Xia Li and Nancy Crane, *Jukebox and Robotic Libraries for Computer Mass Storage* by Sanjay Ranade, *The New TV: A Comprehensive Survey of High-Definition Television* (edited by Lou CasaBianca), *The Virtual Library: Visions and Realities* (edited by Laverna Saunders), and *Virtual Reality: Theory, Practice, and Promise* (edited by Sandra K. Helsel and Judith Paris Roth).

Meckler distributes its own products.

Query letters and SASEs should be directed to:

Alan M. Meckler, President and Publisher

Tony Abbott, Senior Vice President

MESORAH PUBLICATIONS

(See Directory of Religious, Spiritual, and Inspirational Publishers)

METEOR PUBLISHING CORPORATION

3369 Progress Drive
Bensalem, PA 19020
215-245-1489

Meteor Publishing Corporation (founded in 1989) produces category romance novels. Their list emphasis changes from series to series as the market shifts; please query the house to obtain author guidelines and to confirm which series are on the lookout for new writers.

The primary strength of Meteor sales and distribution is through venues such as mail order and subscription services rather than via bookstore trade.

Query letters and SASEs should be directed to:

Kate Duffy, Editorial Director

MICROSOFT PRESS

One Microsoft Way
Redmond, WA 98052-6399
206-882-8080
800-677-7377

Microsoft Press (founded in 1983) is a division of the Microsoft Corporation; the press specializes in solution-oriented computer books—especially those relating to the corpus of Microsoft products. Areas cover the MS-DOS operating system and the Windows graphical user interface environment as well as selected titles pertaining to the Apple Macintosh world. Microsoft Press lists titles in general personal computer applications, programming, and general-interest computing areas. The house brochure features books, book-and-software packages (including diskettes and CD-ROMs), and training videos. The Cobb Group imprint features guides for sophisticated users.

Microsoft Press titles are constantly updated and released in newly revised versions in order to anticipate advances in hardware and software systems as well as in the underlying technology to which they pertain. The house aims to produce information that is reliable, timely, and easy to use, so that readers can get their work done faster and without frustration.

Series from Microsoft Press include Step by Step, Running, Companion, Field Guide, and WYSIWYG (What You See Is What You Get), Microsoft Programming, and Microsoft Professional Editions. The Desktop Publishing by Design line of primers comprises separate titles keyed to major publishing software programs.

Sample Microsoft Press titles: *Running Word for Windows* by Russell Borland, *Running Microsoft Works for Windows* by JoAnne Woodcock, *Microsoft Publisher by Design* by Luisa Simone, *Adventures in a Space Simulator* by Grant Fjermedal, *A Field Guide to Microsoft Windows* by Steven L. Nelson, *Microsoft Word for the Macintosh Step by Step* by the Microsoft Corporation, and *The Way Multimedia Works* by Simon Colin.

A representative general reference work is *Microsoft Press Computer Dictionary*.

Microsoft Press distributes its own books; the list is also available through electronic mail via CompuServe.

Query letters and SASEs should be directed to:

Susanne M. Freet, Acquisitions Coordinator

MILKWEED EDITIONS

430 First Avenue North
Suite 400
Minneapolis, MN 55401-1743
612-332-3192

The Milkweed publishing program encompasses titles in fiction, essays and literature, images and words, poetry anthologies, poetry, and art volumes, as well as nonfiction works that address social and cultural issues. Milkweeds for Young Readers is the house's children's line. Milkweed Editions (instituted in 1984) presents a personalized small-house approach that accents good writing and beautiful books.

Milkweed was founded as a nonprofit literary arts organization (in 1979) with the approach that literature is a transformative art. Under Emilie Buchwald (Publisher/CEO) the house maintains its position to make a humane impact on society. Milkweed Editions offers an award-winning list of distinctive literary voices, with a line of handsomely designed, visually dynamic volumes that address ethical, cultural, and aesthetic issues.

The company's continued marketing success augments the publisher's stance in support of exceptional books with appeal to discerning readers. Milkweed Editions hosts a substantial backlist of hardcovers, paperbacks, and chapbooks.

Characteristic of Milkweed fiction and literary works: *Somebody Else's Mama* by David Haynes, *Justice* by Larry Watson (a prequel to *Montana 1948*), *Confidence of the Heart* by David Schweidel, *Homestead* by Annick Smith, *The Long Experience of Love* (poems) by Jim Moore, *Firekeeper: New and Selected Poems* by Pattiann Rogers, *The Phoenix Gone, the Terrace Empty* (poems) by Marilyn Chin, and *Drive, They Said: Poems about Americans and Their Cars* (edited by Kurt Brown).

Culture and criticism from the Milkweed purview: *What Makes Pornography "Sexy"?* by John Stoltenberg, *Planning to Stay: Learning to See the Physical Features of Your Neighborhood* by William R. Morrish and Catherine R. Brown, and *Transforming a Rape Culture* (sociocultural anthology; edited by Emilie Buchwald, Pamela Fletcher, and Martha Roth).

Milkweed is the publisher of Susan Straight's acclaimed *Aquaboogie: A Novel in Stories* (among a number of novels-in-stories projects), *The Historian: Six Fantasies of the American Experience* by Eugene K. Garber (with paintings by Kathryn Nobbe, and *Minnesota Gothic* (in the Seeing Double series of collaborative books; poetry by Mark Vinz; photography by Wayne Gudmundson).

Contact the editorial department for information pertaining to the Milkweed Prize for Children's Literature and the Milkweed National Fiction Prize.

Books from Milkweed Editions are available via direct order from the publisher; the house's titles are distributed to the trade through Publishers Group West.

MILKWEEDS FOR YOUNG READERS

Milkweeds for Young Readers produces children's books of literary merit that embody humane values. Books that ask the most of us as young readers, the publisher maintains, have the staying power to influence us for a lifetime. Milkweed also produces a series of teaching guides.

Titles from Milkweed's children's program: *The Secret of the Ruby Ring* by Yvonne MacGrory, *A Bride for Anna's Papa* by Isabel Marvin, *Minnie: A Novel for Children* by Annie M. G. Schmidt, *I Am Lavina Cumming: A Novel for Young Readers* by Susan Lowell, and *Gildaen: The Heroic Adventures of a Most Unusual Rabbit* by Emilie Buchwald (illustrations by Barbara Flynn).

Query letters and SASEs should be directed to:

Elisabeth Fitz, First Reader

MIS: PRESS. INC.
(See Henry Holt)

THE MIT PRESS
(See Directory of University Presses)

WILLIAM MORROW & COMPANY, INC.

Avon Books
1350 Avenue of the Americas
New York, NY 10019
212-261-6500

William Morrow & Company and Avon Books are the two primary book-publishing wings of the privately held Hearst Corporation media company. This large publishing operation features multiple imprints that run the spectrum of mainstream commercial trade publishing in fiction and nonfiction, as well as children's books. The house publishes hardcover, trade paper, and mass-market paperback editions. Morrow &

Company and Avon Books are distinct divisions with their own extensive individual programs. (Please see separate subentries below.)

WILLIAM MORROW & COMPANY

1350 Avenue of the Americas
New York, NY 10019
212-261-6500

Morrow excels in commercial nonfiction and frontlist fiction covering the full gamut of trade categories. William Morrow & Company (founded in 1926) is a big house, upholding the tradition established in earlier (and smaller) days as a publisher of books that are selected attentively and promoted with care, so that individual titles achieve maximum market potential. Morrow books earn slots on best-seller lists (national, regional, specialist) with compelling regularity.

Morrow imprints include Hearst Books, Hearst Marine Books, Fielding Travel Books, Quill (trade paperbacks), and AvoNova (science fiction and fantasy). Also included is a children's division that encompasses Morrow Junior Books; Tambourine Books; Mulberry Books; Beech Tree Books; Greenwillow Books; and Lothrop, Lee & Shepard Books (please see subentries below for Morrow children's lines, as well as for Avon's Camelot and Flare juveniles imprints).

Rob Weisbach gained acclaim as an editor with uncommon commercial savvy who, during his stint at Bantam, produced a number of celebrity-driven titles that shot straight up the best-seller charts. Weisbach's arrived at Morrow as head of his own publishing regime—the imprint known as Rob Weisbach Books—with an eye cocked toward high-edge projects including celebrity biographies, popular culture, and juicy investigative scenarios.

Exemplifying the popular eclecticism of Morrow's trade nonfiction program: *Tragic Failure: Racial Integration in America* by Tom Wicker, *Humanity's Descent: An Ecological Epic* by Rick Potts, *Fit over Forty: A Revolutionary Plan to Achieve Lifelong Physical and Spiritual Health and Well-Being* by James M. Rippe, *Phil Simms on Passing: Fundamentals of Throwing the Football* by Phil Simms with Rick Meier, *Don't Know Much about the Civil War: Everything You Need to Know about America's Greatest Conflict but Never Learned* by Kenneth C. Davis, *Louisiana Real and Rustic* by Emeril Lagasse and Marcelle Bienvenu (photographs by Brian Smale), and *Savoring Spices and Herbs: Recipe Secrets of Flavor, Aroma, and Color* by Julie Sahni.

Morrow fiction is selective and dramatically frontlist. In addition to popular contemporary literature, the house hits heavily through the major mainstream categories of mystery and suspense, science fiction and fantasy, and women's lead fiction. Among Morrow's fiction authors are Kathleen E. Woodiwiss, Trevor Barnes, Lynda La Plante, Faye Kellerman, Ken Follett, Ed McBain, Kinky Friedman, Piers Anthony, Sidney Sheldon, and John Irving.

Reflecting Morrow's vigorous fiction list: *Tumbling* by Diane McKinney Whetstone, *Final Victim* by Stephen J. Cannell, *Darkness, Take My Hand* by Dennis Lehane, *Simple Simon* by Ryne Douglas Pearson, *Let the Drum Speak: A Novel of Ancient*

America by Linda Lay Shuler, *The Vipers' Club* by John H. Richardson, *The Boat Ramp* by Andrew Holleran, and *Sister* by A. Manette Ansay.

William Morrow & Company distributes for all its imprints.

Query letters and SASEs should be directed to:

Paul Bresnick, Senior Editor
Nonfiction: humor, show business, sociology, popular biography and autobiography, cartoons, cultural ephemera.

Henry Ferris, Senior Editor
Politics, current events, social issues.

Zachary Schisgal, Editor
Commercial and literary fiction and nonfiction.

Bob Schuman, Editor
Biography, nonfiction.

(Ms.) Toni Sciarra, Senior Editor
Psychology, health, science, women's issues, relationships, social trends, spirituality.

MORROW CHILDREN'S BOOKS

The children's book divisions of William Morrow includes Morrow Junior Books, which publishes fiction and nonfiction for all ages, from the youngest readers through young adult, as well as picture books primarily for children in the middle grades. Morrow's other children's imprints are editorially independent and include Beech Tree Books; Greenwillow Books; Lothrop, Lee & Shepard Books; Mulberry Books; and Tambourine Books.

Beech Tree produces fiction and nonfiction paperbacks (often reprints) for eight- to fourteen-year-old readers. Representative titles: *Gertie's Green Thumb* by Catherine Dexter, *Lanyard: Having Fun with Plastic Lace* by Camilla Gryski, *Shadow Play* by Bernie Zubrowski (illustrated by Roy Doty), and *Yours Till Banana Splits: 201 Autograph Rhymes* by Joanna Cole and Stephanie Calmenson (illustrated by Alan Tiegren).

Greenwillow Books encompass picture-and-story editions for a younger readership. On the Greenwillow list: *Ironman* by Chris Crutcher, *Liza's Blue Moon* by Diana Stevens, *Protecting Marie* (a novel) by Kevin Henkes, and *The Spellcat* by Diana Wynne Jones.

Lothrop, Lee & Shepard publishes picture books, pop-up specialties, and fiction and nonfiction for middle and older readers. Titles: *Fiona Raps It Up* by Frane Berkiewicz, *Roller Coaster* by Kevin O'Malley, *The Wind Garden* by Angela McAllister and Claire Fletcher, and *What to Do When a Bug Climbs in Your Mouth (and Other Poems to Drive You Buggy)* by Rick Walton (pictures by Nancy Carlson).

Morrow Junior Books publishes titles throughout the range of children's and young-adult categories. From the list at Morrow Junior: *Alie Game* by Catherine Dexter, *Missing Pieces* by Norma Fox Mazer, *Nanta's Lion* by Susie MacDonald, *The Patchwork Girl of Oz* by L. Frank Baum, and *Vanishing Ozone* by Laurence Pringle.

Mulberry Books specializes in popular-priced picture books in paperback. Representative Mulberry titles: *A Weekend with Wendell* by Kevin Henkes, *Tidy Titch* by Pat Hutchins, and *Volcanoes* by Seymour Simon.

Tambourine Books addresses a primarily preschooler readership with a lively, illustrated line. Tambourine titles: *I Pretend* by Heidi Goennel, *Do Angels Sing the Blues?* by A. C. LeMieux, and *Coconut Mon* by Linda Milstein (pictures by Cheryl Munro Taylor).

Query letters and SASEs should be directed to:

Amy Cohn, Editor in Chief, Mulberry Books and Beech Tree Books

Elizabeth Shub, Senior Editor, Greenwillow Books
Juvenile to young adult.

Susan Pearson, Editor in Chief, Lothrop, Lee & Shepard Books
Books for juveniles.

Leonard Hort, Senior Editor, Tambourine Books
Juvenile to young adult.

AVON BOOKS

1350 Avenue of the Americas
New York, NY 10019
212-261-6800

Avon's trade approach includes a mix of belletristic and commercial fiction, along with practical and inspirational nonfiction, with particular emphasis on history, business, health, parenting, how-to, multicultural subjects, memoir, psychology, popular science, gender studies, and light reference.

Avon is part of the privately held Hearst Corporation, which also owns the book-publishing firm William Morrow & Company. Avon Books began as a mass-market paperback reprint house in 1941; since then, Avon has branched out to encompass original fiction and nonfiction in trade paperback and mass-market rack-size editions, as well as reprints. The fall of 1996 sees the kickoff of Avon's hardcover line. (For Avon young readers' division, please see subentry below for Camelot and Flare lines.)

Avon's fiction list embraces commercial frontlist titles as well as high-concept literary works and sweeps the gamut of popular genres: adventure, romance, Westerns, suspense, thrillers, mysteries, science fiction and fantasy, and horror. Avon fiction authors include Patricia Cornwell, Raymond Feist, J. A. Jance, Johanna Lindsey, Elizabeth Lowell, Alison Lurie, Colleen McCullough, and Roger Zelazny. AvoNova is Avon's imprint for premiere science, futurist, and fantasy fiction.

Exemplifying Avon fiction: *Come and Go, Molly Snow* by Mary Ann Taylor-Hall, *Shade: An Anthology of Fiction by Gay Men of African Descent* (edited by Bruce Morrow and Charles Rowell), *The Legend of Bagger Vance: A Novel of Golf and the Game of Life* by Steven Pressfield, *Memoir from Antproof Case* by Mark Helprin, *Hearts and Bones* by Margaret Lawrence, *The Shadow Box* by John R. Maxim, *Tex and Mollie in the Afterlife* by Richard Grant, *Undone* by Michael Kimball, *Moonrise* by Ben Bova, *Quicker Than the Eye* by Ray Bradbury, *Poison* by Kathryn Harrison, *Blood: A Southern Fantasy* by Michael Moorcock, *Bloodsucking Fiends* by Christopher Moore, *Fair Peril* by Nancy Springer, and *Fairyland* by Paul J. McAuley.

A special Avon project is Neon Lit, a series conceived by Bob Callahan and Art Spiegelman (author of *Maus*), which combines the best of modern crime literature with graphic illustrations. Series titles include Paul Auster's *City of Glass* and Barry Gifford's *Perdita Durango*.

Avon has an extensive nonfiction list that covers biography, self-help, psychology, inspirational, New Age, business, humor, lifestyles, sports, current issues, and true crime.

Avon nonfiction includes *The Power of Abstinence* by Kristine Napier, *Emblems of the Mind: The Inner Life of Music and Mathematics* by Edward Rothstein, *Carnal Knowledge: The Sex Trivia Quiz Book* by Don Valve, *Goddess Runes: A Comprehensive Guide to Casting and Divination with a Unique Set of Ancient Nordic Runes* by P. M. H. Atwater, *He Loved Me, He Loves Me Not: A Guide to Fudge, Fury, Free Time and Life Beyond the Breakup* by Lynn Harris (illustrated by Chris Kalb), *Live from Death Row* by Mumia Abu-Jamal, *1939: The Lost World of the Fair* by David Gelertner, *Disaster Blasters: A Kid's Guide to Being Home Alone* by Karin Kasdin and Laura Szabo-Cohen, *Red Scare: Memories of the American Inquisition* by Griffin Fariello, *Blues All Around Me: The Autobiography of B. B. King* by B. B. King with David Ritz, *The Field Guide to Extraterrestrials: Based on Actual Eyewitness Accounts and Sightings* by Patrick Huyghe (illustrated by Harry Trumbore), *Mayan Oracles for the Millennium* by R. T. Kaser, and *The Neanderthal Enigma* by James Shreeve.

The Confident Collector series offers identification and price guides for the serious collector and dealer—covering everything from bottles and quilts to comic books and baseball cards.

Avon handles its own distribution.

Query letters and SASEs should be directed to:

Charlotte Abbott, Editor of Trade Paperbacks
Nonfiction: women's studies, history, popular culture, reference, nature. Literary fiction.

Lou Aronica, Senior Vice President and Publisher
Oversees the Avon program.

Tom Colgan, Associate Executive Editor
Fiction: men's adventure, mysteries, police, espionage. Nonfiction: inspiration, history, business, New Age, biography.

Lisa Considine, Editor of Trade Paperbacks
Nonfiction: psychology, health and childcare, nature, multicultural books, Confident Collector series.

Ellen Edwards, Executive Editor, Romance
Fiction: historical and contemporary romance, women's suspense, general women's fiction.

(Ms.) Carrie Feron, Executive Editor
Fiction: mystery, romance, women's suspense, general women's fiction. Nonfiction: spirituality, health, childcare, pet care.

Trish Lande Grader, Executive Editor
Wide interests in commercial nonfiction and fiction, including mysteries and suspense.

Jennifer Hershey, Executive Editor
Wide range of trade interests in fiction and nonfiction. Atmospheric mysteries with emphasis on character and narrative voice.

Lyssa Keusch, Associate Editor
Fiction: romance, mystery. Nonfiction: Self-help.

Rachel Klayman, Editorial Director of Trade Paperbacks
Nonfiction: women's studies, history, popular reference, psychology, popular science.

Micki Nuding, Assistant Editor
Fiction: historical and contemporary romance, women's suspense, general women's fiction. Commercial nonfiction.

Stephen S. Power, Associate Editor
Mass-market: true crime, mysteries, thrillers. Trade: humor, business.

Ann McKay Thoroman, Assistant Editor
Fiction: mystery, romance, women's suspense, commercial and literary women's fiction. Nonfiction: spirituality, health, psychology, inspirational, parenting, pet care.

Christine Zika, Associate Editor
Fiction: romance. Nonfiction: health, relationships.

AVON CAMELOT AND AVON FLARE

The Avon Camelot imprint produces paperback children's titles (middle readers, ages eight to twelve); the Avon Flare line is directed toward the young-adult readership (age twelve and up). Both lists feature topnotch fiction and otherwise selectively cover the gamut of children's nonfiction categories. Avon addresses the educational-sales market through Avon Paperbacks for Schools and Libraries.

Avon Camelot covers general fiction, including family, peer, and school-related stories. Titles from Camelot: *Ask Me Anything about Baseball* (nonfiction) by Louis Phillips, *Moonshiner's Son* by Carolyn Reeder, *Ramona the Brave* by Beverly Cleary, and *Slime Lives! And Other Wierd Facts That Will Amaze You* (nonfiction) by Robin Keats.

Avon Flare publishes general fiction (coming of age, family, and peer stories), as well as historical novels, horror, and suspense titles. Romance can be a strong story element, but Flare does not publish genre romance as such.

From Avon Flare: *Evil in the Attic* by Linda Piazza, *Farewell Kiss* (in the Final Cruise series) by Nichole Davidson, *It Seemed Like a Good Idea at the Time* by Martin Godfrey, *Prom Night* by Jesse Osburn, and *Rats in the Attic and Other Stories to Make Your Skin Crawl* by G. E. Stanley.

Query letters and SASEs should be directed to:

Gwen Montgomery, Editorial Director

Stephanie Siegel, Assistant Editor

THE MOUNTAINEERS BOOKS

300 Third Avenue West
Seattle, WA 98119
206-223-6303

Mountaineers produces guidebooks, instructional texts, historical works, natural history guides, and works on environmental conservation. The Mountaineers (founded in 1906) is a conservation and outdoor-activity group with a mission to explore, study, preserve, and enjoy the natural beauty of the outdoors. The Mountaineers Books was founded in 1961 as a nonprofit publishing program of the club. The Mountaineers sponsors the Barbara Savage/Miles From Nowhere Memorial Award competition for outstanding unpublished nonfiction adventure-narrative manuscripts. The initial title offered by Mountaineers Books, *Mountaineering: The Freedom of the Hills,* is still in print in a fully revised edition.

Mountaineers titles: *K-2: The Story of the Savage Mountain* by Jim Curran, *Best Hikes with Children in San Francisco's North Bay* by Bill McMillon, *Bicycle Touring in Australia* by Leigh Hemmings, *Camp Four: Recollections of a Yosemite Rock-climber* by Steve Roper, *Cascade Alpine Guide: Climbing and High Routes* by Fred Beckey, *Columbia River Gorge: A Complete Guide* (edited by Philip Jones), *Exploring Colorado's Wild Areas* by Scott Warren, *GPS Made Easy: Global Positioning Systems in the Outdoors* by Lawrence Letham, *Heroic Climbs* (edited by Chris Bonnington), *Hold the Heights: The Foundations of Mountaineering* by Walt Unsworth, *Mexico's Volcanoes: A Climbing Guide* by R. J. Secor, *Photography Outdoors: A Field Guide for Travel and Adventure Photographers* by Mark Gardner and Art Wolfe, *The Crystal Horizon: Everest—the First Solo Ascent* by Reinhold Messner, and *Trekking in Nepal: A Traveler's Guide* by Stephen Bezruchka.

A winner of the aforementioned Barbara Savage/Miles From Nowhere competition is *Himalayan Passage: Seven Months in the High Country of Tibet, Nepal, China, India, and Pakistan* by Jeremy Schmidt (with photographs by Patrick Morrow).

The Mountaineers Books distributes its list via direct orders and also utilizes the services of regional and national wholesalers and trade representatives.

Query letters and SASEs should be directed to:

Margaret Foster, Editor in Chief

Cindy Bohn, Editorial Manager

MOYER BELL LIMITED

Kymbolde Way
Wakefield, RI 02879
401-789-0074

Moyer Bell Limited specializes in literary works, reference works, and books in art and design. Many general-interest nonfiction works from this smaller house evidence a high-interest cultural or public-issues slant. Within this specialty arena, Moyer Bell has a program that encompasses original titles, reprints, and translations. The house also has a strong commitment to poetry. The Asphodel Press imprint was founded as a nonprofit organization in 1990 and concentrates on fine literary titles.

Moyer Bell Limited was established in 1984 by Jennifer Moyer and Britt Bell; this notably independent house (with a U.K. base in London in addition to its U.S. operations) has received worldwide accolades for its roster of fine writers and stylish product.

Among Moyer Bell offerings: *Playing God: Deciding Your Life and Death* by Gerald Larue, *Oriental Carpets: A Buyer's Guide* by Essie Sakhai, *The Legend of Good Women: The Liberation of Women in Medieval Cities* by Erika Uitz, *The Mystery of Consciousness: A Prescription for Human Survival* by Ruth Nanda Anshen, *Virgins and Other Endangered Species* (memoir) by Dorothea Straus, *Walking toward the Milpa: Living in Guatemala with Armies, Demons, Abrazos, and Death* (narrative non-fiction) by Marcos McPeek Villatoro, *The Sun and the Moon* (novel) by Niccolò Tucci, *Dreams of Dead Women's Handbags* (collected stories) by Shena Mackay, and *In the Garden of the Three Islands* (poetry) by Maria Luis Cariño.

On Moyer Bell's reference-book list are the periodically revised *Directory of Literary Magazines* issued by the Council of Literary Magazines and Presses, *Grant Seekers Guide* by James McGrath Morris and Laura Adler, and *Directory of American Poetry Books* from Poets House.

Moyer Bell Books are distributed to the trade by Rizzoli International via Rizzoli's arrangement with St. Martin's Press.

Query letters and SASEs should be directed to:

Britt Bell, Publisher

Jennifer Moyer, Publisher

JOHN MUIR PUBLICATIONS

P.O. Box 613
Santa Fe, NM 87504
505-982-4078

John Muir Publications (founded in 1969) produces titles in the areas of adventure and travel; art, crafts, and style; parenting and the family; books for young readers; aeronautics, space, and automotive interest; ski tech; and education.

John Muir books comprise a choice list, of which a high percentage of titles remain in print indefinitely and/or are reissued in updated editions. Among Muir's long-lasting works are *The People's Guide to Mexico* along with the companion volume *The People's Guide to RV Camping in Mexico* by Carl Franz with Steve Rogers (edited by Lorena Havens). Another backlist stalwart is the classic *How to Keep Your Volkswagen Alive: A Manual of Step-by-Step Procedures for the Compleat Idiot* by John Muir himself.

John Muir Publications offers travel lines such as the Unique Travel series, the Undiscovered Islands series, and the 2 to 22 Days itinerary planners. Travel-related titles include *The World Awaits: A Comprehensive Guide to Extended Backpack Travel* by Paul Otteson, *The 100 Best Small Art Towns in America: When to Discover Creative People, Fresh Air and Affordable Living* by John Villani, *Mona Winks: Self-Guided Tours of Europe's Top Museums* by Rick Steves and Gene Openshaw, *The Visitor's*

Guide to the Birds of the Eastern National Parks: United States and Canada by Roland E. Wauer, *Guatemala: A Natural Destination* by Richard Mahler, *Unique New Mexico: A Guide to the State's Quirks, Charisma, and Character* by Sarah Lovett, and *Ranch Vacations: The Complete Guide to Guest and Resort, Fly-Fishing, and Cross-Country Skiing Ranches* by Gene Kilgore.

Automotive works encompass *The Greaseless Guide to Car Care* by Mary Jackson, *How to Keep Your Toyota Pickup Alive: A Manual of Step-by-Step Procedures for the Compleat Idiot* by Larry Owens, and *Off-Road Emergency Repair and Survival* by James Ristow. A representative title in ski tech is *Ski Tech's Guide to Equipment, Skiwear, and Accessories* (edited by Bill Tanler).

JOHN MUIR KIDS BOOKS

John Muir publishes a strong children's list, including series such as Rainbow Warrior Artists, Extremely Weird, Environmental Books for Young Readers, X-Ray Vision, and the family-oriented Kidding Around Travel Guides.

Representative titles here are *Native Artists of Europe* by Reavis Moore, *Rough and Ready Cowboys* by A. S. Gintzler, *Bizarre and Beautiful Ears* by the Santa Fe Writers Group, and *Tracing Our Jewish Roots* by Miriam Sagan.

John Muir Publications is distributed to the trade by Publishers Group West; the house distributes its books worldwide through the offices of a number of regional services.

Query letters and SASEs should be directed to:

Steven Cary, President

MULTNOMAH PRESS

(See listing for Questar in Directory of Religious, Spiritual, and Inspirational Publishers)

MUSTANG PUBLISHING COMPANY

P.O. Box 3004
Memphis, TN 38173
901-521-1406

Mustang produces general trade nonfiction books in hardcover and paperback, with a special emphasis in the fields of how-to, humor, games, outdoor recreation, sports, travel, and careers. Mustang Publishing Company (founded in 1983) is a modest-sized house with a concise publishing vision and compactly tailored list.

Mustang publishes specialty books geared to expansive lifestyles, such as *Paintball! Strategies and Tactics* by Bill Barnes with Peter Wrenn, *Bet on It! The Ultimate Guide to Nevada* by Mary Jane and Greg Edwards, and *The Hangover Handbook: 101 Cures for Humanity's Oldest Malady* by Nic van Oudtshoorn. There's also the immensely popular *The Complete Book of Beer Drinking Games* by Andy Griscom, Ben Rand, and Scott Johnson—as well as *Beer Games II: The Exploitative Sequel.*

The touring and travel list includes *Europe for Free* by Brian Butler, *Festival Europe! Fairs and Celebrations Throughout Europe* by Margaret M. Johnson, *London for Free* by Brian Butler, *The Nepal Trekker's Handbook* by Amy R. Kaplan with Michael Keller, *Europe on 10 Salads a Day* by Mary Jane and Greg Edwards, and the hilariously revised and expanded edition of *Let's Blow Thru Europe: How to Have a Blast on Your Whirlwind Trip Through Europe* by Thomas Neenan and Greg Hancock.

Representative career titles: *Working in T.V. News: The Insider's Guide* by Carl Filoreto with Lynn Setzer. A solid group of Mustang books targets an audience bound for higher education, including series for students and graduate-school applicants, often geared toward particular professional curricula, such as *The One Hour College Applicant* by Lois Rochester and Judy Mandell, *Medical School Admissions: The Insider's Guide* by John A. Zebala and Daniel B. Jones, and the Essays That Worked series that helps prepare readers to apply for business and law school admission.

Mustang also offers Alan and Theresa von Altendorf's general reference *ISMs: A Compendium of Concepts and Beliefs From Abolitionism to Zygodactylism.*

Writers should note that Mustang welcomes book proposals on almost any nonfiction topic. The publisher prefers to see an outline and two to three sample chapters—and urges authors to be sure to enclose a self-addressed stamped envelope (the ubiquitous SASE) with each submission. No phone calls, please.

Mustang's books are distributed through National Book Network.

Query letters and SASEs should be directed to:

Rollin Riggs, Publisher

THE MYSTERIOUS PRESS
(See Warner Books)

THE NAIAD PRESS

P.O. Box 10543
Tallahassee, FL 32302
904-539-5965

Naiad publishes lesbian and feminist fiction, essays, poetry, short stories, humor, translations, and bibliographies. The Naiad emphasis in category fiction includes stylish and traditional mysteries, espionage thrillers, adventure yarns, science fiction, fantasy, romances, historical fiction, erotica, and Westerns. Naiad Press (established in 1973) is the oldest and largest lesbian publishing company in the world.

Naiad has been particularly innovative among book-publishing operations in the development of specialized target-marketing techniques. The house has expanded its media presence to become active in the wider arena of audio books, videos, and theatrical film. The romantic fiction *Claire of the Moon* by Nicole Conn (writer and director of the feature film of the same name) represents a groundbreaking Naiad project that embraces documentary, music, and storytelling in cinema, video, audiocassette, CD, and print.

On Naiad's roster of authors are Jane Rule, Lee Lynch, Diane Salvatore, Denise Ohio, Sarah Aldridge, Amanda Kyle Williams, Gertrude Stein, and Patricia Highsmith (writing as Claire Morgan).

Naiad nonfiction: *For Love and for Life: Intimate Portraits of Lesbian Couples* by Susan E. Johnson, *Sapphistry: The Book of Lesbian Sexuality* by Pat Califia, *Parents Matter: Parents' Relationships with Lesbian Daughters and Gay Sons* by Ann Muller, *Lesbian Crossroads* by Ruth Baetz, and *Happy Endings: Lesbian Writers Talk About Their Lives and Work* by Kate Brandt.

Naiad fiction and literature includes *Faultline* by Sheila Ortiz Taylor, *Bar Girls* by Lauran Hoffman, *Night Songs* (a Gianna Maglione mystery) by Penny Mickelbury, *Cabin Fever* by Carol Schmidt, *Flashpoint* by Katherine V. Forrest, *A Rage of Maidens* (a Caitlin Reece mystery) by Lauren Wright Douglas, *Soul Snatcher* by Camarin Grae, *Murder at Red Rook Ranch* by Dorothy Tell, *Old Dyke Tales* by Lee Lynch, and *Say Jesus and Come to Me* by Ann Allen Shockley.

The basic goal of Naiad Press is to make sure that someday, any woman, any place, can recognize her lesbianism and walk into a bookstore and pick up a book that says to her: "Yes, you are a lesbian and you are wonderful." With that aim in mind, Naiad has adopted the following slogan for use in its potent mailing list campaigns: Lesbians always know; if it's a book by Naiad Press, it's a book you want to own.

Naiad Books maintains a comprehensive backlist. Books are available directly from the publisher via a toll-free telephone order number as well as to the trade through a network of distribution services including Bookpeople, Bookslinger, Ingram, and Inland.

Query letters and SASEs should be directed to:

Barbara Grier, Chief Executive Officer

NATIONAL TEXTBOOK COMPANY
(See NTC Publishing Group)

NAVAL INSTITUTE PRESS
(See Directory of University Presses)

THOMAS NELSON
(See Directory of Religious, Spiritual, and Inspirational Publishers)

NELSON-HALL PUBLISHERS

111 North Canal Street, Suite 399
Chicago, IL 60606
312-930-9446

Nelson-Hall holds major focus on business, criminology, psychology, journalism, history, political science, sociology, educational travel, African-American studies, how-to, and self-help. Nelson-Hall Publishers (founded in 1909) produces educational, scholarly, and professional books; college textbooks; and a line of general-interest nonfiction trade crossovers.

Sample Nelson-Hall titles: *The Decision-Making Process in Journalism* by Carl Hausman, *Personal Valuing: An Introduction* by Dale D. Simmons, *Food Power: A Doctor's Guide to Common Sense Nutrition* by L. Earle Arnow, *Philosophers Look at Science Fiction* (edited by Nicholas D. Smith), *What Handwriting Tells You—About Yourself, Your Friends, and Famous People* by M. N. Bunker, *The Arts in Therapy* by Bob Fleshman and Jerry L. Fryrear, *The Classic Clitoris: Historic Contributions to Scientific Sexuality* (edited by Thomas Power Lowry), and *Blind Mazes: A Study of Love* by George W. Kelling.

Nelson-Hall Publishers handles its own distribution.

Query letters and SASEs should be directed to:

Libby Rubenstein, Senior Editor

Richard Meade, Acquisitions Editor

NEW AMERICAN LIBRARY/NAL

(See Penguin USA)

NEW AMSTERDAM BOOKS

101 Main Street
P.O. Box C
Franklin, NY 13775
212-685-6005

Areas of New Amsterdam publishing interest include art and art history, literature and fiction, biography and letters, food and drink, drama, travel, photography, architecture, archaeology, Islamic studies, publishing, and design.

New Amsterdam Books (begun in 1987) is a small house that publishes a preferred list of trade fiction and nonfiction titles. Featured on the New Amsterdam list are books of an eclectic European cultural viewpoint, as well as American editions of European books. New Amsterdam editions are produced in paperback and clothbound formats.

Characteristic of the New Amsterdam list: *British Landscape Watercolors, 1750–1850* by Jane Munro, *Life and Food in the Caribbean* by Cristine Mackie, *Alastair Sawday's Guide to French Bed & Breakfast* (updated edition by arrangement with Alastair Sawday Publishing), *Victorian Theatre: The Theatre of Its Time* (edited by Russell Jackson), and *The Story of Western Furniture* by Phyllis Bennett Oates (illustrated by Mary Seymour).

From New Amsterdam's well-honed backlist: *Mrs. Delany, Her Life and Her Flowers* by Ruth Hayden, *Anarchism and Anarchists* by George Woodcock, *Typefaces for Books* by James Sutton and Alan Bartram, *The Whiskies of Scotland* by R. J. S. McDowell, and *The Great Fire at Hampton Court* by Michael Fishlock (with foreword by HRH the Prince of Wales).

Of special literary note: *Killing the Mandaris* (fiction) by Juan Alonso, *The Three-Arched Bridge* (literary novel) by Albanian writer Ismail Kildare, *Tennyson: An Illustrated Life* by Norman Page, and *Walt Whitman's New York: From Manhattan to Montauk* (edited by Henry M. Christman).

New Amsterdam issues the illustrated historical series Manuscripts in the British Library.

New Amsterdam Books handles its own distribution.

Query letters and SASEs should be directed to:

Emile Capouya, Managing Director

New Horizon Press

34 Church Street
Liberty Corners, NJ 07938
908-604-6311

mailing address:
P.O. Box 669
Far Hills, NJ 07931

The New Horizon list addresses topics of social concern, including corporate and professional responsibility, behavioral diversity, and politics, as well as personal self-help, how-to, and business books in the mainstream vein.

New Horizon Press (established in 1983) was originally an imprint of Horizon Press; now a separate publishing entity, New Horizon Press is remarkable for its pinpoint commercial vision in the arena of nonfiction accounts of courageous individuals. These incredible stories of real people display an intense human-interest appeal and often embody an investigative journalistic stance that probes related public issues. The house maintains a solid backlist that is particularly strong in the self-help arena.

New Horizon is configured as a small press: Projects are often initiated with restrained author advances; more money accrues to the writer through subsequent sales. The publisher has had conspicuous success in expanding the scope of its projects via targeted promotion, advertising, touring, and subsidiary rights, both in print via book-club selections and in the electronic arena in the form of related television docudramas, talkshow appearances by authors, and feature items on television journals.

Highlighting the New Horizon list: *Evil Web: A True Story of Cult Abuse and Courage* by Mary Rich and Carol Jose, *I Shared the Dream: First Black Woman Senator from Kentucky, Confidant of Martin Luther King, Jr.* by Georgia Davis Powers, *Lifeline: Five Desperate People Fight for Their Lives* by Mary Zimmeth Schomaker, *Sisterhood of the Night: One Woman Battles a Sinister Force* by Becky Usry, *To Love a Child: A Reluctant Father Adopts a "Forgotten" Child* by Ted Schwarz, *Chameleon: The Lives of Dorothy Proctor from Street Criminal to International Special Agent* by Dorothy Proctor and Fred Rosen, *Cutoffs: How Families Who Sever Relationships Can Reconnect* by Carol Netzer, *60 Second Menopause Management: 60-Second Answers to Women's Menopause Questions* by Carol R. Schulz and Mary Jenkins, *Telemedicine: What the Future Holds When You're Ill* by Mariann Karinch, and *You're a Stepparent . . . Now What?* by Joseph Cerquone.

Small Horizons is an imprint offering self-help books for children written by teachers and mental-health professionals. From Small Horizons: *Up and Down the Mountain: Helping Children Cope with Parental Alcoholism* by Pamela Leib Higgins (art by Gail Zawacki), *The Words Hurt* by Chris Loftus (art by Catherine Gallagher), and *The Empty Place: A Child's Guide Through Grief* by Roberta Temes (art by Kim Carlisle).

New Horizon Press distributes its own list.

Query letters and SASEs should be directed to:

Joan S. Dunphy, Editor in Chief

NEWMARKET PRESS

18 East 48th Street
New York, NY 10017
212-832-3575

Newmarket concentrates on general nonfiction, accenting categories such as contemporary issues, history and biography, humor, psychology, parenting, health, nutrition, cooking, personal finance, business, film, and music. Newmarket also issues a small number of children's titles (Newmarket Medallion imprint) as well as occasional works of high-interest fiction (the house was the original publisher of the hardcover edition of Michael Blake's novel *Dances with Wolves*).

Newmarket Press (founded in 1981) is a division of Newmarket Publishing and Communications Company. The house produces books in hardcover, trade paper, and mass-market paperback editions.

Representative of Newmarket nonfiction: *Gifting to People You Love: An Intergenerational Financial Guide* by Adriane G. Berg, *Love Is A Happy Cat* by Michael W. Fox (illustrated by Harry Gans), *Smart Muffins, Cookies, Biscuits and Breads: The Heavenly, Healthy Cookbook for High-Fiber, Low-Fat, No-Sugar Baked Goods* by Jane

Kinderlehrer, *Shalom, Friend: The Life and Legacy of Yitzhak Rabin* by the Staff of *The Jerusalem Report*, and *Discovering Great Music: A Listener's Guide to the Top Composers and Their Master Works* by Roy Hemming.

A special Newmarket program accents tie-ins with film and other media productions. Titles here include *The Birdcage: The Shooting Script* by Elaine May, *The Sense and Sensibility Screenplay and Diaries* by Emma Thompson, *A Midwinter's Tale: The Shooting Script* by Kenneth Branagh, and *Panther: The Illustrated History of the Black Panther Movement and Story Behind the Film* (introduction by Melvin Van Peebles; afterword by Mario Van Peebles).

Newmarket distributes its list through Random House and maintains a network that utilizes a number of regional sales representatives.

Query letters and SASEs should be sent to:

Esther Margolis, President and Publisher

THE NEW PRESS

450 West 41st Street
New York, NY 10036
212-629-8802

The New Press promotes a full-scale not-for-profit forum for publishing hardcover and trade paperback books and other materials in cultural criticism, American politics, history, education, social policy, the arts, and world literature.

The New Press (founded in 1992) is an independent publisher in the most absolute sense. Established in the face of increasing corporate control of commercial publishing, the New Press is committed to publishing, in innovative ways, works of educational, cultural, and community value. Operating in the public interest rather than for private gain, works from the New Press inform public debate and reach out to audiences that are not generally priority markets for mainstream publishing firms.

The New Press program is tempered toward contemporary issues, and courts the controversial. Indeed, plans for the inception of the press are said to have been engendered by director André Schiffrin immediately upon his resignation as head of Pantheon Books in response to what was interpreted as the Random House ownership's plan to redirect Pantheon's emphasis toward the commercial mainstream.

The New Press does have its own brand of commercial prescience as well as attendant market niche. The house is blessed with legendary small-press savvy, as well as personnel with solid corporate backgrounds and extensive industry contacts. Studs Terkel led off a heavy-hitting initial list with *Race: How Blacks & Whites Think & Feel About the American Obsession*, which became a national best-seller; other New Press authors have followed suit and achieved high-profile media recognition and substantial sales.

Among New Press nonfiction features: *The Vampire State and Other Myths and Fallacies about the U.S. Economy* by Fred Block; *Families and Freedom: A Docu-*

mentary History of African American Kinship in the Civil War Era (edited by Ira Berlin and Leslie S. Rowland); *The Spears of Twilight: Three Years among the Jívaro Indians of South America* by Philippe Descola (translated by Janet Lloyd); *The War on the Poor: A Defense Manual* by Randy Albelda, Nancy Folbre, and the Center for Popular Economics; *China Pop: How Soap Operas, Tabloids, and Bestsellers Are Transforming a Culture* by Jianying Zha; *Shades of L.A.: A Family Album* (photoessay) by Carolyn Kozo Cole and Kathy Kobayashi; *The Art of Ancient Egypt: A Portfolio—Masterpieces from the Brooklyn Museum* by the Brooklyn Museum; *The World Out There: Becoming Part of the Lesbian and Gay Community* by Michael Thomas Ford; and *Smoke and Mirrors: Violence, Television, and Other American Cultures* by John Leonard.

New Press expression in fiction and literature is exemplified by *The Thought Gang* by Tibor Fischer, *Paradise* by Abdulrazak Gurnah, *If I Could Write This in Fire: An Anthology of Literature from the Caribbean* (edited by Pamela Maria Smorkaloff), and *Coming of Age in America: A Multicultural Anthology* (edited by Mary Frosch).

Trade distribution for the New Press is handled through W. W. Norton.

Query letters and SASEs should be directed to:

André Schiffrin, Director

NEW YORK UNIVERSITY PRESS
(See Directory of University Presses)

THE NOBLE PRESS
213 West Institute Place, Suite 508
Chicago, IL 60610
312-642-1168

Noble Press accents trade nonfiction keyed to social, political, and environmental issues. The press owns a niche in the arena of socially relevant books aimed at a wide popular readership.

The Noble Press (founded in 1988) is a progressive nonfiction publishing house dedicated to producing high-quality hardcover and trade paperback books. The house slates sizable print runs for its lead titles and is capable of attaining a level of media interest usually viewed as more characteristic of international commercial publishers. Noble competes for and attracts books by proven authors as well as talented newer writers.

Noble has announced the inauguration of a romance fiction line geared toward a multicultural audience. Prospective authors are advised to query the house with regard to writer's guidelines.

Representing the Noble list in nonfiction: *Volunteer Slavery: My Authentic Negro Experience* by Jill Nelson, *The San Quentin Massacre: A True Story of Race and Violence in the Radical New Left* by Paul Liberatore, *The New Untouchables: How*

America Sanctions Police Violence by John DeSantis, *The Doctor, the Murder, the Mystery: The True Story of the Dr. John Branion Murder Case* by Barbara D'Amato, *Staying Well in a Toxic World: Understanding Environmental Illness, Multiple Chemical Sensitivities, Chemical Injuries, and Sick Building Syndrome* by Lynn Lawson, *Black and Single: Meeting and Choosing a Partner Who's Right for You* by Larry E. Davis, and *Woolgathered and Fitified: A Native American People's Struggle for Identity* by Karen Coronado and Richard Mathis.

The Noble Press list is represented to the trade by Consortium.

Query letters and SASEs should be directed to:

Douglas Seibold, Executive Editor

NOLO PRESS
950 Parker Street
Berkeley, CA 94710
510-549-1976

Nolo Press is renowned for a glittering array of self-help titles in law and business and has moved into the related arenas of lifestyle, recreation, travel, and retirement. The house also produces law-form kits, legal software, electronic books, and videotapes.

Nolo's consumerist perspective includes selections in areas such as homeowners, landlords, and tenants; going to court; money matters; estate planning and probate; business; legal reform; patents, copyrights, and trademarks; employee rights and the workplace; family matters; immigration; research and reference; older Americans; and humor.

Nolo Press (instituted in 1971) was founded by two Legal Aid lawyers who were fed up with the public's lack of access to affordable legal information and advice. Convinced that with good, reliable information Americans could handle routine legal problems without hiring an attorney, they began writing plain-English law books for the general readership.

Nolo led off its first list with *How to Do Your Own Divorce in California* and has been going strong since with a steady stream of titles addressing consumer needs in a wide range of general and specialist areas. Whereas lawyers have historically sold information only to the few who can afford their services, Nolo aims to provide comprehensive low-cost information to the public at large.

Many Nolo publications are regularly revised and are issued in updated editions, and the publisher maintains a hardy backlist. Most Nolo titles are written by practicing attorneys who are specialists in their fields of authorship. A major portion of the Nolo list exhibits a national orientation, while some titles are specifically geared to regional markets.

Highlights of the Nolo list: *Get a Life: You Don't Need a Million to Retire Well* by Ralph Warner, *How to Mediate Your Dispute: Find a Solution You Can Live with Quickly and Cheaply Outside the Courtroom* by Peter Lovenheim, *Trouble-Free*

Travel . . . and What to Do When Things Go Wrong by Stephen Colwell and Ann Shulman, *Mad at Your Lawyer: What to Do When You're Overcharged, Ignored, Betrayed, or a Victim of Malpractice* by Tanya Starnes, *Make Your Own Living Trust* by Denis Clifford, and *The Employer's Legal Handbook* by Fred S. Steingold.

Social, community, career, and issues-oriented titles: *Sexual Harassment on the Job* by William Petrocelli and Barbara Kate Repa; *The Copyright Handbook: How to Protect and Use Written Works* by Stephen Fishman; *Getting Started as an Independent Paralegal* by Ralph Warner; *Stand Up to the IRS* by Frederick W. Daily; *Dog Law* by Mary Randolph; *Neighbor Law: Fences, Trees, Boundaries & Noise* by Cora Jordan; and *A Legal Guide for Lesbian and Gay Couples* by Hayden Curry, Denis Clifford, and Robin Leonard.

Representative of the humor category: *29 Reasons Not to Go to Law School* by Ralph Warner, Toni Ihara, and Barbara Kate Repa; *Poetic Justice: The Funniest, Meanest Things Ever Said About Lawyers* (edited by Jonathan and Andrew Roth); and *The Devil's Advocates: The Unnatural History of Lawyers* by Andrew and Jonathan Roth.

Nolo Press distributes its own books to the trade (along with selected titles from other publishers) and also utilizes several distribution services. In addition, Nolo sells to consumers via direct mail and operates its own bookstore in Berkeley.

Query letters and SASEs should be sent to:

Stanley Jacobsen, Acquisitions Editor

Barbara Repa, Senior Editor

W. W. NORTON AND COMPANY, INC.

500 Fifth Avenue
New York, NY 10110
212-354-5500

Norton publishes trade nonfiction, commercial fiction and belles-lettres, and works for professional and academic markets. W. W. Norton (founded in 1923) offers prime-caliber trade books in all areas of its programs in fiction and nonfiction; the house is equally esteemed for its line of college texts and professional reference titles.

W. W. Norton produces hardcover and trade paperback editions under its celebrated gliding seagull colophon as well as through a variety of imprints including Liveright and Countryman. Norton nourishes a comprehensive backlist of books in all areas of its publishing interest.

Norton nonfiction accents trade titles in topics of current public interest, with a range of works featuring the popular as well as scholarly approach to fields including history, cultural criticism, biography, psychology, natural history, and the sciences, as well as art, photography, and lifestyle. Norton also offers a line of books for enthusiasts of sailing and publishes Blue Guide travel books.

Titles here: *Dumbing Down: The Strip-Mining of American Culture* (edited by Katharine Washburn and John Thornton), *Teachings from the Worldly Philosophy* by

Robert Heilbroner, *The Tri-Color Diet: A Miracle Breakthrough in Diet and Nutrition for a Longer, Healthier Life* by Martin Katahn, *A River Lost: The Life and Death of the Columbia* by Blaine Harden, *Leaster Beall: Trailblazer of American Graphic Design* by R. Roger Remington, *Boomerang: Clinton's Health Security Effort and the Turn against Government in U.S. Politics* by Theda Skocpol, *The Solution-Oriented Woman: Creating the Life You Want* by Pat Hudson, *Flesh and Stone: The Body and the City in Western Civilization* by Richard Sennett, *Fundamentals of Sailing, Cruising, and Racing* by Stephen Colgate, and *Intimate Terrorism: The Deterioration of Erotic Life* by Michael Vincent Miller.

In fiction and literary writing Norton publishes novels, poetry (including the Norton Anthologies series), and short story collections—from established, distinguished scribes and from a select few marketable new voices. In addition, the house publishes critical essays, biographies, and literary histories. The Norton fiction list covers classical, modern, contemporary, and experimental styles, as well as novels showing a mainstream commercial profile. The Norton program also encompasses mystery and suspense fiction.

Characteristic of Norton fiction: *Dry Fire* by Catherine Lewis, *What Falls Away* by Tracy Daugherty, *Anger* by May Sarton, *Tularosa* by Michael McGarrity, *The Hide* by Barry Unsworth, *Hope's Cadillac* by Patricia Page, *The Commodore* by Patrick O'Brian, *A Little Yellow Dog* by Walter Mosley, *Seduction Theory* (stories) by Thomas Beller, and *Sudden Fiction (Continued): 60 New Short-Short Stories* (edited by Robert Shepard and James Thomas).

Norton poetry: *Mother Love* by Rita Dove, *My Father Was a Toltec and Selected Poems* by Ana Castillo, *Poetry in Motion: 100 Poems from the Subways and Buses* (edited by Elise Paschen, Molly Peacock, and Neil Neches), *Brink Road* by A. R. Ammons, *Connecting the Dots* by Maxine Kumin, and *Crash's Law* by Karen Volkman.

Works of venturesome literary configuration: *The Coral Sea* (poetry, fiction, and essay) by Patti Smith, *In Short: A Collection of Brief Creative Nonfiction* (edited by Judith Kitchen and Mary Paumier Jones), *When the Air Hits Your Brain: Tales of Neurosurgery* by Frank Vertosick, *Wise Women: Over 2,000 Years of Spiritual Writing by Women* (edited by Susan Cahill), and *Holy Land: A Suburban Memoir* by D. J. Waldie.

W. W. Norton distributes its own list and handles distribution for a number of other publishers, including the Ecco Press, the Taunton Press, the New Press, New Directions Books, Pushcart Press, and Thames and Hudson.

Query letters and SASEs should be directed to:

Edwin Barber, Vice Chairman and Director
Acquires for the full range of house interests.

Jill Bialosky, Associate Editor
Literary fiction. Biographies, memoirs. Some poetry.

(Ms.) Amy Cherry, Editor
History, biography, women's issues, African-American, health.

(Mr.) Hilary Hinzmann, Editor
Current affairs, culture high and low, history, science, fiction.

(Ms.) Carol Houck Smith, Editor-at-Large
Literary fiction, travel memoirs, behavioral sciences, nature.

(Mr.) Gerald Howard, Editor and Vice President
Acquires nonfiction and literary fiction for the trade.

(Mr.) Starling Lawrence, Editor in Chief
Acquires for the full range of house interests.

(Ms.) Alane Mason, Editor
Serious nonfiction for a general audience, particularly cultural and intellectual history, psychology, philosophy, and religion. Literary fiction and memoir.

(Mr.) W. Drake McFeely, President
Nonfiction of all kinds, particularly science and social science.

COUNTRYMAN PRESS
FOUL PLAY PRESS
BACKCOUNTRY PUBLICATIONS

Box 175
Woodstock, VT 05091
802-457-1049

Countryman specializes in regional history, mystery and suspense, classic reprints, recreation, travel, gardening, nature, environment, how-to, regional hiking, walking, bicycling, fishing, cross-country skiing, and canoeing guides. Imprints include Countryman Press, Foul Play Press, and Backcountry Publications.

Countryman (founded in 1973) has been on the cusp of the small, regional press initiative that has enriched the North American publishing scope through editorial acumen and niche-marketing panache. Now part of W. W. Norton, Countryman remains editorially independent.

Representative Countryman titles: *Alaska on Foot: Wilderness Techniques for the Far North* by Erik Molvar, *The Lake Champlain Corridor: Touring Historic Battle Sites from Saratoga to Quebec* by Howard Coffin and Will and Jane Curtis, *Covered Bridges of Vermont* by Ed Barna, *The Maze: A Desert Journey* (literary travel fiction) by Lucy Rees, and *The Architecture of the Shakers* by Julie Nicoletta (photographs by Bret Morgan).

Backcountry Publications: *Walks and Rambles in Ohio's Western Reserve: Discovering Nature and History in the Northeastern Corner* by Jay Abercrombie; *25 Mountain Bike Tours in the Hudson Valley* by Peter Kick; and *50 Hikes in Connecticut: From the Berkshires to the Coast* by David, Sue, and Gerry Hardy.

From Foul Play: *Slaughter Music* by Russell James, *Penance* (a Holland Taylor mystery) by David Housewright, *Astride a Grave* by Bill James, *Fête Fatale* by Robert Barnard, and *Family Business* by Michael Z. Lewin.

Sales and distribution for Countryman are handled by the parent corporation, W. W. Norton.

Query letters and SASEs should be directed to:

Helen Whybrow, Editor in Chief

NTC PUBLISHING GROUP
PASSPORT BOOKS
NATIONAL TEXTBOOK COMPANY

4255 West Touhy Avenue
Lincolnwood, IL 60646
708-679-5500

NTC Publishing Group (founded in 1982 as National Textbook Company) boasts comprehensive offerings in the areas of business and career, professional how-to, and travel, as well as books of general nonfiction interest and reference works of broad appeal.

The structure of NTC Publishing Group (stamped with the staunch emblem of an eagle perched in profile) embraces business and professional divisions that incorporate the formerly independent Crain Books, as well as NTC Business Books and VGM Career Books. The trade logo of Passport Books is a globe in an open book, which covers titles in travel-related fields; Passport also functions as a crossover imprint for some of NTC's books in the area of international business culture. General reference works are issued under the rubric of National Textbook Company.

NTC books in the reference arena include foreign-language references, phrase books, and dictionaries (French, Italian, German, Polish, Russian); resources in the English language (*NTC's Thesaurus of Everyday American English* and *Essentials of English Grammar*); and general-interest works such as *NTC's Dictionary of Shakespeare*.

NTC Publishing Group handles its own distribution.

NTC BUSINESS BOOKS
VGM CAREER BOOKS

NTC Business Books accents business how-to, advertising, promotion, and marketing, and displays an extensive interest in the fields of international business, media planning and use, and general business reference. Formerly a part of the Crain family publishing empire, Crain Books was acquired by NTC and its backlist folded into the NTC Business Books imprint.

NTC Business Books include *The Media Handbook* by Helen Katz, *Power Direct Marketing* by "Rocket" Ray Jutkins, *How to Write a Successful Marketing Plan* by Roman G. Hiebing Jr. and Scott W. Cooper, *Green Marketing: Challenges and Opportunities for the New Marketing Age* by Jacquelyn A. Ottman, *Customer Bonding: Pathway to Lasting Customer Loyalty* by Richard Cross and Janet Smith, *Business Magazine Publishing* by Sal Marino, and *Advertising in Society: Classic and Contemporary Readings on Advertising's Role in Society* by Roxanne Hovland and Gary Wilcox.

NTC Business Books Passport line of intercultural guides to the global marketplace are keyed to a number of geographic locales, including China, Germany, Mexico, and Japan.

VGM Career Books are resources and how-tos covering a variety of professional and career opportunities and specialties. Some titles: *How to Run Your Own Home*

Business by Coralee Smith Kern, *Careers in Communications* by Shonan F. R. Noronha, and *Beating Job Burnout: How to Turn Your Work into Your Passion* by Paul Stevens. Series items include *Getting a Raise Made Easy*, *Great Jobs for English Majors*, and *Careers for History Buffs.*

Query letters and SASEs should be directed to:

Mark R. Pattis, President

Richard Hagle, Editor, Business Books.

PASSPORT BOOKS

Passport Books is known as a publisher of titles in the field of travel. Series from Passport include Essential Travel Guides, Trip Planner, Handbooks of the World, Regional Guides of Italy, and Illustrated Travel Guides from Thomas Cook.

Examples from the various Passport lines: *Toronto's Best-Kept Secrets (and New Views of Old Favorites)* by Mike Michaelson, a set of food-and-wine travel guides, and *Essential Travel Guide to Orlando and Disney World.*

Query letters and SASEs should be directed to:

John Nolan, Executive Editor, Passport Books

OHIO UNIVERSITY PRESS

(See Directory of University Presses)

ORCHARD BOOKS

(See Grolier Incorporated)

ORYX PRESS

4041 North Central at Indian School Road
Phoenix, AZ 85012
602-265-2651

Oryx is a specialist press with a broad range of interest. The house covers reference and informational publications in fields such as business and careers, medicine and consumer health, popular culture, popular science (including nature and environment), technical science, sports, elderly population and services, social services, education, human growth and development, gender studies, multicultural studies, international government and politics, and regional or period American history.

Oryx Press (founded in 1975) targets the informational marketplace, specializing in directories, databases, CD-ROMs, periodicals, loose-leaf services, library and information science readers, and educational texts, as well as general reference works. Many Oryx releases are geared toward the library, corporate, institutional, educational, academic, and technical research arenas. The press issues special catalogs for the school market and for series in higher education.

This independent, innovative house is on the lookout for books with greater high-profile trade potential. Oryx wants books that can carry high prices, stay in print for long periods of time, and deliver royalties consistently.

Oryx core publications include *Holidays of the World Cookbook for Students* by Lois Sinaiko Webb, *Multicultural Folktales for the Feltboard and Readers' Theater* by Judy Sierra, *Women's Rights* by Christine A. Lunardini, *Child Care Choices: A Corporate Initiative for the 21st Century* by Margery Leveen Sher and Madeline Fried, *Business Information: How to Find It, How to Use It* by Michael R. Lavin, *Tapping the Government Grapevine: The User-Friendly Guide to U.S. Government Information Services* by Judith Scheik Robinson, and *Stress and Burnout in Library Service* by Janette S. Caputo.

Illustrating the specialist range of the Oryx program: *Meeting the Needs of People with Disabilities: A Guide for Librarians, Educators, and Other Service Professionals* by Ruth A. Velleman, *How to Write and Publish a Scientific Paper* by Robert A. Day, *Contemporary Thesaurus of Social Science Terms and Synonyms: A Guide for Natural Language Computer Searching* (compiled and edited by Sara D. Knapp), and *From Idea to Funded Project: Grant Proposals That Work* by Jane C. Belcher and Julia M. Jacobsen.

The Oryx Press handles its own distribution.

Query letters and SASEs should be directed to:

Phyllis Steckler, President

Art Stickney, Director of Acquisitions
Both acquire in all areas consistent with publisher description.

THE OVERLOOK PRESS

149 Wooster Street
4th Floor
New York, NY 10012
212-477-7162

The Overlook house concentration is in general nonfiction, including biography, crafts, how-to, fine arts, architecture and design, Hudson Valley regionals, cookbooks, and natural history, with a few titles directed toward the young reader. Overlook also publishes titles in fiction, belles lettres, and poetry.

The Overlook Press (founded in 1971) is a smaller publisher with a diverse and select list. Under its enigmatic logo (a mythical beast in cartouche that calls to mind winged elephantine species), Overlook produces books in special fine editions, hard-cover, and trade paperback. The house nurtures a thriving backlist that features titles such as the business–martial arts classic *Book of Five Rings* (by Miyamoto Musashi; translated by Victor Harris), *The Gormenghast Trilogy* by Mervyn Peake, and *Tiny Houses* by Lester Walker.

Indicative of the Overlook publishing scope: *Chanel: The Couturière at Work* by Amy De La Haye and Shelley Tobin, *100 Great Albums of the Sixties* by John Tobler, *Diagnosis for Disaster: The Devastating Truth about False Memory Syndrome and Its Impact on Accusers and Families* by Claudette Wassil-Grimm, *World Cinema: Diary of a Day* (edited by Peter Cowie), *Designs for Window Treatments: Over 100 Styles for Curtains and Other Soft Furnishings* by Lady Caroline Wrey, *Walk Aerobics* by Les Snowdon and Maggie Humphreys, and *The Zen of Cooking: Creative Cooking With and Without Recipes* by Claire Hyman and Lucille Naimer.

Overlook's literary emphasis is on vanguard fiction, poetry, biography, memoirs, travel, and criticism. Entrants here include *X-Ray: The Unauthorized Autobiography* by Ray Davies, *Brother of Sleep* (fiction) by Robert Schneider, *The Boy in the Well* (poetry) by Daniel Mark Epstein, *The Ukimwi Road: From Kenya to Zimbabwe* by Dervla Murphy, *In Catskill Country: Collected Essays on Mountain History, Life and Lore* by Alf Evers, *Chroma* by Derek Jarman, *Nico: The End* by James Young, and *Transylvania and Beyond* by Dervla Murphy.

Overlook Press is distributed by Penguin USA.

Query letters and SASEs should be directed to:

(Ms.) Tracy Karns, Editor

OXFORD UNIVERSITY PRESS
(See Directory of University Presses)

OXMOOR HOUSE
P.O. Box 2262
Birmingham, AL 35201
800-366-4712

Among Oxmoor's areas of general book-publishing interest are cooking, gardening, decorating, home improvement, crafts, art, sports, hobbies, travel, how-to, and personal finance. Many Oxmoor titles are issued in tandem with how-to videos; the house also produces software products. Leisure Arts is an Oxmoor imprint that produces a line of attractive, reasonably priced volumes covering roughly the same domain as Oxmoor's program.

Oxmoor House (started in 1968) is a subsidiary of Southern Progress Corporation, which is a division of Sunset Publishing Corporation, a part of the Time Warner communications conglomerate. Within this corporate domain, Oxmoor House remains essentially a smaller publisher of general adult nonfiction.

Most Oxmoor titles are originated in house, with a large percentage of its titles representing the book-publishing incarnation of several massively circulated and specialist magazines including *Money*, *Sports Illustrated*, *Southern Living*, *Sunset*, *People*, and *Time*.

Oxmoor, thus, is not a likely home for an original trade-book publishing project, but it constitutes another place to investigate when spelunking for freelance writing gigs.

Characteristic of the Oxmoor list: *Quick Quilts from the Heart* by Marianne Fons and Liz Porter, *Fitting Finesse* by Nancy Zieman, *The Cookie Jar*, *Alma-Lynne's Cross-Stitch for Special Occasions*, and the word-and-picture volume *Wayfarer* by James Dickey and William A. Bake.

Oxmoor House is distributed by Sunset Publishing Corporation.

Query letters and SASEs should be directed to:

Nancy Fitzpatrick, Vice President and Editor in Chief
Crafts, including cross-stitch, quilting, bazaar crafts.

Ann Harvey, Editor
Special publications.

Susan Payne, Senior Food Editor
Cookbooks.

PALADIN PRESS
Box 1307
Boulder, CO 80306
303-443-7250

Paladin issues new titles and reprints in categories such as new identity and personal freedom, espionage and investigation, explosives and demolitions, weapons, military science, ninjutsu, revenge and humor, special forces, survival, martial arts, action careers, sniping, knives and knife fighting, locksmithing, self-defense, police science, terrorism, silencers, and history and culture relating to the above fields, as well as selected general-interest books. Paladin also purveys a video library. Paladin Press (established in 1970) is a division of Paladin Enterprises.

Certain Paladin titles exhibit a markedly subversive approach, and are intended as high-edge, satiric amusement. It should be further noted that particular works on the Paladin list contain material that may be restricted in some jurisdictions and are sold for academic, research, or informational reference purposes only.

From the Paladin catalog: *The One-Round War: USMC Scout-Snipers in Vietnam* by Peter R. Senich, *Body for Sale: An Inside Look at Medical Research, Drug Testing, and Organ Transplants and How You Can Profit From Them* by Ed Brassard, *Bodyguarding: A Complete Manual* by Burt Rapp and Tony Lesce, *How to Investigate by Computer* by Ralph D. Thomas, *The On-Line Expert: Get the Best Results with On-*

Line Searches by Ralph D. Thomas, *Speed Training: How to Develop Your Maximum Speed for Martial Arts* by Loren Christensen, and *Swiss Money Secrets: How You Can Legally Hide Your Money in Switzerland* by Adam Starchild.

Highlights from the backlist: *Private Eyes: What Private Investigators Really Do* by Sam Brown and Gini Graham Scott, *Secrets of Successful Process Serving: How to Start a Successful Service of Process Business and Make It Grow* by Nelson Tucker, *Zips, Pipes, and Pens: Arsenal of Improvised Weapons* by J. David Truby, *Life after Debt: The Complete Credit Restoration Kit* by Bob Hammond, and *Scram: Relocating Under a New Identity* by James S. Martin.

Paladin Press is looking for original manuscripts on combat shooting, firearms and exotic weapons, personal and financial freedom, military science, and other action topics. For more information, call or write the publisher for a copy of the *Author Style Guide* and *Insider Newsletter.*

Paladin Press distributes its own list and also services individual orders via toll-free ordering numbers.

Query letters and SASEs should be directed to:

Jon Ford, Editorial Director

PARAGON HOUSE PUBLISHERS

370 Lexington Avenue
New York, NY 10017
212-953-5950

Paragon House focuses on an interdisciplinary approach to philosophy, critical thought, and religious culture. The Paragon line is further typified by concentration in categories such as issues in philosophy, ethics and morality, philosophy and society, world religions, religion and society, spirituality, and reference.

Paragon House titles in philosophy and religion are distributed primarily in the academic and scholarly market; also on the roster are general trade books in popular areas related to the house's core interests. The house (founded in 1982) publishes trade paperback and hardcover editions.

From the Paragon list: *Critical Theory: The Essential Readings* (edited by David Ingram and Julia Simon-Ingram), *Enemies without Guns: The Catholic Church in China* by James T. Myers, *First Person Mortal* by Lucy Bregman and Sara Thiermann, *From Behind the Wall: Commentary on Crime, Punishment, Race, and the Underclass by a Prison Inmate* by Mansfield B. Frazier, *Nature's Web: Rethinking Our Place on Earth* by Peter Marshall, *Path of the Kabbalah* by David Sheinkin, *The Soul: An Owner's Manual* by George Jaidar, *Through the Moral Maze: Searching for Absolute Values in a Pluralistic World* by Robert Hilary Kane, and *Work and Employment* (edited by David Marsland),

Paragon House distributes through Continuum Publishing Group, in care of Publisher Resources (800-937-5557).

Query letters and SASEs should be directed to:

Michael Giampaoli, Publisher
Spirituality, New Age books.

Roy Carlisle, Senior Editor
Philosophy and religion.

PARAMOUNT COMMUNICATIONS
PARAMOUNT PUBLISHING

(See Simon & Schuster)

PASSPORT BOOKS

(See NTC Publishing Group)

PATHFINDER PRESS

410 West Street
New York, NY 10014
212-741-0690

The Pathfinder program catalogs areas such as black and African studies; women's rights; the Cuban revolution in world politics; revolutionaries and working-class fighters; fascism, big business, and the labor movement; Russia, Eastern Europe, and the Balkans; scientific views of politics and economics; trade unions: past, present, and future; United States history and political issues; Latin America and the Caribbean; the Middle East and China; and art, culture, and politics.

Pathfinder Press (established in 1940) issues books, booklets, pamphlets, posters, and postcards keyed to issues affecting working people worldwide. Pathfinder titles often suggest a perspective associated with such academic and popular movements and streams of thought as populism, internationalism, utopianism, socialism, and communism. Pathfinder publishes the journal *New International*.

The Pathfinder Mural adorning the company's editorial and manufacturing digs in Manhattan's Far West Village features a depiction of a gargantuan printing press in action as well as portraits of revolutionary leaders whose writings and speeches are published by Pathfinder. This community cultural landmark represents the work of more than eighty artists from twenty countries.

Representative Pathfinder books: *Bolivian Diary* by Ernesto (Che) Guevara (in a new translation by Inti Peredo); *The Changing Face of U.S. Politics: Working-Class*

Politics and the Trade Unions by Jack Barnes; *Peru's Shining Path: Anatomy of a Reactionary Sect* by Martín Koppel; *Sexism and Science* by Evelyn Reed; *Origins of Materialism* by George Novack; *The Truth About Yugoslavia: Why Working People Should Oppose Intervention* by George Fyson, Argiris Malapanis, and Jonathan Silberman; and *Lenny Bruce: The Comedian as Social Critic and Secular Moralist* by Frank Kofsky.

Special Pathfinder series include Malcolm X: Speeches and Writings, as well as written works and spoken words from James P. Cannon, Eugene V. Debs, Farrell Dobbs, Carlos Fonseca, Mother Jones, Rosa Luxemburg, Nelson Mandela, Fidel Castro, and Ernesto (Che) Guevara. The house also publishes the works of Karl Marx, Frederick Engels, V. I. Lenin, and Leon Trotsky. Pathfinder produces titles in a number of languages, including Spanish, French, Farsi, Icelandic, Swedish, and Russian.

Pathfinder runs a number of bookstores around the world and offers membership in a readers' club for an annual fee (entitling members to enjoy special discounts). Individual orders are payable via Visa and Mastercard. Pathfinder Press distributes its own publications in the United States and worldwide primarily through its own fulfillment centers.

Query letters and SASEs should be directed to:

Michael Baumann, Editorial Director
Projects consistent with the Pathfinder list.

PAULIST PRESS

See Directory of Religious, Spiritual, and Inspirational Publishers)

PEACHPIT PRESS

2414 Sixth Street
Berkeley, CA 94710
510-548-4393

Peachpit is a specialist computer-publishing house with a list that accents personal computing and desktop publishing for business and recreational users. Peachpit publishes books and book/software packages (including CD-ROM products) that tackle basic practical tasks and troubleshooting as well as advanced applications.

Peachpit catalogs titles in the areas of introductory books, general Macintosh, Macintosh Bible series, desktop publishing, graphics, Windows and Windows applications, word processing, and related topics. Many Peachpit releases are keyed to particular proprietary products.

Peachpit's editorial approach to the computing world is make it relevant, make it dramatic, make it fun. Peachpit authors are at the forefront of ongoing technological developments and trends in computer hardware and software development, and masterful at teasing out the nuances of end-user potential in print.

Peachpit Press (founded in 1986) was acquired by Addison-Wesley in late 1994; the house maintains its independent editorial stance and gains financial and distributional leverage to benefit its worthy list.

Peachpit is not only in the book business, and not only a player on the computer-business stage: Peachpit is also in the teaching business. In addition to trade bookstores and computer venues, Peachpit hits a variety of market sectors such as schools and educational enterprises (including evening classes and adult ed); library, institutional and corporate consumers; and end-user and professional groups.

Sample titles from Peachpit: *Electronic Highway Robbery: An Artist's Guide to Copyrights in the Digital Era* by Mary Carter, *Aether Madness: An Offbeat Guide to the Online World* by Gary Wolf and Michael Stein, *Zap! How Your Computer Can Hurt You—and What You Can Do about It* by Don Sellers, *How to Boss Your Fonts Around* by Robin Williams, *Silicon Mirage: The Art and Science of Virtual Reality* by Steve Aukstakalnis and David Blatner, and *The Computer Privacy Handbook* by André Bacard.

Peachpit Press is distributed through the parent Addison-Wesley Publishing Company.

Query letters and SASEs should be directed to:

Ted Nace, Publisher

PEACHTREE PUBLISHERS, LTD.

494 Armour Circle Northeast
Atlanta, GA 30324
404-876-8761

Peachtree publishes general trade nonfiction and commercial literary fiction, and offers a substantial and growing children's list. Peachtree has a concentration in markedly innovative books in self-help, self-awareness, and self-improvement, as well as parenting, cooking and gardening, and humor. A special area of Peachtree publishing interest encompasses regional topics including the American South in general and the state of Georgia in particular. Peachtree is also known for its storytelling series.

Peachtree Publishers (established in 1978) is a midsize house that produces books in hardcover and trade paperback editions and offers selected works in electronic recorded formats. Peachtree hosts a hardy backlist.

From Peachtree: *Archival Atlanta: Electric Street Dummies, the Great Stonehenge Explosion, Nerve Tonics and Bovine Laws* by Perry Buffington and Kim Underwood, *The Hiking Trails of North Georgia* by Tim Homan with the Georgia Conservancy, *Margaret Mitchell & John Marsh: The Love Story Behind Gone With the Wind* by Marianne Walker, *Cooking in the New South: A Modern Approach to Traditional Southern Fare* by Anne Byrne, *Humor At Work: The Guaranteed, Bottom-Line, Low-*

Cost, High-Efficiency Guide to Success through Humor by Esther Blumenfeld and Lynne Alpern, and *The Single Mother's Book: A Practical Guide to Managing Your Children, Career, Home, Finances, and Everything Else* by Joan Anderson.

Individualist Peachtree projects: *Out to Pasture* by Effie Leland Wilder (illustrated by Laurie Klein) is a humorous and perceptive coming-of-age tale for older adults. *Growing Up Cuban in Decatur, Georgia* by Carmen Agra Deedy combines the rich traditions of her southern upbringing and her Latin American culture in a blend of delightful stories, many of which have been heard on National Public Radio's "All Things Considered." *The New Austerities* by Tito Perdue features a dramatic antimodernist approach to going-home-to-Alabama fiction.

Peachtree distributes its own list to the trade with the assistance of regional sales representatives.

PEACHTREE CHILDREN'S BOOKS

Children's editions from Peachtree encompass award-winning frontlist illustrated storybooks for younger readers as well as a select group of works directed toward parents. Peachtree Jr. is a line of chapter books targeted for ages eight years and up. The AllStar SportStory series combines contemporary tales with sports history and statistics.

Titles of note: *Teaching Your Child the Language of Social Success* by Marshall Duke, Stephen Nowicki Jr., and Elizabeth Martin; *Herman & Marguerite* (an environmental story) by Jay O'Callahan (illustrated by Laura O'Callahan); *Kishina: A True Story of Gorilla Survival* by Maxine Rock; *The Tree That Owns Itself and Other Adventure Tales from Out of the Past* by Loretta C. Hammer and Gail Kanwoski (illustrated by James Watling); and *T. J.'s Secret Pitch* (in the AllStar SportStory series) by Fred Bowen (illustrated by Jim Thorpe).

Backlist favorites: *Once Upon a Child: Writing Your Child's Special Story* by Debbie McChesney (illustrated by Sarah Carter), *When You Were a Baby* (written and photographed by Deborah Shaw Lewis and Gregg Lewis), *Orange Cheeks* (written by Jay O'Callahan and illustrated by Patricia Raine; issued along with a line of audios from storyteller Jay), and *When Someone Dies* (written by Sharon Grenlee and illustrated by Bill Drath).

Query letters and SASEs should be directed to:

Margaret M. Quinlin, President and Publisher

PELICAN PUBLISHING COMPANY

P.O. Box 3110
1101 Monroe Street
Gretna, LA 70053
504-368-1175

Pelican Publishing Company (founded in 1926) is primarily a nonfiction publisher with general trade interests and a specialty list in travel and lifestyle guides, Americana, cookbooks, art and architecture, photography, humor, sports, motivational and inspirational titles, as well as children's books. Many Pelican titles offer a regional or cultural perspective in areas such as the American South, Civil War history, Louisiana and the New Orleans environs, and Scottish-American heritage. Pelican also publishes a select group of fiction works, many of which have a regional or historical twist.

Pelican's travel series include the Maverick Guides, International Guides, and Marmac Guides. Other Pelican series include New Orleans Architecture, the Best Editorial Cartoons of the Year, and the Clovis Crawfish series for Cajun kids.

From Pelican: *Oswald Talked: The New Evidence in the JFK Assassination* by Ray and Mary La Fontaine, *Why Not Freedom! America's Revolt against Big Government* by James Ronald Kennedy and Walter Donald Kennedy, *The Psychology of Persuasion: How to Persuade Others to Your Way of Thinking* by Kevin Hogan, *One on One: The Secrets of Professional Sales Closing* by Ian Seymour, *Golf at St. Andrews* by Keith Mackie, *The Tomato Cookbook* by Roy F. Guste Jr., *Bad Back: Coping for Life* by Lucy M. Dobkins, *Why Cowboys Sleep with Their Boots On* by Laurie Lazzaro Knowlton (illustrated by James Rice), *Mardi Gras Indians* by Michael P. Smith, and *The Best Editorial Cartoons of the Year* (a collection issued yearly; edited by Charles Brooks).

Pelican children's books include these backlist favorites: *Toby Belfer's Seder: A Passover Story Retold* by Gloria Teles Pushker (illustrated by Judith Hierstein), *Eyr the Hunter: A Story of Ice-Age America* by Margaret Zehmer Searcy (illustrated by Joyce Haynes), and *Little Freddie at the Kentucky Derby* by Kathryn Cocquyt (illustrated by Sylvia Corbett).

Pelican Publishing Company handles its own distribution.

Query letters and SASEs should be sent to:

Milburn Calhoun, Publisher

Penguin USA
Viking
Dutton
Donald I. Fine Books

375 Hudson Street
New York, NY 10014
212-366-2000

Penguin USA is a major publishing group that encapsulates what are essentially two large divisions: Viking Penguin and Dutton/Signet. Under this stunning set of wings, Penguin USA offers a wealth of distinctive and distinguished lines and imprints. The house produces books in hardcover, trade paper, and mass-market paperback editions.

Penguin USA maintains an industry presence with a list that is clearly commercial in orientation while offering selected literary titles. Within the Penguin USA establishment are Viking, Penguin, and Studio (which make up the Viking Penguin division).

The Dutton/Signet division comprises Dutton, Mentor, New American Library, Obelisk, Onyx, Plume, Roc, Signet, and Topaz.

Included in the Penguin USA lineup are several children's-book divisions, among them Cobblehill, Dial Books for Young Readers, Dutton Children's Books, Lodestar, Puffin, and Viking Children's Books (please see subentry below for Penguin USA children's divisions).

Penguin USA is also home to the Frederick Warne imprint, Arkana, Virago Modern Classics, and the autonomous imprint Truman M. Talley Books, as well as the subsidiary Stephen Greene Press. The formerly independent publishing house Donald I. Fine is owned by Penguin USA (please see subentry below for Donald I. Fine/Dutton).

Penguin USA mass-market originals are published under a variety of specialty imprints as part of the Dutton program that includes Signet, Obelisk, Onyx, Roc, Topaz, and the affiliated DAW Books (please see also the subentry below for Dutton, as well as separate DAW Books Inc. main entry). These imprints produce a vast selection of mass-market category novels in areas such as historical romance, horror, science fiction and fantasy, mystery and suspense, and Westerns.

Penguin USA distributes for all divisions and imprints in the group and also handles books published by a number of houses including Sports Illustrated, Hamish Hamilton, and Michael Joseph.

The Viking Penguin program does not accept unsolicited manuscripts *or queries*. Any materials sent to the house with SASE is returned *unread*. Anything without SASE is recycled. The house accepts only agented or otherwise solicited work. *The acquisitions contacts listed below are for information and reference purposes.*

VIKING

Viking fields of interest encompass the trade spectrum, with fiction in all the mainstream literary categories including a fine line in mystery and suspense, and nonfiction titles in current events, popular and academic history, personal finance, cooking and food, lifestyle and design, travel, health, music, popular philosophy, self-help, women's studies, history, general reference, essays, biography and autobiography, and literary criticism. Viking's output includes books for young readers (please see below under Penguin USA children's divisions).

Viking (an imprint of the Viking Penguin division of Penguin USA) publishes hardcover trade fiction and nonfiction under its captivating, illustrious logo of a seafaring dragon ship. Viking's publishing program is manifold, spinning off many of its originals in paper editions via Penguin (see Penguin subentry below for representative titles).

Query letters and SASEs should be directed to:

Barbara Grossman, Publisher
Wide-ranging nonfiction interests; some fiction.

Pamela Dorman, Executive Editor
Commercial fiction, especially women's fiction and suspense. Nonfiction interests include self-help and psychology, investigative stories and narrative nonfiction, popular inspiration, popular reference, and women's issues.

Dawn Drzal, Senior Editor
Food, cooking, and wine; science, mathematics, and technology; nature and environment.

Donald Fehr, Senior Editor
Nonfiction, especially biography.

Al Silverman, Editor at Large
Mysteries and thrillers, American history (political, literary, social), twentieth century biography, military history, current events, sports.

Wendy Weil, Senior Editor
Nonfiction, especially music, culture, humor.

Mindy Werner, Executive Editor
Women's issues, Judaism, contemporary issues, health, true crime, and parenting. Literary and commercial fiction.

PENGUIN

Penguin (founded in 1935) is an imprint of the Viking Penguin division of Penguin USA. Penguin was initiated with the vision of making great books available—and affordable—to a broad audience. Publishing under the widely recognized imprint of its emblematic penguin cartouche, the house retains a paperback orientation and operates a program that encompasses both originals and reprints, with a broad scope in fiction and nonfiction. Many Viking hardcover books are reprinted in Penguin paperback.

In addition to the celebrated Penguin Classics line, the imprint features the Viking Portable series, the Viking Critical Library, the Penguin Nature Classics, the Penguin Travel Library, and Penguin Twentieth-Century Classics. Penguin offers an acclaimed assortment of poetry that accents contemporary voices (including titles in the Penguin Poets line). The Arkana imprint is devoted to spirituality and philosophy. Penguin is always on the lookout for strong, original trade-paperback titles.

In 1996, Penguin launched Penguin Ediciones, a paperback line of books written in Spanish; authors include Carlos Fuentes, Gabriel Garcia Marques, and Manuel Puig.

Representative Viking Penguin nonfiction: *The Money Diet* by Ginger Applegarth, *Ms. Miller's Etiquette for Cats* by Melissa Miller, *How to Find the Work You Love* by Laurence C. Boldt, *Daniel Johnnes's Top 200 Wines* by Daniel Johnnes, *The Budget Gardener* by Maureen Gilmer, *From Paperclips to Printers* (cost-cutting home-office how-to) by Dean and Jessica King, *Speaking with the Devil: A Dialogue with Evil* by Carl Goldberg, *Going Global: Four Entrepreneurs Map the New World Marketplace* by William C. Taylor and Alan M. Webber, *Lost and Found: The 9,000 Treasures of Tros—Heinrich Schliemann and the Gold That Got Away* by Caroline Moorehead, and *Combat Golf: The Competitor's Field Manual for Winning against Any Opponent* by Captain Bruce Warren Ollstein.

Among Viking Penguin fiction and literary highlights are *How Stella Got Her Groove Back* by Terry McMillan, *Because We Are Here* by Chuck Wachtel, *The Possessions of a Lady* by Jonathan Gash, *Soultown* (a Whitney Logan mystery) by Mercedes Lambert, *Biggest Elvis* by P. F. Kluge, *Trail of Secrets* by Eileen Goudge,

The Woman Who Walked into Doors by Roddy Doyle, *Nice Girls Finish Last* (a Robin Hudson Mystery) by Sparkle Hayter, *The Serpent Garden* by Judith Merkle Riley, *The Frog* by John Hawkes, *Keith Haring: Journals* by Keith Haring, *A Boy Named Phyllis: A Suburban Memoir* by Frank DeCaro, *The Penguin Book of Erotic Stories by Women* (edited by Richard Glynn Jones and A. Susan Williams), *My First White Friend: Confessions on Race, Love, and Forgiveness* by Patricia Raybon, and *Volcano and Miracle: A Selection of Fiction and Nonfiction from the Journal Written at Night* (edited by Gustaw Herling).

Strong sellers in fiction destined for reprint success: *Felicia's Journey* by William Trevor, *The Cunning Man* by Robertson Davies, *Redeye* by Clyde Edgerton, *Songs in Ordinary Time* by Mary McGarry Morris, *Rose Madder* by Stephen King, *Speaking in Tongues* by Jeffrey Deaver, and *At Home in Mitford* by Jan Karon.

Query letters and SASEs should be directed to:

Kathryn Court, Publisher
Literary and commercial fiction, including Third World and European fiction. Nonfiction interests include humor, travel writing, biography, current affairs, business, nature, women's issues, and true crime.

Marion Maneker, Editor
History, politics, business, current affairs.

Michael Millman, Senior Editor
Oversees the Penguin Classics and Twentieth-Century Classics, the Viking Portable Library, and the Penguin Nature Classics series.

Kristine Puopolo, Assistant Editor
Commercial projects in nonfiction and fiction.

David Stanford, Senior Editor
Nonfiction paperback originals with backlist potential in several areas: popular culture, music, humor, current events, environment. Also hardcover and/or paperback originals for the Arkana imprint, which publishes spiritual literature in areas including mythology, Zen, Tibetan Buddhism, women's spirituality, and Western traditions. Oversees Penguin Poets, which publishes six original poetry works per year.

Jane von Mehren, Executive Editor
Health and social issues, self-help, child care and parenting, nature, popular culture, and personal stories, as well as contemporary and historical commercial fiction.

Caroline White, Editor
Literary fiction, women's issues, memoirs, sociology, religion, film and television, popular culture.

STUDIO BOOKS

Studio publishes commercial, illustrated publications (primarily books, as well as related merchandise such as calendars) for adults in all subject categories and in all price ranges. Studio titles tend toward high-interest frontlist offerings in art and culture, fashion and design, lifestyle, and sports, with interests that cross over into arenas such as health and nutrition, popular psychology and inspiration, humor, works with social and historical themes, and literary writing.

Representing the Studio lineup: *The Complete Book of Irish Country Cooking: Traditional and Wholesome Recipes from Ireland* by Darina Allen, *The Healing Bath: Holistic Bubbles and Soothing Soaks* by Maribeth Riggs (paintings by Sir Lawrence Alma-Tadema), *Glorious American Quilts: The Quilt Collection of the Museum of American Folk Art* by Elizabeth V. Warren and Sharon L. Eisenstat, *Kitchens for Cooks: Planning Your Perfect Kitchen* by Deborah Krasner, *The Blue Dog Art Calendar* by George Rodrigue, *The Complete Home Office* by Alvin Rosenbaum, *The Romanov Legacy* by Zoia Belyakova, *Amen: A Gathering of Forty Prayers and Blessings from Around the World* by Emily Gwathmey and Suzanne Slesin, and *Mud Hens and Mavericks: The Illustrated Travel Guide to the Minor Leagues* by Judith Blahnik and Philip S. Schulz.

Query letters and SASEs should be directed to:

Michael Frangonito, Publisher
Music, history, sports, nostalgia, social issues and current events, science and technology, humor, and how-to.

Barbara Williams, Executive Editor
The occult; women's issues; popular culture, reference, medicine, psychology, and health; food and cooking; decorating and design; illustrated fiction.

Cyril Nelson, Senior Editor
Folk art and crafts, gardening, quilting, collecting, antiques, and architecture.

Sarah Scheffel, Associate Editor
Interests consistent with the house list.

Martha Schueneman, Associate Editor
All popular illustrated-book subjects; child care and parenting, art, and photography.

Christopher Sweet, Executive Director

DUTTON

Dutton spans the spectrum of trade categories in fiction and nonfiction. The house produces a substantial list in mainstream and contemporary fiction, with an emphasis in top-rank suspense and mystery novels, science fiction and fantasy, Westerns, and literary works. Dutton is also a major player in popular nonfiction areas, including current events, biography and memoirs, business and careers, parenting and the family, psychology and inspiration, cultural studies, history, science, and reference.

The Dutton division of Penguin USA is a corporate incarnation of the former E. P. Dutton. Under the Dutton umbrella are a number of imprints, including Signet, Onyx, Topaz, Truman Talley Books, and the William Abrahams line.

Plume publishes primarily trade paperback nonfiction and fiction, original titles as well as reprints. Plume accents commercial nonfiction and selected high-interest contemporary fiction, as well as classics and literary works. Plume also produces a variety of television and film tie-ins and a strong line of popular nutrition, health, and self-improvement titles.

Indicative of the Dutton program in fiction, literary works, and letters: *The World on Blood* by Jonathan Nasaw, *Millionaires Row* by Norman Katkov, *Gossip* by Christopher Bram, *Touched* by Carolyn Haines, *Streets of Fire* by Soledad Santiago, *Fearful Symmetry* by Greg Bills, *Infamous* by Joan Collins, *No Use Dying over Spilled Milk: A Pennsylvania Dutch Mystery with Recipes* by Tamar Myers, *Bad Angel* by Helen Benedict, and *First Cases: First Appearances of Classic Private Eyes* (edited by Robert J. Randisi).

Dutton has published authors such as Nancy Taylor Rosenberg, Helena Maria Viramontes, Lisa Appignanesi, Lisa Alther, Dorothy Allison, Joyce Carol Oates, Julia Alvarez, Max Allan Collins, Joan Hess, Lawrence Block, and Christopher Bram.

Representative Dutton nonfiction: *What Women Want* by Patricia Ireland, *Harriet Roth's Deliciously Healthy Jewish Cooking: 350 New Low-Fat, Low-Cholesterol, Low-Sodium Recipes for Holidays and Every Day* by Harriet Roth, *Facing the Wolf: Inside the Process of Deep Feeling Therapy* by Theresa Sheppard Alexander, *The Directory of Saints: A Concise Guide to Patron Saints* by Annette Sandoval, *Howard Hughes: The Untold Story* by Peter Harry Brown and Pat H. Broeske, *Behind Blue Eyes: The Life of Pete Townshend* by Geoffrey Giuliano, *Split Image: The Life of Anthony Perkins* by Charles Winecoff, *Growing Myself: A Spiritual Journey through Gardening* by Judith Handelsman, *Faith of Our Fathers: African-American Men Reflect on Fatherhood* (edited by Andre Willis), *Mama's Boy: The True Story of a Serial Killer and His Mother* by Richard T. Pienciak, and *Orion's Legacy: A Cultural History of Man As Hunter* by Charles Bergman.

Query letters and SASEs should be directed to:

Rosemary Ahern, Senior Editor
Scholarly/academic books. Literary fiction.

Peter Borland, Senior Editor
Film and television tie-ins.

Deb Brody, Senior Editor
Self-help and popular psychology.

Matthew Carnicelli, Editor
General nonfiction, popular business.

Arnold Dolin, Editorial Director
General nonfiction ranging from business to psychology, contemporary political and social issues, theater, and the entertainment media. Literary fiction.

Carole DeSanti, Executive Editor
Cookbooks, diet, women's issues.

Dierdre Mullane, Senior Editor
Serious nonfiction, science, multicultural literary fiction.

(Ms.) Michaela Hamilton, Editorial Director, Signet and Onyx
True crime, popular psychology, subjects pertinent to relationships. Commercial fiction.

Audrey LaFehr, Executive Editor
Women's fiction.

Constance Martin, Senior Editor
Women's fiction.

Julia Moshin, Editor
Cookbooks, Signet classics, literary fiction.

Danielle Perez, Editor, Dutton/Signet
Commercial fiction, mysteries and suspense. General nonfiction, spirituality.

Joe Pittman, Editor
Thrillers, mysteries, fiction.

Hugh Rawson, Editorial Director, Penguin Reference
Reference, military history.

(Ms.) Hilary Ross, Associate Executive Editor
Women's fiction and romances.

Jennifer Sawyer, Senior Editor, Dutton/Signet
Romance, commercial women's fiction, mysteries, suspense, thrillers; would consider a truly outstanding concept in horror. Looking for writers who show freshness and an edge.

Truman M. Talley, Publisher, Truman M. Talley Books
Business, general history, biography.

DONALD I. FINE BOOKS/DUTTON

Dutton's Fine imprint (formerly the independent house Donald I. Fine, Inc.) hosts a topflight genre list in the fiction categories of mysteries, technothrillers, suspense, and science fiction, along with a selection of high-interest nonfiction.

Donald I. Fine, founder and former publisher of Arbor House, created Donald I. Fine, Inc., in 1983. The company grew to become a medium-sized producer of hardcover and trade paperback books with a discriminating list of adult fiction and nonfiction works. The Fine persona was among an elect group of publishers with an editorial sense that exhibited both literary depth and commercial appeal. With the acquisition by Penguin USA (in late 1995), the imprint maintains a considerable brace of successful volumes on an extensive backlist.

Fiction from Fine includes *Grand Jury* by Philip Friedman, *The Geezer Factory Murders* by Corinne Holt Sawyer, *The Third Sister* (a sequel to Jane Austen's *Sense and Sensibility*) by Julia Barrett, *True Confessions: The Novel* by Mary Bringle, *Green Lake* by S. K. Epperson, and *The Devil's Menagerie* by Louis Charbonneau.

From the Fine nonfiction portfolio: *La Moreau: A Biography of Jeanne Moreau* by Marianne Gray, *Nimitz: The Man and His Wars* by Randall Brink, *The Huntress: The True Saga of Dottie and Brandi Thorson, Modern Day Bounty Hunters* by Christopher Keane with Dottie Thorson, and *Seasons in Hell: With Billy Martin, Whitey Herzog, and "the Worst Baseball Teams in History," the 1973–1975 Texas Rangers* by Mike Shropshire.

The Primus imprint issues a line of original paperbacks as well as reprints, including the Primus Library of Contemporary Americana. Titles here are *A Sistermony* by Richard Stern, *Bardot: An Intimate Portrait* by Jeffrey Robinson, *In the Place of Fallen Leaves* by Tim Pears, *Widow's Walk: One Woman's Spiritual and Emotional Journey to a New Life* by Anne Hoasansky, and *How to Give Good Phone* by Lisa Collier Cool.

Query letters and SASEs should be directed to:

Donald I. Fine, Editor in Chief

Jason Poston, Editor

PENGUIN USA CHILDREN'S DIVISIONS

The Penguin children's book-publishing operations offer a panoply of distinctive divisions, imprints, and affiliates of Penguin's component houses, including Cobblehill Books, Dial Books for Young Readers, Dutton Children's Books, Lodestar Books, Puffin Books, and Viking Children's Books. Each imprint publishes a wide range of titles in a variety of formats, and each children's house is a recognized name in the industry. Taken together, this Penguin lineup represents a powerhouse in the young-reader arena.

The Cobblehill Books affiliate accents picture books with stories to tell, as well as nonfiction for the range of youthful readership. Among Cobblehill titles: *When the Wolves Return* (photoessay) by Ron Hirschi (photography by Thomas D. Mangelsen), *Kids In and Out of Trouble* by Margaret O. Hyde, *The Chicks' Trick* (written and illustrated by Jeni Bassett), *Emeka's Gift: An African Counting Story* (written and photographed by Ifeoma Onyefulu), and *The Haunting of Holroyd Hill* by Brenda Seabrooke.

Dial Books for Young Readers is a division that publishes for the spectrum from preschoolers through older readers. On the Dial list: *Boundless Grace* by Mary Hoffman, *It's a Spoon, Not a Shovel* by Caralyn Buehner (pictures by Mark Buehner), *Titanic Crossing* by Barbara Williams, *The Secret Code Book* (with press-out code-busters) by Helen Huckle, and *Do the Whales Still Sing?* by Dianne Hofmeyr (pictures by Jude Daly).

The Dutton Children's Books program includes humorous and serious titles for the youngest readers through young adults. Indicative of the Dutton list are *Jeremy Kooloo* by Tim Mahurin, *Dinner at Magritte's* (written and illustrated by Michael Garland), *Jimmy, the Pickpocket of the Palace* by Donna Jo Napoli (illustrated by Judith Byron Schachner), and *It's for You: An Amazing Picture-Puzzle Book* by John Talbot.

Lodestar Books offers a vigorous approach to fiction and nonfiction for all age groups, as well as an innovative line of activity books and specialty items. Lodestar fiction and nonfiction titles often have a social-issue edge and deal with phenomena such as ethnic experience, gender relations, art and culture, and sexual preference.

Representative Lodestar titles are *For Home and Country: A Civil War Scrapbook* by Norma Bolotin and Angela Herb, *Toads and Diamonds* (retold and illustrated by Robert Bender), *Paco and the Witch: A Puerto Rican Folktale* (retold by Felix Pitre; illustrations by Christy Hale; also available in Spanish as *Paco y la Bruja*, translated by

Osvaldo Blanco), and *Earth, Sky, and Beyond: A Journey through Space* by Jean-Pierre Verdet (illustrations by Pierre Bon).

Puffin Books is a division that produces the gamut of mainstream children's categories with an emphasis on popular-priced paperback picture-book editions for the youngest readers and novels and nonfiction for the older group. Sample Puffin entrants: *Glasses—Who Needs 'Em?* by Lane Smith, *The Day the Goose Got Loose* by Reeve Lindbergh (illustrated by Steven Kellogg), *Springtime* by Ann Schweninger, *Cats in the Sun* by Lesley Ann Ivory, and *The Sea Lion* by Ken Kesey (illustrated by Neil Waldman). Puffin Classics issues a line of traditional children's works in new editions. The house also produces Spanish-language books.

F. Warne & Company concentrates on reissues of works by historic masters such as Beatrix Potter and Cicely Mary Barker.

Viking Children's Books publishes a well-rounded list that includes picture books for the youngest readers as well as works aimed toward middle and older readership in fiction and nonfiction (some keyed to high-interest contemporary topics). The house also produces a respected reference line. Titles here are *Taking Flight: My Story* by Vicki Van Meter with Dan Gutman, *Two's Company* by Amanda Benjamin, *Dinosaurs: The Fastest, the Fiercest, the Most Amazing* by Elizabeth McLeod (illustrated by Gordon Sauvé), *The Encyclopedia of Native America* (edited by Trudy Griffin-Pierce), and *Undone! More Mad Endings* by Paul Jennings.

Query letters and SASEs should be directed to:

Jo Ann Daly, Editorial Director, Cobblehill Books

Rosanne Lauer, Executive Editor, Cobblehill Books

Virginia Buckley, Editorial Director, Lodestar Books

Phyllis Fogelman, Executive Editor, Dial Books for Young Readers

Cindy Kane, Senior Editor, Dial Books for Young Readers

Toby Sherry, Senior Editor, Dial Books for Young Readers
Acquires hardcover and paperbacks, gifts, and novelty products.

Tracy Tang, Publisher, Puffin Books

Regina Hayes, Publisher, Viking Children's Books

Deborah Brodie, Executive Editor, Viking Children's Books

PENTLAND PRESS, INC.

5124 Bur Oak Circle
Raleigh, NC 27612
919-782-0281
800-948-2786

Pentland is active in the areas of general fiction and nonfiction, including history, military, mystery, religion, science fiction, short stories, Westerns, autobiography, memoirs, music, poetry, romance, self-help, philosophy, and psychology.

Sample titles: *East of Tucson* (Western novel) by Walter Andrea, *Sweet' ning Relationships* (popular family psychology) by Thomas A. Gregg, *Maria* (historical women's fiction) by Margaret Haswell, and *The Saga of Phil and the Red Piece of Meat* (narrative poetry) by David Lindamood.

The house was formed in 1982 in Edinburgh, Scotland, as Pentland Press, Ltd., and has advanced to establish offices in Cambridge and Durham, England, in addition to its American offices (opened in 1993). Pentland is not known for grandiose advances; publishing contracts may involve cooperative investment or a subsidization commitment from the author.

Pentland Press is a member of COSMEP, Publishers Association of the South, and Southeast Booksellers Association Pentland's wholesale representation is through Baker and Taylor.

Query letters and SASEs should be directed to:

Arlene Calhoun, Editorial Director

THE PERMANENT PRESS/SECOND CHANCE PRESS

R.D. 2
Noyac Road
Sag Harbor, NY 11963
516-725-1101

Founded in 1978 by copublishers Judith and Martin Shepard, the Permanent Press mandate is to produce expressive, vital, and exciting nongenre fiction. The sine qua non here for titles is that they be artfully written. The Permanent Press publishes twelve books a year in cloth editions only. Selected out-of-print books are released in reprint under the Second Chance Press imprint.

The publishers present a handpicked list in which they firmly believe. Such dedication is not without payoff: Permanent Press titles generate considerable, favorable word of mouth among readers and booksellers, and reap the kinds of reviews that pique wide interest (particularly in the realm of subsidiary rights).

On the house roster: *Castle Garden* by Bill Albert, *Dear Otto* by Christopher Brookhouse, *Dobryd* by Amm Charney, *Cool's Ridge* by Ursula Perrin, *Smoking Hopes* by Victoria Alexander, *And the Angels Sing* by J. Madison Davis, *Night Train Blues* by Edward Hower, *Home Is the Exile* by Hilary Masters, *Chasing Shadows* (nonfiction) by Fred Wilcox, *The Stepman* by David Margolis, *Passing Off* (basketball/eco-terrorism) by Tom LeClair, *East Justice* by Melanie Braverman, and *Peregrine's Rest* (a Halloween story) by Jennifer Gostin.

News from the sub-rights front: *Résumé with Monsters* (science fiction) by William Browning Spencer has garnered foreign rights in at least two countries: Germany and Italy. The film option for *An Occasional Hell* (mystery) by Randall Silvis became an official purchase when the cameras started to roll.

Permanent Press handles its own distribution and is very active in the subsidiary rights arena.

Query letters and SASEs should be directed to:

Judith Shepard, Editor and Copublisher

PERSEA BOOKS, INC.

60 Madison Avenue
New York, NY 10010
212-779-7668

Persea's categories include essays, memoirs, literary criticism, novels and stories, fine arts and art history, scholarly works, social sciences, and gender and cultural studies.

Persea Books (founded by Michael Braziller in 1975) is an independently owned press that produces a discriminating list in trade and reference nonfiction, fiction and belles lettres, and poetry. Persea's contemporary literature has an international cast of eminent writers. Ontario Review Press is a Persea imprint that focuses on fiction and literary works.

Representative of the Persea program: *The Heart Knows Something Different: Teenage Voices from the Foster Care System* by Youth Communication (edited by Al Desetta), *The Shovel and the Loom* (novel) by Carl Friedman (translated from the Dutch by Jeannette Ringold), *Things Shaped in Passing: More "Poets of Life" Writing from the AIDS Pandemic* (edited by Michael Klein and Richard McCann), *Beyond Telling: Stories* by Jewel Mogan, *Paper Dance: 55 Latino Poets* (edited by Victor Hernández Cruz, Leroy V. Quintana, and Virgil Suarez), *Rhapsodies of a Repeat Offender: Poems* by Wayne Koestenbaum, and *Show Me a Hero: Great Contemporary Stories about Sports* (edited by Jeanne Schinto).

Ontario Review Press entrants include: *Women, Animals, and Vegetables: Essays and Stories* by Maxine Kumin and *Doris Lessing: Conversations* (edited by Earl G. Ingersoll).

Persea shares office space with and is distributed by George Braziller, Inc.

Query letters and SASEs should be sent to:

Karen Braziller, Editorial Director

PETERSON'S

P.O. Box 2123
Princeton, NJ 08543
609-243-9111

Peterson's accents the fields of college admissions, standardized-test preparation, graduate and professional studies, educational administration, job hunting and career opportunities, executive education, educational travel and adventure, and continuing education. Publications cover international work and study opportunities and also offer general resources for kids, teenagers, and families. Peterson's markets strongly to libraries and institutions, as well as to the corporate arena.

Peterson's (founded in 1966) is a leading publisher of educational and career resource and reference materials. Peterson's publications feature books, data services, and computer software (including CD-ROM). Peterson's initially specialized in guides to colleges and graduate schools; currently the house offers a broad selection of specialty reference works (many updated annually) and publishes information in a wide arena.

The Peterson's program highlights the best-selling *Guide to Four-Year Colleges* (updated annually; packaged with College Application Planner software). Also of note: *The Ultimate College Survival Guide* by Janet Farrar Worthington and Ronald Farrar, *Guide to Tennis Camps and Clinics* by Shirley A. Thompson and Joanie Stearns Brown, *The Working Mom's Book of Hints, Tips, and Everyday Wisdom* by Louise Lague, and *I Went to College for This?* by Garrett Soden.

Peterson's/Pacesetter is an imprint that covers "thinking books for thinking businesspeople." On the Pacesetter roster: *Conservative Innovation: Kicking the Newness Habit* by Ron Beyma, *Breaking Boundaries: Public Policy vs. American Business in the World Economy* by Joseph E. Pattison, *Runamok: A Novel about the Realities of Small Business* by Tom Park, *Business Briefs: 165 Guiding Principles from the World's Sharpest Minds* by Russell Wild, *Women Breaking Through: Overcoming the Final 10 Obstacles at Work* by Deborah J. Swiss, and *Quantum Companies II: 100 More Cutting-Edge, High-Growth Companies to Track into the 21st Century* by A. David Silver.

Peterson's handles its own distribution.

Query letters and SASEs should be directed to:

Jim Gish, Editor in Chief, Trade

Carol Hupping, Executive Editor
Education, careers, family.

Ian Gallagher, Senior Editor, Test Preparation

Pfeiffer & Company

8517 Production Avenue
San Diego, CA 92121-2280
619-578-5900

Pfeiffer's trade business list expands each season in areas such as career/personal development and general business/management. Pfeiffer also produces a dynamic array of training games, simulation/experiential-learning leader's manuals, computer software/CD-ROM, and audio- and videocassettes.

Pfeiffer & Company is an international house that specializes in business topics directed particularly toward trainers, consultants, and managers. With offices is Amsterdam, Johannesburg, London, Sydney, and Toronto, in addition to its United States home in San Diego, the Pfeiffer & Company scope is adamantly global.

Representing the Pfeiffer list: *Flawless Consulting* by Peter Block, *Healing the Wounds: Overcoming the Trauma of Layoffs and Revitalizing Downsized Organizations* by David M. Noer, *Intervention Skills: Process Consultation for Small Groups and Teams* by W. Brendan Reddy, *Jumpstarting Your New Team: Establishing Norms* by Ken S. Keleman, *Learning Organization Practices Profile* by Michael J. O'Brien, *Manager's Official Guide to Team Working* by Jerry Spiegel and Cresencio Torres, and *Networking: How to Enrich Your Life and Get Things Done* by Donald R. Woods and Shirley D. Ormerod.

Pfeiffer & Company distributes its own list; selected titles and lines are also available through business trade-book specialist imprints with which Pfeiffer engages in conjoint-publishing arrangements.

Query letters and SASEs should be directed to:

Joanne Paddet, Managing Editor

PFEIFFER-HAMILTON PUBLISHERS

210 West Michigan Street
Duluth, MN 55802
218-727-0500

Pfeiffer-Hamilton produces publications in self-awareness, motivation, and improvement, and also inspirational works and select children's titles. An additional Pfeiffer-Hamilton focus is on gift books about the Minnesota north country.

Pfeiffer-Hamilton Publishers (founded in 1985), along with its sibling company Whole Person Associates, develops stress-management and wellness training materials, including books, audiotapes, and videotapes. The house has achieved a number of major publishing hits. P-H's marketing strategy is to concentrate promotional efforts regionally prior to inaugurating national campaigns.

Some P-H successes: *Old Turtle* by Douglas Wood (a children's book with over a quarter-million copies sold, as well as the spin-off volume *Old Turtle Peace Journal*, edited by Nancy Tubesing), *The Duct Tape Book* (inspiration) by Jim and Tim (along with the follow-up book *Duct Tape 2: Real Stories*), *Overcoming Panic Attacks* (popular psychology) by Shirley Babior, and *Trailside Botany* (appreciation of the natural world) by John Bates.

Pfeiffer-Hamilton Publishers oversees its own distribution.

Query letters and SASEs should be directed to:

Ronald Tubesing, President

PINNACLE BOOKS

(See Kensington Publishing Corporation)

PIÑON PRESS

P.O. Box 35007
Colorado Springs, CO 80935
719-531-3556
800-955-3336 (catalog requests)

Piñon Press (founded in 1991) publishes in the areas of health and nutrition, psychology, self-awareness, parenting and the family, contemporary social issues, and lifestyle, as well as occasional works of fiction and literature. The house produces books in hardcover and trade paperback, and also purveys book-and-tape packages. Piñon releases a short list of new titles seasonally and maintains a full backlist.

Featured from Piñon: *Escaping the Coming Retirement Crisis: How to Secure Your Financial Future* by R. Theodore Benna with William Proctor, *Adult ADD: A Reader Friendly Guide to Identifying, Understanding, and Treating Adult Attention Deficit Disorder* by Thomas A. Whiteman and Michele Novotni, *Adopting the Hurt Child: Hope for Families with Special Needs Kids* by Gregory C. Keck and Regina M. Kupecky, *Who's to Blame? How to Deal with a Victim without Becoming One Yourself* by Carmen Renee Berry and Mark W. Baker, and *Food Smart! Eat Your Way to Better Health* by Cheryl Townsley.

Fiction and literary works include *I Went to the Animal Fair: A Journey through Madness to Meaning* by Heather Harpham, *Writing the River* (poetry) by Luci Shaw, and *Forgiving August* (novel) by Dudley J. Delffs.

Piñon Press handles its own distribution.

Piñon is in the process of redirecting its editorial direction, scope, and emphasis—as well as its personnel. Please inquire at the publisher directly before making any query or submission.

POCKET BOOKS

(See Simon & Schuster)

CLARKSON POTTER

(See Crown Publishing Group under Random House)

PRAEGER PUBLISHERS

(See Greenwood Publishing Group)

PRENTICE HALL
(See Simon & Schuster)

PRESIDIO PRESS
505B San Marin Drive, Suite 300
Novato, CA 94945-1340
415-898-1081

Presidio is known for works in areas such as general military history, American history, aviation, biography and memoirs, World Wars, Korean War, Vietnam, African-American studies, military theory, and professional studies. Presidio also issues a small number of superior fiction titles (often on the Lyford Books imprint) that favor a military-historical or action-adventure milieu.

Presidio Press (founded in 1974) is among America's foremost trade publishers of works in the military-services arena. The house emphasizes both popular and scholarly works, especially those with potential for backlist endurance. Presidio publishes in hardcover and quality paperback editions.

Presidio Press publications include *Lions of July: Prelude to War, 1914* by William Jannen Jr., *Soldiering: The Civil War Diary of Rice C. Bull* (edited by K. Jack Bauer), *Wahoo: The Patrols of America's Most Famous WWII Submarine* by Richard H. O'Kane, *On Strategy: A Critical Analysis of the Vietnam War* by Harry G. Summers, *Swimmers among the Trees: SEAL Operations in Vietnam, 1964–1972* by Joel Hutchins, *They Had a Dream: The Story of African-American Astronauts* by J. Alfred Phelps, and *Elvis in the Army: The King of Rock 'n' Roll As Seen by an Officer Who Served with Him* by William J. Taylor Jr.

Presidio fiction and literary works: *Tell Me a Tale* (historical African-American literature) by James McEachin, *Eagles* by Ray Rosenbaum (Book Four of the Wings of War saga), *Fenwick Travers and the Forbidden Kingdom: An Entertainment* by Raymond M. Saunders, *1901* (a what-if alternative history novel) by Robert Conroy, *Nantucket Revenge* (a Jake Eaton mystery) by Larry Maness, and *Cut-Out* (contemporary thriller) by Bob Mayer.

Presidio's Gulf War memoir, *She Went to War: The Rhonda Cornum Story* by flight surgeon Rhonda Cornum as told to Peter Copeland, garnered considerable subsidiary-rights interest—including a high-profile television-movie option.

Presidio Press titles, as well as those of associated imprints (such as British military publisher Greenhill Books), are distributed to the book trade in the United States and Canada by the Berkley Publishing Group.

Query letters and SASEs should be directed to:

(Mr.) E. J. McCarthy, Executive Editor

PRICE STERN SLOAN
(See Putnam Berkley Group)

PRIMA PUBLISHING

3875 Atherton Road
Rocklin, CA 95765
916-632-4400

Prima Publishing (founded in 1984) is an independent trade publisher with three principal lines—computer products division (CPD), entertainment, and lifestyles. Prima is among the fastest growing independent publishers in North America.

The Prima editorial operation embraces the areas of popular culture, current affairs and international events, business and entrepreneurship, careers, legal topics, biography, computer books (business and professional as well as games and edutainment), cooking, health, parenting and education, natural history and environmental issues, sports, music, psychology and self-help, and writing and reference.

The foremost publisher of electronic entertainment books under its Secrets of the Games imprint, Prima has produced the best-selling official strategy guides for *Myst*, *DOOM II*, and *The 7th Guest*. Prima's entertainment division also publishes fiction based on popular electronic and paper role-playing games under the Proteus imprint.

Prima's computer products division publishes computer productivity, programming, and Internet titles. The Visual Learning Guides series consists of easy-to-understand application guides geared to the layperson. Prima Online, the division's Internet series, includes the title *Build a Web Site: The Programmer's Guide to Creating, Building, and Maintaining a Web Presence* by net.Genesis and Devra Hall.

The company's lifestyle division specializes in general trade books in the parenting, personal finance, cooking, self-help, and health categories. Representative titles include the best-selling *Mary Kay: You Can Have It All* by Mary Kay Ash, the *Lean and Luscious* series of cookbooks by Bobbie Hinman and Millie Snyder, *The Wealthy Barber* by David Chilton, *Preventing and Reversing Osteoporosis: Every Woman's Essential Guide* by Alan R. Gaby, and *World Class Manager* by Gerhard Plenert. Prima is also the publisher of the book you are now reading, *Writer's Guide to Book Editors, Publishers, and Literary Agents* by Jeff Herman.

This year Prima introduced Forum, its serious nonfiction imprint. Topics covered include current affairs, public policy, libertarian/conservative thought, high-level management, individual empowerment, and historical biography. Forum titles include *Break These Chains: The Battle for School Choice* by Daniel McGroarty, *PBS: Behind the Screen* by Laurence Jarvik, *The Race Card* edited by Peter Collier and David Horowitz, and *Stalin: Triumph and Tragedy* by Dmitri Volkogonov.

Prima has its own national sales force and handles warehouse and fulfillment services through the Ballantine Publishing Group, a division of Random House.

Query letters and SASEs should be directed to:

Juliana Aldous, Acquisitions Editor, Entertainment Division

Jennifer Basye Sander, Senior Acquisitions Editor, Lifestyles Division

Daniel J. Francisco, Associate Acquisitions Editor, Entertainment Division

Alan Harris, Senior Acquisitions Editor, Computer Products Division

Georgia Hughes, Acquisitions Editor, Lifestyles Division

Debra Kempker, Publisher, Entertainment Division

Paula Munier Lee, Associate Publisher, Lifestyles Division

Steven K. Martin, Forum, Managing Editor, Lifestyles Division

Don Roche, Jr., Publisher, Computer Products Division

Ian Sheeler, Acquisitions Editor, Computer Products Division

Susan D. Silva, Acquisitions editor, Lifestyles Division

Amy Watson, Acquisitions Editor, Computer Products Division

PRINCETON UNIVERSITY PRESS
(See Directory of University Presses)

PROBUS PUBLISHING COMPANY
(See Irwin Professional Publishing)

PROFESSIONAL PUBLICATIONS, INC.
1250 Fifth Avenue
Belmont, CA 92002-3863
415-593-9119

Professional Publications provides engineering, accounting, and architecture titles, as well as works aimed at the broader business and professional trade arena. The house produces books and educational aids (such as flashcards, audiocassettes, videos, software, and study guides) directed toward the professional market.

Professional Publications (established in 1981) earned remarkable initial success with examination preparation packages (reference manual, ancillary workbooks, flashcards, sample questions) for the professional engineering license examination given to applicants in the major engineering disciplines. Once this niche market was secured, the house branched into wider publishing territory.

Titles from PPI include *Engineer-in-Training Reference Manual* by Michael R. Lindeburg, *Standard Handbook for Civil Engineers* (edited by Frederick S. Merritt), *High-Technology Degree Alternatives: Earning a High-Tech Degree While Working Full Time* by Joel Butler, *345 Solved Seismic Design Problems* by Majid Baradar, *Timber Design for the Civil PE Examination* by Robert L. Brungraber, *Land Surveyor Reference Manual* by Andrew I. Harbin, *Intellectual Property Protection: A Guide for Engineers* by Virginia Shaw Medlen, and *The Expert Witness Handbook: A Guide for Engineers* by D. G. Sunar.

Professional Publications oversees its own distribution; selected titles are offered to the trade through Harcourt Brace.

Query letters and SASEs should be directed to:

Gerry Galbo, Acquisitions Editor

PROMETHEUS BOOKS

59 John Glenn Drive
Amherst, NY 14228
716-691-0133

Prometheus catalogs works with challenging stances on contemporary issues in the areas of politics and current events, health and fitness, philosophy, sports, science, the paranormal, sexuality, literature and literary history, popular culture, and religion, as well as reference works in allied fields and occasional works of fiction. Prometheus also publishes books for young readers and a line of titles on human aging, and serves the educational market with several series of modestly priced classics in reprint (including Great Books in Philosophy and Great Minds). The house offers select works in electronic format.

Prometheus Books (established in 1969) produces an ambitious frontlist that embraces a wide range of perennially popular nonfiction topics; some of the more enduring titles are backlisted indefinitely.

Representative Prometheus projects: *Why I Am an Abortion Doctor* by Suzanne T. Poppema with Mike Henderson, *Brother Tony's Boys: The Largest Case of Child Prostitution in U.S. History* by Mike Echols, *Profiles of Power and Success: Fourteen Geniuses Who Broke the Rules* by Gene E. Landrum, *American Extremists: Militias, Supremacists, Klansmen, Communists, and Others* by John George and Laird Wilcox, *The Book of Wellness: A Secular Approach to Spirituality, Meaning, and Purpose* by Donald B. Ardell, *Prostate Cancer: Treatment and Recovery* by Richard Y. Handy, *Where Did Mary Go? A Loving Husband's Struggle with Alzheimer's* by Frank A. Wall, *Headslap: The Life and Times of Deacon Jones* by John Klawitter and Deacon Jones, and *Dancing Naked in the Material World* (a photodocumentary) by Marilyn Futterman.

Please note: Though known primarily as a house that operates on an advance/royalty arrangement, Prometheus has on occasion offered agreements to authors through which the author invests cooperatively in the costs and thus subsidizes publication.

Prometheus distributes its own list.

Query letters and SASEs should be directed to:

Steven Mitchell, Editorial Director

PUSHCART PRESS

Box 380
Wainscott, NY 11975
516-324-9300

Pushcart Press (established in 1973) is a small, personalized house that is emblematic of the mission to provide useful as well as entertaining trade books and reference volumes directed primarily toward writers, editors, small publishers, and literary aficionados. Pushcart Press is also a dedicated forum for fiction and nonfiction works of literary merit, and the house list includes many award-winning volumes.

Pushcart is known as the house that issues the established annual literary anthology *The Pushcart Prize: Best of the Small Presses*, in addition to the classic *The Publish-It-Yourself Handbook: Literary Tradition and How-To Without Commercial or Vanity Publishers* (both works edited by Pushcart publisher Bill Henderson). *The Pushcart Book of Essays* (edited by Anthony Brandt) expands the house's line of exemplary writing collections.

Ongoing Pushcart Press publishing projects include the Literary Companion series, the Editors' Book Award series, and Pushcart Rediscovery.

Titles from Pushcart: *To a Violent Grave: An Oral Biography of Jackson Pollock* by Jeffrey Potter, *Put That Quill Back in the Goose!* (edited by James Charlton), *Yeshua: The Gospel of St. Thomas* by Alan Decker McNary, *Garden State: A Novel* by Rick Moody, *Imagine a Great White Light* by Sheila Schwartz, *Writing for Your Life* by Sybil Steinberg, the anonymous *Autobiography of an Elderly Woman* (with an afterword by Doris Grumbach), and *The Tale of the Ring: A Kaddish* by Frank Stiffel.

Pushcart Press is distributed by W. W. Norton.

Query letters and SASEs should be directed to:

Bill Henderson, President

THE PUTNAM BERKLEY GROUP
PUTNAM & GROSSET/RIVERHEAD BOOKS/ TARCHER
PRICE STERN SLOAN/BOULEVARD/HP BOOKS

200 Madison Avenue
New York, NY 10016
212-951-8400

Founded in 1838 and subsequently known as G. P. Putnam's Sons, this house achieved renown as one of America's principal publishers. Over the past several decades the company has expanded dramatically. In 1965 Putnam acquired Berkley Books, and in 1975 the augmented enterprise was acquired by the communications conglomerate MCA, itself now part of the Seagram's Corporation wing that also incorporates Universal Studios.

The group's primary trade paper imprint, Perigee Books, was established in 1979, and since then additional divisions have been instituted, including the children's houses Philomel Books and Grosset & Dunlap (see under Putnam & Grosset subentry below). During the early 1990s, two formerly independent entities, Jeremy P. Tarcher and Price Stern Sloan (please see separate subentries below), have been brought under the corporate shield.

The Berkley Publishing Group—which comprises such lines as Berkley, Jove, Ace, and Boulevard—publishes trade and mass-market paperback reprints and originals in nonfiction and fiction, as well as selected hardcover originals.

The nomenclature and categorization of Putnam Berkley lists is flexible; designated projects can assume many different formats and experimental imprints. For example, hardcover genre-fiction releases may bear the Ace/Putnam stamp; Riverhead titles are catalogued under both Putnam (for hardcovers) and Berkley (trade paper originals and reprints); and trade titles in business, finance, and topical spirituality interest are often released as Tarcher/Putnam books.

Putnam New Media was initiated to ride the multimedia tide; for a rash of corporate reasons, during 1995, this division's assets were shifted under the umbrella of another of MCA's media enterprises.

Putnam distributes its own list and provides services for a number of other houses including Farrar Straus & Giroux.

THE PUTNAM PUBLISHING GROUP

200 Madison Avenue
New York, NY 10016
212-951-8400

The Putnam Publishing Group issues a full range of fiction and nonfiction hardcover trade books under the rubric of G. P. Putnam's Sons. Putnam's fiction encompasses frontlist novels, serious commercial fare, and works with contemporary literary flair, as well as topflight entrants in category fiction including mystery, science fiction, suspense, and historical novels. Putnam's nonfiction can embrace any and all areas of major commercial interest.

Special products are issued under such combination imprints as Grosset/Putnam (serious nonfiction), Ace/Putnam (category novels), and Tarcher/Putnam (business and professional; social issues). (See separate subentries below.)

Putnam fiction offers a star-studded lineup of authors, including works such as *That Camden Summer* by LaVyrle Spencer, *McNally's Puzzle* by Lawrence Sanders, *The Dark Room* by Minette Walters, *Man O' War* by William Shatner, *Seduced: The Life and Times of a One-Hit Wonder* by Nelson George, *Honky Tonk Kat* by Karen Kijewski, *Killing Critics* by Carol O'Connell, *Firestorm* by Nevada Barr, *Sudden Prey* by John Sandford, *Cold Fall* by John Gardner, *Drink with the Devil* by Jack Higgins, *Cause of Death* by Patricia Cornwell, and *Rosehaven* by Catherine Coulter.

Putnam produces spectacular omnibus fiction anthologies featuring powerhouse authors such as Tom Clancy, W. E. B. Griffin, Lilian Jackson Braun, Dean Koontz, and LaVyrle Spencer.

The Putnam nonfiction list includes *The Achievement Zone: 8 Skills for Winning All the Time from the Playing Field to the Boardroom* by Shane Murphy, *The Way of the Explorer: An Apollo Astronaut's Journey through the Material and Mystical Worlds* by Edgar Mitchell with Dwight Williams, *Extraordinary Golf: The Art of the Possible* by Fred Shoemaker with Pete Shoemaker, *The Maria Paradox: How Latinas Can Merge*

Old World Traditions with New World Self-Esteem by Rosa Maria Gil and Carmen Inoa Vazquez, *The Alchemy of Love and Lust: Discovering Our Sex Hormones and How They Determine Who We Love, When We Love, and How Often We Love* by Theresa L. Crenshaw, and *Smart Money Moves for African Americans* by Kelvin Boston.

Putnam distributes its own list to the trade.

Query letters and SASEs should be directed to:

Stacy Creamer, Vice President and Senior Editor
Fiction: thrillers, crime and detective novels, horror, medical themes. Nonfiction: true crime.

Liza Dawson, Executive Editor
Commercial fiction and nonfiction. Fiction: mysteries, women-oriented. Nonfiction: wide interests, especially parenting and psychology.

Laura Gaines, Assistant Editor
Serious and commercial fiction and nonfiction.

David Highfill, Senior Editor
Fiction: mysteries and mainstream novels, commercial nonfiction.

Neil Nyren, Publisher, G. P. Putnam's Sons
Serious and commercial fiction and nonfiction.

Christine Pepe, Senior Editor
Fiction: mysteries, thrillers, horror. Nonfiction: business, health, celebrity stories.

Faith Sale, Executive Editor
Serious fiction and nonfiction.

PERIGEE BOOKS

Perigee Books is the Putnam Publishing Group's mainline trade paperback imprint. Perigee acquires originals and reprints in all of the principal Putnam nonfiction categories.

Query letters and SASEs should be directed to:

John Duff, Publisher, Perigee Books
Wide range of commercial nonfiction, cookbooks, popular reference, self-help/how-to, family and parenting issues.

Sheila Curry, Senior Editor, Perigee Books
Spirituality, general nonfiction.

Suzanne Bober, Editor, Perigee Books
Nonfiction, self-help, relationships.

RIVERHEAD BOOKS

Riverhead publishes fiction and nonfiction hardcover and trade paperback originals and reprints. Riverhead fiction and literary works cover an array of serious, lively, and imaginative arenas, explore the frontiers of expression, and resound with the variety and depth of cultural experience. Nonfiction at Riverhead embraces psychology, history, popular culture, and sports; the house is also on the lookout for strong, creative works in religious and spiritual thought.

The Riverhead name was chosen because of its variety of metaphorical themes. *River* expresses the power of moving water to nurture, terrorize, creep, or inundate; *head* resounds with images of authority and unity.

On Riverhead's nonfiction list: *The Color of Water: A Black Man's Tribute to His White Mother* by James McBride, *Brutal Bosses and Their Prey* by Harvey A. Hornstein, *Sex Death Enlightenment: A True Story* by Mark Matousek, *The Cloister Walk* by Kathleen Norris, *Journey into Motherhood: Writing Your Way to Self-Discovery* by Leslie Kirk Campbell, and *Ethics for the Next Millennium* by His Holiness the Dalai Lama and Alexander Norman.

Fiction and literary works from Riverhead: *Going Down* by Jennifer Belle, *The Woman Who Walked on Water* by Lily Tuck, *Depth Takes a Holiday: Essays from Lesser Los Angeles* by Sandra Tsing Loh, *Violette's Embrace* by Michelle Zackheim, *The Romance Reader* (novel) by Pearl Abraham, *High Fidelity* by Nick Hornsby, and *Loving Edith* by Mary Tannen.

Query letters and SASEs should be directed to:

Susan J. Petersen, Publisher

Julie Grau, Senior Editor

Amy Hertz, Senior Editor

Mary South, Senior Editor, Editor in Chief for Trade Paperbacks

Celina (Cindy) Spiegel, Senior Editor

Wendy Carlton, Associate Editor

THE BERKLEY PUBLISHING GROUP

200 Madison Avenue
New York, NY 10016
212-951-8800

The Berkley Publishing Group produces a solid commercial list of fiction and nonfiction, including frontlist titles in trade paper and hardcover editions. The house also accents a mass-market paperback list. Berkley fiction encompasses categories such as romance and women's fiction, action adventure, Westerns, mysteries, science fiction, and fantasy. Nonfiction interests run the gamut of commercial categories. Berkley publishes reprints (many of them originally on the Putnam list) as well as original fiction and nonfiction under the Berkley, Jove, and Ace imprints.

Berkley's nonfiction range includes self-help and awareness, business, true crime, popular culture, and parenting. Boulevard is a media imprint with an accent on popular culture. Perigee concentrates on commercial nonfiction.

Nonfiction titles from Berkley include *Dare to Win* by Jack Canfield and Mark Victor Hansen, *Mo' Yo' Mama* by Snap C. Pop and Kid Rank, *Do-It-Yourself . . . or Not?* by Katie and Gene Hamilton, *The Practically Meatless Gourmet* by Cornelia Carlson,

Generals in Muddy Boots: A Concise Encyclopedia of Combat Commanders by Dan Cragg (edited by Walter J. Boyne), *Eyes of the Sphinx: The Newest Evidence of Alien Contact in Ancient Cultures* by Erich von Daniken, *The Dull Knives of Pine Ridge: A Lakota Odyssey* by Joe Starita, *The Good Nanny Book: How to Find, Hire, and Keep the Perfect Nanny for Your Child* by P. Michelle Riffin, *Diamond in the Rough: The Secret to Finding Your Own Value and Making Your Own Success* by Barry J. Farber, and *A Different Angle: Fly Fishing Stories by Women* (edited by Holly Morris).

Berkley Group fiction authors include Tom Clancy, John Sandford, and LaVyrle Spencer; a significant portion of the list crosses over from Putnam hardcover originals into Berkley paperback reprint editions. Prime Crime is an imprint that emphasizes original frontlist mysteries and suspense fiction. The Berkley romance line includes best-selling writers such as Nora Roberts, Kathleen Sutcliff, Laura Kinsale, and Mary Balogh.

Features from Berkley Prime Crime include *The Death of a Dancing Fool* by Carole Berry, *Murder among the Angels* by Stefanie Matteson, *She Came by the Book* by Mary Wings, and *Most Likely to Die* by Jacqueline Girdner.

The Ace list denotes the forefront of science fiction and fantasy, including original titles as well as reprints. On the Ace list: *The Dragon and the Djinn* by Gordon R. Dickson, *Looking for the Mahdi* by N. Lee Wood, *The Tranquility Alternative* by Allen Steele, and *Cradle of Splendor* by Patricia Anthony.

Jove's interest is in mass-market novels, including romance, historical romance, suspense, action adventure, mysteries, and Westerns.

Query letters and SASEs should be directed to:

Susan Allison, Vice President, Editor in Chief, Ace Books
Science fiction, fantasy, horror.

Ginjer Buchanan, Executive Editor, Ace Books
Horror, science fiction, fantasy, mysteries, psychological suspense.

(Ms.) Hillary Cige, Senior Editor
Commercial nonfiction; business subjects.

Gail Fortune, Editor
Women's fiction, romance, mystery.

Leslie Gelbman, Senior Vice President and Editor in Chief

Laura Ann Gilman, Editor
Science fiction, fantasy, mystery.

Gary Goldstein, Senior Editor
Westerns, horror, general men's fiction.

Jennifer Lata, Assistant Editor
General nonfiction.

Natalie Rosenstein, Vice President, Senior Executive Editor
General fiction, mystery.

Denise Silvestro, Editor
Women's fiction and nonfiction, health, self-help, pop culture, inspirational and New Age books.

Judith Palais, Senior Editor
Women's fiction, general fiction, commercial/literary works, romance.

John Talbot, Senior Editor
Wide range of commercial nonfiction. Fiction: suspense, mysteries, thrillers.

Elizabeth Beier, Senior Editor, Director of Boulevard Books
Movie tie-in books, general nonfiction.

PRICE STERN SLOAN

11150 Olympic Boulevard, Suite 650
Los Angeles, CA 90064
310-477-6100

Price Stern Sloan was founded as an independent in 1964; since 1993 it has been a part of the Putnam Publishing Group. It produces nonfiction titles in crafts, cookery, business, popular psychology, health, gardening, photography, sports, and humor. The house is known for a particularly strong selection of calendars. Price Stern Sloan has also issued titles for children and young adults, featuring activity books, craft kits, pop-ups, audiocassettes, and other specialty publications. As PSS assumes its role within the Putnam operation, its publishing categories and focus continues to evolve.

Query letters and SASEs should be directed to:

Jeanette P. Egan, Editorial Director, Cookbooks
Cookery line.

Bob Lovka, Adult Trade Book Editor
All areas consistent with publisher description, including humor.

Michael Lutfy, Director, Automotive Books
Automotive subjects.

Lisa Rojany, Senior editor, Children's Books
All juvenile books.

TARCHER

200 Madison Avenue
New York, NY 10016
212-951-8800

Tarcher's emphasis is on high-profile commercial titles in popular psychology, healing, self-help/awareness, sexuality, unconventional business books, new directions in scientific thought, and current social issues in topical areas such as gender and health care. The Tarcher imprint is the corporate banner of the formerly independent Jeremy P. Tarcher, Inc. (founded in 1964). The latter grew from a small West Coast house to mid-size as a publisher of hardcover and trade paperback titles in adult trade nonfiction; it also featured a line of innovative philosophical science fiction. Subsequent to Tarcher's acquisition by the Putnam Publishing Group (in 1994), the operation was relocated from its Los Angeles base to Putnam Berkley's New York offices.

On the Tarcher list: *Life, Paint, and Passion: Reclaiming the Magic of Spontaneous Expression* by Michell Cassou and Stewart Cubley, *The High-Performance Mind: Mastering Brainwaves for Insight, Healing, and Creativity* by Anna Wise, *A House Divided: Six Belief Systems Struggling for America's Soul* by Mark Gerzon, *Run Run Run: The Lives of Abbie Hoffman* by Jack Hoffman and Dan Simon, *The End of Work: The Decline of the Global Labor Force and the Dawn of the Post-Market Era* by Jeremy Rifkin, and *Sacred Sorrows: Embracing and Transforming Depression* (edited by John E. Nelson and Andrea Nelson).

Query letters and SASEs should be directed to:

Irene Prokop, Editor in Chief

THE PUTNAM & GROSSET BOOK GROUP

200 Madison Avenue
New York, NY 10016
212-951-8800

The Putnam & Grosset Book Group produces children's books under imprints such as G.P. Putnam's Sons, Philomel Books, Sandcastle Books, Grosset & Dunlap, and Platt & Munk. The list ranges from picture books for toddlers to novels for young adults, including the full spectrum of nonfiction and fiction areas, board books, first reading books, novelty books, miniature editions, foreign-language books, and holiday books.

Titles include *Goodnight, Gorilla* by Peggy Rathmann, *The Ghost of Elvis and Other Celebrity Spirits* by Daniel Cohen, *Mountain Valor* by Gloria Houston (illustrated by Thomas B. Allen), *Nora's Surprise* by Satomi Ichikawa, *The Very Hungry Caterpillar Board Book* by Eric Carle, and *Spot's Big Book of Colors, Shapes, and Numbers* by Eric Hill.

Query letters and SASEs should be directed to:

Jane O'Connor, President, Grosset & Dunlap

Patricia Lee Gauch, Editorial Director, Philomel Books

QUE CORPORATION

(See Macmillan Computer Publishing under Simon & Schuster listing)

RANDOM HOUSE
BALLANTINE PUBLISHING GROUP/CROWN PUBLISHING GROUP
KNOPF PUBLISHING GROUP/PANTHEON/SCHOCKEN
TIMES BOOKS/VILLARD BOOKS/VINTAGE BOOKS

201 East 50th Street
New York, NY 10022
212-751-2600

Random House (founded in 1925) is among the celebrated names of the American book trade. As a major domain of the Newhouse publishing empire, Random House has evolved into an intricate commonwealth of publishing groups, divisions, and imprints with a far-flung web of interests and diverse specialties in virtually all categories of commercial fiction and nonfiction. Random House publishes books in hardcover, trade paperback, and mass-market rack editions.

The house's breadth is indicated by the central trade group that encompasses the mainstream sweep of Random House adult trade books, the resolute commercial orientation of the Villard hardcover imprint, the discriminating trade-paper scheme of Vintage Books, and the Modern Library Classics series. Random House publishing entities include Ballantine Publishing Group, Crown Publishing Group, Knopf Publishing Group/Alfred A. Knopf, Pantheon, Schocken, and Times Books. Random House publishing groups also produce an equally fine medley of lines for young readers. (Please see separate subentries below.)

Random House distributes for itself and its subsidiaries, as well as for a raft of other publishers including National Geographic Books, Prima Publishing, Shambhala Publications, and Sierra Club Books.

RANDOM HOUSE TRADE DIVISION

Assuming a mainstream commercial profile, Random House presents a preferred list of trade fiction and nonfiction titles within its wide-ranging adult trade hardcover lineup.

Random House nonfiction presents topics of popular interest in current events; history, biography, and memoirs; investigative stories and narrative nonfiction; lifestyle and the arts; and popular science. Fiction accents frontlist novels; outstanding mysteries, suspense tales, and thrillers; and commercial literary works.

Random House also publishes large-print editions, audiobooks, and electronic/computer-related works; offers a home-video catalog; and produces a series of reference books covering business, law, and literary areas. The evocative Random House logo of a rambling home is a recognized symbol of unstinting standards in bookmaking.

Random House nonfiction encompasses *Guilty* by Harold Rothwax, *The Best 499 Public Golf Courses in the United States, Canada, Mexico, and the Caribbean* by Robert McCord, *The Private Life of Chairman Mao* by Li Zhisui with Anne F. Thurston, *Ross Perot and Third-Party Politics* by Gerald Posner, *Ghost of a Chance* by Peter Duchin, *The Rogers and Gray Italian Country Cookbook* by Ruth Rogers and Rose Gray, *Massage for Pain Relief* by Peijian Shen, *Man-to-Man* by Michael Korda, *Mr. Truman's War* by J. Robert Moskin, and *Civil War Battlefields and Landmarks* (edited by Frank E. Vandriver).

The Princeton Review line of college directories, academic how-to, and test-preparation guides are popular and valuable items among university students and college-bound readers. Random House also hosts the Paris Review belles lettres product line.

The Random House list in fiction and letters includes *Neanderthal* by John Darnton, *Primary Colors* (satirical political thriller) by Anonymous, *Murder at the National Gallery* by Margaret Truman, *Women Writers at Work* (edited by George Plimpton), *The Shadow Man* by Mary Gordon, *Rose* by Martin Cruz Smith, *The Falconer* by

Elaine Clark McCarthy, *Babel Tower* by A. S. Byatt, *Ants on the Melon* by Virginia Adair, *Dance for the Dead* by Thomas Perry, *And Still I Rise* by Maya Angelou, *The Devil Soldier* by Caleb Carr, *Oswald's Tale* by Norman Mailer, and *The City and the Pillar and Seven Early Stories* by Gore Vidal.

Query letters and SASEs should be directed to:

Deb Futter, Vice President and Executive Editor
Wide-ranging interests consistent with the house list.

Ann Godoff, Executive Editor
Nonfiction: contemporary issues. Commercial and literary fiction.

Jonathan Karp, Editor
Current events, politics, popular culture, fiction.

Robert D. Loomis, Executive Editor
Military and U.S. history, current events, politics, biography. Commercial and literary fiction.

Kate Medina, Executive Editor
Commercial fiction, women's fiction.

David Rosenthal, Executive Editor
Literary and commercial fiction. Nonfiction: current events, politics, contemporary biographies.

RANDOM HOUSE REFERENCE AND INFORMATION PUBLISHING

Random House Reference and Information Publishing offers a tight, well-developed list that accents traditional works alongside new high-profile books and software products. The division is expanding its presence in the computer books and electronic-publishing arena.

Random House reference titles include *Random House Book of Jokes and Anecdotes* by Joe Claro, *Spy Book* by Norman Polmar and Thomas B. Allen, *The Most Challenging Quiz Book Ever* by Louis Phillips, and *The Lenox Hill Hospital Book of Symptoms and Solutions* by Lenox Hill Hospital. In the perennially strong standard-reference arena, with a new twist or two, are *Random House Compact Unabridged Dictionary* (book and CD-ROM) and a revised version of the hardy desktop stand-by *Random House Webster's College Dictionary*.

Random House's computer-books line accents popular trade books in the personal-computing consumer arena, in addition to works of a technical orientation and titles covering business applications. The program has a noteworthy emphasis on younger consumers (topics in cyberpunking and networking).

Computer-oriented titles include *Netspy* by Michael Wolf and Company, Inc., *Multimedia Strategies in the Corporation* (packaged with CD-ROM) by Roger Fetterman (in the New Media Magazine/Apple New Media series), *CompuServe from A to Z: The Ultimate CompuServe Reference* by Charles Bowen, and *The Photoshop*

Filters Toolkit: Amazing Special Effects with Photoshop, Painter and More by Bill Niffenegger.

Query letters and SASEs should be directed to:

Charles Levine, Publisher
Reference titles.

(Ms.) Tracy Smith, Editor in Chief
Practical consumer computer books with contemporary cultural themes. Also acquires for Times Books division (see subentry).

RANDOM HOUSE BOOKS FOR YOUNG READERS

Random House Books for Young Readers publishes books for preschoolers through young adults, with a preponderance of its highly commercial list slated for the younger audience.

Established Random House lines include Babar the Elephant productions, Dr. Seuss titles, Boy Talk, the Betsy Books, and the Sesame Street series. The Pictureback Readers, which appear in English as well as in bilingual Spanish/English editions, are designed to exemplify the type of works that younger readers want to read on their own.

Other Random series include readers geared to specific reader levels and age ranges, as well as a reference line. The house engages in a variety of formats, including peek-a-board books, pop-up books, chunky-shaped books, cuddle-cloth books, scratch-'n'-sniff books, books with phosphorescent ink, mini-storybooks, kits, and book-and-cassette packages.

This division no longer accepts unsolicited manuscripts directly from authors; all projects must go through agents. Query letters and SASEs should be directed to:

Stephanie Spinner, Executive Editor

Jane Gerrer, Executive Editor

Judy Donnelly, Senior Editor

Jennifer Fanelli, Senior Editor

Barbara Katz, Editor

Susan Kassiver, Editor

THE BALLANTINE PUBLISHING GROUP
BALLANTINE/DEL REY/FAWCETT/COLUMBINE
HOUSE OF COLLECTIBLES/ONE WORLD/IVY BOOKS

201 East 50th Street
New York, NY 10022
212-751-2600

The Ballantine Publishing Group is a Random House division that produces trade paperbacks and hardcovers, in addition to its traditionally commanding presence in mass-market paperbacks. The house is active in a full range of commercial fiction and nonfiction areas—originals as well as reprints. Hardcover originals bear the Ballantine or Fawcett logo; general trade paperbacks are likewise released under these two stamps. The other imprints in this division are typified by their respective specialist lines (see below). Ballantine is also home to a number of imprints geared to young-reader interest.

Ballantine and Fawcett fiction accent novels with a popular orientation, including mainstream and category works, with particular emphasis in mysteries, suspense, and thrillers as well as occasional high-concept verse. Representative titles: *The Kindness of Strangers* by Julie Smith, *The Lethal Partner* by Jake Page, *Imagine Love* by Katherine Stone, *A Shred of Evidence* by Jill McGown, *That Day the Rabbi Left Town* by Harry Kemelman, *Pentecost Alley* by Anne Perry, *My Lover Is a Woman: Contemporary Lesbian Love Poems* (edited by Lesléa Newman), and *Buck Naked* by Joyce Burditt.

Ballantine and Fawcett nonfiction plays to the high-interest commercial arena. Titles include *Creating from the Spirit: Living Each Day As a Creative Act* by Dan Wakefield, *Without Child: Challenging the Stigma of Childlessness* by Laurie Lisle, *The 5-Day Miracle Diet* by Adele Puhn, and *Sun Pin: The Art of Warfare* (translated, with an introduction and commentary by D. C. Lau and Roger T. Ames).

Del Rey publishes science fiction and fantasy titles (originals and reprints) in hardcover, trade paper, and mass-market paperback formats, including major series offerings. Titles here are *The Crystal Singer Trilogy* by Anne McCaffrey, *The Ringworld Throne* by Larry Niven, *First King of Shannara* by Terry Brooks, *The Warrior Returns* (an epic fantasy of the Anteros) by Allan Cole, and *Slow River* by Nicola Griffith.

House of Collectibles produces comprehensive reference works in fields such as fine arts, numismatics, music, Hollywood memorabilia, arrowheads, antique jewelry, and garden accessories.

One World is a distinguished imprint that presents commercial and literary writing from authors representing a variety of world cultures. One World books include *Getting Good Loving: How Black Men and Women Can Make Love Work* by Audrey B. Chapman, *Low-Fat Soul* by Jonell Nash, *Messengers of the Wind: Native American Women Tell Their Life Stories* (edited by Jane Katz), *Crossing Over Jordan* by Linda Beatrice Brown, *Brotherman: The Odyssey of Black Men in America—an Anthology* (edited by Herb Boyd and Robert L. Allen), and *Native Wisdom for White Minds: Daily Reflections Inspired by the Native Peoples of the World* by Anne Wilson Schaef.

Ivy Books and Columbine are mass-market paperback imprints that covers a wide range of fiction and nonfiction.

Query letters and SASEs should be directed to:

Joe Blades, Executive Editor, Ballantine
Fiction: hardcover and mass-market originals; mysteries, suspense, espionage.

Joelle Delbourgo, Editor in Chief, Ballantine
Oversees hardcover program and also acquires quality paperbacks. Wide range of how-to/self-help nonfiction titles.

Barbara Dicks, Executive Editor, Ivy
Fiction: romance (primarily Regency, some historicals), contemporary women's fiction. Young-adult fiction for the Juniper imprint.

Virginia Faber, Senior Editor, Ballantine
Psychology, spiritual subjects, serious nonfiction.

Clare Ferraro, Editor, Ballantine
Commercial fiction and nonfiction.

Owen Lock, Editor in Chief, Del Rey and House of Collectibles
Science fiction; price guides.

Leona Nevler, Editor in Chief, Fawcett/Ivy
Commercial fiction.

Susan Randol, Editor, Fawcett, Columbine
Nonfiction: popular reference, infotainment, how-to/self-improvement.

Stephen Sterns, Senior Editor, House of Collectibles
Reference books on antiquing, crafts, and hobbies.

Elisa Wares, Editor, Fawcett
Fiction: commercial women's; Regency romances, some historicals.

Cheryl Woodruff, Senior Editor, Ballantine
Spirituality, religion, New Age.

Joanne Wyckoff, Senior Editor, Ballantine
Nonfiction: history, women's issues, biography, current events. Some literary fiction.

Elizabeth Zack, Editor, Ballantine
Fiction: frontlist commercial. Nonfiction: popular reference, self-help, inspirational.

CROWN PUBLISHING GROUP
HARMONY BOOKS

201 East 50th Street
New York, NY 10022
212-751-2600

Crown publishes a variety of trade-oriented fiction and nonfiction titles in hardcover and paperback. Crown (acquired by Random House in 1988) incorporates a number of Random House imprints and acquisitions that together make up Crown Publishing Group. Crown imprints include Harmony Books (known for commercial versatility, as well as commitment to quality fiction and nonfiction), Crown Arts and Letters, Clarkson Potter/Publishers, Living Language, Bell Tower, and Prince Paperbacks, as well as Fodor's Travel Publications.

Crown's fiction includes commercial novels across the trade spectrum, including mystery and suspense; Harmony Books embraces a typically more vanguard literary tone.

The group's fiction list and works of cultural and literary interest are exemplified by *Spring Collection* by Judith Krantz, *Red Moon Passage* by Bonnie Horrigan, *The Island of the Mapmaker's Wife and Other Tales* by Marilyn Sides, *Poem Crazy* by Susan Wooldridge, *Blood Lines* by Ruth Rendell, *Beauty* by Susan Wilson, *Sister Feelgood* by Donna Marie Williams, *The Piano Man's Daughter* by Timothy Findlay, and *The Information* by Martin Amis.

Crown nonfiction encompasses popular titles in biography, history, art, antiques and collectibles, contemporary culture, crime, sports, travel, languages, cookbooks, and self-help/how-to, as well as popular-reference works.

Cuisine and lifestyle are areas of Harmony and Clarkson Potter emphasis. Releases here include Martha Stewart's coffee-table editions and Lee Bailey's effusive line of savory kitchen-cum-culture excursions.

From Crown nonfiction: *Revised American History* by Edward P. Moser, *Radical Golf* by Michael Laughlin, *A Queer Geography* by Brank Browning, *The Flavors of Sicily* by Anna Tasca Lanza, *The Spiritual Traditions of Sex* by Richard Craze, *Barking at Prozac* by Buck (as told to Tom McNichol), *Perfect Weight* by Deepak Chopra, *Lesbianism Made Easy* by Helen Eisenbach, *Miss Manners Rescues Civilization* by Judith Martin, *Good Girls Don't Eat Dessert* by Rosalyn Meadow and Lillie Weiss, *Chicken Breasts* by Diane Rozas, and *Keeping Kids Reading* by Mary Leonhardt.

Query letters and SASEs should be directed to:

Brandt Aymar, Senior Editor
Many nonfiction interests, including illustrated/coffee-table books.

Michael Denneny, Senior Editor
Gay and lesbian subjects.

Peter St. J. Ginna, Senior Editor
Fiction: literary, suspense. Nonfiction: natural history, history, biographies, practical reference.

(Ms.) Adrienne Ingrum, Executive Editor
Nonfiction trade paperback originals.

Karen Rinaldi, Senior Editor
Broad range of nonfiction interests. Commercial fiction.

Steve Ross, Vice President and Editorial Director
Upscale, commercial nonfiction. Literary and commercial fiction.

Diane Frieden, Assistant Editor
Popular culture, how-to style books, art/architecture, design, and generation X interests.

Eliza Scott, Associate Editor
Health and fitness, nature, nonfiction.

CLARKSON POTTER/PUBLISHERS

Roy Finamore, Editor, Special Projects
Cooking and food, design and architecture, special projects, style and decorating, biography, popular culture.

Annetta Hanna, Senior Editor
Design, gardening, biography, popular culture, how-to style and decorating books.

Pam Krauss, Executive Editor
Cooking and food, self-help, craft, health and fitness, how-to style and decorating books.

Lauren Shakely, Vice President and Editorial Director
How-to style and decorating books, art books, gardening, biography.

Katie Workman, Senior Editor
Cooking and food, popular culture, how-to style and decorating books.

HARMONY BOOKS

Shaye Areheart, Executive Editor
Literary fiction, biographies, humor. Wide general nonfiction interests.

Toinette Lippe, Editorial Director, Bell Tower
Spirituality and inspiration (not reincarnation, astrology, crystals, and the like).

(Ms.) Leslie Meredith, Vice President and Editorial Director
Holistic and alternative healing and wellness, spirituality, Buddhism, relationships and erotica, and pop culture. Literary and quirky fiction.

Sherri Rifkin, Editor
Wide range of commercial and serious nonfiction.
Pop culture, business, humor, women's issues, sex/relationships, alternative health.

Dina Siciliano, Assistant Editor
Wide interests, including popular culture, fiction from contemporary writers.

CROWN BOOKS FOR YOUNG READERS
CLARKSON POTTER JUVENILE BOOKS

Crown's children's list is distinguished by illustrated works in hardcover and paperback, mainly for kids between the ages of three and twelve; the program offers a few nonfiction titles for older grade-school readers including the cutting-edge series Face to Face With Science. Crown has a special emphasis in topnotch science fiction and fantasy titles.

Crown's juveniles division encompasses the imprints Crown Books for Young Readers and Clarkson Potter Juvenile Books. Representative titles from the Crown children's list: *Hammers and Mops, Pencils and Pots: A First Book of Tools and Gadgets We Use Around the House* by True Kelley, *The Third Planet: Exploring the Earth from Space* by Sally Ride and Tam O'Shaughnessy, *Time Flies* by Eric Rohmann, *I Want a Dog* (story and pictures by Dayal Kaur Khalsa), and *Trubloff: The Mouse Who Wanted to Play the Balalaika* by John Burningham.

This house prefers submissions that come through agents. Query letters and SASEs from authors should be directed to Editorial Department; agented submissions may sent to:

Simon Boughton, Publisher

Tracy Gates, Senior Editor

KNOPF PUBLISHING GROUP
ALFRED A. KNOPF

201 East 50th Street
New York, NY 10022
212-751-2600

The publishing firm of Alfred A. Knopf was long associated with fine bookmaking and the literary tradition. The regime of publisher Sonny Mehta (begun in 1990) has brought a best-selling radiance to the house, now astutely positioned in the arena of commercial contemporary letters in its corporate incarnation as Knopf Publishing Group, which, in addition to the Alfred A. Knopf imprint, covers Vintage, Pantheon, and Schocken (see separate Random House subentries). Knopf Books for Young Readers stakes a solid claim in the kids' books domain. Random House corporate marketing and promotion support combines with Knopf editorial and publishing tradition to make for a truly formidable house.

The Knopf roster of eminent authors includes major voices worldwide in virtually every field of fiction and nonfiction. Regardless of the category or genre affiliation or lack thereof, these books are Knopf: The volumes are consummately designed products, and Knopf's running-dog colophon—the illustrious Borzoi—can in and of itself signal a potential reviewer's priorities.

Knopf fiction and literary works express established traditions as well as new domains in popular contemporary writing, including provocatively styled mysteries and suspense fiction, inventive approaches in nonfiction, and literary writing in travel, food, and lifestyle. Knopf has published writers such as Ann Beattie, John le Carré, Sandra Cisneros, Michael Crichton, Brett Easton Ellis, James Ellroy, Carl Hiaasen, P. D. James, Dean R. Koontz, Peter Maass, Cormac McCarthy, Susanna Moore, Toni Morrison, Anne Rice, Donna Tartt, John Updike, and Andrew Vachss.

Titles here include *Intensity* by Dean Koontz, *Servant of the Bones* by Anne Rice, *The Dangerous Old Woman* by Clarissa Pinkola Estés, *The Last Thing He Wanted* by Joan Didion, *My Dark Places* by James Ellroy, *I Was Amelia Earhart* by Jane Mendelsohn, *A Regular Guy* by Mona Simpson, *In the Beginning* by Karen Armstrong, *Tales from Watership Down* by Richard Adams, *Golf Dreams: Writings on Golf* by John Updike, *Selected Stories* by Alice Munro, *Art Objects: Essays on Ecstasy and Effrontery* by Jeanette Winterson, and *Santa Evita* by Tomás Eloy Martínez.

Knopf lists a notable array of poetry, including *The Vixen* by W. S. Merwin, *A Silence Opens* by Amy Clampitt, *Sunday Skaters* by Mary Jo Salter, *Tesserae* by John Hollander, *Collected Poems* by John Updike, *Fire Lyric* by Cynthia Zarin, and *Hotel Lautréamont* by John Ashbery.

Knopf nonfiction accents contemporary culture; issues of public interest; art and architecture; biography and memoir; and titles in health, fitness, and lifestyle. Nevertheless, Knopf titles can roam virtually anywhere across the reaches of the mainstream publishing emporium, including popular reference and humor.

The Knopf list in nonfiction and popular works is represented by *Clint Eastwood: A Biography* by Richard Schickel, *David Brinkley's Homilies* by David Brinkley, *Hitler's Willing Executioners* by Daniel Jonah Goldhagen, *American Foreign Policy* by George

W. Bush and Brent Scowcroft, *Nancy Lancaster: Her Life, Her World, Her Art* by Robert Becker, *The Dictionary of Global Culture* by Kwame Anthony Appiah and Henry Louis Gates Jr., *The Florida Cookbook: 200 Recipes—from Gulf Coast Gumbo to Key Lime Pie* by Jeanne Voltz and Caroline Stuart, *The Book of Jewish Food: An Odyssey from Samarkand to New York* by Claudia Roden, *The Quotable Feline* (an illustrated work) by Jim Dratfield and Paul Coughin, and *Chic Simple Work Clothes* by Kim Johnson Gross and Jeff Stone.

Knopf is home to the National Audubon Society Pocket Guides (field guides) series. The Knopf Guides series includes handbooks regionally keyed to areas of travel interest such as Ireland and the Route of the Mayas. Chic Simple books highlight ingenious approaches to the good life.

Query letters and SASEs should be directed to:

Barbara Bristol, Editor
Historical and literary biography, natural and social history.

Ann Close, Editor
Fiction: contemporary themes; especially interested in Southern or Western settings. Nonfiction: art books.

Robin Desser, Editor
Contemporary fiction; works with international/multicultural outlook; narrative nonfiction, including literary travel.

Gary Fisketjon, Editor at Large
Literary fiction. Varied serious nonfiction interests.

Harry Ford, Senior Editor
Poetry.

Jane Garrett, Editor
United States history, some European and Middle Eastern history, craft and hobby books.

Judith Jones, Senior Editor and Vice President
Literary fiction. Cookbooks.

Susan Ralston, Editor
Biography, cultural history, the arts, contemporary events and issues.

Ken Schneider, Assistant Editor
Contemporary fiction. Nonfiction: cultural history, the arts (drama, music, ballet). Works with Judith Jones.

Jonathan Segal, Senior Editor
Twentieth-century history, contemporary events and issues.

ALFRED A. KNOPF BOOKS FOR YOUNG READERS

The Knopf children's books division produces a hardy list of picture books, books for middle readers, and young adult fiction and nonfiction, along with a slate of special-interest reference series.

The Eyewitness Juniors series, designed for very young naturalists, produces titles geared to special species and interest areas such as snakes and reptiles, frogs and toads, cats, dogs, and amazing poisonous animals. Eyewitness Books, lavishly illustrated volumes on topics such as ancient Egypt and Rome, automobiles, and airplanes, are designed for readers ages ten and up.

Knopf Paperbacks for Kids includes Dragonfly Books (for the very young), Bullseye Books (for middle-grade readers), and Borzoi Sprinters (middle-grade and young adult readers). Umbrella Books offers affordable hardcover picture books.

Unsolicited manuscripts are no longer accepted or considered. All manuscripts are acquired through agents. Query letters and SASEs should be directed to:

Simon Boughton, Publisher

Arthur Levine, Editor in Chief

Tracy Gates, Senior Editor

Lisa Banim, Senior Editor, Borzoi Books

PANTHEON BOOKS

201 East 50th Street
New York, NY 10022
212-751-2600

Pantheon accents nonfiction books in current events, international affairs, contemporary culture, literary criticism and the arts, popular business, psychology, travel, nature, science, and history. The house also has a strong list in contemporary fiction, poetry, and drama. Pantheon also offers Fairytale and Folktale Library.

Pantheon Books was founded in 1942 by German Jewish émigrés and, from its U.S. base, forged an international reputation as a publisher of exemplary titles in fiction and nonfiction, while remaining a viable business entity. Pantheon was bought by Random House in 1990, subsequent to which occurred the famous and abrupt departure of director André Schiffrin, followed by the resignation of members of the editorial staff and the shift of major authors to other houses. Although awestruck literary commentators were quick to offer epitaphs, Pantheon regrouped along a profile similar to that previously pursued; the house continues its product success with seasonally vigorous lists and a refined editorial eye.

Pantheon books include *The Birth of the Beat Generation* by Steven Watson, *All-American Skin Game* by Stanley Crouch, *All Soul's Rising* by Madison Smartt Bell, *The Moor's Last Sigh* by Salman Rushdie, *Breaking the News* by James Fallows, *A Tour of the Calculus* by David Berlinski, *Mr. Wilson's Cabinet of Wonder* by Lawrence Weschler, *Becoming Gay* by Richard A. Isay, and *Black Power, White Blood* by Lori Andrews.

Query letters and SASEs should be directed to:

Dan Frank, Senior Editor, Pantheon Books
Nonfiction: serious subjects, history, science, current issues. Literary fiction.

Erroll McDonald, Executive Editor, Pantheon Books
Literary fiction. Nonfiction: politics, current issues, and contemporary culture.

Shelley Wanger, Senior Editor, Pantheon Books
Picture, illustrated books, biography, film, culture.

SCHOCKEN BOOKS

201 East 50th Street
New York, NY 10022
212-751-2600

With strong footholds in both academic and commercial publishing, Schocken produces titles in cultural, religious, and women's studies; Judaica; literature; science and health; and the social sciences.

Schocken Books was founded in Germany in 1933 by Salman Schocken, a noted bibliophile, Zionist, and department-store kingpin. The house's German division was shut down after Kristallnacht (the formal institution of the full brunt of the Nazi program on November 9, 1938), but much of Schocken's holdings had been moved to Jerusalem and Tel Aviv by that time. In 1945 Schocken opened New York offices and flourished as an independent until acquired by the Pantheon division in 1987.

Under the Random House restructuring, Schocken assumed the stature of an imprint within an imprint, with a lowered profile and restricted publishing operation, giving the impression that the house was viewed primarily as a source of revenue accruing from its classic backlist. Schocken controls the world rights to the works of Franz Kafka, and otherwise includes works by Jean-Paul Sartre, Claude Lévi-Strauss, Susannah Heschel, Gershom Scholem, Elie Wiesel, Primo Levi, and Harold Kushner.

Schocken (under editorial director Arthur Samuelson, a former editor who has, in between Schocken stints, worked at Summit Books and Paragon House) is a major player in the Random House publishing partnership. A strong line of redesigned reissues of Schocken's backlist best-sellers is in full swing. The house has staked new claims in the field of Judaica, and likewise has adopted a robust approach across the contemporary cultural horizon.

To celebrate Schocken's fiftieth year in the United States, the house sports a new logo based on the Bauhaus-style S that was emblematic of Salman Schocken's business enterprises in Germany earlier in the century.

On the Schocken list: *What Darwin Really Said* by Benjamin Farrington, *At World's End: A Daughter's Story* (search for a mysterious father) by Louise Kehoe, *Madame Blavatsky's Baboon* by Peter Washington, *Never the Last Journey* (a Holocaust-survival/business autobiography) by Felix Zandman with David Chanoff, *Murder in the Temple of Love: The Story of Yahweh Ben Yahweh* by Sydney P. Freedberg, and *A Match to the Heart: One Woman's Story of Being Struck by Lightning* by Gretel Ehrlich.

Literary writing includes *The Schocken Book of Contemporary Jewish Fiction* (edited by Ted Solartoff and Nessa Rapoport), *Let 'Em Eat Cake* (novel) by Susan Jedren, *All the Rivers Flow to the Sea* (autobiography) by Elie Wiesel, *Art, Dialogue, and Outrage: Essays on Literature and Culture* by Wole Soyinka, and *Entries* (poetry) by Wendell Berry.

Judaica from Schocken: *A Book That Was Lost and Other Stories* by S. Y. Agnon, *Wrestling with the Angel: Jewish Insights on Death and Mourning* (edited by Jack

Riemer), and *The New Jewish Catalog* by Sharon and Michael Strassfeld. The *Torah* (aka *The Five Books of Moses*, in a riveting translation by Everett Fox) is part of a four-volume project in progress: the *Schocken Bible*.

Query letters and SASEs should be directed to:

Bonnie Fetterman, Editor, Schocken Books
Books about Jewish culture, history, and religion.

TIMES BOOKS

201 East 50th Street
New York, NY 10022
212-751-2600

Times Books publishes general trade nonfiction across the gamut of commercial areas including business and career, finance, current affairs, social issues, science, sports, true crime, how-to, cooking, education, travel, humor, reference, and puzzles and games. Times is particularly strong in the crossword-puzzle publishing arena; the house also produces computer software.

A new imprint, Times Business, incorporates titles in areas such as management, practical career boosters, business biography, business journalism, and investigative business stories into a finely honed and well-directed publishing program. Times Books is the distributor for Kiplinger Books.

Times Books (founded in 1959 by the *New York Times* newspaper) is among the houses acquired by Random House during the latter 1980s.

On the Times Books list: *The Crossword Answer Book* by Stanley Newman and Daniel Stark, *Behind the Crystal Ball* by Anthony Aveni, *Motherguilt* by Diane Eyer, *Modem Nation* by Charles Bowen, *In the Unlikely Event of a Water Landing* by Christopher Noel, *Like Color to the Blind* by Donna Williams, *The Fiske Guide to Colleges* by Edward B. Fiske, and *The American Bar Association Guide to Family Law* (edited by the ABA).

From Times Business: *Real Change Leaders* by Jon R. Katzenbach, *Mean Business: How I Save Bad Companies and Make Good Companies Great* by Albert J. Dunlap, *Hope Is Not a Method: Lessons for Business from the Transformation of America's Army* by Gordon Sullivan and Michael Harzied, *The High-Risk Society* by Michael Mardell, and *The Young Entrepreneur's Guide to Starting and Running a Business* by Steve Mariotti.

Query letters and SASEs should be directed to

Ruth Fecych, Senior Editor
Puzzles, games, and popular culture.

John Mahaney, Executive Editor, Times Business
Special interest in general business, management, marketing, business reference, economics.

Peter Osnos, Publisher
Oversees entire publishing program. Special interests in American politics, business, and journalism.

Elizabeth Rapoport, Senior Editor
Popular science, health, and medicine.

(Ms.) Tracy Smith, Editor in Chief
Technology and business.

Steve Wasserman, Editorial Director
Current events, contemporary history, and international affairs.

Karl Weber, Managing Director, Times Business
General business titles.

VILLARD BOOKS

201 East 50th Street
New York, NY 10022
212-751-2600

Villard leads with titles of high commercial interest in nonfiction and frontlist fiction. Villard nonfiction covers areas such as food; popular psychology; self-enlightenment; humor; inspiration; popular topics in medicine, health, fitness, and sports; true crime; and general reference books. Villard's fiction roster presents mainstream commercial fare as well as mysteries, thrillers, and works of literary interest.

From Villard nonfiction: *Wake Up and Smell the Coffee* by Ann Landers; *Beyond Ritalin* by Stephen W. Garber, Marianne Daniels Garber, and Robyn Freedman Spizman; *George Foreman's Knock-Out-the-Fat Barbecue and Grilling Cookbook* by George Foreman and Cherie Calhoun; *Politically Incorrect's Greatest Hits* by Bill Maher; and *From Beginning to End* by Robert Fulghum.

Villard fiction and works of literary interest: *High and Tight* by Bud Klapisch, *Maiden Voyage* by Cynthia Bass, *Turnaway* by Jesse Browner, *I'm Losing You* by Bruce Wagner, and *Who in Hell* by Sean Kelly and Rosemary Rogers.

Query letters and SASEs should be directed to:

Craig Nelson, Executive Editor

David Rosenthal, Publisher

Annik LaFarge, Associate Publisher

VINTAGE BOOKS

201 East 50th Street
New York, NY 10022
212-751-2600

Vintage trade paperbacks are renowned for high style in design and production standards as well as their substantial content. Vintage accents new titles in the fields of contemporary global and American literature and current-interest nonfiction along with its preponderance of reprints in trade fiction and nonfiction. Among Vintage series are Vintage International, Vintage Contemporaries, Vintage Departures, Vintage Books/

The Library of America, Vintage Classics, Alfaguara•Vintage Español, and Vintage/ Black Lizard Crime.

Indicative of the Vintage list: *The Collected Works of Billy the Kid* by Michael Ondaatje, *Cuba and the Night* by Paco Ayer, *Making Movies* by Sidney Lumet, *My Lead Dog Was a Lesbian* by Brian Patrick O'Donohue, *The Quantity Theory of Insanity* by Will Self, *Walt Whitman's America* by David S. Reynolds, *Jaguars Ripped My Flesh* by Tom Cahill, *Krik? Krak!* by Edwidge Danticat, *Miami Purity* by Vicki Hendricks, *American Dreams* by Sapphire, *The Origin of Satan* by Elaine Pagels, and *The Vintage Book of Contemporary World Poetry* (edited by J. D. McClatchby).

Query letters and SASEs should be directed to:

Laurie Brown, Associate Publisher
Acquires in all areas consistent with house description.

Lu Ann Walther, Vice President
All areas consistent with publisher description.

Edward Kastenmeier, Senior Editor
Acquires in all areas covered in publisher description.

READER'S DIGEST GENERAL BOOKS

260 Madison Avenue
New York, NY 10016
212-953-0030

Reader's Digest General Books (founded in 1961) publishes general nonfiction books in the fields of how-to/do-it-yourself and self-help that cover topics in home maintenance and repair, gardening, crafts and hobbies, cooking, and health. Reader's Digest also produces reference books in law, medicine, money management, English-language usage and vocabulary, history and geography, science and nature, religion and archaeology, travel, and general reference.

Indicative of the Reader's Digest list: *Calligraphy School: A Step-by-Step Guide to the Fine Art of Lettering* by Anna Ravenscroft and Gaynor Goffe, *Decorative Needlepoint: Tapestry and Beadwork* by Julia Hickman, *How a House Works* by Duane Johnson, *Garden Design: How to Be Your Own Landscape Architect* by Robin Williams, *The Art of Watercolor* by Ray Campbell Smith, and *How the Weather Works* by Michael Allaby.

Author credit on many of the house's books is given as the Editors of Reader's Digest; indeed, most titles are originated in-house and are written by consulting writers. Reader's Digest General, thus, is not a likely home for an original publishing project, but when prospecting for assignments, the house might be worth a try for well-qualified freelance writers.

Among such house-authored titles are *Guide to Places of the World*, *Book of Facts*, *Illustrated History of South Africa*, and *Family Handyman: Weekend Improvements*.

Reader's Digest General Books directs a wide marketing and distribution team.

Query letters and SASEs should be directed to:

David Palmer, General Books Editor

REED PUBLISHING (USA)
REED TRADE PUBLISHING
REED REFERENCE PUBLISHING

Reed Trade Publishing:
225 Wildwood Avenue
Woburn, MA 01801
800-366-2665

Reed Reference Publishing:
121 Chanlon Road
New Providence, NJ 07974
908-464-6800

Reed Publishing (USA), along with Reed Reference Publishing, constitutes one of the leading houses in the arena of biographical, bibliographical, and business reference materials. Reed's professional titles cover virtually the entire reference spectrum, from law, medicine, and science to education, history, and the performing arts. Reed is also a leader in electronic publishing, with many titles currently available on CD-ROM.

Reed Reference is a division of Reed Publishing (USA), an international publisher of reference works and directories for trade, institutional, corporate, and library markets, and is a wing of the Reed Elsevier Group. RRP imprints include R. R. Bowker (*Books in Print*), Congressional Information Service, Martindale Hubbell (law directories), Marquis Who's Who, National Register Publishing, K. G. Sauer, Bowker-Sauer, and D. W. Thorpe. Reed Elsevier also owns Heinemann (see separate main entry for Heinemann, along with its Digital Press and Focal Press divisions).

Reed is interested in acquiring new trade books that dovetail with their existing product lines. Fields of special publishing emphasis are self-help, how-to, and other directory/reference works, particularly in the business, legal, and healthcare fields. Catalog areas cover epic adventure, satire, and photography; fantasy, family health, and biography; thrillers, literary works, and popular science; travel, lifestyle, psychology, and inspiration; and popular history and reference.

Representative Reed trade titles: *Kalashnikovs and Zombie Cucumbers* by Nick Middleton, *Positive Parenting* by Elizabeth Hartley-Brewer, *Mind, Body, and Immunity* by Rachel Charles, *The Magistrate's Tale* by Nora Naish, *The Celibate* by Michael Arditti, *Literary Guide to Dublin* by Vivien Igoe, *Claudia Schiffer* by Karl Lagerfeld, *Bulimia* by David Haslam, and *Beating the Blues* by Xandia Williams.

Distribution is overseen by Reed's in-house team via book-trade channels, direct-ordering facilities, and international marketing via Reed subsidiary facilities. RRP delivers its information worldwide in a variety of formats—books, CD-ROM, microfiche, tape leasing, and through on-line accessing of RRP databases.

Query letters and SASEs should be directed to:

Larry Chilnick, Vice President, Editorial Department

REGNERY PUBLISHING, INC.

422 First Street Southeast, Suite 300
Washington, DC 20003
202-546-5005
800-462-6420

Areas of Regnery publishing interest include contemporary politics, current events, public issues, the media, biography, history, and humor. The house is open to projects with broad trade appeal along the gamut of nonfiction categories.

Regnery Publishing Inc. (formerly Regnery Gateway, founded in 1947) is a growing, midsize house that produces primarily nonfiction projects in hardcover and quality paper editions. Regnery Gateway was acquired by Phillips Publishing International and is part of Phillips's Eagle and Regnery Publishing subsidiary, which produces public-policy periodicals and operates the Conservative Book Club. A major accent of Regnery's program is to feature books that offer an inside-the-Beltway Washington-insider purview. The house is also traditionally strong in paperbound reprints for the college market. Regnery Publishing supports a strong backlist.

The Phillips corporate connection enables Regnery to promote titles through venues such as Phillips's *Human Events* newspaper and to take advantage of the parent company's expertise in direct-mail and special-market sales.

Tumbleweed Press is an imprint that highlights narratives of the American frontier. Gateway Editions offers reprints of classics from historic cultures worldwide, as well as contemporary works of international scope in literature, politics, and religion.

On the Regnery Publishing trade list are *Operation Solo: The FBI's Man in the Kremlin* by John Barron, *Blueprint for a New Majority* by Dick Armey, *Goldwater* by Lee Edwards, *Hoover's FBI* by Cartha D. "Deke" DeLoach, *Is Heart Surgery Necessary?* by Julian Whitaker, *Inventing the AIDS Virus* by Peter Duesberg and Bryan Ellison, and *On the Make: The Rise of Bill Clinton* by Meredith L. Oakley.

Representative of the Tumbleweed Press imprint (which offers readers works in the Western and Frontier genres) is *Tackett and the Saloon Keeper* (the third novel of the Tackett Trilogy) by Lyn Nofziger.

Indicative of this house's heritage is founder Henry Regnery's choice of his publishing mark—the gateway that serves as a colophon for books published by Regnery. This gateway is a graphic representation of the *Porta Nigra* in Trier, Germany, a Roman gate constructed about 300 A.D. when Trier was the capital city of Roman Gaul. As such, the gateway symbolizes the passage from barbarous realms into the world of civilization.

Regnery Publishing is distributed to the trade by National Book Network.

Query letters and SASEs should be directed to:

Alfred Regnery, Publisher

Richard Vigilante, Vice President and Executive Editor

FLEMING H. REVELL COMPANY

(See under Baker Book House in the Directory of Religious, Spiritual, and Inspirational Publishers)

RIZZOLI INTERNATIONAL PUBLICATIONS

300 Park Avenue South
New York, NY 10010
212-982-2300

The Rizzoli catalog covers areas such as fine arts, architecture, crafts, culinary arts, decorative arts, design, fashion, gardens, landscaping, travel, and photography. Rizzoli also offers selected titles in sports and the performing arts, as well as a line of children's books.

Rizzoli International (founded in 1976) is one of the exclusive set of cosmopolitan publishers renowned for finesse in the bookmaking craft. The house interest embraces artistic realms worldwide, throughout history as well as the contemporary arena.

Rizzoli's consummately produced volumes display graphics of the highest quality and are offered in hardback and trade paperback editions. Rizzoli's products also include wall calendars, desk diaries, and journals. (Please see separate main entry in this directory for Universe Publishing, an affiliated Rizzoli division.)

From Rizzoli: *Dynasties: Paintings in Tudor and Jacobean England 1530–1630* (edited by Karen Hearn), *Pictorialism to Modernism: The Clarence H. White School of Photography* (edited by Marianne Fulton; text by Bonnie Yochelson and Kathleen A. Erwin), *Morning Glories: Recipes for Breakfast, Brunch and Beyond from an American Country Inn* by Donna Leahy, *Marilyn Monroe: The Life and the Myth* (edited by Giovanbattista Brambilla), *The Ultimate Garden Book for North America* (text by David Stevens and Ursula Buchan in association with the Royal Horticultural Society), *Casa California: Spanish-Style Houses from Santa Barbara to San Clemente* (text by Elizabeth McMillian; photographs by Melba Levick), *Tibetan Portrait: The Power of Compassion* (photographs by Phil Borges; text by the Dahlai Lama; prologue by Jeffrey Hopkins; epilogue by Elie Wiesel), *The Hand of the Poet: 100 Great Poems in Manuscript* (text by Dana Gioia with the New York Public Library), and *Fossils: The Great Halls of the American Museum of Natural History* (text by Lowell Dingus).

Rizzoli International Publications is distributed to the trade by St. Martin's Press. The Rizzoli catalog offers titles from additional publishers in the arts and literary arena, including Artemis, Guggenheim Museum Publications, Gustavo Gili, Marion Boyars, Moyer Bell Limited, PBC International, Scala Books, Solveig Williams Foreign Editions, Sotheby's, and Zwemmer.

The house acquires new projects only on an extremely selective basis.

RIZZOLI CHILDREN'S LIBRARY

Rizzoli Children's Library produces books and activity packages in subject areas and with themes congruent with the overall Rizzoli house interest. The titles entertain in ways that engage cultural and artistic appreciation, with little heed paid to the currently popular gooey and goofy trends.

Rizzoli Children's Library presents: *Carnevalia! African-Brazilian Folklore and Crafts* by Liza Papi, *Edward Lear's Nonsense* (illustrated by James Wines), *The Nightingale and the Wind* (story by Paul Mandelstein; illustrations by Pamela Silin-Palmer), and *The Will and the Way: Paul R. Williams, Architect* by Karen E. Hudson.

A representative Rizzoli series is *A Weekend With the Artist*, visually commanding volumes keyed to individual artists and their worlds. Titles here are *A Weekend with Winslow Homer*, *A Weekend with Picasso*, and *A Weekend with Renoir*.

Query letters and SASEs should be directed to:

Barbara Einzig, Senior Editor
Art and general trade books.

(Ms.) Carole Lalli, Senior Editor
Cookbooks.

David Morton, Senior Editor
Architecture.

RODALE PRESS

33 East Minor Street
Emmaus, PA 18098-0099
610-967-5171

Rodale Press (founded in 1932) specializes in books in the areas of nutrition and healthy cooking, health and fitness, gardening and the home, environment, crafts (including quilting and woodworking), practical spirituality, self-improvement, lifestyle, and selected titles in general reference. Rodale produces hardcover and paperback editions as well as a broad array of video and audio products; the house is geared for entry into the CD-ROM market. In addition, Rodale publishes magazines, among them are *Prevention, Organic Gardening, Runner's World, American Woodworker, Men's Health, Shape, Heart and Soul* (a health magazine for African-American women), *Quilter's Newsletter, Bicycling, Scuba Diver,* and *Backpacker.*

Rodale Press displays tremendous marketing energy; in addition to sales through the bookstore trade, Rodale is highly attuned to the venue of direct marketing. The press itself operates several specialty book clubs, among them Prevention Book Club, Home Improvement Book Club, Creative Needlecrafts Book Club, Woodworker's Guild, Men's Health Book Service, Organic Gardening Book Club, Nature Book Society, and the National Wildlife Federation Book Club. Rodale is among the leaders in addressing the Spanish-language and Latino markets. The company's database contains in the neighborhood of 25 million names.

Another Rodale strength is editorial quality and developmental expertise. Rodale doesn't produce books on a hunch—Rodale researches the market to find out what readers want and then gives it to them. The house is an established leader in its field. As such, Rodale always aims to give readers more than they want—more than they ever thought to ask for or knew they wanted—with products that offer practical value in every sentence. The house's mission statement is "To publish books that empower people's lives." About half of Rodale's titles are agented or packaged; the other half are created by Rodale's in-house staff.

On the Rodale list: *America's Best Quilting Projects: Homespun Plains* (edited by Jane Townswick); *Prevention's Low-Fat Italian Favorites* (edited by Jean Rogers); *Sex: A Man's Guide* by Stefan Bechtel, Laurence R. Stains, and the Editors of *Men's Health* Books; *Houseplants and Container Gardening: Rodale's Successful Organic Gardening* by Cheryl Long and Judy White; *Mental Performance for Peak Performance: Top Athletes Reveal the "Mind Exercises" They Use to Excel* by Steven Ungerleider; *Natural Medicine for Heart Disease* by Glenn S. Rothfield and Susan LeVert; *Sewing Secrets from the Fashion Industry: Proven Methods to Help You Sew Like the Pros* (edited by Susan Huxley); *Jacques Pépin's Simple and Healthy Cooking* (written and illustrated by Jacques Pépin); and *The Woodworkers Visual Handbook* by Joe Arno.

Rodale Press distributes its books directly to readers via routes such as mailing lists and its seven distinct book clubs; St. Martin's Press distributes Rodale titles to the bookstore trade.

Query letters and SASEs should be directed to:

Lois Hazel, Editorial Director, Rodale Books

Debbie Yost, Editorial Director of Health and Fitness Books

Maggie Balitas, Editorial Director of Home and Garden Books

YANKEE BOOKS

Yankee Books covers travel, nature, and the outdoors; cookbooks; tales and mysteries; humor, the forgotten arts (and crafts); literary New England; and genealogy. This press is the publisher of *Yankee* magazine and the annual *The Old Farmer's Almanac.* Formerly an independent regional and specialist house (begun in 1966), Yankee has assumed an expanded range of interests.

Sample Yankee titles: *Vacations in the Maritimes: A Tourbook of Nova Scotia, Prince Edward Island, New Brunswick, Newfoundland, and Labrador* by Laurie Fullerton, *Puddings and Pies: Traditional Desserts for a New Generation* by Barbara J. Grunes, *Hometown Cooking in New England* by Sandy Taylor and the editors of Yankee Books, *Forty Whacks: New Evidence in the Life and Legend of Lizzie Borden* by David Kent, *Favorite Day Trips in New England* by Michael Schuman, and *Dead and Buried in New England: Respectful Visits to the Tombstones and Monuments of 306 Noteworthy Yankees* by Mary Maynard.

Yankee Books distribution is via the marketing division of its parent company, Rodale. Trade distribution for Yankee is through St. Martin's, with *Old Farmer's Almanac* being distributed by Random House.

Query letters and SASEs should be directed to:

Ed Claflin, Managing Editor

ROUTLEDGE, INC.

29 West 35th Street
New York, NY 10001
212-244-3336

Routledge accents trade nonfiction academic works. The house offers noteworthy line-ups in current events, communications and media, cultural studies, education, self-improvement and psychology, world political and cultural studies, philosophical thought, economics, feminist theory, gender studies, history, and literary criticism.

Routledge produces adult nonfiction in the humanities and sciences. Among Routledge specialties are projects that give a vanguard twist to topical issues. Routledge imprints include Theatre Arts Books and Routledge/Thoemmes Press.

Founded in 1977 as Methuen Inc., then as Routledge and Chapman and Hall (as a subsidiary of International Thompson Organization), the house held to the overall profile of a commercial publisher, abreast of trends in scholarship and general public interest as it issued strong lines of trade and academic books. Routledge (with a concentration in the contemporary trade arena) and Chapman and Hall are today separate publishing companies. (Please see the Chapman and Hall entry in this directory).

Representative titles from the Routledge frontlist: *The End of the World: The Science and Ethics of Human Extinction* by John Leslie, *Fugitive Cultures: Race, Violence, and Youth* by Henry Giroux, *The Gender/Sexuality Reader: Culture, History, Political Economy* (edited by Roger Lancaster and Micaela di Leonardo), *Latin for the Illiterati* by Jon R. Stone, *The Near-Death Experience: A Reader* (edited by Lee W. Bailey and Jenny Yates), *The Price You Pay: The Hidden Cost of Women's Relationship to Money* by Margaret Randall, *Religion and Justice in the War Over Bosnia* (edited by G. Scott Davis), and *The Severans: The Changed Roman Empire* by Michael Grant.

Routledge handles its own distribution and also distributes for the U.K. publishing house, Verso.

Query letters and SASEs should be directed to:

Jayne Fargnoli, Editor
Education and sociology.

William Germeno, Editorial Director
Literary and cultural studies, film, communications, theater, classics.

Maureen MacGrogen, Editor

Philosophy and psychoanalysis.

RUNNING PRESS BOOK PUBLISHERS

125 South 22nd Street

Philadelphia, PA 19103

215-567-5080

fax: 215-568-2919

Running Press Book Publishers (founded in 1972) issues hardcover and paperback trade books in general nonfiction. The house shows singular flair in the areas of popular culture and arts, lifestyle, popular science, hobby how-to, and commercial-interest reference titles.

Running Press produces a strong line of specialty items that include ebullient bookstore-counter impulse-sales wares, playful display units for kids' books, and gleaming promotional titles on the Courage Books imprint. In addition, Running Press issues audiocassettes, stylized journals, diaries, calendars, datebooks, bookplates, Miniature Editions, generously appointed educational-entertainment kits, and postcard books. Running Press products often have a sleek production look, and many of its products showcase a humorous or insouciant air. Running Press maintains a staunch backlist.

Running Press accents such titles as the best-selling photoessay book *Sisters* by Carol Seline and Sharon J. Wohlmuth, *Henny Youngman's Big Book of Insults* by Henny Youngman, *The Art and Craft of Wooden Toys* by Ron Fuller, and *The Encyclopedia of Airbrush Techniques* by Michael E. Leek.

Other areas of Running Press interest are typified by *The Little Book of Phobias* (compiled by Joe Kohut), *Skateboarding* by Kevin Wilkins, *Wildflowers: A Romantic History with a Guide to Cultivation* by Fran Hill, *The Encyclopedia of Quilting Techniques* by Katherine Guerrier, and *The Painted Cat* (a Postcard Book).

Running Press distributes its own list.

RUNNING PRESS BOOKS FOR CHILDREN

The Running Press children's list encompasses finely engineered pop-up books, foldouts, small-format editions, kits, coloring books, and how-tos.

Representative of the Running Press children's list: *Knights Treasure Chest* (a discovery kit), *X-Men: The Postcard Book, Kidz Five-Minute Mysteries: Car Sleuth Book and Audiocassette, Start Exploring Places of Mystery: A Fact-Filled Coloring Book* by Emmanuel M. Kramer (illustrations by Helen E. Driggs), *Great Games: More Than 200 Games for All Ages, Bugz: An Extraterrestrial Pop-up Book* (illustrations and paper engineering by Ron van der Meer), and *Where Is Heaven? Children's Wisdom on Facing Death* by Ted Menten.

Query letters and SASEs should be directed to:

Stuart Teacher, President

Nancy Steele, Publisher

Jeff Day, Editorial Director

RUTGERS UNIVERSITY PRESS

(See Directory of University Presses)

ST. MARTIN'S PRESS

175 Fifth Avenue
New York, NY 10010
212-674-5151

St. Martin's produces fiction, general nonfiction, popular special-interest works, scholarly and reference books, and college textbooks. St. Martin's issues hardcover, trade paperback, and mass-market paper editions, and also offers a line of calendars. The house produces a few works for younger readers.

St. Martin's Press (founded in 1952) is an international publisher with a program both broad and comprehensive. St. Martin's has been bought by the German-based international communications conglomerate Verlagsgruppe Georg von Holtzbrinck; within this framework, the house continues to enjoy its long-standing tradition of editorial independence.

Within all categories and fields of publishing interest are published an abundance of works characterized by literary scope; in combination with the house's lively commercial spirit, St. Martin's is a publisher of remarkable depth and strength. The house maintains a strong backlist.

Picador USA is a St. Martin's imprint geared to the international literary scene with a raft of offerings—both originals and reprints—of belletristic writing. (Please see separate Picador USA subentry below.)

St. Martin's is home to a strong list in the areas of lesbian, gay, and gender issues and interest; the house publishes notable works of mainstream fiction and nonfiction in this vein, as well as works with a literary approach. (Please see especially the subentry below for Stonewall Inn Editions.)

St. Martin's Griffin speaks to timely nonfiction and fiction titles in trade paperback. (Please see separate St. Martin's Griffin subentry below.)

Areas of St. Martin's nonfiction interest include current events, popular culture, true crime, cookbooks, business, sports, biography, self-awareness and self-improvement, popular science and psychology, travel and the outdoors, and gardening. St. Martin's instituted a collaborative editorial operation with West Coast–based *Buzz* magazine to develop high-interest titles in the contemporary current-culture arena.

In fiction and literature, St. Martin's publishes top-of-the-line commercial works and is a leader in genres such as mysteries, thrillers, suspense, and historical works, as well as in selected science fiction and fantasy and with some contemporary Westerns (most often in the action-adventure or suspense modes). (For more information regarding category fiction, especially science fiction, fantasy, futurist adventure, horror, and Westerns, please see separate main entry for the St. Martin's affiliate Tor Books.) The publisher's roster embraces cultural biographies and criticism, as well as poetic works and short-story collections.

On the St. Martin's nonfiction list: *Tug of War: Today's Global Currency Crisis* by Paul Erdman, *Accidentally, On Purpose: The Making of a Personal Injury Underworld in America* by Ken Dornstein, *Kashmir in the Crossfire* by Victoria Scofield, *Olympic Politics: Athens to Atlanta, 1896–1996* by Christopher R. Hill, *The Buildings of Europe: Rome* by Christopher Woodward, *Coming into Being: Artifacts and Texts in the Evolution of Consciousness* by William Irwin Thompson, *Hacking the Future: Stories for the Flesh-Eating '90s* by Arthur and Marilouise Kroker, *Sexational Secrets: Erotic Advice Your Mother Never Told You* by Susan Crain Bakos, *Best Words, Best Order* by Stephen Dobyns, *Power and Beauty: Images of Women in Art* by Georges Duby and Michelle Perrot, and *Lebanese Cuisine: More than 250 Authentic Recipes from the Most Elegant Middle Eastern Cuisine* by Anissa Helou.

Representative St. Martin's frontlist fiction and literary titles: *The Vinegar Jar* by Berlie Doherty, *Dog Eat Dog* by Edward Bunker, *The Girl with the Botticelli Eyes* by Herbert Lieberman, *The Darkening Leaf* by Caroline Strickland, *Panda Ray* by Michael Kandel, *Malice Prepense* by Kate Wilhelm, *The Sexual Life of Savages and Other Stories* by Stokes Howell, *Serial Killer Days* by David Prill, *Land Girls* by Angela Huth, *From Bondage: Mercy of a Rude Stream* (volume 3) by Henry Roth, *Snow Wolf* by Glenn Meade, *The Big Blowdown* by George P. Pelicanos, *Murder on the Appian Way* by Steven Saylor, and *A Price for Everything* by Mary Sheepshanks.

In the field of mystery, suspense, and thrillers, St. Martin's shows prowess with a lineup rich and varied, encompassing individual works as well as ongoing series, published in hardcover and trade paper. Dead Letter is St. Martin's sobriquet for an adventurous, eclectic, commercial mass-market paperback list of mystery and suspense, including reprints of successful hardcover titles.

In this arena St. Martin's hosts offerings such as *The Company She Kept* (an Inspector Gil Mayo mystery) by Marjorie Eccles, *The Beekeeper's Apprentice* by Laurie R. King, *Poet in the Gutter* by John Baker, *The Laughing Hangman* by Edward Marston, *The Ghosts of Saigon* by John Maddox Roberts, *Death at Rainy Mountain* by Mardi Oakley Medawar, *Rust on the Razor* (a Tom and Scott mystery) by Mark Richard Zubro, *Past Mischief* by Clare Curzon, and *Dance of the Scarecrows* by Ray Sipherd.

St. Martin's distributes its own books as well as those of houses such as Academy Editions, Audio Renaissance, Boyds Mills Press, Consumer Reports Books, Forge, Rodale Press, Tor Books, Universe Publishing, and World Almanac.

PICADOR USA

St. Martin's Press initiated the Picador USA imprint during the last part of 1994, and the house became an immediate literary presence with an array of titles featuring an international cast of world-class writers. Picador USA publishes in hardcover and trade paperback editions, and highlights original titles as well as reprints.

Picador marketing support encompasses dynamic full-scale promotion and advertising campaigns, author publicity, exposure via major book and literary reviews, and radio spots.

From the Picador portfolio: *The Romantic Movement: Sex, Shopping and the Novel* by Alain de Botton, *Rotten: No Irish, No Blacks, No Dogs* by John Lydon (with Keith and Kent Zimmerman), *Leni Riefenstahl: A Memoir* by Leni Riefenstahl, *The Dog with the Chip in His Neck: Essays from NPR and Elsewhere* by Andrei Codrescu, *Voodoo Dreams: A Novel of Marie Laveau* by Jewell Parker Rhodes, *The Palace Thief* (stories) by Ethan Canin, *Four Hands: A Novel* by Paco Ignacio Taibo II (translated by Laura C. Dail), *The Bird Artist* by Howard Norman, and *Elevator Music: A Surreal History of Muzak, Easy-Listening, and Other Moodsong* by Joseph Lanza.

STONEWALL INN EDITIONS

Stonewall Inn Editions publishes works with a lesbian and gay cultural slant in hardcover and paperback editions. The house addresses trade areas such as current events and public interest, reference works, cultural affairs, and literary anthologies, and produces Stonewall Inn Studio Books (featuring graphically lavish and luxuriously produced gift volumes) and the Stonewall Inn Mysteries line. The scope of St. Martin's lesbian- and gay-interest list is not limited to works issued under the Stonewall Inn imprint.

Featured Stonewall Inn authors have included lights such as Quentin Crisp, Larry Kramer, Paul Monette, Ethan Mordden, Denise Ohio, Randy Shilts, Edmund White, and Mark Richard Zubro.

Titles from Stonewall: *Another Dead Teenager* (a Paul Turner mystery) by Mark Richard Zubro, *Sportsdykes: Stories from On and Off the Field* by Susan Fox Rogers, *The Violet Quill Reader: The Emergence of Gay Writing after Stonewall* (edited by David Bergman), *End of the Empire* (visionary romance-adventure) by Denise Ohio, *Sacred Lips of the Bronx* (a love story) by Douglas Sadonick, and *Dark Wind: A True Account of Hurricane Gloria's Assault on Fire Island* by John Jiler.

ST. MARTIN'S GRIFFIN

St. Martin's Griffin publishes trade paperbacks exclusively, with a strong emphasis in crafts, cooking, modern and contemporary fiction, current culture, biography, and travel. Griffin authors include Douglas Coupland, Studs Terkel, Doris Kearns-Goodwin, Vincent Scully, James Baldwin, and Bob Dylan.

Titles from Griffin: *Generation X* by Douglas Coupland, *Vurt* by Jeff Noon, *The Nancy Drew Scrapbook* by Karen Plunkett-Powell, *England's Dreaming* by Jon Savage, *The Cancer Prevention Diet* by Michio Kushi, *Bread Machine Magic* by Linda Rehberg and Lois Conway, *Route 66* by Michael Wallis, *Critical Path* by R. Buckminster Fuller, and *The World's Most Famous Math Problem* by Marilyn Vos Savant.

Travel titles include the Let's Go Series, currently publishing twenty-four new titles a year and six map guides.

A THOMAS DUNNE BOOK FOR ST. MARTIN'S PRESS

In Thomas Dunne's twenty-five years at St. Martin's Press, he has published virtually every kind of book from run-away bestsellers such as *The Shell Seekers* by Rosamunde Pilcher and *River God* by Wilber Smith to the critically acclaimed nonfiction of Robert Kaplan and Juliet Barker. His imprint produces roughly 150 titles per year and covers a wide array of interests including commercial fiction, mysteries, military histories, biographies, divination systems, politics, philosophy, humor, literary fiction, and current events.

Other Thomas Dunne books include *The Book of Runes* by Ralph Blum, *Snow Wolf* by Glenn Meade, *The It-Doesn't-Matter-Suit* by Sylvia Plath, and *Heart of Justice* by William Coughlin.

A WYATT BOOK FOR ST. MARTIN'S PRESS

Robert B. Wyatt is an editor and publisher whose celebrated career has included stints with Avon and Ballantine. At St. Martin's Press, Wyatt's individualistic imprint is characterized by an enviable editorial eye that encompasses commercial fiction within a vision both vast and deeply personalized.

Wyatt books include *Here, Kitty, Kitty* by Winifred Elze, *Cowkind* by Ray Peterson, *Lorien Lost* by Michael King, *Family Story* by Alison Scott Skelton, *The Virgin Knows* by Christine Palamidessi Moore, *Voices from Silence* by Douglas Unger, *If You Ask Me* by Libby Gelman-Waxner, and *Elena of the Stars* by C. P. Rosenthal.

ST. MARTIN'S SCHOLARLY AND REFERENCE BOOKS

Scholarly and reference books published by St. Martin's Press include works of mainstream-crossover potential keyed to areas of the house's general publishing program, as well as volumes pertinent to particular professional and academic fields.

Some titles here: *The End of the House of Windsor: Birth of a British Republic* by Stephen Haseler, *North Korea and the Bomb: A Case Study in Nonproliferation* by Michael J. Mazarr, *The Classical Vernacular: Architectural Principles in an Age of Nihilism* by Roger Scruton, *Henry James: A Literary Life* by Kenneth Graham, and *The Gates of Gaza: Israel's Road to Suez and Back, 1955–1957* by Mordechai Bar-On.

Query letters and SASEs should be directed to:

Sally Richardson, President and Publisher Trade Division; President, Mass Market Division

Matthew J. Shear, Vice President and Publisher, Mass-Market Division
All mass-market categories in fiction and nonfiction.

(Ms.) Reagan Arthur, Editor
Contemporary fiction, mysteries, media-related nonfiction. Works with the Picador USA imprint. Projects include *I Killed Hemingway* by William McCranor Henderson, *The Lost Diaries of Frans Hals* by Michael Kernan, and *The Ballad of Rocky Ruiz* by Manuel Ramos.

Ruth Cavin, Senior Editor; Associate Publisher, Thomas Dunne Books
Crime fiction, contemporary fiction, anecdotal science and medicine novelties (quotation books). Titles include *The Beekeeper's Apprentice* by Laurie R. King, *Whoever Fights Monsters* by Robert Ressler, and *Four Hands* by Paco Ignacio Taibo II.

Shawn Coyne, Senior Editor
Commercial fiction, mysteries, psychological suspense, sports, true crime, popular culture. Projects include *Salt of the Earth* by Jack Olsen, *Rice* by Jerry Rice and Michael Silver, and *Psychic Warrior* by David Morehouse.

Hope Dellon, Senior Editor
Fiction: mysteries, serious historical novels. Nonfiction: parenting, women's issues, psychology, biography. Titles include *Mary Queen of Scotland and the Isles* by Margaret George, *The Sculptress* by Minette Walters, and *Beyond Jennifer and Jason* by Linda Rosenkrantz & Pamela Redmond Satran.

Thomas L. Dunne, Vice President, Executive Editor; Publisher, Thomas Dunne Books
Eclectic interests; projects have covered commercial women's fiction, mysteries, military histories, biographies, divination systems, politics, philosophy, humor, literary fiction, current events. Titles include *The Shell Seekers* by Rosamunde Pilcher, *The Book of Runes* by Ralph H. Blum, and *Balkan Ghosts* by Robert Kaplan.

(Ms.) Ensley Eikenburg, Associate Editor
Fiction: commercial and literary. Nonfiction: travel, women's issues, sexuality, humor, pop culture, anything controversial. Projects include the best-selling Let's Go travel series, *XXX: A Woman's Right to Pornography* by Wendy McElory, and *Boy Culture* by Matthew Rettenmann.

Jennifer Enderlin, Senior Editor
Women's fiction, psychological suspense, general commercial fiction. Commercial nonfiction (sex, relationships, psychology). Projects include *To Build the Life You Want, Create the Work You Love* by Marsha Sinetar, *End the Struggle and Dance with Life* by Susan Jeffers, and *Just between Us Girls* by Sydney Biddle Barrows.

James Fitzgerald, Executive Editor
Autobiography/biography, music, current culture, fiction. Titles include *Leni Riefenstahl* by Leni Riefenstahl, *Generation X* by Douglas Coupland, and *Rotten* by John Lydon. Responsibilities include overseeing the Buzz Books imprint (featuring primarily a West Coast purview).

Heather Jackson, Editor
Commercial nonfiction of all stripes: health, nutrition, childcare, popular reference, popular culture, psychology/self-help. Titles include *The Ten Commandments of*

Pleasure by Susan Block, *The Kitchen Klutz* by Colleen Johnson, and *Secrets of Serotonin* by Carol Hart.

Keith Kahla, Editor
Gay and lesbian interest, mystery and suspense, literary fiction, cartoon books, anthologies. Projects include *Murder on the Appian Way* by Steven Saylor; *Pawn to Queen Four* by Louis Eighner; and *Beyond Acceptance: Parents of Lesbians and Gays Talk about Their Experiences* by Caroline Griffin, Marian Wirth, and Arthur G. Wirth.

Todd Keithley, Associate Editor
Commercial fiction, mysteries, Westerns, military nonfiction. Projects include *Outlaw Kingdom* by Matt Braun, *The Sundown Riders* by Ralph Compton, and *Mobile Guerrilla Force* by James Donohue.

Amy Kolenik, Assistant Editor
Commercial women's fiction: contemporaries, historicals, suspense, and paranormal.

(Ms.) Marian Lizzi, Associate Editor
Fiction: literary novels and story collections (especially those by new young writers). Nonfiction: pop culture, women's issues, popular history, self-improvement, and an occasional cookbook. Titles include *Funk: The Music, the People, and the Rhythm of the One* by Rickey Vincent, *Welcome to the Jungle* by Geoffrey Holtz, *The Greek Vegetarian* by Diane Kochilas, and *The Vinegar Jar* by Berlie Doherty.

Tom McCormack, Chairman, Editorial Director
Best-seller fiction, controversial current affairs. Titles include *Gospel* by Wilton Barnhardt, *The Silence of the Lambs* by Thomas Harris, and *All Creatures Great and Small* by James Herriot.

Sandra McCormack, Senior Editor
Popular women's fiction, mysteries. Projects include *Family Games* by Jean Stubbs, *Eliza's Daughter* by Joan Aiken, and *Uncertain April* by Betty Palmer Nelson.

Calvert D. Morgan Jr., Editor
Nonfiction: American culture and history, biography, books on music and film, essays. Fiction: Exceptional voices in American fiction, both literary and commercial. Titles include *King of Comedy: The Life and Art of Jerry Lewis* by Shawn Levy, *Blues and Trouble* (short stories) by Tom Piazza, and *The Florence King Reader*.

Kelley Ragland, Assistant Editor
Popular and literary fiction: mysteries—wide range, thrillers, suspense. Serious contemporary or historical women's fiction. Literary nonfiction, especially related to women's or racial issues, also including parenting, psychology, biography; essays. Commercial and serious nonfiction. Open to new writers: Attracted to the quality and craft of the writing; looks for standout characters and unique voice.

Anne Savarese, Editor
Practical and popular nonfiction, travel, women's issues, mystery and contemporary fiction. Projects include *The Country Music Lover's Guide to the U.S.A.* by Janet Byron, *Keep Still* (a Marti MacAlister mystery) by Eleanor Taylor Bland, and *Daughters of Feminists* by Rose L. Glickman.

Charles Spicer, Senior Editor

Commercial fiction: crime, suspense, mysteries. Nonfiction: true crime, biography, history. Titles include *The Other Mrs. Kennedy* by Jerry Oppenheimer, *Topping from Below* by Laura Reese, and *The Rise and Fall of the British Empire* by Lawrence James.

Gordon Van Gelder, Editor

Science fiction, popular culture, mystery/horror, books on writing. Titles include *The Encyclopedia of Science Fiction* by John Clute and Peter Nicholls, *The Psychotronic Video Guide* by Michael J. Weldon, and *The Big Blowdown* by George P. Pelicanos.

Robert Weil, Senior Editor

Nonfiction, biography, popular culture, literary fiction. Projects include *Mercy of a Rude Stream* by Henry Roth, *More Than Words* by Mario Cuomo, and *Mankiller* by Wilma Mankiller.

Jennifer Weis, Executive Editor

Commercial fiction: women's, thrillers, romance. Commercial nonfiction: people books, narrative nonfiction, cookbooks, self-help, health and parenting, humor, popular culture. Projects include *Aaron Spelling: A Prime-Time Life* by Aaron Spelling, *Are You Normal?* by Bernice Kanner, and *Innocence Undone* by Kat Martin.

George Witte, Director, Picador USA and Editor, St. Martin's Press

For Picador: Quality literary fiction and narrative nonfiction of literary or intellectual interest. Titles include *Farewell, I'm Bound to Leave You* by Fred Chappell, *The Book of Secrets* by M. G. Vassanji, and *Hawk Flies Above* by Lisa Norton. For St. Martin's: commercial fiction, business, sports, politics, contemporary issues. Titles include *Dumbing Down Our Kids* by Charles Sykes, *Official Privilege* by P. T. Deutermann, *The On-Line Investor* by Ted Allrich, and *Wrigleyville* by Peter Golenbock.

Robert B. Wyatt, President, A Wyatt Book for St. Martin's Press

Commercial fiction, especially original, new, high-caliber writing. Projects include *Tully* by Paullina Simons, *Saudade* by Katherine Vaz, and *Jennie* by Douglas Preston.

SASQUATCH BOOKS

1008 Western Avenue, Suite 300
Seattle, WA 98104
206-467-4300

Sasquatch specializes in the areas of travel, regional interest, gardening, guidebooks, nature, the outdoors, and food and wine. The publisher is intent on broadening its Pacific Northwest regional concentration and wishes to strengthen its children's list. An additional area of Sasquatch interest is strong literary nonfiction.

Sasquatch Books (founded in 1979) has a string of small-press successes in its skein. Among these: the Best Places travel series (*Northwest Best Places*, *Northern California Best Places*), the Cascadia Gardening series, and the Northwest Mythic Landscape series.

Representative Sasquatch titles: *Red Hot Peppers* (a book/audiocassette/jump rope pack) by Bob and Diane Boardman, *Overstory* (literature) by Robert Leo Heilman, and *O Is for Orca* (photographs by Art Wolfe; text by Andrea Helman).

Query letters and SASEs should be directed to:

Chad Haight, President

Gary Luke, Editorial Director

SCHOLASTIC, INC.

730 Broadway
New York, NY 10003
212-343-6100

Scholastic produces titles for younger readers. Scholastic lists age-range-targeted narrative fiction and general-interest nonfiction as well as instructional materials for use from early childhood through high school.

The house publishes trade and educational lines in hardcover and paperback editions, and owns a niche in electronic publishing. A portion of Scholastic's trade list is intended to appeal to young adults and younger readers alike. In addition, Scholastic, Inc. (founded in 1920) issues magazines, operates classroom book clubs, and offers computer software.

Scholastic offers a wide array of books in series, among them Big Books (picture books), lift-the-flap books, board books, gift sets, ESL (English as a second language) titles, easy readers, middle-grade readers, and a panoply of readers and professional materials for teachers. Scholastic's current enterprise encompasses Spanish-language and bilingual Spanish/English items.

Sample Scholastic projects and imprints are Blue Sky Press, Cartwheel Books, Nightmare Hall, Time Quest Books, The Baby-Sitters Club, Mariposa, and Scholastic Reference. The incredibly successful Goosebumps series of scary stories by R. L. Stine has engendered a line of spin-offs and tie-ins including collectors' novelty items. Scholastic is home to a distinguished roster of writers and illustrators.

Scholastic handles its own distribution.

The editors at Scholastic wish to emphasize that the house accepts *no* unsolicited manuscripts, and that the acquisitions personnel deal only with agented material. Query letters and SASEs should be directed to:

Diane Hess, Executive Editor

Grace Maccarone, Executive Editor, Cartwheel Books

Ann Reit, Executive Editor

SEAL PRESS

3131 Western Avenue, Suite 410
Seattle, WA 98121
206-283-7844

Seal Press (founded in 1976) is a smaller house dedicated to promoting the work of women writers. In addition to its several successful mystery series, Seal publishes a wide range of fiction and poetry, and titles in women's and lesbian studies, sports and the outdoors, popular culture, parenting, self-help, and health.

Seal Press books enjoy a reputation for high literary quality, and the list often features finely designed, well-produced editions in hardcover and trade paperback. Seal Press supports a hardy backlist.

Representative of Seal nonfiction: *Wired Women: Gender and New Realities in Cyberspace* (edited by Lynn Cherny and Elizabeth Reba Weise), *Powerful Invisible Things: A Sportswoman's Notebook* by Gretchen Legler, *Solo: Women Going It Alone in the Outdoors* (edited by Susan Fox Rogers), *New Beginnings: A Creative Guide for Women Who Have Left Abusive Partners* by Sharon Doane, *SurferGirls: Look Ethel! An Internet Guide for Us!* by Laurel Gilbert and Crystal Kile, *She's a Rebel: The History of Women in Rock & Roll* by Gillian G. Gaar (preface by Yoko Ono), and *A Vindication of the Rights of Whores* (edited by Gail Phetersen; preface by Margo St. James).

Seal fiction and literature includes *Night Bites: Vampire Stories by Women* (edited by Victoria A. Brownworth), *Nervous Conditions* by Tsitsi Dangaremba, *The Dyke and the Dybbuk* by Ellen Galford, *The Forbidden Poems* by Becky Birtha, *Another America/Otra America* (poetry) by Barbara Kingsolver (with Spanish translations by Rebeca Cartes), *Egalia's Daughters: A Satire of the Sexes* by Gerd Brantenberg, and *Nowle's Passing* (existential mystery) by Edith Forbes.

Mystery series from Seal include Barbara Wilson's Cassandra Reilly series and Pam Nilsen mysteries, Elisabeth Bowers's Meg Lacey series, Jean Taylor's Maggie Garrett series, and Ellen Hart's Jane Lawless mysteries.

Emblematic of special Seal projects is the volume *She Who Was Lost Is Remembered: Healing from Incest through Creativity* (edited by Louise M. Wisechild), which brings together works from visual artists, musicians, and writers.

Seal Press is distributed to the trade by Publishers Group West.

Query letters and SASEs should be directed to:

Faith Conlon, Publisher

Holly Morris, Editorial Director

SELF-COUNSEL PRESS

1704 North State Street
Bellingham, WA 98225
360-676-4530

Vancouver editorial office:

1481 Charlotte Road
North Vancouver, BC Canada V7J 1H1
604-986-3366

Self-Counsel produces business how-to, legal reference, self-help, and practical popular psychology. Topical areas include entrepreneurship, the legal system and you, business training, the family, and human resources development and management. The house also produces specialty titles geared to lifestyles and to business and legal issues in Florida, Oregon, and Washington.

Self-Counsel Press (founded in 1977) is a smaller house dedicated to providing well-researched, up-to-date books (primarily trade paperbacks) as well as cassettes and work kits. The company's trade motto is "Our business is helping business people succeed." Self-Counsel's expertly written books don't just tell people what to do: They show them—step by step—how to do it. Kick Start Guides is a lineup of pocket-size titles designed for business travelers.

On the Self-Counsel list: *A Small Business Guide to Doing Big Business on the Internet* by Brian Hurley and Peter Birkwood, *No B.S. Time Management for Entrepreneurs* by Dan Kennedy, *Cut Your Losses! A Smart Retailer's Guide to Loss Prevention* by Keith O'Brien, *Write On! Business Writing Basics* by Jane Watson, *Start and Run a Profitable Secondhand Bookstore: A Book-Lover's Step-by-Step Business Plan* by Tracy Jones, *Costa Rica* (a Kick Start guide) by Guy and Victoria Brooks, *A Family Remembers: How to Create a Family Memoir Using Video and Tape Recorders* by Paul McLaughlin, and *Producing a First-Class Newsletter: A Guide to Planning, Writing, Editing, Designing, Photography, Production, and Printing* by Barbara Fanson.

Self-Counsel Press operates its own distributional services.

Query letters and SASEs should be directed to:

Diana R. Douglas, President (Vancouver Office)

Ruth Wilson, Managing Editor (Vancouver Office)

SERPENT'S TAIL/HIGH RISK

180 Varick Street 10th Floor
New York, NY 10014
212-741-8500

Serpent's Tail (founded in 1986) is known for innovative writing in literary fiction, poetry, culture-keyed popular reference, and issues-centered nonfiction. House interest includes gender and sexual expression, the arts, photography, and gift books, cards, and calendars. Serpent's Tail imprints include High Risk, Mask Noir, and Atlas Books. The Midnight Classics line features reprint editions of books that have altered the landscape of American culture. Serpent's Tail offerings are issued in finely designed trade paperback editions. Many Serpent's Tail titles feature European literary voices; the house also operates in the United Kingdom from its London base.

Serpent's Tail fiction and literary works: *Nearly Roadkill: An Infobahn Erotic Adventure* by Caitlin Sullivan and Kate Bornstein, *Slow Death* by Stewart Home, *Somewhere in Advance of Nowhere* (poems) by Jayne Cortez, and *Essays* by Kathy

Acker. The hefty backlist includes such groundbreaking works as *Jack the Modernist* by Robert Glück, *Spinsters* by Pagan Kennedy, *Ghost of Chance* by William S. Burroughs, and *Armed Response* by Ann Rower.

Nonfiction encompasses such titles as *Man Enough to Be a Woman* by Jayne County with Rupert Smith, *The Ultimate Guide to Lesbian and Gay Film and Video* (edited by Jenni Olson), *Ocean of Sound: Aether Talk, Ambient Sound, and Imaginary Worlds* by David Toop, and *Pulp Culture: Hard-Boiled Fiction and the Cold War* by Woody Haut. A special spin-off package is *A Class Apart: The Private Pictures of Montague Glover* (a photographic cultural-historical gift edition) and *Monty's Private Pictures: Thirty Postcards from A Class Apart* (both edited by James Gardener).

Reissues from Midnight Classics include *Inside Daisy Clover* by Gavin Lambert, *Nog* by Rudolph Wurlitzer, and *They Shoot Horses, Don't They?* by Horace McCoy.

Distribution to the book trade for Serpent's Tail is handled through Consortium Book Sales and Distribution.

Query letters and SASEs should be directed to:

Ira Silverberg, Associate Publisher

Pete Ayrton, Publisher

Amy Scholder, Acquisitions Editor

SEVEN STORIES PRESS

632 Broadway 7th Floor
New York, NY 10012
212-995-0908

Seven Stories publishes trade nonfiction, commercial literature, and popular reference works. The house specialty: books with a provocatively high edge in current events, contemporary culture, and biography/personality and memoirs, and those with inventive literary writing (including classic reprints).

Seven Stories Press expands the heritage of publisher Dan Simon, who emigrated from Four Walls Eight Windows (see separate main entry) to originate this press, a move consummated by early 1996. Seven Stories's assets include backlist properties formerly·cataloged by Four Walls.

Sample titles from Seven Stories: *Marilyn: Story of a Woman* (a novel in graphic form) by Kathryn Hyatt, *Censored: The News That Didn't Make the News and Why: The Project Censored Yearbook* by Carl Jensen and Project Censored (introduction by Walter Cronkite), *The Winner of the Slow Bicycle Race: Satirical Writings* by Paul Krassner, *Night Again: Contemporary Fiction from Vietnam* (edited by Linh Dinh), *And We Sold the Rain: Contemporary Fiction from Central America* (edited by Rosario Santos), and *Nonconformity: Writing on Writing* by Nelson Algren.

Distribution to the trade for Seven Stories is handled by Publishers Group West.

Query letters and SASEs should be directed to:

Dan Simon, Publisher

SHAMBHALA PUBLICATIONS

(See Directory of Religious, Spiritual, and Inspirational Publishers)

M. E. SHARPE

80 Business Park Drive
Armonk, NY 10504
914-273-1800

Sharpe publishes across a broad editorial range of the social sciences, including law, literature and literary criticism, area studies, women's studies, multicultural studies, business, comparative politics, and international and developmental economics. Special emphasis is notable in the areas of Asian studies, business (international and domestic), Latin American studies, economics, political science, history, sociology, comparative public-policy analysis, and studies of the formerly Soviet area and Eastern Europe.

M. E. Sharpe (founded in 1959) is a privately held company that produces trade, reference, business, and professional books in hardcover and paperback. Along with the primarily scholarly titles, M. E. Sharpe publishes major single and multivolume reference works under the Sharpe Reference imprint, books aimed at the professional market under the Sharpe Professional imprint, and books aimed at the general reader under the North Castle Books imprint.

Many of M. E. Sharpe's frontlist titles are geared to a general readership, while a large proportion of the list is especially keyed to a scholarly academic and professional audience, with a concentration in the social sciences. The Sharpe list thus encompasses original research, policy studies, translations, reference compendiums, reprints of classics, and books deriving from scholarly disciplines that lend themselves to a slot in the trade market. Sharpe started as a publisher of academic and professional journals and, by the late 1970s, had begun expansion into book publishing.

Sharpe is now on the lookout for more titles of the practical how-to variety to highlight on its professional, technical, and reference lists. Sharpe sells and promotes its titles both nationally and internationally; the house is a recognized industry leader in worldwide distribution. Although a large portion of Sharpe's sales come from direct marketing, it also pursues a variety of means to sell its list—such as libraries, universities, trade and institutional bookstores, and catalogs. First and foremost, however, in order to be given serious consideration, works submitted to Sharpe must have the potential to work as direct-mail items.

In the literary arena, Sharpe's list features works by a number of Nobel laureates, including Wasily Leontief, Vaclav Havel, and Oe Kenzaburo. North Castle Books is an imprint designed to bring the global sweep of knowledge to a broad general audience, principally through trade bookstore distribution. North Castle emphasizes works with literary and cultural significance issued in trade paperback editions.

Representative Sharpe titles are *Freedom Road* (in a new edition) by Howard Fast, *The United Nations at the Crossroads of Reform* by Wendell Gordon, *Moscow DMZ: The Story of the International Effort to Convert Russian Weapons Science to Peaceful Purposes* by Glen E. Schweitzer, *Look for the Union Label* by Gus Tyler, *Hope Is the Last to Die: Coming of Age Under Nazi Terror* by Halina Birenbaum, *Children of the Paper Crane* by Masamoto Nasu (on the North Castle Books imprint), *The Pinch Runner Memorandum* by Kenzaburo Oe, and *The New Pacific Community in the 1990s* by Young Jeh Kim.

M. E. Sharpe orchestrates its own distributional network, including stateside regional sales representatives, library-market specialists, and international wholesalers and reps.

Query letters and SASEs should be directed to:

Peter Coveney, Executive Editor
American history, religion, philosophy, sociology.

Stephen Dalphin, Executive Editor
Textbooks/economics. Latin America studies, world history.

Patricia A. Kolb, Executive Editor
Books about Europe and the former Soviet Union.

Olivia Lane, Executive Editor
Professional business books.

Doug Merwin, Executive Editor
Asian studies.

SHEEP MEADOW PRESS

P.O. Box 1345
Riverdale, NY 10471
718-548-5547

Sheep Meadow publishes a literary list that accents poetry, the shorter prose fictional forms, and the essay, as well as selected nonfiction. Sheep Meadow has on occasion ventured into mainstream trade venues, as with the lifestyle title *Dean Cuisine: The Liberated Man's Guide to Fine Cooking* by Jack Greenberg and James Vorenberg.

Sheep Meadow Press (inaugurated in 1976) sports an international cast of renowned authors and offers small-press dedication to expressive, meaningful writing and fine bookmaking.

From the Sheep Meadow poetry list: *The Ice Lizard* by Judith Johnson, *The Center for Cold Weather* by Cleopatra Mathis, *Collected Poems (1935–1990)* by F. T. Prince, *The Landscape Is Behind the Door* by Pierre Martory (translated by John Ashbery), *Selected Poems* by Diana Der-Hovanessian, and *The Past Keeps Changing* by Chana Bloch.

Indicative of Sheep Meadow's other interests: *Cape Discovery: The Provincetown Fine Arts Work Center Anthology* (edited by Bruce Smith and Catherine Gammon),

Interviews and Encounters by Stanley Kunitz, *Kabbalah and Consciousness* by Allen Afterman, *No Success Like Failure: The American Love of Self-Destruction, Self-Aggrandizement and Breaking Even* by Ivan Solotaroff, and *The Stories and Recollections of Umberto Saba* (translated by Estelle Gilson).

Sheep Meadow titles are available directly from the publisher (call 800-972-4491) and through a variety of trade and library wholesalers, including Inland, Small Press Distribution, Yankee Book Peddler, and Blackwell North American.

All manuscripts must be accompanied by SASEs (reporting time is six months). Projects should be directed to:

Stanley Moss, President and Publisher

SIERRA CLUB BOOKS

100 Bush Street
San Francisco, CA 94104
415-291-1600
fax: 415-291-1602

Sierra Club publishes books in the categories of nature, appropriate technology, outdoor activities, mountaineering, health, gardening, natural history, travel, and environmental issues. Among Sierra Club series are the Adventure Travel Guides, Sierra Club Totebooks, Naturalist's Guides, Natural Traveler, the John Muir Library, and Guides to the Natural Areas of the United States. Sierra Club Books has a strong division that publishes works geared to children and young adults (see separate subentry below).

Founded in 1892 by John Muir, the Sierra Club membership has for over a century been in the forefront of the study and protection of the earth's scenic, environmental, and ecological resources; Sierra Club Books is part of the nonprofit effort the club carries on as a public trust. The house publishes hardcover and paperback books, many of them finely illustrated.

Highlights of the Sierra Club list: *The Sierra Club Green Guide: Everybody's Desk Reference to Environmental Information* by Andrew J. Feldman; *The Sierra Club Wetlands Reader: A Literary Companion* by Sam Wilson and Tom Moritz; *Adventuring in the Pacific* (revised edition) by Susanna Margolis; *The Unsettling of America: Culture and Agriculture* by Wendell Berry; *Mirage: The False Promise of Desert Agriculture* by Russell Clemings; *Baikal* by Peter Mathiessen; and *Ecopsychology* by Theodore Roszak, Mary E. Gomes, and Allen D. Kanner.

Sierra Club Books are distributed to the book trade by Random House.

Query letters and SASEs should be directed to:

James Kohee, Senior Editor
Areas consistent with house list.

Barbara Ras, Senior Editor
Nature writing; environmental issues; nonfiction literary works dealing with nature, environment, cultural anthropology, history, travel, and geography. Fiction and poetry that is clearly related to natural or environmental themes.

SIERRA CLUB BOOKS FOR CHILDREN AND YOUNG ADULTS

Sierra Club Books for Children and Young Adults publishes primarily nonfiction, as well as selected fiction keyed to subject areas that generally reflect the overall Sierra Club house emphasis.

From Sierra Club Books for Children and Young Adults: *Wolf of Shadows* by Whitley Streiber, *What Is an Amphibian?* by Robert Snedden, *Snakes* by Eric S. Grace (from Sierra Club Wildlife Library), *Safari beneath the Sea: The Wonder World of the North Pacific Coast* by Diane Swanson, *Dancers in the Garden* by Joanne Ryder (illustrated by Judith Lopez), and *Ancient Ones: The World of the Old-Growth Douglas Fir* by Barbara Bash.

Sierra Club Books for Children and Young Adults is distributed to the trade by Little, Brown.

Query letters and SASEs should be directed to:

Helen Sweetland, Editor in Chief, Sierra Club Children's Book Division

SILHOUETTE BOOKS

(See Harlequin Books)

SIMON & SCHUSTER
PARAMOUNT COMMUNICATIONS
POCKET BOOKS/SCRIBNER/THE FREE PRESS
MACMILLAN PUBLISHING USA
PRENTICE HALL

New York offices:
1230 Avenue of the Americas
New York, NY 10020
212-698-7000

Simon & Schuster is a leader in consumer books, educational and academic works, business and professional publishing, and reference lines. Simon & Schuster represents an elaborate network of divisions, imprints, and publishing groups that together address virtually all publishing categories and market niches. This powerhouse of publishing operates primarily from editorial environs at several New York addresses, as well as from offices in New Jersey, Virginia, San Francisco, and other United States locations.

S&S imprints and divisions include Simon & Schuster Trade Publishing, Simon & Schuster Children's Publishing Division, Simon & Schuster Interactive, Pocket Books, Scribner, The Free Press, Brassey's (U.S.), Jossey-Bass, Prentice Hall, Silver Burdett Ginn, Allyn & Bacon, Computer Curriculum Corporation, Educational Management Group, and Macmillan Publishing USA.

Simon & Schuster Trade imprints, along with Scribner and Pocket Books programs and the Free Press, cover the commercial trade spectrum. In addition to its trade lineup, Pocket Books maintains a traditional mass-market publishing concentration. Macmillan and Prentice Hall have a commanding presence in professional, business, and academic publishing. Simon & Schuster Children's Publishing Division is a strapping domain of books for young readers.

The Simon & Schuster Trade Division is first and foremost a publisher of popular works, with a vast list that includes imprints such as Simon & Schuster, Touchstone, and Fireside.

Pocket Books publishes commercial works in fiction and nonfiction in hardcover, trade paperback, and mass-market paperback editions, and offers movie and television tie-ins on the Tundra imprint.

Simon & Schuster operates divisions (many under the Macmillan and Prentice Hall designations) devoted primarily to business, professional, and educational offerings. It also offers books in the arenas of hobbies, horticulture, and travel, while additionally addressing the related areas of personal development, lifestyle how-to, and general reference.

Simon & Schuster is the book-publishing flagship of Viacom-owned Paramount Communications. Viacom Inc. is an enormous communications operation—a colossus that straddles the media worlds of electronics and print.

Simon & Schuster (founded in 1924) was among America's largest publishing houses by the time it was acquired by Gulf + Western in 1975. Subsequent to the S&S acquisition, G+W transformed its own corporate tag to Paramount Communications, under which name it operated a megamedia conglomerate that encompassed film and television interests as well as publishing enterprises.

In 1984 Simon & Schuster acquired Prentice Hall, itself a publisher of mammoth size and proven reputation in exceedingly well-targeted professional and educational markets.

The 1994 acquisition of the extensive remnants of the Macmillan Publishing Group by Paramount fit nicely into a corporate tradition of multifaceted change and growth. The former trade-publishing wing of Macmillan was realigned (along with other S&S properties) under the Scribner imprint in 1994; by the middle of 1995, a new trade division emerged, bearing a refreshed Macmillan logo, to concentrate on practical nonfiction, business, and popular reference.

The Paramount Publishing designation was inaugurated in 1993 to cover all Simon & Schuster and Prentice Hall divisions, as well as the operations embraced in the Paramount buyout of Macmillan Publishing Group. Many Paramount Publishing lines continued to be issued under their historic imprints. In light of established trade-name recognition and publishing tradition, in May 1994 the name of the book-publishing umbrella reverted to what it had been—thus the house of Simon & Schuster endures.

Simon & Schuster distributes its many constituent imprints and divisions (please see separate subentries below); S&S also handles distribution services for a number of smaller and midsize houses.

SIMON & SCHUSTER TRADE DIVISION

The Simon & Schuster stamp (an iconic rendition of Jean François Millet's famous sower) signals hardcover and trade paperback books in a wide range of commercial nonfiction and fiction areas, generally selected for potential appeal to the broadest possible spectrum of mainstream and special-interest readerships.

In nonfiction, Simon & Schuster is ever a major player in topical arenas such as popular history and current affairs, popular culture, business, health, self-awareness and improvement, and popular biography and memoirs.

Simon & Schuster nonfiction titles include *Blood Sport* by James B. Stewart, *It Takes a Village* by Hillary Rodham Clinton, *Reasonable Doubts: The O. J. Simpson Case and the Criminal Justice System* by Alan M. Dershowitz, *Where Wizards Stay Up Late: The Story Behind the Creation of the Internet* by Kate Hafner and Matthew Lyon, *Coach: The Life of Paul "Bear" Bryant* by Keith Dunnavant, *La Vera Cucina: Traditional Recipes from the Homes and Farms of Italy* by Carlo Middione, *Will the Real Women . . . Please Stand Up! Uncommon Sense about Self-Esteem, Self-Discovery, Sex and Sensuality* by Ella Patterson, *From the Shadows: The Ultimate Insider's Story of Five Presidents and How They Won the Cold War* by Robert M. Gates, *Bad Guys: America's Most Wanted in Their Own Words* by Mark Baker, *Latino Success: Advice from America's Most Successful Latino Business Executives* by Augusto Failde and William Doyle, and *Hit and Run: How Jon Peters and Peter Guber Took Sony for a Ride in Hollywood* by Nancy Griffin and Kim Masters.

Among Simon & Schuster's fiction authors are popular and critically respected writers such as Maxine Chernoff, Mary Higgins Clark, Jackie Collins, Andrei Codrescu, John Hawkes, Larry McMurtry, and Roxanne Pulitzer. As a group these authors address the mainstream popular readership; S&S titles are usually in the commercial frontlist mode, with topnotch representatives in mystery and suspense, Westerns, women's romances and family sagas, and adventure and espionage thrillers. S&S also produces literary history, biography, and memoirs; investigative narrative nonfiction; and literary inspirational works.

On the Simon & Schuster roster of popular fiction, literary writing, and works of cultural note: *Moonlight Becomes You* (suspense) by Mary Higgins Clark, *Other Women* (novel) by Evelyn Lau, *The Mediterranean Caper* (thriller) by Clive Cussler, *Hacks* (novel) by Christopher S. Wren, *The Spring* (fiction) by Clifford Irving, *Satisfied with Nothin'* (novel) by Ernest Hill, *Exquisite Corpse* (novel) by Poppy Z. Brite, *What's It All About? A Novel of Life, Love, and Key Lime Pie* by William Van Wert, *Last Chants* (a Willa Janson mystery) by Lia Matera, *Kill Me Again* (a Scott Elliott mystery) by Terence Faherty, *The Girls in the Band: Into the Heart of Lesbian America* by Lindsy Van Gelder and Pamela Robin Brandt, *The Book of Jesus: A Treasury of the Greatest Stories and Writings about Christ* by Calvin Miller, *Kickin'*

Balls: The Alexi Lalas Story by Alexi Lalas, and *False Impressions: The Hunt for the Big-Time Art Fakes* by Thomas Hoving.

Query letters and SASEs should be directed to:

Charles F. Adams, Senior Editor
Commercial fiction and nonfiction. Titles include *Armadillos & Old Lace* by Kinky Freidman, *Nobody's Fool* by Martin Gottfreid, *Ray Had an Idea about Love* by Eddie Lewis, and *Off Stage* by Betty Comden.

Dominick Anfuso, Senior Editor
General nonfiction and literary fiction. Titles include *The End of Japan Inc.: And How the New Japan Will Look* by Christopher Wood, *Off the Road: A Walk Down the Pilgrim's Route into Spain* by Jack Hitt, *The Blood Countess: A Novel* by Andrei Codrescu, and *Sailing to Paradise: The Discovery of the Americas in 5000 BC* by Jim Bailey.

Robert Bender, Senior Editor
Popular psychology, natural history, health and fitness, literary biography; wide commercial interests (excluding New Age and celebrity stories). Titles include *The Science of Desire: The Search for the Gay Gene and the Biology of Behavior* by Dean Hamer and Peter Copeland, *Knotted Tongues: Stuttering in History and the Search for a Cure* by Benson Bobrick, *Deadly Medicine* by Thomas Moore, and *Ancestral Passions* by Virginia Morell.

Laurie Bernstein, Senior Editor
Commercial fiction and nonfiction. Projects include *A Tangled Web* by Judith Michael, *Trophy Wife* by Kelly Lange, *Divided Lives: The Public and Private Struggles of Three Accomplished Women* by Elsa Walsh, and *Trunk Show* by Alison Glen.

Bill Rosen, Vice President and Associate Publisher for Illustrated Books for the Simon & Schuster Group
In charge of illustrated books and special projects.

Frederic W. Hills, Vice President and Senior Editor
General nonfiction, including biography and memoirs, modern history, business subjects, health and fitness, self-improvement. Titles include *The Monster Under the Bed* by Stan Davis and Jim Botkin; *When Your Doctor Doesn't Know Best* by Richard N. Podell, M.D., and William Proctor; *Love, Miracles, and Animal Healing* by Allen M. Schoen, DVM and Pam Proctor; and *The Slightly Older Guy* by Bruce Jay Freidman.

Alice Mayhew, Editorial Director, Simon & Schuster Trade Division
Politics, current events, contemporary biographies and memoirs. Projects include *Beyond the Promised Land* by Glenn Frankel, *Mandate of Heaven* by Orville Schell, *In Love with Daylight* by Wilfrid Sheed, and *Darwin's Dangerous Idea* by Daniel C. Dennett.

Paul McCarthy, Senior Editor
Acquires for Simon & Schuster trade division as well as for Pocket Books. Fiction for both S&S and Pocket: mainstream, commercial, suspense, historical novels. Fiction for Pocket: espionage, military, and law-enforcement novels; computer novels. Nonfiction for S&S: serious nonfiction, history, biography. Nonfiction for Pocket: investigative

journalism, current affairs, politics, health, crime, narrative computer nonfiction, narrative psychology, military history, language, popular reference, espionage and law enforcement, autobiography.

Bob Mecoy, Editor
Commercial fiction. Nonfiction in psychology, science, and technology. Titles include *Talking From 9 to 5* by Deborah Tannen, *Six Messiahs* by Mark Frost, and *You Belong to Me* by Johanna Lindsey.

Mary Ann Naples, Senior Editor
Quality fiction. Nonfiction: cultural issues, psychology, celebrity, music, pop culture, biography, and spiritual books. Projects include *Beyond Dreams and Beasts: Computers and the Culture of Simulation* by Sherry Turkle.

Jeff Neuman, Senior Editor
Sports stories and biographies. Titles include *From Red Ink to Roses* by Rick Telander, *Follow the Wind* by Bo Links, *Postcard from Hell* by Rex Dancer, and *I Was Right on Time* by Buck O'Neil.

Rebecca Saletan, Senior Editor
Psychology, popular science, journalism, women's issues, fiction. Titles include *Cuisine of the Water Gods* by Patricia Quintana, *Fire Your Shrink!* by Michele Weiner-Davis, *American Knees* by Shawn Wong, and *Sweet Talk* by Susan Ferraro.

Eric Steel, Editor
Projects include *Biting the Dust* by Dirk Johnson, *Nightswimmer* by Joseph Olshan, *On the Way to the Venus de Milo* by Pearson Marx, and *Toby's Lie* by Daniel Vilmure.

SIMON & SCHUSTER TRADE PAPERBACKS
FIRESIDE BOOKS/ TOUCHSTONE BOOKS

1230 Avenue of the Americas
New York, NY 10020
212-698-7000

Fireside, Simon & Schuster's principal trade paperback imprint, covers the entire slate of commercial nonfiction categories. The house emphasis includes current affairs, popular culture, business and finance, fitness and health, sports, games (including crossword puzzles), lifestyle and hobbies, and parenting. Fireside Books concentrates on original nonfiction (mainly in trade paper with some hardcover) and trade paperback reprints covering the mainstream commercial field.

Simon & Schuster's Touchstone Books imprint emphasizes popular nonfiction in trade paper and mass-market reprint editions, many of which were originally published in hardcover by Simon & Schuster. Touchstone also issues selected original titles.

Editors at the trade paper division can acquire for the following imprints: Fireside, Touchstone, Scribner Paperback Fiction, and Free Press Paperbacks; editors also acquire hardcover for Simon & Schuster, Scribner, and Free Press.

Representative Simon & Schuster trade paperback titles: *A Penny Saved* by Neale Godfrey, *Naked Under Our Clothes* by Dr. Dre and Ed Lover, *Dark Sun* by Richard Rhode, *The End of the Nation State* by Kenichi Ohmae, *Next American Nation* by

Michael Lind, *Greater Expectations* by Michael Damon, *Radical Son* by David Horowitz, *Faith in the Valley* by Iyanla Vanzant, *Flesh and Blood* (novel) by Michael Cunningham, and *The Riders* (fiction) by Tim Winton.

Query letters and SASEs should be directed to:

Trish Todd, Vice President and Editor in Chief
Areas consistent with the house description, particularly popular and commercial works in the areas of psychology, sociology, social history, biography, and self-help.

Sarah Baker, Associate Editor
Political issues, current events, psychology/self-help, music, women's subjects, fiction. Projects include *A Voice of Her Own* by Marlene Schiwy, *Dancing at the Rascal Fair* by Ivan Doig, and *Having an Abortion* by K. Kaufmann.

Becky Cabaza, Senior Editor
General self-help, popular reference, health and fitness, humor, and fiction. Projects include *Maternal Fitness: Preparing for a Healthy Pregnancy, The Homebrewer's Recipe Guide, and Selena's Secret: The Real Story Behind Her Tragic Death.* Fiction titles include *A Place Where the Sea Remembers* by Sandra Benitez (winner of the Barnes & Noble Discover Award) and *The Shipping News* by E. Annie Proulx (winner of the Pulitzer Prize and National Book Award). Looking for projects for the Simon & Schuster Aguilar Libros en Español list.

Dawn M. Daniels, Editor
Black, Latino, and Asian studies; literary fiction; health and fitness; career-oriented books; and self-help/motivation topics. Also works with Simon & Schuster Aguilar Libros en Español. Projects include *Acts of Faith: Daily Meditations for People of Color* by Iyanla Vanzant, *About My Sister's Business: The Black Woman's Road Map to Successful Entrepreneurship, Flyy Girl* (fiction) by Omar Tyree, and *To Do, Doing, Done: A Simple Process for Creating Results and Finishing Everything You Start.*

Cynthia L. Gitter, Editor
Serious and lifestyle nonfiction in the categories of psychology; social, race, and gender issues; entertainment, film, television, and the media; and popular culture. Also interested in Asian-American fiction and nonfiction. Titles include *Nick at Nite's Classic TV Companion, All You Need to Know about the Movie and TV Business, How to Prevent Breast Cancer, The Sexual State of the Union* by Susie Bright, *Aphrodite's Daughters* by Jalaja Bonheim, *Sightings* by Susan Michaels, and *Home Life: One Woman's Memoir and Meditation on the Meaning of Home.*

Penny Kaganoff, Senior Editor
Fiction, religion, women's studies, Judaica, history, politics, personal memoir, archaeology, anthropology, film, fitness, and cooking. Titles include *Lies my Teacher Told Me* by James Loewen, *The World of Jewish Cooking* by Gil Marks, *The Concise Conservative Encyclopedia* (edited by Brad Miner), and *Scribner's Best of the Fiction Workshops* (edited by John Kulka and Natalie Danford).

Sydny Weinberg Miner, Executive Editor
Women's issues, family and childcare, education, health, psychology and self-help, inspiration, multicultural projects, food and cooking, science, nature, and fishing. Titles include *The Firefighter's Cookbook* by John Sineno, *A Penny Saved: Teaching Your*

Children the Values and Life Skills They Will Need to Live in the Real World by Neale Godfrey, *The Third Force: A Novel of the Gadget* by Mark Laidwal, and *Re-Envisioning the Earth: A Guide to Opening the Healing Channels between Mind and Nature* by Paul Devereux.

Betsy Radin Herman, Editor

Psychology/self-help, fiction, humor, parenting, pop reference, pet and gift books, and "merch." Titles include *Poems for Life* by the Nightingale-Bradford School, *Exorcising Your Ex: How to Get Rid of Demons from Relationships Past* by Elizabeth Kuster, and *Difficult Questions Kids Ask (and are Afraid to Ask) about Divorce* by Meg Scheider and Joan Zuckerberg. Fiction includes *Winter Birds* by Jim Grimsley and *Water from the Well* by Myra McLarey.

Laureen Connelly Rowland, Associate Editor

Humor/pop culture, business, literary fiction, self-help, and spirituality. Looking for projects written by and geared specifically for the twentysomething audience. Projects include *Moving to a Small Town* by Wanda Urbanska and Frank Levering, *He's Got the Whole World in His Pants (and More Misheard Lyrics)* by Gavin Edwards, and *The Exes* (fiction) by Pagan Kennedy.

Caroline Sutton, Senior Editor

Focus on New Age/spirituality, alternative medicine, and psychology. Also interested in serious fiction, narrative nonfiction—especially personal journeys. Would like to do the right cat book. Projects include *Touching Spirit*, *Mortally Wounded*, and *Beauty* (a first novel) by Susan Wilson.

POCKET BOOKS

1230 Avenue of the Americas
New York, NY 10020
212-698-7000

The Pocket Books division of Simon & Schuster produces commercial fiction and non-fiction in hardcover and trade paperback editions while maintaining its tradition of mammoth mass-market paperback presence. Pocket Books is currently structured into three separate units: adult fiction and nonfiction, Star Trek Books, and Pocket Books for Young Adults.

Nonfiction from Pocket hits all sectors of the popular spectrum, including current issues, contemporary culture, health and fitness, relationships, self-awareness, personal finance, celebrity-based stories, and popular reference.

Pocket Books maintains a powerful category-fiction list that includes originals and reprints in genres such as thrillers and suspense, romance, science fiction (including the Star Trek series), fantasy, action adventure, and horror. In addition, the house produces original commercial and literary fiction (with many of the literary works issued under the Washington Square Press imprint).

Pocket Books offers a line of books for young adults, including a number of solid fiction and nonfiction series.

Nonfiction and popular works from the Pocket Books list: *Hiding My Candy* by the Lady Chablis with Theodore Bouloukos II, *Manhunter* by John Pascucci and Cameron

Stauth, *Corey Pavin's Shotmaking* by Corey Pavin with Guy Yocum, *Leadership Secrets of the Rogue Warrior* by Richard Marchinko, *Raising a Thinking Child* by Myra B. Shure with Theresa Foy Di Geronimo, *The Gods of Golf* by David L. Smith and John P. Holms, *Let's Be Heard* by Bob Grant, *Right Thinking* by James D. Hornfischer, *365 Ways to Make Love* by Lori Salkin and Rob Sperry, and *A Dog in Heat Is a Hot Dog and Other Rules to Live By* by E. Jean Carroll.

Pocket Books fiction and literary writing: *Guinevere* by Laurel Phelan, *Lord of the Dead* by Tom Holland, *Audrey Hepburn's Neck* by Alan Brown, *The Return* by William Shatner with Judith and Garfield Reeves-Stevens (part of the Star Trek line), *Tarnished Gold* by V. C. Andrews, *I Still Miss My Man, But My Aim Is Getting Better* by Sarah Shankman, *Knights* by Linda Lael Miller, *Hoopi Shoopi Donna* by Suzanne Strempek Shea, *Defiance County* by Jay Brandon, and *The Journal of Callie Wade* by Dawn Miller.

Pocket Books (founded in 1937) was America's first publisher to specialize in customized drugstore/newsstand rack-size paperback editions. Today, the house excels in both original titles and reprint lines brought out under its well-known reading-kangaroo logo (what better animal to convey the notion of a pouch-size edition?).

Query letters and SASEs should be directed to:

Emily Bestler, Vice President and Editorial Director
Varied nonfiction including health, family, parenting, inspirational, popular science, lifestyle. Commercial fiction: thrillers, mysteries.

Sue Carswell, Senior Editor at Large
Celebrity books. Film, television, and other media tie-ins.

Tristram Coburn, Editor
Military and political nonfiction. Action-adventure fiction; military and espionage stories. Works with Paul McCarthy.

Amy Einhorn, Senior Editor, Pocket Books and Washington Square Press
Popular nonfiction. Health, sports, popular culture, some humor. Literary fiction: established as well as emerging voices.

Craig Hillman, Editor
Media tie-ins.

Paul McCarthy, Senior Editor
Acquires for Simon & Schuster trade division as well as for Pocket Books. Fiction for both S&S and Pocket: mainstream, commercial, suspense, historical novels. Fiction for Pocket: Espionage, military, and law-enforcement novels; computer novels. Nonfiction for S&S: serious nonfiction, history, biography. Nonfiction for Pocket: investigative journalism, current affairs, politics, health, crime, narrative computer nonfiction, narrative psychology, military history, language, popular reference, espionage and law enforcement, autobiography.

Julie Rubenstein, Executive Editor
Commercial fiction, women's nonfiction. Narrative nonfiction: women's interest, health. Does a lot of reprints.

Amelia Sheldon, Editor
General noncategory commercial novels, as well as mysteries, suspense, thrillers. Stories with strong female lead characters that are fun and exciting to read; also stories

with a bit of a dark edge. Wide range of commercial nonfiction: parenting, relationships, popular psychology, self-help.

Dan Slater, Editor
Media tie-ins.

Tom Spain, Editor
Fiction and nonfiction. Inspirational books.

Dave Stern, Senior Editor
Men's fiction: adventures, mysteries thrillers, cyberfiction. Nonfiction pertaining to the Internet.

Caroline Tolley, Senior Editor
Historical romances.

Pete Wolverton, Editor
Fiction: Genre mysteries. Nonfiction: sports—golf, football.

POCKET BOOKS STAR TREK BOOKS

Query letters and SASEs should be directed to:

Kara Welsh, Vice President and Associate Publisher

Kevin Ryan, Editorial Director

John Ordover, Editor

POCKET BOOKS FOR YOUNG ADULTS

Query letters and SASEs should be directed to:

Patricia MacDonald, Vice President and Editorial Director

Nancy Pines, Vice President and Associate Publisher

Ruth Ashby, Editor

Lisa Clancy, Editor

SCRIBNER

1230 Avenue of the Americas
New York, NY 10020
212-698-7000

Scribner publishes trade fiction and nonfiction, much of it authoritative and accomplished writing. Scribner nonfiction covers current events, cultural history, biography, criticism, science, true crime, and popular reference. Scribner is home to Lisa Drew Books, a feature line with an especially hard-hitting commercial approach to frontlist publishing. The Rawson Associates imprint concentrates on self-awareness, health, and business books. Fiction from Scribner embraces the range of commercial literary interests and tastes; the house is particularly strong in crime fiction and hosts a number of ongoing mystery series.

Scribner often acquires hard/soft with other S&S divisions, including Touchstone, Fireside, and the Scribner Paperback Fiction imprint, as well as with Pocket Books.

The Scribner list bears the name as well as the midnight-reader's oil lamp logo of the former Charles Scribner's Sons, Publishers, originally an independent firm (founded in 1846). The house subsequently became part of Macmillan; following the acquisition of Macmillan by Simon & Schuster, much of the Macmillan trade operation was taken over by the Scribner program. In addition, remnants of the former Atheneum imprint were added to the Scribner lineup.

Scribner nonfiction: *There's a Word for It: A Grandiloquent Guide to Life* by Charles Harrington Elster, *Eagle's Plume: Preserving the Life and Habitat of America's Bald Eagle* by Bruce Beans, *Hep Cats, Narcs, and Pipe Dreams: A History of America's Romance with Illegal Drugs* by Jill Jonnes, *A History of American Life* by Arthur M. Schlesinger Sr. and Dixon Ryan Fox (abridged and revised by Mark C. Carnes and Arthur M. Schlesinger Jr.), *War without Bloodshed: The Middle East: A Brief History of the Last 2,000 Years* by Bernard Lewis, *Name-Dropping: The Lives and Lies of Alan King* by Alan King with Chris Chase, and *Timeless Healing: The Power and Biology of Belief* by Herbert Benson.

Fiction and literary works: *Accordion Crimes* (novel) by E. Annie Proulx, *Go Now* (novel) by Richard Hell, *Lost Laysen: The Newly Discovered Story* by Margaret Mitchell (author of *Gone with the Wind*), *Brendan Prairie* (novel) by Dan O'Brian, *Hidden Latitudes* (novel) by Alison Anderson, *A Lazy Eye* (stories) by Mary Morrissy, *Sarah's Psalm* (novel) by Florence Ladd, *Midlife Queer: Autobiography of a Decade, 1971–1981* by Martin Dubermann, and *Cave Passages: Roaming the Underground Wilderness* by Michael Ray Taylor.

Scribner accents fiction in the mystery and suspense modes. Titles here are *Spent Matches* by Shelly Reuben, *The Best Money Murder Can Buy* (a Stokes Moran mystery) by Neil McGaughey, *Final Jeopardy* by Linda Fairstein, *Death on a Vineyard Beach* (a Martha's Vineyard mystery) by Philip R. Craig, and *A Day for Dying* (an Inspector Luke Thanet novel) by Dorothy Simpson.

Lisa Drew Books hones a select list in the area of current events and high-interest nonfiction, along with some popular fiction. From Lisa Drew: *Where Peachtree Meets Sweet Auburn: The Saga of Two Families and the Making of Atlanta* by Gary Pomerantz, *The Art of Politics* by Eleanor Clift and Tom Brazaitis, and *Quest for Perfection: The Engineering of Human Beings* by Gina Maranto. Backlist items: *Home on the Range: A Century on the High Plains* by James R. Dickenson, *Napoleon and Josephine: An Improbable Marriage* by Evangeline Bruce, and *Wasteland* (crime novel) by Peter McCabe.

Query letters and SASEs should be directed to:

Gillian Blake, Editorial
Commercial and literary fiction and nonfiction consistent with the Scribner list. Projects include *Hidden Latitudes* by Alison Anderson.

Hamilton Cain, Editor
Literary fiction. Is interested in nonfiction consistent with house description. Titles include *Residents: The Perils of Educating Young Doctors* by David Ewing Duncan,

Cave Passages by Michael Ray Taylor, *A Lazy Eye* by Mary Morrissy, *Eagle's Plume* by Bruce Beans, *Hep Cats, Narcs, and Pipe Dreams* by Jill Jonnes.

Lisa Drew, Publisher, Lisa Drew Books
Commercial nonfiction, including high-interest history, celebrity biographies, and current affairs. Popular fiction. Titles include *A History of American Life* (abridged and revised by Mark C. Carnes and Arthur M. Schlesinger Jr.), *Here We Go Again* by Betty White, and *Pope John Paul II* by Tad Szulc.

Nan Graham, Vice President and Editor in Chief
American literary fiction; fiction about clashing cultures—Third World and European. Nonfiction interests include contemporary social and political issues, women's studies, historical and literary biography, and biographies of artists. Projects include *Accordion Crimes* by E. Annie Proulx, *The Black Album* by Hanif Kureishi, and *City Life* by Witold Rybczynski.

Maria Guarnaschelli, Senior Editor
Literary biographies, popular science, cookbooks. Wide range of trade interests, including fiction. Projects include *The Chimera* by Sebastiano Vasalli.

Leigh Haber, Senior Editor
Literary fiction. Nonfiction consistent with house description. Projects include *Midlife Queer* by Martin Duberman, *Go Now* by Richard Hell, *Sarah's Psalm* by Florence Ladd, and *I Was Looking at the Ceiling When I Saw the Sky* by June Jordan.

Susanne Kirk, Senior Editor
Mystery and suspense fiction. Titles include *Oxford Mourning* by Veronica Stallwood, *The Best Money Murder Can Buy* by Neil McGaughey, *Final Jeopardy* by Linda Fairstein, *Mourn Not Your Dead* by Deborah Crombie, *Death on a Vineyard Beach* by Philip R. Craig, and *A Day for Dying* by Dorothy Simpson.

Susan Moldow, Publisher
Areas consistent with house interest. Projects include *Timeless Healing* by Herb Benson, *Three Gospels* by Reynolds Price, and *The Fatigue Artist* by Lynne Sharon Schwartz.

Scott Moyers, Editor
Commercial and literary fiction and nonfiction consistent with the house list. Projects include *Lost Laysen* by Margaret Mitchell and *Gone with the Wind: 60th Anniversary Edition* by Margaret Mitchell.

Bill Rosen, Vice President and Associate Publisher for Illustrated Books for the Simon & Schuster Group
Projects include *The Middle East* by Bernard Lewis, *Something Happening Here* by Robert Lloyd, and *Millennium* by Felipe Fernandez-Arnesto.

Jane Rosenman, Senior Editor
Literary fiction, commercial nonfiction. Projects include *Bliss* by Bob Sloan, *Name-Dropping* by Alan King, *There's a Word for It!* by Charles Harrington Elster, *Tessie and Pearlie* by Joy Horowitz, *Geography of the Heart* by Fenton Johnson, and *In Defense of Government* by Jacob Weisberg.

Tysie Whitman, Editorial
Commercial and literary fiction and nonfiction consistent with the Scribner list. Projects include *Not Much Fun: The Lost Poems of Dorothy Parker* (edited by Stuart Silverstein).

Rawson Associates

1230 Avenue of the Americas
New York, NY 10020
212-698-7000

Rawson Associates produces selected books in health and diet, self-help, popular psychology, and business how-to. Representative Rawson project: *Healing the Child* by Nancy Cain.

Query letters and SASEs should be directed to:

Eleanor Rawson, Publisher

The Free Press

1230 Avenue of the Americas
New York, NY 10020
212-698-7000

The Free Press produces trade nonfiction titles with an emphasis on business, biography, psychology, history, and current affairs—as well as general-interest works that address popular contemporary themes. The Free Press also publishes professional and academic books in the social sciences and humanities.

New Republic Books is a Free Press imprint (published in association with *New Republic* magazine) that specializes in works that explore contemporary social and political issues.

On the Free Press list: *Taking Judaism Personally* by Judy Petsonk, *The Patriot: An Exhortation to Liberate America from the Barbarians* by Gary Hart, *When Someone You Love Is Depressed* by Laura Epstein Rosen and Xavier F. Amador, *The Coming Russian Boom* by Richard Layard and John Parker, *The Landmark Thucydides* (edited by Robert B. Strassler), *The Idea of Decline in Western History* by Arthur Herman, *Shooting the Messenger* by Bruce W. Sanfors, and *The Diversity Machine* by Frederick R. Lynch.

Query letters and SASEs should be directed to:

Susan Arellano, Senior Editor
Psychology and behavioral sciences.

Adam Bellow, Vice President and Editorial Director
Politics, history, current affairs.

Mitch Horowitz, Senior Editor
Politics and current affairs.

Bruce Nichols, Senior Editor
History, economics, military history.

Robert Wallace, Vice President and Senior Editor
Business and economics (not popular or how-to topics).

SIMON & SCHUSTER REFERENCE DIVISIONS

The reference divisions of Simon & Schuster, Macmillan, and Prentice Hall cover books in the areas of general, popular, business, professional, and library reference. A number of individual imprints appear, each staking claim to a piece of the house's diverse reference-publishing turf.

Major lines and imprints include Macmillan General Reference & Travel, Prentice Hall Business, Training & Healthcare Group, Prentice Hall Professional Technical Reference Division, Macmillan Computer Publishing, Macmillan Popular Reference, Macmillan Library Reference, Brassey's, and Jossey-Bass; educational lines continue under the Prentice Hall and Allyn & Bacon imprints. Additional imprints and lines include Audel, Howell Book House, and Schirmer Books.

Subsequent to the Macmillan buyout, the trade designations as well as the organization of the company's reference divisions underwent dramatic changes. Names of groups and individual imprints shifted week by week, if not overnight. The names and components of the divisions profiled below are therefore subject to change, though it is anticipated that their established publishing programs will continue by whatever appellation they are known.

MACMILLAN PUBLISHING USA
MACMILLAN GENERAL REFERENCE USA
MACMILLAN CONSUMER INFORMATION GROUP

1633 Broadway
New York, NY 10019
212-654-1000
212-654-8500

Macmillan Publishing hosts trade, business and professional, and reference divisions within a framework that has been subject to realignment. The reference divisions of Macmillan and Prentice Hall that have been consolidated under the Macmillan General Reference umbrella offer specialized as well as general lines, including commercial trade nonfiction, popular and consumer reference, business and professional reference, and titles slated for the institutional and library market.

Macmillan General Reference publishes a gamut of categories, from dictionaries and stylebooks through titles geared to particular fields such as collecting specialties, touring, standardized-test preparation, computers, and consumer guides, to gazeteers and works focusing on history, technology, and nature.

Macmillan Consumer Information Group (MCIG), a division of Macmillan Reference, publishes a wide range of mostly trade paperbacks under the imprints Arco, J. K. Lasser, Macmillan Spectra, and Alpha Books. Topics featured include test prep, educational guidance, career development, business, personal finance, self-help, and lifestyle.

A portion of the group's list may be classified as general-interest nonfiction trade books, though they most often do fit into a particular reference mold. Such publications encompass cookbooks, horticultural how-to, and travel guides, along with atlases, maps, encyclopedias, and technical automotive reference guides issued on a number of different imprints, some of which were originally separate and independent publishing houses.

Among these are American Heritage Books, Arco, Burpee Gardening Books, Betty Crocker, Reward Books, J. K. Lasser, Monarch Notes, Equestrian Books, Webster's New World, and Maps & Atlases. Travel series include Baedeker, the Economist Business Traveller's Guides, Frommer's, Gault Millau, Les Guides Bleus, and Mobil Travel Guides.

The Audel series is made up of reference books on home repair that provide practical information in areas such as plumbing, house wiring, and pumps, listing titles such as *Questions and Answers for Electricians' Examinations* revised by Paul Rosenberg and *Professional Tiling* by Edwin M. Field and Selma G. Field.

Howell Book House is an imprint that specializes in pet care and training books, as well as equestrian titles. On the Howell list: *Practical Dressage* by Jane Kidd, *Pet Owner's Guide to the Shetland Sheepdog* by Mary Davis, *The Less-Than-Perfect Rider* by Lesley Bayley and Caroline Davis, and the set of pet-care works by Tim Hawcroft that include *First Aid for Birds*, *First Aid for Cats*, and *First Aid for Dogs*.

Schirmer produces books in the area of music, including biographies of musicians. Representative of the Schirmer list are *The Mozart Compendium* and *Opening Night on Broadway*.

Query letters and SASEs should be directed to:

Theresa H. Murtha, Vice President and Publisher, Macmillan Consumer Reference Group
Business, careers, self-help, lifestyles.

Natalie Chapmann, Editor in Chief
General nonfiction.

Janine Bucek, Editor
Sports books.

(Ms.) Traci Cothran, Editor
Humor, general reference.

Blythe Grossberg, Editor
Travel.

Pam Honig, Editor
Cookbooks.

Mary Ann Lynch, Senior Editor
General reference, illustrated books, art books, relationships, spirituality.

John Nelson, Editor
Business titles.

Ira Wilker, Editor
Travel.

J. K. Lasser Division

Elliott Eiss, Editorial Director
Tax, tax-related personal finance.

Macmillan Spectrum

Richard Staron, Editor in Chief
Business, careers, investing, self-improvement.

Debra Englander, Executive Editor
Personal finance, investing.

Arco Division

Chuck Wall, Vice President and Publisher
Test-preparation books, education and guidance, careers.

Linda Bernbach, Editorial Director
Test prep, careers, study aids.

Barbara Gilson, Senior Editor
Study guides, education-reference materials, self-help, popular reference.

Prentice Hall Business, Training & Healthcare Group
Prentice Hall Direct
Prentice Hall Building

113 Sylvan Avenue, Route 9W
Englewood Cliffs, NJ 07632
201-592-2000

Prentice Hall produces an extensive list in hardcover and trade paperback that features a wide range of books keyed to diverse career and business orientations, as well as a noteworthy line of titles in areas such as health, fitness, and lifestyle—geared for direct-mail audiences.

Prentice Hall is a respected publisher in the educational arena, with series in all subject and curricula areas for the youngest students through postgraduates, along with professional reference works in fields such as law and engineering.

This house is not known for strong distribution to the trade; it specializes in direct marketing and sales to the individual, corporate, and institutional markets. The business and professional division is widely known for the targeted mailing lists it compiles; some of these lists contain more than a million names and addresses.

Sample titles: *Budgeting Basics and Beyond: A Complete Step-by-Step Guide for Nonfinancial Managers* by Jae Shim and Joel Siegel, *Doing Business in the New Vietnam* by Christopher Engholm, *The Organization Game* by Craig Hickman, *Speaker's Lifetime Library* by Leonard and Thelma Spinrad, *Do-It-Yourself Business Promotions Kit* by Jack Griffin, *The Art of Winning Conversations* by Morey Stettner, *Paralegal Practices and Procedure* by Deborah Larbalestrier, *The Broker's Edge* by Steven Drosdeck and Karl Gretz, *Trading in the Global Currency Markets* by Cornelius Luca, *Heinerman's Encyclopedia of Healing Juices* by John Heinerman, *Look 10 Years Younger, Live 10 Years Longer . . . A Man's Guide/ . . . A Woman's Guide* by David Ryback, *Helping Yourself with Foot Reflexology* by Mildred Carter, *Your Skin: An Owner's Guide* by Joseph Bark, *A Woman's Guide to the Language of Success: Communicating with Confidence and Power* by Phyllis Mindell, and *Violence at Work: How to Make Your Company Safer for Employees and Customers* by Joseph A. Kinney.

Query letters and SASEs should be directed to:

Eugene F. Brissie, Vice President and Editorial Director, Business and Self-Improvement
Business, management, health, and self-improvement.

Ellen Schneid Coleman, Executive Editor
Professional and personal finance, accounting.

(Mr.) Win Huppuch, Publisher, Education Publishing
Books for teachers.

Douglas Corcoran, Editor
Health and fitness books, with emphasis on natural healing.

Karen Hansen, Senior Editor
Human resources, training, marketing, advertising, sales, secretarial skills, personal self-improvement.

Susan McDermott, Editor
Plant and operations management, environmental management, existing law books.

Tom Power, Senior Editor
General how-to business titles, management, career, spoken and written communications.

Prentice Hall Professional Technical Reference Division

440 Sylvan Avenue
Englewood Cliffs, NJ 07632
201-816-4110

Query letters and SASEs should be directed to:

Stephen G. Guty, Executive Editor
Computer operating systems; software development tools.

MACMILLAN COMPUTER PUBLISHING

Macmillan Computer Publishing comprises several imprints and subsidiaries that produce titles rated all along the beginner-to-advanced user spectrum. As a group, these houses address topic areas such as accounting and finance, audio, computer-aided design (CAD), children's games, databases and integrated systems, desktop publishing, graphics, multimedia, hardware and utilities, Macintosh, networking and communications, operating systems, professional reference, programming, spreadsheets, and word processing.

The several imprints herein all publish computer books exclusively. The editorial orientation of each imprint seeks to define its own specialized market niche. However, there is some overlap, and interested authors (in addition to consulting the current catalogs) might therefore find it advisable to query more than one imprint simultaneously and separately with regard to proposed computer-book projects.

On the Macmillan Computer Publishing list are *New Riders' Official InterNet Yellow Pages*, *Andrew Tobias' Managing Your Money*, *Advanced Digital Audio*, *AutoCAD for Beginners*, *Alpha-Bytes Fun with Computers*, *Introduction to Databases*, *Quick and Dirty Harvard Graphics Presentations*, *IBM Personal Computer Troubleshooting & Repair*, *Cool Mac Clip Art Plus!*, *Workgroup Computing With Windows*, *Using Assembly Language*, and *Introduction to Programming*.

ALPHA BOOKS
BRADY BOOKS
HAYDEN BOOKS
NEW RIDERS PUBLISHING/NRP
QUE
SAMS PUBLISHING

201 West 103rd Street
Indianapolis, IN 46290
317-581-3500

This parcel of specialist publishers—ranging from former independents to new imprints—umbrellas a vast domain of trade computer book publishing within the imprimatur and marketing arm of Macmillan Computer Publishing.

Alpha Books takes the intimidation out of learning computers and has a primary objective to eliminate technophobia. Armed with this approach, Alpha offers readers a full array of friendly, quick how-to solutions designed for all levels of computer users (including specialty lines for kids). Complete Idiot's . . . is a successful line of how-to computer-related books. (Contact: Theresa H. Murtha at Macmillan Consumer Information Group in New York.)

The Brady Books subsidiary produces authoritative works from experts such as Peter Norton, Jim Seymour, and Winn L. Rosch. Brady Books also represent alliances between Brady and the computer industry leaders exemplified by the lines of titles on imprints such as Symantec Books, Lotus Books, Brady Programming Library, and Peter Norton Computing.

Hayden Books believes that computing doesn't have to be boring. The focus here is on Macintosh computing, electronic publishing, and computer-games titles, with increasing emphasis in the areas of computer sound, graphics, and animation.

New Riders Publishing/NRP focuses on titles for experienced users. These readers often have mastery of one or several different kinds of applications and benefit from a creative, advanced look at a given topic area. NRP books accent coverage of operating systems, computer-aided design, Windows graphics, networking, and new technology (such as on-line communications and electronic publishing).

Que is the current incarnation of Que Corporation (which had been a division of Macmillan). Que computer books deliver comprehensive, high-quality products to the computer book publishing market. Que was one of the first computer book publishers and now holds an enviable position in terms of market leadership in customer satisfaction in areas addressing the interests and needs of professional users and programmers in application areas such as business, data processing, and desktop publishing and graphics.

Sams Publishing is the former Howard W. Sams—known for computer and technical books, including guides to popular video games. Sams computer books provide information and instruction on programming languages, operating environments, networking systems, and related topic areas.

Query letters and SASEs should be directed to:

Tracy Turgeson, Senior Acquisitions Editor, New Riders Publishing

Steve Poland, Acquisitions Editor, Alpha Books

Karen Whitehouse, Acquisitions Editor, Hayden Books

Rick Ranucci, Acquisitions Editor, Que

Gregg Bushyeager, Acquisitions Editor, Sams Publishing

BRASSEY'S (U.S.), INC.

1313 Dolley Madison Boulevard, Suite 401
McLean, VA 22101
703-442-4535

Brassey's (U.S.) is a leading publisher in foreign policy, defense, and national and international affairs. The house emphasizes military history, contemporary military culture, and military reference. Brassey also publishes occasional fictional works featuring a military or historical milieu, as well as a few titles in business and management.

Brassey's list includes *Shadow Over Shangri-La: A Woman's Quest for Freedom* by Durga Pokbrel with Anthony Willet; *Minute Men* by John R. Galvin; *Fifty Years at the Front: The Life of War Correspondent Frederick Palmer* by Nathan Haverstock; *Rain of Ruin: A Photographic History of Hiroshima and Nagasaki* by Donald M. Goldstein, Katherine V. Dillon, and J. Michael Wenger; *The Court of Blue Shadows* (novel set in the aftermath of WW II) by Maynard Allington; *Blood in Zion* by Saul Zadka; and *The*

Colonel's Table: Recipes & Tales by Harry Stanhope and Tank Nash with recipes from Brian Jones.

Query letters and SASEs should be directed to:

Don McKeon, Associate Director of Publishing

JOSSEY-BASS, INC., PUBLISHERS
THE NEW LEXINGTON BOOKS

350 Sansome Street
San Francisco, CA 94104
415-433-1740

Jossey-Bass, Inc., Publishers (established in 1967) produces nonfiction in professional and advanced trade categories covering business, management, and administration in public and nonprofit sectors, as well as issues in psychology, social and health sciences, and education. Jossey-Bass sustains an extensive backlist and publishes specialist journals in fields allied to the house's areas of book-publishing scope.

Jossey-Bass has an editorial commitment to provide useful, leading-edge resources grounded in research and proven in practice. These works present substantive ideas that will help individuals and organizations to learn, develop, and improve their effectiveness. The Jossey-Bass publishing niche accents theory-to-practice books for thinking professionals, often in larger corporations, who are progressive and curious in their thinking, and who are in a position to influence their organizations. Most J-B books are grounded in primary research by the authors, and are aimed at the twin concerns of development of the organization as a whole as well as the individuals within the organization.

The New Lexington Books (formerly Lexington Books, a division of D.C. Heath & Co., later part of Macmillan, and recently a component of Simon & Schuster's Free Press imprint) publishes trade, professional, and academic works in the areas of business, economics, international relations, political affairs, popular lifestyle, psychology, and social concerns.

Jossey-Bass sells via a half-dozen channels; about 20 to 25 percent of J-B business and management titles get general-market trade-bookstore distribution, while the balance are sold through direct mail, direct to corporations, via catalog companies, through agency bookstore accounts (mostly large, independent professional booksellers), and for use in college-level courses.

Representative of the list: *The Connective Edge: Leading in an Interdependent World* by Jean Lipman-Blumen; *Learning As a Way of Being: Strategies for Survival in a World of Permanent White Water* by Peter B. Vaill; *A Voice of Our Own: Leading American Women Celebrate the Right to Vote* (edited by Nancy Neuman); *Beyond Blame: A New Way of Resolving Conflicts in Relationships* by Jeffrey A. Kotter; *The Human Side of Change: A Practical Guide to Organizational Redesign* by Timothy J. Galpin; and *School Wars: When World Views Collide* by Barbara B. Gaddy, T. William Hall, and Robert J. Marzano.

Query letters and SASEs should be directed to:

Cedric Crocker, Editor
Business and management.

(Ms.) Gale Erlandson, Senior Editor
Higher and adult education.

Larry Alexander, Senior Editor
Business and management.

(Ms.) Lesley Iura, Senior Editor
Education.

Andy Pasternak, Editor
Health/social and behavioral sciences.

Sarah Polster, Editor
Religion-in-practice.

Alan Rinzler, Senior Editor
Social and behavioral sciences.

Alan Schrader, Senior Editor
Public administration and nonprofit sector.

SIMON & SCHUSTER CHILDREN'S PUBLISHING DIVISION
SIMON & SCHUSTER BOOKS FOR YOUNG READERS
ATHENEUM BOOKS FOR YOUNG READERS
MARGARET K. MCELDERRY BOOKS
ALADDIN PAPERBACKS
LITTLE SIMON
NICKELODEON BOOKS AND NICK JR.
RABBIT EARS BOOK AND AUDIO
LIBROS COLIBRÍ

1230 Avenue of the Americas
New York, NY 10020
212-698-7000

The Simon & Schuster Children's Publishing Division features a robust lineup of non-fiction, fiction, and poetry in all age ranges, plus a rich array of picture books and specialty publications. S&S publishes books for the Spanish-language market under the Libros Colibrí imprint. Rabbit Ears Book and Audio concentrates on book-and-audio packages. The new Nickelodeon Books operation includes television show tie-in titles and general publishing projects under the Nick imprint.

The division was created subsequent to Paramount's acquisition of Macmillan. The Macmillan enterprise had itself been a major force in children's publishing. The newly forged Simon & Schuster Children's Publishing Division has cohered into a powerful performance sphere, with numerous award-winning and best-selling titles.

The Simon & Schuster Books for Young Readers imprint is a primarily hardcover publisher that aims to create high-quality books that sell to both libraries and bookstores and become backlist staples. The house publishes fiction and nonfiction for all readership groups, from preschoolers through young adults. About half the list is made up of picture books (but not board books or novelty books), nonfiction, and storybooks for older readers. The rest of the list features novels, photoessays, and poetry collections for middle-grade readers and young adults.

Representative titles from the Simon & Schuster Books for Young Readers list are *The Faithful Friend* (by Robert D. San Souci; illustrated by Brian Pinckney), *Zin! Zin! Zin! a Violin* (by Lloyd Moss; illustrated by Marjorie Priceman), *Under the Domim Tree* by Gila Almagor, *Forever* by Judy Blume, *Sitti's Secret* by Naomi Shihab Nye, *Past Forgiving* by Gloria D. Miklowitz, *Running Out of Time* by Margaret Peterson Haddix, *Myths and Legends from Around the World* by Sandy Shepherd, *How I Changed My Life* by Todd Strasser, *Summerspell* by Jean Thesman, *Don't Leave an Elephant to Go and Chase a Bird* (by James Berry; illustrated by Ann Grifalconi) and *Duppy Talk: West Indian Tales of Mystery and Magic* by Gerald Hausman. Series include Animal Peek and Pops (by Sadie Fields with illustrations by David Hawcock), Teeny-Popper Books (by B. J. Johnson), Talking with Artists (edited by Pat Cummings), the S&S Reference line, and Nature Adventure Books.

Atheneum Books for Young Readers produces picture books, fiction, and nonfiction that covers the spectrum of reader-age ranges in all genres (except for board books and novelty books). Atheneum books are often richly produced hardcover editions; works that feature illustration and photography are often packaged with fine-art quality graphics. About a third of the list consists of picture books; however, Atheneum is renowned for topnotch titles in fiction and nonfiction. Produced under Atheneum auspices are Jean Karl Books, Anne Schwartz Books, and the Libros Colibrí Spanish-language line.

Representing Atheneum are titles such as *A Place to Call Home* by Jackie French Koller, *Black Swan/White Crow* (by J. Patrick Lewis; illustrated by Chris Manson), *Parallel Journeys* by Eleanor H. Ayer, *Abigail Adams: Witness to a Revolution* by Natalie S. Bober, *The Absolutely True Story . . .* by Willo Davis Roberts, *I See the Moon* by C. B. Christiansen, *Tears of a Tiger* by Sharon Draper, *Mary Wolf* by Cynthia D. Grant, *Virginia's General* by Albert Marrin, *Emperor Mage* by Tamora Pierce, *The Conjure Woman* (by William Miller; illustrated by Terea Shaffer), and *A Gaggle of Geese* (written and illustrated by Philippa-Alys Browne).

Margaret K. McElderry Books publishes original hardcover trade books for children. The McElderry list encompasses picture books, easy-to-read series, fiction and nonfiction for eight- to twelve-year-old readers, science fiction and fantasy, and young adult fiction and nonfiction. McElderry titles include *Yolanda's Genius* by Carol Fenner, *Dog Friday* by Hilary McKay, and *A Sound of Leaves* (by Lenore Blegvad; illustrated by Erik Blegvad).

Aladdin Paperbacks primarily produces reprints of Simon & Schuster Publishing Division hardcover originals. The Aladdin scope covers preschoolers through young adult, including picture books, paperback reprints, novelty books, and fiction and mysteries for kids to the age of twelve. Aladdin originals include selective series and media tie-ins.

Little Simon is a line devoted to novelty books and book-related merchandise. Little Simon addresses a range from birth through eight years. Popular formats include pop-up books, board books, cloth books, bath books, sticker books, and book-and-audio-cassette sets.

Rabbit Ears is an award-winning entertainment company that produces children's videos. The Simon & Schuster Rabbit Ears Book and Audio lineup concentrates on a slate of tales based on the videos, retold and illustrated in high-profile new editions, accompanied by audiocassettes replete with surround-sound design and musical scores for a discerning audience. Representative performing artists involved are Rubén Blades, Holly Hunter, John Hurt, Garrison Keillor, Jack Nicholson, Meg Ryan, and Kathleen Turner; musicians include Mickey Hart, Mark Isham, Tangerine Dream, and Bobby McPherrin.

Nickelodeon Books and Nick Jr. is queued to Nickelodeon cable-channel programming. This line creates books and other products that cross-promote with co-licensees in the arenas of toys, home videos, CD-ROM, and party goods.

Query letters and SASEs should be directed to:

Willa Perlman, President and Publisher, Simon & Schuster Children's Publishing Division

Stephanie Owens Lurie, Vice President and Editorial Director, Simon & Schuster Books for Young Readers
Picture books, chapter books, middle-grade and young-adult fiction, and nonfiction for all age groups. Looks for picture-book manuscripts with a strong story line, middle-grade fiction with an extra sparkle of humor and imagination, and young-adult fiction that is multilayered and sophisticated in both plot and characterization. Likes to publish nonfiction that is as compelling as a good novel and as attractive as the best picture books. Also interested in Judaica.

Virginia Duncan, Executive Editor, Simon & Schuster Books for Young Readers
Picture books (both short texts for younger readers and longer texts for older readers), interesting and fresh nonfiction for all age groups, and middle-grade novels with a distinctive voice. Likes books that are innovative, appealing to children, and built around a strong plot.

David Gale, Senior Editor, Simon & Schuster Books for Young Readers
Middle-grade and young-adult novels, primarily. Looks for sharp writing and fresh voices. Does not want to consider standard young-adult problem novels or romances, but is interested in more unusual, hard-hitting, and literary young-adult novels.

Andrea Davis Pinkney, Editor, Simon & Schuster Books for Young Readers
Picture-book manuscripts that explore significant yet lesser-known nonfiction topics in an exciting way. Likes to see stories about people from different cultures around the world, and fiction that is based on real-life events.

Rebecca Davis, Editor, Simon & Schuster Books for Young Readers
Picture books, middle-grade and young-adult fiction, and unusual nonfiction projects. Particularly fond of poetry, multicultural stories, and historical fiction tales with distinctive characters and a strong sense of time and place.

Jonathan Lanman, Vice President and Editorial Director, Atheneum Books for Young Readers

Marcia Marshall, Senior Editor, Atheneum Books for Young Readers

Jean Karl, Field Editor, Jean Karl Books, an imprint of Atheneum Books for Young Readers

Sarah Caguiat, Editor, Atheneum Books for Young Readers

Ana Cerro, Associate Editor, Atheneum Books for Young Readers

Margaret K. McElderry, Vice President and Publisher, Margaret K. McElderry Books

Emma K. Dryden, Editor, Margaret K. McElderry Books

Ellen Krieger, Vice President and Editorial Director, Aladdin Paperbacks

Ruth Katcher, Senior Editor, Aladdin Paperbacks

Julia Sibert, Editor, Aladdin Paperbacks

Robin Corey, Vice President and Editorial Director, Little Simon; Vice President and Editorial Director, Rabbit Ears

Alison Weir, Senior Editor, Little Simon

Laura Hunt, Editor, Little Simon; Editor, Rabbit Ears

GIBBS SMITH, PUBLISHER
PEREGRINE SMITH BOOKS

P.O. Box 667
Layton, Utah 84041
801-544-9800

Gibbs Smith publishes trade nonfiction with standout lines in home/interior, children's, literature, nature and environment, the cowboy, architecture, gardening, and humor. The house produces books on the Gibbs Smith and Peregrine Smith Books imprints, in fine hardcover and trade paper editions, and offers distinctive lines of gift books keyed to the publisher's interest areas.

Gibbs Smith, Publisher (founded in 1969) is a house with an independent, resourceful spirit. The publisher considers books the continual greening edge of culture, as well as vehicles that carry the dreams and wisdom of the ages. Gibbs Smith looks for new projects that contribute to and refresh this independent spirit, and considers these questions: What makes good writing? What makes good publishing? Gibbs Smith believes that the single most important quality for both writer and publisher is passion: a sense of great purpose; an unusually heightened interest in the subject matter and in the task—whether it be writing or publishing. As Gibbs M. Smith writes in the introduction to the house's trade list: "It is a great privilege to work from our old barn office in the Rocky Mountains and have our books enter the literary bloodstream of the world."

Highlights of the Gibbs Smith lineup: *The Living Wreath* by Teddy Colbert (principal photography by Chad Slattery), *Don't Throw in the Trowel: Tips and Quips on Gardening* by Texas Bix Bender, *Vintage Denim* by David Little (photographs by Larry

Bond), *Romance of the Mission* by Elmo Baca, *The Log Home Book: Design, Past and Present* by Cindy Teipner-Thiede and Arthur Thiede (photography by Jonathan Stoke and Cindy Teipner-Thiede), *Countdown to 2000: A Kid's Guide to the New Millennium* by Bonnie Bader and Tracey West (illustrations by Brad Teare), and *Once There Was a Bull . . . Frog)* by Rick Walton (illustrated by Greg Hally).

A Gibbs Smith vignette: Mackey Hedges, a cowboy in his mid-50s, walked in with the typescript of a work based on the author's experiences as a working cowboy over the last thirty years. With a unique prose style evocative of Jack Kerouac, it proved to be a major literary achievement and made its debut on the Gibbs Smith list as *Last Buckaroo*.

Gibbs Smith, Publisher distributes its own list and utilizes a network of regional sales representatives.

Query letters and SASEs should be directed to:

Madge Baird, Editorial Director
Humor, Western.

Dawn Valentine-Hadlock, Editor
Gift books, humor.

Gail Yngve, Editor
Poetry, literature, home/design, new age.

Carrol Shreeve, Editor
Gardening, cookbooks, craft, architecture.

Theresa Desmond, Editor
Children's.

SOHO PRESS

853 Broadway
New York, NY 10003
212-260-1900

Soho publishes general nonfiction, investigative and international affairs, and historical works. This compact house is also notable for its formidable roster of contemporary fiction (often with a literary bent), mysteries, and historical novels. The Soho spectrum of interest also verges into the areas of travel, autobiography, and the social sciences.

Soho Press (founded in 1986) publishes a superior list of hardcover and softcover trade books. A solid core of Soho titles have achieved marked commercial success.

From Soho's list in literary works: *Tree of Heaven* by R. C. Binstock, *The Liar* by Stephen Fry, *Reich Angel* by Anita Mason, *Maybe in Missoula* by Toni Volk, *Krik? Krak! Stories* by Edwidge Danticat, and *Antonia Saw the Oryx First* by Maria Thomas.

Crime, mystery, and suspense is represented by *What's a Girl Gotta Do?* by Sparkle Hayter, *The Curious Eat Themselves* by John Straley, *The Kiss Off* by Jim Cirni, *The Money Lovers* by Timothy Watts, *Jade Lady Burning* by Martin Limón, *Outsider in Amsterdam* by Janwillem van de Wetering, and *Her Monster* by Jeff Collignon.

The Hera Series presents works of fiction with historical themes that feature strong female characters. Titles here: *Stealing Heaven: The Love Story of Heloise and Abelard* by Marion Meade, *Child of the Morning* by Pauline Gedge, *The Beacon at Alexandria* by Gillian Bradshaw, and *The Corn King and the Spring Queen* by Naomi Mitchison.

On the Soho nonfiction list: *The Other Mother: A Woman's Love for the Child She Gave Up for Adoption* by Carol Shaefer, *The Manhattan Family Guide to Private Schools* by Catherine Hausman and Victoria Goldman, *Taxi From Hell: Confessions of a Russian Hack* by Vladimir Lobas, *Dino, Godzilla and the Pigs: My Life on Our Missouri Hog Farm* by Mary Elizabeth Fricke, and *By Her Own Hand: Memoirs of a Suicide's Daughter* by Signe Hammer.

Soho Press books are distributed to the trade by Farrar Straus & Giroux.

Query letters and SASEs should be directed to:

Laura Hruska, Associate Publisher

Juris Jurjevics, Publisher

THE SPORTING NEWS PUBLISHING COMPANY

1212 North Lindbergh Boulevard
St. Louis, MO 63132
314-997-7111

The Sporting News Publishing Company (founded in 1886) is a subsidiary of Times Mirror. This publisher issues the periodical *The Sporting News* and produces a short list of books that includes annual digests of sports facts, statistical compilations, team registers, and media guides under the rubric of the Sporting News Library.

The house also publishes a select list of feature titles, especially a line dealing with the history and culture of the game of baseball. Virtually all of the books published by the Sporting News are put together by the editorial staff or are specially commissioned works arising in-house rather than proposed by independent authors.

Sample titles: *College Basketball Yearbook*, *Official NBA Rules*, *The Complete Hockey Book*, *Pro Football Guide*, *Fantasy Baseball Owners Manual*, *Official Baseball Rules*, and *Baseball's Golden Age: The Photographs of Charles M. Conlon* by Neal McCabe and Constance McCabe.

Distribution for the Sporting News list of books is handled by its parent company; books may also be ordered directly or through Contemporary Books.

Query letters and SASEs should be directed to:

Gary Brinker, Director of Information Development

STACKPOLE BOOKS

5067 Ritter Road
Mechanicsburg, PA 17055
717-796-0411

Stackpole publishes in the areas of nature and the outdoors, crafts and hobbies, fly fishing, gardening and cooking, sporting literature, carving and woodworking, history (especially military history), military reference, and Americana.

Stackpole Books was established in 1933 as Stackpole Sons, a small family-owned publishing enterprise. The house acquired Military Service Publishing Company in 1935 and has continued gradual corporate expansion while remaining attuned to its original publishing vision.

Stackpole Books publishes editions that are created lovingly, with striking design. When selecting projects to produce, the publisher determines what readers need and how these needs will be met through a proposed project's fresh perspective. Stackpole signs expert authors, juggles production schedules, and commits the personalized verve to make the dream real. Stackpole believes in perfectionism and care—when focused upon the practical—as keys to successful publishing.

Representative Stackpole titles: *Free Climbing with John Bachar* by John Bachar and Steve Boga, *Backyard Birdfeeding* by John F. Gardner, *How to Photograph Animals in the Wild* by Leonard Lee Rue III and Len Rue Jr., *Old Hickory's War: Andrew Jackson and the Quest for Empire* by David S. Heidler and Jeanne T. Heidler, *Woodcarving Step by Step with Rick Bütz: Woodland Warblers* by Rick and Ellen Bütz, *Fly Rodding the Coast* by Ed Mitchell, *For the Love of Wild Things: The Extraordinary Work of a Wildlife Center* by Mary Jane Stretch and Phyllis Hobe, and *Wild Turkey Cookbook* by A. D. Livingston.

Additional areas of Stackpole's publishing interest are represented by *Outdoor Careers: Exploring Occupations in Outdoor Fields* by Ellen Shenk and *How to Start and Run Your Own Bed & Breakfast Inn* by Ripley Hotch and Carl Glassman.

Stackpole distributes its own list as well as military history titles from United Kingdom publishers Greenhill and Osprey; the house utilizes the services of regional distribution houses and sales representatives.

Query letters and SASEs should be directed to:

Sally Atwater, Editor
Nature.

David Uhler, Editor
Outdoor sports and adventure.

Judith Schnell, Editorial Director
Fly fishing and carving.

William C. Davis, Editor
History.

Ann Wagoner, Associate Editor
Military reference.

STANFORD UNIVERSITY PRESS
(See Directory of University Presses)

STERLING PUBLISHING COMPANY

387 Park Avenue South
New York, NY 10016
212-532-7160

Sterling emphasizes general popular reference and information books, science, nature, arts and crafts, architecture, home improvement, history, humor, health, self-help, wine and food, gardening, business and careers, social sciences, sports, pets, hobbies, drama and music, psychology, occult, and military-science books. Sterling also publishes games, puzzles, calendars, and children's books.

The current scope of the Sterling Publishing Company program includes a wide range of nonfiction practical approaches, including informative how-to books in gardening, crafts, and woodworking; books on military history; art and reference titles; and activity and puzzle books for kids. The house (founded in 1949) hosts a formidable backlist.

Representative Sterling titles: *Easy Card Tricks* by Bob Longe; *Nature Crafts with a Microwave: Over 80 Projects* by Dawn Cusick; *Wreaths from the Garden: 75 Fresh and Dried Floral Wreaths to Make* by Leslie Dierks; *Keep Your Bonsai Alive and Well* by Herb L. Gustafson; *New and Traditional Styles of Chip Carving: From Classic to Positive Imaging* by Wayne Barton; *Celtic Key Patterns* by Ian Bain; *The Healing Touch of Massage* by Carlo De Paoli; *Time Travel: Fact, Fiction, and Possibility* by Jenny Randles; *Aztec Astrology: An Introduction* by Michael Colmer; *Irish Toasts, Curses, and Blessings* by Padraic O'Farrell; *The Art of Italian Regional Cooking* by Francesco Antonucci, Marta Pulini, and Gianni Salvaterra; and *World's Most Incredible Puzzles* by Charles Barry Townsend.

On the Sterling juveniles list are *101 Science Surprises: Exciting Experiments with Everyday Materials* by Roy Richards, *Rainforest Animals Dot-to-Dot* by Susan Baumgart (illustrated by Richard Salvucci), and *Five Minute Frights* (short fiction) by William A. Walker Jr. (illustrated by Will Suckow and Martin Charlot).

Sterling handles its own distribution.

Query letters and SASEs should be directed to:

Sheila Barry, Acquisitions Manager

STEWART, TABORI & CHANG

575 Broadway
New York, NY 10003
212-941-2929

Stewart, Tabori, & Chang publishes luxuriously produced titles in art, popular culture, design, home, cuisine, lifestyle, and collecting. The house offers topnotch specialty merchandise such as calendars, cards, journals, and engagement books. Terrail is an imprint in collaboration with Editions Terrail that publishes a line of art books at reasonable prices. The publisher supports an impeccably select backlist.

Stewart, Tabori & Chang books are produced in hardcover and trade paperback editions. Booksellers especially appreciate the quality product signified by the publisher's prancing bison trade logo—when on display in a bookstore these books can draw significant point-of-purchase interest from customers.

Stewart, Tabori & Chang (founded in 1981 by Andy Stewart, Lena Tabori, and Nai Chang), recently part of the publishing stable of Peter Brant (owner of the magazines *Interview*, *Art in America*, and *Antiques*), is now a division of U.S. Media Holdings, Inc.

From the Stewart, Tabori & Chang list: *Home: Chronicle of a North Country Life* by Beth Powning, *The Foods of Thailand* by Wanphen Heymann-Sukphan, *Natural History Dioramas* by Richard Ross, *Casa Mexicana* (Spanish-language edition) by Tim Street-Porter, *Marlon Brando: Portraits and Film Stills 1946–1995* (text by Truman Capote), *Dance Me to the End of Love* (poetry by Leonard Cohen; paintings by Henri Matisse), *Manhattan Dawn and Dusk* (cards) by Jon Ortner, and *Funny Cats and Funny Dogs* (calendars and books edited by J. C. Suarès).

Stewart, Tabori & Chang's books are distributed to the trade via Publishers Resources; in addition, the house uses a network of independent regional sales representatives.

Query letters and SASEs should be directed to:

Linda Sunshine, Senior Editor

Mary Kalamaras, Editor

Alexandra Childs, Assistant Editor

THE SUMMIT PUBLISHING GROUP

One Arlington Center
1112 East Copeland Road
Fifth Floor
Arlington, TX 76011
817-274-1821

Summit showcases general nonfiction, contemporary biography, sports, how-to, education, children's activity books, health, fiction, and humor. The Summit Publishing Group (founded in 1990; formerly Summit Publishing) began as an advertising agency, then moved progressively into its current focus as a publisher of books.

Summit's areas of expertise are evidenced handily in the type of support provided for lead titles. Publicity is among the strong points of the house's marketing strategy; word has it that Summit's salaried publicists may also earn a commission keyed to a book's outstanding performance. Significant marks have been notched by novelty titles such as *Barney Fife's Guide to Life, Love and Self-Defense*, *The Autobiography of Santa Claus: It's Better to Give*, and *Death at Sea* (a murder mystery that includes clues hidden in 3-D images).

On the Summit list: *On the Brink: The Life and Leadership of Norman Brinker* by Norman Brinker and Donald T. Phillips, *Eye-D Picture Challenge* (preschool edition) by Kathy Oszustowicz, *Best Boss, Worst Boss: Lessons and Laughs from the International "Best Boss, Worst Boss" Contest* by Jim Miller, *Why Can't a Woman Be More Like a Man? A Woman's Guide to Revitalizing Her Natural Sex Drive* by Michael P. Bonaventura, *America's Toughest Sheriff: How to Win the War against Crime* by Joe Arpaio and Len Sherman, *The Women of the America's Cup: Leadership, Teamwork, Breaking Barriers* by Anna Seaton Huntington, *Stewardship: God's Plan for Living* by Ben G. Gill, *Something in the Blood: True Stories of Real Vampires* by Jeff Guinn, *I, Jesus: Stories from the Savior* by Robert Darden, and *Jack Binion's Black Book: The Insider's Guide to Gambling* by Jack Binion.

Summit orchestrates its own distribution.

Query letters and SASEs should be directed to:

Len Oszustowicz, President and Publisher

SURREY BOOKS

230 East Ohio Street, Suite 120
Chicago, IL 60611
312-751-7330

Surrey targets the subject areas of business and careers, self-improvement, education, the family, cooking, nutrition, and health. Surrey Books (founded in 1982) is a small publishing house that is successful in reaching special reader-interest markets. Surrey's numerous ongoing series provide a dependable quality baseline for booksellers and readers alike.

The Surrey series roster includes *Skinny Sandwiches* by Desiree Witkowski, *Skinny Italian Cooking* by Ruth Glick and Nancy Baggett, and *Skinny Mexican Cooking* by Sue Spitler (in the "Skinny" series); the Free & Equal Cookbooks by Carole Kruppa (accenting the use of non-sugar sweetening); the How to Get a Job series keyed to specific metropolitan and regional areas; and the Undiscovered Museum series by Eloise Danto.

Other books from Surrey: *The Restaurant Companion: A Guide to Healthier Eating Out* by Hope Warshaw, *The Travel Writer's Handbook* by Louise Purwin Zobel, and *The Teenage Entrepreneur's Guide: 50 Money Making Business Ideas* by Sarah Riehm.

Surrey Books oversees its own distribution services.

Query letters and SASEs should be directed to:

Susan H. Schwartz, Publisher

SYBEX, INC.

1151 Marina Village Parkway
Alameda, CA 94501
510-523-8233

Sybex produces educational and professional books geared to personal computing for business, small business, and individual end users on introductory, intermediate, and advanced levels. The Sybex list offers timely, high-quality tutorials and reference works in areas ranging from desktop publishing to networking to games.

Many Sybex how-to products (including book-and-diskette packages) are geared to specific operating systems and proprietary programs. Areas of particular Sybex technical scope encompass assembly languages, database management, and creative utilization of spreadsheets. Sybex (founded in 1976) issues a solid block of state-of-the-art titles each year and supports a healthy backlist.

The Sybex catalog highlights the Up & Running computer-book series for beginners and intermediate computer users, the introductory lineup of Your First titles, and Novell Press books for users of Novell networks.

The Sybex product-classification roster offers titles in computer-assisted design (CAD), communications, compact guides, computer literacy, database management, desktop presentation, desktop publishing/PC, file utilities, financial management, fun and games, hardware, Macintosh, networking, operating systems, PostScript printing, sound, spreadsheets, technical, word processing, and virus protection.

From the Sybex list: *Corel Ventura Quick and Easy* by Robin Merrin, *Tom McDonald's PC Games Extravaganza!* by T. Liam McDonald, *The Internet Voyeur* by Jim Howard, *The Visual FoxPro Codebook* by Yair Alan Griver, *The Musician's Guide to MIDI* by Christian Braut, and *Microsoft Word for Kids* by Peter Dublin.

Sybex handles its own distribution.

Query letters and SASEs should be directed to the developmental editor/product manager appropriate for the proposal. They are:

Guy Hart-Davis, Network Press
All Networking.

Gary Masters
Operating systems, programming languages, PC hardware, utilities.

Richard Mills
Spreadsheets, financial management, CAD, general computer literacy.

Brenda Kienan
Internet, electronic mail, communications software, computers for children.

Damon Dean
Macintosh (except data bases, spreadsheets, and word processing); desktop graphics and design (Macintosh); multimedia; alternative platforms; games.

Melanie Spiller
Data bases; presentation software (Windows).

James Sumser
Word processing, integrated packages.

Additional Sybex acquisitions contact:

Kristine Plachy, Acquisitions Manager (and general liaison with authors)
Maintains close contact with the developmental editors; any book or series idea may be directed to her. Also responsible for the areas of proprietary-related projects (including

licensing arrangements), new product updates, nondisclosure agreements, software and evaluation copies.

SYRACUSE UNIVERSITY PRESS
(See Directory of University Presses)

TAB BOOKS
(See McGraw-Hill)

JEREMY P. TARCHER
(See Tarcher under the Putnam Berkley Group)

TAYLOR PUBLISHING COMPANY
1550 West Mockingbird Lane
Dallas, TX 75235
214-819-8501

Taylor presents frontlist trade books and targeted-interest practical titles in the areas of celebrity biography, health and fitness, gardening, home improvement, lifestyle, nature and the outdoors, parenting, popular culture, regional, sports, and coffee-table/gift books. TFB Commemorative Press is an imprint that specializes in titles keyed to university and professional sports teams and franchises. Taylor Publishing Company (founded in 1980) is an innovative house that is particularly adept at hitting specialty and international markets.

Titles from Taylor: *Spielberg: The Man, the Movies, the Mythology* by Frank Santello, *Patty Sheehan on Golf* by Patty Sheehan and Betty Hicks, *ADD on the Job: Making Your ADD Work for You* by Lynn Weiss, *How to Win at Rotisserie Baseball* by Peter Golenbrock, *White Trash Gardening* by Rufus T. Firefly as told to Mike Benton, *Renovating with a Contractor* by Kate Kelly and Kelvin Brenner, *Bonnie Blair: A Winning Edge* by Bonnie Blair with Greg Brown (illustrated by Doug Keith), *Tom Cruise: The Unauthorized Biography* by Frank Sanello, *Never Give Up* by Cal Ripken Jr., *Nightwalkers: Gothic Horror Movies* by Bruce Lanier Wright, and *Living on Flood Plains and Wetlands: A Homeowner's Handbook* by Maureen Gilmer.

Taylor Publishing distributes its own list and handles distribution for a variety of other houses.

Query letters and SASEs should be directed to:

Frank Perliski, President

Lynn A. Brooks, Publisher and Editorial Director

Ten Speed Press/Celestial Arts
Tricycle Press

P.O. Box 7123
Berkeley, CA 94707
510-559-1600

Ten Speed/Celestial Arts publishes practical nonfiction in cooking, business and careers, women's issues, parenting, health, self-discovery, leisure and lifestyle, humor, outdoors, house crafts, and popular reference. Tricycle Press (please see separate subentry below) is Ten Speed/Celestial's children's division. Ten Speed publishes hardcover and paperback titles; the house also offers audio literature and produces a line of posters and novelty items.

Ten Speed Press (founded in 1971) gained success with *Anybody's Bike Book* by Tom Cuthbertson—the first book the publisher produced. This classic work has been revised and updated several times and is emblematic of the type of reference book that Ten Speed Press publishes so well. With the acquisition of the Celestial Arts subsidiary (see separate subentry below), the house obtained the midsize status that set the platform for subsequent expansion of the list. Throughout this growth, Ten Speed has been renowned for its small press publishing savvy.

Ten Speed/Celestial is selective in acquiring new works, and procures in part on the basis of projected publication endurance: The hardy backlist and announcements of revised editions read as fresh and bright as many houses' new releases.

A particular Ten Speed inflection is the individualist expression of the American culture voiced by the house's authors. Many Ten Speed titles feature unconventional approaches to the subject matter at hand—making creativity an enduring Ten Speed/Celestial Arts hallmark. Among its perennial sellers, Ten Speed publishes *What Color Is Your Parachute?* and other career-related works by Richard Bolles, as well as *The Moosewood Cookbook* by Mollie Katzen (along with several additional food titles by Ms. Katzen and the Moosewood Collective). *Barcelona: Jews, Transvestites, and an Olympic Season* is a literary travel piece by Richard Schweid (author of the esteemed culinary classics *Catfish and the Delta* and *Hot Peppers*).

From the Ten Speed list: *Garlic Is Life* by Chester Aaron, *The Small Investor* by Jim Gard, *Send This Jerk the Bedbug Letter* by John Bear, *The Damn Good Résumé Guide* by Yana Parker, *What Not to Name Your Baby* by Andy Meiser and Michael Rey, *The Torani Cookbook* by Lisa Lucheta, *The Guide to Florida's Best Restaurants* by Joyce LaFray, *How to Shit in the Woods* by Kathleen Meyer, and *Cuthbertson's All-in-One Bike Repair Manual* by Tom Cuthbertson.

Ten Speed Press/Celestial Arts handles its own distribution.

Query letters and SASEs should be directed to:

Philip Wood, President and Editorial Director

George Young, Editor in Chief

CELESTIAL ARTS

P.O. Box 7327
Berkeley, CA 94707
510-559-1600

Celestial Arts focuses on self-discovery, popular psychology, relationships and healing, pregnancy and parenting, gay and lesbian issues, practical how-to, kitchen arts, and general trade nonfiction.

Celestial Arts was founded as an independent house in 1966 and was acquired by Ten Speed Press in 1983. The house produces an individual line of hardcover and trade paperback books, along with calendars, maps, poster art, personal journals, and engagement books.

Celestial Arts titles: *Tulips* (in the Totally Flowers series) by Matt Damsker, *Anxiety and Stress Self-Help* by Susan M. Lark, *Essays on Creating Sacred Relationships* by Sondra Ray, *Talking Back to Poems* by Daniel Alderson, and *Penguins* by Jonathan Chester.

Celestial Arts is distributed by Ten Speed Press/Celestial Arts.

Query letters and SASEs should be directed to:

David Hines, Editorial Director

TRICYCLE PRESS

Tricycle is devoted to books, posters, and audiotapes for kids and their grown-ups. Tricycle Press was instituted in 1994 and has unified and expanded the children's division (previously divided between Ten Speed and Celestial). Tricycle Press, in addition to its own roster of originals, catalogs appropriate backlist selections from Ten Speed and Celestial Arts.

Tricycle is committed to publishing projects that reflect the creative spirit of the parent company, Ten Speed Press, and its publishing partner, Celestial Arts.

On the Tricycle Press list: *Babysitter's Companion* by Mary Jayne Fogerty, *Lotions, Potions, and Slime: Mudpies and More!* by Nancy Blakey, *A Sky Full of Kites* by Osmond Molarsky (illustrations by Helen Hipshman), *The Best Summer Ever* by Joan Bergstrum, and *A for Antarctica* by Jonathan Chester.

Query letters and SASEs to Tricycle Press should be directed to:

Nicole Geiger, Managing Editor

TEXAS MONTHLY PRESS
(See Gulf Publishing)

THAMES AND HUDSON

500 Fifth Avenue
New York, NY 10110
212-354-3763

Thames and Hudson publishes popular and scholarly works as well as college texts in the fine arts, archaeology, architecture, biography, crafts, history, mysticism, music, photography, and the sciences.

Thames and Hudson (founded in 1977) is an international producer of well-crafted nonfiction trade books in hardcover and trade paperback under its double-dolphin logo. Though a portion of the publisher's list is originated through the New York editorial office, the greater part of Thames and Hudson's titles are imports via the house's United Kingdom branch.

From Thames and Hudson: *Henri Cartier-Bresson: Mexican Noteboooks* (text by Carlos Fuentes), *Balinese Gardens* (text by William Warren; photographs by Luca Invernizzi Tettoni), *The Splendor of Islamic Calligraphy* by Abdelkebir Khatibi and Mohammed Sijelmassi, *Significant Others: Creativity and Intimate Partnership* (edited by Whitney Chadwick and Isabelle de Courtivron), *Our Boots: An Inuit Women's Art* by Jill Oakes and Rick Riewe, *The Medieval Cookbook* by Maggie Black, *The Avebury Cycle* by Michael Dames, *The Private Realm of Marie-Antoinette* by Marie-France Boyer (photographs by Francois Halard), *The True History of Chocolate* by Sophie D. and Michael D. Coe, *Ports of Entry: William S. Burroughs and the Arts* by Robert A. Sobieszek (with the Los Angeles County Museum of Art), and *Art Deco and Modernist Ceramics* by Karen McReady.

Real Kids/Real Science is a series of children's books covering areas such as marine biology, entomology, and invertebrate zoology.

Thames and Hudson is distributed to the trade by W. W. Norton. The house also offers an 800 ordering number and has in-house fulfillment services for purchases by individual consumers.

Query letters and SASEs should be directed to:

Peter Warner, President

THUNDER'S MOUTH PRESS
MARLOWE

(See Marlowe & Thunder's Mouth)

TIMES BOOKS

(See Random House)

TOR BOOKS/FORGE BOOKS

175 Fifth Avenue
14th Floor
New York, NY 10010
212-388-0100

Tor and Forge cover general trade nonfiction and commercial fiction. Tor publishes a list of mass-market and trade paperbacks, as well as trade hardcovers. Tor's mountain-top logo adorns standout titles in horror, science fiction and fantasy, mystery and suspense, and American historicals (including Westerns), as well as general commercial fiction and nonfiction. The Forge Books imprint (see subentry below) tends toward the center of the trade spectrum. In addition, Tor offers books for younger readers (some of which are intended for the educational market). Tor/Forge (founded in 1980) is a subsidiary of Tom Doherty Associates, an affiliate of St. Martin's Press.

From the Tor program: *A Crown of Swords* by Robert Jordan, *Black Carousel* by Charles Grant, *Bloodletter* by Warren Newton Beath, *Count Geiger's Blues* by Michael Bishop, *Goodlow's Ghosts* by T. M. Wright, *Slow Funeral* by Rebecca Ore, *Steps to Midnight* by Richard Matheson, *The Furies* by Suzy McKee Charnas, and *The Girl Who Heard Dragons* by Anne McCaffrey.

Tor mass-market editions feature paperback books with foiled and embossed covers, and the publisher provides attractive floor displays to booksellers for some of its major releases. Tor's list is distributed to the trade by St. Martin's Press.

FORGE BOOKS

The books that carry the Forge emblem (a stylized flaming anvil) run the gamut of commercial fiction and nonfiction. At Forge the various genres and categories are well represented (often with frontlist sensibility), and many titles honor mainstream conventions even as they exhibit their own individualistic bent.

Forge fiction: *The Cutting Hours* by Julia Grice, *Steroid Blues* by Richard La Plante (author of *Mantis* and *Leopard*), *Speak Daggers to Her* by Rosemary Edgehill, *Presumed Dead* by Hugh Holton, *Play It Again* by Stephen Humphrey Bogart, *False Promises* by Ralph Arnote, and *Cat on a Blue Monday* (a Midnight Louie mystery) by Carole Nelson Douglas.

Forge nonfiction: *The October Twelve: Five Years of Yankee Glory* by Phil Rizzuto and Tom Horton, *Zoo Book: The Evolution of Wildlife Conservation Centers* by Linda Koebner, and *Deke! My Thirty-Four Years in Space* by Donald K. Slayton with Michael Cassutt.

Query letters and SASEs should be directed to:

Natalia Aponte, Associate Editor
Women's fiction, romances, mysteries.

Greg Cox, Editor
Science fiction, fantasy, and horror.

Claire Eddy, Editor
Women's fiction, romances, mysteries.

David Hartwell, Senior Editor
Science fiction.

Patrick Nielsen Hayden, Senior Editor, Manager of Science Fiction
Science fiction, fantasy.

Beth Meacham, Executive Editor, Science Fiction

Melissa Ann Singer, Senior Editor
Women's fiction, romances, mysteries.

Andrew Zack, Consulting Editor
P.O. Box 247
Westfield, NJ 07091-0247

Commercial fiction (excluding women's fiction); thrillers in every shape and form—
international, serial killer, scientific/technological/computer, medical, psychological,
erotic, military, environmental, legal; action novels in the David Morrell or Clive
Cussler tradition.

J. N. TOWNSEND

12 Greenleaf Drive
Exeter, NH 03833
603-778-9883

J. N. Townsend (founded in 1986) is a small publisher with a successful line of titles
about living with animals. Townsend initially published in softcover format only and
issued its first hardcover title in 1994. The house has been able to thrive on the basis of
short press runs and by keeping titles alive on a full backlist.

From Townsend: *Good Companions* by Era Ziztel, *Operation Pet Rescue: Animal
Survivors of the Oakland, California Firestorm* by Gregory N. Zompolis, *Sharing a
Robin's Life* by Linda Johns, *How Do You Spank a Porcupine?* by Ronald Rood, *Sasha's
Tail: Lessons from a Life With Cats* by Jacqueline Damian, and *Nana's Adoption Farm:
The Story of Little Rachell* by Tryntje Horn (illustrated by Dana Lacroix).

Townsend is distributed through C. Hood & Company.

Query letters and SASEs should be directed to:

(Ms.) Jeremy Townsend, Publisher

2.13.61 PUBLICATIONS, INC.
TWO THIRTEEN SIXTY-ONE PUBLICATIONS

P.O. Box 1910
Los Angeles, CA 90078
213-969-8043
213-969-8791

2.13.61 Publications offers new fiction and creative narratives, creative prose nonfiction, poetry, cultural events and critical works, photographic books, and audiovisual products. The house was founded in 1988.

Sample titles: *Eye Scream* by Henry Rollins, *Openers II—the Lyrics of Roky Erikson* by Roky Erickson, *Reach* by Don Bajema, *The Consumer* (short, dark fictions) by M. Gira, *Fuck You Heroes* by Glen E. Friedman (photographic excursion into skateboarder/hardcore punker/rap music culture), *Dream Baby Dream: Images from the Blank Generation* (historical photoessay) by Stephanie Chernikowski, *Rock and the Pop Narcotic* by Joe Carducci, and *Letters to Rollins* by R. K. Overton.

Query letters and SASEs should be directed to:

Gary Ichihara, Director

TURNER PUBLISHING
1059 Techwood Drive Northwest
Atlanta, GA 30318
404-885-4114

Turner publishes primarily popular nonfiction, with occasional, extremely selective, frontlist fiction. Turner Publishing (instituted in 1989) is a book-producing wing of the Turner Communications media conglomerate. Among Turner Publishing projects are tie-ins to other Turner properties and enterprises, such as the film classics of MGM Studios and television programming, both broadcast and cable. Turner Publishing products include lavishly produced items, profusely illustrated and with generous use of color. In addition to books, Turner's list includes calendars and pop-up volumes.

Sample Turner titles: *Andy Lakey: Art, Angels, and Miracles* by Andy Lakey and Paul Robert Walker (foreword by James Redfield), *Dinotopia Lost* by Alan Dean Foster, *Ian Fleming: The Man Behind James Bond* by Andrew Lycett, *Balance of Power: Presidents and Congress from the Era of McCarthy to the Age of Gingrich* by Jim Wright (former Speaker of the House), *Level 4: Virus Hunters of the CDC* by Joseph McCormick with Leslie Alan Horvitz, *Roots of Country: The Legends Look Back* by Robert C. Oermann, *The Goblin Companion: A Field Guide to Goblins* by Terry Jones (illustrated by Brian Froud), and *The Couple Book: Reaching New Levels of Sexual Excitement through Body Exercises and Relationship Renewal* by Jack Rosenberg and Beverly Kitaen-Morse.

A feature fiction title is *Outlaws* (suspense) by Tim Green (NFL analyst for Fox television and author of *Ruffians* and *Titans*). More Turner fiction: *Tesla* by Tad Wise (based on the life of visionary inventor Nikola Tesla), *Natural Enemies* (action novel) by Sara Cameron, and *Necessary Risks* (inspirational drama) by Janet Keller.

Turner Publishing is distributed by Andrews and McMeel.

Query letters and SASEs should be directed to:

Alan Axelrod, Director of Development

Katherine Buttler, Editor

UNIVERSE PUBLISHING

300 Park Avenue South
New York, NY 10010
212-982-2300

Universe produces books in art history and appreciation, architecture and design, photography, and the occasional human- or social-interest title in illustrated format.

Universe's concentration (including a number of series) is in works of scholarly and general interest in the arts, and in artists of the Western and European tradition from prehistoric to contemporary times. Imprints include Universe, Children's Universe, Universe Calendars, and Universe Publishing. Among Universe's products are illustrated gift books, children's books, children's paper products, calendars, address books, and diaries.

Universe Publishing (founded in 1956; formerly known as Phaidon Universe) is an affiliate division of Rizzoli International.

From Universe: *America* (photographs by Jake Rajas), *Olympic Dreams: 100 Years of Excellence* (text by Douglas Collins; an official publication of the United States Olympic Committee), *Fabergé: Fantasies and Treasures* by Géza von Habsburg, *The Gilded Age: Edith Wharton and Her Contemporaries* by Eleanor Dwight, *Whitman's Men: Walt Whitman's Calamus Poems Celebrated by Contemporary Photographers* (with essays by David Groff and Richard Berman), *Catwalk: Inside the World of the Supermodels* by Sandra Morris, and *The Film Lover's Address Book.*

CHILDREN'S UNIVERSE

Children's Universe produces a variety of inventive products, ranging from book-and-toy packages to story books, from hide-and-seek books (with moveable parts) to cut-out puppets, posters, masks, and make-it-yourself gift boxes. These publications feature fine design and are produced in sturdy editions to withstand carefree handling.

Representative works from Children's Universe: *Skateboard Monsters* by Daniel Kirk, *Ravita and the Land of Unknown Shadows* (story by Marietta and Peter Brill; illustrations by Laurie Smollett Kutscera), *Head Trips* by Sara Schwartz, *First Steps in Paint: A New and Simple Way to Learn How to Paint* by Tom Robb, *Dinosaur Cowboys Puppet Theatre* by Judy Lichtenstein, and *The ABC's of Art* (along with a wall frieze version) by National Gallery of Art, London (with flash cards by National Gallery of Art, Washington, DC).

Universe is distributed to the trade by St. Martin's.

Query letters and SASEs should be directed to:

Charles Miers, Publisher
Calendars, graphic products; Children's Universe projects.

James Stave, Senior Editor
Art, architecture, women's studies.

UNIVERSITY OF ARIZONA PRESS
(See Directory of University Presses)

UNIVERSITY OF ARKANSAS PRESS
(See Directory of University Presses)

UNIVERSITY OF CALIFORNIA PRESS
(See Directory of University Presses)

UNIVERSITY OF CHICAGO PRESS
(See Directory of University Presses)

UNIVERSITY OF HAWAII PRESS
(See Directory of University Presses)

UNIVERSITY OF ILLINOIS PRESS
(See Directory of University Presses)

UNIVERSITY OF IOWA PRESS
(See Directory of University Presses)

UNIVERSITY OF MICHIGAN PRESS
(See Directory of University Presses)

UNIVERSITY OF MISSOURI PRESS
(See Directory of University Presses)

UNIVERSITY OF NEBRASKA PRESS
(See Directory of University Presses)

UNIVERSITY OF NEW MEXICO PRESS
(See Directory of University Presses)

UNIVERSITY OF NORTH CAROLINA PRESS
(See Directory of University Presses)

UNIVERSITY OF OKLAHOMA PRESS
(See Directory of University Presses)

UNIVERSITY OF TEXAS PRESS
(See Directory of University Presses)

UNIVERSITY OF WASHINGTON PRESS
(See Directory of University Presses)

UNIVERSITY OF WISCONSIN PRESS
(See Directory of University Presses)

UNIVERSITY PRESS OF NEW ENGLAND/WESLEYAN UNIVERSITY PRESS
(See Directory of University Presses)

VIKING

(See Penguin USA)

WALKER AND COMPANY

435 Hudson Street
New York, NY 10014
212-727-8300

Walker publishes trade fiction and nonfiction. Frontlist fiction accents mysteries and Westerns. Nonfiction emphasis includes science, sports, nature, self-help, business and entrepreneurship, travel, education and parenting, and marriage and family. Walker produces a list of large-print Judaica and Christian inspirational titles; books for children range from preschool picture books to books for young adults (please see separate subentry below for Walker and Company Books for Young Readers).

Walker and Company (established in 1959) is a compact powerhouse with a hard-hitting, diverse list; especially strong are Walker's market niches in mysteries, Westerns, large-print religious and inspirational titles, and children's books chosen to complement a broad, carefully chosen selection of adult nonfiction titles.

Walker operates on the publishing credo that what often separates the success of one book from another is the ability to execute an effective marketing strategy; what then separates one house from another is the ability to execute many such strategies—often simultaneously—season after season.

Walker and Company was founded by the intrepid Sam Walker, whose expressed the view "there cannot be a surfeit of good taste." Such faith in editorial content remains at the heart of the firm today, under the current leadership of publisher George Gibson. Underlying the house's publishing strategy is a commitment to product quality. This two-pronged assault on the marketplace thus relies on compositional and literary depth as well as the ability to capitalize on the potential appeal of such works.

Among Walker nonfiction titles: *Longitude: The True Story of a Lone Genius Who Solved the Greatest Scientific Problem of His Time* by Dava Sobel (a New York *Times* best-seller), *Epilepsy: A New Approach—What Medicine Can Do, What You Can Do for Yourself* by Adrienne Richard and Joel Reiter, *Money Harmony: Resolving Money Conflicts in Your Life and Your Relationships* by Olivia Mellan, *The Joy of Keeping Score: How Scoring the Game Has Influenced and Enhanced the History of Baseball* by Paul Dickson, and *My First Year as a Journalist* (edited by Dianne Selditch).

In fiction Walker is widely admired for topflight category books (a significant number of which are first novels) in mysteries and Westerns. (Walker discontinued its lines in such genres as thrillers, romances, and adventure novels.) Walker also publishes standout mainstream novels.

On Walker's fiction list: *When Well Horses Die* by Sandra West Prowell, *The Innocents* by Richard Barre, *Who in Hell Is Wanda Fuca* (a Leo Waterman mystery) by

G. M. Ford, *The Long Drift* by Sam Brown (sequel to *The Big Lonely*), *The Devil on Horseback* by Lauran Paine, and *The Last Free Range* by James A. Ritchie.

Walker's guidelines for manuscript submission to their genre lists include valuable hints for fiction authors in general and category writers in particular. The sheet for Walker mysteries notes that the mystery novel is a game between author and reader, an entertaining puzzle to be savored and solved; therefore, the mystery must be primary (with nuances such as romantic interest secondary). The story line of the mystery novel must be rooted in the real world (and not imbued with supernatural overtones). In general, manuscripts should respect the conventions of the genre.

Because Walker does welcome unsolicited submissions, the publisher emphasizes the importance of including a stamped, self-addressed envelope as well as maintaining the other customary manuscript-related courtesies—contact the publisher for detailed submission guidelines. Authors please note: Materials submitted without a self-addressed stamped envelope (SASE) will *not* be returned.

Walker handles marketing, sales, and distribution for its own list.

Query letters and SASEs should be directed to:

George Gibson, Publisher

Nonfiction in all Walker areas, including science, nature, parenting, education, business, health, sourcebooks.

Jacqueline Johnson, Editor

Westerns.

Michael Seidman, Editor

Mysteries. No romantic suspense or horror stories.

WALKER AND COMPANY BOOKS FOR YOUNG READERS

Walker and Company Books for Young Readers maintains a sturdy backlist in addition to offering new books in a variety of young-reader markets from preschooler picture books to fiction and nonfiction for young adults.

Representative titles include *Seven Little Rabbits* by John Becker (illustrated by Barbara Cooney), *The Ever-Living Tree: The Life and Times of a Coast Redwood* by Linda Viera (with illustrations by Christopher Canyon), *Sand and Fog: Adventures in Southern Africa* by Jim Brandenburg, *Crime Lab 101: Experimenting with Crime Detection* by Robert Gardner, *The Harvey Girls: The Women Who Civilized the West* by Juddi Morris, *They Dreamed of Horses: Careers for Horse Lovers* by Kay Frydenborg (with photographs by Tanya Wood), and the novel *One Foot Ashore* by Jacqueline Dembar Greene.

Query letters and SASEs should be directed to:

Emily Easton, Editorial Director

Soyung Pak, Editor

Robin Ben-Joseph, Assistant Editor

The above three editors acquire children's books. They are specially interested in young science, photoessays, historical fiction for middle grades, biographies, current affairs, and young-adult nonfiction.

WARNER BOOKS

Time & Life Building
1271 Avenue of the Americas
New York, NY 10020
212-522-7200

Warner Books publishes a wide range of commercial fiction and nonfiction in mass-market, trade paperback, and hardcover originals as well as reprints. Among Warner's nonfiction categories are biography, business, cooking, current affairs, history, house and home, humor, popular culture, psychology, self-help, sports, games books and crosswords, and general reference. Warner fiction in general accents the popular approach and includes works in the categories of mystery and suspense, fantasy and science fiction, action thrillers, horror, and contemporary and historical romance.

Warner's commercial acumen can seem downright visionary. The works of Robert James Waller have paved the way for women's-interest romantic-philosophical fiction that just happens to be written by men. *The Celestine Prophecy* by James Redfield has been termed a spiritual adventure-quest; whether the work is a fluke or a self-contained genre, it has spawned industry-wide interest in sussing out its appeal and developing whatever market it detected (or perhaps created).

The Aspect imprint accents suspense, thrillers, action adventure, future fiction, science fiction, and fantasy. Warner Vision books are generally high-profile mass-market releases. Books on cassette are the domain of Time Warner AudioBooks. A specialized Warner division is the formerly independent Mysterious Press, which publishes a distinguished list of mystery, suspense, and crime novels as well as true crime (see separate subentry below).

Warner Books (founded in 1961) is a division of Time Warner Communications.

From the Warner nonfiction list: *Mountain, Get Out of My Way* by Montel Williams with David Paisner, *Victory of the Spirit: Meditations on Black Quotations* by Janet Cheatham Bell, *The Investment Club Book* by John F. Wasik, *Jump Start Your Brain* by Doug Hall with David Wecker, *Drive Your Woman Wild in Bed* by Staci Keith, *Buns of Steel* by Leisa Hart, and *Curries without Worries: An Introduction to Indian Cuisine* by Sudha Koul.

Among major novelists who have appeared on the Warner imprint are Sidney Sheldon, Scott Turow, Rebecca Brandywyne, and Alexandra Ripley.

Representative Warner fiction: *Exclusive* by Sandra Brown, *The Grid* by Philip Kerr, *Hang Time* by Zev Chafets, *Absolute Power* by David Baldacci, *Iced* by Carol Higgins Clark (copublished with Dove), *The Tenth Insight* by James Redfield (author of *The Celestine Prophecy*), and novels by Robert James Waller (author of *The Bridges of Madison County, Slow Waltz at Cedar Bend, Border Music,* and *Puerto Vallarta Squeeze*).

Warner Books handles its own distribution and distributes book products from other publishers.

Query letters and SASEs should be directed to:

Joann Davis, Executive Editor
Wide commercial fiction and nonfiction interests.

Maureen Egen, Senior Vice President and Publisher
Presides over the Warner Books program.

Rick Horgan, Vice President and Executive Editor
Biographies, pop culture, true crime, general nonfiction. Fiction: Thrillers and mysteries.

Colleen Kapklein, Editor
Health, self-help, general commercial nonfiction. Literary fiction.

Karen Kelly, Senior Editor
General nonfiction; suspense fiction.

Rob McQuilkin, Assistant Editor

Rob McMahon, Assistant Editor

Betsy Mitchell, Editor
Science fiction.

Jessica Papin, Editorial Assistant
Commercial fiction, popular fiction. Commercial nonfiction, including popular science.

Danielle Dayan, Editor
Women's fiction, romances.

(Ms.) Jamie Raab, Executive Editor
General nonfiction. Commercial fiction.

Diane Stockwell, Assistant Editor

Susan Sandler, Senior Editor
Commercial fiction and nonfiction.

Susan Suffes, Senior Editor
Nonfiction: Business, self-help, diet, nutrition, health, popular psychology, Judaica, women's interest.

Rick Wolff, Senior Editor
Business, sports.

Claire Zion, Executive Editor
Women's fiction, including romance.

THE MYSTERIOUS PRESS

Mysterious features novels of crime and suspense, detective fiction, and thrillers, as well as anthologies within these fields. The house also produces literary criticism, some true crime, and reference works for writers and aficionados of mystery and detection. Mysterious Press issues titles in hardcover, trade paperback, and mass-market paper formats, and also releases opulent series of slipcased editions signed by the authors. The Mysterious Press was founded as an independent house in 1976.

Mysterious Press publishes works by writers such as Robert Campbell, Jerome Charyn, George C. Chesbro, Mary Higgins Clark, Janet Dailey, Aaron Elkins, Nicolas Freeling, Elmore Leonard, Charlotte MacLeod, Margaret Maron, Marcia Muller,

Elizabeth Peters, Ellis Peters, Ruth Rendell, Julie Smith, David Stout, Donald E. Westlake, Teri White, and Margaret Yorke.

Mysterious Press fiction titles include *Death of a Charming Man* by M. C. Beaton, *Double* by Marcia Muller and Bill Pronzini, *Electric City* by K. K. Beck, *Life Itself* by Paco Ignacio Taibo II, *Smoke* by Donald E. Westlake, and *Two Bear Mambo* by Joe R. Lansdale.

Time Warner Electronic Publishing and Simultronics Corporation launched *Modus Operandi*, an on-line, multiplayer computer mystery game series, with interactive plots based on scenarios created by authors and editors of Mysterious Press.

The Mysterious Press list is distributed by Warner Books.

Query letters and SASEs should be directed to:

William Malloy, Editor in Chief

Sara Ann Freed, Executive Editor

WATSON-GUPTILL PUBLICATIONS

1515 Broadway
New York, NY 10036
212-764-7300

Watson-Guptill produces titles in art instruction and technique, graphic design, fine arts, photography, crafts, environmental and interior design, architecture, music, theater, and film. Manuals and handbooks abound on the Watson-Guptill booklist, as do annual design reviews geared to specialized fields. Watson-Guptill's imprints are Whitney Library of Design, Amphoto, Billboard Books, Back Stage Books, and RAC Books. A significant portion of the Watson-Guptill list comprises reissues and reprints; the publisher maintains an extensive backlist and is a leading publisher in its areas of interest. Watson-Guptill Publications (founded in 1937) is a division of Billboard Publications.

The Watson-Guptill imprint addresses art instruction and graphic design. Whitney Library of Design issues titles in architecture, interior design, and planning. Amphoto produces instructional volumes from leading photographers. Billboard Books hawks authoritative, up-to-the-minute books on every aspect of music and entertainment. Back Stage Books purveys informative reference and instruction books in the field of performing arts. RAC Books offers a complete line of titles for radio amateurs.

Watson-Guptill distributes its own list.

Query letters and SASEs should be directed to:

Candace Raney, Senior Acquisitions Editor
Graphic design and art instruction.

(Ms.) Robin Simmen, Senior Editor
Amphoto.

Roberto de Alba, Senior Editor
Whitney Library of Design.

Paul Lukas, Senior Editor
Billboard and Back Stage.

Franklin Watts Inc.
(See Grolier Incorporated)

Samuel Weiser, Inc.
(See Directory of Religious, Spiritual, and Inspirational Publishers)

Westminster/John Knox Press
(See Directory of Religious, Spiritual, and Inspirational Publishers)

Westview Press
5500 Central Avenue
Boulder, CO 80301
303-444-3541

Westview Press (founded in 1975) is a subsidiary of SCS Communications. Westview produces a large list of works that cross over from the academic arena into areas of mainstream interest in current affairs and popular culture. The house also publishes scholarly books in social sciences and applied natural sciences, international relations, area studies, domestic and international development, military affairs, political science, history, anthropology, sociology, government, economics, philosophy; health sciences, environment, energy, agriculture, earth sciences, biology; college texts, reference, professional books, and scientific symposia.

Representative titles from Westview Press: *Blood into Ink: South Asian and Middle Eastern Women Write War* (edited by Miriam Cooke and Roshni Rustomji-Kerns), *Culture and the Ad: Exploring Otherness in the World of Advertising* by William M. O'Barr, *Deathright: Culture, Medicine, Politics, and the Right to Die* by James M. Hoefler with Brian E. Kamoie, *Race and Ethnic Relations: Contending Views on Prejudice and Ethnoviolence* (edited by Fred L. Pincus and Howard J. Ehrlich), *Surrogate Motherhood: Conception in the Heart* by Helena Ragoné, and *Women Creating Lives: Identities, Resilience, and Resistance* (edited by Carol E. Franz and Abigail J. Stewart).

Westview Press handles its own distribution through its in-house operation as well as through a network of international sales representatives and distribution services.

Query letters and SASEs should be directed to the Editorial Director.

JOHN WILEY & SONS

605 Third Avenue
New York, NY 10158
212-850-6000

Wiley has strong trade presence with titles of broad commercial interest in areas such as history, reference, current events, health, science, nature, young adult, biography, and psychology. The publisher maintains a reputation for publishing top-drawer professional and popular books in the areas of business, computers, careers, investment, and personal finance, in addition to academically oriented works in business and the sciences. Wiley publishes in hardcover and trade paperback editions.

John Wiley & Sons (established in 1807) is a press with a historic tradition: Through a sequence of partnership shifts and business incarnations over the years (Charles Wiley, Wiley & Halsted, Wiley & Long, Wiley & Putnam), the house has been a player in a broad range of activity (for example, as publishers of writers such as Edgar Allan Poe, Elizabeth Barrett Browning, and James Fenimore Cooper). Today, Wiley is an independent house that produces books for the general trade as well as for specialized professional, scientific, and college markets.

Highlights from the Wiley trade list: *Managed Trading* by Jack D. Schwager, *Infopreneurs: Online and Global* by H. Skip Weitzen, *Trading 101* by Sunny Harris, *A Dose of Sanity: Mind, Medicine, and Misdiagnosis* by Sydney Walker III, *High-Performance Nutrition* by Susan M. Kleiner and Maggie Greenwood-Robinson, *Black Holes: A Traveler's Guide* by Clifford A. Pickover, *The Red Orchestra: The Soviet Spy Network Inside Nazi Europe* by V. E. Tarrant, *A Complex Fate: Gustav Stickley and the Craftsman Movement* by Barry Sanders, *The New Cooking of Britain and Ireland* by Gwenda L. Hyman, *The Last Comanche Chief: The Life and Times of Quanah Parker* by Bill Neeley, and *Valley of the Spirits: A Journey into the Realm of the Aymara* by Alan A. Kolata.

John Wiley & Sons handles its own distribution.

WILEY CHILDREN'S BOOKS

Wiley Children's Books are issued with the house motto: "Discovering the world up close." Wiley titles offer an in-depth approach to the subject at hand, be it the natural world, science and technology, or witty fun-and-game experimental projects. Branches in the Wiley children's family include the Earth-Friendly series, Janice VanCleave's distinctive group of science series (including the Science for Every Kid line), Flying Start, and The House of Science.

Representative titles here: *Online Kids: A Young Surfer's Guide to Cyberspace* by Preston Gralia, *Janice VanCleave's 202 Oozing, Bubbling, Dripping, and Bouncing*

Experiments by Janice VanCleave, *Detective Science: 40 Crime-Solving, Case-Breaking, Crook-Catching Activities for Kids* by Jim Wiese, and *Student Science Opportunities: Your Guide to Over 300 Exciting National Programs, Competitions, Internships, and Scholarships* by Gail Grand.

Query letters and SASEs should be directed to:

Jim Bissent, Editor
General business and management topics.

Kate Bradford, Editor
Science, nature, children's nonfiction.

Jeff Brown, Senior Publisher
Accounting.

Jim Childs, Editor
General business and management topics.

Janet Coleman, Editor
General business and management topics.

(Ms.) P. J. Dempsey, Senior Editor
Popular reference, how-to/self-help, health.

Carole Hall, Associate Publisher and Editor in Chief, Professional and Trade Division

Mike Hamilton, Senior Editor
Career development, small businesses, real estate.

Gerard Helferich, Publisher, General Interest and Children's books.

Hana Lane, Senior Editor
History, current affairs, biography.

Emily Loose, Editor
Economics, sociology, serious nonfiction.

Judith McCarthy, Associate Editor
Popular reference, how-to/self-help, women's interest, parenting, health.

Ruth Mills, Editor
General business and management topics.

Kara Raezer, Assistant Editor
General trade books.

Herb Reich, Senior Editor
Psychology, counseling.

Tim Ryan, Editor
Trade computer books.

Katherine Schowalter, Publisher
Trade computer books.

Myles Thompson, Executive Editor
Investing, banking, business reference.

Pam van Geissen, Editor
Financial and investment subjects.

WILLIAMSON PUBLISHING COMPANY

P.O. Box 185
Church Hill Road
Charlotte, VT 05445
802-425-2102

Williamson Publishing Company (founded in 1983) accents activity books for kids and highlights topics within the subject areas of parenting and the family. The house also produces titles in the fields of business and career, education, travel, cooking, country living, and livestock husbandry. Williamson publications often feature an enthusiastic, upbeat, purposeful how-to approach. Williamson publishes primarily in trade-paperback format. The house offers a strong backlist.

On the list in children's books and works in education and parenting: *Stop, Look, and Listen: Exploring the World Around You* by Sarah A. Williamson, *Super Science Concoctions: 50 Mysterious Mixtures for Fabulous Fun* by Jill Frankel Hauser, *Kids Make Music! Clapping and Tapping from Bach to Rock* by Avery Hart and Paul Mantell, *Tales Alive! Ten Multicultural Folk Tales with Art, Craft, and Creative Experiences* by Susan Milord, *SAT Preparatory Flash Cards: With 500 Math and Vocabulary Questions and Answers* by David Jaffe, *Doing Children's Museums: A Guide to 265 Hands-On Museums* by Joanne Cleaver, and *Parents Are Teachers, Too: Enriching Your Child's First Six Years* by Claudia Jones.

Indicative of the range of William trade nonfiction: *The Women's Job Search Handbook: With Issues and Insights into the Workplace* by Gerri Bloomberg and Margaret Holden, *Retirement Careers: Combining the Best of Work and Leisure* by DeLoss L. Marsh, *Dining on Deck: Fine Foods for Sailing and Boating* by Linda Vail, *Building a Multi-Use Barn: For Garage, Animals, Workshop, or Studio* by John Wagner, and *The Sheep Raiser's Manual* by William K. Kruesi.

Williamson Publishing distributes its list, and works through a number of regional book sales representatives.

Query letters and SASEs should be directed to:

Jack Williamson, President

WORD PUBLISHING

(See Directory of Religious, Spiritual, and Inspirational Publishers)

WORKMAN PUBLISHING COMPANY

708 Broadway
New York, NY 10003
212-254-5900

Workman publishes primarily in the area of general commercial nonfiction with an accent on titles that strike a contemporary note in the lifestyle areas of cooking, food and wine, health and exercise, how-to, sports, pregnancy and childcare, cats, popular culture, and gift books. The house proffers a line of children's books as well as a precisely targeted selection of specialty merchandise such as calendars, journals, and diaries.

Workman also lists titles in popular science, some science fiction and general fiction, satire and humor, self-discovery, fun and games, hobbies and handicrafts, gardening and the home, and travel. Workman produces electronic publishing products, including software, multimedia, and interactive products, often copublished with or distributed for such firms as Turner Interactive and Swfte International.

Workman Publishing Company (started in 1967) is admired for its marketing style that encompasses effects such as particularly eye-catching counter displays for booksellers. In 1988 Workman acquired Algonquin Books of Chapel Hill (see separate subentry below), which specializes in American fiction and nonfiction.

Highlights from Workman: *Nicole Ruthier's Fruit Cookbook: Sweet and Savory, Luscious, Ripe and Zesty, Soups to Roasts* by Nicole Routhier; *Kirby Puckett's Baseball Games* by Kirby Puckett; *The Potting Shed* by Linda Joan Smith; *Memos from the Chairman* by Alan C. (Ace) Greenburg (introduction by Warren Buffett); *The What to Expect When You're Expecting Pregnancy Organizer* by Arlene Eisenberg, Heidi E. Murkoff, and Sandee E. Hathaway; and *Up Your Score: The Underground Guide to the SAT* (updated periodically) by Larry Berger, Michael Colton, Manek Mistry, Paul Rossi, and Lisa Exler.

Workman's Artisan imprint specializes in lifestyle titles. On the Artisan list are *A Cook's Book of Mushrooms: With 100 Recipes for Common and Uncommon Varieties* by Jack Czarnecki (photographs by Louis B. Wallach) and *Grains, Rice, and Beans* by Kevin Graham (photographs by Ellen Silverman). Artisan is the publisher of the Audubon Society's calendar line and distributes books for Eating Well Books (from *Eating Well* magazine).

Workman Publishing Company handles its own distribution.

Query letters and SASEs should be directed to:

Sally Kovalchick, Editor
Humor, quirky popular science and culture.

Suzanne Rafer, Editor
Cookbooks, humor, family issues. Children's activity books.

Peter Workman, President
Oversees entire program. Acquires in all areas consistent with list, including health.

ALGONQUIN BOOKS OF CHAPEL HILL

P.O. Box 2225
Chapel Hill, NC 27515

This division of Workman Publishing Company has a primarily literary orientation in commercial nonfiction and fiction. The house list represents the American tradition, ranging from the homespun to the avant-garde. Algonquin Books of Chapel Hill presents its titles in hardcover and trade paper editions with a look and feel befitting the publisher's emphasis on both the classical and the contemporary—books designed to be comfortably handled when read. The Algonquin editorial staff operates from both the Chapel Hill and the New York Workman offices.

The Algonquin nonfiction list includes *Singing for Your Supper: Entertaining Ways to Be a Perfect Guest* by Edith Hazard, *In My Father's Garden* by Kim Chernin, and *Cobb: A Biography* by Al Stump.

Algonquin fiction offers works such as *The Passion of Ellie O'Barr* (romance) by Cindy Bonner, *The Strange Death of Mistress Coffin* (mystery) by Robert J. Begiebing, and *Omnivores* (contemporary sexual satire) by Lydia Millet.

Front Porch Paperbacks is a list specializing in the work of respected literary voices as well as in new writers. A representative title here is *Sugar Among the Freaks* (short stories) by Lewis Nordan.

Algonquin Books of Chapel Hill is distributed by the parent Workman Publishing Company.

Query letters and SASEs should be directed to:

Shannon Ravenel, Editorial Director

Elizabeth Scharlatt, Publisher

THE WRIGHT GROUP

P.O. Box 218
Cool, CA 95614
916-889-0932
fax: 916-889-0016

The Wright Group (founded in 1980) is a leading publisher of educational books for elementary school and junior high curricula. Wright features the "whole language" approach to reading, and hosts a wide range of books in science and social studies, as well as professional books for educators. The house has a full slate of books geared to the Spanish-language market.

Representative Wright titles: *And What Else?* by Joanne Massam and Anne Kulik, *Language is Fun: Teacher's Book* (in three levels) by Brian Cutting, *Media Scenes and Class Acts* by Jack Livesley, *Ready . . . Set . . . Teach!* by Kathy Patterson, *Stories to Read Aloud* by David Booth, and *Teaching Writing: The Nuts and Bolts of Running a Day-to-Day Writing Program* by Jo Phenix.

The Wright Group handles its own distribution.

Query letters and SASEs should be directed to:

Rebel Williams, Vice President, Project Development

THE WRITER, INC.

120 Boylston Street
Boston, MA 02116
617-423-3157

The Writer, Inc. publishes a selection of books in hardcover and paperback on all phases of writing and selling a written work; these publications are written and edited by experienced and successful authors. Since 1887 both aspiring and professional writers have looked to *The Writer* magazine ("the pioneer magazine for literary workers") as a practical guide to instruct, inform, and inspire them in their work. The Writer is renowned for the annually updated reference resource *The Writer's Handbook,* edited by Sylvia K. Burack. The house also publishes *Plays: The Drama Magazine for Young People* with an attendant list in books. (See separate subentry below.)

The house list includes *Writing and Revising Your Fiction* by Mark Wisniewski, *Write on Target* by Dennis E. Hensley and Holly G. Miller, *The Elements of Mystery Fiction* by William G. Tapply, *Writing Poetry: Where Poems Come From and How to Write Them* by David Kirby, *Preparing Your Manuscript* by Elizabeth Preston, *Guide to Fiction Writing* by Phyllis A. Whitney, *Writing Books for Young People* by James Cross Giblin, *Write and Sell Your Free-Lance Article* by Linda Buchanan Allen, and *The Thirty-Six Dramatic Situations* by Georges Polti.

The Writer distributes its own books.

PLAYS, INC., PUBLISHERS

Plays, Inc., Publishers is a wing of the Writer that targets younger performers in theater. This imprint's list also includes a solid slate of resource materials of value to professionals who work in the theater with children.

Book publications from Plays include *The Big Book of Skits* by Silvia E. Kamerman, *Plays From African Tales* by Barbara Winther, *Costume: An Illustrated Survey From Ancient Times to the 20th Century* by Margot Lister, *The Puppet Book* by Claire Buchwald (illustrations by Audrey Jacubiszyn), *Mime: Basics for Beginners* by Cindie and Mathew Straub (photographs by Jeff Blanton), and *Modern Educational Dance* by Valerie Preston-Dunlop.

Query letters and SASEs should be directed to:

Sylvia K. Burack, Editor

WRITER'S DIGEST BOOKS
F&W PUBLICATIONS
NORTH LIGHT BOOKS/BETTERWAY BOOKS/STORY PRESS

1507 Dana Avenue
Cincinnati, OH 45207
513-531-2222

Writer's Digest/F&W produces books to help writers, poets, artists, songwriters, and photographers develop their talent, hone their professional skills, and—of course—sell their work. The publisher pursues this mission by issuing a list of guidebooks and how-to, reference, and professional titles in hardcover and paperback editions.

Writer's Digest Books (founded in 1919) is a division of F&W Publications, publisher of *Writer's Digest* magazine. The house produces titles for artists and musicians under the aegis of its North Light division, and addresses the home, sports, and small-business markets via Betterway Books (see separate subentries below). Writer's Digest/F&W maintains a comprehensive backlist.

WRITER'S DIGEST BOOKS

The Writer's Digest list covers virtually all commercial writing fields; many of these works are high on the professional-writer's recommendation list. Writer's Digest Books features a series of annually updated resource guides including *Writer's Market*.

Writer's Digest titles include *How to Write Attention-Grabbing Query and Cover Letters* by John Wood, *Travel Writing: A Guide to Research, Writing and Selling* by L. Peat O'Neill, *Writing for Money* by Loriann Hoff Oberlin, *National Writers Union Guide to Freelance Rates and Standard Practice* by National Writers Union, *The Writer's Legal Guide* by Tad Crawford and Tony Lynons, and *Discovering the Writer Within: 40 Days to More Imaginative Writing* by Bruce Ballenger and Barry Lane.

Additional titles are honed to writers' needs in the realms of comedy, horror, historical fiction, science fiction, Westerns, suspense fiction, popular songwriting, business writing, and children's/young-adult books. The Howdunit series has met with particular success and features works geared for writers in the fields of mystery, suspense, and true crime.

Sample titles: *Malicious Intent: A Writer's Guide to How Criminals Think* by Sean P. Mactire, *Modus Operandi: A Writer's Guide to How Criminals Work* by Mauro V. Corvasce and Joseph R. Paglino, *Armed and Dangerous: A Writer's Guide to Weapons* by Michael Newton, *The Writer's Guide to Everyday Life in the Middle Ages* by Sherrilyn Kenyon, and *Aliens and Alien Societies* by Stanley Schmidt.

Distribution for Writer's Digest Books is through the marketing network of corporate umbrella F&W publications.

Query letters and SASEs should be directed to:

Bill Brohaugh, Editorial Director, Writer's Digest Books
How-to books for writers and photographers.

NORTH LIGHT BOOKS

The North Light Books division of F&W Publications produces how-to books geared to the areas of drawing, painting, clip art, printing, desktop publishing, and graphic arts, along with a line of titles for young readers.

On the North Light list: *Creating Textures in Colored Pencil* by Gary Greene, *The Graphic Designer's Sourcebook* by Poppy Evans, *Drawing Nature* by Stanley Maltzman, *Realistic Oil Painting Techniques* by Kurt Anderson, *Freshen Your Paintings with New Ideas* by Lew Lehrman, *Painting with the White of Your Paper* by Judi Wagner and Tony van Hasselt, and *Jewelry and Accessories* by Juliet Bawden.

North Light Books is distributed by F&W Publications; the house also catalogs the lists of Coast to Coast Books and Rockport Publishers.

Query letters and SASEs should be directed to:

Rachel Wolf, Editor for Fine Arts
How-to books for fine artists and graphic designers.

Lynn Haller, Editor
Graphic design.

Betterway Books

Betterway Books (founded in 1980) is a former independent that is now part of F&W Publications. Betterway is a midsized imprint in the interest areas of home-building and remodeling, resource guides and handbooks, small business and personal finance, self-help, theater crafts, collectibles, sports, and reference.

On the Betterway list: *How to Have a 48-Hour Day* by Don Aslett, *Interview Strategies That Will Get You the Job You Want* by Andrea Kay, *Quick and Easy Remodeling Projects to Customize Your Home* by Jack Kramer, *The Complete Guide to Designing Your Own Home* by Scott Ballard, *Woodworker's Source Book* by Charles Self, *Stage Costume Step-by-Step* by Mary T. Kidd, and *Youth Baseball: The Guide for Coaches and Parents* by John P. McCarthy (in the Coaching Kids series).

Betterway Books is distributed through the network of F&W Publications, the parent company.

Query letters and SASEs should be directed to:

William Brohaugh, Editorial Director
How-to and reference books on sports, recreation, consumer information, weddings, theater, performing arts, genealogy.

David Lewis, Editorial Director
How-to and reference books on home building and remodeling, small business and personal finance, hobbies, collectibles, and woodworking.

Wynwood Press

(See under Baker Book House in Directory of Religious, Spiritual, and Inspirational Publishers)

Yale University Press

(See Directory of University Presses)

Yankee Books

(See Rodale Press)

ZEBRA BOOKS

(See Kensington Publishing Corporation)

ZIFF-DAVIS PRESS

5903 Christie Avenue
Emeryville, CA 94608
510-601-2000

Ziff-Davis specializes in computer books and book/software products. The publisher catalogs titles in the areas of general computing, word processing, spreadsheets, operating systems, databases, project management, business presentations, graphics, accounting, and connectivity and communications.

The house issues an assortment of up-to-date guides keyed to particular proprietary computer products, as well as selected titles for children. Also on the Ziff-Davis list are selected general-interest computer titles.

Ziff-Davis Press (founded in 1990) is a division of Ziff Communications.

On the Ziff-Davis list: *How Computers Work* by Ron White, *Computer Crafts for Kids* by Margy and Ann Kuntz, *How to Use Windows* by Doug Hergert, *MacWEEK Guide to Desktop Video* by Eric Holsinger, and *This Old PC* by Dale Lewallen.

Representing general-interest productions are *Your Personal Fitness Trainer* by David H. Bass, along with *How Your Body Works.*

Ziff-Davis Press oversees its own distribution services.

Query letters and SASEs should be directed to:

Cheryl Applewood, Publishing Director

Juliet Langley, Associate Publisher

Stacy Hiquet, Publisher

ZOLAND BOOKS

384 Huron Avenue
Cambridge, MA 02138
617-864-6252

Zoland Books (founded in 1987) is a small independent publishing house that produces fiction, poetry, and books of literary interest as well as literary and art criticism. A significant portion of the Zoland list accents the interrelationship between the written and the visual arts. The house also issues audiotape renditions of selected works, especially poetry. Zoland nurtures a staunch backlist.

Zoland publishes small a group of new titles from year to year, usually not geared to any particular seasonal business goals; projects are acquired on an extremely selective basis.

Representing the Zoland list: *Seeing Eye* (short stories) by Michael Martone, *The Instinct for Bliss* (short stories) by Melissa Pritchard, *The Circles I Move In* (short stories) by Diane Lefer, *The Country Road* (poetry) by James Laughlin, *Offspring* (a novel) by Jonathan Strong, and *Talking Pictures: The Photography of Rudy Burckhardt, 1933–1988* by Rudy Burckhardt and Simon Pettet.

Zoland is distributed to the trade by National Book Network.

Query letters and SASEs should be directed to:

Roland Pease, Editor/Publisher

ZONDERVAN PUBLISHING HOUSE

(See Directory of Religious, Spiritual, and Inspirational Publishers)

University Presses

ARTE PÚBLICO PRESS
(See Directory of United States Publishers)

CAMBRIDGE UNIVERSITY PRESS
40 West 20th Street
New York, NY 10011
212-924-3900
800-872-7423

The Cambridge list includes hardcover and paperback titles of topical contemporary general interest as well as academic import in the fields of literature; art; music; religion; history; philosophy; economics; the classics; mathematics; and the behavioral, biological, physical, social, and computer sciences. One of publishing's old guard, Cambridge University Press (founded in 1534) is a now major international operation that holds fast to a long commitment to quality.

Special imprints include Cambridge Film Classics and the popularly priced Canto line. Cambridge also produces some titles for young readers and publishes a full range of academic and popular reference works. Cambridge is strong in the reprint area, offering editions of anthologies and compilations as well as individual classic works. The Cambridge United States office is editorially independent of the British home office.

Cambridge books include *The Crisis of Vision in Modern Economic Thought* by Robert Heilbroner and William Milberg, *The Evolution and Extinction of the Dinosaurs* by David E. Fastovsky and David B. Westhampel, *Masters of War: Military Dissent and Politics in the Vietnam Era* by Robert Buzzanco, *Search and Destroy: African American Males in the Criminal Justice System* by Jerome G. Miller, *The Clock of Ages: Why We Age—How We Age—Winding Back the Clock* by John J. Medina, *To Rule Jerusalem* by Robert Friedland and Richard Hecht, and *Charles Darwin's Letters: A Selection, 1825–1859* (edited by Frederick Burkhardt; foreword by Stephen Jay Gould).

The house hosts a strong reference list, including *The Cambridge International Dictionary of English* (edited by Paul Procter).

Cambridge University Press handles its own distribution.

Query letters and SASEs should be directed to:

Barbara Colson, Director

Julia Hough, Editor
Psychology and computer science.

Lauren Kowles, Editor
Mathematics and computer science.

(Mr.) Terry Moore, Executive Editor
Philosophy and humanities.

Florence Padgett, Editor
Physical sciences.

Beatrice Rehl, Editor
Fine arts and media studies.

Mary Vaughn, Executive Editor
ESL (English as a second language) books.

Frank Smith, Executive Editor
History and social sciences.

CLEVELAND STATE UNIVERSITY POETRY CENTER

1983 East 24th Street
Cleveland, OH 44115
216-687-3986

Cleveland State University Poetry Center was begun in 1962 at Fenn College (which became Cleveland State in 1964). The center initiated its book-publishing program in 1971. The press publishes poets of local, regional, and international reach, generally under the aegis of one or another of the center's ongoing series. Under its flying-unicorn logo, CSU Poetry Center most often publishes trade paper editions, but it also offers some titles in hardbound. The press generally produces a limited number of new titles each year. In addition, the house maintains a full backlist.

CSU Poetry Center presents a variety of styles and viewpoints—some with evident sociopolitical bent, others with broadly inspirational themes, and others notable for their strong individualistic inflections. The Poetry Center sponsors the Poetry Forum workshop and presents programs of public readings.

Books from CSU Poetry Center Press include award-winning volumes from established bards and releases from accomplished new writers. On the CSU list are *Blood Stories* by Martha Ramsey, *Beastmorfs* by Leonard Trawick, *Order, or Disorder* by Amy Newman, *The Household Gods* by Daniel Bourne, *Flatlands* by Jeff Gundy, *Hyena* by Jan Freeman, *Refinery* by Claudia Keelan, *Nothing in Nature Is Private* by Claudia Rankine, *Dangerous Neighborhoods* by Marnie Prange, *Fugitive Colors* by Chrystos, and *Lives of the Saints and Everything* by Susan Firer.

Indicative of the center's backlist are *The Long Turn Toward Light* by Cleveland poet and artist Barbara Tanner Angell, *At Redbones* by Thylias Moss, *The Rapture of Matter* by Frankie Paino, and *The Sioux Dog Dance: shunk ah weh* by Red Hawk.

The center sponsors an annual poetry contest; please contact the CSU Poetry Center for submissions guidelines.

Poetry Center books are distributed through Bookslinger, Inland, and Spring Church Book Company.

The Poetry Center will accept unsolicited manuscripts *only from December 1 to March 1* ($15 entry fee; full manuscripts only). For complete guidelines send request plus SASE. Query letters and SASEs should be directed to:

Leonard Trawick, Editor

David Evett, Member, Editorial Committee

COLUMBIA UNIVERSITY PRESS

562 West 113th Street
New York, NY 10025
212-666-1000

Columbia hosts a roster of specialty reference titles, including distinguished lines in media studies, journalism, and film. Columbia's publishing interest also includes current events, public issues, popular culture and fine arts, gay and lesbian studies, history, the sciences, literature, and Asian studies. Columbia University Press (established in 1893) publishes a slate of general-interest titles in addition to its established list of scholarly, academic, and scientific works. The press produces books in hardcover and trade paperback editions and nurtures a healthy backlist.

Among Columbia highlights: *Slick Spins and Fractured Facts: How Cultural Myths Distort the News* by Caryl Rivers, *An Evening at the Garden of Allah: A Gay Cabaret in Seattle* by Don Paulson with Roger Simpson, *Ben-Gurion's Spy: The Story of the Political Scandal That Shaped Modern Israel* by Shabtai Teveth, *Friends or Rivals? The Insider's Account of U.S.–Japan Relations* by Michael H. Armacost, *Queen Victoria's Secret* by Adrienne Munich, *Bloomsbury Recalled* by Quentin Bell, *The Resurrection of the Body in Western Christianity, 200–1338* by Carolyn Walker Bynum, and *Poetry of the American West* (edited by Alison H. Deming).

From Columbia reference: *The Columbia Anthology of American Poetry* (edited by Jay Parini) and *The Columbia Guide to Standard American English* by Kenneth G. Wilson.

Columbia University Press distributes its own list and handles distribution for a number of other academically oriented publishers, including Free Association Books, East European Monographs, University of Tokyo Press, American University in Cairo Press, and Edinburgh University Press.

Query letters and SASEs should be directed to:

Jennifer Crewe, Publisher
Humanities.

Edward E. Lugenbeel, Executive Editor
Science.

Ann Miller, Associate Executive Editor
Gay and lesbian studies, art history, philosophy, journalism, media.

James Raines, Editorial Director, Reference

John Michel, Associate Executive Editor
Sociology, anthropology, psychology, psychiatry, social work.

Kate Wittenberg, Editor in Chief
Political science, international affairs, modern studies, history.

CORNELL UNIVERSITY PRESS

Sage House
512 East State Street
Ithaca, NY 14850
607-277-2338

Cornell publishes trade nonfiction and selected fiction, literary works, and poetry in addition to a wide berth of academic and scholarly titles. Cornell's list is anchored by strong interest in literary and art criticism, philosophy, classics, history, political science, agriculture, and science. The press's Comstock Books series continues a tradition of excellence in natural history. Cornell University Press (begun in 1869) is the oldest university press in the United States.

Representing the Cornell trade list: *Land of Women: Tales of Sex and Gender from Early Ireland* by Lisa M. Bitel, *Stranger in Our Midst: Images of the Jew in Polish Literature* (edited by Harold B. Segel), *Reproducing Persons: Issues in Feminist Bioethics* by Laura M. Purdy, *Classical Bronzes: The Art and Craft of Greek and Roman Statuary* by Carol C. Mattusch, and *Working Sober: The Transformation of an Occupational Drinking Culture* by William J. Sonnenstuhl.

Cornell University Press distributes its own list.

Query letters and SASEs should be directed to:

John Ackerman, Director

Peter A. Agree, Editor
United States history, law, agriculture, social sciences, rural sociology.

Roger Haydon, Editor
Studies of the former Soviet Union and Eastern Europe, philosophy, political history, history of science, documentary series in American social history, series in international political economy, immigration history, regional studies.

Bernard Kendler, Executive Editor
Literary criticism.

(Ms.) Rob Reavill, Editor
Science.

DUKE UNIVERSITY PRESS

Box 90660
Durham, NC 27708
919-687-3600

Areas of Duke publishing scope include cultural studies; literary studies; Latin American and Caribbean studies; legal studies; history; Eastern European, Soviet, and post-Soviet studies; German studies; environmental studies; and history of economics. Post-Contemporary Interventions is a series that features imaginative world-class thinkers on culture, media, and global society.

Duke University Press (founded in 1921) publishes scholarly, trade, and textbooks in hardcover and trade paperback editions and maintains a strong backlist. Duke also publishes a number of academic journals, including *MLQ: Modern Language Quarterly.*

On the Duke list: *Ernest Tubb: The Texas Troubadour* by Ronnie Pugh, *Beyond the Whiteness of Whiteness: Memoir of a White Mother of Black Sons* by Jane Lazarre, *The Third Eye: Race, Cinema, and Ethnographic Spectacle* by Fatimah Tobing Rony, *Vampires, Mummies, and Liberals: Bram Stoker and the Politics of Popular Fiction* by David Glover, *Pop Out: Queer Warhol* (edited by Jennifer Doyle, Jonathan Flatley, and José Esteban Muñoz), *Guilty Pleasures: Feminist Camp from Mae West to Madonna* by Pamela Robertson, and *Rhythm and Noise: An Aesthetics of Rock* by Theodore Gracyk.

Duke University Press oversees its own distribution.

Query letters and SASEs should be directed to:

Peter Guzzardi, Editorial Director

THE FEMINIST PRESS AT THE CITY UNIVERSITY OF NEW YORK

311 East 94th Street
New York, NY 10128
212-360-5790

The publishing purview at the Feminist Press includes biographies, cross-cultural studies, fiction, health and medicine, history/sociology, interdisciplinary texts, literary anthologies, art and music, resources and reference works, educational materials, children's books, and women's studies (including several notable series). The house hosts a reprint program as well as its renowned originals, and also supports several feminist journals. The Feminist Press publishes in hardcover and paperback editions and moves a backlist both heady and deep through special sales including holiday mailings.

The Feminist Press maintains its aim to express and celebrate differences within the cultural context of humanity; in so doing the house has held the publishing forefront with a series of important works that brings fresh dimensions to the attention of readers. Founded in 1970 at the crest of the second wave of American feminism, the press led off with a list that concentrated on a program to reestablish hitherto overlooked women's literary classics, aligned with an additional focus on literature of United

State's working-class women. The house's agenda has expanded gradually to encompass themes such as growing up female, women artists, and the family, as well as the publication of academic and general-interest works with an international cast of authors in varied disciplines and literary forms.

Highlights from Feminist Press are *China for Women: Travel and Culture* (combination travel/women's studies; edited by Feminist Press), *Black and White Sat Down Together: Reminiscences of an NAACP Founder* by Mary White Ovington, *Motherhood by Choice: Pioneers in Women's Health and Family Planning* by Perdita Huston, *Get Smart! What You Should Know (But Won't Learn in Class) About Sexual Harassment and Sex Discrimination* by Montana Katz and Veronica Vieland, and *Women Composers: The Lost Tradition Found* by Diane Peacock Jezic.

On the Feminist Press literary list are the African novel *Changes* by Ama Ata Aidoo; the Japanese-American story collection *Songs My Mother Taught Me* by Wakako Yamauchi; a collection of stories by Italian writers titled *Unspeakable Women* (edited and translated by Robin Pickering-Iazzi); a bilingual edition of *The Answer/La Repuesta* by "the first feminist of America," the Mexican Sor Juana Inéz de la Cruz; Maureen Brady's novel *Folly*, set among black and white women in a North Carolina mill town; and *What Did Miss Darrington See? An Anthology of Feminist Supernatural Fiction* (edited by Jessica Amanda Salmonson).

A noteworthy Feminist Press educational project is *Women of Color and the Multicultural Curriculum* (edited by Liza Fiol-Matta and Miriam K. Chamberlain), which includes essays and course outlines.

A special-production volume from Feminist Press is *Long Walks and Intimate Talks*, with stories and poems by Grace Paley and paintings by Vera B. Williams.

Feminist Press books may be ordered directly from the publisher; the list is distributed to the trade in the United States via Consortium Book Sales & Distribution.

Query letters and SASEs should be directed to:

Jean Casella, Senior Editor

GALLAUDET UNIVERSITY PRESS

800 Florida Avenue Northeast
Washington, DC 20002
202-651-5488

The Gallaudet list offers titles in diverse categories such as communication, language arts, deaf culture and history, employment and law, audiology and speechreading, instructional materials, literature, parenting, and professional books, as well as a special concentration in sign language (including American Sign Language). The publisher maintains an extensive backlist.

Imprints of Gallaudet University Press include Clerc Books and Kendall Green Publications. Among areas of current publishing emphasis are audiology, sociolegal issues in special education, English as a second language (ESL), and signed children's books in English. The house also markets a line of videotapes.

The publishing program of Gallaudet University Press (founded in 1968) exemplifies the educational impulse of Gallaudet University through an accent on issues pertinent to deafness. Gallaudet University Press publishes scholarly, educational, and general-interest titles, as well as children's books, along with the magazine *Perspectives in Education and Deafness.*

Among Gallaudet features are *Seeing Language in Sign: The Work of William J. Stokoe* by Jane Mather, *The Politics of Deafness* by Owen Wrigley, and *The Silents* (a memoir of growing up with deaf parents) by Charlotte Abrams.

Representative of the Gallaudet backlist are *The Week the World Heard Gallaudet* by Jack R. Gannon, *Deaf President Now!* by John B. Christiansen and Sharon N. Barnartt, *Language in Motion* by Jerome D. Schein and David A. Stewart, *Kid-Friendly Parenting with Deaf and Hard of Hearing Children* by Denise Chapman Weston, *The Handshape Dictionary of American Sign Language* by Richard Tennant, *A Study of American Deaf Folklore* by Susan Rutherford, *Legal Rights of Hearing-Impaired People* (revised edition) by the National Center for Law and Deafness, *Growing Up Sexually* by Angela Bednarczyk, *No Walls of Stone: An Anthology of Literature by Deaf and Hard of Hearing Writers*, edited by Jill Jepson, and *Gopen's Guide to Closed Captioned Video* by Stuart Gopen.

Children's books include *Animal Signs: A First Book of Sign Language* by Debby Slier, *Sleeping Beauty* by Robert Newby, *Sesame Street Sign Language ABC* with Linda Bove, and *Silent Observer*, written and illustrated by Chrisy MacKinnon.

Gallaudet University Press handles distribution for its own list. The Gallaudet University Bookstore catalogs additional titles in the deafness area from other publishers, as well as a line of gift items.

Query letters and SASEs should be directed to:

Ivey Wallace, Managing Editor

HARVARD BUSINESS SCHOOL PRESS

Morgan 41
Soldiers Field Road
Boston, MA 02163
617-495-6700

Harvard Business School Press publishes trade and professional books for the business and academic communities. Areas of publishing interest embrace organizational behavior/human-resource management, finance, marketing, production and operations management, accounting and control, business history, and managerial economics. Harvard Business publishes the Baker Library line of reference books and offers series on videocassette, as well as HBS Press Expanded Books on diskette. The press also issues the journal *Harvard Business Review* along with a line of books on the Harvard Business Review imprint.

Harvard Business School Press is the publishing division of Harvard University Business School. The press was founded in 1984 as an elaboration of the increasingly successful line of business titles published by Harvard University Press. With the established aim of influencing the way readers think and act, HBS Press has a mandate to publish books that represent the best of contemporary thinking and research in business and that advance the practice of management.

Noteworthy Harvard Business School Press books: *The Loyalty Effect: The Hidden Force Behind Growth, Profits, and Lasting Value* by Frederick F. Reichheld, *Team Talk: The Power of Language in Team Dynamics* by Anne Donnellon, *Broken Promises: An Unconventional View of What Went Wrong at IBM* by D. Quinn Mills and G. Bruce Friesen, *The Internet Strategy Handbook: Lessons from the New Frontier of Business* (edited by Mary J. Cronin), and *Beyond Certainty: The Changing Worlds of Organizations* by Charles Handy.

The Harvard Business Review book imprint features titles such as *First Person: Tales of Management Courage and Tenacity* (edited and with an introduction by Thomas Teal), *Fast Forward: The Best Ideas on Managing Business Change* (edited and with an introduction and epilogue by James Champy and Nitin Nohria), and *The Product Development Challenge: Competing through Speed, Quality, and Creativity* (edited by Kim B. Clark and Steven C. Wheelright).

Harvard Business School Press Operations Department oversees the distribution of the house's publications; the house list is also available to the trade through McGraw-Hill.

Query letters and SASEs should be directed to:

Nicholas Philipson, Senior Acquisitions Editor

HARVARD UNIVERSITY PRESS

79 Garden Street
Cambridge, MA 02138
617-495-2600

Harvard's publishing categories include current events, cultural affairs, the arts, history, psychology, literary studies (including selected poetry), the sciences, legal studies, and economics. Harvard special series have included lines such as The Twentieth Century Fund, the Global AIDS Policy Coalition, and the Developing Child series.

Harvard University Press (started in 1913) is currently the largest academic press in the United States. Harvard University Press produces a large number of trade-oriented general-interest books for an eclectic readership, while maintaining its core program to provide a balanced offering of scholarly works in a range of academic fields. Harvard's extensive list is published in hardcover and trade paperback editions.

Featured Harvard trade titles are *Good Natured: The Origins of Right and Wrong in Humans and Other Animals* by Frans de Waal, *The Trouble with Blame: Victims, Perpetrators, and Responsibility* by Sharon Lamb, *Dubious Conceptions: The Politics of Teenage Pregnancy* by Kristin Luker, *Temptations of a Superpower* by Ronald Steel, *Vanishing Diaspora: The Jews in Eastern Europe Since 1945* by Bernard Wasserstein, *The Culture of Education* by Jerome Bruner, *Private Myths: Dreams and Dreaming* by

Anthony Stevens, *The Sex Revolts: Gender, Rebellion, and Rock 'n' Roll* by Simon Reynolds and Joy Press, *The Discovery of the Greek Bronze Age* by J. Lesley Fitton, and *On Flirtation* by Adam Phillips.

Harvard University Press handles its own distribution.

The publisher will not consider unsolicited poetry or fiction. Query letters and SASEs should be directed to:

Michael A. Aronson, Senior Editor, Social Sciences
Economics, political science, sociology, law, some business.

Aida Donald, Assistant Director and Editor in Chief
History, sociology with historical emphasis, women's studies with historical emphasis.

Michael Fisher, Executive Editor for Science and Medicine
Medicine, science (except astronomy), neuroscience.

Margaretta Fulton, General Editor for the Humanities
Classics (including Loeb Classics), religion, music, art, Jewish studies, women's studies.

Elizabeth Suttell, Senior Editor
East Asian studies.

Angela von der Lippe, Senior Editor for the Behavioral Sciences
Behavioral sciences, earth sciences, astronomy, neuroscience, education.

(Mr.) Lindsay Waters, Executive Editor for the Humanities
Literary criticism, philosophy, film studies, cultural studies.

Stephanie Gouse, Paperbacks and Foreign Rights

Joyce Seltzer, Senior Executive Editor (New York)
History, contemporary affairs.

Contact at:
150 Fifth Avenue, Suite 625
New York, NY 10011
212-337-0280

THE JOHNS HOPKINS UNIVERSITY PRESS

2715 North Charles Street
Baltimore, MD 21218
410-516-6900

The Johns Hopkins University Press (founded in 1878) issues a strong list of contemporary-interest titles and fiction as well as academic, scholarly, technical, and professional works in diverse academic areas such as literary criticism, ancient studies, Jewish studies, economics, political science, and history of and current trends in medicine, science, and technology.

Johns Hopkins titles include *The Devil's Disciples: Makers of the Salem Witchcraft Trials* by Peter Charles Hoffer, *Dinosaurs of the East Coast* by David B. Weishampel and Luther Young, *Leaning Sycamores: Natural Worlds of the Upper Potomac* by Jack Wennerstrom, *The Guide to Living with HIV Infection* (developed at the Johns Hopkins AIDS Clinic) by John G. Bartlett and Ann K. Finkbeiner, *The Act of Bargaining* by Richard Ned Lebow, *Bodies Under Siege: Self-Mutilation and Body Mortification in Culture and Psychiatry* by Armando R. Favazza, *When the Colts Belonged to Baltimore: A Father and a Son, a Team and a Time* by William Gildea, *Woodholme: A Black Man's Story of Growing Up Alone* by DeWayne Wickham, *Old Order Amish: Their Enduring Way of Life* (photographs by Lucian Niemeyer; text by Donald B. Kraybill), *The Betrayed Profession: Lawyering at the End of the Twentieth Century* by Sol M. Linowitz with Martin Meyer, and *Inventing Times Square: Commerce and Culture at the Crossroads of the World* (edited by William R. Taylor).

The Johns Hopkins literary scope is illustrated by *I Am Dangerous* (stories) by Greg Johnson, *In the Crevice of Time: New and Collected Poems* by Josephine Jacobsen, *The Bad Infinity* (drama collection) by Mac Wellman, *Home at Last* (stories) by Jean McGarry, *The Geographical History of America* by Gertrude Stein, and *The Johns Hopkins Guide to Literary Theory and Criticism* (edited by Michael Groden and Martin Kreiswirth).

Johns Hopkins produces a number of specialty lines, such as the collection of works by microhistorian Carlo Ginzburg, the American Land Classics series of facsimile reprints, and Complete Roman Drama in Translation.

The Johns Hopkins University Press handles its own distribution with the support of regional sales representatives.

The press will not consider unsolicited poetry or fiction. Query letters and SASEs should be directed to:

Douglas Armato, Editor and Manager of Book Division
Classics and ancient studies, film studies, American studies, theater.

Robert Brugger, History Editor
American history, history of science and technology, regional titles, documentary editions.

Wendy Harris, Medical Editor
Medicine (hard science for medical professionals), public health.

Robert Harington, Science Editor
Sciences; especially mathematical sciences, earth, planetary and life sciences.

Willis Regier, Director
Humanities, literary theory and criticism.

George F. Thompson, Project Editor
Geography and environmental studies, Anabaptist studies, urban planning.

Henry Y. K. Tom, Executive Editor
Economics, development, European history.

Jacqueline C. Wehmueller, Acquisitions Editor
Trade medical books for an educated general audience; Caribbean studies; books in higher education; history of medicine; reference books.

HOWARD UNIVERSITY PRESS

1240 Randolph Street Northeast
Washington, DC 20017
202-806-4935

A major sector of the Howard University Press publishing scope covers issues and traditions pertaining to Africa—including African-related cultural expressions worldwide, geopolitical topics, and historical studies, in addition to the African-American purview. Howard University Press (founded in 1972) produces scholarly and general nonfiction works in the areas of history, biography, economics, sociology, political science, education, contemporary affairs, communications, the arts, and literature. It also produces a strong line of general-reference books. HU Press generally publishes a select group of new titles per year in hardcover and trade paperback editions. The press maintains a diverse backlist.

Indicative of the Howard University Press publishing program are *The Jamaican Crime Scene: A Perspective* by Bernard Headley, *Pathways to Success* (edited by Lloyd Ren Sloan), *Basic Currents of Nigerian Foreign Policy* by Mae C. King, *We Paid Our Dues: Women Trade Union Leaders of the Caribbean* by A. Lynn Bolles, *African Americans and U.S. Policy Toward Africa* by Elliott P. Skinner, *Captain Paul Cuff's Logs and Letters, 1808–1817: A Black Quaker's Voice from Within the Veil* (edited by Rosalind Wiggins), *An African Victorian Feminist: The Life and Times of Adelaide Smith Casely Hayford, 1869–1960* by Adelaide Cromwell, *The Demography of America* by James Tarver, *Cocoa and Chaos in Ghana* by Gwendolyn Mikell, and *One Third of a Nation* (edited by Lorenzo Morris and Jean Oyemade).

On the literary, cultural, and artistic front are *Social Rituals and the Verbal Art of Zora Neale Hurston* by Lynda Marion Hill, *The Dramatic Vision of August Wilson* by Sandra Shannon, *Ancient Songs Set Ablaze: The Theatre of Femi Osofisan* by Sandra L. Richards, *Black Drama in America* (edited by Darwin T. Turner), *Modern Negro Art* by James A. Porter, and *The New Cavalcade: African American Writing From 1700 to the Present* (edited by Arthur P. Davis, J. Saunders Redding, and Joyce Ann Joyce).

Howard University Press handles distribution through its own in-house marketing department; fulfillment is handled through Johns Hopkins University Press.

Query letters and SASEs should be directed to:

Edwin Gordon, Director of the Press

INDIANA UNIVERSITY PRESS

601 North Morton Street
Bloomington, IN 47404
812-855-4203

Indiana University Press (founded in 1950) publishes books of serious trade interest as well as titles directed toward scholarly and academic audiences. The press addresses subjects such as regional and cultural studies, military history, criminology, political science and international affairs, popular culture and the arts, semiotics, journalism, business and economics, science and technology, environmental issues and natural history, literary criticism, and gender studies. Indiana University Press also publishes short-story collections and fiction in translation. IUP produces hardcover and paperback editions.

Indiana University Press issues a number of prestigious series, among them Theories of Representation and Difference, Theories of Contemporary Culture, Blacks in the Diaspora, Arab and Islamic Studies, and Medical Ethics. The house is home to a variety of academic journals, including *The Middle East Journal*, *Discourse*, and a number of journals in feminist studies.

On the IUP list are *Black Police in America* by W. Martin Delaney, *Frontiers of the Roman Empire* by Hugh Elton, *Vietnam Protest Theatre: The Television War on Stage* by Nora M. Alter, *Ethics for Fundraisers* by Albert Anderson, *Ohio Place-Names* by Larry L. Miller, *A Cynthia Ozick Reader* by Cynthia Ozick (edited by Elaine M. Kauvar), *Following Djuna: Women Lovers and the Erotics of Loss* by Carolyn Allen, *The Well-Tempered Announcer: A Pronunciation Guide to Classical Music* by Robert Friedkin, *The Longest Shadow: In the Aftermath of the Holocaust* by Geoffrey H. Hartman, *Bike Boys, Drag Queens, and Superstars: Avant-Garde, Mass Culture, and Gay Identities in the 1960s Underground Cinema* by Juan D. Suárez, *Drawn from African Dwellings* by Jean-Paul Bourdier and Trinh T. Minh-ha, and *Mexican Cinema* (edited by Paulo Antonio Parangua; translated by Ana Lopéz).

Indiana University Press publishes *Guidelines for Bias-Free Writing* by Marilyn Schwartz and the Task Force on Bias-Free Language of the Association of American University Presses. IUP also recommends to potential authors the popular writing-reference stylebook *The Handbook of Nonsexist Writing* by Casey Miller and Kate Swift.

Indiana University Press distributes its own list, as well as books produced by the Cleveland Museum of Art, the Indiana Historical Society, and the British Film Institute. IUP also serves as regional sales representative for several other university presses.

Query letters and SASEs should be directed to:

Joan Catapano, Senior Sponsoring Editor
Women's studies, film, folklore, black studies, literary theory, regional studies, cultural history and theory.

John Gallman, Director
All areas.

Janet Rabinowich, Senior Sponsoring Editor
Russian and East European studies, African studies, Middle Eastern and Judaic studies, philosophy, and art.

Robert Sloan, Sponsoring Editor
Science, business, medical ethics, history, drama and performance, religion, and political studies.

Natalie Wrubel, Editor and Music Sponsor
Music studies, studies in Russian music.

LOUISIANA STATE UNIVERSITY PRESS

P.O. Box 25053
Baton Rouge, LA 70894-5053
504-388-6294

Areas of Louisiana State University Press interest include Southern history, the American Civil War, African-American history, United States history, Latin American history, European history, philosophy and politics, art, architecture and design, photography, literary voices of the South, American literature, general criticism and European literature, music, natural history, and medicine. LSU offers a wide variety of regional books (not limited to Louisiana environs) as well as concentrations in contemporary fiction, poetry, and literary criticism. The house produces hardcover and trade paperback editions and maintains a solid backlist. Louisiana State University Press (founded in 1935) publishes a primarily academic and scholarly list, along with a good number of general-interest titles.

Among LSU titles: *Manchac Swamp: Louisiana's Undiscovered Wilderness* (photographs by Julia Sims), *Two Months in the Confederate States: An Englishman's Travels through the South* by W. C. Corsan (edited and with an introduction by Benjamin H. Trask), *Along the River Road: Past and Present on Louisiana's Historic Byway* by Mary Ann Sternberg, *Angels, Anarchists, and Gods* (photography by Christopher Felver), *The Coachmen of Nineteenth-Century Paris: Service Workers and Class Consciousness* by Nicholas Papayanis, *Under Their Own Vine and Fig Tree: The African-American Church in the South—1865–1900* by William E. Montgomery, *The Official Louisiana Seafood & Wild Game Cookbook* (edited by Wade Byrd; illustrated by Wayne Miller), and *Electing Jimmy Carter: The Campaign of 1976* by Patrick Anderson.

Fiction, literature, and the arts includes *Brassaï: Images of Culture and the Surrealist Observer* by Marja Warehime, *Talking about William Faulkner: Interviews with Jimmy Faulkner and Others* by Sally Wolf with Floyd C. Watkins, *Almost Innocent* (novel) by Sheila Bosworth, *Something in Common: Contemporary Louisiana Stories* (edited by Ann Brewster Dobie), *Folk Roots and Mythic Wings in Sarah Orne Jewett and Toni Morrison: The Cultural Function of Narrative* by Marilyn Sanders Mobley, and *The Shimmering Maya and Other Essays* by Catherine Savage Brosnan.

Poetry includes *Passages* by Catherine Savage Brosman, *God's Loud Hand* by Kelly Cherry, *The Fire in All Things* by Stephen Yenser, *Resurrection* by Nicole Cooley, and *A History of the River* by James Applewhite.

Louisiana State University Press oversees a distributional network that utilizes the services of regional university presses and book-distribution companies as well as independent sales representatives.

Query letters and SASEs should be directed to:

Maureen Hewitt, Editor in Chief

THE MIT PRESS

55 Hayward Street
Cambridge, MA 02142
617-253-5646

The MIT Press publishes nonfiction trade and reference titles in the forefront of fields such as contemporary art, architectural studies, urban management and design, computer science and artificial intelligence, cognitive and neurological sciences, linguistics, and economic science and finance. The house also produces works attuned to more traditional approaches within the disciplines of philosophy, engineering, and the physical sciences. The press also produces scholarly and professional works, as well as advanced educational textbooks. The MIT Press was founded in 1961 as the publishing wing of the Massachusetts Institute of Technology.

Featured MIT offerings are *The Masters of Truth in Archaic Greece* by Marcel Detienne, *The Evolution of Allure: Sexual Selection from the Medici Venus to the Incredible Hulk* by George L. Hersey, *The Architect: Reconstructing Her Practice* (edited by Francesca Hughes), *The Dancing Column: On the Orders of Architecture* by Joseph Rykwert, *The Closed World: Computers and the Politics of Discourse in Cold War America* by Paul N. Edwards, *Queer Science: The Use and Abuse of Research on Homosexuality* by Simon LeVay, *The Simple Science of Flight: From Insects to Jumbo Jets* by Henk Tennekes, *Getting It Right: Markets and Choices in a Free Society* by Robert J. Barro, and *The Origins of Grammar: Evidence from Early Language Comprehension* by Kathy Hirsh-Paek and Roberta Michnick Golinkoff.

The MIT Press also produces educational lines and publishes a number of specialist journals such as *TDR The Drama Review: A Journal of Performance Studies*, *The Washington Quarterly*, and *October*, a journal of art and activist theory, as well as the October Book Series. Bradford Books accents titles representing the frontiers of areas such as cognitive science, philosophy, and linguistics.

The MIT Press distributes its own list and handles distribution for several other publishers (including houses that specialize in architecture and design).

Query letters and SASEs should be directed to:

Larry Cohen, Science Editor

Roger Conover, Architecture and Design Editor

Amy Pierce, Linguistics Editor and Bradford Books

Robert Prior, Computer Science Editor

Douglas Sehry, Computer Science Editor

Elizabeth Stanton, Cognitive Science Editor and Bradford Books
Philosophy.

Henry Stanton, Cognitive Science Editor and Bradford Books
Fiona Stevens, Neuroscience Editor

Madeline Sunley, Environmental Sciences Editor

Terry Vaughn, Economics Editor

NAVAL INSTITUTE PRESS

118 Maryland Avenue
Annapolis, MD 21402-5035
410-268-6110

Naval Institute Press features trade books in addition to the house's targeted professional and reference titles. Areas of NIP interest include how-to books on boating and navigation, battle histories, and biographies, as well as occasional selected titles in fiction (typically with a nautical adventure orientation). Specific categories encompass fields such as seamanship, naval history and literature, the Age of Sail, aviation and aircraft, World War II naval history, World War II ships and aircraft, current naval affairs, naval science, and general naval resources and guidebooks. Bluejacket Books is a trade-paperback imprint that includes time-honored classics as well as original titles. Naval Institute Press also publishes a line of historical and contemporary photographs and poster art.

Naval Institute Press, situated on the grounds of the United States Naval Academy, is the book-publishing imprint of the United States Naval Institute, a private, independent, nonprofit professional society for members of the military services and civilians who share an interest in naval and maritime affairs. USNI was established in 1873 at the Naval Academy in Annapolis; the press inaugurated its publishing program in 1898 with a series of basic guides to United States naval practice.

Representative Naval Institute Press books: *Sailing on the Silver Screen: Hollywood and the U.S. Navy* by Lawrence Suid, *"Good to Go" The Rescue of Scott O'Grady from Bosnia* by Mary Pat Kelly, *Female Tars: Women Aboard Ship in the Age of Sail* by Suzanne J. Stark, *A History of the Confederate Navy* by Raimondo Luraghi, *Immortal Images: A Personal History of Two Photographers and the Flag Raising on Iwo Jima* by Tedd Thomey, *Katyñ: Stalin's Massacre and the Seeds of Polish Insurrection* by Allen Paul, *Mother Was a Gunner's Mate: World War II in the WAVES* by Josette Dermody Wingo, *Sea Power: A Global Journey* with text and photography by Luc Cuyvers (companion volume to the Public Television documentary), *Building Plank-on-Frame Ship Models* by Ron McCarthy, *Our War Was Different: Marine Combined Action Platoons in Vietnam* by Al Hemingway, and *Chinese Intelligence Operations* by Nicholas Eftimiades.

The house publishing scope is illustrated by successful backlist items such as *The Golden Thirteen: Recollections of the First Black Naval Officers* (edited by Paul Stillwell; foreword by Colin L. Powell), *Brigade, Seats!: The Naval Academy Cookbook* by Karen Gibson, and *Small Boat Emergencies: A Sailor's Guide* by John M. Waters Jr.

Fiction includes *Rising Wind* by Dick Couch, *The Black Sea* by Richard Setlowe, and *The Right Kind of War* by John McCormick. Representative reprint fiction is *"Up Periscope!" and Other Stories* by Alec Hudson, an author whose innovative style paved the way for the modern technothriller.

Naval Institute Press handles its own distribution.

Query letters and SASEs should be sent to:

Paul Wilderson, Executive Editor

Mark Gatlin, Senior Acquisitions Editor

New York University Press

70 Washington Square South
New York, NY 10012
212-998-2575

New York University Press covers the fields of literature and literary criticism, gender studies, psychology, law and politics, history, American history, Jewish studies, Middle Eastern studies, business, finance, economics, and journalism, as well as popular culture, fine arts, and the decorative arts.

New York University Press (founded in 1916) offers a list laden with works of wide contemporary appeal for the general reader; NYU also maintains a strong presence in the scholarly and professional arena. Major series include titles cataloged under Fast Track (general-interest contemporary issues and affairs), International Library of Essays in Law & Legal Theory, Essential Papers in Psychoanalysis, and Cutting Edge: Lesbian Life and Literature. NYU publishes hardcover and paperback editions and supports a vigorous backlist.

From the NYU program are *High Hopes: The Clinton Presidency and the Politics of Ambition* by Stanley A. Renshon, *The Coming Race War? And Other Apocalyptic Tales of America after Affirmative Action and Welfare* by Richard Delgado, *The Road to Athletic Scholarship: What Every Student-Athlete, Parent & Coach Needs to Know* by Kim McQuilken, *Unspeakable Acts: Why Men Sexually Abuse Children* by Douglas W. Pryor, *Privilege Revealed: How Invisible Preference Undermines America* (sociolegal issues) by Stephanie M. Wildman (with contributions by Margalynne Armstrong, Adrienne D. Davis, and Trina Grillo), *The Conquest of the Reich: D-Day to VE Day—a Soldiers' History* by Robin Neillands, *Pregnancy in a High-Tech Age* by Alice C. Andrews and James W. Fonseca, and *The Gay, Lesbian, and Bisexual Student's Guide to Colleges, Universities, and Graduate Schools* by Jan-Mitchell Sherrill and Craig Hardesty.

Literature, art, and cultural studies include *Freakery: Cultural Spectacles of the Extraordinary Body* (edited by Rosemarie Garland Thomson), *Sexual Investigations* by Alan Soble, *Girls! Girls! Girls! Critical Essays on Women and Music* (edited by Sarah Cooper), *Drag: A History of Female Impersonation in the Performing Arts* by Roger Baker, *Lesbian Erotics* (edited by Karla Jay), *Female Fetishism* by Lorraine Gamman and Merja Makinen, and *Sodomy and the Pirate Tradition: English Sea Rovers in the Seventeenth-Century Caribbean* by B. R. Burg.

Bobst Literary Award winners include *Bird-Self Accumulated* (fiction) by Don Judson, *Crazy Water: Six Fictions* (short stories) by Lori Baker, and *Rodent Angel* (poetry) by Debra Weinstein.

New York University Press handles distribution through its own sales office as well as a network of regional sales and marketing representatives.

Query letters and SASEs should be directed to:

Timothy Bartlett, Editor
Psychoanalysis, psychology, and literature.

Jennifer Hammer, Associate Editor

Colin Jones, Director
History.

Niko Pfund, Editor in Chief
Economics, politics, Jewish and women's studies.

Eric Zinner, Editor
Literary criticism and cultural studies.

Ohio University Press

Scott Quadrangle
Athens, OH 45701
614-593-1155

Ohio University Press areas of interest encompass biography, literary criticism, philosophy, African studies, history, economics, international regional and cultural studies, Western Americana, and natural history. The press also publishes fiction reprints and anthologies. Poetry issued through the Swallow Press imprint certifies the house's outstanding presence in this literary niche.

Ohio University Press (established in 1964) produces scholarly and academic works as well as a line of general-interest titles. OU Press publishes in hardcover and paperback. The house backlist is comprehensive.

On the OU Press list: *The Realm of Prester John* by Robert Silverberg, *Forests of Gold: Essays on the Akan and the Kingdom of Asante* by Ivor Wilks, *A User's Guide to Bypass Surgery* by Ted Klein, *Grammercy Park: An American Bloomsbury* by Carole Klein, *Goldfield: The Last Gold Rush on the Western Frontier* by Sally Zanjani, *Bobcat Pride: Ohio University Basketball* by Lee Caryer, and *The Ohio Gardening Guide* by Jerry Minnich.

In the area of arts and letters, Ohio University Press has issued *Womanist and Feminist Aesthetics: A Comparative Review* by Tuzyline Jita Allan, *Sight Unseen: Major Contemporary Dramatists on Radio* by Elissa S. Guralnick, *Discovering Eve* (short stories) by Jane Candia Coleman, *The Complete American Fantasies* by poet-playwright James Schevill, *In My Own Sweet Time: A Memoir* by Blanche Cooney, *Afrika My Music* (autobiography) by Es'kia Mphahlele, *A Spy in the House of Love* by Anaïs Nin (foreword by Gunther Stuhlman), *Beltane at Aphelion: Longer Poems* by John Matthias, and *Isak Dinesen: Critical Views* (edited by Olga Anastasia Pelensky).

Ohio University Press oversees its own sales and distribution.

Query letters and SASEs should be directed to:

Holly Panich, Managing Editor

Oxford University Press

198 Madison Avenue
New York, NY 10016
212-726-6000

Oxford's list is especially prominent in the subject areas of current affairs, world history (both ancient and modern), and United States history. Popular and classical music constitutes another area of Oxford focus; the house's books on jazz are especially well known. In addition, Oxford is strong in literary studies and historical and contemporary cultural expression.

Oxford University Press (founded in 1478) is an international publisher of trade, scholarly, professional, and reference titles in the humanities, the arts, science, medicine, and social studies in hardcover and paperback editions.

Representative Oxford titles include *Religion in the Modern World: From Cathedrals to Cults* by Steve Bruce, *The Strange Case of the Spotted Mice and Other Classic Essays on Science* by Peter Medawar, *Golf Anecdotes* by Robert Sommers, *Sound Choices: Guiding Your Child's Musical Experiences* by Wilma Machover and Marienne Uszler, *Hannah's Heirs: The Quest for the Genetic Origins of Alzheimer's Disease* by Daniel A. Pollen, *Malign Neglect: Race, Crime, and Punishment in America* by Michael Tonry, *Packaging the Presidency: A History and Criticism of Presidential Campaign Advertising* by Kathleen Hall Jamieson, *Am I Thin Enough Yet? The Cult of Thinness and the Commercialization of Identity* by Sharlene Hesse-Biber, *Games, Strategies, and Managers: How Managers Can Use Game Theory to Make Better Business Decisions* by John McMillan, *Colonial New York: A History* by Michael Kammen, *Forbidden Friendships: Homosexuality and Male Culture in Renaissance Florence* by Michael Rocke, *Saints and Schemers: Opus Dei and Its Paradoxes* by Joan Estruch, and *Chasing Dirt: The American Pursuit of Cleanliness* by Suellen Hoy.

Literary works and the house's cultural interest are exemplified by *Software of the Self: The Arts and Cultural Technology* by Anthony Smith, *Living Our Stories, Telling Our Truths: Autobiography and the Making of the African-American Intellectual Tradition* by Vincent Paul Franklin, *Buzz: The Science and Lore of Alcohol and Caffeine* by Stephen Braun, *Goddess: Myths of the Female Divine* by David Leeming and Jake Page, *The Appalachian Trail Reader* (edited by David Emblidge), *The Hard-Boiled Detective: An Anthology of American Crime Stories* (edited by Jack C. Adrian and Bill Pronzini), *Modern Music and After: Directions Since 1945* by Paul Griffiths, *Hot Jazz and Jazz Dance* by Roger Pryor Dodge, and *Too Marvelous for Words: The Life and Genius of Art Tatum* by James Lester.

The Oxford line of dictionaries and general-reference works is among the most prominent in the field, among them *The Oxford English Dictionary* and *The Oxford Dictionary of the American Language*. Other titles here include *A Dictionary of Euphemisms* by R. W. Holder, *The Oxford English Grammar* by Sidney Greenbaum, and *The Oxford Companion to Irish Literature* (edited by Robert Welch and Bruce Stewart). Oxford also publishes college textbooks, Bibles, music, English as a second language (ESL) educational materials, and children's books, as well as a number of journals. The Twentieth Century Fund series accents works in the public interest that consider contemporary political, governmental, cultural, and international issues.

Oxford's New York division is editorially independent of the British home office and handles distribution of its own list as well as titles originating from Oxford outposts worldwide.

Query letters and SASEs should be directed to:

Herbert Addison, Vice President, Executive Editor
Business and economics from academic and theoretical viewpoints; religion; Bibles.

Beth Kaufman Barry, Senior Editor
Clinical medicine.

Joyce Berry, Senior Editor
Medicine, science, geology, geography, art and architecture.

Joan Bossert, Editor
Psychology and medicine.

Claude Conyers, Editorial Director, Academic Reference

Jeff House, Vice President
Medicine.

Don Jackson, Vice President, Executive Editor
Science and medicine.

Kirk Jensen, Senior Editor
Life sciences.

Donald Kraus, Senior Editor
Bibles.

Nancy Lane, Senior Editor
World history.

Elizabeth Maguire, Senior Editor
Comparative literature.

Helen McInnis, Vice President, Executive Editor
Humanities and social sciences.

Sheldon Meyer, Senior Vice President, Special Editorial
Trade-directed areas including American history, Americana, sports, jazz.

Robert Miller, Senior Editor
Philosophy, classics.

Maribeth Payne, Executive Editor
Music.

Cynthia Read, Senior Editor
Religion, linguistics.

Jeffery Robbins, Editor
Physical sciences.

Robert Rogers, Senior Editor
Chemistry.

David Roll, Editor
Political science and sociology.

Nancy Toff, Executive Editor
Children's and young-adult books.

PRINCETON UNIVERSITY PRESS

41 William Street
Princeton, NJ 08540
609-258-4900

Princeton University Press has a particularly strong focus in areas such as popular culture and fine arts, current affairs, literary biography, European history, political science, economics, and natural history. Princeton University Press (founded in 1905) publishes trade and general-interest books in addition to a list of scholarly and scientific works that spans the academic spectrum. Princeton publishes hardcover and paperback editions and hosts a comprehensive backlist.

Princeton titles include *The Nature of Space and Time* by Stephen Hawking and Roger Penrose, *The Harmony of Illusions: Inventing Post-Traumatic Stress Disorder* by Allan Young, *Creating the National Pastime: Baseball Transforms Itself, 1903–1953* by G. Edward White, *The Attentive Listener: Three Centuries of Music Criticism* (edited by Harry Haskell), *A Space on the Side of the Road: Cultural Poetics in an "Other" America* by Kathleen Stewart, *The Rise of Christianity: A Sociologist Reconsiders History* by Rodney Stark, *Spies without Cloaks: The KGB's Successors* by Amy Knight, *Religions of China in Practice* (edited by Donald S. Lopez Jr.), *Liberalism's Crooked Circle* by Ira Katznelson, *Science, Jews, and Secular Culture* by David A. Hollinger, and *Against the Tide: An Intellectual History of Free Trade* by Douglas A. Irwin.

The Bollingen Series, established in 1941, is sponsored by the Bollingen Foundation and has been published by Princeton since 1967. Bollingen titles are works of original scholarship, translations, and new editions of classics. An ongoing Bollingen project is Mythos: The Princeton/Bollingen series in world mythology. Titles here are *Psychology of Kundalini Yoga* by C. G. Young, *On the Laws of the Poetic Art* by Anthony Hecht, *The Survival of the Pagan Gods: The Mythological Tradition and Its Place in Renaissance Humanism and Art* by Jean Seznec, and *The Legend of Baal-Shem* by Martin Buber.

Books from the Princeton Science Library include *Infinity and the Mind* by Rudy Rucker, *A Natural History of Shells* by Geerat J. Vermeij, and *Total Eclipses of the Sun* by J. B. Zirker.

Princeton University Press handles distribution through the offices of California/Princeton Fulfillment Services, as well as through regional sales representation worldwide.

Query letters and SASEs should be directed to:

Robert Brown, Editor
Poetry translations.

Malcolm DeBevoise, Political Science Editor
Political science, international relations, law, cognitive science.

Peter Dougherty, Economics Editor
Economics; some sociology.

Walter Lippincott, Director
Political science, anthropology, opera.

Trevor Lipscomb, Physical Sciences Editor
Mathematics, physics, astronomy, computer science.

Mary Murrell, Sociology and Anthropology Editor
Sociology, anthropology; women's and gender studies, film studies.

Elizabeth Powers, Editor
Fine arts (excluding opera), archaeology, art history, music.

Sara Van Rheenen, Assistant Science Editor
Life sciences, earth sciences.

Ann Wald, Editor
Philosophy, political theory, religion.

Emily Wilkinson, Editor in Chief
Life sciences and history of science.

William E. Woodcock, Editor at Large (West Coast editor; contact through New Jersey office)
Physical anthropology, paleoanthropology, archaeology, life sciences, earth sciences.

RUTGERS UNIVERSITY PRESS

109 Church Street
New Brunswick, NJ 08901
908-932-7762

Rutgers subject areas include African studies, American history, anthropology, art and architecture, biography, communications, environment and ecology, European history, film, gay and gender studies, geography, health, history of medicine and science, humor, literature and literary criticism, New Jerseyana, peace studies, poetry, religion, and sociology. The press also issues selected fiction titles.

Rutgers University Press (founded in 1936) publishes a list of general-interest trade books in addition to scholarly titles in the humanities and social sciences, as well as books with a regional American bent.

Representing the Rutgers nonfiction list: *The Myth of Scientific Literacy* by Morris Shamos, *The Cure of Childhood Leukemia: Into the Age of Miracles* by John Laszlo, *Codes of Conduct: Race, Ethics, and the Color of Our Character* by Karla F. C. Holloway, and *Changing Differences: Women and the Shaping of American Foreign Policy, 1917–1994* by Rhodri Jeffreys-Jones.

Showing the Rutgers literary and cultural scope: *Favored Strangers: Gertrude Stein and Her Family* by Linda Wagner-Martin, *Esky: The Early Years at Esquire* by Hugh Merrill, *Telling Women's Lives: The New Biography* by Linda Wagner-Martin, *Apocalyptic Overtures: Sexual Politics and the Sense of an Ending* by Richard Dellamora, and volumes by creative writers such as Rachel Hadas and Alice Walker.

Rutgers features the Touring North America guidebook series that offers an accent on regional landscape with works such as *Beyond the Great Divide: Denver to the Grand Canyon* and *Megalopolis: Washington, D.C. to Boston.*

New Jerseyana from Rutgers includes *Roadside New Jersey* by Peter Genovese and *Murdered in Jersey* by Gerald Tomlinson.

Rutgers University Press handles its own distribution.

Query letters and SASEs should be directed to:

Leslie Mitchner, Editor in Chief
Literature, film, communications.

Karen Reeds, Science Editor
Sciences.

Martha Heller, Editor
Social sciences.

STANFORD UNIVERSITY PRESS

Stanford, CA 94305-2235
415-723-9598

Stanford produces a notable line of titles in the fields of new technology, the global political and natural environment, postmodern philosophy and psychology, gender studies, international issues, as well as a number of books (many in translation) dealing with current cultural and literary theory. A major Stanford publishing concentration is in the Asian-American and Pacific Rim fields of studies.

Stanford University Press (started in 1925) produces trade and scholarly books in literature, the social sciences, religion, history, political science, anthropology, and natural science in hardcover and paperback editions.

Highlights from the Stanford list: *The Media and Modernity: A Social Theory of the Media* by John B. Thompson; *Democracy and the Global Order: From the Modern State to Cosmopolitan Governance* by David Held; *The Enigma of Health: The Art of Healing in a Scientific Age* by Hans Georg Gadamer (translated by Jason Geiger and Nick Walker); *Dinosaurs, Diamonds, and Things from Outer Space: The Great Extinction* by David Brez Carlisle; *Caring for Patients: A Critique of the Medical Model* by Allen Barbour; *Uncertain Partners: Stalin, Mao, and the Korean War* by Sergei N. Goncharov, John W. Lewis, and Xue Litai; *Vichy France and the Jews* by Michael R. Marrus and Robert O. Paxton; and *The Armature of Conquest: Spanish Accounts of the Discovery of America, 1492–1589* by Beatriz Pastor Bodmer (translated by Lydia Longstreth Hunt).

Works in literature and cultural criticism include *Oedipus Ubiquitous: The Family Complex in World Folk Literature* by Allen W. Johnson and Douglass Price-Williams, *Breaking the Codes: Female Criminality in Fin-de-Siècle Paris* by Ann-Louise Shapiro, *Headhunting and the Social Imagination in Southeast Asia* (edited by Janet Hoskins), *Beethoven's Kiss: Pianism, Perversions, and the Mastery of Desire* by Kevin Kopelson, *Outing Goethe and His Age* (edited by Alice A. Kuzniar), *The Annotated Baseball Stories of Ring W. Lardner, 1914–1919* (edited by George W. Hilton), and *The*

Little Book of Unsuspected Subversion by Edmond Jabès (translated by Rosmarie Waldrop).

Stanford University Press distributes its own books.

Query letters and SASEs should be directed to:

Muriel Bell, Senior Editor
Asian studies, political science, anthropology.

Norris Pope, Director
Latin American studies, history, Victorian studies, natural sciences.

Helen Tartar, Humanities Editor
Philosophy, literary criticism and theory.

John Ziemer, Senior Editor
Asian literature.

SYRACUSE UNIVERSITY PRESS

1600 Jamesville Avenue
Syracuse, NY 13244
315-443-5534

Syracuse University Press (founded in 1943) hosts a publishing program that accents scholarly, general, and regional (New York and New England) nonfiction interests, as well as literature and criticism. Syracuse has particular presence in Irish studies, Iroquois studies, Middle Eastern studies, studies in peace and conflict resolution, history of the medieval period, and historical American utopianism and communitarianism.

On the Syracuse nonfiction list: *Harlem at War: The Black Experience in WWII* by Nat Brandt, *Beyond Eurocentrism: A New View of Modern World History* by Peter Gran, *The Nation of Islam: An American Millenarian Movement* by Martha F. Lee, *Incredible New York: High Life and Low Life from 1850–1950* by Lloyd Morris, *Bonfire of the Humanities: Television, Subliteracy, and Long-Term Memory Loss* by David Marc, *Orchids of the Northeast: A Field Guide* by William K. Chapman, *River of Mountains: A Canoe Journey Down the Hudson* by Peter Lourie, *Irish High Crosses: With the Figure Sculptures Explained* by Peter Harbison, and *The Women and the Warriors: The United States Section of the Women's International League for Peace and Freedom, 1915–1946* by Carrie Foster.

Literature and critical works from Syracuse include *Anticipations: Essays on Early Science Fiction and Its Precursors* (edited by David Seed), *Robert Lowell and the Sublime* by Henry Hart (foreword by Jay Parini), *Daring to Dream: Utopian Fiction by United States Women before 1950* (edited by Carol Farley Kessler), *Foreign Correspondence: The Great Reporters and Their Times* by Jan Hohenberg, *The Whole Matter: The Poetic Evolution of Thomas Kinsella* by Thomas Jackson, *The Economy of Ulysses: Making Both Ends Meet* by Mark Osteen, and *All Things Herriot: James Herriot and His Peaceable Kingdom* by Sanford Sternlicht.

Syracuse University Press distributes its list via its own in-house offices and also utilizes a variety of distribution services worldwide.

Query letters and SASEs should be directed to:

Cynthia Maude-Gembler, Executive Editor

TEXAS A&M UNIVERSITY PRESS

Drawer C
College Station, TX 77843
409-845-1436

Texas A&M University Press (founded in 1974) publishes scholarly nonfiction, regional studies, art, economics, government, history, environmental history, natural history, social science, United States–Mexican borderlands studies, veterinary medicine, women's studies, and military studies. A special portion of the Texas A&M list accents Texas photography, history, and literature.

Texas A&M nonfiction includes *Legend and Lore of Texas Wildflowers* by Elizabeth Silverthorne, *Caught in the Net: The Conflict between Shippers and Conservationists* by Anthony V. Margavio and Craig J. Forsyth with Shirley Laska, *The Caddo Indians: Tribes at the Convergence of Empires, 1542–1854* by F. Todd Smith, *Torpedoes in the Gulf: Galveston and the U-Boats, 1942–1943* by Melanie Wiggins, *Now the Wolf Has Come: The Creek Nation in the Civil War* by Christine Schultz White and Benton R. White, *13 Days to Glory: The Siege of the Alamo* by Lon Tinkle, *Buddhism and the Art of Psychotherapy* by Hayao Kawai, *Galveston Architecture Guidebook* by Stephen Fox and Ellen Beasley, and *Quicksilver: Terlingua and the Chisos Mining Company* by Kenneth Baxter Ragsdale.

On the literary and cultural front: *Caballero: A Historical Novel* by Jovita González and Eve Raleigh (edited by José E. Limón and María Cotera), *Nueva Granada: Paul Horgan and the Southwest* by Robert Franklin Gish, *Tales of the Big Bend* by Elton Miles, and *American Women Afield: Writings by Pioneering Women Naturalists* (edited by Marcia Myers Bonta).

Texas A&M University Press manages its own distribution network and handles distribution for several other regional academically oriented presses.

Query letters and SASEs should be directed to:

Noel Parsons, Editor in Chief

UNIVERSITY OF ARIZONA PRESS

1230 North Park Avenue, Suite 102
Tucson, AZ 85719
602-621-1441

University of Arizona Press (founded in 1959) publishes works of general as well as academic interest related primarily to the scholarly emphasis of the university's programs in Southwest regional culture and natural history. Fields of publishing concentration include general nonfiction about Arizona, the American West, and Mexico; wider categories encompass the American Indian and Latin America. The house also publishes individual and collected works of fiction and poetry—often with a regional, folkloric, or literary tone—as well as belletristic nonfiction.

Representative of the Arizona program are *Paths of Life: American Indians of the Southwest and Northern Mexico* (edited by Thomas E. Sheridan and Nancy J. Parezo), *Miracles on the Border: Retablos of Mexican Migrants to the United States* by Jorge Durand and Douglas S. Massey, *Frank Lloyd Wright: The Phoenix Papers* (three volumes, edited by Kim Shetter), *Eating on the Wild Side: The Pharmacologic, Ecologic, and Social Implications of Using Noncultigens* (edited by Nina K. Etkin), *Lewis H. Morgan on Iroquois Material Culture* by Elisabeth Tooker, *Sharing the Desert: The Tohono O'odham in History* by Winston P. Erickson, and *Sourcing Prehistoric Ceramics at Chodistaas Pueblo, Arizona: The Circulation of People and Pots in the Grasshopper Region* by María Nieves Zedeño.

Literature and fiction on the Arizona list includes *El Milagro and Other Stories* by Patricia Preciado Martin, *The Frontiers of Women's Writing: Women's Narratives and the Rhetoric of Westward Expansion* by Brigitte Georgi-Findlay, *Luminaries of the Humble* (poetry) by Elizabeth Woody, *Night Train to Tuxtla: New Poems and Stories* by Juan Felipe Herrera, *Good Years for the Buzzards* by John Duncklee, *There Was a River: Essays on the Southwest* by Bruce Berger, and *Ranch Wife* by Jo Jeffers.

University of Arizona Press handles its own distribution and also distributes titles originating from the publishing programs of enterprises and institutions such as Arizona Highways, the Phoenix Art Museum, and the Mexican American Studies and Research Center.

Query letters and SASEs should be directed for further routing to:

Stephan Cox, Director

Joanne O'Hare, Senior Editor

UNIVERSITY OF ARKANSAS PRESS

201 Ozark Avenue
Fayetteville, AR 72701
501-575-3246

University of Arkansas Press (begun in 1980) features titles in general humanities, biography, fiction, poetry, translation, literary criticism, history, business, regional studies, natural science, political science, and popular culture. The house issues a moderate list of new books each season (in hardcover and paperback editions) while tending a hardy backlist. University of Arkansas Press hosts an electronic-publishing program with a selection of software editions.

Indicative of the Arkansas list are *It's About Time: The Dave Brubeck Story* by Fred M. Hall, *Ozark Vernacular Houses: A Study of Rural Homeplaces in the Arkansas Ozarks, 1830–1930* by Jean Sizemore, *Black Charlestonians: A Social History, 1822–1885* by Bernard E. Powers Jr., *Bill Clinton on Stump, State, and Stage: The Rhetorical Road to the White House* (compiled and edited by Stephen A. Smith), *Supervision & Management: A Guide to Modifying Work Behavior* by John N. Marr and Richard T. Roessler, *A Corner of the Tapestry: A History of the Jewish Experience in Arkansas, 1820s–1990s* by Carolyn Gray LeMaster, and *The Expedition of Hernando de Soto West of the Mississippi, 1541–1543* (edited by Gloria A. Young and Michael P. Hoffman).

The Arkansas program in literature and cultural studies includes *A New Geography of Poets* (compiled and edited by Edward Field, Gerald Locklin, and Charles Stetler), *Overgrown with Love* (stories) by Scott Ely, *Big Blue Train* (poems) by Paul Zimmer, *Some Days* (poems) by Garnette Mullis, *After the Reunion* (poems) by David Baker, *At Every Wedding Someone Stays Home: Poems* by Dannye Romine Powell (Arkansas Poetry Award winner), *Atomic Love: A Novella and Eight Stories* by Joe David Bellamy, *The Hero's Apprentice* (essays) by Laurence Gonzales, *Sappho to Valéry* (poems in translation by John Frederick Nims), and *The Best of Fisher: 28 Years of Editorial Cartoons from Faubus to Clinton* by George Fisher.

In the area of folklore Arkansas has produced *Roll Me in Your Arms* and *Blow the Candle Out* by Vance Randolph (edited by G. Legman) and *The Arkansas Folklore Sourcebook* (edited by W. K. McNeil and William M. Clements).

University of Arkansas Press supports the Arkansas Poetry Award (details of the competition are available from the press on request). The Timelines catalog features titles of wider interest in the areas of history and biography.

University of Arkansas Press distributes its own list.

Query letters and SASEs should be directed to:

Miller Williams, Press Director

Debbie Self, Managing Editor

UNIVERSITY OF CALIFORNIA PRESS

2120 Berkeley Way
Berkeley, CA 94720
510-642-4247

University of California Press (founded in 1893) publishes a solid general-interest list in addition to its substantial contribution in academic publishing. The house maintains a broad program that encompasses scholarly and classical studies, humanities and the arts, medicine and science, the environment, popular historical and contemporary culture and issues, and language and linguistics. The press has major concentrations in specialty areas such as California and the West, the Pacific Ocean region including the Pacific Rim, Asian studies, Oceania, and Latin America. University of California Press also produces literary fiction, letters, and poetry.

University of California titles include *Speak Low (When You Speak Love): The Letters of Kurt Weil and Lotte Lenya* (edited and translated by Lys Symonette and Kim H. Kowalke), *Dreaming: Hard Luck and Good Times in America* by Carolyn See, *The Making of Byzantium, 600–1025* by Mark Whitlow, *The Activist's Handbook: A Primer for the 1990s and Beyond* by Randy Shaw, *Blackface, White Noise: Jewish Immigrants in the Hollywood Melting Pot* by Michael Rogin, *Benjamin Franklin and His Enemies* by Robert Middlekauff, and *The San Francisco School of Abstract Expressionism* by Susan Landauer.

University of California Press distributes its own list.

Query letters and SASEs should be directed to:

Doug Abrams Arava, Editor
Religious studies.

Deborah Kirshman, Editor
Fine arts.

Doris Kretchmer, Executive Editor
Humanities, music.

Mary Lamprech, Editor
Classics.

Sheila Levine, Editorial Director
Asian studies (East and Southeast Asia), history (East and Southeast Asia), France.

Monica McCormick, Editor
African studies, history.

Naomi Schneider, Executive Editor
Sociology, politics, gender studies, ethnic studies, Latin American studies.

Lynne Withey, Associate Director
South Asian studies, Middle Eastern studies; history (South Asian and Middle East).

Los Angeles office:
405 Hilgard Avenue
Los Angeles, CA 90024
310-794-8147

Edward Dimendberg, Editor
Philosophy, film.

Stan Holwitz, Assistant Director
Anthropology, Judaica, history.

UNIVERSITY OF CHICAGO PRESS

5801 South Ellis Avenue
Chicago, IL 60637
312-702-7700

University of Chicago Press (founded in 1891) specializes in the arts, humanities, and social sciences. Above all a scholarly and academic house, Chicago nonetheless has a noteworthy list of books intended for a wider readership. Major areas of Chicago publishing interest are history, regional Chicago and Illinois books, literary studies, philosophy and linguistics, anthropology, archaeology, art, architecture, music, religion, business and economics, media studies, political science, sociology, psychology, education, legal studies, gender studies, popular culture, and publishing, along with selected titles in the biological and physical sciences.

Representative titles from University of Chicago Press are *Inventing the Public Enemy: The Gangster in American Culture, 1918–1934* by David E. Ruth, *Jammin' at the Margins: Jazz and the American Cinema* by Krin Gabbard, *Home and Work: Negotiating Boundaries through Everyday Life* by Christena E. Nippert-Eng, *American Gay* by Stephan O. Murray, *The Colors of Violence: Cultural Identities, Religion, and Conflict* by Sudhir Kakar, *Ill-Gotten Gains: Evasion, Blackmail, Fraud, and Kindred Puzzles of the Law* by Leo Katz, *The Challenger Launch Decision: Risky Technology, Culture, and Deviance at NASA* by Diane Vaughan, *Moral Politics: What Conservatives Know That Liberals Don't* by George Lakoff, and *The Life of God (As Told by Himself)* by Franco Ferrucci.

The press publishes the professional reference work *The Chicago Manual of Style* as well as the annually updated resource for academic writers *Association of American University Presses Directory*.

University of Chicago Press distributes its own list.

Query letters and SASEs should be directed to:

Susan Abrams, Editor
Biological science, history of science.

T. David Brent, Editor
Anthropology, philosophy, psychology.

Kathleen Hansell, Editor
Music.

Geoffrey Huck, Editor
Economics, linguistics.

Penelope Kaiserlian, Editor
Geography.

Douglas Mitchell, Editor
Sociology, history.

Alan Thomas, Editor
Literary criticism and theory, religious studies.

John Tryneski, Editor
Political science, law, education.

Karen Wilson, Editor
Art, architecture, classics, women's studies.

University of Georgia Press

330 Research Drive
Athens, GA 30602
706-369-6130

University of Georgia Press (established in 1938) publishes a solid list of mainstream-interest books in addition to its specialized roster of academic, scholarly, and scientific publications. Georgia trade-book titles accent fiction and literature, biography and memoirs, history, current affairs, and regional titles; the house academic emphasis overlaps these areas of concentration, in a program that features scholarly nonfiction, poetry, short fiction, regional studies, and novels. The press publishes hardcover and trade paperback editions.

Representative of the Georgia nonfiction list: *Classic Natchez: History, Homes, and Gardens* by Randolph Delehanty and Van Jones Martin, *Civil Rights and the Idea of Freedom* by Richard H. King, *American Plants for American Gardens: Plant Ecology—the Study of Plants in Relation to Their Environment* by Edith A. Roberts and Elsa Rehmann, and *Jesus and the Law* by Alan Watson (the third volume of a provocative series that probes the historical roots of Jesus).

The New Georgia Guide is filled with essays, tours, maps, and other resources keyed to Georgia's heritage and culture.

Fiction, literature, and critical studies on the Georgia list include *The Sweet Everlasting* (novel) by Judson Mitcham, *Crossing to Sunlight* (poems) by Paul Zimmer, *Large Animals in Everyday Life* (stories) by Wendy Brenner, *Cherokee Editor: The Writings of Elias Boudinot* (edited by Theda Perdue), and *The Green Breast of the New World: Landscape, Gender, and American Fiction* by Louise H. Westling.

University of Georgia Press sponsors the Flannery O'Connor Award for Short Fiction. (Please call or write for entry requirements and submission guidelines.)

University of Georgia Press oversees its own distribution.

Query letters and SASEs should be directed to:

Karen Orchard, Executive Editor

University of Hawaii Press

2840 Kolowalu Street
Honolulu, HI 96822
808-956-8255

Areas of University of Hawaii Press publishing interest include cultural history, economics, social history, travel, arts and crafts, costume, marine biology, natural history, botany, ecology, religion, law, political science, anthropology, religion, and general reference. Particular UHP emphasis is on regional topics relating to Hawaii, East Asia, South and Southeast Asia, and Hawaii and the Pacific.

University of Hawaii Press (started in 1947) publishes books for the general trade as well as titles keyed to the academic market. UHP also issues a series of special-interest journals. The house maintains an established backlist.

On the University of Hawaii list are *Sihanouk: Prince of Light, Prince of Darkness* by Milton Osborne, *Rapanui: Tradition and Survival on Easter Island* by Grant McCall, *The Snorkeller's Guide to the Coral Reef from the Red Sea to the Pacific Ocean* by Paddy Ryan, *Camping Hawai'i: A Complete Guide* by Richard McMahon, *Fragile Traditions: Indonesian Art in Jeopardy* (edited by Paul Michael Taylor), *Staying on the Line: Blue-Collar Women in Contemporary Japan* by Glenda D. Roberts, and *Yoshiwara: The Glittering World of the Japanese Courtesan* by Cecilia Segawa Seigle.

On the literary front, Hawaii has published *Five Years on a Rock* by Milton Murayama, *Twilight over Burma: My Life As a Shan Princess* by Inge Sargent, and *Chaos and All That* by Liu Sola (translated by Richard King).

A notable UHP series is Talanoa: Contemporary Pacific Literature, which makes the writing of Pacific Islanders available to a wider audience. Sample titles here are those by Milton Osborne, *Tales of the Tikongs* by Epeli Hau'ofa, *Deep River Talk: Collected Poems* by Hone Tuwhere, *Once Were Warriors* by Alan Duff, and *Leaves of the Banyan Tree* by Albert Wendt.

The University of Hawaii Press handles its own distribution via a network that includes in-house fulfillment services as well as independent sales representatives.

Query letters and SASEs should be directed to:

William Hamilton, Director

University of Illinois Press

1325 South Oak Street
Champaign, IL 61820
217-333-0950

University of Illinois Press (founded in 1918) publishes books of general and scholarly nonfiction, with strong emphasis on American studies (especially history, literature, music), communications, film studies, folklore, gender studies, African-American studies, regional studies, ecology, law and political science, religion and philosophy, labor studies, and athletics. The press also publishes poetry and short fiction.

Representative of the University of Illinois program are *From Grunts to Gigabytes: Communications and Society* by Dan Lacy, *Green Nature/Human Nature: The Meaning of Plants in Our Lives* by Charles A. Lewis, *The Holocaust and the Jews of Marseille: The Enforcement of Anti-Semitic Policies in Vichy France* by Donna F. Ryan, *Wanted Dead or Alive: The American West in Popular Culture* (edited by Richard Aquila), *History by Hollywood: The Use and Abuse of the American Past* by Robert Brent Toplin, *Good-bye Piccadilly: British War Brides in America* by Jenel Virden, *Doowop: The Chicago Scene* by Robert Pruter, *Steppin' on the Blues: The*

Visible Rhythms of African American Dance by Jaqui Malone, *Same-Sex Dynamics Among Nineteenth-Century Americans: A Mormon Example* by D. Michael Quinn, *Out in the Field: Reflections of Lesbian and Gay Anthropologists* (edited by Ellen Lewin and William L. Leap), *Pederasty and Pedagogy in Archaic Greece* by William Armstrong Percy III, and *Ground Rules: Baseball and Myth* by Deeanne Westbrook.

Of literary note: *Taking it Home: Stories from the Neighborhood* by Tony Ardizzone, *Flights in the Heavenlies* (stories) by Ernest J. Finney, and *The New World* (stories) by Russell Banks. A particularly lavish production is *Walter Burley in America* (photographs and essay by Mati Maldre; essay, catalog, and selected bibliography by Paul Kruty).

University of Illinois Press distributes its own list as well as books from other university publishers, including Vanderbilt University Press.

Query letters and SASEs should be directed to:

Elizabeth G. Delany, Associate Director
Western Americana, religious studies, archaeology, anthropology.

Karen M. Hewitt, Associate Editor
Women's studies, environmental studies, film studies.

Ann Lowry, Journals Manager and Senior Editor
Literature.

Judith M. McCulloh, Executive Editor
Music, folklore, pop culture.

Richard J. Martin, Executive Editor
Political science, sociology, law, philosophy, architecture, economics.

Richard L. Wentworth, Director
American history, black history, communications, sports history, and regional books.

UNIVERSITY OF IOWA PRESS

University of Iowa
Iowa City, IA 52242
319-335-2000

University of Iowa Press (established in 1938) produces a solid list in selected categories that include scholarly works; general-interest nonfiction; and regional titles in the areas of archaeology, anthropology, and history. The house also produces short stories, literary criticism, and poetry.

Iowa series include American Land and Life, Singular Lives: The Iowa Series in North American Autobiography, and publications from the annual Iowa Poetry Prize competition.

Iowa nonfiction includes *History, Power, and Identity: Ethnogenesis in the Americas, 1492–1992* (edited by Jonathan D. Hill), *Kinship with the Land: Regionalist Thought in Iowa, 1894–1942* by E. Bradford Burns, *Okoboji Wetlands: A Lesson in*

Natural History by Michael J. Lannoo, and *The Anthropology of Iceland* (edited by E. Paul Durrenberger and Gíslli Pálsson).

Literature and the arts are areas in which Iowa has traditionally produced a strong list. Titles here include *Emily Dickinson's Gothic: Goblin with a Gauge* by Daneen Wardrop, *Textual and Theatrical Shakespeare: Questions of Evidence* (edited by Edward Pechter), and *The Great Machines: Poems and Songs of the American Railroad* (edited by Robert Hedin). Iowa offers a new edition of *The Writing Path: An Annual of Poetry and Prose from Writers' Conferences*, a series edited by Michael Pettit. Winners of the Iowa Poetry Prize include *Furious Cooking* by Maureen Seaton and *Swamp Candles* by Ralph Burns.

University of Iowa Press oversees its own distributional services, including representation to the trade by Baker & Taylor.

Query letters and SASEs should be directed to:

Paul Zimmer, Director

Holly Carver, Assistant Director and Managing Editor

University of Michigan Press

839 Greene Street
Box 1104
Ann Arbor, MI 48106-1104
313-764-4388

Fields of University of Michigan publishing interest include African-American studies, anthropology, archaeology, Chinese studies, classical studies, criticism and theory, economics, education, German studies, history, human development, language and linguistics, law, literary biography, literature, mathematics and engineering, Michigan and the Great Lakes region, music, natural and physical sciences, philosophy and religion, poetry, political science, psychology, sociology, theater and drama, and women's studies.

University of Michigan Press (founded in 1930) publishes a large-sized list primarily of scholarly interest in general nonfiction areas such as textbooks, monographs, academic literature, and professionally oriented works in the behavioral and biological sciences as well as humanities. University of Michigan Press publishes in hardcover and paperback editions. Ann Arbor Paperbacks is an imprint geared toward the general trade market.

Representative of the Michigan list: *Unsportsmanlike Conduct* by Walter Byers, *Medical Malpractice and the American Jury* by Neil Vidmar, *The Gay Critic* by Hubert Fichte, *Early French Cookery* by Eleanor D. Scully and Terence Scully, *The Spiral of Memory* (a literary work) by Joy Harjo, *The American Poet at the Movies: A Critical History* by Laurence Goldstein, *Wild Men in the Looking-Glass: The Mythic Origins of European Otherness* by Roger Bartra (translated by Carl T. Berrisford), *Lake Country* (literary essays) by Kathleen Stocking, and *Let the Good Times Roll: The Story of Louis Jordan and His Music* by John Chilton.

University of Michigan Press handles distribution through a worldwide network of independent sales representatives.

Query letters and SASEs should be directed to:

Ellen Bauerle, Editor
Classics, archaeology, history.

Colin Day, Director
Economics.

Mary Erwin, Editor
ESL (English as a second language), regional.

LeAnn Fields, Executive Editor
Literature, theater, women's studies.

Kevin Henninger, Assistant Editor
Ann Arbor Paperbacks.

Malcolm Litchfield, Editor
Political science, law.

Susan Whitlock, Desk Editor
Anthropology, series.

UNIVERSITY OF MINNESOTA PRESS

111 Third Avenue South
Minneapolis, MN 55401
612-624-2516

University of Minnesota Press (founded in 1927) focuses on scholarly, professional, and reference works; university-level textbooks; regional nonfiction; special fiction series; cultural theory, media studies, and literary theory; and gay and lesbian studies.

Among Minnesota's general nonfiction offerings are *Too Much of a Good Thing: Mae West As a Cultural Icon* by Ramona Curry, *Mapping Multiculturalism* (edited by Avery F. Gordon and Christopher Newfield), *Media Matters: Race and Gender in U.S. Politics* by John Fiske, *Word's Out: Gay Men's English* by William L. Leap, *God and Caesar at the Rio Grande: Sanctuary and the Politics of Religion* by Hilary Cunningham, and *Professor Wellstone Goes to Washington: The Inside Story of a Grassroots U.S. Senate Campaign* by Dennis J. McGrath and Dane Smith.

Cultural and literary works are represented by *Queer Noises: Male and Female Homosexuality in Twentieth-Century Music* by John Gill, *The Murmuring Coast* (a novel) by Lídia Jorge (translated by Natália Costa and Ronald W. Sousa), *Further Selections from the Prison Notebooks* by Antonio Gramsci (edited and translated by Derek Boothman), and *A Concise Dictionary of Minnesota Ojibwe* by John D. Nichols and Earl Nyholm. A noteworthy Minnesota series is Emergent Literature.

University of Minnesota Press distributes through several independent services worldwide.

Query letters and SASEs should be directed to:

Micah Kleit, Acquisitions Editor

Carrie Mullen, Acquisitions Editor

Todd Orjala, Acquisitions Editor

UNIVERSITY OF MISSOURI PRESS

2910 LeMone Boulevard
Columbia, MO 65201
314-882-7641

University of Missouri Press accents scholarly books, general-interest trade titles, fiction, poetry, music, art, and regional works. Specific areas within the UMP publishing range include African-American studies, cultural studies, economics, education, folklore, gender studies, intellectual history, journalism, and photography. University of Missouri Press (founded in 1958) publishes in hardback and trade paper editions.

Highlights of the Missouri line: *The Unmaking of Adolf Hitler* by Eugene Davidson, *The Chain Gang: One Newspaper versus the Gannett Empire* by Richard McCord, *The Trail of Tears Across Missouri* by Joan Gilbert, *Dancing to a Black Man's Tune: A Life of Scott Joplin* by Susan Curtis, and *On Shaky Ground: The New Madrid Earthquakes of 1811–1812* by Norma Hayes Bagnall.

In the UMP literary arena are *Second Sight: Poems for Paintings by Carol Cloar* by Dabney Stuart, *The Golden Labyrinth: Poems* by Maurya Simon, *This Waking Unafraid: Poems* by David Swanger, *A Visit to Strangers: Stories* by Gladys Swan, *Playing Out of the Deep Woods: Stories* by G. W. Hawkes, *Goodnight Silky Sullivan: Stories* by Laurie Alberts, *Writing the World* (belles lettres) by Kelly Cherry, and *Small Caucasian Woman: Stories* by Elaine Fowler Palencia.

University of Missouri Press handles its own distributional services.

Query letters and SASEs should be directed to:

Beverly Jarrett, Director and Editor in Chief

(Mr.) Clair Willcox, Acquisitions Editor

UNIVERSITY OF NEBRASKA PRESS

312 North 14th Street
Lincoln, NE 68588-0484
402-472-3581

The program at University of Nebraska Press encompasses agriculture and natural resources, anthropology, history, literature and criticism, musicology, philosophy, psychology, wildlife and environment, and general reference works. The house further accents the literature and history of the Trans-Missouri West, the American Indian, contemporary and modern literary trends, sports, and the environment (especially emphasizing Western U.S. and American Indian tie-in topics).

University of Nebraska Press (founded in 1941) publishes general trade titles in hardcover and paperback, as well as selected fiction and scholarly nonfiction. Many UNP titles and subject areas overlap categories, and thus are provided wider marketing exposure. University of Nebraska Press has successfully established niches in each of its targeted market sectors; a solid showcase of Nebraska titles has garnered book-club sales in both mainstream and specialty venues.

Representative of the Nebraska publishing program: *The Italians and the Holocaust: Persecution, Rescue, and Survival* by Susan Zuccotti, *Small Wars: Their Principles and Practice* by Colonel C. E. Callwell, *The Guitar in Jazz: An Anthology* (edited by James Sallis), *Daughter of the Regiment: Memoirs of a Childhood in the Frontier Army, 1878–1898* by Mary Leefe Laurence (edited by Thomas T. Smith), *Basketball: Its Origin and Development* by James Naismith (introduction by William J. Baker), *The Man in the Dugout: Fifteen Big League Managers Speak Their Minds* by Donald Honig, *The Cubist Poets in Paris: An Anthology* edited and translated by LeRoy C. Breunig, and *Mass Rape: The War Against Women in Bosnia-Herzegovina* (edited by Alexandra Stiglmayer).

The University of Nebraska literary horizon brims with leading-edge criticism and theory, works keyed to the American West and the American Indian, and historical as well as current writers worldwide, including Latin American, British and Scottish, European women, French feminist, and international literature of political and religious import. The house offers a strong selection of scholarly writings on the life and works of Willa Cather.

University of Nebraska Press produces the Books of the West series, which accents biography, autobiography, and memoirs; the Women in the West series; Western history and literature; art and photography; film; American Indian topics; and the great outdoors. Bison Books is Nebraska's imprint for popularly oriented trade titles featuring a line of Western classics in reprint.

Nebraska American Indian studies include biography and memoirs, literature and legend, society and culture, and history, as well as a line of titles for young readers. Series listed in this area are American Indian Lives, Sources of American Indian Oral Literature, Studies in the Anthropology of North American Indians, Indians of the Southeast, and American Tribal Religions. The press offers the North American Indian Prose Award in conjunction with the Native American Studies Program at the University of California, Berkeley. (Detailed information is available from the publisher on request.) A recent winner of this award is *Completing the Circle* by Virginia Driving Hawk Sneve.

University of Nebraska Press distributes its own list.

Query letters and SASEs should be directed to:

Dan Ross, Director

Doug Clayton, Editor in Chief

UNIVERSITY OF NEW MEXICO PRESS

1720 Lomas Boulevard Northeast
Albuquerque, NM 87131
505-277-2346

University of New Mexico Press (begun in 1929) is a publisher of general, scholarly, and regional trade books in hardcover and paperback editions. Among areas of strong New Mexico interest are archaeology, folkways, literature, art and architecture, photography, crafts, biography, women's studies, travel, and the outdoors. New Mexico offers a robust list of books in subject areas pertinent to the American southwest, including native Anasazi, Navajo, Hopi, Zuni, and Apache cultures; Nuevomexicano (New Mexican) culture; the pre-Columbian Americas; and Latin American affairs. UNP also publishes works of regional fiction and belles lettres, both contemporary and classical. The press commands a staunch backlist.

Representative of the University of New Mexico Press list: *Best Plants for New Mexico Gardens and Landscapes* by Baker Morrow, *Literacy, Education, and Society in New Mexico, 1693–1821* by Bernardo Gallegos, *Language on the Job: Balancing Business Needs and Employee Rights* by Bill Piatt, *Coercion and Market: Silver Mining in Colonial Potosí, 1662–1826* by Enrique Tandeter, *Bert Geer Phillips and the Taos Art Colony* by Julie Schimmel and Robert R. White, *Ceramics and Ideology: Salado Polychrome Pottery* by Patricia L. Crown, *The Colonial Architecture of Mexico* by James Early, and *The Last Cowboys: Closing the Open Range in Southeastern New Mexico, 1890s–1920s* by Connie Brooks.

New Mexico literary horizons emphasize regional literary expression, as well as works in the broader areas of criticism and biography. Titles include *After Hours: Conversations with Lawrence Block* by Lawrence Block and Ernie Bulow, *Broken Bars: New Perspectives from Mexican Women Writers* by Kay S. García, *Spud Johnson and Laughing Horse* by Sharyn Udall, *Lighting the Corners: On Art, Nature, and the Visionary* by Michael McClure, and *Poet-Chief: The Native American Poetics of Walt Whitman and Pablo Neruda* by James Nolan.

University of New Mexico Press is home to the literary journal *Blue Mesa Review*. The Pasó por Aquí series makes available texts from the Nuevomexicano literary heritage (many editions in bilingual format). Diálogos is a series in Latin American studies, specializing in books with crossover potential in both academic and general markets.

University of New Mexico Press handles distribution for its own list and also works through regional sales representatives.

Query letters and SASEs should be directed to:

Elizabeth Hadas, Director

Dianne Edwards, Assistant to the Director

David V. Holtby, Associate Director and Editor

Barbara Guth, Managing Editor

Dana Asbury, Editor

Larry Durwood Ball, Editor

Andrea Otañez, Editor at Large

Anne Tyler, Technical Editor

Leslie Wagner, Editorial Assistant

UNIVERSITY OF NORTH CAROLINA PRESS

P.O. Box 2288
Chapel Hill, NC 27515
919-966-3561

University of North Carolina Press publishing interest encompasses African-American studies, American studies, British history, business history, Civil War, folklore, Latin American studies, lifestyle, literary studies, anthropology, world history, nature, political science, social issues, legal history, sports and sports history, and gender studies.

University of North Carolina Press (founded in 1922) publishes works of general nonfiction, scholarly titles, and regional books, as well as a selection of general-interest trade titles. The house has a broad array of books on a firm backlist.

North Carolina nonfiction includes *Mothers of Invention: Women of the Slaveholding South in the American Civil War* by Drew Gilpen Faust; *Freshwater Fishes of the Carolinas, Virginia, Maryland, and Delaware* by Fred C. Rhode, Rudolf G. Arndt, David G. Lindquist, and James F. Parnell; *The Amerasia Spy Case: Prelude to McCarthyism* by Harvey Klehr and Ronald Radosh; *Race and the Shaping of Twentieth-Century Atlanta* by Ronald H. Bayor; *Moonlight, Magnolias, and Madness: Insanity in South Carolina from the Colonial Period to the Progressive Era* by Peter McCandless; *Hillbillyland: What the Movies Did to the Mountains and What the Mountains Did to the Movies* by J. W. Williamson; and *The Fredericksburg Campaign: Decision on the Rappahannock* (edited by Gary W. Gallagher).

Representing the literarily oriented portion of the North Carolina list are *Blasphemy: Verbal Offense against the Sacred, from Moses to Salman Rushdie* by Leonard W. Levy, *The Party at Jack's: A Novella* by Thomas Wolfe, *U.S. History as Women's History: New Feminist Essays* (edited by Linda K. Kerber, Alice Kessler-Harris, and Kathryn Kish Sklar), and *Joe Alsop's Cold War: A Study of Journalistic Influence and Intrigue* by Edwin M. Yoder Jr.

University of North Carolina Press handles its own distribution with the assistance of regional sales representatives.

Query letters and SASEs should be directed to:

Lewis Bateman, Executive Editor
American and European history, legal and business history.

David Perry, Editor in Chief
Southern regional studies, Latin American studies.

Kate Torrey, Director
American studies, gender studies.

(Ms.) Sian Hunter White, Assistant Editor

UNIVERSITY OF OKLAHOMA PRESS

1005 Asp Avenue
Norman, OK 73019
405-325-5111

University of Oklahoma Press highlights the fields of Americana, regional topics (especially the American west), anthropology, archaeology, history, military history, political science, literature, classical studies, and women's studies. University of Oklahoma Press series include the Western Frontier Library, the American Indian Literature and Critical Studies series, and the Bruce Alonzo Goff Series in Architecture.

University of Oklahoma Press (founded in 1928) publishes a wide range of scholarly nonfiction, with crossover trade titles primarily in popular history and the arts. The house's prowess is particularly renowned in the arena of the native cultures of North, Central, and South America—the extensive backlist as well as new and current offerings in these fields embrace a wellspring of over 250 titles.

The Oklahoma nonfiction list includes *Triggernometry: A Gallery of Gunfighters* by Eugene Cunningham, *Running with Bonnie and Clyde: The Ten Fast Years of Ralph Fults* by John Neal Phillips, *The Life and Legacy of Annie Oakley* by Glenda Riley, *When Indians Became Cowboys: Native Peoples and Cattle Ranching in the American West* by Peter Iverson, *International Encyclopedia of Horse Breeds* by Bonnie L. Hendricks, *The Cross and the Serpent: Religious Repression and Resurgence in Colonial Peru* by Nicholas Griffiths, *At The Edge of the World: Caves and Late Classic Maya World View* by Karen Bassie-Sweet, *In the Realm of 8 Deer: The Archaeology of the Mixtec Codices* by Bruce E. Byland and John M. D. Pohl, *Hieroglyphs and the Afterlife in Ancient Egypt* by Werner Forman and Stephen Quirke, *China: Ancient Culture, Modern Land* (edited by Robert E. Murowchick), and *The Golden Age of Movie Musicals and Me* by Saul Chaplin.

Fiction and literary titles include *Bone Game* by Louis Owens, *Smith and Other Events: Tales of the Chilcotin* by Paul St. Pierre, *Girl on a Pony* by LaVerne Hanners, and *The WPA Oklahoma Slave Narratives* (edited by T. Lindsay Baker and Julie P. Baker). The Oklahoma program includes a roster of works in the American Indian Literature and Critical Studies series.

University of Oklahoma Press distributes its own books with the assistance of regional sales representatives.

Query letters and SASEs should be directed to:

John N. Drayton, Editor in Chief
Western history.

Ron Chrisman, Acquisitions Editor
Paperbacks.

Kimberley Wiar, Acquisitions Editor
Literary criticism, classics.

UNIVERSITY OF SOUTH CAROLINA PRESS

1716 College Street
Columbia, SC 29208
803-777-5243

The emphasis of University of South Carolina Press covers the areas of Southern studies, military history, contemporary and modern American literature, maritime history, international relations, religious studies, speech and communication, international business, and industrial relations. University of South Carolina Press (founded in 1944) publishes a strong academic and scholarly list, with some crossover general trade titles. The press publishes in hardcover as well as trade paperback, and maintains an extensive backlist.

Indicative of the South Carolina program are *Plantations and Outdoor Museums in America's Historic South* by Gerald and Patricia Gutek, *Winning and Losing in the Civil War: Essays and Stories* by Albert Castel, *One Dies, Get Another: Convict Leasing in the American South, 1866–1928* by Matthew J. Mancini, *The Georgia Gold Rush: Twenty-Niners, Cherokees, and Gold Fever* by David Williams, *Profits and Politics in Paradise: The Development of Hilton Head Island* by Michael N. Danielson, *The New Religious Right: Piety, Patriotism, and Politics* by Walter H. Capps, and *World Health and World Politics: The World Health Organization and the UN System* by Javed Siddiqi.

The South Carolina literary scope is represented by *Katherine Anne Porter's Poetry* (edited by Darlene Harbour Unrue), *United Artists* (poems) by S. X. Rosenstock, *Mamba's Daughters: A Novel of Old Charleston* by DuBose Heyward, *The Doctor to the Dead: Grotesque Legends and Folk Tales of Old Charleston* by John Bennett, *America's Greatest Game Bird: Archibald Rutledge's Turkey-Hunting Tales* (edited by Jim Casada), and *The Falling Hills* by Perry Lentz (a novel based on the Civil War's Fort Pillow massacre).

University of South Carolina Press oversees its own distribution.

Query letters and SASEs should be directed to:

Warren Slesinger, Acquiring Editor

UNIVERSITY OF TENNESSEE PRESS

Communications Building
Knoxville, TN 37996
423-974-3321

Areas addressed by the University of Tennessee Press catalog include African-American studies, American government, American history, Appalachian studies, arts and culture, Civil War studies, constitutional studies, earth science, education, guidebooks, history of journalism, literary criticism, material culture, poetry studies, policy studies, political science, presidential studies, religion, Southern studies, Tennessee studies, vernacular architecture, and women's studies. University of Tennessee Press (established in 1940) specializes in carefully produced scholarly books and monographs, as well as in exemplary general nonfiction, and in popular works of regional interest. The house hosts a staunch backlist.

Representative Tennessee titles: *When Dempsey Fought Tunney: Heroes, Hokum, and Storytelling in the Jazz Age* by Bruce J. Evensen, *Savory Suppers and Fashionable Feasts: Dining in Victorian America* by Susan Williams, *Creoles of Color of the Gulf South* (edited by James H. Dormon), and *A Most Indispensable Art: Native Fiber Industries from Eastern North America* (edited by James B. Petersen).

Voices of the Civil War (Frank L. Byrne, general editor) is a Tennessee series that has introduced works such as *A Southern Boy in Blue: The Memoir of Marcus Woodcock, 9th Kentucky Infantry (U.S.A.)* (edited by Kenneth W. Noe), *From Huntsville to Appamattox: R. T. Coles's History of 4th Regiment, Alabama Volunteer Infantry, C.S.A., Army of Northern Virginia* (edited by Jeffrey D. Stocker), and *Valleys of the Shadow: The Memoir of Confederate Captain Reuben G. Clark* (edited by Wilene B. Clark).

The Outdoor Tennessee series includes *From Ridgetops to Riverbottoms: A Celebration of the Outdoor Life in Tennessee* by Sam Venable, *Hiking Trails of the Great Smoky Mountains: A Comprehensive Guide* by Kenneth Wise, *Tennessee's Historic Landscapes* by Carroll Van West, *Oakseeds: Stories from the Land* by Gary W. Cook, and *A Geologic Trip Across Tennessee by Interstate 40* by Harry L. Moore.

University of Tennessee Press is distributed via Chicago Distribution Center.

Query letters and SASEs should be directed to:

Meredith Morris-Babb, Acquisitions Editor

UNIVERSITY OF TEXAS PRESS
Box 7819
Austin, TX 78713
512-471-7233

Areas of University of Texas Press publishing scope include international politics and regional studies, gender studies, Latin America, American Southwest, Texana, Mesoamerica, linguistics, literature (including Latin American and Middle Eastern works in translation), the environment and nature, cuisine and lifestyle, art and architecture, film studies, social sciences, and humanities.

University of Texas Press (founded in 1950) is among the largest American university presses and publishes in a wide range of general nonfiction fields, offering titles of popular, scholarly, and academic interest in hardcover and trade paperback.

On the UTP nonfiction list: *Snake Lovers' Lifelist and Journal* by Chris Scott, *Humanature* by Peter Goin, *Texan Iliad: A Military History of the Texas Revolution* by Stephen L. Hardin, *Unwrapping a Mummy* by John H. Taylor, *The Birth of the Penitentiary in Latin America: Essays on Criminology, Prison Reform, and Social Control, 1830–1940* (edited by Ricardo D. Salvatore and Carlos Aguirre), *Native American Mathematics* (edited by Michael R. Closs), *The Dirt Doctor's Guide to Organic Gardening* by J. Howard Garrett, *Peppers* by Jean Andrews, and *Shore Ecology of the Gulf of Mexico* by Joseph C. Britton and Brian Morton.

Literature, the arts, and cultural studies are represented by *I Am Annie Mae: A Black Texas Woman in Her Own Words* by Annie Mae Hunt and Ruthe Winegarten, *The Stone and the Thread: Andean Roots of Abstract Art* by César Paternosto (translated by Esther Allen), *Deleites de la Cocina Mexicana/Healthy Mexican American Cooking* (a bilingual cookbook) by Maria Luisa Urdaneta and Daryl F. Kanter, *Art and the Higher Life: Painting and Evolutionary Thought in Late Nineteenth-Century America* by Kathleen Pyne, *Cinema and Painting: How Art Is Used in Film* by Angela Dalle Vacche, *Texan Jazz* by Dave Oliphant, *The Writings of Carlos Fuentes* by Raymond Leslie Williams, *Maya Textiles of Guatemala* by Margot Blum Schevill, and *Covarrubias* by Adriana Williams.

University of Texas Press handles its own distribution; the house catalog includes books issued by the Menil Foundation, Menil Collection, and Rothko Chapel.

Query letters and SASEs should be directed to:

Theresa J. May, Assistant Director and Executive Editor
Social sciences, Latin American studies.

Joanna Hitchcock, Director
Humanities and classics.

Shannon Davies, Acquisitions Editor
Sciences.

UNIVERSITY OF WASHINGTON PRESS
Box 50096
Seattle, WA 98145
206-543-4050

The program at University of Washington Press is particularly strong in some of the fields of the publisher's major academic concentrations, which encompasses fine arts (including a special interest in the arts of Asia), regional America (with an emphasis on Seattle and the Pacific Northwest), and Native American studies. University of Washington Press maintains a solid backlist.

University of Washington Press (established in 1920) is a midsized house with a primarily scholarly list that features select titles geared toward the general-interest trade market. The house produces books in hardcover and paperback (including reprint editions), and distributes adjunct visual resources (including videotapes, films, and filmstrips). University of Washington also handles a line of scholarly imports (primarily fine arts titles). UWP enters into joint-publication projects with a variety of museums and cultural foundations, and produces a large number of fine arts books and exhibition catalogs.

On the Washington general-nonfiction list: *Whispered Silences: Japanese Americans and World War II* (essay by Gary Y. Okihiro; photographs by Joan Myers); *Science and Dissent in Post-Mao China: The Politics of Knowledge* by H. Lyman Miller; *Louis Armstrong: A Cultural Legacy* by Mark Miller, Richard A. Long, Dan Morganstern, and Donald Bogle (published in conjunction with the Queens Museum of Art); *Zakhor: Jewish History and Jewish Memory* by Yosef Hayim Yerushalmi; and *The Essence of Chaos* by Edward N. Lorenz.

The Native American and regional cultural arena is represented by *The Living Tradition of Yup'ik Masks: Agayuliyararput, Our Way of Making Prayer* by Ann Fienup-Riordan (translations by Marie Meade; photography by Barry McWayne); *A Legacy of Arctic Art* by Dorothy Jean Ray; *Inuit Women Artists* by Odette Leroux, Marion E. Jackson, and Minnie Aodla Freeman; *Haa Kusteeyí (Our Culture): Tlingit Life Stories* (edited by Nora Marks Dauenhauer and Richard Dauenhauer); *Seeing Seattle* by Roger Sale (photographs by Mary Randlett); *Shaping Seattle Architecture: A Historical Guide to the Architects* (edited by Jeffrey Karl Ochsner); *Why Not? The Art of Ginny Ruffner* by Bonnie J. Miller; *A Wealth of Thought: Franz Boaz on Native American Art* (edited by Aldona Jonaitis).

University of Washington Press handles its own distribution via its home office and a number of regional sales representatives. It also distributes for a number of other specialist publishers and arts institutions, including the Tate Gallery, Asian Art Museum of San Francisco, Reaktion Books, the Columbus Museum of Art, National Portrait Gallery of the Smithsonian Institution, Exhibitions International, and the Idaho State Historical Society.

Query letters and SASEs should be directed to:

Naomi Pascal, Editor in Chief

UNIVERSITY OF WISCONSIN PRESS

114 North Murray Street
Madison, WI 53715
608-262-4928

University of Wisconsin Press catalogs fields such as African studies, African-American studies, agriculture, American studies, anthropology and folklore, biography, contemporary issues, economics, environmental studies, European studies, gay studies, geography, history, history of science, Latin American studies, law, literature and criticism, medicine, music, philosophy, poetry, political science, rhetoric, sociology, statistics, Wisconsin regional studies, and women's studies. The press hosts a steadfast backlist.

University of Wisconsin Press (founded in 1937) is a midsize house that specializes in nonfiction and scholarly books and journals, with a short list of crossover titles geared to mainstream trade interest.

Titles from the Wisconsin program include *The Print in the Western World: An Introductory History* by Linda C. Hults, *The History of Alta California: A Memoir of Mexican California* by Antonion María Oso (translated, edited, and annotated by Rose Marie Beebe and Robert M. Sencowicz), *Organ Transplantation: Meanings and Realities* (edited by Stuart J. Youngner, Renée C. Fox, and Laurence J. O'Connell), *Green Culture: Environmental Rhetoric in Contemporary America* (edited by Carl G. Herndl and Stuart C. Brown), *People of the Book: Thirty Scholars Reflect on Their Jewish Identity* (edited by Jeffrey Rubin-Dorsky and Shelley Fisher Fishkin), *Post-Theory: Reconstructing Film Studies* (edited by David Bordwell and Noël Carroll), *The Tangled Web They Weave: Truth, Falsity, & Advertisers* by Ivan L. Preston, and *Romantic Motives: Essays on Anthropological Sensibility* by George W. Stocking Jr.

A special Wisconsin series is the acclaimed Life Course Studies, which represents a broad interdisciplinary spectrum of inquiry into the nature of human timetables and biographies—the human biocultural life course.

Distribution for University of Wisconsin Press publications is through the house's customer service office; trade sales are garnered nationwide by the press's formidable lineup of regional field representatives.

Query letters and SASEs should be directed to:

Rosalie Robertson, Senior Acquisitions Editor

Mary Elizabeth Braun, Assistant Acquisitions Editor

UNIVERSITY PRESS OF NEW ENGLAND
WESLEYAN UNIVERSITY PRESS

110 Mount Vernon Street
Middletown, CT 06457-0433
860-685-2420

The University Press of New England/Wesleyan University Press program is known for individualistic works that often exhibit an interdisciplinary focus, as well as titles keyed to particular scholarly fields. The house focuses on fiction and literature, public issues, poetry and the arts, history, biography, social sciences, gender studies, cultural studies, law and social policy, and southern Africa.

University Press of New England is a publishing consortium comprising a number of educational establishments, including Brandeis University, Dartmouth College, Middlebury College, the National Gallery of Art, Tufts University, University of Connecticut, University of New Hampshire, University of Rhode Island, Salzburg Seminar, and University of Vermont, as well as Wesleyan University. University Press of New England (started in 1970) and Wesleyan University Press (founded in 1957) share editorial offices.

On the UPNE/Wesleyan nonfiction list: *A New Name for Peace: International Environmentalism, Sustainable Development, and Democracy* by Philip Shabecoff, *Up River: The Story of a Maine Fishing Community* (photographs and text by Olive Pierce; word pictures by Carolyn Chute), *The Heretic's Feast: A History of Vegetarianism* by Colin Spencer, and *Looking for Heroes in Postwar France* by Neal Oxenhandler.

Fiction, literature, culture, and the arts play a large part in the UPNE/Wesleyan program. Titles here include *Club Cultures: Music, Media, and Subcultural Capital* by Sarah Thornton, *Musicage: Cage Muses on Words, Art, Music* (John Cage in conversation with Joan Retallack), *Voices in the Wilderness: American Nature Writing and Environmental Politics* by Daniel G. Payne, *So Fine a Prospect: Historic New England Gardens* by Alan Emmet, *The Front Matter, Dead Souls* (an experiment in literary form) by Leslie Scalpino, *Edge Effect: Trails and Portrayals* (poetry) by Sandra McPherson, *No More Nice Girls: Countercultural Essays* by Ellen Willis, and *The Substance of Style: Perspectives on the American Arts and Crafts Movement* (edited by Bert Denker).

The dandelion logo signifies A Hardscrabble Book, an imprint that highlights imaginative New England literature. Sample titles: *Wherever That Great Heart May Be* (stories) by W. D. Wetherell, *J. Eden* (novel) by Kit Reed, *The Best Revenge* (stories) by Rebecca Rule, *The Hair of Harold Roux* (a National Book Award winner) by Thomas Williams, and *Live Free or Die* (novel) by Ernest Herbert.

High-profile items from UPNE/Wesleyan include *Neon Vernacular* by Yusef Komunyakaa (winner of the Pulitzer Prize for poetry), *Atlantis* by Samuel L. Delany (a suite of novellas that dramatize the African-American literary experience), and *Rider* (poetry) by Mark Rudman (National Book Critics Circle award). A headline-garnering project was Wesleyan's acquisition of the controversial final novel of Jean Genet, a pro-Palestinian homoerotic quasi-philosophical work called *Prisoner of Love*.

University Press of New England provides distribution services for all its associated imprints.

Query letters and SASEs should be directed to:

Eileen McWilliam, Director of Wesleyan University Press

YALE UNIVERSITY PRESS

302 Temple Street
New Haven, CT 06520
203-432-0960

The Yale publishing program offers both trade and academically oriented titles in the fields of the arts, the humanities, and the social sciences. Particular general-interest areas include contemporary issues, culture, and events; architecture, art criticism, and art history; history of America (with additional focus on the American West); literature and literary criticism; and political science, economics, and military studies. Yale produces hardcover and trade paper editions.

Yale University Press sponsors the annual Yale Younger Poets Competition and publishes the winning manuscript. Yale series include Composers of the Twentieth Century and Early Chinese Civilization.

Yale University Press (established in 1908) is at the forefront of university publishing. The house is one of the major academic houses, and Yale's commercial presence is evident in the catalogs of book clubs as well as on national, regional, and specialty best-seller lists.

The Yale list includes *The Enchanted World of Sleep* by Peter Lavie, *Journey of Purpose: Reflections on the Presidency, Multiculturalism, and Third Parties* by Paul E. Tsongas, *Rise of the New York City Skyscraper, 1865–1913* by Sara Bradford Landau and Carl W. Condit, *What Every Woman Needs to Know About Menopause: The Years Before, During, and After* by Mary Jane Minkin and Carol V. Wright, *Lola Montez: A Life* by Bruce Seymour, *Sin and Censorship: The Catholic Church and the Motion Picture Industry* by Frank Walsh, *Virtual Justice: The Flawed Prosecution of Crime in America* by H. Richard Uviller, *Invented Cities: The Creation of Landscape in Nineteenth-Century New York and Boston* by Mona Domosh, *Modern Art in the Common Culture* by Thomas Crow, *Young, Poor, and Pregnant: The Psychology of Teenage Motherhood* by Judith S. Musick, *Marihuana, the Forbidden Medicine* by Lester Grinspoon and James B. Bakalar, *Remembrance and Reconciliation: Encounters between Young Jews and Germans* by Björn Krondorfer, and *Comrade Criminal: The Rise of the New Russian Mafia* by Stephen Handelman.

Yale University Press handles its own distribution.

Query letters and SASEs should be directed to:

Jean E. Thomson Black, Editor
Science and medicine.

Jonathan Brent, Executive Editor
Classics, literature, philosophy, poetry.

John S. Covell, Senior Editor
Economics, law, political science.

Charles Grench, Editor in Chief
Anthropology, archaeology, history, Judaic studies, religion, women's studies.

Harry Haskell, Editor
Music and performing arts.

Judy Metro, Senior Editor
Art, art history, architecture and history of architecture, geography, landscape studies.

John G. Ryden, Director

Gladys Topkis, Senior Editor
Education, psychiatry, psychology, psychoanalysis, sociology.

The University As Publisher: From Academic Press to Commercial Presence

WILLIAM HAMILTON

You see the advertisements in book-review publications, you are aware of the spots on radio and television, and you see and hear the authors on interview shows. So you know today's university presses publish much more than scholarly monographs. While the monograph is—and will always be—the bread and butter of the university press, several factors over the past quarter century have compelled university presses to look beyond their primary publishing mission of disseminating scholarship. The reductions in financial support from parent institutions, library budget cutbacks by federal and local governments, and the scarcity of grants to underwrite the costs of publishing monographs have put these presses under severe financial pressure. The watchword for university presses, even in the 1970s and early 1980s, was survival.

While university presses were fighting for their lives, their commercial counterparts were also experiencing difficult changes. The commercial sector responded by selling off unprofitable and incompatible lists or merging with other publishers; many were bought out by larger concerns. Publishers began to concentrate their editorial and marketing resources on a few titles that would generate larger revenues. Books that commercial publishers categorized as financial risks, the university presses saw as means of entry into new markets and opportunities to revive sagging publishing programs.

Take a look through one of the really good bookstores in your area. You'll find university press imprints on regional cookbooks, fiction, serious nonfiction, calendars, literature in translation, reference works, finely produced art books, and a considerable number of upper-division textbooks. Books and other items normally associated with commercial publishers are now a regular and important part of university press publishing.

There are approximately 100 university presses in North America, including branches of the venerable Oxford University Press and Cambridge University Press here in the United States. Of the largest American university presses—Chicago, Harvard, California, Columbia, MIT, Princeton, Texas, and Yale—each publishes well over 100 books per year. Many are trade books that are sold in retail outlets throughout the world. The medium-sized university presses—approximately 20 fit this category—publish between 50 and 100 books a year. Presses such as Washington, Indiana, Cornell, North Carolina, Johns Hopkins, and Stanford are well established as publishers of important works worthy of broad circulation. All but the smallest university presses have developed extensive channels of distribution, which ensure that their books will be widely available in bookstores and wherever serious books are sold. Small university presses usually retain larger university presses or commissioned sales firms to represent them.

UNIVERSITY PRESS TRADE PUBLISHING

The two most common trade areas in which university presses publish are (1) nonfiction titles that reflect the research interests of their parent universities and (2) regional titles.

For example, University of Hawaii Press publishes approximately thirty new books a year with Asian or Pacific Rim themes. Typically eight to ten of these books are trade titles. Recent titles have presented Japanese literature in translation, a lavishly illustrated book on Thai textiles, books on forms of Chinese architecture, and a historical guide to ancient Burmese temples. This is a typical university press trade list: a diverse, intellectually stimulating selection of books that will be read by a variety of well-informed, responsive general readers.

For projects with special trade potential, some of the major university presses enter into copublishing arrangements with commercial publishers—notably in the fields of art books and serious nonfiction with a current-issues slant—and there seems to have been more of these high-profile projects lately.

Certain of the medium-sized and larger university presses have in the past few years hired editors with experience in commercial publishing in order to add extra dimensions and impact to the portion of their program with a trade orientation.

It's too early to know if these observations represent trends and, if so, what the repercussions will be. Obviously, with the publishing community as a whole going through a period of change, it pays to stay tuned to events.

UNIVERSITY PRESS AUTHORS

Where do university press authors come from? The majority of them are involved in one way or another with a university, research center, or public agency, or are experts in a particular academic field. Very few would list their occupation as author. Most of the books they write are the results of years of research or reflect years of experience in their fields.

The university press is not overly concerned about the number of academic degrees following its trade book authors' names. What matters is the author's thoroughness in addressing the topic, regardless of his or her residence, age, or amount of formal education. A rigorous evaluation of content and style determines whether the manuscript meets the standards of the press.

UNIVERSITY PRESS ACQUISITION PROCESS

Several of the other essays in this volume provide specific strategies for you to follow to ensure that your book idea receives consideration from your publisher of choice: But let me interject a cautionary note. The major commercial publishers are extremely difficult to approach unless you have an agent. And obtaining an agent can be more difficult than finding a publisher! The commercial publishers are so overwhelmed by unsolicited manuscripts that you would be among the fortunate few if your proposal or manuscript even received a thorough reading. Your unagented proposal or manuscript will most likely be read by an editorial assistant, returned unread, or thrown on the slush pile unread and not returned.

An alternative to the commercial publisher is the university press. Not only will the university press respond, the response will generally come from the decision maker— the acquisitions editor.

Before approaching any publisher, however, you must perform a personal assessment of your expectations for your book. If you are writing because you want your book to be on the best-seller list, go to a medium-to-large commercial press. If you are writing in order to make a financial killing, go to a large commercial publisher. If you are writing in the hope that your book will be a literary success, contribute to knowledge, be widely distributed, provide a modest royalty, and be in print for several years, you should consider a university press.

SHOULD A UNIVERSITY PRESS BE YOUR FIRST CHOICE?

That depends on the subject matter. It is very difficult to sell a commercial publisher on what appears on the surface to be a book with a limited market. For example, Tom Clancy was unable to sell *The Hunt for Red October* to a commercial publisher because the content was considered too technical for the average reader of action-adventure books. Clancy sent the manuscript to a university press that specialized in military-related topics. Naval Institute Press had the foresight to see the literary and commercial value of Clancy's work. As they say, the rest is history.

Tom Clancy created the present-day technothriller genre and has accumulated royalties well into the millions of dollars. Once Clancy became a known quantity, the commercial publishers began courting him. All of his subsequent books have been published by commercial houses.

How do you find the university press that is suitable for you? You must research the industry. Start by finding out something about university presses. In addition to the listings in the directory of publishers and editors appearing in this book, most university presses are listed in *Literary Market Place*.

A far better and more complete source is *The Association of American University Presses Directory*. The AAUP directory offers a detailed description of each AAUP member press with a summary of its publishing program. The directory lists the names and responsibilities of each press's key staff, including the acquisitions editors. Each press states its editorial program—what it will consider for publication. A section on submitting manuscripts provides a detailed description of what the press expects a proposal to contain. Another useful feature is the comprehensive subject grid, which identifies over 125 subject areas and lists the university presses that publish in each of them. An updated directory is published every fall and is available for a nominal amount from the AAUP central offices in New York City or through its distributor, University of Chicago Press.

Most university presses are also regional publishers. They publish titles that reflect local interests and tastes and are intended for sale primarily in the university press's local region. For example, University of Hawaii Press has over 250 titles on Hawaii. The books—both trade and scholarly—cover practically every topic one can think of. Books on native birds, trees, marine life, local history, native culture, and an endless variety of other topics can be found in local stores, including the chain bookstores.

This regional pattern is repeated by university presses throughout the country. University of Washington Press publishes several titles each year on the Pacific Northwest and Alaska; Rutgers University Press publishes regional fiction; University of New Mexico Press publishes books on art and photography, most dealing with the desert Southwest; Louisiana State University Press publishes Southern history and literature; Nebraska publishes on the American West; and almost all university presses publish important regional nonfiction. If your book naturally fits a particular region, you should do everything possible to get a university press located in that region to evaluate your manuscript.

Do not mistake the regional nature of the university press for an inability to sell books nationally—or globally. As mentioned earlier, most university presses have established channels of distribution and use the same resources that commercial publishers use for book distribution. The major difference is that the primary retail outlets for university press books tend to be bookstores associated with universities, smaller academic bookstores, specialized literary bookstores, and independent bookstores that carry a large number of titles. Matching books to buyers is not as difficult as you might think. Most patrons of university press bookstores know these stores are likely to carry the books they want.

Traditionally, very few university press titles are sold through major chain bookstores outside their local region. Even so, this truism is subject to change. Some of the biggest bookstore chains are experimenting with university press sections in their large superstores.

WHAT TO EXPECT AT A UNIVERSITY PRESS

You should expect a personal reply from the acquisitions editor. If the acquisitions editor expresses interest, you can expect the evaluation process to take as long as six to eight months. For reasons known only to editorial staffs—commercial as well as those of university presses—manuscripts sit and sit and sit. Then they go out for review, come back, and go out for review again! Once a favorable evaluation is received, the editor must submit the book to the press's editorial board. It is not until the editorial board approves the manuscript for publication that a university press is authorized to publish the book under its imprint.

A word about editorial boards. The imprint of a university press is typically controlled by an editorial board appointed from the faculty. Each project presented to the editorial board is accompanied by a set of peer reviews, the acquisitions editor's summary of the reviews, and the author's replies to the reviews. The project is discussed with the press's management and voted on. Decisions from the editorial board range from approval, through conditional approval, to flat rejection. Most university presses present to the editorial board only those projects they feel stand a strong chance of acceptance—approximately 10 to 15 percent of the projects submitted annually. So if you have been told that your book is being submitted to the editorial board, there's a good chance that the book will be accepted.

Once a book has been accepted by the editorial board, the acquisitions editor is authorized to offer the author a publishing contract. The publishing contract of a university press is quite similar to a commercial publisher's contract. The majority of the paragraphs read the same. The difference is most apparent in two areas: submission of the manuscript and financial terms.

University presses view publishing schedules as very flexible. If the author needs an extra six to twelve months to polish the manuscript, the market is not going to be affected too much. If the author needs additional time to proofread the galleys or page proofs, the press is willing to go along. Why? Because a university press is publishing for the long term. The book is going to be in print for several years. It is not unusual for a first printing of a university press title to be available for ten or more years. Under normal circumstances the topic will be timeless, enduring, and therefore of lasting interest.

University presses go to great lengths to ensure that a book is as close to error-free as possible. The academic and stylistic integrity of the work is foremost in the editor's mind. Not only the content but the notes, references, bibliography, and index should be flawless. It does not matter if the book is a monograph or serious nonfiction. The university press devotes the same amount of care to the editorial and production processes to ensure the book is as accurate and complete as possible. This leads us to the second difference: financial terms.

Commercial publishers follow the maxim that time is money. The goal of the organization is to maximize shareholder wealth. Often the decision to publish a book is based solely on financial considerations. If a book must be available for a specific season in order to meet its financial goals, the marketing department may apply pressure to the editorial office, and editorial will in turn put pressure on the author to meet the agreed-upon schedule. This pressure may result in mistakes, typos, and inaccuracies—but will also assure timely publication and provide the publisher with the opportunity to earn its expected profit. At the commercial publishing house, senior management is measured by its ability to meet annual financial goals.

University presses are not-for-profit organizations. Their basic mission is to publish books of high merit that contribute to universal knowledge. Financial considerations are secondary to what the author has to say. A thoroughly researched, meticulously documented, and clearly written book is more important than meeting a specific publication date. The market will accept the book when it appears.

Do not get the impression that university presses are entirely insensitive to schedules or market conditions. University presses are aware that certain books—primarily textbooks and trade titles—must be published at specific times of the year if sales are to be maximized. But less than 20 percent of any year's list would fall into such a category.

UNIVERSITY PRESSES AND AUTHOR REMUNERATION

No and yes. No royalties are paid on a predetermined number of copies of scholarly monographs—usually 1,000 to 2,000.

A royalty is usually paid on textbooks and trade books. The royalty will be based on the title's sales revenue (net sales), and will usually be a sliding-scale royalty ranging from as low as 5 percent to as high as 15 percent.

As with commercial publishers, royalties are entirely negotiable. Do not be afraid or embarrassed to discuss them with your publisher. Just remember that university presses rarely have surplus funds to apply to generous advances or high royalty rates. However, the larger the university press, the more likely you are to get an advance for a trade book.

Never expect an advance for a monograph or supplemental textbook.

WHEN CONSIDERING A UNIVERSITY PRESS

When you're deciding where to submit your manuscript, keep the following in mind: University presses produce approximately 10 percent of the books published in the United States each year. University presses win approximately 20 percent of the annual major book awards. Yet university presses generate just 2 percent of the annual sales revenue.

So if you want to write a book that is taken seriously, that will be carefully reviewed and edited; if you want to be treated as an important part of the publishing process; if you want your book to have a good chance to win an award; and if you are not too concerned about the financial rewards, then a university press may very well be the publisher for you.

Religious, Spiritual, and Inspirational Publishers

ABINGDON PRESS

201 Eighth Avenue South
Nashville, TN 37202
615-749-6290

Abingdon Press is the book-publishing division of the United Methodist Publishing House (founded in 1789). Abingdon produces hardcover, trade paperback, and mass-market paperback editions covering a wide range of religious specialty, religious trade, and popular markets. Areas of concentration include professional reference and resources for the clergy, academic and scholarly works in the fields of religious and biblical history and theory, inspirational and devotional books, and titles with contemporary spiritual and ethical themes intended for a wider readership. Abingdon's publishing presence includes software and works on CD-ROM.

Abingdon also issues several series of books for children, resources for Sunday school and general Christian education, as well as church supplies (posters, calendars, certificates, maps, buttons, music, and dramatic scripts). Dimensions for Living is an Abingdon imprint dedicated to titles with a popular orientation (see separate subentry below). Abingdon reprints a number of its best-selling titles in mass-market paperback editions and tends a formidable backlist.

Abingdon's frontlist includes *Sacred Cows Make Gourmet Burgers: Ministry Anytime, Anywhere, by Anyone* by William M. Easum, *Ten Strategies for Preaching in a Multimedia Culture* by Rhomas H. Troeger, *Love Letters from Cell 92: The Correspondence between Dietrich Bonhoeffer and Maria Von Wedemeyer, 1943–45* (edited by Ruth-Alice Von Bismarck and Ulrich Kabitz; translated by John Brownjohn), *Faithquakes* by Leonard Sweet, *Cries from the Cross: Sermons on the Seven Last Words of Christ* by Leighton Farrell, *A Community of Joy: How to Create*

Contemporary Worship by Timothy Wright, and *The Liberating Pulpit* by Justo L. Gonzalez and Catherine G. Gonzalez.

Academic and scholarly titles—some with crossover religious trade appeal—are represented by *The Wounded Heart of God: The Asian Concept of Han and the Christian Doctrine of Sin* by Andrew Sun Park, *Wesley and the People Called Methodists* by Richard P. Helzenrater, and *Religion, Politics, and Oil: The Volatile Mix in the Middle East* by Charles A. Kimball.

Professional reference and how-to include *Parables from the Back Side: Bible Stories with a Twist* by J. Ellsworth Kalas, *The Abingdon Preaching Annual* (compiled and edited by Michael Duduit), *Abingdon Clergy Income Tax Guide* (periodically revised and updated), *The Abingdon Women's Preaching Annual* (compiled and edited by Jana L. Childers and Lucy A. Rose), and *The Storyteller's Companion to the Bible* (commentary by Mary Donovan Turner; edited by Michael E. Williams).

Children's books and titles in Christian education include *Abingdon's Speeches and Recitations for Young Children* by Libby Malloy-Kisseih, *Lost and Found: A Musical Story Based on the Parables of the Lost Coin, the Lost Sheep, and the Prodigal Son* by Nyleas L. Butler-Moore and Carol F. Krau, and *Choral Therapy: Techniques and Exercises for the Church Choir* by Lloyd Pfautsch.

In addition to distributing its own books, Abingdon Press handles the lists of several other smaller religious publishers.

Query letters and SASEs should be directed to:

Mary Catherine Dean, Editor, Trade Books
Nonfiction books that "help families and individuals live Christian lives"; contemporary social themes of Christian relevance.

Dr. Paul Franklyn, Editor, Professional Books
Methodist doctrine and church practices for clergy and laity.

Dr. Rex D. Matthews, Editor, Academic Books
Books for Sunday and parochial schools and seminaries.

Jack Keller, Editor, Reference Books
Dictionaries and general reference guides relevant to Methodist history and policy.

DIMENSIONS FOR LIVING

Dimensions for Living is an Abingdon imprint devoted to general-interest religious trade books on practical Christian living. Dimensions for Living publishes in the popular categories of inspiration, devotion, self-help, home, and family, as well as producing gift volumes. The concept behind the Dimensions for Living imprint—"quality books that celebrate life"—was developed in response to market research. The editorial approach is to combine contemporary themes with mainstream Christian theology.

Dimensions for Living titles encompass works such as *Meditations to Make You Smile* by Martha J. Beckman (illustrated by John McPherson), *True Intimacy: 52 Devotions for Married Couples* by Jeanette C. Lauer and Robert H. Lauer, *Empty Nest, Full Life* by Anne Marie Drew, and *Family Time* by Debbie Trafton O'Neal.

Query letters and SASEs should be directed to:

Sally Sharpe, Editor, Dimensions for Living
Quality books that celebrate life and affirm the Christian faith.

AMANA BOOKS

58 Elliot Street
Brattleboro, VT 05301
802-257-0872

Amana Books (founded in 1984) publishes scholarly and religious titles with an editorial emphasis on topics of particular concern with respect to the Middle East geographic area. Amana categories include Middle Eastern studies, Islamic studies, and works of general interest. The house publishes a select number of new titles each year and maintains a solid backlist.

In Arabic, the word *Amana* signifies "that which is placed in trust"—meaning faith and commitment to humanitarian justice for all peoples in all lands. Amana Books supports this cause through the publication of books that provide analyses of political, historical, cultural, and religious issues and traditions. The publishing house explores the causes and effects of oppression, injustice, and misunderstanding, while offering original insights and possible solutions. By challenging established conceptions, works from Amana contribute vigorously to the public debate on social and political conditions throughout the world.

Representative Amana titles: *Princes & Emperors: International Terrorism in the Real World* by Noam Chomsky, *Taking Sides: America's Secret Relations with a Militant Israel* by Stephen Green, *Warriors at Suez: Eisenhower Takes America into the Middle East in 1956* by David Neff, *Through the Hebrew Looking Glass: Arab Stereotypes in Children's Literature* by Fouzi El-Asmar, *Saudi Arabia: Forces of Modernization* by Bob A. Abdrabboh, *Islam, Christianity, and African Identity* by Sulayman S. Nyang, *Journeys Back to Arab Spain* by Habeeb Salloum, *Conversations with Contemporary Armenian Artists* by Jackie Abramiam, *Alfonsina Storni: Selected Poems* translated by Dorothy Scott Loos, and Deborah Shea's literary reflection *Giving Up the Dream.*

Amana publishes *The Qur'an: Translation and Commentary* by Thomas B. Irving in two editions: hardcover in both the Arabic and English languages, and paperback in the English language only.

Amana Books handles its own distribution.

Query letters and SASEs should be directed to:

S. A. Rabbo, Publisher

AMERICAN FEDERATION OF ASTROLOGERS

6535 South Rural Road
Box 22040
Tempe, AZ 85285-2040
602-838-1751

American Federation of Astrologers (founded in 1938) is the world's largest astrological member organization in addition to being a leading publisher of astrological books, cassette tapes, astrological software, charts and other astrological aids, and related supplies. American Federation of Astrologers, as an organization, aims to further astrological education and research. AFA encourages and promotes the science and art of astrology and advocates freedom of thought and speech in the astrological arena; the house offers a monthly membership bulletin and hosts periodic conventions. The organization's publishing program has generally produced a short list of new titles each year and supports an extensive publications backlist.

American Federation of Astrologers catalogs works such as *Introduction to Political Astrology* by Charles Carter, *The Eagle and the Lark* by Bernadette Brady, *Secret Symbolism and the Sacred Tarot* by Doris C. Doane, *Dynamics of Aspect Analysis* by Bill Tierney, *Case Studies in Horary Astrology* by Joan Titsworth, *Horoscope of Murder* by Doris V. Thompson, *Christian Hermetic Astrology* by Robert Powell, *The Yin and Yang of Astrology* by Elizabeth Greenwood, *Sexual Behavior in the Zodiac* by Chancey King, *Star Wheel Technique* by Thyrza Escobar, *Pronunciation Guide: Astrology and Astronomy* by T. Patrick Davis, *Healing Pluto Problems* by Donna Cunningham, and *Let's Learn Astrology: The First Astrology Workbook for Beginners* by Patricia G. Crossley.

Additional professional reference titles include *Time Changes in the USA* by Doris Chase Doane, the key word text *The Rulership Book* by Rex. E. Bills, and the four-volume astrological instruction set by C. and E. Grant titled *The Grant Textbook Series*.

Authors please note: American Federation of Astrologers considers for publication completed manuscripts only; they do not consider queries, outlines, samples, or proposals. Manuscripts may be submitted along with copies on diskette (other than Macintosh). Subject matter should appeal only to the sophisticated astrologer; Sunsign material geared to the amateur or to a popular audience is not suited for the house's publishing program.

American Federation of Astrologers distributes its own list as well as publications of other houses.

Complete manuscripts and/or diskettes (with SASEs) should be directed to:

Kris A. Riske, Publications Manager

JASON ARONSON INC., PUBLISHERS

230 Livingston Street
Northvale, NJ 07647
201-767-4093

Jason Aronson Inc., Publishers (founded in 1965) produces a strong list of works in the field of Jewish interest, covering contemporary currents of Jewish thought as well as traditional Judaica. The house interest embraces popular, scholarly, and literary works—original titles and reprints. The well-nurtured Aronson backlist includes a lineup of established classics. (For Aronson's program in psychotherapy, please see Directory of U.S. Publishers.)

Highlights from the Aronson list include *In the Image of God: A Feminist Commentary on the Torah* by Judith S. Antonelli, *The Animal Kingdom in Jewish Thought* by Shlomo Pesach Toperoff, *Celebrating the New Moon: A Rosh Chodesh Sourcebook* by Susan Berrin, *Total Immersion: A Mikvah Anthology* (edited and with an introduction by Rikvah Slonim), *Why Me God? A Jewish Guide for Coping with Suffering* by Lisa Aiken, *The Jewish Guide to the Internet* by Diane Romm, *Demystifying the Mystical: Understanding the Language and Concepts of Chasidism and Jewish Mysticism* by Chaim Dalfin, and *Women in Chains: A Sourcebook on the Agunah,* compiled by Jack Nusan Porter.

Aronson supervises its own distribution, which, in addition to a network of regional and national trade-fulfillment services, features a direct-mail catalog operation. Aronson also oversees the operations of the Jewish Book Club.

Query letters and SASEs should be directed to:

Arthur Kurzweil, Publisher

AUGSBURG FORTRESS PUBLISHING

426 South Fifth Street
P.O. Box 1209
Minneapolis, MN 55440
612-330-3300

Augsburg Fortress Publishing (founded in 1890) is a subsidiary of the Publishing House of the Evangelical Lutheran Church in America. In addition to a wide range of Bibles and titles in popular and professional religious categories, Augsburg Fortress produces computer software, recordings, artwork, and gift items. Augsburg Fortress also vends a line of liturgical vestments and supplies.

Augsburg Fortress's ecumenical emphasis enables the house to address a broad range of issues and views within a diversified booklist. Augsburg Fortress produces works of interest to general readers in addition to books that appeal primarily to a mainstream religious readership, as well as titles geared to professional clergy and practitioners of pastoral counseling. Categories include theology and pastoral care, biblical and historical academic studies, the life and tradition of Martin Luther, self-improvement and recovery, and books for younger readers from nursery and preschoolers through young adult. The Fortress Press imprint accents issues of contemporary cultural, theological, and political impact.

Representative of the Augsburg list are *Our Hope for Years to Come* by Martin and Micah Marty, *The Everyday, Anytime Guide to Prayer* by Walt Kallestad, *Journey of the Heart: Reflections on Life's Way* by Gerhard Frost, *We Will Meet Again in Heaven: One Family's Remarkable Struggle with Life and Death* by Christel and Isabell Zachert, *New Father's Survival Guide: Devotions for the First Year of Parenthood* by Dean Nelson, *Longing for a Child: Coping with Infertility* by Bobbie Reed, and

A Garden's Blessing: Refreshment for the Soul by Lois Trigg Chaplin (a gift book; photographs by Van Chaplin and Beth Maynor).

Children's selections include the line of Good News Explorers Sunday school curriculum series, the Rejoice series, and the Witness series, as well as individual titles such as *Ms. Pollywog's Problem-Solving Service* by Ellen Javernick (illustrated by Meredith Johnson), *Swamped!* by Nathan Aaseng, and *So I Can Read* by Dandi Mackall (illustrations by Deborah A. Kirkeeide).

Authors should note: Augsburg Fortress prefers to receive a proposal rather than a completed manuscript; the house receives over 3,000 submissions per year. A finely honed book proposal may therefore be considered essential.

Augsburg Fortress has a potent distribution network with sales representatives operating via offices nationwide.

FORTRESS PRESS

Fortress Press is an imprint that focuses on the ever-changing religious worldview of the contemporary world. Fortress's trade- and religious-trade-oriented list is keyed to issues of topical interest, tackled with vision and precision. These works address political and cultural issues, and are often on the cusp of current religious debate.

Titles from Fortress Press include *X-odus: An African-American Male Journey* by Garth Kasimu Baker-Fletcher, *The Paradoxical Vision: A Public Theology for the Twenty-First Century* by Robert Benne, *God Beyond Gender: Feminist Christian God Language* by Gail Ramshaw, *The Spirituality of African Peoples: The Search for a Common Moral Discourse* by Peter J. Paris, *Womanism and Afrocentrism in Theology* by Cheryl J. Sanders, *The Crucifixion of Jesus: History, Myth, Faith* by Gerard S. Sloyan, and *Theology for a Scientific Age: Being and Becoming—Natural, Divine, and Human* by Arthur Peacocke.

Query letters and SASEs should be directed to:

Ronald Klug, Director of Publications

Robert Klausmeier, Senior Acquisitions Editor

Alice Peppler, Children's Book Editor

AURORA PRESS

300 Catron Road, Suite B
Santa Fe, NM 87501
505-989-9804
fax: 505-982-8321

Mailing address:
P.O. Box 573
Santa Fe, NM 87504

Aurora titles specialize in astrology, health, metaphysical philosophies, and the emerging global consciousness. Aurora Press (founded in 1982) publishes works that catalyze personal growth, balance, and transformation. The press aims to make available to the book-buying public writings that promote an innovative synthesis of ancient wisdom and twentieth-century resources, and thus integrate esoteric knowledge with daily life. Aurora Press typically issues a limited number of new titles each season; the house backlist includes many perennial sellers.

Aurora selects manuscripts for publication on the following basis: The information presented must be beneficial in a practical way; new to the general public; and helpful in exploring inner potential, expanding consciousness, or improving the quality of life.

The outstanding sales of Aurora's titles (including many foreign-language editions) has validated the Aurora publishing stance that it is possible to produce high-quality books without compromising personal ideals or values.

From the Aurora list: *The I Ching and the Genetic Code: The Hidden Key to Life* by Martin Shonberger, *Uninvited Guests: A Documented History of UFO Sightings, Alien Encounters, and Coverups* by Richard Hall, *The Sabian Symbols in Astrology: Illustrated by 1000 Horoscopes of Well-Known People* by Marc Edmund Jones (in a new edition), *Coming Home: A Guide to Dying at Home with Dignity* by Deborah Duda, and *Silver Dental Fillings: The Toxic Time Bomb* by Sam Ziff.

Series from Aurora include works by Elisabeth Haitch (*Sexual Energy & Yoga, Wisdom of the Tarot*) and Dane Rudhyar (*The Planetarization of Consciousness, An Astrological Triptych*).

Aurora Press is distributed to the trade and individual customers via the Samuel Weiser fulfillment and distribution center.

Aurora Press does not accept unsolicited manuscripts. Query letters and SASEs should be directed to:

Barbara Somerfield, President

Michael King, Director

BAHÁ'Í PUBLISHING

415 Linden Avenue
Wilmette, IL 60091
708-251-1854
800-999-9019 (catalog requests)

Bahá'í Publishing Trust (founded in 1902) is a subsidiary of the National Spiritual Assembly of the Bahá'ís of the United States. The house publishes books pertaining to the Bahá'í religion; interest areas include history, juveniles, scholarly works, and multimedia materials.

Representative titles: *Release the Sun* by William Sears, *Developing Genius: Getting the Most Out of Group Decision-Making* by John Kolstoe, *Songs for the Phoenix* by Michael Fitzgerald, *Journey to Mount Eternity* by Cindy Savage, *Created Rich: How Spiritual Attitudes and Material Means Work Together to Achieve Prosperity* by Patrick Barker, *Wings of a Bird* by Bambi Betts, *The Great Adventure* by Florence Mayberry, and *Sexuality, Relationships, and Spiritual Growth* by Agnes Ghaznavi.

The house's Bahá'í Distribution Service wing handles trade and personal order fulfillment.

Query letters and SASEs should be directed to:

Larry Bucknell, General Manager

BAKER BOOK HOUSE
FLEMING H. REVELL/CHOSEN BOOKS
SPIRE BOOKS/WYNWOOD BOOKS

Twin Brooks Industrial Park
6030 East Fulton Road
Ada, MI 49301
616-676-9185

Baker Book House (founded in 1939) produces works across the spectrum of general religious subject areas (from Protestant and ecumenical perspectives). Baker Book House is a preeminent distributor in the religious-publishing field; in addition to books, Baker carries audiovisual materials.

Baker Book House distributes its own list (including its diverse imprints) and catalogs selected works from other publishing firms.

In addition to its comprehensive distribution services, Baker Book House has taken over the lists of several divisions of the former Gleneida Publishing Group, including Fleming H. Revell, Chosen Books, Spire Books, and Wynwood Books.

BAKER BOOK HOUSE

The publishing division of Baker Book House issues titles of general trade interest as well as a wide selection of books for ministers, students, schools, libraries, and church workers.

On the Baker Book House list are *Journey into the Light: Exploring Near Death Experiences* by Richard Albanes, *Christian Marriage: A Handbook for Couples* by Michael and Myrtle Boughen, *Dynamic Fingertip Devotions* by Amy Bolding, *Bouncing Back: Handling the Humor and Heartaches of Frustration* by Brent D. Earles, *Deserted by God?* by Sinclair B. Ferguson, *The Male Temperament* by Tim LaHaye, *A Time to Weep* (historical novel) by Gilbert Morris, *Web of Deception* (Victorian suspense) by Jane Peart, *Roman Catholics and Evangelicals* by Norman Geisler and Ralph MacKenzie, *The Goddess Revival* (edited by Aida Besancon Spencer), *The Darwin Legend* by James Moore, and *The Poor Have Faces: Loving Your Neighbor in the 21st Century* by John and Sylvia Ronsvalle.

Among titles for younger readers and the entire family (including fiction) are *See the Wind, Mommy* by Marsha Crockett, *After the Tassel Is Moved* by Louis Caldwell, *The Jack and Jill Syndrome: Healing for Broken Children* by Patricia Rushford, *One Wintry*

Night by Ruth Bell Graham (illustrated by Richard Jesse Watson), *Guys and a Whole Lot More* by Susie Shellenberger, *Shawn Hawk: A Novel of the 21st Century* by Roger Elwood, *Eagles Flying High* by Linda Rae Rao, and *Amee-Nah: Zuni Boy Runs the Race of His Life* by Kenneth Thomasma.

FLEMING H. REVELL
CHOSEN BOOKS
SPIRE BOOKS

This Baker wing specializes in spiritually oriented works for the popular religious audience, including a wide range of fiction. Offerings from the Revell program include the Treasury of Helen Steiner Rice line of inspirational titles (including the Precious Moments series). The Chosen Books imprint produces evangelical Christian books for personal growth and enrichment. Spire accents an inspirational list of personal stories told through autobiography and memoir.

Representative titles: *Making Peace with Your Inner Child* by Rita Bennett, *Silent Hunger: A Biblical Approach to Overcoming Compulsive Eating and Overweight* by Arthur and Judy Halliday, *Angels All Around Me* by Sarah Hornsby, *God Is* by Robert H. Schuller, *Christy* (special abridged version) by Catherine Marshall, *Forbidden Legacy* (Western historical novel) by Barbara Masci Goss, *School Daze: Helping Parents Cope with the Bewildering World of Public Schools* by Bill Sanders, and *Angel Unaware* by Dale Evans Rogers.

Representative children's titles: *You're Grounded for Life! And 49 Other Crazy Things Parents Say* by Joey O'Connor, *Simplicity: Kingdom Living through the Eyes of a Child* by Betty Malz, and *The Cross and the Switchblade* by David Wilkerson (with John and Elizabeth Sherrill).

WYNWOOD PRESS

Wynwood Press represents a primarily nonfiction trade list in self-awareness and self-improvement. The Wynwood Press program currently produces new titles only occasionally. Wynwood's extensive backlist includes cookbooks and works on language and lexicography, as well as select titles in mystery and suspense fiction (Wynwood was the original publisher of John Grisham's first novel, *A Time to Kill*).

Query letters and SASEs should be directed to:

Jane Schrier, Adult Fiction Acquisitions Editor

Paul Engle, Professional Books Acquisitions Editor

Allan Fisher, Director of Publications

Bill Petersen, Senior Acquisitions Editor

Dan Van't Kerkhoff, General Trade Acquisitions Editor

Jim Weaver, Academic and Reference Books Acquisitions Editor

BEAR & COMPANY PUBLISHING

P.O. Box 2860
Santa Fe, NM 87504
505-983-5968

Bear & Company (founded formally in 1980) publishes a wide array of titles in historical and contemporary spiritual traditions, healing, and energetic medicine. Bear's list in health and medicine accents revolutionary techniques that incorporate elements such as emotion, intuition, channeling, herbs, and crystals.

Conceived over a kitchen table in the fall of 1979, Bear & Company originally highlighted titles in creation spirituality. The publisher has built a substantial backlist in this field (including Matthew Fox's *Original Blessing: A Primer in Creation Spirituality*)—and publishes works exhibiting an increasingly diverse spectrum of thought.

A natural outgrowth of the original Bear & Company approach is a remarkable lineup in Native American spirituality, including works that expand the interpretation of pre-Columbian traditions into the contemporary arena. Bear's benchmark title in this area is *The Mayan Factor: Path Beyond Technology* by José Argüelles.

The house insignia—a rambling bear under a full moon—marks a roster of thoughtful, vivid, and evocative explorations into who we are, where we came from, and the destiny of the species, as illuminated by the company's trade slogan: "Books to celebrate and heal the Earth."

Representative titles show artistry continues to waft from the Bear & Company kitchen: *Beyond My Wildest Dreams: Diary of a UFO Abductee* by Kim Carlsberg, *The Trickster, Magician & Grieving Man: Reconnecting Men with the Earth* by Glen A. Mazis, *The Woman with the Alabaster Jar: Mary Magdalen and the Holy Grail* by Margaret Starbird, *Sexual Peace: Beyond the Dominator Virus* by Michael Sky, *Journey to the Four Directions: Teachings of the Feathered Serpent* by Jim Berenholtz, *Dolphins, ETs & Angels: Adventures Among Spiritual Intelligences* by Timothy Wyllie, and *Accepting Your Power to Heal: The Personal Practice of Therapeutic Touch* by Dolores Krieger.

A Bear hallmark is the divination series, which features illustrated books and sets of cards. Packages include *The Mayan Oracle: Return Path to the Stars* by Ariel Spilsbury and Michael Bryner (illustrations by Donna Kiddie), *Inner Child Cards: A Journey into Fairy Tales, Myth & Nature* by Isha Lerner and Mark Lerner (illustrated by Christopher Guilfoil), and *Medicine Cards: The Discovery of Power Through the Ways of Animals* by Jamie Sams and David Carson (illustrations by Angela Werneke).

Bear's best-selling backlist includes *Ancient Voices, Current Affairs: The Legend of the Rainbow Warriors* by Steven McFadden, *Bringers of the Dawn: Teachings from the Pleiadians* by Barbara Marciniak, *Gift of Power: The Life and Teachings of a Lakota Medicine Man* by Archie Fire Lame Deer and Richard Erdoes, *Liquid Light of Sex: Understanding Your Key Life Passages* by Barbara Hand Clow, and *The Earth Chronicles* series of titles by Zecharia Sitchin.

Bear & Company distributes its list via a network that includes several distribution services and wholesalers.

Query letters and SASEs should be directed to:

Barbara Hand Clow, Editorial Director

BETHANY HOUSE PUBLISHERS

6820 Auto Club Road
Minneapolis, MN 55438
612-829-2500

Bethany House Publishers (founded in 1956) issues hardcover and trade paperback titles in evangelical Christian fiction (with an accent on historicals) and nonfiction, as well as a youth line. Areas of Bethany House nonfiction interest include devotional works, relationships and family, and biblical reference. The house's trade credo is: "God's light shining through good books." Bethany's traditional devotion to bookmaking is evident in its enduring backlist.

Bethany's fiction authors include best-selling authors such as Janette Oke, Judith Pella, and Gilbert Morris. The line features titles with American prairie and Western themes, historical romances, and works with contemporary settings; the house also offers boxed series sets. Titles here include *Dreamers* (a novel of faith and love in ancient Egypt) by Angela Elwell Hunt, *Song in a Strange Land* (in the Liberty Bell series) by Gilbert Morris, *A Vow to Cherish* by Deborah Raney, *Winds of Allegiance* (in the Great Northwest series) by Linda Chaikin, *The Bluebird and the Sparrow* by Janette Oke, and *Warrior's Song* by Judith Pella. *Toward the Sunrising* is part of the Reconstruction-era Cheney Duvall, MD, series by the father/daughter writing team Lynn Morris and Gilbert Morris.

Indicative of Bethany nonfiction: *The Death of Truth: Finding Your Way Through the Maze of Multiculturalism, Inclusivism, and the New Postmodern Diversity* (edited by Dennis McCallum), *Becoming a Vessel God Can Use* by Donna Partow, *Growing a Family Where People Really Like Each Other* by Karen Dockrey, *The Healing Power of a Healthy Mind: How Truth Can Enhance Your Immune System* by William Backus, *If God Loves Me, Why Can't I Get My Locker Open?* by Lorraine Peterson, *Questions to Ask Your Mormon Friend: Effective Ways to Challenge a Mormon's Arguments Without Being Offensive* by Bill McKeever and Eric Johnson, and *The Family Under Siege: What the New Social Engineers Have in Mind for You and Your Children* by George Grant.

Fiction for children and young adults includes *Mandie and Her Missing Kin* by Lois Gladys Leppard (twenty-five titles so far in the Mandie series, with over 4 million copies sold), *Whispers Down the Lane* by Beverly Lewis, and *Betrayed* (in the Jennie McGrady mystery series) by Patricia Rushford.

Bethany House distributes to the trade through Ingram, Baker & Taylor, and other wholesalers.

In accord with its current acquisitions policy, Bethany House is not considering unsolicited manuscripts or proposals. Query letters and SASEs should be directed to:

Gary Johnson, Publisher

BROADMAN & HOLMAN PUBLISHERS

127 Ninth Avenue North
North Nashville, TN 37234
615-251-2000

Broadman & Holman is a division of the Southern Baptist Convention that publishes books for a wide general readership as well as for the religious professional market. The house publishes a frontlist keyed to contemporary social, cultural, and religious interests; an array of inspirational and self-improvement titles, textbooks, and historical views of the Baptist church and theology; as well as works for younger readers. Broadman & Holman's catalog also lists audiovisual materials, as well as liturgical and other church-related supplies. Broadman & Holman represents the merger of Broadman Press (founded in 1891) and Holman Bible Publishers.

Broadman & Holman books of mainstream religious trade interest: *Been There. Done That. Now What?* by Ed Young, *The Walk: The Measure of Spiritual Maturity* by Gene A. Getz (foreword by Charles Swindoll), *Choices: Making Sure Your Everyday Decisions Move You Closer to God* by Ronnie W. Floyd, *Seasons of a Woman's Life* by Normajean Hinders, *Grandparenting by Grace: A Guide Through the Joys and Struggles* by Irene Endicott, and *Reclaiming Your Family: Seven Ways to Take Control of What Goes on in Your Home* by Robert and Debra Bruce.

Academic and professional works from Broadman & Holman include *Gods of This Age or God of the Ages?* by Carl F. H. Henry, *Evangelism: A Concise History* by John Mark Terry, *User-Friendly Greek: A Commonsense Approach to the Greek New Testament* by Kendall H. Easley, *The Southern Baptist Convention: A Sesquicentennial History* by Jesse C. Fletcher, and *Healing the Earth: A Theocentric Perspective on Environmental Problems and Their Solutions* by Richard A. Long. Broadman & Holman produces the multivolume scholarly work, *The New American Commentary*, keyed to particular scriptural texts.

Broadman & Holman distributes its own list.

Query letters and SASEs should be directed to:

Vicki Crumpton, Acquisitions Editor
General religious topics, trade books on Christian living.

John Landers, Editor of Academic Books

Richard P. Rosenbaum Jr., Editorial Director

Charles A. Wilson, Publisher

Janis Whipple, Acquisitions Editor
Devotional, juvenile, inspirational material.

Trent Butler, Editor
Reference books and Bibles.

BUDDHA ROSE PUBLICATIONS

Box 548
Hermosa Beach, CA 90254
310-543-9673

Buddha Rose Publications (founded in 1989) is a subsidiary of Buddha Rose International. The press produces a variety of print materials ancillary to its book-publishing program. The Buddhist Books imprint publishes works that explore and enlighten from the Buddhist perspective.

Buddha Rose handles its own distribution.

Query letters and SASEs should be directed to:

Scott Shaw, President and Editor in Chief

Elliott Sebastian, Editor

Chariot/Victor Publishing
Chariot Family Publishing
Victor Books

4050 Lee Vance View
Colorado Springs, CO 80918
719-536-0100
719-536-3271

Chariot/Victor Publishing marks the merger (in July of 1996) of Chariot Family Publishing and Scripture Press Publications/Victor Books, along with the operation's relocation from Illinois to Colorado.

The house is in the process of editorial and corporate reorganization, and the following subentries are based on the traditional programs of the formerly independent wings of Chariot/Victor.

It is of course prudent to check with the publisher regarding projects intended for submission, including imprint and divisional emphasis and editorial updates.

Chariot/Victor distribution utilizes a network of field representatives and services that includes its own in-house catalog and marketing operations.

Chariot Family Publishing

Chariot produces a strong list of titles with a religious orientation in the publishing areas of juveniles, poetry, inspirational and devotional, reference (including many works expressly designed for young readers), and Sunday school curriculum, as well as works for a general readership. Chariot markets a line of illustrated Bibles and illustrated inspirational and devotional readings. Chariot Family Publishing was operated as a division of Cook Communications (formerly David C. Cook Publishing—"Serving His Church since 1875").

Imprints include LifeJourney Books (fiction and nonfiction for adults), Christian Parenting, Chariot Children's Books, and Bible Discovery. Rainfall Toys offers gift and educational items that are inspirational and fun.

LifeJourney fiction is strong in the area of frontier adventure, historical romance, and mystery genres. The list includes *Turner's Crossroads* by Penelope J. Stokes, *Innocent Prey* by D. Whitesmith, and *Bitter Night, Sweet Dawn* by Janet Bedley.

Nonfiction from LifeJourney accents the personal-growth category. Titles of note are *Caregiving for Your Loved Ones* by Mary Vaughn Armstrong, *Heaven* by Joe Bayly, *When I Relax I Feel Guilty* by Tim Hansel, and *The Woman God Can Use* by Pamela Hoover Heim.

Christian Parenting Books offers titles such as *How to Enjoy Raising Your Children* by Harold Sala, *Common-Sense Discipline* by Roger Allen and Ron Rose, and *Mothering: The Complete Guide for Mothers of All Ages* by Grace Ketterman.

Chariot titles include *Jesus Loves the Little Children* by Debby Anderson, *Sidewalk Squares and Triangle Birds* by Glenda Palmer, *Trouble in the Deep End* by Nancy Simpson Levene, and *In Focus: Devotions to Help You Stand Firm in a Changing World* by Kim Boyce with Ken Abraham. *The Picture Bible Dictionary* by Berkeley Mickelsen and Alvera Mickelsen is a Bible Discovery book.

Query letters and SASEs should be directed to:

Julie Smith, Managing Editor

Marcy Balogh, Assistant Editor

VICTOR BOOKS
SCRIPTURE PRESS PUBLICATIONS

Scripture Press Publications (founded in 1934) and Victor Books are noteworthy for a wide range of books keyed to spiritual, religious, philosophical, and social topics for the adult and youth markets, as well as for educational materials and supplies. The Scripture Press list features a Bible-based orientation, with many titles offering an evangelical Christian perspective.

Categories of publishing interest include family, men's studies, women's studies, books of the Bible, Bible characters, group builder resources, and general topics. The Victor Books imprint marks the trade-directed portion of the Scripture Press program.

Representing the Scripture/Victor list: *Cynic, Sage or Son of God?* by Gregory A. Boyd, *Prayer Powerpoints* (edited by Randall Roth), *Defeating Those Dragons* by David E. Seemuth, *Body Language* by Jill Briscoe, *On the Brink of Divorce* by Judy Hamlin, *God: Coming Face to Face with His Majesty* by John MacArthur Jr., *Be a Motivational Leader* by LeRoy Elms, *How the Bible Became a Book* by Terry Hall, *The Leadership Style of Jesus* by Michael Youssef, and *Training Manual for Small Group Leaders* by Julie A. Gorman.

Books for young readers include *Anne and Gran* and *Dan and Gramps*, both by Jean Watson (illustrated by Toni Goffe).

Query letters and SASEs should be directed to:

David Horton, Acquisitions Editor

CROSSROAD PUBLISHING COMPANY

370 Lexington Avenue
New York, NY 10017
212-532-3650

Crossroad Publishing Company (founded in 1980) publishes scholarly and general-interest titles in religion, philosophy, spirituality, and personal improvement. Crossroad offers books in spirituality, religion, and counseling for general and popular religious markets. The Crossroad Herder imprint publishes books in theology, religious studies, and religious education for professionals and active members of Catholic and mainline Protestant churches.

Crossroad and sibling imprint Crossroad Herder (formerly Herder & Herder) is a United States–based wing of the international firm Verlag Herder (founded in 1798). The programs of Crossroad and Crossroad Herder offer books by some of the most distinguished authors in the United States and abroad in the fields of theology, biblical studies, spirituality, religious education, women's studies, world religions, psychology, and counseling. Crossroad supports a strong backlist.

Crossroad and Continuum, now two completely separate entities sharing the same address, were corporate affiliates within the Crossroad/Continuum Publishing Group from 1980 through the early 1990s. Even through the dual-house years, each publisher retained its distinct identity. (For Continuum, please see the entry in the directory of United States Publishers.)

Crossroad is an entrepreneurial house of modest size, with a tightly focused program that takes advantage of diverse marketing channels—as such, this publisher provides an excellent environment for authors looking for personalized and long-term publishing relationships.

Frontlist titles include *Caring for Elderly Parents* by Ruth Whybrow, *Let Someone Hold You* by Paul Morrissey, *The Growth of Mysticism* by Bernard McGinn, *Rediscovering the Sacred: Spirituality in America* by Phyllis Tickle, *Violence Unveiled* by Gil Bailie, *Dear Heart, Come Home: The Path of Midlife Spirituality* by Joyce Rupp, *The Price of Wisdom: The Heroic Struggle to Become a Person* by James McMahon, *Raising Abel: The Rediscovery of the Eschatological Imagination* by James Allison, *Hidden Women of the Gospels* by Cathy Coffey, and *Parables and the Enneagram* by Clarence Thompson.

Selections from the backlist are *The Zen Teachings of Jesus* by Kenneth S. Leong, *A Singing Something: Womanist Reflections on Anna Julia Cooper* by Karen Baker-Fletcher, *Medicine Wheels: Native American Vehicles of Healing* by Roy I. Wilson, and *In the Courts of the Lord: A Gay Priest's Story* by James Ferry.

An ongoing Crossroad line is the Adult Christian Education Program, which issues series titles in Scripture study, theology and church history, Christian living, and world religious traditions.

Crossroad has sponsored the Crossword Women's Studies Award and the Crossroad Counseling Book Award, both of which bestow publication under the house imprimatur. (Details are available on request from the publisher.)

Crossroad distributes via Publisher Resources.

Query letters and SASEs should be directed to:

Michael Leach, Publisher

Bob Heller, Editor

CROSSWAY BOOKS

1300 Crescent Boulevard
Wheaton, IL 60187
708-682-4300

Crossway Books (founded in 1938) is a division of Good News Publishers. Crossway produces a midsize seasonal list of books with a Christian perspective aimed at both the religious and the general audience, including issues-oriented nonfiction, evangelical works, inspiration, self-awareness, and fiction. Crossway also issues a line of audiobooks.

Representative of the Crossway list are *Telling the Truth: How to Revitalize Christian Journalism* by Marvin Olasky, *No More Excuses: Be the Man God Made You to Be* by Tony Evans, *God in the Dark* by Os Guiness, *A Woman's Walk with God: A Daily Guide for Prayer and Spiritual Growth* by Sheila Cragg, and *Ten Secrets for a Successful Family* by Adrian Rogers.

Fiction from Crossway includes *Fated Genes* by Harry Lee Krauss Jr., *The Gathering Storm* by W. E. Davis, *Code of the West* by Stephen Bly, and *Wells of Glory* by Mary McReynolds.

Sample children's books: *Annie Henry and the Secret Mission* by Susan Olasky, *Children of the King* by Max Lucado, and *Hattie Marshall and the Dangerous Fire* by Debra Smith.

The house handles its own distribution.

Query letters and SASEs should be directed to:

Leonard G. Goss, Editorial Director

CONTINUUM PUBLISHING GROUP

(See Directory of United States Publishers)

DHARMA PUBLISHING

2425 Hillside Avenue
Berkeley, CA 94704
510-548-5407

Mailing address:
2910 San Pablo Avenue
Berkeley, CA 94702
800-873-4276

Dharma Publishing (founded in 1972) is a specialist house active in a variety of formats. Dharma publishes trade paperbacks and journals; distribution includes subscription and mail order. Areas of interest include art, history, biography, literature, philosophy, psychology, spiritual, scholarly, cosmology, and juveniles.

Sample titles: *Wisdom of Buddha: The Samdhinirmocana Sutra* (translated by John Powers), *The Voice of the Buddha* (translated by Gwendolyn Bays), *Tibet in Pictures* by Li Gotami Govinda, *Skillful Means: Patterns for Success* by Tarthang Tulku, and *Tibetan Buddhism in Western Perspective* by Herbert V. Guenther.

Dharma Publishing reflects the Odiyan style of Dharma, a form of Buddhism that practices a blend of spiritual concerns with independence, individual responsibility, and down-to-earth knowledge. The publishing house considers projects from sectarians only, and rarely publishes books from outside writers.

Query letters and SASEs should be directed to:

Tarthang Tulku, President and Editor

DIMENSIONS FOR LIVING
(See Abingdon Press)

DISCIPLESHIP RESOURCES
1908 Grand Avenue
P.O. Box 840
Nashville, TN 37202-0840
615-340-7068

Discipleship Resources (founded in 1951) is the publishing component of the General Board of Discipleship, one of the major program boards of the United Methodist Church. Areas of publishing interest encompass United Methodist history, doctrine, and theology, as well as Bible study, Christian education, ethnic church concerns, evangelism, ministry of the laity, stewardship, United Methodist men, and worship.

Discipleship Resources issues a varied inventory including books; booklets; manuals; audiovisuals; packets; and supplies directed to local church members and leaders, lay and clergy, men and women, children, youth, and adults—as well as to district and conference leaders and others serving the congregation. Some resources guide the leader of an area of work or particular program, while others are aimed toward individual study and enrichment.

Titles include *Serving with Christ: A Study of Jesus' Farewell Commission to His Disciples* by R. Wade Paschal Jr., *Don't Shoot the Horse ('Til You Know How to Drive the Tractor): Moving from Annual Fund Raising to a Life of Giving* by Herb Mather, *Needing, Kneeling, Knowing: A Workbook of Spiritual Development for Church School Teachers* by Judy Gattis Smith, *Beyond the Walls: A Congregational Guide for Lifestyle Relational Evangelism* by Jim Hollis, and *Come and See: Biblical and Contemporary Encounters with Christ* by Shirley F. Clement.

Writers who wish to submit materials to Discipleship Resources for publishing consideration may acquire editorial guidelines on request from the publisher. The guide includes versatile tips that are broadly applicable to manuscript preparation in general.

Discipleship Resources handles its own sales and distribution.

Query letters and SASEs should be directed to:

Craig Gallaway, Managing Editor

WILLIAM B. EERDMANS PUBLISHING COMPANY

255 Jefferson Avenue Southeast
Grand Rapids, MI 49503
616-459-4591

William B. Eerdmans Publishing Company (founded in 1911) publishes books of general interest; religious, academic, and theological works; juvenile literature; regional history; and American religious history. The Eerdmans publishing purview offers a Christian perspective in areas such as anthropology, biblical studies, biography, African-American studies, church administration, music, philosophy, psychology, science, social issues, current and historical theology, and women's interest.

On the Eerdmans list: *The Bible for Everyday Life* (edited by George Carey), *The Astonished Heart: Reclaiming the Good News from the Lost-and-Found of Church History* by Robert Farrar Capon, *Celtic Women: Women in Celtic Society and Literature* by Peter Berresford Ellis, *The Dead Sea Scrolls Translated: The Qumran Texts in English* by Florentino Garcia Martinez, *Sworn on the Altar of God: A Religious Biography of Thomas Jefferson* by Edwin S. Gaustad, *St. Francis* by Brian Wildsmith, and *Handbook of European History, 1400–1600: Late Middle Ages, Renaissance, and Reformation* (edited by Thomas A. Brady Jr., Heiko A. Oberman, and James D. Tracy).

A special Eerdmans project is the beautifully produced *The Leningrad Codex: A Facsimile Edition* (Astrid B. Beck, managing editor; David Noel Freedman, general editor; James A. Sanders, publication editor).

The Eerdmans catalog also highlights general reference works, such as Bible commentaries and theological dictionaries, as well as titles in Old and New Testament studies.

Titles for younger readers include *An Introduction to the Liturgical Year* by Inos Biffi (illustrations by Franco Vignazia), *Sebgugugu the Glutton: A Bantu Tale from Rwanda* retold by Verna Aardema (illustrations by Nancy L. Clouse), and *The Story of Zacchaeus* by Marty Rhodes (illustrations by Cat Bowman Smith).

William B. Eerdmans Publishing Company distributes its own list with the assistance of regional sales representatives.

Query letters and SASEs should be directed to:

Jon Pott, Editor in Chief

Amy Eerdmans, Children's Book Editor

Charles van Hof, Managing Editor

FELDHEIM PUBLISHERS

200 Airport Executive Park
Spring Valley, NY 10977
914-356-2282

Feldheim Publishers (founded in 1954) is among the leading houses in areas of publishing activity that include works of contemporary authors in the field of Orthodox Jewish thought, translations from Hebrew of Jewish classical works, dictionaries and general reference works, textbooks, and guides for sabbaths and festivals, as well as in literature for readers ages three and up (Young Readers Division). The Feldheim publishing program is expanding, and the house releases an increasing number of new titles each season. Feldheim retains a comprehensive backlist.

Representative Feldheim offerings are *Blue Star over Red Square* by Carmela Raiz, *Be Fruitful and Multiply* (edited by Richard V. Grazi, MD), *Designer World* by Avraham Katz, *My Friends, We Were Robbed!* by Uri Zohar, *The Nineteen Letters: The World of Rabbi S. R. Hirsch* by Joseph Elias, *Ethics From Sinai* by Irving M. Burim, *Guardian of Eden* by Yisroel Miller, *Shabbat and Electricity* (compiled by Dovid Oratz from the writings of L.Y. Halperin), *S'Shah Tovah: The Jewish Woman's Clinical and Halachic Guide to Pregnancy and Childbirth* by Baruch and Michal Finkelstein, and *A Weed Among the Roses* by Eva Vogiel.

Books of interest to younger readers include *School for One* by Judith Weil, *Anything Can Happen* by Libby Lazewnik, and *Baila Wants a Bicycle Bell* by Ruth Finkelstein.

Feldheim Publishers handles its own distribution as well as offering books of other publishers, including American Yisroel Chai Press and Targum Press.

Query letters and SASEs should be directed to:

Yitzchak Feldheim, President

FRIENDSHIP PRESS

475 Riverside Drive
New York, NY 10115
212-870-2383

The Friendship list encompasses religious books as well as titles in the public-interest realm that address contemporary topics such as cultural pluralism, the media, global awareness, health and wholeness, technology and the environment, human rights, and world peace. Friendship also issues special ecumenical program materials intended for the use of adults, youths, and children, as well as producing videos, maps, notecards, and informational posters.

Friendship Press was established in 1902 as a missionary education movement in the United States and Canada. Now part of the National Council of the Churches of Christ USA, Friendship Press is a leading ecumenical publisher of educational materials for schools and parishes.

Friendship catalogs titles such as *Welcome the Child: A Child Advocacy Guide for Churches* by Shannon P. Daley and Kathleen A. Guy, *The Caribbean: Culture of Resistance, Spirit of Hope* (edited by Oscar Bolioli), *Remembering the Future: The Challenge of the Churches in Europe* (edited by Robert C. Lodwick), *Angle of Vision: Christians and the Middle East* by Charles A. Kimball, *We Belong Together: The Churches in Solidarity with Women* (edited by Sarah Cunningham), *Haiku, Origami, and More: Worship and Study Resources from Japan* by Judith May Newton and Mayumi Tabuchi, *The Indian Awakening in Latin America* (edited by Yves Materne), *Torch in the Night: Worship Resources from South Africa* by Anne Hope, *Keeping Covenant with the Poor: Study Guide on Poverty in North America* by Nancy A. Carter, and *Justice and the Intifada* (edited by Kathy Bergen, David Neuhaus, and Ghassan Rubeiz).

Friendship Press publishes a limited number of new titles per season—most of which are commissioned additions to curriculum lines. Friendship is, however, open to considering manuscripts by authors written from an embracing global cultural perspective.

Friendship Press distributes its own list.

Query letters and SASEs should be directed to:

Margaret Larom, Curriculum Editor

Audrey Miller, Executive Director

GLENEIDA PUBLISHING GROUP
(See Baker Book House and Liguori Publications)

GOSPEL LIGHT PUBLICATIONS
2300 Knoll Drive
Ventura, CA 93003
805-644-9721

Gospel Light, along with its Regal Books division, accents titles in general religious interest, religious education, and juveniles; the house also offers video and audio selections. Regal Books (founded in 1933) specializes in resources for evangelism, discipleship, and Christian education.

The publisher's mission is to equip Christians, their churches, their communities, and their world with the good news of Jesus Christ. The Gospel Light/Regal trade motto is "Bright ideas to help you grow."

Gospel Light/Regal Books highlights include *Pastors of Promise* by Jack Hayford, *Secrets of a Lasting Marriage: Building a Love That Will Last Forever* by H. Norman Wright, *Helping Others Find Freedom in Christ: Connecting People in God through Discipleship Counseling* by Neil T. Anderson, and *Drugproof Your Kids* by Stephen Arterburn and Jim Burns.

On the Regal list of children's and youth books are *Busting Free: Helping Youth Discover Their Identity in Christ* by Neil T. Anderson and Dave Park, *What Hollywood Won't Tell You about Love, Sex, and Dating* by Susie Shellenberger and Greg Johnson, and *How to Be a Christian Without Being Religious* by Fritz Ritenour.

Gospel Light oversees its own distribution.

Unsolicited manuscripts are not accepted.

Query letters and SASEs should be directed to:

Kyle Duncan, Acquisitions

HARPER SAN FRANCISCO

1160 Battery Street
San Francisco, CA 94111
415-477-4400

Harper San Francisco is strong in a variety of general trade and specialist areas: psychology, self-awareness, and self-help; inspiration and meditation; writing, journaling, and creativity; gender studies and the field of sexual identity and expression; spirituality worldwide (historical traditions and contemporary trends); Judaica; Gnosticism; the historical Jesus; gift books; parenting; wellness and recovery; health and fitness; alternative therapies; biography; society and culture; ethics and philosophy; science; environment and nature; Native American studies; spiritual journeys; mysticism; witchcraft and the occult; mythology; Celtic studies; music; and cookbooks. In addition, the publisher offers occasional works of fiction and books with themes of popular interest.

HSF focuses on books that inspire and nurture the mind, body, and spirit; explore the essential religious, spiritual, and philosophical questions; present the rich and diverse array of cultures and their wisdom traditions; and support readers in their ongoing personal discovery and enrichment.

Harper Edge is a new imprint at HSF, for which plans are to take full advantage of the house's West Coast presence, with titles that spotlight the interface between culture and technology.

Harper San Francisco is a division of the international HarperCollins corporate family of publishers. Harper San Francisco is an imprint of HarperCollins Adult Trade Division (which includes imprints emanating from the HarperCollins New York offices). Harper

San Francisco benefits directly from the core HarperCollins marketing and sales power, and retains its editorial independence and identity.

HSF has featured works by Martin Luther King Jr., Norman Vincent Peale, the Dalai Lama of Tibet, C. S. Lewis, Matthew Fox, and Melodie Beattie. The house is also represented by the Hazelden imprint (for selected books copublished with Hazelden Educational Materials) and is also corporately affiliated with the editorially independent Zondervan subsidiary of HarperCollins (see separate Hazelden and Zondervan listings). A Pillow Book is the tag for a line of works that embrace the varieties of sexual experience.

On Harper San Francisco: *By the River Piedra I Sat Down and Wept* by Paul Coelho (translated by Alan R. Clarke), *It's Not All in Your Head: The New Psychiatry for Women* by Susan Swedo and Henrietta Leonard, *The Multi-Orgasmic Man: Sexual Secrets Every Man Should Know* by Mantak Chia and Douglas Abrams Arava, *The Spirit of a Man: A Vision of Transformation for Black Men and the Women Who Love Them* by Iyanla Vanzant, *The Dance of the Dissident Daughter: A Woman's Journey from Christian Tradition to the Sacred Feminine* by Sue Monk Kidd, *Sex between Men: An Intimate History of the Sex Lives of Gay Men Postwar to Present* by Douglas Sadownick, *The Country of Marriage: Discovering the Secrets of Enduring Love* by Cathleen Rountree, *Expect a Miracle: The Miraculous Things That Happen to Ordinary People* by Dan Wakefield, *The Jew in the Lotus* by Rodger Kamenetz, *E. T. 101: The Cosmic Instruction Manual for Planetary Evolution* cocreated by Mission Control and Zoev Jho, and *Mystic Cats: A Celebration of Cat Magic and Feline Charm* by Roni Jay (illustrated by Lorraine Harrison).

A special HSF set is *The Music of Silence: Entering the Sacred Space of Monastic Experience* by David Steindl-Rast with Sharon Lebell (packaged with a CD of Benedictine Monk music).

The house invites prospective authors to correspond first via a brief query letter describing the essential character of the projected work, along with author qualifications and any previous books published or professional credentials. Detailed guidelines for submissions are available on request from the editorial department.

Harper San Francisco handles distribution through independent fulfillment offices; the house direct-mail catalog incorporates an extensive backlist. Harper San Francisco titles are also available through the offices of the parent company, HarperCollins Publishers.

Query letters and SASEs should be directed to:

Lisa Bach, Editor
Popular psychology and self-help; women's studies/feminist spirituality; gay and lesbian studies; alternative spirituality and inspiration. Projects include A Course in Love by Joan Gattuso, Chasing Grace by Martha Manning, Prayers of the Saints by Woodeene Koenig-Bricker, and The Optimystic's Handbook by Terry Lynn Taylor and Mary Beth Crain.

Kevin Bentley, Associate Editor
Gay and lesbian spirituality, memoir, and general nonfiction; popular psychology; personal growth; writing; alternative/New Age; packaged projects and paperback reprints

in all Harper San Francisco publishing areas. Projects include *Revelations for a New Millennium* by Andrew Ramer, *Sex between Men* by Douglas Sadownick, and *Totems* by Brad Steiger.

Clayton Carlson, Senior Vice President
Acquires consistent with house list.

Mark Chimsky, Executive Editor
Religious studies, popular spirituality, psychology, sexuality, gay and lesbian studies, popular culture. Projects include *Honest to Jesus* by Robert Funk; *A Commentary on the Torah* by Richard Elliott Friedman; and *The Dead Sea Scrolls: A New Translation* by Michael Wise, Martin Abegg Jr., and Edward Cook.

Thomas Grady, Executive Editor
World religions, Christian spirituality and mysticism, alternative spirituality; psychology and personal growth. Projects include *The Essential Rumi* by Coleman Barks, *The Faithful Gardener* by Clarissa Pinkola Estés, and *The Joy of Living and Dying in Peace* by the Dalai Lama.

Patricia Klein, Senior Editor
Books on all aspects of Christian life, ranging across the entire spectrum of the Christian tradition from conservative Evangelical to progressive Catholic, including (but not limited to) spirituality, devotion, personal growth, spiritual renewal, family life, Christian thought and teaching, and the Bible. Projects include *Glimpses of Grace: Daily Thoughts and Reflections* by Madeleine L'Engle, *Streams of Living Water* by Richard Foster, and *The Power Behind Positive Thinking* by Eric Fellman.

John V. Loudon, Executive Editor
Religious studies, psychology/personal growth, inspiration, Eastern religions, Jewish and Christian spirituality. Books include *By the River Piedra I Sat Down and Wept* by Paulo Coelho, *The Real Jesus* by Luke Timothy Johnson, and *Entering the Circle* by Olga Kharatidi.

Caroline Pincus, Editor
Psychology/self-help; Jewish spirituality; alternative and complementary health; lesbian and gay studies; multicultural studies. Titles include *Prayer Is Good Medicine* by Larry Dossey, *Everyday Sacred* by Sue Bender, *Journey to the Heart* by Melodie Beattie, and *Suzanne White's Guide to Love* by Suzanne White.

Susan Reich, Vice President and Publishing Director
Acquires in areas consistent with house list.

HARVEST HOUSE PUBLISHERS

1075 Arrowsmith
Eugene, OR 97402
503-343-0123

Harvest House Publishers (founded in 1974) produces religious-oriented works in trade nonfiction and fiction, Bible study and theological thought, and educational and devotional resources in hardcover trade paperback and mass-market paperback editions. Harvest House frontlist titles often address topics of current general interest with widespread implications on the social religious front. Subjects include media, technology, and politics; parenting, youth, relationships, and the family; Christian living and contemporary values; cults and the occult; personal awareness, inspiration, and spiritual growth; Christian history and heritage; and humor.

The publisher's nondenominational list features many works that offer an Evangelical Christian perspective and includes many notable individualist author voices. The house issues a number of strong lines directed toward the child and youth market (please see separate subentry below) and also produces books in the Spanish language. Also featured are audiobooks, calendars, and daily planners.

Examples of Harvest House nonfiction: *Living Water: The Power of the Holy Spirit in Your Life* by Chuck Smith, *Quiet Times for Parents: A Daily Devotional* by H. Norman Wright, *Encyclopedia of New Age Beliefs* by John Ankerberg and John Weldon, *The Mark of the Beast: Your Money, Computers, and the End of the World* by Peter Lalonde and Paul Lalonde, *Daily in Christ: A Devotional* by Neil Anderson and Joanne Anderson, *His Imprint, My Expression* by Kay Arthur, *A Place Called Simplicity: The Quiet Beauty of Simple Living* by Claire Cloninger, and *Sodom's Second Coming: Equipping You and Your Family for the Coming Homosexual Assault* by F. LaGard Smith.

Fiction from Harvest House includes mainstream novels with a religious accent, historical adventure tales, Bible-based stories, books with a focus on women's readership (including romances), occult thrillers, mystery and suspense fiction, and futuristic works. Among them: *Where the Wild Rose Blooms* (part of the Rocky Mountain Memories series) by Lori Wick, *Return to the Heartland* (the conclusion to the Heartland Heritage series) by June Masters Bacher, *The Wolf Story* by James Byron Huggins, *Samson* by Ellen Gunderson Traylor, and the international thriller *Sanctuary of the Chosen* by Dave Hunt (who also authors some of Harvest House's popular nonfiction works).

Harvest House manages its own distributional network.

HARVEST HOUSE BOOKS
FOR CHILDREN AND YOUNG ADULTS

Harvest House produces a solid selection of books directed toward a youthful readership, as well as titles of interest to teachers and parents. The list includes coloring books, picture books, storybooks, interactive books, joke books, general nonfiction, and novels (including a number of successful series).

Indicative of the Harvest House list for children and youth are *Friends No Matter What* by Mark Littleton, *A Change of Heart* by Ginny Williams, and *Jest Another Good Clean Joke Book* by Bob Phillips.

Query letters and SASEs should be directed to the Manuscript Coordinator.

Hazelden Publishing Group

15251 Pleasant Valley Road
P.O. Box 176
Center City, MN 55012
612-257-4010

Hazelden Publishing Group issues books for a general and professional readership in areas such as awareness, discovery, wholeness and transformation, meditation, recovery, personal and spiritual growth, self-help, spirituality, substance abuse, and compulsive behaviors. The house's backlist represents all areas of the Hazelden publishing program.

The Hazelden publications and marketing vision encompasses books, pamphlets, audiocassettes and videocassettes, computer software, calendars, organizers, and books for young readers, along with a gift line.

Hazelden was established as a publishing operation (in 1954, as Hazelden Educational Materials) with the hardcover release of *Twenty-Four Hours a Day* by Rich W (still in print in hardcover and paperback editions). Hazelden is a division of the Hazelden Foundation, which also operates a network of recovery centers. The publisher has a major concentration in materials related to the 12-Step approach.

In early 1994, Hazelden purchased CompCare and Parkside, two former niche publishers (both with strong backlists) in areas consistent with Hazelden's publishing range—particularly in treatment and recovery titles, as well as the broader general-interest trade arena. Hazelden also bought PIA (Psychiatric Institute of America), a publisher with similar scope. The titles of these publishers have been folded into the Hazelden list, thereby augmenting Hazelden's preeminence in this particular publishing arena.

In addition to the aforementioned *Twenty-Four Hours a Day,* Hazelden's best-selling trade entrants include *Codependent No More* and *The Language of Letting Go* (both by Melody Beattie), as well as *Each Day a New Beginning.*

Representative Hazelden titles are *Embodying Spirit: Coming Alive with Meaning and Purpose* by Jacquelyn Small (licensed with Harper San Francisco), *Dancing Backwards in High Heels: How Women Master the Art of Resilience* by Patricia O'Gorman, *Lighting a Candle: Quotations in the Spiritual Life* by Molly Young (licensed with Harper San Francisco), *Winning a Day at a Time* by John Lucas (an autobiography of the National Basketball Association coach), and *My Mind Is Out to Get Me: Humor and Wisdom in Recovery* by Dr. Ron B.

Highlights of the Hazelden children's program have included *The Cat at the Door and Other Stories to Live By: Affirmations for Children* by Anne D. Mather and Louise B. Weldon (illustrated by Lyn Martin), *Making the Most of Today: Daily Readings for Young People on Self-Awareness, Creativity, and Self-Esteem* by Pamela Espeland and Rosemary Wallner, and *Starry Night* (written and illustrated by David Spohn).

Hazelden publications appear in the mainstream book trade market through projects sponsored conjointly with Harper San Francisco. Hazelden also furnishes its titles to the bookstore trade directly, and has made inroads into the gift-distribution world.

Additional marketing avenues for Hazelden trade titles include the house's direct-to-the-consumer mail-order business. Hazelden books are popular items worldwide, with a foreign distribution network that includes Russia and Canada.

Other areas to which Hazelden markets include: structured care (Hazelden develops and markets print, audio, and visual materials for treatment centers, hospitals, and professional markets); prevention, education, and professional training (the publisher accesses the markets of primary and secondary schools, counselor-training programs, and community prevention and treatment programs); and corrections (the publisher addresses the needs of county, state, and federal corrections facilities).

Hazelden books and series are available to the trade via Hazelden, and through Harper San Francisco.

Query letters and SASEs should be directed to the Editorial Department or to:

Betty Christiansen, Associate Editor

HEBREW PUBLISHING COMPANY

P.O. Box 157
Rockaway Beach, NY 11693
718-945-3000

Hebrew Publishing Company (established in 1901) offers a wide range of titles in categories such as reference and dictionaries; religion, law, and thought; rabbinical literature; literature; history and biography; children's books; Hebrew language textbooks and Hebrew culture; Yiddish; Bible, Hebrew/English; Bible, English only; prayers and liturgy—daily, Hebrew only and Hebrew/English; prayers and liturgy—Sabbath, high holidays, and festivals; prayers and liturgy—memorial; prayers and liturgy—Purim; general prayers and liturgy; Hanukkah items; Haggadahs; educational materials; sermons and aids for the rabbi; and calendars. The house publishes a limited number of new titles and maintains an established backlist.

The HPC list includes *Rahel Varnhagen: The Life of a Jewess* by Hannah Arendt, *Encyclopedia of Jewish Concepts* by Philip Birnbaum, *Business Ethics in Jewish Law* (Jung/Levine), *Acharon Hamohikanim (The Last of the Mohicans)* by James Fenimore Cooper, and *Torah and Tradition* by Orenstein and Frankel.

Hebrew Publishing Company oversees its own distribution, utilizing services of independent fulfillment and distribution firms.

Query letters and SASEs should be directed to:

Charles Lieber, Editor in Chief

HEBREW UNION COLLEGE PRESS

3101 Clifton Avenue
Cincinnati, OH 45220
513-221-1875

Hebrew Union College Press (founded in 1921) publishes a select list of new titles covering a full range of scholarly Judaica, with frontlist titles of broader appeal. Within the HUC scope are books representing a variety of divisions, institutions, and programs, including Klau Library, Skirball Museum, *Kuntresim* (Hebrew texts copublished with Ben-Zion Dinur Center of the Hebrew University), the journals *Hebrew Union College Annual* and *American Jewish Archives*, and special-interest projects (such as books and videotapes) from HUC-UC Ethics Center. Hebrew Union College Press engages in copublishing projects with other institutions, including Harvard University Press, KTAV Publishing House, University of Alabama Press, and Yale University Press.

Representing the HUC Press list are *Karaite Separatism in Nineteenth-Century Russia* by Philip Miller, *Reason and Hope: Selections from the Jewish Writings of Hermann Cohen* (translated, edited, and with an introduction by Eva Jospe), *To Write the Lips of Sleepers: The Poetry of Amir Gilboa* by Warren Bargad, *The Merit of Our Mothers: A Bilingual Anthology of Jewish Women's Prayers* compiled by Tracy Guren Klirs, *Jewish Lore in Manichaean Cosmogony: Studies in the Book of Giants Traditions* by John C. Reeves, *The Jews of Dynastic China: A Critical Bibliography* by Michael Pollak, and *Tolerance and Transformation: Jewish Approaches to Religious Pluralism* by Sandra B. Lubarsky.

HUC welcomes the submission of scholarly manuscripts in all areas of Judaica. For further information, contact Professor Michael E. Meyer, Chair, Publications Committee, at the publisher's address.

Hebrew Union College Press is distributed by Behrman House.

Query letters and SASEs should be directed to:

Michael A. Meyer, Chair, Publications Committee

Barbara Selya, Managing Editor

HERALD PRESS

616 Walnut Avenue
Scottsdale, PA 15683
412-887-8500

Herald Press (established in 1908) is the trade division of the Mennonite Publishing House, the official publishing agency of the Mennonite Church. Areas of Herald Press publishing interest include the family, cookbooks, biography and personal experience, fiction, peace and social concerns, devotional works, Bible study, Bible and theology, church life and missions, Mennonite history and culture, songbooks, publications for younger readers, and non–English-language publications (primarily in Spanish).

Titles include *Enter the River: Healing Steps from White Privilege Toward Racial Understanding* by Jody Miller Shearer, *Global Gods: Exploring the Role of Religions in Modern Societies* by David W. Shenk, *Cherish the Earth: The Environment and Scripture* by Janice E. and Donald R. Kirk, *Sexual Abuse in Christian Homes and Churches* by Carolyn Holderread Heggen, *Extending the Table: A World Community*

Cookbook by Joetta Handrich Schlabach, *Called to Care: A Training Manual for Small Group Leaders* by Palmer Becker, and *Bioethics and the Beginning of Life: An Anabaptist Perspective* (edited by Roman Miller and Beryl Brubaker).

HERALD PRESS PUBLICATIONS FOR YOUNG READERS

Children's books from Herald Press include *Shadow at Sun Lake* by Esther Bender, *Let's Make a Garden* by Tamara Awad, *The Mystery of Sadler Marsh* by Kim D. Pritts (illustrations by Matthew Archambault), and the collage-illustrated creation story *And It Was Good* by Harold Horst Nofziger.

Series for an audience of teens and adults include the Bible-based historical novels by James R. Schott under the banner People of the Promise, Mary Christner Borntrager's contemporary stories published as the Ellie's People line, and Carrie Bender's continuing epistolary family romance/saga Miriam's Journal.

Writers may request editorial guidelines from the publisher—the pamphlet includes information on writing for journals of the Mennonite Publishing House.

Herald Press handles its own distribution, including trade fulfillment, direct mail, and its chain of Provident Bookstores.

Query letters and SASEs should be directed to:

Michael King, Editor

David Garber, Editor

HORIZON PUBLISHERS

50 South 500 West
P.O. Box 490
Bountiful, UT 84011
801-295-9451

Horizon Publishers (founded in 1971) is a smaller house that produces hardcover and paperback works emphasizing the areas of religion, inspiration, health foods, self-sufficient living, music, marriage and family, children's activities, cross-stitch and needlework design and instruction, and general youth and adult fiction and nonfiction.

Horizon is a privately owned corporation with no official ecclesiastical ties; the major readership of the house's theologically oriented books is Latter-Day Saint (Mormon), and religious works that Horizon issues are compatible with that basic doctrinal perspective. A wide range of Horizon's publishing interests are encompassed within that purview—from books on doctrine and church history to children's religious teaching stories to religious music. The Horizon list includes religious humor, faith-promoting experiences, historical works, biographies of well-known leaders, doctrinal studies, and religious fiction. Horizon also produces a line of inspirational and doctrinal cassette tapes.

The house's pamphlet detailing guidelines for authors is filled with apt advice for all writers.

Representative of the range of Horizon's list are *Amazing But True Mormon Stories* by Joan Oviatt, *How to Write Your Personal History* by Diane S. Crowther, *Journeys Beyond Life—True Accounts of Next-World Experiences* by Arvin S. Gibson, *Ancient American Indians—Their Origins, Civilizations & Old-World Connections* by Paul and Millie Chessman, *Mastering Management—Practical Procedures for Business Control* by A. Leslie Derbyshire, *New Age Menace—The Secret War against the Followers of Christ* by David N. Balmforth, *The Black Powder Plainsman—A Beginner's Guide to Muzzleloading and Reenactment on the Great Plains* by Randy Smith, *Stalking Trophy Mule Deer* by Walt Prothero, *Aliens and UFOs—Messengers or Deceivers?* by James L. Thompson, *Dutch Oven Secrets* by Lynn Hopkins, *The Desert Shall Blossom—A Comprehensive Guide to Vegetable Gardening in the Mountain West* by David E. Whiting, *Music Reading: Quick and Easy—A Singer's Guide* by Duane S. Crowther, and *Retiring First Class* by Clint Combs and Larry Bradshaw.

Fiction titles include *Cracked Wheat for Christmas* by Ted C. Hindmarsh, *Cody—a Novel That Motivates Towards Success* by David K. Draper, and *The Feather of the Owl* by Lee Dalton.

Family-oriented books include *Play With Me—Crafts for Preschoolers* by Barbara Miles, *God's Special Children—Helping the Handicapped Achieve* by Keith J. Karren and Sherril A. Hundley, and *It Makes Cents—The Family Thrift Book* by Vi Judge.

Horizon Publishers handles its own distribution.

Query letters and SASEs should be directed to:

Liza M. Baker, Editorial Assistant

HUMANICS LTD.
(See Directory of United States Publishers)

INNER TRADITIONS INTERNATIONAL

1 Park Street
Rochester, VT 05767
802-767-3174

Inner Traditions publishes in subject areas such as acupuncture, anthroposophy, aromatherapy, the arts, astrology, bodywork, cookbooks, crafts, cultural studies, Earth studies, Egyptian studies, gemstones, health and healing, homeopathy, indigenous cultures, African-American traditions, inner traditions of the West and the East, myth and legend, massage, natural medicine, self-transformation, sacred sexuality, spirituality, and travel.

Inner Traditions International (founded in 1975) produces hardcover trade books and trade paperbacks, illustrated gift books, and mass-market paperback editions, as well as a line of audioworks and selected videotapes. The house also packages specialty items such as boxed sets and tarot decks.

Special imprints include Destiny Books, Destiny Recordings, Healing Arts Press, and Park Street Press. Inner Traditions en Español is a line published in the Spanish language. Inner Traditions India issues works aimed at the Indian market. The house has announced a forthcoming slate of multimedia titles in the works. Inner Traditions International publishes a medium-sized list each year and maintains a strong backlist.

The Inner Traditions imprint accents works that represent the spiritual, cultural, and mythic traditions of the world, focusing on inner wisdom and the perennial philosophies.

Destiny Books are contemporary metaphysical titles for a popular audience with special emphasis on self-transformation, the occult, and psychological well-being. Destiny Recordings are cassettes and compact discs of spiritual and indigenous music traditions. Destiny Audio Editions include Inner Traditions books on tape as well as original spoken-word cassettes.

Healing Arts Press publishes works on alternative medicine and holistic health that combine contemporary thought and innovative research with the accumulated knowledge of the world's great healing traditions.

Park Street Press produces books on travel, psychology, consumer and environmental issues, archeology, women's and men's studies, and fine art.

Inner Traditions en Español is the house's Spanish-language publishing program, in cooperation with Lasser Press of Mexico City. This line includes popular titles from a variety of Inner Tradition imprints.

Inner Traditions India is a series comprising selections from the Inner Traditions International list, along with projects that arise in India; these works are produced in India for the Indian market.

Representative works from Inner Traditions: *Kava: Medicine Hunting in Paradise* by Chris Kilham, *Harmonic Experience: Tonal Harmony from its Natural Origins to Its Modern Expression* by W. A. Matthieu, *The Healing Bath: Using Essential Oil Therapy to Balance Body Energy* by Milli D. Austin, *The Mythic Imagination: The Quest for Meaning through Personal Mythology* by Stephen Larsen, *The Philosophy of Classical Yoga* by Georg Feuerstein, *The Mystery of the Grail: Initiation and Magic in the Quest for the Spirit* by Julius Evola, *Alternative Science: Challenging the Myths of the Scientific Establishment* by Richard Milton, *Secret Places of the Lion: Alien Influences on Earth's Destiny* by George Hunt Williamson, *Two Ravens: The Life and Teachings of a Spiritual Warrior* by Louis Two Ravens Irwin and Robert Liebert, and *Whole Food Facts: The Complete Reference Guide* by Evelyn Roehl.

Areas of topical interest are suggested by *People of the Earth: The New Pagans Speak Out* (edited by Ellen Evert Hopman and Lawrence Bond), *The Great Book of Hemp: The Complete Guide to the Commercial, Medicinal, and Psychotropic Uses of the World's Most Extraordinary Plant* by Robert A. Nelson, *Celebrating the Great Mother: A Handbook of Earth-Honoring Activities for Parents and Children* by Cait Johnson and Maura D. Shaw, *The Phallus: Sacred Symbol of Male Creative Power* by Alain Daniélou, *The Yoni: Symbol of the Universal Feminine* by Rufus C. Camphausen, and *Less Is More: The Art of Voluntary Poverty* (edited by Goldian VandenBroek). A literary slant is offered in *The Prophet of Campostela: Apprenticeship and Initiation into the Mysteries of the Cathedrals* (a novel) by Henri Vicenot

Kits and gift packages include *The Book of Doors Divination Deck* by Athon Veggi and Allison Davidson, *The Lakota Sioux Sweat Lodge Cards* by Chief Archie Fire

Lame Deer and Helene Sarks, and *Leela: The Game of Self-Knowledge* by Harish Johari.

Inner Traditions supervises its own distribution.

Query letters and SASEs should be directed to:

Rowan Jacobsen, Managing Editor

INTERVARSITY PRESS

5206 Main Street
Box 1400
Downers Grove, IL 60515
708-964-5700

InterVarsity Press publications embrace the main fields of Bible study guides, reference books, academic and theological books, popularly written and story-oriented books, and issues-oriented books of general interest to educated Christians. IVP produces lines for children and young adults in addition to its adult list.

Nonfiction categories in areas of contemporary religious interest include titles in self-improvement, spirituality, and interpersonal relations. IVP fiction focuses on fantasy and science fiction and includes titles in other popular mainstream categories (but no romance or historical novels). The house produces a solid list in humor.

InterVarsity Press (founded in 1954) is the publishing arm of InterVarsity Christian Fellowship of the USA. The press operates within IVCF's framework and publishes interdenominational books (in hardback and paperback) under the banner "for those who take their Christianity seriously."

Indicative of the InterVarsity Press nonfiction frontlist are *What on Earth Is the Church? An Exploration into New Testament Theology* by Kevin Giles, *Temptations Families Face* by Tom L. Eisenman, *The Battle of Beginnings: Why Neither Side Is Winning the Creation-Evolution Debate* by Del Ratzsch, *Woman of Influence: Ten Traits of Those Who Want to Make a Difference* by Pam Farrel, *When God Interrupts: Finding New Life through Unwanted Change* by M. Craig Barnes, *Politics for the People* by Bruce Barron, *Black Man's Religion* by Craig S. Keener and Glenn Usry, *Straight and Narrow? Compassion and Clarity in the Homosexuality Debate* by Thomas E. Schmidt, and *After Life: What the Bible Really Says* by Douglas Connelly.

On the InterVarsity fiction list are *A Time to Speak* by Linda Shands, *The Mystery of the Campus Crook* by John Bibee, and *Stolen Identity* (suspense) by Brian Regrut.

The Saltshaker Books imprint underscores its mission of meeting the needs of mind and heart by addressing contemporary nuances of women's life. LifeGuide Bible Studies introduces new titles that focus on particular scriptural areas and specific books of the Bible.

That the InterVarsity Press list is intended for those who take their Christianity seriously certainly applies to the IVP approach to humor: The house issues a notable line of cartoon books including *Attack of the Zit Monster & Other Teenage Terrors* by Randy Glasbergen, *Murphy's Laws of Marriage* by Steve Dennie and Rob Suggs, and

As the Church Turns by Ed Koehler. Charlene Ann Baumbich's *How to Eat Humble Pie & Not Get Indigestion* exhibits lively yet pointed writing on relationships.

A full set of guidelines for manuscript submission to InterVarsity Press is available on request from the publisher.

InterVarsity Press distributes its own list.

Query letters and SASEs should be directed to:

Andrew T. Le Peau, Editorial Director

JEWISH LIGHTS PUBLISHING

P.O. Box 237
Sunset Farm Offices—Route 4
Woodstock, VT 05091
802-457-4000

Jewish Lights Publishing (founded in 1990) shows a vigorous approach to titles relevant to Jewish tradition, theology, history, and contemporary culture, all within the trade motto "Words for the soul—made in Vermont." Jewish Lights offers books in hardcover, quality paperback, and gift editions.

The house's principal goal is to stimulate thought and help all people learn about who the Jewish people are, where they come from, and what the future may hold. People of the diverse Jewish heritage are the publisher's primary audience; however, Jewish Lights books are directed to people of all faiths and all backgrounds, with the aim that they engage, educate, and spiritually inspire their audience from the touchstone traditions of Jewish wisdom.

Jewish Lights features authors at the forefront of spiritual thought. Each voice is unique, and each speaks in a way readers can hear. Jewish Lights books are judged as successful not only by whether they are beautiful and commercially successful, but also by the difference they make in their readers' lives.

Jewish Lights titles include *God & the Big Bang: Discovering Harmony between Science & Spirituality* by Daniel C. Matt, *How to Be a Perfect Stranger: A Guide to Etiquette in Other People's Religious Ceremonies* (edited by Arthur J. Magida), *Godwrestling—Round 2: Ancient Wisdom, Future Paths* by Arthur Waskow, *Invisible Lines of Connection: Sacred Stories of the Ordinary* by Lawrence Kushner, *Self, Struggle and Change—Family Conflict Stories in Genesis and Their Healing Insights in Our Lives* by Norman J. Cohen, *Being God's Partner: How to Find the Hidden Link between Spirituality and Your Work* by Jeffrey K. Salkin (introduction by Norman Lear), *Healing of Soul, Healing of Body* (edited by Simkha Weintraub), *But God Remembered* by Sandy Eisenberg Sasso, and *Lifecycles: Jewish Women on Life Passages and Personal Milestones* by Debra Orenstein.

The press publishes the award-winning Kushner Series: Classics of Modern Jewish Spirituality by Lawrence Kushner. A related special-edition project is *The Book of Letters: A Mystical Hebrew Alphabet* (designed by Lawrence Kushner).

The Jewish Lights program for children and family includes *In God's Name* by Sandy Eisenberg Sasso (illustrations by Phoebe Stone), *When a Grandparent Dies: A Child's Own Workbook for Dealing with Shiva and the Year Beyond* by Nechama Liss-Levenson, and *The New Jewish Baby Book: A Guide to Choices for Today's Families* by Anita Diamant.

Jewish Lights Publishing handles its own distribution.

Query letters and SASEs should be directed to:

Stuart M. Matlins, Editor

THE JEWISH PUBLICATION SOCIETY

1930 Chestnut Street
Philadelphia, PA 19103
215-564-5925

The Jewish Publication Society specializes in hardcover and trade paperback books of Jewish interest as well as works of general interest in the areas of history and culture, religious thought, graphically lavish gift and art books, and literature that includes historical as well as contemporary fiction and poetry. JPS publishes editions of traditional religious works (including the Torah) as well as relevant commentaries; the house also produces children's books for readers from preschool to young adult.

The Jewish Publication Society (founded in 1888) upholds a commitment to the English-speaking Jewish community by publishing works of exceptional scholarship, contemporary significance, and enduring value. The publisher traditionally assumes a demanding balancing act among the various denominations of Jewish institutional life, between academic and popular interests, between past and present visions of Judaism.

On the JPS nonfiction list are *Preparing Your Heart for the Holy Days: A Guided Journal* by Kerry M. Olitzky and Rachel T. Sabath, *The View from Jacob's Ladder: One Hundred Midrashim* by David Curzon, *In the Year 1096: The First Crusade and the Jews* by Robert Chazen, *Coat of Many Cultures: The Joseph Story in Spanish Literature, 1200–1492* by Michael McGaha, *Reclaiming the Dead Sea Scrolls* by Lawrence Schiffman, *From Jerusalem to the Edge of Heaven: Meditations on the Soul of Israel* by Ari Elon, *On the Possibility of Jewish Mysticism in Our Time* by Gershom Scholem, *On Family and Feminism* by Blu Greenberg, *Jewish Law* by Menahem Elon, *Swimming Lessons in the Sea of Talmud* by Gershon Schwartz and Michael Katz, and *Blessings* (a prayer book) by Melanie Greenberg.

Works in the field of literature and the arts include *Genesis: The Beginning of Desire* by Avivah Gottlieb Zornberg, *Emma Lazarus in Her World: Life and Letters* by Bette Roth Young, *Shaking Eve's Tree: Short Stories of Jewish Women* (edited by Sharon Niederman), *Look to the Hills* (historical fiction of the American West) by Hazel Krantz, *The Blessing and the Curse* (a contemporary novel) by Linda Bayer, *Ruby of Cochin: An Indian Jewish Woman Remembers* by Ruby Daniel and Barbara Johnson, and the illustrated work *A Jewish Bestiary: A Book of Fabulous Creatures Drawn from Hebraic Legend and Lore* by Marc Podwall.

The Jewish Publication Society is a not-for-profit educational institution that distributes its own list and, through its book club, offers to its membership Judaica from other publishers as well.

THE JEWISH PUBLICATION SOCIETY CHILDREN'S BOOKS

The dynamic children's books branch of the Jewish Publication Society develops projects in four categories: preschool, primary, middle readers, and young adults. The kids' list encompasses picture books, storybooks, biographies, general nonfiction, and works with specific religious or cultural themes.

Sample titles: *David and Max* by Gary Provost and Gail Levine-Provost; *The Great Jewish Quiz Book* by Barbara Spector; and a set of titles by Melanie Hope Greenberg: *Celebrations: Our Jewish Holidays* and *Blessings: Our Jewish Ceremonies*.

For readers of all ages, JPS offers *We Are Children Just the Same: Vedem, the Secret Magazine by the Boys of Terezin* (edited by Paul Wilson), a collection of excerpts from *Vedem*, a clandestine journal produced by youths imprisoned at Theresienstadt during the Holocaust.

Query letters and SASEs should be directed to:

Dr. Ellen Frankel, Editor in Chief

Bruce Black, Editor, Children's Books

KAR-BEN COPIES

6800 Tildenwood Lane
Rockville, MD 20852
301-984-8733

Kar-Ben Copies (founded in 1976) offers a growing Jewish library for young children (and the family, in addition to teachers). The house's list encompasses presentations keyed to high holidays, Sabbath, culture and tradition, and general-interest concepts. Kar-Ben's children's books are handsomely produced volumes that often incorporate fine illustrative work. The Kar-Ben catalog also highlights books especially for toddlers, as well as a reference line for youngsters (My Very Own Jewish Library). The house also offers audiocassettes and calendars.

Representing the Kar-Ben list are *Jeremy's Dreidel* by Ellie Gellman (illustrated by Judith Friedman); *Sammy Spider's First Passover* by Sylvia Rouss; *Thank You, God* by Judith Groner and Madeleine Wikler; *Only Nine Chairs* by Debby Miller and Karen Ostrove; *Jewish Holiday Crafts for Little Hands* by Ruth Esrig Brinn; and *Tell Me a Mitzvah—Little and Big Ways to Repair the World* by poet, philosopher, and activist Danny Siegel.

A special Kar-Ben release is a group of book-and-cassette packages, with accompanying leader's guides for family services keyed to the high holidays (Selichot, Rosh Hashanah, and Yom Kippur), written by Judith Z. Abrams, designed and illustrated by Katherine Janus Kahn, with original music by Frances T. Goldman.

Kar-Ben welcomes comments, kudos, and manuscripts.

Kar-Ben has its own expanded order-fulfillment facility; many Kar-Ben titles are also available through Baker & Taylor as well as other trade-book distributors.

Query letters and SASEs should be directed to:

Madeleine Wikler, Editor in Chief

H. J. Kramer, Inc.

P.O. Box 1082
Tiburon, CA 94920
415-435-5367

Kramer's publishing emphasis is in the areas of spiritual life, interpersonal relationships, resources for good health, and self-awareness and guidance. The Starseed Press imprint publishes books for younger readers (see subentry below). Kramer books are finely produced editions in trade paperback and hardcover. The house typically issues a small number of new titles seasonally and sustains a strong backlist.

H. J. Kramer, Inc. (founded in 1984 by Hal and Linda Kramer) holds a commitment to publish books that touch the heart, open the spirit, and accentuate the view that who we are makes a difference—that personal choices change the world. Kramer books, old and new, are intended to support the reader's personal vision. A number of Kramer books sell exceedingly well in the mainstream market and garner translation rights worldwide as well as domestic book club sales.

Featured on the Kramer list: *Into a Timeless Realm: A Metaphysical Adventure* (the final volume in the Worlds Beyond Quartet) by Michael J. Roads, *Tara's Angels: One Family's Extraordinary Journey of Courage and Healing* by Kirk Moore, and *The Laws of Spirit: Simple, Powerful Truths for Making Life Work* by Dan Millman.

Backlist favorites include *Creating with the Angels: An Angel-Guided Journey into Creativity* by Terry Lynn Taylor, *Son-Rise The Miracle Continues* by Barry Neil Kaufman, *The Blue Dolphin* (a parable) by Robert Barnes, *Creating Money: Keys to Abundance* by Sanaya Roman and Duane Packer, *The Complete Guide to Aromatherapy: Self-Help with Essential Oils* by Erich Keller, and Christopher Bird's investigative foray *The Persecution and Trial of Gaston Naessens: The True Story of the Efforts to Suppress an Alternative Treatment for Cancer, AIDS, and Other Immunologically Based Diseases.*

A Kramer hallmark is Dan Millman's renowned set of writings (including *Way of the Peaceful Warrior*) that, in addition to audiocassette rendering, has now branched into a children's series. Kramer has also published a number of works on José Silva's mind-control method.

Starseed Press

Starseed Press children's books from H. J. Kramer are illustrated works slated for trade as well as educational markets. Starseed books embody the principles of education through the power of story and incorporate myths, legends, fables, fairy tales, folklore, and original author visions into volumes of contemporary appeal. Starseed's lineup encompasses award-winning picture books that build self-esteem, inspire nonviolence, and encourage positive values.

Titles include *Dragon Soup* by Arlene Williams (illustrated by Sally J. Smith), *Today I Am Lovable: 365 Positive Activities for Kids* by Diane Loomans, *By Day and By Night* by Karen Pandell (illustrated by Marty Noble), and *Grandfather Four Winds and Rising Moon* by Michael Chanin (illustrated by Sally J. Smith).

Backlist benchmarks include *Secret of the Peaceful Warrior* (in the Peaceful Warrior children's series) by Dan Millman (illustrated by T. Taylor Bruce), *The Lovables in the Kingdom of Self-Esteem* by Diane Loomans (illustrated by Kim Howard), and *The Land of the Blue Flower* by Frances Hodgson Burnett (author of *The Secret Garden* and *The Little Princess*) in an edition illustrated by Judith Ann Griffith.

H. J. Kramer's list is distributed to the trade by Publishers Group West, Bookpeople, New Leaf Distributing Company, and Inland Book Company.

Prospective authors please note: Kramer's list is selective and is, generally speaking, fully slated several publishing seasons in advance. Kramer and Starseed are thus essentially closed to unsolicited submissions.

Query letters and SASEs should be directed to:

Hal Kramer, President

Jan Phillips, Acquisitions Editor

KTAV PUBLISHING HOUSE INC.

P.O. Box 6249
900 Jefferson Street
Hoboken, NJ 07030
201-963-9524

KTAV Publishing House (founded in 1924) features books of Jewish interest, including scholarly Judaica, sermonica, textbooks, and books for a younger readership. KTAV also markets religious educational materials (including books), as well as gifts and decorative items. Many KTAV titles in the scholarly vein relate the history of Jewish thought and culture within the context of broader issues—some of global scope—and are of appeal to the interested general reader.

KTAV's catalog embraces the categories of Judaica, Biblica, Torah study, Jewish law, contemporary Halachic thought, sermonica, Jewish history, Jewish thought, contemporary Jewry, and Torah and science.

Titles from KTAV include *God and Evil: A Jewish Perspective* by David Birnbaum, *Orthodoxy Confronts Modernity* (edited by Jonathan Sacks), *In the Beginning: Biblical Creation and Science* by Nathan Aviezer, *The Path of the Righteous: Gentile Rescuers of Jews During the Holocaust* by Moredecai Paldiel, *From Text to Tradition: A History of Second Temple and Rabbinic Judaism* by Lawrence H. Schiffman, *Voices in Exile: A Study in Sephardic Intellectual History* by Marc D. Angel, and *Modern Medicine and Jewish Ethics* (in a revised and augmented edition) by Fred Rosner.

Diverse historical and cultural perspectives are presented in titles such as *Roots and Boots: From Crypto-Jew in New Spain to Community Leader in the American Southwest* by Floyd S. Fierman, *Ordained to Be a Jew: A Catholic Priest's Conversion to Judaism* by John David Scalamonti, and *The Jewish Woman in Time and Torah* by Eliezar Berkovits.

KTAV distributes its own list; in addition, the house distributes the books of Yeshiva University Press.

Query letters and SASEs should be directed to:

Bernard Scharfstein, President

LIGUORI PUBLICATIONS
TRIUMPH BOOKS

One Liguori Drive
Liguori, MO 63057
314-464-2500

New York area office:
333 Glen Head Road
Old Brookville, NY 11545
516-759-7402

Liguori Publications and its trade imprint Triumph Books represents a twofold approach to religious publishing. Liguori initiated its book program in 1968 and met with immediate success with *Good Old Plastic Jesus* by Earnest Larsen and *Keeping Your Balance in the Modern Church* by Hugh O'Connell. Liguori (run by Redemptionist priests) produces books and pamphlets focused on the needs of Catholic parishes and specialized religious bookstore markets, and publishes *Liguorian* magazine. Triumph Books publishes for the mainstream religious-trade-book market. Under the rubric of Liguori Faithware, the publisher supplies computer resources for Catholics.

Though Liguori is assuredly a business, it is primarily a ministry. Through its publications—in print and through electronic media—Liguori is able to reach people in ways that are not available in ordinary day-to-day ministry. Authors interested in Liguori or Triumph may request from the publisher a brochure covering submissions guidelines.

Highlights from Liguori include *Mother Teresa: In My Own Words* by Mother Teresa, *The Healing Power of Prayer* by Bridget Mary Meehan, and *The Courage to Choose: Change Your Attitude, Change Your Life* by Marilyn Gustin.

Also indicative of the Liguori program are *Dangerous Prayer: Being Vulnerable to God* by William J. O'Malley, *Morning Star: Christ's Mother and Ours* by Oscar Lukefahr, *Self-Esteem: Key to Happiness* by Russell M. Abata, *Family Planning: A Guide for Exploring the Issues* by Charles and Elizabeth Balsam, and *Sex and the Christian Teen* by Jim Auer.

Liguori's 1994 edition of *Catechism of the Catholic Church* (along with the Spanish-language *Catecismo de la Iglesia Católica*) rose to the coveted rank of number-one best-seller in the religious-books list.

From Liguori Faithware comes *How to Survive Being Married to a Catholic* (an interactive CD-ROM/book combination).

Liguori Publications promotes and markets through vehicles such as catalog mailings and listings in *Liguorian* magazine, circulates bookstore and parish newsletters, and utilizes fliers and self-mailers.

TRIUMPH BOOKS

Triumph Books emphasizes an ecumenical perspective in the religious trade market. Triumph reaches a wide readership through books in a variety of areas including psychology, spirituality, inspiration, awareness, theology, and Christian living.

Triumph Books asserts that social and cultural developments impact readers' values and religious faith. The house's publishing program, reflecting this vision, accents topics of contemporary controversy and debate. Triumph was formerly part of Gleneida Publishing Group.

On the Triumph list: *The Confession of Saint Patrick* (edited and translated by D. R. Howlett), *Being Priest to One Another* by Michael Dwinell, *To Hell and Back with Dante: A Modern Reader's Guide to the Divine Comedy* by Joseph Gallagher, *Toward God: The Ancient Wisdom of Western Prayer* and *Sacred Reading: The Ancient Art of Lectio Divina* (both titles by Michael Casey), *Sean's Legacy: An AIDS Awakening–A Father Remembers His Only Son* by Robert Hopkins, *Overcoming Depressive Living Syndrome: How to Enjoy Life, Not Just Endure It* by Earnie Larsen with Cara A. Macken, and *Celibacy: A Way of Living, Loving, and Serving* by A. W. Richard Sipe.

The house has inaugurated the Women's Wisdom series. Among the entrants: *In a High Spiritual Season* by Joan Chittister, *Beauty at Dawn: Notes to My Sisters* by Paula Bendry Larsen, and *"Gammaw . . . Gammaw . . ." Thunder in an Infant's Voice* by Paula Bendry Larsen.

Triumph offers a line of titles from the world-renowned guru J. P. Vaswani, including *The Way of Abhyasa: Meditation in Practice* and *The Good You Do Returns: A Book of Wisdom Stories*. A noteworthy Triumph edition is the popularly oriented classic, *Peace of Soul* by Fulton J. Sheen.

Query letters and SASEs should be directed to:

Rev. Robert Pagliari, Editor in Chief, Book and Pamphlet Department (Liguori, MO)

Kass Dotterweich, Managing Editor, Triumph Books (Liguori, MO)

(Ms.) Pat Kossmann, Executive Editor (Old Brookville, NY)

Joan Marlow Golan, Administrative Editor (Old Brookville, NY)

LLEWELLYN PUBLICATIONS

P.O. Box 64383
St. Paul, MN 55164
612-291-1970

Llewellyn Publications (established in 1897) is a venerable house with a historical emphasis on the practical aspects of what today is termed New Age science—how it works and how to practice it. Traditional areas of Llewellyn publishing concentration include astrology, magick, the occult, self-improvement, self-development, spiritual science, alternative technologies, nature religions and lifestyles, spiritist and mystery religions, divination, phenomena, and tantra. These works are brought out under the lustrous Llewellyn logo: a crescent moon. Llewellyn's trade motto is "new worlds of mind and spirit," indicating the publisher's openness to explore new territory.

Llewellyn catalogs a full stock of new seasonal releases along with a prolific backlist in hardcover, trade paper, and mass-market editions. Llewellyn also issues tarot decks and divination kits. The house's expanded program includes Spanish-language trade paperbacks.

Representing the Llewellyn list: *A Kitchen Witch's Cookbook* by Patricia Telesco, *Sexuality in the Horoscope* (edited by Noel Tyl), *The Sabbats: A New Approach to Living the Old Ways* by Edain McCoy, *How to Develop and Use Psychometry* by Ted Andrews, *Hawaiian Religion and Magic* by Scott Cunningham, *The Healing Earth Tarot* by Jyotie McKie and David McKie, *The Tarot of the Orishas* (created by Zolrak; illustrated by Durkon), *Secrets of a Natural Menopause* by Edna Copeland Ryneveld, *Dancing with Dragons: Invoke Their Ancient Wisdom and Power* by D. J. Conway, *The Handbook of Celtic Astrology: The 13-Sign Lunar Zodiac of the Ancient Druids* by Helena Paterson, *Faery Wicca* by Kisma K. Stepanich, *The Grail Castle: Male Myths and Mysteries in the Celtic Tradition* by Kenneth Johnson and Marguerite Elsbeth, *The Once Unknown Familiar: Shamanic Paths to Unleash Your Animal Powers* by Timothy Roderick, *Egyptian Magick: Enter the Body of Light & Travel the Magickal Universe* by Betty Schueler, and *Holistic Aromatherapy: Balance the Body and Soul with Essential Oils* by Ann Berwick.

Llewellyn is currently exploring the fiction market with titles such as *Walker between the Worlds*, a spiritually based thriller by Diana DesRochers published in mass-market paperback. Additional fiction includes *The Rag Bone Man* by Charlotte Lawrence and *The Celtic Heart* by Kathryn Marie Cocquyt.

Llewellyn is a specialty house and looks for projects (books and audiotapes, as well as videos and computer software) that will have extended sales viability. Llewellyn is not geared toward academic or scholarly publishing and its products are aimed at general audiences without specialist knowledge or training. Authors may request writers' guidelines from the house, which contain valuable tips generally applicable to structuring and proposing publishing projects.

An aggressive marketer and promoter, Llewellyn publications and authors are given full house support, including arranging author interviews and appropriate advertising and subsidiary rights—often incorporated into the schedule is placement in Llewellyn's magazines (*New Times*) and primarily promotional venues (*New Worlds*). Llewellyn's marketing network encompasses distributional arrangements worldwide.

Query letters and SASEs should be directed to:

Nancy Mostad, Acquisitions Manager

LOTUS LIGHT PUBLICATIONS

P.O. Box 325
Twin Lakes, WI 53181
414-889-8561
800-824-6396

Lotus Light Publications (founded in 1981) is a division of Lotus Brands, Inc. Lotus Light produces works in the fields of health, yoga, and Native American and New Age metaphysics. In addition to books, Lotus Light produces video and audio materials, as well as incense and other related sideline materials such as essential oils, body-care products, charts, artwork, jewelry, chimes, and crystals.

From the Lotus Light list: *Aromatherapy: To Heal and Tend the Body* by Robert Tisserand, *Ayurvedic Cooking for Westerners* by Amadea Morningstar, *New Eden: For People, Animals, Nature* by Michael W. Fox (illustrated by Susan Seddon Boulet), *Spirit Stones* by Douglas Brodoff, *Rainforest Remedies: One Hundred Healing Herbs of Belize* by Rosita Arvigo and Michael Balick, *Stargazer: A Native American Inquiry into Extraterrestrial Phenomena* by Gerald Hausman, *Abundance through Reiki: Universal Life Force Energy As Expression of the Truth That You Are—The 42-Day Program to Absolute Fulfillment* by Paula Horan, *Secrets of Precious Stones* by Ursula Klinger Raatz, *Bhagavad Gita and Its Message* by Sri Aurobindo, and *Cosmo-Biological Birth Control* by Shalila Sharamon and Bodo Baginski.

Lotus Light Publications distributes primarily through special product outlets such as health-food stores and spiritual-interest booksellers.

Query letters and SASEs should be directed to:

Niran Kar

LURAMEDIA, INC.

7060 Miramar Road, Suite 104
San Diego, CA 92121
619-578-1948

LuraMedia editorial interest encompasses self-discovery, relationships, cooking and nutrition, parenting and child development, writing and journaling, healing and inspiration, transition and renewal, Bible study, and meditation. LuraMedia (founded in 1982) is a small house that operates as a creative publishing forum to select, design, produce, and distribute books, tapes, and journaling programs that feature the areas of personal growth with spiritual and feminine dimensions. The publisher's goal is to provide materials that foster healing and hope, balance and justice.

Emblematic of the LuraMedia list: *Raising Peaceful Children in a Violent World* by Nancy Lee Cecil with Patricia L. Roberts, *Rattling Those Dry Bones: Women Changing the Church* (edited by June Steffensen Hagen), *Keeper of the Night: A Portrait of Life in the Shadow of Death* by Lee Modjeska, *Nobody Owns Me: A Celibate Woman*

Discovers Her Sexual Power by Francis B. Rothluebber, *Feeding the Whole Family: Down-to-Earth Cookbook and Whole Foods Guide* by Cynthia Lair, *Seven Times the Sun: Guiding Your Child through the Rhythms of the Day* by Shea Darian, and *Guerrillas of Grace: Prayers for the Battle* by Ted Loder (drawings by Ed Kerns).

A Weaving of Wonder is a special project that includes *Fables to Summon Inner Wisdom* by Charlotte Rogers Brown and *Integration Reflections* by Karolyn Smith Rogers in a single volume that demonstrates the how-to and how-it-was-done aspects of self-discovery through writing.

LuraMedia handles its own distribution; its books are available through a variety of regional and national fulfillment services.

Query letters and SASEs should be directed to:

Lura Jane Geiger, Publisher

MESORAH PUBLICATIONS

4401 Second Avenue
Brooklyn, NY 11232
718-921-9000

Mesorah Publications (founded in 1976) publishes hardcover and paperback editions within a wide-ranging program that includes works of contemporary cultural and popular interest in addition to traditional Judaica, Bible study, liturgical materials, history, and juveniles. Mesorah also produces series on audiocassette. The Art Scroll Library series is produced with special attention to design and production.

Highlights of the general-interest side of Mesorah's catalog include *It's About Time: The Guide to Successful Jewish Homemaking* by Chaya Levine and Nechamah Berg, *Self Improvement?—I'm Jewish!* by Abraham J. Twerski, *On Judaism—Conversations on Being Jewish in Today's World* by Emanuel Feldman, *Fingerprints on the Universe—Searching for Belief and Meaning in Today's Turbulent World* by Louis Pollack, and *The Complete Service for the Period of Bereavement* by J. J. Schacter and David Weinberger.

Mesorah's stalwart backlist includes popular titles such as Raphael Sackville's swashbuckling historical novel *Prince of Akko, Herald of Destiny: The Story of the Jews in the Medieval Era, 750–1650* by Berel Wein (in deluxe hardcover coffee-table format), and *Lieutenant Birnbaum: A Soldier's Story* by storyteller Meir Birnbaum with Yonason Rosenblum.

Liturgical works include *The Stone Edition of the Chumash* and *The Art Scroll Siddur.*

Mesorah children's books include *Say It with Zest* by Mindy Shapiro, *My Book: A Comprehensive Family Album for the Jewish Child* (designed by Yaffa Ganz; illustrated by Liat Benyamini Ariel), and *Dovy and the Surprise Guests* by Goldie Goldin (illustrated by Linda Snowden).

Mesorah Publications distributes its own list as well as selections from other houses such as Orthodox Union/NCSY and Shaar Press.

Query letters and SASEs should be directed to:

Abraham Biderman, Acquisitions Editor

MOODY PRESS

820 North La Salle Drive
Chicago, IL 60610
312-329-2101

In addition to general-interest titles with a religious inclination (Bible-based inter-denominational), Moody produces a medium-to-large list that includes Bibles, books for children and youths, novels, biographies, educational resources, and works for religious professionals. Moody's books are issued in clothbound editions, trade paper, and mass-market paperback. Moody also catalogs computer software, audiotapes, and videocassettes. Moody Press (founded in 1894) serves as the publishing ministry of Moody Bible Institute.

Moody produces a number of well-targeted and successful lines that encompass the spectrum of the house's publishing interests. This portion of the Moody program offers series such as Men of Integrity, Moody Acorns, Golden Oldies, Healing for the Heart, Quiet Time Books for Women, and Salt & Light Pocket Guides.

Highlights from Moody: *How You Can Be Sure That You Will Spend Eternity with God* by Erwin Lutzer, *Love for All Seasons: Eight Ways to Nurture Intimacy* by John Trent, *Made for His Pleasure: Ten Benchmarks for a Vital Faith* by Alistair Begg, *The Way to God* by Dwight L. Moody, *Breaking Down Walls: A Model for Reconciliation in an Age of Racial Strife* by Raleigh Washington and Glen Keherein, *Purity and Passion: Authentic Male Sexuality* by Rick Ghent and Jim Childerston, *The Adversary: The Christian versus Demon Activity* by Mark I. Bubeck, and *Sound Mind Investing: A Step-by-Step Guide to Financial Stability and Growth* by Austin Pryor.

Fiction from Moody includes *The Fields of Bannockburn: A Novel of Christian Scotland from Its Origins to Independence* by Donna Fletcher Crow, *The Hofburg Treasures* (high-tech espionage) by Stephen P. Adams, *The Lambda Conspiracy* by Spenser Hughes, *Final Thunder* by Janice Miller, *Port Royal* (in the Buccaneers series) by Linda Chaikin, and Sandy Dengler's Jack Prester mystery series.

Larry Burkett Products is a line of books and tapes accenting the social/financial sphere. Titles here include *Women Leaving the Workplace, The Coming Economic Earthquake, Debt-Free Living: How to Get Out of Debt (and Stay Out),* and *Using Your Money Wisely: Biblical Principles Under Scrutiny.*

MOODY CHILDREN & YOUTH

Moody produces a variety of publications geared toward a younger readership, including picture books, biographies, Bible stories, read-aloud volumes, and gift editions. In the Moody Children & Youth lineup are *The Bible in Pictures for Little Eyes* by Kenneth N. Taylor, *When I'm a Mommy* by Ginger Adair Fulton, *The Soldier Boy's Discovery* (in the Bonnets and Bugles series) by Gilbert Morris, *Sex: It's Worth Waiting For* by Greg Speck, and *Winners and Losers: Quiet Times Between Teens and God* by Stephen Bly and Janet Bly.

Moody Children & Youth series include Children's Bible Basics (authored by Carolyn Nystrom), Dallas O'Neil and the Baker Street Sports Club (by Jerry B. Jenkins), Patricia St. John Books (inspirational novels), and Sensitive Issues Books (by Carole Gift Page).

Query letters and SASEs should be directed to:

Jim Bell, Editorial Director

MOORINGS

As of spring 1996, Random House/Ballantine ceased publishing under the Moorings imprint.

MULTNOMAH PRESS

(see Questar Publishers)

THOMAS NELSON

Nelson Place at Elm Hill Pike
P.O. Box 141000
Nashville, TN 37214
615-889-9000

Thomas Nelson (founded in 1961) produces Christian trade books in hardcover and trade paperback in the areas of health, inspiration, self-help, psychology, family concerns, parenting, contemporary issues and interest, and healing and recovery. Nelson also issues a line of titles for young readers. The house offers a strong, select list of adult and young-adult fiction. Thomas Nelson produces magazines and journals and is among the largest publishers of Bibles and Scripture commentaries in the United States. Oliver-Nelson is a trade-oriented imprint.

Already among the major players in the religious-publishing arena, Nelson enjoys its current phase of corporate exuberance. The house bought Here's Life Publishers from Campus Crusade for Christ and expanded their evangelism and discipleship markets. Nelson addresses the growing Spanish Christian readership in the United States and abroad through their Editorial Caribe and Editorial Betania divisions (both acquired in 1994). Thomas Nelson also owns the editorially independent Word Publishing (see separate main entry in this directory).

Indicative of the Nelson list are *Champions Again! An Inside Look at UCLA and the 1994–95 NCAA Championship Season* by Keith Erickson (foreword by John Wooden), *When Life Doesn't Turn Out Like You Planned* by Bill Butterworth, *The Glorious Journey: Insight, Encouragement, and Guidance for Your Walk of Faith* by Charles Stanley, *Dear Mom: If I Could Tell You Anything* by Robin Webster and Doug Webster, *Challenging the Status Quo: From City Hall to Congress* by Congresswoman Sue Myrick with Sandy Dengler, *Tee-ology: 18 Inspirational Lessons for Golfers* by John Freeman, and *A Touch of Georgia: Where to Go and What to Do in the Peach State* (a Region by Region Guide).

Fiction includes historical and contemporary novels, as well as futurist thrillers. Among them: *The Legend of Storey County* by Brock Thorne, *The Fourth Millennium* by Paul Meier and Robert L. Wise, *Sharon's Hope* by Neva Cole, *It Happened at the Sunset Grille* by Will Cunningham, *The Hope of Herrick House* by Carole Gift Page, *Mortal Intent* by Bob Massie, and *The Price of Love* by Christine S. Drake.

A lead Nelson publishing project is the production of a series of family-oriented works from Carolyn Coats and Pamela Smith; titles here include *Things Your Mother Told You But You Didn't Want to Hear*, *Things Your Dad Always Told You But You Didn't Want to Hear*, and *My Grandmother Always Said That*.

Nelson children's titles include *Dr. Shivers Carnival of Terror* (in the Spine Chillers series) by Fred E. Katz, *God Loves You* (a pop-up book) by Vlasta Van Kempen, and the Itty Bitty Books line.

Thomas Nelson handles its own distribution.

Query letters and SASEs should be sent to:

Rick Nash, Acquisitions Editor

NEWCASTLE PUBLISHING COMPANY

13419 Saticoy Street
North Hollywood, CA 91605
213-873-3191

Newcastle Publishing Company (established in 1970) purveys paperback originals and reprints (cataloged under the banner "quality books for the discerning reader") in a broad range of areas that include art therapy and journaling; self-help and psychology; health and nutrition; personal transformation and spirituality; numerology; palmistry; handwriting analysis; tarot books and decks; Celtic lore; mythology; education and child rearing; how-to books for senior citizens and older adults; as well as selected general-interest occult nonfiction. Imprints include Forgotten Fantasy Library, the Living Well Collection, the Newcastle Tarot Library, and Greenbrier Books.

Indicative of the Newcastle list are *Living the Wheel: Working with Emotion, Terror, and Bliss Through Imagery* by Annabelle Nelson, *Foot Analysis: The Foot Path to Self-*

Discovery by Avi Grinberg, *Lambda Gray: A Practical, Emotional, and Spiritual Guide for Gays and Lesbians Who Are Growing Old* (conceived and compiled by Karen Westerberg Reyes), *Love Styles: How to Celebrate Your Differences* by Tina B. Tessina, *The Magic and Mysteries of Mexico: The Arcane Secrets and Occult Lore of the Ancient Mexicans and Maya* by Lewis Spence (a Newcastle Classic), *The Essence of Magic: Tarot, Ritual, and Aromatherapy* by Mary K. Greer, *Expressions of Healing: Embracing the Process of Grief—A Compassionate Workbook* by Sandra Graves, *Roll Away the Stone: An Introduction to Aleister Crowley's Essays on the Psychology of Hashish* by Israel Regardie (including the complete text of Aleister Crowley's *The Herb Dangerous*), and *Schemes and Scams: A Practical Guide for Outwitting Today's Con Artist for the 50+ Consumer* by Douglas P. Shadel and the pseudonymous former con artist John T.

Newcastle Publishing Company is distributed by Borgo Press.

Query letters and SASEs should be directed to:

Al Saunders, President and Publisher

Gina Gross, Editor

NEW LEAF PRESS

P.O. Box 726
Green Forest, AR 72638
501-438-5288

Areas of New Leaf interest include Christian living, ethics, prophecy and eschatology, biography, theology, applied Christianity, history, Bible study, family/home/marriage, friendship and love, education, evangelism, devotional works (including daily readings), humor, and fiction. The house has a solid backlist.

New Leaf Press (founded in 1975) publishes primarily for the Christian religious market, with some trade-religious crossover titles. New Leaf produces in hardcover and paperback (trade paper and mass-market); many New Leaf books are priced economically.

Characteristic titles from New Leaf: *Parenting: What's It All About?* by David and Elizabeth Heller, *Lessons from the Gridiron: Inspirational Stories from the Gridiron for Young and Old Alike* by Rita McKenzie Fisher, *Vital Signs of Christ's Return: The 77 Most-Asked Questions of Christ's Return* by Ray W. Yerbury, *Quit Playing with Fire: It's Time to Get Serious about the Issues Facing Teens Today* by Ron Luce, *Moments for Sisters: Unforgettable Memories from the Bonds of Love* by Robert Strand, *The Shepherd's Man* (fiction) by David F. Gray, *Church Chuckles* (humor) by Dick Hafer, and *Life After Lucy: The True Story of* I Love Lucy's *Little Ricky* by Keith Thibodeaux with Audrey T. Hingley.

New Leaf titles for younger readers include *Columbus and Cortez, Conquerors for Christ* by John Eidsmoe.

New Leaf Press distributes its own list; New Leaf also provides distribution services for other publishers with related market outlooks.

Query letters and SASEs should be directed to:

Jim Fletcher, Editor

NORTH ATLANTIC BOOKS/FROG, LTD.

P.O. Box 12327
Berkeley, CA 94701
510-644-2116

North Atlantic and Frog share areas of publishing scope, embracing topics such as holistic health, herbalism, homeopathy, psychology, internal martial arts (particularly t'ai chi ch'uan and aikido), sports, somatics and bodywork, anthropology and shamanism, food and cooking, studies of the Martian enigmas, Western occult, Buddhism, and Eastern thought. Areas of recent concentration include political and social commentaries on spiritual and ecological issues. Works are generally in the nonfiction arena, with selected works featuring a literary approach, and there is occasional fiction. The house backlist is comprehensive.

North Atlantic Books (founded in 1964; trade publisher since 1977) and Frog, Ltd. represent the publishing division of Society for the Study of Native Arts and Sciences.

Representative titles: *Bruce Lee: Fighting Spirit* by Bruce Thomas, *The Ultimate Egoist: The Complete Stories of Theodore Sturgeon (Volume 1)* (edited by Paul Williams), *The Double Mirror: A Skeptical Journey into Buddhist Tantra* by Stephen T. Butterfield, *Inventing the AIDS Virus: The Fallacy of the HIV–AIDS Connection* by Peter Duesberg, *The Mentals: Personality Profiles of the Homeopathic Constitutional Types* by Philip M. Bailey, *Action Theater: The Improvisation of Presence* by Ruth Zaporah, *The Organic Gourmet* by Barbara Kahn, *Retooling on the Run: The Executive Warrior* by Stuart Heller and David Sheppard Surrenda, *The Monuments of Mars: A City on the Edge of Forever* (revised edition) by Richard C. Hoagland, and *We Came to Play: Writings on Basketball* (edited by Q. R. Hand and John Ross).

North Atlantic/Frog handles its own distribution.

Query letters and SASEs should be directed to:

Richard Grossinger, Pubisher

Lindy Hough, Publisher

Marianne Dresser, Senior Editor

Kathy Glass, Senior Editor

NUMATA CENTER

2620 Warring Street
Berkeley, CA 94704
510-843-4128

Numata Center for Buddhist Translation and Research is a nonprofit organization established by Mr. Yehan Numata, founder of the Mitutoyo Corporation, international manufacturer of precision measuring instruments. Numata projects the translation and publication of the Chinese Buddhist canon, as well as additional works, in finely produced English-language editions.

Numata has engaged a variety of scholars and writers to participate in this landmark program, and the initial volumes have been received heartily by the library market, as well as by specialty and trade booksellers.

Sample titles: *The Lotus Sutra* (translated by Kubo Tsugunari and Yuyama Akira), *The Summary of the Great Vehicle* (translated by John P. Keenan), *Letters of Master Rennyo* (translated by Minor Rogers), and *Essentials of the Eight Traditions* (translated by Leo Pruden).

Query letters and SASEs should be directed to:

Reverend Kiyoshi Yamashita, Director

Orbis Books

Walsh Building
Maryknoll, NY 10545
914-941-7636

Orbis Books (founded in 1970) is a division of Maryknoll Fathers and Brothers. The house addresses topics such as theology, global religious issues, social justice, interreligious matters, mission theology, spirituality, politics, ecology, and African-American studies. Orbis also offers audio and video products.

Featured on the Orbis list are *The Hidden Heart of the Cosmos: Humanity and the New Story* by Brian Swimme, *Spirit of Fire: The Life and Vision of Teilhard de Chardin* by Ursula King, *Were You There? Godforsakenness in Slave Religion* by David Emmanuel Goatley, *Dialogue of Life: A Christian among Allah's Poor* by Bob McCahill, *Women Healing Earth: Third-World Women on Ecology, Feminism, and Religion* (edited by Rosemary Radford Reuther), *Nonviolent Story: Narrative Conflict Resolution in the Gospel of Mark* by Robert R. Beck, and *When War Is Unjust: Being Honest in Just-War Thinking* by John Howard Yoder.

Orbis Books is distributed by Westminster/John Knox Press

Query letters and SASEs should be directed to:

Robert Ellsberg, Editor in Chief

Paragon House Publishers

(See Directory of United States Publishers)

PAULIST PRESS

997 Macarthur Boulevard
Mahwah, NJ 07430
201-825-7300

Paulist Press publishes Roman Catholic as well as ecumenical titles in Bible study, biography, women's studies, spirituality, current issues, self-help and personal growth, Catholicism, liturgy, theology, philosophy, ethics, Jewish–Christian relations, world religions, youth ministry, and education, along with a selected list in fiction. The Paulist list ranges from popularly oriented traditionalist works to provocative frontiers of religious thought. In addition to books, Paulist vends a video and audio line.

Paulist Press (founded in 1866) is a publishing division of the Missionary Society of St. Paul the Apostle.

Featured Paulist Press titles: *Mary of Magdala: Apostle and Leader* by Mary R. Thompson, *Driftwood: Prayers for Beached Travelers* by Don Kimball, *The Advent Kitchen* by Barbara Benjamin and Alexandra Damascus Vali, *Experiencing Mystagogy: The Sacred Pause of Easter* by Gerard F. Baumbach, *Urgings of the Heart: A Spirituality of Integration* by Wilkie Au and Noreen Cannon, *God on the Job: Finding God Who Waits at Work* by Thomas Smith, *Euthanasia: Moral and Pastoral Perspectives* by Richard M. Gula, *Bringing Dreams to Life: Learning to Interpret Your Dreams* by George R. Slater, *Caregiver's Gethsemane: When a Loved One Longs to Die* by Cecile Bauer, and *A Dictionary of the Jewish–Christian Dialogue* (expanded edition; edited by Leon Klenicki and Geoffrey Wigoder).

Children's books include *Sharing the Sun* by Lee Klein (illustrated by Bruce Gebert), *The Boy Jesus Goes A-Walking and Other Stories* by Mary Richardson (illustrated by Hilda Joanna), and *It Takes Courage* by Christine L. Schmitt (illustrated by Jami Moffett).

Paulist Press distributes its own list and catalogs selected titles from other publishing houses.

Query letters and SASEs should be directed to:

Donald Brophy, Managing Editor

PILGRIM PRESS

700 Prospect Avenue East
Cleveland, OH 44115
216-736-3700

Pilgrim publishes general trade books (with cultural or religious themes), religious books, and curriculum aids. Pilgrim Press (founded in 1957) is the book-publishing banner of United Church Press, the publishing wing of the United Church of Christ.

The house has a tradition of publishing books and other resources that challenge, encourage, and inspire, crafted in accordance with fine standards of content, design, and production.

Indicative of the Pilgrim list: *Reclaiming the Soul: The Search for Meaning in a Self-Centered Culture* by Jeffrey Boyd, *Common Ground: A Priest and a Rabbi Read Scripture Together* by Andrew M. Greeley and Jacob Neusner, *The Turn of the Millennium: An Agenda for Christian Religion in an Age of Science* by Jeffrey G. Sobosan, *Boundary Wars: Intimacy and Distance in Healing Relationships* by Katherine Hancock Ragsdale, *Why Write Letters: Ten Ways to Simplify—and Enjoy—Your Life* by Donna E. Schaper, *Eros Breaking Free: Interpreting Sexual Theo-Ethics* by Anne Bathurst Gilson, and *Not Without a Struggle: Leadership Development for African American Women in Ministry* by Vashti M. McKenzie.

A new Pilgrim series is the Pilgrim Library of Ethics. Titles here include *Abortion: A Reader* (edited by Lloyd Steffen).

Pilgrim oversees its own distribution.

Query letters and SASEs should be directed to:

Richard Brown, Senior Editor

Lynne M. Deming, Publisher

Sidney Fowler, Curriculum Editor

QUESTAR PUBLISHERS
MULTNOMAH BOOKS

305 West Adams
P.O. Box 1720
Sisters, OR 97759
503-549-1144

Questar offers programs in Christian-oriented self-awareness and improvement, popular spirituality and theology, and fiction. Questar Publishers (founded in 1987) initially gained recognition for the line of Gold'n'Honey books for children. The house was started by Donald C. Jacobson, previously of Multnomah Press (which is now part of the Questar publishing family).

From Questar: *The Beginner's Bible* by Karen Henley, *One Small Sparrow* by Jeff Leeland, *Locking Arms* by Stu Weber, and *To Know Him by Name* by Kay Arthur.

Children's books (including Gold'n'Honey favorites): *Once Upon a Parable* by Mack Thomas (illustrated by Hilber Nelson), *The Nursery Bible Bedtime Book* by L. J. Sattgast (illustrated by Trish Tenud), *Songs and Rhymes for Wiggle Worms* by Mary Hollingsworth, and *Are Tigers Ticklish?* by Debby Anderson.

The Questar list is handled by the house's personal account representatives; titles can also be ordered through Spring Arbor.

MULTNOMAH BOOKS

Multnomah produces books and audiocassettes with a contemporary flavor in Christian living and family enrichment, as well as devotional titles, gift books, and children's books. Multnomah Books (now part of Questar) was founded in 1969 as Multnomah Press, a division of Multnomah School of the Bible.

Indicative of the Multnomah program: *Six Hours One Friday: Anchoring to the Power of the Cross* by Max Lucado, *Choices: For Women Who Long to Discover Life's Best* by Mary Farrar, *Future Grace: Experiencing God's Awesome Power* by John Piper, *Come . . . and Behold Him: An Invitation to Christmas Worship* by Jack Hayford, *Designing a Woman's Life: Discovering Your Unique Purpose and Passion* by Judith Couchman, *Guard Your Heart: Growing Strong from the Inside Out* by Charles Swindoll, and *Lifestyle Evangelism: Crossing Traditional Boundaries to Reach the Unbelieving World* by Joe Aldrich.

Multnomah offers a strong list of fiction, including contemporary and historical novels, romances, sagas, and thrillers. Representative Multnomah fiction titles are *The President* by Parker Hudson, *Tears of the Sun* (Book Four in the Journeys of the Stranger series) by Al Lacy, *Stonehaven* by Amanda MacLean, and *The Call of the Green Bird* by Alberta Hawse.

Query letters and SASEs should be directed to the Editorial Department or to:

Lisa T. Bergren, Managing Editor

REGAL BOOKS
(See Gospel Light Publications)

ST. ANTHONY MESSENGER PRESS
1615 Republic Street
Cincinnati, OH 45210
513-241-5615

Areas of St. Anthony Messenger publishing interest include Catholic identity, family life, morality and ethics, parish ministry, pastoral ministry, prayer helps, sacraments, saints and Christian heroes, Scripture, seasonal favorites, small-group resources, spirituality for every day, and youth ministry. St. Anthony Messenger Press (founded in 1970) publishes Catholic religious works and resources for parishes, schools, and individuals; the house produces books (hardcover and paperback, many in economically-priced editions), magazines, audiotapes, and videocassettes as well as educational programs.

On the St. Anthony Messenger list are *Lights: Revelations of God's Goodness* by Jack Wintz, *Radical Grace: Daily Meditations by Richard Rohr* (edited by John Bookser Feister), *Holy Bells and Wonderful Smells: Year-Round Activities for Classrooms and Families* by Jeanne Hunt, *The Sacraments: How Catholics Pray* by Thomas Richstatter, *The Heart's Healing Journey: Seeking Desert Wisdom* by Gloria Hutchinson, *The Wind Harp and Other Angel Tales* by Ethel Pochocki.

A special project is *A Retreat With . . .*, a series (edited by Gloria Hutchinson) that features the words of historical figures such as Thomas Merton, Gerard Manley Hopkins, and Hildegard of Bingen interwoven with daily prayer, dialogue, and deepening acquaintance.

Backlist favorites include *Swimming in the Sun: Discovering the Lord's Prayer with Francis of Assisi and Thomas Merton* by Albert Haase, *The Wild Man's Journey: Reflections on Male Spirituality* by Richard Rohr and Joseph Martos, and *Prayers for Caregivers* by Patti Normile.

St. Anthony Messenger Press handles its own distribution.

Query letters and SASEs should be directed to:

Lisa Biedenbach, Managing Editor

SCRIPTURE PRESS PUBLICATIONS/VICTOR BOOKS

(See Chariot/Victor Publishing)

SHAMBHALA PUBLICATIONS

Horticultural Hall
300 Massachusetts Avenue
Boston, MA 02115
617-424-0030

Shambhala publishes hardcover and paperback titles in creativity, philosophy, psychology, medical arts and healing, mythology, folklore, religion, art, literature, cooking, martial arts, and cultural studies. Shambhala generally issues a modest list of new titles each year and tends a flourishing backlist; the house periodically updates some of its perennial sellers in revised editions.

The house packages a number of distinct lines including gift editions and special-interest imprints. Shambhala Dragon Editions accents the sacred teachings of Asian masters. Shambhala Centaur Editions offers classics of world literature in small-sized gift editions. The New Science Library concentrates on titles relating to science, technology, and the environment. Shambhala copublishes C. G. Jung Foundation Books with the C. G. Jung Foundation for Analytical Psychology. Shambhala Redstone Editions are fine boxed sets comprising books, postcards, games, art objects, and foldouts. Shambhala Lion Editions are spoken-word audiotape cassette presentations. Little Barefoot Books features children's literature (much of it classic) in miniature illustrated editions.

Shambhala Publications is a foremost representative of the wave of publishers specializing in the arena of contemporary globalized spiritual and cultural interest. Since Shambhala's inception (the house was founded in 1969), the field has blossomed into a still-burgeoning readership, as underscored by the many smaller independent presses and large corporate houses that tend this market.

Among Shambhala highlights are *Hard Travel to Sacred Places* by Rudolph Wurlitzer, *The Beat Book: Poems and Fiction from the Beat Generation* (compiled by Anne Waldman; foreword by Allen Ginsberg), *Earth Angels: Messengers of the Creative Spirit* by Shaun McNiff, *Deep Ecology* by George Sessions, *A Brief History of Everything* by Ken Wilber, *The Erotic Spirit: An Anthology of Poems of Sensuality, Love, and Longing* (edited by Sam Hamill), *The Body: An Encyclopedia of Archetypal Symbolism* by George R. Elder, *Opening the Inner Gates: New Paths in Kabbalah and Psychology* (edited by Edward Hoffman), *Spiritual Path, Sacred Place: Myth, Ritual, and Meaning in Architecture* by Thomas Barrie, and *Alchi—Ladakh's Hidden Buddhist Sanctuary: The Sumtsek* (text by Roger Cooper; photographs by Jaroslav Poncar).

Shambhala's strong backlist includes *Awakening the Hidden Storyteller: How to Build a Storytelling Tradition in Your Family* by Robin Moore, *The Blank Canvas: Inviting the Muse* by Anna Held Audette, *The Female Ancestors of Christ* by Ann Belford Ulanov, *The Forbidden Self: Symbolic Incest and the Journey Within* by John Perkins, and *Same-Sex Love: And the Path to Wholeness* (edited by Robert H. Hopke, Karen Lofthus Carrington, and Scott Wirth).

Shambhala Redstone Editions offers the boxed sets *José Guadalupe Posada: Mexican Popular Prints* (edited by Julian Rothstein), *A Gambling Box* (edited by Kate Pullinger), and *Surrealist Games* (compiled by Alistair Brotchie and edited by Mel Gooding).

Little Barefoot titles include *The Outlandish Adventures of Orpheus and the Underworld* by Paul Newham with illustrations by Elaine Cox, *The World Is Round* by Gertrude Stein with illustrations by Roberta Arenson, and *The Brownies' Merry Adventures* by Palmer Cox (illustrated by the author).

Shambhala's own fulfillment department services individual and special orders. Shambhala's list is distributed to the trade by Random House.

Query letters and SASEs should be directed to:

Carolyn Allison, Editorial Assistant

Samuel Bercholz, President and Editor in Chief

Emily Hilburn Sell, Editor

Signature Books

564 West 400 North Street
Salt Lake City, UT 84116
801-531-1483

Signature Books (established in 1981) publishes contemporary literature as well as scholarly works relevant to the Intermountain West. The Signature list emphasizes topics that range from outlaw biographies to speculative theology, from demographics to humor; the common objective is to provide alternatives to the institutional agendas that underlie many of the publications in the region. In addition to a wide range of nonfiction, Signature publishes novels and collections of poetry.

Representative of Signature nonfiction: *Friendly Fire: The ACLU in Utah* by Linda Sillitoe, *Culture Clash and Accommodation: Public Schooling in Salt Lake City, 1890–1994* by Frederick S. Buchanan, *In Sacred Loneliness: The Plural Wives of Joseph Smith* by Todd Compton, *Mahonri Young: His Life and Art* by Thomas E. Toone, *Park City Underfoot: Self-Guided Tours of Historic Neighborhoods* by Brent D. Corcoran, *Black Saints in a White Church: Contemporary African-American Mormons* by Jessie L. Embrie, *Sacred Lands, Sacred View: Navajo Perceptions of the Four Corners Region* by Robert S. McPherson, *Set in Stone, Fixed in Glass: The Great Mormon Temple and Its Photographers* by Nelson B. Wadsworth, and *Early Mormonism and the Magic World View* by D. Michael Quinn.

Indicative of Signature interest in fiction and the literary arts are *Spirits in the Leaves* (memoir) by Jerry Johnston, *"A Schoolmarm All My Life" : Personal Narratives from Frontier Utah* (edited by Joyce Kinkead), *Love Chains* (stories) by Margaret Blair Young, *Special Living Lessons for Relief Society by Sister Fonda AlaMode* (humor by Laurie Johnson), *Haste* (poetry) by Lisa Orme Bickmore, *The Way We Live: Stories by Utah Women* (edited by Ellen Fagg), *An Environment for Murder* (suspense) by Rod Decker, *Beyond the River* (mainstream fiction) by Michael Fillerup, *Washed by a Wave of Wind: Science Fiction from the Corridor* (edited by M. Shayne Bell), *What Do Ducks Do in Winter? and Other Western Stories* by Lewis Horne, and *Tending the Garden: Essays on Mormon Literature* (edited by Eugene England and Lavina Fielding Anderson). Cartoon humor with a local purview is evident through *Utah: Sex and Travel Guide* by Calvin Grondahl.

Signature Publications oversees distribution of its titles via in-house ordering services and a national network of wholesalers.

Query letters and SASEs should be directed to:

Gary Bergera, Director of Publishing

SWEDENBORG PUBLISHING HOUSE

P.O. Box 549
West Chester, PA 19381
215-430-3222
800-355-3222

Swedenborg Publishing House is part of Swedenborg Foundation, Inc. (founded in 1849). Swedenborg produces a limited list of books and videos relating to the theological works and insights of Emanuel Swedenborg (1688–1772), as well as a line of Swedenborg's complete theological works. The house publishes the trade series, Chrysalis Reader, which features stories, essays, poetry, and art that explores themes of spiritual development.

On the Swedenborg list: *Testimony to the Invisible: Essays on Swedenborg* (edited by James F. Lawrence), *Gold from Aspirin: Spiritual Views on Chaos and Order from*

Thirty Authors (in the Chrysalis Reader series; edited by Carol S. Lawson), *Swedenborg and Esoteric Islam* by Henry Corbin (translated by Leonard Fox), and *Angels in Action: What Swedenborg Saw and Heard* by Robert H. Kirven.

Query letters and SASEs should be directed to:

George F. Dole, Acquisitions

JEREMY P. TARCHER, INC.

(See listing under the Putnam Berkley Group in the directory of United States book publishers)

TRIUMPH BOOKS

(See Liguori Publications)

TYNDALE HOUSE PUBLISHERS

Box 80
351 Executive Drive
Wheaton, IL 60189
708-668-8300

Tyndale offers a comprehensive program in Christian living, devotional, inspirational, and general nonfiction, from a nondenominational Evangelical perspective. Tyndale publishing interest also encompasses religious fiction. The house also offers a strong line of Bibles. Tyndale House Publishers (founded in 1962) produces hardcover, trade paperback, and mass-market paperback originals as well as reprints. Tyndale also catalogs audio and video products.

Indicative of Tyndale nonfiction: *Family Shock: Keeping Families Strong in the Midst of Earthshaking Change* by Gary R. Collins, *Fight Like a Man: Redeeming Manhood for Kingdom Warfare* by Gordon Dalbey, *You Gotta Believe!* by George Shinn (owner of the NBA Charlotte Hornets), *Choices for a Lifetime: Determining the Values That Will Shape Your Future* by Stuart Briscoe, *Five Lies of the Century: How Many Do You Believe?* by David T. Moore, and *Does God Care If I Can't Pay My Bills? Practical Help and Encouragement for Weathering Your Financial Crisis* by Linda K. Taylor.

Tyndale fiction includes mainstream novels as well as a number of inspirational romance series, including works set in Revolutionary War and Civil War milieus. The house is interested in Evangelical Christian–theme romance in other historical periods (including Regency), as well as those with a humorous twist. On the fiction list are

Nightwatch (espionage thriller) by Jon Henderson, *As Sure As the Dawn* by Francine Rivers (part of the Mark of the Lion series), and *A Rose Remembered* by Michael Phillips.

The Tyndale program of books for children and young adults is in a transitional phase; currently the house is not interested in fiction geared for this younger age group.

Tyndale House oversees its own distribution. It does not accept unsolicited manuscripts.

Query letters and SASEs should be directed to the Editorial Department or to:

Karen Ball, Senior Editor

UNION OF AMERICAN HEBREW CONGREGATIONS/UAHC PRESS

838 Fifth Avenue
New York, NY 10021
212-249-0100

Union of American Hebrew Congregations/UAHC Press publishes in the areas of religion (Jewish), Reform Judaism, textbooks, audiovisual materials, social action, biography, and ceremonies. In trade categories UAHC Press accents juvenile fiction and adult nonfiction books as well as titles in basic Judaism and inspirational works. The house catalogs books, audiocassettes, videotapes, and multimedia products.

Founded in 1873, UAHC Press is a division of Union of American Hebrew Congregations. The UAHC Press publishing program includes *Reform Judaism* magazine.

The UAHC list includes *What We Believe . . . What We Do . . . A Pocket Guide for Reform Jews* by Simeon J. Maslin, *The Book of the Jewish Year* by Stephen M. Wylen, *Our Sacred Texts: Discovering the Jewish Classics* by Ellen Singer with Bernard M. Zlotowitz, *If I'm Jewish and You're Christian, What Are the Kids? A Parenting Guide for Interfaith Families* by Andrea King, *Shalom/Salaam: A Resource for Jewish–Muslim Dialogue* (edited by Andrea Weiss and Gary M. Bretton-Granatoor), *The Other Side of the Hudson: A Jewish Immigrant Adventure* by Kenneth Roseman, and *America: The Jewish Experience* by Sondra Leiman (with a companion guide for teachers).

On the UAHC Press children's list: *The Tattooed Torah* by Marvell Ginsburg (illustrated by Martin Lemelman), *Listen to the Trees: Jews and the Earth* by Molly Cone (illustrated by Ray Doty; companion teacher's guide by Gavriel Goldman), *A Thousand and One Chickens* by Seymour Rossel (illustrated by Vlad Guzner), *The Little Menorah Who Forgot Chanukah* (story and music by Jerry Sperling; illustrated by Giora Carmi), and *A Candle for Grandpa: A Guide to the Jewish Funeral for Children and Parents* (by David Techner and Judith Hirt-Manheimer; illustrated by Joel Iskowitz).

UAHC Press handles its own distribution.

Query letters and SASEs should be directed to:

Aron Hirt-Manheimer, Acquisitions Editor, Trade

David Kasakove, UAHC Education Department
Textbooks, preschool through adult.

VEDANTA PRESS

1946 Vedanta Place
Hollywood, CA 90068
213-465-7114

Vedanta publishing interest includes meditation, religions and philosophies, women's studies, devotional songs and poetry, biography, history, myth, and children's books. In addition to its list of titles imported from the East (primarily India), Vedanta's program embraces works of Western origin. The publisher catalogs titles from other publishers and also sells audiotapes and videotapes.

The house publishes books on the philosophy of Vedanta, with an aim to engage a wide variety of temperaments, using a broad spectrum of methods, in order to attain the realization of each individual personality's divinity within. Vedanta Press (founded in 1947) is a subsidiary of the Vedanta Society of Southern California.

Representative titles: *Women Saints: East and West* (edited by Swami Ghanananda and Sir John Stewart-Wallace), *Man As Microcosm in Tantric Hinduism* by Grace Cairns, *Encountering God: A Spiritual Journey from Bozeman to Banares* by Diana Dick, *Wherever You Go, There You Are* by John Kabat-Zinn, *Vedic Mathematics* by Swami Bharati Krishna Tirthaji, *Learning the Sanskrit Alphabet* by Thomas Egenes, and *Swami Vivekananda in the West: New Discoveries* by Mary Louise Burke.

Vedanta publishes many classic Vedic works in a variety of editions and translations. Among them: *Bhagavad Gita: The Song of God* (translated by Swami Prabhavananda and Christopher Isherwood; introduction by Aldous Huxley).

Vedanta Press handles its own distribution.

Vedanta's books originate in house, though the publisher is open to considering additional projects that may fall within its program. Vedanta does not wish to receive unsolicited manuscripts. Query letters and SASEs should be directed to:

Robert Adjenian, Manager

VICTOR BOOKS

(See Chariot/Victor Publishing)

SAMUEL WEISER, INC.

P.O. Box 612
York Beach, ME 03910
207-363-4393

Samuel Weiser specializes in books relating to all facets of the secret and hidden teachings worldwide. Areas of publishing interest include self-transformation, alternative healing methods, meditation, metaphysics, consciousness, astrology, tarot, astral projection, kabbalah, earth religions, oriental philosophy and religions, Buddhism, t'ai chi, healing, and Tibetan studies.

Many Weiser titles revamp age-old themes into vibrant works of contemporary sensibility. In addition to new titles, Weiser publishes classic references and tracts in reprint; Weiser also offers a particularly distinguished selection relevant to the works of Aleister Crowley as well as Gurdjieff studies. The house publishes in hardcover and paperback editions and maintains a thriving backlist. Samuel Weiser, Inc. was founded in 1955.

Representative Weiser titles are *Serpent of Fire: A Modern View of Kundalini* by Darrel Irving, *Cutting the Ties That Bind* by Phyllis Krystal, *Magical Hearth: Home for the Modern Pagan* by Janet Thompson, *I Am Woman by Rite: A Book of Women's Rituals* by Nancy Brady Cunningham, *The Winged Prophet from Hermes to Quetzalcoatl: An Introduction to Mesoamerican Deities through the Tarot* by Carol Miller and Guadalupe Rivera, *Taming Our Monkey Mind: Insight, Detachment, Identity* by Phyllis Krystal, *Psycho-Regression: A New System for Healing & Personal Growth* by Francesca Rossetti, *The Handbook of Yoruba Religious Concepts* by Baba Ifa Karade, *Symbolism of the Celtic Cross* by Derek Bryce, *The Consulting Astrologer's Guidebook* by Donna Cunningham, and *Emasculation of the Unicorn: The Loss and Rebuilding of Masculinity in America* by C. T. B. Harris.

Samuel Weiser handles its own distribution and distributes selected titles from other houses; the Weiser distribution catalog lists titles from over 200 publishers. Weiser as well utilizes the services of several national trade distributors.

Query letters and SASEs should be directed to:

Eliot Stearns, Editor

WESTMINSTER/JOHN KNOX PRESS

100 Witherspoon Street
Louisville, KY 40202
502-569-5000

Westminster/John Knox publishes general-interest religious trade books as well as academic and professional works in biblical studies, theology, philosophy, ethics, history, archaeology, personal growth, and pastoral counseling. Among Westminster/John Knox series are Literary Currents in Biblical Interpretation, Family Living in Pastoral Perspective, Gender and the Biblical Tradition, and The Presbyterian Presence: The Twentieth-Century Experience.

Westminster/John Knox Press represents the publications unit of the Presbyterian Church (USA). The house unites the former independents, Westminster Press and John Knox Press, which were originally founded as one entity in 1838, then separated into distinct enterprises, and again merged following the reunion of the Northern and Southern Presbyterian Churches in 1983.

Among Westminster/John Knox Press titles are *Family, Freedom, and Faith: Building Community Today* by Paula M. Cooey, *Dictionary of Feminist Theologies* (edited by Letty M. Russell and J. Shannon Clarkson), *We Were Baptized Too: Claiming God's Grace for Lesbians and Gays* by Marilyn Bennett Alexander and James Preston, *What Really Happened to Jesus: A Historical Approach to the Resurrection* by Gerd Lüdemann (in collaboration with Alf Özen; translated by John Bowden), *Old Testament Prophecy: From Oracles to Canon* by Ronald E. Clements, *Breaking the Fall: Religious Readings of Contemporary Fiction* by Robert Detweiler, and *Reading the Fractures of Genesis: Historical and Literary Approaches* by David M. Carr.

On the WJK backlist are *The Truth Under Lock and Key? Jesus and the Dead Sea Scrolls* by Klaus Berger, *Sexuality and the Sacred: Sources for Theological Reflection* (edited by James B. Nelson and Sandra P. Longfellow), *The Life of Moses: The Yahwist as Historian in Exodus-Numbers* by John Van Seters, *Helpmates, Harlots, and Heroes: Women's Stories in the Hebrew Bible* by Alice Ogden Bellis, *Survivor Prayers: Talking with God about Childhood Sexual Abuse* by Catherine J. Foote, and *Ending Auschwitz: The Future of Jewish and Christian Life* by Mark H. Ellis.

Westminster/John Knox distributes its list through Spring Arbor. The house also represents titles from other publishers, including Orbis Books, Pilgrim Press, Saint Andrew Press, and the United Church Publishing House of Canada.

Query letters and SASEs should be directed to:

Stephanie Egnotovich, Managing Editor

WISDOM PUBLICATIONS

361 Newbury Street
Boston, MA 02115
617-536-3358

Wisdom's publishing arena centers on Buddhism, Tibet, and related East–West themes. Wisdom titles are published in appreciation of Buddhism as a living philosophy and with the commitment to preserve and transmit important works from all the major Buddhist traditions. The house offers books and tapes, as well as the journal *Tricycle: The Buddhist Review.* Wisdom Publications (founded in 1975) is a nonprofit organization initiated by Lama Thubten Yeshe around the time he established the international Foundation for the Preservation of the Mahayana Tradition (FMPT).

Representative titles: *The Fine Arts of Relaxation, Concentration, and Meditation: Ancient Skills for Modern Minds* by Joel and Michelle Levey, *Tibetan Thangka Paintings: Methods and Materials* by David and Janis Jackson, *Thank You and OK! An American Zen Failure in Japan* by David Chadwick, and *The World of Tibetan Buddhism: An Overview of Its Philosophy and Practice* by the Dalai Lama (translated by Geshe Thupten; foreword by Richard Gere).

Wisdom Publications handles its own distribution.

Query letters and SASEs should be directed to:

Tim McNeill, President

WORD PUBLISHING

1501 LBJ Freeway
Suite 650
Dallas, TX 75234
214-488-9673

Word Publishing offers a list with a predominantly nondenominational Christian orientation. Word's field of interest encompasses biography, inspirational and spiritual works, contemporary issues, fiction, counseling and psychology, love and marriage, divorce, men, women, parenting and family living, singles, youth, music, evangelical and the mission, theology and doctrine, and Bibles and biblical studies. Word also accents series such as Contemporary Christian Counseling, Word Biblical Commentary, WordSoft Bible Software, and Communicator's Commentary. Word Music specializes in songbooks, choral arrangements, and musical performance resources.

The publisher's intonation is basically academic and professional; however, the program of best-selling crossover titles for the religious-trade and general audience provide the house with a high public profile. Word Publishing produces hardcovers and trade paperbacks, as well as audiotapes and videotapes, computer software, and educational products. Word Publishing (founded in 1951) is owned by Thomas Nelson. Word was previously a subsidiary of Capital Cities/ABC Inc.

On the Word list are *The Scout: Searching for the Best in Baseball* by Red Murff with Mike Capps, *The Applause of Heaven* by Max Lucado, *The Grace Awakening* by Charles Swindoll, *Upstaging God: Restoring Superstar Status to Jesus Alone* by Pelle Karlsson, *Family Health & Medical Guide* by the American Academy of Family Physicians, *Searching for God in America* by Hugh Hewitt (in conjunction with the PBS series), *I'm So Glad You Told Me What I Didn't Wanna Hear* by Barbara Johnson (author of *Stick a Geranium in Your Hat . . .* and *Mama, Get the Hammer*), *The Family Manager* by Kathy Peel, *Blinded by the Light: Exposing the Truth about Near Death Experiences* by Raymond Quigg Lawrence Jr., and *Out of Control* (humor) by Mark Lowry.

Word's fiction lineup includes *Split Ticket* (political thriller) by H. L. Richardson, *Wings of a Dove* by Beverly Bush Smith, *Blood Ties* by Sigmund Brouwer, and *The Revolt* by S. Wise Bauer.

Word Kids! has a publishing profile for younger readers similar to that of the adult division, with many of the same authors appearing here. Among them: *Paw Paw Chuck's Big Ideas in the Bible* by Charles R. Swindoll, *All the Children of the World* by Karen M. Leimert, *Spider Sisters: We'll Always Have Each Other* by John Trent, and the Cooper Kids Adventure Series by Frank Peretti.

WordSoft Bible Software encompasses an advanced study system (that incorporates text in Greek and Hebrew), simplified Bible search tools and databases, dictionaries, and several versions of the Bible.

Word Publishing oversees its own distribution.

In accord with current acquisitions policy, Word Publishing does not consider unsolicited manuscripts or proposals.

Query letters and SASEs should be directed to:

Lynn Wheeler, Assistant to the Vice President, Trade Publishing

WYNWOOD PRESS

(See Baker Book House)

YESHIVA UNIVERSITY PRESS

500 West 185th Street
New York, NY 10033
212-960-5400

Yeshiva University Press (founded in 1960) produces a select list that includes original academic works as well as titles of mainstream reader interest; the house also issues scholarly Judaica in reprint.

Representing the Yeshiva University list: *Faith after the Holocaust* by Eliezer Berkovits, *A Treasury of Sephardic Laws and Customs* by Herbert C. Dobrinsky, *Ashkenaz: The German Jewish Heritage* (edited by Gertrude Hirschler), *Jewish Woman in Jewish Law* by Moshe Meiselman, *The Renaissance of the Torah Jew* by Saul Bernstein, and *Modern Medicine and Jewish Ethics* by Fred Rosner.

Books from Yeshiva University Press are distributed through KTAV Publishing House.

Query letters and SASEs should be directed to the editorial offices of KTAV Publishing House (please see entry for KTAV in this section of the directory).

ZONDERVAN PUBLISHING HOUSE

5300 Patterson Avenue Southeast
Grand Rapids, MI 49530
616-698-3487

Zondervan produces nonfiction books addressing contemporary issues in spirituality including counseling, inspirational novels, juveniles, humor, Bibles, and Bible study guides, as well as entries in the form of computer software, audiotape, and videotape. Zondervan Publishing House (founded in 1931) is among the most potent publishers specializing in evangelical Christian titles.

Zondervan exhibits immense promotional prowess; its public persona includes eye-catching bookseller floor displays, posters, advertising schedules, and tie-ins via other media outlets including programming on the Zondervan Radio Network. Zondervan authors are among the most enterprising in this area of publishing. Zondervan's HarperCollins connection (the house has been an editorially independent subsidiary of HarperCollins since 1988) makes for a brawny marketing arm, and Zondervan's readership and distribution is extraordinary.

Among Zondervan features: *Spirituality in an Age of Change* by Alistair McGrath, *The Silence of Adam: Becoming Men of Courage in a World of Chaos* by Larry Crab (with Don Hudson and Al Andrews), *Jesus Under Fire: Modern Scholarship Reinvents the Historical Jesus* (edited by Michael J. Wilkins and J. P. Moreland), *Stress Fractures: Advice and Encouragement for Handling Your Fast-Paced Life* by Charles Swindoll, and *Lambs among Wolves: Is It Possible for Christians to Influence Today's Culture? These People Did and So Can You* by Bob Briner.

Series for younger readers include Jane Peart's The Brides of Montclair and the Holly's Heart novels by Beverly Lewis. Sports Heroes is a series by Mark Littleton (including these titles: *Baseball, Basketball, Football,* and *Track and Field*). Other youth-oriented works include *Geek-Proof Your Faith* by Greg Johnson and Michael Ross, *Teach 'Toons* by Rick Bundschuh and Tom Finley, and *Help! I'm a Volunteer Youth Worker! 50 Easy Tips to Help You Succeed with Kids* by Doug Fields.

HarperCollins handles Zondervan's distribution to the book trade.

Zondervan asks that interested authors write to request submissions guidelines before submitting manuscripts or other material. Query letters and SASEs should be directed to:

Scott W. Bolinder, Publisher, Trade Books

David Lambert, Editor
Youth books and fiction.

Sandy Vander Zeicht, Editor
Self-help and other nonfiction trade books.

The Writer's Journey: Themes of the Spirit and Inspiration

Deborah Levine

If you have decided to pursue writing as a career instead of as a longing or a dream, you might find yourself falling into a pattern of focusing on the goal instead of on the process. When you have a great book idea, you may envision yourself on a book-signing tour or as a guest on *Oprah* before you've written a single word.

It's human nature to look into your own future, but too much projection can get in the way of what the writing experience is all about. The process of writing is like a wondrous journey that can help you cross a bridge to the treasures hidden within your own subconscious. Some people believe that it's a way for you to link with the collective or universal consciousness, the storehouse of all wisdom and truth, as it has existed since the beginning of time.

There are many methods of writing that bring their own rewards with them. Some people produce exceptional prose by using their intellect and their mastery of the craft of writing. They use research and analytical skills to help them produce works of great importance and merit.

Then there are those who have learned to tap into the wellspring from which all genius flows. They are the inspired ones who write with the intensity of an impassioned lover. They are the spiritual writers who write because they must. They may not want to, they may not know how to, but something inside them is begging to be let out. It gnaws away at them until they find a way to set it free.

Although they may not realize it, spiritual writers are engaged in a larger spiritual journey toward ultimate self-mastery and unification with God.

Spiritual writers often feel as if they're taking dictation. It is as though their thoughts have a life of their own and the mind is merely a receiver. Some people refer to this as "channeling" and believe disembodied spirits take over and write through them. Although I sincerely doubt that Gandhi or other notables have authored as many channeled books as people have been claiming, truly spiritual writing does have an otherworldly feeling and can often teach the writer things he or she would otherwise not have known.

Writing opens you up to new perspectives, much like self-induced psychotherapy. Although journals are the most direct route for self-evaluation, fiction and nonfiction also serve as vehicles for a writer's growth. Writing helps the mind expand to the limits of the imagination.

Anyone can become a spiritual writer. There are many benefits from doing so, not the least of which is the development of your soul. On a more practical level, it is much less difficult to write with flow and fervor than it is to be bound by the limitations of logic and analysis. If you tap into the universal source, there is no end to your potential creativity.

The greatest barrier to becoming a spiritual writer is the human ego. We treat our words as if they were our children—only we tend to be neurotic parents. A child is not owned by a parent, but rather must be loved, guided, and nurtured until he or she can carry on, on his or her own.

The same is true for our words. If we try to own and control them like property, they will be limited by our vision for them. We will overprotect them and will not be able to see when we may be taking them into the wrong direction for their ultimate well-being.

Another ego problem that creates a barrier to creativity is our need for constant approval and our tendency toward perfectionism. We may feel the tug toward free expression, but will erect blockades to ensure appropriate style and structure. We write with a schoolmarm looking over our shoulder waiting to tell us what we are doing wrong.

Style and structure are important to ultimate presentation, but that is what editing is for. Ideas and concepts need to flow like water through a running stream.

The best way to become a spiritual writer is to relax and have fun. If you are relaxed and are in a basically good mood, you'll be open to intuition. Writers tend to take themselves too seriously, which causes anxiety, which exacerbates fear, which causes insecurity, which diminishes our self-confidence and leads ultimately to mounds of crumpled papers and lost inspiration.

If you have faith in a Supreme Being, the best way to begin a spiritual writing session is with the following writer's prayer:

> Almighty God (Jesus, Allah, Great Spirit, etc.), Creator of the Universe, help me to become a vehicle for your wisdom so that what I write is of the highest purpose and will serve the greatest good. I humbly place my (pen/keyboard/dictaphone) in your hands so that you may guide me.

Prayer helps to connect you to the universal source. It empties the mind of trash, noise, and potential writer's blocks. If you are not comfortable with formal prayer, a few minutes of meditation will serve the same purpose.

Spiritual writing as a process does not necessarily lead to a sale. The fact is that some people have more commercial potential than others, no matter how seemingly unimportant their message might be. Knowledge of the business of writing will help you make a career of it. If you combine this with the spiritual process, it can also bring you gratification and inner peace.

If you trust the process of writing and allow the journey to take you where it will, it may bring you benefits far beyond your expectations.

Canadian Publishers

BANTAM BOOKS CANADA
DOUBLEDAY CANADA LIMITED

105 Bond Street
Toronto, ON M5B 1Y3
416-340-0777

This publishing operation is the corporate cousin to the New York firm Bantam Doubleday Dell. Bantam Books Canada releases a significant frontlist of hardcover editions; the house also produces a large number of trade paperbacks (originals as well as reprints) and mass-market paperback editions (primarily reprints). Doubleday Canada is primarily a hardcover operation. Doubleday produces a broad list that encompasses commercial and literary fiction, children's titles, and an array of nonfiction categories, including politics, history, autobiography, current affairs, arts, sports, travel, and cookbooks. Doubleday Canada has a strong Canadian orientation, and emphasizes Canadian authors.

Corgi, Dell, and Seal concentrate on trade and mass-market paperbacks. These houses all publish a solid selection of works by Canadian writers (particularly the McClelland-Bantam line), as well as authors from throughout the British Commonwealth nations.

Bantam Doubleday Dell Canada, which also includes allied imprints McClelland-Bantam and Delacorte, inhabits a historic office building in the heart of downtown Toronto. The component divisions share interlocking ownership and operate virtually as a single editorial entity.

Representative of the list: *Exposure* by Evelyn Anthony, *The Modern Canoe* by Ted Bissland and Stephen Pellerin, *The Canadian Patient's Book of Rights* by Lorne Rozovsky, *A Spanish Lover* by Joanna Trollope, *Women and Ghosts* by Alison Lurie, *Dead Meat* by Philip Kerr, and *An Imaginative Experience* by Mary Wesley.

Bantam Doubleday Dell Seal Books Canada handles its own Canadian distribution; United States distribution is through the Bantam Doubleday Dell order-processing department.

Queries with SASEs only—Doubleday accepts no unsolicited manuscripts. Query letters and SASEs from United States writers should be directed to the New York office of Bantam (see Bantam Doubleday Dell in the Directory of United States Publishers).

DOUGLAS & MCINTYRE PUBLISHERS

1615 Venables Street
Vancouver, BC V5L 2H1
604-254-7191

Toronto office:
585 Bloor Street West
2nd Floor
Toronto, ON M6G 1K5
416-537-2501

Douglas & McIntyre Publishers (founded in 1964) offers a publishing program with Canadian emphasis—often with a specifically British Columbian inflection. The house produces hardcover and paperback books in both fiction and nonfiction. Nonfiction areas of interest include native art, current affairs, history, travel, and nature studies. Douglas & McIntyre fiction tends toward literary works, serious popular fiction, and tales of mystery and suspense.

Douglas & McIntyre nonfiction titles include *The Pacific Province: A History of British Columbia* (edited by Hugh Johnston), *Chiefly Feasts: The Enduring Kwakiutl Potlatch* by Aldona Jonaitis, *Letter from Vienna: A Daughter Uncovers Her Family's Jewish Past* by Claudia Cornwall, *Stone, Bone, Antler, and Shell: Artifacts of the Northwest Coast* by Hilary Stewart, *Mondays Are Yellow, Sundays Are Grey: A Mother's Fight to Save Her Children from the Nightmare of Sexual Abuse* by Ellen Prescott, and *The Canadian Fish Cookbook* by A. Jan Howarth.

Fiction and literary works include *Sex of the Stars* by Monique Proulx (translated by Matt Cohen), *Local Colour: Writers Discovering Canada* (edited by Carol Martin), *A Story As Sharp As a Knife: An Introduction to Classical Haida Literature* by Robert Bringhurst, *Notes from the Century Before: A Journal from British Columbia* by Edward Hoagland (illustrations by Claire Van Vliet) and *In the Navel of the Moon: A Tale From Mexico* by Paul St. Pierre.

Tales of mystery and suspense include *Blood Vessel* by Paul Grescoe, and *Deadly Appearances* by Gail Bowen.

The Greystone Books imprint offers travel guides; one-day getaways; regional histories; sports books (especially hockey); and titles in hiking, camping, and outdoor recreation. Sample Greystone books: *Day Trips from Vancouver* by Jack Christie, *Fishing in the West* by David Carpenter, and *52 Weekend Activities around Vancouver* by Sue Lebrecht and Judi Lees.

Douglas & McIntyre handles its own distribution, as well as purveying books from additional houses and institutions including the Canadian Museum of Civilization, the Mountaineers, the New Press, Sierra Club Books, and Thames and Hudson.

DOUGLAS & MCINTYRE CHILDREN'S DIVISION

Within its children's division, Douglas & McIntyre offers several special imprints. Groundwood Press publishes titles for preschoolers through young adults. Earthcare Books is an environmental series for middle-grade readers, which includes *For the*

Birds, written by Canadian novelist Margaret Atwood. First Discovery is a series of nature books for toddlers and early readers. Rounding out Douglas & McIntyre's juveniles list are fiction for young adults, picture books, the Walker imprint's nonfiction and picture books (some of which are targeted for appeal to the entire family), and Meadow Mouse paperbacks.

Representative titles include *Dreamers* (a young-adult novel) by Mary-Ellen Lang Collura, *Hiccup Champion of the World* by Ken Roberts, *Dressing* (a baby board book) by Helen Oxenbury, and *Easy Peasy* by Sarah Hayes (illustrated by John Bendall-Brunello).

Query letters and SASEs should be directed to the Acquisitions Editor; correspondence will be redirected in house. The Toronto office handles fiction and children's books; the rest of the Douglas & McIntyre list is issued from the Vancouver office.

FIREFLY BOOKS

3680 Victoria Park Avenue
Willowdale, Ontario
Canada M2H 3K1
416-499-8412
800-387-5085

Firefly Books produces trade nonfiction in areas such as popular biography, popular science, lifestyles, the natural world, hobbies and crafts, gardening, food, sports, recreation, and health.

Representative of the Firefly list: *Rise and Dine* by Marcy Claman, *Nature Photography* (National Audubon Society Guide) by Tim Fitzharris, *In Quest of the Big Fish* by Henry Waszuk and Italo Labignan, *The New Northern Gardener* by Jennifer Bennett, *The Complete Breast Book: Everything You Need to Know about Breast Disease* by June Engel, *Soccer: What's It All About?* by Dick Howard, and *Mike Tyson: The Release of Power* by Reg Gutteridge and Norman Giller.

Firefly Books handles its own distribution.

Query letters and SASEs should be directed to:

Lionel Koffler, President

FITZHENRY & WHITESIDE LTD.

195 Allstate Parkway
Markham, ON L3R 4T8
905-477-9700

Fitzhenry & Whiteside Ltd. (founded in 1966) specializes in trade nonfiction (producing books in both English and French), works of fiction and literature (much of it showing a Canadian bent), and also offers a textbook list. Fitzhenry & Whiteside nonfiction titles range through Canadian history, architecture, biography, gardening, art (including puzzles and how-to), native studies, nature, and guides to collectibles and antiques. Fitzhenry & Whiteside also publishes children's books, emphasizing books for preschoolers and young schoolchildren. The house typically publishes a small number of new seasonal titles.

On the Fitzhenry & Whiteside nonfiction list: *Trees in Canada* by John Laird Farrar, *100 Best Restaurants of Canada: Canada's National Restaurant Guide to Fine Dining* by John McCann, *Toronto in Art: 150 Years through Artists' Eyes* by Edith Firth, *Contemporary Canadian Architecture: The Mainstream and Beyond* by William Bernstein and Ruth Cawker, and *Dr. Alan Brown: Portrait of a Tyrant* by B. Foster Kingsmill.

Fitzhenry & Whiteside fiction and literature includes *Celebrating Canadian Women* by Greta Hofmann Nemiroff, *The Poetry of Lucy Maude Montgomery* (selected by Kevin McCabe and John Ferns), *The Fitzhenry & Whiteside Fireside Book of Canadian Christmas* (edited by Patrick Crean), and *Tuppence Ha'Penny Is a Nickel* by Francis X. Atherton.

On the children's list: *Ladybug Garden* (written and illustrated by Celia Godkin); also of interest: *Understanding and Appreciating Your Child's Art* by Mia Johnson.

Fitzhenry & Whiteside Ltd. distributes its own list and provides distribution services in Canada for a number of United States publishers.

Query letters and SASEs should be directed to:

Robert Fitzhenry, Chairman
Adult trade books.

Sharon Fitzhenry, President

HARLEQUIN ENTERPRISES LIMITED
WORLDWIDE LIBRARY

225 Duncan Mill Road
Don Mills, ON M3B 3K9
416-445-5860

The Harlequin Enterprises home base in Ontario, Canada, issues the greater portion of Harlequin Books series, while the New York office issues several Harlequin series as well as the Silhouette list (please see listing for Harlequin Books in the directory of United States Publishers and Editors). Harlequin Enterprises also produces the Worldwide Library, which concentrates on titles in the mystery/suspense mode.

HARLEQUIN BOOKS

The Harlequin series of romance novels published in Canada, like their American counterparts, each stake out particular market-niche segments of reader interest within the overall categories of romance fiction and women's fiction.

The editorial acquisitions departments for Harlequin Romance and Harlequin Presents are located at the operation's United Kingdom offices. What follows are overviews of some of the editorial guidelines supplied to authors.

Mira Books is dedicated to mainstream single-title women's fiction in hardcover and mass-market paperback editions. Mira titles assume no particular genre designation, though the works are considered to be of interest to a primarily women's readership. Mira Books hosts a wide variety of authors and approaches.

Harlequin Temptation introduces strong, independent heroines and successful, sexy heroes who overcome conflict inherent to their heated relationships, and in the end decide to marry. The books in this series are known for their wit as well as emotional strength.

Harlequin Superromances are the longest books of the Harlequin series (approximately 350 manuscript pages) and therefore require a more complex plot and at least one fully developed subplot. This series is generally mainstream in tone, with romance of course being the propelling theme. Love scenes may be explicit so long as they exhibit good taste.

Harlequin Regency Romances are set in England during the Regency period (1811 to 1820) and the writer should be able to provide accurate details of dress, speech, and customs of that historical period. These stories are in general lighthearted and lively, often feature elements of intrigue and adventure, and offer a minimum of sexual activity.

Detailed information is available on request from the publisher. Harlequin will send prospective authors full editorial guidelines with suggested heroine and hero profiles, as well as information pertaining to manuscript length, setting, and sexual approach and content.

Make sure your query is clear as to which line it is intended for: Harlequin Romance, Harlequin Presents, Harlequin Temptation, Harlequin Superromance, or Harlequin Regency Romances. Query letters and SASEs should be directed to:

Brenda Chin, Assistant Editor
Harlequin Temptation.

Paula Eykelhof, Senior Editor
Harlequin Superromance.

Ilana Glaun, Assistant Editor
Mira Books.

Wendy Blake Kennish, Assistant Editor
Superromance, Harlequin Temptation.

Dianne Moggy, Senior Editor and Editorial Coordinator
Mira Books.

Amy Moore, Associate Editor
Mira Books.

Jane Robson, Editor
Superromance.

Susan Sheppard, Editor
Harlequin Temptation, Love and Laughter.

Zilla Soriano, Editor
Superromance.

Maureen Stonehouse, Editor
Harlequin Regency Romances and Harlequin Superromances.

Birgit David Todd, Senior Editor
Harlequin Temptation.

Malle Vallick, Editor
Harlequin Temptation, Love and Laughter.

Marsha Zinberg, Senior Editor and Editorial Coordinator, Special Projects

HARLEQUIN MILLS & BOON
HARLEQUIN PRESENTS
HARLEQUIN ROMANCE
MILLS & BOON/HARLEQUIN ENTERPRISES LTD.

Eton House, 18-24 Paradise Road
Richmond, Surrey TW9 1SR
United Kingdom

To query the U.K. divisions, write (and enclose SASE) care of the Editorial Department (especially to request guidelines), or direct inquiries to the following editors:

Tessa Shapcott, Senior Editor
Harlequin Presents (contemporary romances).

Linda Fildew, Senior Editor
Harlequin Romance (contemporary romances).

Sheila Hodgson, Senior Editor
All Mills & Boon series.

Elizabeth Johnson, Senior Editor
Love on Call (medical romances).

Karen Stoecker, Editorial Director
All Mills & Boon series.

Samantha Bell, Editor
All Mills & Boon series.

Gillian Green, Editor
All Mills & Boon series.

Marysia Juszczakievicz, Editor
All Mills & Boon series.

WORLDWIDE LIBRARY

225 Duncan Mill Road
Don Mills, ON M3B 3K9
416-445-5860

The Worldwide Library division of Harlequin Enterprises hosts two major imprints: Worldwide Mystery and Gold Eagle Books. Worldwide Library emphasizes genre fiction in the categories of mystery/suspense, action-adventure, futuristic fiction, war drama, and post-holocaust thrillers. The house gives its titles (primarily mass-market paperbacks) solid marketing and promotional support.

The Worldwide Mystery imprint produces primarily mainstream mystery and detective fiction in reprint. This imprint has not been issuing previously unpublished, original fiction. However, Worldwide is an important venue to keep in mind regarding potential reprint-rights sales.

Titles in reprint at Worldwide include *Time of Hope* by Susan B. Kelly, *A Fine Italian Hand* by Eric Wright, *Zero at the Bone* by Mary Willis Walker, *Hard Luck* by Barbara D'Amato, *Murder Takes Two* by Bernie Lee, and *The Hour of the Knife* by Sharon Zukowski.

Gold Eagle Books is known for a fast-and-furious slate of men's action adventure series with paramilitary and future-world themes. Series include Deathlands, the Destroyer, the Executioner, and Stony Man. Gold Eagle also publishes Super Books keyed to the various series—longer novels with more fully developed plots. Prospective authors should be familiar with the guidelines and regular characters associated with each series.

Query letters and SASEs should be directed to:

(Mr.) Feroze Mohammed, Senior Editor and Editorial Coordinator
Gold Eagle Books.

Randall Toye, Editorial Director
Gold Eagle-Worldwide Library.

KEY PORTER BOOKS LTD.

70 The Esplanade, 3rd Floor
Toronto, ON M5E 1R2
416-862-7777

Key Porter Books Ltd. (founded in 1981) is a midsize house that publishes a primarily nonfiction list with a Canadian twist. Key Porter produces titles in current affairs, science and health, travel, the environment, ecology, politics, and sports, and also a solid line of money books and entrepreneurial guides. Windsor Books is a Key Porter division that specializes in travel guides. Key Porter also issues books for children and young adults. In addition, the house offers coffee-table and gift editions, as well as occasional fiction and literary works.

Frontlist Key Porter titles are provided full promotional support that spotlights targeted review venues, national media exposure, magazine advertising (including co-op arrangements), and foreign-rights sales. The house maintains a strong backlist.

Among Key Porter highlights: *Canada: Romancing the Land* (created by Lorraine Monk; poetry by Miriam Waddington), *The Complete Breast Book* (Your Personal Health series) by June Engel, *Skate: 100 Years of Figure Skating* by Steve Milton (principal photography by Barbara McCutcheon), *In Quest of the Big Fish* by Henry Wasczuk and Italo Labignan, *Elizabeth: A Biography of the Queen* by Sarah Bradford, and *The Quest for the Fourth Monkey: A Thinking Person's Guide to Psychic and Spiritual Phenomena* by Sylvia Fraser.

Representative of the Key Porter backlist: *Maximum, Minimum, Medium: A Journey through Canadian Prisons* by Julius Melnitzer, *Ducks in the Wild: Conserving Waterfowl and Their Habits* by Paul A. Johnsgard, and *Starting a Business: A Complete Guide to Starting and Managing Your Own Company* (revised edition) by Gordon Brockhouse.

KEY PORTER KIDS

Key Porter Kids is an imprint that specializes in works for younger readers, including pop-ups, board books, story books, novels, and reference works. The house publishes science books for children under the imprint Greey de Pencier/Books from Owl.

Titles here are *Songs for Survival: Songs and Chants from Tribal Peoples around the World* (edited by Nikki Siegen-Smith; illustrated by Bernard Lodge), *Animal Hideaways* (text by Anita Ganeri; illustrations by Halli Verrinder), *Creepy Crawlies in 3-D!* by Rick and Susan Sammon (photography by David Burder), *How on Earth? A Question-and-Answer Book about How Our Planet Works* by Ronald Orenstein, and *Anne of Green Gables* (pop-up dollhouse with dolls).

Key Porter handles its own distribution.

Query letters and SASEs should be directed to:

Susan Renouf, Editor in Chief

LESTER PUBLISHING LIMITED

56 The Esplanade
Toronto, ON M5E 1A7
416-362-1032

Lester Publishing Limited (founded in 1991) produces a compact list of trade non-fiction and fiction and offers lines in children's and young-adult books. Lester titles have garnered an admirable array of publishing awards.

Nonfiction from Lester: *The Illustrated History of Canada* (edited by Craig Brown), *North Star to Freedom: The Story of the Underground Railroad* by Gena K. Gorrell, *Bad Blood: The Tragedy of the Canadian Tainted Blood Scandal* by Vic Parsons, *Great Moments in Canadian Baseball* by Brian Kendall, and *False God: How the Globalization Myth Has Impoverished Canada* by James Laxer.

Lester fiction and literature includes *Truly Grim Tales* (stories) by Priscilla Galloway, *A Place Not at Home* (autobiographical novel) by Eva Wiseman, *A Gift of Rags* (novel) by Abraham Boyarsky, *Travels by Night* (memoir of the 1960s) by Douglas Fetherling, *The Animals' Waltz* (novel) by Cary Fagan, and *The Rose Tree* (lyrical fiction) by Mary Walkin Keane.

Lester's list for children and young adults includes *The Night Voyagers* (novel) by Donn Kushner, *The Sugaring-Off Party* (a picture book) by Jonathan London (illustrated by Gilles Pelletier), and *Saying Good-Bye* (stories) by Linda Holeman.

Lester Publishing books are marketed and distributed to the trade by Key Porter Books.

Query letters and SASEs should be directed to:

Malcolm Lester, Publisher

Kathy Lowinger, Executive Editor

Janice Weaver, Assistant Editor

LITTLE, BROWN AND COMPANY CANADA LIMITED

148 Yorkville
Toronto, ON M5R 1C2
416-967-3888

Little, Brown and Company Canada Limited (founded in 1953) publishes original titles of Canadian interest as well as works for the wider English-speaking market. The house also purchases the Canadian rights to books published in the United States. When asked if they were interested in books by United States writers, Ann Ledden replied, "We would love to find a good new American writer." Little, Brown issues a seasonal list of new books in hardcover and trade paperback; the publisher maintains a substantial backlist.

On the Little, Brown fiction list are *The Hole That Must Be Filled* (stories) by Kenneth J. Harvey, *Theory of War* by Joan Brady, *A Suitable Boy* (a saga of India) by Vikram Seth, *Water Damage* (thriller) by Gregory Ward, *Serenity House* (satirical fable) by Christopher Hope, and *Much Improved by Death* (a Matthew Prior mystery) by Anthony Quogen.

Nonfiction from Little, Brown includes *Just a Minute: The Great Canadian Heritage Quiz Book* by Marsha Boulton, *Ribbon of Highway: The Trans-Canada Coast to Coast by Bus* by Kildare Dobbs, *The Daycare Handbook: A Parent's Guide to Finding and Keeping Quality Daycare in Canada* by Barbara Kaiser and Judy Sklar Rasminsky, *Sunburned: Memoirs of a Newspaperman* by Douglas Creighton, and *The People of the Pines: The Warriors and the Legacy of Oka* by Geoffrey York and Loreen Pindera.

Little, Brown and Company (Canada) Limited distributes its own list as well as those of United Kingdom and Commonwealth-based publishers and smaller Canadian presses.

Query letters and SASEs should be directed to:

Kim McArthur, President

MACFARLANE WALTER & ROSS

37A Hazelton Avenue
Toronto, ON M5R 2E3
416-924-7595

Macfarlane Walter & Ross specialties include current events, futurist works, social trends, and sports; a good percentage of Macfarlane books evidence a marked humorous edge. MW&R emphasizes Canadiana, especially biographies, business, history, politics, travel, and culture. The house also boasts a hefty selection of literary fiction and criticism.

Macfarlane Walter & Ross (founded in 1988) typically publishes a small seasonal list that nonetheless covers a wide range of nonfiction. MW&R publishes original titles of Canadian interest and also buys the Canadian rights to books from United States publishers. The house supports a solid backlist.

Macfarlane Walter & Ross nonfiction includes *Toronto for Kids: The Complete Family Travel Guide to Attractions, Sites and Events* by Anne Holloway, *Frank Ogden's New Book: Roadmaps for the Future* by Frank Ogden (packaged with a CD-ROM version), *Where the Jobs Are: Career Survival for Canadians in the New Global Economy* by Colin Campbell, and *Road Games: A Year in the Life of the NHL* by Roy MacGregor.

In the Macfarlane Walter & Ross literary and cultural lineup are *City to City* by Jan Morris, *A Fool in Paradise* and *The Good Wine* (a two-volume autobiography by artist Doris McCarthy), *Photographs That Changed the World* by Lorraine Monk, *The Gates of Paradise: The Anthology of Erotic Short Fiction* (edited by Alberto Manguel), and a full slate of titles by John McPhee.

Macfarlane Walter & Ross is distributed by Stoddart Publishing.

Query letters and SASEs should be directed to the Acquisitions Editor.

MACMILLAN CANADA

29 Birch Avenue
Toronto, ON M4V 1E2
416-963-8830

Macmillan Canada is especially strong in books with a Canadian connection. Nonfiction subject areas include business, sports, biographies, politics, true crime, cookbooks, history, and general reference works with a Canadian flavor. Macmillan Canada publishes selected works of fiction geared to the literary and commercial mainstream, including mysteries, suspense, and thrillers. The company also produces a line of calendars. Macmillan Canada is corporately affiliated with the British publisher Macmillan.

Representative of Macmillan Canada nonfiction: *Big, Bold, and Beautiful: Living Large on a Small Planet* by Jackqueline Hope, *Goin' the Distance: Canada's Boxing Heritage* by Murray Greig, *The Ontario Harvest Cookbook: An Exploration of Feasts and Flavours* by Anita Stewart and Julia Aitken, *Feel Fantastic: Maye Musk's Good Health Clinic* by Maye Musk, and *The Ultimate Book of Household Hints & Tips* by Cassandra Kent.

Fiction and literary works from Macmillan Canada include *Desert Kill* by Philip Gerard, *How to Start a Charter Airline* by Susan Haley, and *Genetic Soldier* by George Turner.

On the children's-interest list: *My Rainy Day Activity Book* and *The Children's Step-by-Step Cookbook* (both by Angela Wilkes), and *Sharing the Secrets: Teach Your Child to Spell* by Ruth Scott and Sharon Siamon.

Macmillan Canada distributes its own list and handles Canadian distribution for a number of international houses including IDG Books, Irwin Professional Publications, Microsoft Press, and William Morrow.

Query letters and SASEs should be directed to:

Shannon Potts, Editorial Assistant

MCCLELLAND & STEWART

481 University Avenue, Suite 200
Toronto, ON M5G 2E9
416-598-1114

McClelland & Stewart (established in 1906) publishes a wide-ranging and respected program in fiction and nonfiction, with hardcover and trade paperback lines. The house trade motto is "the Canadian publishers," signaling the fine array of Canadian authors between McClelland & Stewart covers.

Trade nonfiction areas encompass general-interest works of topical interest in current events and public issues, lifestyle and travel, medicine, religion, history, memoirs and biography, true crime, and the arts. In fiction, the McClelland & Stewart list includes mainstream and category titles as well as literary fiction. The house also publishes literary nonfiction as well as poetry. New Canadian Library is a paperback line covering Canada's literary tradition, past and present. McClelland & Stewart offers a line for young readers and vends the Audio Renaissance series of book tapes.

McClelland & Stewart nonfiction books include *Capital Walks: A Walking Guide to Ottawa* by Katharine Fletcher, *The Loyalists: Revolution, Exile, Settlement* by Christopher Moore, *Sasquatch/Bigfoot: The Search for North America's Incredible Creature* by Don Hunter with Rene Dahinden, *Blue Jays Trivia Quiz Book* by Bob Elliot, *Sculpture of the Inuit* by George Swinton, *The Uncommon Touch: An Investigation of Spiritual Healing* by Tom Harpur, and *Line Screw: My 12 Riotous Years Working Behind Bars in Some of Canada's Toughest Jails* by J. Michael Yates.

Indicative of McClelland & Stewart fiction and literary interest: *Tales from the Canadian Rockies* (edited by Brian Patton), *The Canadian Cowboy: Stories of Cows, Cowboys, and Cayuses* by Andy Russell (illustrations by Don Brestler), *For Those Who Hunt the Wounded Down* by David Adams Richards, and *George Bowering Selected Poems: 1961–1992* (edited by Roy Miki).

The house publishes *The Canadian Writer's Market: An Extensive Guide for Freelance Writers* by Jem Bates and Adrian Waller.

McClelland & Stewart distributes its own titles and handles Canadian distribution for a number of international publishing firms, such as Atlantic Monthly Press, I. B. Tauris & Company, and St. Martin's Press.

Query letters and SASEs should be directed to the Editorial Board.

McGill–Queen's University Press

Montreal office:
McGill University
3430 McTavish Street
Montreal, PQ H3A 1X9
514-398-3750

Kingston office:
Queen's University
Kingston, ON K7L 3N6

Publications from McGill–Queen's University Press include works in architecture, biography, British studies, business history, Canadian history, Canadian politics, economics, environment, French history, housing policy, international history, Irish history, Judaica, literature and literary criticism, Loyalist history, native studies, philosophy, political economy, psychology, Quebec history, sociology, urban geography, and women's studies, and also general-interest works primarily in areas of current interest in international and cultural affairs. McGill–Queen's publishes no hard sciences.

McGill–Queen's University Press (founded in 1969) produces trade books with scholarly market crossover, as well as titles geared specifically for the academic market. The press is a conjoint publishing endeavor of Queen's University (Kingston) and McGill University (Montreal). Many McGill–Queen's books have a Canadian subject slant; in addition, the house is strong in a variety of fields in the international arena as well as in the social sciences and humanities. McGill–Queen's publishes in the French and English languages.

On the McGill–Queen's list in nonfiction: *The Cassock and the Crown: Canada's Most Controversial Murder Trial* by Jean Monet, *Top Secret Exchange: The Tizard Mission and the Scientific War* by David Zimmerman, *Reasonable Self-Esteem* by Richard Keshen, *The Moral Foundations of Canadian Federalism: Paradoxes, Achievements, and Tragedies of Nationhood* by Samuel V. LaSelva, *Ontario Hydro at the Millennium: Has Monopoly's Moment Passed?* (edited by Ronald Daniels), *The Secession of Quebec and the Future of Canada* by Robert A. Young, and *The Glory of Ottawa: Canada's First Parliament Buildings* by Carolyn A. Young.

The McGill–Queen's literary purview embraces criticism, autobiography, biography, and letters. Offerings here include *Cold Comfort: My Love Affair with the Arctic* by Graham W. Rowley, *Mapping Our Selves: Canadian Women's Autobiography* by Helen M. Buss, *Pierrot in Petrograd* by J. Douglas Clayton, *The Birth of Modernism: Ezra Pound, T. S. Eliot, W. B. Yeats, and the Occult* by Leon Surette, and *Fear and Temptation: The Image of the Indigene in Canadian, Australian, and New Zealand Literatures* by Terry Goldie.

Distribution for McGill–Queen's University Press is handled by the University of Toronto Press.

Query letters and SASEs should be directed to:

Peter Blaney, Editor (Montreal)
All areas.

Philip Cercone, Director of Press and Acquisitions Editor (Montreal)
All areas.

NC PRESS LIMITED

345 Adelaide Street West
Toronto, ON M5V 1R5
416-593-6284

Titles on the NC Press list engage a broad range of topics that cover the spectrum of general trade interest in areas such as cooking, health, Canadian history, politics, poetry, art and performance, literature and literary criticism, folkways and lifeways, the natural world, self-help, and popular psychology.

NC Press Limited (incorporated in 1970) is a trade publisher of Canadian books dedicated to the social, political, economic, and spiritual health of the human community. This is a small press—currently publishing a frontlist of six to ten new books each year—with an expansive vision: "To make a difference." NC Press thus strives to present complex ideas in ways accessible to a wide readership. Among NC Press books are numerous literary-award winners. The press has served as agent for non-Canadian publishers, and catalogs a substantial backlist.

In 1988 Gary Perly, president of Perly's Maps, purchased a majority interest in NC Press Limited; the house now produces the Perly's map and atlas series, which offers a strong line of urban atlases and street guides to environs such as Toronto, Montreal, and Quebec City.

NC Press books include *Ninety-Nine Days: The Ford Strike in Windsor in 1945* by Herb Colling, *Living and Learning with a Child Who Stutters: From a Parent's Point of View* by Lise G. Cloutier-Steele, *A Woman in My Position: The Politics of Breast Implant Safety* by Linda Wilson with Dianne Brown, and *Eating Bitterness: A Vision Beyond Prison Walls* by Arthur Solomon.

Literary and cultural works include *One Animal Among Many: Gaia, Goats and Garlic* by David Walter-Toews, *Voices from the Odeyak* by Michael Posluns, *Folktales of French Canada* by Edith Fowke, and *Images: Thirty Stories by Favorite Writers* (with paintings by Len Gibbs).

NC Press books are distributed via the publisher's network, which involves independent sales representatives worldwide and the fulfillment services of University of Toronto Press.

Query letters and SASEs should be directed to:

Caroline Walker, President and Publisher

PENGUIN BOOKS CANADA LIMITED

10 Alcorn Avenue, Suite 300
Toronto, ON M4V 3B2
416-925-2249

Penguin Books Canada Limited (founded in 1974) operates independently of its American affiliate Penguin USA. Penguin Canada's mandate is to publish Canadian authors; the house does so with fine style, covering the general trade nonfiction mother lode as well as mainstream and category fiction and literary works.

The publisher also purveys via its catalog and distribution network featured titles from the parent company's various divisions including Penguin USA, Bloomsbury, Viking Australia, and Viking UK. Among Penguin Canada's offerings is a major concentration of works from Commonwealth-based writers. The Viking Canada imprint hosts a select list of fiction and nonfiction. Penguin Puffin and Viking Kestrel are the house's juvenile imprints. Penguin Canada markets the Highbridge audio line of books on cassette.

From the Penguin Canada list: *The Windsor Castle: Official Guide* by Michael Joseph, *Shakedown: How the Government Screws You from A to Z* by James Bovard, *The Puck Starts Here: The Origin of Canada's Great Winter Game—Ice Hockey* by Garth Vaughn, *The Sacred Earth* (a gift volume featuring the photography of Courtney Milne), *The Pilgrim's Guide to the Sacred Earth* (travel reference) by Sherrill Miller, *Dead Silence: The Greatest Mystery in Arctic Discovery* by John Geiger and Owen Beattie, *From Here to Paternity: An Intimate View of a Father's Day* by Jay Teitel, and *The Night Inside: A Vampire Thriller* by Nancy Baker. Penguin also offers works by Mordechai Richler and Peter C. Newman, among other Canadian scribes.

Penguin Books Canada Limited utilizes the services of its own distribution center.

PENGUIN BOOKS CANADA BOOKS FOR YOUNG READERS

Penguin Books Canada publishes a full slate of books for young readers, which covers reading levels from preschool through young adult (with the focus of the program in the range of preschool through grade six). The house produces easy-readers, lift-the-flap books, mini editions, giant books, board books, pop-up books, joke books, fiction, folklore, poetry, music, and plays as well as general nonfiction. Imprints include Puffin, Kestrel, and NAL Young Adult.

Young readers' titles from Penguin Books Canada include *Coming to Tea* by Sarah Garland, *Elephant Pie* by Hilda Offen, *Rent a Genius* by Gillian Cross, *Nini at Carnival* by Errol Lloyd, *Why Mosquitoes Buzz in People's Ears: A West African Tale* by Verna Aardema, and *Just Too Cool* by Jamie Callan.

In accordance with its current acquisitions policy, Penguin Books Canada is not accepting unsolicited manuscripts. Query letters and SASEs should be directed to:

Cynthia Good, Publisher

RANDOM HOUSE OF CANADA LIMITED

1265 Aerowood Drive
Mississauga, ON L4W 1B9
416-624-0672

Random House of Canada Limited (founded in 1944) is a subsidiary of Random House, Inc., the United States publisher. The house produces a list of new titles from its Canadian offices, with a major concentration in books of appeal to the Canadian market.

Random House of Canada operates its own marketing network and handles Canadian distribution for the Random House U.S. divisional imprints and client companies, such as National Geographic Books, Prima Publishing, Shambhala Publications, and Sierra Club Books.

Query letters and SASEs should be directed to:

Douglas Pepper, Executive Editor

STODDART PUBLISHING CO. LTD.

34 Lesmill Road
Don Mills, ON M3B 2T6
416-445-3333

Stoddart nonfiction category areas include humor, history, military history, politics, biography, cooking, environment, nutrition, and business and consumer guides. Stoddart also publishes a solid fiction line that encompasses mainstream novels and genre categories including mysteries and thrillers. Stoddart Publishing (founded in 1984) is the trade-publishing arm of General Publishing Company and produces a wide range of titles with a Canadian orientation or by Canadian authors.

Nonfiction on Stoddart: *From the Cop Shop: Hilarious Tales from Our Men and Women of the Badge* by Peter V. MacDonald, *The Mighty River* by Claude Villeneuve (illustrated by Frédéric Back; translated by Fred Reed), *Money to Burn: Trudeau, Mulroney, and the Bankruptcy of Canada* by D'Arcy Jenish, *Contracting Your Own Home: A Step-by-Step Guide* (revised edition) by David Caldwell, and *Freenet: Canadian On-line Access, the Free and Easy Way* by Pierre Bourque and Rosaleen Dickson.

Stoddart fiction and literature includes *Sandman Blues* (novel) by Stéphane Bourguignon (translated by David Homel), *A Shriek in the Forest Night: Wilderness Encounters* by R. D. Lawrence, and *The Third Illustrated Anthology of Erotica* (compiled and edited by Charlotte Hill and William Wallace).

Stoddart handles its own distribution, as well as distribution for books issued by Anansi, the Boston Mills Press, and Macfarlane Walter & Ross.

STODDART JUVENILES

Stoddart produces Canada's largest list of young-adult paperbacks, including those in the Gemini and Junior Gemini lines. Stoddart Young Readers are for preschoolers through young adults, and include picture books, pop-up books, fairy tales, and science titles for young adults.

Query letters and SASEs should be directed to:

Don Bastian, Managing Editor

UNIVERSITY OF BRITISH COLUMBIA PRESS

6344 Memorial Road
Vancouver, BC V6T 1Z2
604-822-3259

Categories of University of British Columbia Press interest include Canadian culture and history, political science, Asian studies, native studies with an accent on the Northwest Coast, Pacific Rim studies, global geography, fisheries and forestry, environmental studies, Northern studies, and Canadian sociology.

University of British Columbia Press (founded in 1971) publishes academic books, as well as general-interest works, with an emphasis on Canadian subjects.

On the University of British Columbia Press list: *Canada and Quebec: One Country, Two Histories* by Robert Bothwell; *A Persistent Spirit: Towards Understanding Aboriginal Health in British Columbia* (edited by Peter H. Stephenson, Susan J. Elliott, Leslie T. Foster, and Jill Harris); *Outlines of Classical Chinese Grammar* by Edwin G. Pulleyblank; *Killer Whales: The Natural History and Genealogy of* Orcinus orca *in British Columbia and Washington State* by John K. B. Ford, Graeme M. Ellis, and Kenneth C. Balcomb; *Morals and the Media: Ethics and Canadian Journalism* by Nicholas Russell; and *Haida Monumental Art: Villages of the Queen Charlotte Islands* by George F. MacDonald.

University of British Columbia Press handles its own distribution.

Query letters and SASEs should be directed to:

Jean Wilson, Senior Editor

UNIVERSITY OF TORONTO PRESS

10 Saint Mary Street, Suite 700
Toronto, ON M4Y 2W8
416-978-2239

University of Toronto Press publishes in a range of fields including history and politics; women's studies; health, family, and society; law and crime; economics; workplace communication; theory/culture; language, literature, semiotics, and drama; medieval studies; Renaissance studies; Erasmus; Italian-language studies; East European studies; classics; and nature. The list includes topical titles in Canadian studies, native studies, sociology, anthropology, urban studies, modern languages, and music, as well as travel and touring guides.

University of Toronto Press produces titles for the general trade as well as academic works. UTP issues a series of specialist journals of note including *Scholarly Publishing*. The house produces no original contemporary fiction or poetry.

Representing the University of Toronto list: *In a Crystal Land: Canadian Explorers in Antarctica* by Dean Beeby; *Everybody Does: Crime by the Public* by Thomas Gabor; *Bankrupt Education: The Decline of Liberal Education in Canada* by Peter C. Emberley and Waller R. Newell; *Sexual Assault in Canada: A Decade of Legal and Social Change* (edited by Julian V. Roberts and Renate M. Mohr); *Historical Atlas of East Central Europe* by Paul Robert Magocsi (with cartographic design by Geoffrey J. Matthews); and *The Crucible of War, 1939–1945: The Official History of the Royal Canadian Air Force* (third volume) by Brereton Greenhous, Stephen J. Harris, William C. Johnston, and William G. P. Rawling.

Publications in the arts and literature include *Allusion: A Literary Graft* by Allan H. Pasco, *Discoveries of the Other: Alliterity in the Work of Leonard Cohen, Hubert Aquin, Michael Ondaatje, and Nicole Brossard* by Winifred Siemerling, *Naming Canada: Essays on Place Names from Canadian Geographic* by Alan Rayburn, *The Political Writings of Mary Wollstonecraft* (edited by Janet Todd), *Sounding Differences: Conversations with Seventeen Canadian Women Writers* by Janice Williamson, *The Logic of Ecstasy: Canadian Mystical Painting 1920–1940* by Ann Davis, and *Northern Voices: Inuit Writing in English* (edited by Penny Petrone).

University of Toronto Press oversees a distributional network encompassing offices and sales agents worldwide; the house handles titles from other book publishers as well as for institutions such as the Royal Ontario Museum and Canadian Museum of Nature.

Query letters and SASEs should be directed to:

Joan Bulger, Editor
Art and classics, architecture.

Virgil Duff, Executive Editor
Social sciences, scholarly medical books, law and criminology, women's studies.

Gerald Hallowell, Editor
Canadian history and Canadian literature.

Ron Schoeffel, Senior House Editor
Romance languages, native languages, religion and theology, education, philosophy.

Kieran Simpson, Editor, Department of Directories

Suzanne Rancourt, Editor
Medieval studies, medieval and Old English Literature.

Book Publishing for
the Canadian Market

GREG IOANNOU

Canadian and United States writers who are considering submitting inquiries to Canadian publishers should keep a few important points in mind. In most cases, Canadian book publishers are looking for material of Canadian interest. However, this does not mean that they are not interested in queries from writers who reside in or are native to other countries. Indeed, there is a rich current in the publishing stream that features the Canadian experience from outlander or expatriate perspectives. Appropriate queries (see the listings for these publishers) will be considered. Keep in mind the markets as well as the mandates of each of these houses.

Publishing in Canada is markedly different from the industry in the United States. A large percentage of Canadian-owned publishing houses are small to medium sized, with net sales that seem low to those who are accustomed to the standards of the U.S. marketplace. (Remember, the English-language Canadian market is only one-tenth the size of the U.S. market.)

Canada *is* a separate market, and some writers are able to sell the Canadian rights to their books separately from the U.S. rights. Before you sign a contract for "North American rights," consider whether your book would likely sell enough copies in Canada that it would be of interest to a Canadian publisher.

Don't just blithely sell the Canadian rights to a hockey book or a biography of a Canadian celebrity (such as Faye Wray, Neil Young, or Peter Jennings) to a U.S. publisher for the blanket "foreign rights" or "world English-language rights" rate—the Canadian rights alone may be worth more than the U.S. or rest of the worldwide rights are!

The Canadian government directly subsidizes the book industry to help ensure that Canadian writers get their works published domestically and to keep the national market from being overwhelmed by the publishing giants to the south. The grant system makes possible a greater independence on the part of Canadian-owned houses, which comprise the creative heart of publishing in Canada.

Never send an unsolicited manuscript to a Canadian publisher. Many Canadian publishers will send them back unopened because of a court ruling that forced Doubleday Canada to pay a writer thousands of dollars in compensation for losing the only copy of an unsolicited manuscript. Send query letters only!

It is a nice touch for American writers to remember that Canada is *not* part of the United States, so Canadian publishers cannot use U.S. stamps to return anything sent to them. Use International Reply Coupons (available at any post office) instead.

PART TWO

Writer's Guide Directory of Literary Agents

AEI
ATCHITY EDITORIAL/ENTERTAINMENT INTERNATIONAL, INC.
LITERARY MANAGEMENT AND EXECUTIVE PRODUCTION

9601 Wilshire Boulevard
Box 1202
Beverly Hills, CA 90210
213-932-0407
fax: 213-932-0321
e-mail: aeikja@lainet.com
website: http://www.lainet.com/~aeikja

Manager names: Kenneth Atchity, president; Chi-Li Wong, partner and vice president of development and production; Andrea McKeown, director of development, books; Sidney Kiwitt, business affairs (NY). Writer's Lifeline associates: David Angsten, Paul Aratow, Monica Faulkner (senior editor), Sherry Gottlieb, Michelle Ozolsa, Ed Stackler, Bill Thompson, and Alan Williams.

> *Personal information pertaining to Ken Atchity:*
> **Born:** Eunice, Louisiana; January 16, 1944.
> **Education:** B.A., Georgetown; Ph.D. in comparative literature, Yale.
> **Career history:** Professor of comparative literature, Occidental College; instructor, UCLA Writer's Program (1970–1987). Author of thirteen books, including *A Writer's Time: A Guide to the Creative Process, from Vision Through Revision* (Norton), *The Mercury Transition: Career Change Through Entrepreneurship* (Longmeadow), *The Renaissance Reader* (HarperCollins), and *Greenlighting Your Story Idea* (with Chi-Li Wong; forthcoming Owl Books). Producer of twenty films for video, television, and theater, including *Champagne for Two* (Cinemax-HBO), *Amityville: The Evil Escapes* (NBC), *Shadow of Obsession* (NBC), and *Falling Over Backwards.*
> **Hobbies/personal interests:** Collecting author-autographed books; pitchers; tennis; travel.
> **Subjects/categories most enthusiastic about managing:** Nonfiction: Strong main-stream nonfiction, especially true and heroic stories with TV or film potential; business books, especially with entrepreneurial orientation; previously published books with solid sales records. Fiction: Mainstream commercial novels (action, horror, thrillers, suspense, mainstream romance, espionage, outstanding science fiction with strong characters) that can also be made into TV or feature films. Scripts: For TV: strong female leads. For Film: all kinds, especially action, romantic comedy, thrillers, science fiction, and horror.
> **Subjects/categories not interested in managing:** Drug-related; fundamental religious; category romance; category mystery or Western; poetry; children's; "interior" confessional fiction.
> **Best way for a prospective client to initiate contact:** Query letter (with SASE) and twenty-five sample pages.
> **Reading-fee policy:** No reading fee. $150 one-time fee charged for expenses, on signing, to writers who have not yet previously published a book. AEI's Writers'

Lifeline, an affiliated company, offers an analysis service with fees ranging from $250 to $650. We offer this service only to writers requesting specific feedback for their careers or seeking to enter our Writer's Lifeline consulting service for one-on-one coaching by editors experienced in the methods outlined in *A Writer's Time*.

Client representation in the following categories: Nonfiction 45%; fiction 45%; screenplays 10%.

Commission: Books: 15% of all domestic sales, 25% foreign, Scripts: 10%. If we exercise our option to executive produce a project for film or television, commission on dramatic rights sale is reduced to 5%.

Number of titles sold during the past year: 21.

Approximate percentage of all submissions (from queries to manuscripts) that are rejected: 95%.

Representative titles sold:

Fiction:

180 Seconds at Willow Park by Rick Lynch (New Line Pictures).

Megalodon by Steve Allen (Walt Disney Pictures).

Sign of the Watcher by Brett Bartlett (Propaganda Films).

Signs of the Mother, Telephone Tag, Moral Obligations by Cheryl Saban (Dove Books).

The Hong Kong Sanction by Mitch Rossi (Kensington/Pinnacle).

The Cruelest Lie by Milton Lyles (Barclay House).

An Invitation to Sanctuary by George Klembith and Tammy Schwartz (Barclay House).

Chokecherry Roots by Floyd Martinez (Arte Público).

Nonfiction:

Success through Cashflow Reengineering by Jim Sagner (American Management Association).

The Rag Street Journal: A Guide to Thrift Shops in North America by Elizabeth Mason (Owl).

Anatomy of Deceit by Jerry M. Blaskovich (Barclay House).

Simply Heavenly: The Monastery Vegetarian Cookbook by Abbott George Burke (Macmillan).

The Hollywood Facelift by Nola Rocco (Barclay House).

Atchity's Encyclopedia of American Folklore (Random House).

Marilyn by Moonlight by Jack Allen (Barclay House).

Description of the Client from Hell: He or she is so self-impressed it's impossible to provide constructive criticism; makes his or her package impossible to open, and provides return envelope too small to be used.

Description of Dream Client: He or she comes in with an outstanding novel, plus an outline for two more, and is delighted to take commercial direction on the writing and the career.

The most common mistakes potential clients make when soliciting an agent to represent them: The most costly mistake is remaining ignorant of where your work fits into the market, and of who your reader might be. Don't send kinds of work (romances, light mysteries, poetry, episodic scripts) we're specifically *not* looking for.

What writers can do to enhance their chances of getting an agent (besides being good writers): Be a great writer and a determined, optimistic client ready for an exciting, new lifelong career. And think "high concept": Would this story make a block-buster film?

Why did you become a manager? Nearly two decades of teaching literature and creative writing at Occidental College and UCLA Writers Program, reviewing for the *Los Angeles Times Book Review*, and working with the dreams of creative people through Dreamworks (which I cofounded) provided natural foundation for my new career. I made the transition from academic life through producing, but continued my publishing-consulting business by connecting my authors with agents. As I spent more and more time developing individuals' writing careers, as well as working directly with publishers in my search for film properties, it became obvious that literary management was the next step. True or fiction, what turns me on is a good story.

What might you be doing if you weren't a manager? If I weren't a literary manager and producer, I'd be doing the same thing and calling it something else.

Comments: Dream big. Don't let anyone define your dream for you. Risk it. The rewards in this new career are as endless as your imagination, and the risks, though real, are not greater than the risk of suffocating on a more secure career path. Begin by learning all you can about the business of writing, publishing, and producing, and recognizing that as far-off and exalted as they may seem, the folks in these professions are as human as anyone else. We're enthusiasts, like you: Make me enthused!

MARCIA AMSTERDAM AGENCY

41 West 82nd Street, Suite 9A
New York, NY 10024
212-873-4945

Agent: Marcia Amsterdam.
  Education: B.A., English and journalism, Brooklyn College.
  Career history: Editor; agent (1960–present).
  Hobbies/personal interests: Reading, theater, movies, art, travel, discovering wonderful new writers.
  Subjects/categories most enthusiastic about agenting: An eclectic list of mainstream and category fiction and popular nonfiction. I enjoy medical and legal thrillers, character-driven science fiction, mysteries, horror, historical romance, contemporary women's fiction, and quality young-adult fiction.
  Subjects/categories not interested in agenting: Children's books, poetry, short stores, technical books, thrillers about drug cartels.
  Best way for a prospective client to initiate contact: A query letter (with SASE).
  Reading-fee policy: No reading fee.
  Client representation in the following categories: Nonfiction, 5%; Fiction, 95%.
  Commission: 15% domestic; 20% on foreign sales and movie and television sales (split with subagents); 10% on screenplays.

Number of titles sold during the past year: A fair number.

Approximate percentage of all submissions (from queries through manuscripts) that are rejected: Alas, most.

Representative titles sold:

Free Fall (Dell).

Back Slash (Kensington).

Children of the Dawn (Warner).

The X-Files Trivia Book (Kensington).

The most common mistakes potential clients make when soliciting an agent to represent them: Spelling and grammar still count, as does a comfortable, legible typeface.

What writers can do to enhance their chances of getting an agent (besides being good writers): A smartly written query letter that makes me smile, that asks a surprising question, that presents an original idea in an interesting voice.

Description of the Client from Hell: I wouldn't know. I've never had one.

Description of Dream Client: One who trusts the reader, is professional, adaptable, has a sense of humor, and has confidence in my judgment.

Why did you become an agent? When I was an editor, other editors often came to me for suggestions about books they were working on. I found that I enjoyed giving editorial and career advice. One editor said, "You keep selling my books. Why don't you become an agent?" So I did.

What might you be doing if you weren't an agent? Reading published books more, traveling more.

ARCADIA

20A Old Neversink Road
Danbury, CT 06811
203-797-0993

Agent: Victoria Gould Pryor.

Born: August 14, 1945.

Education: B.A., Pembroke College in Brown University; M.A., NYU.

Career history: John Cushman Agency, Sterling Lord Agency, Harold Matson Agency, Literistic Ltd., Arcadia.

Hobbies/personal interests: Science, medicine, nature, foreign affairs, fine fiction, thrillers, children, education, law, art, classical music, business, current affairs, gardening.

Subjects/categories most enthusiastic about agenting: Literary and commercial fiction. Nonfiction in science, true crime, true business, current affairs, plus anything else that is intriguing and wonderful.

Subjects/categories not interested in agenting: Science fiction, fantasy, children's/young adult, humor, how-to and self-help.

Best way for a prospective client to initiate contact: Detailed query letter with sample material plus SASE.

Reading-fee policy: No reading fee.

Client representation in the following categories: Nonfiction, 75%; Fiction, 25%.

Commission: 15% for new clients.

Number of titles sold during the past year: 10.

Approximate percentage of all submissions (from queries through manuscripts) that are rejected: 99.9%.

Representative titles sold:

A Sense of Time: The Search for the Clock Gene (Knopf).

When the Air Hits Your Brain: Tales of Neurosurgery (Norton).

No Visible Wounds: Emotional Battering of Women (Contemporary).

Spy Operations That Changed the Course of the 20th Century (Wiley). Espionage.

Listening Now (Random House). Fiction.

Sacred Places: Science and the Study of Ancient Intangibles (Addison-Wesley).

Description of the Client from Hell: The Client from Hell delivers extremely late or not at all, insists on calling after hours or on weekends, usually to deliver complex information that should be put in writing. He/she knows best, whatever information or advice is offered, and overvalues his/her own work. Fortunately, I've never had first-hand experience with this kind of author.

Description of Dream Client: Like most of the authors I work with, a dream client behaves like a professional, has intriguing ideas, delivers top writing on time and is a mensch.

The most common mistakes potential clients make when soliciting an agent to represent them: Study the market carefully before you choose your subject. Look at what exists already in your field and learn from it; know your field and find your niche. Too many writers show their work half-cocked and make it easy for an agent to say no. Fiction writers don't need to demonstrate that their subject is timely; a true writer knows that timeliness does not necessarily mean worthiness. And a good agent has some sense of what is happening in the world and in the book business.

What writers can do to enhance their chances of getting an agent (besides being good writers): A professionally prepared presentation leaps out from whatever else is on one's desk at the time. It is thorough, thoughtful, intelligent. The writer has clearly done his/her homework and has lovingly and carefully prepared a document that is provocative and enticing. It grabs you in your heart and gut, demands your respect, and will not let you say no.

Why did you become an agent? The luck of the draw: I stumbled onto the perfect field for me, combining a love of writing, people and business, with a little bit of law and social work thrown in on the side.

What might you be doing if you weren't an agent? I'd be an unhappy and prosperous doctor or lawyer, or a happy and starving woodworker.

Comments: It's a jungle out there. Prepare yourself for anything and everything. Have a sturdy spouse (preferably one who is independently wealthy or at least works full-time) and a sturdier ego. Work hard, have a high threshold for frustration, and a well-developed sense of adventure and humor. You'll need it all.

THE AUTHOR'S AGENCY

3355 North Five Mile Road, Suite 332
Boise, ID 83713-3925
208-376-5477

Agent: Rhonda J. Winchell.

Born: San Diego, California.

Education: B.A., anthropology, Pacific Lutheran University (summa cum laude).

Career history: We are in our second year of agenting. As such, we bring enthusiasm for our authors to the editors when we pitch them.

Hobbies/personal interests: Reading and movies, movies and reading, Reggae music, trout fishing.

Subjects/categories most enthusiastic about agenting: Because our personal tastes and interests are broad, we are open to almost anything. We most enjoy the writer who opens a door we might not have if left to our personal tastes.

Subjects/categories not interested in agenting: No such subject.

Best way for a prospective client to initiate contact: Writers are welcome to contact us in the manner that best suits them. Phone calls are welcome. Letters are welcome. Manuscripts are welcome. Our door is open to any writer who is professional and courteous in contacting us. We believe writers contribute greatly to society and are vital to the health of a society.

Reading-fee policy: No reading fee.

Client representation in the following categories: Nonfiction, 33 1/3%; Fiction, 33 1/3%; Scripts, 33 1/3%.

Commission: 15%.

Number of titles sold during the past year: Confidential.

Approximate percentage of all submissions (from queries through manuscripts) that are rejected: We never use the "r" word.

Representative titles sold: We provide this information to our authors when offering a contract.

The most common mistakes potential clients make when soliciting an agent to represent them: Because we do not expect authors to be marketing people, it is not possible to make a mistake in contacting us. If they've written a terrific book/script, we'll read it off a brown paper bag.

What writers can do to enhance their chances of getting an agent (besides being good writers): We feel very spoiled when a writer encloses a résumé or a brief note about their background. Clean, crisp pages are heavenly. Enclosing SASE makes us swoon.

Description of the Client from Hell: We do not have any clients from hell.

Description of Dream Client: Our dream client is one who realizes that the agent is worth the 15 percent and then some. A couple of our dream clients stay ahead of their deadlines and are always plotting/planning their next book.

Why did you become an agent? I became an agent after realizing that I did not have the patience to spend my life as a writer (although I've had nonfiction published in national magazines). However, as a literary person since childhood, agenting is a natural choice for my advocative personality.

What might you be doing if you weren't an agent? If I were not an agent, I would be a movie producer.

Comments: We are greatly appreciative of the authors who place their work with us. Books are the foundation of a civilization, and the freedom to express ourselves through the medium of printed words remains the most powerful presence of individual rights in the world.

LORETTA BARRETT BOOKS INC.

101 Fifth Avenue
New York, NY 10003

Agent: Loretta A. Barrett.

Education: B.A., M.A., (teaching), University of Pennsylvania.

Career history: Executive editor, vice president, Doubleday. Has had own literary agency since 1990.

Hobbies/personal interests: All outdoor activities; loves to travel.

Subjects/categories most enthusiastic about agenting: Nonfiction interests in psychology, New Age, women's issues, general. Fiction interests in women's fiction, mysteries, thrillers.

Subjects/categories not interested in agenting: Unsolicited manuscripts, children's books, mainstream romance, science fiction/fantasy, horror, reference, textbooks.

Best way for a prospective client to initiate contact: Query letter (with SASE).

Reading-fee policy: No reading fee.

Client representation in the following categories: Nonfiction, 60%; Fiction, 40%.

Commission: 15%.

Number of titles sold during the past year: 45.

The most common mistakes potential clients make when soliciting an agent to represent them: Not sending an SASE; rambling, long letters; sending an unsolicited manuscript.

What writers can do to enhance their chances of getting an agent (besides being good writers): A short, to-the-point letter including a brief synopsis of the work. A separate page with credentials is also appreciated.

Why did you become an agent? I like working with authors and developing projects.

What might you be doing if you weren't an agent? I would be an editor, as I had been previously.

THE WENDY BECKER LITERARY AGENCY

530-F Grand Street, Suite 11-H
New York, NY 10002
Telephone/fax: 212-228-5940
e-mail: dulf86a@prodigy.com

Agent: Wendy Becker.

　　Education: B.S., psychology, SUNY at Albany.

　　Career history: Associate editor, McGraw-Hill. Editor, John Wiley & Sons. Agency begun 1994.

　　Hobbies/personal interests: Reading (what else?), music/opera, travel.

　　Subjects/categories most enthusiastic about agenting: Nonfiction (trade): business, biography, history, current events, parenting/psychology. Selective "genre" fiction: mystery, romance, science fiction.

　　Subjects/categories not interested in agenting: Poetry, literary fiction, short stories, children's books, anything in the college market.

　　Best way for a prospective client to initiate contact: Query letter (with SASE), to include outline, table of contents, author résumé, and up to three sample chapters. Do *not* call. Do *not* send complete manuscripts.

　　Reading-fee policy: No reading fee.

　　Client representation in the following categories: Nonfiction, 80%; Fiction, 20%.

　　Commission: 15%.

　　The most common mistakes potential clients make when soliciting an agent to represent them: Never approach an agent initially via telephone, because there is no way to properly evaluate an author without seeing his/her work.

BERMAN, BOALS AND FLYNN

225 Lafayette Street, Suite 1207
New York, NY 10012
212-343-1244

Agents: Lois Berman, Judy Boals, Jim Flynn.

　　Career history: Agency is over 20 years old.

　　Subjects/categories most enthusiastic about agenting: Dramatic and black comedies. (Works for theater and screen.)

　　Subjects/categories not interested in agenting: Works exhibiting extreme violence and/or that are abusive to anyone.

　　Best way for a prospective client to initiate contact: Query letter (with SASE), biography, current work available.

　　Representation: Dramatic only.

　　Commission: 10%.

　　Approximate percentage of all submissions (from queries through manuscripts) that are rejected: 98%.

　　The most common mistakes potential clients make when soliciting an agent to represent them: Too many phone calls. With no track record, claims a similarity in talent to well-established writers.

　　Description of Dream Client: Keeps writing, trying new things, grows.

　　Why did you become an agent? Love theater. Enjoy putting together creative people.

　　What might you be doing if you weren't an agent? Producing theater.

MEREDITH BERNSTEIN LITERARY AGENCY, INC.

2112 Broadway, Suite 503A
New York, NY 10023
212-799-1007
fax: 212-799-1145

Agents: Meredith Bernstein; Elizabeth Cavanaugh, associate.

Born: Bernstein: July 9, 1946; Hartford, Connecticut; Cavanaugh: October 16, 1962.

Education: Bernstein: B.A., University of Rochester, 1968; Cavanaugh: B.A., literature and creative writing, Ohio University, Athens, Ohio.

Career history: Bernstein: Many jobs before becoming an agent: freelance reader, story editor, and worked for another agency for five years before starting my own in 1981. Cavanaugh: Before working in publishing, held a number of positions that were "book" related, including a period as a librarian; began in publishing, with the Bernstein agency in the mid-1980s, and was instrumental in the development of our foreign rights activity.

Hobbies/personal interests: Bernstein: I am a collector of vintage and contemporary costume jewelry and clothing, so fashion is a strong interest; sports of all kinds; almost any cultural event—I'm an avid theater goer; spending time with friends; travel, adventure, and personal growth work. Cavanaugh: I am interested in all forms of art and love museums, movies, dance, music (I studied the violin for 10 years), and, of course, reading. I am also an avid cook, love gardening, and am currently renovating a 70-year-old house. I am a strong environmentalist and love animals and nature and enjoy camping, hiking, and canoeing.

Subjects/categories most enthusiastic about agenting: Bernstein: personal memoirs, women's issues, medical and psychological subjects, almost any strong *narrative* nonfiction; good novels; literary fiction; creative projects. Cavanaugh: narrative nonfiction, parenting, pop-science, general nonfiction, mysteries, literary fiction, mainstream fiction.

Subjects/categories not interested in agenting: Bernstein: Anything too technical, science fiction, children's books. Cavanaugh: science fiction, children's, poetry, or screenplays.

Best way for a prospective client to initiate contact: A query letter with SASE.

Reading-fee policy: No reading fee.

Client representation in the following categories: Nonfiction, 50%; Fiction, 50%.

Commission: 15% domestic; 20% on foreign sales (split with subagents).

Number of titles sold during the past year: Many!

Approximate percentage of all submissions (from queries through manuscripts) that are rejected: Unsure, but probably fairly high, because we must truly believe in the projects we represent and, therefore, we are selective about what we request to see.

Representative titles sold:

Bernstein:

Gray Matter by David Jacobs (Simon & Schuster).

Beauty Politics by Rebecca Carroll (Crown).

Things I Wish I'd Known Sooner by Jaroldeen Edwards (Pocket).

Antiques Across America by Nancy McCarthy (Avon).
Lessons from the Heart by Samantha Gieri and Mary Pesaresi (Prima).
Three titles by Sharon Sola (Mira).
Cavanaugh:
Our Forever Family by Maggie Conroy (nonfiction) (Kensington Hardcover).
Cannibal King by Marilyn Campbell (fiction) (Oryx).

The most common mistakes potential clients make when soliciting an agent to represent them: Bernstein: Poor presentation, no SASE. Cavanaugh: Poorly researched projects (which includes not knowing the market in terms of what is already on the shelves for the type of book they are writing), sloppy presentation.

What writers can do to enhance their chances of getting an agent (besides being good writers): Bernstein: Be a great storyteller! Present a good idea. Be a person well versed in his/her field, well prepared, and enthusiastic. Cavanaugh: Submit a clean, professional presentation with something fresh and new to say or with a unique voice in which to tell the tale.

Description of the Client from Hell: Bernstein: Pushy, demanding, inflexible, calls too much, sloppy presentation of material, egomaniacal. Cavanaugh: For me, a difficult client is one who does not listen well.

Description of Dream Client: Bernstein: Professional, courteous, sees our relationship as teamwork, respects how hard I work for him/her. Cavanaugh: A Dream Client is first and foremost a gifted writer (and researcher), whose talent and passion for his/her work brings the project to life. Second, dream writers take a professional approach to their career.

Why did you become an agent? Bernstein: I was born to do this! Cavanaugh: As an agent, the diversity of projects I represent allows me to work within the creative process in *many* different genres and with many different publishers.

What might you be doing if you weren't an agent? Bernstein: I wouldn't mind running another creative business—fashion, public relations, or maybe a store. Something that requires vision, sales ability, and gives visible results. Cavanaugh: It would most likely involve some aspect of books or publishing (maybe editing or even writing) or perhaps be as far afield as environmental science or catering.

Pam Bernstein & Associates Inc.

790 Madison Avenue
New York, NY 10021
212-288-1700

Agent: Pam Bernstein.

Career history: Director, foreign rights, William Morris Agency, 1978–1992.

Hobbies/personal interests: Reading, sports skiing, sailing, horseback riding, cooking, gardening.

Subjects/categories most enthusiastic about agenting: Nonfiction: adult, women's issues. Fiction: adult, women's. Also, espionage thrillers; biography; health, medicine, self-improvement; Jewish projects; spiritual.

Subjects/categories not interested in agenting: Science fiction, horror, "coffee table" books.

Best way for a prospective client to initiate contact: Query letter with an SASE.

Reading-fee policy: No reading fee.

Client representation in the following categories: Nonfiction, 60%; Fiction, 40%.

Commission: 15%.

Number of titles sold during the past year: 20.

Approximate percentage of all submissions (from queries through manuscripts) that are rejected: 90%.

Representative titles sold:

Recovery of Sacred Psychology by Peter Rinehart (Addison-Wesley).

Rabbi, Rabbi by Andrew Kane (St. Martin's Press).

A Jury of Her Peers by Jean Hanff Korlity (Crown).

JobSmarts For 20-Somethings by Bradley Richardson (Vintage/Random House).

The Virgin Homeowner by Janice Papolos (Norton).

The Perfect Setting by Peri Wolfman and Charles Gold (Clarkson Potter).

Tumbling by Diane McKinney-Whetstone (William Morrow).

Angry All the Time by Scott Wetzler (Harper Collins)

Friends for Life: Mothers and Their Adult Daughters by Susan Jonas and Marily Nissenson (Morrow)

The most common mistakes potential clients make when soliciting an agent to represent them: Repeated phone calls, badly typed letters, smelly manuscripts, are all no-nos! Why do writers send pictures?!

What writers can do to enhance their chances of getting an agent (besides being good writers): Submit strong proposals, display organizational talents and clear thinking, and have impressive writing credentials.

Description of the Client from Hell: The person with unrealistic dreams about his talent, his advance, and his importance with his publisher. It takes time to build an author's career.

Description of Dream Client: My Dream Client is a warm, appreciative, talented writer who understands that we both have different roles in this relationship, and who respects the differences.

Why did you become an agent? I love the creative process of working with authors—reading, selling, finding the right marriage of editor and author.

DANIEL BIAL AGENCY

41 West 83rd Street, 5-C
New York, NY 10024
212-721-1786

Bial.

B.A., English, Trinity College.

ory: Editor for 15 years, including 10 years at HarperCollins. Founded 2.

ersonal interests: Travel, cooking, music, parenting.

categories most enthusiastic about agenting: Nonfiction: popular reference, popular culture, science, history, humor, Judaica, sports, psychology, ction: quality fiction, mysteries.

Subjects/categories not interested in agenting: Nonfiction: academic treatises, crafts, gift books. Fiction: romances, horror, medical thrillers, children's books, poetry, novels by authors with no publishing credits.

Best way for a prospective client to initiate contact: Query letter with SASE.

Reading-fee policy: No reading fee.

Client representation in the following categories: Nonfiction, 90%; Fiction, 10%.

Commission: 15% domestic. 20% foreign.

Number of titles sold during the past year: 26.

Representative titles sold:

Song of Songs (Simon & Schuster).

Encyclopedia of Modern Wicca (Harper San Francisco).

Encyclopedia of UFOs (Contemporary).

Politically Correct Bible Stories (Crown).

Sci Fi Video Guide (Billboard).

Econoguide (series) (Contemporary).

Gay USA (Fodor's).

Great Female Athletes (series) (Chelsea House).

The most common mistakes potential clients make when soliciting an agent to represent them: A surprising number of writers devote time in their query letter to telling me about their previous failures. They essentially reject themselves.

What writers can do to enhance their chances of getting an agent (besides being good writers): Savvy writers research their field and rate the competition's strengths and weaknesses. They highlight why their book is going to be new, different, better. They explain why they are the best writer on the topic. And they display an enthusiasm that suggests it will survive all the ups and downs of the publishing process.

Description of the Client from Hell: Clients from Hell are almost always wrapped up in private grievances and needs. They talk when they should listen, try force when they should use tact, and get involved in personal gamesmanship when much of publishing calls for team play. They suspect the worst and often cause crises simply through their own closed-mindedness.

Description of Dream Client: Dream clients produce trim, tight, ready-to-sell material. They know the business and how to get ahead. They recognize the importance of marketing and that good intentions don't sell books—hard work does. They take pride in their work and in their relationships.

Why did you become an agent? I became an agent for the same reason I first became an editor: because I loved the discovery of new authors and books, loved helping create a sellable project, and loved negotiating big advances. I switched desks because I wanted to be my own boss.

The Blake Group

8609 Northeast Plaza Drive, Suite 300
Dallas, TX 76225
214-373-2221
fax: 214-361-7200

Agents: Dr. Albert H. Halff, President; Mrs. Lee Halff, Consulting Editor; Hal Copeland, Marketing/PR Consultant

Subjects/categories most enthusiastic about agenting: Virtually any fiction or nonfiction subject or category may be considered by the Blake Group

Best way for a prospective client to initiate contact: Send us a strong query letter with two or three chapters. Persuade us to request your complete manuscript. Include some information about yourself and an SASE. Mail is always preferred to fax or telephone calls.

Reading-fee policy: No fee.

Commission: 15% domestic; 20% foreign

Number of titles sold during the past year: N.A.

Approximate percentage of all submissions (from queries through manuscripts) that are rejected: 85%

Representative titles sold: Our published clients include Edward Bradley; Betty Bunker; Paul Dempsey; Harold Durham; Elizabeth Dunn and Laura Hays; Te Edwards; Frank Goodwyn; Lloyd Hill; Peggy Hitchcock; Deanna Hudak and Rougeau; Linda McKenzie and son; Bonnie Neely; Pam Russell and Debbie Good; Charles Pugh; Lannon Reed; Pamela Sanchez; Maynard Smith; John Wright and Julie Yarbrough.

Publisher sales include Algonquin Books, Augsburg Fortres, Ballantine, Harbinger House, Hazeldon/Compcare, Holloway House, McFarland and Co., Pelican Publishing, Pendragon Press, Pilot Books, SRA/McGraw Hill, Texas A&M University Press, University of Pennsylvania Press and Zebra Books.

Blassingame—Spectrum Corporation
Spectrum Literary Agency

111 Eighth Avenue, Suite 1501
New York, NY 10011
212-691-7556

Agent: Lucienne Diver.

Education: Degree in English/writing and anthropology, summa cum laude, State University of New York, Potsdam.

...al interests: Hobbies: reading, writing, painting, mandolin, theater. ...forensics, anthropology, environmental issues.

...ries most enthusiastic about agenting: Fantasy, science fiction, ...on't want to limit myself, so whatever catches my interest.

...rospective client to initiate contact: Query letter with an SASE,

...cy: No reading fee.

...on mistakes potential clients make when soliciting an agent to **represent them:** The biggest turn-off is ego. An author convinced that his/her first novel will become a *New York Times* best-seller is likely to be disappointed and difficult to deal with.

One very basic mistake is the failure to include an SASE with a submission. Many agencies and publishing houses will not even look at material that does not come with a response envelope. Many writers underestimate the importance of the cover letter, which is, after all, the first impression the reader gets.

What writers can do to enhance their chances of getting an agent (besides being good writers): The two most important things are how the writer expresses him/herself and whether or not the synopsis of the novel catches my interest.

Description of the Client from Hell: Has unrealistic expectations (first novel will break all sales records first week on the shelves and be made into a major motion picture grossing billions).

Description of Dream Client: Someone who has taken the time to learn something of the business, and who can make informed decisions.

Why did you become an agent? I can get *paid* to read books! I love books, was always excited by the prospect of a job in publishing, and I love working with creative and intelligent people.

What might you be doing if you weren't an agent? I considered going to graduate school for forensic anthropology. Publishing won out!

THE JOAN BRANDT AGENCY

788 Wesley Drive Northwest
Atlanta, GA 30305
404-351-8877

Agent: Joan Brandt.

Career history: 21 years in business, established own agency in 1990, moved to Atlanta in 1992.

Subjects/categories most enthusiastic about agenting: Fiction: contemporary issues; detective, police, mystery, crime; literary; mainstream. Nonfiction: popular or topical.

Best way for a prospective client to initiate contact: Well-written query letter (with SASE).

Reading-fee policy: No reading fee.

Client representation in the following categories: Nonfiction, 34%; Fiction, 66%.

Commission: 15% domestic; 20% foreign.

Comments: Just as not every competent pianist is of concert caliber, so I wish people would not assume that just because they have produced 350+ double-spaced, spell-checked and computer-printed pages, that automatically puts them in the running for publication. Sometimes—more often than not—it's enough that they've accomplished a book for themselves, for their families and friends, and have had a lot of fun in the process.

BROCK GANNON LITERARY AGENCY

172 Fairview Avenue
Cocoa, FL 32967
407-633-6217

Agent: Louise Peters.

Born: Over 21.

Education: B.S., Radford University.

Career history: Teacher, editor, agent.

Hobbies/personal interests: Sailing.

Subjects/categories most enthusiastic about agenting: Fiction.

Subjects/categories not interested in agenting: Open to all subjects.

Best way for a prospective client to initiate contact: Query.

Reading-fee policy: We only charge for postage, long distance calls, photocopying, etc. We *don't* critique, edit, evaluate, etc.

Client representation in the following categories: Fiction, 20%; nonfiction, 70%; children's/young adult, 10%; textbooks, 0%.

Commission: 10%.

Number of titles sold during the past year: One (we're a new agency).

Approximate percentage of all submissions (from queries through manuscripts) that are rejected: 90%.

Representative titles sold:

New Jerusalem, Lang Marc.

Description of the Client from Hell: Someone who calls often for no reason and consume a great deal of time.

Description of Dream Client: A good writer.

The most common mistakes potential clients make when soliciting an agent to represent them: Sending inappropriate material. Not having the manuscript edited. Not having a cover letter. Not knowing the market for the book.

What writers can do to enhance their chances of getting an agent (besides being good writers): Follow directions.

Why did you become an agent? The written word can be a thing of beauty.

What might you be doing if you weren't an agent? Teaching.

Comments: I accept no censorship. When I have something to say, I say it and believe this is everyone's right.

ANDREA BROWN LITERARY AGENCY, INC.

P.O. Box 429
El Granada, CA 94018
415-728-1783

Agent: Andrea Brown.

Education: B.A., journalism and English, Syracuse University.

Career history: Editorial assistant, Dell; editorial assistant, Random House; assistant editor (all children's books), Knopf; started agency in 1981.

Hobbies/personal interests: Golf, theater, gardening, travel.

Subjects/categories most enthusiastic about agenting: Chapter books, funny middle-grade fiction, science, high-tech nonfiction.

Subjects/categories not interested in agenting: No general adult fiction or nonfiction. No rhyming picture books.

Best way for a prospective client to initiate contact: Query letter (with SASE) or phone-call query.

Reading-fee policy: No reading fee.

Client representation in the following categories: Children's, 95% (Nonfiction, 40%; Fiction, 60%).

Commission: 15% domestic; 20% foreign.

Number of titles sold during the past year: Too many to count.

Approximate percentage of all submissions (from queries through manuscripts) that are rejected: 95%.

Representative titles sold:

The Bully Brothers at the Beach (Scholastic).

One April Morning (Lothrop, Lee & Shephard).

Slime (Millbrook).

The most common mistakes potential clients make when soliciting an agent to represent them: Faxing queries. I hate that. Or long calls asking lots of questions before I'm even interested. And calling after I've said no already. Or resending with minor changes after we have rejected it. It closes the door on any future interest I may have in the writer.

What writers can do to enhance their chances of getting an agent (besides being good writers): Provide straightforward information about material. I like plain, honest excitement about the project with a low-key, professional presentation.

Description of the Client from Hell: One who has to talk to his agent on a daily basis, who always thinks his work is perfect as it is and that the editor is always wrong.

Description of Dream Client: One who works hard and takes his career seriously and respects that an agent has many clients to represent, but still remembers to mention that he appreciates the time and effort on his behalf.

Why did you become an agent? I loved publishing as a business and working with authors, but hated publishing houses and their attitudes about authors.

What might you be doing if you weren't an agent? Teaching or still being a book editor, or laying on my deck or beach.

Comments: Children's books are in a period of change and turmoil. The publishers have glutted the market, and now the authors are suffering as well, with cutbacks and cancellations. Writers must write terrific books that are also commercial. I worry about the quality of children's literature in the future, as publishers are forced to cut fiction and their midlist.

Curtis Brown Ltd.

Ten Astor Place
New York, NY 10003
212-473-5400

Branch Offices:
1750 Montgomery Street,
San Francisco, CA 94111
415-954-8566

1235 Bay Street, Suite 400
Toronto, ON M5R 3K4 Canada
802-362-5165.

Agents: Perry H. Knowlton, chairman & CEO; Peter L. Ginsberg, president; Timothy F. Knowlton, COO. Books: Laura J. Blake, Ellen Geiger, Peter L. Ginsberg, Emilie Jacobson, Ginger Knowlton, Perry H. Knowlton, Marilyn E. Marlow, Andrew Pope, Jess Taylor, Maureen Walters, Mitchell S. Waters. Film, TV & Multimedia Rights: Timothy Knowlton, Jess Taylor. Audio Rights: Christopher McKerrow. Translation Rights: Dave Barbor.

The following information pertains to Perry Knowlton:

Born: Unknown. Some think I'm in my sixties, but I'm actually going to be 140 some time next year. I owe the unusually advanced age to the ingestion of yogurt since birth (my mother's suggestion). Some say that yogurt also stimulates the imagination.

Education: Prep school (Exeter), college (Princeton), no graduate schooling.

Career history: Teacher (English), editor (Scribner's), agent (Curtis Brown) 1959 to present day.

Hobbies/personal interests: Boating, dogs, cats, birds, collecting (various, but including money, also spending it!). Reading for pleasure (when there's time), genealogy (mine), children (mine, mostly), grandchildren (again mine, mostly).

Subjects/categories most enthusiastic about agenting: I find the question confusing.

Subjects/categories not interested in agenting: Poetry. I have represented poets in the past, but it's no longer possible economically.

Best way for a prospective client to initiate contact: The best way is to persuade a friend, who also happens to be a client of mine, to read the work and let me know what he or she thinks of it. Failing that, try the usual query-letter approach (return envelope, etc.). Keep in mind that on my next birthday I'll be 140 years old, so I'm trying to be as selective as possible.

Reading-fee policy: No reading fee.

Client representation in the following categories: Nonfiction, 49^1/$_2$%; Fiction, 49^1/$_2$%; Juvenile and young adult, 1%.

Commission: 15% domestic; 20% foreign.

Number of titles sold during the past year: A fair number.

Approximate percentage of all submissions (from queries through manuscripts) that are rejected: Approximately 98%.

Representative titles sold recently: This is a difficult one for me. What, for instance, does "recently" mean? Some of the books I've sold that don't yet have titles or publication dates, were sold to publishers that now belong to another publisher, and some of them were sold only a year or two back, others longer ago than that, and some to publishers whose names are no longer recognizable to the average writer. When asked, I tend to avoid listing the names of my authors for three reasons. The first is simply that I'm afraid of leaving out the name of an author who might resent not being on the list; the second is the obverse side of that coin, fear of listing an author who'd rather not be listed; and the third is that I know there are hundreds of eager agents out there who have been waiting patiently for me to make this particular mistake so they can then have the opportunity to raid the pantry, so to speak, and slake their piranha-like hunger. After all, many of these people are my friends, and I'd hate to lose them. I refer to the agents, of course. My clients would never leave me.

A costly mistake potential clients make when soliciting you to represent them: A letter whose last paragraph concludes with, "Just between you and *I*, you'll never regret taking me on."

What writers can do to enhance their chances of getting an agent (besides being good writers): My enthusiasm tingles when some young genius—talented, of course—says "Just between you and *me*, you're going to make a fortune through the representation of my work. I Guarantee it!"

Description of the Client from Hell: A client who decided to be an exception to the above.

Description of Dream Client: Any one of my clients.

Why did you become an agent? I don't think about it very much at this stage of my long life, but I do know that I switched from the publishing side because, as an editor in the employ of a publisher, my conscience forced my loyalty towards my authors, not my employer, and I didn't like the schizoid position I found myself occupying. And that was a long time ago when I was at Scribner's, and Scribner's was owned and operated by a Scribner, a good man who was a friend of mine as well as my boss. I try not to think too much about what it would be like today.

What might you be doing if you weren't an agent? I might consider a life as a peregrine falcon or as an eagle—a golden eagle, I think. Although I still enjoy a relatively full head of hair, the idea of that glistening white head on the bald eagle would seem a bit redundant.

The following information pertains to Peter L. Ginsberg:
Subjects/categories most enthusiastic about agenting: Nonfiction: history, business, biography, religion, current affairs. Fiction: mystery, literary.
Subjects/categories not interested in agenting: Science fiction, romance, how-to nonfiction.
Best way for a prospective client to initiate contact: Query letter (with SASE).
Client representation in the following categories: Nonfiction, 80%; Fiction, 20%.
Approximate percentage of all submissions (from queries through manuscripts) that are rejected: 95%.
Description of Dream Client: Responsive, creative, enterprising, patient.

The following information pertains to Emilie Jacobson:
Subjects/categories most enthusiastic about agenting: General trade fiction and nonfiction. Some material for older children (no picture books).
Subjects/categories not interested in agenting: Technical and/or textbooks, poetry, science fiction, prizefighting.
Best way for a prospective client to initiate contact: Query letter (with SASE). Please, *not* by fax!
Reading-fee policy: No reading fee.
Commission: 15% domestic; 20% Canada/overseas.
Approximate percentage of all submissions (from queries through manuscripts) that are rejected: 97%.
Description of the Client from Hell: Eternal complainer, telephones constantly, delivers manuscript Christmas Eve so I can read it over the holiday. Alienates all editors.
Description of Dream Client: Has confidence in my ability. Trusts me to be in touch when there is anything to report. Writes like an angel. Understands the publishing business.

The following information pertains to Maureen Walters:
Subjects/categories most enthusiastic about agenting: Women's fiction, mysteries and suspense, self-help nonfiction.
Subjects/categories not interested in agenting: Science fiction and fantasy.
Best way for a prospective client to initiate contact: Query letter (with SASE).
Reading-fee policy: No reading fee.
Client representation in the following categories: Nonfiction, 20%; Fiction, 70%; Children's, 10%.
Commission: 15%.

The following information pertains to Laura J. Blake:
Born: Not yesterday.

Education: B.A., English, Vassar College.

Career history: I served as an intern at Curtis Brown while I was still in college, began work at CB two weeks after graduation, and have been here ever since.

Hobbies/personal interests: Film, theater, reading, gardening, regional equestrian competitor, the outdoors.

Subjects/categories most enthusiastic about agenting: Anything outstanding. Nonfiction: history, biography, current affairs, health issues, satire. Fiction: Anything exceptionally written.

Subjects/categories not interested in agenting: Poetry, science fiction and fantasy.

Best way for a prospective client to initiate contact: The best way is through a referral from either a client of mine or an editor with whom I work.

Reading-fee policy: No reading fee.

Client representation in the following categories: Nonfiction, 45%; Fiction, 45%; Children's, 10%.

Commission: 15% domestic; 20% foreign.

Approximate percentage of all submissions (from queries through manuscripts) that are rejected: 98%.

The most common mistakes potential clients make when soliciting an agent to represent them: Authors who call are unwelcome. Send an intelligent, professional query letter.

Description of Dream Client: A talented writer who knows the idiosyncrasies of the publishing business yet nonetheless remains determined to be a part of it; a writer with the skills and patience to participate in an often frustrating and quirky industry.

Why did you become an agent? I have a great love of books, and I love fighting for the little guy.

What might you be doing if you weren't an agent? Teaching, or riding horses.

The following information pertains to Ginger Knowlton:

Education: B.A., child development; minors in communication studies and English.

Career history: Preschool teacher and director; office manager of a bed-and-breakfast inn.

Hobbies/personal interests: Tennis, sailing, skiing, golf, reading, playing.

Subjects/categories most enthusiastic about agenting: Middle-grade and young-adult fiction and nonfiction; historical fiction.

Subjects/categories not interested in agenting: Pornography, self-help.

Best way for a prospective client to initiate contact: If it's a picture book, send the whole manuscript with a letter. If it's anything else, send the first two chapters or a proposal along with a letter. Of course, always include an SASE.

Reading-fee policy: No reading fee.

Client representation in the following categories: Adult nonfiction, 2^1/$_2$%; Adult fiction, 2^1/$_2$%; Children's, 95%.

Commission: 15%.

Approximate percentage of all submissions (from queries through manuscripts) that are rejected: 95%.

The most common mistakes potential clients make when sol... represent them: Form letters that begin "Dear Agent" or "Dear Curtis Brown"; grammatical and spelling errors in the query letter script); someone who writes, "I've tested this on my grandchildren (c students or whatever) and they loved it."

What writers can do to enhance their chances of getting an agent (l good writers): A professional approach, especially one with humor.

Description of the Client from Hell: Fortunately, I don't have firsthand with "Clients from Hell" so I don't want to jinx myself by describing one.

Description of Dream Client: One who writes well, trusts me implicitly, ar ...akes millions of dollars.

What might you be doing if you weren't an agent? Volunteering in my local library or grammar school. Playing tennis 'til I drop.

The following information pertains to Ellen Geiger:
Born: March 24, 1949, New York, New York.

Education: Graduate degrees in education and anthropology; broad eclectic interests.

Career history: Background in film production; was public television executive prior to becoming literary agent.

Hobbies/personal interests: Film, theater, pop culture, tennis, France, history, psychology, and others—too many to mention.

Subjects/categories most enthusiastic about agenting: Serious fiction and nonfiction, politics, social issues, history, biography, gender studies, psychology, pop culture, current affairs, health, self-help. Also commercial fiction—mysteries, thrillers, and big commercial women's novels.

Subjects/categories not interested in agenting: Romance, science fiction, children's.

Best way for a prospective client to initiate contact: Send query letter and sample chapters and/or outline (with SASE).

Reading-fee policy: No reading fee.

Client representation in the following categories: Nonfiction, 75%; Fiction, 25%.

Approximate number of previously unpublished authors signed during the past year: 5.

Commission: 15%.

Approximate number of writers currently represented: 30 to 35.

Approximate percentage of all submissions (from queries through manuscripts) that are rejected: 90%.

Representative titles sold:
Hot Jobs: Interviews with Young People with Really Cool Careers (HarperCollins).
The Trouble with Thin Ice (HarperCollins). Mystery.
Reflections of a Wall Street Psychiatrist (Simon & Schuster).
The Abortionist (Free Press).
Asian Herbal Medicine (Crown).
The Traditional Bible (Harvard).

The Question of Equality (companion book to PBS series) (Scribner).
Classic TV (St. Martin's).
Dreamworks: The Making of the New Studio (Dutton).

The most common mistakes potential clients make when soliciting an agent to represent them: Faxing a long proposal; calling every day or few days to check up; misspellings or sloppy writing errors in their proposal; sending something out that isn't their best effort.

What writers can do to enhance their chances of getting an agent (besides being good writers): Present a thoughtfully written letter and a good proposal or chapter outline, and/or an original idea (hard to find). Whatever you do, don't use a form letter to query an agent.

Description of the Client from Hell: Someone who can't be pleased, who is dissatisfied no matter what happens.

What might you be doing if you weren't an agent? I'd raise horses and live on a farm.

Comments: I'm very interested in cutting-edge issues—for example, sex, race, class, gender, health. I'm happier if I can meet the potential client to see if we would get along.

The following information pertains to Andrew Pope:
Born: January 20, 1971.
Education: A.B., English literature, University of Georgia.
Career history: Started in the business as assistant to the CEO of Curtis Brown (Perry Knowlton), moved up to agenthood a couple of years later.
Hobbies/personal interests: Reading, writing, drawing.
Subjects/categories most enthusiastic about agenting: Solid fiction—either literary or commercial. I like odd, quirky, dark, and humorous things. Southern fiction and short-story collections appeal to me as well. As far as nonfiction goes, I look for history, humor, and biography (especially literary) among other things.
Subjects/categories not interested in agenting: Horror, science fiction, children's books.
Best way for a prospective client to initiate contact: A simple, straightforward letter works best.
Reading-fee policy: No reading fee.
Client representation in the following categories: Nonfiction, 40%; Fiction, 60%.
Commission: 15%.
Approximate percentage of all submissions (from queries through manuscripts) that are rejected: 98%.
The most common mistakes potential clients make when soliciting an agent to represent them: Query letters that are riddled with misspellings and sixth-grade grammar fouls never fail to mystify me. Embarking on a career as a writer without learning to write a decent piece of mail strikes me as a rather costly mistake.
What writers can do to enhance their chances of getting an agent (besides being good writers): That's a tough question.
Description of Dream Client: Patient, confident, realistic, ambitious, easy-going.

What might you be doing if you weren't an agent? I'd be looking for one, I suppose.

The following information pertains to Jess Taylor:

Born: March 11, 1960.

Education: B.A., English and American literature, Harvard; M.A., English and comparative literature, Columbia.

Career history: Three years in development for TV and features; agent with Curtis Brown from 1989 to present.

Hobbies/personal interests: Stories in all forms; novels, movies, plays. Poetry, painting, stained-glass windows, sitcoms, TV commercials, and songs.

Subjects/categories most enthusiastic about agenting: Anything that tells a story. Fiction, nonfiction; books and screenplays.

Subjects/categories not interested in agenting: Anything that doesn't tell a story.

Best way for a prospective client to initiate contact: 1. By referral from (a) a client, (b) a friend, (c) an editor or a producer. 2. A letter describing a project, that tells just enough to prompt me to want to read the rest of the story.

Client representation in the following categories: Nonfiction, 20%; Fiction, 70%; Children's, 10%.

Approximate percentage of all submissions (from queries through manuscripts) that are rejected: 99%.

The most common mistakes potential clients make when soliciting an agent to represent them: I'm turned off by the way most writers approach me. Most commonly, they don't bother to learn anything about me or Curtis Brown Ltd., before trying to get my attention.

What writers can do to enhance their chances of getting an agent (besides being good writers): I like it when they've clearly done their homework, know something about the agent they're approaching, have come up with an intelligent, memorable, and intriguing way to encapsulate the premise of a story, and have armed me in advance with a pitch.

Description of the Client from Hell: I wouldn't have time.

Description of Dream Client: Articulate, disciplined, self-reliant, opinionated, funny, daring, considerate, attentive, diplomatic, blunt, passionate about stories, and *above all* concise on the telephone.

Why did you become an agent? It was a job and the rent was due. (My own question: Why have you *remained* an agent? I've got great clients.)

What might you be doing if you weren't an agent? Editing commercial fiction and narrative nonfiction for a trade publishing house; operating a small hotel in the Galapagos Islands.

The following information pertains to Mitchell S. Waters:

Born: June 19, 1957.

Education: A.B.D., English literature, Fordham University; BA., English literature, Fairleigh Dickinson University (1982).

Career history: Tennis instructor; college composition and literature instructor.

...sonal interests: Tennis, painting, music, acting, theater (opera, ballet, ...al), skating, film.

...categories most enthusiastic about agenting: Nonfiction: history, biog- ...nt affairs, health, pop culture, gender studies, gay studies. Fiction: literary, ...ay, romance, young adult.

...ts/categories not interested in agenting: Science fiction, poetry, pic- ...ks.

...way for a prospective client to initiate contact: Query letter (with SASE).

Reading-fee policy: No reading fee.

Client representation in the following categories: Nonfiction, 45%; Fiction, 45%; Children's, 10%.

Commission: 15% domestic, 20% foreign.

Approximate percentage of all submissions (from queries through manuscripts) that are rejected: 98%.

The most common mistakes potential clients make when soliciting an agent to represent them: Sloppily written letters, no SASE, faxed submissions.

What writers can do to enhance their chances of getting an agent (besides being good writers): An elegantly written letter that shows they've done their homework about both their material and the agent they're approaching.

Why did you become an agent? I love books and being an advocate.

What might you be doing if you weren't an agent? Teaching literature.

SHEREE BYKOFSKY ASSOCIATES, INC.

11 East 47th Street
New York, NY 10017
212-308-1253

Agent: Sheree Bykofsky.

Born: September, 1956; Queens, New York.

Education: B.A., State University of New York, Binghamton; M.A., Columbia University (English and comparative literature).

Career history: Executive editor/book producer, The Stonesong Press (1984 to present); freelance editor/writer (1984 to present); general manager/managing editor, Chiron Press, 1979–1984. Author of six books and co-executive editor of *The New York Public Library Desk Reference.*

Hobbies/personal interests: Tournament Scrabble, poker, racquetball, movies, bridge.

Subjects/categories most enthusiastic about agenting: Popular reference, adult nonfiction (hardcovers and trade paperbacks), quality fiction (highly selective).

Subjects/categories not interested in agenting: Genre romances, science fiction, Westerns, occult and supernatural, children's books.

Best way for a prospective client to initiate contact: Send a well-written, detailed query letter with SASE.

Reading-fee policy: No reading fee.

Client representation in the following categories: Nonfiction, 80%; Fiction, 20%.
Commission: 15%.

Number of titles sold during the past year: 31.

Approximate percentage of all submissions (from queries through manuscripts) that are rejected: 95%.

Representative titles sold:

Movie Time: A Chronological History of the Movies and the Movie Industry by Gene Brown (Macmillan/Prentice Hall).

Debt Free: Bankruptcy Without Guilt by James Caher and John Caher (Holt).

Handbook for the Soul by Richard Carlson and Benjamin Shield, eds. (Little Brown).

People vs. Crime by Tucker Carlson (Forum).

Multicultural Manners by Norine Dresser (Wiley).

More Oral Sadism and the Vegetarian Personality by Glenn Ellenbogen (Brunner/Mazel).

The Parent's Dictionary by Merrill Furman (humor) (Contemporary).

Public Speaking for the Painfully Shy by Don Gabor (Crown).

Vital Touch: The Role of Touch in Infant Development, An Evolutionary Perspective by Sharon Heller (Holt).

The Executive Toolbox: 60 Power Breaks by James Joseph (Berkley).

All Aboard: The Comprehensive Guide to North American Train Travel by Jim Loomis (Prima).

Life's Little Frustration Book by G. Gaynor McTigue (St. Martin's).

Lavender Light: Meditations for Gay Men in Recovery by Adrian Milton (Perigee).

Jimmy Carter: A Prophet Scorned by Kenneth Morris (University of Georgia).

500 Things You Should Never Do by Ed Morrow (Contemporary).

The Hidden Face of Shyness by Frank Schneier and Lawrence Welkowitz (Avon).

No Human Involved by Barbara Seranella (fiction) (St. Martin's).

Men Are Lunatics and Women Are Nuts! by Ron Shwartz (Running Press).

The most common mistakes potential clients make when soliciting an agent to represent them: Excessive hubris; not explaining what the book is about; paranoia (we're not going to steal your idea); sloppy grammar, punctuation, and spelling.

What writers can do to enhance their chances of getting an agent (besides being good writers): I love a query letter that is as well written as the proposed book, or a polished, perfect, professional proposal.

Description of the Client from Hell: I only take on an author if I feel we can work well together.

Description of Dream Client: One who is not only a talented writer but who is a professional in every sense—from writing the proposal to promoting the book. Also, one who appreciates my hard work on his/her behalf. So far, all of my clients have proven to be dream clients.

Why did you become an agent? It suits me, and I feel I have the talent and experience to do it well.

What might you be doing if you weren't an agent? Writing and editing.

Comments: In addition to being an agent, I am a book packager and author. This gives me *and my clients* a perspective that most agents do not have.

Martha Casselman, Literary Agent

P.O. Box 342
Calistoga, CA 94515
707-942-4341

Agent: Martha Casselman.

Born: June 8, 1935; New York City.

Education: B.A., English and education, Jackson College of Tufts University; attended Radcliffe Publishing Procedures Course.

Career history: Magazines, editorial assistant, copyeditor, editor (*Good Housekeeping*, *Show* magazine, *Holiday* magazine); freelance editor and reader (Book-of-the-Month Club, Viking, etc.)—in New York before move to California in 1976.

Hobbies/personal interests: Can you believe—reading? (Belongs to reading group.)

Subjects/categories most enthusiastic about agenting: Food books, some nonfiction, some young adult; other exciting books too wonderful to turn away.

Subjects/categories not interested in agenting: Poetry, textbooks, religion, almost all kids' books (except as above).

Best way for a prospective client to initiate contact: Write brief letter (with SASE), and be straightforward about what other contacts are being made; make proposal/query so good it's impossible for me *not* to go after it (but expect long-distance calls to be collect if you make a query by phone).

Reading-fee policy: No reading fee.

Client representation in the following categories: Nonfiction, 89%; Fiction, 1%; Children's, 10%.

Commission: 15%, plus some copying, overnight mail expenses; 20% if using sub-agents.

Number of titles sold during the past year: Confidential.

Approximate percentage of all submissions (from queries through manuscripts) that are rejected: 99%.

Representative titles sold: Confidential.

The most common mistakes potential clients make when soliciting an agent to represent them: For nonfiction: not enough research on the market of books already in print.

What writers can do to enhance their chances of getting an agent (besides being good writers): Make your proposal *so* good (for nonfiction) that when I get an editor to take it to the publishing board the editor could keel over in the hall and the proposal could sell itself to the editors at that meeting. Fiction: Excellence, excitement, and imagination—in the sample material, *not* the cover letter.

Description of the Client from Hell: The client signs a contract, then spends the next three years complaining about its clauses; also, the client who has something under submission from this office and then gets sweet-talked into accepting a contract without the agent's guidance.

What might you be doing if you weren't an agent? Teaching/tutoring in the local grade school or high school. (Is being *prosperous* what makes an agent happy? You bet—that's why we need great material.)

Comments: It's not getting any easier.

CASTIGLIA LITERARY AGENCY

1155 Camino Del Mar, Suite 510
Del Mar, CA 92014
619-753-4361

Agent: Julie Castiglia.

Education: Educated in England.

Career history: Published writer (three titles), freelance editor (10 years), agent (last eight years).

Hobbies/personal interests: Traveling, hiking, skiing, gardening, animals, decorative arts, books.

Subjects/categories most enthusiastic about agenting: Mainstream, literary and ethnic fiction. Nonfiction: psychology, science and health, biography, women's issues, niche books, contemporary issues.

Subjects/categories not interested in agenting: Horror and science fiction, contemporary genre romance.

Best way for a prospective client to initiate contact: A query (with SASE).

Reading-fee policy: No reading fee.

Client representation in the following categories: Nonfiction, 75%; Fiction, 25%.

Commission: 15% domestic; 20% foreign.

Number of titles sold during the past year: 26.

Approximate percentage of all submissions (from queries through manuscripts) that are rejected: 95%.

Representative titles sold:

The Path: Finding Your Mission in Life Work by Laurie Beth Jones (Hyperion/Disney).

Serafina's Wild Horse Ballet by Margarita Engle (Harmony Books).

The Shaman Bulldog by Renaldo Fischer with Michelle St. George (Warner Books).

Dreamscape by Nicholas Heyneman (Simon & Schuster).

Hemingway A–Z by Charles Oliver (Facts on File).

Night Train by Jess Mowry (Holt).

Babylon Boyz by Jess Mowry (Simon & Schuster).

The Way Is Within by Ron Rathbun (Berkley).

Prentice Hall's Directory of Online Business Information by Chris Engholm and Scott Grimes (Prentice Hall).

Dead Snails Leave No Trails by Loren Nancarro and Janet Taylor (Ten Speed).

The most common mistakes potential clients make when soliciting an agent to represent them: Impoliteness, calling too often, talking too much.

What writers can do to enhance their chances of getting an agent (besides being good writers): Attitude, credentials, and obvious knowledge of the publishing business.

Description of the Client from Hell: Loquacious, untrustworthy, grumpy, promises but does not perform, doesn't meet deadlines. Talks but doesn't write!

Description of Dream Client: Trustworthy, intelligent, hard working—understands the business. All the clients I work with have become good friends. They trust my judgment and appreciate what I do for them—they are my dream clients.

Why did you become an agent? I've always loved books and knew the publishing business well, having sold my own three books and edited other writers' work. It was a natural step.

What might you be doing if you weren't an agent? Writing and traveling.

CISKE & DIETZ LITERARY AGENCY

P.O. Box 555
Neenah, WI 54957
414-722-5944

Milwaukee office:
10605 West Wabash
Milwaukee, WI 53224
414-355-8915

Agents: Francine Ciske, Andrea Boeshaar (Milwaukee office).

Subjects/categories most enthusiastic about agenting: Ciske: Romance—contemporary, historical, including all category imprints; nonfiction (with the exception of self-help subjects). Boeshaar: Inspirational (for the Evangelical Christian market only) which includes fiction, nonfiction, with a special interest in romance.

Subjects/categories not interested in agenting: Ciske: New Age, poetry, short-story collections, science fiction/fantasy, alternative spirituality, mysticism, or fiction novels that contain an element of romance. Boeshaar: Anything that does not target the Evangelical Christian market, poetry, short stories.

Best way for a prospective client to initiate contact: Ciske: Query letter (with SASE), brief outline, first 5 to 10 pages of manuscript: Boeshaar: Query letter (with SASE), brief outline, and first three chapters of manuscript.

Reading-fee policy: No reading fee.

Client representation in the following categories: Nonfiction, 30%; Fiction, 70%.

Commission: 15% domestic; 20% foreign.

Approximate percentage of all submissions (from queries through manuscripts) that are rejected: 90%.

The most common mistakes potential clients make when soliciting an agent to represent them: Ciske: Sending random sections of their manuscript instead of the first 5 to 10 pages. Insisting I read the entire manuscript instead of a partial because they feel the action picks up toward the middle of the book. Submissions sent by certified or express mail. Querying me with a confusing, jumbled letter regarding several untitled projects. Not including SASE (self-addressed, stamped envelope). If we make a suggestion or offer advice when we reject a manuscript, and the writer agrees and makes changes, we welcome them to resubmit. However, this does not mean we are offering a critique-by-mail service. It means we will be happy to look at another submission. Boeshaar: Not including SASE. Sending randomly chosen chapters instead of the first three chapters.

What writers can do to enhance their chances of getting an ag**good writers):** Queries that sum up the book in one paragraph, inc setting, and clearly stating what it is (fiction, nonfiction, historical SASE enclosed.

Why did you become an agent? I love to sell, negotiate, read a strong desire to help talented, professional writers reach their g

What might you be doing if you weren't an agent? I would ing moment considering the idea of becoming an agent.

CONNIE CLAUSEN & ASSOCIATES LITERARY AGENCY

250 East 87th Street
New York, NY 10128
212-427-6135
fax: 212-996-7111

Agents: Connie Clausen, Founder; Stedman Mays, Principal Associate
Education: Stedman Mays: M.A. in English, University of Virginia.

The following information pertains to Connie Clausen:
Career history: MGM Studios, Production Dept. and Head of Special Promotion; Senior Editor *Haire's Infant and Children's Review*; TV Spokeswoman: *Live Like a Millionaire* (co-host), the Colonial Airline show, Arm & Hammer, Vel, Beech-Nut (with Dr. Spock), Coca-Cola, Ponds, Gleem; Dramatic roles: *The Gambler* (Broadway), *Love of Life*, *Goodyear Theater, Danger*, and *Suspense* (all TV); Author of the autobiographical memoir *I Love You Honey, But the Season's Over* (Holt) and various articles; Publicist, Publicity Director, Head of Marketing, and Vice President at Macmillan; Founder of Connie Clausen & Associates, 1976.

Subjects/categories most enthusiastic about agenting: (Mostly Nonfiction): memoirs, biography, autobiography, true stories, medical, health/nutrition, psychology, how-to, financial, women's issues, spirituality, true crime, fashion/beauty, style, humor, rights for books optioned for TV movies and feature films.

Subjects/categories not interested in agenting: We normally do not represent fiction.

Best way for a prospective client to initiate contact: A query letter or a proposal, including SASE.

Reading-fee policy: No fees.

Client representation in the following categories: Nonfiction, 100%; Children's: 10%.

Commission: 15%.

Approximate percentage of all submissions (from queries through manuscripts) that are rejected: 90%.

Representative titles sold:
Looking for the Other Side: A Skeptic's Odyssey, Sherry Suib Cohen (Clarkson Potter).
Resident Alien: The New York Diaries, Quentin Crisp (Alyson).

Permanent Remissions: Life Extending Diet Strategies, Robert Haas (Pocket Books).

The Pocket Doctor, Michael LaCombe, M.D. (Andrews & McMeel).

The Pocket Pediatrician, Michael LaCombe, M.D. (Andrews & McMeel).

Drawing Angels Near: Children Tell of Angels in Words and Pictures, Mimi Doe and Garland Waller (Pocket Books).

The Rules: Time-Tested Secrets for Capturing the Heart of Mr. Right, Ellen Fein and Scherrie Schneider (Warner Books).

What the IRS Doesn't Want You to Know, Marilyn Kaplan and Naomi Weiss (Villard—revised periodically).

Growing Myself: A Spiritual Journey through Gardening, Judith Handelsman (Dutton).

The Book of Luck, Stefan Bechtel and Laurence Roy Stains (Workman).

Access 2 for Dummies, Scott Palmer (IDG Books).

Filling the Void: Six Steps from Loss to Fulfillment, Dorothy Bullitt (Rawson/Scribner).

The Way of the Scout, Tom Brown (Berkley).

"I Love Him, But . . .": The Things Men Do That Drive Their Wives Crazy, Merry Bloch Jones (Workman).

"I Love Her, But. . . .": The Things Women Do That Drive Their Husbands Crazy, Robert Llewellyn Jones (Workman).

The Common Sense Kitchen Advisor, Deborah Krasner (Harper Collins).

Healing the Child: A Mother's Story, Nancy Cain (Rawson/Scribner).

The Chiropractor's Health Book, Leonard McGill (Clarkson Potter).

Shadows of the King: The Secret Bonds Between Gay Men and Their Fathers, Guy Kettelhack (Crown).

Dancing Around the Volcano: Freeing Our Erotic Lives, Guy Kettelhack (Crown).

Pilaf, Risotto, and Other Ways with Rice, Sada Fretz (Little, Brown).

Angels of Emergency: True Life Rescue Stories from America's Paramedics and EMTs, Dary Matera and Donna Theisen (Harper Collins).

Description of the Dream Client: An author who has read and digested Strunk and White; who has read a book or two about how to get published, about how to write a query letter and a proposal; who listens to constructive suggestions and revises accordingly.

Why did you become an agent? Love publishing—learn with every book.

THE COHEN AGENCY

331 West 57th Street, #176
New York, NY 10019

Agent: Rob Cohen.

Education: B.A., Union College.

Career history: Assistant in small publishing company (2 years); agent with Richard Curtis Associates (9 years); Cohen Agency (1 1/2 years).

Hobbies/personal interests: Writing, skiing, traveling, photography, camping, theater, museums, music (not new), and old movies.

Subjects/categories most enthusiastic about agenting: Women's fiction, romance, suspense, horror, anything with female protagonist as well as mainstream and literary women's fiction.

Subjects/categories not interested in agenting: Academic works, juvenile and young adult, poetry, short stories, action adventure, and category Westerns.

Best way for a prospective client to initiate contact: Send first 50 pages of book and short synopsis.

Reading-fee policy: No reading fee.

Client representation in the following categories: Nonfiction, 10%; Fiction, 90%. **Commission:** 15%.

Number of titles sold during the past year: 33.

Approximate percentage of all submissions (from queries through manuscripts) that are rejected: 90%.

Representative titles sold:

Wasted Space by Elizabeth Moon (St. Martin's Press).

Tin Lizzy by Margaret Brownley (New American Library).

Nowhere to Turn by Rachel Gibson (Avon Books).

Amber by Bette Ford (Zebra/Arabesque).

Risky Games by Olga Bilos (Pinnacle).

The Desert Waits by Margaret Fulb (Zebra Books).

Remember Love by Susan Phonluft (Berkley Books).

Post Pregnancy Workout by Rob Pan (Berkley Books).

The most common mistakes potential clients make when soliciting an agent to represent them: I don't need an author's evaluation of their own work. A comparison to another published author or their personal favorites does not bother me, but a statement such as "This is great writing" is off-putting. I feel I can judge that for myself.

What writers can do to enhance their chances of getting an agent (besides being good writers): Usually if authors appear to be somewhat knowledgeable about the industry in general and their specific markets, I find that their research extends to their care in their writing.

Description of the Client from Hell: Authors who treat publishing industry professionals as *the enemy* and who have trouble separating their personal goals from professional evaluation.

Description of Dream Client: An author who works well with me and others and whose work itself is extremely appealing to me personally.

Why did you become an agent? I enjoyed working for and with authors and books.

What might you be doing if you weren't an agent? Editing, perhaps, or some other aspect of publishing.

Comments: To whom, the aspiring author? Don't worry about writing what you know, write what you feel, but write it for yourself. The publishing industry is becoming more frighteningly corporate every day and art is less and less appreciated. Publishing your work is a bonus—writing it is the achievement.

RUTH COHEN, INC.

P.O. Box 7226
Menlo Park, CA 94025
415-854-2054

Agent: Ruth Cohen.

Subjects/categories most enthusiastic about agenting: Women's fiction, Regencies, current "themes" of modern women, mysteries (different settings with fascinating characters), juvenile literature (quality picture books, middle-grade fiction/ nonfiction, young-adults showing "special" writing skills).

Subjects/categories not interested in agenting: Films, poetry, books in verse, science fiction, Westerns, how-to books.

Best way for a prospective client to initiate contact: Send a query letter (with SASE), which also includes the opening 10 to 15 pages of the manuscript. Please, *no* unsolicited *full manuscripts*.

Reading-fee policy: No reading fee, except for foreign mailings and faxes.

Client representation in the following categories: Nonfiction, 5%; Fiction, 60%; Children's, 35%.

Commission: 15% domestic; 20% foreign.

Number of titles sold during the past year: 87.

Representative titles sold:
The Dinosaur Stomp (Candlewick).
The Vampire Viscount (NAL).
Quake! (Scholastic).

What writers can do to enhance their chances of getting an agent (besides being good writers): Submit a well-written, well-crafted, well-disciplined manuscript.

Description of the Client from Hell: There aren't really any clients from hell. There are clients who grow disappointed and who despair of the publishing world as it merges and alters and leaves fewer opportunities for new writers to succeed in work they love—writing.

Description of Dream Client: Clients who understand that our combined efforts generally will advance both our careers, and that patience and stamina are the preferred attributes for getting published well—now and always.

Comments: Keep trying—and keep trying to detach yourself from your own writing so that you can view it objectively. Then reassess, revise, rework, and resubmit.

COLLINS PURVIS, LTD.

P.O. Box 626
East Amherst, NY 14051
716-639-0713
e-mail: litagency@aol.com

Agent: Michael C. Purvis.

Born: January 1, 1959; Laurel, Mississippi.

Education: B.A., psychology, Louisiana State University, 1979; M.A. film & communications, University of New Orleans, 1981; Juris Doctor, Southwestern University School of Law, 1984; admitted to practice law in California, New York, and District of Columbia.

Career history: General counsel for a major corporation. Prior to that was an attorney for the Walt Disney Company for four years. Prior to that, I was a trial attorney.

Hobbies/personal interests: Foreign travel, movies, animals, politics.

Subjects/categories most enthusiastic about agenting: Nonfiction, including current affairs, politics and social issues, investigative journalism, controversial topics, biographies, entertainment and the media, popular culture, popular science, psychology, women's issues, business, popular reference, and academic and scientific textbooks.

Fiction: We are interested in action/adventure, suspense, and thrillers.

Subjects/categories not interested in agenting: No metaphysics, recovery, abuse, addiction, poetry, sports, beauty/fashion, medicine, cookbooks, or religion. Nothing involving *angels*.

Best way for a prospective client to initiate contact: Please send a query letter first with a brief synopsis of the work, along with SASE for a reply. No unsolicited manuscripts or sample chapters will be accepted. Please do not phone. We are now recommending that you query via e-mail.

Reading-fee policy: No reading fee.

Client representation in the following categories: Nonfiction, 70%; Fiction, 30%.

Commission: 15% domestic, 20% foreign.

Number of titles sold during the past year: Not available.

Approximate percentage of all submissions (from queries through manuscripts) that are rejected: 99%.

Representative titles sold: Not available.

The most common mistakes potential clients make when soliciting an agent to represent them: Too vague about their work—that is, fails to submit an adequate synopsis. Sends whole manuscript or sample chapters. Fails to enclose SASE or tries to contact us by phone. Poorly written query letter. Tells us the story is based on the author's life.

What writers can do to enhance their chances of getting an agent (besides being good writers): Clear, concise, and polished query letter and synopsis of work.

Description of the Client from Hell: One who telephones constantly and expects to hear back from publishers on a daily basis. Thankfully, we don't have any clients like this.

Description of Dream Client: One who is highly talented and is productive, pleasant, and patient. This writer would also polish the substance and presentation of his/her work until it leaps off the page.

Why did you become an agent? I like the interaction between art and commerce, that is between *show* and *business*. I also like the prospect of bringing a work to fruition (birthing it, so to speak) so that the general public can be exposed to something new and exciting. The personal interaction with interesting people is also great, as is the opportunity to address cutting-edge issues.

What might you be doing if you weren't an agent? I would probably be a journalist or working as a political consultant.

Comments: Who better to represent you than an attorney? Hey, we're not all bad!

RICHARD CURTIS ASSOCIATES, INC.

171 East 74th Street
New York, NY 10021
212-772-7363

Agent: Richard Curtis.

Born: June 23, 1937.

Education: B.A., American studies, Syracuse University; M.A., American studies, University of Wyoming.

Career history: Foreign rights manager, Scott Meredith Literary Agency (1959–1966); freelance author (1967–1975); started own agency (1975); incorporated Richard Curtis Associates, Inc. (1979); first president of Independent Literary Agents Association (1980): treasurer (1991–1995) and president (1995–1996) of Association of Authors' Representatives.

Hobbies/personal interests: Watercolor painting, softball, racquetball, classical music.

Subjects/categories most enthusiastic about agenting: Although best known for categories such as science fiction, thrillers, Westerns, and romance, I've become more and more interested in mainstream fiction, commercial nonfiction, and software/multimedia.

Subjects/categories not interested in agenting: See last question.

Best way for a prospective client to initiate contact: One-page query letter plus no more than one-page synopsis of proposed submission. Must be accompanied by SASE or we won't reply. No faxed queries; no e-mail queries. No submission of material unless specifically requested. If requested, submission must be accompanied by SASE or we assume you don't want your submission back.

Reading-fee policy: No reading fee.

Client representation in the following categories: Nonfiction, 10%; Fiction, 90%.

Commission: 15% on basic sale to U.S. publisher; 15% on dramatic (movies, television, audio, multimedia); 20% on British and foreign publication rights.

Number of titles sold during the past year: Approximately 150.

Approximate percentage of all submissions (from queries through manuscripts) that are rejected: 99%.

Representative titles sold:

Ignition by Kevin Anderson and Doug Beason (Tor Books, Universal Pictures).

Blood Relations by Barbara Parker (Dutton/Penguin Publishers).

Exquisite Corpse by Poppy Z. Brite (Simon & Schuster).

The Crook Factory by San Simmons (Avon Books).

Two romance novels by Jennifer Blake (Harlequin/Mira).

Four Western novels by Matthew Braun (St. Martin's Paperbacks).
Two untitled novels by Megan Chance (Harper Paperbacks).
Three untitled novels by Dave Duncan (Avon Books).
Four novels by Greg Keyes (Del Rey Books).

The most common mistakes potential clients make when solic **represent them:** Phone queries instead of a letter. Want to see us l material. Don't proofread their work.

What writers can do to enhance their chances of getting an agent (besides being good writers): Simple letter; well-described synopsis of work to be submitted.

Description of the Client from Hell: High PITA factor. PITA stands for *Pain In The Ass*. Divide commissions earned into time listening to complaints.

Description of Dream Client: Low PITA factor.

Why did you become an agent? Love authors, love publishers, love books, love being in the middle.

What might you be doing if you weren't an agent? A pianist, an artist, a catcher for the New York Mets, a linebacker for the New York Giants, a volleyball player on a California beach, a psychotherapist, a rabbi, a playwright.

Comments: Anyone thinking of going into writing or publishing must become adept with a computer. The writer of tomorrow will create with images and sounds, like a one-person movie producer.

DH LITERARY, INC.

P.O. Box 990
Nyack, NY 10960
212-753-7942

Agent: David Hendin.

Born: December 16, 1945.

Education: B.S., biology, education, University of Missouri (1967); M.A., journalism, University of Missouri (1967).

Career history: United Feature Syndicate/United Media; senior vice president and chief operating officer of United Feature Syndicate; president and chief operating officer of World Almanac, Pharos Books (1970–1993). Author of 11 nonfiction books including *Death As a Fact of Life* (Norton, Warner) and *The Life Givers* (Morrow), and coauthor of *The Genetic Connection* (Morrow, Signet).

Hobbies/personal interests: Archaeology.

Subjects/categories most enthusiastic about agenting: Strong nonfiction, inspirational and how-to nonfiction, medical and psychology nonfiction, women's interest nonfiction, thrillers and unusual mysteries, literary fiction. I also represent comic strips and columns for newspaper syndication (very selectively).

Subjects/categories not interested in agenting: Genre fiction, children's.

Best way for a prospective client to initiate contact: Query letter (with SASE) or one-page e-mail query.

Reading-fee policy: No reading fee.

Client representation in the following categories: Nonfiction, 75%; Fiction, 20%; Textbooks 5%.

Commission: 15%.

Number of titles sold during the past year: 24.

Approximate percentage of all submissions (from queries through manuscripts) that are rejected: 90%.

Representative titles sold:

Hug the Monster by David Smith and Sandy Leicester (Andrews & McMeel).

Miss Manners Rescues Civilization by Judith Martin (Crown).

Talking Tall by Jeff McQuain (Random House).

The Thin You Within You by Dr. Abraham Twerski (St. Martin's).

Norton Anthology of Rock'N'Roll by William McKeen and Dave Marsh (W. W. Norton).

Legend of St. Nicholas by R.O. Blechman (Stewart, Tabori & Chang).

Eating the Bear by Carole Fungaroli (Farrar Straus Giroux).

His Promised Land: The Memoir of John P. Parker, Escaped Slave and Conductor on the Underground Railroad (W. W. Norton/Tri-Star for Jonathan Demme to direct).

The most common mistakes potential clients make when soliciting an agent to represent them: Send too much material before being asked; don't write a good query letter; don't enclose SASE; start the query by telling me they have 14 unpublished projects . . .

What writers can do to enhance their chances of getting an agent (besides being good writers): Great ideas and superb query letters.

Description of the Client from Hell: I have no clients from hell.

Description of Dream Client: Great ideas, prompt delivery, at least a passing interest in the business side of publishing.

Why did you become an agent? I have been a newspaper columnist, book author, and president of a publishing company. Becoming an agent was the next logical extension of my professional life—not to mention that some of my best friends are writers!

What might you be doing if you weren't an agent? Excavating ruins in the Middle East or teaching journalism at a university (both of which I've done).

Comments: Writers—send me your fabulous ideas. I have a relatively small number of clients and love to work on projects I like.

DHS LITERARY, INC.

Twin Sixties Tower
6060 North Central Expressway, Suite 624
Dallas, TX 75206
214-363-4422
fax: 214-363-4423

Agent: David Hale Smith, president.

Born: July 9, 1968.

Education: B.A., English, Kenyon College, 1990.

Career history: Copy editor, one year, Southwest NewsWire, Inc., Dallas; agent/agent, three years, Dupree/Miller & Associates, Dallas; founded DHS Li Agency, March 1994.

Hobbies/personal interests: Reading, writing, camping, hiking, travel.

Subjects/categories most enthusiastic about agenting: Mainstream fiction: thrillers, suspense, mystery, and historical fiction; literary fiction; Westerns. Business nonfiction. Multicultural interests. Pop culture, music, film and television, technology. General nonfiction and gift books.

Subjects/categories not interested in agenting: Children's, young-adult, short stories, poetry.

Best way for a prospective client to initiate contact: Query with synopsis and *SASE*. Material sent without SASE will not be acknowledged or returned. Direct queries to V. Michele Lewis, Submissions Director.

Reading-fee policy: No reading fee.

Client representation in the following categories: Nonfiction, 50%; Fiction, 50%.

Commission: 15% domestic sales; 25% on foreign (via subagents).

Number of titles sold during the past year: About 30, including film options and rights sales.

Approximate percentage of all submissions (from queries through manuscripts) that are rejected: As a new agency, we are extremely selective. We reject 90–95% of all submissions.

Representative titles sold:

A Flash of Red by Clay Harvey (Putnam).

Hollywood Hi-Fi by George Gimarc and Pat Reeder (St. Martin's).

Could You Love Me Like My Cat? by Beth Fowler (Fireside/Simon & Schuster).

Kontum Diary by Paul Reed and Ted Schwarz (Summit).

The Babysitter's Companion by Mary Jayne Fogerty (Ten Speed/Tricycle).

Lone Star Song by Rick Koster (St. Martin's).

The *"Moving To"* Series by Bookworks (four book deal) (Macmillan/Alpha Books).

The most common mistakes potential clients make when soliciting an agent to represent them: The biggest mistake I see people making is coming on too strong without backing up their claims of "sure-fire" success. I think that people *must* be aggressive to get noticed in this business—but if you're all style and no substance it is a waste of everybody's time. Another common blunder I see is just a general lack of preparedness. Spend some time learning about the business *before* contacting agents and publishers.

What writers can do to enhance their chances of getting an agent (besides being good writers): When someone says, "I've got something that will knock your socks off," and it *does*, that excites me.

There is nothing quite like the experience of reading a brilliant cover letter, and then tearing into an even better manuscript.

: Unprofessional people who think that once
...and selling their work is finished. I had a client
...agency was his personal secretarial and counsel-
...I the time we spent talking to him and doing his
...I selling his stuff. He is no longer a client.
...professional in every phase of the business, who
...onship is a team endeavor. A successful publishing
...rative effort. I work extremely hard for my clients—
...who make it easier for me to do my job by working

...nt? I have always loved books, reading good ones and
...people—that's the best part of the job. When I learned
...d stuff even before the publishers do, that's where I

What ...... g if you weren't an agent? I am in awe of good writers,
and I have always ... o be one. I know some pretty good stories, and I plan on
taking a crack at writing them down someday.

I would also like to sail around the world with my family one day.

Comments: *Always* read the book first, then go see the movie!

SANDRA DIJKSTRA LITERARY AGENCY

1155 Camino del Mar, Suite 515
Del Mar, CA 92014
619-755-3115

Agents: Sandra Dijkstra; Amy Rennert, associate; Kathryn Miller, associate.

Born: Dijkstra: New York City; Rennert: Brooklyn, New York; Miller: Long Island,
New York.

Education: Dijkstra: B.A., English; M.A., comparative literature; Ph.D., French literature; Rennert: B.A. English, Colorado College; Miller: B.A. English, UCLA.

Career history: Dijkstra: Former professor of literature; Rennert: Former Editor in
Chief of San Francisco Focus; Miller: Former sales manager at CD-ROM production
and distribution company.

Hobbies/personal interests: Dijkstra: reading; Rennert: reading, movies, theater,
bicycling, cooking, boogie boarding; Miller: reading, movies, computers, traveling,
horseback riding.

Subjects/categories most enthusiastic about agenting: Literary and commercial
fiction of all kinds; nonfiction, especially biography; business; health; history; memoirs; nature; popular culture; psychology; science; self-help and sports; children's books.

Subjects/categories not interested in agenting: No screenplays, plays, poetry, or
short works not intended for book-length publication.

Best way for a prospective client to initiate contact: Send us a professional, and well-thought-out cover letter, accompanied by the first 50 pages of the work, a one page summary of the project, and an SASE for return and/or response.

Reading-fee policy: No reading fee.

Client representation in the following categories: Nonfiction, 60–65%; Fiction, 35–40%; Children's, 2%.

Commission: 15% domestic; 20% foreign (to be split with our foreign agents).

Number of titles sold during the past year: 50.

Approximate percentage of all submissions (from queries through manuscripts) that are rejected: 90%.

Representative titles sold:

The Hundred Secret Senses by Amy Tan (Putnam).

Mistress of Spices by Chitra Divakaruna (Anchor).

The Falconer by Elaine Clark McCarthy (Random House).

The Main Corpse by Diane Mott Davidson (Bantam).

Verdi by Janell Cannon (Harcourt Brace).

The Opening of the American Mind by Lawrence Levine (Beacon).

Red Azalea by Anchee Min (Pantheon).

Tessie and Pearlie by Joy Horowitz (Scribner).

Everyday Sacred by Sue Bender (Harper/San Francisco).

Like Mother, Like Daughter by Debra Waterhouse (Hyperion).

The most common mistakes potential clients make when soliciting an agent to represent them: They sabotage their presentation by bullying or harassing the people with whom they speak on the phone, by trying to sell themselves over the phone, or by not being aware of other books published in their field or genre. This lack of professionalism undermines their case (i.e., by faxing in their queries and/or expecting their submission to be read in 24 hours).

What writers can do to enhance their chances of getting an agent (besides being good writers): Have a professional presentation and manner, a knowledge of other writers and recent books in their field or genre, a passion for their subject or craft, and a lot of determination and patience. Professionalism is a highly valued commodity in this business, and an understanding of the publishing industry and how it functions can only help a writer. Also, it never hurts to have recommendations from other better-known writers, reviewers, booksellers, etc. But the best way is to demonstrate strong writing and to present a unique point of view and a fresh voice.

Description of the Client from Hell: A client who is never happy—with his agent, editor, publicist, publisher. This hellion expends more energy pointing out what's *wrong* with the way others are handling his/her book than with helping to figure out positive and exciting ways to make this effort right. Clients from Hell write nasty letters, call incessantly, and never offer a kind word. Fortunately, about 99% of our authors are *not* Clients from Hell, but that 1 percent can certainly make us feel like they are a majority!

Description of Dream Client: Dream clients are those who call us to fill us in when they have news or to make legitimate requests (but not daily). They have a professional,

owledge of the sometimes archaic workings of publishing. They
appreciative of our work and our feedback. They keep to their
course, continue to write wonderful books.

an agent? Because we love to read and take great pleasure in
get discovered and find their readership.

oing if you weren't an agent? College professor of literature.
our way, conglomerates would not be allowed to buy up pub-
uld go back to editing, and marketing people would not be the
publishing. In our perfect world, books would be valued as
again, and authors/writers respected for their craft rather than their personality!

JIM DONOVAN LITERARY

6022 Winton Street
Dallas, TX 75206
214-826-1251

Agent: Jim Donovan.

Born: December 6, 1954.

Education: B.S., University of Texas.

Career history: In books since 1981 as a bookstore manager; chain-store buyer; published writer (*Dallas: Shining Star of Texas*, 1994, Voyageur Press); freelance editor; and senior editor, Taylor Publishing, 6 years. Literary agent since 1993.

Subjects/categories most enthusiastic about agenting: Any book with something fresh to say, whether it's fiction or nonfiction.

Subjects/categories not interested in agenting: Children's, poetry, short stories, romance, religious, technical books, computer books.

Best way for a prospective client to initiate contact: Query first with brief synopsis, first chapter, and SASE.

Reading-fee policy: No reading fee.

Client representation in the following categories: Nonfiction, 80%; Fiction, 20%.

Commission: 15%.

Number of titles sold during the past year: 11

Approximate percentage of all submissions (from queries through manuscripts) that are rejected: 97%.

Representative titles sold:

Hogan by Curt Sampson (Rutledge Hill).

Inside the Dragon: The Jackie Chan Story by Clyde Gentry (St. Martin's).

Taking Charge of Dyslexia by Kathleen Nosek (Taylor).

King of the Cowboys: The Life and Times of Jerry Jones by Jim Dent (Adams Publishing).

The most common mistakes potential clients make when soliciting an agent to represent them: The top ten query letter turnoffs: (1) Don't use a form letter that begins with "to whom it may concern" or "dear editor." (2) Don't say your writing is better than best-selling writers. (3) Don't mention your self-published books unless they've sold several thousand. (4) Don't refer to your "fiction novel." (5) Don't brag about how great or how funny your book is. (6) Don't quote rave reviews from your relatives, friends, or editors whom you've paid. (7) Don't tell the agent how you're positive your book will make both of you rich. (8) Don't say it's one of five novels you've finished. (9) Don't tell editors that they'll be interested because it will make a great movie. (10) Don't ask for advice or suggestions (if you don't think it's ready, why should they?).

What writers can do to enhance their chances of getting an agent (besides being good writers): Provide a clear, well-thought-out query letter or proposal that describes the book, why there's a need for it, how it does something better than or different from the competition, and why the author is the perfect person to write the book.

What might you be doing if you weren't an agent? A publisher.

Jane Dystel Literary Management

One Union Square West, Suite 904
New York, NY 10003
212-627-9100

Agent: Jane Dystel.

Education: B.A., New York University. Attended, but did not graduate from Georgetown Law School.

Career history: Permissions editor at Bantam Books; managing and acquisitions editor at Grosset & Dunlap; Publisher of *World Almanac* and founder of *World Almanac* publications; partner at Acton and Dystel Inc.; partner at Acton, Dystel, Leone and Jaffe; founder and owner of Jane Dystel Literary Management.

Hobbies/personal interests: Golf, gardening, cooking, ice skating, travel.

Subjects/categories most enthusiastic about agenting: Literary and commercial fiction; serious nonfiction; cookbooks.

Subjects/categories not interested in agenting: Genre fiction (i.e., romance, sci-fi, Westerns), poetry, children's books.

Best way for a prospective client to initiate contact: Submit a query letter accompanied by an outline and a couple of sample chapters (with SASE).

Reading-fee policy: No reading fee.

Client representation in the following categories: Nonfiction, 80%; Fiction, 20%.
Commission: 15%.

Number of titles sold during the past year: About 50.

Approximate percentage of all submissions (from queries through manuscripts) that are rejected: 95%.

Representative titles sold:
Ben & Jerry's: The Inside Scoop by Fred Lager.
Our Health, Our Lives by Dr. Eileen Hoffman.

Fatal Justice by Fred Bost and Jerry Potter.

The Price of a Child by Lorene Cary.

I Never Forget a Meal by Michael Tucker.

The Tiger's Tail by Gus Lee.

The Splendid Table by Lynne Rossetto Kasper.

Guilty by Harold Rothwax.

Don't Pee on My Leg and Tell Me It's Raining by Judy Sheindlin and Josh Getlin.

Inner Simplicity by Elaine St. James.

Living Posthumously by Andrew Schmookler.

What the Deaf-Mute Heard by Dan Gearino.

The most common mistakes potential clients make when soliciting an agent to represent them: Flashy, self-important letters full of hype and cuteness. Authors who refer to their work as "fictional novels."

Most common and costly mistakes have to do with bad grammar, sloppy presentation, illegible material (exotic fonts or single spacing), and lack of proofreading.

What writers can do to enhance their chances of getting an agent (besides being good writers): Intelligent, well-written queries that show originality.

Description of the Client from Hell: Someone who calls incessantly wanting updates and hand-holding. Someone who whines about everything. Someone who is dishonest and unpleasant.

Description of Dream Client: Someone who is talented and asks intelligent questions. Someone who is patient and understanding of the fact that selling books can be a slow process. Someone who takes rejection in his/her stride.

Why did you become an agent? Having worked in many other areas of publishing, it seemed like an exciting new field to explore. I was intrigued by the increasing importance of the agent–author relationship in the publishing world.

What might you be doing if you weren't an agent? I'd be in some area of law or public service.

Comments: People should read more and read better books.

ANN ELMO AGENCY, INC.

60 East 42nd Street
New York, NY 10165
212-661-2880

Agent: Lettie Lee.

Subjects/categories most enthusiastic about agenting: Romance, juvenile, nonfiction.

Subjects/categories not interested in agenting: Poetry.

Best way for a prospective client to initiate contact: Query letter.

Commission: 15%.

FELICIA ETH LITERARY REPRESENTATION

555 Bryant Street, Suite 350
Palo Alto, CA 94301
415-375-1276
fax: 415-375-1277

Agent: Felicia Eth.
  Born: December 17, 1952; New York City.
  Education: B.A., Brandeis University.
  Career history: Felicia Eth Literary Representation; St. Martin's Press, West Coast editor; Writers House, Inc., New York; Warner Brothers, story editor: Palomar Pictures, assistant, TV and feature development.
  Hobbies/personal interests: Travel, art, gardening.
  Subjects/categories most enthusiastic about agenting: Fiction: contemporary well-written mainstream fiction, including psychological novels, feminist novels, suspense/adventure (though not on the global level). Nonfiction: intelligent, cutting-edge, or well crafted, in diverse areas including psychology, women's issues, health, popular science, biography, investigative journalism, narrative nonfiction, ecology, travelogue.
  Subjects/categories not interested in agenting: Most fiction, romance, science fiction, children's, Westerns.
  Best way for a prospective client to initiate contact: Send query letter (with SASE); for nonfiction, proposal is fine.
  Reading-fee policy: No reading fee.
  Client representation in the following categories: Nonfiction, 90%; Fiction, 10%.
  Number of titles sold during the past year: 10. Many of my clients are new writers. I tend to work with fewer books than many agents, and prefer to spend a good deal of time on each title.
  Commission: 15%.
  Representative titles sold:
  What It's Like to Live Now by Maran (Bantam).
  Caught up in the Rapture by Jackson (Simon & Schuster).
  A Chosen Death by Shavelson (Simon & Schuster).
  Comments: It's hard to make a general statement. I have quirky tastes, but if I get excited about a book, I'm raring to go. I look for smart authors with something fresh and new to say—something that's worth saying, and might really make a difference. I'm also inclined to writers based on the West Coast who need a connection to New York, but who don't necessarily want things done in the traditional way.

JOYCE A. FLAHERTY, LITERARY AGENT

816 Lynda Court
St. Louis, MO 63122
314-966-3057

Agents

(Member: AAR).

y of Wisconsin, Madison; Webster University, St. Louis, B.A.

ournalist; executive director for nonprofit business organization; onsultant, which included publishing clients. Founded literary agency

personal interests: Reading and tracking books in bookstores.

cts/categories most enthusiastic about agenting: Commercial fiction: en's fiction, genre fiction, thrillers, contemporary and historical romance. nfiction: self-help or how-to for commercial publishing markets, investigative reporting and Americana. We are interested in a broad range of fiction and nonfiction.

Subjects/categories not interested in agenting: Science fiction, erotica, children's books, poetry, collections of short stories or articles, syndicated materials, screenplays—except for the books sold.

Best way for a prospective client to initiate contact: Query first with brief synopsis, first chapter, and SASE.

Reading-fee policy: No reading fee. $50 marketing fee for unpublished book authors or for published authors writing in areas different than published books.

Client representation in the following categories: Nonfiction, 20%; Fiction, 80%.

Commission: 15% domestic, 15% plus foreign co-agents' fees.

Number of titles sold during the past year: 63.

Approximate percentage of all submissions (from queries through manuscripts) that are rejected: 99%.

Representative titles sold:

Prairie Rose by Susan E. Kirby (Avon).

101 Things a College Girl Should Know by Stephanie Edwards (Andrews & McMeel).

Talisman by Charlene Cross (Pocket Books).

The most common mistakes potential clients make when soliciting an agent to represent them: Queries don't give enough information to evaluate the submission. Cover letters don't give word counts or phone number where the writer can be reached. Author doesn't include SASE.

What writers can do to enhance their chances of getting an agent (besides being good writers): Great letter, great first chapter, and wonderful commercial ideas that give a fresh, new slant or twist. Everything mentioned in the letter or proposal is pertinent.

Description of the Client from Hell: We have wonderful, professional clients.

Description of Dream Client: Turns in clean copy, always meets deadlines, pleasant natured and great writing with fresh, commercial ideas.

Why did you become an agent? I have always loved books and have been interested in publishing and writers. It's such a fascinating business. Sometimes tough, but always a challenge.

What might you be doing if you weren't an agent? A bookstore owner.

Comments: It's been a tough market for new authors. The wholesale market seems to be consolidating. Yet new authors continue to appear on the shelves, and so I would advise authors to keep on searching for the right agent. Don't give up! Although at this time we have no unpublished book authors, we always look for special new talent.

THE FOGELMAN LITERARY AGENCY

7515 Greenville Avenue, Suite 712
Dallas, TX 75231
214-361-9956

Agents: Evan M. Fogelman, Linda Diehl Kruger.

Born: Fogelman: May 1, 1960.

Education: Fogelman: B.A. with honors (1982), Juris Doctor (1985), Tulane University; Stanford Publishing Course. Kruger: B.A., media theory and criticism, University of Texas at Austin (1989).

Career history: Fogelman: Entertainment attorney, book reviewer, author publicist. Kruger: Production manager for a national advertising agency.

Hobbies/personal interests: Fogelman: poetry; opera; French bulldogs; step aerobics; laughter; literary theory; and, of course, reading. Kruger: Exercising, movies, crafts, travel, dogs, cooking, reading.

Subjects/categories most enthusiastic about agenting: Fogelman: Women's fiction (both category and mainstream, including romance, mysteries), popular business, psychological self-help, nonfiction geared for the women's market, political biography, author biography. Kruger: All categories of romance. Our agency works primarily with published authors of the romance genre. However, I invite unpublished romance authors to query with an SASE. Nonfiction: subjects that target a female audience, pop culture, some self-help, mainly commercial nonfiction.

Subjects/categories not interested in agenting: Fogelman: Police procedurals, technothrillers, science fiction, fantasy, shoot-'em-up Westerns, cyberpunk novels, children's books, poetry, short stories. Kruger: Poetry, short stories, true Westerns, science fiction, historical fiction, action adventure, New Age, mysteries.

Best way for a prospective client to initiate contact: Fogelman: Query letter (with SASE). Kruger: A query letter with SASE will be responded to within five business days. Published authors are invited to call. No unsolicited material, please.

Reading-fee policy: No reading fee.

Client representation in the following categories: Fogelman: Nonfiction, 50%; Fiction, 50%; Kruger: Nonfiction, 30%; Fiction, 70%.

Commission: 15% domestic, including all agency-negotiated subsidiary-rights deals; 10% foreign.

Number of titles sold during the past year: 40+.

Approximate percentage of all submissions (from queries through manuscripts) that are rejected: Fogelman: 99.5%. Kruger: 99.5%.

Representative titles sold:

Fogelman:

Green Lake by S. K. Epperson (NAL).

Willful Injustice by Bob Dietz (Regnery).

Untitled contemporary romance by Katherine Sutcliffe (Berkley).

Untitled historical romance by Katherine Sutcliffe (Berkley).

Two untitled romantic suspense novels by Helen R. Myers (Mira).

Kruger:

Bitterroot and *Miracle of Love* by Victoria Chancellor (Leisure).

Midnight Confessions and *Framed* by Karen Leabo (Silhouette).

The Bride Wore Tie-Dye by Karen Leabo (Silhouette).

Four category romance titles by Karen Leabo (Bantam)

Wedding Rings and Baby Things and *Casey and the Cowboy* by Teresa Southwick (Silhouette).

Chasing Baby by Pam McCutcheon (Harlequin).

Quicksilver by Pam McCutcheon (Leisure).

Still Remembering You by Bobby Sherman and Dena Hill (Contemporary).

What to Do about Baby by Martha Hix (Silhouette).

Three Regency romance titles by April Kihlstrom (Signet).

The most common mistakes potential clients make when soliciting an agent to represent them: Fogelman: Gratuitous hostility or scrupulous meanness, sloppiness, gimmicks, and uninformed impatience. Kruger: When a writer cannot tell me what type of a book he/she has written. One writer described his books as (and this is an actual quote): "a non-genre erotic contemporary mainstream men's fantasy action/adventure romantic sexual comedy novel, or, if you really need a category, call it Romance Novel, Male Division." In helping a writer categorize his/her book, I always ask one question: If you had one copy of your manuscript and you had to put it on one bookshelf at the bookstore, where would it go? Also, I hate unsolicited material.

What writers can do to enhance their chances of getting an agent (besides being good writers): Fogelman: Published authors who can plainly and informatively articulate what they want make me enthusiastic. Saying, "I want to write best-sellers" does nothing for me. Saying, "I know I need an editor who wants me to write best-sellers" sends me into an enthusiastic and delightful orbit—it's what the business is based on. Kruger: When writers research what I'm looking for and deliver, upon request, a professional, clean presentation of their work. Also, when writers are enthusiastic about their work, it catches my attention.

Description of the Client from Hell: Fogelman: Anyone who assumes the publishing business will reward him/her just for being intelligent. Kruger: A writer who does not realize that this is a creative, yet *professional* business. I don't want a client wrapped up in gossip or contests or anything that would distract him/her from his/her writing career.

Description of Dream Client: Fogelman: Someone who understands writing is a wonderful, difficult business that requires focus; an ability to deal with rejection; and, most importantly, the devoted persistence to finish what he/she starts. Kruger: Someone who keeps the lines of communication open. This is a two-way relationship. As for the creative process, my dream client creates characters and then releases those characters to tell the story.

Why did you become an agent? Fogelman: I completely enjoy the crossroads of art and commerce. Kruger: There are many reasons I became an agent, but what keeps me in this business is the chance to work with such creative individuals. This is an exciting business, one unlike any other profession. The atmosphere of our agency is always entertaining and challenging. I wouldn't change a thing.

What might you be doing if you weren't an agent? Fogelman: Oil-well wildcatter. Kruger: Eating a lot of barbecue.

Comments: Fogelman: If you're reading this because you're writing, good. If you're reading this *instead* of writing, bad. Kruger: When sending a query, or a partial or completed manuscript to an agent or editor, put your best work first. This is the all-important first impression, so never send a *rough draft*. Believe in your writing, your work, proof and re-proof, and never let your enthusiasm die. Best of luck!

SHERYL B. FULLERTON ASSOCIATES

1010 Church Street
San Francisco, CA 94114
415-824-8460

Agent: Sheryl Fullerton.

Born: March 24, 1948.

Education: B.A., English, University of Utah, Phi Beta Kappa, magna cum laude.

Career history: Production editor, Prentice Hall (college textbooks) (1971–1974); development editor, Wadsworth Publishing Company (college textbooks (1974–1978); acquisitions editor (music, sociology, religion, anthropology), Wadsworth (1979–1988); editorial manager, Wadsworth (1988–1993); literary agent (1994 to present).

Hobbies/personal interests: Cooking, gardening, travel.

Subjects/categories most enthusiastic about agenting: Psychology, psychotherapy, business, management, social and cultural issues, popular culture, religion/spirituality, women's issues, gay and lesbian issues, health and wellness, current affairs, pop culture, selected reference, self-help and how-to, some niche fiction.

Subjects/categories not interested in agenting: Science, technology, computers, nature/environment, most fiction.

Best way for a prospective client to initiate contact: By mail—a strong query letter (with SASE) will get a prompt response. Prefer *not* to get calls or unsolicited manuscripts.

Reading-fee policy: No reading fee.

Client representation in the following categories: Nonfiction, 90%; Fiction, 5%; Textbooks, 5%.

Commission: 15% domestic, 20% foreign.

Number of titles sold during the past year: 10.

Approximate percentage of all submissions (from queries through manuscripts) that are rejected: 60–70%. I am very willing to work with relatively inexperienced writers.

Representative titles sold:

Leading from the Heart: Discovering Spirit in America's Workplaces by Kay Gilley (Butterworth-Heinemann).

The World As a Whole: Returning Heart and Human Spirit to Our Lives by Gail Holland (Conari Press).

What's That From? The Ultimate Quiz Book of Memorable Movie Lines Since 1969 by Jay Nanda (St. Martin's).

The Golden Ghetto: The Psychology of Affluence by Jessie O'Neill (Hazelden Publishers).

Beyond Recovery: Eye Movement Desensitization Reprocessing (EMDR), The Breakthrough Trauma Therapy by Laurel Parnell (W. W. Norton).

Sacred Heritage: Explorations in Psychology and Contemporary Shamanism by Donald Sandner and Steven Wong (Routledge).

Reclaiming the Heartland: Lesbian and Gay Male Voices From the Midwest by William Spurlin and Karen Osborne (University of Minnesota, due out June, 1996).

Hung Jury: Diary of a Menendez Juror by Hazel Thornton (Temple University Press).

The most common mistakes potential clients make when soliciting an agent to represent them: No SASE, phoning rather than writing a strong query letter, not being up front about talking to other agents at the same time. Most costly mistake: Not doing their homework up front concerning the market for their book (e.g., competing books, bookselling realities).

What writers can do to enhance their chances of getting an agent (besides being good writers): A strong, well-written query letter accompanied by a realistic and enthusiastic proposal that indicates market savvy will get my attention every time.

Description of the Client from Hell: People with the highly unattractive and unpleasant combination of ignorance about the publishing business and arrogance about themselves and their work, which often taints the author–agent relationship with distrust and suspicion.

Description of Dream Client: Someone with a great idea that has been checked against realities, passion and persistence, willingness to work and learn as a writer, personal credibility (does what she says she'll do), excellent writing skills and more than one book idea, and strong connections (professional) that will help sell the book. (I represent mostly nonfiction authors.)

Why did you become an agent? I love working with authors and being part of the world of ideas. I also love the autonomy of having my own business and working with and developing authors' careers.

What might you be doing if you weren't an agent? I would probably be an editor or an author myself—possibly writing on food/wine/restaurants (not really a surprise, considering I live in the *foodie* capital of the West).

Comments: Writers need to understand the realities of contemporary publishing and bookselling. The more educated they are and the more they understand the importance of selling and marketing themselves and their ideas, the more likely their chances of success. Get over the illusion that publishers are waiting eagerly for manuscripts—they

are busy, skeptical, and harried—so the better job the agent and author do of
their decisions easier, the better the process works for everybody.

FORTHWRITE LITERARY AGENCY

3579 East Foothill Boulevard, Suite 327
Pasadena, CA 91107
818-798-0793

Agent: Wendy L. Zhorne.
  Born: October 2, 1964.
  Education: Journalism, Arizona State University.
  Career history: Journalism and sales.
  Hobbies/personal interests: Mothering my daughter, épée fencing, reading, and
gardening.
  Subjects/categories most enthusiastic about agenting: Business, self-help, pop
psychology, how-to, health, computer, and consumer reference on a variety of subjects!
  Subjects/categories not interested in agenting: No fiction, true crime, poetry, syn-
dicated, shorts, or cartoon books.
  Best way for a prospective client to initiate contact: (1) Get a referral from one of
our satisfied editors or clients. (2) Have the credentials to write on your subject and say
so in your query letter (with SASE!).
  Reading-fee policy: No reading fee.
  Client representation in the following categories: Nonfiction, 100%.
  Commission: 15% domestic; 20% foreign.
  Number of titles sold during the past year: 34.
  **Approximate percentage of all submissions (from queries through manuscripts)
that are rejected:** 90–95%.
  Representative titles sold:
  Heart at Work by Jack Canfield (coauthor of *Chicken Soup for the Soul*) and
Jacqueline Miller (McGraw-Hill).
  Success Secrets of the Motivational Masters by Michael Jeffreys (Prima).
  Alternative Therapies A–Z by Dr. Mark Kastre (Holt).
  The Art of Japanese Vegetarian Cooking by Max Jacobson (Prima).
  **The most common mistakes potential clients make when soliciting an agent to
represent them:** The first mistake authors make is to choose not to send SASE with
the query. But the *costliest* mistake by far is sending entire manuscripts to agents who
don't even handle your type of book! Beyond those egregious errors, I would say calling within six weeks of submission to request an answer is most unpleasant.
  **What writers can do to enhance their chances of getting an agent (besides being
good writers):** An author who knows and is passionate about the subject and who has
the credentials to write it makes me gleeful. If that writer can also write well and promote well, I am ecstatic!

nt from Hell: The ones who don't read; who think the fact
...gh to make it unique; authors who are not living an abun-
...to live one; authors who are poor who write on how to be-
...ho cannot write well but insist they can.

lient: Most of my clients are Dream Clients! They have
...d in their niche; write well (or work well with a ghost!);
...published; and never, ever, ever ask for loans, to borrow
...heir publisher or editor!

ent? I *love* being an agent because there are those in-
...book the world needs comes from a wonderful writer and
...a terrific, enthusiastic, creative editor. That synergy makes me high. I'm
an agent because I'm addicted!

What might you be doing if you weren't an agent? I'd be running a center for
bereaved parents' recovery near Edinburgh, Scotland, in some drafty old castle lined
with books.

Comments: Agents are the luckiest people in the world! We get to meet interesting
people; handle important, worthy, and/or helpful books; deal with the intricate and
ever-changing, exciting world of publishing (in the U.S. and abroad, all types of
rights—electronic, foreign, audio, etc.); and we get to make a major contribution to humanity through our efforts.

MAX GARTENBERG, LITERARY AGENT

521 Fifth Avenue, Suite 1700
New York, NY 10175
212-860-8451

Agent: Max Gartenberg.
 Born: New York City.
 Education: B.A., New York University; M.A., Brown University.
 Career history: As an English major with a graduate degree, I drifted into college
teaching, then realized that I wanted to be where the action was, not where it had been
in the past. I was living in the Midwest when that lightning bolt struck—about the same
time I had to go to New York on family business. The rest is commentary.
 Subjects/categories most enthusiastic about agenting: Although I will occasionally take on a new novelist whose talent seems to me superior, fiction writers might be
well advised to look elsewhere. I am most interested in solid nonfiction—books that
present fresh and significant information or viewpoints—regardless of subject area,
whether for trade, paperback, or reference.
 Subjects/categories not interested in agenting: I am not interested in category fiction, novelty books, and personal memoirs.
 Best way for a prospective client to initiate contact: With a one- or two-page,
first-class letter describing any relevant background information, accompanied by a

SASE if the writer wishes for any sort of reply. I usually don't read sample pages or chapters if these are included. And I am absolutely turned off by cold calls and faxed queries.

Reading-fee policy: No reading fee.

Commission: 15% on initial sale; thereafter 10% on sales in the U.S., 15–20% elsewhere.

Approximate percentage of all submissions (from queries through manuscripts) that are rejected: 95%.

Representative titles sold:

Phantom Illness by Carla Cantor (Houghton Mifflin).

The Complete Art of War by Ralph D. Sawyer (Westview Press).

Answers to Lucky by Howard Owen (HarperCollins).

In Search of the Old Ones by David Roberts (Simon & Schuster).

Description of the Client from Hell: The client who demands unceasing attention, who is never satisfied with the deal I bring him (he always has friends whose agents got twice as much), who delivers his manuscript late and in such disorder that the publisher rejects it and demands return of the advance—and who, on top of everything, blames me for the mess. This is not an imaginary character.

Description of Dream Client: A writing professional who can be counted on to produce a well-made, literate, enlightening, and enjoyable book with a minimum of *Sturm und Drang*. Fortunately, this is not an imaginary character, either.

The most common mistakes potential clients make when soliciting an agent to represent them: What most turns me off is a solicitation which tells me almost nothing about the writer or his material but requests detailed information about myself and my services which are readily available in such books as the *Writer's Guide*.

What writers can do to enhance their chances of getting an agent (besides being good writers): A sense that the writer knows his subject, has reviewed the literature which has come before, and has written a book that is genuinely fresh and new.

Why did you become an agent? I love good books. They are the pillars of our civilization. It is a privilege to work with those who create them.

THE SEBASTIAN GIBSON AGENCY

Literary, Musical, and Performing Artist
Talent and Athlete Agency
125 Tahquitz Canyon Way, Suite 200
Palm Springs, CA 92262
619-322-2200
fax: 619-322-3857

Agent: Sebastian Gibson.

Born: December 8, 1950.

Education: B.A., cum laude, UCLA; L.L.B., magna cum laude, University College Cardiff, Great Britain; J.D., University of San Diego School of Law.

Career history: The author of two novels, six screenplays, the lyrics and music to a stage musical, and hundreds of copyrighted songs. Author of published legal articles in both the United States and England. Performed as a stage musician on tour in the U.S. and Europe, and in a national television special. Obtained law degrees in both the U.S. and Great Britain. Practiced law in San Diego for four years, subsequently in England and the Middle East, and in 1984 began the Law Offices of Sebastian Gibson in Palm Springs, California. Presently practices law and represents literary and entertainment clients and sports figures from law offices in Palm Springs and Palm Desert, California.

Hobbies/personal interests: Reading well-written books, traveling to book fairs, discovering new talent.

Subjects/categories most enthusiastic about agenting: All categories of fiction, particularly novels with interesting characters and well-woven plots. Especially interested in legal and psychological thrillers, historical novels, mystery/suspense and action/adventure or espionage with romance subplots and interesting twists, crime/police with humorous/gritty elements, medical dramas, women's fiction, sagas, and any well-written novel with unusual characters. Nonfiction with unusual approaches or written by celebrities, cookbooks or photography with a novel twist, humorous diet books, controversial issues, biographies, current affairs, "kiss and tell" books, and women's issues. Also children's, juvenile, young adult, stage plays, musicals, television scripts, and screenplays.

Subjects/categories not interested in agenting: Poetry, textbooks, essays, short stories, how-to books, books in verse, computer, gardening, porn, travel, autobiographies by non-celebrities, drug recovery, parenting.

Best way for a prospective client to initiate contact: Fiction: Send book proposal with outline and three sample chapters or up to 50 pages with SASE. Do not send unsolicited manuscripts. They will be trashed. No disks, please. Sample chapters should already be edited and without typographical errors or incorrect grammar.

Reading-fee policy: No reading fee as such. We do, however, request a bush-league, small potato, hardly-worth-mentioning handling fee of $7.50 per submission to pay for whoopee cushions to keep the staff in line, harassing phone calls to publishers, and trips to Tahiti for those all-important Tahitian writer conferences.

Client representation in the following categories: Nonfiction, 30%; Fiction, 60%; Children's, 10%.

Commission: 10% domestic; 20% foreign (split with foreign agents).

Number of titles sold during the past year: Confidential, as some clients are represented by the Law Offices of Sebastian Gibson.

Approximate percentage of all submissions (from queries through manuscripts) that are rejected: 95–98%.

Representative titles sold: Confidential, as some clients are represented by the Law Offices of Sebastian Gibson.

Description of the Client from Hell: We don't have any overly demanding clients with unrealistic expectations. Five years ago we buried them all alive in killer ant anthills in the desert.

Description of Dream Client: A best-selling author who leaves his or her present uncaring agent for the personal care our agency can provide.

The most common mistakes potential clients make when soliciting an agent to represent them: Sending first drafts, no SASE, unsolicited manuscripts, incessant calls, autobiographies, and travel memoirs of trips to Orlando or Tijuana.

What writers can do to enhance their chances of getting an agent (besides being good writers): Bribes. Seriously, book proposals and manuscripts already well edited and thoughtfully and creatively written.

Why did you become an agent? With a background in music, literature, sports, and the law, it was a natural progression to add a literary, talent, and athlete agency to our law firm.

What might you be doing if you weren't an agent? Sipping piña coladas on a beach in Greece, far away from telephones, car phones, beepers, pagers, and comptuers.

Comments: The world needs more good books. An author with something to say that pulls on one's emotions and sparks one's interest can have a profound effect on others. Share your strength, your intellect, and don't be afraid to bare the soul of your characters, as long as it's done in an interesting way.

Irene Goodman Literary Agency

521 Fifth Avenue
New York, NY 10175
212-682-1978
fax: 212-490-6502

Agent: Irene Goodman.

Born: November 29, 1949; Detroit, Michigan.

Education: B.A., University of Michigan, 1971; M.A., University of Michigan, 1973.

Career history: Editorial assistant at T. Y. Crowell, 1975–1976; assistant at Kirby McCauley Agency, 1976–1978; established own agency in 1978.

Hobbies/personal interests: Theater, opera, cooking, Nantucket, the Berkshires, *Doonesbury*, figure skating (watching, not doing), politics, movies, hanging out with small children, watching cooking shows on weird cable channels.

Subjects/categories most enthusiastic about agenting: All types of women's fiction, romance novels, mysteries, biographies, some popular nonfiction.

Subjects/categories not interested in agenting: Literature, esoteric nonfiction, technothrillers, macho genre books, psychobabble, feminist diatribes. I don't handle children's books because I like to leave something sacred.

Best way for a prospective client to initiate contact: The very best way is through a referral by a client.

Reading-fee policy: No reading fee.

Client representation in the following categories: Nonfiction, 5%; Fiction, 95%.

Commission: 15% until the author sells a book for $25,000 or more, or until the author brings in $50,000 in a calendar year, then the commission goes permanently to 10%.

Number of titles sold during the past year: 56.

Approximate percentage of all submissions (from queries through manuscripts) that are rejected: 98%.

Representative titles sold:

My Outlaw by Linda Lael Miller (Pocket).

The Love Charm by Pamela Mursi (Avon)

The Matter of Marriage by Debbie Macumber (Mira).

The most common mistakes potential clients make when soliciting an agent to represent them: The biggest problem is a general one and it concerns the sheer volume. No one I know in the business can seriously devote any real attention to the "slush pile," simply because there is too much of it. While I look at everything, I do it very rapidly, often giving only seconds to each piece. This means that I'm probably missing something in there that's good, but it still isn't worth it to me to spend the time. The odds are about one in a thousand, and that doesn't justify the time spent.

What writers can do to enhance their chances of getting an agent (besides being good writers): People who find an appropriate way to separate themselves from the masses. This can mean outstanding quality, being useful and visible at a conference, or getting referred by someone I know and respect. It definitely means having something that is salable as opposed to something that needs a lot of work or is completely off the mark or not what I represent.

Description of the Client from Hell: Someone who wants me to be mother, psychiatrist, best friend, sounding board, loan officer, editor, accountant, and lawyer—all rolled into one. I am none of those things in my work. What I am is an agent.

Description of Dream Client: I have several real dream clients. It is my privilege to work with them. Here's what they all have in common: They work hard, they don't whine, they have a terrific sense of humor, they are intelligent, they have lives and expect me to have one, and—oh, yes—they have talent. They are responsible for themselves, they know how to say thank you, they know how to laugh at themselves (and at me occasionally, when I deserve it), and they like to give people the benefit of the doubt. They enrich my life and give as much back to me as I give to them.

Why did you become an agent? I became an agent because it was my destiny. That sounds pompous, but consider this: I don't like working in large companies because I can't tolerate the politics. I like to be a part of a working community, but I also need to fly solo. Autonomy is stimulating to me; it motivates me to get things done. I love making deals, I love books, and I love having an equal partnership with a very talented author. Bureaucracy makes me crazy, and I love being in a position where I can cut through it.

What might you be doing if you weren't an agent? When I was in my 20s, I was considering two career options: pursuing an advanced degree in medieval studies or studying gourmet cooking in Paris. The third option was to come to New York and go into book publishing, which is obviously what I did.

I like the news and I like writing fast under deadline, so I might have been a journalist or political strategist. Or I might have been an author. When I first came to New York, I wanted to be an editor, but that was before I learned what agents did. When I saw agents at work, I was very attracted to it and wanted to be one. The fact that I actually am one is mostly because I'm not very patient and I refused to give up.

If you could say anything you wanted, without censor, what would you say?
Absolutely nothing. That's why I'm a good agent.

SANFORD J. GREENBURGER ASSOCIATE, INC.

55 Fifth Avenue
New York, NY 10003
212-206-5612
fax: 212-463-8718

Founded: 1932.

Agents: Heide Lange, Vice President; Faith Hamlin; Beth Vesel; Theresa Park; Elyse Cheney; Daniel Mandel.

International Rights Agent: Christine Harcar.

Best way for a prospective client to initiate contact: Query letter with a SASE.

Reading-fee policy: No reading fee policy.

Client representation in the following categories: Fiction, 40%; Nonfiction, 60%.

Commission: 15% domestic; 20% international.

Number of titles sold during the past year: Hundreds.

The following information pertains to Heide Lange:
Born: July 21, 1949.

Education: BA, Hunter College, CUNY.

Career history: I started working at the agency while attending college. As Sanford Greenburger's assistant, I ws fortunate enough to learn the business from a "publishing gentleman" with an international reputation, and it's been my home for 28 years. My books have generally reflected my background, interests and stages in life. Married, two children, I've handled general nonfiction from art, which was my college major (*Drawing on the Right Side of the Brain* was my first bestseller), to relationships and sex (*The G Spot*), pregnancy and childbirth, parenting, women's health and other issues, current events, controversy, biographies, memoirs, journalism, some general reference, how-to, self improvement.

Hobbies/personal interests: Reading, gardening, bicycling, rollerblading and any other activities I can share with the family before our children are off to college (in a flash, it seems).

Subjects/categories most enthusiastic about agenting: See above and representative titles below, but basically, if an author is passionate about and experienced in the subject he or she is writing about, I'm prepared to be enticed by it.

Subjects/categories not interested in agenting: Category fiction, children's books.

Representative titles sold:

Let Me Hear Your Voice: A Family's Triumph Over Autism by Catherine Maurice (Knopf).

Emotional Wisdom by Jean Grasso Fitzpatrick (Viking).

Raising Your Spirited Child by Mary Kurcinka (HarperCollins).

Swim with the Dolphins: How Women Can Succeed in Corporate America on Their Own Terms by Connie Glaser and Barbara Smalley (Warner).

The Multi-Orgasmic Man: How Any Man Can Experience Multiple Orgasms and Dramatically Enhance His Sexual Relationship by Mantak Chia and Douglas Abrams Arava (Harper San Francisco).

The Random House Work Menu by Stephen Glazier (Random House).

Life's Big Instruction Book: The Almanac of Indispensable Information by Carol Madigan and Ann Elwood (Warner).

Encyclopedia of the Renaissance edited by Paul Grendler (Scribner's).

Lauren Groveman's Kitchen: Nurturing Foods for Family and Friends by Lauren Groveman (Chronicle).

Italian Food and Drink: An A to Z Guide by John Mariani (Broadway Books).

Why did you become an agent? The fact that I love to read was really my entry into this business and sometimes I still can't believe I can make money doing what I love. That, and the clients I can help realize their dreams, makes this very gratifying work.

The following information pertains to Faith Hamlin:

Born: Pre-Babyboomer.

Education: Boston University—Speech Therapy and Psychology.

Career history: Two children, bookstore buyer/manager, sales rep for several publishers, sales manager for Macmillan, Atheneum, Scribner, Free Press; agent for 10 years.

Subjects/categories most enthusiastic about agenting:

Adults—Most non-fiction, especially health, medical, psychology, parenting, women's issues, sports, biography/autobiography, gay/lesbian, science, humor, the arts, and books by journalists. I look for people with strong credentials, a point of view and excellent writing skills.

Children's—Picture books, middle grade, YA, commercial but not cartoon characters; illustrators and photographers who can also write text. With the flood of submission I receive, I can consider only writers with a track record.

Subjects/categories not interested in agenting:

Adult—fiction, except mysteries

Children's—No science fiction

Representative titles sold:

Adult

Behind the Crystal Ball by Anthony Aveni (Times Books).

Wilder Times by Kevin Lally (Henry Holt).

Curse of Rocky Colavito by Terry Pluto (Simon & Schuster).

Rudy Tomjanovich Autobiography by Rudy T and Robert Flakoff (Simon & Schuster).

Jackie Under My Skin by Wayne Koestenbaum (FSG/Plume).

Body in the Bog by Katherine Hall Page (William Morrow).

Attorney for the Damned by Denis Woychuk (Free Press).

Raising a Thoughtful Teenager by Rabbi Ben Kamin (Dutton).

Maria Tallchief: Native American Dancer by Maria Tallchief/Larry Kaplan (Henry Holt).

Allegra Kent by Allegra Kent (St. Martin's Press).

Women's Crisis Handbook by Lauren Hartman (Houghton Mifflin).

Dr. Spock Biography by Thoman Maier (Harcourt Brace).

Songs for Myself by Jack Maguire (Jeremy Tarcher).

Prostate Cancer: A Guide for Women and the Men They Love by Sandra Haber, Barbara Wainrib, and Jack Maguire

It's About Time by Linda Sapadin and Jack Maguire (Penguin).

Dr. Mom's Breastfeeding Guide by Marianne Neifert, M.D. (Dutton).

Christmas Cookies by Maria Robbins, St. Martin's Press).

Children's books:

Rainy Days and Saturdays by Linda Hetzer (Workman).

Rodeo by Ken Robbins, (Henry Holt).

Thunder on the Plains by Ken Robbins (Scholastic).

Earth, Air, Water and Fire by Ken Robbins (Henry Holt).

Red Bird by Doreen Rappaport (Dial).

Wild Colorado by Richard Maurer (Crown).

Hostae by Ed Myers (Hyperion).

Christie and Company by Katherine Hall Page (Avon).

How They Sleep by Cor Hazelaar (FSG).

The Signpainter's Dream by Roger Roth (Crown).

What's a Vomit Comet by Astronaut Mike Mullane (Wiley).

The following information pertains to Beth Vesel:

Education: BA, English/Political Theory, UC Berkeley; Graduate work in Comparative literature, UC Berkeley.

Career history: Senior agent, Greenburger Associates since 8/88.

Assistant to Gloria Loomis/Watkins Loomis, 1/85–8/88.

Assistant, Little Brown subsidiary rights/special sales, 11/83–12/84.

Subjects/categories most enthusiastic about agenting: Serious psychology, psychology; cultural criticism; gender/gay/lesbian studies; extraordinary fiction.

Subjects/categories not interested in agenting: Self-help; genre fiction

Best way for a prospective client to initiate contact: Through a current client or an editor with whom I work.

Reading-fee policy: No fees.

Client representation in the following categories: Fiction, 30%; Nonfiction, 70%.

Commission: 15%.

Representative titles sold:

The Secret Language of Eating Disorders by Peggy Claude-Pierre (Times/Vintage).

Getting a Life (Sequel to *Your Money or Your Life)* by David Heitmiller and Jaquelynn Blix (Viking).

From Menarche to Menopause by Deborah Sischel, M.D. and Jeanne Driscoll, R.N. (Morrow/Avon).

Desire Lines by Christina Balar-Kline (Morrow) novel.

Why did you become an agent? Because I love books and care about authors. I was once a writer myself.

The following information pertains to Theresa Park:

Education: BA, University of California, Santa Cruz; JD, Harvard Law School.

Career history: Previously an attorney with Cooley Goaward Castro Huddleson and Tatum (Palo Alto, CA); joined Sanford Greenburger Associates in 1994.

Subjects/categories most enthusiastic about agenting: Commercial fiction; serious non-fiction (including cultural studies, science, history, international issues, multicultural/cross-cultural issues, memoir, social narrative, serious psychology, law & business); literary fiction; Asian American work; cookbooks.

Subjects/categories not interested in agenting: Science fiction, humor.

Approximate percentage of all submissions (from queries through manuscripts) that are rejected: 97%.

Representative titles sold:

The Notebook by Nicholas Sparks (Warner Books).

Torchlight by Robert Louis Stevenson III (Putnam).

Blood Lines: From Ethnic Pride to Ethnic Cleansing by Vamik Volkan, M.D. (Farrar, Straus, & Giroux).

The Simple Living Guide by Janet Luhrs (Broadway Books).

A Table: Inviting the Seasons into the Kitchen by Monique Hooker and Tracy Richardson (Henry Holt).

Why did you become an agent? I love books, I love to work with people, and I love to do deals! Also, with my background as a transactional lawyer, it seemed like the right area of publishing to get into. One of the best thing about being a lawyer was having clients—I enjoy getting to know people and working closely with them on their manuscripts and proposals; the personal rewards of watching a client's career blossom are the best part of my job.

What might you be if you weren't an agent? I don't know—I love being an agent so much that I can't imagine doing anything else right now.

The following information pertains to Elyse Cheney:

Born: December 23, 1967.

Education: University of Pennsylvania; BA in English literature.

Career history: Art curator; agent at Connie Clausen 1992–1995.

Hobbies/personal interests: Tennis, politics, crime, women's issues.

Subjects/categories most enthusiastic about agenting: Academics with trade cross-over potential, lifestyle, high-quality journalism, serious psychology, social issues, current events, history, personality-driven books. Thrillers, women's fiction, some literary fiction.

Subjects/categories not interested in agenting: Science fiction, right-wing, children's.

Best way for a prospective client to initiate contact: Query letter with SASE.

Reading-fee policy: No reading fee.

Client representation in the following categories: Nonfiction, 80%; Fiction, 20%.

Commission: 15%.

Number of titles sold during the past year: 10.

Approximate percentage of all submissions (from queries through manuscripts) that are rejected: 95%.

Representative titles sold:

Who's Insane? by Dr. Barbara Kirwin (Little, Brown).

Potted Gardens by Rebecca Cole (Clarkson Potter).

Webonomics: Nine Business Principles of the World Wide Web by Evan Schwartz

Description of the Client from Hell: Imperious and lazy.

The most common mistakes potential clients make when soliciting an agent to represent them: Handing in bad writing.

What writers can do to enhance their chances of getting an agent (besides being good writers): Be totally professional and submit great writing.

Why did you become an agent? I like reading, writing, editing, and selling. I like the entrepreneurial aspect of the profession.

The following information pertains to Daniel Mandel:

Education: BS, Cornell University.

Career history: Associate, Diane Cleaver, Inc.

Subjects/categories most enthusiastic about agenting: Fiction, art, politics, popular culture.

What might you be if you weren't an agent? I would, of course, be a writer.

THE CHARLOTTE GUSAY LITERARY AGENCY

10532 Blythe Avenue
Los Angeles, CA 90064
310-559-0831

Agent: Charlotte Gusay.

Education: BA, California State University, San Bernardino (literature and theater, and a degree in education). Also attended University of Oregon, University of Uppsala (Sweden), and UCLA.

Career history: Taught in secondary schools for several years. Interest in filmmaking developed. Founded (with partners) a documentary-film company in the early 1970s. Soon became interested in the fledgling audio-publishing business. Became the managing editor for the Center for Cassette Studies/Scanfax, producing audio programs, interviews, and documentaries.

In 1976 founded George Sand, Books in West Hollywood, one of the most prestigious and popular book shops in Los Angeles. It specialized in fiction and poetry, and sponsored readings and events. Patronized by the Hollywood community's glitterati and literati, George Sand, Books was the place to go when looking for the "best" literature and quality books. It was here that the marketing of books was preeminent. It closed in 1987. Two years later the Charlotte Gusay Literary Agency was opened.

Hobbies/personal interests: Gardens and gardening, magazines (a magazine junkie), good fiction reading, anything French, anything Greek.

Subjects/categories most enthusiastic about agenting: I enjoy both fiction and non-fiction. Prefer commercial, mainstream—but quality—material. Especially like books that can be marketed as film material. Also material that is innovative, unusual, eclectic, nonsexist. Will consider literary fiction with crossover potential. TCGLA is a signatory to the Writers' Guild, and so represents screenplays and screenwriters selectively. I enjoy unusual children's books and illustrators but have begun to limit children's projects.

Subjects/categories not interested in agenting: Does not consider science fiction or horror, poetry or short stories (with few exceptions), or the romance genres per se.

Best way for a prospective client to initiate contact: Send one-page query (with SASE). Then if we request your material (book, proposal, whatever it is), note the following guidelines: For Fiction: send approximately first 50 pages and a synopsis, along with your credentials (i.e., list of previous publications, and/or list of magazine articles, and/or any pertinent information, education and background). For Nonfiction: send a proposal consisting of an overview, chapter outline, author biography (including complete credentials), sample chapters, marketing and audience research, and survey of the competition. Two important notes: (1) Material will not be returned without SASE correct in size and postage. (2) In order to better serve our clients, we do not accept queries, new projects, proposals, or any materials between June 15 and September 15.

Reading-fee policy: No reading fee.

Client representation in the following categories: Nonfiction, 40%; Fiction, 15%; Children's, 10%; Books to film/screenplays, 35%.

Commission: 15% books; 10% screenplays.

Representative titles sold:

Walking in the Sacred Manner (Touchstone/Simon & Schuster).

A Garden Story (Faber & Faber).

Groucho Marx and Other Short Stories and Tall Tales (Faber and Faber).

Love, Groucho (Faber and Faber).

10 Pearls of Wisdom: For Achieving Your Goals and Capturing Your Dreams (Kensington Publishing).

A Young People's Survival Guide to Natural Disasters (Magination Press/Brunner-Mazel).

Entertainment rights:

The Fall Line (Kensington Publishing).

Carnival of Saints (Ballantine Books).

Dead Languages (Knopf; optioned by Sanford/Pillsbury).

Les Travailleurs de la Mer (Screenplay based on Victor Hugo novel).

Drop-off, Big Fish, Drowned Man's Key (St. Martin's, optioned by Warner Brothers).

The Roar of a Lion: The Life of Antonio Ligabue (Capra Press).

Description of the Client from Hell: The one who does not understand the hard work we do for our clients. Or the one who refuses to build a career in a cumulative manner, but rather goes from one agent to the next and so on. Or the one who circulates his/her manuscript without cooperating with his agent. Or the one who thinks it all happens by magic. Or the one who does not understand the nuts and bolts of the business.

Description of Dream Client: The one who cooperates. The one who appreciates how hard we work for our clients. The one who submits everything on time, in clean, edited, proofed, professional copies of manuscripts and professionally prepared proposals. The one who understands the crucial necessity of promoting his/her own books until the last one in the publisher's warehouse is gone. The one who works hard on his/her book-selling campaign in tandem with the agent. The author/agent relationship, like a marriage, is a cooperative affair and it is cumulative. The Dream Client will happily do absolutely whatever is necessary to reach the goal.

The most common mistakes potential clients make when soliciting an agent to represent them: (1) Although I contend with it, I am not fond of multiple submissions. In fact, I think it smacks a bit of an inhumane arrogance. Agent/author relationships, I often describe as a *marriage* in which the offspring is the book. Would you shop for a husband or a wife by multiple submission? (2) Writers who don't understand the role of an agent and are really not ready for an agent. Clients must understand the role of agents and that agents represent only the material they feel they can best handle. Potential clients must understand that any given agent may or may not be an editor, a sounding board, a proposal writer, or guidance counselor. Because of the enormous amount (some 20–50 per day, plus or minus) of submissions, queries, and proposals, the agent most often has only the time to say yes or no to your project. Above all, when clients don't understand why in the world I can't respond to a multiple submission with regard to their 900-page novel within a few days, all I can do is shake my head and wonder if that potential client realizes that I am human.

What writers can do to enhance their chances of getting an agent (besides being good writers): The first requisite is always that writers be courteous, respectful, and professional. Then they should be ready to describe their work or project in a few dynamite words and be knowledgeable about where and how their work fits into the trade market. Then I'm impressed and my enthusiasm begins to build.

Why did you become an agent? I became an agent because I know how to sell books and movies. Above all, I am knowledgeable and experienced, and I love agenting.

What might you be doing if you weren't an agent? I would write a book. I would travel to Istanbul and become a foreign agent. I would finish all of Proust. I would reread Jane Austen. I would work in my garden, play the piano, tap dance, sew dresses for my beautiful daughter, and much more.

If you could say anything you wanted, without censor, what would you say? (I love this question. It is so existential.) So here's my confession: It's about a curious mindset in the *literary milieu*. Clients think that agents should do their work for free. When, as it becomes necessary for various of life's services, authors pay their plumber, their mechanic, their baby-sitters, their gardeners, their dentists, *their lawyers*. Why do authors come to a professional agent and expect services to be gratis? I do not charge reading fees. (I am prohibited by the WGA signatory rules, in any case.) But do ponder for a moment, how many 900-page novels am I able to read in any given week and how shall I be paid for *my time?*

Answer: I yearn to be able to humbly ask the client for a simple, minimal processing fee for each query I answer. Were that possible, how much better I could serve my clients is untold. (As a matter of note, the Agent's Access Program, sponsored by the WGA, itself charges writers a minimal processing fee to screen material.) Voila! There you have it. What an odd and archaic business this is! *Something's wrong with this picture. And the queries stack up; the reading pile grows; the frustration level rises. I ask myself, why didn't I become a dermatologist?*

REECE HALSEY AGENCY

8733 Sunset Boulevard, Suite 101
Los Angeles, CA 90210
310-652-2409 (Halsey)
fax: 310-652-7595

Note: Contact Dorris Halsey by referral only. All new submissions and SASEs should be directed to Kimberly Cameron.

Reece Halsey North:
98 Main Street, Suite 704
Tiburon, CA 94920
415-789-9177 (Cameron)
fax: 415-789-9177

Agents: Dorris Halsey, Kimberley Cameron.

Education: Halsey: educated in France. Cameron: Marlborough School, Humboldt State University, Mount St. Mary's College.

Career history: Halsey: worked with her husband, Reece, who was head of the literary department at William Morris. They opened this office in 1957. Cameron: former publisher, Knightsbridge Publishing Company. Has been working with Dorris Halsey since 1993.

Hobbies/personal interests: Reading for the sheer pleasure of it.

Subjects/categories most enthusiastic about agenting: Literary fiction, writing that we feel is exceptional in its field.

Subjects/categories not interested in agenting: Children's fiction, poetry, cookbooks.

Best way for a prospective client to initiate contact: Ms. Halsey works with referrals only. Please send an SASE with all queries to Kimberley Cameron at Reece Halsey North.

Reading-fee policy: No reading fee.

Client representation in the following categories: It depends completely on the material we decide to represent. It changes often. The most accurate breakdown is: Nonfiction, 30%; Fiction, 70%.

Commission: 15% domestic; 20% foreign.

Number of titles sold during the past year: We don't feel this should be public information.

Approximate percentage of all submissions (from queries through manuscripts) that are rejected: 98%.

Representative titles sold: Dorris Halsey has the distinguished honor of representing the Aldous Huxley Estate. HarperCollins is publishing all his works, marking the centennial of his birth (1894–1963).

Dorris has sold many celebrity biographies, nonfiction works, and fiction to most major houses and smaller houses, including Knightsbridge.

The most common mistakes potential clients make when soliciting an agent to represent them: We are always impressed by politeness, in a well-written letter or otherwise. Their most costly mistake is using too many rhetorical adjectives to describe their own work.

What writers can do to enhance their chances of getting an agent (besides being good writers): Show patience, understanding, politeness, and trust.

Description of the Client from Hell: One who calls too often and asks "What's new?"

Description of Dream Client: A *patient* author who understands the publishing business and knows what it takes to get a book sold.

Why did you become an agent? We both love books and what they have to teach us. We both understand how important and powerful the written word is, and appreciate what it takes to be a good writer.

What might you be doing if you weren't an agent? Reading.

Comments: This business, especially today, is all uphill. We work extremely hard at what we're doing, and the love of books is what keeps us going. I don't think many agents do what they do every day for the money. We feel an exceptional amount of responsibility for our authors, and I just wish they could see and hear what we do for them. We have the highest regard for the process of writing, and do the best we can with the material in our hands.

What more can one do?

JEANNE K. HANSON LITERARY AGENCY

5111 Wooddale Avenue South
Edina, MN 55424
612-922-9471

Agent: Jeanne Hanson.

Born: August 12, 1944.

Education: B.A., Wellesley College (philosophy and English); M.A.T., Harvard University (English); M.A., University of Minnesota (journalism); Radcliffe publishing course (1984).

Career history: Teacher for two years; journalist for fifteen years; literary agent for ten years.

Hobbies/personal interests: Reading, aerobic exercise of all kinds, talking, negotiating things in all aspects of life.

Subjects/categories most enthusiastic about agenting: Any kind of nonfiction book that a journalist might write—all my clients are journalists. For example, the following subjects are of interest: humor, business, travel, journalistic books, food, science, nature, medical, psychology, self-help, illustrated books, pop reference, pop culture, and so on!

Subjects/categories not interested in agenting: Commercial fiction (glitzy type), memoirs of any kind, category fiction.

Best way for a prospective client to initiate contact: A letter (with SASE).

Reading-fee policy: No reading fee. 15% on projects placed with publishers.

Client representation in the following categories: Nonfiction, 97%; Fiction, 1%; Children's, 2%.

Commission: 15%.

Number of titles sold during the past year: 27.

Approximate percentage of all submissions (from queries through manuscripts) that are rejected: 98%.

Representative titles sold:

Three travel guides (Fielding).

Eating-disorders book (Simon & Schuster).

Humor book (Workman).

Nature book (Morrow).

Pop reference book (Warner).

Nature book (NorthWord).

Sports book (Simon & Schuster).

Psychology book (Houghton Mifflin).

Science book (St. Martin's Press).

The most common mistakes potential clients make when soliciting an agent to represent them: Sending a query to multiple agents. Also, faking it by saying, "I got your name from someone who admired your work" or some such.

Description of the Client from Hell: Someone who approaches me for the first time by addressing the letter "Dear Sir" or "To whom it may concern." Someone who is rude.

Description of Dream Client: A superb journalist who comes to me out of the blue or via an existing client. Someone with an idea so "on-target" in the culture that I just gasp!

Why did you become an agent? Because I love books, love one-on-one interactions with people about ideas, and love negotiating and organizing.

What might you be doing if you weren't an agent? I guess being a journalist again.

Comments: Let's get those damn publishers to do a better job selling the books once the authors work so hard writing them!

CHADWICK ALLEN HARP

119 Lincoln Terrace
Jeffersonville, PA 19403
610-631-9795
610-631-9793
E-mail: wickmode@aol.com

Agent: Chadwick Allen Harp.

Born: March 24, 1969, Norristown, PA.

Education: BA (history and philosophy), *cum laude,* The George Washington University, 1991; JD, The Dickinson School of Law, 1996.

Career history: My career history can be divided into the areas of writing, medicine, and law. Writing: My articles and essays have appeared in magazines and newspapers across the country, including *The Arizona Republic, The Cumberland County Sentinel, Cape Cod Life, The Minneapolis Star Tribune, The Montgomery Advertiser, Pennsylvania Heritage, The San Francisco Chronicle, The Tampa Tribune, The Tampa Times, The Washington Post,* and *The Washington Times.* Medicine: I spent five years serving in various administrative positions at the George Washington University Medical Center. Law: Since 1994 I have prepared tax returns and worked in the areas of estate planning and estate administration, tax law, and entertainment law.

Hobbies/personal interests: I enjoy writing, visiting with friends and family, traveling, and dining. I am a member of the Board of Directors of the Children's Aid Society of Montgomery County, PA. I am interested in child welfare and child abuse issues and issues surrounding children and their families. Volunteering my time and talents is an important part of my life.

Subjects/categories most enthusiastic about agenting: I will consider all ideas and projects regardless of the genre of subject matter. I want to represent writers who have solid, professional writing skills and who can tell a story. Please proofread an polish everything that you write.

Subjects/categories not interested in agenting: Again, I will consider all projects or ideas that are accompanied by solid, professional writing skills.

Best way for a prospective client to initiate contact: I prefer that prospective clients contact me by sending a query packet. The packer should include the following items. First, send me a 1-2 page cover letter describing your project, your ideas, and the status of the project. You may also wish to tell my why you believe that we will work well together and why you decided to send a query package to me. Second, include your resume, biography, or other document that will tell me about your background. Third, include the first 20 to 30 pages of the project and, if appropriate, the table of contents of a 1 to 2 page synopsis. Please do not fax this to me. Please do not call me. You may send this via e-mail. I will respond to your query within 4-6 weeks. Always enclose a return envelope with sufficient postage.

It is worth stating that I expect a professionally prepared query packet. If you send me garbage, I will recycle it. I will not waste the time of Mike, my mailman, to return garbage to you.

Reading-fee policy: I do not charge a reading feel. I feel that charging a reading fee is unprofessional and unethical. My recycling policy allows me to separate quickly those projects I will and will not consider.

Client representation in the following categories: Fiction, 30%; nonfiction, 30%; children's/young adult, 20%; and textbooks, 20%;

Commission: I charge a 10% commission on all contracts I negotiate for a client. This includes any and all contracts, including, for example, book contracts for domestic or foreign sales, contracts for television or theatrical motion picture productions, and contracts concerning merchandising. To prevent our relationship from appearing or becoming adversarial, I prefer that oral understandings (not written words) establish and govern our respective duties, responsibilities, and obligations.

Number of titles sold during the past year: The basis of my professional relationships is confidentiality. I neither confirm nor deny who I do and do not represent. I do not discuss any aspect of my professional relationships. Therefore, I will not disclose the titles that I have sold during the past year.

Approximate percentage of all submissions (from queries through manuscripts) that are rejected: All the writers I represent began our relationship with a professionally prepared query packet. I will initiate a professional relationship with a new client in precisely the same manner.

Representative titles sold:
Confidential.

Description of the Client from Hell: The client from hell forgets the limitations and the responsibilities of our respective roles. As an agent, my responsibility is to contact appropriate editors, to negotiate contracts and the terms thereof, to encourage the authors I represent, and to act as the advocate of my client. As a writer, your responsibility is to write with care and professionalism, to meet reasonable deadlines, and to listen to the advice of others. A client from hell breaches these duties or imposes others beyond our professional relationship. A client from hell acts unprofessionally. I will end my relationship with a client from hell.

Description of Dream Client: A dream client is a good writer who understands our respective duties and obligations. A dream client has a good sense of humor, is patient, works hard, listens to my counsel, and seeks to build our relationship based on trust and good faith. A dream client proofreads and polishes everything he or she writes.

The most common mistakes potential clients make when soliciting an agent to represent them: The most costly mistake a writer can make is a poor first impression. As my mother taught me, I have only one first impression. If a first impression is poor, it is very difficult to ameliorate by subsequent conduct. A poor impression is made when a writer sends my garbage, when a writer calls me without an invitation to do so, or when a writer sends me a 40 page FAX. Here are some helpful hints. Purchase good quality letterhead for your cover letters. Send a polished, professionally prepared cover letter and manuscript. Make sure all your printing is of laser quality. I will recycle all query packets—and not bother Mike the mailman—if they are prepared unprofessionally.

What writers can do to enhance their chances of getting an agent (besides being good writers): I am enthusiastic about fresh ideas presented by a writer who approaches the craft and our relationship in a professional manner. I am excited about discovering talent and helping an author during his or her career. Writers who are compassionate and sensitive, caring and kind, honest and thoughtful, passionate and brave are most likely to work well with me.

Why did you become an agent? I became an agent because I love discovering new talent. I love books—collecting them and reading them. As an agent, my responsibility is to find good projects and to help writers. My responsibility is to assume some of the administrative responsibilities involved with professional writing so that my client can concentrate on his or her craft.

What might you be if you weren't an agent? If I was not an agent, the time I spend doing so would be spent on other pursuits. I enjoy very much the time I spend as an agent. As an entrepreneurial, creative person, with empathy and compassion, I understand the thoughts and concerns of authors. I know that many concerns do not involve money or contracts. And yet I offer counsel in the administrative areas surrounding the wonderful world of writing. I feel a sense of accomplishment when I voluntarily assume some of the details of a writer's life so that he or she may focus time and energy upon writing.

Comments: Nothing. To do so would be unprofessional and uncouth.

JOHN HAWKINS & ASSOCIATES

71 West 23rd Street, Suite 1600
New York, NY 10010
212-807-7040

Agents: Moses Cardona, J. Warren Frazier, William Reiss, Elly Sidel.

Born: Cardona: October 8, 1966; Reiss: September 14, 1942.

Education: Cardona: B.S., marketing, New York University (1988); Frazier: Princeton; Reiss: B.A., Kenyon College; Sidel: B.A. Bennington College.

Career history: Cardona: bookkeeper/officer manager; foreign rights agent, literary agent (also handling agency's foreign rights and subsidiary rights). Reiss: Freelance researcher; editorial assistant to Lombard Jones (a graphic designer and editor); encyclopedia editor, Funk & Wagnalls Standard Reference Library; literary agent. Sidel: I have had a long, varied career in publishing, film, and television, as well as raising two children as a single mom and working as a certified chemical-dependency counselor at Hazelden in Minnesota. Also vice president of movies and mini-series, Warner Brothers; television director of special projects, CBS Entertainment, New York; vice president of production, 20th Century Fox Film Corporation; senior editor, Bantam Books; manager of subsidiary rights, Bantam Books; etc.

Hobbies/personal interests: Cardona: Tennis, rollerblading, jigsaw puzzles. Sidel: reading, going to the ballet, movies, theater, watching television, especially ice skating, *Cops* and *Seinfeld*, hanging out, playing with friends and family, walking, swimming, politics, travel.

Subjects/categories most enthusiastic about agenting: Cardona: science fiction, horror-supernatural, fantasy, mysteries. Frazier: Fiction: culture, mystery, literary. Nonfiction: biography, travel. Reiss: biographies, nonfiction historical narratives, archaeology, science fiction and fantasy, mysteries and suspense, true-crime narrative, natural history, children's fiction, adult fiction. Sidel: literary and commercial fiction, narrative nonfiction, psychology (pop and otherwise), popular culture, women's issues, journalism.

Subjects/categories not interested in agenting: Cardona: children's, military, poetry. Frazier: romance. Reiss: romance novels, poetry, plays. Sidel: cookbooks, children's, science fiction.

Best way for a prospective client to initiate contact: Cardona: Query letter with a few sample chapters. Frazier: Letter with personality, half-page synopsis of book with first 3–4 chapters. Reiss: telephone, or send a letter describing project with a few sample pages to provide a sense of writing style. Sidel: The very best way of contact is through a referral or a query letter (with SASE).

Reading-fee policy: No reading fee.

Client representation in the following categories: Frazier: Nonfiction, 50%; Fiction, 50%.

Commission: 15%

Approximate percentage of all submissions (from queries through manuscripts) that are rejected: Frazier: 95%.

Representative titles sold:

William Reiss:

Edith Wharton: An Extraordinary Life by Eleanor Dwight (Abrams).

Wicked by Gregory Maguire (Regan Books/HarperCollins).

Walking Towards Walden by John Hanson Mitchell (Addison-Wesley).

Tiger, Tiger Burning Bright by Ron Koertge (Orchard Books).

The Lost Diaries of Frans Hals by Michael Kernan (St. Martin's).

The most common mistakes potential clients make when soliciting an agent to represent them: Sidel: Someone who is too pushy and aggressive and won't take no for an answer.

What writers can do to enhance their chances of getting an agent (besides being good writers): Frazier: Somebody whose letter shows both intelligence and a sense of humor.

Description of the Client from Hell: Sidel: Pushy, demanding, inflexible, argumentative, dumb person with unrealistic expectations.

Description of Dream Client: Sidel: A talented, flexible, creative professional writer who understands that this is a process. Someone with a sense of humor and a Pulitzer Prize.

Why did you become an agent? Cardona: I fell into the profession. A friend who was a client helped me find this position starting at the agency, and I grew through the years to appreciate this industry. I realized there were few Latino professionals and wanted to give a voice and presence to the world of publishing. Sidel: Good way to integrate all of my professional and personal experience; use my contacts; work with ideas and smart, creative people; as well as earn a living.

What might you be doing if you weren't an agent? Sidel: Traveling around the world.

HEACOCK LITERARY AGENCY, INC.

1523 Sixth Street, Suite 14
Santa Monica, CA 90401-2514
310-451-8523
310-393-6227
e-Mail: GraceBooks@aol.com

Agents: Rosalie Heacock, Robin Lea Henning.

Born: Heacock: Girard, Kansas; Henning: Manhasset, New York.

Education: Heacock: B.A., fine arts/English; M.A., humanities, California State University. Henning: B.A., Afro-American Studies, University of California at Los Angeles.

Career history: Heacock: editor, Green Hut Press; executive editor, Kids & Company; sole founder of the Shelley Muir Agency in 1973, which became the Heacock Literary Agency in 1978, the latter cofounded with James B. Heacock (b. 1924; d. 1994). Member, Association of Authors' Representatives, Women's National Book Association, Author's Guild, American Booksellers' Association.

Hobbies/personal interests: Heacock: reading; all aspects of art, *en plein air* (on site) landscape painting, choral singing, hiking in the Santa Monica mountains, dogs, birds, gardening, sailing, traveling. Founding member, 1987, the Plein Air Artists of the Santa Monica Mountains and Seashore. Henning: Music, children, facing racism, church service, reading.

Subjects/categories most enthusiastic about agenting: Well-written books on timely subjects, particularly books which make a contribution.

Subjects/categories not interested in agenting: Science fiction, true crime, horror, books that would better be magazine articles (including bad-news books and other *downers*).

Best way for a prospective client to initiate contact: We prefer letters to telephone calls or faxes. Send us a one-page query letter (with SASE). Include writing experience, why you have written the book, and brief biographical data.

Reading-fee policy: No reading fee.

Client representation in the following categories: Nonfiction, 95%; Fiction, 2.5%; Children's, 2.5%.

Commission: 15%.

Number of titles sold during the past year: 17.

Approximate percentage of all submissions (from queries through manuscripts) that are rejected: 90%.

Representative titles sold:

Bright and Early Thursday Evening by Don and Audrey Wood (Harcourt Brace).

Waking the World by Allan Chinen, M.D. (Jeremy Tarcher/Putnam).

Racing Against Time by Antony C. Anjoubault (Barclay House).

The Gift of Touch by Helen Colton (Kensington Trade Paperback).

Panic Free by Lynne Freeman, Ph.D. (Barclay House).

The Flying Dragon Room by Audrey Wood (Scholastic/Blue Sky Press).

Making It! Wealth-Building Secrets from Two Great Entrepreneurial Minds by E. Joseph and William A. Cohen (Prentice Hall).

Red Racer by Audrey Wood (Simon & Schuster).

The most common mistakes potential clients make when soliciting an agent to represent them: Authors who address letters "to whom it may concern," demand an immediate reply, make multiple queries without revealing the fact, call the day after the material has reached the agency, send SASE later, and those who send inserts to be added to the original submission.

What writers can do to enhance their chances of getting an agent (besides being good writers): I am enthusiastic about writers who present original ideas which are well expressed, and those who have credentials in the subjects they have chosen for their books. We read everything we represent, and the clients under contract have first priority for our time. Queries must wait, but all will be read and responded to, in the order in which they have been received. When reading a well-written, one-page query letter on a timely subject, we will not hesitate to invite more.

Description of the Client from Hell: Someone too self-involved to understand the value of courtesy and patience. In this business, both are treasured virtues. Others we avoid: the writer who does not enclose SASE and then calls to see why we have not given an immediate response; one who is rude and demanding and feels the world owes him or her an instant forum.

Description of Dream Client: The dream client who values what we do and occasionally says so; understands the difficulties of placing work in today's marketplace; and is courteous, patient, and has a good sense of humor. (Why cry when you can laugh?)

Why did you become an agent? Heacock: Once an agent remarked to me, when I said I was considering a career as a literary agent, "Why? You don't *look* like a masochist." What's more, I'm not! I became an agent because the value of good books cannot be overestimated. Good books need an advocate, and I love being one.

What might you be doing if you weren't an agent? Heacock: Traveling the world, with my paint box at the ready.

Comments: The world is undergoing great and exciting change. While some may find the present transformations disturbing (with the media's emphasis on its negativity), much is for the good. Writers have the opportunity to help us move into that good through the power and influence of their words and ideas. It is an important responsibility and also a joy. While it may take time to gain your forum, you should not give in to discouragement. Read all you can, learn to see your mistakes and correct them, polish your work until it has a jewel's radiance—and remember to occasionally laugh at yourself and at the world.

Here's my answer to the question "Why should a client choose your agency?": You should choose my agency because you deserve an agent who has integrity, who appreciates good authors, and who will invest time to get your works into print. We give our best efforts to our authors.

RICHARD HENSHAW GROUP

264 West 73rd Street
New York, NY 10023
212-721-4721

Agent: Rich Henshaw.

Born: September 18, 1964; New York, New York.

Education: B.A., Franklin & Marshall College.

Career history: Independent since 1995; 1987–1995, agent and director of foreign rights, Richard Curtis Associates; 1992–1995, partner in the Content Company, an agency specializing in new media.

Hobbies/personal interests: My family, books, cooking, wine, travel, skiing.

Subjects/categories most enthusiastic about agenting: Mainstream and genre fiction, including mysteries and thrillers, science fiction, fantasy, horror, historical, literary, and young adult. Nonfiction areas of interest are business, celebrity biography, computer, current events, health, history, how-to, movies, popular culture, popular reference, popular science, psychology, self-help, and sports. I am also interested in working with books that lend themselves to adaptation to CD-ROM and other new media formats.

Subjects/categories not interested in agenting: Fiction: category romance, Westerns, poetry, short stories. Nonfiction: coffee-table books, cookbooks, scholarly books.

Best way for a prospective client to initiate contact: Query letter and first 50 pages (with SASE) for fiction. Query letter (with SASE) for nonfiction. I also accept queries by e-mail, not to exceed one page. My Internet address is RHGAGENTS@ aol.com.

Reading-fee policy: No reading fee.

Client representation in the following categories: Nonfiction, 20%; Fiction, 80%.

Commission: 15% domestic 20% foreign.

Number of titles sold during the past year: 15.

Approximate percentage of all submissions (from queries through manuscripts) that are rejected: 95%.

Representative titles sold:

Trick Me Twice by Stephen Solomita (Bantam)

Witchy Woman by Steve Brewer (St. Martin's).

You're Dead, David Borelli by Susan Brown (Atheneum).

Drop Shot by Harlan Coben (Dell).

The Eternal Guardians (series) by Ronald Anthony Cross (TOR).

Blood Will Tell by Dana Stabenow (Putnam).

John Stanley's Creature Features Movie Guide by John Stanley (Berkley/ Boulevard).

The most common mistakes potential clients make when soliciting an agent to represent them: No SASE. Unpolished manuscripts. Bound manuscripts. Slick queries that say little about the characters, plot, subject, or style of the work.

Description of the Client from Hell: Blames agent for all pitfalls in the publishing process. Never expresses gratitude or appreciation for a job well done.

Description of Dream Client: Informed, courteous, loyal, professional.

Why did you become an agent? Since I wrote my first (terrible) short story in college and attempted to market it, I've been fascinated by the creative process involved in writing and the manner in which books and other intellectual property are commercially exploited. I've always been an agent and I can't imagine doing anything else.

What might you be doing if you weren't an agent? I might start my own publishing company.

THE JEFF HERMAN AGENCY, INC.

140 Charles Street, Suite 15A
New York, NY 10014
212-941-0540

Agent: Jeff Herman.

Born: December 17, 1958.

Education: Bachelor of Science, Syracuse University.

Career history: Full-time literary agent since 1988. Before that ran my own public relations agency. During postadolescence: cleaned toilets in public parks, agricultural work, restaurant work, etc.

Hobbies/personal interests: Not showing up for work; reading stuff that's unrelated to work. Staring into space without a clear purpose and without a deadline.

Subjects/categories most enthusiastic about agenting: I am genuinely open to being pitched on most concepts and ideas. In the end, I need to have a positive feeling about selling it.

Subjects/categories not interested in agenting: See preceding answer.

Best way for a prospective client to initiate contact: Letters (with SASE), naturally, are most convenient for me. But any methods that succeed are, in the final analysis, "best."

Reading-fee policy: No reading fee. If I think you're rich and stupid, I may be tempted. To date, I have not sold out.

Client representation in the following categories: Nonfiction, 85+%; Fiction, <5%; Textbooks, <5%; Children's, <5%. (For most fiction and special nonfiction projects, see listing for Jamie Forbes directly below.).

Commission: 15% on domestic sales; 10% on foreign sales when subagent is used.

Number of titles sold during the past year: 50+.

Approximate percentage of all submissions (from queries through manuscripts) that are rejected: Most.

Representative titles sold:

Successful Intelligence by Robert Sternberg (Simon & Schuster).

The Aladdin Factor by Jack Canfield and Mark Victor Hansen. (Berkley).

The Everyday Enneagram by Tom Condon (Harper San Francisco).

Joe Montana on the Art and Magic of Playing Quarterback by Joe Montana (Henry Holt).

Wealth in a Decade by Brett Machtig (Irwin).

Walk Like a Giant, Sell Like a Madman by Ralph Roberts (HarperBusiness).

Description of the Client from Hell: Lots of sizzle, no nourishment. Lots of consumption, no growth. Lots of expectation, no satisfaction.

Description of Dream Client: Someone I can learn from.

The most common mistakes potential clients make when soliciting an agent to represent them: Arrogant. Demanding. Negative.

What makes you enthusiastic about the way some writers solicit you? Gracious. Appreciative. Sincere. Positive.

Why did you become an agent? It's what I happened to be doing when I turned 30. Seriously, it's mentally arousing, and rewards creativity and independence.

What might you be doing if you weren't an agent? Anything but an editor.

Jamie M. Forbes represents selected projects for the Jeff Herman Agency, Inc.

Born: Chevy Chase, Maryland.

Education: B.A. from Washington University (St. Louis); master's degree in psychology from the Graduate Faculty of Political and Social Science at the New School for Social Research (New York).

Career history: Musician, metals broker, performance artist, sensory-evaluation consultant for the food industry. Worked for publishers and book packagers (both in-house corporate as well as freelance and consultant) in editorial capacities, project development, and publicity and promotion. Wrote dozens of hardcore flesh novels (under various pseudonyms—and anonymously). Reviewed manuscripts for literary agencies. Book doctor; ghostwriter.

Hobbies/personal interests: Sports that use blades, legs, projectiles, brains; food with delirious seasonings; books!

Subjects/categories most enthusiastic about agenting: Investigative stories and critical works of serious, penetrating, and high-edge societal and cultural significance; incisive biographical interpretations of established celebrities or cult icons; astonishing new directions in health, nutrition, popular psychology, and creative spirituality; on-field accounts from the political, financial/business, and military arenas. Imaginative works that flout conventional distinctions among fiction and nonfiction categories and are marketable *because* they are so remarkably well done.

Commercial fiction. Particularly suspense fiction, which includes thrillers and mysteries. Trailblazing works from new voices with astounding points of view. Literary works: In order to sell commercially, literary writing must embody, if not predict, rising cultural tides and show strong concept development (not necessarily action-heavy plotting).

Subjects/categories not interested in agenting: Whatever causes gag reflex from market overexposure.

Best way for a prospective client to initiate contact: Query letter that sells the concept and demonstrates that the author knows how to excite editorial response (with SASE).

Reading-fee policy: No reading fee.

Client representation in the following categories: Fiction: 30%; nonfiction: 30%; the rest divvied up among creative and investigatory works that neither are strictly traditional fictional forms nor do they necessarily slot nicely into predefined categories of nonfiction.

Commission: 15% domestic; 10% on foreign sales (when going through the offices of a subagent).

Approximate percentage of all submissions (from queries through manuscripts) that are rejected: 99+%.

Description of the Client from Hell: Generally, this translates to someone who would attempt to impose self-absorbed, whimsical notions of what publishing *should* be onto an entire industry that could hardly care less about them.

Description of Dream Client: Superb word stylist and exceptional market researcher who can make a reader's head dance—and induce publishers to cough up bounteous advances.

The most common mistakes potential clients make when soliciting an agent to represent them: Writers often (and perhaps unwittingly) undermine their own presentations in a number of ways. Among the most common: Flagrant knock-off of an overpublished motif or cookie-cutter version of an established writer's signature approach—brandishing other writers' hard-won gold as if it's their lode to mine. Or the contrary approach of saying certain renowned writers suck—therefore their own work will blow everyone away instantly (and there's no back-up by way of offering an outstanding original project). Rambling, virtually pointless queries.

What writers can do to enhance their chances of getting an agent (besides being good writers): Bring bankable book-publishing credits to the project. Acquire celebrity status in a field with marketable tie-ins to book publishing.

Failing the above high-profile classifications, show you have the potential to sell extremely well—so that publishers are convinced they must take a chance on you as a new author. Attractively packaged and well-organized presentations pinpoint your publicity, promotional, and marketing flair. Elements such as press clippings, interviews, reviews of previous work, lists of your previous publications, performances, workshops, seminars—all these details can suggest to an agent or editor that other media professionals share enthusiasm for the author's product, which underscores author's aplomb in the public eye and, hence, the impression of viability as a publishing persona.

Why did you become an agent? I want to rule Hell.

What might you be doing if you weren't an agent? Divine.

Comments: I'm looking for something that jazzes the reader's juices. Maybe even something scary, maybe something with which people can disagree vehemently—for in the deflated space of electronic global economy, creative works that play to terror, suspicion, and controversy are rewarded with precious return in media/entertainment venues. Tips: Invent the next sizzling true-life issue and portray it in a compelling, humanized manner. Fiction: Tell great tales and know what sells.

Want a taste of what it's like on the corporate side? Buy stock in paper-manufacturing companies. Invest in publicly traded international communications entities and/or publishing firms. Sit back, track your money for a few months. In your leisure time, contact freelance editors, book designers, typesetters, printers, and distributors—get a rough idea of the resources required to get your work to the marketplace (especially dig those paper prices). Then ask yourself: Would I publish my book?

HULL HOUSE LITERARY AGENCY

240 East 82nd Street
New York, NY 10028
212-988-0725
fax: 212-794-8758

Agent: David Stewart Hull.

Born: March 21, 1938; Oshkosh, Wisconsin.

Education: B.A., Dartmouth College, 1960; University of London, School of African and Oriental Studies, 1960–1962.

Career history: 1966–1968, East Coast story editor, MCA–Universal Pictures; 1968–1970, editor, Coward, McCann Publishers; 1970–1981, partner, vice president, James Brown Associates, Inc.; literary agency sold to Curtis Brown (U.K.) in 1978; 1981–1987, agent, Peter Lampack Agency, Inc.; 1987 to present, president, Hull House Literary Agency.

Hobbies/personal interests: Collecting and researching American nineteenth-century painting. I have been a guest curator at the New York Historical Society.

Subjects/categories most enthusiastic about agenting: Fiction: crime novels, commercial fiction—but will consider literary fiction. Nonfiction: biography, true crime, history (particularly military), books on arts.

Subjects/categories not interested in agenting: Juveniles, young adult, short stories, science fiction, Westerns, poetry, New Age, historical novels except those set in the U.S., screenplays/teleplays, humor.

Best way for a prospective client to initiate contact: Write a one-page letter outlining the project, also listing prior book-length publications, if any. All queries *must* be accompanied by an SASE.

Reading-fee policy: No reading fee.

Client representation in the following categories: Nonfiction, 40%; Fiction, 60%.

Commission: 15% domestic; 20% foreign (split with foreign agent).

Number of titles sold during the past year: We do not give out this information.

Approximate percentage of all submissions (from queries through manuscripts) that are rejected: Just for the hell of it, we kept a record of the number of query letters received during 1995. The total was 3,104! And during the first two months of 1996, the number of queries increased by approximately 30% over last year's monthly figures.

From that appalling 1995 total, we asked to see about 15 manuscripts, and took on 5 for representation here. A couple of authors didn't reply to our request to see their manuscripts, which is bad manners. While it is understandable that multiple-agent queries might generate several requests from agents to see a manuscript, it is common courtesy to let an agent know that it is being reviewed or represented elsewhere.

Representative titles sold: We do not give out this information.

The most common mistakes potential clients make when soliciting an agent to represent them: Writing a letter with bad grammar! I am astonished at the misuse of apostrophes and inability to distinguish between *lie* and *lay*. (The last misuse of this was observed in a letter from a writer with a degree in English, which makes one wonder.) And I don't take too kindly to being addressed by my first name by writers unknown to me. While the fax machine is one of man's greatest inventions, sending a lengthy query letter by this method is certain to get my attention in a way you don't want it.

What writers can do to enhance their chances of getting an agent (besides being good writers): Produce good writing on interesting subject matter.

Description of the Client from Hell: Over the last 25 years in this business, I have had remarkably little difficulty with my clients, but there have been a few exceptions. Not too long ago, an author disagreed with my recommendations on placing of a second novel and effectively sabotaged a most promising career. Disregarding the advice of an experienced agent is not a wise thing to do.

Description of Dream Client: A writer who understands the publishing process.

Why did you become an agent? My first two jobs in New York City involved dealing with agents, and it seemed to me that what they were doing was more interesting than my own work. So after considerable investigation, I became a partner in an existing agency, and eventually formed my own firm.

What might you be doing if you weren't an agent? I think I might have become a dealer in American painting.

Comments: This agency is always willing to consider the work of unpublished writers. While the majority of our clients have previously published book-length works, a number of them started with us without a publication history. We firmly believe in the encouragement of quality writing, and there is obviously a lot of it out there.

We are very active in the foreign-language sales of books by our clients. In one case, a book has been sold in 13 foreign languages including Bulgarian (a first for us). We also work closely with motion picture agents on the West Coast, and during the past year three books by our clients have been optioned for major sums.

We are painfully aware of the lack of traditional editorial functions at some publishing houses. We are always willing to give comments of a limited nature to clients on their manuscripts. If, in our opinion, a promising manuscript needs more editorial work than we can carry out on the agency level, we recommend a number of freelance editorial services which we know have benefited our other clients.

SHARON JARVIS & COMPANY
TOAD HALL, INC.

Rural Route 2, Box 16B
Laceyville, PA 18623
717-869-2942

Agent: Sharon Jarvis.
  Born: October 1, 1943; Brooklyn, New York.
  Education: B.F.A., Hunter College, 1964.
  Career history: Book editor for Ace, Popular Library, Doubleday, Ballantine, and Playboy for 13 years; an agent for 13 years; co-authored two novels, edited six non-fiction books.
  Hobbies/personal interests: Anything strange and unusual.
  Subjects/categories most enthusiastic about agenting: Genre fiction, popular nonfiction.
  Subjects/categories not interested in agenting: No plays, scripts, articles, short stories.
  Best way for a prospective client to initiate contact: Query letter only, with SASE.
  Reading-fee policy: No fee if we request material.
  Client representation in the following categories: Nonfiction, 20%; Fiction, 80%.
  Number of titles sold during the past year: 15.
  Approximate percentage of all submissions (from queries through manuscripts) that are rejected: 99%.
  Representative titles sold:
  Eyes of the Empress by Camille Bacon-Smith (DAW).
  Hawk Woman by Tela Starhawk Lake (M. Evans & Company).
  The most common mistakes potential clients make when soliciting an agent to represent them: Unpublished writers who assure me they've written a major best-seller and who imply I'm a fool if I don't agree with them. And I don't care if it's written on an IBM-compatible computer in WordPerfect. *Nobody* cares. Also people who write "I've decided to let you be my agent."
  What writers can do to enhance their chances of getting an agent (besides being good writers): Produce a well written completed manuscript that fits a category or a niche.
  Description of the Client from Hell: Someone who calls every week and wants to know why I haven't convinced an editor to buy his book. (As though I have the power to do that.)
  Description of Dream Client: Someone I hear from once every four months and who understands the marketplace (meaning I can sell their work).
  Why did you become an agent? God knows.
  What might you be doing if you weren't an agent? A plumber, like my uncles.
  Comments: I get 25 queries a week from people who can't write and have no concept of how to write a marketable book. Nobody does their homework. They all think they can just sit down and write brilliantly. Even the ones with a rudimentary grasp of English. Even the ones for whom English is a second language.

Nobody knows how to describe their book properly. They confuse a synopsis with sell copy. I can understand not knowing how to describe a book in two or three paragraphs because that takes years of practice. But they can't even tell me what category their book is in. They forget to give me word lengths, so I can't judge if their book is category or mainstream (not that they know the difference).

I don't know who's giving these people advice, but I can tell when I get some kind of form letter (especially the ones that tell me what computer program the book is written in). I hate form letters that obviously went out to lots of agents at the same time (the ones that aren't personalized or where my name has been typed in).

The ones I really want to set fire to are the ones whose friends and relatives really loved their book; the ones who assure me their book is the best thing since sliced bread; the ones who want me to convince them I should be their agent; the ones who want me to send them money for a copy of their manuscript; the ones who get my name wrong or who call me Sharon when I've never met them; the published authors whose last book was published in 1978; nonfiction writers first trying their hand at fiction (why ruin a perfectly good career?).

JCA LITERARY AGENCY

27 West 20th Street
New York, NY 10011
212-807-0888

Agent: Jeff Gerecke.

Career history: publicity, sub rights at University of California Press (1980–1983); foreign scout at Lynn Franklin Associates (1983–1987); literary agent (1987 to present).

Hobbies/personal interests: Computers, sports.

Subjects/categories most enthusiastic about agenting: Crime fiction and thrillers; literary fiction; general nonfiction: business, history, politics; pop culture.

Best way for a prospective client to initiate contact: Query letter (with SASE). Sample chapters acceptable.

Reading-fee policy: No reading fee.

Client representation in the following categories: Nonfiction, 25%; Fiction, 75%.

Commission: 15%.

Approximate percentage of all submissions (from queries through manuscripts) that are rejected: 90%.

Representative titles sold:
A Lesson Before Dying by Ernest J. Gaines (Knopf).
Betrayal by Gwen Hunter (Pocket).
The Gourmet Detective by Peter King (St. Martin's).
Interior Designs by Marge Burman (Dutton Signet).

The most common mistakes potential clients make when soliciting an agent to represent them: Don't compare your book to anything written more than 10 years ago. Don't *hype* your agent; tell the truth about past submission experiences.

What writers can do to enhance their chances of getting an agent (besides being good writers): Professional and informative letters.

Description of the Client from Hell: Anyone who describes their books as a sure-fire best-seller. Anyone who tells me their friends love their book, so it must be good. Anyone who tells me it has great possibilities as a CD-ROM.

Description of Dream Client: A writer who reads the kinds of books he/she is writing and knows the market. A writer who understands the value of an editorial critique and can work with someone else to polish his/her book.

Why did you become an agent? I enjoy working with writers on their books.

J. KELLOCK AND ASSOCIATES LTD.

11017 80th Avenue
Edmonton, AB T6G 0R2 Canada
403-433-0274

Agent: Joanne Kellock.

Education: B.A. with honors in English, University of Alberta; M.A. (incomplete), University of Alberta; graduate studies, Harvard/Radcliffe.

Career history: Sales representative, while still at university, for Penguin, Pan, Fontana, Van Nostrand Reinhold, Macmillan Canada (university text market); Bantam publicist: author promotion. Marketing manager: Government of Canada, National Museums of Canada, Ottawa, Ontario. Literary Agent full time since 1987.

Hobbies/personal interests: Classical music, collect paintings and sculpture, cooking for guests.

Subjects/categories most enthusiastic about agenting: Literary fiction, all categories of works for children, creative nonfiction, extraordinarily well-written commercial genre.

Subjects/categories not interested in agenting: Poetry, essays, short stories (unless from a previously published writer), esoteric, New Age, texts.

Best way for a prospective client to initiate contact: Query letter—no initial telephone calls please.

Reading-fee policy: Yes, a fee is charged for previously unpublished writers, or published writers of, say, nonfiction, who have now written a novel or a work for children.

Fee Schedule: $140 U.S., for three chapters plus a brief synopsis. If style works with subject or subject is something selling today, balance read free of charge. $100 U.S. for picture books for children.

Client representation in the following categories: Nonfiction, 30%; Fiction, 30%; Children's/young adult, 40%.

Commission: 15% North America; 20% foreign and U.K. unless subject is one I handle myself in U.K. (i.e., works for children, fiction, and some nonfiction).

Number of titles sold during the past year: 15.

Approximate percentage of all submissions (from queries through manuscripts) that are rejected: 90%.

Representative titles sold:
Campfire Tales by Andy Russell (McClelland & Stewart, Canada). Nonfiction.
Adventures in Pirate Cove by Martyn Godfrey (Avon Books, New York). Three-book series.
Emma's Eggs by Barbara Spurll (Stoddart Publishing, Canada). Illustrations only.
Bird Song and *Shadow Dance* by Tololwa M. Mollel (Clarion Books, New York) Picture Books.
Mom, the School Flooded by Ken Rivard (Annick Press, Canada). Picture book.
Kitiko's Journey by Tololwa Mollel (Stoddart Publishing, Canada). Picture book.
Do You Want Fries with That? by Martyn Godfrey (Scholastic, Canada).
Why Just Me? Mass-market rights (Scholastic, Canada).

The most common mistakes potential clients make when soliciting an agent to represent them: Initial telephone query calls; cover letter carelessly written and mistake ridden; manuscript carelessly written, filled with typos, spelling errors, grammar errors, and that old saw, errors in logic.

What writers can do to enhance their chances of getting an agent (besides being good writers): They are not guilty of any of the most common mistakes (see above question).

Description of the Client from Hell: Those who do not read the complete listing in Jeff Herman's *Writer's Guide to Book Editors, Publishers, and Literary Agents.*

Description of Dream Client: The client that presents me with a *knock your socks off* novel or creative work of nonfiction. The client who behaves professionally and does not barrage me with letters, faxes, telephone calls soon after a submission. The client who always encloses SASE, plus necessary postage for responses to queries, or toing and froing with material, or return of material, and knows (having read the complete listing), that first, I do require a fee from all previously unpublished writers—magazine, newspaper, periodical publications are not a book—and also know that I cannot mail to the U.S. with U.S. postage.

Why did you become an agent? Evolution—it seems to me that anyone who starts out anywhere in the publishing industry stays. Most of us seem to move around within the industry. I have a sincere love of literature.

What might you be doing if you weren't an agent? Running an art gallery; doing an honors degree in seventeenth-century history, but I would rather be reading Jane Austen.

Comments: "Rather, I would ask, why is it everyone today thinks they can write a book? So, you want to write a novel, are you prepared to spend the next ten years of your life learning how?" (Quote from W. O. Mitchell, well-known Canadian novelist, from a workshop on the novel I attended.)

THE JETT LITERARY AGENCY

7123 East Jan Avenue
Mesa, Arizona 85208
602-985-9400 phone and fax

Agent: Dawn M. Snyder.

 Born: July 22, 1964; Baltimore, MD.

 Education: University of Maryland.

 Career history: Freelance writer for eight years; Editor for several publishing houses and agents.

 Hobbies/personal interests: Traveling, writing, my husband and my children.

 Subjects/categories most enthusiastic about agenting: Adult fiction and nonfiction, scripts, children's fiction with a message.

 Subjects/categories not interested in agenting: Technical (electrical, mechanical manuals, etc.).

 Best way for a prospective client to initiate contact: 1) Query letter with SASE; 2) Send manuscript with SASE and reading fee.

 Reading-fee policy: Reading fee: $50 for children's and scripts, $75 for all others; charges one time $200 marketing fee.

 Client representation in the following categories: Fiction, 25%; nonfiction, 50%; children's/young adult, 10%; and scripts, 15%.

 Commission: 15% on domestic sales; 20% on foreign sales.

 Description of the Client from Hell: Someone sho constantly calls, is unrealistic in his expectations, and *knows* he has the next bestseller.

 Description of Dream Client: Professional, patient, understanding—all of which you must be in this business.

 The most common mistakes potential clients make when soliciting an agent to represent them: A writer who calls to pitch their manuscript over the phone. A big mistake one writer made was calling the agency to tell us he was sending a manuscript he wrote, and he knew we would represent him because he was friends with another client. Big mistake!

 What writers can do to enhance their chances of getting an agent (besides being good writers): Professionalism—follows agency requirements.

 Why did you become an agent? It was suggested to me by publishing houses and agents I edited for. I always admired the work of agents.

 What might you be if you weren't an agent? Still writing for the corporate world.

NATASHA KERN LITERARY AGENCY, INC.

P.O. Box 2908
Portland, OR 97208-2908
503-297-6190

Agent: Natasha Kern.

 Born: Lindsey, California.

Education: University of North Carolina, Chapel Hill; Columbia University, New York; graduate work, New York University.

Career history: editor for Simon & Schuster, Bantam, and Ballantine; publicist for Bob Woodward, Arnold Schwarzenegger, etc.; acquisitions editor for New York agents prior to forming own agency ten years ago.

Hobbies/personal interests: Activities involving my children and our Shiba Inu; gardening; swimming; cooking; and, of course, reading.

Subjects/categories most enthusiastic about agenting: Fiction: commercial and literary; mainstream women's; romances, historicals, thrillers and mysteries. Nonfiction: health, science, feminism, parenting, psychology, self-help, gardening, current issues, gay topics, celebrity biographies, business, controversial, reference.

Subjects/categories not interested in agenting: Fiction: horror and science fiction, children's or young adult. Nonfiction: sports or scholarly.

Best way for a prospective client to initiate contact: Send a detailed, one-page query with an SASE. Include the submission history (publishers/agents), your writing credits, and information on how complete the project is.

Reading-fee policy: $45.

Client representation in the following categories: Nonfiction, 45%; Fiction, 55%.

Commission: 15% domestic; 20% foreign and film.

Number of titles sold during the past year: 42.

Approximate percentage of all submissions (from queries through manuscripts) that are rejected: 99% unsolicited; 85% solicited partials, proposals, and manuscripts. From 3,000 queries every year, approximately 10 writers are accepted for representation. Write a good query!

Representative titles sold:

Herbal Prescriptions for Better Health by Don Brown (Prima).

Misbegotten by Tamara Leigh (HarperCollins).

Fertile Ground by Charles Wilson (St. Martin's).

Sons Without Fathers by Kennedy and Terdal (Carol Publishing).

Hollywood Be Thy Name by Cass Warner Sperling and Cork Millner (Prima).

Breast Cancer: What Your Doctor May Not Tell You by Steve Austin (Prima).

Phoenix Sub Zero and *Barracuda, Final Bearing* by Mike DiMercurio (Donald I. Fine/NAL).

Plainswomen by Irene Brown (Ballantine).

Live Ten Years Longer; Look Ten Years Younger by David Ryback (Simon & Schuster).

Bette Midler by George Mair (Carol Publishing).

The Power of Anger Management by Gary Hankins (Warner).

Between Love and Hate by Lois Gold (NAL).

My Kind of Place by Eric and Margaret Burnette (Chronicle).

Enchant the Dream by Kathleen Morgan (Kensington).

No Pictures in My Grave by Susan Lloyd (Mercury).

Conor's Way by Laurie Guhrke (HarperCollins).

Kiss Me, Katie by Robin Hatcher (HarperCollins).

The Learned Lady by Joan Overfield (Avon).

Mortal Sins by Greg Iles (Dutton/Signet).
Watermelon Summer by Anne Avery (Penguin USA).
River of Our Return by Gladys Smith (HarperCollins).
Lesbian Gulls and Gay Giraffes by Bruce Bagemihl (HarperCollins).
Aphrodite's Daughters by Jalaja Bonheim (Simon & Schuster).
Ryan's by Barbara Freethy (Avon).

The most common mistakes potential clients make when soliciting an agent to represent them: It does not appeal to me when writers tell me their mom, friends, or children love their book and their writing is better and will make more money than that of the current number-one best-selling author. Writers need to study how to write a great query letter; many elements are often missing, such as: length of manuscript, genre, if it is completed, publishing credits. Also don't just say "here's a book I've written" and attach a ten-page synopsis—it won't get read. Obviously, errors in grammar or spelling are unacceptable. The worst are queries that are threatening, bizarre, obscene, plain weird, or arrive by fax. No SASE means no response.

What writers can do to enhance their chances of getting an agent (besides being good writers): In nonfiction, the author's passionate belief in the subject as well as expertise and a defined audience are very appealing. If there are writing problems, I will get them help in producing a book. In fiction, a wonderful, fresh authorial voice, a page-turning plot, character depth, well-structured chapters, and strong imaginative prose. The writing is everything in fiction.

Description of the Client from Hell: A client who truly does not want to delegate anything to the agent; calls a dozen times every day (especially evenings and weekends); submits dot-matrix manuscripts; misses deadlines; breaches contracts; and is demanding, arbitrary, unwilling to work as part of a team, and sends 50-page faxes!

Description of Dream Client: One who participates in a mutually respectful business relationship, is clear about needs and goals, and communicates about career planning. This client has a gift for language and storytelling, a commitment to a writing career, and a passion for excellence. How wonderful that so many of my clients are dream clients.

Why did you become an agent? When I left New York, I knew that I wanted to stay in publishing. However, editorial work was not sufficiently satisfying by itself. I knew I could acquire and develop salable properties and that my background gave me expertise in sales and running a company. I wanted to work with people long term and not just on a single project or phase of one. Plus, I had an entrepreneurial temperament, and experience negotiating big-money deals from raising venture capital for high-tech firms. When I developed literary projects for other agents that did not sell, I knew I could sell them myself—so I did. I've never regretted that decision. Agenting combined my love of books, my affinity for deal making, and my preference for trusting my own intuition. I sold 28 books the first year the agency was in business.

What might you be doing if you weren't an agent? I did everything else I ever wanted to do before becoming an agent. Agenting is truly a calling for me, and I would not be as happy doing anything else. It is a case of "do what you love (and are good at) and the money follows."

Comments: Believe in yourself and your own gifts. Keep in mind that the challenge for every writer is twofold—to have something to say and to have the mastery of the craft to say it well. Study and practice plotting, pacing, point of view, etc., so you can express exactly what you want to say. Nothing is more important than being true to your own artistic vision and understanding the requirements of the medium you have chosen to express it in, whether you are writing a symphony, haiku, or a novel. Keep in mind that in imitating other writers you can only be second rate at being them. Expressing your own inner thoughts, feelings, and stories in your own way is the only path to real success. Your world, your history, your experiences, your insights cannot be duplicated by anyone else. Bring us in to share your vision, your imagination. No one can do it better than you can, because the truth of your uniqueness is what you are here to offer everyone else. It is what moves us and takes us outside our own lives when we read what you have written.

KIDDE, HOYT & PICARD

335 East 51st Street
New York, NY 10022
212-755-9461

Agents: Kay Kidde; Laura Langlie, associate agent (telephone: 212-755-9465).

Born: Kidde: August 30, 1930; Montclair, New Jersey. Langlie: January 21, 1964.

Education: Kidde: Chatham Hall, Virginia (1948); B.A., Vassar College (1952). Langlie: University of Iowa.

Career history: Kidde: Has taught, worked as editor, senior editor at NAL, Putnam/Coward McCann, Harcourt. Langlie: Assistant to the publisher at Carroll & Graf Publishers, Inc.; associate production manager at Kensington Publishing Corporation.

Hobbies/personal interests: Kidde: Published poet, writer, tennis, ocean swimming, sailing. Langlie: Theater going, film watching, cooking, and reading.

Subjects/categories most enthusiastic about agenting: Kidde: Mainstream/literary fiction, mainstream nonfiction, romantic fiction. Langlie: General nonfiction, biographies, mainstream/literary fiction, nature writing, mystery and suspense fiction, historical romances.

Subjects/categories not interested in agenting: Male adventure, porn, science fiction, young adult, juvenile, poetry, unpublished short stories.

Best way for a prospective client to initiate contact: Write a query letter (with SASE), preferably one to three pages, including a synopsis, past publishing credits, and other writing experience.

Reading-fee policy: No reading fee. Author is responsible for photocopying, some long-distance telephone and fax expenses, and postage expenses for manuscripts being returned to the author.

Client representation in the following categories: Nonfiction, 25%; Fiction, 75%.

Commission: 15% for new clients.

Number of titles sold during the past year: 15.

Approximate percentage of all submissions (from queries through manuscripts) that are rejected: 90%.

Representative titles sold:
Closing Distance by Jim Oliver (Putnam).
Profile by C. J. Koehler (Carroll & Graf).
Something to Hide by Pat Robinson (St. Martin's).
Stolen Splendor by Diana Hairland (Zebra).
Pacific Passions by Frank Sherry (Morrow).
Aquamarine by Nancy Christiansen (Zebra).
Love in Full Bloom by Margaret Fowler and Priscilla McCutcheon (Ballantine).
Horses of the Night by Michael Cadnum (Carroll & Graf).
See How They Run by Sally McCluskey (Bantam).

The most common mistakes potential clients make when soliciting an agent to represent them: Kidde: Insistence; the coy, undisciplined, lack of straight presentation of selves. Langlie: An incomplete presentation of their book projects. Presumptuousness.

What writers can do to enhance their chances of getting an agent (besides being good writers): Kidde: Write a beautiful novel with agape in it. Langlie: Be original and get to know the market. Read!

Description of the Client from Hell: The prospective Client from Hell is one who is pushy, loud, not a stylist, unpublished.

Why did you become an agent? Kidde: Because I love good books. Langlie: I enjoy putting people together. I'm a good matchmaker in business.

What might you be doing if you weren't an agent? Kidde: Writing more. Langlie: Somehow, I'd be involved with authors and publishing. This always has been what I've wanted to do.

Comments: Go for good values; go for love, style, and reality.

HARVEY KLINGER INC.
301 West 53rd Street
New York, NY 10019
212-581-7068

Agents: Harvey Klinger; Laurie Liss, associate; Carol McCleary, associate.

The following information pertains to Harvey Klinger:
Born: April 1, 1951.
Education: B.A., New College; M.A., the Writing Seminars, John Hopkins University.
Career history: Began as Doubleday trainee; founded own agency in 1977.
Hobbies/personal interests: Travel, water sports, collecting, exercise, theater, my own country house.
Subjects/categories most enthusiastic about agenting: Mainstream and literary fiction. Nonfiction: psychology, self-improvement, important biography, science, current issues.
Subjects/categories not interested in agenting: Category romance, historicals, science fiction, fantasy, Westerns, computers, children's.

Best way for a prospective client to initiate contact: Query letter with brief description/synopsis (plus SASE). *Do not telephone*!

Reading-fee policy: No reading fee.

Client representation in the following categories: Nonfiction, 50%; Fiction, 50%.

Commission: 15% domestic; 25% foreign (subagent collects 10%).

Number of titles sold during the past year: 50+.

Approximate percentage of all submissions (from queries through manuscripts) that are rejected: 90%.

Representative titles sold:

Relic (Tor).

Shadow Soul (Pocket).

Real Moments (Delacorte).

The Christmas Box (Simon & Schuster).

Eye Contact (Bantam).

The Seasons of Beento Blackbird (Little, Brown).

You Can *Look Younger at Any Age* (Holt).

Fruit Acids for Fabulous Skin (St. Martin's).

The most common mistakes potential clients make when soliciting an agent to represent them: Too many phone calls and faxes. Trying to sell themselves, rather than letting the material speak for itself.

What writers can do to enhance their chances of getting an agent (besides being good writers): Be referred by people whose opinions I respect.

Description of the Client from Hell: Someone who *kvetches* all the time, but doesn't want to listen to constructive advice.

Description of Dream Client: The opposite.

Why did you become an agent? To use both my creative and legal (I come from a family of lawyers) sides.

What might you be doing if you weren't an agent? Writing a novel!

Comments: If you've truly got talent, *persevere*. Unfortunately, there's just not much great talent out there, especially among younger would-be writers who grew up on TV and video games, rather than on the printed word. They think they know how to write; they don't!

BARBARA S. KOUTS, LITERARY AGENT

P.O. Box 558
Bellport, NY 11713
516-286-1278

Agent: Barbara S. Kouts.

Born: October 24, 1936.

Education: B.A., English, New York University; M.A., English, SUNY at Stony Brook.

Career history: Freelance editorial work at book publishers and magazines; began working in literary agency 1980; founded own agency in 1991.

Hobbies/personal interests: Walking, swimming, reading, bicycle riding, gardening, spending time with my family and friends.

Subjects/categories most enthusiastic about agenting: Children's, literary novels, psychology, parenting, interpersonal relationships. Mysteries and fast-moving movie tie-in novels. Novels with depth in ideas and characters. Health, sports, and gardening.

Subjects/categories not interested in agenting: Science fiction and romance novels. Mass-market children's books.

Best way for a prospective client to initiate contact: Query letter and description of project (with SASE).

Reading-fee policy: No reading fee (only photocopying expenses).

Client representation in the following categories: Nonfiction, 20%; Fiction, 20%; Children's, 60%.

Commission: 10%.

Number of titles sold during the past year: Lost count!

Approximate percentage of all submissions (from queries through manuscripts) that are rejected: 90% of new submissions and queries.

Representative titles sold:

Dawn Land by Joseph Bruchac (Fulcrum Publishers).

The Faithful Friend by Robert Sans Souci (Simon & Schuster).

How to Get A Good Job in 30 Days by Hal Gieseking (Simon & Schuster).

Minty by Alan Schroeder.

The most common mistakes potential clients make when soliciting an agent to represent them: Calling on the phone over and over again to find out about everything! Constantly! Sending sloppy and unprofessional work!

What writers can do to enhance their chances of getting an agent (besides being good writers): They are professional in all aspects of their query letter and phone conversations. Real pros stand out!

Description of the Client from Hell: Expecting much too much—instant reads, instant dollars, instant attention! A feeling of mistrust, quibbling over everything.

Description of Dream Client: Hard-working, reliable, consistent in writing, willing to rewrite and revise, kind and considerate. Upbeat and cheerful.

Why did you become an agent? Great love of books! And good reads! I love to see a manuscript turn into a published book.

What might you be doing if you weren't an agent? Working with books or writing in some other capacity. Getting a Ph.D. in English. Reading all the great classics!

Comments: Keep on writing—never give up! "To one's own self be true." *Hakuna matata.*

IRENE KRAAS AGENCY

220 Copper Trail
Santa Fe, NM 87505
505-474-6216

Agent: Irene W. Kraas.

Born: August 16; is this necessary?

Education: B.A., psychology; M.Ed., educational psychology.

Career history: Career counselor; management consultant and trainer to business, universities, and government; literary agent (1990 to present).

Hobbies/personal interests: Reading, hiking, and enjoying life.

Subjects/categories most enthusiastic about agenting: Fiction: especially science fiction, mysteries, and all genre and good literature.

Subjects/categories not interested in agenting: Poetry, young children's (I do young adult), and most nonfiction.

Best way for a prospective client to initiate contact: Send me a short cover letter, the first 50 pages of a *completed* manuscript, and return postage.

Reading-fee policy: No reading fee.

Client representation in the following categories: Fiction, 100% (Young Adult, 30%).

Commission: 15%.

Number of titles sold during the past year: 12.

Approximate percentage of all submissions (from queries through manuscripts) that are rejected: 95%.

Representative titles sold:

Spider World Tales by Duncan Long (Harper) Young adult, 3-book series.

Iroshi, The Glaive and *Penseus* by Cary Osborune (Berkley/Ace) 3-book series.

Quantum Moon and *Opalite Moon* by Denise Vitula (Berkley/Ace).

The Leaving Summer by Donal Harding (Morrow Young Adult).

The Faery Convention and *The Hair of the Dog* by Brett David (Baen).

The most common mistakes potential clients make when soliciting an agent to represent them: No cover letter or no return postage. Envelope too small. I can ignore everything if it's a great manuscript.

What writers can do to enhance their chances of getting an agent (besides being good writers): I have to admit that I'm really only interested in the manuscript, so if the writer just sends the 50 pages and SASE, I'm a happy camper.

Description of the Client from Hell: I'll take the Fifth, thanks.

Description of Dream Client: Great writers who trust me to do the very best for them.

Why did you become an agent? I went from 20 years in business consulting to becoming the great American writer to agenting. I love using my business acumen in helping first authors get a break.

What might you be doing if you weren't an agent? I've done what I've wanted all along and this is the ultimate. However, if I had to choose, I would be a rich publisher and publish all those great books which I've had rejected!

MICHAEL LARSEN/ELIZABETH POMADA LITERARY AGENTS

1029 Jones Street
San Francisco, CA 94109
415-673-0939

Agents: Michael Larsen, Elizabeth Pomada.

Born: Larsen: January 8, 1941; New York, New York. Pomada: June 12, 1940; New York, New York.

Education: Larsen: City College of New York, 1965. Pomada: Cornell University, 1962.

Career history: Larsen: Worked at William Morrow, Bantam, and Pyramid (now Berkley). Pomada: Worked at Holt, David McKay, and the Dial Press.

Hobbies/personal interests: Larsen: Technology and the future, jazz and classical musical, the media convergence, movies, and reading books between covers without the phone ringing. Pomada: France, traveling and writing about it, reading for pleasure.

Subjects/categories most enthusiastic about agenting: Larsen: Nonfiction; Business, technology, trends, visions of the future, how-to's, health, spirituality, architecture, belly-laugh humor, promotable illustrated books, new ideas with social or aesthetic value that will interest the general public. Pomada: Women's interests, travel, food, biographies, the arts.

Subjects/categories not interested in agenting: Articles, short stories, poetry, scripts, young adult or children's books, textbooks. Also Westerns and hard-core science fiction unless they break out of the genre and sweep Elizabeth away. People don't want to spend $25 to get depressed; don't sell a problem, sell a solution.

Best way for a prospective client to initiate contact: Fiction: After you have finished and polished a novel, send the first 30 pages and a brief synopsis with SASE and phone number. Nonfiction: After you have read Michael's book on proposals, but before you start writing, call between 9 A.M. and 5 P.M. California time Monday to Friday. Michael will advise you on how to make your proposal as salable as possible. For a free brochure, "How To Make Yourself Irresistible to an Agent or Publisher" based on Michael's newly published *Literary Agents: What They Do, How They Do It and How to Find and Work with the Right One for You*, send a #10 SASE.

Reading-fee policy: No fees.

Client representation in the following categories: Nonfiction, 70%; Fiction, 30%.

Commission: 15% domestic; 20% foreign.

Number of titles sold during the past year: 15–20.

Approximate percentage of all submissions (from queries through manuscripts) that are rejected: More than 90%.

Representative titles sold:

Complete Confidence by Sam Horn, the author of *Tongue Fu!* (St. Martin's Press).

How High Can You Bounce? The Nine Keys to Personal Resilience by Roger Crawford (Bantam).

I'm Not As Old As I Used to Be by Frances Weaver (Hyperion).

It Was the Vacation of a Lifetime Until I Forgot to Wear My Underwear on a Glass Bottomed Boat by Susan & Peter Fenton (St. Martin's Press).

Pangaea by Lisa Mason (a science fiction novel) (Bantam/Spectra).

The Random House Quotationary by Leonard Roy Frank (Random House).

Red Wyvern by Katharine Kerr (the ninth volume in the Deverry Series) (Bantam/Spectra).

The Royal Treatment: Taking Home the Secrets of the World's Greatest Spas by Stephen Capellini (Dell).

Sub Zero by John Campbell (a technothriller) (Avon).

TV Dinners: An Entertainment Guide To Food, Fun, and Games from Your Favorite TV Shows by Pat & Barry Katzmann (Berkley).

The Way of the Guerrilla by Jay Conrad Levinson (Houghton Mifflin).

When Life Becomes Precious: A Comprehensive Guide for Friends, Loved Ones, and Co-Workers of Cancer Patients by Elise Needell Babcock (Bantam).

Your Next 50 Years: Smart Retirement Strategies for Baby Boomers by Ginita Wall and Victoria Felton-Collins (Holt).

The most common mistakes potential clients make when soliciting an agent to represent them: Sloppy, unprofessional letters and queries that are obviously mass multiple submissions and not really meant for us. The most costly mistake a writer can make is what a Random House editor calls "premature emission"—sending a novel or proposal out before it's ready to be seen by a professional agent or editor.

What writers can do to enhance their chances of getting an agent (besides being good writers): We are most enthusiastic about writers who have done their homework, who have studied and have a realistic view about the profession they are trying to enter—publishing. These writers have then polished their craft and submitted an exciting new idea, in a new, well-written voice, in a professional manner that shows that they are totally committed to their writing career.

Description of Dream Client: Dream writers are grateful, faithful, creative in coming up with fresh ideas, conscientious in writing and rewriting, tireless in promoting, and patient. Also, they have a positive but realistic perspective on agenting and publishing, know their literary and financial goals, and are totally committed to developing their craft and career. They understand that, since they can leave us at any time, we want them to be satisfied with our efforts, become life-long friends, and inspire us to be Dream Agents.

Why did you become an agent? We became agents because we loved working with books and discovered that there were no publishing jobs available in California when we moved here, so we had to create our own jobs.

What might you be doing if you weren't an agent? If Michael were not an agent, he would be publishing and writing books that can help make the world a better place. He still believes that the right book can change the world. If Elizabeth were not an agent, she would be traveling the world and writing about it.

If you could say anything you wanted, without censorship, what would you say? We like to handle books that we like, by people we like, and sell them to editors we like. Our business depends on us finding new writers. We love to get excited about new books and writers, and are as eager to find promising new writers as they are to be published.

Writing and selling a book is easy compared to making it successful. Your ability to promote your work will be a major factor in determining the editor, publisher, and deal you get for your books.

The right book will change the world. Writers are the most important people in publishing because they make it go. Now is the most exciting time ever to be alive and the best time to be a writer. The age of information is the age of the writer.

There are more agents, publishers, and formats for your books to be published in, more ways to get your books published, and more ways to promote and make money from them than ever. Be professional but relentless. Persistence rewards talent.

LEVANT & WALES LITERARY AGENCY, INC.

108 Hayes Street
Seattle, WA 98109
206-284-7114

Agent: Elizabeth Wales.

Born: March 30, 1952.

Education: B.A., Smith College; graduate work in English and American literature at Columbia University.

Career history: Worked in the trade sales departments at Oxford University Press and Viking Penguin; worked in city government and served a term on the Seattle school board; also worked as a bookseller and publisher's representative.

Hobbies/personal interests: Reading, theater, cooking/eating, visual arts—all that Seattle has to offer in "the arts." Walking, hiking/backpacking, camping.

Subjects/categories most enthusiastic about agenting: Sponsors a wide range of narrative nonfiction titles: especially interested in projects that might be termed difficult or risky, or could have a progressive cultural or political impact. In fiction, looking for talented mainstream storytellers, both new and established. Especially interested in writers from the Northwest, Alaska, the West Coast, and what have become known as the Pacific Rim countries.

Subjects/categories not interested in agenting: Children's books, almost all genre projects (romance, historicals, true crime, horror, action/adventure).

Best way for a prospective client to initiate contact: Send query letter with writing sample(s) and a brief description of the book project with SASE to the agency for consideration.

Reading-fee policy: No reading fee.

Client representation in the following categories: Nonfiction, 80%; Fiction, 20%.

Commission: 15% domestic.

Number of titles sold during the past year: 12.

Approximate percentage of all submissions (from queries through manuscripts) that are rejected: Most of our projects and authors come from referrals, but several times a year we "discover" a beauty of a book from the submissions pile.

Representative titles sold:

Callous Hands: Searching for a Grandfather by David Mas Masumoto (W. W. Norton, 1997).

Disappearance: A Map, A Meditation on Death and Loss from the High Latitudes by Sheila Nickerson (Doubleday, 1996).

The Memoirs of Ben Graham: The Dean of Wall Street by Benjamin Graha (McGraw-Hill, 1996).

Zen Masters of Old by C. C. Tsai, translated by Brian Bruya (Anchor, 1998).

Savage Love by Dan Savage (Dutton, 1997/98).

What writers can do to enhance their chances of getting an agent (besides being good writers): It's hard to miss writing talent. It stands out.

Why did you become an agent? For the adventure and the challenge; also, I am a generalist—interested in variety.

Comments: I am particularly interested in writers who are dedicated to writing, and/or who have a particularly compelling story to tell.

ELLEN LEVINE LITERARY AGENCY

15 East 26th Street, Suite 1801
New York, NY 10010-1505
212-889-0620
No phone queries accepted. Please query by letter.

Agent: Diana Finch.

Born: September 16, 1954, Hanover, New Hampshire.

Education: B.A., Harvard University, 1976; M.A., University of Leeds, Leeds, England, 1977.

Career history: Sanford A. Greenburger Associates, assistant agent, 1981–1984; St. Martin's Press, assistant editor, 1978–1981. In addition to representing my own clients, I handle translation and magazine rights and attend the Frankfurt Book Fair annually, so I am always looking out for opportunities for my clients to be published in magazines and in other countries.

Hobbies/personal interests: Sports, including skiing, soccer, and field hockey—as participant. Theater.

Subjects/categories most enthusiastic about agenting: Serious nonfiction.

Subjects/categories not interested in agenting: Romance fiction, mysteries.

Best way for a prospective client to initiate contact: By query letter with SASE.

Reading-fee policy: No reading fee.

Client representation in the following categories: Nonfiction, 50%; Fiction, 30%; Children's, 20%.

Commission: 15%

Number of titles sold during the past year: 15 (not including foreign sales).

Approximate percentage of all submissions (from queries through manuscripts) that are rejected: 95%. I receive many queries.

Representative titles sold:

Finding Part-Time Work That Pays by Cindy Tolliver and Mary Ann Alwan (Avon).

Homesource by Prudence McCullough (HarperCollins).

Marketing Online by Marcia Yudhin (Plume).

Golf's Mental Hazards by Alan Shapiro Ph.D. (Simon & Schuster).

When Black Couples Work Together by Anita Diggs and Vera Paster Ph.D. (Kensington).

Circle of Stones: A Novel of our Earliest Beginnings by Joan Lambert (Pocket Books).

The most common mistakes potential clients make when soliciting an agent to represent them: Writers who emphasize their desire to be famous and rich when they have not yet published even one book or who stress the marketing possibilities without equal attention to the content of their work turn me off.

What writers can do to enhance their chances of getting an agent (besides being good writers): They are recommended by writers or editors whose judgment I trust. They present polished material that is in final form. They write about their work in a clear and inspired way.

Description of the Client from Hell: I am delighted to say: currently none of mine. Perhaps someone who does not allow for the time it can take for an agent to give good feedback or collect correct information.

Description of Dream Client: Inspired, intelligent writers who communicate their concerns to me clearly and stay involved in all aspects of writing and publishing.

Why did you become an agent? I was an editor first, and I became an agent to be 100% on the writer's side.

What might you be doing if you weren't an agent? Teaching or editing.

JAMES LEVINE COMMUNICATIONS, INC.

330 Seventh Avenue, 14th Floor
New York, NY 10001
212-268-4846
fax: 212-465-8637

Agents: James A. Levine, Arielle Eckstut, Jack Hailey, Daniel Greenberg.

Born: Levine: April 20, 1946. Hailey: December 13, 1945. Greenberg: October 13, 1970.

Education: Levine: B.A., Amherst College; M.A. (C.Phil. in English literature), University of California at Berkeley; Ed.D., Harvard University. Eckstut: B.A., University of Chicago. Hailey: B.A. (English), Amherst College; Ph.D. (English), Cornell University. Greenberg: B.A. (history), University of Wisconsin at Madison.

Career history: Levine: Spent much of my career doing what I do now: putting together ideas, people, and money; identifying, nurturing, and marketing talent; creating projects that make a difference. As an entrepreneur in the not-for-profit and academic sectors, including a decade as Vice President for Product Development at the Bank Street College of Education, I channeled people's expertise into a variety of media: print, software, video, and audio. Have also written 6 books, 2 software manuals, and over 60 articles for leading magazines. Eckstut: Pastry chef prior to becoming literary agent. Hailey: In addition to agenting, I have been involved with literature and writing for most of my working life as an educator and as a consultant to government school districts and to foundations. Greenberg: Dutton Books, subsidiary rights; Roberto Sautachiara Literary Agency (Italian subagent).

Hobbies/personal interests: Levine: Jazz, sports (playing them), photography, travel, voracious reading. Eckstut: I'm a member of an improvisational theater group. I also love to cook, bake, make art (I have a design background), and I'm an avid movie goer. Greenberg: Sports, music, Italian cooking, Irish history.

Subjects/categories most enthusiastic about agenting: Levine: A very wide range, as long as it's well written, including psychology, business, parenting, narrative nonfiction, literary fiction, technology, medical, how-to, social issues. Eckstut: Narrative nonfiction, food (cookbooks and philosophy of), urban studies, psychology, health, gardening, science, social sciences, and literary fiction (adult and young-adult). Hailey: Literary fiction, mysteries, true crime, cultural studies, young adult fiction. Greenberg: Fiction, sports, history.

Subjects/categories not interested in agenting: Levine: Anything that's poorly written. Eckstut: Self-help, popular fiction, romance, children's, true crime, academic and professional books. Greenberg: Romances.

Best way for a prospective client to initiate contact: Query letter (with SASE), with outline, sample chapter, and credentials.

Reading-fee policy: No reading fee.

Client representation in the following categories: Nonfiction, 95%; Fiction, 5%; (Children's, 15% of all titles).

Commission: 15%.

Number of titles sold during the past year: 35.

Approximate percentage of all submissions (from queries through manuscripts) that are rejected: 98%.

Representative titles sold:

Undercurrents: A Life Beneath the Surface (Harper San Francisco).

The Beer Lover's Rating Guide (Workman).

The Genesis of Ethics (Crown).

Inside the Tornado (HarperBusiness). *Business Week* best-seller.

It's Not All in Your Head (Harper San Francisco).

The Midwife's Apprentice (Clarion). Newbery Award winner

The Couple Who Became Each Other and Other Tales of Healing from a Master Hypnotherapist (Bantam).

Everyday Soul (Riverhead).

The Soul Solution (Dutton/Plume).

The Parent's Journal Guide to Raising Great Kids (Bantam).

The Hispanic Guide to the Internet (Henry Holt).

Someday My Prince Will Come: A Virgin's Memoir (Warner).

The most common mistakes potential clients make when soliciting an agent to represent them: Sends a whole manuscript, unsolicited, with no SASE (the only worse scenario is the person who keeps calling—wanting to know why they have not gotten their manuscript back). Insists they've written the next great American novel. Says their friends and family like it (not even *love* it!). Says their murder mystery is funny and cute! Gives no biography that says who they are or why they're qualified to write what they've written.

What writers can do to enhance their chances of getting an agent (besides being good writers): Levine: I love the challenge of working with smart people with great ideas. Eckstut: First, great writing. Second, great recipes. Greenberg: For fiction, any piece of solid writing interests me, no matter the genre. I also look at credentials and publishing history. I keep my eyes open for a sharp sense of humor.

Description of the Client from Hell: Calls all the time for unnecessary reasons, is rude, haughty, disorganized, takes for granted everything you do, and never once says thanks!

Description of Dream Client: Organized, thoughtful, easy to get along with, conscientious, reliable, cordial, and fun!

Why did you become an agent? Levine: I was an agent before I ever knew I was an agent. Eckstut: Pure luck. Greenberg: I enjoy working with talented and interesting people. There is also nothing quite as exciting as the huge deal!

What might you be doing if you weren't an agent? Levine: Writing and working in some other organizational setting to develop people's talent. Eckstut: Architect? Actor? Chef? Who knows!

Comments: We feel passionately about feeling passionately about the projects we take on.

KAREN LEWIS & COMPANY

P.O. Box 741623
Dallas, TX 75374-1623
214-342-3885
fax: 214-340-8857

Agent: Karen K. Lewis

Education: M.A., journalism.

Subjects/categories most enthusiastic about agenting: Fiction: Literary and genre. Nonfiction: self-help, psychology, health, women's issues.

Subjects/categories not interested in agenting: Poetry, short stories, juveniles.

Best way for a prospective client to initiate contact: Query letter (with SASE), brief synopsis, and first chapter.

Reading-fee policy: No reading fee. Charge for copies, overseas calls, and postage.

Client representation in the following categories: Nonfiction, 40%; Fiction, 60%.

Commission: 15% domestic, 20% foreign.

Approximate percentage of all submissions (from queries through manuscripts) that are rejected: 95%.

Description of the Client from Hell: A writer who lacks the ability to judge his or her own work objectively.

Description of Dream Client: A client who is patient and looks for creative ways to make positive things happen.

Why did you become an agent? I love to read and to work with promising writers.
What might you be doing if you weren't an agent? College professor of literature.

THE LITERARY GROUP INTERNATIONAL

270 Lafayette Street, Suite 1505
New York, NY 10012
212-274-1616

Austin branch office:
1300 Guadalupe Street, Suite 208
Austin, TX 78701
Phone queries are not encouraged; please initiate contact in writing.

Agents: Scott Waxman, Jim Hornfischer.

The following information pertains to Scott Waxman (New York office):
Born: June 19, 1967.
Education: Fieldston High School (Bronx, NY); Cornell University (English major).
Career history: Assistant editor at HarperCollins (1990–1993); agent, the Literary Group International (1993 to present).
Hobbies/personal interests: Piano, golf, tennis, biking.
Subjects/categories most enthusiastic about agenting: Sports, biographies, health, commercial fiction.
Subjects/categories not interested in agenting: Investment, poetry, children's science.
Best way for a prospective client to initiate contact: Query letter (with SASE).
Reading-fee policy: No reading fee.
Client representation in the following categories: Nonfiction, 90%; Fiction, 10%.
Commission: 15%.
Number of titles sold during the past year: 14.
Approximate percentage of all submissions (from queries through manuscripts) that are rejected: 90%.
Description of the Client from Hell: One who won't trust my judgment and uses other people's poor advice to refute what I say.
Description of Dream Client: One with faith in my judgment, a wealth of great ideas, and strong contacts in their field.
The most common mistakes potential clients make when soliciting an agent to represent them: Don't like queries that try to shock. If the idea is good, I'll read it.
What makes you enthusiastic about the way some writers solicit you? A good, succinct query letter with solid sales points.
Why did you become an agent? I love books, I love talent, and I love making deals.
What might you be doing if you weren't an agent? Too terrifying to ponder.
Comments: I'm tired of pretentious agents in their octogenarian years pushing their weight around, and their outrageous incredulity when young agents push back.

The following information pertains to Jim Hornfischer (Austin branch office):
Born: November 18, 1965.

Education: B.A. (Phi Beta Kappa), international relations/German, Colgate University.

Career history: Editorial positions in the McGraw-Hill general books division (1987–1989) and the HarperCollins adult trade division (1989–1992). Agent, Literary Group International, (1993 to present).

Hobbies/personal interests: Fishing, travel, chess, typography/graphic design, military history and hardware, sports, and NHL '95 on Sega Genesis (just ask Frank Weimann).

Subjects/categories most enthusiastic about agenting: Fiction: quality mainstream and literary; distinctive, writerly prose. Nonfiction: biography, current events, history, politics, polemics, memoirs, African-American/Native American/Hispanic issues, business, humor, relationship guides, general-interest science, medicine/health, academic/professional writing for a general audience.

Subjects/categories not interested in agenting: Books I can't be proud of. Books without readerships.

Best way for a prospective client to initiate contact: A concise, intelligent query letter, brief biography or C.V., and news clippings or reviews, where appropriate, will do the trick.

Reading-fee policy: No reading fee.

Client representation in the following categories: Nonfiction, 95%; Fiction, 5%.

Commission: 15%.

Number of titles sold during the past year: My (and my clients') business affairs are kept in confidence.

Approximate percentage of all submissions (from queries through manuscripts) that are rejected: The same parade-drenching number as the rest of them.

Representative titles sold:

Good Days and Mad by Dick DeBartolo (Thunder's Mouth).

Luck by Nicholas Rescher (Farrar Straus Giroux).

Selena! by Clint Richmond (Pocket) The four-week #1 New York Times bestseller.

Lady Bird Johnson by Jan Jarboe (Scribner).

Himpressions by Valerie Shaw (HarperCollins) A national bestseller in the author's self-published edition.

The Reckless Decade: America in the 1980s by H. W. Brands (St. Martin's/Thomas Dunne).

Theodore Roosevelt by H. W. Brands (Basic).

Convicted in the Womb: One Man's Journey From Prisoner to Peacemaker by Carl Upchurch (Bantam).

Rebel Private: Front and Rear by William A. Fletcher (Dutton).

Mother Knew Best: Wit and Wisdom from the Moms of Celebrities by Elsa and David Hornfischer (Penguin/Plume). The authors perceptively write, "When you have son who is a literary agent, it is dangerous to suggest an idea for a book."

Father Knew Best: Wit and Wisdom from the Dads of Celebrities . . . and Doubly So.

The Lost History of the Canine Race by Mary Elizabeth Thurston (Andrews & McMeel) Book-of-the Month Club, QPB.

Right Thinking: Conservative Common Sense Through the Ages by James D. Hornfischer (Pocket). A plug for my own little book there.

Raising Safe Kids in an Unsafe World by Jan Wagner (Avon).

War's End by Major General (USAF-retired) Charles W. Sweeney (Avon). A memoir by the commander of the Nagasaki mission.

The Assassination of the Black Male Image by Earl Ofari Hutchinson (Simon & Schuster).

Not Now Honey, I'm Watching the Game by Kevin Quirk (Simon & Schuster).

Barbara Jordan: A Biography by Mary Beth Rogers (Bantam).

The most common mistakes potential clients make when soliciting an agent to represent them: Telephoning and (invariably) making a bad (i.e., obnoxious, suspicious, or needy) impression; real writers write—and reserve for relatives the need to *reach out and touch someone*. Dropping by the office and insisting on *just a moment of your time*. Exhibiting mistrust of their parcel carrier by *just checking in* repeatedly after submitting their work. Requiring me to audition for the role of their agent before I'm even remotely interested. Not enclosing return postage.

What makes you enthusiastic about the way some writers solicit you? They grasp the rudiments of the business, temper their ambition with patience, conduct themselves in good faith, and oh yeah, *write well*.

Description of the Client from Hell: The perpetually paranoid, disaster-mongering, frequent-phoner. (As of this writing, I have, thankfully, none.)

Description of Dream Client: She simply *can't help* herself from turning out tight, compelling prose and keeping an open ear for good advice. Genetically driven to professionalism, follow-through, and positive mental attitude.

Why did you become an agent? I'm your basic book junkie and wanted to work on a greater variety of projects than one can as an editor.

What might you be doing if you weren't an agent? Flying an F-16, playing first base for the Bosox, or writing a curmudgeonly column for a village weekly newspaper.

Comments: Memo to T. Clancy, J. Grisham, S. King, D. Steel, and R. J. Waller: Any of you folks want to grab a little lunch?

TONI LOPOPOLO LITERARY AGENCY

P.O. Box 1484
Manhattan Beach, CA 90266
310-546-6690
fax: 310-546-2930

Deliveries to:
1150 Manhattan Beach Boulevard, Suite 8
Manhattan Beach, CA 90266

Agents: (Ms.) Toni Lopopolo; Nikki Ballard, senior editor (see Comments section).

Born: All gifts accepted on or around July 18.

Education: B.A., State University of San Francisco; graduate work, University of California at Berkeley and New York University.

Career history: Literary agent (1990 to present); executive editor, St. Martin's Press (1981–1990), Macmillan (1978–1981); marketing director, Houghton Mifflin (1975–1978); promotion director, Harcourt Brace (1973–1975); publicity associate, Bantam Books (1970–1973).

Hobbies/personal interests: My four-legged pals: a Whippet, a French bulldog, and a cat. Operatic Divas: collecting CDs of their best tunes. Traveling to/reading about Italy, especially the 100 cities. Growing orchids.

Subjects/categories most enthusiastic about agenting: Mystery/thrillers with unusual or ethnic elements (Hispanic, Asia, black, Italian, etc.), female protagonist. Genre fiction, women's commercial fiction, family sagas (especially ethnic), police work, biography (unusual lives of women who have made a mark on the world), American History, family economics, family health and pregnancy, psychological self-help, women's interest, personal management, and drama rights.

Subjects/categories not interested in agenting: Try us.

Best way for a prospective client to initiate contact: With a well-written, *personalized* query letter that includes SASE, publishing credentials, and biography. For nonfiction: include expertise in the subject. For fiction: include a one-page synopsis of the plot, where and how (private study or classes) the writer has perfected the skills that make up the craft of fiction writing, and the last ten novels read.

Reading-fee policy: Unpublished clients are charged a marketing fee, when an agency agreement is signed, to cover out-of-pocket agency expenses. First-time novelists who show promise but need to polish fiction-writing skills can join our editorial program if desired. Fees depend on work involved and length of draft.

Client representation in the following categories: Nonfiction, 75%; Fiction, 25%.

Commission: 15%.

Number of titles sold during the past year: 25.

Approximate percentage of all submissions (from queries through manuscripts) that are rejected: 90%

Representative titles sold:

Attracting Terrific People by Dr. Lillian Glass (St. Martin's Press, 1997). Sixth book from the "First Lady of Communication."

Do Not Go Gently by Judith Smith-Levin (HarperCollins, 1997). First novel featuring black women homicide detectives.

Leader of the Pack by Nancy Baer and Steve Duno (HarperCollins, 1996). Animal behaviorists and trainers help dog owners establish just who is Alpha Dog in the family pack.

Eye of the Agency: A Sadie Greenstreet Mystery by Richard W. Moquist (St. Martin's Press, 1997). Set in the Midwest of the 1870s, featuring a perky journalist married to a Pinkerton, this illustrated mystery is set on a riverboat traveling down the Mississippi.

Stein on Writing by Sol Stein (St. Martin's Press, 1995). The great guru of fiction writing and dynamic prose presents the best book for writers ever.

The most common mistakes potential clients make when soliciting an agent to represent them: Those who feel they can *sell* their books to me over the phone. The *wannabee* who sends an unsolicited manuscript, or anything unsolicited except a query letter. The first novelist who has not mastered the skills that make up the craft of fiction and who needs instruction, not an agent. The costly mistakes usually come from fiction writers who have no idea of the market, who want an agent to read uncut and/or unedited, very long manuscripts. Unpublished writers who feel their agent should also act as their writing teacher, *gratis*. Writers who want to meet to discuss their novels before I have read anything they have written. People who say they want to write a novel but have not read one since high school. People who feel they can write fiction because their nonfiction has been published. Those who do not find out how to solicit an agent before doing so.

Failing to enclose the SASE means that submissions will be discarded, unread. *Sending certified mail, or anything requiring a signature, to a post office box is thoughtless.* Why should anyone take precious time to wait in line for mail that is unsolicited and unexpected? Enclose a 20¢ self-addressed postcard. Wastes no time and helps the insecure to know their submission arrived. Or, find out the physical address of the agency.

What writers can do to enhance their chances of getting an agent (besides being good writers): Nonfiction: The query letter is directed to me, personally, telling why they have chosen my agency; this writer has done his/his homework and researched what this agency is interested in representing. The writer is the appropriate person to write the book because of his or her expertise and background, and is savvy about the publishing business and how an agent operates. This writer also knows the value of an ideal, complete proposal and needs very little instruction and advice from me.

Fiction: No signs of the amateur; know how to present their novels in a succinct style and in the correct length for a first novel; show they are well read, and bring quotes from published writers or other respected authorities endorsing the novel. And, they have mastered the skills required to write good fiction and have the talent and security to create an original story within a standard format.

Description of the Client from Hell: Those who do not honor their deadlines. Those who do not help promote their own books. Those who phone too often when they know if I had any important information, they would be the first to know.

Description of Dream Client: Clients who have done their homework, aren't constantly needing reassurance, who carefully copyedit their work before sending it to me for evaluation, who respect my personal time, who research the market and help with ideas for promoting their books, who have day jobs and don't depend solely on their books for income (especially before their books sell in big numbers), who realize an agency has other clients besides them, who respect my work day and night, and who are appreciative of my efforts on their behalf.

Why did you become an agent? I became an agent because I worked in the book business for the better part of my adult life, and it's what I know best. Also, discovering a new writer and selling that writer's book is a thrill and a satisfaction for me. I can't picture my life outside of book publishing so I will always be connected somehow.

What might you be doing if you weren't an agent? My backup job has always been helping to run the family vineyards and orchards in the San Joaquin Valley. So far, I've avoided this. Also, I'd still be studying for the Opera as a coloratura. I'd love to be growing orchids, writing my own novels, and teaching fiction writing to the very talented.

Comments: Because the unsolicited mail received here is so unrelenting and abundant, we may soon have to take on new clients by referral only, especially first novels. If only would-be novelists would learn their craft before trying to convince an agent to read still-raw fiction they insist is ready for *marketing*. Fiction writing is not often a God-given talent. One must study and master the skills involved, read voraciously, not just as a reader, but as a writer, and understand that fiction writing is mainly rewriting, many times over. There must be an investment of time and money for lessons, editorial work, and objective critical evaluations, and there must be practice, practice, practice. People who send unsolicited mail to an agent should understand there is little obligation on the agent's part to serve them. Demanding quick attention, as though from a government clerk, is inappropriate. Unless you are a signed client, you have no cause for righteousness and criticism. Response from an agent is a courtesy.

Comments from Nikki Ballard, senior editor and associate agent: Always read carefully what the agent asks you to send. Construct a brief but complete chapter-by-chapter outline and a terse book synopsis. Spend nearly as much time on these as you do on your submission. Neither should end: . . . *and then in a plot twist so stunning and original you'll need to read it to believe it, the hero wraps up the story!* We don't need to know your computer is capable of graphic gymnastics (i.e., don't send cover ideas, dummy ads, or book mockups). We *do* need to know you are committed to perfecting your craft through constructive criticism, extensive rewriting, and abundant reading.

LOWENSTEIN-MOREL ASSOCIATES

121 West 27th Street, Suite 601
New York, NY 10001
212-206-1630
fax: 212-727-0280

Agent: Eileen Cope.

Education: Degrees in political science and journalism.

Career history: Editor with the Putnam Berkley Group.

Subjects/categories most enthusiastic about agenting: Areas of interest include literary and multicultural fiction, comparative religions, psychology, ethics, contemporary social issues, contemporary ethnic and cultural issues, Asian studies, history, anthropology, sexuality, politics, and the arts (particularly music, theater, and art history).

Subjects/categories not interested in agenting: All category fiction, children's, young adult.

Best way for a prospective client to initiate contact: Please send a query letter and C.V. (with SASE).

Reading-fee policy: No reading fee.
Client representation in the following categories: Nonfiction, 80%; Fiction, 20%.
Commission: 15% domestic, 20% foreign.
Representative titles sold:
A partial listing of Eileen Cope's acquisitions and sales for 1995 include:
Awakening The Buddha Within: Timeless Teachings for a Western World (Broadway Books).
The Mozart Effect: Using the Power of Music to Heal the Body, Strengthen the Mind, and Unlock the Creative Spirit (Avon Hardcover).
Fasting the Body; Finding the Spirit: The Three-Day Life Detox Program (HarperCollins).
A Radiant Life: Bringing Sacred Traditions and Spiritual Practices Into Everyday Living (Harper San Francisco).
Agency recent sales include:
Salud! A Latina's Guide to Total Health—Mind, Body, and Spirit (HarperCollins).
Black Lies, White Lies: The Truth According to Tony Brown (William Morrow).
Sister CEO's: A Black Women's Guide to Starting a Business (Viking Penguin).
Leaving Deep Water: Asian-American Women at the Crossroads of Two Cultures (Dutton).
Return to the Center: Finding our Spiritual Rooms in the Second Half of Life (Doubleday/Anchor).
Stand on a Tightrope by Suzanne Vega (Avon Hardcover).

LUKEMAN LITERARY MANAGEMENT LTD.

205 West 80th Street, Suite 4C
New York, NY 10024
212-874-5959

Agent: Noah Lukeman.
Born: November 28, 1973.
Education: BA, Brandeis; Higo Honors English and Creative Writing, Cum Laude
Career history: Worked short editorial stints at William Morrow; Farrar, Straus, Giroux; and Delphinium Books.
Subjects/categories most enthusiastic about agenting: Open to all categories.
Subjects/categories not interested in agenting: Poetry, children's books.
Best way for a prospective client to initiate contact: Send in work with an SASE.
Reading-fee policy: No fees.
Client representation in the following categories:
Fiction, 50%; Nonfiction, 50%.
Commission: 15.%
Description of the Client from Hell: Pushy, impatient, controlling.
Why did you become an agent? To help writers.

DONALD MAASS LITERARY AGENCY

157 West 57th Street, Suite 1003
New York, NY 10019
212-757-7755

Agent: Donald Maass, president; Jennifer Jackson, associate.

Born: Maass: 1953; Columbus, Georgia. Jackson: 1971, Cambridge, N

Education: Maass: B.A., St. Lawrence University, 1975. Jackson. B.A., St. Lawrence University, 1993.

Career history: Maass: 1977–1978, editor, Dell Publishing; 1979, agent, Scott Meredith Literary Agency, Inc.; 1980, founded Donald Maass Literary Agency. Jackson: 1993–1994, editorial assistant; 1994–1995, assistant agent; 1995 to present, associate agent, Donald Maass Agency.

Hobbies/personal interests: Maass: Reading, theater, sailing, squash, antiques, stock market. Author of 14 pseudonymous novels. Jackson: reading, writing, Web-page design, book collecting, home brewing, hiking and camping in the Adirondacks, horseback riding.

Subjects/categories most enthusiastic about agenting: Maass: Fiction specialist. Concentration in science fiction, fantasy, mystery, suspense, horror, frontier, mainstream, and literary. Jackson: Fiction specialist: concentration in science fiction, fantasy, romance, mystery, suspense, horror, mainstream, literary, and women's fiction.

Subjects/categories not interested in agenting: Pop psychology, how-to, true crime, humor/novelty, juvenile.

Best way for a prospective client to initiate contact: Concise (one-page!) query letter that includes prior short story, novel, article, and/or nonfiction book credits.

Reading-fee policy: No reading fee.

Client representation in the following categories: Nonfiction, 5%; Fiction, 95%.

Commission: 15% domestic; 20% foreign.

Number of titles sold during the past year: 75.

Approximate percentage of all submissions (from queries through manuscripts) that are rejected: 99%.

Representative titles sold:

Weighed in the Balance and *Ashworth House* by Anne Perry (Fawcett Columbine).
Fairyland by Paul McAuley (Morrow).
God's Fires by Patricia Anthony (Berkley/ACE).
The Wizard and the Floating City by Christopher Rowley (NAL/ROC).
Timespell by Robert Charrette (HarperPrism).
Voices of Hope by David Feintuch (Warner/Aspect).
Seeds of Time by Kay Kenyon (Bantam/Spectra).
Dear Diary #2: Second Best by Cheryl Lanham (Berkley).
First Dawn and *Second Fire* by Mike Moscoe (Berkley).
The Players by Stephanie Cowell (W. W. Norton).
The Confidential Casebook of Sherlock Holmes edited by Marvin Kaye (St. Martin's Press).

The most common mistakes potential clients make when soliciting an agent to represent them: One common turnoff: Query letters that try too hard. Keep it simple. Who are you? What have you got? What do you want in an agent? Avoid long summaries; I usually skim them.

What writers can do to enhance their chances of getting an agent (besides being good writers): Display a professional manner, original ideas, great storytelling, and ambition coupled with realism about the business.

Description of the Client from Hell: Neurotic, afraid to grow, in a hurry, feels that publishers are the enemy.

Description of Dream Client: Patient, passionate, dedicated to craft, writes for the joy of it, works well with others, enjoys the publishing game.

Why did you become an agent? Maass: I got into this profession by chance, but have stayed in it because I am an analyst, a strategist, and a risk taker. Jackson: An innate love of books and the creative process. It was an extremely natural decision.

What might you be doing if you weren't an agent? Maass: Oh, Lord, it's too late to think about that now. Jackson: I'd probably be at home reading a big, fat paperback novel and baking chocolate-chip cookies (from scratch, of course).

Comments: Maass: Interested writers may want to read my book, *The Career Novelist,* published in 1996 by Heinemann. Jackson: Work hard, play hard, keep submitting, and invite me to your writer's group conferences.

CAROL MANN AGENCY

55 Fifth Avenue
New York, NY 10003
212-206-5635

[handwritten: Did not send]

Agent: Carol Mann.
  Born: July 23, 1949; Cambridge, Massachusetts.
  Education: University High, Chicago; Smith College.
  Career history: Teacher, the Brearley School; educational marketing, Avon Books.
  Hobbies/personal interests: Tennis, film, social history.
  Subjects/categories most enthusiastic about agenting: Fiction: Authors Paul Auster, Marita Golden. Nonfiction: history, psychology, health and fitness, alternative medicine, sociology, anthropology, political science, American social history, popular culture, biography, memoir, true crime.
  Best way for a prospective client to initiate contact: Query letter (with SASE).
  Reading-fee policy: No reading fee.
  Commission: 15%.
  Representative titles sold:
  All God's Children: The Bosket Family and the American Tradition of Violence by Fox Butterfield (Knopf).
  Gathering Storm by Morris Dees (HarperCollins).
  The Good Marriage by Dr. Judith Wallerstein (Houghton Mifflin, Warner).

The Holistic Pediatrician by Dr. Kathi Kemper (HarperCollins).
Mr. Vertigo by Paul Auster (Viking).
When Work Disappears by William Julius Wilson.

MARCH TENTH, INC.

4 Myrtle Street
Haworth, NJ 07641
201-387-6551

Agent: Sandra Choron.

Education: B.A., Lehman College, New York.

Career history: Having "grown up" at a small publisher (Hawthorn Books) and then moved on to a large firm (Dell) where I was a senior editor, I have had experience in all aspects of book publishing.

Hobbies/personal interests: Popular culture, music, folk art, painting, writing, spying on kids to find out what the next generation is *really* up to.

Subjects/categories most enthusiastic about agenting: Popular culture, history, fine fiction, general nonfiction, music, self-help (keep it original, please!), new trends, biography, novelty projects.

Subjects/categories not interested in agenting: Politics, personal memoirs of people who never did anything interesting, special interest, juvenile, short fiction, poetry.

Best way for a prospective client to initiate contact: Submit a query letter (with SASE).

Reading-fee policy: No reading fee.

Client representation in the following categories: Nonfiction, 98%; Fiction, 1%; Children's, 1%.

Commission: 15% domestic; 20% foreign or dramatic rights.

Number of titles sold during the past year: 20.

Approximate percentage of all submissions (from queries through manuscripts) that are rejected: 90%.

Representative titles sold:

If: Questions for the Game of Life by James Saywell and Evelyn McFarlane (Villard).

The New Book of Rock Lists by Dave Marsh (Simon & Schuster).

Shock Value by John Waters (Thunder's Mouth/Marlowe).

Hank Williams by Colin Escott (Little Brown).

The Book of Lists for Kids by Sandra and Harry Choron (Houghton-Mifflin).

Keith Moon by Tony Fletcher (Avon).

Boldly Live as You've Never Lived Before: Life Lessons from Star Trek by Richard Raben and Hiyaguha Cohen (Morrow).

The most common mistakes potential clients make when soliciting an agent to represent them: They fail to describe the project in a concise way. They fail to state their credentials. No SASE (these do not receive a reply). I don't like being hyped. Facts and sales ammunition are great, but if there are three exclamation points in your first paragraph, my shit-detector goes crazy!

What writers can do to enhance their chances of getting an agent (besides being good writers): They include large amounts of money with their submissions.

Description of the Client from Hell: Someone who is convinced that "everyone" will buy his book.

Description of Dream Client: Tall, dark . . .

What might you be doing if you weren't an agent? I'd be running a publishing company, making a large sum of money.

Comments: Publishing a book is an incredibly gratifying experience. It can also be unbelievably grueling. Enter at your own risk!

DENISE MARCIL LITERARY AGENCY, INC.

685 West End Avenue, 9C
New York, NY 10025
212-932-3110
fax: 212-932-3113

Agent: Denise Marcil.

Born: Troy, New York.

Education: B.A., Skidmore College (major: English; minor: art history).

Career history: Avon Books, editorial assistant; Simon & Schuster, assistant editor; literary agency president, 1977 to present.

Hobbies/personal interests: Entertaining, cooking, ballroom dancing, fly fishing, attending theater and ballet.

Subjects/categories most enthusiastic about agenting: Women's commercial fiction; thrillers; mainstream suspense; medical thrillers; popular reference nonfiction, especially by experts with national exposure in seminars, workshops, and speaking engagements; some business books; parenting; personal finance; health; popular psychology; and spirituality.

Subjects/categories not interested in agenting: Men's action adventure; science fiction/fantasy; young adult or children's; most serious narrative nonfiction. I take on very little literary fiction.

Best way for a prospective client to initiate contact: One-page query letter with SASE. Do not send sample material or manuscript.

Reading-fee policy: No reading fee.

Client representation in the following categories: Nonfiction, 25%; Fiction, 75%.

Number of titles sold during the past year: 68.

Approximate percentage of all submissions (from queries through manuscripts) that are rejected: 95%.

Representative titles sold:

The Pregnancy Book and *The High Needs Child* by Dr. William Sears and Martha Sears, R.N. (Little, Brown).

A Rare Chance by Carla Neggers (Pocket Books).

Lethal Practice by Dr. Peter Clement (Ballantine Publishing Group).

Beguiled by Arnette Lamb (Pocket Books).

Makeovers by Catherine Todd (Avon Books).

The most common mistakes potential clients make when soliciting an agent to represent them: When a potential author doesn't follow instructions for submitting material, that tells me I couldn't work with him or her. For example, if I ask for the first chapter or three chapters and I receive half the manuscript or the entire manuscript, I know I'm in trouble. Also, not including an SASE with a letter or SAS mailer with a manuscript is a serious mistake.

Potential clients who are pushy or arrogant are a turn-off.

Also, if a writer is submitting his or her work to more than one agent, this should be stated in the letter. There's nothing worse than taking the time to read something only to learn the author has already signed up with another agent. It's discourteous to the other agents.

What writers can do to enhance their chances of getting an agent (besides being good writers): Be courteous, honest, and ethical. Tell me their expectations and communicate openly and reasonably with me.

Description of the Client from Hell: Someone who fails to keep me informed of his needs or problems (or change of address), assuming I know what he wants or that he is dissatisfied. My office is set up with systems in place to serve authors efficiently. I consider an author unreasonable if he expects always to be the exception to the rule, and makes demands for services I don't normally render unless circumstances require.

Description of Dream Client: Someone who is aware of and appreciates the hard work I put in for him. He communicates openly and honestly and writes the best book he's capable of.

Why did you become an agent? Having worked as an editor, I realized that I could offer my clients the extra skill and service of editorial feedback in addition to selling their work and managing their careers. I love books, and my favorite part of this job is discovering new authors and selling their first books.

What might you be doing if you weren't an agent? Frankly, I can't imagine working in another field.

Comments: Authors should know that their agents are their advocates. For an author to view the author/agent relationship as adversarial can only hurt him.

MARGRET MCBRIDE LITERARY AGENCY

7744 Fay Avenue, Suite 201
La Jolla, CA 92037
619-454-1550
fax: 619-454-2156

…t McBride; Winifred Golden, vice president, associate agent; Susan
…e agent.

…tegories most enthusiastic about agenting: Mainstream fiction and

…ategories not interested in agenting: Children's books, poetry, genre
romance, scientific/professional (non-trade) books, textbooks, magazine

…/ for a prospective client to initiate contact: Query letter with SASE.

…g-fee policy: No reading fee.

Client representation in the following categories: Nonfiction, 75%; Fiction, 25%.

Commission: 15% domestic; 25% foreign.

Number of titles sold during the past year: 20.

Approximate percentage of all submissions (from queries through manuscripts) that are rejected: 97%.

Representative titles sold:

Youth in Revolt (Doubleday). Fiction.

Devil's Hole (HarperCollins). Fiction.

Ain't Gonna Be the Same Fool Twice (Hyperion). Fiction.

Everyone's a Coach (HarperCollins). Nonfiction.

The Grammar Bible (Ballantine). Nonfiction.

From Panic to Power (HarperCollins). Nonfiction.

Platinum Rule (Warner). Nonfiction.

The most common mistakes potential clients make when soliciting an agent to represent them: Calling to set up an appointment to meet, prior to submitting work. Verbal/telephone queries seldom work.

GERARD McCAULEY AGENCY

P.O. Box 844
Katonah, NY 10536
914-232-5700

Agent: Gerard F. McCauley.

Born: April 9, 1934.

Education: B.A., University of Pittsburgh; graduate studies, Columbia University.

Career history: Editor, college texts, Alfred A. Knopf; associate editor, trade texts, Little Brown; literary agent, Curtis Brown Ltd.; Founded own agency in 1970.

Hobbies/personal interests: Baseball, reading, golf, writing letters.

Subjects/categories most enthusiastic about agenting: History, biography, general nonfiction.

Subjects/categories not interested in agenting: Fiction, how-to books, business books.

Best way for a prospective client to initiate contact: Recommendation by editor or another writer.

Reading-fee policy: No reading fee.

Client representation in the following categories: Nonfiction, 80%; Textbook, 15%; Children's, 5%.

Commission: 15%.

Number of titles sold during the past year: 42.

Approximate percentage of all submissions (from queries through manuscripts) that are rejected: 95%

Representative titles sold:

Foreign Policy by Walter McDougall (Houghton Mifflin).

Lewis & Clark by Ken Burns (Knopf).

Lyndon Johnson by Charles Wood (Free Press).

Fresh Start by Julie Rosso (Crown).

A World History by William McNeill and John R. McNeill (Norton).

The most common mistakes potential clients make when soliciting an agent to represent them: A phone call where portions of the proposal are read aloud. Any unsolicited manuscript sent Federal Express without SASE, which is sent to 50 editors and agents simultaneously.

What writers can do to enhance their chances of getting an agent (besides being good writers): Intelligent and well-written proposals.

Description of the Client from Hell: Evening and weekend calls. Needs response to 300-page manuscript within a week. Presents own proposals to editors without my knowledge. Suffers from writer's cramp as soon as contract is signed.

Description of Dream Client: One who views relationship as a partnership, which is true of 90% of the clients I represent.

Why did you become an agent? I like writers.

What might you be doing if you weren't an agent? Editor or unemployed with the time to read the work of several novelists free of the distraction of reading unsolicited manuscripts.

Comments: Ninety percent of the writers submitting book proposals or manuscripts have little talent for writing, but the tenacity to type well.

McIntosh and Otis, Inc.

310 Madison Avenue
New York, NY 10017
212-687-7400

Agent: Renée Cho.

Career history: McIntosh and Otis, Inc., has the oldest juvenile department of any agency.

Subjects/categories most enthusiastic about agenting: We are looking for well-written, thoughtful books on all subjects from baby books to young-adult, fiction and nonfiction. We like to see the work of writers who are willing to take risks either in natter. We are looking for material that is fresh, original, and

pective client to initiate contact: For picture books, please ript. For older fiction or nonfiction, we prefer a query letter and e SASE).

y: No reading fee.

o.

ion mistakes potential clients make when soliciting an agent to We prefer short introductory or query letters. It is unnecessary to de- a picture book and to suggest marketing strategies or potential to sell sion. The manuscript must speak for itself.

DORIS S. MICHAELS LITERARY AGENCY, INC.

20 West 64th Street, Apartment 29-R
New York, NY 10023
212-769-2430

Agent: Doris S. Michaels.

Born: May 1955, Lodi, California.

Education: B.A., English and German literature, University of California at Santa Cruz; M.A.T., German and English, University of California at Berkeley; Certificate in Computer Technology, Columbia University; Certificate in Book and Magazine Publishing, Summer Publishing Institute, New York University.

Career history: Acquisitions Editor for Prentice-Hall, 1982–1984; Technology Consultant and Trainer for PHINET and Prudential-Bache 1984–1987; International Information Center Manager for Union Bank of Switzerland based in Zurich 1987–1992; Independent Literary Agent based in NYC 1994 to present.

Hobbies/personal interests: Reading, music, especially listening to classical music and playing the violin. Sports, especially mountain biking, skiing, and swimming. Computers.

Subjects/categories most enthusiastic about agenting: Fiction: commercial fiction, literary fiction, women's fiction, novels with strong screen potential. Adult nonfiction (hardcovers and trade paperbacks): Biographies, business, classical music, sports, women's issues. Multimedia electronic works for computers.

Subjects/categories not interested in agenting: Science fiction, fantasy, mysteries, thrillers, romances, Westerns, occult and supernatural, horror stories, poetry, textbooks, religion, film scripts, cookbooks, diet books, short stories, articles, humor, professional manuals.

Best way for a prospective client to initiate contact: Query first with SASE. Please, no calls.

Reading-fee policy: No reading fee.

Client representation in the following categories: Nonfiction, 30%; Fiction, 70%.
Commission: 15%.

Number of titles sold during the past year: 4

Approximate percentage of all submissions (from queries through manuscripts that are rejected: 98%.

Representative titles sold:

The Dollar Bill Knows No Sex by Wendy Rue and Karin Abarbanel (McGraw-Hill).

The Heart Asks Pleasure by Anna Tuttle Villegas (St. Martin's Press).

The Neatest Little Guide to Mutual Fund Investing by Jason Kelly (Dutton/Penguin USA).

Better Vocabulary in 30 Minutes a Day by Edith Schwager (Career Press).

The most common mistakes potential clients make when soliciting an agent to represent them: They send an unprofessional query letter without an SASE. Nonfiction projects arrive without a clearly written proposal.

What writers can do to enhance their chances of getting an agent (besides being good writers): The writers who do their homework and check the market for the project create a much better impression. Only the best possible representation of the work should be sent.

Description of the Client from Hell: I only work with clients with whom I can develop a good working relationship.

Description of Dream Client: Someone who has talent, understands the publishing process, appreciates the hard work I do, and listens carefully.

Why did you become an agent? I enjoy reading good fiction and the process of helping talented writers get published.

What might you be doing if you weren't an agent? Touring as a concert violinist.

Comments: Having lived and worked in Europe (Germany, Switzerland, and England) for over six years and being a first-generation American enables me to represent books that can appeal to a broader, more international market.

JEAN V. NAGGAR LITERARY AGENCY

216 East 75th Street, 1E
New York, NY 10021
212-794-1082

Agents: Anne Engel, Frances Kuffel, Jean V. Naggar.

Born: Kuffel: 1956.

Education: Engel: Bachelor of Laws, London University. Kuffel: B.A., English, B.A., religious studies, University of Montana; M.F.A. creative writing, Cornell University. Naggar: B.A. with honors, London University.

Career history: Engel: 20 years as an editor in British publishing houses. Kuffel: left Ph.D. program in English to get a life and have been with this agency ever since. Naggar: writer, editor, translator, book reviewer.

Hobbies/personal interests: Engel: looking at cities. Kuffel: reading, history (especially World War II), biography, nineteenth-century English novels, cooking and entertaining, writing. Naggar: parenting, reading, music, business, travel, cooking. Wide-ranging other interests that do not include sports and politics.

...s most enthusiastic about agenting: Engel: Science, biography. ...ion with a strong, probably masculine, storyline. Serious nonfic-... history, women's studies, cultural studies. Naggar: Fiction: strong, ...ream fiction, literary fiction, contemporary, suspense, historical fic-...onfiction: biography, literary autobiography or memoirs, science for ...ychology and sophisticated self-help.

...egories not interested in agenting: Engel: fiction, children's books. ...ige anything; genre books: science fiction, romance, fantasy, mystery, ...rns. Naggar: sports, politics, category fiction, most science fiction, ...merican drug-cartel espionage.

Best w... for a prospective client to initiate contact: Engel: An enthusiastic, balanced letter. Kuffel: Query letter. Naggar: Query letter.

Reading-fee policy: No reading fee.

Client representation in the following categories: Engel: Nonfiction, 100%. Kuffel: Nonfiction, 33%; Fiction, 33%, Children's, 33%. Naggar: Nonfiction, 45%; Fiction, 45%; Children's, 10%.

Commission: 15% domestic; 20% international.

Number of titles sold during the past year: Kuffel: 18. Naggar: 47.

Approximate percentage of all submissions (from queries through manuscripts) that are rejected: Kuffel: 98%. Naggar: 96%.

Representative titles sold:

Frances Kuffel:

Rebuilding the Indian by Fred Haefele (Riverhead).

Become Rosemary by Frances Wood (Bantam Doubleday Dell Books for Young Readers).

Why Lapin's Ears Are Long and Other Louisiana Tales by Sharon Arms Doucet (Orchard Books).

Women Living Single by Lee Reilly (Faber & Faber).

The Boy with Paper Wings by Susan Lowell (Milkweed).

Cindy Ellen by Susan Lowell (Joanna Cotler Books/HarperCollins).

Fun with Hand Shadows by Sati Achath (Contemporary Books).

Jean V. Naggar:

Happily Ever After by Betsy Stone (Doubleday), nonfiction.

Catch Your Breath by Jessica Auerbach (Putnam's).

The Thirteenth Hour by Barbara Sofer (Dutton/NAL).

I Love You, I Love You, I Love You by Bryn Collins (Contemporary Books). Nonfiction.

The Burning Man by Phillip Margolin (Doubleday).

Breach of Trust by Bonnie MacDougal (Pocket Books).

The Living Sea by Carl Safina (Henry Holt). Nonfiction.

Songs of Ordinary Time by Mary McGarry Morris (Viking).

Pryor Rendering by Gary Reed (Dutton/NAL).

Virus Ground Zero by Ed Regis (Pocket Books). Nonfiction.

Lessons From The Trial by Gerald Uelman (Andrews & McMeel). Nonfiction.

Mother of Pearl by Mary Morrissy (Scribner).

The most common mistakes potential clients make when soliciting an agent to represent them: Kuffel: Telling me in the query letter what their writing means, rather than what it's about; telling me how *strong, powerful, dynamic*, etc., their writing and story is; telling me how much other readers have loved it. Telling me about themselves at more length and before describing the plot of subject matter. Oh—and hearing from a wife about her husband's book! Naggar: Not doing any background research on agents *before* contacting; asking, *Do you want to see my work?* without describing it; calling every five minutes to *check up on things*—a sure precursor of the Client from Hell!

What writers can do to enhance their chances of getting an agent (besides being good writers): Kuffel: A writer who *briefly* conveys his or her storyline and prose style; subject matter that's different and makes *me* interested in something new. Naggar: Professional queries that identify and define reasons why I might want to read the book.

Description of the Client from Hell: Kuffel: One who expects a phone call even when there is nothing to discuss; one who is unreasonable or suspicious about what I can achieve for them. A *loose pistol*—acting independently of my efforts and without telling me! Naggar: An author who has chosen me as an agent but never quite trusts me.

Description of Dream Client: Kuffel: One who has a sense of humor and a sense of reality about how long things take in publishing; one who trusts me to do my job; one who takes criticism of their work well, and quickly. A writer with very literary capabilities and a healthy dose of cynicism about precious writing for its own sake. Naggar: Talented, appreciative, intelligent, knowledgeable.

Why did you become an agent? Kuffel: I'm nuts about books, and in what other job can you be involved with everything from the goofiest projects and children's books to scholarship? Naggar: I love reading and respect writers. I enjoy being an advocate for writers I respect.

What might you be doing if you weren't an agent? Kuffel: Stand-up comic; adjunct professor in some grim little English department; secretary in an insurance office in Montana.

Comments: Kuffel: Stop whining and get a real job—the world does *not* owe you a living you can perform in your pajamas!

RUTH NATHAN LITERARY AGENCY

80 Fifth Avenue
New York, NY 10011
212-675-6063

Agent: Ruth Nathan.
Born: New York City.
Education: B.A., Radcliffe College.
Career history: Theatrical producer, trade book publisher, story editor for film studios and independent producers.

interests: Theater, film, history (especially medieval), cooking,

ies most enthusiastic about agenting: Show Biz, historical fic-
decorative arts, specialties in each field only.

ories not interested in agenting: Male adventure, romance, chil-
ence fiction, fantasy, technothrillers, serious political material.

a prospective client to initiate contact: No unsolicited manuscripts.
essential as is SASE.

ee policy: No reading fee.

presentation in the following categories: Nonfiction, 80%; Fiction, 20%.
Commission: 15%.

Number of titles sold during the past year: 4.

**Approximate percentage of all submissions (from queries through manuscripts)
that are rejected:** 95%.

Representative titles sold:

King of Comedy (biography of Jerry Lewis) by Shawn Levy (St. Martin's).

No Good Deed and *Protocol for Murder* by Paul Nathan, mystery novels.

Book of Days by Stephen Rider (Carroll & Graf USA, Macmillan UK).

**The most common mistakes potential clients make when soliciting an agent to
represent them:** Sending unsolicited work or misrepresenting material not researched.

**What writers can do to enhance their chances of getting an agent (besides being
good writers):** Cooperate.

Description of the Client from Hell: Impatient, illiterate, ignorant, and deals with
other agents at same time. I do not allow this!

Description of Dream Client: Civilized, modest, and above all, a *good* writer.

Why did you become an agent? Propinquity.

What might you be doing if you weren't an agent? Producing writing seminars
with various colleges (will welcome inquiries about this).

Comments: Remember—I am selective and cranky!

NEW BRAND AGENCY GROUP
A DIVISION OF ALTER-ENTERTAINMENT LLC

205 Wildberry Lane
Nashville, TN 37209
615-353-8829

Agent: Eric D. Alterman.

Born: April 4, 1963.

Education: Undergraduate, Tufts University; Law School, Washington College of
Law, American University.

Career history: Attorney, owner-operator of radio broadcasting company, legal and
marketing consulting, literary agent.

Hobbies/personal interests: Guitar, golf, reading.

Subjects/categories most enthusiastic about agenting: Original and exciting contemporary fiction. Nonfiction that has an interesting or novel presentation of ideas relating to subject matter that will appeal to a wide audience. Thrillers, mysteries, romance, young adult novels.

Subjects/categories not interested in agenting: Hard-core science fiction and fantasy.

Best way for a prospective client to initiate contact: Send 50 pages, summary, and SASE to our address. We'll get back to you within a few weeks.

Reading-fee policy: No reading fee.

Client representation in the following categories: Nonfiction, 50%; Fiction, 40%; Children's, 10%.

Commission: 15%.

Number of titles sold during the past year: 3.

Approximate percentage of all submissions (from queries through manuscripts) that are rejected: 90%.

Representative titles sold:

Multiple mystery novels by Rae Foley (Thorndike Press, Chivers Press).

The Complete Guide to Buying Your Shelter Dog.

The most common mistakes potential clients make when soliciting an agent to represent them: Writers should be sure to follow submission instructions. It is frustrating when no SASE is enclosed, etc. One of the biggest mistakes a new writer can make is submitting a hard-to-read manuscript (should be 12-point, double-spaced, clear printing, etc.).

What writers can do to enhance their chances of getting an agent (besides being good writers): Strong, clear, confident letter with short, but comprehensive, summary of the manuscript.

Description of the Client from Hell: Doesn't take care in checking his/her manuscript for errors; doesn't include SASE with submissions; expects publishers to respond overnight; forgets my birthday.

Description of Dream Client: Polite best-selling author who remembers my birthday.

Why did you become an agent? At some point in her or his career, every lawyer must ask the question, *Is there some other way I might make a living?* I love working with new writers who have lots of energy and a drawer full of fresh ideas.

What might you be doing if you weren't an agent? I might be sitting around somewhere spending all day reading published books instead of unpublished books (it wouldn't be as fun).

Comments: Find an agent that seems to care about your work. There is no substitute for enthusiasm.

NEW ENGLAND PUBLISHING ASSOCIATES, INC.

P.O. Box 5
Chester, CT 06412
203-345-7323
fax: 203-345-3660

Agents: Elizabeth Frost Knappman, president; Edward W. Knappman, vice president; Larry Hand, managing editor; Rebecca Barardy; Victoria Harlow.

Born: EFK: October 1, 1943. EWK: November 17, 1943

Education: EFK: B.A., anthropology, George Washington University (1965); completed all course work for an M.A. in this field. EWK: B.A., history, George Washington University (1965); M.S., journalism, Columbia University (1966).

Career history: EFK: Senior editor, William Morrow; senior editor, Doubleday; editor, William Collins & Sons (London); editor, Natural History Press. Author of *Women's Suffrage in America* (with Kathryn Cullen-Du Pont), *The Bully Pulpit*, *World Almanac of Presidential Quotations*, *ABC-CLIO History of Women's Progress in America*, *The Quotable Lawyer* (with D. Shraeger). EWK: Publisher of Facts On File; executive vice president of Facts On File.

Hobbies/personal interests: EFK: Writing in the area of women's history, singing, knitting, gardening, and tennis. EWK: Reading in the areas of history and politics and keeping up with computer developments.

Subjects/categories most enthusiastic about agenting: EFK: Women's subjects, biographies, true crime, literature. EWK: Reference, history, information, self-help, biographies.

Subjects/categories not interested in agenting: Personal memoirs, fiction, children's books, screenplays.

Best way for a prospective client to initiate contact: Send a well-thought-out proposal with a sample chapter and résumé.

Reading-fee policy: No reading fee.

Client representation in the following categories: Nonfiction, 90%.

Commission: 15%, unless co-agents must be employed for dramatic or foreign rights.

Number of titles sold during the past year: 35.

Approximate percentage of all submissions (from queries through manuscripts) that are rejected: 95%.

Representative titles sold:

The Cinnamon Lake Mysteries (Concordia).

Susan Sontag (Norton).

Eudora Welty (Doubleday).

Detective Lane Frank Mysteries (Bantam).

Women's Rights on Trial (Gale Research).

Elements of Expression (Holt).

Carey McWilliams (Crown).

Beyond the Conscious Mind (Plenum).

Edna Ferber (Prometheus).

Guide to Concise Writing (Writer's Digest).

Rebecca West: A Biography (Scribner's).

Let's Hear It for the Girls (Viking-Penguin).

Drink-Link Moderation Program (Carroll).

After Shanghai (St. Martin's Press).

The Financially Independent Woman (Carroll).

Penguin Dictionary of English Usage.
Back to Butler Creek (Random House).

The most common mistakes potential clients make when soliciting an agent to represent them: It's important to put in the time and effort to perfect a proposal. It's a mistake to try to wing it. The market has never been more competitive, and authors who ignore this are making an error. The key is to carefully research your competition, not just in the bookstores, but in the libraries, union catalog, and *Books in Print.*

What writers can do to enhance their chances of getting an agent (besides being good writers): Be friendly people who can sum up their book idea and why it's different with brevity. Writers must not mind revising proposals and working hard. Produce a well-crafted proposal that anticipates all the questions an editor or agent might ask: target audience, competition, qualifications for writing the book, the angle for the work, and how it is organized.

Description of the Client from Hell: There are no Clients from Hell, just people anxious to make a living from their writing.

Description of Dream Client: Professional, flexible about revisions, patient, friendly.

Why did you become an agent? After many years as an editor (EFK) and publisher (EWK), we needed to find a way to remain in the industry we loved while having our own business. Our combined literary agency, book-producing business, and consulting operations allow us to do this. What started as a small business in 1982 has grown to a good-sized one, with 8 employees to serve clients.

What might you be doing if you weren't an agent? EFK: Writing books in the area of women's history. EWK: Publishing books from the concept stage to their marketing and distribution. Both of us might be traveling to various countries we have not yet visited.

Comments: We would suggest that authors persevere, and not get discouraged about their writing. Somewhere there is a publisher for your work, or a way to continue writing, even if a book publisher seems uninterested. Writers' groups and professional associations can be very helpful—as are friends who are writing professionally. A subscription to *Publishers Weekly* and regular visits to bookstores and libraries to see what is being published are indispensable. But always remember, it's a good idea to keep your day job.

EDWARD A. NOVAK III LITERARY REPRESENTATION

711 North Second Street, Suite 1
Harrisburg, PA 17102
717-232-8081

Agent: Ed Novak.
Born: May 27, 1958; Long Beach, California.
Education: B.A., Georgetown University; M.A., University of Chicago.
Career history: Editorial director, Acton & Dystel Literary Agency; editor, Macmillan Publishing and Charles Scribner's Sons.

...onal interests: Reading, writing, parenting, nonprofit and church ...golf, watching televised sporting events and CNN, scanning gossip ...plaining about government.

...categories most enthusiastic about agenting: Sports; business/legal; ...biography; history/sociology; self-help and inspiration; popular science; ...l, mystery, and romance fiction.

...ts/categories not interested in agenting: Science fiction, New Age, poetry, ...how-to.

...way for a prospective client to initiate contact: Write me a simple query letter (with SASE) that answers three questions: (1) What's going to be in the book? (2) Who would want to read it and why? (3) Why are you the best author for it?

Reading-fee policy: Fee for unsolicited work. Send outline and three chapters. Writer will receive 500-word critique within a month. I will read everything and write back. Fee for this service is $50.

Client representation in the following categories: Nonfiction, 85%; Fiction, 15%.

Commission: 15% on domestic licenses; 19% on all foreign licenses.

Number of titles sold during the past year: 12.

Approximate percentage of all submissions (from queries through manuscripts) that are rejected: 99%.

Representative titles sold:

Tim Allen (unauthorized biography) by Mike Arkush (Avon Books).

Elvis in the Army by Colonel Bill Taylor (Presidio Press).

Bear Bryant: The Legend and the Man by Keith Dunnavant (Simon & Schuster).

Rogue's Isles: A Michael Carolina Murder Mystery by Thomas G. Briody (Dunne/St. Martin's Press).

The Race by Hunter R. Clark and Thomas Lee Wright (Times Books).

Untitled biography of coach Bob Knight by Lee Daniel Levine (Simon & Schuster).

The Savage and *The Warrior* by Nicole Jordan (Avon Books).

The most common mistakes potential clients make when soliciting an agent to represent them: They fail to make the connection between writing a good query letter and writing a good manuscript. They fail to describe their qualifications or how they came to the subject. They spend too much time describing the plot. They don't think about why anyone would spend money to read *their* book.

What writers can do to enhance their chances of getting an agent (besides being good writers): Imaginative writing, great writing, unexplored ideas, terrific writing.

Description of the Client from Hell: The same way I'd describe the Agent from Hell: when they stop returning your phone calls.

Description of Dream Client: Most of my clients are dreamy: professional, know their jobs, aren't afraid to ask questions, flatter their editors and publicists, and acknowledge their agent in the book.

Why did you become an agent? Because I'm the kid who spent school vacations in the public library—I love making books happen.

What might you be doing if you weren't an agent? Philanthropist.

Comments: Get the #?@/!! back to your keyboard!

Oriole Literary Agency

P.O. Box 1540
Alpine, CA 91903-1540
619-445-4735
fax: 619-445-6786

Agent: Steve Albrecht.

Born: February 22, 1963.

Education: B.A., English, University of San Diego; M.A., security management, Webster University.

Career history: 12 years as an author and 3 years as a literary agent.

Subjects/categories most enthusiastic about agenting: Business and management books.

Subjects/categories not interested in agenting: Books not related to business or management.

Best way for a prospective client to initiate contact: We accept one-page query letters or faxes. Please don't send writing samples, chapters, or complete manuscripts. You must include SASE to get your material answered.

Reading-fee policy: No reading fee.

Client representation in the following categories: Nonfiction, 100%.

Commission: 15%.

Approximate percentage of all submissions (from queries through manuscripts) that are rejected: We are very focused on business-related books. We reject everything else.

Representative titles sold:

We have good relationships with the top 15 business book publishers.

The most common mistakes potential clients make when soliciting an agent to represent them: Don't tell me, "We are both going to make lots of money" or "This will be an instant best-seller."

What writers can do to enhance their chances of getting an agent (besides being good writers): Good clients go to the bookstores to see what is on the shelves (or not) in their fields.

Description of the Client from Hell: He or she won't take no for an answer.

Description of Dream Client: He or she writes salable proposals and demonstrates both writing competence and business experience.

Why did you become an agent? I love writing and the art of business.

Fifi Oscard Agency, Inc.

24 West 40th Street
New York, NY 10018
212-764-1100

S. Murray.

Bennington College, The Sorbonne, Sarah Lawrence, B.A.

ategories most enthusiastic about agenting: Cookbooks, travel, sports,
r nonfiction.

or a prospective client to initiate contact: Query letter (with SASE).
ee policy: No reading fee.
ion: 15%.

OTITIS MEDIA LITERARY AGENCY

1926 Dupont Avenue South
Minneapolis, MN 55403
612-377-4918

Agents: B. R. Boylan, Hannibal Harris, Greg Boylan, Ingrid DiLeonardo.
The following information pertains to B. R. Boylan:
Born: December 11, 1936.
Education: Loyola University, Chicago.
Career history: After several years in Chicago as a reporter then an editor, I moved to New York and started a freelance career in book writing. My first book, a medical how-to manual, *The New Way to Live with Diabetes*, ultimately had more than one million copies in print. A few books later, I took on marriage, divorce, sex, and the gaggle of how-to marriage and sex experts (and their ghosts), in my book, *Infidelity*. I spent several months on the road promoting this book, and it was excerpted or serialized in numerous newspapers and magazines.

A few years later, I published a book dealing with one of my passions, history, in *Benedict Arnold: The Dark Eagle*. This was only the third biography of Arnold written in the twentieth century, and it added a whiff of revisionism to the stew. Predictably, it was denounced by academicians, treated fairly by dozens of other reviewers, and had the amazing effect of drawing from the closet all the Benedict Arnold fanatics.

During the intervening years, I have researched and written about the American Revolution, the French Revolution, the American Civil War, and the survival of fugitive Nazi war criminals, mainly in South America. It was there, in 1977, that I met and talked with Dr. Josef Mengele. I continued to work on books, book reviews, and scripts.

An editor of mine, to whom I had referred several authors with talent and ideas, seven of whom he signed up, urged me to get into the literary agency business on the side. During this same period of time, several other published authors, playwrights, and film writers were complaining, as was I, at Hollywood's refusal to consider any script not repped by an agency. That ultimately led to Otitis Media Literary Agency.

Hobbies/personal interests: Reading and researching historical projects, listening to opera and classical music, book collecting, photography, and theater.

Subjects/categories most enthusiastic about agenting: Nonfiction: History, music, biography, satire, comedy, anthropology/archeology, true crime. Fiction: Adventure, history, action, time-travel, multi-layered mystery, erotic, travel, crime, satire, and comedy.

Subjects/categories not interested in agenting: Children's books, self-help, poetry, academic treatises, science fiction, college textbooks, young adult, positivism, theology, coming of age, short stories, diatribes, new age, nutritional quackery, occult, outdoor, cookbooks.

Best way for a prospective client to initiate contact: We'll take a *brief* telephone call from an experienced pro who wants to know if we are interested in the manuscript or script he has written. But anyone without a professional track record should use the mails to send a query letter, which consists of a *brief* (3–4 sentences) synopsis of the story, along with a brief biography listing published or produced works, with names and dates essential. If nothing has been published commercially, a bit about their credits, training, classes, and personal interests. The first 25 pages of the work are *all* that we will accept. Unsolicited complete manuscripts rarely are read, and no SASE means nothing will be read or returned.

Reading-fee policy: No reading fee.

Commission: 15% domestic, 20% foreign.

Number of titles sold during the past year: Confidential.

Approximate percentage of all submissions (from queries through manuscripts) that are rejected: 96%.

Representative titles sold: Confidential.

The most common mistakes potential clients make when soliciting an agent to represent them: This is an easy one. The wannabe who insists he is a *writer* or an *author*, yet produces drivel. The wannabe who calls or writes us with a demand that we audition for him, manuscript and track record unseen, demanding to know the names of all the books and screenplays we have sold, for how much, and to whom. Requesting references from our contacts in film and publishing! Telling us what the real role of agent is: "You guys get rich off the money we make for you."

The most costly mistakes? Sending a query letter announcing they have written the next socko hit novel/screenplay, and inviting us to get rich with them. Another is the query letter that barely mentions the project but tells us what a splendid writer the author is and how he *loves to write!* That is a statement that clearly separates the amateurs from the professionals.

What writers can do to enhance their chances of getting an agent (besides being good writers): When they are low-key but professional in their initial contact, then continue to act that way. When they can sense the right time to check in with us, and seem to know intuitively when to suggest a second project. Also, those who approach us with a whiff of personality in what they send, and then are cordial and enthusiastic on the phone, in their fax, or letter. That spirit can be infectious.

Description of the Client from Hell: Writers to whom we describe our submission guidelines, but who then ignore them blatantly, arguing that their work cannot be understood without reading it all. We don't have time to plow through every script and manuscript that rolls in. If it's worthwhile, we'll know by the fifth page, definitely by the tenth. Also, the beginners who ignore correct formats, refuse to revise or improve their proposals, call us constantly, expect an immediate reaction, or waste their query letter with references to their support/critique groups, assuring us that everyone who has read it just loves it and predicts a glowing future of success, fame, and lots of money.

Other clients from hell demand a written critique of the book from the editor who just said no, or demand a list of editors, publishers, and phone numbers, then drive the stake deeper into their hearts by calling that editor or producer and arguing. There is the writer who, if we express interest in a particular proposal, then inundates us with his 12 other unpublished novels, poetry, and screenplays. We are particularly turned off by the whiner who calls every day, wanting hand-holding or psychotherapy.

Description of Dream Client: A good writer who moves from one project to the next, understanding the patience required to circulate and sell books. This client can accept rejection without help from his therapist, noting any specific remarks offered by the editor. The dream client does not second guess us or the editors, based on what his relatives or friends tell him.

Why did you become an agent? My years as a theatrical director, when I was pulling all the strings in order to produce the best possible performance, gave me a sense of overall responsibility for a good project. After suffering a brief burnout from doing too much writing, I found agenting a splendid way to regain a healthy perspective. I suddenly was overwhelmed with the good, the awful, and the pedestrian. I early on ran into the client from hell, followed shortly by the dream client, and was rolling. Agenting is a difficult packaging job, harder than almost anything I had tried before. As a result, my own writing enthusiasm returned with a whoosh, and I found myself enjoying that which I have always dreaded—selling.

What might you be doing if you weren't an agent? Photography, especially historical. Running an opera company, directing plays, musicals, and opera.

Comments: Americans are bombarded by pushy special-interest publishers, the colleges, the adult-education courses, the writing *schools* and schlocky agents—all of whom declare that *anyone* can learn to write, and that every sucker should give it a try to "free your inner spirit, give growth to your creative unconsciousness . . . become a writer! And make lots of money!"

My personal belief is that writers are born with a creative gift, one that often calls for great efforts to develop. The rest of the world are born without the gift, and no matter how hard they try, how conscientious their studies and workshops, they are unlikely to ever become professional writers.

Unfortunately, there is no test or talent marathon to determine who has and who has not the gift. Literary agents often are in a position to do so, as are editors, but the untalented are so numerous that picking the gifted few is a very exacting, demanding art. It also is repulsive to see the great horde of unwashed politicians, generals, and celebrities listed as *authors* of their own autobiographies. How about a national policy of *truth in bylines?*

THE RICHARD PARKS AGENCY

138 East 16th Street, Suite 5B
New York, NY 10003
212-254-9067

Agent: Richard Parks.

    Education: B.A., Duke University; M.A., University of North Carolina.

    Career history: Curtis Brown, Ltd. (1970–1978); United Artists Corporation (1978–1981); Alexander, Smith & Parks (1981–1988); The Richard Parks Agency (1989 to present).

    Best way for a prospective client to initiate contact: Fiction: by referral only. Nonfiction: by referral or query letter.

    Reading-fee policy: No reading fee.

    Client representation in the following categories: Nonfiction, 50%; Fiction, 50%.

    Commission: 15% domestic, 20% foreign.

    The most common mistakes potential clients make when soliciting an agent to represent them: No calls or faxed queries, please.

PELHAM LITERARY AGENCY

2290 East Fremont Avenue, Suite C
Littleton, CO 80122
303-347-0623

Agent: Howard Pelham.

    Born: February 21, 1927.

    Education: Advanced degrees in English and social anthropology.

    Career history: Teaching and writing. Published 15 Western novels.

    Hobbies/personal interests: Reading and writing.

    Subjects/categories most enthusiastic about agenting: Young adult, Western, genre fiction of all kinds.

    Subjects/categories not interested in agenting: Film scripts.

    Best way for a prospective client to initiate contact: Either by telephone or query by mail. Do not send manuscript before querying.

    Reading-fee policy: No reading fee.

    Client representation in the following categories: Nonfiction, 10%; Fiction, 90%.

    Commission: 15%.

    Number of titles sold during the past year: 2.

    Approximate percentage of all submissions (from queries through manuscripts) that are rejected: 80% of the queries I respond to send me a manuscript not ready to be submitted.

    Representative titles sold:

Foreign Adoption by Barbara Bascomb and Carole McKelvey (Pocket Books).

Death of a Gunslinger by Howard Pelham (Thomas Bourgey, Inc.).

    The most common mistakes potential clients make when soliciting an agent to represent them: Those who assume what they haven written is a boon to the publishing business and set an advance figure before anyone bids on the manuscript.

    Description of the Client from Hell: I haven't met one yet, but I don't like clients who send me manuscripts cold and then keep calling me about them before I have a chance to read them.

Description of Dream Client: One who writes blockbuster best-sellers and is patient.

Why did you become an agent? I sold my own books for 15 years. The next natural step was to sell books by others.

What might you be doing if you weren't an agent? Writing.

PERKINS ASSOCIATES

5800 Arlington Avenue, Suite 18J
Riverdale, NY 10471
212-304-1607
718-543-5344

Agents: Lori Perkins, Peter Rubie.

Born: Perkins: April 8, 1959; Rubie: May 3, 1950.

Education: Perkins: B.A., journalism, New York University, 1980. Rubie: journalism degree, NCTJ, England.

Career history: Perkins: Publisher and founder, *Uptown Dispatch*, an Upper Manhattan weekly; adjunct professor of journalism, New York University; agent with Barbara Lowenstein 1986–1989. Rubie: Fleet Street newspapers (England); BBC radio news (England); fiction editor, Walker & Company (New York City); book doctor (New York City); literary agent; published novelist and nonfiction writer.

Hobbies/personal interests: Perkins: Parenting, journal writing, modern art. Rubie: Movies, chess, politics/world affairs, music, science.

Subjects/categories most enthusiastic about agenting: Perkins: Pop culture, Hispanic culture and fiction, gay fiction and nonfiction. Rubie: Cutting-edge, well-characterized stories and strong nonfiction.

Subjects/categories not interested in agenting: Perkins: Westerns, screenplays, short stores, poems, romance. Rubie: Westerns, romance, children's.

Best way for a prospective client to initiate contact: Perkins: Query letter (with SASE). Rubie: Query letter (with SASE) and proposal.

Reading-fee policy: No reading fee.

Client representation in the following categories: Perkins: Nonfiction, 80%; Fiction, 20%; Rubie: Nonfiction, 75%; Fiction, 25%.

Commission: 15% domestic; 20% foreign.

Number of titles sold during the past year: Perkins: 50; Rubie: 40.

Approximate percentage of all submissions (from queries through manuscripts) that are rejected: Perkins: 99%; Rubie: 95%.

Representative titles sold:

Perkins:

Death Wore a Smart Little Outfit by Orland Outland (Berkley).

Darkness and Light: The Authorized Biography of Dean Koontz by Katherine Ransland (HarperCollins).

Future Noir: The Making of Blade Runner by Paul Sammon (HarperCollins).

Rubie:

Keeper by Greg Rucka (Bantam).

Sing the Light by Louise Ranley (Berkley).

How to Keep Your Cool with Your Kids by Lon Makarowski (Perigee).

How the Tiger Lost Its Stripes by Cory Meacham (Harcourt Brace).

Jaco by Bill Milkooski (Miller Freemand).

Witchhunter by Katheryn Lyon (Avon).

The most common mistakes potential clients make when soliciting an agent to represent them: Perkins: Too many projects to consider at once. Expects that once s/he has an agent, the book is sold. Rubie: Overly *cute* approach, putting form over substance, belligerent and aggressive, pleading and whining, unprofessional.

What writers can do to enhance their chances of getting an agent (besides being good writers): Perkins: They have researched the kind of books I do and know my abilities. Rubie: Strong, direct writing and story idea, simply but powerfully presented, and thorough professionalism.

Description of the Client from Hell: Perkins: Daily phone calls. A new project idea every day. Rubie: Unprofessional, unreal expectations, no knowledge of the publishing industry, calls every day for *news*, does not listen to advice, and a *control* freak.

Description of Dream Client: Perkins: Knows the market and how to present his/her material; takes editorial input well; has patience. Rubie: Calls every six weeks or so, works with agent as part of an effective team, responsive, responsible, thoroughly professional.

Why did you become an agent? Perkins: I love to read. Rubie: To help discover new talent and help further the careers of established writers. As a writer, I try to be the sort of agent *I* would like to have.

What might you be doing if you weren't an agent? Perkins: Running a newspaper. Rubie: Writing full time; music.

Comments: Perkins: I wish more writers considered themselves professionals and looked at their careers accordingly. Rubie: To understand my philosophy of writing, read my book *The Elements of Storytelling* (John Wiley, 1996).

JAMES PETER ASSOCIATES, INC.

P.O. Box 772
Tenafly, NJ 07670
201-568-0760
fax: 201-568-2959
e-mail: bholtje@attmail.com

Agent: Bert Holtje.

Born: February 24, 1931.

Education: B.S.; M.A., experimental psychology.

Career history: Founded James Peter Associates, Inc., in 1971. Author of 27 published books.

Hobbies/personal interests: Amateur radio, W2TQS; used to play clarinet, sax, and bass; history and politics; used to fly.

Subjects/categories most enthusiastic about agenting: All nonfiction, but especially interested in: history, politics, current affairs, pop culture, health, general reference, business, science, biography.

Subjects/categories not interested in agenting: Fiction, children's and young adult books.

Best way for a prospective client to initiate contact: Query letter (with SASE) with brief outline and description.

Reading-fee policy: No reading fee. Member of AAR (Association of Authors' Representatives).

Client representation in the following categories: Nonfiction, 100%.

Commission: 15% domestic, 20% foreign.

Number of titles sold during the past year: 33.

Approximate percentage of all submissions (from queries through manuscripts) that are rejected: 90%.

Representative titles sold:

Trade and reference titles:

Balance of Power: Power and Politics From the Era of McCarthy to the Age of Gingrich by Jim Wright, former Speaker, U.S. House of Representatives (Turner Publishing).

No Holds Barred: The Strange Life and Crimes of John DuPont by Carol Turkington (Turner Publishing).

Women's Guide to Self-Protection: Protecting Yourself Under the Law by Patricia Phillips, J.D., and George Mair (Macmillan).

The Coping Life Series by Frank Bruno, Ph.D. (Macmillan). Includes *Stop Worrying, Conquer Loneliness, Stop Procrastinating, Overcome Shyness, Defeat Depression, Get a Good Night's Sleep.*

Who Is Eleanor Rigby and 1,001 More Questions and Answers About the Beatles by Brandon Toropov (HarperCollins).

Great Cities to Get Started In by Sandra Gurvis (Macmillan).

The Complete Idiot's Guide to Getting the Job You Want by Marc Dorio (Macmillan).

The Complete Idiot's Guide to American History by Alan Axelrod (Macmillan).

The Complete Idiot's Guide to Wine by Philip Seldon (Macmillan).

The Art and Skill of Dealing with People by Brandon Toropov (Simon & Schuster).
Business books:

The Executive Assistant's Employment Almanac by Melba Duncan (McGraw-Hill).

The Business Communicator's Library by James Holtje (Simon & Schuster).

Talking It Out: The Supervisor's Instant Access Desk Reference by Ray Dreyfack (Prentice-Hall).

The most common mistakes potential clients make when soliciting an agent to represent them: Writers who send material that we don't handle.

What writers can do to enhance their chances of getting an agent (besides being good writers): Their own enthusiasm coupled with a realistic notion of the potential of their books.

Description of the Client from Hell: The client who refuses to ac[cept]
of commercial publishing today.

Description of Dream Client: A person with good ideas who ca[n]
clearly, entertainingly, and with enthusiasm.

Why did you become an agent? I like writing. I am the author of [2]
writers. And I like the give and take of negotiation.

What might you be doing if you weren't an agent? Be an architect.

Comments: *Don't print this!* Publishers are heading in the wrong dir[ec]
ing too much decision responsibility to sales and marketing people. Teach editors the
basics of marketing.

PMA LITERARY AND FILM MANAGEMENT, INC.

132 West 22nd Street, 12th Floor
New York, NY 10011
212-929-1222

Agent: Peter Miller.

Born: August 15, 1948.

Education: A.S., Atlantic Community College; B.A., Monmouth College.
Additional courses: MFA program, Rutgers University; NYU; and the New School.

Career history: Founded Writers House, a literary agency, 1972; founded the Peter
Miller Agency, 1974 and incorporated agency in 1981; founded PMA Literary and Film
Management, Inc., 1992. Have now been in business for 25 years.

Hobbies/personal interests: Traveling, gourmet food and wine, reading, fishing,
playing with my daughters (Jeanne and Margo).

Subjects/categories most enthusiastic about agenting: Action suspense fiction,
history, serious journalism and current events, pop culture.

Best way for a prospective client to initiate contact: A query letter written to my
attention detailing essence of the book and why it is commercial, along with biography
of the author.

Reading-fee policy: PMA does not have obligatory evaluation fee. However, if desired by an author, PMA has a non-obligatory evaluation and editorial service.

Client representation in the following categories: Nonfiction, 48%; Fiction, 49%;
Children's, 1%.

Commission: 15% domestic; 10–15% film rights; 20–25% foreign.

**Approximate percentage of all submissions (from queries through manuscripts)
that are rejected:** 90–95% of all unsolicited manuscripts are rejected.

Representative titles sold:

The Chieftains by John Glott (Random House U.K.).
The Killer's Game by Jay Bonansruga (Simon & Schuster).
The Fifth Canon by Michael Ebenhandt (Dutton).
Erotic Astrology by Olivia (Ballantine).
Women Behind Bars by Wensley Clarkson (St. Martin's).

Untitled investment book by David Newman (Simon & Schuster).

The most common mistakes potential clients make when soliciting an agent to represent them: Many authors express a negative attitude toward agents and the publishing industry in general. What a way to win your potential agent's confidence.

What writers can do to enhance their chances of getting an agent (besides being good writers): Professional, well-thought-out query letter with polished synopsis and/or manuscript presentation.

Description of the Client from Hell: The client sends you a handwritten manuscript and calls you every day to see if you have read it.

Description of Dream Client: A client who trusts your judgment and lets you work for them. After all, I've been selling books for 25 years and have sold over 700, so I must be doing something right.

Why did you become an agent? It happened, and I'm glad it did because I think I'm good at it.

What might you be doing if you weren't an agent? Be a publisher or film producer.

Comments: Writers, write on!

SUSAN ANN PROTTER, LITERARY AGENT

110 West 40th Street, Suite 1408
New York, NY 10018
212-840-0480

Agent: Susan Ann Protter.

Education: B.A., 1961; M.A., NYU, 1965.

Career history: French teacher, Lawrence High School, Cedarhurst, New York, 1963–1964; publishing assistant, *Report Magazine*, New York, 1964–1965; associate director, subsidiary rights department, Harper & Row Publishers Inc., 1966–1970; consultant, Addison-Wesley Publishers, Reading, MA, 1970–1971; founded Susan Ann Protter agency 1971.

Hobbies/personal interests: Sailing, opera, travel, movies, languages.

Subjects/categories most enthusiastic about agenting: Fiction: thrillers, mysteries, science fiction. Nonfiction: women's health, science, medicine, popular psychology, biography, parenting, how-to.

Subjects/categories not interested in agenting: Westerns and romance.

Best way for a prospective client to initiate contact: Query letter (with SASE).

Reading-fee policy: No reading fee.

Client representation in the following categories: Nonfiction, 40%; Fiction, 60%.

Commission: 15%.

Number of titles sold during the past year: 15.

Approximate percentage of all submissions (from queries through manuscripts) that are rejected: 96%.

Representative titles sold:

Freeware by Rudy Rucher (Morrow/AvoNova).

Life Happens by Kathleen McCoy, Ph.D. and Charles Wibblesman, M

Pirates of the Universe by Terry Bisson.

Strange Brains by Clifford A. Pickover (Plenum).

Beware the Butcher Bird by Lydia Adamson (Dutton).

Twenty Teachable Virtues by Barbara C. Unell and Jerry L. Wyckoff, Ph.D. (Perigee).

The most common mistakes potential clients make when soliciting an agent to represent them: When the query letter has clearly been written without the agent in mind but is some general overwritten pitch. Letters should be kept short and to the point, as we receive hundreds of them monthly. Also, a writer must include an SASE if they want a reply.

What writers can do to enhance their chances of getting an agent (besides being good writers): I appreciate it when the query letters are clear, to the point, and indicate how and why they have chosen this agency.

Description of the Client from Hell: Calls all the time and tells me how to run my business.

Description of Dream Client: A creative, disciplined writer with an ability to write with a clear audience in mind, who takes editorial comments and criticism constructively and delivers on time.

RAINES & RAINES

71 Park Avenue
New York, NY 10016
212-684-5160

Agents: Theron Raines, Joan Raines, Keith Korman.

Best way for a prospective client to initiate contact: One-page letter (with SASE).

Reading-fee policy: No reading fee.

Commission: 15% domestic, 20% foreign.

Approximate percentage of all submissions (from queries through manuscripts) that are rejected: Most.

Representative titles sold:

Works of Winston Groom (*Forrest Gump*).

Works of Cynthia Ozick.

Works of Roderick Thorp (*Die Hard*).

HELEN REES LITERARY AGENCY

308 Commonwealth Avenue
Boston, MA 02115
617-262-2401

Agent: Helen Rees.

Born: October 2, 1936.

Education: B.A., history, George Washington University.

Career history: Director of Office of Cultural Affairs, City of Boston (1978–1982); literary agent (1983 to present).

Hobbies/personal interests: Horseback riding, opera, theater, hiking.

Subjects/categories most enthusiastic about agenting: Literary fiction, history, psychology, business.

Subjects/categories not interested in agenting: Children's books, young adult, science fiction, poetry, cookbooks, gardening books, photography.

Best way for a prospective client to initiate contact: Query letter (with SASE) with 3 chapters and a synopsis.

Reading-fee policy: No reading fee.

Commission: 15% domestic; 20% foreign.

Number of titles sold during the past year: 14.

Approximate percentage of all submissions (from queries through manuscripts) that are rejected: 85%.

Representative titles sold:

The Advocate's Devil by Alan Dershowitz.

Bankruptcy 1995 by Harry Figgie.

Reengineering the Corporation by Michael Hammer and James Champy.

Thriving in Transition by Marcia Perkins-Reed.

The most common mistakes potential clients make when soliciting an agent to represent them: In a query letter, they unrealistically hype their material.

What writers can do to enhance their chances of getting an agent (besides being good writers): Produce an original idea and execute it well.

Description of the Client from Hell: Someone who sends a manuscript over and calls an hour later to see if I've read it.

Description of Dream Client: Someone who listens and is talented.

REMINGTON LITERARY ASSOCIATES, INC.

10131 Coors Road Northwest, Suite 12-886
Albuquerque, NM 87114
505-898-8305
fax: 505-890-0486
Jeffrey Poston pager: 505-884-4797

Agents: Kay Lewis Shaw (also known as "Happy" Shaw), Jeffrey A. Poston.

Born: Shaw: December 11, 1948. Poston: June 6, 1958.

Education: Shaw: B.S., art education, University of Georgia (1972). Poston: BSEE, aerospace science and engineering.

Career history: Shaw: In the 1970s, I taught art in public schools and for a private museum in northern Georgia. After moving to New Mexico in 1978, I taught private art lessons. In 1982, I became a founding member of Southwest Writers Works, went on to serve as its treasurer (twice), vice president and president in 1987. I began studying writing in 1982 and began teaching it professionally in 1988. I considered to be a master teacher of genre novel structure, and currently "Literature of New Mexico" for the University of New Mexico's Center on Aging's Elderhostel Programs. Poston: seventeen-year Air Force career, retired as an officer and engineer. Twelve-year fiction writing/speaking career.

Hobbies/personal interests: Shaw: I love going to the movies and analyzing why they work or not. When I have the time, I like to read for pleasure, decorate, sew, create artwork, and collect blue-and-white china and wicker furniture. Currently, I also teach for UNM's Elderhostel Programs because I love teaching people from all over about the West and about our popular authors who have lived or still do live in New Mexico. Poston: Outdoor, nature activities such as camping and hiking are always personal favorites. I also enjoy volleyball, in-line skate racing, movies, reading, and writing.

Subjects/categories most enthusiastic about agenting: Shaw: Remington represents all categories of adult and young-adult genre novels, but we are extremely selective in the horror genre. We also look at children's picture books and commercially targeted nonfiction for both adults and children. Poston: Fiction: I prefer action in almost any category but concentrate on Western, men/women's action-adventure, near-future science fiction and hard-core science fiction (especially Star Trek). Nonfiction: Self-help, computer, men's health/awareness.

Subjects/categories not interested in agenting: Shaw: No thrillers or horror written totally from the villain's point of view. No autobiographical novels from authors who have not studied writing. We would rather see material from writers who know what they have written—where it would go in a bookstore. It is extremely difficult to market something that is a little bit of this and a little bit of that. Poston: Sorry, but Romance makes me gag, although others in the agency accept that category.

Best way for a prospective client to initiate contact: Shaw: We would rather meet clients at writers' conferences or workshops or review novels in our annual Search for a Bestseller Contest. We do read all query letters and respond. However, please do not send material with your query letter. We will let you know if we want to see anything or not. We do not like phone queries, as many people can talk a story but cannot do anything on paper. Please send a professionally written business letter. We would prefer a mailed query rather than a faxed one. We use our fax for our clients' business concerns and would rather not have it tied up with receiving query letters. Poston: Send a query letter with a brief (2-page maximum) description of work. For nonfiction, include credentials. But, please, don't call unless I invite you to on my reply. I *always* respond to queries, usually in 2–3 weeks.

Reading-fee policy: Occasionally, we charge a $75 reading fee for materials sent in unsolicited. Normally, there is no reading fee if the author has been referred by an editor, other agent, a client, or we have met them at a writers' conference. If we read the partial once and it has lots of potential but also lots of problems, we give a critique but ask for the reading fee on the second time around *if* we are willing to look at it again. All of our clients pay a $150 marketing fee and any expenses that exceed that amount for postage, copying, or long distance calls. Clients receive copies of receipts, bills, etc., showing how their marketing fees are used. Rarely, we will edit material if it shows *exceptional* promise. Fees are based on the amount of work needed.

Client representation in the following categories: Nonfiction, 10%; Fiction, 60%; Children's 40%.

Commission: 15% domestic; 20% foreign; 20% movie, dramatic, electronic, and audio rights.

Number of titles sold during the past year: Remington produces its own newsletter, and a current list of titles sold may be obtained by writing the agency directly. Please enclose three first-class stamps to cover the postage on the newsletter.

Approximate percentage of all submissions (from queries through manuscripts) that are rejected: 90%.

Representative titles sold:

Please request our newsletter for a current list of titles sold. Please enclose three first-class stamps to cover the postage on the newsletter.

The most common mistakes potential clients make when soliciting an agent to represent them: Shaw: I really hate being told by the author that he or she is a wonderful writer. I am really turned off when someone isn't professional enough to enclose SASE with a query letter or partial submission that we are reviewing. I dislike writers who corner editors or agents at conferences. That really makes a bad impression all around. People who cannot take criticism should think about going into some other business. A writer should expect criticism from agents, editors, and readers, for that is the true nature of publishing one's work. If the person argues with an agent or editor, I have no desire to work with them as a client. Yes, it is always the author's work, but editors and agents are in the business of knowing what has a greater chance of selling and what doesn't.

Poston: Some writers seem to expect the agent to be their private personal editor. They get too personal in what should *always* start out as a business relationship. Especially, never get so personal that you submit incomplete or unprofessional work. This wastes your money and my time and can even damage the relationship.

What writers can do to enhance their chances of getting an agent (besides being good writers): Shaw: When I see a professionally written query that is followed up on my request by professionally presented material, I am excited, for I know that this person realizes that this is a business. If the person has studied writing from published writers rather than stated they have an English, creative writing, or journalism degree, I am even more excited, as no one can teach novelists, especially, how to handle their craft better than those who are successful at it. Degrees are great to improve your mind, but most academic teachers don't have a clue as to how to make their material accessible to the average bookbuyer.

Poston: When a writer realizes that I am first a businessman and also someone who can help them realize their goal of getting published, I really get excited, especially with new writers. It helps immensely when the writer realizes that agents aren't power-hungry, critical, writer bashers *only* looking for a best-seller.

Description of the Client from Hell: Shaw: The author claims to want an agent, but then doesn't let the agent do the job. People who do not realize that this is a business and call after normal business hours and drunk on top of that! People who must check with their *unpublished* friends on everything that the agent says. People who are untrusting, unprofessional, and downright rude. Remington weeds out anyone who proves to be any of these.

Poston: My Client from Hell falls into one of two categories: (1) He/she wants detailed critique/advice repeatedly at no charge. Or (2) he/she is unpublished, but can't accept criticism, preferring instead to defend every little word or counter every comment suggested that might make the work marketable. He/she wants an agent, then questions the agent's professionalism because that agent won't market the work *as is*.

Description of Dream Client: Shaw: All of our clients are now dream clients. They have no problem with revisions and tackle them in a highly professional manner. They produce quality work in correct format. They are polite, express thanks for any help that we give them, and are a delight to work with. If compromise is called for, they have no problem with talking and working through things. Poston: The dream client *wants* to get published and gracefully accepts criticism, even though it may be painful. This client realizes that he/she is the creator while we (the agency) are the polishers. These client work the win–win scenario and are willing to do whatever is necessary to get published without sacrificing the integrity of their creation (or themselves).

Why did you become an agent? Shaw: I've studied writing for over ten years and have been teaching it professionally for seven. Becoming an agent seemed to be a logical step. Poston: I have a personal mission to mentor people and help people achieve their goals. Of course, finding a potential bestseller helps a bit!

What might you be doing if you weren't an agent? Shaw: I would be a minister in the Church of Religious Science, or at least a practitioner, helping people to learn that life is a wonderful experience and how to turn negatives into positives. Or, I would be running a retreat center for creative people—writers and artists. Or, I would run a bookstore or an antique store. Or, I would be a best-selling author. Or, all of them. Poston: If I weren't an agent, I would spend more time being a writer.

Comments: Shaw: Writing professionally takes more than owning the latest computer equipment and putting words on paper. Like any professional business, publishing has its rules, taboos, and insider information. To believe in yourself is not enough. I have read hundreds of partials, etc., in the past year written by people who believe in themselves but don't have a clue as to what it takes to create salable work. If you want to succeed and become a published writer, study the craft in the area in which you wish to sell. Writing adult novels is different from writing for children, and nonfiction has its own structure. Why should anyone publish work that shows no awareness of what publishers feel they can sell to a book-buying reader? Commitment goes beyond belief in oneself. Commit to doing anything you have to do—buying writing books, taking classes, going to conferences, and writing, writing, writing until you *know*, not believe, it is publishable.

Finally, read. Read what it is that you say you want to write. I can't even count the number of times that people have said that they wanted to write a romance or a mystery or whatever, but when asked if they read that type of novel, they admitted that they did not. This seems an awful lot like saying that you want to fly planes so you take driving lessons. A multi-published novelist friend once told a group of writers, "Whatever time you have to write use half of it to read." Commit yourself to your profession. Nothing else works.

Poston: Remember, the writer's job is to create. The agent's job is to market. Try to consider objectively all comments by the agent to polish and improve your work. While every individual's opinions are unique, try to filter through the comments that are personal preferences of the agent and those that are based on sound judgment and experience. After all, the agents have their finger on the pulse of the publishing world—where you want your book to be. But, if you think you can write perfectly and don't want to rewrite, don't waste your time. Best-selling authors can get virtually any editor/agent/publisher they want, but they are all wise enough to accept professional critiques. Unless your agent proves to be incompetent, trust him/her and have faith in his/her judgment. Only then can he/she help you achieve your goal.

JUDITH RIVEN LITERARY AGENT

250 West 16th Street, 4F
New York, NY 10011
212-255-1009

Agent: Judith Riven.
  Education: B.A. and M.A.
  Career history: Twenty-four years in publishing; majority of them spent as an acquiring editor in various major trade publishing houses; have in-depth experience in both paperback and hardcover, reprint and original, fiction and nonfiction; have been agenting for $2\frac{1}{2}$ years.
  Subjects/categories most enthusiastic about agenting: Health, both conventional medical and alternative nutrition, practical or prescriptive. Nonfiction: Social issues, women's issues, narrative nonfiction, well-textured fiction with a strong emotional component, natural history, personal finance.
  Subjects/categories not interested in agenting: Science fiction, cyberpunk, gratuitous violence, romances.
  Best way for a prospective client to initiate contact: Query letter accompanied by SASE. *No SASE, no response.*
  Reading-fee policy: No reading fee. Standard expenses are billed back (copying, messengers, Federal Express, etc.).
  Client representation in the following categories: Nonfiction, 85%; Fiction, 15%.
  Commission: 15%.
  Number of titles sold during the past year: About 17.
  Approximate percentage of all submissions (from queries through manuscripts) that are rejected: 90–95%.
  Representative titles sold:
  Money Makeovers (Doubleday). A descriptive and prescriptive work on why women are more risk adverse about investing than are men.
  Breathe Right Now (W. W. Norton). A medical reference on breathing disorders.
  Wrath of Angels (Basic Books). A narrative (nonfiction) history of the anti-abortion movement.

The most common mistakes potential clients make when soliciting an agent to represent them: Anyone who tells me what a great opportunity is being offered me sets off a warning signal. The most costly mistake can be being aggressively persistent, as opposed to good follow-up.

What writers can do to enhance their chances of getting an agent (besides being good writers): A well-written query about a well-thought-out project by someone with strong credentials will always evoke an enthusiastic response from me.

Description of the Client from Hell: Someone who is unable to trust his/her agent or editor or publisher and consequently is always sure that not enough is being done for his/her work or that what is being done isn't being done properly.

Description of Dream Client: Someone with whom I have good chemistry, who is eager to make the project successful but respects boundaries, someone who can take direction or give it, who understands that the agent/client relationship is a collaboration that can be rewarding and fun for both.

Why did you become an agent? It was a natural segue from being an acquiring editor and I had been considering making the switch for some time.

What might you be doing if you weren't an agent? Editing.

Comments: If anyone is serious about writing a book, she has to be prepared for rejection; interminable delays; inadequate payment; and, often, poor distribution and display of the book once it's published. Everything beyond that is gravy.

ROSENSTONE/WENDER

Three East 48th Street
New York, NY 10017
212-832-8330

Agents: Phyllis Wender, Susan Cohen.

    Subjects/categories most enthusiastic about agenting: Adult and children fiction and nonfiction.

    Best way for a prospective client to initiate contact: Send letter of inquiry (with SASE).

    Reading-fee policy: No reading fee.

    Commission: 15% domestic, 20% foreign.

THE ROTH AGENCY

138 Bay State Road
Rehoboth, MA 02769
508-252-5818

Agent: Shelley Roth.

    Born: November 18, 1958, New York.

    Education: B.A., Brandeis University, summa cum laude; University of London.

Career history: Seventeen years in book publishing as in-house editor (Little, Brown, G.K. Hall); sales; freelance editor; agent. Also was professional folk musician.

Hobbies/personal interests: Books, film, Cajun and swing dancing, music (blues, folk, New Orleans, and Broadway), theater, psychology, biking, travel, gardening.

Subjects/categories most enthusiastic about agenting: A broad range of serious nonfiction including, in part, psychology, contemporary social issues, health, women's issues, investigative journalism, political and cutting-edge issues, music/theater/film, multicultural issues, popular culture, family and parenting, history, biography, nature and environment, excellent narrative nonfiction. Fiction: Literary and quality mainstream.

Subjects/categories not interested in agenting: Science fiction/futuristic, fantasy, action/adventure, espionage/technothrillers, Westerns, computer/technical.

Best way for a prospective client to initiate contact: Nonfiction: Query letter along with an SASE, brief annotated table of contents, author biography with publishing credits, submission history of proposal/manuscript. Fiction: Query letter along with an SASE, one-page (or less) plot synopsis, author biography with publishing credits, and submission history of manuscript. No phone calls, please.

Reading-fee policy: No reading fee.

Commission: 15% domestic; 20% foreign.

Approximate percentage of all submissions (from queries through manuscripts) that are rejected: 95%.

Representative titles sold:

How Good Parents Raise Great Kids by Dr. Alan Davidson (Warner).

The Legend of the Barefoot Mailman by John Fleming (Faber and Faber). Literary fiction.

Put Your Heart on Paper by Henriette Klauser (Bantam).

Are You Alone On Purpose? by Nancy Werlin (Houghton Mifflin).

The most common mistakes potential clients make when soliciting an agent to represent them: Phoning instead of querying by letter; giving a long and detailed account of their manuscript on the phone; sending an entire manuscript instead of the amount requested; no SASE.

What writers can do to enhance their chances of getting an agent (besides being good writers): The more writers know their market and audience, and the more they've familiarized themselves with the publishing process, the better. This, plus thoroughly researching the competition, is crucial for the new nonfiction writer. Let agents know how you were referred to them; whether you've published before; and, if so, where you've been published.

Comments: The concept as well as the execution of your manuscript (and, for nonfiction, the proposal) must both be excellent, or at least have the potential to be so. Quality writing, a professional attitude, and a sense of humor (you need one in this industry) are important. Credentials and writing credits are a definite plus.

For new writers: Read about publishing and talk to other writers to understand the quirks and nuances of the publishing business. For nonfiction writers: Learn all you can about writing proposals (from books on the subject, etc.) and send your best effort. Don't be lazy, or hasty, when making a first impression.

As of this writing, we're signing on more nonfiction than fiction. Our standards are high; any new fiction must be truly outstanding to distinguish itself from the pack.

PESHA RUBINSTEIN LITERARY AGENCY, INC.

1392 Rugby Road
Teaneck, NJ 07666
201-862-1174
fax: 201-862-1180

Agent: Pesha Rubinstein.
  Born: September 5, 1955.
  Education: B.A., Bryn Mawr College.
  Career history: 1990 to present, independent agent; 1981–1990, editor, Zebra Books; 1980–1981, editor, Leisure Books; 1979–1980, assistant, Rolling Stone Press; 1978–1979, assistant, Simon & Schuster.
  Hobbies/personal interests: My children, sewing, walking.
  Subjects/categories most enthusiastic about agenting: Commercial fiction and children's picture book artists.
  Subjects/categories not interested in agenting: Men's adventure, Westerns, young adult fiction, science fiction, poetry.
  Best way for a prospective client to initiate contact: Query letter (with SASE) and first 10 pages of manuscript.
  Reading-fee policy: No reading fee. Yes, photocopying reimbursement.
  Client representation in the following categories: Fiction, 70%; Children's, 30%.
  Commission: 15% domestic; 20% foreign.
  Number of titles sold during the past year: Approximately 25.
  Approximate percentage of all submissions (from queries through manuscripts) that are rejected: Most of them.
  Representative titles sold:
  Cheer Squad by Linda Joy Singleton (Avon). Middle-grade series.
  The Perfect Body by Amanda Maketsky (Harper Paperbacks).
  Clown Child by Amy Littlesugar (Philomel).
  The Eagle's Gift illustrated by Tatsuro Kiuchi (Putnam).
  Storyteller's Beads by Jane Kurtz (HB).
  Noble and Ivy by Carole Howey (Leisure).
  Romancing Anna by Nikki Rivers (Harlequin).
  Historical romances by Tanya Crosby (Avon).
  The most common mistakes potential clients make when soliciting an agent to represent them: Writers sometimes still submit manuscripts that are single-spaced and typed on both sides of the paper and don't enclose SASE! An author's costliest mistake, aside from the above, is misspelling words and not knowing how to use *lay* and *lie* properly.

What writers can do to enhance their chances of getting an agent (besides being good writers): I get a buzz from a clean manuscript that grabs me from the first paragraph.

Description of the Client from Hell: The one with horns and a tail.

Description of Dream Client: Prompt delivery of manuscript. One who accepts rather than fights constructive criticism. A client who understands that self-promotion is part of the writing process today.

Why did you become an agent? I need to be my own boss and there's nothing I love more than reading. Voilà! An agent is born!

What might you be doing if you weren't an agent? A tinker, a tailor, a soldier, a sailor . . .

Comments: Persist, persist, persist! Even with 30 rejections behind him/her, an author just has got to keep on writing. Good luck!

RUSSELL-SIMENAUER LITERARY AGENCY, INC.

P.O. Box 43267
Upper Montclair, NJ 07043
201-746-0539
201-992-4198
fax: 201-746-0754

Agents: Jacqueline Simenauer, Margaret Russell.

Born: Simenauer: February 23, 1948. Russell: December 8, 1949.

Education: Simenauer: Fordham University. Russell: M.A., Columbia University.

Career history: Simenauer: Editor, World Wide Features, Inc.; president, Psychiatric Syndication Service, Inc.; freelance writer and co-author: *Beyond the Male Myth* (Times Books), *Husbands and Wives* (Times Books), *Singles: The New Americans* (Simon & Schuster), *Not Tonight Dear* (Doubleday). Russell: Director of publicity, Ticknor & Fields; director of publicity, Basic Books; associate director of publicity, Simon and Schuster; co-author *Nachemia: German and Jew in the Holocaust* (New Horizon Press).

Hobbies/personal interests: Simenauer: Traveling the world. Russell: Music, gardening.

Subjects/categories most enthusiastic about agenting: Popular psychology by psychologists and psychiatrists, how-to/self-help, women's issues, health, alternative health concepts, fitness, medical, diet, nutrition, current issues, true crime, business, celebrities, specialized cookbooks.

Literary and mainstream commercial fiction. First novels welcome.

We are willing to handle any subject that we consider suitable for the general public where the author has the expertise and the credentials.

Subjects/categories not interested in agenting: Poetry, crafts.

Best way for a prospective client to initiate contact: By query letter (with SASE) with a good description of the book.

Reading-fee policy: No reading fee. We will read all material submitted to us free of charge. We do have a special Breakthrough Program for the first-time author who would like an in-depth critique of his/her work by our freelance editorial staff. There is a charge of $2 per page for this service, and it is *completely optional.*

Client representation in the following categories: Nonfiction, 98%; Fiction, 2%.
Commission: 15%
Number of titles sold during the past year: 25.
Approximate percentage of all submissions (from queries through manuscripts) that are rejected: 95%.
Representative titles sold:
The Benzo Blues by Edward Drummond, M.D. NAL/Dutton).
The Joys of Fatherhood by Marcus J. Goldman, M.D. (Prima).
The Endometriosis Sourcebook by the Endometriosis Association (Contemporary Books).
The Healing Mind by Eileen Oster (Prima).
The Bride's Guide to Emotional Survival by Rita Bigel-Casher, Ph.D. (Prima).

The most common mistakes potential clients make when soliciting an agent to represent them: A hand-written, practically illegible query letter; a carelessly typed, single-spaced, and/or incomplete query or proposal; the handing down of a time limit, usually nonviable, for the sale of his/her work to a publisher; the stipulation of daily updates on the status of the manuscript. These are all costly mistakes because we usually will not handle manuscripts under these circumstances.

What turns you on? Wit and warmth do wonders. The terrific presentation of ideas and excellent credentials do even bigger wonders.

Description of the Client from Hell: Arrogant writer who doesn't understand why his manuscript wasn't snapped up by a publisher yesterday, and who doesn't understand why agents "deserve" commission.

Description of Dream Client: We have lots of them!

Why did you become an agent? Simenauer: To paraphrase Douglas MacArthur, "Old editors never die; they just become literary agents." Russell: Having been triple threats as publicist, editor, and author, I thought I would combine them and become formidable.

What might you be doing if you weren't an agent? Simenauer: An investment banker. Russell: A bed-and-breakfast host on Cape Cod.

Comments: Simenauer: Literary agents are more often than not yanked between the demands of the authors and the demands of the publishing houses, finding themselves rendering services *above and beyond,* which often goes unappreciated. That is when I think of becoming an investment banker. Russell: Any writer who doesn't love Mozart need not apply to the Russell-Simenauer Literary Agency.

RUSSELL & VOLKENING, INC.

50 West 29th Street, #7E
New York, NY 10001
212-684-6050

Agents: Joseph Regal, Jennie Dunham.

Education: Regal: English, magna cum laude, Columbia College. Dunham: Princeton University (anthropology major).

Career history: Regal: entire career spent with Russell Volkening. Dunham: Before getting my position at Russell and Volkening, I worked for John Brockman Associates and Mildred Marmur Associates. I have always been on the agency side of the business.

Hobbies/personal interests: Regal: music (classical, jazz, hard rock, blues, etc.), sports (basketball, tennis, running), art, and, of course, books. Also interested in science, especially as it applies to the nature of time and the physics of our existence.

Dunham: book arts and paper making, movies, photography, Old English, language and linguistics, feminist/women's studies, travel, science, and religion.

Subjects/categories most enthusiastic about agenting: Regal: mainly interested in fiction, both literary and crime, but no romance or science fiction (which I like but do not agent). Also a fan of well-written nonfiction that tells me something about our culture or another culture—exploration of who we are and what our future promises (or threatens). Dunham: quality fiction, nonfiction, children's.

Subjects/categories not interested in agenting: Regal: no romance or science fiction, no poetry (agents are more or less useless in that field); I also don't do screenplays or plays, though I do handle those rights if they stem from a book I represent. Dunham: romance, science fiction, poetry, horror, individual short stories.

Best way for a prospective client to initiate contact: Query letter (with SASE) and short description of the book. Dunham: Write a letter describing the project and the author's qualifications for the project and enclose the customary SASE for a response. If the project seems as if I might be interested, I will request it. Please do not send sample material unless requested.

Reading-fee policy: No reading fee. When we receive money for a client, we recover expenses we incur which specifically related to projects by the author. For example, we will recover the cost of sending copies of an author's books abroad to coagents or for photocopying.

Client representation in the following categories: Regal: Nonfiction, $33 1/3$%; Fiction, $66 2/3$%; Dunham: Nonfiction, 40%; Fiction, 25%; Textbooks, 5%; Children's, 30%.

Commission: 10% domestic; 15% motion picture or other dramatic contracts; 20% foreign.

Number of titles sold during the past year: 10.

Approximate percentage of all submissions (from queries through manuscripts) that are rejected: Regal: 98%; Dunham: the majority.

The most common mistakes potential clients make when soliciting an agent to represent them: Regal: I immediately stop reading if someone sends a query letter telling me they have written the next big best-seller. Also, if they have a long, profitable career ahead of them and seek a like-minded agent to act in synergy—well, who is seeking a dysfunctional, unprofitable relationship? I am also ever amazed at the number of query letters that arrive with typos. What kind of writer pays so little attention to his/her writing? Dunham: In this day of computers, I think it's a mistake to send a form query letter without a specific person's name in the salutation. Also, sometimes writers address agents familiarly as if they knew them, which really should be reserved for people who do know them personally.

What writers can do to enhance their chances of getting an agent (besides being good writers): Regal: many queries are clever, with multicolored paper clips or exciting stationery, et cetera, but in the end, the only thing that matters is the idea and the writing. If that is there and is clearly presented, I am enthusiastic. Dunham: Professionalism, good writing, and good ideas.

Description of the Client from Hell: Regal: There is no Client from Hell. I am straightforward with each client from the start and so far that has prevented any impossible expectations or enraging situations. It can be annoying when someone is not aware of the limitations of the agent's powers: If an editor does not want to buy the book, we cannot make him or her buy it. Dunham: The client from hell is the exact opposite of the dream client—unproductive, unsuccessful, uninteresting, and unpleasant.

Description of Dream Client: Again, there is no Dream Client; we are all human and by and large rational creatures. I do prefer clients who are realistic about their writing and the market. Dunham: A client who is productive, successful, interesting, and pleasant is a good client.

Why did you become an agent? Regal: I've always loved books, and in an agent's position I get to be more involved with every stage of the writing and development and publication than in any other job. It excites me to look for the next John Irving, or even to know that I have eased a writer's life and made them feel safe and comfortable. Dunham: I collect books, and as an agent I like helping bring books to the world. I like the variety of book projects I handle as an agent. I receive great satisfaction in protecting authors by negotiating contracts for them. Ever since my first job as an agent, I knew that this is what I wanted for a career.

What might you be doing if you weren't an agent? Regal: Selling vacuum cleaners door-to-door. Dunham: Maybe I would be an anthropologist or a professor (English/folklore/communications). Maybe I would try to do business in a foreign country.

Comments: Regal: I would like to plug small agencies. (Here I admit that Russell & Volkening, founded in 1940, has only three agents). I can understand why writers would be attracted to bigger agencies—the lure of being at a place with 30 other best-selling authors, the lure of having legions of people working on various rights for you—but I strongly believe small agencies serve writers better. When I represent an author, I am involved with every aspect of his/her career. S/he is not a little fish in a big sea, nor are other people who may not like his/her book as much as I do working on various rights. When I make a commitment to a writer, it is more serious (and thus we choose more carefully) than if an agent with 50 other authors decides to try you and see how it goes. The relationship between author and agent is probably the most important in the business these days, and you should make sure that you have a communicative, honest, dedicated agent and that the connection is fulfilling.

THE SAGALYN LITERARY AGENCY

4825 Bethesda Avenue, Suite 302
Bethesda, MD 20814
301-718-6440
fax: 301-718-6444

Agent: Raphael Sagalyn.

   Best way for a prospective client to initiate contact: Send a cover letter.

   Representative titles sold:

   The Invention That Changed the World: A History of Radar by Robert Buderi (Simon & Schuster).

   The Moral Animal by Robert Wright (Pantheon).

   Rising Ride: The Mississippi River Flood of 1927 by John Barry (Simon & Schuster).

   The Second Curve by Dr. Ian Morrison (Ballantine).

   Bowling Alone by Professor Robert D. Putnam (Simon & Schuster).

   The Individualized Corporation by Christopher Bartlett and Sumantra Ghoshal (Harper Business).

   Two untitled novels by David Ignatius (Random House).

Victoria Sanders Literary Agency

241 Avenue of the Americas
New York, NY 10014
212-633-8811

Agent: Victoria Sanders.

   Born: November 21, 1960.

   Education: B.F.A., New York University, 1983; J.D., Benjamin N. Cardozo School of Law, 1988.

   Career history: WNET/Channel 13 (PBS); Simon & Schuster Inc.; Carol Mann Agency; Charlotte Sheedy Agency; founded own agency in 1992.

   Subjects/categories most enthusiastic about agenting: Fiction: literary and commercial. Nonfiction: history biography, politics, sociology, psychology. Special interests: African-American, Latin, women's, gay and lesbian work.

   Subjects/categories not interested in agenting: Hard science, children's, textbooks.

   Best way for a prospective client to initiate contact: Query letter with SASE.

   Reading-fee policy: No reading fee.

   Client representation in the following categories: Nonfiction, 50%; Fiction, 50%.

   Commission: 15% straight; 20% if coagented foreign; 20% if coagented to film, TV (though I tend to handle my own, and then it's 15%).

   Approximate percentage of all submissions (from queries through manuscripts) that are rejected: 90%.

   Representative titles sold:

   Sisters and Lovers by Connie Briscoe (HarperCollins). Commercial novel.

   Big Girls Don't Cry by Connie Briscoe (HarperCollins). Commercial novel.

   Bertice: The World According to Me by Dr. Bertice Berry (Scribner). Inspirational memoir.

   Flight of the Blackbird by Faye McDonne Smith (Scribner). Commercial fiction.

   He Say/She Say by Yolanda Joe (Doubleday). Commercial fiction.

Caribe by Evangline Bianco (Doubleday). Literary fiction.

The most common mistakes potential clients make when soliciting an agent to represent them: Don't query if you are unsure or hesitant about submitting without additional information on the agency or current clients.

What writers can do to enhance their chances of getting an agent (besides being good writers): The project is the most important part. A good novel or nonfiction project idea is always exciting.

Why did you become an agent? It's the best of both worlds. I get to read manuscripts and negotiate deals. I came from L.A. and film, and, after getting a law degree, realized that the best part of the entertainment business was in bridging the gap between the writer or artist and the producer or publisher. I love being the representative and friend of my clients.

What might you be doing if you weren't an agent? A producer.

HAROLD SCHMIDT LITERARY AGENCY

343 West 12th Street, Suite 1B
New York, NY 10014
212-727-7473

Agent: Harold Schmidt.
   Born: Cincinnati, Ohio.
   Education: University of Southern California, B.A., and graduate studies.
   Career history: Creative Management Associates, 1974–1975; International Creative Management, 1975–1979; William Morris Agency, Inc., 1979–1983.
   Subjects/categories not interested in agenting: Juveniles, romances.
   Best way for a prospective client to initiate contact: Please send a query with SASE before submitting manuscript.
   Reading-fee policy: No reading fee.
   Client representation in the following categories: Nonfiction, 40%; Fiction, 60%.
   Commission: 15% of domestic, dramatic; 20% on U.K. and foreign translation.
   Approximate percentage of all submissions (from queries through manuscripts) that are rejected: 98%.
   Representative titles sold:
   The Gangster of Love by Jessica Hagedorn (Houghton Mifflin).
   Coming Out of Shame by Gershen Kaufman and Lev Raphael (Doubleday).
   The Outer World by John Wynne (City Lights).
   The Gifts of the Body by Rebecca Brown (HarperCollins).
   How to Start and Run a Successful Consulting Business by Gregory and Patricia Kishel (John Wiley).
   The most common mistakes potential clients make when soliciting an agent to represent them: Sending manuscripts without being asked. Calling to pitch their books.
   What writers can do to enhance their chances of getting an agent (besides being good writers): A detailed, carefully thought-out and professionally presented query letter is very important.

Description of the Client from Hell: A client with unrealistic expectations about his work and/or a client who is too impatient with the amount of time it takes to evaluate material, find a publisher, and negotiate an agreement.

What might you be doing if you weren't an agent? I am confident I would be involved with books and probably motion pictures in one capacity or another. And there's a part of me that has always wanted to own a used-book store.

SEBASTIAN LITERARY AGENCY

333 Kearny Street, Suite 708
San Francisco, CA 94108
415-391-2331

Agent: Laurie Harper.
   Born: September, 1954.
   Education: Business and finance, with pre-law studies.
   Career history: The literary agency was founded in 1985. It evolved simultaneously with the closing of my small Bay Area regional publishing company (Sebastian Publishing), which published gift books, selling to B. Dalton, Waldenbooks, and independents throughout the West Coast. After I placed books with other publishers for authors I could not publish, I discovered my strengths as an agent. I briefly experienced the author's side of publishing (very enlightening) writing a media biography of a legendary radio personality (*Don Sherwood: The Life and Times of the World's Greatest Disc Jockey,* Prima Publishing, 1989), which enjoyed 12 weeks on the *San Francisco Chronicle's* best-seller list. Prior to publishing, I was in banking (operations and lending) with a major California bank for 8 years.
   Hobbies/personal interests: Apparently my real interests simply lie with people: who they are, what they are doing, where they have been, how they think. My insatiable curiosity is about how people live their lives, whether shown in books, film, the arts, or as discussed in local cafes. Being an agent is not only what I do, it's who I am in the sense that it reflects my true interests.
   Subjects/categories most enthusiastic about agenting: Business (management, financial/investment, entrepreneurial, career issues, marketing and sales, human resource), biographies (historical, media-related, professional, or political; not family memoirs), consumer reference, health/nutrition, psychology/self-help, gift/inspirational, popular culture, social issues/current affairs, humor, sports.
   Subjects/categories not interested in agenting: No fiction at this time. No poetry, children's or young adult, original screenplays, New Age, or scholarly.
   Best way for a prospective client to initiate contact: Please send a query letter explaining the project, who you are, and why you are doing this book. Feel free to include the proposal, outline, and a sample chapter. And, of course, the SASE. I do not want phone calls unless the author has been referred to me by a client or colleague.
   Reading-fee policy: No reading fee or *editorial* fee. I do charge my clients a $100 annual administration fee, which is a nominal contribution to phone and postage ex-

penses incurred on their behalf, which I do not charge back. Once a client has earnings, the annual fee is rarely charged.

Client representation in the following categories: Nonfiction, 99%; Fiction, 1%.

Commission: 15% domestic; 20–25% foreign translation licensing, depending on the territory/subagent; 20% dramatic/film licensing.

Number of titles sold during the past year: It usually averages 15–20.

Approximate percentage of all submissions (from queries through manuscripts) that are rejected: 95%. The majority of new clients come from referrals from my clients or industry professionals and colleagues. However, every submission is read and considered on its own merit.

Representative titles sold:

Good Intentions: The Nine Unconscious Mistakes of Nice People by Duke Robinson (Warner).

David Copperfield's Tales of the Impossible created by Janet Berliner, coedited by Janet Berliner and David Copperfield (Harper Collins/Prism). Two-volume fiction anthology.

The Little Book of Big Profits by William Buchsbaum (Macmillan).

Opal: The Diary of an Understanding Heart by Opal Whiteley, adapted by Jane Boulton (Crown/Clarkson Potter).

Eating Well for a Healthy Menopause by Elaine Moquette-Magee (John Wiley).

Natural Beauty for All Seasons by Janice Cox (Henry Holt).

Virtual Meetings: How New Technologies Are Changing the Way We Meet and Work by James Creighton and James Adams (AMACOM).

A Crisis of Spirit: Our Search for Integrity by Anita Spence, Ph.D. (Plenum/Insight Books).

Grandmothers Are Like Snowflakes: No Two Are Alike by Janet Lanese (Dell).

Index Mutual Funds by Jerry Tweddell and Jack Pierce (AMACOM).

The most common mistakes potential clients make when soliciting an agent to represent them: It is a costly mistake to use anything other than the current year's resource material when exploring potential agents. Too many changes in the constant motion of publishing and agencies to use last year's guide. It is also counterproductive to query without providing the agent sufficient orientation and information. We are reading the proposal cold. The author has to make it make sense; give it a proper framework. Demonstrate that you know the market for your book: what's been published, how your book fits into the scheme of things. You must answer the obvious questions: Who cares? Why? Are these book-buying people? How many are there? Can anyone find them? What do you specifically have to offer a publisher who would invest in this project? Publishing is, after all, first and foremost a business . . . not an endowment for the arts or for hobbyists.

What writers can do to enhance their chances of getting an agent (besides being good writers): A solid, well-thought-out and well-written package that presents a professional, intelligent book and author. Even if I can't take that author, I will try to give the professional writer information or suggestions for other agents.

Description of the Client from Hell: The first thing has to be unrealistic expectations; financial and promotional expectations that are simply not realistic for as-yet-unproven authors. For previously unpublished authors, it's understandable that they don't know the industry, but it is incumbent on each prospective author to inform him/herself of the basics. Attend some conferences; do some reading; talk to other published authors. I'm happy to coach an author about strategy or problem solving, to help plan out a realistic publishing career path, but the agent can't be in charge of teaching Publishing 101. Another difficulty comes if the author expects the agent to perform miracles: We can't sell what isn't salable. It is the author's responsibility to consider and reflect on the feedback given by agents and publishers, and to use that to improve the manuscript's potential for publication. I expect my clients to be mature professional adults, capable of approaching this process positively and constructively. No whining allowed.

Description of Dream Client: I fortunately have many. They can be described as committed; deeply thoughtful and caring, both about the writing of their books and about cultivating all the relationships inherent in a publishing *team;* honest and straightforward in their dealings; responsible in doing what they promise, when they promise it. This client is mindful and appreciative of the fact that the agent represents many clients and the editors have many authors, each of whom expect and deserve honest, focused, productive efforts to be made on their behalf. These clients make it all worthwhile, for everyone, and we go the extra mile for them.

Why did you become an agent? I love books-reading and learning, and I enjoy each of the diverse challenges of publishing. Books are fundamental to our society, and I take pride in being part of their contribution. There is enormous satisfaction from creating a successful team—making the right match between author and publisher, negotiating a fair contract that promotes a successful venture, and assisting in every way to build long-lasting relationships.

What might you be doing if you weren't an agent? I would most likely be in contract law, perhaps working for the Authors Guild.

Comments: There is much that can be criticized and ridiculed in this industry. It's no secret that it isn't a well-run business, per se, or that there is precious little logic to it. But it is a constantly evolving business and each of us in it are charged with making our own contribution, as authors, agents, or publishers. It serves no constructive purpose to sit around bashing and trashing everything that goes wrong. I would like to see and hear more about what goes right and see a greater sharing of helpful information and experience. If you don't like the challenges of publishing, don't do it. If you enjoy the challenge, make a contribution to the best interests it serves. Don't worry about what everyone else does or doesn't do; do what you think is right and good.

THE SEYMOUR AGENCY

17 Rensselaer Avenue
Heuvelton, NY 13654
315-344-7223
fax: 315-344-7223

Agents: Mary Sue Seymour, Michael J. Seymour.
  Born: MSS: September 21, 1952. MJS: August 19, 1948.

Education: MSS: B.S., State University at Potsdam, New York; postgraduate work with Potsdam State, Ithaca College, Azusa Pacific College. MJS: B.S., Siena College, NY; M.S., St. Lawrence University; M.A., SUNY at Potsdam.

Career history: MSS: Taught 11 years in the public school system; professional artist; currently teach part-time; freelance writer published in several national magazines. MJS: Taught over 20 years; columnist for newspaper group and regional editor for a magazine; Coast Guard captain—run fishing charter service seasonally.

Hobbies/personal interests: MSS: Piano, reading, alpine skiing, swimming, hiking, camping in the Adirondacks(!). MJS: Fishing, hunting—and then there's writing about fishing and hunting.

Subjects/categories most enthusiastic about agenting: Both agents: any women's fiction or romance; non-fiction proposals of any type; any quality fiction.

Subject/categories not interested in agenting: children's books, screenplays, short stories.

Best way for a prospective client to initiate contact: one- to two-page query letter with first three chapters and a three- to four-page synopsis. (Enclose SASE.)

Reading-fee policy: *No* reading fee, handling fee, management fee, or charge for office expenses (phone calls).

Client representation in the following categories: Nonfiction 25%, Fiction 75%.

Commission: 15% prepublished authors (commission for our published authors is negotiable); 20% foreign sales.

Number of titles sold during the past year: Several.

Approximate percentage of all submissions (from queries to manuscripts) that are rejected: 90%.

Representative titles sold:
Warrior Bride by Tamara Leigh (Bantam, lead title).
Virgin Bride by Tamara Leigh (Bantam Fanfare).
Pagan Bride by Tamara Leigh (Bantam Fanfare).
Saxon Bride by Tamara Leigh (Bantam Fanfare).
Fools' Paradise by Tori Phillips (Harlequin Historicals). Maggie Winner!
Silent Knight by Tori Phillips (Harlequin Historicals).
Whispers of the River by Tom Hron (Signet).
Whispers of the Mountain by Tom Hron (Signet).
Whispers of the Wind by Tom Hron (Signet).
Summer of Fire by Jill Shaluis (Robinson Publishing, London, England).
Color Me Loved by Jill Shaluis (Robinson Publishing, London, England).

Description of the Client from Hell: Never had one.

Description of Dream Client: A Dream Client is one who writes a lot, uses suggestions, is enthusiastic about her/his writing, appreciates what we try to do for him/her, and sends us a book we can sell.

The most common mistakes potential clients make when soliciting an agent to represent them: Unfocused queries, sending samplings of various chapters, faxing queries instead of enclosing SASE with correspondence.

What writers can do to enhance their chances of getting an agent (besides being good writers): A dynamic lead, dark print with easy to read type, focused query, realistic expectations, and professionalism.

Why did you become an agent? We are published authors and have had agency representation from three different agencies and left. We knew something about the profession, judged writing contests, and wanted to help those "almost" writers get started.

What might you be doing if you weren't an agent? MSS: giving private piano lessons; a professional watercolorist. MJS: teaching full-time.

Comments: Thousands of musicians are out of work in this country but that doesn't diminish the quality of their music. Rejections don't diminish writers as people. Writing is a process. If you are willing to stay with it and endure the frustration of constant rewrites, you might make it. Not everyone gets a book published, but no one can accurately predict who will and who won't.

THE ROBERT E. SHEPARD AGENCY

4111 18th Street, Suite 3
San Francisco, CA 91114
415-255-1097

Agent: Robert Shepard.

Born: 1961, Ridgewood, New Jersey.

Education: B.A. and M.A., English, University of Pennsylvania.

Career history: After writing speeches and doing research for a prominent professor of urban studies, I clawed my way into trade publishing, remaining at Addison-Wesley for nearly nine years. I spent time on the editorial, sales, and marketing sides of the business (ultimately in charge of a multimillion-dollar sales department), and later did some business consulting. But I missed my literary roots and am glad to be working with authors again.

Hobbies/personal interests: Hiking, biking, trains, and diagramming sentences.

Subjects/categories most enthusiastic about agenting: Nonfiction: especially subjects from the *social science* side of the aisle; current affairs, sociology, psychology, sexuality (especially gay/lesbian nonfiction), health, history, biography, business, and the *soft* side of science. But I regularly digress.

Subjects/categories not interested in agenting: I love fiction but do not represent it. In general, I stay away from works aimed solely at professional or academic audiences, and I'm extremely wary of collections and highly autobiographical works—although sometimes I can be convinced.

Best way for a prospective client to initiate contact: E-Mail (<sfbiblio@ well.com>) is the best way. Otherwise, query letter (with SASE).

Reading-fee policy: No reading fee.

Client representation in the following categories: Nonfiction, 100%; Fiction, 0%.

Commission: 15% domestic.

Number of titles sold during the past year: 7. The practice is young, but I intend to keep the client base small in any case. I am happy to work with new authors (or with published authors who are new to the trade side of publishing) and am glad to put in the time to cultivate strong proposals.

Approximate percentage of all submissions (from queries through manuscripts) that are rejected: 95%.

Representative titles sold:

New Men: Inside the Lives of American Seminarians at the Vatican (Grosset/Putnam).

The TwentySomething Guide to Creative Self-Employment (Prima).

Wild and Outside (Walker). Literary nonfiction about baseball.

The Healing Art of T'ai Chi (Sterling).

The most common mistakes potential clients make when soliciting an agent to represent them: A big one is failing to share the proposal with a friend, another writer, or a trusted advisor before sending it out. Not to sound like the English teacher I sometimes think I should have been, but bad spelling and grammar spell doom. And a loyal ally can sometimes give you valuable feedback. I also dislike the classic proposal clichés: "There is no competition," "This is just like a Tracy Kidder/Peter Mayle/Martha Stewart/Tom Peters book," etc. And I require SASE, but I hate to put that in the same league.

What writers can do to enhance their chances of getting an agent (besides being good writers): Go to a good, independent bookstore. It's essential for authors to have some perspective on their work, and that means knowing all about books that are similar, or that an agent might mistake as being similar, and (in another vein) being able to talk about authors you respect whose work is in some ways akin to yours. There's nothing more helpful to me than a short overview that answers questions like these: Why did you write this book? What need does it fill? What audience do you envision? What are some books like yours, even if they are terrible (and say why)? Why are you the right person to write this book? What would you like your work to achieve that hasn't been achieved before? Browsing in bookstores, and buying and reading a few recent works, can be very helpful as you answer those questions. I recommend libraries, too, but it's essential to stay current.

Description of the Client from Hell: One who's good at selling an agent or editor on a book but doesn't want to actually write it. Writing is tough and an agent tries to help, but in the end the responsibility is the author's.

Description of Dream Client: One who is passionate about writing, passionate about his or her subject, and appreciative when things go right.

Why did you become an agent? I love books and believe they can and should still be central to our cultural life. But at a time when we're producing ever more titles, I think many of them are poorly crafted, in every sense. I see authors who still feel the creative urge but whose experiences in publishing have soured them to the whole enterprise, and I see editors who love what they do but feel overextended and underappreciated in the difficult business climate of the 1990s. In such an environment, I think an agent can be more than just someone who sells books, but rather one who can restore the health to some of those relationships that, for better or worse, are keys to the *business* of publishing. I try to create ongoing author–editor dialogues and play the role of moderator when it's helpful or necessary. When everything works, we can end up with books that are well written, well edited, and well marketed, and everyone can walk away ready and enthusiastic to do it again.

be doing if you weren't an agent? It could go one of three ways:
k and get that Ph.D. and write papers on nineteenth-century au-
1ely prominent in their day but paradoxically have become to-
due to bad marketing), or I would be conducting a symphony
riding trains somewhere in an attempt to escape my job as pub-
terary nonfiction house. I'm not picky.

LEE SHORE AGENCY, LTD.

Sterling Building
440 Friday Road
Pittsburgh, PA 15209
412-821-0440
800-898-7886 (for brochure and guidelines requests *only*)
e-mail: LeeShore1@aol.com
Website: http://www.olworld.com/olworld/m_1shore/ (use for instant access to brochure and guidelines)

Agent: Cynthia Sterling.
Born: June 21, 1953; Johnstown, Pennsylvania.
Education: University of Pittsburgh.
Career history: Departmental assistant of nuclear medicine and cardiopulmonary functions; writing instructor.
Hobbies/personal interests: Chairman for Sterling Foundation (nonprofit, tax exempt), which assists writers and artists; authoring and coauthoring on a variety of subjects; collecting art and antiques; gardening.
Subjects/categories most enthusiastic about agenting: Trade, textbooks, scholarly, good fiction, both mass-market and genre; true stories.
Subjects/categories not interested in agenting: Children's, poetry, plays, articles.
Best way for a prospective client to initiate contact: Phone, personal letter with brief synopsis, stop by office (an appointment is necessary).
Reading-fee policy: No fee for established authors. $125 evaluation fee for unpublished writers.
Client representation in the following categories: Nonfiction, 34%; Fiction, 55%; Textbooks, 10%; Children's, 1%.
Commission: 15% domestic; 20% foreign.
Number of titles sold during the past year: 65.
Approximate percentage of all submissions (from queries through manuscripts) that are rejected: 80%.
Representative titles sold:
The View from Rampart Street by Mary Lou Widmer (Pelican Publishing).
Against All Odds by Bill Shanklin (Barclay House).
Hero's Journey in Literature by Evans Lansing Smith (University Press of America).
Una's Song by Megan Davidson (Zebra).

Hell's Creation by John Russo (Ravenmor).

End the Pain by Dr. Lynn Hawker and Terry Bicehouse (Zinn Publishing Group).

Getting Your Manuscript Sold by Sterling and Davidson (Barclay).

The Rescue of Jennifer Lynn (made-for-TV movie) (Benchmark Pictures).

The most common mistakes potential clients make when soliciting an agent to represent them: Maybe it's that maturity thing, but around this agency we give all writers the benefit of the doubt. After all, not all the advice or information the writer receives from many sources is necessarily the way the real world works. Once in a while, I'll read to the staff a letter that is particularly off-base. We'll all shake our heads, then give the writer the same polite consideration we give all prospective clients.

What writers can do to enhance their chances of getting an agent (besides being good writers): Have a professional approach with respect for my time and expertise—a rarity indeed.

Description of the Client from Hell: Once upon a time I could give a vivid description of clients from both Heaven and Hell. After being in the business as long as I have, meeting the people I've met, and traveling to various countries in pursuit of manuscripts and education, I suppose I've grown a little wiser. Now I see my clients as people who, for their own set of reasons, act and react the way they do. I try to communicate clearly both my praises and my concerns regarding their attitude and listen to their concerns as well. After all, in the end, the client has the choice to seek representation elsewhere. I'm proud to say that most clients choose to stay with us.

Description of Dream Client: I would describe my dream client as being John Grisham, or Stephen King, or Tom Clancy, or any top-selling author of their caliber. If they're looking for an agent, I'm here. (I can dream, can't I?) Now, back to an obtainable dream. A dream client is one who, first and foremost, can write; knows his audience; is willing to learn rules and play by them; has a business side; can talk with (not to) his agent; understands that there are certain things in the industry that just *are* and cannot be changed, thereby making some points nonnegotiable; who is courteous, friendly, has a sense of humor, sends me expensive gifts, and realizes that I am the Queen. . . . I just slid way back to La La Land.

Why did you become an agent? My main purpose is to establish a writers' and artists' retreat. To do so, I needed to understand everything about writers, publishers, distributors, the art of writing, and running a business. The agent is like the hub in a wheel: As the wheel turns, each spoke brings in new information.

What might you be doing if you weren't an agent? I'd be an author full-time, taking another path to establish the writers' and artists' retreat.

Comments: Writing is a creative process, of course, but writing is also a craft. To learn that craft takes time, patience, and courage. The road to mastery is at least 10 years long, and most writers never become masters. But that does not mean you cannot get published at an earlier stage in your development. Remember, creativity without structure is chaos. So enjoy what you write, but work at your craft and know your audience. Once you understand the conventions of writing, then you can experiment, create something new and different. If you are calling your work new and different just because you don't understand the conventions of writing, in the end (like a newspaper at the bottom of a bird cage) you'll have crap. Oops—I mean a mess.

MICHAEL SNELL LITERARY AGENCY

P.O. Box 1206
Truro, MA 02666-1206
508-349-3718

Agent: Michael Snell, President.
Born: August 16, 1945.
Education: B.A., DePauw University, Phi Beta Kappa.
Career history: Editor, Wadsworth Publishing Company (1967–1978); executive editor, Addison-Wesley (1978–1979); owner, Michael Snell Literary Agency (1979 to present).
Hobbies/personal interests: Tennis, golf, shellfishing, fishing.
Subjects/categories most enthusiastic about agenting: Specialize in all types of business books, from low-level career, how-to, and self-help to sophisticated advanced professional and reference. Careers, management, leadership, small business, entrepreneurial, finance (personal and corporate), technology. Computer books, both trade and professional, and business technology. Popular psychology, especially how-to, self-help, and health/fitness. Pets and animals.
Subjects/categories not interested in agenting: New age, personal memoirs, poetry, noncommercial fiction and nonfiction, religion.
Best way for a prospective client to initiate contact: Send a one-page query letter (with SASE) outlining the topic and the author's credentials.
Reading-fee policy: No reading fee, except for added percentages for developmental editing and writing from author's advances and royalties, if and when agreed on in advance of a publisher's contract. The publisher, not the author, pays these additional percentages according to the publisher's contract.
Client representation in the following categories: Nonfiction, 15%; Fiction, 15%; Textbooks, 15%; Children's, 15%.
Commission: 15% of advances and royalties.
Number of titles sold during the past year: 36.
Approximate percentage of all submissions (from queries through manuscripts) that are rejected: 90%.
Representative titles sold:
The Color-Blind Career by Ollie Stevenson and Dana Heubler (Peterson's).
60 Second Pain Relief by Peter Lehndorff and Brian Tarcy (New Horizons).
Digital Image Processing by Howard Burdick (McGraw-Hill).
The Digital Corporation by Jim Best (Wiley).
Leadership IQ by Emmett Murphy (Wiley).
Finding and Keeping Your Dream Dog by Myrna Milani (Contemporary).
Heart Zone Training by Sally Edwards (Adams).
Turbocharge Your Career by Ron Yeaple (Macmillan).
Bulletproofing Windows 95 by Glen Weadock (McGraw-Hill).
Marketing Straight to the Heart by Barry Feig (AMACOM).
Advertising Methods That Work by Fred Hahn (Prentice-Hall).

Analytical Tools for Financial Advisors by Ed McCrathy (Urwin).

Selling to Tough Customers by Josh Gordon (AMACOM).

The Jericho Agenda by Bill Atkinson (Berrett-Kohler).

Reinventing the Business Meeting by Ava Butler (McGraw-Hill).

Futursex by Ken Maxwell (Plenum).

Vestpocket Guide to Business Writing by Deborah Dumaine (Prentice Hall).

The Ten Commandments of Successful Businesswomen by Pam Gilberd (Macmillan).

Insider's Guide to Growing a Small Business by Pete Richamn (Macmillan).

The Science Almanac by Ed Francis (Plenum).

Get Published! by Michael Snell and Kim Baker (Prima).

Powerpoint Presentations by Glenn and Emily Weadock (IDG Books).

The most common mistakes potential clients make when soliciting an agent to represent them: The author who insists that her/his book will be an automatic best-seller but has not created a compelling proposal or manuscript. Many authors fail to analyze their market, their audience, and their competition fully. Authors who depend on friends, family, and amateurs for approval of their work but fail to obtain professional evaluation often live in a world of illusion and do not improve their work sufficiently. Others turn us off by acting as if they are considering hiring us, when the opposite is true: We are considering whether or not to invest valuable time, money, and expertise in advising them and helping their success.

What writers can do to enhance their chances of getting an agent (besides being good writers): We like writers who know their limitations with respect to understanding how publishing really works and who appreciate the need for joining with us in a partnership ruled by a clear division of labor, where they do their job (learning to develop winning material) and we do ours (providing developmental advice, marketing, and contract negotiation). We respond to brief query letters that get to the point about the topic and the author's background. A sense of humor, an eagerness to learn, a desire to affect people's lives in a positive and lasting way always helps. Our hearts go out to *pragmatic idealists.*

Description of the Client from Hell: The expert on a subject who thinks she/he is an expert on publishing. The ambitious writer who will not listen to, and learn from, our 30 years of publishing experience. The author who is in a big hurry and cannot come to terms with the slow process of publishing a book. The author who wants so desperately to make money that she/he pays too little attention to shaping an excellent book proposal and manuscript that will appeal to editors and readers: Those who write to make money seldom do, but those who write to change people's lives often do (and make money automatically).

Description of Dream Client: A person who knows a subject intimately, possesses professional credentials in that subject, and can write reasonably well. Someone who knows how to listen, learn, and take direction from publishing professionals. An author so committed to the subject that she/he will promote it tirelessly, regardless of the publisher's promotional budget. *A sense of humor.*

Why did you become an agent? A lifelong love of books, a belief that books can make a big difference in people's lives, and 13 years working successfully as an editor/publisher. Bringing a book to market is like growing a garden or birthing a child:

the harvest, the birth provides a deep satisfaction no amount of money can buy. We make a good living helping writers achieve both personal and financial satisfaction. The work gives us a perfect blend of idealism, lasting influence, and wealth creation.

What might you be doing if you weren't an agent? I suppose my impulse to grow and develop books could find a satisfying outlet in many fields, especially teaching or business. The art of turning an idea into a tangible product consumers find useful or uplifting applies not just to books but to everything from computers to farming. The joy of watching a student grow and develop could come from almost any educational endeavor, from software instruction to shaping bonsai trees.

Comments: We have grown increasingly weary of all the hype surrounding computers and the so-called information superhighway, because we believe that the *quality* of content will always be more important than the channel of distribution via which that content reaches people. We've published computer books since 1967, so we keep abreast of the field, but the quality of submitted material has declined while the quantity of material has skyrocketed. We continue to work hard to help writers generate the intellectual properties from which they can derive both personal satisfaction and income regardless of the means whereby their audience will obtain those properties.

Our advice to authors: Worry about content; worry about clear and concise and interesting communication; develop your subject matter and writing credentials; work with and learn from publishing professionals; and remain patient, perseverant, and humble as you do so. Your computer won't make you smarter. And electronic distribution of your work will not make it more creative, more useful, or even more valuable.

We keep stressing the old-fashioned qualities that make a book (or any sort of communication) valuable: work, work, work, learn, learn, learn, revise, revise, revise.

Elyse Sommer, Inc.

110-34 73rd Road
P.O. Box 751133
Forest Hills, NY 11375-8733
718-263-2668

Agent: Elyse Sommer.

Education: Graduate, major: journalism, minor: marketing, New York University.

Career history: Founded my own agency just four years out of college after a stint as a magazine editor. Agency has always been and remains a one-person operation.

Hobbies/personal interests: Reading, writing, computers, music, skiing.

Subjects/categories most enthusiastic about agenting: Nonfiction books: thoroughly researched, well-thought out, and organized.

Subjects/categories not interested in agenting: Science fiction, poetry, children's picture books.

Best way for a prospective client to initiate contact: A query letter that outlines your book, its stage of completion, your credentials, the nature of the submission (multiple or to me only), marketing history, if any. Since it's hard to judge a project from just a letter, a table of contents and writing sample (with SASE for its return) would be helpful.

Reading-fee policy: No reading fee.

Client representation in the following categories: Nonfiction, 80%.

Commission: 15% on manuscripts sold for an advance between $5,000 and $25,000; 10% on advances exceeding $25,000; 20% on advances under $5,000.

Number of titles sold during the past year: This is a small agency. We average a sale a month.

Approximate percentage of all submissions (from queries through manuscripts) that are rejected: As a one-person agent, I am highly selective in what I take on.

The most common mistakes potential clients make when soliciting an agent to represent them: *Fishing expedition* calls about a project on which the writer has done absolutely no work or proposals claiming to be unique when a quick search of the bookshelf or the Internet shows it has indeed been done (and usually better).

What writers can do to enhance their chances of getting an agent (besides being good writers): An interesting, lively style, and a proposal that anticipates questions.

Why did you become an agent? I loved books, and still do. I loved (and still do) seeing an idea turn into something that will entertain and inform many.

Philip G. Spitzer Literary Agency

50 Talmadge Farm Lane
Easthampton, NY 11937
516-329-3650
fax: 516-329-3651

Agent: Philip Spitzer.

Born: August 6, 1939, New York City.

Education: M.A., New York University Graduate Institute of Book Publishing; M.A., French, University of Paris, France.

Career history: New York University Press, 1961–1962; McGraw-Hill Book Company, trade sales, sales promotion manager, art book department, 1963–1966; John Cushman Associates/Curtis Brown Ltd. Literary Agency, 1966–1969; Philip G. Spitzer Literary Agency, 1969 to present.

Hobbies/personal interests: Sports, travel, etc.

Subjects/categories most enthusiastic about agenting: Fiction: literary and suspense. Quality nonfiction including sports, biography, current events.

Subjects/categories not interested in agenting: Most category fiction, most how-to.

Best way for a prospective client to initiate contact: Query letter (with SASE).

Reading-fee policy: No reading fee.

Client representation in the following categories: Nonfiction, 50%; Fiction, 50%.

Commission: 15% domestic; 20% foreign.

Number of titles sold during the past year: 30.

Approximate percentage of all submissions (from queries through manuscripts) that are rejected: 95%.

Representative titles sold:

Trunk Music by Michael Connelly (Little, Brown).

Cimarron Rose by James Lee Burke (Hyperion).

Dancing after Hours by Andre Dubus (Knopf).

The Blue Wall by Kenneth Abel (Delacorte).

Dark Witness: Why Black People Must Die by Ralph Wiley (Ballantine).

The Game of Their Lives by Geoffrey Douglas (Holt).

Bearing Secrets by Richard Barre (Walker).

The most common mistakes potential clients make when soliciting an agent to represent them: Telephoning is a mistake.

Description of the Client from Hell: Daily phone calls; impossible to satisfy; if book doesn't sell—either to publisher or subsequently in bookstores—agent is to blame.

Description of Dream Client: Informed; respectful; loyal.

Why did you become an agent? Best job I could find at the time. Started my own business because a publishing friend printed up stationery and business cards.

What might you be doing if you weren't an agent? Book sales representative.

STADLER LITERARY AGENCY

P.O. Box 182
3202 East Greenway, Suite #1307-182
Phoenix, AZ 85032
602-569-2481
fax: 602-569-2265

[handwritten: Did not solicit]

Agent: Rose Stadler.

Born: November 23, 1944.

Education: BacSW, University of Minnesota, 1979; MSW, Arizona State University (currently enrolled, anticipated graduation May 1997).

Career history: 20+ years as a social worker; 14+ of those years as a Child Welfare Specialist involved with all areas of neglect and abuse with adoptions, foster care, and developmental disabilities. Statewide training officer. Certified counselor with the Arizona Board of Behavioral Health and Certified College Instructor. Taught social work at the undergraduate level for 5 years and taught (noncredit) fiction writing for 13 years at local community colleges. Presenter for national and local child-abuse prevention seminars.

Hobbies/personal interests: Writing, teaching both writing and social work, camping, photography.

Subjects/categories most enthusiastic about agenting: Fiction: historicals, literary fiction, mysteries, suspense, thrillers, children's literature, anything with movie potential. Nonfiction and social issues also interest me.

Subjects/categories not interested in agenting: Romance, science fiction, fantasy, short stories, war stories, high-tech, or sports. I refuse to accept or handle pornography.

Best way for a prospective client to initiate contact: Query letter with sample chapters and SASE.

Reading-fee policy: Yes; $75 for a full-length manuscript (average length 100,000 words, or 300–350 pages). The fee covers my time at a minimum wage, marketing, copying, postage expenses.

Client representation in the following categories: Fiction: 50%; Nonfiction: 50%.

Commission: 15% domestic, 20% foreign.

Number of titles sold during the past year: Since I'm the new kid on the block, I haven't actually sold anything as of this writing. *But,* I have seven authors who look like they might get publishing contracts and four others that are highly promising.

Approximate percentage of all submissions (from queries through manuscripts) that are rejected: Guesstimate: 75%.

What writers can do to enhance their chances of getting an agent (besides being good writers): I love a good laugh, and I love a well-written query letter. When I see professionalism, I respond as fast as I can. Good writing always gets my attention, but when a personal touch is added, it makes the writer more than a piece of paper.

The most common mistakes potential clients make when soliciting an agent to represent them: Nothing beats a well-written query with adequate SASE, address, home phone number, and daytime phone number. It bothers me when writers say, "I have this really great idea . . . and I want *you* to write it for me." A few things bother me about the way some people try to get my attention. One of them is dropping in with twenty pounds of manuscript that they want me to handle, right now! Another thing is poorly packaged manuscripts or boxes that fall apart in the mail.

I would strongly recommend that writers follow the rules of general business. Don't call in the middle of the night. Don't call collect. Don't "pop in" with manuscripts. Always enclose adequate SASE. Don't be rude, overbearing, or pushy. Don't send your grandmother to me on your behalf.

Being insulting or establishing an adversarial relationship with an agent is *not* a good way to do business. Not many, but a few writers think that if they insult their way to the top, they will publish faster. A lot of authors are temperamental and close to the edge, but being rude far outweighs the value of their work.

Description of the Client from Hell: The Client from Hell is a know-it-all who won't take criticism, won't rewrite, turns in sloppy work, won't get things back to me in a timely manner and then blames me for his or her deficits. The client from purgatory is one who forgets the SASE or just adds SASE to cover the cost of a #10 envelope, thinking that if he or she doesn't send the entire SASE, a rejection will not be forthcoming. Nail-biters, telephone callers, pacers bug me, but I can work around these impatient souls better than the know-it-alls.

Description of Dream Client: The ideal client is one who is takes his craft seriously, can take criticism, gets edits and rewrites done in a timely manner, and is pleasant to represent.

Why did you become an agent? I became an agent for several reasons. (1) I had taught fiction writing for 12+ years and have seen 106 of my former students experience the thrill of publication. (2) One of my students camped on my doorstep and begged me to represent him. (I was working full time as a social worker, going to school, teaching, and trying to work on my own writing. It couldn't be done.) (3) I finally said, "Oh, all right." (4) A local newspaper picked up on my fly-by-the-seat-of-my-pants part-time job and two days later I had 187 phone calls. And (5) the most important reason of all, I've had my share of rejections, lost manuscripts, agents or publishers who let their dog sleep on my work. So I took a chance. I still love social work, but this combines the love of writing with my "people" skills.

What might you be doing if you weren't an agent? No doubt about it, I'd still be a social worker, dreaming about "someday."

Comments: To publishers, I would say: "Please give the new writer a chance. Everyone has to start somewhere. Sometimes an agent has to jump through the flaming hoops just to get thirty seconds of your time." To publishers I would also say this: "After a specific editor has accepted a proposal from me, it ends up in the 'unsolicited' slush pile? Why? Wouldn't it be easier to say 'no' at the onset and save us both the trouble?"

To aspiring authors, I would say: "Listen to what the experts have to say to you. Learn something and be willing to murder your darlings when necessary. Be persistent."

STEPPING STONE LITERARY AGENCY

59 West 71st Street, Suite 9B
New York, NY 10023
212-362-9277
fax: 212-501-8240

*Did not
reload*

Agents: Sarah Jane Freymann, president; Katharine Sands, associate; Steven Schwartz, associate.

Personal information for Sarah Jane Freymann:

Born: London, England.

Education: Although educated mostly in New York, I went to a French school—the Lycée Francais—which is why I am fluent in many languages; and I traveled a great deal from a very early age.

Career history: My first job was with the United Nations. I also worked as a model, and as an editor.

Hobbies/personal interests: Spiritual paths and journeys with a special interest in those of women; adventures of all kinds which ultimately provide insight, growth, and a greater appreciation of our world; mind/body well being, wondrous food, shared with good friends and family; exercise; experiencing different cultures and lifestyles; opera; my daughter.

Subjects/categories most enthusiastic about agenting: Spiritual, psychology/pop psychology, women's/men's issues, mind/body health, cookbooks, biography, travel, natural science, commercial/literary fiction, pop culture, current events. Special interest in Asian-American, Latino-American, Native-American, African-American fiction and nonfiction.

Subjects/categories not interested in agenting: Science fiction, fantasy, horror, genre romance, genre mysteries, screenplays, anything channeled.

Best way for a prospective client to initiate contact: Via a query letter (with SASE). Not by phone. Not by fax.

Reading-fee policy: No reading fee,

Client representation in the following categories: Nonfiction, 79%; Fiction, 19%; Children's, 2%.

Commission: 15%.

Approximate percentage of all submissions (from queries through manuscripts) that are rejected: 75%.

Representative titles sold:

Judging Time (Bantam). Fiction.

A Place to Dream (Warner). Nonfiction.

Children of the Troubles in Northern Ireland (Pocket Books). Nonfiction.

Reflections on a California Pool (Rizzoli). Nonfiction.

Killing Time: Who Killed Nicole Brown Simpson and Ron Goldman (Macmillan). Nonfiction.

The Seven Deadly Sins: A Handbook (Macmillan) Nonfiction.

Flavors: The Market Table Cookbook.

Owning It: Zen and the Act of Facing Life (Kodansha). Nonfiction.

Perfect Pitch (Warner). Nonfiction.

The most common mistakes potential clients make when soliciting an agent to represent them: We do not keep an accounting of "costly mistakes"—we all make mistakes. I used to say, however, that nothing in particular turned us off. Experience has made me qualify that statement. I am "turned off" by writers who are arrogant and belligerent and by writers who invariably feel that the publisher is their enemy.

What writers can do to enhance their chances of getting an agent (besides being good writers): I want writers who are experts in their fields for nonfiction and willing to admit that they might need a coauthor if necessary if their writing skills are not well honed. I like to see a well-written proposal and 2–3 chapters. With fiction, we prefer writers who have been previously published. They need solid, well-honed writing skills, a great story, and a fresh "voice."

Description of the Client from Hell: I wouldn't know—we've never had one.

Description of Dream Client: One who not only writes beautifully, with passion and intelligence, but who is also a nice human being—a "mensch." Someone with a sense of humor. Someone who has the patience and willingness to rewrite and rework their material, if necessary. And last, but not least, clients who have the confidence not to call us too often and who realize that, if we spend all our time talking to them on the phone, we won't have that time to spend selling their work.

Why did you become an agent? Probably in the genes. I'm a natural matchmaker and a physician's daughter. I like to think that, thanks to my intervention, this author and that publisher met, formed a relationship, and that I am the midwife to this wonderful book.

What might you be doing if you weren't an agent? An actress, a spiritual teacher, a marathon runner, a writer, an opera singer, the mother of 15 children, a nineteenth-century explorer, a doctor, a filmmaker—all of which I may still do!

Comments: Life is all about feeling engaged and connected. I love being able to make that kind of heart and mind commitment to authors and to their work. That is what makes the *business* of selling books become the *joy* of selling books. Seeing my authors successfully, creatively, and happily published is my goal as an expert. I delight in the knowledge that, out of this relationship, something came into being that people can both benefit from and find enjoyment in.

SUSAN TRAVIS LITERARY AGENCY

1317 North San Fernando Boulevard, #175
Burbank, CA 91504
818-557-6538

Agent: Susan Travis.

Education: B.A., English literature, University of California, Berkeley.

Career history: Prior to establishing my agency in 1995, I spent four years with the Margaret McBride Literary Agency, most recently as an associate agent. Before joining the McBride Agency, I worked in the managing editorial department of Ballantine Books, New York.

Subjects/categories most enthusiastic about agenting: I represent an even mix of fiction and nonfiction and truly enjoy working on both. For fiction, I am currently representing literary and mainstream fiction and am interested in reading just about anything, provided the writing is good and there is depth to the work. My nonfiction interests encompass a wide area. In the past, I've handled cookbooks, self-help/psychology, health, and business. I would like to receive more nonfiction submissions for books targeted at a general audience, not those aimed at an exclusive or limited market.

Subjects/categories not interested in agenting: I do not represent children's or young-adult works, poetry or screenplays, and I do very little with science fiction and fantasy.

Best way for a prospective client to initiate contact: Fiction: A query letter that gives a brief synopsis or overview of the project and any pertinent information about the author. The letter should be concise. My interest is usually piqued more by a description of the underlying themes in a project rather than a blow-by-blow plot summary. The first 15–20 pages of the manuscript may be enclosed with the query.

Nonfiction: A query letter giving a brief overview of the project and a brief description of the author's credentials or expertise. Or, a complete proposal may be sent. If the manuscript is complete, the author should query first rather than sending the entire manuscript. *A SASE with correct postage must be enclosed for a reply and return of material.*

Reading-fee policy: No reading or marketing fees.

Client representation in the following categories: Nonfiction, 50%; Fiction, 50%. **Commission:** 15% domestic, 20% foreign.

Approximate percentage of all submissions (from queries through manuscripts) that are rejected: 90%.

The most common mistakes potential clients make when soliciting an agent to represent them: Verbal/telephone queries seldom work. If an author is trying to market writing, then let the writing speak for itself. Authors have to make the effort to pitch their work using the written work. One of the most costly mistakes an author can make is to market work prematurely. I usually base decisions on an *as is* basis, not the hidden potential. Unpolished manuscripts can rarely compete with those by authors who have taken the extra time to polish their projects and make a professional submission.

What writers can do to enhance their chances of getting an agent (besides being good writers): I'm looking for good writing, not gimmicks.

Description of Dream Client: Dream clients are those who are professional, business-like, yet friendly, who appreciate input and advice but don't require constant hand-holding.

SUSAN P. URSTADT INC. AGENCY

103 Brushy Ridge Road
New Canaan, CT 06840
203-972-8226

Agent: Susan P. Urstadt; Jeanne Fredericks.

Education: Urstadt: B.A., Wheaton College, 1964. Fredericks: B.A., Mount Holyoke College, 1972; Radcliffe Publishing Procedures Course; M.B.A., New York University Graduate School of Business Administration, 1979.

Career history: Urstadt: Foreign-publisher's representative and literary scout (1970–1985); incorporated literary agency in 1975. Fredericks: assistant to editorial director and foreign/subsidiary rights director, Basic Books (1972–1974); managing editor and acquisitions editor, Macmillan (1974–1980); editorial director, Ziff-Davis Books (1980–1981); literary agent, Susan P. Urstadt Agency (1990 to present).

Hobbies/personal interests: Urstadt: Reading, art, antiques, decorative arts, theater, horses, travel, food, social history, literature, gardening, conservation. Fredericks: family activities, tennis, skiing, swimming, coaching soccer, reading, cooking, traveling, biking, gardening, casual entertaining.

Subjects/categories most enthusiastic about agenting: Urstadt: history, biography, food and wine, gardening, art, antiques, decorative arts, natural science, conservation, performing arts, travel, education, health, careers, business, outstanding artists for juvenile and adult; popular reference. Fredericks: practical, popular reference by authorities, especially in health, sports, science, business, cooking, parenting, travel, women's issues, plus an occasional outstanding juvenile or novel.

Subjects/categories not interested in agenting: Horror, occult fiction, celebrity biographies; in juveniles, no formula characters.

Best way for a prospective client to initiate contact: Please query (with SASE) by mail, with outline, description of project, author biography, sample writing. No phone calls. No fax.

Reading-fee policy: No reading fee.

Client representation in the following categories: Nonfiction, 90%; Fiction, 5%; Children's, 5%.

Commission: 15% domestic.

Number of titles sold during the past year: 20–25.

Approximate percentage of all submissions (from queries through manuscripts) that are rejected: 95%.

Representative titles sold:

The Brewmaster's Bible by Stephen Snyder (HarperCollins).

Whole Healing by Elliott Dacher, M.D. (Dutton).

How to Get the Home You Want by Carolyn Janik (Kiplinger).

Landscape Magic by Doug Green (Chapters).

Traditions by Emyl Jenkins (Crown).

The Secret Wars of Leslie Groves by Stanley Goldberg (Steerforth).

What writers can do to enhance their chances of getting an agent (besides being good writers): Submit a complete, professional proposal. Be respectful of agent's time and other commitments. A good agent's first responsibility is to current clients.

Why did you become an agent? Love of books.

What might you be doing if you weren't an agent? Might have enjoyed a career in magazines or journalism.

THE RICHARD R. VALCOURT AGENCY

177 East 77th Street PPHC
New York, NY 10021
212-570-2340
fax: use same number.

[handwritten: Did not select]

Agent: Richard R. Valcourt.

Born: November 29, 1941, Fall River, Massachusetts.

Education: B.A., Roger Williams College; M.A., New York University; A.B.D., City University Graduate School; L.L. B., LaSalle Extension University.

Career history: Radio-television journalist (1961–1980); program administration, City University of New York (1980–1995); instructor, Department of Political Science, Hunter College (1981–1995); managing editor, International Journal of Intelligence (1986 to present); founded Richard Valcourt Agency (1995).

Hobbies/personal interests: Reading, films, baseball.

Subjects/categories most enthusiastic about agenting: Government and politics, national security issues, biography, social concerns, historical and political fiction.

Subjects/categories not interested in agenting: Vulgar and violent novels, works of marginal interest.

Best way for a prospective client to initiate contact: Letter of inquiry (with SASE), brief biography, summary of material.

Reading-fee policy: No reading fee. Charge for photocopying and phone calls if excessive.

Client representation in the following categories: Nonfiction, 70%; Fiction, 30%.
Commission: 15% domestic, 20% foreign.

Number of titles sold during the past year: New agency, will list next year.

Approximate percentage of all submissions (from queries through manuscripts) that are rejected: Approximately one-third. I try to work with author to improve manuscript and resubmit before rejecting outright.

Representative titles sold:

Will list next year.

The most common mistakes potential clients make when soliciting an agent to represent them: Sending incomplete materials, or expecting immediate results. Or failing to inform me that they are querying several agents simultaneously.

What writers can do to enhance their chances of getting an agent (besides being good writers): Most writers really want their works to be published, and earnestly seek assistance from an agent. They are looking for someone who will care about them and their work, and help them achieve their goals. From them I receive courteous and comprehensive submissions.

Description of the Client from Hell: Someone who has too high an opinion of his/her writing and is overconfident about its potential for publication. Happy to report very few problems in this area so far.

Description of Dream Client: A good writer who, having researched the field, sends in a professionally acceptable manuscript and accompanying information, and patiently awaits the outcome, knowing that it usually takes time.

Why did you become an agent? My love for books is lifelong. Working with authors as an editor, I developed a sense of their styles and needs. From helping them publish articles, I now assist them in publishing their works as books.

What might you be doing if you weren't an agent? Probably sitting on the other side of the desk as the owner of a small publishing house.

Comments: Despite all the hyperbole, computer technology will never replace the personal intimacy of a real book. Nor should it.

DAVID VIGLIANO AGENCY LTD.

654 Madison Avenue, Suite 809
New York, NY 10021

Agent: David Vigliano; Noah T. Lukeman.

Born: Vigliano: June 18, 1959; Lukeman: November 28, 1973.

Education: Vigliano: B.A., Hunter; M.B.A., Harvard. Lukeman: B.A., Brandeis University.

Career history: Vigliano: Worked at Warner Books, where I originated the idea of an in-house packager, and put together such bestselling books as *McMahon* and *What They Really Teach You at Harvard Business School*. Lukeman: Worked brief stints at William Morrow, Delphinium Books, and Farrar Straus Giroux.

Subjects/categories most enthusiastic about agenting: Vigliano: Literary and commercial fiction, nonfiction. Lukeman: Literary fiction.

Subjects/categories not interested in agenting: Children's.

Best way for a prospective client to initiate contact: A one-page query letter, giving a brief synopsis of work and publication credits.

Reading-fee policy: No reading fee.

Client representation in the following categories: Nonfiction, 50%; Fiction, 50%.

Commission: 15%.

Number of titles sold during the past year: 75.

Approximate percentage of all submissions (from queries through manuscripts) that are rejected: 99%.

Representative titles sold:

Home for the Holidays (Pocket).

Hiya, Kid: Valerie Harper's Memoirs (Dutton).

Refuse to Lose by John Califari (Ballantine).

The Mao Game by John Milica (Regan Books).

Another Day in Paradise by Eddie Little (Viking).

Girl by Blake Nelson (Fireside).

Days of Our Lives Scrapbook by Laraine Zenka (HarperCollins).

Alt.Culture by Stephen Daly and Nathaniel Wice (HarperCollins).

Go Now by Richard Hell (Scribner).

Bless Me, Father by Marie Kriegel (Doubleday).

The most common mistakes potential clients make when soliciting an agent to represent them: Not being patient.

Description of the Client from Hell: Pushy and impatient.

Description of Dream Client: Relaxed and uncontrolling.

JOHN A. WARE LITERARY AGENCY

392 Central Park West
New York, NY 10025

Agent: John A. Ware.

Born: May 21, 1942.

Education: B.A., philosophy, Cornell University; graduate work, English literature, Northwestern University.

Career history: Editor, eight years, Doubleday & Company; literary agent, one year, James Brown Associates/Curtis Brown Ltd.; founded John A. Ware Literary Agency in 1978.

Hobbies/personal interests: Music, choral singing and blues bands; running.

Subjects/categories most enthusiastic about agenting: Biography and history, investigative journalism *in re* social commentary and contemporary affairs, memoir and bird's-eye views of phenomena, literary and suspense fiction, Americana and folklore, nature and science.

Subjects/categories not interested in agenting: Technothrillers mances; men's action-adventure; how-to's, save the area of medicine books and cookbooks; hard-core science fiction.

Best way for a prospective client to initiate contact: Query le

Reading-fee policy: No reading fee. Only for Xeroxing, auth and books, and unusual mailing expenses.

Client representation in the following categories: Nonfiction, 80%; 1

Commission: 15% on all sales, save foreign, which are 20%.

Approximate percentage of all submissions (from queries through manuscripts) that are rejected: 90%.

Representative titles sold:

Booth: A Novel and Photographs by David Robertson (Anchor/Doubleday).

Into the Wild by Jon Krakauer (Willard/Random House).

Hoops Nation by Christopher Ballard (Holt).

Lay Low and Don't Make the Big Mistake: The Lazy Person's Guide to Corporate Success by Brian Harris and Rich Herschlag (Simon & Schuster).

Now That I'm Out, What Do I Do? by Brian McNaught (St. Martin's).

Four Corners by Kenneth A. Brown (HarperCollins).

What writers can do to enhance their chances of getting an agent (besides being good writers): Selectively, preferably one-on-one, rather than shopping among 20 agents (or so) via word processor and fax.

Description of the Client from Hell: Untrusting, and accordingly, nudging.

Description of Dream Client: Professional at all aspects of his/her chosen writing area; trusting; in possession of a sense of humor.

Why did you become an agent? I like working with writers, editorially and otherwise, outside the corporate realms of meetings and red tape, inside of which I worked as an editor.

What might you be doing if you weren't an agent? Teaching philosophy or working as a sportswriter, or in some position in race relations.

Comments: In what remains of our genteel world of books, I would encourage a shoring up of the realm of common courtesy, returning phone calls, saying please and thank you, etc.

WATERSIDE PRODUCTIONS, INC.

2191 San Elijo Avenue
Cardiff-by-the-Sea, CA 92007
619-632-9190

Agents: David Fugate, Margot Maley, Matthew Wagner.

The following information pertains to David Fugate:

Born: June 11, 1969.

Education: B.A., literature with honors, University of California at San Diego.

Career history: I've worked in a bookstore; as a sporting goods salesman; as a night manager of a lodge in Vail, Colorado; and was manager of submissions with the Margret McBride Literary Agency before joining Waterside in 1994.

Hobbies/personal interests: Sports of all kinds (except baseball and hockey), reading, crime and mob films, travel.

Subjects/categories most enthusiastic about agenting: Computer books, compelling nonfiction in the areas of business, management, technology, sports, true crime. Fiction with an edge, including crime stories and thrillers.

Subjects/categories not interested in agenting: New Age, self-help, children's, romance, poetry, short stories.

Best way for a prospective client to initiate contact: Nonfiction: Query letter or proposal. Fiction: Query letter and synopsis.

Reading-fee policy: No reading fee.

Client representation in the following categories: Nonfiction, 95%; Fiction, 5%.

Commission: 15% domestic, 20% film, 25% foreign.

Number of titles sold during the past year: 36.

Approximate percentage of all submissions (from queries through manuscripts) that are rejected: 98%.

Representative titles sold:

The Schwa World Operations Manual by Bill Barker (Chronicle).

The New Financial Metrics by Bill Simon (Van Nosttrand Reinhold).

Danny Goodman's Guide to Javascript by Danny Goodman (IDG Books).

Game Programming with Java by John Withers (John Wiley & Sons).

Computer Telephony Strategies by Jeffrey Shapiro (IDG Books).

High Powered C++ Programming by Steve Holzner (MIS Press).

The Beginner's Guide to Netscape by Elizabeth Parker (Charles River Media).

The most common mistakes potential clients make when soliciting an agent to represent them: Those who I can tell haven't researched their market thoroughly have little chance of success. I'm also turned off by anyone who wants to meet with me before showing me any of their materials.

What writers can do to enhance their chances of getting an agent (besides being good writers): Those who have compelling, marketable ideas, who understand their audience and are willing to do what it takes to succeed. I'm especially impressed by authors who have taken the time to produce a quality proposal or treatment before they contact me.

Description of the Client from Hell: Someone who is arrogant; demands an immediate response on everything; isn't willing to put in the work to produce a quality book or proposal; fails to meet deadlines; consistently overestimates their value in the marketplace; is litigious; and has some horrible, infectious disease.

Description of Dream Client: A talented writer who is professional, understands the business, meets deadlines, is easy to work with, has good relationships with his or her editor, and appreciates the value that a good agent can provide for his or her career.

Why did you become an agent? I like books and words and ideas, and the agency I did an internship with in college asked me to stay on when I graduated. It was very natural.

What might you be doing if you weren't an agent? I would be the sixth man for some mediocre professional basketball team in Greece, or a nomadic ski bum, or a project-development person in Tarantino's production company, or on the editorial side of the publishing industry.

Comments: The world is no longer a stage. It's a courtroom, and everything you say will be used against you.

The following information pertains to Margot Maley:
Born: June 18, 1970.
Education: Literature, University of California at San Diego.
Career history: Waterside Productions for four years.
Hobbies/personal interests: Skiing, tennis, biking, acting, cooking, riding horses.
Subjects/categories most enthusiastic about agenting: Computer books, sports books, business, women's issues, cookbooks, and general nonfiction.
Subjects/categories not interested in agenting: Fiction, New Age, religious.
Best way for a prospective client to initiate contact: Through a query letter or a phone call.
Reading-fee policy: No reading fee.
Client representation in the following categories: Nonfiction, 100%.
Commission: 15%.
Number of titles sold during the past year: 65.
Approximate percentage of all submissions (from queries through manuscripts) that are rejected: 90%.
Representative titles sold:
A Dose of Sanity by Dr. Sydney Walker (John Wiley & Sons).
Internet Security Secrets by John Vacca (IDG Books).
Virtual College by Pam Dixon (Petersons).
Web Hacking with Javascript by Nick Arnett and David Land (O'Reilly and Associates).
Cheapskate's Vacation Guide by Stephen Tannenbaum (Carol Publishing).
The Case for Business on the Internet by Jill Ellsworth (John Wiley & Sons).
The most common mistakes potential clients make when soliciting an agent to represent them: A poorly written proposal or query letter or too many phone calls to *check on the status* of their proposal.
What writers can do to enhance their chances of getting an agent (besides being good writers): A specifically addressed letter and proposal, a writer who is professional and enthusiastic and has a great idea.
Description of the Client from Hell: A rude, arrogant, pushy, and impatient person who has completely unrealistic expectations.
Description of Dream Client: A great writer with good ideas who meets deadlines and is friendly and pleasant to deal with.
Why did you become an agent? Growing up I always seemed to have either a book or a phone in my hand.
What might you be doing if you weren't an agent? I would be leading safaris in East Africa.

The following information pertains to Matthew Wagner:
Born: July 12, 1962.
Education: B.A., literature/creative writing, University of California at Santa Cruz.
Career history: I've been a library clerk, a book binder, a bookstore clerk and buyer. I've been a literary agent for six years.
Hobbies/personal interests: Yoga, tennis, golf, *lots* of reading.
Subjects/categories most enthusiastic about agenting: Computer books, Internet-specific programming titles, sports, culture and technology, general how-to, business, and management.
Subjects/categories not interested in agenting: Fiction, poetry, self-help.
Best way for a prospective client to initiate contact: Query letter.
Reading-fee policy: No reading fee.
Client representation in the following categories: Nonfiction, 95%; Textbooks, 5%.
Commission: 15%.
Number of titles sold during the past year: 150.
Approximate percentage of all submissions (from queries through manuscripts) that are rejected: 90%.
Representative titles sold:
Parenting for Dummies (IDG).
Real Life Windows (IDG).
Free Throw (HarperCollins).
The Flexible Enterprise (Wiley).
Windows 95 for Dummies (IDG).
Netscape Publishing (Ventura).
The most common mistakes potential clients make when soliciting an agent to represent them: Telling me the book is sure to sell several million copies because the market is *everyone*. Insufficient market research.
What writers can do to enhance their chances of getting an agent (besides being good writers): Professionalism and passion. Really great ideas. New wrinkles on old topics.
Description of the Client from Hell: Someone prone to projection who thinks he or she is always right.
Description of Dream Client: Professional, open minded, creative, honest, and disciplined.
Why did you become an agent? Probably because I can talk *really* fast. Also, I love books and like dealing with writers and publishers. It helps to be on the cutting edge.
What might you be doing if you weren't an agent? Editor, publisher, or packager. I would love to run a bookstore someday.

RUTH WRESCHNER, AUTHORS' REPRESENTATIVE

10 West 74th Street
New York, NY 10023
212-877-2605

Agent: Ruth Wreschner.

Born: Frankfurt, Germany.

Education: B.A., McGill University, Montreal, Canada.

Career history: Assistant editor (medical division, 1973–1978) and executive assistant (science division, 1961–1973), John Wiley & Sons.

Hobbies/personal interests: Music (classical), art, travel, literature.

Subjects/categories most enthusiastic about agenting: Nonfiction: all areas, except erotica; special interest in popular medicine/psychology, parenting, business, health, science, biography, history. Fiction: primarily mainstream; secondary genre (mysteries, contemporary and historical romances, suspense/thrillers).

Subjects/categories not interested in agenting: Erotica and science fiction.

Best way for a prospective client to initiate contact: Nonfiction: Query letter (with SASE) containing detailed proposal. Fiction: Query letter (with SASE) containing brief synopsis; if I am interested, I will ask for sample chapters.

Reading-fee policy: No reading fee.

Client representation in the following categories: Nonfiction, 80%; Fiction, 20%. Children's, Nonfiction, 80%; Fiction, 20%.

Commission: 15% domestic; 20% foreign.

Number of titles sold during the past year: 12.

Approximate percentage of all submissions (from queries through manuscripts) that are rejected: 97–98%.

Representative titles sold:

The Perfect Match by Chris Walkowicz (Howell/Macmillan). Dog book.

Seven Secrets of Successful Parents by Randy C. Wolfe (Contemporary).

Wide-Angle Vision by Wayne Burkan (Wiley). Business book.

Pirouette Club by Berit Haahr (Avon). Ballet young-adult series.

Wall Street's Picks: 100 Best Stocks and Mutual Funds 1996 by Kirk Kazanjian (Dearborn). To become an annual.

The Super Attractive Emerging Corporation by Gabe Baumann (McGraw-Hill). Business book.

Lupus by Daniel Wallace, M.D. (Oxford University Press).

The most common mistakes potential clients make when soliciting an agent to represent them: Not including SASE with their queries. Their most costly mistakes might be to submit work in an unprofessional manner: sloppy, handwritten, without a cover letter.

What writers can do to enhance their chances of getting an agent (besides being good writers): Primarily their subject matter and credentials. And for fiction writers, it is all, of course, *on the page*. It is always a moment of ecstasy when really exciting fiction arrives.

Description of the Client from Hell: People who are overly demanding of my time, particularly when they have totally unsalable work. Clients who go on relentless phone campaigns. *When I get an offer from a publisher, I call!*

Description of Dream Client: Someone who is pleasant and courteous to deal with, who trusts me, who submits a really professional proposal, and who meets deadlines and other obligations.

Why did you become an agent? I had worked in publishing for most of my career. I love the challenge; the people I meet; and, first and foremost, I love the written word.

What might you be doing if you weren't an agent? I honestly don't know. If I were *super rich* I might devote time to charity (community work) and spend more time traveling than I have time to do now.

Comments: I am disturbed, as I am sure many agents are, by the incredibly high advances publishers pay for so-called *big books*—which often don't pan out. All this at the expense of a new and gifted writer.

WRITERS HOUSE

21 West 26th Street
New York, NY 10010
212-685-2400

Agents: Susan Ginsburg, Albert J. Zuckerman, Fran Lebowitz, Merrilee Heifetz, Amy Berkower, Susan Cohen, Liza Landsman.

Born: Ginsburg: New York. Lebowitz: September 23, 1963, Baltimore.

Education: Ginsburg: Yale University. Zuckerman: D.F.A., dramatic literature, Yale. Lebowitz: Franklin and Marshall College; University of Maryland. Heifetz: B.A., Sarah Lawrence College.

Career history: Ginsburg: editor in chief, Atheneum; executive editor, St. Martin's; executive editor, Simon & Schuster/Pocket Books. Zuckerman: naval officer; foreign service officer, U.S. State Department; assistant professor of playwrighting, Yale Drama School; winner of Stanley Drama Prize for best new American play of 1964; author of two published novels and of *Writing the Blockbuster Novel;* writer for *The Edge of Night* on TV; Broadway producer. Lebowitz: Lowenstein Associates, 1 year; William Morris, 2 years; Writers House, 2 years. Heifetz: Teaching writing to children, literary agent.

Hobbies/personal interests: Zuckerman: Helping writers; antique textiles and furniture. Lebowitz: Dangerous sports. Heifetz: Cooking, art, sports.

Subjects/categories most enthusiastic about agenting: Ginsburg: Fiction: commercial fiction of any type and literary fiction that is accessible. Nonfiction: broad range of topics chosen purely by interest and marketability. True crime, women's issues, science, biography/autobiography, cookbooks. Zuckerman: Fiction: wonderful novels of all kinds, especially those accessible and attractive to a large readership. Nonfiction: history, biography, narrative nonfiction. Lebowitz: Children's books (middle grade), and young-adult novels. Adult novels. Heifetz: Fiction with an edge, distinctive mysteries, wonderful historical women's fiction, well-written but commercial fantasy; cyberbooks, new technology.

Subjects/categories not interested in agenting: Ginsburg: Children's books, science fiction. Zuckerman: Scholarly, professional, screenplays. Lebowitz: Financial self-help. Heifetz: Men's adventure.

Best way for a prospective client to initiate contact: Ginsburg: Through written correspondence—query letter (with SASE). Zuckerman: An interesting, intelligent letter (with SASE). Lebowitz: Letter (with SASE) and small chunk of work or entire proposal. Heifetz: Letter (with SASE).

Reading-fee policy: No reading fee.

Client representation in the following categories: Agency as a whole has about 300 clients. Ginsburg: 40–50 clients; Nonfiction, 60%; Fiction 40%. Zuckerman: about 70 clients; Nonfiction, $33^1/3\%$; Fiction, $66^2/3\%$. Lebowitz: 20–30 clients; Nonfiction, 10%; Fiction, 15%; Children's/young adult, 75%. Heifetz: Nonfiction, 10%; Fiction, 80%; Children's, 10%.

Commission: 15%.

Number of titles sold during the past year: Agency: More than 200. Lebowitz: 25 to 30. Heifetz: About 30.

Approximate percentage of all submissions (from queries through manuscripts) that are rejected: Lebowitz: 98%. Heifetz: Unsolicited, 99%. Other, 75%.

Representative titles sold:

A Place Called Freedom by Ken Follett (Crown).

Blessing in Disguise by Eileen Goudge (Viking).

Green River Rising by Tim Willocks (Morrow).

The Select by F. Paul Wilson (Morrow).

Black Holes and Baby Universes by Stephen Hawking (Bantam).

The First Wives' Club by Olivia Goldsmith (Simon & Schuster).

Stardust: Illustrated Fantasy by Neil Gaiman and Charles Jess (DC Comics).

Other well-known clients are: Octavia E. Butler, Nora Roberts, Barbara Delinsky, Ridley Pearson, Michael Lewis, Ann Martin, Francine Pascal, James Howe, Bruce Sterling, Joan Vinje, Craig Thomas, Cynthia Voight, Colin Wilson.

The most common mistakes potential clients make when soliciting an agent to represent them: Lebowitz: Calling a day after sending submission. Heifetz: Harassing the agent.

What writers can do to enhance their chances of getting an agent (besides being good writers): Zuckerman: Be talented, study books that are having some success, and be willing to work their butts off. Lebowitz: Make the cover letter short, place no value judgments on their writing, and give me the hook I'd need to sell it to an editor.

Description of the Client from Hell: Heifetz: I don't have any.

Description of Dream Client: Heifetz: Talented, professional, pleasant to deal with.

Why did you become an agent? Heifetz: I like reading and I like writers.

What might you be doing if you weren't an agent? Heifetz: Living in Italy.

THE GAY YOUNG AGENCY, INC.

700 Washington Street, Suite 3 Upper
New York, NY 10014
212-691-3124
fax: 212-807-9772
E-Mail: GYAgency@aol.com

Agent: Gay Young.

Born: April 13, 1955.

Education: B.A., Wellesley College (1975); J.D., New York University (1978).

Career history: Former Wall Street lawyer, left to join the Charlotte Sheedy Literary Agency and learn publishing.

Hobbies/personal interests: Computers and technology.

Subjects/categories most enthusiastic about agenting: New media (Internet, on-line services, CD-ROM), business, and children's books.

Subjects/categories not interested in agenting: Fiction (other than for children), science fiction.

Best way for a prospective client to initiate contact: Send a query letter outlining the project and include name, address, telephone number, and SASE.

Reading-fee policy: No reading fee.

Client representation in the following categories: Nonfiction, 60%; Children's, 40%.

Commission: 15%.

Representative titles sold:

The Elements of Interactive (Holt).

The Skwinkles (Avon).

Dermatology CD-ROM.

What writers can do to enhance their chances of getting an agent (besides being good writers): I get excited about working with people who have a sense of professionalism.

Description of the Client from Hell: Someone who promises material and then doesn't deliver or return phone calls.

Description of Dream Client: Focused, with appropriate skills to implement her/his project, and polite.

Why did you become an agent? I love being around new ideas and creative people.

What might you be doing if you weren't an agent? I would be miserably doing corporate law.

THE ANDREW ZACK LITERARY AGENCY

P.O. Box 247
Westfield, NY 07091-0247
908-518-0318

Agent: Andrew Zack.

Born: March 16, 1966, Quincy, Massachusetts.

Education: B.A., English and political science, University of Rochester, 1988.

Career history: Eight years in book publishing, including two and a half as an agent for Scovil Chichak Galen Literary Agency, Inc. Worked as an editor, in-house or freelance, for Warner Books, Donald I. Fine, the Berkley Publishing Group, Dell Publishing, Avon Books, and Tom Doherty Associates. I remain a Consulting Editor to Tom Doherty Associates.

Hobbies/personal interests: Biking, movies, investing, computers, jazz, reading.

Subjects/categories most enthusiastic about agenting: History, particularly military history and intelligence services history; politics/current affairs; new media technology and issues; science and technology—how they affect society and business; narrative accounts of how big breakthroughs were achieved; new works that shatter old beliefs; natural science—geology, paleontology, biology, etc.; business—narrative accounts and management how-to; marketing; biography/autobiography; media-related (celebrity biography) and political; personal finance/investing; humor; narrative, topical and celebrity-related; commercial fiction (excluding *women's fiction*); thrillers in every shape and form—international, serial killer, scientific/technological/computer, medical, psychological, erotic, military, environmental, legal; mysteries and crime novels—less cozy, more hard-edged, but not necessarily hard-boiled; action novels in the David Morrell or Clive Cussler tradition.

Best way for a prospective client to initiate contact: Nonfiction: query letter with résumé and a 2–3 page introduction to the project. Fiction: 3 chapters and a synopsis, along with history of previously published works, if any. Always include SASE for the return of any material.

Reading-fee policy: No reading fee.

Client representation in the following categories: Fiction, 60%; Nonfiction, 40% (I want more nonfiction).

Commission: 15% domestic, 20% foreign.

Approximate percentage of all submissions (from queries through manuscripts) that are rejected: 98%.

Representative titles sold:

Crota by Owl Goingback (Donald I. Fine Books).

Deadly Vintage by William Relling Jr. (Walker & Co.).

Cutting Edge and *Just Instinct* by Robert Walker (The Berkley Publishing Group).

Using Excel for Windows 95 by Joshua Nossiter (Que).

The Future Is Ours by John Bartlett, editor (Henry Holt & Co.).

The most common mistakes potential clients make when soliciting an agent to represent them: Phoning instead of writing; having a poorly written synopsis; making repeated telephone calls to check on the status of their submissions; not sending SASE.

What writers can do to enhance their chances of getting an agent (besides being good writers): Nonfiction writers have to be recognized experts in their subject areas, or proven journalists who have written with great success about a number of different subjects. Novelists should be, first and foremost, real *wordsmiths*. Understand *how* to write, not just type, a work of fiction. Then, know your marketplace. The combination of good writing and a commercial story will always sell.

Comments: The agent/author relationship is a business partnership. The agent has his or her role and the author has his or her role. Neither is an *employee* of the other. Interestingly enough, I never hear about agents or authors *hiring* each other, but I hear about them firing one another all the time. Agents, obviously, are business people. Authors need to be business people too. Authors should do their best to be as informed as possible about the nature of the publishing business. They should subscribe to

Publishers Weekly, or at least read it in the library every week. They should talk to their local independent bookseller (and if they *really* want to learn a few things, they should get a part-time job working in a bookstore). My best client is an *educated* client. I find the hardest thing about the agent/author relationship is communication. E-mail has become an important mode of communication for me. It's quick and easy and almost instantaneous as a form of communication. Authors should be able to ask their agents all the questions they want, and if an author's agent disagrees with that, it's time to find another agent. But authors also need to recognize that every minute spent on the phone with them is a minute that could be spent selling their projects. As long as an author understands the job he or she has and the job the agent has in the author/agent relationship, the business partnership will flourish and be profitable.

SUSAN ZECKENDORF ASSOCIATES, INC.

171 West 57th Street, Suite 11B
New York, NY 10019
212-245-2928

Agent: Susan Zeckendorf.
  Born: New York City.
  Education: B.A., Wellesley College; M.Ed., Columbia University Teachers College.
  Career history: Counseling psychologist (1980–1988).
  Hobbies/personal interests: Reading, music, film.
  Subjects/categories most enthusiastic about agenting: Literary fiction, mysteries, thrillers, women's commercial fiction, social history, biography, music, psychology, science.
  Subjects/categories not interested in agenting: Romance, science fiction, New Age.
  Best way for a prospective client to initiate contact: Query letter (with SASE).
  Reading-fee policy: No reading fee.
  Client representation in the following categories: Nonfiction, 25%; Fiction, 75%.
  Commission: 15%.
  Approximate percentage of all submissions (from queries through manuscripts) that are rejected: 90%.
  Representative titles sold:
  Cry for Help by Karen Hanson Stuyk (Berkley).
  Maybelleen by Kathleen Wallace King (Holt). Literary fiction.
  Fifth Avenue (a social history with photographs) by Jerry E. Patterson (Abrams).
  Morning Glory: The Mary Lou Williams Story by Linda Dahl (Schimer/Macmillan). A music biography.
  Not in Our Stars by Una-Mary Parker (Hodder/Headline).
  False Promises by Una-Mary Parker (Hodder/Headline).
  Time is Now by Una-Mary Parker (Hodder/Headline).

Streetlights: Illuminations of the Urban Black Experience, edited by Doris Austin and Martin Simmons (Viking). Fiction anthology.

How to Write a Damn Good Novel II: Advanced Techniques by James W. Frey (St. Martin's).

The most common mistakes potential clients make when soliciting an agent to represent them: Sending gimmicky letters. *Not* sending an SASE.

What writers can do to enhance their chances of getting an agent (besides being good writers): Submit a short query letter that is to the point—with an SASE.

Description of the Client from Hell: An unpublished writer who wants an auction and a six-figure advance for a mediocre project.

Description of Dream Client: Honest and considerate.

Why did you become an agent? Because I have great admiration and respect for those who have writing talent.

What Makes This Agent Directory Special?

Jeff Herman

No other listing of literary agents comes anywhere close to this one. We don't just tell you who the agents are and where to find them; we get the agents to actually talk to you and reveal a slice of their personalities. These surveys also reveal what each agent wants to represent (and doesn't want to), when and where they were born and educated; their career history, and their agenting track record. Memorize some of these tidbits and you can be something of a gossip.

About 125 exceptionally well-qualified agents are included in this listing. Each year I invite the 200+ members of the Association of Author Representatives, as well as a couple dozen excellent nonmember agents, to be in the book. As you might expect, many of the most successful agents are not overly hungry for unsolicited new submissions, and therefore do not wish to participate. We listed no one against his or her wishes, and we allowed all of our agent contributors to be as terse or expansive as they pleased.

There are surely many superb agents of whom I am not aware and therefore didn't reach out to for inclusion. My staff and I have done our best to include only legitimate agents who can, and do, get the job done for their clients. Although we can't guarantee it, we trust that the surveys were answered accurately and honestly. Let us know if you discover otherwise.

PART THREE

Writer's Guide
Road Maps to Your Success

Over the Transom and into Print

The Battle of the UNs (Unagented/Unsolicited Submissions)

JEFF HERMAN

Most major publishing houses claim to have policies that prevent them from even considering unagented/unsolicited submissions. *Unagented* means that the submission was not made by a literary agent. *Unsolicited* means that no one at the publisher asked for the submission.

It's possible that you, or people you know, have already run into this frustrating roadblock. You may also be familiar with the rumor that it's more difficult to get an agent than it is to get a publisher—or that no agent will even consider your work until you *have* a publisher. On the surface, these negatives make it seem that you would have a better shot at becoming a starting pitcher for the Yankees, or living out whatever your favorite improbable fantasy might be. But, as you will soon learn, these so-called policies and practices are often more false than true. Especially if you develop creative ways to circumvent them.

I have dubbed the above obstacle course the Battle of the UNs. If you're presently unagented/unsolicited, you're one of the UNs. Welcome! You're in good company. Nobody is born published. There is no published author who wasn't at one time an UN. Thousands of new books are published each year, and thousands of people are needed to write them. You can be one of them.

In this chapter I'll show you how to win the Battle of the UNs. But first let me clarify an important distinction. When I use the word *win* here, I don't mean to say that you'll necessarily get your work published. What I mean is this: You'll gain reasonable access to the powers that be for your work, and you'll learn how to increase the odds—dramatically—that your work will be acquired.

Please be realistic. For every published writer, there are, at minimum, several thousand waiting in line to get published. "Many are called, but few are chosen."

It's completely within your power to maximize your chances of getting published. It's also within your power to minimize those chances. There are reasons why some highly talented people habitually underachieve, and those reasons can often be found within them. If you fail, fail, and fail, you should look within yourself for possible answers. What can you do to turn it around? If you find some answers, then you haven't failed at all, and the lessons you allow yourself to learn will lay the groundwork for success in this and in other endeavors.

Having an agent greatly increases the likelihood that you will be published. For one thing, on the procedural level, an established agent can usually obtain relatively rapid (and serious) consideration for his or her clients. One basic reason for this is that editors view agents as a valuable screening mechanism; that is, when a project crosses the editor's desk under an agent's letterhead, the editor knows it's undergone vetting from someone in the industry who is familiar with the applicable standards of quality and market considerations.

I usually recommend that unpublished writers first make every attempt to get an agent before they start going directly to the publishers. It's significantly easier to get an agent than it is to get a publisher—not the other way around. Most agents I know are always on the lookout for fresh talent. Finding and nurturing tomorrow's stars is one of our functions.

However, one of my reasons for writing and researching this book is to reveal to you that, as a potential author, not having an agent does not necessarily disqualify you from the game automatically. Before I show you ways to win the Battle of the UNs, I'd like you to have a fuller understanding of the system.

YOU ARE THE EDITOR

Imagine that you're an acquisitions editor at one of America's largest publishing firms in New York City. You have a master's degree from an Ivy League college and you, at least, think you're smarter than most other people. Yet you're earning a lot less money than most of the people who graduated with you. Your classmates have become lawyers, accountants, bankers, and so forth, and they all seem to own large, well-appointed apartments or homes—whereas you, if you fall out of bed, might land in the bathtub of your minuscule New York flat.

On the other hand, you love your job. For you, working in publishing is a dream come true. As in other industries and professions, much of your satisfaction comes from advancement—getting ahead.

To move up the career ladder, you must acquire at least a few successful titles each year. To find them you'll be competing with many editors from other publishers, and perhaps even with fellow editors within your own firm. As in any other business, the people who make the most money for the company will get the choice promotions and the highest salaries. Those who perform less impressively will tend to be passed over. (Of course, being a good editor and playing politics well are also important.)

There are two tried-and-true sources for the titles that publishers acquire: literary agents and direct solicitations.

Literary Agents

As an editor on the move, you'll cultivate relationships with many established literary agents. You'll want them to know what you like and what you don't like. And, by showing these agents you're disposed to acquiring new titles to build your position in the company, you'll encourage them to send you projects they think are right for you.

When you receive material from agents, you usually give it relatively fast consideration—especially if it's been submitted simultaneously to editors at other houses, which is usually the case. When something comes in from an agent, you know it's been screened and maybe even perfected. Established agents rarely waste your time with shoddy or inappropriate material. They couldn't make a living that way because they'd quickly lose credibility with editors.

Direct Solicitations

If you're an ambitious editor, you won't just sit back passively and wait to see what the agents might bless you with. When you're resourceful, the opportunities are endless. Perhaps you'll contact your old American history professor and ask her to do a book showcasing her unique perspectives on the Civil War.

Or maybe you'll contact that young fresh fiction writer whose short story you just read in a leading literary journal. You might even try reaching that veteran United States Senator who just got censured for sleeping with his young aides.

One place you'll tend *not* to use is the *slush pile*. This is the room (more like a warehouse) where all the unagented/unsolicited submissions end up. Looking through the slush pile isn't a smart use of your limited time and energy. The chances that anything decent can be found there are much less than one percent. You have less-than-fond memories of your first year in the publishing business, when, as an editorial assistant (which was basically an underpaid secretarial job), one of your tasks was to shovel through the slush. Once in a great while, something promising was found, but most of the stuff wasn't even close. At first, you were surprised by how unprofessional many of the submissions were: Many weren't addressed to anyone in particular; some looked as if they had been run over by Mack trucks; others were so poorly printed they were too painful for tired eyes to decipher—the list of failings is long.

No, the slush pile is the last place—or perhaps no place at all—to find titles for your list.

Now you can stop being an editor and go back to being whoever you really are. I wanted to show you why the system has evolved the way it has. Yes, though it's rational, it's cold and unfair, but these qualities aren't unique to publishing.

You're probably still wondering when I'm going to get to that promised modus operandi for winning the Battle of the UNs. Okay, we're there.

OUT OF THE SLUSH

The following steps are intended to keep you out of the infamous slush pile. Falling into the slush is like ending up in jail for contempt of court; it's like being an untouchable in

India; it's like being Frank Burns on *M*A*S*H*. My point is that nobody likes the Slushables. They're everyone's scapegoat and nobody's ally.

Once your work is assigned to the slush pile, it's highly unlikely that it will receive effective access. Without access, there can be no acquisition. Without acquisition, there's no book.

Let's pretend that getting published is a board game. However, in this game you can control the dice. Here are several ways to play:

Get the Names!

If you submit to nobody, it will go to nobody. Sending it to "The Editors," "Gentlemen," or the CEO of a $100-million publishing house equals sending it to no one. Instead, use the directory in this book to get the names of the suitable contacts.

In addition to using this directory, there are two other proven ways to discover who the right editors are:

1. Visit bookstores and seek out recent books that are in your category. Check the Acknowledgments section of each one. Many authors like to thank their editors here (and their agents). If the editor is acknowledged, you now have the name of someone who edits books like yours. Then call to confirm that the editor still works at that publishing house.

2. Or, call the publisher and ask for the editorial department. More often than not, the phone will be answered by a young junior editor who will say something like "Editorial." Like people who answer phones everywhere, these people may sound as if they are asleep, as if they are harried, or even as if they're making the most important declaration of their lives. Luckily for you, publishers plant few real secretaries or receptionists in their editorial departments, since it's constantly confirmed that rookie editors will do all that stuff for everyone else—and for a lot less money! Hence, real editors (although low in rank) can immediately be accessed.

   Returning to the true point of this—once someone answers the phone, ask, "Who edits your business books?" (Or whatever your category is.) You can also ask who edited a specific and recent book that's similar to yours. Such easy but vital questions will bring forth quick and valuable answers. Ask enough times and you can build a list of contacts that competes with the one in this book.

Don't Send Manuscripts Unless Invited to Do So!

Now that you're armed with these editors' names, don't abuse protocol (editors yell at *me* when you do—especially when they know where you've gotten their names). Initiate contact by sending a letter describing your work and encouraging the editor to request it. This letter, commonly referred to as a query letter, is in reality a sales pitch or door opener. (Please see the material in this book about query letters for a full overview of this important procedure.) In brief, the letter should be short (less than 1 1/2 pages), easy to read and to the point, personalized, and well printed on professional stationery. Say what you have, why it's hot, why you're a good prospect, and what's available for review upon request.

In addition to the letter, it's okay to include a résumé/bio that highlights any writing credits or relevant professional credentials; a brief summary (two to three pages) if the book is nonfiction, or a brief synopsis if it's fiction; a photo, if you have a flattering one; and promotional materials. Be careful: At this stage your aim is merely to whet the editor's appetite; you don't want to cause information overload. Less is more.

Also include a self-addressed stamped envelope (SASE). This is an important courtesy; without it, you increase your chances of getting no response. Editors receive dozens of these letters every week. Having to address envelopes for all of them would be very time consuming. And at 32 cents a pop, it's not worth doing. The SASE is generally intended to facilitate a response in the event of a negative decision. If the editor is intrigued by your letter, he may overlook the missing SASE and request to see your work—but don't count on it.

You may be wondering: If I have the editor's name, why not just send her my manuscript? Because you're flirting with the slush pile if you do. Even though you have the editor's previously secret name, you're still a UN, and UNs aren't treated kindly. An editor is inundated with reams of submissions, and her problem is finding good stuff to publish. If you send an unsolicited manuscript, you'll just be perceived as part of that problem. She'll assume you're just another slushy UN who needs to be sorted out of the way so she can go on looking for good stuff. A bad day for an editor is receiving a few trees' worth of UN manuscripts; it deepens her occupational neurosis.

On the other hand, a professional letter is quite manageable and is, at least, likely to be read. It may be screened initially by the editor's assistant, but will probably be passed upstairs if it shows promise.

If the editor is at all intrigued by your letter, she will request to see more material, and you will have earned the rank of being solicited. Even if your work is not ultimately acquired by this editor, you will have at least challenged and defeated the UNs' obstacle course by achieving quality consideration. Remember: Many people get published each year without the benefits of being agented or initially solicited.

It's okay, even smart, to query several editors simultaneously. This makes sense because some editors may take a very long time to respond, or, indeed, may never respond. Querying editors one at a time might take years. If more than one editor subsequently requests and begins considering your work, let each one know that it's not an exclusive. If an editor requests an exclusive, that's fine—but give him a time limit (four weeks is fair).

Don't sell your work to a publisher before consulting with all those who are considering it to see if they're interested. If you do sell it, be sure to give immediate written and oral notification to everyone who's considering it that it's no longer available.

The query-letter stage isn't considered a submission. You only need to have follow-up communications with editors who have gone beyond the query stage, meaning those who have requested and received your work for acquisition consideration. If you don't hear back from an editor within six weeks of sending her your letter, it's safe to assume she's not interested in your work.

If you send multiple queries, don't send them to more than one editor at the same house at the same time. If you don't hear back from a particular editor within six weeks of your submission, it's probably safe to query another editor at that house. One editor's reject is another's paradise; that's how both good and bad books get published.

We've just covered a lot of important procedural ground, so don't be embarrassed if you think you've forgotten all of it. This book won't self-destruct (and now, presumably, you won't either).

Cold Calls Breed Cold Hearts

One more thing: It's best not to cold-call these editors. Don't call them to try to sell them your work. Don't call them to follow-up on query letters or submissions. Don't call them to try to change their minds.

Why not? Do you like it when someone calls you in the middle of your favorite video to sell you land in the Nevada desert, near a popular nuclear test site?

Few people like uninvited and unscheduled sales calls. In some businesses, such as public relations, calling contacts is a necessary part of the process—but this is not so in publishing. Furthermore, this business is based on hard copy. You may be the greatest oral storyteller since Uncle Remus, but if you can't write it effectively and engagingly nobody is going to care. You'll end up soliciting their hostility. Of course, once they *are* interested in you on the basis of your hard copy, your oral and physical attributes may be of great importance to them.

On the other hand, some people are so skilled on the telephone that it's a lost opportunity for them not to make maximum use of it as a selling method. If you're one of these extremely rare and talented people, you should absolutely make use of whatever tools have proven to work best for you.

Everything I've said is my opinion. This is a subjective industry, so it's likely—no, it's certain—that others will tell you differently. It's to your advantage to educate yourself to the fullest extent possible (read books, attend workshops, and so forth) and in the end use your own best instincts about how to proceed. I'm confident that my suggestions are safe and sound, but I don't consider them to be the beginning and the end. The more you know, the simpler things become; the less you know, the more complex and confusing they are.

BREAKING THE RULES

Taken as a whole, this book provides a structure that can be considered a set of guidelines, if not hard-and-fast rules. Some people owe their success to breaking the rules and swimming upstream—and I can certainly respect that. Often such people don't even know they're breaking the rules; they're just naturally following their own unique orbits (and you'll find a few illustrations of this very phenomenon elsewhere in these essays). Trying to regulate such people can often be their downfall.

On one hand, most of us tend to run afoul when we stray from established norms of doing business; on the other hand, a few of us can't succeed any other way (Einstein could have written an essay about that). If you're one of those few, hats off to you! Perhaps we'll all learn something from your example.

Keep reading!

How to Write the
Perfect Query Letter

DEBORAH LEVINE

The query is a short letter of introduction to a publisher or agent, encouraging him or her to request to see your fiction manuscript or nonfiction book proposal. It is a vital tool often neglected by writers. If done correctly, it can help you to avoid endless frustration and wasted effort. The query is the first hurdle of your individual marketing strategy. If you can leap over it successfully, you're well on your way to a sale.

The query letter is your calling card. For every book that makes it to the shelves, there are thousands of worthy manuscripts, proposals, and ideas knocked out of the running by poor presentation or inadequate marketing strategies. Don't forget that the book you want to sell is a product that must be packaged correctly to stand above the competition.

A query letter asks the prospective publisher or agent if she would like to see more about the proposed idea. If your book is fiction, you should indicate that a manuscript or sample chapters are available on request. If nonfiction, you should offer to send a proposal and, if you have them, sample chapters.

The query is your first contact with the prospective buyer of your book. To ensure that it's not your last, avoid these common mistakes. The letter should be concise and well written. You shouldn't try to impress the reader with your mastery of all words over three syllables. Instead, concentrate on a clear and to-the-point presentation with no fluff. Think of the letter as an advertisement. You want to make a sale of a product, and you have very limited space and time in which to reach this goal.

The letter should be only one page long if possible. It will form the basis of a query package that will include supporting materials. Don't waste words in the letter describing material that can be included separately. Your goal is to pique the interest of an ditor who has very little time and probably very little patience. You want to entice her to keep reading and ask you for more.

The query package can include a short résumé, media clippings, or other favorable documents. Do not get carried away, or your package will quickly come to resemble junk mail. Include a self-addressed stamped envelope (SASE) with enough postage to return your entire package. This will be particularly appreciated by smaller publishing houses and independent agents.

For fiction writers, a short (one to five pages), double-spaced synopsis of the manuscript will be helpful and appropriate.

Do not waste money and defeat the purpose of the query by sending an unsolicited manuscript. Agents and editors may be turned off by receiving manuscripts of 1,000+ pages that were uninvited and are not even remotely relevant to what they do.

The query follows a simple format (which can be reworked according to your individual preferences): (1) lead, (2) supporting material/persuasion, (3) biography, and (4) conclusion/pitch.

YOUR LEAD IS YOUR HOOK

The lead can either catch the editor's attention or turn him off completely. Some writers think getting someone's attention in a short space means having to do something dramatic. Editors appreciate cleverness, but too much contrived writing can work against you. Opt instead for clear conveyance of thoroughly developed ideas and get right to the point.

Of course you don't want to be boring and stuffy in the interest of factual presentation. You'll need to determine what is most important about the book you're trying to sell, and write your letter accordingly.

You can begin with a lead similar to what you'd use to grab the reader in an article or a book chapter. You can use an anecdote, a statement of facts, a question, a comparison, or whatever you believe will be most powerful.

You may want to rely on the journalistic technique of the inverted pyramid. This means that you begin with the strongest material and save the details for later in the letter. Don't start slowly and expect to pick up momentum as you proceed. It will be too late.

Do not begin a query letter like this: "I have sent this idea to twenty agents/publishers, none of whom think it will work. I just know you'll be different, enlightened, and insightful, and will give it full consideration." There is no room for negatives in a sales pitch. Focus only on positives—unless you can turn negatives to your advantage.

Some writers make the mistake of writing about the book's potential in the first paragraph without ever stating its actual idea or theme. Remember, your letter may never be read beyond the lead, so make that first paragraph your hook.

Avoid bad jokes, clichés, unsubstantiated claims, and dictionary definitions. Don't be condescending; editors have egos, too, and have power over your destiny as a writer.

SUPPORTING MATERIAL: BE PERSUASIVE

If you are selling a nonfiction book, you may want to include a brief summary of hard evidence, gleaned from research, that will support the merit of your idea. This is where you convince the editor that your book should exist. This is more important for nonfiction than it is for fiction, where style and storytelling ability are paramount. Nonfiction writers must focus on selling their topic and their credentials.

You should include a few lines showing the editor what the publishing house will gain from the project. Publishers are not charitable institutions; they want to know how they can get the greatest return on their investment. If you have brilliant marketing ideas, or know of a well-defined market for your book where sales will be guaranteed, include this rather than other descriptive material.

In rereading your letter, make sure you have shown that you understand your own idea thoroughly. If it appears half-baked, the editors won't want to invest time fleshing out your thoughts. Exude confidence so that the editor will have faith in your ability to carry out the job.

In nonfiction queries, you can include a separate table of contents and brief chapter abstracts. Or it can wait for the book proposal.

YOUR BIOGRAPHY IS NO PLACE FOR MODESTY

In the biographical portion of your letter, toot your own horn, but in a carefully calculated, persuasive fashion. Your story of winning the third-grade writing competition (it was then that you knew you wanted to be a world-famous writer!) should be saved for the documentary done on your life after you reach your goal.

In the query, all you want to include are the most important and relevant credentials that will support the sale of your book. You can include, as a separate part of the package, a résumé or biography that will elaborate further.

The separate résumé should list all relevant and recent experiences that support your ability to write the book. Unless you're fairly young, your listing of academic accomplishments should start after high school. Don't overlook hobbies or activities not related to your job if they correspond to your book story or topic. Those experiences are often more valuable than academic achievements.

Other information to include: any impressive print clippings about you, a list of your broadcast interviews and speaking appearances, and copies of articles and reviews about any books you have written. This information can never hurt your chances and could make the difference in your favor.

There is no room for humility or modesty in the query letter and résumé. When corporations sell toothpaste, they list the product's best attributes and create excitement about the product. If you can't find some way to make yourself exciting as an author, you'd better rethink your career.

HERE'S THE PITCH

At the close of your letter, ask for the sale. This requires a positive and confident conclusion with phrases such as "I look forward to your speedy response." Phrases such as "I hope" and "I think you will like my book" sound too insecure. This is the part of the letter where you go for the kill.

Be sure to thank the reader for his or her attention in your final sentence.

FINISHING TOUCHES

When you're finished, reread and edit your query letter. Cut out any extraneous information that dilutes the strength of your arguments. Make the letter as polished as possible so that the editor will be impressed with you as well as with your idea. Don't ruin your chances by appearing careless; make certain your letter is not peppered with typos and misspellings. If you don't show pride in your work, you'll create a self-fulfilling prophecy; the editor will take you no more seriously than you take yourself.

Aesthetics are important. If you were pitching a business deal to a corporation, you would want to present yourself in conservative dress, with an air of professionalism. In the writing business, you may never have face-to-face contact with the people who will determine your future. Therefore your query package is your representative.

If an editor receives a query letter on yellowed paper that looks as if it's been lying around for twenty years, he or she will wonder if the person sending the letter is a has-been or a never-was.

You should invest in state-of-the-art letterhead—with a logo!—to create an impression of pride, confidence, and professionalism. White, cream, and ivory paper are all acceptable, but you should use only black ink for printing the letter. Anything else looks amateurish.

Don't sabotage yourself by letting your need for instant approval get the best of you. Don't call the editor. You have invited him or her to respond, so be patient. Then prepare yourself for possible rejection. It often takes many nos to get a yes.

One final note: This is a tough business for anyone—and it's especially so for greenhorns. Hang in there.

Query Letter Tips

Jeff Herman

If you have spent any time at all in the publishing business, the term *query letter* is as familiar to you as the back of your hand—perhaps even more so. Yet, no matter how many courses you've attended and books you've read about this important part of the process, you may still feel inadequate when you try to write a query that sizzles. If it's any consolation, you're far from being alone in your uncertainty.

The purpose of the query letter is to formally introduce your work and yourself to potential agents and editors. The immediate goal is to motivate them to promptly request a look at your work, or at least review a portion of it.

In effect, the letter serves as the writer's way over the first hurdle. It's a relatively painless way for agents and editors to screen out unwanted submissions without the added burden of having to root through a deluge of unwanted manuscripts. Editors and agents are more relaxed if their in-boxes are filled with fifty unanswered queries, as opposed to fifty uninvited 1,000-page manuscripts. The query is an effective way to control the quality and quantity of the manuscripts that arrive at the office. And that's why you have to write good—no, make that *outstanding*—queries.

The term query letter is part of the lexicon and jargon of the publishing business. This term isn't generally used in other industries. I assume it has ancient origins. I can conjure up images of an Egyptian scribe poised thoughtfully over a scroll of papyrus; a Chinese writer refining the elegance of an opening line; and a Mesopotamian poet burning the oil till dawn, revising one clay tablet after another. Ah, yes, I can picture an English gentleman with a fluffy quill pen composing a most civilized letter to a prospective publisher for the purpose of asking for his work to be read and, perchance, published. Our environments may change, but the nature of our ambitions remain the same.

Let's get contemporary. Whenever you hear the term query letter you should say to yourself "pitch" or "sales" letter. Because that's what it is. You need the letter to sell.

Here are some fundamental guidelines:

- *Don't be long-winded.* Agents and editors receive lots of these things, and they want to mow through them as swiftly as possible. Ideally, the letter should be a single page with short paragraphs. (I must admit I've seen good ones that are longer than a page.) When you lose your reader, you've lost your opportunity.
- *Get to the point. Don't pontificate.* Too many letters go off on irrelevant detours, which makes it difficult for the agent/editor to determine what's actually for sale other than the writer's soapbox.
- *Make your letter attractive.* When making a first impression, the subliminal impact of aesthetics cannot be overestimated. Use high-quality stationery and a readable, attractive typeface. The essence of your words are paramount, but cheap paper and poor print quality will only diminish your impact.
- *Don't say anything negative about yourself or your attempts to get published.* Everyone appreciates victims when it's time to make charitable donations, but not when it's time to make a profit. It's better if you can make editors/agents think that you must fight them off.

Q & A

Q: Why can't I bypass the query hurdle by simply submitting my manuscript?

A: You may—and no one can litigate against you. But if you submit an unsolicited manuscript to a publisher it's likely to end up in the so-called slush pile and may never get a fair reading. If sent to an agent, there is a chance nothing negative will come of it (this chance may be remote or fair, depending on the timing and the agent). However, most agents prefer to receive a query first.

Sending unsolicited nonfiction book proposals is in the gray zone. Proposals are much more manageable than entire manuscripts, so editors/agents may not particularly mind. But you may want to avoid the expense of sending unwanted proposals. After all, the query is also an opportunity for you as an author to screen out those agents and editors who clearly have no interest in your subject. Also, you shouldn't be overly loose with your ideas and concepts.

These pointers, in combination with the other good information in this book and other accessible resources, should provide a solid foundation as you develop your own approach for creating a dynamic query letter.

The Knockout Nonfiction Book Proposal

Jeff Herman

The nonfiction book proposal should be viewed as a sales brochure. If you keep this in mind as you write it, you will gain more than a mere leg up on your competition: It will invariably make the difference between success and failure. This is because of the proposal's primary importance in the process of editorial acquisition and book publishing in general.

Before agents and publishers will accept a work of fiction (especially from a newer writer), they require a complete manuscript. However, nonfiction projects are different: A proposal alone can do the trick. This is what makes nonfiction writing a much less speculative and often more lucrative endeavor (relatively speaking) than fiction writing.

Instead of devoting five years of long evenings to writing a 1,000-page fiction manuscript only to receive a thick pile of computer-generated rejections, why not spend a few weeks developing a nonfiction project? Then send a proposal to an interested editor or agent. If you can't sell it to anyone, you'll find out soon enough and without losing a few years of your life in the process.

On the other hand, writing fiction does have its own perks: It is often an emotionally driven endeavor in which rewards are gained though the act of writing and are not necessarily based on rational, practical considerations. Fiction writing, whether it be pulp or literary, is one of the most creative things a person can do. In fact, many successful nonfiction writers fantasize about being fiction writers.

And there is a market for fiction: Millions of Americans read fiction voraciously. As is covered elsewhere in this book, the fiction market has a category structure through which agents and publishers can be approached. Nevertheless, as an author, you should understand that writing nonfiction is the easier road to getting published. And it all starts with the proposal.

As you'll learn, the proposal's structure, contents, and size can vary substantially, and it's up to you to decide the best format for your purposes. Still, the guidelines given below serve as excellent general parameters. In addition, an excellent model proposal is featured in the next chapter.

APPEARANCE COUNTS

- Your proposal should be printed in black ink on clean letter-sized (8 1/2" × 11") white paper.
- Avoid slick-surfaced computer paper. Be sure to type or print out your manuscript on bond paper—and to separate and trim the pages if they are generated from a fanfold, tractor-fed printer.
- Letter-quality printing is by far the best. Make sure the ribbon, toner, or ink cartridge is fresh and that all photocopies are dark and clear enough to be read easily. Be wary of old manual typewriters—have the proposal retyped on up-to-date equipment if necessary. Publishing is an image-driven business, and you will be judged, perhaps unconsciously, on the physical and aesthetic merits of your submission.
- Always double-space, or you can virtually guarantee reader antagonism—eye-strain makes people cranky.
- Make sure your proposal appears fresh and new and hasn't been dog-eared, marked-up, and abused by previous readers. No editor will be favorably disposed if she thinks that everyone else on the block has already sent you packing. You want editors to suppose that you have lots of other places you can go, not nowhere else to go.
- Contrary to common practice in other industries, editors prefer not to receive bound proposals. If an editor likes your proposal, she will want to photocopy it for her colleagues, and your binding will only be in the way. If you want to keep the material together and neat, it's best to use a paper clip; if it's a lengthy proposal, perhaps it will work best to clip each section together separately.

THE TITLE PAGE

The title page should be the easiest part, and it can also be the most important, since, like your face when you meet someone, it's what is seen first.

Try to think of an attention getting title that effectively communicates your book's concept. A descriptive subtitle, following a catchy title, can help to achieve both goals. It's very important that your title and subtitle relate to the book's subject, or an editor might make an inaccurate judgment about your book's focus and automatically dismiss it. For instance, if you're proposing a book about gardening, don't title it *The Greening of America.*

Examples of titles that have worked very well are:

How to Win Friends and Influence People by Dale Carnegie.

Think and Grow Rich by Napoleon Hill.

Baby and Child Care by Dr. Benjamin Spock.

How to Swim with the Sharks without Being Eaten Alive by Harvey Mackay.

And, yes, there are notable exceptions: An improbable title that went on to become a perennial success is *What Color Is Your Parachute?* by Richard Bolles. Sure, you may gain freedom and confidence from such exceptional instances, and by all means let your imagination roam during the brainstorming stage. However, don't bet on the success of an arbitrarily conceived title that has nothing at all to do with the book's essential concept or reader appeal.

A title should be stimulating and, when appropriate, upbeat and optimistic. If your subject is an important historic or current event, the title should be dramatic. If a biography, the title should capture something personal (or even controversial) about the subject. Many good books have been handicapped by poor titles, and many poor books have been catapulted to success by good titles. A good title is good advertising. Procter & Gamble, for instance, spends thousands of worker hours creating seductive names for its endless array of soap-based products.

The title you choose is referred to as the "working title." Most likely, the book will have a different title when published. There are two reasons for this: (1) A more appropriate and/or arresting title may evolve with time; and (2) the publisher has final contractual discretion over the title (as well as a lot of other things).

The title page should contain only the title; your name, address, and telephone number; and the name, address, and phone number of your agent, if you have one. The title page should be neatly and attractively spaced. Eye-catching and tasteful computer graphics and display-type fonts can contribute to the overall aesthetic appeal.

OVERVIEW

The overview portion of the proposal is a terse statement (one to three pages) of your overall concept and mission. It sets the stage for what's to follow. Short, concise paragraphs are usually best.

BIOGRAPHICAL SECTION

This is where you sell yourself. This section tells who you are and why you're the ideal person to write this book. You should highlight all your relevant experience, including media and public-speaking appearances, and list previous books and/or articles published by and/or about you. Self-flattery is appropriate—so long as you're telling the truth. Many writers prefer to slip into the third person here, to avoid the appearance of egomania.

MARKETING SECTION

This is where you justify the book's existence from a commercial perspective. Who will buy it? For instance, if you're proposing a book on sales, state the number of people who earn their livings through sales; point out that thousands of large and small companies depend on sales and spend large sums on sales training; and mention that all sales professionals are perpetually hungry for fresh, innovative books on sales.

Don't just say something like "My book is for adult women and there are more than fifty million adult women in America." You have to be much more demographically sophisticated than that.

COMPETITION SECTION

To the uninitiated, this section may appear to be a set-up to self-destruction. However, if handled strategically, and assuming you have a fresh concept, this section will win you points rather than undermine your case.

The competition section is where you describe major published titles with concepts comparable to yours. If you're familiar with your subject, you'll probably know those titles by heart; you may have even read most or all of them. If you're not certain, check *Books in Print*—available in virtually every library. It catalogs all titles in print in every category under the sun. Don't list everything published on your subject—that could require a book in itself. Just describe the leading half-dozen titles or so (backlist classics as well as recent books) and *explain why yours will be different.*

Getting back to the sales-book example, there is no shortage of good books on sales. There's a reason for that—there's a sizable market for them. You can turn that to your advantage by emphasizing what a substantial, insatiable demand there is for sales books. Your book will feed that demand with its unique and innovative sales success program. Salespeople and companies dependent on sales are always looking for new ways to enhance sales skills (it's okay to reiterate key points).

PROMOTION SECTION

Here you suggest possible ways to promote and market the book. Sometimes this section is unnecessary. It depends on your subject and on what, if any, realistic promotional prospects exist.

If you're proposing a specialized academic book such as *The Mating Habits of Octopi*, the market is a relatively limited one, and elaborate promotions would be wasteful. But if you're proposing a popularly oriented relationship book along the lines of *The Endless Orgasm in One Easy Lesson*, the promotional possibilities are almost endless. They would include most major electronic broadcast and print media outlets, advertising, maybe even some weird contests. You want to guide the publisher toward seeing realistic ways to publicize the book.

CHAPTER OUTLINE

This is the meat of the proposal. Here's where you finally tell what's going to be in the book. Each chapter should be tentatively titled and clearly abstracted. Some successful proposals have fewer than one hundred words per abstracted chapter, others have several hundred words per chapter. Sometimes the length varies from chapter to chapter. There are no hard-and-fast rules here; it's the dealer's choice. Sometimes less is more, at other times an outline that brief inadequately represents the project.

At their best, the chapter abstracts should read like minichapters, as opposed to stating "I will do . . . and I will show. . . ". Visualize the trailer for a forthcoming movie; that's the tantalizing effect you want to create. Also, it's a good idea to preface the outline with a table of contents so the editor can see your entire road map at the outset.

SAMPLE CHAPTERS

Sample chapters are optional. A strong, well-developed proposal will often be enough. However, especially if you're a first-time writer, one or more sample chapters will give you an opportunity to show your stuff. They will also help dissolve an editor's concerns about your ability to actually write the book, thereby increasing the odds that you'll receive an offer—and you'll probably increase the size of the advance, too.

Nonfiction writers are often wary of investing time to write sample chapters, since they view the proposal as a way of avoiding speculative writing. This can be a shortsighted position, however, for a single sample chapter can make the difference between selling and not selling a marginal proposal. Occasionally a publisher will ask you to write one or two sample chapters before making a decision about a particular project. If the publisher seems to have a real interest, writing the sample material is definitely worth the author's time, and the full package can then be shown to additional prospects too.

Many editors say that they look for reasons to reject books, and that being on the fence is a valid reason for rejecting a project. To be sure, there are cases where sample chapters have tilted a proposal on the verge of rejection right back onto the playing field!

Keep in mind that the publisher is speculating that you can and will write the book upon contract. A sample chapter will significantly reduce the publisher's concerns about your ability to deliver a quality work beyond the proposal stage.

WHAT ELSE?

There are a variety of materials you may wish to attach to the proposal to further bolster your cause. They include the following:

- Laudatory letters and comments about you.
- Laudatory publicity about you.
- A headshot (not if you look like the Fly, unless you're proposing a humor book or a nature book).
- Copies of published articles you've written.
- Videos of TV or speaking appearances.
- Any and all information that builds you up in a relevant way. (But be organized about it—don't create a disheveled, unruly package.)

LENGTH

The average proposal is probably between 15 and 30 double-spaced pages, and the typical sample chapter is an additional 10 to 20 double-spaced pages. But sometimes proposals reach 100 pages, and sometimes they're 5 pages total. Extensive proposals are not a handicap. Include whatever it takes!

Note: Readers of *Writer's Guide* who wish to do more research on the topic of book proposals should read *Write the Perfect Book Proposal: 10 Proposals That Sold and Why* by Jeff Herman and Deborah Adams (John Wiley & Sons). This work contains samples of successful book proposals along with pertinent commentary and coaching on the techniques writers can employ to develop the sort of book projects agents find salable—and publishers find marketable.

Model Successful
Nonfiction Book Proposal

JEFF HERMAN

In this chapter is a genuine proposal that won a healthy book contract. It's excerpted from *Write the Perfect Book Proposal* by Jeff Herman and Deborah Adams (Wiley), and includes an extensive critique of its strongest and weakest points. All in all, it's an excellent proposal and serves as a strong model.

The book is titled *Heart and Soul: A Psychological and Spiritual Guide to Preventing and Healing Heart Disease* and it is written by Bruno Cortis, M.D. This project was sold to the Villard Books division of Random House. Every editor who saw this proposal offered sincere praise. Ironically, several of these editors regretted not being able to seek the book's acquisition. From the outset I was aware this might happen. The past few years have given us numerous unconventional health and healing books— many of which are excellent. Most publishers I approached felt that their health/spirituality quota was already full and that they would wind up competing with themselves if they acquired any more such titles.

Experienced agents and writers are familiar with the market-glut problem. In many popular categories it's almost endemic. If you're prepared for this reality from the outset there are ways to pave your own road and bypass the competition. Dedicated agents, editors, and writers want to see important books published regardless of what the publishers' lists dictate. Further, it is not necessary for every publisher to want your book (though that is the proven way to maximize the advance). In the end, you need only the right publisher and a reasonable deal. Let's look at the title page from the book proposal.

HEART AND SOUL

(This is a good title. It conjures up dramatic images similar to a soulful blues melody. And it has everything to do with what this proposal is about. The subtitle is scientific and provides a clear explanation for the patients.)

**A Psychological and Spiritual Guide to
Preventing and Healing Heart Disease
by
Bruno Cortis, M.D.
Book Proposal**

**The Jeff Herman Agency, Inc.
500 Greenwich Street
Suite 501c
New York, NY 10013
212-941-0540**

(The title page is sufficient overall. But it would have been better if the software had been used to create a more striking cover sheet. To a large degree, everything does initially get judged by its cover.)

OVERVIEW

(One minor improvement would have been to shift the word "Overview" to the center of the page, styling such headings with a special typeface throughout the proposal to make them stand out from the body text.)

Heart disease is the number-one killer of Americans over the age of forty. The very words can sound like a death sentence. Our heart, the most intimate part of our body, is under siege. Until now, most experts have advised victims of the disease, as well as those who would avoid it, to change avoidable risk factors, like smoking, and begin a Spartan regimen of diet and exercise. But new research shows that risk factors and lifestyle are only part of the answer. In fact, it is becoming clear that for many patients, emotional, psychological, and even spiritual factors are at least as important, both in preventing disease and in healing an already damaged heart.

(This is a powerful lead paragraph. The author knows there are a lot of books about heart disease. The first paragraph of the overview immediately distinguishes this book proposal and draws attention to "new research." Anything that is potentially cutting edge is going to catch the eye of a prospective publisher.)

Like *Love, Medicine, and Miracles* by Bernie Siegel, which showed cancer patients how to take charge of their own disease and life, *Heart and Soul* will show potential and actual heart patients how to use inner resources to form a healthy relationship with their heart, actually healing circulatory disorders and preventing further damage.

(The paragraph above contains the central thesis for the project, and it is profoundly important. In retrospect this could have worked exceedingly well as the first paragraph of the proposal, thereby immediately setting the table. This is also a clever comparison to a highly successful book. It indicates an untapped market that has already proven itself in a similar arena. Instead of merely making unsubstantiated claims based on the success of Dr. Siegel's work, the author shows what this book will do to merit the same type of attention.)

The author, Bruno Cortis, M.D., is a renowned cardiologist whose experience with hundreds of "exceptional heart patients" has taught him that there is much more to medicine than operations and pills.

(It is good to bring the author's credentials into the overview at this juncture. A comparison has been made with a highly successful and marketable doctor/ author, which will immediately raise questions as to whether this author has similar potential. The author anticipates this line of editorial reasoning and here makes some strong statements.)

Dr. Cortis identifies three types of heart patients:

- Passive Patients, who are unwilling or unable to take responsibility for their condition. Instead, these patients blame outside forces, withdraw from social contacts, and bewail their fate. They may become deeply depressed, and tend to die very soon.
- Obedient Consumers, who are the "A" students of modern medicine. Following doctors' orders to the letter, these patients behave exactly as they are "supposed to," placing their fates in the hands of the experts. These patients tend to die exactly when medicine predicts they will.
- Exceptional Heart Patients, who regard a diagnosis of heart disease as a challenge. Although they may have realistic fears for the future, these patients take full responsibility for their situation and actively contribute to their own recovery. While they may or may not follow doctors' orders, these patients tend to choose the therapy or combination of therapies that is best for them. They often live far beyond medical predictions.

(This is an exceptional overview—especially where it defines the three patient types.)

It is Dr. Cortis' aim in this book to show readers how to become exceptional heart patients, empowering them to take responsibility for their own health and well-being.

(The remaining paragraphs of this overview section show a highly focused and well-thought-out plan for the book. The writing collaborator on this project had to condense and assimilate boxes and boxes of material to produce this concise and to-the-point overview that leaves no questions unanswered. Although it took a great deal of effort for the writer to write such a good proposal, there is no struggle for the editor to understand exactly what is being proposed and what the book is going to be about.)

Although Dr. Cortis acknowledges the importance of exercise, stress management, and proper nutrition—the standard staples of cardiac treatment—he stresses that there is an even deeper level of human experience that is necessary in order to produce wellness. Unlike other books on heart disease, *Heart and Soul* does not prescribe the same strict diet and exercise program for everyone. Instead it takes a flexible approach, urging readers to create their own unique health plan by employing psychological and spiritual practices in combination with a variety of more traditional diet and exercise regimens.

While seemingly revolutionary, Dr. Cortis' message is simple: You can do much more for the health of your heart than you think you can. This is true whether you have no symptoms or risk factors whatsoever, if you have some symptoms or risk factors, or if you actually already have heart disease.

MARKET ANALYSIS

Heart and Soul could not be more timely. Of the 1 1/2 million heart attacks suffered by Americans each year, nearly half occur between the ages of forty and sixty-five. Three-fifths of these heart attacks are fatal. While these precise statistics may not be familiar to the millions of baby boomers now entering middle age, the national obsession with oat bran, low-fat foods, and exercising for health shows that the members of the boomer generation are becoming increasingly aware of their own mortality.

(The writer would be well advised to ease off the use of the term "baby boomer." It is used so often in book proposals that many editors are undoubtedly sick of it—and some have said so. It might be better merely to describe the exceptional number of people in this pertinent age bracket, without attempting to sound trendy. Good use of facts, trends, and the public's receptivity to what some would characterize as an unorthodox treatment approach.)

This awareness of growing older, coupled with a widespread loss of faith in doctors and fear of overtechnologized medicine, produces a market that is ready for a book emphasizing the spiritual component in healing, especially in reference to heart disease.

Most existing books on the market approach the subject from the physician's point of view, urging readers to follow doctor's orders to attain a healthy heart. There is very little emphasis in these books on the patient's own responsibility for wellness or the inner changes that must be made for the prescribed regimens to work. Among the best known recent books are the following:

(Not a big deal in this instance, but ordinarily it would be better to identify this portion of the proposal as the competition section and set it off under a separate heading.)

Healing Your Heart, by Herman Hellerstein, M.D., and Paul Perry (Simon and Schuster, 1990). Although this book, like most of the others, advocates proper nutrition, exercise, cessation of smoking, and stress reduction as the road to a healthy heart, it fails to provide the motivation necessary to attain such changes in the reader's lifestyle. Without changes in thinking and behavior, readers of this and similar books will find it difficult, if not impossible, to follow the strict diet and exercise program recommended.

In *Heart Talk: Preventing and Coping with Silent and Painful Heart Disease* (Harcourt Brace Jovanovich, 1987), Dr. Peter F. Cohn and Dr. Joan K. Cohn address the dangers of "silent" (symptomless) heart disease. While informative, the book emphasizes only one manifestation of heart disease, and does not empower readers with the motivational tools needed to combat that disease.

(This section is termed the market analysis, which in this proposal actually departs from the approach of the typical marketing section of most proposals. Instead of telling the publisher how to sell the book, the writing collaborator (see the About the Authors section below) shows special insight into the target audience. The key is that this analysis is not merely a statement of the obvious. This type of in-depth analysis of the potential reader can be very persuasive.)

The Trusting Heart, by Redford Williams, M.D. (Times Books, 1989), demonstrates how hostility and anger can lead to heart disease, while trust and forgiveness can contribute to wellness. While these are important points, the holistic treatment of heart disease must encompass other approaches as well. The author also fails to provide sufficient motivation for behavioral changes in the readers.

(The author does a good job of demonstrating the invaluable uniqueness of this particular project—especially important when compared with the strong list of competitors.)

The best book on preventing and curing heart disease is *Dr. Dean Ornish's Program for Reversing Heart Disease* (Random House, 1990). This highly successful book prescribes a very strict diet and exercise program for actually reversing certain types of coronary artery disease. This still-controversial approach is by far the best on the market; unfortunately, the material is presented in a dense, academic style not easily accessible to the lay reader. It also focuses on Dr. Ornish's program as the "only way to manage heart disease," excluding other, more synergistic methods.

(The writer collaborator directly analyzed the competition, highlighting the most relevant books on the market without listing every one directly. Although you do not want to present the editor with any unnecessary surprises, if there are too many similar books out in your particular subject area you might want to use this approach. The writer confronts the heaviest competition directly by finding specific distinguishing factors that support the strength of her proposed project.)

APPROACH

Heart and Soul will be a 60,000- to 70,000-word book targeted to health-conscious members of the baby boom generation. Unlike other books on heart disease, it will focus on the connection between the mind and the body as it relates to heart disease, showing readers how to use that connection to heal the heart. The book will be written in an informal but authoritative style, in Dr. Cortis' voice. It will begin with a discussion of heart disease and show how traditional medicine fails to prevent or cure it. Subsequent chapters will deal with the mind–body connection and the role in healing of social support systems, self-esteem, and faith. In order to help readers reduce stress in their lives, Dr. Cortis shows how they can create their own "daily practice" that combines exercise, relaxation, meditation, and use of positive imagery. Throughout the book, he will present anecdotes that demonstrate how other exceptional heart patients have overcome their disease and gone on to lead healthy and productive lives.

In addition to a thorough discussion of the causes and outcomes of coronary artery disease, the book will include tests and checklists that readers can use to gauge their progress, and exercises, ranging from the cerebral to the physical, that strengthen and help heal the heart. At the end of each chapter readers will be introduced to an essential "Heartskill" that will enable them to put the advice of the chapter into immediate practice.

Through example and encouragement *Heart and Soul* will offer readers a variety of strategies for coping with heart disease, to be taken at once or used in combination. Above all an accessible, practical book, *Heart and Soul* will present readers with a workable program for controlling their own heart disease and forming a healthy relationship with their hearts.

(This is a good summary statement of the book.)

ABOUT THE AUTHORS

Bruno Cortis, M.D., is an internationally trained cardiologist with more than thirty years' experience in research and practice. A pioneer of cardiovascular applications of lasers and angioscopy, a Diplomate of the American Board of Cardiology, and a contributor of more than seventy published professional papers, Dr. Cortis has long advocated the need for new dimensions of awareness in health and the healing arts. As a practicing physician and researcher, his open

[handwritten margin note: UC will approach it differently → back to basics, other books are for after you're organized]

acknowledgment of individual spirituality as the core of health puts him on the cutting edge of those in traditional medicine who are beginning to create the medical arts practices of the future.

(This is a very good description of the author. The writing collaborator establishes Dr. Cortis as both an expert in his field and a compelling personality. All of this material is relevant to the ultimate success of the book.)

Dr. Cortis has spoken at conferences in South America, Japan, and Australia, as well as in Europe and the United States. His firm, Mind Your Health, is dedicated to the prevention of heart attack through the development of human potential. Dr. Cortis is the cofounder of the Exceptional Heart Patients program. The successful changes he has made in his own medical practice prove he is not only a man of vision and deeds, but also an author whose beliefs spring from the truths of daily living.

(A formal vita follows in this proposal. It is best to lead off with a journalistic-style biography and follow up with a complete and formal résumé—assuming, as in this case, the author's professional credentials are inseparable from the book.)

Kathryn Lance is the author of more than thirty books of nonfiction and fiction (see attached publications list for details). Her first book, *Running for Health and Beauty* (1976), the first mass-market book on running for women, sold half a million copies. *The Setpoint Diet* (1985), ghosted for Dr. Gilbert A. Leveille, stayed on the *New York Times* bestseller list for several weeks. Ms. Lance has written widely on fitness, health, diet, and medicine.

(Though she wasn't mentioned on the title page, Lance is the collaborator. This brief bio and the following résumé reveal a writer with virtually impeccable experience. Her participation served to assure editors that they could count on the delivery of a high-quality manuscript. Her bio sketch is also strong in its simplicity. Her writing credits are voluminous, but she does not use up space here with a comprehensive listing. Instead she showcases only credits that are relevant to the success of this particular project.

Comprehensive author resumes were also attached as addenda to the proposal package.)

Heart and Soul
by
Bruno Cortis, M.D.
Chapter Outline

(Creating a separate page (or pages) for the entire table of contents is a useful and easy technique to enable the editor to gain a holistic vision for the book before delving into the chapter abstracts. In retrospect, we should have had one here.)

(The following is an exceptional outline because it goes well beyond the lazy and stingy telegram approach that many writers use, often to their own detriment. [Telegrams once were a popular means of communication that required the sender to pay by the word.] Here each abstract reads like a miniature sample chapter unto itself. It proves that the writers have a genuine command of their subject, a well-organized agenda, and superior skills for writing about it. Together they are a darn good team. Whatever legitimate reasons a publisher may have had for rejecting this proposal, it had nothing to do with its manifest editorial and conceptual merits. Some writers are reluctant to go to this editorial distance on spec. However, if you believe in your project's viability and you want to maximize acquisition interest and the ultimate advance, you'll give the proposal everything you've got.)

Table of Contents
Introduction: Beating the Odds: Exceptional Heart Patients
(See sample chapter.)

CHAPTER ONE. YOU AND YOUR HEART
Traditional medicine doesn't and can't "cure" heart disease. The recurrence rate of arterial blockage after angioplasty is 25 to 35 percent, while a bypass operation only *bypasses* the problem, but does not cure it. The author proposes a new way of looking at heart disease, one in which patients become responsible for the care and well-being of their hearts, in partnership with their physicians. The author presents a brief, understandable discussion of the physiology of heart disease and heart attack, then follows with additional topics including:

(This is a good technique for a chapter abstract. The writer organizes the structure as a listing of chapter topics and elaborates with a sample of the substance and writing approach that will be incorporated into the book. The editor cannot of course be expected to be an expert on the subject but after reading this abstract he or she will come away with a good sense of the quality of the chapter and the depth of its coverage.)

  Heart disease as a message from your body. Many of us go through life neglecting our bodies' signals, ignoring symptoms until a crisis occurs. But the body talks to us and it is up to us to listen and try to understand the message. The heart bears the load of all our physical activity as well as our mental activity. Stress can affect the heart as well as any other body system. This section explores the warning signs of heart disease as "messages" we may receive from our hearts, what these messages may mean, and what we can do in response to these messages.

Why medical tests and treatments are not enough. You, the patient, are ultimately responsible for your own health. Placing all faith in a doctor is a way of abdicating that responsibility. The physician is not a healer; rather, he or she sets the stage for the patient's body to heal itself. Disease is actually a manifestation of an imbalance within the body. Medical procedures can help temporarily, but the real solution lies in the patient's becoming aware of his own responsibility for health. This may involve changing diet, stopping smoking, and learning to control the inner life.

(Although the abstracts are directed to the editor who reviews the proposal, the writer incorporates the voice to be used in the book by speaking directly to the reader. This is an effective way to incorporate her writing style into the chapter-by-chapter outline.)

Getting the best (while avoiding the worst) of modern medicine. In the author's view, the most important aspect of medicine is not the medication but the patient/physician relationship. Unfortunately, this relationship is often cold, superficial, professional. The patient goes into the medical pipeline, endures a number of tests, then comes out the other end with a diagnosis that is like a flag he has to carry for life. This view of disease ignores the patient as the *main* component of the healing process. Readers are advised to work with their doctors to monitor their own blood pressure and blood sugar and cholesterol levels, and to learn what these numbers mean. They are further advised how to enlist a team of support people to increase their own knowledge of the disease and to discover the self-healing mechanisms within.

How to Assess Your Doctor. Ten questions a patient needs to ask in order to assure the best patient–doctor relationship.

Taking charge of your own medical care. Rather than being passive patients, readers are urged to directly confront their illness and the reasons for it, asking themselves: How can I find a cause at the deepest level? What have I learned from this disease? What is good about it? What have I learned about myself? Exceptional heart patients don't allow themselves to be overwhelmed by the disease; rather, they realize that it is most likely a temporary problem, most of the time self-limited, and that they have a power within to overcome it.

Seven keys to a healthy heart. Whether presently healthy or already ill of heart disease there is a great deal readers can do to improve and maintain the health of their hearts. The most important component of such a plan is to have a commitment to a healthy heart. The author offers the following seven keys to a healthy heart: respect your body; take time to relax every day; accept, respect, and appreciate yourself; share your deepest feelings; establish life goals; nourish your spiritual self; love yourself and others unconditionally. Each of these aspects of heart care will be examined in detail in later chapters.

Heartskill #1: *Learning to take your own pulse.* The pulse is a wave of blood sent through the arteries each time the heart contracts; pulse rate therefore provides important information about cardiac function. The easiest place to measure the pulse is the wrist: place your index and middle finger over the underside of the opposite wrist. Press gently and firmly until you locate your pulse. Don't use your thumb to feel the pulse, because the thumb has a pulse of its own. Count the number of pulse beats in fifteen seconds, then multiply that by four for your heart rate.

This exercise will include charts so that readers can track and learn their own normal pulse range for resting and exercising, and be alerted to irregularities and changes that may require medical attention.

(The inclusion of this technique shows how specific and practical information will be included in the book—important for a nonfiction book proposal. Editors look for what are called the program aspects of a book, because they can be used in promotional settings—and may also be the basis for serial-rights sales to magazines.)

CHAPTER TWO. YOUR MIND AND YOUR HEART

This chapter begins to explore the connection between mind and body as it relates to heart disease. Early in the chapter readers will meet three Exceptional Heart Patients who overcame crushing diagnoses. These include Van, who overcame a heart attack (at age 48), two open heart surgeries, and "terminal" lung cancer. Through visualization techniques given him by the author, Van has fully recovered and is living a healthy and satisfying life. Goran, who had a family history of cardiomyopathy, drew on the support and love of his family to survive a heart transplant and has since gone on to win several championships in an Olympics contest for transplant patients. Elaine, who overcame both childhood cancer and severe heart disease, is, at the age of twenty-four, happily married and a mother. The techniques used by these Exceptional Heart Patients will be discussed in the context of the mind–body connection.

(The authors do not save the good stuff for the book. If you have interesting case studies or anecdotes, include them in your abstracts: The more stimulating material you include, the more you will intrigue your editor. In general, this chapter-by-chapter synopsis is exceptionally detailed in a simplified fashion, which is important for this type of book.)

How your doctor views heart disease: Risk factors versus symptoms. Traditional medicine views the risk factors for heart disease (smoking, high blood cholesterol, high blood pressure, diabetes, obesity, sedentary lifestyle, family history of heart disease, use of oral contraceptives) as indicators of the likelihood of developing illness. In contrast, the author presents these risk factors as *symptoms* of an underlying disease and discusses ways to change them. Smoking, for example, is not the root of the problem, which is, rather, fear, tension, and stress. Smoking is just an outlet that the patient uses to get rid of these basic elements that he or she believes are uncontrollable. Likewise high cholesterol, which is viewed by the medical establishment as largely caused by poor diet, is also affected by stress. (In a study of rabbits on a high-cholesterol diet, narrowing of arteries was less in rabbits that were petted, even if the diet remained unhealthful.) Other elements besides the traditional "risk factors," such as hostility, have been shown to lead to high rates of heart disease.

A mind/body model of heart disease. It is not uncommon to hear stories like this: They were a very happy couple, married fifty-two years. Then, suddenly, the wife developed breast cancer and died. The husband, who had no previous symptoms of heart disease, had a heart attack and died two months later. All too often there is a very close relationship between a traumatic event and serious illness. Likewise, patients may often become depressed and literally will themselves to die. The other side of the coin is the innumerable patients who use a variety of techniques to enlist the mind–body connection in helping to overcome and even cure serious illnesses, including heart disease.

Rethinking your negative beliefs about heart disease. The first step in using the mind to help to heal the body is to rethink negative beliefs about heart disease. Modern studies have shown that stress plays a most important role in the creation of heart disease, influencing all of the "risk factors." Heart disease is actually a disease of self, caused by self, and is made worse by the belief that we are its "victims." Another negative and incorrect belief is that the possibilities for recovery are limited. The author asserts that these beliefs are untrue, and that for patients willing to learn from the experience, heart disease can be a path to recovery, self-improvement, and growth.

The healing personality: tapping into your body's healing powers. Although the notion of a "healing personality" may sound contradictory, the power of healing is awareness, which can be achieved by anyone. The author describes his own discovery of spirituality in medicine and the realization that ultimately the origin of disease is in the mind. This is why treating disease with medicine and surgery alone does not heal: These methods ignore the natural healing powers of the body/mind. How does one develop a "healing personality"? The starting point is awareness of the spiritual power within. As the author states, in order to become healthy, one must become spiritual.

Writing your own script for a healthy heart. Before writing any script, one must set the stage, and in this case readers are urged to see a cardiologist or physician and have a thorough checkup. This checkup will evaluate the presence or absence of the "risk factors," and assess the health of other body organs as well. Once the scene is set, it is time to add in the other elements of a healthy heart, all of which will be explored in detail in the coming chapters.

Making a contract with your heart. We see obstacles only when we lose sight of our goals. Therefore it is important to make out (either mentally or on paper) a contract with one's heart that promises to take care of it. Each individual reader's contract will be somewhat different; for example, someone who is overweight might include in the contract the desire that in six months she would weigh a specific amount. The point is to set realistic, achievable goals. Guidelines are provided for breaking larger goals down into small, easily achievable steps. Creating goals for the future makes them a part of the present in the sense that it is today that we start pursuing them.

What to say when you talk to yourself. In the view of the author, the greatest source of stress in life is the negative conversations we have with ourselves. These "conversations," which go on all the time without our even being aware of them, often include negative suggestions such as "When are you going to learn?" "Oh, no, your stupid idiot, you did it again!" When we put ourselves down we reinforce feelings of unworthiness and inadequacy, which leads to stress and illness. Guidelines are given for replacing such negative self-conversation with more positive self-talk, including messages of love and healing.

Heartskill #2: *Sending healing energy to your heart.* In this exercise, readers learn a simple meditation technique that will help them get in touch with their natural healing powers and begin to heal their hearts.

CHAPTER THREE. THE FRIENDSHIP FACTOR: PLUGGING INTO YOUR SOCIAL SUPPORT SYSTEM

Heart disease is not an isolated event, and the heart patient is not an isolated human being. Among the less medically obvious "risk factors" involved in coronary disease is social isolation. In this chapter the author discusses the importance of maintaining and strengthening all the social support aspects of the patient's life, including family, friendship, community, and sex. He shows how intimacy and connection can be used not just for comfort but as actual healing tools.

Sexual intimacy: the healing touch. Following a heart attack, many patients may lose confidence due to a fear of loss of attractiveness or fear of death. Citing recent studies, the author points out that there is a difference between making sex and making love. The desire for sex is a human need and is not limited to healthy people. Anybody who has had a heart problem still has sexual needs and ignoring them may be an additional cause of stress. Guidelines for when and how to resume sexual activity are offered. Other topics covered in this chapter include:

Keeping your loved ones healthy, and letting them keep you healthy

How you may be unwittingly pushing others out of your life

The art of nondefensive, nonreactive communication

Accepting your loved ones' feelings and your own

How to enlist the support of family and friends

Joining or starting your own support group

Heartskill #3: *Mapping your social support system.*

CHAPTER FOUR. OPENING YOUR HEART: LEARNING TO MAKE FRIENDS WITH YOURSELF

In addition to enlisting the support of others, for complete healing it is necessary for the patient to literally become a friend to himself or herself. This may entail changing old ways of thinking and responding, as well as developing new, healthier ways of relating to time and other external stresses. In this chapter the author explores ways of changing Type A behavior, as well as proven techniques for dealing with life's daily hassles and upsets. An important section of the chapter shows readers how to love and cherish the "inner child," that part of their personality that needs to be loved, to be acknowledged, and to have fun. Equally important is the guilt that each of us carries within, and that can lead not only to unhealthy behaviors but also to actual stress. The author gives exercises for learning to discover and absolve the hidden guilts that keep each of us from realizing our true healthy potential. Topics covered in this chapter include:

A positive approach to negative emotions

Checking yourself out on Type A behavior: a self-test

Being assertive without being angry

Keeping your balance in the face of daily hassles and major setbacks

Making a friend of time

Identifying and healing your old childhood hurts

Letting go of hurts, regrets, resentments, and guilt

Forgiving yourself and making a new start

The trusting heart

Heartskill #4: *Forgiveness exercise.*

CHAPTER FIVE: IDENTIFYING AND ELIMINATING STRESS IN YOUR LIFE

The science of psychoneuroimmunology is beginning to prove that the mind and body are not only connected, but inseparable. It has been demonstrated that changes in life often precede disease. Lab studies have shown that the amount of stress experienced by experimental animals can induce rapid growth of a tumor that would ordinarily be rejected. For heart patients, the fact of disease itself can become another inner stress factor that may worsen the disease and the quality of life. One out of five healthy persons is a "heart reactor," who has strong responses under stress that induce unhealthful physiological changes such as narrowing of the coronary arteries, hypertrophy of the heart muscle, and high blood pressure. In this chapter the author shows readers how to change stress-producing negative beliefs into constructive, rational beliefs that reduce stress. Included are guidelines to the five keys for controlling stress: diet, rest, exercise, attitude, and self-discipline. Additional topics include:

Why you feel so stressed-out
Where does emotional stress come from and how does it affect your heart?
Your stress signal checklist
Staying in control
Calculating your heart-stress level at home and on the job
Stress management
Heartskill #5: *Mapping your stress hot spots.*

CHAPTER SIX. YOUR FAITH AND YOUR HEART

As the author points out, there are few studies in the field of spirituality and medicine, because physicians, like most scientists, shy away from what is called "soft data." Soft data are anything outside the realm of physics, mathematics, etcetera: the "exact sciences." As a physician, the author has grown ever more convinced of the body's natural healing power, which is evoked through mind and spirit. No matter how "spirit" is defined, whether in traditional religious terms or as a component of mind or personality, the truth is that in order to become healthy, it is necessary to become spiritual.

In a ten-month study of 393 coronary patients at San Francisco General Hospital, it was proven that the group who received outside prayer in addition to standard medical treatment did far better than those who received medical treatment alone. Those in the experimental group suffered fewer problems with congestive heart failure, pneumonia, and cardiac arrests, and had a significantly lower mortality rate. This chapter explores the possible reasons for this startling result and illuminates the connection between spirit and health.

The difference between spirituality and religion. A discussion of the differences between traditional views of spirituality and the new holistic approach that sees mind, body, and spirit as intimately connected and interdependent.

Faith and heart disease. The healing personality is that of a person who takes care of his own body. He may also use other "paramedical" means to get well such as physical exercise, a proper diet, prayer, meditation, positive affirmations, and visualization techniques. The author surveys these techniques that have been used for centuries to contribute to the healing of a wide variety of diseases. Other topics exploring the connection between faith and a healthy heart include:

Tapping into your personal mythology
Forgiving yourself for heart disease
Keeping a psychological–spiritual journal
Heartskill #6: *Consulting your inner advisor.*

CHAPTER SEVEN. PUTTING IT ALL TOGETHER: HOW TO DEVELOP YOUR OWN DAILY PRACTICE FOR A HEALTHY HEART

Daily Practice as defined by the author is a personalized program in which readers will choose from among the techniques offered in the book to create their own unique combination of mental and physical healing exercises. Each component of the daily practice is fully explained. The techniques range from the familiar—healthful diet and exercise—to the more spiritual, including prayer, meditation, and visualization. Included are examples of each of these techniques as practiced by Exceptional Heart Patients. Other topics in this chapter include:

The benefits of daily practice

Meditation: how to do it your way

Stretching, yoga, and sensory awareness

Hearing with the mind's ear; seeing with the mind's eye

The psychological benefits of exercise

Healthy eating as a meditative practice

The healing powers of silent prayer

Creating your own visualization exercises

Creating your own guided-imagery tapes

Using other types of positive imagery

Heartskill #7: *Picking a practice that makes sense to you.*

CHAPTER EIGHT. LEARNING TO SMELL THE FLOWERS

In our society, pleasure is often regarded as a selfish pursuit. We tend to feel that it is not as important as work. And yet the key element in health is not blood pressure, or cholesterol, or blood sugar; instead it is peace of mind and the ability to enjoy life. Indeed, this ability has been proven to prevent illness. In this chapter the author focuses on the ability to *live* in the moment, savoring all that life has to offer, from the simple physical pleasures of massage to the more profound pleasures of the spirit. Topics covered in this chapter include a discussion of Type B behavior, which can be learned. The secrets of this type of behavior include self-assurance, self-motivation, and the ability to relax in the face of pressures. The author shows how even the most confirmed Type A heart patient can, through self-knowledge, exchange outwardly directed goals for inward ones, thus achieving the emotional and physical benefits of a Type B lifestyle. Other topics discussed in this chapter include:

Getting the most out of the present moment

Taking an inventory of life's pleasures

Counting down to relaxation

Hot baths, hot showers, hot tubs, and saunas

Touching: feeding the skin's hunger for human touch

Pets, plants, and gardens as healing helpers

Heartskill #8: *Building islands of peace into your life.*

CHAPTER NINE. CREATING YOUR FUTURE

The heart may be viewed in many different ways: as a mechanical pump, as the center of circulation, as the source of life. The author suggests viewing the heart above all as a spiritual organ, the center of love, and learning to figuratively fill it with love and peace. A *positive* result of heart disease is the sudden knowledge that one is not immortal and the opportunity to plan for a more worthwhile, fulfilling life in the future. In this final chapter, Dr. Cortis offers guidelines for setting and achieving goals for health—of mind, body, and spirit. For each reader the goals, and the means to achieve them, will be different. But as the author points out, this is a journey that everyone must take, patients as well as doctors, readers as well as the author. No matter how different the paths we choose, we must realize that truly "our hearts are the same." Additional topics discussed include:

The Art of Happiness

Choosing your own path to contentment

Goals chosen by other exceptional heart patients

Developing specific action steps

Reinforcing and rethinking your life goals

Finding your own meaning in life and death

Heartskill #9: *Helping others to heal their hearts.*

RECOMMENDED READING

APPENDIX I. FOR FRIENDS AND FAMILY: HOW TO SUPPORT AN EXCEPTIONAL HEART PATIENT

APPENDIX II. ON FINDING OR STARTING A SELF-HELP GROUP

APPENDIX III. ABOUT THE EXCEPTIONAL HEART PATIENT PROJECT

AUTHOR'S NOTES

ACKNOWLEDGMENTS

INDEX

(Appendixes are always a valuable bonus.)

(It is great to be able to include an actual endorsement in your proposal package. Quite often, writers mention those from whom they intend to request endorsements, but do not actually have them lined up. Perhaps this is unnecessary to say, but it is valuable to reiterate: editors and agents are not overly impressed by such assertions. They do, however, respect those authors who demonstrate that they can deliver on their claims. The inclusion of at least one such blurb creates tremendous credibility.)

GERALD G. JAMPOLSKY, M.D.
Practice Limited to Psychiatry
Adults and Children

21 Main Street
Tiburon, California 94920
(415) 435-1622

April 1, 1997

Mr. Jeff Herman
The Jeff Herman Agency, Inc.
500 Greenwich Street, Suite 501C
New York, NY 10013

Dear Jeff:

You may use the following quote for Bruno's book:

"Dr. Bruno Cortis writes from the heart—for the heart. This is a much-needed and very important book."

Gerald Jampolsky, M.D.
Coauthor of *Love Is the Answer*

With love and peace,

Jerry

Gerald Jampolsky, M.D.

(The author, Dr. Cortis, is very well connected in his field. He solicited promises from several prominent persons to provide cover endorsements like this one. Having these promises to provide such blurbs at the time I marketed the proposal further enhanced the agency's sales position.)

Rejected . . . Again

The Process and the Art of Perseverance

JEFF HERMAN

Trying to sell your writing is in many ways similar to perpetually applying for employment: It's likely you will run into many walls. And that can hurt. But even the Great Wall of China has a beginning and an end—it's simply an external barrier erected for strategic purposes. In my experience, the most insurmountable walls are the ones in our own heads. Anything that is artificially crafted can and will be overcome by people who are resourceful and determined enough to do it.

Naturally, the reality of rejection cannot be completely circumvented. It is, however, constructive to envision each wall as a friendly challenge to your resourcefulness, determination, and strength. There are many people who got through the old Berlin Wall because for them it was a challenge and a symbol—a place to begin, not stop.

The world of publishing is a potentially hostile environment, especially for the writer. Our deepest aspirations can be put to rest without having achieved peace or satisfaction. But it is within each of us to learn about this special soil, and blossom to our fullest. No rejection is fatal until the writer walks away from the battle leaving dreams and goals behind.

WHY MOST REJECTION LETTERS ARE SO EMPTY

What may be most frustrating are the generic word processed letters that say something like: "not right for us." Did the sender read any of your work? Did she have any personal opinions about it? Could she not have spared a few moments to share her thoughts?

As an agent, it's part of my job to reject the vast majority of the submissions I receive. And, with each rejection, I know I'm not making someone happy. On the other hand, I don't see spreading happiness as my exclusive purpose. Like other agents and editors, I make liberal use of the generic rejection letter.

Here's why: Too much to do, too little time. There just isn't sufficient time to write customized, personal rejection letters. To be blunt about it, the rejection process isn't a profit center; it does consume valuable time that otherwise could be used to make profits. The exceptions to this rule are the operations that charge excessive reading fees and who make a handsome profit with each rejection.

In most instances, the rejection process is "giveaway" time for agents and editors, since it takes us away from our essential responsibilities. Even if no personal comments are provided with the rejections, it can require many hours a week to process an ongoing stream of rejections. An understaffed literary agency or publishing house may feel that it's sufficiently generous simply to assign a paid employee the job of returning material as opposed to throwing it away. (And some publishers and literary agencies do in practice simply toss the greater portion of their unsolicited correspondence.) Agents and editors aren't Dear Abby, though many of us wish we had the time to be.

Therefore, your generic rejection means no more and no less than that particular agent/editor doesn't want to represent/publish you and (due to the volume of office correspondence and other pressing duties) is relaying this information to you in an automated, impersonal way. The contents of the letter alone will virtually never reveal any deeper meanings or secrets. To expect or demand more than this might be perceived as unfair by the agent/editor.

KNOW WHEN TO HOLD; KNOW WHEN TO FOLD

It's your job to persevere. It's your mission to proceed undaunted. And it's your option to determine the ways your judgment comes into play. Regardless of how many books about publishing you've read, or how many writers' conferences you've attended, it's up to no one but you to figure out how and when to change your strategy if you want to win at the book-publishing game.

If your initial query results are blanket rejects, then it may be time to back off, reflect, and revamp your query presentation or overall approach. If then there are still no takers, you may be advised to reconceive your project in light of its less-than-glamorous track record. Indeed, there might even come a time for you to use your experience and newfound knowledge of what does and doesn't grab attention from editors and agents and move on to that bolder, more innovative idea you've been nurturing in the back of your brain.

AN AUTHENTIC SUCCESS STORY

Several years ago, two very successful, though unpublished, gentlemen came to see me with a nonfiction book project. My hunch was that it would make a lot of money. The writers were professional speakers and highly skilled salespeople, so I arranged for them to meet personally with several publishers, but to no avail.

All told, we got more than twenty rejections—the dominant reason being that editors thought the concept and material were weak. Not ones to give up, and with a strong belief in their work and confidence in their ability to promote, the authors were ultimately able to sell the book for a nominal advance to a small Florida publishing house—it was out there at last, published and in the marketplace.

As of this writing, *Chicken Soup for the Soul*, by Jack Canfield and Mark Victor Hansen, has sold millions of copies and has been a *New York Times* bestseller for a couple of years straight. Furthermore, this initial success has generated several best-selling sequels.

We all make mistakes, and the book rascals in New York are definitely no exception. Most importantly, Canfield and Hansen didn't take no for an answer. They instinctively understood that all those rejections were simply an uncomfortable part of a process that would eventually get them where they wanted to be. And that's the way it happened.

Whatever It Takes

A Relentless Approach to Selling Your Work

Jeff Herman

There's a very telling story about Jack Kerouac, a tale from which we can all learn. Kerouac was a celebrated (as well as controversial) literary figure who reached his professional peak in the 1950s. Although Jack K is no longer with us on a physical plane, a flourishing Kerouac revival has brought his name (and sales) to new levels of worldwide acclaim. Jack Kerouac remains one of the icons of the Beat Generation and is perhaps best remembered for his irreverent and manic travel-memoir-as-novel *On the Road*.

SALES TALES FROM THE BEAT GENERATION

The story begins when Kerouac was a young and struggling writer, ambitiously seeking to win his day in the sun. Jack was a charismatic man and had acquired many influential friends. One day Kerouac approached a friend who had access to a powerful publishing executive. Kerouac asked the friend to hand-deliver his new manuscript to the executive, with the advice that it be given prompt and careful consideration.

When the friend handed the manuscript to the executive, the executive took one glance and began to laugh. The executive explained that two other people had hand-delivered the very same manuscript to him within the last few weeks.

What this reveals is that Kerouac was a master operator. Not only did he get his work into the right face, he finagled to reinforce his odds by doing it redundantly. Some might say he was a manipulator, but his works were successfully published, and he did attain a full measure of fame in his own day, which even now retains its luster.

. . . AND FROM THE BEATEN

I will now share a very different sort of story. It starts in the 1940s, when a best-selling Pulitzer Prize–winning young-adult book was published. Titled *The Yearling*, and

675

written by Marjorie Kinnan Rawlings, this work was made into an extremely popular film starring Gregory Peck. The book continues to be a good backlist seller.

In the 1990s a writer in Florida, where *The Yearling*'s story takes place, performed an experiment. He converted the book into a raw double-spaced manuscript and changed the title and author's name—but the book's contents were not touched. He then submitted the entire manuscript to about twenty publishers on an unagented/unsolicited basis. I don't believe the submissions were addressed to any specific editors by name.

Eventually this writer received many form rejections, including one from the book's actual publisher. Several publishers never even responded. A small house in Florida did offer to publish the book.

What is glaringly revealed by this story? Sure, there may be several layers of meaning here (such as changes in reader taste and market trends), but the essential dynamic is that even a work of Pulitzer Prize quality will not see the light of day if the writer doesn't use his brain when it's time to sell the work.

How to Beat Yourself—and How Not To

People who are overly aggressive do get a bad rap. As an agent and as a person, I don't like being hounded by salespeople—whether they're hustling manuscripts or insurance policies. But there are effective ways to be heard and seen without being resented. Virtually anyone can scream loud enough to hurt people's ears. Only an artist understands the true magic of how to sell without abusing those who might buy. And each of us has the gift to become an artist in his or her own way.

Here's an example of what not to do:

It's late in the day and snowing. I'm at my desk, feeling a lot of work-related tension. I answer the phone. It's a first-time fiction writer. He's unflinchingly determined to speak endlessly about his work, which I have not yet read. I interrupt his meaningless flow to explain courteously that, while I will read his work, it's not a good time for me to talk to him. But he will not let me go; he's relentless. Which forces me to be rude and cold as I say "bye" and hang up. I then resent the thoughtless intrusion on my space and time. And I may feel bad about being inhospitable to a stranger, whatever the provocation.

Clearly the above scenario does not demonstrate a good way to initiate a deal. I'm already prejudiced against this writer before reading his work.

Here's a more effective scenario:

Same conditions as before. I answer the telephone. The caller acknowledges that I must be busy, and asks for only thirty seconds of my time. I grant this. He then begins to compliment me; he's heard I'm one of the best, and so forth. I'm starting to like this conversation; I stop counting the seconds. Now he explains that he has an excellent manuscript that he is willing to give me the opportunity to read, and would be happy to send it right over. He then thanks me for my time and says good-bye. I hang up, feeling fine about the man; I'll give his manuscript some extra consideration.

In conclusion, relentless assertiveness is better than relentless passivity. But you want your style to be like Julie Andrews's singing voice in *The Sound of Music*, as opposed to a 100-decibel boombox on a stone floor.

The Literary Agency from A to Z
How Literary Agents Work

JEFF **H**ERMAN

Literary agents are like stockbrokers, marketing or sales directors, or real-estate agents: They bring buyers and sellers together, help formulate successful deals, and receive a piece of the action (against the seller's end) for facilitating the partnership.

Specifically, literary agents search for talented writers, unearth marketable nonfiction book concepts, and discover superior fiction manuscripts to represent. Simultaneously, agents cultivate their relationships with publishers.

When an agent detects material she thinks she can sell to a publisher, she signs the writer as a client, works on the material with the writer to maximize its chances of selling, and then submits it to one or more appropriate editorial contacts.

The agent has the contacts. Many writers don't know the most likely publishers. Even if the writers do have a good overview of the industry, and even some inside contacts, the typical agent knows many more players and also knows which editors like to see what material. And the agent may even be aware of finesse elements such as recent shifts in a publisher's acquisition strategy.

HOW AGENTS WORK FOR THEIR CLIENTS

A dynamic agent achieves the maximum exposure possible for the writer's material, which greatly enhances the odds that the material will be published—and on more favorable terms than a writer would receive by soliciting the publisher herself.

Having an agent gives the writer's material the type of access to the powers that be that it might otherwise never obtain. Publishers assume that material submitted by an agent has been screened and is much more likely to fit their needs than the random material swimming in the slush pile.

If and when a publisher makes an offer to publish the material, the agent acts on the author's behalf and negotiates the advance (the money paid up front), table of royalties, control of subsidiary rights, and many other important and marginal contract clauses that may prove to be important down the line. The agent acts as the writer's advocate with the publisher for as long as the book remains in print or licensing opportunities exist.

The agent knows the most effective methods for negotiating the best advance and other contract terms, and is likely to have more leverage with the publisher than the writer does.

There's more to a book contract than the advance-and-royalty schedule. There are several key clauses that the writer may know little or nothing about but would accept with a cursory perusal in order to expedite the deal. Striving to close any kind of agreement can be intimidating if you don't know much about the territory; ignorance is a great disadvantage during a negotiation. An agent, however, understands every detail of the contract and knows where and how it should be modified or expanded in your favor.

Where appropriate, an agent acts to sell subsidiary rights after the book is sold to a publisher. These rights can include serial rights, foreign rights, dramatic and movie rights, and audio and video rights, and also a range of syndication and licensing possibilities. Often, a dynamic agent will be more successful at selling the subsidiary rights than the publisher would be.

THE AGENT'S PERSPECTIVE

No agent sells every project she represents. Even though an author is signed on the basis of their work's marketability, agents know from experience that some projects with excellent potential are not necessarily quick-and-easy big-money sales. And, yes, every agent has been as bewildered as the author when a particularly promising package receives no takers. Some projects, especially fiction, may be marketed for a long time before a publisher is found (if one ever is).

THE AUTHOR'S EXPECTATIONS

What's most important to you as an author is that you feel sure the agent continues to believe in the project and is actively trying to sell it.

For his work, your agent receives a commission (usually 15%) against your advance and all subsequent income relevant to the sold project.

Although this is an appreciable chunk of your work's income, the agent's involvement should end up netting you much more than you would have earned otherwise. The agent's power to round up several interested publishers to consider your work opens up the possibility that more than one house will make an offer for it, which means you'll be more likely to get a higher advance and also have more leverage regarding the various other contractual clauses.

The writer–agent relationship can become a rewarding business partnership. An agent can advise you objectively on the direction your writing career should take. Also, through her contacts, an agent may be able to get you book writing assignments you would never have been offered on your own.

FINDING THE BEST AGENT FOR YOU

There are many ways to get an agent; your personal determination and acumen as a writer will be one of your most important assets. The best way to gain access to potential agents is by networking with fellow writers. Find out which agents they use, and what's being said about whom. Maybe some of your colleagues can introduce you to their agents, or at least allow you to drop their names when contacting their agents. Most agents will be receptive to a writer who has been referred by a current and valued client.

This book features a directory of literary agencies, including their addresses, the names of specific agents, and agents' specialty areas, along with some personal remarks and examples of recent titles sold to publishers.

QUERY FIRST

The universally accepted way to establish initial contact with an agent is to send a query letter. Agents tend to be less interested in—if not completely put off by—oral presentations. Be sure the letter is personalized: Nobody likes generic, photocopied letters that look like they're being sent to everyone.

Think of the query as a sales pitch. Describe the nature of your project and offer to send additional material—and enclose a self-addressed stamped envelope (SASE). Include all relevant information about yourself—along with a résumé if it's applicable. When querying about a nonfiction project, many agents won't mind receiving a complete proposal. But you might prefer to wait and see how the agent responds to the concept before sending the full proposal.

For queries about fiction projects, most agents prefer to receive story-concept sheets and/or plot synopses; if they like what they see, they'll request sample chapters or ask you to send the complete manuscript. Most agents won't consider manuscripts for incomplete works of fiction because few publishers are willing to do so.

If you enclose an SASE, most agents will respond to you, one way or another, within a reasonable period of time. If the agent asks to see your material, submit it promptly with a polite note stating that you'd like a response within four weeks on a nonfiction proposal, or eight weeks on fiction material. If you haven't heard from the agent by that time, write or call to find out the status of your submission.

CIRCULATE WITH THE FLOW

You're entitled to circulate your material to more than one agent at a time, but you're obligated to let each agent know that such is the case. If and when you do sign with an agent, immediately notify other agents still considering your work that it's no longer available.

At least 200 literary agents are active in America, and their individual perceptions of what is and isn't marketable varies widely—which is why a few or even several rejections should never deter writers who believe in themselves.

Buyer and Seller Reversal

When an agent eventually seeks to represent your work, it's time for her to begin selling herself to you. When you're seeking employment, you don't necessarily have to accept the first job offer you receive; likewise, you do not have to sign immediately with the first agent who wants you.

Do some checking before agreeing to work with a particular agent. If possible, meet the agent in person. A lot can be learned from in-person meetings that can't be gathered from telephone conversations. See what positive or negative information you can find out about the agent through your writers' network. Ask the agent for a client list and permission to call certain clients. Find out the agent's specialties.

Ask for a copy of the agent's standard contract.* Most agents today will want to codify your relationship with a written agreement; this should protect both parties equally. Make sure you're comfortable with everything in the agreement before signing it. Again, talking with fellow writers and reading books on the subject are excellent ways to deepen your understanding of industry practices.

When choosing an agent, follow your best instincts. Don't settle for anyone you don't perceive to be on the level, or who doesn't seem to be genuinely enthusiastic about you and your work.

Self-Representation: A Fool for a Client?

Agents aren't for everyone. In some instances, you may be better off on your own. Perhaps you actually do have sufficient editorial contacts and industry savvy to cut good deals by yourself. If so, what incentive do you have to share your income with an agent?

Of course, having an agent might provide you the intangible benefits of added prestige, save you the hassles of making submissions and negotiating deals, or act as a buffer through whom you can negotiate indirectly for tactical reasons.

You might also consider representing yourself if your books are so specialized that only a few publishers are potential candidates for them. Your contacts at such houses might be much stronger than any agent's could be.

Attorneys: Literary and Otherwise

Some entertainment/publishing attorneys can do everything an agent does, though there's no reason to believe they can necessarily do more. A major difference between

---

*Please see sample agency contract in this book.

the two is that the lawyer may charge you a set hourly fee or retainer, or any negotiated combination thereof, instead of an agency-type commission. In rare instances, writer–publisher disputes might need to be settled in a court of law, and a lawyer familiar with the industry then becomes a necessity.

BOTTOM-LINE CALCULATIONS

The pluses and minuses of having an agent should be calculated like any other business service you might retain—it should benefit you more than it costs you. Generally speaking, the only real cost of using an agent is the commission. Of course, using the wrong agent may end up causing you more deficits than benefits, but even then you may at least learn a valuable lesson for next time.

Your challenge is to seek and retain an agent who's right for you. You're 100 percent responsible for getting yourself represented, and at least 50 percent responsible for making the relationship work for both of you.

Points of Inquiry from the Writer's Side

Questions and Answers About Agents, Editors, and the Publishing Industry

Jeff Herman

In the course of my ongoing participation in publishing workshops, seminar presentations, and panels at writers' conferences, there are certain questions that arise time and again. Obviously, this implies widespread areas of interest and concern. Many of these oft-voiced requests for information zing straight to the heart of the world of book publishing. Indeed, these commonly raised points of inquiry touch on matters of great importance to my own day-to-day work.

The following questions are asked from the gut and replied to in kind. In order to be of value to the author who wishes to benefit from an insider view, I answer these serious queries in unvarnished terms, dispensing with the usual sugar coating in order to emphasize the message of candor.

Q: Is it more difficult to get an agent than it is to get a publisher?

A: I believe it's substantially easier to get an agent than it is to get a publisher.

The primary reason for this is that no agent expects to sell 100 percent of the projects she chooses to represent. Not because any of these projects lack merit (though some of them may), but because only so many titles are published per year—and many excellent ones just won't make the cut. This is especially true for fiction by unknown or unpublished writers, or for nonfiction in saturated categories. As a result, many titles will be agented but never published.

Naturally, a successful agent prefers to represent projects that she feels are hot and that publishers will trample each other to acquire. But few if any agents have the luxury of representing such sure-bet projects exclusively. In fact, the majority of their projects may be less than "acquisition-guaranteed," even though they are of acquisition quality. The agent assumes that many of these projects will eventually be sold profitably, but probably doesn't expect all of them to be. Every experienced agent knows that some of the best cash cows were not easily sold.

Make no mistake—it's not easy to get a reputable agent. Most agents reject 98 percent of the opportunities that cross their desks. They accept for representation only material they believe can be sold to a publisher. That is, after all, the only way for them to earn income and maintain credibility with publishers. If an agent consistently represents what a publisher considers garbage, that will become her professional signature— and her undoing as an agent.

But don't despair. This is a subjective business, composed of autonomous human beings. One agent's reject can be another's gold mine. That's why even a large accumulation of rejections should never deter you as a writer. Some people get married young, and some get married later!

Q: Is there anything I can do to increase my odds of getting an agent?
A: Yes.

First consider the odds quoted in the previous answer. The typical agent is rejecting 98 percent of everything he sees. That means he's hungry for the hard-to-find 2 percent that keeps him in business. If you're not part of that 2 percent, he'll probably have no use for you or your project. Your challenge is to convince him that you're part of that select 2 percent.

Q: What do agents and editors want? What do they look for in a writer? What can I do to become that kind of writer?
A: Let's back up a step or two and figure out *why* agents want to represent certain projects and *why* editors want to buy. This industry preference has little to do with quality of writing as such.

Many highly talented writers never get published. Many mediocre writers do get published—and a number of them make a lot of money at it. There are reasons for this. The mediocre writers are doing things that more than compensate for their less-than-splendid writing. And the exceptional writers who nevertheless underachieve in the publishing arena are (regardless of their talents) most likely doing things that undermine their presentation; their potential; and, most importantly, their profitability in the eyes of the agents they contact.

In other words, being a good writer is just part of a complex equation. Despite all the criticism the educational system in the United States has received, America is exceedingly literate and has a mother lode of college graduates and postgraduates. Good, knowledgeable writers are a dime a dozen in this country. *Profitable* writers, however, are a rare species. And agents and editors obviously value them the most. Once more: Being an excellent writer does not necessarily coincide with being a financially successful writer. Ideally, of course, you want to be both.

To maximize your success as a writer you must do more than hone your ability to write; you must also learn the qualifiers and the disqualifiers for success. Obviously you wish to employ the former and avoid the latter. Publishing is a business, and agents tend to be the most acutely business oriented of all the players. That's why they take the risk of going into business for themselves (most agents are self-employed).

If you wish, wear your artist's hat while you write. But you'd better acquire a business hat and wear it when it's time to sell. This subtle ability to change hats separates the minority of writers who get rich from the majority who do not. In my opinion, rich writers didn't get rich from their writing (no matter how good it is); they get rich by being good at business.

Many good but not-so-wealthy writers blame various internal or external factors for their self-perceived stagnation. My answer to them is: Don't blame anyone, especially yourself. To lay blame is an abdication of power. In effect, when you blame, you become a car with an empty gas tank, left to the elements. The remedy is to fill the tank yourself. Learn to view mistakes, whether they be yours or those of the people you relied on, as inconvenient potholes—learning to move around them will make you an even better driver.

Observe all you can about those who are successful—not just in writing, but in all fields—and make their skills your skills. I'm not saying that making money is or should be your first priority. Your priorities, whatever they are, belong to you. But money is a widely acknowledged and sought-after emblem of success.

If an emphasis on personal gain turns you off, you may of course pursue other goals. Many successful people in business find the motivation to achieve their goals by focusing on altruistic concepts—such as creating maximum value for as many people as possible. Like magic, money often follows value even if it wasn't specifically sought. If you're unfortunate enough to make money you don't want, there's no need to despair: There are many worthy parties (including charities) that will gladly relieve you of this burden.

Here are specific ways to maximize your ability to get the agent you want:

- *Don't start off by asking what the agent can do for you.* You're a noncitizen until the agent has reason to believe that you may belong to that exclusive 2 percent club the agent wants to represent. It's a mistake to expect the agent to do anything to sell herself to you during that initial contact. You must first persuade her that you're someone who's going to make good money for her business. Once you've accomplished that, and the agent offers you representation, you're entitled to have the agent sell herself to you.
- *Act like a business.* As you're urged elsewhere in this book, get yourself professional letterhead and state-of-the-art office equipment. While rarely fatal, cheap paper and poor-looking type will do nothing to help you—and in this business you need all the help you can give yourself.

    Virtually anyone—especially the intellectually arrogant—is apt to be strongly affected on a subliminal level by a product's packaging. People pay for the sizzle, not the steak. There is a reason why American companies spend billions packaging, naming, and advertising such seemingly simple products as soap. We would all save money if every bar of soap were put into a plain paper box and just labeled "Soap." In fact, the no-frills section does sell soap that way—for a lot less. But few people choose to buy it that way. Understand this human principle, without judging it, and use it when packaging yourself.

- *Learn industry protocol.* I never insist that people follow all the rules. As Thomas Jefferson wisely suggested, a revolution every so often can be a good thing. But you should at least know the rules before you break them—or before you do anything.

  For instance, most agents say they don't like cold calls. I can't·say I blame them. If my rejection rate is 98 percent, I'm not going to be enthusiastic about having my ear talked off by someone who is more than likely part of that group. Just like you, agents want to use their time as productively as possible. Too often, cold calls are verbal junk mail. This is especially true if you are a writer selling fiction: Your hard copy is the foot you want to get through the door.

  Speaking for myself, most cold calls have a neutral effect on me (a few turn me off, and a few rouse my enthusiasm). I try to be courteous, because that's how I would want to be treated. I will allow the caller to say whatever he wants for about one minute before I take over to find out what, if anything, the person has in the way of hard copy. If he has some, I invite him to send it with an SASE. If he doesn't have any, I advise him to write some and then send it. Usually I don't remember much about what he said on the phone; I may not even remember that he called. But that doesn't matter; it's the hard copy that concerns me at first. This is the way it works with most agents. We produce books, not talk.

  An agent's time is an agent's money (and therefore his clients' money). So don't expect any quality access until the agent has reason to believe you're a potential 2 percenter. If you're the CEO of General Motors, for instance, and you want to write a book, then all you need to do is call the agent(s) of your choice and identify yourself; red carpets will quickly appear. But the vast majority of writers have to learn and follow the more formalized procedures.
- *As explained elsewhere in this book, view the query letter as a sales brochure.* The best ones are rarely more than one-and-a-half pages long and state their case as briefly and efficiently as possible.

Here are the most common query mistakes:

1. Long, unfocused paragraphs.
2. Pontificating about irrelevancies (at least matters that are irrelevant from the agent's perspective).
3. Complaining about your tribulations as a writer. We all know it's a tough business, but nobody likes losers—least of all shrewd agents. Always be a winner when you're selling yourself, and you'll be more likely to win.

Most agents are hungry for that golden 2 percent, and they dedicate a great deal of time shoveling through mounds of material looking for it. You must be the first to believe that you are among the publishing elite, and then you must portray yourself that way to others. Reality begins in your own head, and is manifested primarily through your own actions—or lack thereof.

Every agent and editor has the power to reject your writing. But only you have the power to be—or not to be—a writer.

Q: Should I query only one agent at a time?

A: Some of my colleagues disagree with me here, but I recommend querying five to ten agents simultaneously, unless you already have your foot in the door with one. I suggest this because some agents will respond within ten days, while others may take much longer or never respond at all. Going agent by agent can eat up several months of valuable time before a relationship is consummated. And then your work still must be sold to a publisher.

To speed up this process, it's smart to solicit several agents at a time, though you should be completely up front about it. If you go the multiple-submissions route, be sure to mention in your query letters to each agent that you are indeed making multiple submissions (though you needn't supply your agent list).

When an agent responds affirmatively to your query by requesting your proposal or manuscript, it's fine then to give the agent an exclusive reading. However, you should impose a reasonable time frame—for example, two weeks for a nonfiction proposal and four weeks for a large manuscript. If it's a nonexclusive reading, make sure each agent knows that's what you want. And don't sign with an agent before talking to all the agents who are reading your work. (You have no obligation to communicate further with agents who do not respond affirmatively to your initial query.)

Most agents make multiple submissions to publishers, so they should be sensitive and respectful when writers have reason to use the same strategy agents have used with success.

Q: How do I know if my agent is working effectively for me? When might it be time to change agents?

A: As I remarked earlier, agents don't necessarily sell everything they represent, no matter how persistent and assertive they may be. In other words, the fact that your work is unsold doesn't automatically mean that your agent isn't doing his job. To the contrary, he may be doing the best job possible, and it may be incumbent on you to be grateful for these speculative and uncompensated efforts.

Let's say ninety days pass and your work remains unsold. What you need to assess next is whether your agent is making active and proper attempts to sell your work.

Are you receiving copies of publisher rejection letters regarding your work? Generally, when an editor rejects projects submitted by an agent, the work will be returned within a few weeks, along with some brief comments explaining why the project was declined. (In case you're wondering, the agent doesn't have to include a SASE; the editors *want* agent submissions.) Copies of these rejection letters should be sent to you on a regular basis, as they are received by the agent. While no one expects you to enjoy these letters, they at least document that your agent is circulating your work.

If you have received many such rejection letters within these ninety days, it's hard to claim that your agent isn't trying. If you've received few or none, you might well call the agent for a status report. You should inquire as to where and when your work has been submitted, and what, if anything, the results of those submissions have been. In the end, you will have to use your own best judgment as to whether your agent is performing capably or giving you the run-around.

If it ever becomes obvious that your agent is no longer seriously trying to sell your work (or perhaps never was), you should initiate a frank discussion with the agent about what comes next. If the agent did go to bat for you, you should consider the strong possibility that your work is presently unmarketable, and act to preserve the agent relationship for your next project. Remember, if your work remains unsold, your agent has lost valuable time and has made no money.

If the evidence clearly shows that your agent has not been performing from day one, then your work has not been tested. You should consider withdrawing it and seek new representation.

Agent-hopping by authors is not rampant, but it's not uncommon either. Often the agent is just as eager as you—or more so—for the break-up to happen. One veteran colleague once told me that when he notices he hates to receive a certain client's phone calls, then it's time to find a graceful way to end the relationship.

The wisdom of agent-jumping must be assessed on a case-by-case basis. The evidence shows that many writers have prospered after switching, while others have entered limbo or even fallen far off their previous pace.

Before you decide to switch agents, you should focus on why you are unhappy with your current situation. It may be that if you appeal to your agent to discuss your specific frustrations—preferably in person, or at least by phone—many or all of them can be resolved, and your relationship will be given a fresh and prosperous start.

Agents are not mind readers. You only have one agent, but your agent has many clients. It is therefore mostly your responsibility as a writer client to communicate your concerns and expectations effectively to your agent. Your relationship may require only occasional adjustments, as opposed to a complete break-up.

Q: Who do agents really work for?
A: Themselves! Always have and always will.

True, agents serve their clients, but their own needs and interests always come first. Of course, this is the way it is in any business relationship (and in too many personal ones). You should never expect your lawyer, accountant, or stockbroker (and so on) to throw him- or herself into traffic to shield you from getting hit.

As long as the interests of the agent and the writer are in harmony, everything should work out well. However, on occasion the writer may have expectations that could be detrimental to the agent's own agenda (not to mention state of mind). Writers must never lose sight of the truth that publishers are the agent's most important customers. Only a foolish agent would intentionally do serious damage to her relationships with individual editors and publishing houses. It should be further noted that there is, therefore, a fine line that an agent will not cross when advocating for her clients.

Q: What do agents find unattractive about some clients?
A: Agents are individuals, so each will have his own intense dislikes. But, generally speaking, there is a certain range of qualities that can hamper any and all aspects

of an agent's professional association with a client—qualities that often have similarly negative effects in realms other than publishing. Here's a litany of displeasing client types and their characteristics.

- *The Pest.* Nobody likes a nag, whether at home or at the office. A squeaky wheel may sometimes get the grease—not than anyone likes the effect—but more often they get the shaft.
- *The Complainer.* Some people can never be satisfied, only dissatisfied. It seems to be their mission in life to pass along their displeasure to others. These folks are never any fun—unless you're an ironic observer.
- *The BS artist.* These clients believe everything even remotely connected with themselves is the greatest—for example, their fleeting ideas for books should win them millions of dollars up front. Of course, if they actually produce the goods, then the BS part of the term doesn't apply to them.
- *The Screw-Up.* These clients miss trains, planes, and deadlines. Their blunders can create major hassles for those who count on them.
- *The Sun God.* Some people believe they are more equal than others, and will behave accordingly. It's a real pleasure to see Sun Gods humbled.
- *The Liar.* Need I say more?

Sometimes these wicked traits combine, overlap, and reinforce themselves in one individual to create what an agent may rate as a veritable Client from Hell. Enough said on this subject for now, except that I would be remiss if I did not insist that no trade or professional class is immune to this nefarious syndrome—not even literary agents.

Q: How does someone become an agent?
A: For better or worse, anyone in America can be declared an agent at any time. But what someone says and what he or she does are different things. Legitimate literary agents earn most or all of their income from commissions. The less-than-legitimate agencies most often depend on reading and management fees for their cash, with few if any actual book sales to their credit.

Most agents earn their stripes by working as editors for publishers. But that is by no means the only route, nor is it necessarily the most effective training ground. Good agents have emerged from a variety of environments and offer a broad range of exceptional credentials. What's most important is the mix of skills they bring to their agenting careers, such as the following.

- Strong relationship skills—the ability to connect with people and earn their confidence.
- Sales and marketing skills—the ability to get people to buy from them.
- Persuasion and negotiating skills—the ability to get good results in their dealings.
- An understanding of the book market and what publishers are buying.
- An ability to manage many clients and projects at the same time.

Q: Who owns book publishing?
A: Many decades ago, book-publishing entities were customarily founded by individuals who had a passion for books. Though they obviously had to have business

skills to make their houses survive and thrive, money was not necessarily their primary drive (at least not in the beginning), or they would have chosen more lucrative endeavors.

The vestiges of these pioneers can be found in the family names still extant in the corporate designations of most of today's publishing giants. But apart from the human-sounding names, these are very different companies today. Much of the industry is owned by multinational, multibillion-dollar conglomerates who have priorities other than the mere publication of books. The revenues from book operations are barely noticeable when compared with such mass-market endeavors as movies, TV/cable, music, magazines, sports teams, and character licensing. Stock prices must rise, and shareholders must be optimally satisfied for these firms to feel in any way stable.

Q: How does this type of ownership affect editors and the editorial-acquisition process?

A: This rampant corporate ownership translates into an environment in which book editors are pressured to make profitable choices if their careers are to prosper. At first glance, that doesn't sound radical or wrongheaded, but a downside has indeed developed—editors are discouraged from taking risks for literary or artistic rationales that are ahead of the market curve, or even with an eye toward the longer term development and growth of a particular writer's readership.

The bottom line must be immediately appeased by every acquisition, or the nonperforming editor's career will crumble. The editor who acquires blockbusters that the culturally elite disdain is an editor who is a success. The editor whose books lose money but are universally praised by critics is an editor who has failed.

Of course, the above comparison is extreme. Most editors are not single-minded moneygrubbers, and they do their best to acquire meaningful books that also make commercial sense. Where the cut becomes most noticeable is for the thousands of talented fiction writers who will never write big money-makers. While slots still exist for them, large publishers are increasingly reluctant to subsidize and nurture the careers of these marginally profitable writers. Commercially speaking, there are better ways to invest the firm's resources.

Q: What, if any, are a writer's alternatives?

A: Yes, the big kids are dominant on their own turf and intend to extend their claim to as much of book country as they can. But this isn't the end of the story. The heroes are the thousands of privately owned "Mom and Pop" presses from Maine to Alaska who only need to answer to themselves. Every year, small presses, new and old, make an important contribution to literate culture with books that large publishers won't touch. It's not uncommon for some of these books to become best-sellers. University presses also pump out important (and salesworthy) books that would not have been published in a rigidly commercial environment.

Q: Is there anything positive to say about the current situation?

A: I don't mean to imply that the corporate ownership of the bulk of the book industry is absolutely bad. Indeed, it has brought many benefits. Publishers are learning to take advantage of state-of-the-art marketing techniques and technologies, and have more capital with which to do it. The parent entertainment and communications firms enable the mainstream commercial publishers to cash in on popular frenzies, as with dinosaur mania, the latest and most salacious scandals, fresh interest in the environment or fitness, or celebrity and other pop-culture tie-ins such as *Gump* and *Madonna* books.

The emergence of superstores enables more books to be sold. The stores create very appealing environments that draw much more traffic than conventional old-style bookstores. Many people who hang out at the superstores were never before motivated to go book shopping. But once they're in one of these well-stocked stores—whether at the bookshelves, ensconced in reading seats, or perched with a steaming mug at an in-store cafe—they're likely to start spending.

The unfortunate part is that many small independent bookshops cannot compete with these new venues. However, many others are finding clever ways to hang on by accenting special reader-interest areas or offering their own individual style of hospitality.

Q: *How profitable is publishing?*

A: One way to measure an industry's profitability is to look at the fortunes of those who work in it. By such a measure, the book business isn't very profitable, especially when compared to its twentieth-century sisters in entertainment and information industries: movies, television, music, advertising, and computers. Most book editors require a two-income family if they wish to raise children comfortably in New York or buy a nice home. The vast majority of published authors rely on their day jobs or spouse's earnings.

A handful of authors make annual incomes in the six and seven figures but it's often the movie tie-ins that get them there, and in turn push even more book sales.

A fraction of book editors will climb the ranks to the point at which they can command six-figure incomes, but most never attain this plateau. Almost all writers just starting in the business earn barely above the poverty level for their initial publishing endeavors—if that.

A well-established literary agent can make a lot of money. The trick is to build a number of backlist books that cumulatively pay off healthy commissions twice a year, while constantly panning for the elusive big-advance books that promise short-term (and perhaps long-term) windfalls.

In many ways, the agents are the players best positioned to make the most money. As sole proprietors they're not constrained by committees and can move like lightning. When everything aligns just right, the agent holds all the cards by controlling access to the author (product) and the publisher (producer).

The publishing companies themselves appear at least adequately profitable, averaging about 5 to 10 percent return on revenues (according to their public balance sheets). The larger companies show revenues of between $1 billion and $2 billion, sometimes nudging higher.

These are not sums to sneeze at. But most of those sales derive from high-priced non-bookstore products like textbooks and professional books. Large and midsize publishers alike depend on their cash-cow backlist books for much of their retail sales. These books entail virtually no risk or investment, since their customer base is essentially locked in for an indefinite period, and the publisher has long ago recouped the initial investment. Many backlist books are legacies from editors and business dynamics that current employees may know nothing about.

The real risk for the current regime is their *frontlist*, which is the current season's crop. Large houses invest tens of millions of dollars to acquire, manufacture, market, and distribute anywhere from fifty to a few hundred "new" books. A small number of big-ticket individual titles will by themselves represent millions of dollars at risk. Most titles will represent less than $50,000 in risk on a pro-rata basis.

In practice, most of these frontlist titles will fail. The publisher will not recoup its investment and the title will not graduate to the exalted backlist status. But, like the fate of those innumerable turtle eggs laid in the lake, it's expected that enough spawn will survive to generate an overall profit and significant backlist annuities well into the future.

In the fairness of a broader picture, it is known that most motion pictures and television shows fail, as do most new consumer products (such as soap or soft drinks) that have engendered enormous research-and-development costs. It's the ones that hit—and hit big—that make the odds worth enduring for any industry.

Free versus Fee
The Issue of Literary Agency Fees

JEFF HERMAN

Many literary agencies charge a fee to read unsolicited manuscripts, although the majority of well-established agencies don't charge such fees—yet.

There's a good deal of internal debate within the literary agency community about the ethics of charging reading fees, especially since many highly reputable agents have begun to charge relatively modest fees. Effective January 1, 1996, no members of the Association of Authors' Representatives are permitted to charge any kind of fees. While this addition to the organization's Canon of Ethics had an effect on only a fraction of its membership, it is too early to see whether the formerly fee-charging members put more stock in their fees or in their membership. (Fee-charging agencies, numbering a few hundred, are currently nonmembers of the AAR.)

Fees per se are a gray area, not necessarily right or wrong—although some *are* clearly wrong. The correctness of fee assessment must be judged on a case-by-case basis. How much is the fee? What's being provided in return for the fee? And, most importantly, what is the writer being led to believe he's getting for the fee?

FEES RANGE FROM TWENTY-FIVE TO SEVERAL HUNDRED DOLLARS

When a reputable agency does charge a fee, it's usually modest—$50 to $100 for reading a complete manuscript. These agencies defend their fees by maintaining that they're merely breaking even on such charges, since the fees cover the costs of reading the manuscript cover-to-cover and providing a detailed and useful critique—even if the work is rejected (which it usually is).

It's morally incumbent upon these agencies to make it abundantly clear to the writer that payment of the fee guarantees only a fair reading and constructive comments, and does *not* mean that the writer will be offered representation. Better yet, these agencies might even reveal approximately what percentage of prospective clients are in fact offered representation.

A much more controversial scenario involves agencies that charge writers hundreds of dollars for single readings, or into the thousands of dollars for what is portrayed as in-depth editorial feedback or additional literary services. It's obvious that among these agencies are those who reap significant profits simply by reading and, almost always, rejecting manuscripts written by often-vulnerable writers.

These agencies defend themselves by asserting that even though they reject more than 95 percent of the manuscripts, their extensive critiques greatly enhance the writer's chances of success down the line. Many writers claim that the critiques from some of these firms, while indeed wordy, aren't overly useful. Attending a weekend writing workshop might well be a better use of the money—that's for the writer to decide.

Some fee-charging agencies require monthly or yearly retainers (typically running into at least several hundred dollars annually). The usual justification is that, particularly when handling new writers, the agency incurs enormous expenses and, in exchange for expending their efforts and skills on long shot (but worthy) properties, they more than earn their money.

That may be true—but how can a writer be sure there is honest application behind the operation, and not just perfunctory rendering of generic services? One eye-opening giveaway may be when, in response to a query for a nonfiction book or a short synopsis or chapter selection for a novel, a contract is almost instantly sent to the writer, along with a fee schedule. If this happens to you, get a friend to send in another copy of the same material (with only the author name and address changed) and watch what happens. Barring inadvertent office miscues, if there's a contract in the offing, there's another clue for you. Maybe even send in a sheaf of printed-out gibberish and see if that earns an offer of agent representation (in exchange for cash). If it does, it's time to say "Bingo!"—and time to move on in your search for an agent.

It should be noted that established, reputable literary agencies customarily bill their clients (or are reimbursed) for such amenities as manuscript copying, messenger service, and express correspondence and deliveries. But such fees are spelled out and agreed to in an agency representation agreement, and there are no highly visible (or invisible) items (such as those sometimes termed "management fees") over and above the agency commission on sale of the author's literary properties.

IS THE CRITIQUE WORTH THE CASH?

Many agents resent those agents who charge fees. They feel that the entire profession's image is negatively affected by such practices, and that it's wrong for agents to earn money from anything other than commissions.

Agents who do not charge reading fees are unlikely to spend much time reading and analyzing a manuscript once they've decided to reject it. The writer is likely to receive only a terse computer-generated rejection letter. It may sometimes appear that the manuscript hasn't even been read, since many agents do stop reading if the first few pages are a turn-off. On a bad-to-mediocre day, an agent may view all manuscripts as junk mail until proven otherwise.

It is therefore understandable that battle-weary writers are tempted by the siren song of fee-charging agencies. At least they promise to acknowledge that there's a living, breathing writer alive within you, and their customized comments on official stationery are like manna—yes, it's just another rejection, but one with candy on top.

WHO CHARGES FOR WHAT—WITH NO GUARANTEES?

Just because some agents charge for a service does not make them impostors or knaves. Conversely, just because others are excellent literary advisors with strings of impressive credits does not mean they are able to turn your idea into a big-money plum regardless of how well-honed the writing is.

To fee or not to fee is a complicated issue, one that does not subscribe to cut-and-dried guidelines. Yes, there are combination editor/agents as well as editorial services that charge fees up front and have respectable, even estimable track records. The question for the potential client is how to separate the scamsters from the worthy professionals.

For that there is no easy answer. It is almost a given that in order to be able to judge whether an editorial service is of topnotch commercial quality the writer is probably superbly accomplished (on some level) already. Freelance editors, ghostwriters, and publishing consultants have been known to remark that their best and most appreciative clients are often those whose original writing ideas or other materials show the most professionalism.

Some flourishing freelance editors and book doctors (believe it or not) actually turn down a potential client's work (even if the editor isn't rich) unless they think the client's material has a solid shot at eventual publication. It may be in the consultant's best interest to concentrate on gigs that will earn that freelancer visible publishing credits and the prospect of happy referrals down the road—rather than glomming short-term bucks from someone who'll complain when their fantasy of literary glory is shot down in a shrapnel haze of computer-generated rejection sheets, regardless of how well the consultant has served the project.

One key here is that for the most part these freelance editors, literary advisors, book doctors, and publishing consultants do not represent themselves as literary agents per se. However, when these freelancers have a range of publishing contacts, they may be able to refer or recommend a project to an agent or publisher of their acquaintance. Again—it's a delicate task to weed out the riffraff from the respected professionals, and there are no guarantees.

I will not pass judgment on the propriety of literary agencies that charge reading fees. But if I were a writer, I'd first try my luck with the many excellent agencies that don't charge anything.

For further insight into this issue, please read the chapter titled "The Literary Agent Trade Association," which includes the Association of Authors' Representatives Canon of Ethics.

A SAMPLE SEDUCTION . . .

The following is an actual pitch letter from a fee-charging agency with only the names and other identifying information changed. Such correspondence is typical of the alluring invitations writers often receive in response to their agent submissions. There's nothing illegal about this reverse solicitation, nor, in all fairness, should such a practice automatically be deemed morally reprehensible. It's possible that a worthwhile service is indeed being provided for the money requested. However, $1,650 (or $500 or $3,000) is real money.

If a writer chooses to explore this route, there are preliminary steps I strongly advise following:

1. Ask for references. You're being asked to shell out hundreds of dollars to a virtual stranger. Get to know those who would spend your money.
2. Ask for a list of titles sold. Find out whether the so-called agency actually has an agenting track record. Or is this particular operation just a high-priced reading service with an agency facade?
3. Better yet, call or write agents who don't charge a fee and ask them to recommend book doctors, collaborative writers, or editorial freelancers whom they use to shape and develop their own clients' works. This may be a better place to spend your money.

The We-Charge-a-Fee Agency
Candyland, USA 77777

April 1, 19§§

Ms. Desi Parrot
123 Hungry Street
Birdland, USA 00000

Dear Ms. Parrot:

I read with interest your letter of April 1, synopsis, and excerpts from your novel, *The Child-Eater*, for which you are proposing agency representation. As you know, we specialize in this genre; from my experience, I can tell you that there is definite interest by publishers in novels like yours.

We believe that every writer can benefit from representation by a full-service literary agency in providing up-to-date information on editorial/media buying trends; in associations with editors and producers; and in dealing with options, contract terms, advances, royalties, and ancillary rights. The *odds against* publication by an unrepresented writer are considerable. We have the experience to identify markets for your writing, anticipate where problems are likely to arise, and work as an advocate for your ambitions and interests.

The first step toward representation and publication is a careful reading and market analysis of your material. This involves an evaluation of the literary and commercial prospects of your work by an experienced editor. If the material is immediately marketable, we will proceed to a representation contract and undertake to sell your work worldwide. If editing is needed, we will provide specific guidelines and unlimited consultative services to you in the revising or polishing of your work. Our goal is to help you become a *published* author.

If you have had minimal or no trade sales (i.e., book-length fiction), our consulting fee is $1,650.00. As you know, some agencies advertise free appraisals, but these "come-ons" mask the services of very high priced editing services with little influence in the market. We *do not* charge monthly representation fees and your initial fee is refunded on sale of the work. You may pay by check or money order, or by Visa, MasterCard or Discover; please include card number and expiration date and note that there is an additional five (5) percent charge for the use of credit cards. The fee is fully refundable on sale of the manuscript.

We are accepting a limited number of new clients and look forward to reading your complete manuscript. Please read and sign the enclosed Material Submission Release Form. Once we make a sale for you, we will accept further material on our professional commission terms, eliminating all fees. Please drop me a line, Ms. Parrot, if I can answer any questions. I look forward to being of service to you with *The Child-Eater.*

Sincerely,

Doreem On

Doreem On,
President

Enclosed as an accompaniment to the letter on the previous page, this coupon reveals how some literary agents have come to employ modern marketing techniques to entice authors.

$150   **$150**

Fee-Reduction Certificate

This certificate entitles the author to a fee reduction of $150.00 from the standard consultation fee of $1,650.00. Please enclose this certificate with your manuscript and deduct $150.00 from your fee.

(Check or money order should be payable to "Doreem On.")

The manuscript must be submitted within sixty (60) days from this date.

Doreem On	
FOR THE AGENCY	AUTHOR
April 1, 1988	
DATE	TITLE

$150   **$150**

When the Deal Is Done

How to Thrive After Signing a Publishing Contract

Jeff Herman

Congratulations! You've sold your book to an established publishing house. You've gained entry to the elite club of published authors. You'll discover that your personal credibility is enhanced whenever this achievement is made known to others. It may also prove a powerful marketing vehicle for your business or professional practice.

Smell the roses while you can. Then wake up and smell the coffee. If your experience is like that of numerous other writers, once your book is actually published, there's a better-than-even chance you'll feel a bit of chagrin. Some of these doubts are apt to be outward expressions of your own inner uncertainties. Others are not self-inflicted misgivings—they are most assuredly caused by outside circumstances.

Among the most common author complaints are the following: (1) Neither you nor anyone you know can find the book anywhere. (2) The publisher doesn't appear to be doing anything to market the book. (3) You detest the title and the jacket. (4) No one at the publishing house is listening to you. In fact, you may feel that you don't even exist for them.

As a literary agent, I live through these frustrations with my clients every day, and I try to explain to them at the outset what the realities of the business are. But I never advocate abdication or pessimism. There are ways for every author to substantially remedy these endemic problems. In many cases this means first taking a deep breath, relaxing, and reaching down deep inside yourself to sort out the true source of your emotions. When this has been accomplished, it's time to breathe out, move out, and take charge.

What follows are practical means by which each of these four common failures can be preempted. I'm not suggesting that you can compensate entirely for what may be a publisher's defaults; it's a tall order to remake a clinker after the fact. However, with lots of smarts and a little luck you can accomplish a great deal.

A PHILOSOPHY TO WRITE BY

Let me introduce a bit of philosophy that applies to the writer's life as well as it does to the lives of those who are not published. Many of you may be familiar with the themes popularized by psychotherapists, self-awareness gurus, and business motivators that assert the following: To be a victim is to be powerless—which means you don't have the ability to improve your situation. With that in mind, avoid becoming merely an author who only complains and who remains forever bitter.

No matter how seriously you believe your publisher is screwing up, don't fall into the victim trap. Instead, find positive ways to affect what is or is not happening for you.

Your publisher is like an indispensable employee whom you are not at liberty to fire. You don't have to work with this publisher the next time, but this time it's the only one you've got.

There are a handful of perennially best-selling writers, such as John Grisham, Anne Rice, Mary Higgins Clark, and Michael Crichton, whose book sales cover a large part of their publisher's expense sheet. These writers have perhaps earned the luxury of being very difficult, if they so choose (most of them are reportedly quite the opposite).

But the other 99.98% of writers are not so fortunately invested with the power to arbitrate. No matter how justified your stance and methods may be, if you become an author with whom everyone at the publishing house dreads to speak, you've lost the game.

The editors, publicists, and marketing personnel still have their jobs, and they see no reason to have you in their face. In other words: Always seek what's legitimately yours, but always try to do it in a way that might work *for* you, as opposed to making yourself persona non grata till the end of time.

ATTACKING PROBLEM NO. 1: NEITHER YOU NOR ANYONE YOU KNOW CAN FIND THE BOOK ANYWHERE

This can be the most painful failure. After all, what was the point of writing the book and going through the whole megillah of getting it published if it's virtually invisible?

Trade book distribution is a mysterious process, even for people in the business. Most bookstore sales are dominated by the large national and regional chains, such as Waldenbooks, B. Dalton, Barnes and Noble, and Crown. No shopping mall is complete without at least one of these stores. Publishers always have the chain stores in mind when they determine what to publish. Thankfully, there are also a few thousand independently owned shops throughout the country.

Thousands of new titles are published each year, and these books are added to the seemingly infinite number that are already in print. Considering the limitations of the existing retail channels, it should be no surprise that only a small fraction of all these books achieves a significant and enduring bookstore presence.

Each bookstore will dedicate most of its visual space to displaying healthy quantities of the titles they feel are safe sells: books by celebrities and well-established authors, or books that are being given extra-large printings and marketing budgets by their publishers, thereby promising to create demand.

The rest of the store will generally provide a liberal mix of titles, organized by subject or category. This is where the backlist titles reside and the lower profile newer releases try to stake their claims. For instance, the business section will probably offer two dozen or so sales books. Most of the displayed titles will be by the biggest names in the genre, and their month-to-month sales probably remains strong, even if the book was first published several years ago.

In other words, there are probably hundreds of other sales books written in recent years that, as far as retail distribution is concerned, barely made it out of the womb. You see, the stores aren't out there to do you any favors. They are going to stock whatever titles they feel they can sell the most of. There are too many titles chasing too little space.

It's the job of the publisher's sales representative to lobby the chain and store buyers individually about the merits of her publisher's respective list. But here, too, the numbers can be numbing. The large houses publish many books each season, and it's not possible for the rep to do justice to each of them. Priority will be given to the relatively few titles that get the exceptional advances.

Because most advances are modest, and since the average book costs about $20,000 to produce, some publishers can afford to simply sow a large field of books and observe passively as some of them sprout. The many that don't bloom are soon forgotten, as a new harvest dominates the bureaucracy's energy. Every season, many very fine books are terminated by the publishing reaper. The wisdom and magic these books may have offered is thus sealed away, disclosed only to the few.

I have just covered a complicated process in a brief fashion. Nonetheless, the overall consequences for your book are in essence the same. Here, now, are a few things you may attempt in order to override such a stacked situation. However, these methods will not appeal to the shy or passive:

- Make direct contact with the publisher's sales representatives. Do to them what they do to the store buyers—sell 'em! Get them to like you and your book. Take the reps near you to lunch and ball games. If you travel, do the same for local reps wherever you go.
- Make direct contact with the buyers at the national chains. If you're good enough to actually get this kind of access, you don't need to be told what to do next.
- Organize a national marketing program aimed at local bookstores throughout the country.

There's no law that says only your publisher has the right to market your book to the stores. (Of course, except in special cases, all orders must go through your publisher.) For the usual reasons, your publisher's first reaction may be "What the hell are you doing?" But that's okay; make them happy by showing them that your efforts work. It would be wise, however, to let the publisher in on your scheme up front.

If your publisher objects—which she may—you might choose to interpret those remarks as simply the admonitions they are, and then proceed to make money for all. This last observation leads to ways you can address the next problem.

ATTACKING PROBLEM NO. 2: THE PUBLISHER DOESN'T APPEAR TO BE DOING ANYTHING TO MARKET THE BOOK

If it looks as if your publisher is doing nothing to promote your book, then it's probably true. Your mistake is being surprised and unprepared.

The vast majority of titles published receive little or no marketing attention from the publisher beyond catalog listings. The titles that get big advances are likely to get some support, since the publisher would like to justify the advance by creating a top seller.

Compared to those in other Fortune 500 industries, publishers' in-house marketing departments tend to be woefully understaffed, undertrained, and underpaid. Companies like Procter & Gamble will tap the finest business schools, pay competitive salaries, and strive to nurture marketing superstars. Book publishers don't do this.

As a result, adult trade book publishing has never been especially profitable, and countless sales probably go unmade. The sales volumes and profits for large, diversified publishers are mostly due to the lucrative—and captive—textbook trade. Adult trade sales aren't the reason that companies like Random House can generate more than $1 billion in annual revenues.

Here's what you can do:

Hire your own public relations firm to promote you and your book. Your publisher is likely to be grateful and cooperative. But you must communicate carefully with your publishing house.

Once your manuscript is completed, you should request a group meeting with your editor and people from the marketing, sales, and publicity departments. You should focus on what their marketing agenda will be. If you've decided to retain your own PR firm, this is the time to impress the people at your publishing house with your commitment, and pressure them to help pay for it. At the very least, the publisher should provide plenty of free books.

Beware of this common problem: Even if you do a national TV show, your book may not be abundantly available in bookstores that day—at least not everywhere. An obvious answer is setting up 800 numbers to fill orders, and it baffles me that publishers don't make wider use of them. There are many people watching *Oprah* who won't ever make it to the bookstore, but who would be willing to order then and there with a credit card. Infomercials have proven this.

Not all talk or interview shows will cooperate, but whenever possible you should try to have your publisher's 800 number (or yours) displayed as a purchasing method in addition to the neighborhood bookstore. If you use your own number, make sure you can handle a potential flood.

If retaining a PR firm isn't realistic for you, then do your own media promotions. There are many good books in print about how to do your own PR. (A selection of relevant titles may be found in this volume's Suggested Resources section.)

ATTACKING PROBLEM NO. 3: YOU DETEST THE TITLE AND JACKET

Almost always, your publisher will have final contractual discretion over title, jacket design, and jacket copy. But that doesn't mean you can't be actively involved. In my opinion you had better be. Once your final manuscript is submitted, make it clear to your editor that you expect to see all prospective covers and titles. But simply trying to veto what the publisher comes up with won't be enough. You should try to counter the negatives with positive alternatives. You might even want to go as far as having your own prospective covers professionally created. If the publisher were to actually choose your version, the house might reimburse you.

At any rate, don't wait until it's after the fact to decide you don't like your cover, title, and so forth. It's like voting: Participate or shut up.

ATTACKING PROBLEM NO. 4: NO ONE AT THE PUBLISHING HOUSE SEEMS TO BE LISTENING TO YOU

This happens a lot—although I bet it happens to certain people in everything they do. The primary reasons for this situation are (1) the people you're trying to access are incompetent, (2) you're not a priority for them, or (3) they simply hate talking to you.

Here are a few things you might try to do about it:

- If the contact person is incompetent, what can he really accomplish for you anyway? It's probably best to find a way to work around this person, even if he begins to return your calls before you place them.
- The people you want access to may be just too busy to give you time. Screaming may be a temporary remedy, but eventually they'll go deaf again. Obviously their time is being spent somewhere. Thinking logically, how can you make it worthwhile for these people to spend more time with you? If being a pain in the neck is your best card, then perhaps you should play it. But there's no leverage like being valuable. In fact, it's likely that the somewhere else they're spending their time is with a very valuable author.
- Maybe someone just hates talking to you. That may be their problem. But, as many wise men and women have taught, allies are better than adversaries. And to convert an adversary is invaluable. Do it.

CONCLUSION

This essay may come across as cynical, but I want you to be realistic and be prepared. There are many publishing success stories out there, and many of them happened because the authors made them happen.

For every manuscript that is published, there are probably a few thousand that were rejected. To be published is a great accomplishment—and a great asset. If well tended, it can pay tremendous dividends.

Regardless of your publisher's commitment at the outset, if you can somehow generate sales momentum, the publisher will most likely join your march to success and allocate a substantial investment to ensure it. In turn, they may even assume all the credit. But so what? It's to your benefit.

Ghost with the Most
Mastering Ghostwriting and Collaboration

Gene Busnar

If you're looking for a writing career with a never-ending source of opportunities, you might consider ghostwriting or collaborating on books. I've learned that there's an almost inexhaustible supply of would-be coauthors who are convinced that they're sitting on a bestseller—be it some kind of unique personal experience, a revolutionary new way of growing tulips, or a secret of the universe that's going to improve our lives.

Many of these unheralded giants are driven by an inflated sense of their own vision and self-importance. But, fortunately, quite a few potential collaborators actually do have commercially viable nonfiction book ideas. All they need is a professional writer to take care of a few "minor details," which can be paraphrased by the following:

- I have the ideas, but lack the writing skills.
- I don't have the time to write the book myself.
- I don't have an agent or book-publishing contacts.

Now, if these were the only reasons people needed collaborators or ghostwriters, this business would be a lot simpler. Anyone with a great story or a wonderful idea for a how-to book could hire a professional writer to put things in proper literary form. In theory, the book's content—its very soul—already exists, so the writer's job should be relatively simple.

Unfortunately, things usually don't turn out that way. Professional ghostwriters and collaborative writers are expected to know what book companies are buying at any given time, and to anticipate the inherent problems in a particular book idea—especially if it's being sold in proposal form.

A publisher or agent may come to you with a fully conceived project by an articulate, promotable coauthor. But this is relatively rare—especially when you are in the early stages of your career.

There have been times when I've had to reshape the idea, change the principal's voice and language, and find a better title for the book. If you happen to possess these skills, coauthors shouldn't be all that hard to find. But first you must get some publishing credits under your belt.

If you haven't yet published a book, try writing articles for magazines and local newspapers. But don't expect your first assignments to pay well. Think of them as vehicles that can propel you to a higher level.

It may be possible to short-circuit the steps most authors go through by coming up with an innovative book concept and putting together a proposal that indicates you can deliver the goods. But the skimpier and less relevant your credits, the more you'll be expected to prove before people will treat you with consideration—much less shell out some serious bucks for your effort.

Maybe you've heard inspirational stories of people who struck it rich on their first try. Such cases are rare. The vast majority of successful nonfiction writers work extremely hard at improving their craft and building their business—over the course of a number of projects and years.

For this chapter, I've chosen to focus primarily on the business aspects of collaboration and ghosting—since this is an area where many talented new writers need help. Frankly, I think it's ridiculous to enter such a difficult and competitive field unless you possess the necessary talent. So before you go any further, it might be worthwhile to take a few minutes to think about some of the issues on the following talent evaluation questionnaire.

Do You Have What It Takes?

1. What experience do you have (professional or otherwise) as a writer?
2. Have you ever received feedback about your writing from an agent or editor?
3. What was the thrust of that feedback?
4. Have you ever won any contests or received any writing awards? List them.
5. Have you worked with a teacher or mentor who encouraged you to pursue a professional writing career?
6. Are you open to constructive criticism of your writing?
7. Can you think of an instance where such criticism helped you to improve your writing?
8. Do your writing talents fit into a commercial category?
9. If not, are you willing to take steps to present them in more commercial ways?
10. What sets your writing apart from or makes it superior to that of your competitors?

If you honestly feel the talent is there, you may be off to a running start. But remember, even the greatest talent doesn't guarantee success.

It's a truism that many fine writers aren't good at business, but that's not surprising. Most people enter this field because they like to write—not because they expect to get rich.

If money is the primary motivation, you'd be better advised to seek out a career in law, copywriting, or any number of more financially lucrative fields. Still, if you're going to succeed—or at least survive—you'd better accept the fact that business and marketing skills are at least as important as literary talent. This is especially true in collaborative and ghostwriting work—fields that require a good deal of negotiation and personal interaction.

If you want to write just for pleasure, that's one thing. But the moment you decide to earn money at your craft, you become a businessperson. If you want to make it professionally, start thinking of yourself not just as a writer, but also as someone who's in the *business* of writing. Here are four suggestions to help point your career in that direction:

1. Take a business-minded approach.
2. Present yourself powerfully.
3. Position yourself advantageously.
4. Price your services for profit.

TAKE A BUSINESS-MINDED APPROACH

Don't make the mistake of thinking that, because you're good, clients will find you. You've got lots of competitors out there who are aggressively pursuing work, so you can't afford to be too laid back. It's part of your job to make potential clients aware of you. Potential clients include not only co-writers, but agents and editors who can direct projects your way.

Most successful nonfiction writers do all sorts of things to generate work and develop new contacts. No matter where you are in your career, consider devoting time and energy to the following activities:

- Join professional societies and attend their meetings.
- Associate with as many agents, editors, and potential collaborators as possible.
- Stay in touch with peers who have similar interests.
- Sign up for relevant courses, lectures, and seminars—especially those conducted by reputable people in your field.
- Read trade publications.
- Keep up with economic and other trends that influence our business.

In the final analysis, your success as a writer can hinge as much on how creative you are in your business as it does on your actual work. That's why it's essential that you understand and assume responsibility for the business side of your writing career as early in the game as possible.

PRESENT YOURSELF POWERFULLY

Whenever you submit a manuscript, proposal, or résumé to an editor, agent, or potential collaborator, it's essential to look at those presentation materials from the other person's point of view. When you present your work to people in a position to buy your services, you're selling yourself as well as the materials at hand.

Professionalism in your work and manner communicates that you are someone people ought to take seriously—even if they don't buy the immediate project. The creation of a professional image includes the following:

Looking Like a Pro

- Appropriate and well-organized materials.
- Dependability and promptness.
- A willingness to accept critical feedback.

Of all these factors, an openness to criticism and tolerance for rejection may be the most difficult. Here, especially, you need to get out of your own skin for a moment and imagine how you'd feel if you were an agent or an editor. One of the toughest things is telling other people that their work doesn't measure up—whatever the reason.

Criticism and rejection can be even more difficult when you're on the receiving end. Still, when you communicate a willingness to accept constructive criticism, you invite feedback that can help you make valuable refinements in your presentation. At the same time, you let people know that they're dealing with a confident professional— one who has a genuine interest in meeting their needs.

POSITION YOURSELF ADVANTAGEOUSLY

One key to presenting yourself professionally is giving potential clients a clear-cut picture of what you do. Since your potential clients have the option of choosing the writer who best fills their specific needs, it's your job to see to it that you occupy that particular niche in their minds. In advertising, this concept is called positioning. It's a principle that applies especially well to the business of writing.

Positioning saves your potential clients a good deal of time. You can assume that anyone who's in a position to give you paying work has certain requirements and categories in mind. It's your job to meet those criteria. If you don't, someone else will.

Many good writers are capable of collaborating or ghosting in a number of areas. Unfortunately, that's not what most agents and editors want to hear. Their lives are already too cluttered up with superfluous people and irrelevant information. If you try to hit them with all your credentials at once, they may find it difficult to remember anything about you.

Once you have an idea of what specific clients are looking for, you can present only the information that is most relevant. The best way to make that determination is to research potential clients before you approach them.

Let's say, for example, that you want to ghostwrite political autobiographies, and you're trying to interest an agent who specializes in that area. He asks you to send some samples of your work. How do you decide which materials to include and which ones to leave out?

As a rule, the best presentations are the most concise. That's why it's best to present potential clients with only those materials that relate to the job at hand. As you develop more of a relationship with agents and editors, you can make them aware of your other skills. But be careful not to overwhelm them with too much material.

If you tell an agent who perceives you as a political writer that you also have skills in the medical area, he may file that information away for future reference. But if a call for a medical writer comes in, he's most likely to go with someone who has positioned herself or himself primarily in that area.

Of course, there are exceptions to the rule. For example, the agent may not be able to get the medical writer he or she wants at that particular moment. The memory that you had some background in that area may surface—and suddenly your phone is ringing.

PRICE YOUR SERVICES FOR PROFIT

You may have never thought about it in this light, but in most professions, pricing is determined by positioning and perception rather than by any objective measure.

Have you ever wondered, for example, why your car mechanic charges $20 an hour, while your attorney can charge $200 an hour?

The reasons for this huge difference in pricing can't be measured in any real terms. But the fact is, nobody would pay $200 an hour to get their car fixed. And if an attorney asked for a mere $20 an hour, you'd probably question the guy's competence.

Unfortunately, pricing guidelines in the book-writing business are not nearly so well established as in lawyering or repairing cars. That's why it's essential to establish yourself as a business person who puts a high value on your hours.

Personally, I see no objective reason why the services of a good writer should be worth less than those of a mediocre attorney. But because writing is thought of as a glamour profession, people sometimes expect you to work for nothing—especially when you start out. Let them know that you're in this business for profit—not glamour.

I'll never forget how offended one celebrity became when I told him that I actually expected to be paid—and paid well—for working with him on his book proposal. This made a profound impression on me, and I've since made it a policy to regard people who take this attitude as a threat to my very survival.

In writing, as in any business, there are times when it may be worthwhile to accept a low-paying project. Just make sure that you have a clear idea of what's in it for you.

I've listed six compensating factors that can offset a low price. You may want to use them as negotiating points in deciding whether to accept a particular project:

What to Ask for When the Price Is Wrong

- The prominent appearance of your name on the cover and in all publicity for the book.
- A generous allowance for expenses and supplies.
- Greater creative freedom.
- A larger portion of the advance up front.
- A better deal on subsidiary or ancillary rights.
- A larger number of author's copies of the book.

Most writers take on work for a combination of three reasons: to make money, to be creative and expressive, and to build credibility—which will hopefully lead to making more money.

Once you accept these as the general business goals of collaboration and ghost-writing, it behooves you to look for projects that are fulfilling, well paying, and career enhancing.

If you can find a project that meets all three of these criteria, go for it. If a project allows you to achieve any two of these goals, it's certainly worth considering. One out of three would be a marginal call at best. But if the project doesn't satisfy any of these three tests, the decision is simple: Forget it, and move on to something more rewarding.

Gene Busnar can be reached at: Collaboration Consultants, Ltd., P.O. Box 826, Keyport, NY 07735.

The Youth Market
Books for Children and Young Adults

Jamie M. Forbes

Publishing programs geared toward children and young adults show splendid life in several important categories. Light reference and entertainingly educational non-fiction books are a traditionally strong area of sales across all age groups. There's vigorous interest in children's titles based on multicultural folk tales, well told and finely illustrated. Mystery and horror are strong genres for ages ranging from the very earliest readers through young adults. Major publishers that are members of communications conglomerates have access to an array of licensed characters with built-in exposure to potential readers through television and film counterparts.

All this is by way of a major cautionary note: The market is tight for new talent, and it's tougher now for a greenhorn to break in. Established creators can be expected to protect their hard-won turf. Is everybody is going to gang up and play meanie to all the new kids on the block? The rules of play may be changing, but this does not necessarily signal the game's over; it is, rather, a notice for the rookie players to pump up a notch and by all means keep hustling.

Good-bye Yellow Brick Road

Everyone who's had a kid (or been one) believes they can write for the children's and young-adult market—or so it appears to editors and agents who are swamped with proposals they deem far off the mark. Though this scheme of visionary would-be-author unreality is not much different from the world of adult trade publishing (where it seems everyone has a how-to/inspirational book inside them, or a hook for a sizzling new thriller), it is an exceptionally excruciating phenomenon in the realm of kid's lit—it is immediately, abundantly clear when a prospective author has not done a bit of homework.

Publishers often have certain preferences for queries and submissions. Part of your homework is to find out from your target houses whether to include sample material with your query—and if so how much to include. Call the publisher and inquire about such protocols from someone in the editorial department—whatever information you have seen in print is subject to change, and requirements for individual series and lines are bound to vary.

If you have in mind an original series, it might be best to suggest this indirectly by first presenting a strong character whose escapades beg to be turned into a series, rather than stating your intent outright. Perhaps you can couch your ultimate goals somewhere in the presentation package subtly, without appearing bombastic or rude. As for novelizations and television/movie spin-offs, publishers often keep writers on tap for these projects; query publishers to find out what you can do to become part of their crew.

Skip the trip down the yellow brick road: If you want to write for children or young-adult readers, a nuts-and-bolts approach is called for at the outset. The routine of conceiving and structuring your work according to brutal publishing demands can be overbearing and numbing at first, and even confusing to the novice writer. However, as the guidelines are comprehended, they become a source of confidence that you're on the right track. Research in the field results in flights of insight that can guide the prospective author into shaping a proposal worthy of consideration rather than one that's ripe to hit the trash can.

CHILDREN'S LITERATURE AS CORPORATE ENTERPRISE

In corporate-style children's publishing, many successful projects are now originated in house, or by those outside the company who can bring to bear considerable experience (and contacts) in writing, illustration, editing, design, manufacturing of product, and the marketing of same.

Many lines intended for children's and young-adult markets are handled by independent book packagers or book producers that specialize in this field. These typically small, entrepreneurial operations mastermind ideas, develop concepts (perhaps in tandem with their corporate clients), and commission work from artists, designers, and writers. Many freelancers work through book packagers, rather than through agents or publishers, with varying arrangements pertaining to compensation (flat fees, hourly rates, royalties) and author credit.

As a writer or illustrator for hire, you might not be an accredited author as such (at least when you start out), but you work for money, not on spec. In some established series with strict specifications or in start-up lines, it might not be much of a free-market atmosphere, but (and this part bears repeating) your creative labors are rewarded in currency, if not renown.

Children's publishing has traditionally been more open to unagented/unsolicited submissions than has the adult-publishing sphere; however, it is increasingly the case that acquisitions departments in major children's houses do not accept *any* unsolicited manuscripts directly from authors. All projects they consider are those that go through the screening process at literary agencies—and the agents whose author submissions get respect are themselves specialists in books for younger readers.

Not every agent listed in writer's-resource directories is skilled in addressing the nuances of the ever-changing children's/young-adult market. As a writer or illustrator it behooves you to seek out those agents who have expertise in this area and are open to new recruits.

In addition, it can be well worth your while (and worth your money) to avail yourself of the services of an independent editorial consultant with a solid background in children's publishing. Referrals to qualified professionals may be obtained through writers' organizations, editorial associations, or some of the more amiable literary agencies.

Aside from the major commercial publishers, there are numerous smaller, regional presses that have solid children's divisions or that specialize in works directed toward certain age groups. Check these guys out (there are a number of such publishers listed in the directories in this book); you might be surprised and gratified to know how open some of them are to new authors.

MARKETING BY DESIGN

No one in commercial publishing will let you forget that the primary objective is to circulate product—and create profit. As an artist or writer who wishes to participate financially in the publishing industry, please bear in mind at all times that you are in the research-and-development wing of what is essentially a manufacturing and marketing enterprise.

That means, as an intelligent creator, you must know your market and understand what it takes to reach your buyer. Apart from the niceties of promotion and distribution (to which your publishing overview should be attuned), knowledge of the special requirements of your selected area can make or break your project at the concept stage.

Illustrators must familiarize themselves with the prevailing conventions of books for young kids as they apply to the rendering of animals who dress up in clothing and speak, for the right mix of innocence and affection between young lovers who never kiss, for ways to portray action scenes in ways that are not overly scary.

Artists must also be experts in print technology, and be able to execute their designs expressively within the confines of layout requirements, with elements of shading, line, and color separation well-defined in the backs of their minds before they begin their work.

For writers, there are particular sets of standards to be met in terms of readership level (such as vocabulary, sentence structure, and content). You've got one strong market made up of titles for tots who do not themselves read—here you want to write books that are inviting *to be read aloud to them.*

There are also the questions of who is buying the book and why. Obviously the adult caretaker is going to plunk down the bucks for products targeted at the youngest age groups. However, even here, the kids themselves have enormous input, gauged by their responses while browsing around children's sections (which, in some of the more lavish bookstores, are set up to resemble play areas).

Publishers design some children's lines to be read by younger readers on their own, because the kids themselves want to read them. Other series are keyed to the demands of the educational market, to be read in large part because they are assigned by teachers. Even though there is some sales overlap—school libraries represent an important market sector—the emphasis on individual creativity varies enormously within the overall readability guidelines.

Because the field is geared to specific age ranges, the actual makeup of each market sector changes as readers progress through the various levels. This implies that children's publishers are wise to be aware of subtle cultural shifts that are sometimes much more slowly reflected in adult trade divisions. The trend toward books published in the Spanish language in addition to their English counterparts, as well as in bilingual Spanish/English editions, was evident in the arena of books for younger readers before the major commercial houses began to dance to that same tune.

In line with this view, children's books were multimedia affairs—in the tangibly physical sense—long before the advent of electronic versions. In order to tickle the fancy of admirably antic kids, children's books engage a variety of formats not strictly limited to type and pictures. Among established approaches are peek-a-board books, pop-up books, chunky-shaped books, cuddle-cloth books, mini-storybooks, glow-in-the-dark books with phosphorescent ink; books with puzzle-pages, ribbons, bows, and gilt; books boxed with wearable accessories; books in tandem with activity kits; and book-and-audio packages. Publishers construe such projects as unlikely to arise from the whimsical ideas and grandiose sheaves of notes that sometimes appear miraculously at writer's conferences.

In order to publish complex packages successfully, each element is handled by seasoned professionals. Of course artists and writers play important roles, but there is more variety of publishing skill, expertise, and expense involved in bringing these products out beautifully than there is when translating the words of adult literary masters into printed type, no matter how elegantly designed.

Children's-publishing houses make use of an array of personnel equipped with exquisite design skills, eagle editorial eyes, and consummate aesthetic sense; they require ingenious technicians familiar with the latest means of production and print, with a robust command of engineering concepts and manufacturing processes.

AIN'T NO PLAYPEN

At major publishing firms, there are fewer venues for the first-time writer or prospective illustrator, and an increasing emphasis is placed on developing brand-name lines and series—particularly those with spin-off potential in other media, as well as into toyland and wearable apparel. If divisions and imprints with specialties in the arena of younger readers seem to be closing off the traditional avenues used by rookie talent to get to them, it's due to circumstances that have much to do with corporate consolidation at the larger houses, as well as insider advantages of personal contacts at smaller start-up operations.

Fun and games may be the end products of some children's and young-adult publishing projects, but getting to play in the first place is no lark for the aspiring writer and illustrator. As a personal pastime, many people enjoy composing sets of rhymes, developing storylines combined with pictures, or conceiving text-and-photographic layouts. With some copies of their creations printed and bound, these people are amply rewarded by the response of young readers in their personal circles.

If, however, you are determined to vie with the big kids in the publishing biz, it is essential to see the world of children's publishing up close as publishers view it—not in the golden light of far-off fantasies derived from half-forgotten images of childhood bliss. You are, at this level, in competition with all the others out there with the same dream. In order to get a toe in, you not only must step out from the rest of the pack, you also must show accomplishment on the order of that of those with professional credentials. You may well have to master the requisite skills on your own, but there is a community of like-minded individuals and programs out there to assist you.

Be resourceful. This means literally taking advantage of the substantial resources at hand. That includes studying some of the many excellent books on the subject of writing for children and young adults, joining writers' groups, attending conferences, and making use of any and all networking connections you can negotiate. With a solid combination of refined skills, unflagging determination, and a growing mesh of contacts, you too can break through.

Novel Truths
Revealing the Secret World of Fiction

JAMIE M. FORBES

You know you like it when you read it—but do you know what it is you've read? Maybe you like *this* writer (most of the time), or books from *that* publisher (some of the time), but never read any of *that* kind of stuff. Indeed, it might be said that you'd read even more than you already do if they published more of what you enjoy.

You know plenty of other people who feel the same way you do. Maybe you'd be mortified to find out that publishers want to view you as part of a specific market, with the books that please you ideally seen in terms of categories, genres, brand-name authors, and high-identity imprints.

You're an individual with personal tastes and a distinct style—give a babe a break once in a while! Since you're asking what you can do about this state of affairs, why don't you write a story about it? The kind others of your ilk will buy in droves.

What kind of book is that, bub?

A good one—just one hell of a novel.

You've got to tell us more than that to get it into print.

THE WAY OF THE WORD WARRIOR

Why classify your fiction in mercenary terms? As an accomplished writer, you've earned the right for the text to stand on its own. After all, you've got a riveting story complete with rich characters and exquisite atmosphere. Guess what: Regardless of how well honed a plot you've got, it's not enough. What, then, if anything, is gained by slapping on a label? It's certain that many folks suffer plenty in life from being pigeon-holed, but remember: Life is tough, and writing is tougher.

Whether a novel is a heartfelt work of art or commercial calculation on the author's part, it finally does have to stand on its own as an experience worthy of the reader's buck. However, in order to get to the reader, your work will be categorized for much the same reason any other product is packaged and named: A book is not a book until it's brought to the market ready to be bought.

MAP THE LITERARY LANDSCAPE

Browse through some of the bookseller superchains, take a peek into specialty bookstores: You will see that all books have to be someplace. And some are racked in a couple different places—certain popular fiction titles are also stocked in mystery or horror sections, or sometimes even under a sign bearing, of all things, the word *Literature*.

All well and good, some writers may say. Booksellers and publishers are the marketing professionals; that's their game, and they can play it any way they want—so long as they do a good job selling books. Writers are the prose pros, and let's just leave it that way.

No chance.

For writers, bookselling is not a spectator sport. Nor should marketing be solely the province of publishers and booksellers. An author is in charge the instant the idea for a work springs forth. It quickly becomes apparent to fledgling writers that a marketing hook is as important in the initial query letter as it is in the finished book or promotional tour.

Writers are often advised to study the market (or markets), to gear their work for a particular slot and to learn how to position their work in the publishing emporium. Such stratagems sound sweet and dandy, but where to begin? One key to enlightenment is through the concept of category. Understanding how your novel fits within the category structure of contemporary fiction publishing may spell the difference between literary success and oblivion.

BE AWARE—AND GET THERE

Consider the following buzzterms: hard-boiled, cozy, psychological horror, vampire romance, contemporary Western, medical–legal thriller, spiritual adventure. Sound like anything you've written, by chance—or would choose to read? If so, lovely; if not, look around, there are plenty of other categories, genres, and subgenres to be found, each with its own special appeal and its own readership niche.

Though some classifications seem evident on the surface, plenty of pitfalls lurk underfoot. There are several different approaches to the horror story, and many forms of mysteries. Is *literary fiction* a category or simply a description, or is it both? Is a work categorized according to genre, or is genre fiction itself a category?

A customary breakdown of the fiction market describes three broad sectors. (1) There is category (or genre) fiction, wherein books are typified by genre or category (such as with detective fiction, horror, romance, suspense, thriller, or Western) and are marketed as such. (2) Commercial fiction (the high end of mainstream fiction) is expected to find a wide readership that supersedes or cuts across genres; the most marketable of these works are designated lead titles, or frontlist books (often literally placed at the front of the catalog listings). (3) Literary works are characterized by accomplishment in the art and craft of writing, and may otherwise represent a genre (or not), have cult appeal (not limited to the academy), or even be considered commercial.

You as writer can of course choose to write whatever you want, however you want—and by all means dream on during the idea stages. Nonetheless, please bear in mind that your chances of being published are incalculably greater if your work is seen clearly as having a conspicuous place in the category scheme of commercial publishing.

Booksellers and publishers are fond of pronouncements that put the market in perspective—their perspective. You may hear there is little crossover between the readership of horror and mystery; there is said to be more of a blend (but not much more) between aficionados of science fiction and avant-garde suspense. The evidence to support such claims may in actuality be scant, and your own anecdotal experience may seem to point out new and different readership trends.

However, publishers sign authors and sell books on the basis of what they have already sold successfully. If your work is a crossover piece, it's best to play it as commercially as possible, which by some definitions means watering down the specific genre attributes and pumping up your story with universal passions, intensifying the human interaction, and interlacing your plot elements with boffo schemes of fear and greed, intrigue and romance.

Riddle Me This: The Fiction Query

Once you've got your product polished enough to hawk, you need to find a place to sell it. Unless you're betting on Internet distribution or planning to flog your own home-printed copies at the local flea market, your most likely venue is through the publishing establishment of editors and agents. You reach them, first of all, through the dreaded and ubiquitous query letter—with which publishing houses and literary agencies are deluged daily.

When you query an agent or editor, be sharp as a buccaneer's cutlass, and as stealthy as a sea-rover prowling for quarry. The initial aim of all paper pirates is to lure the reader to request the full manuscript. Make sure the dynamic appeal of your tale is portrayed in a conceptual hook of as few words as possible, up front, very likely in the opening sentence: The query lead whets the edge in order to make a breach in the impassive reader's defenses.

There are any number of ways to do this. Even the most obliquely suggested examples would undoubtedly result in an overwhelming tilt toward certain query approaches that have in the past proven to be eye-openers, and these techniques would quickly lose their edge, so you won't find any real recommendations here. You may choose to take a stand and be creative and original, or to be pointed and precise. A fiction query is both a demonstration of writing agility and a business letter. It can work at either extreme or anywhere along the continuum.

Now that you've poked that opening, you're ready for the follow-through.

Embroider the opening gambit with a succinct depiction of the story's primary selling points. If you haven't done so in the lead, state how the work fits into the book-publishing industry's category structure and also what makes *this* piece so unique that it screams to be published. Do it all in a sentence or two, regardless of how elaborate the actual story is.

Then you may highlight one or two further aspects of character, plot, or setting that accent the story's allure. Be careful: If this part of the query threatens to run more than two or three paragraphs, try to shave it down; the extra copy expended here risks diluting the impact (the material you cut might be used to better effect in a synopsis).

The space you save can be used to rattle off a few pertinent personal notes, such as prior publication or special career or professional expertise brought to bear in the story. Writing tightly can allow a one-page query to pack more of a wallop than a glossy, brochure-sized writer's packet that contains diffuse credits and irrelevant fanfare.

Red Flags and Jolly Rogers

Valid or not, certain approaches send out red flags in the eyes of agents and editors. Where original fiction is concerned, people in publishing tend not to be impressed by the invocation of big-money books or hugely popular movies with which an inquiring writer's work is to be compared. "So what? That's been done before," they'll say, "the market is saturated already." When your work is truly innovative, you've done yourself a grave disservice with a derivative presentation.

Likewise, citing topical societal motifs or current political fiascoes as if they existed intrinsically to sell a particular author's novel is inclined make a bad moon rise in a reader. Surely, finessing the context of contemporary culture can augment a book's appeal, but a query letter that runs far afield from the work at hand is apt to be read as preposterous posturing from a resounding blowhard. That's enough to make a reader suspect the manuscript is more of the same.

Don't get spooked by these protocols. Agents and editors are well aware that to get the big picture you have to read the whole story; they know that a query is in essence a sales pitch. They'll begin to appreciate your subtlety and breadth when they read the full piece (or get a taste in the sample chapters or short synopsis you enclose). Your query convinces them that their extra reading is likely to be worthwhile.

As a writer you can oversimplify your story to the point of gross misrepresentation if you say your book is, for instance, a medical thriller (by god, it's about my *characters*!); but such a description shows the agent or editor you're not unfamiliar with such niceties as bookstores and book reviews: You indicate you are aware of industry dictates (however confining), and know a thing or two about positioning a product in the marketplace.

A final caveat: Don't advertise something that isn't there; your manuscript must be all you claim it to be—and more.

Readership Base: Safe Haven or Stranded by Success?

Calling your manuscript a literary sci-fi mystery thriller showcasing elements of sword-and-sorcery fantasy in an erotic action-adventure scenario may encompass your grand achievement very accurately. But such a description can also cover a work with lack of focus, unsteady vision, and terrifying scarcity of storytelling precision. A crossover concept, if it is not seen as highly commercial (regardless of the quality of writing), limits rather than expands potential appeal in the eyes of publishers, which equals no deal. (PS: The aforementioned work is likely one that can be presented more marketably as a science-fiction adventure.)

Be aware that, once published, authors, like their output, are classified by genre or category, and writers may encounter flak from editors and agents when they wish to break out of the mold created by their success in one arena. A way around this perhaps enviable predicament is for a writer to use different pen names as brand names for certain series or lines, in much the same manner publishers devise special imprint names like Berkley Prime Crime, Warner Aspect, or Vintage Contemporaries.

Through genre hopping, the writer may lose hard-won name recognition gained in one field and have to build a new readership virtually from the beginning—lower anticipated sales for a bankable author are a major reason for resistance from the publishing community, and low (if any) advances are an anticipated stance. The reverse is the case when a writer is moved from category classification to frontlist commercial status, for then the publisher is confident the writer is ready and able to break into a wider market and still retain an established readership base.

YOUR OWN COMPASS

Navigating the literary seas can be treacherous indeed for the writer who is adrift; these are turbulent, murky waters, where fierce waves crash, whirlpools gyrate, and rocks await to dash your craft. In order to chart your course, it is prudent to take out a map of the literary landscape before you begin your manuscript in earnest. Then compass your route to the marketplace during the initial stages of development, rather than after a complete draft, when major revisions (or an entirely new start) are required to bring your story into port rather than being tossed and forgotten on a forlorn beach.

If your premise and plot structure don't fit the established category format, you may be in for a real ordeal when trying to find a publisher, at least in the mainstream commercial arena. However, when the writing voice is strong, with sufficient resourcefulness and good fortune, a suitable publisher can be found.

Anne Rice's *Interview with the Vampire* didn't slide nicely into quaint horror formulas, and some might not classify it as proper literature. Knopf bought it, and millions of fans couldn't care less how her work is categorized. Did Tom Clancy invent the technothriller? Regardless of that subgenre's current popularity, it was Naval Institute Press, and not a commercial house, that initially brought out Clancy's *Hunt for Red October*. Did John Grisham break new legal-thriller ground with *The Firm*? (Grisham's first novel, *A Time to Kill*, was introduced by Wynwood, a primarily religious house.) James Redfield's *The Celestine Prophecy* would seem, on description, to be a defiantly uncategorizable mélange of genres—the book's commercial success shows how wise the writer was to follow through on his vision. Full-blooded romance in tandem with philosophical pursuits says rejection-slip wallpaper to many—to Robert James Waller it said: *Bridges of Madison County* and a full skein of subsequent bestsellers.

Books. Hooks. Premise and plot. That's a lot to think about when you start a new project. Once you begin, the whole shebang becomes internalized as you lose all trepidation and move along undaunted. It's downright glorious when you realize that, whether working in line with or in defiance of category guidelines, your writing is energized by your industry awareness.

Keep in mind that the sign on the spine of a paperback or the blurb on the back of a hardcover tells the bookseller where to rack the package. The prospective reader knows where to browse, look around, and pick up your book on the basis of its catchy title or snazzy design—if not yet on the basis of your burgeoning literary renown. This hungry book lover will then flip through those lush pages, be agog at your individuality and personal style (even though it is clearly being marketed as a category work), and head for the counter ready to buy your book.

For an unfettered treatment of the category structure of contemporary fiction publishing, please see the chapter that follows: "Fiction Dictionary."

Fiction Dictionary

Jamie M. Forbes

In book publishing, people describe works of fiction as they relate to categories, genres, and other market concepts, which, coming from the mouths of renowned industry figures, can make it sound as if there's a real system to what is actually a set of arbitrary terminology. Categories are customarily viewed as reflecting broad sectors of readership interest. Genres are either subcategories (classifications within categories) or types of stories that can pop up within more than one category—although *genre* and *category* are sometimes used interchangeably.

For instance, suspense fiction (as a broad category) includes the jeopardy story genre (typified by a particular premise that can just as easily turn up in a supernatural horror story). Or, again within the suspense fiction category, there's the police procedural (a subcategory of detective fiction, which is itself a subcategory of suspense that is often seen as a separate category). The police procedural can be discussed as a distinct genre with its own special attributes. There are also particular procedural genre types, such as those set in the small towns of the American plains. As a genre story type, tales of small-town American life also surface in the context of categories as disparate as literary fiction, horror stories, Westerns, and contemporary and historical romance.

As we can see, all of this yakety-yak is an attempt to impose a sense of order onto what is certainly a muddy creative playing field.

The following listing of commonly used fiction descriptives gives an indication of the varieties of writing found within each category. This is not meant to be a strict taxonomy. Nor is it exhaustive. The definitions associated with each category or genre are fluid and personalized in usage and can seem to vary with each author interview or critical treatise or with each spate of advertising copy or press release, or they can shift during the course of a single editorial conference. One writer's "mystery" may be a particular editor's "suspense," which can then be marketed to the public as a "thriller."

Then, too, individual authors do come up with grand, original ideas that demand publication and thereby create new categories, or decline to submit to any such designation. But that's another story—maybe it's yours.

ACTION ADVENTURE

The action-oriented adventure novel is best typified in terms of premise and scenario trajectory. These stories often involve the orchestration of a journey that is essentially exploratory, revelatory, and (para)military. There is a quest element—a search for a treasure in whatever guise—in addition to a sense of pursuit that crosses over into thrillerdom. From one perspective, the action-adventure tale, in story concept if not explicit content, traces its descent from epic-heroic tradition.

In modern action-adventure we are in the territory of freebooters, commandos, and mercenaries—as well as suburbanites whose yen for experience of the good life, and whose very unawareness in the outback, takes them down dangerous trails. Some stories are stocked with an array of international terrorists, arms smugglers, drug dealers, and techno-pirates. Favorite settings include jungles, deserts, swamps, and mountains—any sort of badlands (don't rule out an urban environment) that can echo the perils that resound through the story's human dimension.

There can be two or more cadres with competing aims going for the supreme prize—and be sure to watch out for lots of betrayal and conflict among friends, as well as the hitherto unsuspected schemer among the amiably bonded crew.

Action-adventures were once thought of as exclusively men's stories. No more. Writers invented new ways to do it, and the field is now open.

COMMERCIAL FICTION

Commercial fiction is defined by sales figures, either projected (prior to publication, even before acquisition) or backhandedly through actual performance. Commercial properties are frontlist titles, featured prominently in a publisher's catalog and given good doses of publicity and promotion.

If an agent or editor says a manuscript is commercial, the question in response is apt to be: How so? Many books in different genres achieve best-seller potential after an author has established a broad-based readership and is provided marketing support from all resources the publisher commands.

Commercial fiction is not strictly defined by content or style; it is perhaps comparative rather than absolute. Commercial fiction is often glitzier, more stylishly of the mode in premise and setting; its characters strike the readers as more assuredly glamorous (regardless of how highbrow or lowlife).

A commercial work offers the publisher a special marketing angle, which changes from book to book or season to season—this year's kinky kick is next year's ho-hum. For a new writer in particular, to think commercially is to think ahead of the pack and not jump on the tail-end of a bandwagon that's already passed. If your premise has already played as a television miniseries, you're way too late.

Commercial works sometimes show elements of different categories, such as detective fiction or thrillers, and may cut across or combine genres to reach out toward a vast readership. Cross-genre books may thus have enticing hooks for the reading public at large; at the same time, when they defy category conventions they may not satisfy genre aficionados. If commercial fiction is appointed by vote of sales, most popular mysteries are commercial works, as are sophisticated best-selling sex-and-shopping oh-so-shocking wish-it-were-me escapades.

CRIME FICTION

Related to detective fiction and suspense novels, in subject matter and ambiance, are stories centered on criminal enterprise. Crime fiction includes lighthearted capers that are vehicles in story form for portrayal of amusingly devious aspirations at the core of the human norm. Crime stories can also be dark, black, *noir*, showing the primeval essence of tooth-and-nail that brews in more than a few souls.

Some of the players in crime stories may well be cops of one sort or another (and they are often as corrupt as the other characters), but detection per se is not necessarily the story's strong suit. It is just as likely that in the hands of one of the genre's masters the reader's lot will be cast (emotionally at least) in support of the outlaw characters' designs.

DETECTIVE FICTION

Varieties of detective fiction include police procedurals (with the focus on formal investigatory teamwork); hard-boiled, poached or soft-boiled (not quite so tough as hard-boiled); and the cozy (aka tea-cozy mysteries, manners mysteries, manor house mysteries).

Detectives are typically private or public pros, or related professionals whose public image at least involves digging under the surface (reporters, journalists, computer hackers, art experts, psychotherapists, and university academics including archaeologists). They may even be rank amateurs who are interested or threatened via an initial plot turn that provides them with an opportunity (or the necessity) to assume an investigatory role.

The key here is that the detective story involves an ongoing process of discovery that forms the plot. Active pursuit of interlocking clues and other leads is essential—although sometimes an initial happenstance disclosure will do in order to kick off an otherwise tightly woven story.

The manifold denominations of modern detective fiction (also called mysteries, or stories or novels of detection) are widely considered to stem from the detective tales composed by the nineteenth-century American writer Edgar Allan Poe. Though mysterious tracks of atmosphere and imagery can be traced in the writings of French symbolists (Charles Baudelaire was a big fan of Poe), the first flowering of the form was in Britain, including luminaries such as Arthur Conan Doyle, Agatha Christie, and Dorothy L. Sayers. Indeed, in one common usage, a traditional mystery (or cozy) is a story in the mode initially established by British authors.

The other major tradition is the American-grown hard-boiled detective story, with roots in the tabloid culture of America's industrial growth and the associated institutions of yellow journalism, inspirational profiles of the gangster-tycoon lifestyle, and social-action exposés.

The field continues to expand with infusions of elements such as existentialist character conceits, the lucidity and lushness of magic-realists, and the ever-shifting sociopolitical insights that accrue from the growing global cultural exchange.

Occasionally detective fiction involves circumstances in which, strictly speaking, no crime has been committed. The plot revolves around parsing out events or situations that may be construed as strange, immoral, or unethical (and are certainly mysterious), but which are by no means considered illegal in all jurisdictions.

Fantasy Fiction

The category of fantasy fiction covers many of the story elements encountered in fables, folk tales, and legends; the best of these works obtain the sweep of the epic and are touched by the power of myth. Some successful fantasy series are set within recognizable museum-quality frames, such as those of ancient Egypt or the Celtic world. Another strain of fantasy fiction takes place in almost-but-not-quite archeologically verifiable regions of the past or future, with barbarians, nomads, and jewel-like cities scattered across stretches of continental-sized domains of the author's imagination.

Fair game in this realm are romance, magic, and talking animals. Stories are for the most part adventurous, filled with passion, honor, vengeance—and *action*. A self-explanatory subgenre of fantasy fiction is termed sword-and-sorcery.

Horror

Horror has been described as the simultaneous sense of fascination and terror, a basic attribute that can cover significant literary scope. Some successful horror writers are admired more for their portrayal of atmosphere than for attention to plot or character development. Other writers do well with the carefully paced zinger—that is, the threat-and-delivery of gore. In the hands of skilled practitioners, sometimes not much more is needed to produce truly terrifying effects.

The horror genre has undergone changes—there is overall less reliance on the religiously oriented supernatural, more utilization of medical and psychological concepts, more sociopolitical and cultural overtones, and a general recognition on the part of publishers that many horror aficionados seek more than slash-and-gore. Not that the readers aren't bloodthirsty—it is just that in order to satisfy the cravings of a discerning audience a writer must create an augmented reading experience.

The horror itself can be supernatural in nature, psychological, paranormal, or techno (sometimes given a medical–biological slant that verges on sci-fi), or can embody personified occult/cultic entities. In addition to tales of vampires, were-creatures, demons, and ghosts, horror has featured such characters as the elemental slasher/stalker (conceived with or without mythic content), a variety of psychologically tormented souls, and just plain folks given over to splatterhouse pastimes. Whatever the source of the horror, the tale is inherently more gripping and more profound when the horrific beast, force, or human foe has a mission and is a character with its own meaningful designs and insights—when something besides single-minded bloodlust is at play.

At times the horror premise is analogous to a story of detection (especially in the initial setup), often the horror plot assumes the outlines of the thriller (particularly where there is a complex chase near the end), and sometimes the horror-story scenario ascribes to action-adventure elements. However, rather than delineating a detailed process of discovery (as in a typical mystery) or a protracted hunt throughout (as in the thriller), the horror plot typically sets up a final fight to the finish (until the sequel) that, for all its pyrotechnics and chills, hinges on something other than brute force.

LITERARY FICTION

The term *literary* describes works that feature the writer's art expressed at its most refined levels; literary fiction describes works of literature in forms such as the novel, novella, novelette, short story, and short-shorts (also known as flash fiction). In addition to these fictional formats, literary works include poetry, essays, letters, dramatic works, and superior writing in all nonfiction varieties covering areas such as travel, food, history, current affairs, and all sorts of narrative nonfiction as well as reference works.

Literary fiction can adhere to the confines of any and all genres and categories, or suit no such designation. A work of fiction that is depicted as literary can (and should) offer the reader a multidimensional experience. Literary can designate word selection and imagery that is careful or inspired, or that affects an articulated slovenliness. A literary character may be one who is examined in depth, or is sparsely sketched to trenchant effect. Literature can postulate philosophical or cultural insights, and portray fresh ideas in action. Literary works can feature exquisitely detailed texture or complete lack of sensory ambiance.

Structurally, literary fiction favors story and plot elements that are individualistic or astonishingly new rather than tried-and-true. In some cases the plot as such does not appear important, but beware of quick judgment in this regard: Plotting may be subtle, as in picking at underlying psychology or revelation of character. And the plot movement may take place in the reader's head, as the progressive emotional or intellectual response to the story, rather than demonstrated in external events portrayed on paper.

To say that a work is literary can imply seriousness. Nonetheless many serious works are not particularly sober, and literary reading should be a dynamic experience—pleasurably challenging, insightful, riveting, fun. A work that is stodgy and boring may not be literary at all, for it has not achieved the all-important aim of being fine reading.

Obviously, a book that is lacking engaging characters, consciousness of pace, and story development but features fancy wordplay and three-page sentences hardly exemplifies literary mastery. Though such a work may serve as a guidepost of advanced writing techniques for a specialized professional audience, it is perhaps a more limited artifice than is a slice-and-dice, strip-and-whip piece that successfully depicts human passion and offers a well-honed story.

Commercial literature, like commercial fiction in general, is essentially a back-definition; commercial literature indicates works of outstanding quality written by authors who sell well, as opposed to just plain literature, which includes writers and works whose readership appeal has not yet expanded beyond a small core. Non-commercial literary works are staples of the academic press and specialized houses, as well as selected imprints of major trade publishers.

When a literary author attracts a large readership, or manages to switch from the list of a tiny publisher to a mammoth house, the publisher might decide a particular project is ripe for a shot at the big time and slate the writer for substantial attention, accompanied by a grand advance. If you look closely, you'll note that literary authors who enter the commercial ranks are usually not just good writers: Commercial literary works tap into the cultural pulse, which surges through the editorial avenues into marketing, promotion, and sales support.

In day-to-day commercial publishing discourse, to call a piece of work literary simply means it is well written. As a category designation, literary fiction implies that a particular book does not truly abide by provisos of other market sectors—though if the work under discussion does flash some category hooks, it might be referred to in such catch-terms as a literary thriller or literary suspense.

MAINSTREAM FICTION

A mainstream work is one that can be expected to be at least reasonably popular to a fairly wide readership. In a whim of industry parlance, to various people in publishing the label mainstream signifies a work that is not particularly noteworthy on any count. It's a work of fiction that's not literary according to circumscribed tastes, and not something easily categorized with a targeted, predictable base of readership. Maybe not particularly profitable, either, especially if the publishing house is bent on creating best-sellers. A mainstream work may therefore be seen as a risky proposition rather than as a relatively safe bet.

Let this be a cautionary note: In some publishing minds, a plain-and-simple mainstream book signifies midlist, which equals no sale. In a lot of publishing houses midlist fiction, even if it's published, gets lost; many commercial trade houses won't publish titles they see as midlist (see Midlist Fiction).

A mainstream work may be a good read—but if that's all you can say about it, it's a mark against its prospects in the competitive arena. When a story is just a good story, the publisher doesn't have much of a sales slant to work with; in publishing terms that makes for a dismal enough prognosis for an editor or agent to pass.

If a manuscript must sell on storytelling merits or general interest alone, it most likely won't sell to a major publisher at all. If mainstream fiction is what you've got, the writer is advised to return to the workshop and turn the opus into a polished piece with a stunning attitude that can be regarded as commercial, or redesign the story line into a category format such as mystery, suspense, or thriller. A mainstream mystery or mainstream thriller may contain characters who aren't too wacko and milieus that aren't overly esoteric. Such works are eminently marketable, but you might suppress the mainstream designation in your query and just call your work by its category or genre moniker.

If you've got the gifts and perseverance to complete a solid story, and you find your-self about to say it's a mainstream book and no more, you'll be farther along faster if you work to avoid the midlist designation. Think commercially and write intrepidly.

Please note: Many editors and agents use the term *mainstream fiction* as more or less synonymous with *commercial fiction* (which see, please).

MIDLIST FICTION

Midlist books are essentially those that do not turn a more-than-marginal profit. That they show a profit at all might testify to how low the author's advance was (usually based on projected sales). Midlist books may be category titles, literary works, or main-stream books that someone, somewhere believed had commercial potential (yet to be achieved).

The midlist is where no one wants to be: You get little if any promotion, few reviews, and no respect. Why publish this kind of book at all? Few publishers do. A midlist book was most likely not intended as such; the status is unacceptable unless the writer is being prepped for something bigger, and is expected to break through *soon*. When a writer (or series) stays midlist too long, she's gone—the publishers move on to more profitable use of their resources.

If the publishers don't want you, and the readers can't find you, you're better off going somewhere else too. (See Commercial Fiction or any of the other category designations.)

MYSTERY

Many people use the term *mystery* to refer to the detective story (see Detective Fiction). When folks speak of traditional mysteries, they often mean a story in the British cozy mold, which can be characterized—but not strictly defined—by an amateur sleuth (often female) as protagonist, a solve-the-puzzle story line, minimal body count (with all violence performed offstage), and a restrained approach to language and tone. Sometimes, however, a reference to traditional mysteries implies not only cozies but also includes stories of the American hard-boiled school, which are typified by a pri-vate eye (or a rogue cop), upfront violence as well as sex, and vernacular diction.

On the other hand, mysteries are seen by some to include all suspense fiction cate-gories, thereby encompassing police procedurals, crime capers, and thrillers—even going so far afield as horror and some fantasy fiction.

In the interests of clarity, if not precision, here we'll say simply that a mystery is a story in which something of utmost importance to the tale is unknown or covert at the outset and must be uncovered, solved, or revealed along the way. (See Crime Fiction, Detective Fiction, Fantasy Fiction, Horror, Suspense Fiction, and Thriller.)

ROMANCE FICTION

The power of love has always been a central theme in literature, as it has in all arts, in all life. For all its importance to the love story genre, the term *romance* does not pertain strictly to the love element. The field can trace its roots through European medieval romances that depicted knights-errant and women in distress, which were as much tales of spiritual quest, politics, and action as love stories. The Romantic movement of the nineteenth century was at its heart emblematic of the heightened energy lent to all elements of a story, from human passion, to setting, to material objects, to psychological ramifications of simple acts.

Thanks to the writers and readers of modern romances, they've come a long way from the days of unadulterated heart stopping bodice-rippers with pampered, egocentric heroines who long for salvation through a man. Today's romance most often depicts an independent, full-blooded female figure in full partnership with her intended mate.

Modern romance fiction is most assuredly in essence a love story, fueled by the dynamics of human relationships. From this core, writers explore motifs of career and family, topical social concerns, detective work, psychological suspense, espionage, and horror, as well as historical period pieces (including European medieval, Regency, and romances set in the American West) and futuristic tales. Romance scenarios with same-sex lovers are highlighted throughout the ranks of vanguard and literary houses, though this theme is not a priority market at most trade publishers or romance-specialist presses.

Among commercial lead titles tapped for best-seller potential are those books that accentuate the appeal of romance within the larger tapestry of a fully orchestrated work. (See also Women's Fiction.)

SCIENCE FICTION

Take humankind's age-old longings for knowledge and enlightenment and add a huge helping of emergent technology, with the twist that science represents a metaphysical quest—there you have the setup for science fiction. Though the basic science fiction plot may resemble that of action-adventure tales, thrillers, or horror stories, the attraction for the reader is likely to be the intellectual or philosophical questions posed, in tandem with the space-age glitter within which it's set. In terms of character interaction, the story line should be strong enough to stand alone when stripped of its technological trimmings.

In the *future fiction* genre, the elements of science fiction are all in place, but the science tends to be soft-pedaled, and the story as a whole is character based. In a further variation, the post-apocalyptic vision presents the aftermath of a cataclysm (either engendered by technology or natural in origin) that sets the survivors loose on a new course that demonstrates the often-disturbing vicissitudes of social and scientific evolution. Such scenarios are generally set in the not-too-distant future and are usually Earth-based, or barely interstellar, with recognizable (but perhaps advanced) technology as the norm.

Purity of genre is at times fruitless to maintain or define. Is Mary Shelley's *Frankenstein* a science fiction tale or a horror story, or is it primarily a literary work? Is Jules Verne's *20,000 Leagues under the Sea* science fiction, a technothriller, or a futuristic action adventure?

Stories of extraterrestrial exploration, intergalactic warfare, and other exobiological encounters are almost certain to be placed within the science fiction category, until the day when such endeavors are considered elements of reality.

SUSPENSE FICTION

Suspense fiction embraces many literary idioms, with a wide range of genres and sub-divisions categorized under the general rubric of suspense. Indeed, in broad terms, all novels contain suspense—that is, if the writer intends the reader to keep reading way into the evening and beyond.

Suspense fiction has no precise formula that specifies certain character types tied to a particular plot template. It is perhaps most applicable for a writer to think of suspense as a story concept that stems from a basic premise of situational uncertainty. That is: Something horrible is going to happen! Let's read! Within suspense there is consider-able latitude regarding conventions of style, voice, and structure. From new suspense writers, editors look for originality and invention and new literary terrain, rather than a copycat version of last season's breakout work.

However, that said, writers should note that editors and readers are looking for works in which virtually every word, every scene, every blip of dialog serves to heighten sus-pense. This means that all imagery—the weather, the social setting, and even the food ingested by the characters—is chosen by the writer to induce a sense of unease. Each scene (save maybe the last one) is constructed to raise questions or leave something unresolved. Every sentence or paragraph contains a possible pitfall. A given conversa-tional exchange demonstrates edgy elementals of interpersonal tension. Everything looks rosy in one scene? Gotcha! It's a setup to reveal later what hell lurks underneath. Tell me some good news? Characters often do just that, as a prelude to showing just how wrong things can get.

The *jeopardy* story (or, as is often the case, a *woman-in-jeopardy* story) reflects a premise rather than being a genre per se. A tale of jeopardy—a character under contin-uous, increasing threat and (often) eventual entrapment—can incorporate what is oth-erwise a psychological suspense novel, a medical thriller, an investigatory trajectory, or a slasher-stalker spree.

Additional subdivisions here include *romantic suspense,* in which a love relation-ship plays an essential or dominant role—see Romance Fiction); *erotic suspense,* which is not necessarily identical to neurotic suspense; and *psychological suspense* (see immediately below).

PSYCHOLOGICAL SUSPENSE

When drifts of character, family history, or other psychodynamics are central to a sus-pense story's progress and resolution, the tale may aptly be typified as psychological. Sometimes superficial shticks or gimmicks suffice (such as when a person of a certain gender turns out to be cross-dressed—surprise!), but such spins work best when the suspense is tied to crucial issues the writer evokes in the heads of the characters and readers and then orchestrates skillfully throughout the story line.

There are, obviously, crossover elements at play here, and whether a particular work is presented as suspense, psychological suspense, or erotic suspense can be more of an advertising copywriting decision than a determination on the part of editor or author.

THRILLER

The thriller category is exemplified more by plot structure than by attributes of character, content, or story milieu. A thriller embodies what is essentially an extended game of pursuit—a hunt, a chase, a flight worked fuguelike through endless variations.

At one point in the history of narrative art, thrillers were almost invariably spy stories, with international casts and locales, often set in a theater of war (hot or cold). With shifts in political agendas and technical achievement in the real world, the thriller formula has likewise evolved. Today's thriller may well involve espionage, which can be industrial or political, domestic or international. There are also thrillers that favor settings in the realms of medicine, the law, the natural environs, the human soul, and the laboratory. This trend has given rise to the respective genres of legal thriller, medical thriller, environmental thriller, thrillers with spiritual and mystical themes, and the technothriller—assuredly there are more to come.

The thriller story line can encompass elements of detection or romance, and certainly should be full of suspense; but these genre-specific sequences are customarily expositional devices, or may be one of many ambient factors employed to accentuate tension within the central thriller plot. When you see a dust jacket blurb that depicts a book as a mystery thriller, it likely connotes a work with a thriller plot trajectory that uses an investigatory or detective-work premise to prepare for the chase.

WESTERN FICTION

The tradition of Western fiction is characterized as much by its vision of the individualist ethic as it is by its conventional settings in the frontier milieu of the American West during the period from the 1860s to the 1890s, sometimes extending into the early 1900s. Though the image of the lone, free-spirited cowpoke with an internalized code of justice has been passed down along the pulp-paper trail, it has long been appreciated by historians that the life of the average itinerant ranch hand of the day was anything but glamorous, anything but independent.

Whatever the historical record, editors by and large believe readers don't want to hear about the lackluster aspects of saddle tramps and dustbusting ruffians. Nevertheless, there have been inroads by books that display the historically accurate notions that a good chunk of the Western scene was inhabited by women and men of African-American heritage, by those with Latino cultural affinities, by Asian expatriates, by European immigrants for whom English was a second language, as well as by a diversity of native peoples.

Apart from the traditional genre Western, authors are equipped for a resurgence in a variety of novels with Western settings, most notably in the fields of mystery, crime, action-adventure, suspense, and future fiction. Among the newer Western novels are those replete with offbeat, unheroic, and downright antiheroic protagonists; the standardized big-sky landscape has been superseded by backdrops that go against the grain.

Family sagas have long included at least a generation or two who drift, fight, and homestead through the Western Frontier. In addition, a popular genre of historical romance is set in the American West (see Romance Fiction).

Many contemporary commercial novels are set in the Western U.S., often featuring plush resorts, urban and suburban terrain, as well as the remaining wide country. The wide variety of project ideas generated by writers, as well as the reader response to several successful ongoing mystery series with Western elements, indicates a lively interest out there.

WOMEN'S FICTION

When book publishers speak of women's fiction, they're not referring to a particular genre or story concept (even if they think they are). This category—if it is one—is basically a nod to the prevalence of fiction readers who are women. Women's fiction is a marketing concept. As an informal designation, women's fiction as a matter of course can be expected to feature strong female characters and, frequently, stories offered from a woman's perspective.

As for the writers, many (if not most) are women, but certainly not all of them are; the same observation applies to readers. Men can and do read these works too—and many professional male writers calculate potential readership demographics (including gender) as they work out details of story and plot. In essence, what we've got is storytelling that can appeal to a broad range of readers but may be promoted principally to the women's market.

Furthermore, many women writers consider their work in abstract compositional terms, regardless of to whom it is marketed. Other women writers are publicized as cultural pundits, though they personally don't see their stance as particularly women oriented. Some women writers adopt the pose of the literary firebrand or outlaw as they claw their way through dangerous domains of unseemly characterization, engage in breakthrough storytelling techniques, and explore emergent modes of sexuality without identifying their writing by gender. Any and all of these female wordsmiths may find themselves publicized as women authors.

Romantic fiction constitutes one large sector of the women's market, for many of the conventions of romance tap into culturally significant areas of the love relationship of proven interest to women bookbuyers.

Descriptive genre phrases pop in and out of usage; some of them trip glibly from the tongue and are gone forevermore, while others represent established literary norms that endure: kitchen fiction, mom novels, domestic dramas, lipstick fiction, family sagas, historical romances, erotic thrillers. When these titles are written and/or promoted in ways intended to pique the interest of women readers, they're automatically women's fiction.

The New Poetry
Barkers, Chargers, and Performance Artists

Jamie M. Forbes

Poetry has once again changed its face, and media moguls are put on notice of an audience at the brink. Long out of grace in commercial book-publishing circles, poetry's current growth has been initially established in the realms of live performance, video, and audio presentations rather than in print. What's this mean for the poet who wants a book contract? Too soon to tell for certain, but prospects look better than they have in a long spell.

WHY PUBLISHERS ARE AVERSE TO VERSE

Commercial publishers do not emphasize poetry due to one huge factor, and for a host of rationales related to that big one: Money. That is, poetry usually doesn't make much, if any. Poetry programs from major publishers are often maintained as prestige lines that at best can be expected to break even or be marginally profitable.

When a book of poetry does render a hefty sum, publishers want to know why it does, in terms that translate into a successfully replicable marketing strategy. If a publisher deems it unlikely that a given type of work will sell profitably, why the hell buy it from the author in the first place?

It's not that publishers don't take chances. Publishers have found that breaking through with a work of nonfiction of high current interest by a first-time author, or a novel by a writer with a new voice in an established fiction category, while chancy, represents a better bet —in large part because those markets are already strong. Poems from hitherto little-known poets have virtually no retailing presence, regardless of how good the work is, unless the author is in some manner promotable. An example of this line of reasoning occurs when the poet is a celebrity, a recognized name you can take to the bank—which is not to say a person necessarily renowned as a poet.

DEATH AND TRANSFIGURATION

During this century, through a quirk of literary fashion, the practice of poetry for a time resembled a cult of personality, wherein the poet's biography was essential to full appreciation of a personalized vision set within increasingly rarefied expression in verse. As formal poetry lost its universality and poets became less viable commodities, poetics—seen as academic and elitist—was the province of specialty publishers with restricted lists. At the same time, what had been a major cultural function of verse was taken over by popular literature (novels and short fictional forms), popular music, and other performance vehicles of mass appeal (including the movies, video, and modeling).

Lest you think poetry as a profession has dug its own way to cultural extinction, in a blink of the eye it's resurrected from within its original bardic tradition as a performance art, often in the context of music and movement. To those with a bookish inclination, it is enlightening to see today's poets stride forth as performers in their own right, go *mano a mano* with the masses, and earn a widening audience. In the resultant groundswell, verse is reinvigorated and once again promotable; even book publishers are opening up their lists, albeit slowly, to the new field of contenders.

THE TRADITION THAT NEVER WAS

When discussing the tradition of academic poetry, we're in the realm of a perceptual figment. Bear in mind that the poet's assignation to the conservatory is an aberration, the theme of only a fragment of the twentieth century. For most of poetry's history it has been a popular form, practiced in public as well as in letters and print.

The meter and substance of verse were perhaps first derived from the settings of pasture and polis—poetry has always featured both pastoral and urban approaches, dealt with both the workaday world and refined pursuits. It is in no way surprising that the texture of today's most popular lyric formats is from the malls and the streets, the airports and the highways, with cadences resounding to the beat of found sounds—of music, electronics, and industry, of shoot-outs and party shouts.

In much the same way, writers of earlier generations warped their environments into poetic forms. Works from T. S. Eliot, Vachel Lindsay, Sylvia Plath, Allen Ginsberg, and Gregory Corso emanated from the milieus of the blues, Dixieland, swing, be-bop, and modern jazz. Now our poetics embrace the range of hard-core, grunge, techno, and hip-hop. Looking back over the timeline of a poet's career, the difference between an old master and a young bastard is who is speaking and when.

Virtuosos of verse appear in such guises as contributors to pop-culture fan magazines (in areas not queued primarily to poetry), in cyberspace exchanges, and in performance and poetry events (such as the slam circuit). In addition, the literary phase endures in the profusion of small and academic presses and literary journals, many with their own sponsored competitions.

WORDS WITH WINGS

Look over the rosters of trade publishing houses; there's poetry there. Every major publisher produces at least a few editions in the field, though they're rarely highlighted at the front of the catalog. The poetry book that does achieve the rank of lead title is most likely one with a commercial hook over and above that of its poetics. *The Book of Birth Poetry* edited by Charlotte Otten (Bantam) shows how a definite marketing angle that overlays a strong selection of poetic work can be positioned for a mainstream audience.

Poetry produced by commercial trade programs also includes point-of-purchase novelty volumes, often incorporating illustrations or other enticing trinkets such as posters, cards, or bubble gum gewgaws. This is not to decry the state. Some poets who take their unadorned words very seriously may look down on this notion; readers, however, are almost never dissuaded by such baubles—they simply see more reward to the package they are buying. Not so incidentally, word-and-picture packages are no less successful an approach when adopted by publishers in the fine arts or by literary presses. There's more than one way to fit your words with wings.

Devotees of straitlaced poetry publishing are sometimes resentful (not to say envious) of the relatively free rein occasionally given those who have not paid substantial poetic dues. Many bookbuyers, on the other hand, would be hard put to believe that a cloistered academic's synthetic vision is automatically more riveting than the life experience at the heart of the volume *Always a Reckoning* by Jimmy Carter (issued through Times Books, with a Random House audiobook spinoff). Even though Carter is without a master of fine arts degree in poetry and doesn't have much of a track record in literary magazines or poetry competitions, it is heartening to all poets that the man has acknowledged the practice of verse as worthy of one with his manifold global accomplishments.

Similarly, *Collected Poems* by John Updike (Knopf) might not have seen such high-profile publication if the author had not achieved renown as a popular prose literateur. In addition, Updike's volume may be seen in publishing terms as a lead-in to the house's slate of offerings by such respected versifiers as Cynthia Zarin, Mary Jo Salter, Carolyn Olds, John Hollander, and John Ashbery.

STATE-OF-THE-ART OR FALSE START?

The public declamation of verse enjoys a tradition that extends back to the earliest human gatherings, and on-stage poetry performance continues unabated into the current age. Around the globe, poetry presentations, often in the form of competitions, are drawing many happy participants and listeners to cafés, bars, galleries, and salons.

One of the longest-running and most famed venues for this type of expression made it into book-length publication from a major house: *Aloud: Voices from the Nuyorican Poets Cafe*, an anthology edited by Mogul Algerian and Bob Dolman (Henry Holt). Though it took the Nuyoricans two decades of enduring presence to gain the requisite level of public awareness and media clout to garner a commercial publishing contract, this publication signaled the breakout of renewed publisher attention.

To wit: A poetry slam with a gay theme has been presented in print through the pages of *Gents, Bad Boys, and Barbarians* edited by Rudy Kikel (Alyson Publications). Since then, popular poetry titles have been prominently displayed in a wide variety of bookstores, and there are more marquee poetry projects coming down the publishing pipeline.

Whether this revived interest in poetry is a flash-in-the-pan concept intended to cash in on fleeting public fancies or is indicative of a swelling, sustainable trend remains to be seen. The future of poetry publishing hinges on how poets and publishers seize the moment. Muddy marketing of sloppy product will surely kill the lights. One way poets can work to prevent such a dire fate is to ensure there's a more-than-adequate supply of fine verse from which publishers can select the best and most potentially market-grabbing entrants.

POETS ANONYMOUS NO LONGER

How do you make a publisher hunger for your verse? As with any school of industry, you want to work hard to research and develop your standout product. In this case, it means writing a lot of poetry, and then taking it to an audience. Enter competitions for written works and present yourself live and in-person at poetry slams. See what the response is and gear your ongoing poetic enterprise accordingly, to maximize your potential appeal. Get yourself published in literary journals and popular magazines. In short, make a name for yourself.

There are resources available for this line of endeavor. To name just a couple, which are updated periodically, Dustbooks offers *Directory of Poetry Publishers*, and Writer's Digest produces the volume *Poet's Market*. Familiarize yourself with the many niche publishers (well over a thousand in the United States alone) oriented toward interests such as multicultural, gender, and sociopolitical issues, in addition to humor, homespun, regional, religious, splatterpunk, and aesthetic word-art, as well as mainline verse. Read these magazines and journals to gauge how your work fits in with what others are doing and to get a sense of what makes your work distinctive.

When you can see your poetic output in this light, you'll know where and how to submit your work (some publishers have extremely explicit and strict guidelines, whereas others are more free spirited). Some editors like to see several pieces, others just one; the response time is often months (up to half a year or longer). There are competitions you will want to be aware of, and theme-oriented editions of journals in the planning stages a year in advance, so watch for notices. *Be sure to enclose a self-addressed stamped envelope (the ubiquitous SASE) for return of your material.*

Cover letters should be as brief as possible. Provide a short, sweet encapsulation of your approach and appeal; list the poem(s) by title; slip in some bio material (including previous publications, awards, workshop or performance experience)—then over and out. If you haven't heard anything *after a few months*, feel free to query your submission's status via a short note with self-addressed stamped postcard.

Please be advised that many journals pay no money at all, and some of the best-known shell out a small honorarium at most—there's minimal remuneration in this publishing field, but it does get your work out there.

Another avenue to address is indicated by the publication from Poets & Writers titled *Author & Audience: A Readings and Workshops Guide*. In this arena you can hone your persona further. Some poets take an impresario approach and curate series of readings at bookstores, galleries, cafés, parks, or anywhere there's an open space. If they're the sort who can make themselves public point-persons, these carnival barkers are the ones listed as editors of books that include their own work in addition to that of their hard-charging star performers.

If you have a musical propensity, look real good, and your words work well as soundbursts, you might wish to team with a few other like-minded individuals and enter the fray in jazz, rock, hip-hop, or a musical approach of your own invention, and gain the opportunity to stake your claim to a cult following on which to build. The words of musically inclined writers as diverse as Jim Carroll, Leonard Cohen, and Patti Smith (all affirmed poets) are published in book form.

However you've done it, once you've achieved a recognizable identity, you (or your agent) can approach a commercial publisher with a skein of work and a proven record with many of the same attributes and sales venues available to the authors of business how-tos, self-help, and awareness titles (many of whom conduct workshops, appear at symposia, and are public speakers—that is, they're performance artists).

If your work and reputation is more suited to smaller literary houses, once you've had dozens of works published in recognized journals, you can select a representative package intended for book-length publication. Many literary and university presses sponsor poetry competitions in which the top prizes include publication—so check these out, especially if you're not yet published in book form.

Literary, not-for-profit operations have marketing considerations analogous to those found in the commercial trade, so your best shot is to organize your work according to a definable style or theme that grabs hold of an area of reader interest and is sure to inspire catalog copy.

Another option for poets is publication in chapbook format—slimmer folios of work, most often in soft paper binding. Many small presses produce titles in this form, and every year individuals and groups of poets fund their own chapbook publications, often with the intent of getting a distribution deal either through a literary press or through an independent distribution service (and thus be available to the bookstore trade).

Yes, poetry is, as ever, changing and on the move. It behooves the creator to be inventive and indefatigable, and in the current environment to think in terms that are not bound by the vision of a book of verse. Performance is assuredly public; appearances on computer networks are by definition electronic publication; lyrics of pop music represent an established form of marketable verse. Think of a new way to do it, and you can be there first.

The Producer's Niche
Book Packagers and Superauthors— Creative Ways for Writers to Profit

Jamie M. Forbes

Book producer. Sounds rather Hollywood to some—like a power-broking agent who packages film projects replete with star performers, name directors, and genius screenwriters. Indeed, book producers do the same thing as these major players in film production; the difference is they package books, not movies. And, again like those wheeler-dealers of the silver screen, the role of a book packager is to bring together the talent necessary (including writers) to carry through the vision at hand.

A Land of Opportunity or Just Another Writer's Block?

The foregoing glitter masks the actual raw business talk about money and work and how a writer can get some of both—and, yes, there is much to be had. The good news begins just a bit farther along. The bad part comes up immediately following, and will be over before you know it. As the benefits of hard knowledge begin to sink in, the potential dividends for writers who explore the book-producing field will become greatly apparent. And remember: On the playing fields of free enterprise, book producers are among the freest players.

To the writer who wants to jump-cut across the maze of agents, editors, and publishers and head straight toward successful publication (and who wouldn't?): Don't expect to approach a book producer cold with your original idea, have the producer beam at you gratefully, offer you a contract, a celebratory drink, and then handle all the hassles necessary to present you a juicy check. It's no bet. Don't hold your breath in anticipation. Don't even think of such a course as the last straw you grasp.

But don't screenwriters do that and sometimes the movie is made? And isn't book producing kind of like Hollywood fantasies, only in the book trade? Occasionally—so much so as to be a real rarity. All is not lost, however. With the explosion of unrealistic flights of fancy comes clear vision into the realms of actual potential for writers, including recognition of authorship and royalties to go with it.

Writers are essential to any book project, whether it is a traditionally written, conventionally published work or a complex volume representing the state of the book-making art—book producers package the entire gamut. With this in mind, be aware that a book producer is far more likely to pursue the initial developmental and creative work with people who are not writers who nevertheless do have ideas for books.

Why is that? No single answer applies, for the types of projects book producers carry out are extremely varied. For the purpose of considering book-production operations as fields of opportunities for writers, let's break down the atypical world of book producers into three broad categories and cite why it is unlikely that an outside writer will be included on the ground floor of a given project, as well as note vital roles writers play along the way. At least one of these roles may surprise as well as inspire you.

First of all, these nonwriters with whom book producers work may be potential sponsors for the project—such as celebrity performers, athletes, politicians, or business leaders with a story to tell. Or these sponsors may well be corporate entities (including nonprofit cultural or policy foundations in addition to commercial interests) with a lot of internal materials they'd like to see turned into a book. In these cases a book producer can hire a professional ghostwriter or coauthor, or commission someone who is credited full-fledged authorship to actually research and write the entire manuscript. We are talking about opportunities for writers here.

Second, book producers often work closely with publishing houses, for example to develop or expand a series or line of books, or compose a single specialty title the publisher wishes to farm out rather than do in-house. In such instances the book producer interfaces with writers the same way that the sponsoring publisher would if the books were produced in the publishing house. More slots for wordsmiths to shoot for.

And the third reason a writer is not likely to be needed to ignite a project is that the book producer is often a writer too. This observation applies to one-person book-production firms as well as to people working within larger ensembles.

Someone who considers idea generation and project development as strong professional suits may wish to explore this field with an eye toward developing talents along this line. Ultimately this person might consider whether it would be potentially advantageous to turn a trick packaging entire projects—in lieu of or perhaps in addition to unadorned literary pursuits.

A WORLD WHERE RULES ARE FEW

If you're still hazy about who, what, or where book producers are, and unable to circumscribe what it is book producers do, please know that the industry is right there with you. It's not that book producers as a group aren't anything you can describe: They are and will do almost anything imaginable in the book-publishing realm.

This shouldn't baffle anyone when industry definitions are far less than clear and may appear to be redefined throughout a given day, when skeptics speak of certain authors who are too busy to do any actual writing themselves, when editors do not have time to edit, and when publishers have duties more pressing than the nuts-and-bolts of publishing. Someone must do all this scribbling, this editorial work; somehow the manuscript must be produced—otherwise there wouldn't be any books to have parties over.

With increasing frequency and success, book producers have stepped opportunely into publishing industry gaps, staking claims to territory in the research-and-development area as well as any and all aspects of editing, design, production, and manufacture. Yes, book producers can do it all, which is why they defy typology.

WHO BOOK PRODUCERS ARE

Book producers usually comprise one to several people on a full-time basis. As with other aspects of being a book producer, there are notable exceptions to this account, and a few book producers offer positions to as many personnel as are employed by good-sized publishers. Regardless of core size, the book producer's staff can be expanded or contracted to embrace any number of freelancers and consultants as the project load demands.

WHAT BOOK PRODUCERS DO

Simply put, book producers are service operations that undertake different tasks warranted as they perform functions otherwise typically rendered by book publishers, literary agents, and authors. It is this shape-shifting aspect that gives book producers their flexibility and strength and that, perhaps more than anything else, accounts for their increasing vigor in the publishing marketplace—estimates run in the neighborhood of one out of every five to six books published in the United States are brought out through a book producer.

A book producer can take on the entire spectrum of editorial and production work—a process traditionally overseen by the publisher. Where the book producer almost invariably bows out is in areas pertaining to marketing, sales, and distribution. Here, too, arise situations that belie the rule, as when the book producer works with the publisher to develop sales and marketing approaches, as well as to probe promotional venues and publicity angles. Careful now—too much of this sort of business and the book producer becomes just another publisher.

A book producer might as a matter of course try to reserve the rights to projects originated by the producer in house. That is, subsidiary rights—ordinarily handled by either the publisher or literary agent—may be most profitably retained and purveyed by a skillful and active book producer (who is by far the most interested party in such schemes). These sub rights can encompass territorial translation and reprint rights divvied up worldwide, serial rights, dramatic and screen rights, and electronic rights (including CD-ROM and multimedia adaptation).

Most definitely, book packagers function as their own brokers and managers. Book producers sell literary properties and deal with publishers on the same basis of person-to-person interaction and paperwork rituals as do those who go by the sobriquet of literary agent.

Book producers are also the equivalent of superauthors. In addition to their roles as originators of book ideas and the writing capabilities of particular individuals, book producers are true authors of a project, providing editorial material either directly, indirectly, or a combination of both—as well as directing the entire creative team. In the case of complex works this can involve commissioning different writers for different sections and hiring copyeditors, indexers, proofreaders, artists, designers, photographers, and production personnel.

Some book producers have a full-time staff to handle editing, production, and research and development and to attend to protocols such as writing the project proposals. Other packagers personally do as much of the work as feasible. This is especially characteristic of small book-producer operations wherein, for instance, one of the associates is adept in layout and design and works with a partner who can write. Rather than having a staff as such (they may even perform their own office support, including filing and shipping duties), these producers utilize the services of freelancers on an as-needed basis.

WHERE BOOK PRODUCERS ARE LOCATED

Commercial publishers often operate from highly visible corporate headquarters in skyscrapers bearing their house logos or the banner of the communications conglomerate that owns them. Small presses can be veritable cottage industries, with components set up in basements, side rooms, and garages. As one might by now anticipate, where book producers are is a many-layered question with a multi-tiered response.

Often as not, a book producer does not inhabit a single place. There may be a homey den where the packager per se does anything but hibernate, or an entire suite of offices and production facilities. Members of a project team may be found in other offices, in other suites, in ateliers of artists and workshops of graphics consultants, as well as in studios of individual writers. Especially when equipped with electronic communications, members of these book production teams are by no means confined to the same locality.

HOW BOOK PRODUCERS PACKAGE BOOKS

Book producers (alone or in league with a potential sponsoring participant) come up with the original idea for a publishing project, shape the proposal, sell the proposed work to the publisher, and supply the editorial and production talent to bring the project to fruition. How book producers package books might best be viewed from the vantage of how it is that book ideas come to be packaged.

Publishers are most certainly interested in a proposal that sets forth an easily categorized product. For commercial trade publishers, the most highly prized work is one that can be tightly marketed through mainstream bookstore chains, sell well on its merits as communicated via word of mouth and a smattering of reviews, be picked up by a specialty book club or two, and benefit cost-effectively from a modicum of advertising push and sales force vigor. As entrepreneurs, book producers position their packages with those considerations in mind, just as any author is advised to do.

In many publishing deals, the chances for closure increase with the ability of the author or book producer team to bring as much to the table as possible—especially in terms of elements that support the project's access to markets. The book producer, as the fulcrum for the project, is in position to orchestrate these elements.

To illustrate, let's conceive of a complex project, a series of international business guides that include sections offering travel tips; lifestyle reportage; cultural, political, and historical notes; practical business advice; and information keyed to contingencies such as health care and automobile emergencies. Lots of research here. Lots of writing. Jobs for photographers and designers too—these volumes will be lavish.

Lots of expenses.

The book producer fronts the coinage to cover the book proposal. That's part of the producer's act. As for the rest of the package, let's see how many beneficiaries we can bring in. There's the not-for-profit educational wing of a financial institution that would love to underwrite (in part) a high-profile, top-quality project. How high profile is it? Since the financial institute is a potential player, there are corporate sponsorships in the works—as well as talk of a series geared to broadcast on noncommercial television.

The published books will of course point out the participation of those who gave goods and services—airlines, hotels, film companies, computer firms, sportswear outfitters, food and beverage councils, manufacturers of pharmaceuticals, windscreens, sunscreens, and weather-proof make-up. All sponsors benefit from publicity and promotional value.

If the public TV series goes blooey, let's try for an infomercial on cable and tailor the repositioned project more toward a for-profit home-study/seminar course (perhaps packaged with complementary audiotapes, videotapes, or computer software)—in which case the not-for-profiteer underwriter's got to walk. In either event, a major trade book publisher we know has already informally shown interest. If we go the infomercial route, a publisher with proven direct-mail sales expertise might prove an excellent partner.

WATCHWORDS AND BYLINES

As we have seen, there is no such thing as a typical packaged book. The book producer can be called on to coordinate complicated books, or can offer a publisher the straightforward advantages of expanded services—in which case the book producer becomes a virtual extended editorial staff through which a particular publisher can issue more books.

There are no givens as to what constitutes a book package or the deals book packagers make with publishers and writers. As Stephen R. Ettlinger, of Ettlinger Editorial Projects, remarks: "What is the common denominator is that we make books happen. We turn ideas into books. We do that by assembling the creative team necessary—of which, of course, the writer is an element."

One should never forget that the publisher is the projected source for the book producer's money on any and all given projects. The book packager puts up money for proposals, but not beyond that. The basic agreement between a publisher and a book producer is similar or identical to that drafted for an author–publisher contract.

What this implies is very important: Agreements between book producers and writers can take any form that's appropriate for a given project.

Sometimes book producers have their own original projects that require expert writers in a given category. Which means lots of times the producer is the author, contractually and actually, or else the book producer will hire one or more writers. In such cases book producers act essentially as editors. Some people write up the book proposals. Some write the books. Some have bylines. Some are ghosts. Sometimes the writing is work-for-hire, with other parties the copyright holders. Some writers get royalties, or what amounts contractually to equivalent compensation.

Some packaging projects are based on a flat fee to the book producer for a specified number of manufactured volumes; this means the book producer oversees the project through printing and binding. Other commissions can be keyed to anything from completed manuscript—edited, copyedited, and styled—or any other production stage up through electronic mechanicals. Occasionally book producers consult all the way to setting up the distribution end.

Deals with writers range from the book producer paying a writer a flat fee, to an hourly rate, to a contractually delineated even split of the royalties, to the idea that the book producer acts as a glorified agent with compensation at a slightly higher rate if the project was the packager's idea.

Of universal interest to writers is the question of who holds copyright—with implications regarding compensation in areas such as royalties and reprint rights. Regardless of the general run of cocktail chatter, at no point should anyone ever say definitively which parties should or shouldn't control the copyright without first examining the overall history of the project, and whether the writer's work has been commissioned as work-for-hire, as coauthor, or as sole writer. Again, there are no firm rules, only guidelines derived from experience. Who holds copyright? Perhaps the writer does, even if the book was the producer's original idea. In such instances royalties may still accrue to both book producer and author, with the breakdown provisional depending on eventualities such as future sales.

THE WRITER'S APPROACH

For newer writers as well as veterans there is the lush scenario that runs as follows: A timely referral to you personally when a book producer is in need of someone with your precise abilities and areas of expertise. Of course, you've worked hard to position yourself to accept just such a challenge, in many cases by means of more prosaic but equally time-honored techniques, including a cold first encounter.

The best way to approach a book producer cold is with a query letter and résumé or page or so of sample writing; point out you are a writer available for hire. Do some research beforehand to ascertain whether a particular producer pursues projects in your particular range, and target your queries accordingly.

This technique is not meant to be a last-gasp career saver: Your query and writer's kit most likely go into the book producer's resource files for future reference. Few book producers have tremendous volume (as compared with commercial publishers), but many book producers have a wide variety of projects they encounter as time goes on. Others have concentrated focus over a long haul (such as series novels or reference lines) that may necessitate calling in fresh troops—meaning you.

On the professional networking front, the American Book Producers Association (ABPA) offers an annual seminar (generally in October); this engagement is appropriate to attend if you want to become a book producer or wish to make contact with one regarding your skills as writer, designer, agent, or editor. The Association holds monthly luncheon meetings (often with guest speakers) that are open to the public and sometimes announced in *Publishers Weekly*.

The ABPA also maintains a freelancer database for use by book producers. Inquire at the ABPA office about how to send in information to be added to this database, as well as to obtain details regarding the aforementioned seminar and meetings, in addition to the Association's membership directory, which lists book producers' specialties, contact persons, and representative projects.

American Book Producers Association
160 Fifth Avenue, Suite 604
New York, NY 10010
212-645-2368

ESTABLISHING AND MAINTAINING A WORKING RELATIONSHIP

In the case of producers who specialize, once a writer gets a chance to give a best shot and comes up a winner, chances are excellent for that writer to establish ongoing or long-term associations. These book producers look for writers who have interests pertinent to the producer's scope and appreciate when a writer is particularly good at writing in these specialty areas—be they travel and lifestyle, fitness and health, or fiction for young adults. One manner of specialty can be standout excellence in a particular important ancillary task—gain notice as a book doctor or proposal writer and you have one big foot in the door.

If a writer is versatile—can also do research, edit, and copyedit, or do worthy writing in a number of fields—chances are good for developing a continuing relationship. That versatile publishing person is inherently valuable to versatile book producers, who, it may be expected, can place great value on others' adaptability.

In addition to specific professional prerequisites, an important aspect of initiating a relationship between a book producer and a writer is the anticipated texture of the working relationship. As is true in many endeavors, business and pleasure often run together. It makes a positive difference if a writer's presentation portrays a person with whom it is fun and easy to work, if the book producer and writer are indeed made for each other.

In order to sustain a working relationship, this impression of ease must always be backed up by performance reliability. This may entail the writer to be on call—to be available to come in for meetings or work in-house. The writer should be equipped with such amenities as a computer and communications facilities. The writer should be the sort who can achieve tight deadlines; who can work well as part of a team; who can share special expertise and use others' ideas effectively toward the project's ends; who, in short, can get things done under the gun, both within a structure or by dispensing with one, simultaneously if need be.

How do book producers choose a writer? Often a balancing act. "She's fast but not that good a writer. He's a good writer but not that fast." Which writer would you ask first? Depends on the nature of the project, of course.

In a previous life, Stephen Ettlinger was a picture editor. He asked a colleague to describe what a good picture was, and her response applies to writers as well as photographers: "For me a good picture is one that's on my desk before the deadline as opposed to one that isn't." All else—however fine the quality—can be useless if the work is not delivered on time.

Book producers cite other types of problems that can arise, such as with writers who don't like answering machines or who ignore the basics of computer usage and have no back-ups available in the pinch.

Getting back to that essential literary imperative, money: Many of the worst eventualities can be avoided entirely when the writer has a thorough understanding of the financial arrangements among writer, book producer, and publisher. Expectations of financial return that were not set down in writing can be a personal and professional nightmare for both writer and producer. Again, if you were a book producer, which kind of writer would you choose?

EXPANDING THE WRITER'S ENVELOPE

As with hunting in any unknown territory, writers who hope to gain from an association with a book producer may heed the following. Explore the landscape thoroughly; stalk, watch, wait till you sight your quarry; and as you close in, be wary, wily, patient, and vigilant to your own interests.

Book publishing represents free enterprise at its best, especially in the sense that bookmaking tradition embodies the business ideals of imagination, creativity, resourcefulness, and quality—as well as teamwork in action. With regard to the process of developing and producing publishing product, the answers to many everyday questions about the industry may once have seemed pretty cut and dried, even if they were not always the obvious response. What is a writer's job? What does a publisher do?

In an era of increasing fluidity and change (both technological and entrepreneurial), opportunities abound in all arenas central and tangential to print publishing. Writers and allied professionals who like to get gritty playing with ideas and who have the bravado to do whatever it takes to make a product have an open field on which to play. To the usual round of questions has been added: Who or what is a book producer? And what do they do? The answers are up to you.

By way of inspiration, here's what someone else did. A writer named Paisley reached a level of success few writers achieve. Paisley has written, coauthored, collaborated on, and ghostwritten numerous articles, books, and corporate communications. Never one to be complacent, Paisley occasionally expressed to me a sense of stagnation even in light of these formidable accomplishments.

Along came another nonfiction book-collaboration assignment Paisley set to work on, this one commissioned by an entrepreneurial professional. As it happened, even with a glittery book-proposal package and stunning sample chapters, this particular project did not garner the type of offer from commercial publishers that impressed the author–entrepreneur sufficiently to give the go-ahead. Instead, after batting around a number of options (including accepting a publisher's small advance), the entrepreneur decided to pursue a glamorized version of self-publication by starting a small press—with one single title on its list.

The entrepreneur knew enough about publishing to recognize that such a project could likely be handled through a network of freelancers and consultants, with one person designated as project director. At this juncture, the one person in publishing the entrepreneur knew best (and trusted implicitly) was Paisley. Though coordinating this type of production was technically beyond the scope of Paisley's previous experience, the entrepreneur exuded the sort of confidence that proved contagious. As it happened, Paisley's contacts in the publishing industry were a solid base from which to work, and Paisley took the entrepreneur's book successfully through the writing and editorial phases, into production and manufacture, and was instrumental in working out a distribution deal through a firm that handled a group of small presses.

Oilá! Paisley is now a book packager (in addition to being a writer), someone with experience in all phases of the publishing arts. Paisley can add many more diverse and remunerative credits to an already-glossy portfolio.

Should the varied roles book producers assume appeal to you? If ideas and their development and presentation are among your strong points, or if you manage projects outstandingly and find dealing with the business aspects of publishing invigorating, you might want to go the whole route. Package, produce—even write if you want to—and be a superauthor too.

Thanks go to Stephen R. Ettlinger, former president of American Book Producers Association and president of Ettlinger Editorial Projects, for his gracious and much-appreciated interview input and research contributions that provided much of the information and resources utilized in the preparation of this essay.

Mirror, Mirror . . .

Self-Publishing and Vanity Publishing—Advantages and Differences

JEFF HERMAN

Achieving publication through the sale of an author's work to a major commercial trade publisher may not always be feasible, possible, or even the most desirable route into the literary marketplace for a given project. Some books may be excellent candidates for the list of a smaller press with artfully targeted audiences (such as business, religious, or literary houses), while others fall naturally into the publishing sphere of the university press, or the array of independent scientific, professional, and scholarly publishers that cater to specialist interests.

Literary success is all about reaching the audience that best appreciates the work at hand; commercial success by definition is keyed to finding and selling to that primary readership economically, and expanding the readership base as cost efficiently as possible.

Certain publishing options have special appeal to entrepreneurial authors—and others who, at least in theory, wish to control the outcome of their book to the greatest possible degree. Some authors wish to have final say over the creative and editorial content of the product; they prefer to oversee the means of production, manufacture, and distribution; and they plan to step lively as they orchestrate their own publicity and promotional endeavors. Assuming these various tasks, responsibilities, and risks should result in programs wherein the author–publisher stands to gain the greatest rate of financial return possible.

Such ventures, when appropriate, can be accomplished on the cheap; other projects may well justify the investment of money and labor of the same order that a publisher might put into a comparable project. Alternate publishing options are also available for those who wish to subsidize publication through firms that produce books and offer attendant publishing services more or less on order.

Self-publishing (often with the assistance of independent contractors and consultants) and publishing through the offices of a vanity press may sound similar in concept, but important distinctions must be recognized—these pertain as much to business practices of individual companies as they do to traditions associated with the author as self-publisher and the subsidy publisher.

VANITY PUBLISHING

Vanity publishing is more formally referred to as subsidy publishing (primarily in the promotional literature of its practitioners). In this context the term subsidy does not, of course, mean that the publication of a book is subsidized by a governmental or corporate agency, or funded by an arts or humanities council. Though this form of publishing does have many variations, in the strictest usage it is the author who subsidizes publication by paying the press to publish his or her book.

Vanity publishing is a controversial industry. Sometimes it's a perfectly legitimate means of seeing one's writings in print, and the author is fully satisfied with the results. However, there are many instances in which the author has misunderstood the process and is terribly disappointed—and in the hole for a lot of money.

Few conventional commercial publishers will engage in anything that smacks of vanity publishing. (*Note*: An author who promises to buy back many copies of a published book, and to spend a lot of his or her own money on marketing, can often induce even the most prestigious publishing house to publish a book that it would not otherwise publish.)

There are a number of companies, some quite large and well established, that function solely as vanity presses. Many of these publishers promote their services by means of a variety of outlets, including brochures sent through the mail to lists of the likely, and classified as well as display advertisements in selected publications. *Writer's Digest* magazine is one of the more logical and frequently used advertising channels; the classified section of the *New York Times Book Review* has over the years logged quite a roster of listings for vanity houses and allied services.

KNOW EXACTLY WHAT SERVICES WILL BE PROVIDED

In vanity or subsidy publishing, the way the arrangement often works is that the writer pays a flat fee to have a set number of books produced. Some subsidy publishers provide worthy editorial, production, design, marketing, and distribution assistance. Some make exaggerated claims regarding the value and caliber of these services—whereas others make no such claims at all, maintaining that these functions are the author's responsibility.

Over the years some practitioners of the vanity trade have discovered that they snag more customers when they can glibly deflect any discussion of the possible pitfalls of the process—even in response to a potential customer's direct questions. In addition, with increased volume and increasingly lower production costs (and standards), the profit margin is all that much higher. For the foregoing reasons, an uninformed and less-than-curious consumer is the vanity house's most valued customer.

In all cases, the more the writer knows about the publishing process in general—and is aware of the limited or nonexistent clout a vanity press has regarding book distribution—the better situated the author is to determine any advantages one particular subsidy publisher's program may have over another's, as well as how subsidy publishing stacks up against other available options, such as self-publishing.

Among several worst-case vanity press scenarios is one wherein the publisher simply prints the books and delivers them casually to the writer's doorstep. ("Yours to do with as you please, thank you! We're out of it now—no marketing or distribution services provided.") The writer could probably have engaged a printing house to do virtually the same thing for a fraction of the cost.

In another popular variation of the vanity-publishing approach, the contractual fee is set at a price that provides the publisher with a healthy profit even without the sale of so much as one copy of the published title—even though numerous (but decidedly perfunctory and ineffectual) promotion and marketing services are specified in the contract.

In this case, the publisher may have little motivation to promote or market a given published work. However, according to the terms of the agreement the publisher will derive further income from any sales, even if the sales are really due to the successful independent marketing efforts of the paying writer.

This is all well within the bounds of everyday hard-nosed business practices perhaps, and a secure way to turn a profit if done right. So long as the vanity house's contractual obligations are met in full, the question here is rather of the nature of the publisher's come-on. Visions of potential glamour and literary recognition that subsidy house brochures proclaim may not be dark and devious schemes to lure the naive (doesn't all advertising trade in similar notions?); however, such forms of hype appear calculated to offer shadows and gray areas in which hitherto obscure fantasies of the potential customer may feel free to take full beguiling shape.

If the writer knows up front exactly what he or she can and can't expect from the vanity publisher, then everything is square. But if the company has encouraged or knowingly allowed the writer to have unrealistic expectations, then a crime has been committed—morally and ethically at least, if not legally. Vanity publishers that grossly mislead writers while taking their money are guilty of fraud. In 1990, one of the largest vanity presses in the country lost a million-dollar class-action suit, and hundreds of hoodwinked writers were granted refunds.

Even so, most suits against vanity presses are based on the assertion of fraud in the execution of contractual services, and any rewards to the authors are small potatoes compared with the kind of money conceivably involved if the complainant can prove a claim of fraud in the inducement of an agreement—a complaint that, no matter how heartfelt, is most difficult to substantiate.

BEWARE OF SHARKS!

The following correspondence is genuine, though all names and titles have been altered. My purpose for exposing these ever-so-slightly personalized form letters isn't to condemn or ridicule anyone. I simply wish to show how some subsidy publishers hook their clients. Again, as long as the writer truly understands the facts, no one has the right to cast any stones at this particular publishing option.

SHARK HOUSE
PUBLISHERS

Mr. Bourne Bate
Brooklyn Bridge
East River, NY 00000

Dear Mr. Bate:

Your manuscript *A Fish's Life* is written from an unusual perspective and an urgent one. In these trying economic times which have created despair and anguish, one must give thought to opportunities, and this upbeat and enthusiastic book makes us realize that those opportunities are out there! My capsule critique: Meticulous aim! With a surgeon's precision we're taught how to work through everything from raising money to targeting areas. There is a sharp eye here for all of the nuances, studded with pointers and reasoning, making it a crucial blueprint.

What can I say about a book like this? It stopped me in my tracks. I guess all I can do is thank you for letting me have the opportunity to read it.

The editors that read this had a spontaneous tendency to feel that it was imbued with some very, very good electricity and would be something very special for our list and saw such potential with it that it was given top priority and pushed ahead of every other book in house. The further problem is that publishing being an extremely rugged business, editorial decisions have to be based on hard facts which sometimes hurt publishers as much as authors. Unfortunately, we just bought several new non-fiction pieces . . . yet, I hate to let this one get away. Publishing economics shouldn't have anything to do with a decision, but unfortunately it does and I was overruled at the editorial meeting.

Still I want you to know that this is a particularly viable book and one that I really would love to have for our list. Further, this might be picked up for magazine serialization or by book clubs because it is so different. Our book, *Enraptured* was serialized six times in *International Inquirer* and sold to Andorra. *The Devil Decided* sold well over 150,000 copies, and we have a movie option on it. *Far Away* was serialized in *Places* magazine and *Cure Yourself* was taken by a major book club.

I really want this book for our list because it will fit into all the areas that we're active in. Therefore, I'm going to make a proposition for you to involve yourself with us. What would you think of the idea of doing this on a cooperative basis? Like many New York publishers these days, we find that sometimes investors are interested in the acquisition of literary properties through a technique which might be advantageous under our tax laws. There is no reason that the partial investor cannot be the writer, if they so choose. Tax advantages may accrue.

I'd be a liar if I promised you a best seller, but I can guarantee that nobody works as hard promoting a book as we do: nag paperback, book clubs, magazines, and foreign publishers with our zeal and enthusiasm. We do our PR work and take it seriously because this is where we're going to make the money in the long run. One of our authors hired a top publicist on his own for $50,000. He came limping back to us saying they didn't do the job that we did, and which we don't charge for. This made our office feel very proud of all our efforts.

I feel that your book deserves our efforts because it is something very special. Think about what I've written you, and I will hold the manuscript until I hear from you. I truly hope that we can get together because I really love this book and believe it is something we can generate some good action for vis-à-vis book clubs, foreign rights, etc., because it is outstanding and has tremendous potential.

Sincerely,

Eda U. Live

Eda U. Live
Executive Editor

The writer of *A Fish's Life* wrote back to Shark House (all names have been changed) and informed the vanity press that he did not want to pay any money to the publisher to have his book published. The vanity house responded with the following letter. This publisher has probably learned from experience that some exhausted writers will return to them with open wallets after fruitless pursuit of a conventional commercial publishing arrangement.

 **SHARK HOUSE PUBLISHERS**

Mr. Bourne Bate
Brooklyn Bridge
East River, NY 00000

Dear Mr. Bate:

I have your letter in front of me and I want you to know that I think very highly of the book. Before I go any further, I want to tell you that it is a topnotch book and it hits the reader.

In order for us to do a proper job with a book, there is a great deal of PR work involved and this is very costly. To hire an outside agent to do a crackerjack job would cost you upwards of $50,000. Yet, here we do not charge for it because it is part of our promotion to propel a book into the marketplace and it is imperative that this be done. The author has to be booked on radio and TV, stores have to be notified, rights here and abroad have to be worked on, reviewers contacted, autograph parties, and myriad details.

In view of this, why did I ask you to help with the project? I think the above is self-explanatory especially when we are in the midst of a revolution between books and television. Publishers are gamblers vying for the same audience. Just because a publisher loves a book is no guarantee that the public is going to love it. In times when bookstores are more selective in the number of books they order, the best of us tremble at the thought of the money that we must put out in order to make a good book a reality.

Be that as it may, I have just come from another editorial meeting where I tried to re-open the case for us, but unfortunately, the earlier decision stands.

As a result, I have no choice but to return the manuscript with this letter. I would also like to tell you that you must do what the successful writers do. Keep sending it out. Someone will like it and someone will buy it.

I wish you every success. Live long and prosper.

Sincerely,

Eda U. Live

Eda U. Live
Executive Editor

SELF-PUBLISHING

Vanity publishing shouldn't be confused with self-publishing. If you can't find a commercial house to publish your book (or don't want them to), you can publish it yourself. In fact, many successful titles that eventually found their ways onto mainstream publishers' trade lists were initially self-published. As already mentioned, the basic production costs of doing it yourself should be much less than paying a vanity house essentially to "self-publish" it for you.

The key to the productivity of this choice is the answer to the question: What will you do with the books after you've printed them?

It's exceptionally difficult (but not impossible) for a sole proprietor to achieve meaningful bookstore distribution—though you should at least check out the option of commissioning one of the regional or small press distribution services who send catalogs and offer representation on a regional or nationwide basis.

On the other hand, if you're a born promoter who can achieve ample media visibility, or if you have an active seminar business, you can sell numerous copies of your book via back-of-the-room sales and 800 numbers.

Your per-unit profits will be many times greater than your per-unit royalties would have been if you'd used a commercial publisher. Once your up-front production costs have been met, your reprint costs can be very low (depending on quantity ordered); the profit margin can be relatively astronomic if manufacturing volume can be matched closely to projected sales figures. As publishing houses well know, marketing and promotional efforts can entail the outlay of significant amounts of money, so discretion and prudence should be watchwords here.

If the author knows the intended audience well and has written a work geared to that familiar readership, that author may prove far more adept at reaching that readership than a given publishing house's expert but thinly spread staff would have been.

One more cautionary note about vanity houses is pertinent here: With publication under a vanity arrangement, even an ambitious author's promotional and marketing agenda may prove to be futile. Please realize that the names of the largest and most successful vanity presses are well known to booksellers and book reviewers. The jacket design and overall slack production quality of the typical vanity house's package is likely to draw snickers and sneers from industry professionals and may be more than subliminally noticeable to even casual browsers. If a bookstore were to stock such a shoddy item, it might reflect poorly on the quality of an outlet's other stock.

In a reverse-case scenario of name recognition, when faced with a volume issued under an ignominious vanity imprimatur, most bookstores or critics will have nothing to do with the work in question. If on close inspection the work is indeed worthy, it's too bad—it's all over already. A bookstore buyer or book reviewer won't even take it that far.

You're much better off with a well-packaged product under a newly minted name of your own device that, though it may be unrecognized, at least has no one soured on it yet.

Self-publishing can be not only a boon in itself, it can also be an asset with potential windfall ramifications. Successful self-publishers have licensed trade distribution rights to their books to major publishers in deals that have turned tidy profits for one and all.

The Literary Agent Trade Association

Jeff Herman

Unlike members of some august professions, such as the law or medicine, literary agents have no institutionalized industry trade groups to regulate who can and cannot practice legally. Thus anyone can declare himself to be a literary agent—even if he's incarcerated, since so much of the work is done by phone.

But the industry does have the Association of Authors' Representatives (AAR). The group was formed in October of 1991 through the merger of the Independent Literary Agents Association and the Society of Authors' Representatives.

The AAR has approximately 250 members. It has no policing or enforcement powers, other than the power to rule on membership status. To be a member of the AAR, the agent must meet minimum professional performance standards, and must agree to adhere to a written code of professional practices. (Please see the AAR Canon of Ethics and the organization's Television Packaging Disclosure Statement, both reprinted by permission below.)

It is unlikely that an illegitimate or discreditable agent would be able to gain membership to AAR. On the other hand, many perfectly qualified agents have, for a variety of reasons, opted not to join the AAR. An agent's lack of membership in the organization should never automatically be seen as a black mark against that agent.

The primary functions of the AAR are to serve as a formal and informal network for agents to share information; to create a unified and forceful way for agents to advocate for their positions within the industry, which, in turn, generally benefits their clients; and to establish a code of ethics and standards for the agenting business. (As I've said, there is no enforcement power beyond granting or withholding membership.)

You may write to the AAR to obtain their membership list, brochure, and Canon of Ethics (include a check for $5 and SASE with 55¢ postage).

Association of Authors' Representatives, Inc.
Ten Astor Place
Third Floor
New York, NY 10003

CODE OF ETHICS

The following is the code of ethics that all AAR members must agree, in writing, to uphold.

ASSOCIATION OF AUTHORS' REPRESENTATIVES, INC.
CANON OF ETHICS

1. The members of the Association of Authors' Representatives, Inc., are committed to the highest standard of conduct in the performance of their professional activities. While affirming the necessity and desirability of maintaining their full individuality and freedom of action, the members pledge themselves to loyal service to their clients' business and artistic needs, and will allow no conflicts of interest that would interfere with such service. They pledge their support to the Association itself and to the principles of honorable coexistence, directness, and honesty in their relationships with their co-members. They undertake never to mislead, deceive, dupe, defraud, or victimize their clients, other members of the Association, the general public, or any other person with whom they do business as a member of the association.

2. Members shall take responsible measures to protect the security and integrity of clients' funds. Members must maintain separate bank accounts for money due their clients so that there is no commingling of clients' and members' funds. Members shall deposit funds received on behalf of clients promptly upon receipt, and shall make payments of domestic earnings due clients promptly, but in no event later than ten business days after clearance. Revenues from foreign rights over $50 shall be paid to clients within ten business days after clearance. Sums under $50 shall be paid within a reasonable time of clearance. However, on stock and similar rights, statements of royalties and payments shall be made not later than the month following the member's receipt, each statement and payment to cover all royalties received to the 25th day of the previous calendar month. Payments for amateur rights shall be made not less frequently than every six months. A member's books of account must be open to the client at all times with respect to transactions concerning the client.

3. In addition to the compensation for agency services that is agreed upon between a member and a client, a member may, subject to the approval of the client, pass along charges incurred by the member on the client's behalf, such as copyright fees, manuscript retyping, photocopies, copies of books for use in the sale of other rights, long

distance calls, special messenger fees, etc. Such charges shall only be made if the client has agreed to reimburse such expenses.

4. A member shall keep each client apprised of matters entrusted to the member and shall promptly furnish such information as the client may reasonably request.

5. Members shall not represent both buyer and seller in the same transaction. Except as provided in the next sentence, a member who represents a client in the grant of rights in any property owned or controlled by the client may not accept any compensation or other payment from the acquirer of such rights, including but not limited to so-called "packaging fees," it being understood that the member's compensation, if any, shall be derived solely from the client. Notwithstanding the foregoing, a member may accept (or participate in) a so-called "packaging fee" paid by an acquirer of television rights to a property owned or controlled by a client if the member: a) fully discloses to the client at the earliest practical time the possibility that the member may be offered such a "packaging fee" which the member may choose to accept; b) delivers to the clients at such time a copy of the Association's statement regarding packaging and packaging fees; and c) offers the client at such time the opportunity to arrange for other representation in the transaction. In no event shall the member accept (or participate in) both a packaging fee and compensation from the client with respect to the transaction. For transactions subject to Writers Guild of America (WGA) jurisdiction, the regulations of the WGA shall take precedence over the requirements of this paragraph.

6. Members may not receive a secret profit in connection with any transaction involving a client. If such profit is received, the member must promptly pay over the entire amount to the client.

7. Members shall treat their clients' financial affairs as private and confidential, except for information customarily disclosed to interested parties as part of the process of placing rights as required by law, or, if agreed with the client, for other purposes.

8. The AAR believes that the practice of literary agents charging clients or potential clients fees for reading and evaluating literary works (including outlines, proposals, and partial or complete manuscripts) is subject to serious abuse that reflects adversely on our profession. For this reason the AAR discourages that practice. New members and members who had not, before October 30, 1991, registered their intent to continue to charge reading fees shall not charge such fees. The term "reading fees" in the previous sentence includes any request for payment other than to cover the actual cost of returning materials. *Effective January 1, 1996, all AAR members shall be prohibited from directly or indirectly charging such fees or receiving any financial benefit from the charging of such fees by any other party.*

Until January 1, 1996, AAR members who, *in accordance with the registration provisions of the previous paragraph*, do charge such fees are required to comply with the following:

A. Before entering into any agreement whereby a fee is to be charged for reading and evaluating any work, the member must provide to the author a written statement that clearly sets forth (i) the nature and extent of the services to be rendered, including whether the work will be read in whole or in part and whether a written report is to be provided and, if so, the nature and extent of that report; (ii) whether the services are to be rendered by the member personally, and if not, a description of the professional background of the person who will render the services; (iii) the period of time within which the services will be rendered; (iv) under what circumstances, if any, the fee charged will be refunded to the author; (v) the amount of the fee, including any initial payment as well as any other payments that may be requested by the member for additional services, and how that fee was determined (e.g., hourly rate, length of work reviewed, length of report, or other measure); and (vi) that the rendering of such services shall not guarantee that the member will agree to represent the author or will render the work more salable to publishers.

B. Any member who charges fees for such services and who seeks or facilitates the member's inclusion in any published listing of literary agents shall, if the listing permits, indicate in that listing that the member charges such fees. Apart from such listings, members shall not solicit reading fee submissions.

C. The rendering of such services for a fee shall not constitute more than an incidental part of the member's professional activity.

Signature of AAR Member   *Date*

Please print or type your name here

TELEVISION PACKAGING DISCLOSURE STATEMENT

The following is the Television Packaging Disclosure Statement referred to in the AAR Canon above.

ASSOCIATION OF AUTHORS' REPRESENTATIVES, INC.
TELEVISION PACKAGING DISCLOSURE STATEMENT

The Association of Authors' Representatives requires all of its member agents to send this disclosure statement to their clients when the member agent is planning or expecting to share in a "packaging fee" from the sale of television rights in material represented by that agent. The purpose of this statement is to give such clients a general understanding of the issues raised by the practice of "packaging" in the television industry. This requirement does not apply, however, to deals which are subject to the jurisdiction of the Writers Guild of America.

Decades ago certain talent agencies working in the television industry established a practice of demanding a fee for their services, as opposed to a commission on their clients' income, when such agencies "attached" various elements (such as a screenwriter, director and star, almost all of whom are usually represented by that agency) to a particular property. This process is called "packaging" and the fees involved are called "packaging fees." The agencies pointed out that such projects were more likely to be produced as a result of their packaging efforts, which from our observation is certainly true, and therefore they were entitled to direct compensation for their services. Since most agencies don't take a commission on their clients' income if they receive a packaging fee (in many cases, primarily with clients who are members of various unions such as the Writers Guild of America, the Screen Actors Guild, and the Directors Guild the agencies are specifically prohibited from doing so), the packaging agents also argue that the process is beneficial to their clients because the client doesn't pay a commission to the agency. Obviously, one could argue that any services performed by an agency for the benefit of its clients' projects, including the process of "packaging" a project, are a logical extension of their services for such clients and that such agents are already compensated by their commission(s) on their clients' fees. Additionally, there is a potential conflict of interest since the agency would clearly have a financial incentive which is less closely allied with its clients' interests. For example, a packaging agent might choose to attach one of its directing clients to a particular project, in order to receive a packaging fee, rather than attach a more appropriate—perhaps even *better*—director who happens to be represented by another agency. As another example, the agent might not negotiate for the client as aggressively since the agent's compensation is not tied directly to the client's fees. This could be dangerous since the agent's potential participation in the packaging fee could create an incentive for the agent to grant concessions to a producer, for example, whose interests are directly at odds with the client's. On the other hand, the deals for each element of a package are often subject to especially close scrutiny, all the more so when a high profile actor, director or producer is involved, and most talent agents are particularly cautious about the possibility of conflicts of interest in packaging situations. As a result, the terms of each deal in a package, including that for the underlying rights, tend to be among the best possible.

Whatever the arguments (and there are many more on both sides of the issue), packaging has become a well-established practice in the television industry and packaging fees, often five to ten percent of the budget of the television movie, can be quite large, sometimes greater than the fee paid to the author of the underlying work (or the screenwriter, director, etc.). Additionally, the circumstances under which an agency might receive a packaging fee are less clearly defined than they were initially. In the early years after the networks and producers accepted the principle of packaging, a packaging agent was expected to provide at least three of the talent elements (e.g. screenwriter, producer, and star) to be entitled to the packaging fee. Now it is possible for an agency to receive a packaging fee merely for representing the one element, say a very high profile actor or actress, who is the principal reason the project was scheduled for actual production (as opposed to development). The lines have become so blurred that it is possible for an agency to perform the majority of the "packaging" work only to find another agency demanding the packaging fee (or a large share of it) because of one "green-lighting" client. As a result, many of the talent agencies are also willing to pool their resources on particular projects and share the packaging fees. This practice of sharing packaging fees has been extended to literary agents as well.

Although the Association of Authors' Representatives has reservations about the practice of packaging as it has developed in the television industry, the AAR does recognize the reality of that practice in the television industry and realizes that there might be projects where an AAR member's participation in a packaging arrangement may be beneficial to the member's client.

Paragraph 5 of the AAR's Canon of Ethics contains the following language:

> Members shall not represent both buyer and seller in the same transaction. Except as provided in the next sentence, a member who represents a client in the grant of rights in any property owned or controlled by the client may not accept any compensation or other payment from the acquirer of such rights, including but not limited to so-called "packaging fees," it being understood that the member's compensation, if any, shall be derived solely from the client. Notwithstanding the foregoing, a member may accept (or participate in) a so-called "packaging fee" paid by an acquirer of television rights to a property owned or controlled by a client if the member: a) fully discloses to the client at the earliest practical time the possibility that the member may be offered such a "packaging fee" which the member may choose to accept; b) delivers to the clients at such time a copy of the Association's statement regarding packaging and packaging fees; and c) offers the client at such time the opportunity to arrange for other representation in the transaction. In no event shall the member accept (or participate in) both a packaging fee and compensation from the client with respect to the transaction. For transactions subject to Writers Guild of America (WGA) jurisdiction, the regulations of the WGA shall take precedence over the requirements of this paragraph.

Clients of the members of the AAR are encouraged to explore fully with their agents all of the relevant factors of a potential package and the AAR members are expected to be as helpful as possible in answering their clients' questions and otherwise helping their clients reach a decision concerning the packaging of a particular project. Questions which such clients might wish to direct to their agents include:

- To whom was the material submitted and with what strategy?
- Was the material submitted to any other packaging agents?
- Are there any agencies, directors, stars, etc., who might be more appropriate?
- How large is the potential packaging fee?

The issues and potential conflicts of packaging are extremely complex. Each author should carefully weigh the specific details of the particular packaging arrangement. The AAR's Canon of Ethics and this statement have been developed by the AAR to help prevent questionable behavior by the members of the AAR on behalf of their clients and to provide some guidelines to help their clients understand the advantages and disadvantages of packaging. However, the AAR cannot prevent such behavior and this statement is not intended to be a comprehensive analysis of the practice of packaging in the television industry.

Reprinted by permission of the Association of Authors' Representatives, Inc.
Copyright © by the Association of Authors' Representatives, Inc.

The Author–Agent Agreement

Jeff Herman

The author–agent relationship is a business relationship. Substantial sums and complex deals may be involved. It's to everyone's advantage to explicitly codify the rules and parameters of the relationship in a brief, plain-English agreement. It's true that the author–agent relationship can become unusually cozy. Still, there's no reason why even the best of friends can't have written business agreements without diminishing their mutual trust and affection. From at least one perspective, explicitly written agreements can be seen to go hand in hand with—and serve to underscore or amplify—existing bonds of confidence, faith, and friendship.

Some agents prefer oral understandings and handshakes, but most use a standard written agreement. It's unlikely that any two agencies will use the same agreement, but most agreements overlap each other closely in their intent and spirit.

There are several aspects of the author–agent arrangement covered by the typical agreement. Here are some of the major points of consideration, along with some key questions you might reflect on as you peruse the materials your prospective agent has submitted to you.

REPRESENTATION

What precisely will the agency be representing? Will it be a per-project representation? Or will it include all future works as well? Will it automatically cover all nonbook sales, such as magazine or newspaper articles? The extent of the representation should be spelled out so that there are no memory lapses or misunderstandings down the line.

AGENCY COMMISSION

The agency will receive a commission for all sales it makes against the work's advance, and on any subsequent income derived from royalties and the licensing of various rights. According to a recent study by the Authors' Guild, most agencies charge new clients 15 percent for domestic sales. Many agencies charge 20 to 30 percent for foreign sales, since the commission often must be split with local subagents (the agent in the foreign country who actually expedites the sale).

DURATION AND POTENTIAL TERMINATION OF THE AGREEMENT

When does the agreement end? How can the author or agency act to terminate the agreement? What happens after it's terminated?

Are agency agreements negotiable? Probably. It's a case-by-case situation. Don't be afraid to question, or attempt to reword, some aspects of the agreement. It will be better if such discussions are held in a friendly manner, directly between you and the agent. As a cautionary note, it is a common observation that the involvement of third parties—especially lawyers—can backfire and ignite issues that are irrelevant to the traditional ground rules of the author–agent understanding. It's fine to consult a lawyer, but you should be the point person.

The following is the standard agreement that I use with my clients. It's provided for your reference. It's not the only way an agreement can be or should be.

SAMPLE LETTER OF AGREEMENT

This Letter of Agreement between THE JEFF HERMAN AGENCY, INC., (Agency) and
_____ (Author), entered into on _____ (date), puts into effect the following terms and conditions:

REPRESENTATION

- The Agency is hereby exclusively authorized to seek a publisher for the Author's work, hereby referred to as the "Project," on a per-project basis. The terms and conditions of this Agreement will pertain to all Projects the Author explicitly authorizes the Agency to represent, through oral and written expression, and that the Agency agrees to represent. Separate Agreements will not be necessary for each single project, unless the terms and conditions differ from this Agreement.

COMMISSION

- If the Agency sells the Project to a publisher, the Agency will be the Agent-of-Record for the Project's income-producing duration and will irrevocably keep 15% of all the Author's income relevant to sold Project. The due Agency commission will also pertain to all of the Project's subsidiary rights sales, whether sold by the Agent, Author, or Publisher. In the event the agency uses a subagent to sell foreign or film rights, and the subagent is due a commission, the Agency commission for such will be 10%, and the subagent's commission will not be more than 10%. All Project income will be paid by the publisher to the Agency. The Agency will pay the Author all due monies within a reasonable time, upon receipt and bank clearance, with full accounting provided. The Agency will not be required to return any legitimately received commissions should the Author–Publisher contract be terminated or if the Author's work is unacceptable to the Publisher. There will be an Agency Clause in the Author–Publisher contract stating the Agency's status, the wording of which shall be subject to Author approval. These terms will be binding on the Author's estate in the event of his/her demise.

EXPENSES

- The Agency will be entitled to receive reimbursement from the Author for the following specific expenses relevant to its representation of the Project: manuscript/proposal copying costs; long-distance telephone calls and telefaxes between Author and Agency; necessary overnight deliveries and local messenger costs; postage and handling for manuscripts, foreign shipping, and communications costs. An itemized accounting and records of all such items will be maintained by the Agency and will be shown to the Author. No significant expenses (in excess of $25.00) will be incurred without the Author's prior knowledge and consent. The Agency will have the option either to bill the Author for these expenses, regardless of whether or not the Project in question is sold to a publisher, or to charge such expenses against the Author's account.

PROJECT STATUS

- The Agency agrees to forward to the Author copies of all correspondence received from publishers in reference to the Author's Project(s).

REVISIONS

- This Agreement can be amended or expanded by attaching Rider(s) to it, if all parties to this agreement concur with the terms and conditions of the Rider(s) and sign them.

TERMINATION

- This Agreement can be terminated in writing by any party to it by writing to the other parties at any time following its execution. However, the Agency shall remain entitled to due commissions which may result from Agency efforts implemented prior to the termination of this Agreement, and will remain entitled to all other due monies as stated in this Agreement. Termination of the Agency representation of one or more Author Projects will not imply termination of this Agreement, unless such is specifically requested in writing.

Signatures below by the parties named in this Agreement will indicate that all parties concur with the terms and conditions of this Agreement.

THE JEFF HERMAN AGENCY, INC.	AUTHOR
	Social Security No.:
	Date of birth:

Specific project(s) being represented at this time:

Q & A

Q: If you, Mr. Herman, were the writer, what are some of the key points that would most concern you about an agent's agreement?

A: As a writer, I would prefer to see the following incorporated into my agreement with the literary agency:

1. I would want the representation to be on a per-project basis. I would not want to be automatically obligated to be represented by the agent on my next project.
2. I would want a liberal termination procedure. If at any point after signing the agreement I change my mind, I want the ability to immediately end the relationship.

Of course, I realize that the agent will be entitled to his commission relevant to any deals I accept that result from his efforts on the project's behalf—even if the deal is consummated after my termination of the agent.

The Collaboration Agreement

Jeff Herman

Any book that is written by two or more writers is a collaborative effort. Such collaborative endeavors are predominately nonfiction works, though collaborative fiction is by no means unheard of (typically a novel featuring a celebrity author that is for the most part written by someone else, or two best-selling novelists looking to synergize their reader base). There are several reasons why a writer might choose to collaborate with another, as opposed to writing the book alone; the most common reasons follow.

On one hand, a person may have the essential expertise, professional status, and promotability to author a book, but may lack the time, ability, and/or interest to do the actual writing. Therefore, retaining someone to do the writing is a sensible—even preferable—alternative.

On the other hand, some nonfiction projects, especially academic or professionally oriented ones, cover a broad range of material, and few individuals have the requisite depth to write the book unilaterally. Therefore, two or more writers with complementary specializations may team up. For exceptionally technical books, such as medical texts, there can be several collaborators.

Many writers earn handsome incomes writing other people's books. When they are collaborative writers, their names are flashed along with the primary author of the project (and given second billing, usually preceded by "and," "with," or "as told to"). If they are true ghostwriters, they may well have the same level of input and involvement as collaborators, but will generally receive no public recognition for their work (other than perhaps a subtle pat on the back in the acknowledgments section).

WHAT ARE COLLABORATION AGREEMENTS?

As with any business relationship, it's wise for the collaborators to enter into a concise agreement (written in plain English) that spells out all the terms and conditions of the relationship—especially each party's respective responsibilities and financial benefits.

A collaboration agreement can run from one to more than twenty pages, depending on how much money is at issue and the complexity of the other variables. Most of the time industry insiders can keep these agreements down to an easy-to-read two pages. It's probably not necessary to go to the expense of retaining a lawyer for this task. If you have an agent, he can probably draw up an agreement for you, or at least show you several samples.

The following is a sample collaboration agreement that is similar to ones used by many of my clients. Please note: This sample collaboration agreement is intended only as a reference guide.

SAMPLE COLLABORATION AGREEMENT

This collaboration agreement (Agreement), entered into on [*date*], by and between John Doe (John) and Jane Deer (Jane), will put into effect the following terms and conditions, upon signing by both parties.

(1) Jane will collaborate with John in the writing of a book about [*subject or brief description goes here*].

(2) In consultation with John, Jane will prepare a nonfiction book proposal and sample chapter for the purpose of selling the book to a publisher.

(3) Jane and John will be jointly represented by [*name of literary agent/agency*].

(4) John will be the book's spokesperson. John's name will appear first on the cover and in all publicity, and his name will be more prominently displayed than Jane's.

(5) Following the sale of the project proposal to a publisher, if, for any reason, Jane does not wish to continue as a collaborator, she shall be entitled to [*monetary amount goes here*] against the book's first proceeds in consideration of her having written the successful proposal, and she will forfeit any future claims against the book and any connection thereto.

(6) Jane's and John's respective estates will be subject to the terms and conditions of this Agreement, in the event of either's demise.

(7) John agrees to indemnify and hold harmless Jane from any liability, claim, or legal action taken against her as a result of her participation in the book proposal or book. Such exoneration includes but is not limited to costs of defending claims including reasonable counsel fees. John agrees that any funds derived from sale of the proposal or book may be utilized to pay such claims.

(8) This Agreement can be amended or expanded by attaching riders to it, if such riders are signed by Jane and John.

(9) No other claims or representations are made by either party; both agree that this Agreement fully integrates their understanding. No other representations, promises, or agreements are made except as may be in writing and signed by the party to be held responsible.

(10) Jane shall receive the first [*monetary amount goes here*] of the book's proceeds when sold to a publisher. John shall receive the next [*monetary amount goes here*]. All income thereafter shall be evenly received (50/50). All subsidiary rights income shall be split 50/50.

(11) John will own the book's copyright.

(12) John will be responsible for paying expenses relevant to the preparation of the proposal (photocopying; telephone; deliveries; travel; etc.). Upon the book's sale to a publisher and the receipt of the first part of the advance, John will be reimbursed for 50% of these expenses by Jane. John and Jane will equally split (50/50) costs relevant to writing the book following its sale to a publisher.

_____   _____

Jane Deer   John Doe

Q & A

Q: What about agent representation if it's a collaborative effort?
A: There are two possibilities:

1. *The same agent will represent both parties.* However, this requires the agent to be equal in her dealings with both parties. For instance, the agent should avoid tilting toward John while he's negotiating the collaboration agreement with Jane.

   What I do is provide both parties with accurate advice, and then step aside as they—hopefully—work things out between themselves and then come back to me with all issues resolved.

   More important, the agent should not "double-dip." In other words, my commission will only pertain to the work's income. I will not touch any money that one collaborator may pay to the other, even if such payments exceed the work's advance.

2. *Some collaborations can be coagented.* Each collaborator may already have a different agent. Or it may be felt that there will be a conflict of interest for the same agent to represent both parties.

   When this happens, both agents will negotiate the collaboration agreement with each other in behalf of their respective clients. All parties will then work out a strategy to determine which agent is to be out front selling and negotiating the deal. Each agent will receive a commission only against her client's respective share.

As with any other business relationship, collaboration agreements generally have the best chance to produce a productive and successful outcome when they reasonably and realistically reflect the rights, responsibilities, special talents, and good interests of all involved parties.

Overcoming Writer's Roadblocks

Writer's Guide to a Wholesome Outlook and a Sound Mind

JEFF HERMAN AND JAMIE M. FORBES

Trying to make it as a writer can drive anyone crazy, and may have already sent you over the edge. Regardless of your sanity rating, telling people you're a writer cuts you a lot of slack. They expect you to be a bit bizarre, if not an absolute miscreant. Since you're given this license to Nutsville, why not use it in ways that will let you vent your frustration?

We know that world-class athletes practice visualization techniques to enhance their performance mindset. Some counselors and psychologists use systems such as creative fantasy, role-playing, artistic manipulation, and personal journals to root through their clients' psyches and bring out the best that they can be.

Of course, we have to hedge on this a bit, and are therefore obligated to say that the ideas provided here are for entertainment or inspirational purposes only. Here are some scenarios to get your creative juices bubbling:

CREATIVE WAYS TO GAIN RICHES, FITNESS, FAME, AND LOVE

- Put wet cement into book-shaped boxes and send it to people who rejected your work, along with a cover note asking them to read your masterpiece. Change your pen name and *don't* remember to include an SASE.

  You might also want to make a contribution to the U.S. Postal Service Hernia Fund, to protect your karma.

- Cut out photos of models from *Cosmopolitan* or *GQ* magazines, and include them in your submission packages—don't say anything about them in your attached correspondence. If and when editors and agents offer you contracts because they think you're a hunk/babe, who are they to complain? You told no lies. (If you ever have to meet these editors or agents in person, you don't know what they're talking about.)
- On the assumption that many in the effete trade of publishing come from landed gentry, threaten to surgically mutilate pedigreed livestock, tramp out crop circles visible from the country house, implant alien colonies underneath organic vineyards, and abduct extended aristocratic families en masse to other galaxies if certain editors reject you. Of course, government agents might pay you a surprise visit, and they are a notoriously humorless lot—you would be too if you were being tailed by all those black helicopters.

  Although you can unnerve the entire New York editorial corps with such a campaign, various restraining orders might bar you from ever entering the city again. This will, however, be an opportunity to get a lot of publicity, which could be parlayed into book and movie deals. At the very least, you'll be able to appear on TV talk shows—maybe even Court TV.
- Legally change your name to an established, published brand name, such as Atwood, Chopra, Follett, Oates, Rice, Tan, Mosley, or Zelazny. These names, as well as dozens of others you can choose, have subliminal power to evoke contractual echoes in the halls of publishing.
- Agents and editors are mercenary tramps anyway—so who's to say you couldn't do it better yourself? Beat the creeps at their own game: Send drab first drafts to the offices of various hotshot literary agencies and big-name publishers. You should soon accumulate plenty of rejection slips—many of them will be printed on official letterhead stationery.

  Produce computer mock-ups of these letterheads and compose notes that say thus-and-such literary agency wants you to sign with them. Write memos to *other* agencies saying that you'd rather sign with *them*, even though you have these other fine offers (include copies of your forged notes from other agencies to buttress your case).
- If you don't sway a literary agency this way, all is by no means lost. Send your most calculatedly commercial manuscript around to a select group of renowned editors with a cover letter printed on the letterhead of the agency you feel is most impressive—be sure to insert your own telephone number (bill yourself under a snot-nosed alias, with the title "agent at large" or somesuch ritzy moniker that will lend credence to your branch office address).

  Wait for the offers to roll in. If they don't (or even if they do), remember the literary image that typifies the publishing game as a Monopoly board. As your newfound expertise bleeds into other notorious schemes, you may soon get to prove your worth as a highly respected jail house lawyer as you research the prison library and write your own appeals. Or maybe negotiate book deals for other inmates.

- Put together a full-fledged press kit, complete with photographs, reviews, interviews, articles about you, and a tape of video clips. If these do not yet exist, invent an entire career for yourself and submit it as a book-proposal package—call it *How to Become a Celebrity in Seventeen Seconds* or say it's an avant-garde novel.
- Take a fancy lunch with someone you trust, then take a nap.
- Stop writing.
- Start writing.
- Eat well and prosper.

Glossary

A

abstract   A brief profile of chapters in a nonfiction book proposal (also called a **synopsis**); a point-by-point summary of an article or essay. In academic and technical journals abstracts often appear with (and may serve to preface) the articles themselves.

adaptation   A rewrite or reworking of a piece for another medium, such as the adaptation of a novel for the screen. (See **screenplay**.)

advance   Money paid (usually in installments) to an author by a publisher prior to publication. The advance is paid against royalties: If an author is given a $5000 advance, for instance, the author will collect royalties only after the royalty monies due exceed $5000. A good contract protects the advance if it should exceed the royalties that are ultimately due from sales.

advance orders   Orders received before a book's official publication date, and sometimes before actual completion of the manufacture of the book.

agent   The person who acts on behalf of the author to handle the sale of literary properties. Good literary agents are as valuable to publishers as they are to writers; they select and present manuscripts appropriate for particular houses or of interest to particular acquisitions editors. Agents are paid on a percentage basis from the monies due their author clients.

American Booksellers Association (ABA)   The major trade organization for retail booksellers, chain and independent. The annual ABA convention and trade show offers a chance for publishers and distributors to display their wares to the industry at large, and provides an incomparable networking forum for booksellers, editors, agents, publicists, and authors.

American Society of Journalists and Authors   A membership organization for professional writers. ASJA provides a forum for information exchange among writers and others in the publishing community, as well as networking opportunities. (See **Dial-a-Writer**.)

anthology   A collection of stories, poems, essays, and/or selections from larger works (and so forth), usually with a unifying theme or concept, by different authors or by a single author. Anthologies are compiled as opposed to written; their editors (as opposed

777

to authors) are responsible for securing the needed reprint rights for the material used, as well as supplying (or providing authors for) pertinent introductory or supplementary material and/or commentary.

attitude   A contemporary colloquialism that describes a characteristic temperament common among individuals who consider themselves superior. Attitude is rarely deemed an attribute, whether in publishing or elsewhere.

auction   Manuscripts a literary agent believes to be hot properties (such as possible best-sellers with strong subsidiary rights potential) will be offered for confidential bidding from multiple publishing houses. Likewise, the reprint, film, and other rights to a successful book may be auctioned off by the original publisher's subsidiary rights department.

authorized biography   A history of a person's life written with the authorization, cooperation, and, at times, participation of the subject or the subject's heirs.

author's copies/author's discount   Author's copies are the free copies of their books the authors receive from the publisher; the exact number is stipulated in the contract, but it is usually at least ten hardcovers. The author will be able to purchase additional copies of the book (usually at 40 percent discount from the retail price) and resell them at readings, lectures, etc. If large quantities are bought, author discounts can go as high as 70 percent.

author tour   Travel and promotional appearances by an author on behalf of the author's book.

autobiography   A history of a person's life written by that same person, or, as is typical, composed conjointly with a collaborative writer ("as told to" or "with"; see **coauthor**, **collaboration**) or **ghostwriter**. Autobiographies by definition entail the authorization, cooperation, participation, and ultimate approval of the subject.

B

backlist   Books published prior to the current season and still in print. At some publishing houses, such titles represent the publisher's cash flow mainstays. Some backlist books continue to sell briskly, some remain best-sellers over several successive seasons, and others sell slowly but surely through the years. Although many backlist titles may be difficult to find in bookstores that stock primarily current lists, they can be ordered either through a local bookseller or directly from the publisher.

backmatter   Elements of a book that follow the text proper. Backmatter may include the appendix, notes, glossary, bibliography and other references, list of resources, index, and colophon.

best-seller   Based on sales or orders by bookstores, wholesalers, and distributors, best-sellers are those titles that move in the largest quantities. Lists of best-selling books can be local (newspapers), regional, or national (*Publishers Weekly* or the *New*

York Times), as well as international. Fiction and nonfiction are usually listed separately, as are hardcover and paperback, and sometimes additional classifications (such as how-to/self-improvement) are used. In addition, best-seller lists can be keyed to particular genre or specialty fields (such as best-seller lists for mysteries, science fiction, or romance novels, and for historical works, business books, or religious titles).

bibliography   A list of books, articles, and other sources that have been used in the writing of the text in which the bibliography appears. Complex works may break the bibliography down into discrete subject areas, such as general history, the twentieth century, or trade unions.

binding   The materials that hold a book together (including the cover). Bindings are generally denoted as hardcover (featuring heavy cardboard covered with durable cloth and/or paper) or paperback (using a pliable, resilient grade of paper). In the days when cloth was used more lavishly, hardcover volumes were conventionally known as cloth-bound; in the very old days, hardcover bindings sometimes featured tooled leather and real gold and silver leaf ornamentation.

biography   A history of a person's life. (See **authorized biography, autobiography, unauthorized biography**.)

blues (or bluelines)   Photographic proofs of the printing plates for a book used to inspect the set type, layout, and design before it goes to press.

blurb   A piece of written copy or extracted quotation used for publicity and promotional purposes, as on a flyer, in a catalog, or in an advertisement (see **cover blurbs**).

book club   A book club is a book-marketing organization that ships selected titles to subscribing members on a regular basis, sometimes at greatly reduced prices. Sales to book clubs are negotiated through the publisher's subsidiary rights department (in the case of a best-seller, they can be auctioned off). Terms vary, but the split of royalties between author and publisher is often 50/50. Book club sales are seen as blessed events by author, agent, and publisher alike.

book contract   A legally binding document that sets the terms for the advance, royalties, subsidiary rights, advertising, promotion, publicity, and a host of other contingencies and responsibilities. Writers should therefore be thoroughly familiar with the concepts and terminology of the standard book-publishing contract.

book distribution   The method of getting books from the publisher's warehouse into the reader's hands—traditionally via bookstores, but can include means such as telemarketing and mail-order sales. Publishers use their own sales forces as well as independent salespeople, wholesalers, and distributors. Many large and some small publishers distribute for other publishers, which can be a good source of income. A publisher's distribution network is extremely important, because it not only makes possible the vast sales of a best-seller but also affects the visibility of the publisher's entire list of books.

book jacket (See **dust jacket**.)

book producer or **book packager** An individual or company that can assume many of the roles in the publishing process. A book packager or producer may conceive the idea for a book (most often nonfiction) or series, bring together the professionals (including the writer) needed to produce the book(s), sell the individual manuscript or series project to a publisher, take the project through to manufactured product—or perform any selection of those functions, as commissioned by the publisher or other client (such as a corporation producing a corporate history as a premium or giveaway for employees and customers). The book producer may negotiate separate contracts with the publisher and with the writers, editors, and illustrators who contribute to the book.

book review A critical appraisal of a book (often reflecting a reviewer's personal opinion or recommendation) that evaluates aspects such as organization and writing style; possible market appeal; and cultural, political, or literary significance. Before the public reads book reviews in the local and national print media, important reviews have been published in respected trade journals such as *Publishers Weekly*, *Kirkus Reviews*, *Library Journal*, and *Booklist*. A rave review from one of these journals will encourage booksellers to order the book; copies of these raves will be used for promotion and publicity purposes by the publisher and will encourage other book reviewers nationwide to review the book.

Books in Print Listings, published by R. R. Bowker, of books currently in print; these yearly volumes (along with periodic supplements such as *Forthcoming Books in Print*) provide ordering information including titles, authors, ISBN numbers, prices, whether the book is available in hardcover or paperback, and publisher names. Intended for use by the book trade, *Books in Print* is also of great value to writers who are researching and market-researching their projects. Listings are provided alphabetically by author, title, and subject area.

bound galleys Copies of uncorrected typesetter's page proofs or printouts of electronically produced mechanicals that are bound together as advance copies of the book (compare **galleys**). Bound galleys are sent to trade journals (see **book review**) as well as to a limited number of reviewers who work under long lead times.

bulk sales The sale at a discount of many copies of a single title (the greater the number of books, the larger the discount).

byline The name of the author of a piece, indicating credit for having written a book or article. Ghostwriters, by definition, do not receive bylines.

C

casing Alternate term for binding (see **binding**).

category fiction Also known as genre fiction. Category fiction falls into an established (or newly originated) marketing category (which can then be subdivided for more precise target marketing). Fiction categories include action-adventure (with such further designations as military, paramilitary, law enforcement, romantic, and martial arts), crime novels (with points of view that range from deadpan cool to literary-visionary, including humorous capers as well as gritty urban sagas), mysteries or detective fiction (hard-boiled, soft-boiled, procedurals, cozies), romances (including historicals as well as contemporaries), horror (supernatural, psychological, or technological), thrillers (tales of espionage, crisis, and the chase), Westerns, science fiction, and fantasy. (See **fantasy**, **horror**, **romance fiction**, **science fiction, suspense fiction**, and **thriller**.)

CD or **computer CD**   High-capacity compact disks for use by readers via computer technology. **CD-ROM** is a particular variety; the term is somewhere between an acronym and an abbreviation—CD-ROMs are compact computer disks with read-only memory, meaning the reader is not able to modify or duplicate the contents. When issued by publishers, these are viewed as books in electronic format. (See **multimedia**.)

children's books   Books for children. As defined by the book-publishing industry, children are generally readers age 17 and younger, though many houses adhere to a fine but firm editorial distinction between titles intended for younger readers (under 12) and young adults (generally ages 12 to 17). Children's books (also called juveniles) are produced according to a number of categories, each with particular requisites regarding elements such as readability ratings, length, and inclusion of graphic elements. Picture books are often for the very young, with designations such as toddlers (who do not themselves read) and preschoolers (who may have some reading ability). Other classifications include easy story books (for younger school children), middle-grade books (for elementary to junior high school students), and young adult (abbreviated YA, for readers through age 17).

coauthor   One who shares authorship of a work. Coauthors all have bylines. Coauthors share royalties based on their contributions to the book. (Compare **ghostwriter**.)

collaboration   Writers can collaborate with professionals in any number of fields to produce books outside the writer's own areas of strictly credentialed expertise (for example, a writer with an interest in exercise and nutrition may collaborate with a doctor on a health book). Though the writer may be billed as a coauthor (see **coauthor**), the writer does not necessarily receive a byline (in which case the writer is a **ghostwriter**), and royalties are shared based on respective contributions to the book (including expertise or promotional abilities as well as the actual writing).

colophon   Strictly speaking, a colophon is a publisher's logo; in bookmaking, the term may also refer to a listing of the materials used, as well as credits for the design, composition, and production of the book that are sometimes included in the backmatter or as part of the copyright page.

commercial fiction   Fiction written to appeal to as broad-based a readership as possible.

concept   A general statement of the idea behind a book.

cool   A modern colloquial expression that indicates satisfaction or approval, or signifies calm within a whirlwind. A fat contract for a new author is definitely cool.

cooperative advertising (co-op)   An agreement between a publisher and a bookstore. The publisher's book is featured in an ad for the bookstore (sometimes in conjunction with an author appearance or other special book promotion); the publisher contributes to the cost of the ad, which is billed at a lower (retail advertising) rate.

copublishing   Joint publishing of a book, usually by a publisher and another entity such as a foundation, a museum, or a smaller publisher. An author can copublish with the publisher by sharing the costs and decision making and, ultimately, the profits.

copyeditor   An editor, responsible for the final polishing of a manuscript, who reads primarily in terms of appropriate word usage and grammatical expression, clarity and coherence of the material as presented, factual errors and inconsistencies, spelling, and punctuation. (See **editor**.)

copyright   The legal proprietary right to reproduce, have reproduced, publish, and sell copies of literary, musical, and other artistic works. The rights to literary properties reside with the author from the time the work is produced—regardless of whether a formal copyright registration is obtained. However, for legal recourse in the event of plagiarism, the work must be registered with the U.S. Copyright Office, and all copies of the work must bear the copyright notice. (See **work-for-hire**.)

cover blurbs   Favorable quotes from other writers, celebrities, or experts in a book's subject area, which appear on the dust jacket and are used to enhance the book's point-of-purchase appeal to the potential book buying public.

crash   Coarse gauze fabric used in bookbinding to strengthen the spine and joints of a book.

curriculum vitae (or c.v.)   Latin expression meaning "course of life"—in other words, the **résumé** (which see).

D

deadline   In book publishing, this not-so-subtle synonym for the author's due date for submission of the completed manuscript to the publisher can be as much as a full year before official publication date, unless the book is being produced quickly to coincide with or follow up a particular event.

delivery   Submission of the completed manuscript to the editor or publisher.

Dial-a-Writer   Members of the American Society of Journalists and Authors can be listed with the organization's project-referral service, Dial-a-Writer, which can provide accomplished writers in most specialty fields and subjects.

direct marketing   Advertising that involves a "direct response" (an equivalent term) from a consumer—for instance an order form or coupon in a book-review section or in the back of a book, or mailings (direct-mail advertising) to a group with a special interest in a particular book.

display titles   Books that are produced to be eye-catching to the casual shopper in a bookstore setting are termed display titles. Often rich with flamboyant cover art, these publications are intended to pique book buyer excitement about books in general. Many display titles are stacked on their own freestanding racks; a book shelved with its front cover showing is technically a display title. Promotional or **premium** titles are likely to be display items, as are mass-market paperbacks and hardbacks with enormous best-seller potential. Check your local bookstore and find a copy of this edition of *Writer's Guide*—if not already racked in display manner, please adjust the bookshelf so that the front cover is displayed posterlike to catch the browser's eye (that's what *we* do routinely).

distributor   An agent or business that buys books from a publisher to resell, at a higher cost, to wholesalers, retailers, or individuals. Distribution houses are often excellent marketing enterprises, with their own roster of sales representatives and house catalogs. Skillful use of distribution networks can give a small publisher considerable national visibility.

dramatic rights   Legal permission to adapt a work for the stage. These rights initially belong to the author but can be sold or assigned to another party by the author.

dust jacket (also **dustcover** or **book jacket**)   The paper wrapper that covers the binding of hardcover books, designed especially for the book either by the publisher's art department or by a freelance artist. Dust jackets were originally conceived to protect the book during shipping, but now their function is primarily promotional—to entice the browser to actually reach out and pick up the volume (and maybe even open it up for a taste before buying)—by means of attractive graphics and sizzling promotional copy.

dust jacket copy   Synopses printed on the dust jacket flaps. They may be written by the book's editor, but are often either recast or written by in-house copywriters or freelance specialists. Editors send advance copies (see **bound galleys**) to other writers, experts, and celebrities to solicit quotable praise that will also appear on the jacket.

E

editor   Editorial responsibilities and titles vary from house to house (often being less strictly defined in smaller houses). In general, the duties of the editor in chief or executive editor are primarily administrative: managing personnel, scheduling, budgeting, and defining the editorial personality of the firm or imprint. Senior editors and acquisitions editors acquire manuscripts (and authors), conceive project ideas and find writers to carry them out, and may oversee the writing and rewriting of manuscripts. Managing editors have editorial and production responsibilities, coordinating and scheduling the book through the various phases of production. Associate and assistant editors edit; they are involved in much of the rewriting and reshaping of the manuscript. Copyeditors read the manuscript and style its punctuation, grammar, spelling, headings and subheadings, etc. Editorial assistants, laden with extensive clerical duties and general office work, perform some editorial duties as well—often as springboards to senior editorial positions.

Editorial Freelancers Association   This organization of independent professionals offers a referral service, through both its annotated membership directory and its job phone line, as a means for authors and publishers to connect with writers, collaborators, and research and editorial experts in virtually all general and specialist fields.

el-hi   Books for elementary and/or high schools.

endnotes   Explanatory notes and/or source citations that appear either at the end of individual chapters or at the end of a book's text; used primarily in scholarly or academically oriented works.

epilogue   The final segment of a book, which comes "after the end." In both fiction and nonfiction, an epilogue offers commentary or further information, but does not bear directly on the book's central design.

F

fantasy   Fantasy is fiction that features elements of magic, wizardry, supernatural feats, and entities that transcend conventional laws of reality. Fantasy can resemble prose versions of epics and rhymes, may be informed by mythic cycles or folkloric material derived from cultures worldwide, or may be guided by the author's own personal shamanistic imagery and creative archetypes. Fantasies that involve heroic–erotic roundelays of the death-dance are often referred to as the sword-and-sorcery subgenre.

film rights   Like **dramatic rights**, these belong to the author, who may sell or option them to someone in the film industry—a producer or director, for example (or sometimes a specialist broker of such properties)—who will then try to gather the other professionals and secure the financial backing needed to convert the book into a film. (See **screenplay**.)

footbands   (See **headbands**.)

footnotes   Explanatory notes and/or source citations that appear at the bottom of a page. Footnotes are rare in general-interest books, the preferred style being either to work such information into the text or to list informational sources in the bibliography.

foreign agents   Persons who work with their United States counterparts to acquire rights for books from the U.S. for publication abroad. They can also represent U.S. publishers directly.

foreign market   Any foreign entity—a publisher, broadcast medium, etc.—in a position to buy rights. Authors share royalties with whomever negotiates the deal, or keep 100 percent if they do their own negotiating.

foreign rights   Translation or reprint rights that can be sold abroad. Foreign rights belong to the author but can be sold either country-by-country or en masse as world rights. Often the U.S. publisher will own world rights, and the author will be entitled to anywhere from 50 to 85 percent of these revenues.

foreword   An introductory piece written by the author or by an expert in the given field (see **introduction**). A foreword by a celebrity or well-respected authority is a strong selling point for a prospective author or, after publication, for the book itself.

Frankfurt Book Fair   The largest international publishing exhibition—with five hundred years of tradition behind it. The fair takes place every October in Frankfurt, Germany. Thousands of publishers, agents, and writers from all over the world negotiate, network, and buy and sell rights.

Freedom of Information Act   Ensures the protection of the public's right to access to public records—except in cases violating the right to privacy, national security, or certain other instances. A related law, the Government in the Sunshine Act, stipulates that certain government agencies announce and open their meetings to the public.

freight passthrough   The bookseller's freight cost (the cost of getting the book from the publisher to the book seller). It is added to the basic invoice price charged the bookseller by the publisher.

frontlist   New titles published in a given season by a publisher. Frontlist titles customarily receive priority exposure in the front of the sales catalog—as opposed to backlist titles (usually found at the back of the catalog), which are previously published titles still in print.

frontmatter   The frontmatter of a book includes the elements that precede the text of the work, such as the title page, copyright page, dedication, epigraph, table of contents, foreword, preface, acknowledgments, and introduction.

fulfillment house   A firm commissioned to fulfill orders for a publisher—services may include warehousing, shipping, receiving returns, and mail-order and direct-marketing functions. Although more common for magazine publishers, fulfillment houses also serve book publishers.

G

galleys   Printer's proofs (or copies of proofs) on sheets of paper, or printouts of the electronically produced setup of the book's interior—the author's last chance to check for typos and make (usually minimal) revisions or additions to the copy (see **bound galleys**).

genre fiction   (See **category fiction**.)

ghostwriter   A writer without a byline, often without the remuneration and recognition that credited authors receive. Ghostwriters often get flat fees for their work, but even without royalties experienced ghosts can receive quite respectable sums.

glossary   An alphabetical listing of special terms as they are used in a particular subject area, often with more in-depth explanations than would customarily be provided by dictionary definitions.

H

hardcover   Books bound in a format that uses thick, sturdy, relatively stiff binding boards and a cover composed (usually) of a cloth spine and finished binding paper. Hardcover books are conventionally wrapped in a dust jacket. (See **binding**, **dust jacket**.)

headbands   Thin strips of cloth (often colored or patterned) that adorn the top of a book's spine where the signatures are held together. The headbands conceal the glue or other binding materials and are said to offer some protection against accumulation of dust (when properly attached). Such bands, placed at the bottom of the spine, are known as footbands.

hook   A term denoting the distinctive concept or theme of a work that sets it apart—as being fresh, new, or different from others in its field. A hook can be an author's special point of view, often encapsulated in a catchy or provocative phrase intended to attract or pique the interest of a reader, editor, or agent. One specialized function of a hook is to articulate what might otherwise be seen as dry albeit significant subject matter (academic or scientific topics; number-crunching drudgery such as home bookkeeping) into an exciting, commercially attractive package.

horror   The horror classification denotes works that traffic in the bizarre, awful, and scary in order to entertain as well as to explicate the darkness at the heart of the reader's soul. Horror subgenres may be typified according to the appearance of were-creatures, vampires, human-induced monsters, or naturally occurring life forms and spirit entities—or absence thereof. Horror fiction traditionally makes imaginative literary use of paranormal phenomena, occult elements, and psychological motifs. (See **category fiction**, **suspense fiction**.)

how-to books   An immensely popular category of books ranging from purely instructional (arts and crafts, for example), to motivational (popular psychology, self-awareness, self-improvement, inspirational), to get rich quick (such as in real estate or personal investment).

hypertext   Works in hypertext are meant to be more than words and other images. These productions (ingrained magnetically on computer diskette or CD) are conceived to take advantage of readers' and writers' propensities to seek out twists in narrative trajectories and to bushwalk from the main path of multifaceted reference topics. Hypertext books incorporate documents, graphics, sounds, and even blank slates on which readers may compose their own variations on the authored components. The computer's capacities to afford such diversions can bring reader and hypertext literateur so close as to gain entry to each other's mind-sets—which is what good books have always done.

I

imprint   A separate line of product within a publishing house. Imprints run the gamut of complexity, from those composed of one or two series to those offering full-fledged and diversified lists. Imprints as well enjoy different gradations of autonomy from the parent company. An imprint may have its own editorial department (perhaps consisting of as few as one editor), or house acquisitions editors may assign particular titles for release on appropriate specialized imprints. An imprint may publish a certain kind of book (juvenile, paperback or travel books), or have its own personality (such as a literary or contemporary tone). An individual imprint's categories often overlap with other imprints or with the publisher's core list, but some imprints maintain a small-house feel within an otherwise enormous conglomerate. The imprint can offer the distinct advantages of a personalized editorial approach, while availing itself of the larger company's production, publicity, marketing, sales, and advertising resources.

index   An alphabetical directory at the end of a book that references names and subjects discussed in the book and the pages where such mentions can be found.

instant book   A book produced quickly to appear in bookstores as soon as possible after (for instance) a newsworthy event to which it is relevant.

international copyright   Rights secured for countries that are members of the International Copyright Convention (see entry below for **International Copyright Convention**) and respect the authority of the international copyright symbol, ©.

International Copyright Convention   Countries that are signatories to the various international copyright treaties. Some treaties are contingent on certain conditions being met at the time of publication, so an author should inquire before publication into a particular country's laws.

introduction   Preliminary remarks pertaining to a piece. Like a foreword, an introduction can be written by the author or an appropriate authority on the subject. If a book has both a foreword and an introduction, the foreword will be written by someone other than the author; the introduction will be more closely tied to the text and will be written by the book's author. (See **foreword**.)

ISBN (International Standard Book Number)   A ten-digit number that is keyed to and identifies the title and publisher of a book. It is used for ordering and cataloging books and appears on all dust jackets, on the back cover of the book, and on the copyright page.

ISSN (International Standard Serial Number)   An eight-digit cataloging and ordering number that identifies all U.S. and foreign periodicals.

J

juveniles   (See **children's books**.)

K

kill fee   A fee paid by a magazine when it cancels a commissioned article. The fee is only a certain percentage of the agreed-on payment for the assignment (no more than

50 percent). Not all publishers pay kill fees; a writer should make sure to formalize such an arrangement in advance. Kill fees are sometimes involved in work-for-hire projects in book publishing.

L

lead The crucial first few sentences, phrases, or words of anything—be it a query letter, book proposal, novel, news release, advertisement, or sales tipsheet. A successful lead immediately hooks the reader, consumer, editor, or agent.

lead title A frontlist book featured by the publisher during a given season—one the publisher believes should do extremely well commercially. Lead titles are usually those given the publisher's maximum promotional push.

letterhead Business stationery and envelopes imprinted with the company's (or, in such a case, the writer's) name, address, and logo—a convenience as well as an impressive asset for a freelance writer.

letterpress A form of printing in which set type is inked, then impressed directly onto the printing surface. Now used primarily for limited-run books-as-fine-art projects. (See **offset**.)

libel Defamation of an individual or individuals in a published work, with malice aforethought. In litigation, the falsity of the libelous statements or representations, as well the intention of malice, has to be proved for there to be libel; in addition, financial damages to the parties so libeled must be incurred as a result of the material in question for there to be an assessment of the amount of damages to be awarded to a claimant. This is contrasted to slander, which is defamation through the spoken word.

Library of Congress The largest library in the world is in Washington, DC. As part of its many services, the LOC will supply a writer with up-to-date sources and bibliographies in all fields, from arts and humanities to science and technology. For details, write to the Library of Congress, Central Services Division, Washington, DC 20540.

Library of Congress Catalog Card Number An identifying number issued by the Library of Congress to books it has accepted for its collection. The publication of those books, which are submitted by the publisher, are announced by the Library of Congress to libraries, which use Library of Congress numbers for their own ordering and cataloging purposes.

literature Written works of fiction and nonfiction in which compositional excellence and advancement in the art of writing are higher priorities than are considerations of profit or commercial appeal.

Literary Market Place (*LMP*) An annual directory of the publishing industry that contains a comprehensive list of publishers, alphabetically and by category, with their addresses, phone numbers, some personnel, and the types of books they publish. Also included are various publishing-allied listings, such as literary agencies, writer's conferences and competitions, and editorial and distribution services. *LMP* is published by R. R. Bowker and is available in most public libraries.

logo A company or product identifier—for example, a representation of a company's initials or a drawing that is the exclusive property of that company. In publishing usage, a virtual equivalent to the trademark.

M

mainstream fiction Nongenre fiction, excluding literary or avant-garde fiction, that appeals to a general readership.

marketing plan The entire strategy for selling a book: its publicity, promotion, sales, and advertising.

mass-market paperback Less-expensive smaller-format paperbacks that are sold from racks (in venues such as supermarkets, variety stores, drugstores, and specialty shops) as well as in bookstores. Also referred to as rack (or rack-sized) editions.

mechanicals Typeset copy and art mounted on boards to be photocopied and printed. Also referred to as paste-ups.

midlist books Generally mainstream fiction and nonfiction books that traditionally formed the bulk of a publisher's list (nowadays often by default rather than by intent). Midlist books are expected to be commercially viable but not explosive best-sellers— nor are they viewed as distinguished, critically respected books that can be scheduled for small print runs and aimed at select readerships. Agents may view such projects as a poor return for the effort, since they generally garner a low-end advance; editors and publishers (especially the sales force) may decry midlist works as being hard to market; prospective readers often find midlist books hard to buy in bookstores (they have short shelf lives). Hint for writers: Don't present your work as a midlist item.

multimedia Presentations of sound and light, words in magnetically graven image— and any known combination thereof as well as nuances yet to come. Though computer CD is the dominant wrapper for these works, technological innovation is the hallmark of the electronic-publishing arena, and new formats will doubtless come of age and expand the market potential. Multimedia books are publishing events; their advent suggests alternative avenues for authors as well as adaptational tie-ins with the world of print. Meanwhile, please stay tuned for virtual reality, artificial intelligence, and electronic end-user distribution of product.

multiple contract A book contract that includes a provisional agreement for a future book or books. (See **option clause.**)

mystery stories or **mysteries** (See **suspense fiction.**)

N

net receipts   The amount of money a publisher actually receives for sales of a book: the retail price minus the bookseller's discount and/or other discount. The number of returned copies is factored in, bringing down even further the net amount received per book. Royalties are sometimes figured on these lower amounts rather than on the retail price of the book.

new age   An eclectic category that encompasses health, medicine, philosophy, religion, and the occult—presented from an alternative or multicultural perspective. Although the term has achieved currency relatively recently, some publishers have been producing serious books in these categories for decades.

novella   A work of fiction falling in length between a short story and a novel.

O

offset or **offset lithography**   A printing process that involves the transfer of wet ink from a (usually photosensitized) printing plate onto an intermediate surface (such as a rubber-coated cylinder) and then onto the paper. For commercial purposes, this method has replaced letterpress, whereby books were printed via direct impression of inked type on paper.

option clause/right of first refusal   In a book contract, a clause that stipulates that the publisher will have the exclusive right to consider and make an offer for the author's next book. However, the publisher is under no obligation to publish the book, and in most variations of the clause the author may, under certain circumstances, opt for publication elsewhere. (See **multiple contract**.)

outline   Used for both a book proposal and the actual writing and structuring of a book, an outline is a hierarchical listing of topics that provides the writer (and the proposal reader) with an overview of the ideas in a book in the order in which they are to be presented.

out-of-print books   Books no longer available from the publisher; rights usually revert to the author.

P

package   The package is the actual book; the physical product.

packager   (See **book producer**.)

page proof   The final typeset copy of the book, in page-layout form, before printing.

paperback   Books bound with a flexible, stress-resistant, paper covering material. (See **binding**.)

paperback originals   Books published, generally, in paperback editions only; sometimes the term refers to those books published simultaneously in hardcover and paperback. These books are often mass-market genre fiction (romances, Westerns, Gothics, mysteries, horror, and so forth) as well as contemporary literary fiction, cookbooks, humor, career books, self-improvement, and how-to books—the categories continue to expand.

paste-ups   (See **mechanicals**.)

permissions   The right to quote or reprint published material, obtained by the author from the copyright holder.

picture book   A copiously illustrated book, often with very simple, limited text, intended for preschoolers and very young children.

plagiarism   The false presentation of someone else's writing as one's own. In the case of copyrighted work, plagiarism is illegal.

preface   An element of a book's frontmatter. In the preface, the author may discuss the purpose behind the format of the book, the type of research on which it is based, its genesis, or its underlying philosophy.

premium   Books sold at a reduced price as part of a special promotion. Premiums can thus be sold to a bookseller, who in turn sells them to the bookbuyer (as with a line of modestly priced art books). Alternately, such books may be produced as part of a broader marketing package. For instance, an organization may acquire a number of books (such as its own corporate history or biography of its founder) for use in personnel training and as giveaways to clients, or a nutrition/recipe book may be displayed along with a company's diet foods in nonbookstore outlets. (See **special sales**.)

press agent   (See **publicist**.)

press kit   A promotional package that includes a press release, tipsheet, author biography and photograph, reviews, and other pertinent information. The press kit can be put together by the publisher's publicity department or by an independent publicist and sent with a review copy of the book to potential reviewers and to media professionals responsible for booking author appearances.

price   There are several prices pertaining to a single book: The invoice price is the amount the publisher charges the bookseller; the retail, cover, or list price is what the consumer pays.

printer's error (PE)   A typographical error made by the printer or typesetting facility, not by the publisher's staff. PEs are corrected at the printer's expense.

printing plate   A surface that bears a reproduction of the set type and artwork of a book, from which the pages are printed.

producer   (See **book producer**.)

proposal   A detailed presentation of the book's concept, used to gain the interest and services of an agent and to sell the project to a publisher.

publication date or **pub date** A book's official date of publication, customarily set by the publisher to fall six weeks after completed bound books are delivered to the warehouse. The publication date is used to focus the promotional activities on behalf of the title—in order that books will have had time to be ordered, shipped, and be available in the stores to coincide with the appearance of advertising and publicity.

public domain Material that is not copyrighted, whose copyright has expired, or is not copyrightable. The last includes government publications, jokes, titles—and, it should be remembered, ideas.

publicist (press agent) The publicity professional who handles the press releases for new books and arranges the author's publicity tours and other promotional venues (such as interviews, speaking engagements, and book signings).

publisher's catalog A seasonal sales catalog that lists and describes a publisher's new books; it is sent to all potential buyers, including individuals who request one. Catalogs range from the basic to the glitzy, and often include information on the author, on print quantity, and the amount of money slated to be spent on publicity and promotion.

publisher's discount The percentage by which a publisher discounts the retail price of a book to a bookseller, often based in part on the number of copies purchased.

Publishers' Trade List Annual A collection of current and backlist catalogs arranged alphabetically by publisher, available in many libraries.

Publishers Weekly (PW) The publishing industry's chief trade journal. *PW* carries announcements of upcoming books, respected book reviews, interviews with authors and publishing-industry professionals, special reports on various book categories, and trade news (such as mergers, rights sales, and personnel changes).

Q

quality In publishing parlance, the word *quality* in reference to a book category (such as quality fiction) or format (quality paperback) is a term of art—individual works or lines so described are presented as outstanding products.

query letter A brief written presentation to an agent or editor designed to pitch both the writer and the book idea.

R

remainders Unsold book stock. Remainders can include titles that have not sold as well as anticipated, in addition to unsold copies of later printings of best-sellers. These volumes are often remaindered—that is, remaining stock is purchased from the publisher at a huge discount and resold to the public.

reprint A subsequent edition of material that is already in print, especially publication in a different format—the paperback reprint of a hardcover, for example.

résumé A summary of an individual's career experience and education. When a résumé is sent to prospective agents or publishers, it should contain the author's vital publishing credits, specialty credentials, and pertinent personal experience. Also referred to as the curriculum vitae or, more simply, vita.

returns Unsold books returned to a publisher by a bookstore, for which the store may receive full or partial credit (depending on the publisher's policy, the age of the book, and so on).

reversion-of-rights clause In the book contract, a clause that states that if the book goes out of print or the publisher fails to reprint the book within a stipulated length of time, all rights revert to the author.

review copy A free copy of a (usually) new book sent to print and electronic media that review books for their audiences.

romance fiction or **romance novels** Modern or period love stories, always with happy endings, which range from the tepid to the torrid. Except for certain erotic-specialty lines, romances do not feature graphic sex. Often mistakenly pigeonholed by those who do not read them, romances and romance writers have been influential in the movement away from passive and coddled female fictional characters to the strong, active modern woman in a tale that reflects areas of topical social concern.

royalty The percentage of the retail cost of a book that is paid to the author for each copy sold after the author's advance has been recouped. Some publishers structure royalties as a percentage payment against net receipts.

S

SASE (self-addressed stamped envelope) It is customary for an author to enclose SASEs with query letters, with proposals, and with manuscript submissions. Many editors and agents do not reply if a writer has neglected to enclose an SASE with correspondence or submitted materials.

sales conference A meeting of a publisher's editorial and sales departments and senior promotion and publicity staff members. A sales conference covers the upcoming season's new books, and marketing strategies are discussed. Sometimes sales conferences are the basis on which proposed titles are bought or not.

sales representative or **sales rep** A member of the publisher's sales force or an independent contractor who, armed with a book catalog and order forms, visits bookstores in a certain territory to sell books to retailers.

satisfactory clause In book contracts, a publisher will reserve the right to refuse publication of a manuscript that is not deemed satisfactory. Because the author may be forced to pay back the publisher's advance if the complete work is found to be unsatisfactory, in order to protect the author the specific criteria for publisher satisfaction should be set forth in the contract.

science fiction   Science fiction includes the hardcore, imaginatively embellished technological/scientific novel as well as fiction that is even slightly futuristic (often with an after-the-holocaust milieu—nuclear, environmental, extraterrestrial, genocidal).

science fiction/fantasy   A category fiction designation that actually collapses two genres into one (for bookseller-marketing reference, of course—though it drives some devotees of these separate fields of writing nuts). In addition, many editors and publishers specialize in both of these genres and thus categorize their interests with catch phrases such as sci-fi/fantasy.

screenplay   A film script—either original or one based on material published previously in another form, such as a television docudrama based on a nonfiction book or a movie thriller based on an espionage novel. (Compare with **teleplay**.)

self-publishing   A publishing project wherein an author pays for the costs of manufacturing and selling his or her own book and retains all money from the book's sale. This is a risky venture but can be immensely profitable (especially when combined with an author's speaking engagements or imaginative marketing techniques). In addition, if successful, self-publication can lead to distribution or publication by a commercial publisher. Compare with **subsidy publishing**.

self-syndication   Management by writers or journalists of functions that are otherwise performed by syndicates specializing in such services. In self-syndication, it is the writer who manages copyrights, negotiates fees, and handles sales, billing, and other tasks involved in circulating journalistic pieces through newspapers, magazines, or other periodicals that pick up the author's column or run a series of articles.

serial rights   Reprint rights sold to periodicals. First serial rights include the right to publish the material before anyone else (generally before the book is released, or coinciding with the book's official publication)—either for the U.S. or for a wider territory. Second serial rights cover material already published, either in a book or another periodical.

serialization   The reprinting of a book or part of a book in a newspaper or magazine. Serialization before (or perhaps simultaneously with) the publication of the book is called first serial. The first reprint after publication (either as a book or by another periodical) is called second serial.

series   Books published as a group either because of their related subject matter (such as a biographical series on modern artists or on World War II aircraft) and/or single authorship (a set of works by Anaïs Nin). This is a ready-made niche for an industrious author or compiler/editor who is up-to-date on a publisher's program and has a brace of pertinent qualifications and/or contacts. In contemporary fiction, some genre works are published in series form (such as family sagas, detective series, fantasy cycles).

shelf life   The amount of time an unsold book remains on the bookstore shelf before the store manager pulls it to make room for newer incoming stock with greater (or at least untested) sales potential.

short story A brief piece of fiction that is more pointed and more economically detailed as to character, situation, and plot than a novel. Published collections of short stories—whether by one or several authors—often revolve around a single theme, express related outlooks, or comprise variations within a genre.

signature A group of book pages that have been printed together on one large sheet of paper that is then folded and cut in preparation for being bound, along with the book's other signatures, into the final volume.

simultaneous publication The issuing at the same time of more than one edition of a work, such as in hardcover and trade paperback. Simultaneous releases can be expanded to include (though rarely) deluxe gift editions of a book as well as mass-market paper versions.

simultaneous (or multiple) submissions The submission of the same material to more than one publisher at the same time. Although simultaneous submission is a common practice, publishers should always be made aware that it is being done. Multiple submissions by an author to several agents is, on the other hand, a practice that is sometimes not regarded with great favor by the agent.

slush pile The morass of unsolicited manuscripts at a publishing house or literary agency, which may fester indefinitely awaiting (perhaps perfunctory) review. Some publishers or agencies do not maintain slush piles per se—unsolicited manuscripts are slated for instant return without review (if an SASE is included) or may otherwise be literally or figuratively pitched to the wind. Querying a targeted publisher or agent before submitting a manuscript is an excellent way of avoiding, or at least minimizing the possibility of, such an ignoble fate.

software Programs that run on a computer. Word processing software includes programs that enable writers to compose, edit, store, and print material. Professional-quality software packages incorporate amenities such as databases that can feed the results of research electronically into the final manuscript, alphabetization and indexing functions, and capabilities for constructing tables and charts and adding graphics to the body of the manuscript. Software should be appropriate to both the demands of the work at hand and the requirements of the publisher (which may contract for a manuscript suitable for on-disk editing and electronic design, composition, and typesetting).

special sales Sales of a book to appropriate retailers other than bookstores (for example, wine guides to liquor stores). This classification also includes books sold as premiums (for example, to a convention group or a corporation) for promotional purposes. Depending on volume, per-unit costs can be very low, and the book can be custom designed. (See **premiums**.)

spine That portion of the book's casing (or binding) that backs the bound signatures and is visible when the volume is aligned on a bookshelf.

stamping In book publishing, the impression of ornamental type and images (such as a logo) on the book's binding, using a die with raised or intaglioed surface to apply ink stamping or metallic-leaf stamping.

subsidiary rights   The reprint, serial, movie and television, as well as audiotape and videotape rights deriving from a book. The division of profits between publisher and author from the sales of these rights is determined through negotiation. In more elaborately commercial projects, details such as syndication of related articles and licensing of characters may ultimately be involved.

subsidy publishing   A mode of publication wherein the author pays a publishing company to produce his or her work, which may thus appear superficially to have been conventionally published. Subsidy publishing (alias vanity publishing) is generally more expensive than self-publishing, because the subsidy house makes a profit on all its contracted functions, charging fees well beyond basic costs for production and services.

suspense fiction   Fiction within a number of genre categories that emphasize suspense as well as the usual (and sometimes unusual) literary techniques to keep the reader engaged. Suspense fiction encompasses novels of crime and detection (regularly referred to as mysteries—these include English-style cozies; American-style hard-boiled detective stories; dispassionate law-enforcement procedurals; crime stories), action-adventure, espionage novels, technothrillers, tales of psychological suspense, and horror. A celebrated aspect of suspense fiction's popular appeal—one that surely accounts for much of the category's sustained market vigor—is the interactive element: The reader may choose to challenge the tale itself by attempting to outwit the author and solve a crime before detectives do, figure out how best to defeat a demon before the hero does, or parse out the elements of a conspiracy before the writer reveals the whole story.

syndicated column   Material published simultaneously in a number of newspapers or magazines. The author shares the income from syndication with the syndicate that negotiates the sale. (See **self-syndication**.)

syndication rights   (See **self-syndication**, **subsidiary rights**.)

synopsis   A summary in paragraph form, rather than in outline format. The synopsis is an important part of a book proposal. For fiction, the synopsis portrays the high points of story line and plot, succinctly and dynamically. In a nonfiction book proposal, the synopsis describes the thrust and content of the successive chapters (and/or parts) of the manuscript.

T

table of contents   A listing of a book's chapters and other sections (such as the front-matter, appendix, index, and bibliography), or of a magazine's articles and columns, in the order in which they appear; in published versions, the table of contents indicates the respective beginning page numbers.

tabloid   A smaller-than-standard-size newspaper (daily, weekly, or monthly); traditionally, certain tabloids are distinguished by sensationalism of approach and content rather than by straightforward reportage of newsworthy events. In common parlance, *tabloid* is used to describe works in various media (including books) that cater to immoderate tastes (e.g., tabloid exposé, tabloid television; the tabloidization of popular culture).

teleplay   A **screenplay** geared toward television production. Similar in overall concept to screenplays for the cinema, teleplays are nonetheless inherently concerned with such TV-loaded provisions as the physical dimensions of the smaller screen, and formal elements of pacing and structure keyed to stipulated program length and the placement of commercial advertising. Attention to television demands is fundamental to the viability of a project.

terms   The financial conditions agreed to in a book contract.

theme   A general term for the underlying concept of a book. (See **hook**.)

thriller   A thriller is a novel of suspense with a plot structure that conforms to a cat-and-mouse game, with a sense of the hunt being paramount. Thrillers can be spy novels, tales of geopolitical crisis, legal thrillers, medical thrillers, technothrillers. The common thread is a growing sense of threat and the excitement of the chase.

tipsheet   An information sheet on a single book that presents general publication information (publication date, editor, ISBN, etc.), a brief synopsis of the book, information on competing books, and other relevant marketing data such as author profile and advance blurbs. The tipsheet is given to the sales and publicity departments; a version of the tipsheet is also included in press kits.

title page   The page at the front of a book that lists the title, subtitle, author (and other contributors, such as translator or illustrator), as well as the publishing house and sometimes its logo.

trade books   Books distributed through the book trade—meaning bookstores and major book clubs—as opposed to, for example, mass-market paperbacks, which are sold at magazine racks, newsstands, and supermarkets as well.

trade discount   The discount from the cover or list price that a publisher gives the bookseller. It is usually proportional to the number of books ordered (the larger the order, the greater the discount), and typically varies between 40 and 50 percent.

trade list   A catalog of all of a publisher's books in print, with ISBNs and order information. The trade list sometimes includes descriptions of the current season's new books.

trade (quality) paperbacks   Reprints or original titles published in paperback format, larger in dimension than mass-market paperbacks, and distributed through regular retail book channels. Trade paperbacks tend to be in the neighborhood of twice the price of an equivalent mass-market paperback edition and about half to two-thirds the price of comparable hardcover versions.

trade publishers   Publishers of books for a general readership—that is, nonprofessional, nonacademic books that are distributed primarily through bookstores.

translation rights   Rights sold either to a foreign agent or directly to a foreign publisher, either by the author's agent or by the original publisher.

treatment   In screenwriting, a full narrative description of the story, including sample dialogue.

U

unauthorized biography   A history of a person's life written without the consent or collaboration of the subject or the subject's survivors.

university press   A publishing house affiliated with a sponsoring university. The university press is generally nonprofit and subsidized by the respective university. Generally, university presses publish noncommercial scholarly nonfiction books written by academics, and their lists may include literary fiction, criticism, and poetry. Some university presses also specialize in titles of regional interest, and many acquire projects intended for commercial distribution.

unsolicited manuscript   A manuscript sent to an editor or agent without being requested by the editor/agent.

V

vanity press   A publisher that publishes books only at an author's expense—and will generally agree to publish virtually anything that is submitted and paid for. (See **subsidy publishing**.)

vita   Latin word for "life." A shortened equivalent term for *curriculum vitae* (see **résumé**).

W

word count   The number of words in a given document. When noted on a manuscript, the word count is usually rounded off to the nearest 100 words.

work-for-hire   Writing done for an employer, or writing commissioned by a publisher or book packager who retains ownership of, and all rights pertaining to, the written material.

Y

young-adult (YA) books   Books for readers generally between the ages of twelve and seventeen. Young-adult fiction often deals with issues of concern to contemporary teens.

young readers or **younger readers**   Publishing terminology for the range of programs that address the earliest readers through young adults.

Z

zombie or **zombi**   In idiomatic usage, a zombie is a person whose conduct approximates that of an automaton; hence some people in book publishing may be characterized as zombies.

Suggested Resources

The American Heritage Dictionary of the English Language (third edition) (Boston: Houghton Mifflin, 1992; updated periodically). Among American dictionaries intended for desktop use, *The American Heritage Dictionary* stands out as the most careful, comprehensive, and literate. The practicality and charm of this reference volume is reflected in a fine balance of layout, design, and illustrations; combined with articulate definitions, usage notes, and historical details of the American lexicon, *The American Heritage Dictionary* is a rich resource for professional American writers (as well as full-blooded dictionary fans).

Appelbaum, Judith. *How to Get Happily Published* (fourth edition) (New York: Harper & Row, 1988; NAL, 1992). Beyond the mere how-to-get-published primer; sensible advice on generating ideas, putting them into words, and maintaining control over the editing, sales, and marketing of one's work.

Appelbaum, Judith, Nancy Evans, and Florence Janovic. *The Sensible Solutions How to Get Happily Published Handbook* (New York: Sensible Solutions, 1981). Worksheets and additional information for authors of trade books, designed to be used in conjunction with *How to Get Happily Published.*

Aronson, Charles N. *The Writer Publisher* (Arcade, NY: Charles Aronson, 1976). Fascinating, often-horrific, account of the author's experience with a major vanity press; also details the travails of self-publishing. Long out of print masterwork—look for it in used-book bins and specialty book dealer catalogs.

The Associated Press. *The Associated Press Stylebook and Libel Manual* (Reading, MA: Addison-Wesley, 1994). Easy to use, set up in dictionary format; adroit quick-reference guide to contemporary journalistic and mainstream usage. Far from comprehensive, but addresses most frequently encountered day-to-day nuts-and-bolts writing considerations. Treatment of libel issues is a must-read for investigative and opinionative writing. Materials pertaining to gaining resources under the authority of the Freedom of Information Act provides essential background for projects in the public interest. Fully revised and updated edition is edited by Norm Goldstein.

The Association of American University Presses Directory (Chicago: University of Chicago Press, published annually). Detailed description of each AAUP member press with a summary of its publishing program, names and responsibilities of key staff, and requirements for submitting proposals and manuscripts.

Atchity, Kenneth J. *A Writer's Time: A Guide to the Creative Process, from Vision through Revision* (second edition) (New York: Norton, 1995). Comprehensive in approach and scope, this handbook offers a stylish account of how to get in tune, stay attuned, and fine-tune your writing skills. Includes section on effective marketing for writers.

Balkin, Richard. *How to Understand and Negotiate a Book Contract or Magazine Agreement* (Cincinnati: Writer's Digest Books, 1985). Essential reading for every writer who stands to make a sale. Author is an established agent.

Ballon, Rachel. *Blueprint for Writing: A Writer's Guide to Creativity, Craft, and Career* (Los Angeles: Lowell House, 1994). Whether it be a novel, story, or script, carefully crafted narratives require development of such basic elements as structure, plot, and character in order to create depth, focus—and entertainment value. This book helps the professional writer fine-tune a work and demystifies the writing process for rookies. Author is founder and director of the Writer's Center in Los Angeles.

Barzun, Jacques. *Simple & Direct: A Rhetoric for Writers* (revised edition) (Chicago: University of Chicago Press, 1994). Techniques to take a writer's craft to new heights of effectiveness and expressiveness, through diction, syntax, tone, meaning, composition, and revision. Exercises, model passages, and amusing examples of style gone bad.

Bates, Jem, and Adrian Waller. *The Canadian Writer's Market: An Extensive Guide for Freelance Writers* (eleventh revised edition) (Toronto: McClelland & Stewart, 1994). Provides writers with resources keyed to the Canadian market in magazines and book publishing. Includes advice, strategies, and editorial guidelines for thriving in the professional marketplace; information pertaining to writing courses, prizes, and awards; as well as some crossover market listings for the United States industry.

Bernard, André (editor). *Rotten Rejections* (Wainscott, NY: Pushcart Press, 1990). Humorous and harrowing collection of literary rejection letters to such recipients as William Faulkner, Gustave Flaubert, James Joyce, and Vladimir Nabokov. Fine inspiration for writers encountering rejection during any phase of their careers.

Bernstein, Theodore. *The Careful Writer: A Modern Guide to English Usage* (New York: Atheneum, 1965). Lively, accurate, and articulate classic. Mainstream and mass-market writers may view it as too high-toned a tome to grace their shelves, but this work nevertheless addresses their needs accessibly with observations they might well heed.

Bernstein, Theodore. *Miss Thistlebottom's Hobgoblins: The Careful Writer's Guide to the Taboos, Bugbears, and Outmoded Rules of English Usage* (New York: Simon & Schuster, 1984). More apt insights from the author of *The Careful Writer*.

Block, Lawrence. *Telling Lies for Fun and Profit: A Manual for Fiction Writers* (New York: William Morrow/Quill, 1981). Inside look at winning techniques and career strategies by an admired master of both. Introduction to the new edition is by Sue Grafton.

Borcherding, David H. (editor). *Romance Writer's Sourcebook: Where to Sell Your Manuscripts* (Cincinnati: Writer's Digest Books, updated periodically). Illuminating essays and valuable resources to guide writers of romances through the reaches of this vast sector of the fiction market.

Boston, Bruce O. (editor). *Stet! Tricks of the Trade for Writers and Editors* (Alexandria, VA: Editorial Experts, 1986). Supple, interactive collection of articles that sets the writer inside the heads of editors and publishers.

Boswell, John. *The Awful Truth About Publishing: Why They Always Reject Your Manuscript . . . And What You Can Do About It* (New York: Warner Books, 1986). A view from the other side—that is, the inside view from within the large publishing house.

Brown, Rita Mae. *Starting from Scratch: A Different Kind of Writer's Manual* (New York: Bantam, 1988). Courage, philosophy, and practical guidance for holding to and honing your writer's vision through the travails of publishing.

Browne, Renni, and Dave King. *Self-Editing for Fiction Writers* (New York: HarperCollins, 1993). Guidance in an often-overlooked area that is crucial for today's fiction writers. In an age when many editors are too overworked to do it for you, you better know how to do it yourself.

Bunnin, Brad, and Peter Beren. *Author Law and Strategies: A Personal Guide for the Working Writer* (Berkeley: Nolo Press, 1984). The ins and outs of publishing laws, published by specialists in do-it-yourself legal guides.

Burgett, Gordon. *The Writer's Guide to Query Letters and Cover Letters* (Rocklin, CA: Prima Publishing, 1992). Sound and pointed advice, from an expert's perspective, on how to utilize the query and cover letter to sell your writing.

The Chicago Manual of Style (fourteenth edition) (Chicago: University of Chicago Press, 1993). In matters of editorial style—punctuation, spelling, capitalization, issues of usage—this book provides traditional, conservative, and justifiable guidelines. This esteemed work is not, however, a handbook of grammar per se and does not offer writers ready tips for resolving day-to-day creative and compositional questions. The *Chicago Manual* is, rather, a professional reference work for the publishing and editing trades—and in this area it remains the American standard. Many commercial writers and editors characterize the *Chicago Manual* as intricate and arcane relative to their own reference demands.

Clardy, Andrea Fleck. *Words to the Wise: A Writer's Guide to Feminist and Lesbian Periodicals & Publishers* (Ithaca, NY: Firebrand, 1993; updated periodically). Popular pamphlet-sized handbook lists more than 150 United States and Canadian book and periodical publishers, references for children's book and scholarly publishers, and submissions and payment policies—keyed to publishing enterprises that actively acquire women's words.

Collier, Oscar, with Frances Spatz Leighton. *How to Write and Sell Your First Nonfiction Book* (New York: St. Martin's, 1994). Practical, encouraging how-to from industry professionals. Topics include choosing a subject, targeting an audience, proposal writing, researching effectively and conducting interviews, dealing with agents and editors, understanding contracts, and marketing your book.

Curtis, Richard. *Beyond the Bestseller: A Literary Agent Takes You Inside the Book Business* (New York: NAL, 1989; Plume, 1990). Incisive and practical advice, from a literary agent who is also an accomplished writer.

Curtis, Richard. *How to Be Your Own Literary Agent: The Business of Getting Your Book Published* (Boston: Houghton Mifflin, 1984). Insights and how-to; a personal point of view from one who knows the ropes and shows them to you.

Davidson, Jeffrey P. *Marketing for the Home-Based Business* (Holbrook, MA: Bob Adams, 1991). For entrepreneurs of all stripes (including writers) who are based in their homes. Digs beneath the obvious and uncovers ways to project a professional image and transform your computer, telephone, and fax into a dynamic marketing staff.

Dotson, Edisol W. *Putting Out: The Essential Publishing Resource for Lesbian and Gay Writers* (Pittsburgh, PA: Cleis Press, 1995; updated periodically). Specialized reference tool lists book publishers, magazines, newspapers, newsletters, theater groups, and agents—all of them with an interest in publishing, producing, or agenting gay and lesbian writing. Includes nuts-and-bolts submissions guidelines, pertinent publishers' marketing budgets, publishers' selection policies. How-to essays cover project development, contracts, marketing.

Dustbooks (editors). The renowned Small Press Information Library includes four separate books: *The Directory of Small Press Editors & Publishers*; *Directory of Poetry Publishers*; *The International Directory of Little Magazines and Small Presses*; and *Small Press Record of Books in Print* (Paradise, CA: Dustbooks, all volumes published annually). This set of references, geared toward the literary arena, is produced by the publishers of the industry journal *Small Press Review*. These resources for market exploration also provide writers with editorial requirements and procedures for manuscript submission keyed to individual publishers and periodicals.

Fry, Ronald W. (editor). *Book Publishing Career Directory* (Hawthorne, NJ: Career Press, published annually). Descriptions of various publishing jobs by those who actually do them, plus advice on securing those positions.

Gage, Diane, and Marcia Hibsch Coppess. *Get Published: Editors From the Nation's Top Magazines Tell You What They Want* (New York: Henry Holt, 1986). An extensive survey of dozens of national magazines—who they are and what they're looking for.

Gardner, John. *On Becoming a Novelist* (New York: Harper & Row, 1983). Sympathetic and enjoyable account of the education, art, and survival of the beginning writer.

Goldberg, Natalie. *Writing Down the Bones: Freeing the Writer Within* (Boston: Shambhala Publications, 1986). Thought-provoking and practical advice on the art and technique of writing. The author is a Zen Buddhist and writing instructor.

Goldberg, Natalie. *Wild Mind: Living the Writer's Life* (New York: Bantam, 1990). Enlightened counseling and illuminating exercises to get the most from, and into, your craft.

Gross, Gerald (editor). *Editors on Editing: What Writers Need to Know about What Editors Do* (New York: Grove/Atlantic Monthly Press, 1993). Celebrated editor and book doctor Jerry Gross offers a revised and updated edition of this consummate resource classic. Covering virtually every area of trade publishing from the large commercial houses to the small literary presses, top editors offer astute, practical, and provocative discussions of the author/editor relationship. Includes valuable tips on how to prospect, delineates the editorial process, and details what writers can do to benefit most from an editor's attention.

Harman, Eleanor, and Ian Montagnes (editors). *The Thesis and the Book* (Toronto: University of Toronto Press, 1976). Selection of articles about the revision of scholarly presentations into works of broader appeal. The discussion of the demands of specialist audiences versus those of a wider market is pertinent to the development of general nonfiction projects—especially those involving collaboration between writing professionals and academics.

Henderson, Bill. *The Publish-It-Yourself Handbook: Literary Tradition and How-to without Commercial or Vanity Publishers* (New York: Norton/Pushcart, 1987). Eminently readable classic comprising tales—both inspirational and cautionary—by persons who have self-published.

Herman, Jeff, and Deborah M. Adams. *Write the Perfect Book Proposal: 10 Proposals That Sold and Why* (New York: Wiley, 1993). Analysis of successful nonfiction book proposals with pointed and insightful commentary from a team of accomplished industry professionals—New York literary agent Jeff Herman and book-proposal doctor (and author) Deborah Adams. Doesn't just tell you how to do it—this book shows you in detail how it was done.

Hollywood Creative Directory (Santa Monica, CA: HCD, updated periodically). Resources available in print, on diskette, or on-line. HCD also publishes *Hollywood Financial Directory*, *Hollywood Distributors Directory*, *Hollywood Movie Music Directory*, *Hollywood Interactive Entertainment Directory*, and *Hollywood Agents & Managers Directory*—as well as other specialized reference and resource materials, including mailing lists and labels.

Horowitz, Lois. *Knowing Where to Look: The Ultimate Guide to Research* (Cincinnati: Writer's Digest Books, 1984). An invaluable tool for anyone who has to dig up elusive facts and figures.

Huddle, David. *The Writing Habit: Essays* (Layton, UT: Gibbs Smith, 1992). A serious, useful book on the literary craft. Much more than a how-to guide; provides practical, energetic, supportive advice and imaginative approach to learning tricks of the trade.

Hudson, Bob. *Christian Writer's Manual of Style* (Grand Rapids, MI: Zondervan, 1988). Valuable overview and helpful details pertaining to writing expression and stylistic conventions in the field of Christian writing; directed toward the academic and professional market as well as more general readership.

Jacobsohn, Rachel. *The Reading Group Handbook: Everything You Need to Know, From Choosing Members to Leading Discussions* (New York: Hyperion, 1994). Reading groups are proliferating and thriving nationwide; such fellowships are sponsored by bookstores as well as book lovers (including writers) as fun, stimulating, and interactive recreational venues through which (incidentally) to support our home industry. This handbook takes readers through the territory and provides a variety of resource listings.

Judson, Jerome. *The Poet's Handbook* (Cincinnati: Writer's Digest Books, 1980). The art and mechanics of writing poetry by "rule" and example. Also includes tips on getting published.

Judson, Jerome. *On Being a Poet* (Cincinnati: Writer's Digest Books, 1984). A discussion of the art of poetry—both the author's and that of other poets.

Judson, Jerome. *Poet's Market* (Cincinnati: Writer's Digest Books, published annually). Market-research resource for the poet.

Killian, Kristi, and Sheila Bender. *Writing in a Convertible with the Top Down* (New York: Warner Books, 1992). How to quit stalling, shift into creative gear, and speed successfully on your way through the all-terrain territory known as publishing country. Wealth of advice and inspiration—as lively and informal as it is pertinent.

Kilpatrick, James J. *The Writer's Art* (Kansas City, MO: Andrews, McMeel & Parker, 1984). An opinionated discussion of proper usage, style, and just plain good writing from one of the news business's most popular curmudgeons.

Klauser, Henriette Anne. *Writing on Both Sides of the Brain: Breakthrough Techniques for People Who Write* (New York: Harper & Row, 1986). How to refrain from editing while you write; how to edit, mercilessly and creatively, what you've just written.

Klauser, Henriette Anne. *Put Your Heart on Paper: Staying Connected in a Loose-Ends World* (New York: Bantam, 1995). How to communicate, create, and relate through the written word. Invaluable tales and techniques that apply equally to the writer's craft and everyday life.

Kremer, John. *101 Ways to Market Your Books—For Publishers and Authors* (Fairfield, IA: Ad-Lib Publications, 1986). Sensible, innovative, and inspiring advice on producing the most marketable book possible and then marketing it as effectively as possible.

Kremer, John. *Book Publishing Resource Guide* (Fairfield, IA: Ad-Lib Publications, updated periodically). Comprehensive listings for book-marketing contacts and resources—contains a vast bibliography and references to other resource guides.

Lamott, Anne. *Bird by Bird: Some Instructions on Writing and Life* (New York: Pantheon, 1994). Breathtakingly evocative and insightful commentary on commitment, training, and craft, and what it means to be a writer.

Larsen, Michael. *How to Write a Book Proposal* (Cincinnati: Writer's Digest Books, 1985). A clear and no-nonsense—even inspiring—step-by-step guide to the book proposal. Author is West Coast–based literary agent and writer.

Literary Market Place (New York: R.R. Bowker, published annually). Hefty annual directory of the publishing industry, including publishing houses and their personnel, literary agencies, and writers' organizations and events, as well as research, writing, editing, and publishing services nationwide.

Litowinsky, Olga. *Writing and Publishing Books for Children in the 1990s: The Inside Story from the Editor's Desk* (New York: Walker & Company, 1992). A leading editor and literary agent elucidates the world of children's and young-adult publishing. Consummate advice on writing for young readers, and for avoiding the many pitfalls in this hard-to-break-into field.

Long, Duncan. *You Can Be an Information Writer* (Port Townsend, WA: Loompanics, 1991). Irreverent resource manual shows where opportunities and money are in the burgeoning market for technical documentation, specialist articles, topical investigative reports, up-to-the-minute how-to guides, and advertising. Section on research techniques demonstrates ways to shave time and pump up the bucks simultaneously.

Luey, Beth. *Handbook for Academic Authors* (revised edition) (New York: Cambridge University Press, 1990). This reference pinpoints key (and unsuspected) considerations important in the field of academic publishing; valuable information with strategic implications for players in the publish-or-perish game.

Maass, Donald. *The Career Novelist: A Literary Agent Offers Strategies for Success* (Portsmouth, NH: Heinemann, 1996). Straightforward approach to commercial viability and success as a writer of fiction. Remarkable insights into the current (and future) publishing climate as they apply to veteran wordsmiths and aspiring storytellers alike. In addition to being an established literary agent, Donald Maass is the author of numerous published novels.

Mann, Thomas. *A Guide to Library Research Methods* (New York: Oxford University Press, 1987). A practical guide to the most helpful, time-saving, and cost-effective information sources.

McCormack, Thomas. *The Fiction Editor* (New York: St. Martin's Press, 1988). How to fine-tune fiction; every bit as helpful for writers as it is for editors.

McInerny, Ralph. *Let's Write a Mystery*; *Let's Write a Novel*; and *Let's Write Short Stories* (Arlington, VA: Vandamere Press/Quodlibetal Features, 1993). Series of vivid instructional packages on the art and marketing of written works. Individual programs are geared to the areas of mystery writing, mainstream novels, and short fiction. Each title includes a set of audiotapes, tutorial lessons, a workbook, and drafts of unpublished writing in its respective field.

Miller, Casey, and Kate Swift. *The Handbook of Nonsexist Writing* (New York: Harper & Row, 1988). Guidelines for eliminating sexist terms and constructions from all writing.

Niggling resisters to usage reformation still exist among professional scribblers—the printed word has shown, however, that to be lexically correct liberates writers to be both admirably exact and at their exhilaratingly expressive best.

Namanworth, Phillip, and Gene Busnar. *Working for Yourself* (New York: McGraw-Hill, 1986). Everything you need to know about the business and personal side of freelancing and being self-employed. Great tips applicable to orchestrating a writer's business and working life.

Norville, Barbara. *Writing the Modern Mystery* (Cincinnati: Writer's Digest Books, 1986). Excellent overview, from concept to completed work. A framework for development rather than specific how-to, but plenty of tips to aid the writer in following through on fresh ideas.

Oberlin, Loriann Hoff. *Writing for Money* (Cincinnati: Writer's Digest Books, 1995). How your writing talents can supplement your regular income or establish a self-employed career. Supportive guide that covers fields such as writing books and articles, reference writing, teaching courses and seminars, and serving commercial clients.

O'Cork, Shannon. *How to Write Mysteries* (Cincinnati: Writer's Digest Books, 1989). Original approach to detective and crime fiction, from concept through composition. Author OCork is among the exemplary practitioners in this literary field.

O'Gara, Elaine. *Travel Writer's Markets: Where to Sell Your Travel Articles and Place Your Press Releases* (revised edition) (Boston: Harvard Common, 1993). A must for travel writers; provides an abundance of practical information, as useful for field-hardened veterans as it is revelatory for greenhorns. How to submit manuscripts and photographs; how to research your market.

Paludan, Eve. *Romance Writer's Pink Pages* (Rocklin, CA: Prima Publishing, updated periodically). Definitive resource for romance authors and writers of women's fiction. Includes information on marketing your work, publishing trends, networking, and more. Incisive commentary from writers, editors, and agents.

Parinello, Al. *On the Air: How to Get on Radio and TV Talk Shows and What to Do When You Get There* (Hawthorne, NJ: Career Press, 1991). Exciting guide to the electronic media and their use for promotional purposes. Ties in marketing aspects common to diverse fields such as seminars, social activism, and professional training and advancement—and is especially appropriate for authors devoted to the entrepreneurial spirit.

Polking, Kirk, and Leonard S. Meranus (editors). *Law and the Writer* (third edition) (Cincinnati: Writer's Digest Books, 1985). A collection of pieces addressing legal issues that concern writers and their works.

Powell, Walter W. *Getting into Print: The Decision-Making Process in Scholarly Publishing* (Chicago: University of Chicago Press, 1985). An eye-opening, behind-the-scenes look at the operations of two scholarly presses.

Poynter, Dan. *The Self-Publishing Manual* (Santa Barbara, CA: Para Publishing, 1989). Informative and complete step-by-step how-to by the principal of one of the most successful one-person publishing firms.

Poynter, Dan, and Mindy Bingham. *Is There a Book Inside You? How to Successfully Author a Book Alone or through a Collaborator* (Santa Barbara, CA: Para Publishing, 1985). A thought-provoking series of exercises to help you assess your publishing potential.

Preston, Elizabeth, Ingrid Monke, and Elizabeth Bickford. *Preparing Your Manuscript* (Boston: The Writer, 1992). Contemporary guide to manuscript preparation; provides step-by-step advice for professional presentation of work for submission to editors, publishers, agents, television producers. Covers punctuation, spelling, indexing, along with examples of proper formats for poetry, prose, plays; also offers essential information on copyright, marketing, and mailing manuscripts.

Princeton Language Institute (editors). *The 21st Century Manual of Style* (New York: Dell/Laurel, 1993). Dictionary-style reference with a futuristic outlook. Concise presentation of where language and lexical expression are now, directions the lingo is going, and where you as a writer want to be.

The Prolific Writer's Magazine (Oradell, NJ: BSK Communications, published quarterly). Literary/trade publication that provides educationally enriching and entertaining articles, news, blurbs, profiles, interviews, and much more. Assistance and support for the talents of aspiring and professional writers.

Provost, Gary. *The Freelance Writer's Handbook* (New York: NAL/Mentor, 1982). Invaluable reference and resource guide, mainly for writers of short pieces.

Provost, Gary. *Make Your Words Work* (Cincinnati: Writer's Digest, 1990). Astute approach to methods of expression, style, pacing, and compositional problem solving; applicable to nonfiction as well as to fiction. Instructive exercises to deliver the most power with your writing.

Rivers, William L. *Finding Facts: Interviewing, Observing, Using Reference Sources* (Englewood Cliffs, NJ: Prentice-Hall, 1975). A careful inquiry into the demanding research process and the difficulties involved in achieving objectivity.

Roberts, Ellen E. M. *The Children's Picture Book: How to Write It, How to Sell It* (Cincinnati: Writer's Digest Books, 1981). A wise and enthusiastic step-by-step guide by an established children's book editor.

Ross, Marilyn, and Tom Ross. *Marketing Your Books: A Collection of Profit-Making Ideas for Authors and Publishers* (Buena Vista, CO: Communication Creativity, 1990). Fine-tuned, cost-effective, innovative promotional designs. Authors should note: This book accentuates the philosophy that a successful marketing strategy begins at the concept stage—before the book itself is written.

Ross, Tom, and Marilyn Ross. *The Complete Guide to Self-Publishing* (Buena Vista, CO: Communication Creativity, 1990). Up-to-date, step-by-step information and procedures that take your book from the idea stage through production, setting up your publishing business, and into the hands of consumers. Not just for entrepreneurs who self-publish—contains valuable tips for commercially published writers to maximize the success of their titles.

Rubens, Philip (editor). *Science and Technical Writing: A Manual of Style* (New York: Henry Holt, 1992). Comprehensive one-stop style guide for writers and editors in scientific and technical fields (including students). Addresses fundamental issues of style and usage, distinguishes between specialized terminology and technobabble, and provides guidelines for achieving communication with one's audience.

Rubie, Peter. *The Elements of Storytelling: How to Write Compelling Fiction* (New York: Wiley, 1996). Decisive, silver-tongued guide to the art and craft of novelistic writing. Holistic approach to creating enticing characters and plot, sharpening the pacing, developing a graceful style and powerful structure. The author is an accomplished literary agent, writer, and editor.

Schaeffer, Garry, and Dr. Tony Alessandra. *Publish and Flourish—A Consultant's Guide: How to Boost Visibility and Earnings through a Publishing Strategy* (New York: Wiley, 1992). Publishing is a business—and also a great adjunct to one. This book shows entrepreneurs, consultants, and freelancers in all fields how to use a publishing program both as a marketing tool and as a profit-centered part of their own business careers.

Schwartz, Marilyn and the Task Force on Bias-Free Language of the Association of American University Presses. *Guidelines for Bias-Free Writing* (Bloomington, IN: Indiana University Press, 1995). A valuable reference on contemporary style that can be used as a writer's guide to producing hard-hitting prose without being in the least contrite.

Seidman, Michael. *From Printout to Published* (New York: Carroll & Graf, 1992). Engaging and unvarnished consideration of the writer–publisher interface all the way from first draft through finished book. Detailed discussions of manuscript submissions, working with agents, contract negotiation, gaining ample advances, editing, cover design, book marketing, promotion—and more. Authored by a renowned and popular editor.

Seidman, Michael. *Living the Dream: An Outline for a Life in Fiction* (New York: Carroll & Graf, 1992). Sage and sound philosophy and tips-of-the-trade in the what-goes-around-comes-around world of fiction publishing.

Seuling, Barbara. *How to Write a Children's Book and Get It Published* (revised and expanded edition) (New York, Scribner, 1991). Filled with broad truths and subtle nuances to guide authors successfully through the domain of children's publishing.

Seymour-Smith, Martin. *Dictionary of Fictional Characters* (Boston: The Writer, 1992). Updated, reedited, and expanded from the earlier text of Freeman and Urquhart, this new version of a classic work is the definitive writer's reference guide to over 50,000 fictional characters from novels, short stories, poems, plays, and operas.

Spy magazine editors. *Spy Notes on McInerney's* Bright Lights, Big City, *Ellis's* Less Than Zero, *Janowitz's* Slaves of New York . . . *and All Those Other Hip Urban Novels of the 1980s* (New York: Dolphin/Doubleday, 1989). "Becoming the Literary Voice of a Generation" is an astonishing examination of just what it takes to get published and why you may be better off staying undiscovered.

Sterling, C. L., and M. G. Davidson. *Getting Your Manuscript Sold: Surefire Writing and Selling Strategies That Will Get Your Book Published* (New York: Barclay House/Zinn Communications, 1995). With a practical how-to orientation, this book asks pertinent questions about a writer's work and gives illuminating answers to help launch a writing career. Authors are agent Cynthia Sterling and editor Megan Davidson.

Sterling, C. L. and M. G. Davidson. *Writing Aerobics* (New York: Barclay House/Zinn Communications, 1996). Practical and zesty methods that bring into play the entire range of a writer's talent. Insightful observations and imagination-sparking exercises.

Strunk, William, Jr., and E. B. White. *The Elements of Style* (third edition) (New York: Macmillan, 1979). This highly respected, widely read, and well-loved classic is seen by some contemporary writers as sheer stuffed-shirt punditry. It is, however, a slim volume and doesn't take up much space or require much time to read—and modern writers may well find themselves adopting Strunk-and-White principles in spite of themselves.

Stuart, Sally E. (editor). *Christian Writer's Market* (Wheaton, IL: Harold Shaw Publishers, updated annually). Bursting with information about book and periodical publishers, new media opportunities, writers' conferences, and specialized editors and agents. This work is a grand tool for beginning and advanced writers, full-time freelancers, agents, editors, publicists, and writing classes. Computer-disk version available.

Todd, Alden. *Finding Facts Fast* (Berkeley: Ten Speed Press, 1979). Details basic, intermediate, and advanced research techniques; hundreds of ideas for those stuck in a research dead-end.

Volunteer Lawyers for the Arts. *Pressing Business: An Organizational Manual for Independent Publishers* (New York: VLA, 1984). Delineates legal and business concepts applicable to smaller literary and not-for-profit publishing enterprises. Addresses issues writers should be aware of, since for practical (including tax) purposes they are part and parcel to the same industry.

Welty, Eudora. *One Writer's Beginnings* (New York: Warner Books, 1984). "Listening," "Learning to See," and "Finding a Voice"—three beautifully written essays (based on lectures given at Harvard) that trace Ms. Welty's influences and her growth as a young writer in the South.

Wilson, James. *Freelance Writer's Handbook: The Real Story* (Port Townsend, WA: Loompanics, 1988). How to stalk a market, how to command your career, how to get the most money and not get ripped off, how to handle editors, the use of photography, and more. Blithely scathing resource depicts behind-the-scenes publishing machinations as well as dispensing a wealth of advice toward resolving other terrors (writer's block, rejection) part and parcel of the writer's terrain. How-to-do-it manual written by a pro who has done it.

Wisniewski, Mark. *Writing & Revising Your Fiction* (Boston: The Writer, 1995). Hows and whys of the do-or-die process of working your fiction ideas through to publishable form. Author is an accomplished fiction writer, writing teacher, and workshop leader.

Words into Type (Englewood Cliffs, NJ: Prentice Hall, 1974). This esteemed professional reference for the publishing industry covers technical considerations of editing, copyediting, proofreading, and typographic style, which can and should be of tremendous value to writers during manuscript preparation. The explication of what goes on inside the publisher's shop clues the writer in on what to expect from the sometimes-enigmatic production sequence. This reference work is based on studies by Marjorie E. Skillin, Robert M. Gay, and other authorities.

The Writer's Handbook (Boston: The Writer, published annually). One of the most respected, clear-eyed, high-quality reference and resource work in the writing-for-publication field; a pioneering work, now with a long tradition of success. Edited by Sylvia K. Burack.

Writer's Market (Cincinnati: Writer's Digest Books, published annually). A directory of thousands of markets and outlets; best known for its listing of the hundreds of consumer and trade periodicals. Also includes book publishers, book packagers, greeting-card publishers, syndicates, and more. (In addition, Writer's Digest Books offers a catalog of specialist and generalist sourcebooks and guidebooks for writers covering virtually the entire publishing spectrum.)

Zinsser, William. *On Writing Well* (New York: Harper & Row, 1985). How to simplify nonfiction writing and deliver fresh, vigorous prose. An excellent book to keep on hand.

Zobel, Louise Purwin. *The Travel Writer's Handbook* (Chicago: Surrey Books, 1994). Veteran travel writer Louise Zobel explains the practical aspects of travel writing, from pretrip research, to photography, to selling strategies. Includes the most marketable formats for travel writing.

Zuckerman, Albert. *Writing the Blockbuster Novel* (Cincinnati: Writer's Digest Books, 1993). Thorough and incisive book geared toward producing popular "big-book" fiction. Writer–agent author (with a skein of successful clients) provides expert dissection of compositional techniques, narrative structure, character attributes and development, importance of conflict—all keyed to instructional examples from best-selling novels.

Index